Lecture Notes in Computer Science   9529

Commenced Publication in 1973
Founding and Former Series Editors:
Gerhard Goos, Juris Hartmanis, and Jan van Leeuwen

More information about this series at http://www.springer.com/series/7407

Guojun Wang · Albert Zomaya
Gregorio Martinez Perez · Kenli Li (Eds.)

Algorithms and Architectures for Parallel Processing

15th International Conference, ICA3PP 2015
Zhangjiajie, China, November 18–20, 2015
Proceedings, Part II

 Springer

Editors
Guojun Wang
Central South University
Changsha
China

Albert Zomaya
The University of Sydney
Sydney, NSW
Australia

Gregorio Martinez Perez
University of Murcia
Murcia
Spain

Kenli Li
Hunan University
Changsha
China

ISSN 0302-9743   ISSN 1611-3349 (electronic)
Lecture Notes in Computer Science
ISBN 978-3-319-27121-7   ISBN 978-3-319-27122-4 (eBook)
DOI 10.1007/978-3-319-27122-4

Library of Congress Control Number: 2015955380

LNCS Sublibrary: SL1 – Theoretical Computer Science and General Issues

Springer Cham Heidelberg New York Dordrecht London

Printed on acid-free paper

Springer International Publishing AG Switzerland is part of Springer Science+Business Media
(www.springer.com)

Welcome Message from the ICA3PP 2015 General Chairs

Welcome to the proceedings of the 15th International Conference on Algorithms and Architectures for Parallel Processing (ICA3PP 2015), which was organized by Central South University, Hunan University, National University of Defense Technology, and Jishou University.

It was our great pleasure to organize the ICA3PP 2015 conference in Zhangjiajie, China, during November 18–20, 2015. On behalf of the Organizing Committee of the conference, we would like to express our cordial gratitude to all participants who attended the conference.

ICA3PP 2015 was the 15th event in the series of conferences started in 1995 that is devoted to algorithms and architectures for parallel processing. ICA3PP is now recognized as the main regular event in the world that covers many dimensions of parallel algorithms and architectures, encompassing fundamental theoretical approaches, practical experimental projects, and commercial components and systems. The conference provides a forum for academics and practitioners from around the world to exchange ideas for improving the efficiency, performance, reliability, security, and interoperability of computing systems and applications.

ICA3PP 2015 attracted high-quality research papers highlighting the foundational work that strives to push beyond the limits of existing technologies, including experimental efforts, innovative systems, and investigations that identify weaknesses in existing parallel processing technology.

ICA3PP 2015 consisted of the main conference and six international symposia and workshops. Many individuals contributed to the success of the conference. We would like to express our special appreciation to Prof. Yang Xiang, Prof. Andrzej Goscinski, and Prof. Yi Pan, the Steering Committee chairs, for giving us the opportunity to host this prestigious conference and for their guidance with the conference organization. Special thanks to the program chairs, Prof. Albert Zomaya, Prof. Gregorio Martinez Perez, and Prof. Kenli Li, for their outstanding work on the technical program. Thanks also to the workshop chairs, Dr. Mianxiong Dong, Dr. Ryan K.L. Ko, and Dr. Md. Zakirul Alam Bhuiya, for their excellent work in organizing attractive symposia and workshops. Thanks also to the publicity chairs, Prof. Carlos Becker Westphall, Dr. Yulei Wu, Prof. Christian Callegari, Prof. Kuan-Ching Li, and Prof. James J. (Jong Hyuk) Park, for the great job in publicizing this event. We would like to give our thanks to all the members of the Organizing Committee and Program Committee as well as the external reviewers for their efforts and support. We would also like to give our thanks to the keynote speakers, Prof. John C.S. Lui, Prof. Jiannong Cao, Prof. Wanlei Zhou, and Prof. Hai Jin, for offering insightful and enlightening talks. Last but not least, we would like to thank all the authors who submitted their papers to the conference.

November 2015

Guojun Wang
Peter Mueller
Qingping Zhou

Welcome Message from the ICA3PP 2015 Program Chairs

On behalf of the Program Committee of the 15th International Conference on Algorithms and Architectures for Parallel Processing (ICA3PP 2015), we would like to welcome you to join the conference held in Zhangjiajie, China, during November 18–20, 2015.

The ICA3PP conference aims at bringing together researchers and practitioners from both academia and industry who are working on algorithms and architectures for parallel processing. The conference features keynote speeches, panel discussions, technical presentations, symposiums, and workshops, where the technical presentations from both the research community and industry cover various aspects including fundamental theoretical approaches, practical experimental projects, and commercial components and systems. ICA3PP 2015 was the next event in a series of highly successful international conferences on algorithms and architectures for parallel processing, previously held as ICA3PP 2014 (Dalian, China, August 2014), ICA3PP 2013 (Vietri sul Mare, Italy, December 2013), ICA3PP 2012 (Fukuoka, Japan, September 2012), ICA3PP 2011 (Melbourne, Australia, October 2011), ICA3PP 2010 (Busan, Korea, May 2010), ICA3PP 2009 (Taipei, Taiwan, June 2009), ICA3PP 2008 (Cyprus, June 2008), ICA3PP 2007 (Hangzhou, China, June 2007), ICA3PP 2005 (Melbourne, Australia, October 2005), ICA3PP 2002 (Beijing, China, October 2002), ICA3PP2000 (Hong Kong, China, December 2000), ICA3PP 1997 (Melbourne, Australia, December 1997), ICA3PP 1996 (Singapore, June 1996), and ICA3PP 1995 (Brisbane, Australia, April 1995).

The ICA3PP 2015 conference collected research papers on related research issues from all around the world. This year we received 602 submissions for the main conference. All submissions received at least three reviews during a high-quality review process. According to the review results, 219 papers were selected for oral presentation at the conference, giving an acceptance rate of 36.4 %.

We would like to offer our gratitude to Prof. Yang Xiang and Prof. Andrzej Goscinski from Deakin University, Australia, and Prof. Yi Pan from Georgia State University, USA, the Steering Committee chairs. Our thanks also go to the general chairs, Prof. Guojun Wang from Central South University, China, Dr. Peter Mueller from IBM Zurich Research, Switzerland, and Prof. Qingping Zhou from Jishou University, China, for their great support and good suggestions for a successful the final program. Special thanks to the workshop chairs, Dr. Mianxiong Dong from Muroran Institute of Technology, Japan, and Dr. Ryan K.L. Ko from the University of Waikato, New Zealand, and Dr. Md. Zakirul Alam Bhuiyan from Temple University, USA. In particular, we would like to give our thanks to all researchers and practitioners who submitted their manuscripts, and to the Program Committee and the external reviewers who contributed their valuable time and expertise to provide professional reviews working under a very tight schedule. Moreover, we are very grateful to our keynote speakers who kindly accepted our invitation to give insightful and prospective talks.

Finally, we believe that the conference provided a very good opportunity for participants to learn from each other. We hope you enjoy the conference proceedings.

Albert Zomaya
Gregorio Martinez Perez
Kenli Li

Welcome Message from the ICA3PP 2015 Workshop Chairs

Welcome to the proceedings of the 15th International Conference on Algorithms and Architectures for Parallel Processing (ICA3PP 2015) held in Zhangjiajie, China, during November 18–20, 2015. The program this year consisted of six symposiums/workshops covering a wide range of research topics on parallel processing technology:

(1) The 6th International Workshop on Trust, Security and Privacy for Big Data (TrustData 2015)
(2) The 5th International Symposium on Trust, Security and Privacy for Emerging Applications (TSP 2015)
(3) The Third International Workshop on Network Optimization and Performance Evaluation (NOPE 2015)
(4) The Second International Symposium on Sensor-Cloud Systems (SCS 2015)
(5) The Second International Workshop on Security and Privacy Protection in Computer and Network Systems (SPPCN 2015)
(6) The First International Symposium on Dependability in Sensor, Cloud, and Big Data Systems and Applications (DependSys 2015)

The aim of these symposiums/workshops is to provide a forum to bring together practitioners and researchers from academia and industry for discussion and presentations on the current research and future directions related to parallel processing technology. The themes and topics of these symposiums/workshops are a valuable complement to the overall scope of ICA3PP 2015 providing additional values and interests. We hope that all of the selected papers will have a good impact on future research in the respective field.

The ICA3PP 2015 workshops collected research papers on the related research issues from all around the world. This year we received 205 submissions for all workshops. All submissions received at least three reviews during a high-quality review process. According to the review results, 77 papers were selected for oral presentation at the conference, giving an acceptance rate of 37.6 %.

We offer our sincere gratitude to the workshop organizers for their hard work in designing the call for papers, assembling the Program Committee, managing the peer-review process for the selection of papers, and planning the workshop program. We are grateful to the workshop Program Committees, external reviewers, session chairs, contributing authors, and attendees. Our special thanks to the Organizing Committees of ICA3PP 2015 for their strong support, and especially to the program chairs, Prof. Albert Zomaya, Prof. Gregorio Martinez Perez, and Prof. Kenli Li, for their guidance.

Finally, we hope that you will find the proceedings interesting and stimulating.

Mianxiong Dong
Ryan K.L. Ko
Md. Zakirul Alam Bhuiyan

Welcome Message from the TrustData 2015 Program Chairs

The 6th International Workshop on Trust, Security and Privacy for Big Data (TrustData 2015) was held in Zhangjiajie, China.

TrustData aims at bringing together people from both academia and industry to present their most recent work related to trust, security, and privacy issues in big data, and to exchange ideas and thoughts in order to identify emerging research topics and define the future of big data.

TrustData 2015 was the next event in a series of highly successful international workshops, previously held as TrustData 2014 (Dalian, China, March 2012) and TrustData 2013 (Zhangjiajie, China, November, 2013).

This international workshop collected research papers on the aforementioned research issues from all around the world. Each paper was reviewed by at least three experts in the field. We feel very proud of the high participation, and although it was difficult to collect the best papers from all the submissions received, we feel we managed to have an amazing conference that was enjoyed by all participants.

We would like to offer our gratitude to the general chairs, Dr. Qin Liu and Dr. Muhammad Bashir Abdullahi, for their excellent support and invaluable suggestions for a successful final program. In particular, we would like to thank all researchers and practitioners who submitted their manuscripts, and the Program Committee members and additional reviewers for their tremendous efforts and timely reviews.

We hope you enjoy the proceedings of TrustData 2015.

Keqin Li
Avinash Srinivasan

Welcome Message from the TSP 2015 Program Chairs

On behalf of the Program Committee of the 5th International Symposium on Trust, Security and Privacy for Emerging Applications (TSP 2015), we would like to welcome you to the proceedings of the event, which was held in Zhangjiajie, China.

The symposium focuses on trust, security, and privacy issues in social networks, cloud computing, Internet of Things (IoT), wireless sensor networks, and other networking environments or system applications; it also provides a forum for presenting and discussing emerging ideas and trends in this highly challenging research area. The aim of this symposium is to provide a leading edge forum to foster interaction between researchers and developers with the trust, security, and privacy issues, and to give attendees an opportunity to network with experts in this area.

Following the success of TSP 2008 in Shanghai, China, during December 17–20, 2008, TSP 2009 in Macau SAR, China, during October 12–14, 2009, TSP 2010 in Bradford, UK, during June 29–July 1, 2010, and TSP 2013 in Zhangjiajie, China, during November 13–15, 2013, the 5th International Symposium on Trust, Security and Privacy for Emerging Applications (TSP 2015) was held in Zhangjiajie, China, during November 18–20, 2015, in conjunction with the 15th International Conference on Algorithms and Architectures for Parallel Processing (ICA3PP 2015).

The symposium collected research papers on the aforementioned research issues from all around the world. Each paper was reviewed by at least two experts in the field. We realized an amazing symposium that we hope was enjoyed by all the participants.

We would like to thank all researchers and practitioners who submitted their manuscripts, and the Program Committee members and additional reviewers for their tremendous efforts and timely reviews.

We hope you enjoy the proceedings of TSP 2015.

Imad Jawhar
Deqing Zou

Welcome Message from the NOPE 2015 Program Chair

Welcome to the proceedings of the 2015 International Workshop on Network Optimization and Performance Evaluation (NOPE 2015) held in Zhangjiajie, China, during November 18–20, 2015.

Network optimization and performance evaluation is a topic that attracts much attention in network/Internet and distributed systems. Due to the recent advances in Internet-based applications as well as WLANs, wireless home networks, wireless sensor networks, wireless mesh networks, and cloud computing, we are witnessing a variety of new technologies. However, these systems and networks are becoming very large and complex, and consuming a great amount of energy at the same time. System optimization and performance evaluation remain to be resolved before these systems become a commodity.

On behalf of the Organizing Committee, we would like to take this opportunity to express our gratitude to all reviewers who worked hard to finish reviews on time. Thanks to the publicity chairs for their efforts and support. Thanks also to all authors for their great support and contribution to the event. We would like to give our special thanks to the Organizing Committee, colleagues, and friends who worked hard behind the scenes. Without their unfailing cooperation, hard work, and dedication, this event would not have been successfully organized.

We are grateful to everyone for participating in NOPE 2015.

Gaocai Wang

Welcome Message from SCS 2015 Program Chairs

As the Program Chairs and on behalf of the Organizing Committee of the Second International Symposium on Sensor-Cloud Systems (SCS 2015), we would like to express our gratitude to all the participants who attended the symposium in Zhangjiajie, China, during November 18–20, 2015. This famous city is the location of China's first forest park (The Zhangjiajie National Forest Park) and a World Natural Heritage site (Wulingyuan Scenic Area).

The aim of SCS is to bring together researchers and practitioners working on sensor-cloud systems to present and discuss emerging ideas and trends in this highly challenging research field. It has attracted some high-quality research papers, which highlight the foundational work that strives to push beyond limits of existing technologies, including experimental efforts, innovative systems, and investigations that identify weaknesses in the existing technology services.

SCS 2015 was sponsored by the National Natural Science Foundation of China, Springer, the School of Information Science and Engineering at Central South University, and the School of Software at Central South University, and it was organized by Central South University, Hunan University, National University of Defense Technology, and Jishou University. SCS 2015 was held in conjunction with the 15th International Conference on Algorithms and Architectures for Parallel Processing (ICA3PP 2015), which highlights the latest research trends in various aspects of computer science and technology.

Many individuals contributed to the success of this international symposium. We would like to express our special appreciation to the general chairs of main conference, Prof. Guojun Wang, Prof. Peter Mueller, and Prof. Qingping Zhou, for giving us this opportunity to hold this symposium and for their guidance in the organization. Thanks also to the general chairs of this symposium, Prof. Jie Li and Prof. Dongqing Xie, for their excellent work in organizing the symposium. We would like to give our thanks to all the members of the Organizing Committee and Program Committee for their efforts and support.

Finally, we are grateful to the authors for submitting their fine work to SCS 2015 and all the participants for their attendance.

Xiaofei Xing
Md. Zakirul Alam Bhuiyan

Welcome Message from the SPPCN 2015 Program Chairs

On behalf of the Program Committee of the Second International Workshop on Security and Privacy Protection in Computer and Network Systems (SPPCN 2015), we would like to welcome you to join the proceedings of the workshop, which was held in Zhangjiajie, China.

The workshop focuses on security and privacy protection in computer and network systems, such as authentication, access control, availability, integrity, privacy, confidentiality, dependability, and sustainability issues of computer and network systems. The aim of the workshop is to provide a leading-edge forum to foster interaction between researchers and developers working on security and privacy protection in computer and network systems, and to give attendees an opportunity to network with experts in this area.

SPPCN 2015 was the next event in a series of highly successful international conferences on security and privacy protection in computer and network systems, previously held as SPPCN 2014 (Dalian, China, December 2014). The workshop collected research papers on the above research issues from all around the world. Each paper was reviewed by at least two experts in the field.

We would like to offer our gratitude to the general chair, Prof. Jian Weng, for his excellent support and contribution to the success of the final program. In particular, we would like to thank all researchers and practitioners who submitted their manuscripts, and the Program Committee members and additional reviewers for their tremendous efforts and timely reviews.

We hope all of you enjoy the proceedings of SPPCN 2015.

Mianxiong Dong
Hua Guo
Tieming Cheng
Kaimin Wei

Welcome Message from the DependSys 2015 Program Chairs

As the program chairs and on behalf of the Organizing Committee of the First International Symposium on Dependability in Sensor, Cloud, and Big Data Systems and Applications (DependSys2015), we would like to express our gratitude to all the participants attending the international symposium in Zhangjiajie, China, during November 18–20, 2015. This famous city is the location of China's first forest park (The Zhangjiajie National Forest Park) and a World Natural Heritage site (Wulingyuan Scenic Area).

DependSys is a timely event that brings together new ideas, techniques, and solutions for dependability and its issues in sensor, cloud, and big data systems and applications. As we are deep into the Information Age, we are witnessing the explosive growth of data available on the Internet. Human beings are producing quintillion bytes of data every day, which come from sensors, individual archives, social networks, Internet of Things, enterprises, and the Internet in all scales and formats. One of the most challenging issues we face is to achieve the designed system performance to an expected level, i.e., how to effectively provide dependability in sensor, cloud, and big data systems. These systems need to typically run continuously, which often tend to become inert, brittle, and vulnerable after a while.

This international symposium collected research papers on the aforementioned research issues from all around the world. Although it was the first event of DependSys, we received a large number of submissions in response to the call for papers. Each paper was reviewed by at least three experts in the field. After detailed discussions among the program chairs and general chairs, a set of quality papers was finally accepted. We are very proud of the high number of participations, and it was difficult to collect the best papers from all the submissions.

Many individuals contributed to the success of this high-caliber international symposium. We would like to express our special appreciation to the steering chairs, Prof. Jie Wu and Prof. Guojun Wang, for giving us the opportunity to hold this symposium and for their guidance in the symposium organization. In particular, we would like to give our thanks to the symposium chairs, Prof. Mohammed Atiquzzaman, Prof. Sheikh Iqbal Ahamed, and Dr. Md Zakirul Alam Bhuiyan, for their excellent support and invaluable suggestions for a successful final program. Thanks to all the Program Committee members and the additional reviewers for their tremendous efforts and timely reviews.

We hope you enjoy the proceedings of DependSys 2015.

Latifur Khan
Joarder Kamruzzaman
Al-Sakib Khan Pathan

Organization

ICA3PP 2015 Organizing and Program Committees

General Chairs

Guojun Wang   Central South University, China
Peter Mueller   IBM Zurich Research, Switzerland
Qingping Zhou   Jishou University, China

Program Chairs

Albert Zomaya   University of Sydney, Australia
Gregorio Martinez Perez   University of Murcia, Spain
Kenli Li   Hunan University, China

Steering Chairs

Andrzej Goscinski   Deakin University, Australia
Yi Pan   Georgia State University, USA
Yang Xiang   Deakin University, Australia

Workshop Chairs

Mianxiong Dong   Muroran Institute of Technology, Japan
Ryan K.L. Ko   The University of Waikato, New Zealand
Md. Zakirul Alam Bhuiyan   Central South University, China

Publicity Chairs

Carlos Becker Westphall   Federal University of Santa Catarina, Brazil
Yulei Wu   The University of Exeter, UK
Christian Callegari   University of Pisa, Italy
Kuan-Ching Li   Providence University, Taiwan
James J. (Jong Hyuk) Park   SeoulTech, Korea

Publication Chairs

Jin Zheng   Central South University, China
Wenjun Jiang   Hunan University, China

Finance Chairs

Pin Liu   Central South University, China
Wang Yang   Central South University, China

Local Arrangements Chairs

Fang Qi   Central South University, China
Qin Liu   Hunan University, China
Hongzhi Xu   Jishou University, China

Program Committee

1. Parallel and Distributed Architectures Track

Chairs

Stefano Giordano   Italian National Interuniversity Consortium
                          for Telecommunications, Italy
Xiaofei Liao   Huazhong University of Science and Technology,
                          China
Haikun Liu   Nanyang Technological University, Singapore

TPC Members

Marco Aldinucci   Universitá degli Studi di Torino, Italy
Yungang Bao   Chinese Academy of Sciences, China
Hui Chen   Auburn University, USA
Vladimir Getov   University of Westminster, UK
Jie Jia   Northeastern University, China
Yusen Li   Nanyang Technological University, Singapore
Zengxiang Li   Agency for Science, Technology and Research,
                          Singapore
Xue Liu   Northeastern University, China
Yongchao Liu   Georgia Institute of Technology, USA
Salvatore Orlando   Universitá Ca' Foscari Venezia, Italy
Nicola Tonellotto   ISTI-CNR, Italy
Zeke Wang   Nanyang Technological University, Singapore
Quanqing Xu   Agency for Science, Technology and Research
                          (A*STAR), Singapore
Ramin Yahyapour   University of Göttingen, Germany
Jidong Zhai   Tsinghua University, China
Jianlong Zhong   GraphSQL Inc., USA
Andrei Tchernykh   CICESE Research Center, Ensenada, Baja California,
                          Mexico

2. Software Systems and Programming Track

Chairs

Xinjun Mao	National University of Defense Technology, China
Sanaa Sharafeddine	Lebanese American University, Beirut, Lebanon

TPC Members

Surendra Byna	Lawrence Berkeley National Lab, USA
Yue-Shan Chang	National Taipei University, Taiwan
Massimo Coppola	ISTI-CNR, Italy
Marco Danelutto	University of Pisa, Italy
Jose Daniel Garcia	Carlos III of Madrid University, Spain
Peter Kilpatrick	Queen's University Belfast, UK
Soo-Kyun Kim	PaiChai University, Korea
Rajeev Raje	Indiana University-Purdue University Indianapolis, USA
Salvatore Ruggieri	University of Pisa, Italy
Subhash Saini	NASA, USA
Peter Strazdins	The Australian National University, Australia
Domenico Talia	University of Calabria, Italy
Hiroyuki Tomiyama	Ritsumeikan University, Japan
Canqun Yang	National University of Defense Technology, China
Daniel Andresen	Kansas State University, USA
Sven-Bodo Scholz	Heriot-Watt University, UK
Salvatore Venticinque	Second University of Naples, Italy

3. Distributed and Network-Based Computing Track

Chairs

Casimer DeCusatis	Marist College, USA
Qi Wang	University of the West of Scotland, UK

TPC Members

Justin Baijian	Purdue University, USA
Aparicio Carranza	City University of New York, USA
Tzung-Shi Chen	National University of Tainan, Taiwan
Ciprian Dobre	University Politehnica of Bucharest, Romania
Longxiang Gao	Deakin University, Australia
Ansgar Gerlicher	Stuttgart Media University, Germany
Harald Gjermundrod	University of Nicosia, Cyprus
Christos Grecos	Independent Imaging Consultant, UK
Jia Hu	Liverpool Hope University, UK
Baback Izadi	State University of New York at New Paltz, USA
Morihiro Kuga	Kumamoto University, Japan
Mikolaj Leszczuk	AGH University of Science and Technology, Poland

Paul Lu	University of Alberta, Canada
Chunbo Luo	University of the West of Scotland, UK
Ioannis Papapanagiotou	Purdue University, USA
Michael Hobbs	Deakin University, Australia
Cosimo Anglano	Università del Piemonte Orientale, Italy
Md. ObaidurRahman	Dhaka University of Engineering and Technology, Bangladesh
Aniello Castiglione	University of Salerno, Italy
Shuhong Chen	Hunan Institute of Engineering, China

4. Big Data and Its Applications Track

Chairs

Jose M. Alcaraz Calero	University of the West of Scotland, UK
Shui Yu	Deakin University, Australia

TPC Members

Alba Amato	Second University of Naples, Italy
Tania Cerquitelli	Politecnico di Torino, Italy
Zizhong (Jeffrey) Chen	University of California at Riverside, USA
Alfredo Cuzzocrea	University of Calabria, Italy
Saptarshi Debroy	University of Missouri-Columbia, USA
Yacine Djemaiel	Communication Networks and Security, Res. Lab, Tunisia
Shadi Ibrahim	Inria, France
Hongwei Li	UESTC, China
William Liu	Auckland University of Technology, New Zealand
Xiao Liu	East China Normal University, China
Karampelas Panagiotis	Hellenic Air Force Academy, Greece
Florin Pop	University Politehnica of Bucharest, Romania
Genoveva Vargas Solar	CNRS-LIG-LAFMIA, France
Chen Wang	CSIRO ICT Centre, Australia
Chao-Tung Yang	Tunghai University, Taiwan
Peng Zhang	Stony Brook University, USA
Ling Zhen	Southeast University, China
Roger Zimmermann	National University of Singapore, Singapore
Francesco Palmieri	University of Salerno, Italy
Rajiv Ranjan	CSIRO, Canberra, Australia
Felix Cuadrado	Queen Mary University of London, UK
Nilimesh Halder	The University of Western Australia, Australia
Kuan-Chou Lai	National Taichung University of Education, Taiwan
Jaafar Gaber	UTBM, France
Eunok Paek	Hanyang University, Korea
You-Chiun Wang	National Sun Yat-sen University, Taiwan
Ke Gu	Changsha University of Technology, China

5. Parallel and Distributed Algorithms Track

Chairs

Dimitris A. Pados	The State University of New York at Buffalo, USA
Baoliu Ye	Nanjing University, China

TPC Members

George Bosilca	University of Tennessee, USA
Massimo Cafaro	University of Salento, Italy
Stefania Colonnese	Universitá degli Studi di Roma La Sapienza, Italy
Raphael Couturier	University of Franche Comte, France
Gregoire Danoy	University of Luxembourg, Luxembourg
Franco Frattolillo	Universitá del Sannio, Italy
Che-Rung Lee	National Tsing Hua University, Taiwan
Laurent Lefevre	Inria, ENS-Lyon, University of Lyon, France
Amit Majumdar	San Diego Supercomputer Center, USA
Susumu Matsumae	Saga University, Japan
George N. Karystinos	Technical University of Crete, Greece
Dana Petcu	West University of Timisoara, Romania
Francoise Sailhan	CNAM, France
Uwe Tangen	Ruhr-Universität Bochum, Germany
Wei Xue	Tsinghua University, China
Kalyan S. Perumalla	Oak Ridge National Laboratory, USA
Morris Riedel	University of Iceland, Germany
Gianluigi Folino	ICAR-CNR, Italy
Joanna Kolodziej	Cracow University of Technology, Poland
Luc Bougé	ENS Rennes, France
Hirotaka Ono	Kyushu University, Japan
Tansel Ozyer	TOBB Economics and Technology University, Turkey
Daniel Grosu	Wayne State University, USA
Tian Wang	Huaqiao University, China
Sancheng Peng	Zhaoqing University, China
Fang Qi	Central South University, China
Zhe Tang	Central South University, China
Jin Zheng	Central South University, China

6. Applications of Parallel and Distributed Computing Track

Chairs

Yu Chen	Binghamton University, State University of New York, USA
Michal Wozniak	Wroclaw University of Technology, Poland

TPC Members

Jose Alfredo F. Costa	Universidade Federal do Rio Grande do Norte, Brazil
Robert Burduk	Wroclaw University of Technology, Poland
Boguslaw Cyganek	AGH University of Science and Technology, Poland
Paolo Gasti	New York Institute of Technology, USA
Manuel Grana	University of the Basque Country, Spain
Houcine Hassan	Universidad Politecnica de Valencia, Spain
Alvaro Herrero	Universidad de Burgos, Spain
Jin Kocsis	University of Akron, USA
Esmond Ng	Lawrence Berkeley National Lab, USA
Dragan Simic	University of Novi Sad, Serbia
Ching-Lung Su	National Yunlin University of Science and Technology, Taiwan
Tomoaki Tsumura	Nagoya Institute of Technology, Japan
Krzysztof Walkowiak	Wroclaw University of Technology, Poland
Zi-Ang (John) Zhang	Binghamton University-SUNY, USA
Yunhui Zheng	IBM Research, USA
Hsi-Ya Chang	National Center for High-Performance Computing, Taiwan
Chun-Yu Lin	HTC Corp., Taiwan
Nikzad Babaii Rizvandi	The University of Sydney, Australia

7. Service Dependability and Security in Distributed and Parallel Systems Track

Chairs

Antonio Ruiz Martinez	University of Murcia, Spain
Jun Zhang	Deakin University, Australia

TPC Members

Jorge Bernal Bernabe	University of Murcia, Spain
Roberto Di Pietro	Universitá di Roma Tre, Italy
Massimo Ficco	Second University of Naples (SUN), Italy
Yonggang Huang	Beijing Institute of Technology, China
Georgios Kambourakis	University of the Aegean, Greece
Muhammad Khurram Khan	King Saud University, Saudi Arabia
Liang Luo	Southwest University, China
Barbara Masucci	Universitá di Salerno, Italy
Juan M. Marin	University of Murcia, Spain
Sabu M. Thampi	Indian Institute of Information Technology and Management – Kerala (IIITM-K), India
Fernando Pereniguez-Garcia	Catholic University of Murcia, Spain
Yongli Ren	RMIT University, Australia
Yu Wang	Deakin University, Australia
Sheng Wen	Deakin University, Australia

Mazdak Zamani   Universiti Teknologi Malaysia, Malaysia
Susan K. Donohue   University of Virginia, USA
Oana Boncalo   University Politehnica Timisoara, Romania
K.P. Lam   University of Keele, UK
George Loukas   University of Greenwich, UK
Ugo Fiore   Federico II University, Italy
Christian Esposito   University of Salerno, Italy
Arcangelo Castiglione   University of Salerno, Italy
Edward Jung   Kennesaw State University, USA
Md. Zakirul Alam Bhuiyan   Central South University, China
Xiaofei Xing   Guangzhou University, China
Qin Liu   Hunan University, China
Wenjun Jiang   Hunan University, China
Gaocai Wang   Guangxi University, China
Kaimin Wei   Jinan University, China

8. Web Services and Internet Computing Track

Chairs

Huansheng Ning   University of Science and Technology Beijing, China
Daqiang Zhang   Tongji University, China

TPC Members

Jing Chen   National Cheng Kung University, Taiwan
Eugen Dedu   University of Franche-Comte, France
Sotirios G. Ziavras   NJIT, USA
Luis Javier Garcia Villalba Universidad Complutense de Madrid (UCM), Spain
Jaime Lloret   Universidad Politecnica de Valencia, Spain
Wei Lu   Keene University, USA
Stefano Marrone   Second University of Naples, Italy
Alejandro Masrur   Chemnitz University of Technology, Germany
Seungmin (Charlie) Rho   Sungkyul University, Korea
Giandomenico Spezzano   ICAR-CNR, Italy
Jiafu Wan   South China University of Technology, China
Yunsheng Wang   Kettering University, USA
Martine Wedlake   IBM, USA
Chung Wei-Ho   Research Center for Information Technology
                             Innovation in Academia Sinica, Taiwan
Xingquan (Hill) Zhu   Florida Atlantic University, USA
Nikos Dimitriou   National Center for Scientific Research Demokritos,
                             Greece
Choi Jaeho   CBNU, Chonju, Korea
Shi-Jinn Horng   National Taiwan University of Science and
                             Technology, Taiwan

9. Performance Modeling and Evaluation Track

Chairs

Deze Zeng	China University of Geosciences, China
Bofeng Zhang	Shanghai University, China

TPC Members

Ladjel Bellatreche	ENSMA, France
Xiaoju Dong	Shanghai Jiao Tong University, China
Christian Engelman	Oak Ridge National Lab, USA
Javier Garcia Blas	University Carlos III, Spain
Mauro Iacono	Second University of Naples, Italy
Zhiyang Li	Dalian Maritime University, China
Tomas Margalef	Universitat Autonoma de Barcelona, Spain
Francesco Moscato	Second University of Naples, Italy
Heng Qi	Dalian University of Technology, China
Bing Shi	Wuhan University of Technology, China
Magdalena Szmajduch	Cracow University of Technology, Poland
Qian Wang	Wuhan University, China
Zhibo Wang	Wuhan University, China
Weigang Wu	Sun Yat-sen University, China
David E. Singh	University Carlos III of Madrid, Spain
Edmund Lai	Massey University, New Zealand
Robert J. Latham	Argonne National Laboratory, USA
Zafeirios Papazachos	Queen's University of Belfast, UK
Novella Bartolini	Sapienza University of Rome, Italy
Takeshi Nanri	Kyushu University, Japan
Mais Nijim	Texas A&M University – Kingsville, USA
Salvador Petit	Universitat Politècnica de València, Spain
Daisuke Takahashi	University of Tsukuba, Japan
Cathryn Peoples	Ulster University, Northern Ireland, UK
Hamid Sarbazi-Azad	Sharif University of Technology and IPM, Iran
Md. Abdur Razzaque	University of Dhaka, Bangladesh
Angelo Brayner	University of Fortaleza, Brazil
Sushil Prasad	Georgia State University, USA
Danilo Ardagna	Politecnico di Milano, Italy
Sun-Yuan Hsieh	National Cheng Kung University, Taiwan
Li Chaoliang	Hunan University of Commerce, China
Yongming Xie	Hunan Normal University, China
Guojun Wang	Central South University, China

Secretariats

Zhe Tang   Central South University, China
Feng Wang   Central South University, China

Webmaster

Xiangdong Lee   Central South University, China

TrustData 2015 Organizing and Program Committees

Steering Chairs

Guojun Wang — Central South University, China
Peter Mueller — IBM Zurich Research Laboratory, Switzerland

General Chairs

Qin Liu — Hunan University, China
Muhammad Bashir Abdullahi — Federal University of Technology, Minna, Nigeria

Program Chairs

Keqin Li — State University of New York at New Paltz, USA
Avinash Srinivasan — Temple University, USA

Publicity Chairs

Shui Yu — Deakin University, Australia
Weirong Liu — Central South University, China

Program Committee

Andrei Tchernykh — CICESE Research Center, Mexico
Baoliu Ye — Nanjing University, China
Bimal Roy — Indian Statistical Institute, India
Chang-Ai Sun — University of Science and Technology, China
Chao Song — University of Electronic Science and Technology of China, China
Christian Callegari — The University of Pisa, Italy
Chunhua Su — Japan Advanced Institute of Science and Technology, Japan
Franco Chiaraluce — Polytechnical University of Marche (UVPM), Italy
Hai Jiang — Arkansas State University, USA
Horacio Gonzalez-Velez — National College of Ireland, Ireland
Imed Romdhani — Edinburgh Napier University, UK
Jianguo Yao — Shanghai Jiao Tong University, China
Joon S. Park — Syracuse University, USA
Kevin Chan — US Army Research Laboratory, USA
Lizhe Wang — Rochester Institute of Technology, USA

TSP 2015 Organizing and Program Committees

Program Chairs

Imad Jawhar	United Arab Emirates University, UAE
Deqing Zou	Huazhong University of Science of Technology

Program Committee Members

Chao Song	University of Electronic Science and Technology, China
David Zheng	Frostburg State University, USA
Feng Li	Indiana University-Purdue University Indianapolis, USA
Haitao Lang	Beijing University of Chemical Technology, China
Huan Zhou	China Three Gorges University, China
Mingjun Xiao	University of Science and Technology of China, China
Mingwu Zhang	Hubei University of Technology, China
Shuhui Yang	Purdue University Calumet, USA
Xiaojun Hei	Huazhong University of Science and Technology, China
Xin Li	Nanjing University of Aeronautics and Astronautics, China
Xuanxia Yao	University of Science and Technology Beijing, China
Yaxiong Zhao	Google Inc., USA
Ying Dai	LinkedIn Corporation, USA
Yunsheng Wang	Kettering University, USA
Youwen Zhu	Nanjing University of Aeronautics and Astronautics, China
Yongming Xie	Changsha Medical University, China

Steering Committee

Wenjun Jiang	Hunan University, China (Chair)
Laurence T. Yang	St. Francis Xavier University, Canada
Guojun Wang	Central South University, China
Minyi Guo	Shanghai Jiao Tong University, China
Jie Li	University of Tsukuba, Japan
Jianhua Ma	Hosei University, Japan
Peter Mueller	IBM Zurich Research Laboratory, Switzerland
Indrakshi Ray	Colorado State University, USA

NOPE 2015 Organizing and Program Committees

Steering Committee Chairs

Wei Li   Texas Southern University, USA
Taoshen Li   Guangxi University, China

Program Chair

Gaocai Wang   Guangxi University, China

Program Committee Members

Dieter Fiems   Ghent University, Belgium
Shuqiang Huang   Jinan University, China
Juan F. Perez   Imperial College London, UK
Haoqian Wang   Tsinghua University, China
Yitian Peng   Southeast University, China
Hongbin Chen   Guilin University of Electronic Technology, China
Jin Ye   Guangxi University, China
Junbin Liang   Hong Kong Polytechnic University, Hong Kong,
                            SAR China
Xianfeng Liu   Hunan Normal University, China
Hao Zhang   Central South University, China
Chuyuan Wei   Beijing University of Civil Engineering and
                            Architecture, China
Hongyun Xu   South China University of Technology, China
Zhefu Shi   University of Missouri, USA
Songfeng Lu   Huazhong University of Science and Technology,
                            China
Yihui Deng   Jinan University, China
Lei Zhang   Beijing University of Civil Engineering and
                            Architecture, China
Xiaoheng Deng   Central South University, China
Mingxing Luo   Southwest Jiaotong University, China
Bin Sun   Beijing University of Posts and Telecommunications,
                            China
Zhiwei Wang   Nanjing University of Posts and Telecommunications,
                            China
Yousheng Zhou   Chongqing University of Posts
                            and Telecommunications, China
Daofeng Li   Guangxi University, China

SCS 2015 Organizing and Program Committees

Steering Chairs

Jie Li   Tsukuba University, Japan
Dongqing Xie   Guangzhou University, China

Program Chairs

Xiaofei Xing   Guangzhou University, China
Md. Zakirul Alam Bhuiyan   Central South University, China
                              and Temple University, USA

Program Committee Members

Marco Aiello   University of Groningen, The Netherlands
David Chadwick   University of Kent, UK
Aparicio Carranza   City University of New York, USA
Mooi Choo Chuah   Lehigh University, USA
Yueming Deng   Hunan Normal University, China
Christos Grecos   Independent Imaging Consultant, UK
Dritan Kaleshi   University of Bristol, UK
Donghyun Kim   North Carolina Central University, USA
Santosh Kumar   University of Memphis, USA
Muthoni Masinde   University of Nairobi, Kenya
Satyjayant Mishra   New Mexico State University, USA
Nam Nguyen   Towson University, USA
Jean-Marc Seigneur   University of Geneva, Switzerland
Hamid Sharif   University of Nebraska, USA
Sheng Wen   Deakin University, Australia

Publicity Chairs

Zeyu Sun   Xi'an Jiaotong University, China
Yongming Xie   Hunan Normal University, China

SPPCN 2015 Organizing and Program Committees

General Chair

Jian Weng   Jinan University, China

Program Chairs

Mianxiong Dong	Muroran Institute of Technology, Japan
Hua Guo	Beihang University, China
Tieming Chen	Zhejiang University of Technology, China
Kaimin Wei	Jinan University, China

Program Committee

Fuchun Guo	University of Wollongong, Australia
Jianguang Han	Nanjing University of Finance and Economics, Nanjing, China
Debiao He	Wuhan University, China
Xinyi Huang	Fujian Normal University, China
Xuanya Li	Chinese Academy of Sciences, China
Fengyong Li	Shanghai University of Electric Power, China
Changlu Lin	Fujian Normal University, China
Chang Xu	Beijing Institute of Technology, China
Tao Xu	University of Jinan, China
Yanjiang Yang	I2R, Singapore
Yang Tian	Beihang University, China
Shengbao Wang	Hangzhou Normal University, China
Wei Wu	Fujian Normal University, China
Xiyong Zhang	Information Engineering University, China
Lei Zhao	Wuhan University, China

DependSys 2015 Organizing and Program Committees

Steering Committee Chairs

Jie Wu	Temple University, USA
Guojun Wang	Central South University, China

General Chairs

Mohammed Atiquzzaman	University of Oklahoma, USA
Sheikh Iqbal Ahamed	Marquette University, USA
Md. Zakirul Alam Bhuiyan	Central South University, China and Temple University, USA

Program Chairs

Latifur Khan	The University of Texas at Dallas, USA
Joarder Kamruzzaman	Federation University and Monash University, Australia
Al-Sakib Khan Pathan	International Islamic University Malaysia, Malaysia

Program Committee Members

A.B.M Shawkat Ali	The University of Fiji, Fiji
A.B.M. Alim Al Islam	Bangladesh University of Engineering and Technology, Bangladesh
A. Sohel Ferdous	University of Western Australia, Australia
A.K.M. Najmul Islam	University of Turku, Finland
Abdul Azim Mohammad	Gyeongsang National University, South Korea
Abdur Rouf Mohammad	Dhaka University of Engineering and Technology, Bangladesh
Afrand Agah	West Chester University of Pennsylvania, USA
Andreas Pashalidis	Katholieke Universiteit Leuven – iMinds, Belgium
Asaduzzaman	Chittagong University of Engineering and Technology, Bangladesh
C. Chiu Tan	Temple University, USA
Changyu Dong	University of Strathclyde, UK
Dana Petcu	West University of Timisoara, Romania
Daqiang Zhang	Tongji University, China
Farzana Rahman	James Madison University, USA
Hugo Miranda	University of Lisbon, Portugal
Jaydip Sen	National Institute of Science and Technology, India
Jianfeng Yang	Wuhan University, China
Jinkyu Jeong	Sungkyunkwan University, South Korea

Kaoru Ota	Muroran Institute of Technology, Japan
Karampelas Panagiotis	Hellenic Air Force Academy, Greece
Lien-Wu Chen	Feng Chia University, Taiwan
Liu Jialin	Texas Tech University, USA
M.M.A. Hashem	Khulna University of Engineering and Technology, Bangladesh
M. Thampi Sabu	Indian Institute of Information Technology and Management, India
Mahbub Habib Sheikh	CASED/TU Darmstadt, Germany
Mahmuda Naznin	Bangladesh University of Engineering and Technology, Bangladesh
Mamoun Alazab	Australian National University, Australia
Manuel Mazzara	Innopolis University, Russia
Md. Abdur Razzaque	University of Dhaka, Bangladesh
Md. Arafatur Rahman	University Malaysia Pahang, Malaysia
Mohammad Asad Rehman Chaudhry	University of Toronto, Canada
Md. Obaidur Rahman	Dhaka University of Engineering and Technology, Bangladesh
Md. Rafiul Hassan	King Fahd University of Petroleum and Minerals, Saudi Arabia
Md. Saiful Azad	American International University, Bangladesh
Mehran Asadi	Lincoln University of Pennsylvania, USA
Mohamad Badra	Zayed University, UAE
Mohamed Guerroumi	University of Sciences and Technology Houari Boumediene, Algeria
Mohammad Asadul Hoque	East Tennessee State University, USA
Mohammad Mehedi Hassan	King Saud University, Saudi Arabia
Mohammad Shahriar Rahman	University of Asia Pacific, Bangladesh
Mohammed Shamsul Alam	International Islamic University Chittagong, Bangladesh
Morshed Chowdhury	Deakin University, Australia
Muhammad Mostafa Monowar	King AbdulAziz University, Saudi Arabia
N. Musau Felix	Kenyatta University, Kenya
Phan Cong	Vinh Nguyen Tat Thanh University, Vietnam
Qin Liu	Hunan University, China
Ragib Hasan	University of Alabama at Birmingham, USA
Raza Hasan	Middle East College, Oman
Reaz Ahmed	University of Waterloo, Canada
Risat Mahmud Pathan	Chalmers University of Technology, Sweden
S.M. Kamruzzaman	King Saud University, Saudi Arabia
Salvatore Distefano	Politecnico di Milano, Italy
Shan Lin	Stony Brook University, USA
Shao Jie Tang	University of Texas at Dallas, USA
Sheng Wen	Deakin University, Australia

Shigeng Zhang	Central South University, China
Sk. Md. Mizanur Rahman	King Saud University, Saudi Arabia
Subrota Mondal	Hong Kong University of Science and Technology, Hong Kong, SAR China
Syed Imran Ali	Middle East College, Oman
Tanveer Ahsan	International Islamic University Chittagong, Bangladesh
Tanzima Hashem	Bangladesh University of Engineering and Technology, Bangladesh
Tao Li	The Hong Kong Polytechnic University, Hong Kong, SAR China
Tarem Ahmed	BRAC University, Bangladesh
Tian Wang	Huaqiao University, China
Tzung-Shi Chen	National University of Tainan, Taiwan
Vaskar Raychoudhury	Indian Institute of Technology Roorkee, India
Wahid Khan	University of Saskatchewan, Canada
Weigang Li	University of Brasilia, Brazil
Weigang Wu	Sun Yat-sen University, China
William Liu	Auckland University of Technology, New Zealand
Xiaofei Xing	Guangzhou University, China
Xuefeng Liu	The Hong Kong Polytechnic University, Hong Kong, SAR China
Xuyun Zhang	University of Melbourne, Australia
Yacine Djemaiel	Communication Networks and Security, Res. Lab, Tunisia
Yifan Zhang	Binghamton University, USA
Yu Wang	Deakin University, Australia

Publication Chairs

Jin Zheng	Central South University, China
Wenjun Jiang	Hunan University, China

Local Arrangements Chairs

Fang Qi	Central South University, China
Qin Liu	Hunan University, China
Hongzhi Xu	Jishou University, China

Finance Chairs

Pin Liu	Central South University, China
Wang Yang	Central South University, China

Web Chair

Min Guo	Central South University, China

Contents – Part II

Parallel and Distributed Algorithms

Big Data and Its Applications

PAHDFS: Preference-Aware HDFS for Hybrid Storage

Wei Zhou, Dan Feng, Zhipeng Tan[(✉)], and Yingfei Zheng

School of Computer Science and Technology, Wuhan National Laboratory for Optoelectronics, Huazhong University of Science and Technology, Wuhan 430074, China
zhipengtan@163.com

Abstract. In order to satisfy requirements of real-time processing and large capacity put forwarded by big data, hybrid storage has become a trend. There's asymmetric read/write performance for storage devices, and asymmetric read/write access characteristics for data. Data may obtain different access performance on the same device due to access characteristics waving, and the most suitable device of data may also change at different time points. As data prefer to reside on device on which they can obtain higher access performance, this paper distributes data on device with highest preference degree to improve performance and efficiency of whole storage system. A Preference-Aware HDFS (PAHDFS) with high efficiency and scalability is implemented. PAHDFS shows good performance in experiments.

Keywords: Hybrid storage · HDFS · Big data · Preference-aware · Access characteristics

1 Introduction

Big data puts forward high demands on data storage. On the one hand, real-time data processing requires quick data access. On the other hand, data volume reaches PB or even EB scale, which demands a lot of storage devices. To improve storage performance and accelerate data process, many new storage devices such as Flash, PCM are widely adopted [1, 2]. But these new storage devices usually have small capacity and high price. In order to satisfy the demand on storage capacity [3], traditional storage devices such as mechanical hard disk are still used in large quantities. For hybrid environment in which a variety of storage devices coexist, how to effective manage data and make full use of every device is a key issue to improve the efficiency of big data storage and process.

But the widely used big data storage platform HDFS [4] hasn't considered efficiently utilizing new type devices such like Flash and PCM. HDFS assumes all storage devices have the same I/O performance, and distributes data evenly across different storage devices according to their free capacity. Consequently the superiority of new type devices can hardly be exploited. Although recent Hadoop 2.6 allows user manually specify storage type, its coarse-granularity and static management makes it hard to take full advantage of new type storage devices under big data environment.

© Springer International Publishing Switzerland 2015
G. Wang et al. (Eds.): ICA3PP 2015, Part II, LNCS 9529, pp. 3–17, 2015.
DOI: 10.1007/978-3-319-27122-4_1

Meanwhile, Hybrid storage system usually contains several types of devices. The performance may not only imbalance between different devices, but also asymmetric between read and write factor of the same device. But existing researches on hybrid storage either lack considering the asymmetric read/write performance of storage devices, or defect on weak scalability. These approaches are difficult to sufficiently satisfy requirements of real-time data process and hyper-large data volume put forwarded by big data.

This paper considers that data prefer to reside on device on which they can obtain higher access performance, and defines preference degree to weight the imbalance access performance between different devices. Then proposes a preference model to calculate preference degree of data according to read/write access frequency, and distributes data on device with highest preference degree. A Preference-Aware HDFS (PAHDFS) based on preference model is implemented, in which efficiency and scalability is also guaranteed.

The rest of this paper is organized as follows. Section 2 presents related works. Section 3 describes the preference model. In Sect. 4, we detail the design of PAHDFS. Section 5 demonstrates the effectiveness of PAHDFS versus HDFS through experiments. And finally Sect. 6 concludes the paper.

2   Related Work

Hadoop Distributed File system (HDFS) is widely used as storage platform of big data process systems such like Hadoop [5], SPARK [6]. But HDFS hasn't considered optimizing for new-type devices from the beginning of designation. With the falling down of price and strengthening of reliability, new-type devices such like Flash SSD are now widely used by data institutions [7–9]. For hybrid storage environment, HDFS just assumes all devices have the same performance, and consequently distributes data evenly across different storage devices only according to their free capacity. As a result, the superiority of new type devices can hardly be exploited. Although recent Hadoop 2.6 allows user manually specify storage type [10], but the configurable granularity is a whole file or directory, and data won't migrate to another device when needed. Consequently, the adapted HDFS can still hardly to take full advantage of new type storage devices under big data environment.

Besides, most policies of HDFS are designed to acceleration read access of large files. But recent researches reveals files as small as several KBs or MBs still account for a certain proportion according to big data load [11]. On another aspect, write requests also occupies a substantial proportion of data access due to some accelerate strategies (such like request merge, caching mechanisms) filtering a large extents of up-level read request [12], and some reliability strategies generating lots of log or backup files [13]. Then HDFS should be adapted to fit these features.

HatS [14] modifies of HDFS to improve efficiency of SSD. It constructs virtual Datanodes for each type of device by run multiple Datanode service threads, and reasonably distribute data across virtual Datanodes to effective utilize devices. But it needs extra manage APIs to distribute data and increases overhead of Namenode.

Literature [15] places SSD and HDD at the same level of storage tier, manages data at the granularity of page and distributes data according to the read/write frequency of page. Data of hot pages with read tender will be allocated to SSD and others allocated to HDD, asymmetric read/write characteristics of SSD and HDD is utilized to improve overall access performance. One defect of this approach is the accumulative recording method of access frequency can't precisely represent the real-time access characteristics when data load fluctuate frequently. Literature [16] proposes a time sensitive SSD and HDD and efficient hybrid storage model to resolve this problem. But these two approaches are all get I/O statistics to determine the data distribution based on pages. On the one hand, metadata will increase rapidly when data volume and memory capacity expand, which makes manage and search of metadata difficult, and can't satisfy the volume and real-time requirements of big data; On the other hand, it is difficult to mine data correlation between adjacent requests at page level which can be utilized to speed up storage performance. Thus these approaches are not suitable to directly apply to the HDFS.

Data management strategies based on access characteristics should efficiently utilize the read performance of SSD, and reduce write and erase operations of SSD with the aid of the Hard disk [17, 18]. I-CASH [19] composes SSD and disk in pairs, using intelligent algorithms to distinguish data with high read frequency but relative rare modify and distribute they on SSD. Modified data to SSD will be firstly stored in hard disk in the way of log to avoid random write to SSD. Read performance will greatly benefit from high random read performance of SSD and high compute ability of multi-core CPU. Hystor [20] implements a logical block device made up of HDD and SSD. Critical data are determined by access frequency and data size, and then stored on SSD. S4D-Cache [21] builds parallel file system respectively composed of HDD servers and file system composed of SSD servers. A cache module is run at client side to decide which file system to store according to data access characteristics.

HDFS lacks support of new-type devices such lick Flash SSD, and the existing researches either lack consideration of the asymmetric I/O performance of storage devices, or defect on weak scalability, therefore can hardly fully satisfy the requirements of real-time data process and hyper-large data volume put forwarded by big data. This paper proposed a preference model to thoroughly utilize storage device characteristics and distribute data on the most suitable device on which they can obtain best access performance. In addition, the implementation of PAHDFS is transparent for client and won't burden the load of Namenode, thus scalability can be guaranteed.

This paper proposed preference model and implements Preference-Aware HDFS for Hybrid Storage (PAHDFS). For hybrid environment composed of variety types of storage devices, PAHDFS tracks read/write characteristics of data, and analyses the most fitting device on which data can obtain best access performance according to device read and write ability of device. So access performance and resource utilization can be improved if data are placed on suitable devices. Beside, data size of access request is considered in preference model, and small files with high access frequency may have priority to store on high performance device such like SSD. So access of small files can also obtain good performance.

3 Preference Model

The volume of big data is usually very huge. But the real-time characteristic requires rapid analyzing and obtaining useful information from massive extent of data with low density of value. This puts forward higher requirements on storage performance and efficiency. Storage devices in hybrid storage environment have imbalance I/O performance, and the access characteristics of different types of data also wave violently. So, state-of-art data distribution and device management is a key issue for improving I/O performance and resource utilization efficiency.

Data prefer to reside on device on which they can obtain higher access performance. There's asymmetric read/write performance for storage devices, and asymmetric read/write access characteristics for data. Data may obtain different access performance on the same device due to access characteristics waving, and the most suitable device of data may also change at different time points. This paper defines preference degree to weight the imbalance access performance between different devices and proposes a preference model to calculate preference degree of data according to their read/write access frequency, then distributes data on device with highest preference degree to improve storage performance and efficiency.

Table 1. Parameters definition

Name	Description
B	Block$\{B_1, B_2, \ldots\}$ is the collection of Data Block
D	Dev$\{D_1, D_2, \ldots\}$ is collection of storage device
S	S_i is the size of Data Block B_i
FR	FR_i is the read frequency of B_i
FW	FW_i is the write frequency B_i
TR	$TR_m(i)$ is the transfer time of reading B_i once when it is distributed on D_m
TW	$TW_m(i)$ is the transfer time of writing B_i once when it is distributed on D_m
C	$C_m(i)$ is the overall cost access time of B_i containing all read and write operations when it is distributed on D_m
PR	PR_m is the read bandwidth of D_m
PW	PW_m is the write bandwidth of D_m
TS	TS_m is the average seek time of D_m
	(SSD has seek time of 0)

To facilitate description, some parameters used during calculating are defined as shown in Table 1.

3.1 Calculation of Preference Degree

The read/write bandwidth (PR, PW), seek time (TS) can be obtained by the performance parameters of device description.

Read time of Data block B_i when it is distributed on D_m is equal to read data transmission time plus seek time,

$$TR_m(i) = S_i/PR_m + TS_m \qquad (1)$$

Write time of Data block B_i when it is distributed on D_m is equal to write data transmission time plus seek time,

$$TW_m(i) = S_i/PW_m + TS_m \qquad (2)$$

The overall access time of Data block B_i on D_m is calculated as read frequency multiply by read time, plus write frequency multiply by write time,

$$C_m(i) = TR_m(i) * FR_i + TW_m(i) * FW_i \qquad (3)$$

If $C_m(I) < C_n(I)$, it indicates the access time of B_i on D_m is shorter, and B_i will get better access performance on D_m, so B_i prefers to resides on D_m. This paper defines the concept of preference degree, which indicates the imbalance access performance of data block when distributed on different devices: According devices D_m and D_n, preference degree of data block B_i to D_m is equal to B_i's Overall access time on D_n minus Overall access time on D_m,

$$P_{m,n}(i) = C_n(i) - C_m(i) \qquad (4)$$

The greater $P_{m,n}(I)$ is, the more block Bi prefers to be distributed on D_m.

If $P_{m,n}(I) > P_{m,n}(j) > 0$, then it implies data block B_i is more eager for being stored on D_m than B_j. For example, assuming a scene as shown in Fig. 1, device D_1 is Flash SSD (PR = 200 MB/s, PW = 125 MB/s, TS = 0 ms), There's only one free block on D_1. Device D_2 is hard disk (PR = 100 MB/s, PW = 100 MB/s, TS = 4 ms). Free blocks of D_2 are adequate. Two data blocks is to be distributed: B_1 (S_1 = 2 MB, FR_1 = 6, FW_1 = 0), B_2 (S_2 = 2 MB, FR_2 = 0, FW_2 = 8). Which block should be distributed on D_1? Calculate $C_1(1)$ = 60 ms, $C_2(1)$ = 144 ms, $C_1(2)$ = 128 ms, $C_2(2)$ = 192 ms, get $P_{1,2}(1)$ = 84 ms, $P_{1,2}(2)$ = 64 ms. Although the access frequency of B_2 is higher, but because the gap of B_2's access time between on D_1 and on D_2 is smaller, data block B_1 gets more priority to be distributed on Flash SSD then B_2.

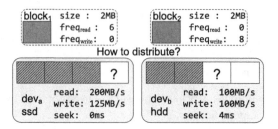

Fig. 1. An example of data distribution

According to access load of big data, files as small as several KBs or MBs still account for a certain proportion. To ensure access performance of small files with high access frequency is very important for guaranteeing overall system performance and improving data processing efficiency.

Substitution parameters of (4), then transform it to (5):

$$
\begin{aligned}
P_{m,n}(i) &= C_n(i) - C_m(i) \\
&= (TR_n - TR_m) * FR_i + (TW_n - TW_m) * FW_i \\
&= (S_i/PR_n + TS_n - S_i/PR_m - TS_m) * FR_i + (S_i/PW_n + TS_n - S_i/PW_m - TS_m) * FW_i \\
&= S_i * [(1/PR_n - 1/PR_m) * FR_i + (1/PW_n - 1/PW_m) * FW_i] + (TS_n - TS_m) * (FR_i + FW_i)
\end{aligned}
\tag{5}
$$

It can be seen from the formula (5) that data block with same access frequency but different size will get different preference degree. That is the bigger block will get larger preference degree. Therefore small files will get small preference degree even though they are frequently accessed, and can't be distributed on high performance devices. To resolve this problem, a correction factor u is used to justify preference degree according to file size,

$$
P_{m,n}(i) = [C_n(i) - C_m(i)] * 2^{u(i)}
\tag{6}
$$

$$
u(i) = \max\{0, 10 - \log_2 S_i\}
\tag{7}
$$

Similar to *reverse bitmap* of Hystor [20], transfer time of small files under 1 MB will be multiplied by the power of correction factor and amplified. And because the seek time (if exist) is also amplified, ultimately calculated preference degree will be larger than files with same access frequency but larges size. So small files with higher access frequency get higher priority to store on high performance devices.

3.2 Data Distribute Algorithm

With the rapid development of material and technology, many kinds of storage devices with different functions emerge in endlessly. For example, Flash SSD classified by interface can be divided into SATA interface, PCI interface, m-SATA interface, M2 interface, etc. The control chips of SSD from different vendors are also distinct. Substantially performance characteristics of these storage devices may vary widely. PAHDFS can precisely choose most effective device from a variety of storage devices for data to store based on preference model, thus improve access performance and resource utilization.

The following steps determine whether a data block is stored on the most suitable device, and whether the data block need to be migrated:

(1) For a data block B_i, according to statistics of read/write frequency obtained by monitor module, calculate it overall access time on each device $C_1(I)$, $C_2(I)$, ...;

(2) assume the minimum access time is obtained on D_{x1}, second on D_{x2}, so on;

Assume block is now distributed on device D_{xm}, if m! = x1, then Bi is not distributed on device with shortest access time, further step is needed to determine whether migration should be taken; Otherwise if m = x1, do not need to take migration, stop.

(3) determine whether B_i can be migrated to D_{x1},

Access characteristics of data may fluctuate over time, if take migrate just at once when discovered access time of B_i on device xm is not the shortest, possibly xm becomes the device with shortest access time after migration completed, then block needs to be migrated again. As a result, overwhelm migrations will cause severe performance shocking, and a large number of resources are occupied by frequent data migration. To avoid this problem, PAHDFS admit data block B_i to migrate from D_{xm} to D_{xi} only when the following two conditions are satisfied at the same time:

(a) The benefit of migration exceed its overhead,

$$P_{xi,xm} > T_{move}$$

It takes time to complete migration, and data access will be affected during migration process. So PAHDFS requires when B_i's preference degree to D_{x1} greater than the migration time, that is the reduced access time after the migration should exceed time cost by migration.

(b) Preference degree of Bi from D_{xi+1} to D_{xi} ($P_{xi, xi+1}(i)$) should exceed the admittance threshold $Slimit_{xi}$ of D_{xi}, migration shouldn't pull block with higher preference degree out of the target device,

$$P_{xi,xi+1} > Slimit_{xi}$$
$$Slimit_{xi} = 0, D_x utility < threshould$$
$$= L, D_x utility >= threshould$$
$$L = min \left\{ P_{x,x+1}(1), P_{x,x+1}(2), ... \right\} * Increment$$

(Assumimg Block $\{B_1, B_2, ...\}$ is the collection of blocks distributed on the target device, Thred C_x is a capacity threshold indicate whether D_x is nearly out of use determined by experience. Increment is a value also determined by experience)

(4) If B_i can be migrated to D_{x1}, then perform migration; if not, go back to step (3) and determine whether it can be migrated to D_{x2}, in turn, determine D_{x3}, D_{x4}, …

Although only two kinds of devices are used during evaluation, the preference model and distribution algorithm is capable of managing variety storage devices.

Preference model firstly distribute data on device on which it can obtain highest access performance. Then if free capacity of a device if inadequate, data which can get most performance growth will be selected to distribute on the device. And an admittance threshold is set to avoid overwhelm migrations cause by access characteristics fluctuation. Hence PAHDFS can distribute data on suitable devices and provides high access performance for hybrid environment in which data access characteristics is fluctuate in endless.

4   Implementation of PAHDFS

As shown in Fig. 2, PAHDFS monitors data blocks operation from Clients and Namenode on Datanode. The monitor module obtains read and write frequencies of data blocks, then the preference degree is calculated by preference model introduced in Sect. 3. Finally, the transform module moves data to device in which data can obtain best access performance. As Datanode proceeds most of works, and Datanode only reports storage device type of blocks to Namenode after transform accomplished, the overhead of Namenode won't be aggravated. Moreover, Datanode provides the same APIs to Clients as HDFS. This architecture is easy scalable and compatible.

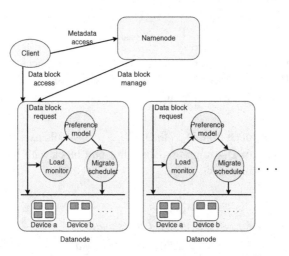

Fig. 2. Architecture of PAHDFS

PAHDFS monitors read and write access frequency of data blocks on Datanode. These statistics are stored in hash table inside memory and periodically flushed to disk. Due to data access characterize fluctuates over time, the preference degree to each device may also dynamic change. Preference model should be sensitive to aware this fluctuation and react quickly. The current approach is to periodically attenuate historical statistics by an attenuation factor. As re-access time window of data is usually long and waves by different big data load (from several minutes to several hours), attenuation factor is adjusted according to specific data load.

When a block is migrated, firstly create a new copy of the block on target device, then modify the block address map table of Datanode, and finally delete the origin block. Read access of block can still process during migration, read requests will be redirected to the new device after migration completed. But write requests will be blocked waiting for migration completion to ensure data consistency.

5 Experiments

5.1 Experiments Platform

Our experiment cluster consists of 1 Namenode and 12 DataNodes. All nodes have two 2.00 GHz Intel Xeon E5-2620 CPU, 16 GB main memory. The storage of each node contains a 600 GB Seagate Savvio 10 K.6 hard drive and a 120 GB Kingston v300 SSD, their detailed specifications are listed in Table 2. Both HDDs and SSDs are connected through an LSI MegaRaid 2108 SAS card. All nodes are connected by 10 GBps Infiniband network. The operating system is RedHat Enterprise 5.0 with Kernel 2.6.18.

Table 2. Specifications of HDD and SSD

	Seagate HDD	Kingston SSD
Capacity	120 GB	600 GB
Interface	SAS	SAS
Read bandwidth	125 MB/s	190 MB/s
Write bandwidth	125 MB/s	130 MB/s

5.2 File Access Performance Test

We design a test tool adapted from HDFS benchmark TestDFSIO to test the file access performance of PAHDFS. This tool can randomly select some files to get higher access frequency rather than TestDFSIO access files with the same probability. So that hot files will randomly appear. In general, the larger the SSD size is, the better the PAHDFS's performance is. We constrained the SSD space in 8 GB to avoid overestimating the performance improvement. To eliminate the influence of memory cache, the available memory of Datanode is restricted in 1 GB.

(1) Read test

Read performance is respectively tested when using different file sizes and the results are shown in Fig. 3. It can be seem PAHDFS obtains higher read throughput than HDFS. When file size is 256 KB, the read throughput of HDFS is 748 MB/s, and read throughput of PAHDFS is 1005 MB/s, improves by 34.4 %; when file size is 1 MB, the read throughput of HDFS is 888 MB/s, and read throughput of PAHDFS is 1663 MB/s, improves by 87.3 %. Because PAHDFS distributes data with high read frequency on SSD, while HDFS ignores the performance gap between SSD and HDD and distributes data evenly across SSD and HDFS. When file size exceeds 16 MB/s, PAHDFS not so superior than HDFS, this is because the read performance gap narrows for continuous big block access. The advantage of PAHDFS at file size of 256 KB is not so obvious than at 1 MB and 4 MB. The reason is client should get metadata from Namenode before get data from Datanode, and communication overhead takes a large amount of the access time of small file.

(2) Write test

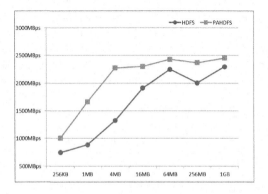

Fig. 3. Result of read test

Figure 4 shows the results of write performance respectively tested when using different file sizes. It can be seem the disparity between PAHDFS and HDFS is not very clear. When file size is 256 KB, the write throughput of HDFS is 403 MB/s, and write throughput of PAHDFS is 448 MB/s, improves by 11.1 %; when file size is 1 MB, the write throughput of HDFS is 872 MB/s, and write throughput of PAHDFS is 1008 MB/s, improves by 15.6 %; when file size exceeds 4 MB, the difference between PAHDFS an HDFS becomes unremarkable. This is because the gap of continuous write performance between the SSD and HDD used during test is not very obvious. Data distribution of PAHDFS and HDFS is quite similar. But on the other side, for small files SSD has relative higher write performance than HDD as it doesn't contain seek time. And the preference model of PAHDFS gives more priority for small files to store on SSD by amplify their preference degree. Consequently PAHDFS has better write performance when file size is small. The reason PAHFS's superiority not very clear is similarly to read experiment, that is because communication overhead takes a large amount of the access time of small file.

(3) Mixed read and write test

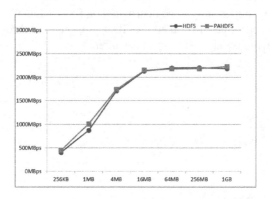

Fig. 4. Result of write test

Performance when read and write are mixed is also tested. Situations read has the proportion of 25 %, 50 %, 75 % are respectively tested. Figure 5 shows the results when read proportion is 25 %. The performance of PAHDFS and HDFS is close. Because write is the dominative operation during test and SSD write has slight impact to SSD read, the test results is very similar to write test in 5.3. It can be clearly seem PAHDFS has more competitive performance than HDFS. When file size is 256 KB, the overall throughput of HDFS is 559 MB/s, and read throughput of PAHDFS is 573 MB/s, improves by 2.5 %; when file size is 1 MB, the read throughput of HDFS is 1107 MB/s, and read throughput of PAHDFS is 1152 MB/s, and improves by 4.0 %.

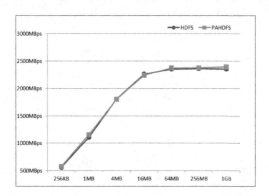

Fig. 5. Result of mixed read and write test (25 %READ)

The results when read proportion is 50 % are showed in Fig. 6. It can be seen PAHDFS has more competitive performance than HDFS. When file size is 256 KB, the overall throughput of HDFS is 630 MB/s, and read throughput of PAHDFS is 810 MB/s, improves by 28.6 %; when file size is 1 MB, the read throughput of HDFS is 1184 MB/

s, and read throughput of PAHDFS is 1624 MB/s, and improves by 37.2 %. The reason can be explained as follows. For the SSD and HDD used during test, the read performance gap is far greater than write performance gap. In PAHDFS, files with high read frequency have more opportunity to be distributed on SSD, while files with high write frequency are inclined to be distributed on HDD. So, the read throughput is greatly improved and the write throughput hasn't been affect.

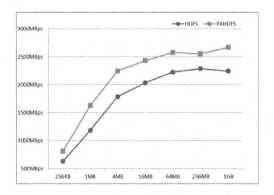

Fig. 6. Result of mixed read and write test (50 %READ)

As shown in Fig. 7, when read proportion increases to 75 %, PAHDFS gains further more priority than HDFS. When file size is 256 KB, the overall throughput of HDFS is 70 MB/s, and read throughput of PAHDFS is 975 MB/s, improves by 38.2 %; when file size is 1 MB, the read throughput of HDFS is 1064 MB/s, and read throughput of PAHDFS is 1816 MB/s, and improves by 70.6 %. As the proportion of read increases, the PAHDFS's profit gained by warranting files with high read frequency have more opportunity to be distributed on SSD is further amplified.

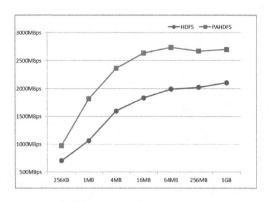

Fig. 7. Result of mixed read and write test (75 %READ)

5.3 Wordcount and Grep

To examine the performance under reality workload, we use *datagenerator* of BigDa-taBench [22] to generate 45 GB wiki data sets, and execute *wordcount* and *grep* on the generated data. The execute time is showed in Fig. 8. For *wordcount*, the execute time of PAHDFS is 750 s which 12.6 % faster than HDFS's 858 s. The improvement seems not very obviously. We consider the reason is there're a lots of write operations, network transfer and computing during wordcount, and the superiority of SSD read is covered. For grep test in which read may take larger amount, PAHDFS takes more advantage. Its execute time is 192 s and 30.4 % than HDFS's 276 s.

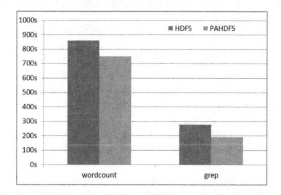

Fig. 8. Comparison of execute time

6   Conclusion

This paper raises that data have their preference to storage devices, and data prefer to reside on devices which most compatible to access characteristics and can provide best access performance. A preference model for data distribution is proposed. Preference degree is defined to weight the imbalance access performance between different devices. Then data are distributed to device with highest preference degree and obtain high access performance. This paper designs and implements PAHDFS (Preference-Aware HDFS), an improved HDFS sufficiently utilizing new-type storage devices to boost big data access and process based on preference model. Also, small files with high access frequency are given priority to distribute on of new type storage devices such as Flash SSDS to improve access efficiency of the whole system. Besides, interfaces maintains the same as original HDFS which users can transparently access as before, and scalability can be guaranteed as there won't be load burden put forwarded to Namenode. Experiments results show that compared to HDFS, PAHDFS's read throughput improves maximum by 87.3 %, write throughput improves maximum by 15.6 %, mixed read and write throughput improves maximum by 70.6 %.

Acknowledgments. This work is supported by National Basic Research 973 Program of China under Grant No. 2011CB302301, National University's Special Research Fee No. 2015XJGH010, NSFC No. 61173043.

References

1. Chen, S, Gibbons, P, Nath, S.: Rethinking database algorithms for phase change memory. In: 5th Biennial Conference on Innovative Data Systems Research (CIDR), pp. 21–31. Asilomar, California, USA (2011)
2. Gao, S., Xu, J.-L., He, B., et al.: PCMLogging: reducing transaction logging overhead with PCM. In: 20th Conference on Information and Knowledge Management (CIKM), pp. 2401–2404. Glasgow, Scotland, UK (2011)
3. Sun, G.-Y., Joo Y, Chen Y-B, Niu D-M, et al.: A Hybrid solid-state storage architecture for the performance, energy consumption, and-lifetime-improvement. In: 16th International Conference on High-Performance Computer Architecture (HPCA), pp. 1–12. Bangalore, India (2010)
4. HDFS Architecture Guide. http://hadoop.apache.org/docs/r1.0.4/hdfs_design.html
5. Apache Hadoop. http://hadoop.apache.org
6. Apache Spark. https://spark.apache.org
7. Chen, S.: FlashLogging: exploiting flash devices for synchronous logging performance. In: 35th SIGMOD International Conference on Management of Data, pp. 73–86. Rhode Island, USA (2009)
8. Lv, Y., Li, J., Cui, B., Chen, X.: Log-compact R-tree: an efficient spatial index for SSD. In: 16th International Conference on Database Systems for Advanced Applications, pp. 202–213. Hong Kong, China (2011)
9. Kang, W.-H., Lee, S.-W., Moon, B.: Flash-based extended cache for higher throughput and faster recovery. Proc. VLDB Endowment 5(11), 1615–1626 (2012)
10. HDFS-2832. https://issues.apache.org/jira/browse/HDFS-2832
11. Harter, T., Dragga, C., Vaughn, M., et al.: A file is not a file: understanding the I/O behavior of apple desktop applications. In: 23rd ACM Symposium on Operating Systems Principles (SOSP), Cascais, Portugal (2011)
12. Chen, Y., Srinivasan, K., Goodson, G., Katz, R.: Design implications for enterprise storage systems via multi-dimensional trace analysis. In: 23rd ACM Symposium on Operating Systems Principles (SOSP), pp. 43–56. Cascais, Portugal (2011)
13. Chen, Y., Alspaugh, S., Katz, R.: Interactive analytical processing in big data systems: a cross-industry study of mapreduce workloads. Proc. VLDB Endowment 5(12), 1802–1813 (2012)
14. Krish, K.R., Anwar, A, Butt, A.R.: hatS: a heterogeneity-aware tiered storage for Hadoop. In: 14th IEEE/ACM International Symposium on Cluster, Cloud and Grid Computing (CCGrid), pp. 502–511. Chicago, Illinois, USA (2014)
15. Ioannis, K., Stratis, V.: Flashing up the storage layer. Proc. VLDB Endowment 1(1), 514–525 (2008)
16. Yang, P.-Y., Jin, P.-Q., Yue, L.-H.: A time-sensitive and efficient hybrid storage model involving SSD and HDD. Chin. J. Comput. 35(11), 2294–2305 (2012)
17. Soundararajan, G., Prabhakaran, V., Balakrishnan, M., Wobber, T.: Extending SSD lifetimes with disk-based write caches. In: 8th USENIX Conference on File and Storage Technologies (FAST), Berkeley, USA (2010)

18. Lu, Y., Shu, J., Zheng, W.: Extending the lifetime of flash-based storage through reducing write amplification from file systems. In: 11th Conference on File and Storage Technologies (FAST), pp. 257–270. San, CA (2013)
19. Yang, Q., Ren, J.: I-CASH: intelligently coupled array of SSD and HDD. In: 17th International Conference on High-Performance Computer Architecture (HPCA), pp. 278–289. San Antonio, Texas (2011)
20. Chen, F., Koufaty, D., Zhang, X.: Hystor: making the best use of solid state drives in high performance storage systems. In: 25th International Conference on Supercomputing, pp. 22–32. Tuscon, Arizona, USA (2011)
21. He, S., Sun, X.-H., Feng, B.: S4D-cache: smart selective SSD cache for parallel I/O systems. In: 34th IEEE International Conference on Distributed Computing Systems (ICDCS), pp. 514–523. IEEE Press, Madrid, Spain (2014)
22. Wang, L., Zhan, J., Luo, C., et al.: BigDataBench: a big data benchmark suite from internet services. In: 20th IEEE International Symposium on High Performance Computer Architecture (HPCA), pp. 488–499. Orlando, Florida, USA (2014)

Urban Traffic Congestion Prediction Using Floating Car Trajectory Data

Qiuyuan Yang[1], Jinzhong Wang[1], Ximeng Song[1],
Xiangjie Kong[1,2,3(✉)], Zhenzhen Xu[1], and Benshi Zhang[1]

[1] School of Software, Dalian University of Technology,
Dalian 116620, China
xjkong@ieee.org
[2] Key Laboratory of System Control and Information Processing,
Ministry of Education, Shanghai 200240, China
[3] Key Laboratory of Control Engineering of Henan Province,
Henan Polytechnic University, Jiaozuo 454000, China

Abstract. Traffic congestion prediction is an important precondition to promote urban sustainable development. Nevertheless, there is a lack of a unified prediction method to address the performance metrics, such as accuracy, instantaneity and stability, systematically. In the paper, we propose a novel approach to predict the urban traffic congestion efficiently with floating car trajectory data. Specially, an innovative traffic flow prediction method utilizing particle swarm optimization algorithm is responsible for calculating the traffic flow parameters. Then, a congestion state fuzzy division module is applied to convert the predicted flow parameters to citizens' cognitive congestion states. We conduct extensive experiments with real floating car data and the experimental results show that our proposed method has advantage in terms of accuracy, instantaneity and stability.

Keywords: Floating car · Particle swarm optimization · Traffic congestion prediction · Traffic flow prediction · Fuzzy comprehensive evaluation

1 Introduction

Urban traffic congestion has become a critical problem that not only reduces residents' life quality, but also restricts the sustainable development of society and economy [1, 2]. Nevertheless, urban traffic flow is complex and constantly changing, which is difficult to acquire the current and future traffic conditions. Especially, there are two major challenges that should be answered to perform urban traffic congestion prediction. Firstly, how to predict traffic congestion in large-scale urban areas? Secondly, how to improve the accuracy, instantaneity and stability of traffic congestion prediction simultaneously?

Fortunately, floating car, namely Global Position System (GPS)-equipped taxi, is an effective way to collect the real-time traffic data in a large-scale road network [3]. In addition, these ubiquitous mobile sensors have lower cost than the fixed sensors which collect data at fixed trunks or major intersections. From this point, we propose a novel method using floating car trajectory data to improve the overall performance of traffic congestion prediction.

© Springer International Publishing Switzerland 2015
G. Wang et al. (Eds.): ICA3PP 2015, Part II, LNCS 9529, pp. 18–30, 2015.
DOI: 10.1007/978-3-319-27122-4_2

The proposed method includes Traffic Flow Prediction (TFP) and Congestion State Fuzzy Division (CSFD) modules. The former predict traffic flow parameters by using Particle Swarm Optimization (PSO) algorithm. The latter converts the predicted traffic flow parameters to citizens' cognitive congestion state using a Fuzzy Comprehensive Evaluation (FCE) method. Furthermore, TFP module is composed by three sub modules: Traffic Volume Prediction (TVP), Traffic Speed Prediction (TSP) and PSO. TVP sub module predicts the traffic volume, while TSP sub module is for predicting average speed. PSO sub module optimizes the punish coefficients and the multi-kernel functions' parameters of Support Vector Machine (SVM) in TVP and TSP sub modules. The reason for choosing PSO algorithm is that it can get the optimum solution in a short time with a low computing complexity which meets the performance requirements of congestion prediction in terms of accuracy, instantaneity and stability.

The rest of this paper is organized as follows. In Sect. 2, we present related works about urban traffic congestion prediction. Then, our proposed congestion prediction method is introduced in Sect. 3. In Sect. 4, experiment results are described. Finally, the paper is concluded in Sect. 5.

2 Related Work

Kong et al. [4] presented a systematic solution to efficiently predict traffic state by extracting the spatio-temporal average velocity from a large number of GPS probe vehicles. The method was based on a curve-fitting and vehicle-tracking mechanism. In order to improve the estimation accuracy, they calculated mean speed at road section from multi-source traffic data to estimate the traffic states [5]. Zhang et al. [6] proposed a weighted approach to estimate traffic state using GPS data by increasing the weights of recent velocity information. Li et al. [7] presented a hybrid learning framework to appropriately combine estimation results of freeway traffic density state from multiple macroscopic traffic flow models. Feng et al. [8] proposed a cooperative approach to estimate arterial travel time states including Bayesian and Expectation Maximization algorithms using GPS probe data. Shankar et al. [9] explored advantages of fuzzy inference systems to evaluate the level of road traffic congestion using traffic density and speed information.

Related to traffic flow and congestion prediction, Xu et al. [10] presented a spati-temporal variable selection method based on Support Vector Regression (SVR) model to predict traffic volume. In this method, the spatial and temporal information of all available road segments was taken into account. Hong et al. [11] presented a SVR traffic flow forecasting model using Gaussian Radial Basis Function (RBF) kernel. In this method, a hybrid Genetic Algorithm (GA) with Simulated Annealing is used to forecast the RBF suitable parameters accurately. Li et al. [12] applied SVR model with Gauss loss function (Gauss-SVR) to forecast urban traffic flow and they proposed a Chaotic Cloud Particle Swarm Optimization algorithm to optimize the parameters of Gauss-SVR model. Wang and Shi [13] proposed a traffic speed forecasting model using chaos–wavelet analysis and SVM to choose the appropriate kernel function. Wang et al. [14] proved that selecting the appropriate SVR parameters improve the prediction of traffic flow in terms of the instantaneity and accuracy performance metrics.

The discussed methods above only considered one kernel function of SVM to improve the accuracy of urban traffic state prediction, while the road traffic congestion cannot be predicted by these methods accurately. The reason is that various SVM kernel functions have different prediction accuracy and adaptability. In addition, the predicted traffic flow cannot intuitively forecast the future traffic congestion for travelers and traffic administrators. To tackle these shortcomings, Chen et al. [15] proposed an accurate particle filter method to predict multi-step traffic state using speed measurements. Similarly, Dunne and Ghosh [16] proposed a regime-based multivariate traffic condition prediction method using an Artificial Neural Network (ANN) structure with adaptive learning strategies. Min and Wynter [17] presented a scalable multivariate spatial-temporal autoregressive model to predict the traffic volume and speed jointly. Zhang et al. [18] proposed a robust traffic congestion prediction method based on hierarchical fuzzy rule-based systems and GA, which combines the variable selection, ranking and lateral tuning of the membership functions with optimization of the rule base.

Closely related to traffic congestion estimation and prediction, Herring et al. [19] proposed two statistical learning algorithms which uses data from GPS-equipped smart phones. In this method, logistic regression and spatio-temporal auto regressive moving average models are employed to estimate and forecast the arterial traffic conditions. Castro et al. [20] proposed a method to construct a model of traffic density based on large scale taxi traces, and used the model to predict future traffic conditions according to the probabilistic transition matrix. To conduct a comprehensive and accurate traffic flow analysis, Zhou et al. [21] proposed a traffic condition estimation and prediction method based on Least Squares Support Vector Machine (LS-SVM) classification and regression using the floating car data.

The above-mentioned methods have not considered the traffic capacity as well as the spatial information of the roads. In addition, most of them only have considered one single performance metric and there is a lack of a systematic method to address accuracy, instantaneity and stability at the same time. In order to tackle this issue, we propose a new method to predict traffic congestion to improve the three performance metrics simultaneously. In the next section, we will describe our proposed method in detail.

3 Traffic Congestion Prediction

In this section, we describe the proposed congestion prediction method, which includes TFP and CSFD modules. TFP module is used to predict the traffic flow parameters and consists of TVP, TSP, and PSO sub modules. TVP sub module is used for predicting traffic volume, while TSP sub module is used for predicting average traffic speed. And PSO sub module is applied to optimize the punish coefficients and the parameters of the multi-kernel functions of SVM in TVP and TSP. Furthermore, CSFD modules converts the predicted traffic flow parameters to citizens' cognitive state with the help of FCE method.

In our method, SVM and PSO algorithms are chosen as optimization methods. This is because SVM has effective nonlinear mapping and generalization abilities, and SVM can solve small sample, over learning and local minimum problems, while PSO is a heuristic algorithm that has an advantage in search speed and stability. Our method can benefit from these excellent features.

3.1   The TFP Module

TFP module includes TVP, TSP, and PSO sub modules. In TVP and TSP sub modules, we use LIBSVM library [22] to calculate ε-Support Vector Regression (ε-SVR). The regression function for prediction is calculated using Eq. (1) as follows:

$$y = f(x) = \sum_{i=1}^{N} \left(a_i - a_i^*\right) K(x_i, x) + b \tag{1}$$

where a_i, a_i^* are the Lagrange multipliers related to punish coefficient c. $K(x_i, x)$ is the kernel function, and b is the bias.

In addition, we use linear in Eq. (2), and radial basis function (RBF) in Eq. (3) as the kernel function $K(x_i, x)$ of Eq. (1) respectively.

$$K(x_i, x) = (x_i \times x) \tag{2}$$

$$K(x_i, x) = \exp\left(-\frac{\|x_i - x\|^2}{2\sigma^2}\right) \tag{3}$$

Most of the existing congestion prediction methods such as [10–14] only consider one kernel function: linear, polynomial, or RBF. Different from these methods, our proposed TFP module considers multiple kernel functions since different kernel functions have different prediction accuracies and fitting abilities.

The TVP Sub Module. Assuming that the current time is denoted by t, we aim to predict the traffic volume of time $t + 1$ at some road sections. The input variables include six parameters AS_{t-2}, AS_{t-1}, AS_t, Vol_{t-2}, Vol_{t-1}, Vol_t and the output variable is Vol_{t+1}. Among these, AS_i indicates the average speed of time i, and Vol_i indicates the traffic volume of time i. Then, the TVP model is trained considering the punish coefficient c and multiple kernel functions. At last, the TVP model is tested using the real floating car data.

The TSP Sub Module. Training and testing methods in TSP sub module are similar to those in TVP sub module, except that the input variables in TSP include Vol_{t-2}, Vol_{t-1}, Vol_t, AS_{t-2}, AS_{t-1}, AS_t and the output variable is AS_{t+1}.

The PSO Sub Module. In this module, we aim to optimize the punish coefficient c and multiple kernel functions based on kernel parameters of the SVM model in TVP and TSP sub module.

- Firstly, we determine the parameters of PSO algorithm such as maximum evolution number, maximum population number, cross validation number, the range of punish coefficient c, the corresponding kernel parameter kp of the selected kernel function, the position and speed of the particle swarm, etc. In this module, the parameters c and kp are selected as the position of the particle swarm.
- Secondly, the parameters c and kp of the current particle are selected as *pbest*, and the optimal value of all particles as *gbest*. Then, the fitness function value is identified in order to construct and update the position and speed using Eqs. (4) and (5) [23] as follows.

$$v_i(t+1) = \omega \times v_i(t) + c_1 \times r_1 \times (p_{best} - x_i(t))$$
$$+ c_2 \times r_2 \times (g_{best} - x_i(t)) \quad\quad (4)$$

$$x_i(t+1) = x_i(t) + v_i(t+1) \quad\quad (5)$$

- Thirdly, if *pvalue* is better than *pbest*, set *pbest = pvalue*.
- Fourthly, if *gvalue* is better than *gbest*, set *gbest = gvalue*.
- Finally, if the evolution number reaches the maximum value, the optimization stops. Otherwise, the procedure returns to the second step.

After PSO optimizes the parameters of SVM in TVP and TSP sub modules, it transmits the parameters back to TVP and TSP. Then, the traffic volume and average traffic speed are predicted in case different kernel functions are selected in the SVM model. We compare the predicted traffic volume in the case of different kernel functions in the SVM model of TVP and select the best result with minimum error. The TSP sub module follows the same process to obtain the best result. In addition, the corresponding kernel parameters in the SVM improve the prediction accuracy and ensure the real-time performance.

3.2   The CSFD Module

We calculate traffic volume and average traffic speed values using TFP which we have introduced in the preceding section. However, the congestion state fuzzy division cannot be performed directly since the predicted parameters do not characterize the traffic congestion state accurately. Considering the length, the lane number of the road section and traffic volume, we calculate the traffic density. Then, the road saturation is calculated using traffic capacity and traffic volume. Finally, congestion state division is applied with the following FCE method using road saturation, traffic density, and average traffic speed.

Traffic Congestion Factor and Evaluation Sets. The traffic congestion factor sets are expressed as $U = \{u_1, u_2, u_3\}$ corresponding to the road saturation, traffic density, and traffic speed. The evaluation sets are also expressed as $V = \{v_1, v_2, v_3, v_4, v_5\}$ corresponding to 'very smooth', 'smooth', 'mild congestion', 'moderate congestion' and 'serious congestion'. Moreover, we denote that $u_1(or\ u_2) \rightarrow \{v_1, v_2, v_3, v_4, v_5\}$ and $u_3 \rightarrow \{v_5, v_4, v_3, v_2, v_1\}$, which mean that the smaller road saturation (or traffic density) indicates the lighter traffic congestion, while the smaller road section average speed indicates more serious traffic congestion.

Determining Weights of the Evaluation Factors. The weights of each evaluation factor is expressed as $W_a = \{w_1, w_2, w_3\}$ and $W_b = \{w_4, w_5, w_6\}$.

Performing the Single Factor Fuzzy Evaluation. For the i_{th} factor in factor set U, we get the membership r_{ij} of the j_{th} evaluation in evaluation set V through the trapezoidal membership function. The single factor fuzzy evaluation set is expressed as $R_i = \{r_{i1}, r_{i2}, r_{i3}, r_{i4}, r_{i5}\}$ in Eq. (6).

$$R = \begin{pmatrix} R_1 \\ R_2 \\ R_3 \end{pmatrix} = \begin{pmatrix} r_{11} & r_{12} & r_{13} & r_{14} & r_{15} \\ r_{21} & r_{22} & r_{23} & r_{24} & r_{25} \\ r_{31} & r_{32} & r_{33} & r_{34} & r_{35} \end{pmatrix} \tag{6}$$

Performing the Fuzzy Comprehensive Evaluation. After identifying the weights and performing the single factor fuzzy evaluation, the fuzzy comprehensive evaluation matrix B is calculated using a fuzzy transformation based on Eqs. (7) and (8) as follows:

$$B = W \circ R = W \circ \begin{pmatrix} r_{11} & r_{12} & r_{13} & r_{14} & r_{15} \\ r_{21} & r_{22} & r_{23} & r_{24} & r_{25} \\ r_{31} & r_{32} & r_{33} & r_{34} & r_{35} \end{pmatrix}$$
$$= (b_1, b_2, b_3, b_4, b_5) \tag{7}$$

$$b_j = \sum_{i=1}^{n} w_i \times r_{ij}, \quad i = 1, 2, \ldots, 6, \quad j = 1, 2, \ldots, 5 \tag{8}$$

where $\circ$ is the fuzzy compositional operation and b_j is the fuzzy comprehensive evaluation index which means the membership of the jth factor of the evaluation object.

Determining the Traffic Congestion State. Based on the maximum membership principle, the biggest membership b_j is calculated as the final evaluation index b, namely traffic congestion state, as follows.

$$b = \max(b_1, b_2, b_3, \ldots, b_5) \tag{9}$$

4   Experiment and Discussion

4.1   The Floating Car Data

The floating car data are the real traffic GPS data collected by 12,000 taxis in Beijing China over a period of one month (November 2012) [24]. The traffic data are recorded once per minute approximately. The format of a GPS data is showed in Fig. 1.

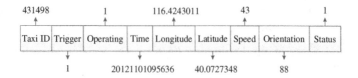

Fig. 1. Data format of a GPS data entry.

In experiments, we select a road section from Lian Hua Qiao to Liu Li Qiao at third ring near Beijing west railway station as the research area, of which exists seriously recurrent traffic congestion. We first preprocess the data in order to eliminate noisy sample points, of which perceived positions are chaotic. In the second step, the sample points with the same vehicle ID are linked to each other according to their time correlate on. Then, we capture the floating car trajectories on the urban road network space. In the next step, map matching is carried out according to the floating car trajectories, the latitude and longitude of the vehicles, and the urban geographic information. Finally, the traffic flow parameters are extracted in five minutes.

The traffic flow parameters include the traffic volume and traffic speed. The traffic volume is equal to the floating car number divided by a floating car detection ratio. The floating car detection ratio equals the total number of floating cars divided by the total number of vehicles on the road. Based on the annual report of Beijing traffic development in 2012 [25], the floating car detection ratio is 19 %. The traffic speed is equal to the average speed of floating car in five minutes. The average speed of each floating car trajectory can be acquired by GPS sample points.

4.2   Performance Indexes

We consider the performance indexes from the TFP and CSFD modules, which include the traffic flow prediction and congestion state division indexes. These concepts are identified in the rest of this subsection.

Traffic Flow Prediction Indexes. The prediction accuracy indexes include mean absolute error (*maerr*) and mean absolute relative error (*mareer*) as shown in Eqs. (10) and (11):

$$maerr = \frac{1}{N} \sum_{t=1}^{N} |P_{redict}(t) - R_{eal}(t)| \tag{10}$$

$$marerr = \frac{1}{N} \sum_{t=1}^{N} \frac{|P_{redict}(t) - R_{eal}(t)|}{R_{eal}(t)} \tag{11}$$

where P_{redict} denotes the predicted value and R_{eal} denotes the real value.

The real-time performance indexes include the time for training model and traffic flow prediction (*tptime*). The stability performance indexes are related to the process of the punish coefficient selection and the prediction accuracy.

Congestion State Division Indexes. The congestion state prediction accuracy is given by the formula that the prediction congestion states divide by the real congestion state. The real-time performance indexes include the time to perform congestion state division.

4.3   Traffic Flow Prediction

Through estimating the traffic congestion, we aim to induce travel cost and prevent congestion from further spreading. To this target, a congestion prediction method is applied, which includes the traffic flow prediction and the congestion state fuzzy division. Thus, we do experiments from these two aspects.

The traffic volume and traffic speed prediction results are explored in our experiments. We compare the results of prediction with different optimization techniques. Specifically, PSO optimization method is used in the RBF kernel function (PSO-R), as well as the linear kernel function (PSO-L) of SVM. In addition, GA optimization method is used in the RBF kernel function (GA-R), as well as the linear kernel function (GA-L) of SVM.

In order to evaluate the performance of PSO and GA optimization methods, their common parameters are set as follows: the maximum evolution number is 100, the maximum population number is 20, the cross validation number of SVM is 3, punish coefficient c is [0.1, 100], RBF kernel parameter is [0.01, 1000]. Moreover, the crossover probability and mutation probability of GA are set to 0.4 and 0.01, respectively.

We compare PSO-R, PSO-L, GA-R, and GA-L methods in terms of four evaluation metrics called *maserr*, *marerr*, *tptime* and stability, respectively. The evaluation results

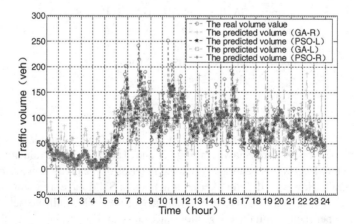

Fig. 2. Comparison among the real traffic volume and prediction results of proposed method with different optimization techniques.

Table 1. Performance comparison among different optimization techniques of proposed method about traffic volume prediction

Metrics	GA_R	PSO_L	GA_L	PSO_R
maerr	37.9212	22.2051	22.2027	21.5979
marerr	1.0464	0.5472	0.5476	0.5370
tptime	1.108 s	1.794 s	1.529 s	0.265 s
c, σ	0.18, 8.2	100, 0.1	91.84	100
Stability	No	Yes	No	Yes

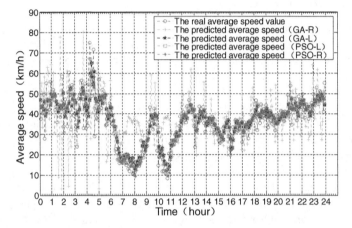

Fig. 3. Comparison among the real average speed and prediction results of proposed method with different optimization techniques.

Table 2. Performance comparison among different optimization techniques of proposed method about average speed prediction

Metrics	GA_R	PSO_L	GA_L	PSO_R
maerr	9.92	4.87	4.86	4.74
marerr	0.36	0.15	0.15	0.14
tptime	2.136 s	1.056 s	2.036 s	0.171 s
c, σ	91.4, 35.2	40.99	100	100, 0.1
Stability	No	No	Yes	Yes

for the traffic volume prediction are shown in Fig. 2 and Table 1. Similarly, the traffic speed prediction results are shown in Fig. 3 and Table 2. The evaluation results demonstrate that PSO-R has better performance in terms of the prediction accuracy and stability metrics. However, different kernel functions in SVM have different prediction accuracies and fitting abilities. We take advantages of the SVM multi-kernel functions to carry out experiments with the congestion state fuzzy division in the next subsection.

4.4 Congestion State Prediction

From the previous subsection, we can acquire the predicted traffic volume and average speed. Then, considering the length and lane number of road section as well as the traffic volume, the traffic density can be acquired with the help of Google Earth. The experiment area is 1.127 km^2 with 8 lanes. The road saturation can also be calculated using the traffic capacity and traffic volume. We acquire the traffic capacity from China highway capacity manual, which defines that the maximum traffic capacity of multi-lane highway designed with 80 km/h is 1800 pcu/h/lane. In other words, the maximum traffic capacity of the explored road in this paper is 150 pcu/5 min/lane. At last, the congestion state division in our proposed FCE method is performed using the road saturation, the traffic density, and the traffic average speed. Accordingly, the weight sets are assigned as $W_a = [0.43, 0.27, 0.3]$ and $W_b = [0.23, 0.17, 0.6]$.

In this step, we present our experiment results of traffic congestion state prediction using the PSO optimization method in SVM by selecting the RBF kernel function (PSO-SVM-R), the linear kernel function (PSO-SVM-RL), genetic algorithm optimizing SVM selecting RBF and linear kernel function (GA-SVM-RL).

We compare PSO-SVM-R, PSO-SVM-RL, and GA-SVM-RL methods in terms of accuracy, instantaneity, and stability metrics. In order to analyze the results of traffic congestion prediction before and after morning and evening peak accurately, one day is divided into five periods which are before morning peak (befmor), morning peak (mor), between morning and evening peak (betmoev), evening peak (eve), and after evening peak (afteve). The evaluation results for the congestion state prediction are shown in Figs. 4, 5 and 6, as well as Table 3.

In summary, the following results are concluded from our experiments:

- The PSO-SVM-RL method has better prediction accuracy than the PSO-SVM-R method, especially in the morning and evening peek.
- The PSO-SVM-RL method outperforms the GA-SVM-RL in terms of prediction accuracy, real-time and stability.

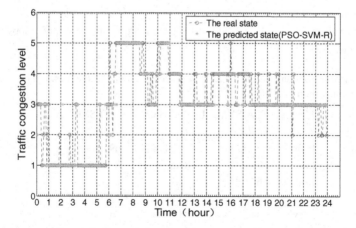

Fig. 4. Comparison between the real congestion state and prediction result of proposed method with PSO-SVM-R.

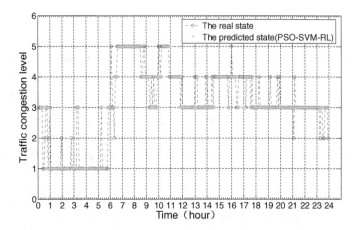

Fig. 5. Comparison between the real congestion state and prediction result of proposed method with PSO-SVM-RL.

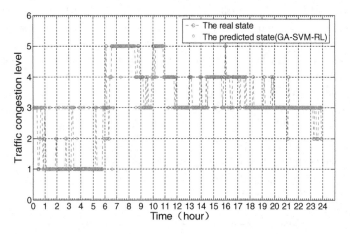

Fig. 6. Comparison between the real congestion state and prediction result of proposed method with GA-SVM-RL.

Table 3. Performance comparison among different optimization techniques of proposed method about traffic congestion prediction

Metrics	GA-SVM-RL	PSO-SVM-R	PSO-SVM-RL
Accuracy	67.25 %	74.22 %	74.91 %
befmor	53.57 %	70.24 %	69.05 %
mor	75.0 %	87.5 %	87.5 %
betmoev	62.5 %	67.71 %	68.75 %
eve	83.33 %	75 %	83.33 %
afteve	84.75 %	84.75 %	84.75 %
Real-time	6.094 s	0.701 s	4.695 s
Stability	No	Yes	Yes

- Both the PSO-SVM-RL and PSO-SVM-R methods outperform the GA-RL method in all the performance metrics.
- The PSO optimization method has better performance on the multi-kernel function of SVM rather than the single kernel function.

The PSO optimization method has better performance on the multi-kernel and single kernel function of SVM in comparison to the GA optimization method.

5 Conclusion

In this paper, we propose a novel traffic congestion prediction method in large scale urban areas which has an advantage in accuracy, instantaneity and stability simultaneously. In order to predict traffic congestion more efficiently, the PSO optimization method is used to optimize the punish coefficients and multiple kernel functions' parameters of SVM in the process of predicting traffic flow parameters. In addition, the FCE method is responsible for helping citizens to make sense of the traffic congestion state based on the predicted flow parameters. In the future, we plan to further improve the comprehensive performance and take more factors into account.

Acknowledgments. This work was partially supported by the Natural Science Foundation of China under Grants No. 61203165 and No. 61174174, the Foundation of Key Laboratory of System Control and Information Processing, Ministry of Education, P.R. China No. SCIP2012001, and the Fundamental Research Funds for Central Universities.

References

1. Zheng, Y., Capra, L., Wolfson, O., et al.: Urban computing: concepts, methodologies, and applications. ACM Trans. Intell. Syst. Technol. (TIST) **5**(3), 38 (2014)
2. Younes, M.B., Boukerche, A.: A performance evaluation of an efficient traffic congestion detection protocol (ECODE) for intelligent transportation systems. Ad Hoc Netw. **24**, 317–336 (2015)
3. Zheng, Y.: Trajectory data mining: an overview. ACM Trans. Intell. Syst. Technol. (2015). doi:10.1145/2743025
4. Kong, Q.J., Zhao, Q., Wei, C., et al.: Efficient traffic state estimation for large-scale urban road networks. IEEE Trans. Intell. Transp. Syst. **14**(1), 398–407 (2013)
5. Kong, Q.J., Li, Z., Chen, Y., et al.: An approach to urban traffic state estimation by fusing multisource information. IEEE Trans. Intell. Transp. Syst. **10**(3), 499–511 (2009)
6. Zhang, J.D., Xu, J., Liao, S.S.: Aggregating and sampling methods for processing GPS data streams for traffic state estimation. IEEE Trans. Intell. Transp. Syst. **14**(4), 1629–1641 (2013)
7. Li, L., Chen, X., Zhang, L.: Multimodel ensemble for freeway traffic state estimations. IEEE Trans. Intell. Transp. Syst. **15**(3), 1323–1336 (2014)
8. Feng, Y., Hourdos, J., Davis, G.A.: Probe vehicle based real-time traffic monitoring on urban roadways. Transp. Res. Part C Emerg. Technol. **40**, 160–178 (2014)

9. Shankar, H., Raju, P.L.N., Rao, K.R.M.: Multi model criteria for the estimation of road traffic congestion from traffic flow information based on fuzzy logic. J. Transp. Technol. **2**, 50 (2012)

10. Xu, Y., Wang, B., Kong, Q., et al.: Spatio-temporal variable selection based support vector regression for urban traffic flow prediction. In: Proceeding of the 93rd Annual Meeting of the Transportation Research Board, Washington, DC, pp. 14–1994 (2014)

11. Hong, W.C., Dong, Y., Zheng, F., et al.: Hybrid evolutionary algorithms in a SVR traffic flow forecasting model. Appl. Math. Comput. **217**(15), 6733–6747 (2011)

12. Li, M.W., Hong, W.C., Kang, H.G.: Urban traffic flow forecasting using Gauss–SVR with cat mapping, cloud model and PSO hybrid algorithm. Neuro Comput. **99**, 230–240 (2013)

13. Wang, J., Shi, Q.: Short-term traffic speed forecasting hybrid model based on chaos-wavelet analysis-support vector machine theory. Transp. Res. Part C Emerg. Technol. **27**, 219–232 (2013)

14. Wang, F., Tan, G., Deng, C., et al.: Real-time traffic flow forecasting model and parameter selection based on ε-SVR. In: Proceedings of the 7th IEEE World Congress on Intelligent Control and Automation, pp. 2870–2875. Chongqing, China (2008)

15. Chen, H., Rakha, H.A., Sadek, S.: Real-time freeway traffic state prediction: a particle filter approach. In: Proceedings of the 14th International IEEE Conference on Intelligent Transportation Systems (ITSC), pp. 626–631. Washington, DC, USA (2011)

16. Dunne, S., Ghosh, B.: Regime-based short-term multivariate traffic condition forecasting algorithm. J. Transp. Eng. **138**(4), 455–466 (2011)

17. Min, W., Wynter, L.: Real-time road traffic prediction with spatio-temporal correlations. Transp. Res. Part C Emerg. Technol. **19**(4), 606–616 (2011)

18. Zhang, X., Onieva, E., Perallos, A., et al.: Hierarchical fuzzy rule-based system optimized with genetic algorithms for short term traffic congestion prediction. Transp. Res. Part C Emerg. Technol. **43**(1), 127–142 (2014)

19. Herring, R., Hofleitner, A., Amin, S., et al.: Using mobile phones to forecast arterial traffic through statistical learning. In: Proceedings of the 89th Transportation Research Board Annual Meeting, pp. 10–2493. Washington DC, USA (2010)

20. Castro, P.S., Zhang, D., Li, S.: Urban traffic modelling and prediction using large scale taxi GPS traces. In: Kay, J., Lukowicz, P., Tokuda, H., Olivier, P., Krüger, A. (eds.) Pervasive 2012. LNCS, vol. 7319, pp. 57–72. Springer, Heidelberg (2012)

21. Zhou, X., Wang, W., Yu, L.: Traffic flow analysis and prediction based on GPS data of floating cars. In: Lu, W., Cai, G., Liu, W., Xing, W. (eds.) Information Technology. LNEE, vol. 210, pp. 497–508. Springer, Heidelberg (2013)

22. Chang, C.C., Lin, C.J.: LIBSVM: a library for support vector machines. ACM Trans. Intell. Syst. Technol. (TIST) **2**(3), 1–27 (2011)

23. Kennedy, J., Eberhart, R.: Particle swarm optimization. Proc. IEEE Int. Conf. Neural Netw. **4**(2), 1942–1948 (1995)

24. http://www.datatang.com/data/44502

25. Beijing Traffic Development Research Center. The transportation development annual report at 2012 of Beijing city. http://www.bjtrc.org.cn/JGJS.aspx?id=5.2&Menu=GZCG (2012)

A Metadata Cooperative Caching Architecture Based on SSD and DRAM for File Systems

Zhisheng Huo[1,2]([⊠]), Limin Xiao[1,2], Qiaoling Zhong[1,2], Shupan Li[1,2], Ang Li[1,2], Li Ruan[1,2], Shouxin Wang[3], and Lihong Fu[3]

[1] State Key Laboratory of Software Development Environment,
Beihang University, Beijing 100191, China
[2] School of Computer Science and Engineering, Beihang University,
Beijing 100191, China
huozhisheng1122@126.com, xiaolm@buaa.edu.cn
[3] Space Star Technology Co., Ltd., Beijing 100086, China

Abstract. The metadata IO plays a critical role in achieving the high IO scalability and throughput to file systems. Due to the resource contention, the performance of the metadata IO is low. Adding the SSD into the storage system is a effective way to improve the performance of file systems, but the current methods mainly focus on the performance of the data server, rarely aim to the performance of the metadata IO. In this paper, we proposed a novel cooperative caching management algorithm based on DRAM and SSD named ACSH. By exploiting the temporal locality widely exhibited in most of the metadata workloads, ACSH can improve the performance of the metadata IO with reducing the write traffic to the SSD, and it includes a adaptive adjustment model, which can adjust the number of the cached metadata according to the locality strength of the metadata workload for improving the perforamcne and reducing the write traffic to the SSD cache layer further. ACSH has been evaluated based on the real-world workloads. Our experiments show that ACSH can reduce the latency by up to 1.5–3X in contrast with the original cache consisting of DRAM which has the same cost with ACSH. Compared with the recent study LARC, it can reduce the write traffic to the SSD by up to 23–30 %.

Keywords: Metadata cache · File system · SSD and DRAM · Cooperative caching architecture · Intensive metadata access · Resource contention

1 Introduction

The file system resides in the IO critical path in storage stack, and consists of three parts: metadata servers, data servers, clients. Due to the increasing amount of data, the amount of metadata is growing, the performance of metadata service plays a critical role in file systems [10]. With the number of users surging [1], the metadata server faces the intensive metadata IO challenge [34]. Due to the

G. Wang et al. (Eds.): ICA3PP 2015, Part II, LNCS 9529, pp. 31–51, 2015.
DOI: 10.1007/978-3-319-27122-4_3

consideration of the cost, the current storage system is comprised of the commodity hardware [29], the metadata storage component mainly consists of hard disk drive (HDD) that causes the IO resource contention. So the performance of metadata IO is very low.

Flash memory has been implemented in file systems over the past few years. Compared with the HDD, the SSD outperforms it by orders of magnitude for random IOs, but it can sustain only a finite number of erase/write cycles. However, the price of SSD is much higher than that of HDD. Thus the SSD is often used as a cache tier between DRAM and HDD [24]. Some researches deployed SSD as buffer out of file systems to absorb intensive write IOs for the data IO [23]. Others proposed a hybrid storage framework based on SSD and HDD to improve the throughput of file systems [16]. LARC used a certain amount of SSD capacity as the ghost cache to filter out the frequently accessed files to reduce the write traffic to the SSD [13].

Although the above cache methods have been somewhat effective for improve the performance of the storage system and improve the lifetime of the SSD. However, there are some challenges to the performance improving of the metadata IO workload.

The first challenge for SSD cache is how to make use of the metadata workload to improve the performance of metadata IO. The SSD was used as buffer out of file systems that only focuses on the performance of data IO and is lack of considering of the metadata workloads to improve the performance of the metadata IO. Compared with the data IO workload, the metadata IO workload has its own characteristics: the metadata IO workload is intensive and small, the metadata IO operation will bring the write traffic SSD more easily due to the fact that the SSD erases a block before writes a page. So it is infeasible that the SSD is simply added into metadata servers like some cache methods [5,23]. A appropriate cache method based on SSD is required for the metadata IO.

The second challenge for SSD cache is how to reduce the write traffic to SSD. A certain amount of SSD cache was used as ghost cache to filter out the popular data [13], but when the size of ghost cache is large, the write traffic to the SSD became heavy again. So a cache method which reduces the write traffic to the SSD without bringing any additional write to SSD again is required.

The third challenge for the SSD cache is how to adjust the number of cached popular metadata according to the temporal locality strength of the metadata workload. The metadata workload always changes over time that will cause the locality strength of the metadata IO to be weak or strong, if the unpopular metadata is cached in the SSD layer that will reduce the hit ratio and bring a great deal of the write operation in the SSD cache layer. So the cache method must adjust the number of cached popular metadata files according to the locality strength of the metadata workload adaptively.

To address the above challenges, we proposed a novel cooperative caching algorithm based on DRAM and SSD named ACSH for improving the performance of the metadata IO in this paper. ACSH can supply a fast response to clients, eliminate resource contention to improve the scalability of file system IO with extending the lifetime of the SSD. Specifically, there are three characteristics of ACSH:

(1) ACSH is inside the metadata servers, it can make full use of the metadata workloads to improve the performance of the metadata IO. Because the SSD layer and the DRAM layer work cooperatively, the intensive metadata IO is absorbed in the DRAM cache layer, so the write traffic to SSD cache layer is reduced greatly.
(2) ACSH is comprised of DRAM and SSD, in order to improve the hit ratio of the SSD cache layer, the DRAM cache is used as the filter to judge the popularity of metadata, the filter does not bring the additional write traffic to the SSD cache layer, when it looks for the popular metadata.
(3) ACSH can adjust the number of the cached popular metadata files according to the temporal locality strength of metadata workload adaptively, when the locality strength is weak, the number of the popular metadata is small, so ACSH will keep more unpopular metadata out of the SSD layer, but when the locality strength is strong, the SSD layer will cache more popular metadata.

ACSH consists of two components: the cooperative caching architecture and the unified management framework.

The Cooperative Caching Architecture. Adding the SSD into the cache can extend the size of cache and improve the performance of file systems. But if SSDs is simply added into file system, this will hurt the lifetime of SSD due to the defect of the SSD. The key idea of the cooperative caching architecture is to identify the seldom accessed metadata files with keeping them out of the SSD cache layer, and to adjust the cached metadata according to the workload locality strength for reducing the write traffic to the SSD. To achieve this, ACSH uses a cooperative caching architecture based on DRAM and SSD, it uses a DRAM filter to judge the popular metadata and cache them in the SSD cache layer, it adaptively adjusts the threshold of the metadata accessing counting according to the strength of temporal locality. Because of the high price of DRAM, when the size of SSD cache is fixed, ACSH can determine a proper proportion of memory as the filter cache.

The Unified Management Framework. The size of DRAM filter impacts the hit rate of the SSD cache layer, when it is less than the reuse distance of most of popular metadata, these popular metadata will be failed to be discover for caching in the SSD layer. In order to improve the hit rate, we proposed a unified management framework to group all metadata servers' filter caches into a logic one that can extend the size of each server's filter cache.

The remainder of the paper is organized as follows. Section 2 discusses the related works, and highlights the metadata IO bottlenecks in the existing methods for further motivation. Then we present the design and implementation of ACSH in Sects. 3 and 4 respectively. Section 5 evaluates its performance with the real-world traces and workloads. We conclude in Sect. 6.

2   Motivation and Relate Work

With the increasing popularity of the SSD, both engineers and researchers have integrated it into storage system that can be put into two categories: the SSD is deployed between DRAM and HDD as the cache, the SSD is implemented with the HDD medium as the hybrid storage.

First, several previous studies focused on using the SSD as the cache for storage systems. Mercury [7] is a persistent and write-through host-side cache framework which is based on SSD to improve the performance of storage systems and reduce latency. The largest-scale high-performance (HPC) systems are stretching the parallel file system to their limits in terms of aggregate bandwidth and numbers of clients, to further sustain the scalability of these file systems, one proposed storage system designing integrate a tier of SSD burst buffers into the storage system at the IO forwarding nodes to absorb the burst write workload [4,5,23]. The SSD can be attached directly to the memory bus and accessed like normal DRAM, it is poised to close the enormous performance gap between persistent storage and main memory, employing superpages to reduce the pressure on memory management resources such as TLB to improve the file system performance [28]. Koller et al. [17] developed and evaluated two consistent write-back caching policies, ordered and journaled, for the SSD cache to ensure the data consistency that perform increasingly better than write-through. Lee et al. [19] present a novel buffer cache architecture that subsumes the functionality of caching and journaling by making use of SSD to avoid logging and provide the same journaling effect by simply altering the state of the cached block to frozen. Hybrid storage solutions use NAND flash memory based Solid State Drives (SSDs), the SSD is divided into the cache space and the over-provisioned space, balancing the two spaces appropriately helps improve the performance of hybrid storage systems [25]. The above studies mainly focuses on the data server performance without taking the SSD's lifetime into consideration, and is lack of considering of the metadata workload for improving the performance of the metadata IO and extending the lifetime of the SSD.

Second, in addition to caching, the storage tiering is another sought-after technology for the hybrid storage. Recently many storage vendors are designing the hybrid storage system based on SSD and HDD that can satisfy multiple server level objectives (SLOs) of different workloads in one storage system, the resource management algorithm based on SLO controls the amount of SSD which is given to a particular workload [30]. Given these trade-offs between HDDs and SSDs in terms of cost, performance, HybridStore [16] proposed a trade-off method that not only makes full use of the SSD, but also improves the lifetime of SSD. Dynamic storage tier (DST) organized SSD and HDD into a multilayer system. Hybrid storage architectures based on DST, dynamically transfer data between SSD and HDD, to improve storage systems performance and scalability [9,12,26,38]. Other researchers had proposed LARC [13] that divided SSD into two parts to improve the lifetime of SSD, one part was used as the ghost cache to filter out the seldom accessed data in order to improve the hit ratio and extend the lifetime of SSD. The above studies can improve the scalability of data servers, some methods can extend the lifetime of the SSD, but they failed to improve the performance of the metadata IO due to its own specific workload characteristics. For example, LARC can somewhat be suitable for improving the performance of the metadata IO, but when the size of ghost cache increased, LARC will bring the heavy write traffic to the SSD again.

The above methods are efficient in their application scenarios, but they are lack of considering of the metadata workload to improve the performance of the metadata IO and extend the lifetime of the SSD, and the methods for reducing the write to the SSD is inefficient, because they may bring the additional write traffic to the SSD again.

The metadata workload has its own characteristics: (1) The size of metadata is small, and the amount of metadata is large. Because of the increasing amounts of data in modern storage system for various high performance computing and Internet applications, the volume of data reaches and even exceeds EB [39,40], this causes the large-scale namespace which has hundreds of billions of directories consisting of the massive small files and exceeds the memory cache capacity overwhelmingly [21]. (2) The metadata IO is intensive, in fact, a higher proportion of file system I/Os are the metadata I/O activities [33], which is more than 50 % [36]. The interval of time between them is less than the response time of HDD [1,8,15,20,27,34]. With the ever increasing number of users, the intensive metadata access faces serious resource contention challenge. So the intensive metadata IO causes the whole performance of file systems degrading greatly. (3) Through the analysis of file system workloads, we can know that the metadata workloads show temporal and spatial locality [1,2,20]. Table 1 shows that the metadata in less than 1 % directories is popular [22].

In view of the above metadata workload characteristics, it is infeasible that the above methods simply make use of the SSD as the cache with regard to the metadata. First, the small size metadata will shorten the lifetime of SSD easily described in the above, some optimization methods [37] can reduce the write to the SSD through the novel data organization, but they will store all metadata in the SSD, so this will be the unpopular metadata's useless write traffic to the SSD. Second, the metadata IO is intensive, so the SSD is a appropriate medium to absorb the intensive IO, but the IO operations for writing the unpopular metadata into the SSD will hurt the lifetime of the SSD. Third, the amount of metadata exceeds the capacity of the DRAM cache, due to the high price of the DRAM, the SSD is a good choice to be used as the extensional cache layer, but the unpopular metadata will bring the heavy write to the SSD due to the low proportion of the popular metadata described in Table 1, the above methods do not make full use of the metadata workload locality to reduce the write traffic to the SSD. (Although some file systems [29] are designed to store the metadata in the memory, but there are still many file systems [31,35] which have a large amount of metadata that the memory cannot accommodate them).

So this motivates us to study the cooperative cache layer consisting of SSD and DRAM, by exploiting the metadata locality characteristic [11], the cooperative

Table 1. Locality analysis of the metadata

Trace	ext	size	uid	ctime
Web [20]	0.000162 %–0.120 %	0.0579 %–0.177 %	0.000194 %–0.558 %	0.000291 %–0.0105 %
Eng [20]	0.00101 %–0.264 %	0.00194 %–0.462 %	0.000578 %–0.137 %	0.000453 %–0.0103 %
Home [20]	0.000201 %–0.491 %	0.0259 %–0.923 %	0.000417 %–0.623 %	0.000370 %–0.128 %

cache can improve the metadata IO performance with reducing the write traffic to the SSD through taking the metadata workload into consideration.

3 ACSH Design

ACSH is a metadata cooperative cache architecture that addresses the problem of low metadata performance and extends the lifetime of SSD cache through making use of the specific metadata workload characteristics. In this section, we present the design goals, concepts of ACSH.

3.1 Design Goals

ACSH is designed to leverage the SSD to extend the cache size of metadata server for providing a better metadata IO performance and extending the lifetime of SSD cache. ACSH meets three design goals: (1) It should make full use of the metadata IO temporal locality to improve the hit rate of SSD cache, and can adjust the number of the cached popular metadata files according to the strength of temporal locality adaptively. So That will improve the performance of the metadata IO and extend the lifetime of the SSD. (2) It can filter out the unpopular metadata without bringing the additional write traffic to the SSD; (3) Because the larger the size of filter cache is, the higher the hit rate of SSD cache is that will lead to a higher performance of the metadata IO, due to the high price of DRAM, the size of the filter cache cannot expand without limit, so it should group all metadata servers's filter caches to extend the size of each server's filter cache to improve the hit ratio of the SSD cache layer, and should give a proper proportion of memory as the filter cache according to the locality strength.

3.2 ACSH Architectural Overview

ACSH is composed of two key components: the metadata cooperative cache architecture based on DRAM and SSD, the unified management framework. Figure 1 illustrates the architecture of ACSH and the overall primary abstractions of design.

The metadata cooperative cache architecture resides in each metadata server, it is comprised of three components: the filter cache consisting of the DRAM, the SSD cache layer, a metadata file replacement algorithm between the filter cache

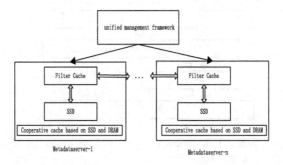

Fig. 1. ACSH Architecture. This figure depicts the architecture of ACSH. In a single metadata server, the cooperative cache based on DRAM and SSD. A unified management framework is proposed for multiple metadata servers.

and the SSD cache. The filter cache can filter out the popular metadata which is demoted to the SSD cache layer. When the filter cache capacity is exhausted, the replacement algorithm actively demotes the metadata to SSD cache layer according to the access counting threshold.

The size of filter cache capacity impacts the hit rate of SSD cache layer. Reuse distance is the number of metadata accessed between two consecutive accesses to one metadata file. When the size of filter cache is larger than or equal to the reuse distance of one file, the metadata file can be found out, so the size of filter cache must be larger than the minimal reuse distance. The greater the size of filter cache is, the more popular metadata will be discovered. The size of filter cache is limited in a single metadata server due to the high price of DRAM, so in order to increase the size of each server's filter cache, we propose a unified management framework, which can group and manage all servers' filter caches as one larger filter cache to extend the size of filter cache for each metadata server.

4   Design Components

In this section, we introduce the detail of ACSH.

4.1   Metadata Cooperative Cache Based on DRAM and SSD

We employ a two-level cache framework not only to improve the performance of the metadata IO, but also to extend the lifetime of the SSD. The first-level cache is called the filter cache consisting of DRAM, the second is the SSD cache. The filter cache and the SSD cache work cooperatively, the filter cache decides which metadata will be cached in the SSD cache layer or written back to the HDD. Specifically, according to the temporal locality of the metadata IO, some metadata files will be accessed frequently, so the cooperative cache architecture must seek them out to store in the SSD cache layer. This has three advantages:

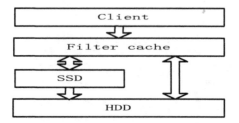

Fig. 2. Cooperative cache. This figure presents the architecture of the cooperative cache, which comprises DRAM and SSD.

(1) The more popular metadata files is in the SSD cache layer, the higher the hit rate is. So the performance of metadata IO is improved greatly. (2) The cache architecture can overcome the short lifetime of SSD problem to some extent, the SSD used as the metadata cache makes feasible. (3) The cache framework can adjust the number of the cached popular metadata according to the locality strength of the metadata workload for improving the performance of the metadata IO and extending the lifetime of the SSD.

Figure 2 shows the architecture of the metadata cooperative cache in a single metadata server. The filter cache is on top of the SSD cache layer, the metadata is stored the filter cache firstly. In this paper, we adopted the counting mechanism to record the accessing times of each metadata. The metadata in the filter cache is demoted to the SSD layer or the HDD layer according to their accessing count. The key idea of the filter cache is to filter out the unpopular metadata and keep them out of the SSD cache layer. To achieve this, the metadata in the filter cache is organized as a queue which is sorted by the descending accessing count. When the filter cache runs out of its capacity, the cached metadata whose access count are greater than or equal to the threshold are moved to the SSD cache.

Figure 3 shows the management architecture of the cooperative cache. Assume that the size of filter cache can hold n metadata files, they are f_1, f_2, ..., f_n, their access counts are c_1, c_2, ..., c_n respectively. When the filter cache reaches its capacity limitation, the metadata replacement algorithm starts working that decides which metadata should be cached in the SSD cache layer.

First, the replace algorithm proactively collects the accessing count of each metadata and sets the replacement threshold:

$$T_r = \left\lceil \frac{c_1 + c_2 + \cdots + c_n}{n} \right\rceil$$

Next, according to T_r, the metadata in the filter cache is divided into two lists:

$$\begin{cases} c_i \geq T_r, & list_1 = \{f_i, \ldots, f_k\} \\ c_j < T_r, & list_2 = \{f_j, \ldots, f_m\} \end{cases}$$

Finally, the metadata in $list_1$ is demoted to the SSD cache layer. When the free space of the filter cache achieves 50 % of the whole space, the replacement algorithm stops to work. This cooperative cache architecture makes full use of the metadata workload locality characteristic, it does not bring the additional write traffic to the SSD cache layer while filtering out the popular metadata.

We know that most of metadata are accessed only one time, if they reside in the filter cache all the time that will waste the capacity of the filter cache and reduce the accuracy rate of T_r causing the unpopular metadata demoted into the SSD cache, this will reduce the performance of the metadata IO. So we proposed a time window based replacement strategy. Set the time window be T, if the access time of the metadata in $list_2$ is less than T_r beyond the time window, the metadata replacement algorithm considerates them never to be accessed again, they are actively written back to the HDD layer.

T_r is set on line, once the capacity of the filter cache is used with saturation, the replacement algorithm collects all metadata accessing counts, T_r is set to equal to the average value of all metadata files access counts. If the SSD cache still has a great deal of free space after a long time, this presents T_r is so high that it prevents the popular metadata from entering into the SSD cache. Because the higher T_r is, the stronger the temporal locality is, so T_r should be decreased. And vice versa, T_r should be increased. The meaning of parameter is described in Table 2.

Table 2. The meaning of parameter

Parameter	Meaning
S_{fc}	The capacity of filter cache
T_r	The average threshold of accessing times
f	The average size of metadata file
S	The free capacity of SSD cache layer
S_D	The size of SSD capacity
m	The number of cached metadata file
T_r'	The adjusted threshold
ρ	The ratio of free space
ρ_1	The threshold of adjusting rate

The adjustment range of T_r is: $T_r' \in [T_r - d, T_r + d]$, when $S = \rho \times S_D (\rho \geq 60\%)$, T_r need to be adjusted to $T_r' = T_r - d$, T_r should be decreased, so more metadata files can enter into SSD cache layer, which will be fully used. $m = \frac{S_{fc}}{f} - T_r'$, so $m \times f = \rho_1 \times S \Rightarrow d = \frac{\rho_1 \times S}{f} - \frac{S_{fc}}{f} + T_r$. When $S = \rho \times S_D (\rho \leq 40\%)$, T_r should be increased to decrease the number of metadata file entering into SSD cache, $T_r' = T_r + d$, so we can get the conclusion that $m \times f = \rho_1 \times S \Rightarrow d = \frac{\rho_1 \times S}{f} - \frac{S_{fc}}{f} - T_r$.

Through the dynamic adjustment of T_r, the real popular metadata can be found out to be cached in the SSD layer. T_r represents the strength of temporal locality. When T_r is high, we can get to know that the workload has a stronger

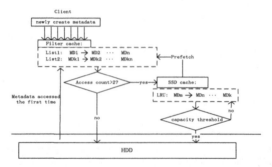

Fig. 3. The management architecture of cooperative cache. SSD use LRU to manage cache space.

temporal locality, T_r should be decreased properly, more popular metadata will be demoted into the SSD cache layer. Conversely, the current workload shows a weaker temporal locality, the popularity of metadata is low, so we should decrease the number of the cached metadata, T_r should be increased. The experiment indicates that $\rho_1 = 1.5\%$ is appropriate.

The SSD cache layer uses LRU to manage the metadata, so the metadata at the end of LRU list is written back to the HDD when the SSD cache runs out of its space.

4.2   Unified Management Framework

The larger the size of the filter cache is, the more the popular metadata will be cached in the SSD cache layer. The size of filter cache in one metadata server is limited due to the high price of DRAM, however, all metadata servers' workloads are unbalance, some metadata servers' filter caches are used tensively, others are idle. In order to improve the hit rate of the SSD cache layer and make full use of the valuable DRAM cache resource. So we proposed a unified management framework to extend the size of each metadata server's filter cache. Specifically, we utilize this framework grouping all metadata server's filter caches into a larger filter cache, when the size of the filter cache is enlarged and greater than most of the metadata's reuse distance, more popular metadata will be discovered, so the hit ratio of the SSD cache layer will be improved.

As shown in Fig. 4, the unified management framework consists of three parts: the filter cache mapping table (MS TABLE), the information collection algorithm (CA), the target address mapping table (TM). MS TABLE is a global data structure, and contains all metadata server's filter cache information except its own. Every record in MS TABLE is comprised of the metadata server's IP and the remaining space of its filter cache. Each metadata server keeps a MS TABLE to look up other metadata servers's remaining space of the filter cache. CA is used to collect the metadata server filter cache information and resides in each metadata server to update the local MS TABLE periodically. CA sends the query requests to other metadata servers after a fixed period of time, these

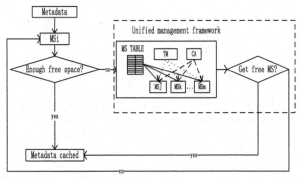

Fig. 4. The unified management framework. All filter caches are grouped into a logical filter cache which is managed uniformly

Table 3. Parameter declaration

Parameter	Meaning
S_{fc}	The capacity of filter cache
n	The number of filter cache
S_f	The average size of metadata file
h_1	The ratio of popular files to SSD through a single filter cache
h_2	The ratio of popular files to SSD cache with the unified framework
k_1	The number of popular files in a single filter cache
k_2	The number of popular files in the unified filter cache framework

metadata servers calculate their remaining space of the filter cache and response this request, and the local MS TABLE is updated. TM table residing in each metadata server is used to record the metadata's target address, when a metadata arrived at the local filter cache in metadata server MS_i, if its filter cache is exhausted, the client would look up the local MS TABLE to find out a metadata server whose filter cache has the maximum remaining space, MS_i records the metadata destination address in TM table, the client transfers the metadata to the corresponding metadata server's filter cache.

When a local metadata server gets to know that all metadata servers' filter caches are exhausted by querying the MS TABLE, it sends the freeing the file cache's space requests to all metadata servers, which ignites the metadata replacement algorithm to free the filter cache space, the metadata replacement algorithm not only demote the local popular metadata to the local SSD cache layer, but also transfer the popular metadata cached in other servers to the local SSD cache layer through TM table. Figure 5 show the pesudo code of the unified management framework management algorithm.

```
1:  client \xrightarrow{MS_i} metafile_i //client request metafile_iin MataServer_i//
2:  if local − FCache_i then //judge whether filter cache has free space//
3:      metafile_i → local − FCache_i
4:  else
5:      Lookup(MS TABLE) → local − FCache_j
6:  end if
7:  Update(MS TABLE, TM) //updating TS TABLE and TM table//
8:  CA(requests) //CA collecting filter information periodically//
9:  for i = 0; i ≤ m; i + + do //m is the number of filter cache//
10:     local − FCache_i == 0 //all filter cache run out
11: end for
12: for i = 0; i ≤ m; i + + do // all filter caches conduct replacement algorithm//
13:     function Replace-Algorithm(local − FCache_i)
14:         local − FCache_i → local − SSD //local metadata files are demoted to
    SSD cache//
15:         Lookup(TM_i)
16:         Nonlocal−FCache → local−SSD //non-local metadata files are demoted
    to SSD through TM//
17:     end function
18: end for
```

Fig. 5. Unified management framework algorithm

Figure 6 shows that when a metadata IO request arrives at a metadata server, the client first lookups the local filter cache and the local SSD cache layer. If there is no hit, the request is redirected to other metadata servers filter cache through the TM table. Otherwise, the local HDD responses the request.

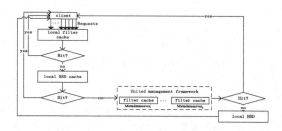

Fig. 6. The metadata accessing process based on ACSH

Now we analyse the performance of the unified management framework quantificationally, the parameters are described in Table 3.

So we can get the following formula: $k_1 = \frac{S_{fc}}{S_f} \times h_1$, $k_2 = \frac{n \times S_{fc}}{S_f} \times h_2$, so the improvement ratio: $\rho = \frac{k_2 - k_1}{k_1} = \frac{n \times h_2 - h_1}{h_1} (h_2 > h_1)$.

In order to indicate the efficiency of the unified management framework, we use the websearch [3] workload to test it. Figure 7 shows that with the growth

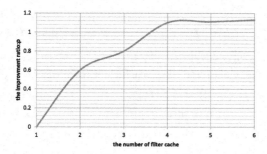

Fig. 7. Relationship between the improvement of hit rate and the number of filter cache

of the number of filter caches, ρ increases too. Because the size of unified cache framework is greater than that of a single filter cache, more popular metadata will be discovered and cached in the SSD cache layer. But when the size of filter cache is greater than the maximum reuse, all the popular metadata have entered into the SSD cache layer, ρ tends to be smooth. In our test process, the configuration of servers are shown in Table 5, when the number of filter caches is more than 4, the popular metadata is almost completely discovered, so ρ changes from steep to smooth.

4.3   The Size of Filter Cache Setting Policy

As the above description, the larger the size of filter cache is, the higher the hit rate of SSD cache is. But the price of DRAM is so high that it is impossible to extend the size of filter cache infinitely, the size of filter cache should be set reasonably to improve the hit rate of SSD cache.

Table 4. Parameter description

Parameter	Meaning
C_S	The size of SSD cache
C_{fc}	The size of filter cache
f	The average size of metadata file
d	The reuse distance of one metadata
P_i	The accessing probability of the metadata
T	The accessing times of one metadata file
i	The rank of metadata file's accessing times

The parameters used in the following part are described in Table 4. The metadata whose reuse distance: $d \leq \frac{C_{fc}}{f}$ can be selected to cache in the SSD cache layer, assume the number of these metadata files is n, their reuse distances are $\{d_1, \ldots, d_n\}$ respectively, the probability of reuse distance d_i obeys IRM model [32] basically: $D(d_i) = P_i(1-P_i)^{(d_i-1)}$, so the probability of reuse distance $d_i \leq \frac{C_{fc}}{f}$: $D(\frac{C_{fc}}{f}) = \sum_{i=1}^{n} P_i D(d_i) = P_i(1-P_i)^{(\frac{C_{fc}}{f}-1)}$. In real environment, the popularity of frequently accessed files satisfies uniform distribution, so $P_i = 1/n$. So $D(\frac{C_{fc}}{f}) = P_i(1-P_i)^{T_r-1}[1 - (1-P_i)^{\frac{C_{fc}}{f}-T_r+1}]$. Because the accessing times of a metadata file and its rank meet Zipf's law [6], so $T = K/i^\alpha$ (K is constant, $\alpha \in [0.5, 1]$), when the replace threshold is T_r, $T_r = K/i_1^\alpha \Rightarrow i_1 = \sqrt[\alpha]{\frac{K}{T_r}}$. In fact, many metadata files are accessed only one time, so $1 = K/i_2^\alpha \Rightarrow i_2 = \sqrt[\alpha]{K}$. We can get the ratio of metadata files whose accessing times $T_r \leq T$: $\rho = i_1/i_2$. The relationship between the maximum hit rate of SSD and the size of SSD cache is $H_{max} = 1 - \frac{1}{\sqrt{C_S}}$. To achieve the maximum hit rate, the size of filter cache must be adjusted, so

$$\rho \times D(\frac{C_{fc}}{f}) \leq H_{max}$$

$$\Rightarrow \frac{1}{\sqrt[\alpha]{T_r}} \times P_i(1-P_i)^{T_r-1}[1-(1-P_i)^{\frac{C_{fc}}{f}-T_r+1}] \leq 1 - \frac{1}{\sqrt{C_S}}$$

$$\Rightarrow (\log_{(1-P_i)}(1 - \frac{(1-\frac{1}{\sqrt{C_S}}\sqrt[\alpha]{T_r})}{P_i(1-P_i)^{T_r-1}}) + T_r - 1) \times f \leq C_{fc}$$

From the above formula, we can know that when the size of SSD cache is fixed, C_{fc} changes with the varying of T_r. T_r is adjusted dynamically, so C_{fc} should be adjusted too. When T_r is fixed, the minimal of C_{fc} can be determined. In the real metadata workload, when T_r is higher, the strength of temporal locality is strong, so C_{fc} should be increased to cache more popular metadata that will improve the hit rate of the SSD cache layer. On the contrary, when T_r is low, the strength of temporal locality is weak, C_{fc} should be decreased to reduce the write traffic to the SSD cache layer.

5   Evaluation

In this section, we evaluate ACSH algorithm with the trace-driven by adding ACSH into PVFS2 [31], we ran several real-life workloads and collected the experimental results.

5.1   PVFS2 Framework

We have added ACSH into PVFS2, which consists of three components: clients, metadata servers containing hybrid cache framework based on SSD and DRAM, data servers. There are a preprocessor and a access interface in the client. The preprocessor converts the traces of different format into the PVFS2's customized format. The access interface is used to replay the workload IO operations.

We implemented ACSH in 1400 lines of C code in PVFS2, we add the ACSH into the PVFS2 metadata IO path, ACSH resides in both the metadata servers

Table 5. Hardware and software configuration for simulator

Configuration	Detail
CPU	AMD Quad-core processors
Memory	$2 \times 4\,GB$ DDR2-667 MHz
SSD	Intel SSDSA2SH064GIGC 80 GB
Operating system	Ubuntu Linux 10.04

and the clients, and provides the cooperative cache mechanism for the original cache of PVFS2. Table 5 describes the configuration of the metadata server. In the process of our experiments, the overhead of network IO is ignored, because PVFS2 is installed in a special LAN without other applications, so the latency of network will bring a little impact to the latency of the metadata IO.

In this section, we experimentally answer the following questions: (1) When all metadata servers's filter cache are grouped into one larger filter cache, is the hit rate of SSD improved? (2) Compared with the traditional DRAM cache which has the same cost with ACSH, can ACSH improve the performance of the metadata IO? (3) LARC [13] is the recent study, which can effectively reduce the write traffic to the SSD, so compared with LARC, can ACSH reduce the write traffic to the SSD cache layer?

5.2 Workloads

We use 4 different I/O traces to test our ACSH algorithm. These traces are directly from real-world systems, represented by websearch, ads, webvm and homes respectively. Websearch is collected from the web search engine and is available at Umass Trace Repository. Ads comes from an online advertisement system. Webvm comes from a webmail proxy and online course management system for a university department. Homes is from an NFS server which includes personal files of scientific researchers.

Table 6 describes detail of 4 traces. All traces are read and write mixed. Among these traces, websearch, ads are read dominant, but webvm and homes are write dominant [13].

Table 6. The traces used by test

Trace	♯ of read	♯ of write	% of read
Websearch [3]	17,253,000	2,000	99.9
Ads [14]	14,089,000	348,000	97.6
Webvm [18]	3,116,000	11,177,000	21.8
Homes [18]	4,053,000	17,110,000	19.1

5.3   Results

In this experimental part, we configure 8 metadata servers, whose configuration are described in Table 5. Figure 8 shows that increasing the number of the filter cache can improve the hit rate of the SSD cache layer in one metadata server, Fig. 8a shows that when the number of filter cache is 2, the average hit rate is 40 % for all servers, and with the increasing of the number of filter caches, the hit rate is increasing. When the number of filter cache is 8, the average hit rate is 69 % for all servers. Figure 8b shows the similar result that uses the Ads workload to conduct the experiment. So we can get a conclusion that the unified management framework is efficient and can improve the performance of the file system, because when the hit ratio is high, this means that the more popular metadata is discovered to be cached in the SSD cache layer.

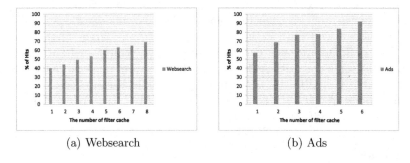

(a) Websearch   (b) Ads

Fig. 8. The hit rate with the number of filter cache

In order to test the effectiveness of ACSH, ACSH is compared with the traditional DRAM cache, which has the same amount cost with ACSH. ACSH represents the cooperative cache based on DRAM and SSD, no-ACSH represents the traditional DRAM caching. We configure the larger/smaller size of memory cache for no-ACSH and ACSH respectively. 2 GB-ACSH means that the size of filter cache is 2 GB, 6 GB-no-ACSH represents the cache only consists of 6 GB DRAM. Similarly, it has the same meaning to 3 GB-ACSH and 7 GB-no-ACSH. Figure 9 shows the average response latency for the intensive metadata accesses. We configurate 20 client servers by making use of the multi-threads to simulate multiple clients' concurrent accessing IOs in PVFS2, the websearch and ads workloads are used to test the performance of ACSH. The experiment result shows that ACSH can reduce the access latency for the intensive accesses, because the filter cache can filter out the popular metadata which is demoted to the SSD cache layer, so the cooperative cache can absorb most of the metadata IO requests. In Fig. 9a, the average latency of ACSH is lower than that of no-ACSH from 100 clients to 1000 clients, 2 GB-ACSH outperforms 6 GB-no-ACSH by 2X, 3 GB-ACSH outperforms 7 GB-no-ACSH by 3X respectively. In Fig. 9b, under the above configuration of DRAM and SSD, we can get the similar result that ACSH outperforms no-ACSH by 2.1X, 1.5X respectively. So we can get a

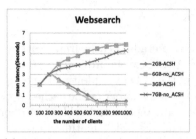 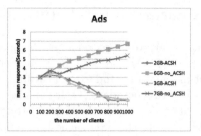

(a) The average latency for web-search test

(b) The average latency for ads test

Fig. 9. Performance test for intensive client accessing

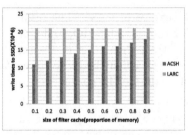 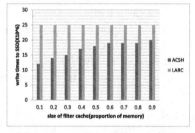

(a) Webvm write traffics to SSD

(b) homes write traffics to SSD

Fig. 10. Test for extending the lifetime of SSD. Using webvm and homes workloads to test ACSH which can reduce the wite traffics to SSD cache

conclusion that not only ACSH can improve the performance of the file system, but also it is a cost-effective way of improving performance.

Webvm and homes are write dominant traces, so we make use of them to test whether or not ACSH can reduce the write traffics to the SSD cache layer. We conduct this test in one metadata server, its configuration is described in Table 5. In Fig. 10, we configure the same size of cache in memory for ACSH and LARC respectively. ACSH means that the DRAM cache layer and the SSD cache layer are managed by ACSH, LARC do not use it. As shown in Fig. 10, the average write traffics of ACSH is lower than that of LARC. In contrast with LARC, ACSH can reduce write traffics to SSD by 23 % and 30 % for webvm and homes respectively. Because LARC [13] needs a part of the SSD cache as the ghost cache to filter out the seldom accessed metadata, when the size of the ghost cache is large, this will brings the additional write traffic to SSD again, but ACSH filters out the popular metadata in the DRAM filter layer, so it does not bring the additional write to the SSD layer. We can also know that with the increasing of the filter cache size, more popular metadata will be discovered, so the write traffic to the SSD cache layer will be getting heavier.

6   Conclusion and Future Work

In this paper, we proposed a novel cooperative metadata cache framework ACSH based on DRAM and SSD for file systems. ACSH can improve the performance of the metadata IO and extend the lifetime of the SSD by exploiting the temporal locality of the metadata IO. It can also adjust the number of the cached popular metadata according to the locality strength of the metadata workload to improve the hit ratio of the SSD cache layer and extend the SSD's lifetime further.

We proposed a unified management framework to multiple metadata servers that groups all metadata server filter caches to one large filter cache. The larger the size of the filter cache is, the higher the hit rate in SSD is. The unified management framework can extend the size of each metadata server's filter cache, so the hit rate of SSD cache is improved.

ACSH has been evaluated based on the real-world traces. The results show that ACSH can improve the performance of the metadata IO, and can reduce the write traffic to the SSD cache layer in contrast with other methods.

We will further study the reliability of ACSH, when the file system crashes due to the power failure, the file system will maintain the consistency.

Acknowledgments. This version has benefited greatly from the many detailed comments and suggestions from the anonymous reviewers. The authors gratefully acknowledge these comments and suggestions. The work described in this paper are supported by the National Natural Science Foundation of China under Grant No. 61370059 and 61232009, the Beijing Natural Science Foundation under Grant No. 4152030, the fund of the State Key Laboratory of Software Development Environment under Grant No. SKLSDE-2014ZX-05, the Open Research Fund of The Academy of Satellite Application under Grant NO. 2014_CXJJ-DSJ_04, the Fundamental Research Funds for the Central Universities under Grant NO. YWF-14-JSJXY-14 and YWF-15-GJSYS-085, the Open Project Program of National Engineering Research Center for Science &Technology Resources Sharing Service (Beihang University).

References

1. Abad, C.L., Roberts, N., Lu, Y., Campbell, R.H.: A storage-centric analysis of mapreduce workloads: file popularity, temporal locality and arrival patterns. In: IEEE International Symposium on Workload Characterization (IISWC), pp. 100–109. IEEE (2012)
2. Adams, I.F., Madden, B.A., Frank, J.C., Storer, M.W., Miller, E.L., Harano, G.: Usage behavior of a large-scale scientific archive. In: Proceedings of the International Conference on High Performance Computing, Networking, Storage and Analysis, p. 86. IEEE Computer Society Press (2012)
3. Application, O.L.T.P.: I/O. UMass Trace Repository
4. Bent, J., Faibish, S., Ahrens, J., Grider, G., Patchett, J., Tzelnic, P., Woodring, J.: Jitter-free co-processing on a prototype exascale storage stack. In: IEEE 28th Symposium on Mass Storage Systems and Technologies (MSST 2012), pp. 1–5. IEEE (2012)

5. Bent, J., Grider, G., Kettering, B., Manzanares, A., McClelland, M., Torres, A., Torrez, A.: Storage challenges at Los Alamos National Lab. In: IEEE 28th Symposium on Mass Storage Systems and Technologies (MSST 2012), pp. 1–5. IEEE (2012)

6. Breslau, L., Cao, P., Fan, L., Phillips, G., Shenker, S.: Web caching and zipf-like distributions: evidence and implications. In: Proceedings of Eighteenth Annual Joint Conference of the IEEE Computer and Communications Societies, INFO-COM 1999, vol. 1, pp. 126–134. IEEE (1999)

7. Byan, S., Lentini, J., Madan, A., Pabón, L., Condict, M., Kimmel, J., Kleiman, S., Small, C., Storer, M.: Mercury: host-side flash caching for the data center. In: IEEE 28th Symposium on Mass Storage Systems and Technologies (MSST 2012), pp. 1–12. IEEE (2012)

8. Carns, P., Harms, K., Allcock, W., Bacon, C., Lang, S., Latham, R., Ross, R.: Storage access characteristics of computational science applications. In: Proceedings of 27th IEEE Conference on Mass Storage Systems and Technologies (MSST) (2011)

9. Chen, F., Koufaty, D.A., Zhang, X.: Hystor: making the best use of solid state drives in high performance storage systems. In: Proceedings of the International Conference on Supercomputing, pp. 22–32. ACM (2011)

10. Devulapalli, A., Ohio, P.: File creation strategies in a distributed metadata file system. In: IEEE International Conference on Parallel and Distributed Processing Symposium, IPDPS 2007, pp. 1–10. IEEE (2007)

11. Gu, P., Wang, J., Zhu, Y., Jiang, H., Shang, P.: A novel weighted-graph-based grouping algorithm for metadata prefetching. IEEE Trans. Comput. **59**(1), 1–15 (2010)

12. Guerra, J., Pucha, H., Glider, J.S., Belluomini, W., Rangaswami, R.: Cost effective storage using extent based dynamic tiering. In: FAST, pp. 273–286 (2011)

13. Huang, S., Wei, Q., Chen, J., Chen, C., Feng, D.: Improving flash-based disk cache with lazy adaptive replacement. In: 29th Symposium on Mass Storage Systems and Technologies (MSST 2013), pp. 1–10. IEEE (2013)

14. Kavalanekar, S., Worthington, B., Zhang, Q., Sharda, V.: Characterization of storage workload traces from production windows servers. In: IEEE International Symposium on Workload Characterization, IISWC 2008, pp. 119–128. IEEE (2008)

15. Kim, Y., Gunasekaran, R., Shipman, G.M., Dillow, D.A., Zhang, Z., Settlemyer, B.W.: Workload characterization of a leadership class storage cluster. In: 5th Petascale Data Storage Workshop (PDSW 2010), pp. 1–5. IEEE (2010)

16. Kim, Y., Gupta, A., Urgaonkar, B., Berman, P., Sivasubramaniam, A.: Hybridstore: a cost-efficient, high-performance storage system combining SSDS and HDDS. In: IEEE 19th International Symposium on Modeling, Analysis & Simulation of Computer and Telecommunication Systems (MASCOTS 2011), pp. 227–236. IEEE (2011)

17. Koller, R., Marmol, L., Rangaswami, R., Sundararaman, S., Talagala, N., Zhao, M.: Write policies for host-side flash caches. In: FAST, pp. 45–58 (2013)

18. Koller, R., Rangaswami, R.: I/o deduplication: utilizing content similarity to improve i/o performance. ACM Trans. Storage (TOS) **6**(3), 13 (2010)

19. Lee, E., Bahn, H., Noh, S.H.: Unioning of the buffer cache and journaling layers with non-volatile memory. In: FAST, pp. 73–80 (2013)

20. Leung, A.W., Pasupathy, S., Goodson, G.R., Miller, E.L.: Measurement and analysis of large-scale network file system workloads. In: USENIX Annual Technical Conference, vol. 1, no. 2, pp. 2–5 (June 2008)

21. Leung, A.W.: Organizing, indexing, and searching large-scale file systems. Dissertations & Theses - Gradworks (2009)
22. Leung, A.W., Shao, M., Bisson, T., Pasupathy, S., Miller, E.L.: Spyglass: fast, scalable metadata search for large-scale storage systems. In: FAST, vol. 9, pp. 153–166 (2009)
23. Liu, N., Cope, J., Carns, P., Carothers, C., Ross, R., Grider, G., Crume, A., Maltzahn, C.: On the role of burst buffers in leadership-class storage systems. In: IEEE 28th Symposium on Mass Storage Systems and Technologies (MSST 2012), pp. 1–11. IEEE (2012)
24. Narayanan, D., Thereska, E., Donnelly, A., Elnikety, S., Rowstron, A.: Migrating server storage to SSDS: analysis of tradeoffs. In: Proceedings of the 4th ACM European Conference on Computer Systems, pp. 145–158. ACM (2009)
25. Oh, Y., Choi, J., Lee, D., Noh, S.H.: Caching less for better performance: balancing cache size and update cost of flash memory cache in hybrid storage systems. In: FAST, vol. 12 (2012)
26. Peters, M.: Compellent harnessing SSDS potential. ESG Storage Systems Brief (2009)
27. Qiang, Z., Chu, L.: Cernet io workloads: analysis and characterization? J. Comput. Inf. Syst. 8(14), 6017–6024 (2012)
28. Qiu, S., Reddy, A.N.: Exploiting superpages in a nonvolatile memory file system. In: IEEE 28th Symposium on Mass Storage Systems and Technologies (MSST 2012), pp. 1–5. IEEE (2012)
29. Ghemawat, S., Gobioff, H., Leung, S.T.: The Google file system. ACM SIGOPS Operating Syst. Rev. 37(5), 29–43 (2003)
30. Sehgal, P., Voruganti, K., Sundaram, R.: Slo-aware hybrid store. In: IEEE 28th Symposium on Mass Storage Systems and Technologies (MSST 2012), pp. 1–6. IEEE (2012)
31. Lasser, C., Lordi, R., Stanfill, C.: U.S. Patent No. 5,897,638. U.S. Patent and Trademark Office, Washington, DC (1999)
32. Vanichpun, S., Makowski, A.M.: The output of a cache under the independent reference model: where did the locality of reference go? In: ACM SIGMETRICS Performance Evaluation Review, vol. 32, pp. 295–306. ACM (2004)
33. Wallace, G., Douglis, F., Qian, H., Shilane, P., Smaldone, S., Chamness, M., Hsu, W.: Characteristics of backup workloads in production systems. In: FAST, p. 4 (2012)
34. Wang, F., Xin, Q., Hong, B., Brandt, S.A., Miller, E.L., Long, D.D., McLarty, T.T.: File system workload analysis for large scale scientific computing applications. In: Proceedings of the 21st IEEE/12th NASA Goddard Conference on Mass Storage Systems and Technologies, pp. 139–152 (2004)
35. Weil, S.A., Brandt, S.A., Miller, E.L., Long, D.D.E., Maltzahn, C.: Ceph: a scalable, high-performance distributed file system. In: Proceedings of the 7th Symposium on Operating Systems Design and Implementation (OSDI), pp. 307–320 (2006)
36. Weil, S.A., Pollack, K.T., Brandt, S.A., Miller, E.L.: Dynamic metadata management for petabyte-scale file systems. In: Proceedings of the 2004 ACM/IEEE Conference on Supercomputing, p. 4. IEEE Computer Society (2004)
37. Welch, B., Noer, G.: Optimizing a hybrid SSD/HDD HPC storage system based on file size distributions. In: IEEE 29th Symposium on Mass Storage Systems and Technologies (MSST 2013), pp. 1–12 (2013)

38. Dufrasne, B., Bauer, W., Careaga, B., Myyrrylainen, J., Rainero, A., Usong, P.: IBM System Storage DS8700 Architecture and Implementation. IBM Redbooks (2011)

39. Xing, J., Xiong, J., Sun, N., Ma, J.: Adaptive and scalable metadata management to support a trillion files. In: Proceedings of the Conference on High Performance Computing Networking, Storage and Analysis, p. 26. ACM (2009)

40. Xu, Q., Arumugam, R.V., Yong, K.L., Mahadevan, S.: Drop: facilitating distributed metadata management in EB-scale storage systems. In: IEEE 29th Symposium on Mass Storage Systems and Technologies (MSST 2013), pp. 1–10. IEEE (2013)

Parallel Training GBRT Based on KMeans Histogram Approximation for Big Data

Rong Gu[1], Lei Jin[1], Yongwei Wu[2], Jingying Qu[2], Tao Wang[2], Xiaojun Wang[2], Chunfeng Yuan[1], and Yihua Huang[1]([⊠])

[1] National Key Laboratory for Novel Software Technology,
Collaborative Innovation Center of Novel Software Technology
and Industrialization, Nanjing University, Nanjing 210023, China
{gurong,jinlei}@smail.nju.edu.cn, {cfyuan,yhuang}@nju.edu.cn
[2] Baidu, Inc., Beijing 100085, China
{wuyongwei03,qujingying,wangtao07,wangxiaojun01}@baidu.com

Abstract. Gradient Boosting Regression Tree (GBRT), one of the state-of-the-art ranking algorithms widely used in industry, faces challenges in the big data era. With the rapid increase in the sizes of datasets, the iterative training process of GBRT becomes very time-consuming over large scale data. In this paper, we aim to speed up the training process of each tree in the GBRT framework. First, we propose a novel KMeans histogram building algorithm which has lower time complexity and is more efficient than the cutting-edge histogram building method. Further, we put forward an approximation algorithm by combining the kernel density estimation with the histogram technique to improve the accuracy. We conduct a variety of experiments on both the public Learning To Rank(LTR) benchmark datasets and the large-scale real-world datasets from Baidu search engine. The experimental results show that our proposed parallel training algorithm outperforms the state-of-the-art parallel GBRT algorithm with near 2 times speedup and better accuracy. Also, our algorithm achieves the near-linear scalability.

Keywords: Learning To Rank · Gradient boosting regression tree · Parallel computing · KMeans histogram · Kernel density estimation

1 Introduction

The past decade has witnessed the rise of the large amount of data generated from the World Wide Web and the Mobile Internet. Information retrieval systems such as search engines, have been playing an important role in allowing users to fast retrieve information from the vast data. The important component of information retrieval systems is the ranking function, which is responsible for returning the retrieved documents in the order of the decreasing relevance to the query. Learning To Rank (LTR) is one of the critical techniques used in information retrieval systems. Learning to rank refers to machine learning techniques in a ranking task [17]. It has also been adopted in a wide range of

© Springer International Publishing Switzerland 2015
G. Wang et al. (Eds.): ICA3PP 2015, Part II, LNCS 9529, pp. 52–65, 2015.
DOI: 10.1007/978-3-319-27122-4_4

fields including Natural Language Processing and Data Mining [7]. A lot of algorithms and frameworks have been proposed to deal with learning to rank such as RankNet [2], ListNet [3], LambdaMART [15], NDCG Boost [14] and GBRT [13]. Among them, GBRT is one of the cutting-edge LTR algorithms [13]. It is an ensemble learning method which combines the gradient boosting framework and regression tree algorithm together [6]. Like many other boosting frameworks, gradient boosting creates a set of weak learners in an iterative manner. It tries to acquire the model by optimizing the loss function in function space rather than parameter space and achieves better results than many traditional methods.

However, efficiently training GBRT model over big data is very challenging [13]. First, the framework of gradient boosting is essentially sequential, which limits the parallelization of the framework. Second, the construction of each regression tree usually involves data sorting, which can be quite time-demanding with large scale datasets [12]. In this paper, we present a novel parallel GBRT training algorithm for efficiently processing big data. We aim to accelerate the training process of each individual regression tree in the gradient boosting framework. During the training process, the histograms representation of the training dataset is learned by the KMeans algorithm in data parallelism fashion. Based on the learned histograms, we further propose the kernel density estimation method to approximate the best split point for each regression tree node. We implement our proposed parallel algorithm on both multi-core and distributed environments. The experimental results on the public LTR benchmark datasets and the real-world large scale datasets of Baidu show that, compared with the state-of-the art parallel GBRT algorithms [13], our method gains near 2 times speedup and achieves even better NDCG accuracy without losing scalability.

2   Background

2.1   Gradient Boosting Regression Tree

The Gradient Boosting is a machine learning technique to learn a regression model. It is actually an extension of parameter optimization in function space [6]. Given the training set $D = \{(x_i, y_i)\}_{i=1}^{N}$, where x_i denotes the feature vector and y_i denotes the regression target. The regression task is to find such a function $F(x; \theta)$ with parameters $\theta = \{\theta_1, \theta_2, ..., \theta_m\}$ to minimize a loss function $L(y, F(x; \theta))$. Gradient Boosting adopts an iterative way of optimizing the loss function in function space. Here, we briefly illustrate the gradient boosting regression framework in Algorithm 1.

2.2   Kernel Density Estimation

Kernel density estimation is a non-parametric method of estimating the possibility distribution function of a random variable in the statistical field. Assume that we have n independent observations $\{x_i\}_{i=1}^{n}$ drawn from the variable X which is subject to an unknown probability distribution $f(x)$. The goal of the

---

Algorithm 1. The framework of GBRT

Require:

    Training set: $\{(x_i, y_i)\}_{i=1}^{N}$; Number of iterations: M;

    Loss function: $L(y, F(x))$; Shrinkage: s.

Ensure:

    The predict function: $F(x)$.

1: $F_0(x) = \arg\min\limits_{\gamma} \sum_{i=1}^{N} L(y_i, \gamma)$.

2: **for** $m = 1$ to M **do**

3:    Update the training target with:

    $y_i' = -\left[\frac{\partial L(y_i, F(x_i))}{F(x_i)}\right]_{F(x)=F_{m-1}(x)}$ $i = 1, ..., N$.

4:    Fit the regression tree model $f_m(x; \alpha_m)$ into the new training set $\{(x_i, y_i')\}_{i=1}^{N}$.

5:    Update the predict model:

    $F_m(x) = F_{m-1}(x) + s * f_m(x; \alpha_m)$.

6: **end for**

7: **return** $F_m(x)$

---

kernel density estimation is to estimate the probability distribution function with the observations as the only information we have. By applying the kernel density estimation method on the observations above, the density function $f(x)$ we estimate becomes:

$$f_h'(x) = \frac{1}{Nh} \sum_{i=1}^{n} K\left(\frac{x - x_i}{h}\right) \tag{1}$$

where K is the kernel function which integrates to one and h is a parameter called bandwidth which has a great impact on the final probability density curve. We usually get an under-smoothed estimation with a smaller bandwidth and an over-smoothed estimation with a larger bandwidth. The kernel density estimation is a very important approach in the density estimation field. In our algorithm, we combine it with histogram methods to improve the accuracy.

3   Related Work

Many research efforts have been devoted to improving the training speed of the GBRT model. Previously, researchers adopt various techniques like task parallelism and data parallelism to speed up the training process of each individual tree [12]. The task parallelism methods speed up the process by parallelizing the construction of different tree nodes. However, this method suffers from the data imbalance problem. The data parallelism accelerates the training process by distributing the training samples among processors, either vertically or horizontally [11]. Each processor conducts the same execution with local data partitions which have similar sizes. In [10], Planet parallelizes the training process in this way on MapReduce [5]. However, MapReduce does not perform well with iterative tasks.

Also, researchers exploit approximation algorithms to accelerate the training process of the GBRT model. For example, histogram approaches are proposed to speed up the construction of a single tree by reducing the time of finding best splits of tree nodes [1]. Since the size of a histogram is considerably smaller than the entire training dataset, this method can speed up the training process a lot. The histogram method is also used in [13] to speed up the training of GBRT for web search rank. The strategy in this paper is an optimized histogram approximation method combining with data parallelism.

4   Parallel GBRT Training Algorithm

To avoid the time-consuming sorting process during the construction of each individual tree in GBRT, we propose a novel KMeans histogram approximation method. To further improve the accuracy of the model, we adopt a kernel density estimation method in our histogram approximation.

4.1   KMeans Histogram Approximation for Regression Tree

The GBRT model is made up of many regression trees which are generated sequentially. A regression tree is created by iteratively splitting its nodes until the stop criteria is satisfied. To split a node, a best split feature and the corresponding split value need to be found over the data in this node and this is also the most time-consuming stage of the construction of a tree. Here, we analyze the process and difficulties in finding the best split value as below.

For the data $D = \{x_i, y_i\}_{i=1}^N$ in a tree node T, where x_i is the feature value (for simplicity, x_i here is a one dimensional value of one feature) and y_i denotes the regression target value or label. In fact, a split value x' splits the data into two subsets $D_1 = \{(x, y)|x < x'\}$ and $D_2 = \{(x, y)|x \geq x'\}$. The best split value x' is usually found in regression tree by minimizing the node impurity criterion. In regression, we minimize the sum of squared residuals:

$$\min_{x'} \sum_{y \in D_1} (y - \bar{y}_L)^2 + \sum_{y \in D_2} (y - \bar{y}_R)^2 \tag{2}$$

$$= \min_{x'} \frac{Y_L^2}{n_L} - 2\frac{Y_L}{n_L} \sum_{i=1}^{n_L} y_i + \frac{Y_R^2}{n_R} - 2\frac{Y_R}{n_R} \sum_{i=n_L+1}^{n_L+n_R} y_i$$

$$= \min_{x'} -\frac{Y_L^2}{n_L} - \frac{Y_R^2}{n_R}$$

As we can see, the node impurity criterion can be rewritten as:

$$-\frac{Y_L^2}{n_L} - \frac{Y_R^2}{n_R} \tag{3}$$

where Y_L and Y_R denotes the sum of the labels of D_1 and D_2, n_L and n_R denotes the number of instances in D_1 and D_2, $\bar{y}_L$ and $\bar{y}_R$ means the average target value in D_1 and D_2. To find the best split value, the original algorithm needs to sort the feature values of the whole D which leads to $O(nlog(n))$ time complexity. This is very time-consuming when the number of training samples and features becomes large both in the single-node and distributed environments.

Here, we adopt the approximation framework based on KMeans histogram to estimate the best split value. By approximating the sum of labels and the number of of instances with feature value smaller the candidate split value x', we can calculate the cost by the tree node impurity criterion above and further get the best split value for the feature. To approximate the node impurity criterion given a specific split point, we need to approximate the value of Y_L(or Y_R) and n_L(or n_R) at first. These values can be approximated by the histogram technics. The histogram can be regarded as the compression of the dataset. During its construction, the data is compressed into a fix-sized histogram which can be used to approximate the best split values. In our approach, we improve the histogram method by adopting the KMeans algorithm to fast generate it. Further, we improve the accuracy of the approximation approach by using the kernel density estimation technics.

The form of a histogram is a set of bins $H = \{(p_1, m_1), (p_2, m_2), \ldots, (p_B, m_B)\}$, where p_i is the bin center and m_i is the statistical variable to approximate. Since we need to approximate the sum of the label Y_L, Y_R and the number of the instance n_L, n_R, these statistical variables are added into the bin. In fact, the KMeans algorithms could also be regarded as a kind of density estimation method. The K clusters can be viewed as K high-density regions and the centers of the clusters are the K bins in histogram. We only need one iteration clustering process to construct the histogram which can be done by the online way. The KMeans histogram construction algorithm is described in Algorithm 2. Without loss of generality, the feature vector here is one dimensional. When constructing histogram of K bins, we first randomly select K bin centers (cluster centers), then the instances are added one by one into the closest bin. Every add action triggers the update of the bin information locally.

Algorithm 2. KMeans Histogram Construction

Require:
   The input dataset: $\{(x_i, y_i)\}_{i=1}^N$;
   The number of bins(clusters) in Histogram: B.
Ensure:
   The histogram: $H = \{(b_i, n_i, Y_i))\}_{i=1}^B$.
1: Randomly select B instances from the dataset to initialize the histogram as: $H = \{(b_i, 1, y_i)\}_{i=1}^B$ where b_i is the ith instance value x_i and y_i is the ith target value.
2: **for** $i = 1$ to $N - B$ **do**
3:    Find the nearest bin center b_j for the ith instance (x_i, y_i).
4:    Update the jth bin information with:
   $\left(\frac{b_j * n_j + x_i}{n_j + 1}, n_j + 1, Y_j + y_i\right)$.
5: **end for**
6: **return** The histogram: H.

Given a dataset of N instances, the time cost of constructing a histogram of b bins is $O(Nb)$. As b is much smaller than N, the time complexity is much lower than pre-sorting method's $O(Nlog(N))$. It is also lower than the $O(Nblog(b))$ time complexity of the original histogram algorithm proposed in [1]. Since the histogram representation can be updated incrementally, it can also be handled in the streaming processing way as well.

Once we get the histograms of each feature, we can use them to approximate the statistical variable it summarizes. For GBRT, the number of instances (the sum of regression targets) left to a split point is needed to be approximated. Therefore, we generate the probability density function first before further generating the cumulative distribution function. A simple but inefficient way for generating the probability density function is applying the kernel function to each training sample and then adding them up. Here, we propose a novel approach by combing the histogram and kernel density estimation together to reduce the time cost of generating the probability density function. Given a histogram of M bins: $H = \{(b_i, n_i, Y_i)\}_{i=1}^{M}$. For a bin (cluster) center b_i, the statistical variable n_i means that there are about n_i instances around the value b_i. Thus, we can just naturally apply the kernel function to each bin center n_i times and add them up to get the probability density function as below:

$$f'(x) = \frac{1}{N} \sum_{i=1}^{M} \frac{n_i}{h_i} K\left(\frac{x - b_i}{h_i}\right) \tag{4}$$

where h_i is the bandwidth of each bin and N is the total number of instances.

The probability density function of the sum of labels can be created in a similar way. However, in order to calculate n_L (or Y_L) given an arbitrary split point a, we need a cumulative distribution function. Thus, our algorithm needs an appropriate kernel function K, whose integral is an elementary function so that we can calculate the definite integral fast during computation. In this paper, we choose the Epanechnikov kernel function:

$$K(u) = \frac{3}{4}\left(1 - u^2\right) I\left(|u| \leq 1\right) \tag{5}$$

Thus, we can rewrite the probability density estimation function as:

$$f'(x) = \frac{1}{N} \sum_{i=1}^{M} \frac{3n_i}{4h_i} \left(1 - \left(\frac{x - b_i}{h_i}\right)^2\right) I\left(\left|\frac{x - b_i}{h_i}\right| \leq 1\right) \tag{6}$$

In this way, we can further calculate the integral of the probability density function $F(x)$. Given a specific split point a, we can calculate n_L in the following manner:

$$n_L \approx N * F(a) = \sum_{i=1}^{M} \frac{n_i}{h_i} * h_i(a) \tag{7}$$

where

$$h_i(a) = \begin{cases} 0 & a < b_i - h_i \\ \frac{3}{4}a - \frac{h_i}{4}\left(\frac{a-b_i}{h_i}\right)^3 & b_i - h_i \le a \le b_i + h_i \\ h_i & a > b_i + h_i \end{cases} \qquad (8)$$

As far as Y_L is concerned, we can approximate it in the same way. Finally, we calculate the node impurity criterion with these approximation methods.

The bandwidth h_i is an important parameter which influences the final probability density curve. For any bin center b_i, the bandwidth is set in the way below and works empirically well.

$$h_i = max\,(b_i - b_{i-1}, b_{i+1} - b_i) \qquad (9)$$

Until now, we have elaborated how to estimate the best split value for each feature. Based on this, we introduce the complete process of splitting a leaf node. For a specific tree node T with the data inside needing to be split, we first construct the histograms for each feature over the data. Then, we adopt the uniform procedure put forward in [1] to calculate the candidate split points set. The uniform procedure attempts to make the number of the instances between any neighboring split points approximately equal. Finally, we adopt the kernel function approximation method to calculate the sum of squared residuals of every candidate split value. Among them, we select the one which minimizes the impurity criterion as the best split value.

Algorithm 3 describes the entire workflow of creating an individual tree based on the KMeans histogram. The training process of GBRT is the iterative construction of every single tree as shown in Algorithm 1. The entire process only requires one scan over the dataset and the computation on each example is rather small. Benefitting from our efficient tree construction method, the total training time of the GBRT model can be reduced.

4.2   Parallelization

To further accelerate the training process, we parallelize the KMeans histogram GBRT in data parallelism way. The histogram information representing a dataset can also be constructed by combining several sub-histograms representing the subsets of the original set [1]. The parallel training framework is the master-worker mode which has one master and multiple workers. The workers execute the tasks in parallel under the coordination of the master. Specifically, we first split the training data horizontally into N parts and distribute them into N different workers. These N workers are only responsible for constructing histograms over the local data partitions. For splitting a tree node, all the workers first construct the sub-histograms over local data partitions and then send these histograms back to the master node. The master then merges all these sub-histograms to construct the histogram of global training data. Different data fragments are partitioned approximately in the same size to avoid draggers.

Algorithm 3. Train Regression Tree Using KMeans Histogram Approximation

Require:

The training dataset: $D = \{(x_i, y_i)\}_{i=1}^{N}$; Number of bins in each histogram: b; Number of candidates: c; The depth of the tree(stop criteria): h.

Ensure:

The trained tree model $F(x; \theta)$.

1: Initialize the tree with only the root node n_0, the train set D is initialized in this node. Add n_0 into node set N.

2: **while** $!N.isEmpty()$ **do**

3:    $n' = N.getFirst()$; $N.removeFirst()$

4:    **if** n' meets the stop criteria **then**

5:       Continue;

6:    **else**

7:       Create histogram $H = \{h_1, h_2, \ldots, h_f\}$ of all f features over the data D' in n' using k-means histogram construction method. Each histogram has b bins.

8:       Construct candidate split points sets $C = \{C_1, C_2, \ldots, C_f\}$, $C_i = \{s_1, s_2, \ldots, s_c\}$ for each feature.

9:       Get the best split feature f_i and the best split value v for n' among C using kernel density approximation.

10:       Split the node n' into two new nodes n_1 and n_2 by the split info and add them into N.

11:       Update the data in n_1 and n_2 by splitting the data D' in n' into D_1 and D_2.

12:    **end if**

13: **end while**

After the global histogram is constructed, the master then adopts the uniform procedure in [1] to construct a set of candidate split values. Further, it uses the approximation method proposed in Sect. 4.1 to select the best split feature and the corresponding value for each leaf node. The best split information will be sent to each worker to guide the split of their corresponding leaf nodes locally. At the worker side, it needs to collect some statistical information and send it back to the master after split. For example, the master needs to know how many instances each leaf node contains to decide whether to stop splitting process. We implement our parallel algorithms both in multi-core and distributed environments using OpenMP and MPI. Our proposed algorithm also naturally fits and can be easily implemented on the data parallel programming models such as MapReduce [5], Spark RDD [16].

5   Evaluation

We evaluate our algorithm, denoted as KH-GBRT(**K**means **H**istoram based **GBRT**), on both the public benchmarks and large-scale realistic data from Baidu, the largest Chinese search engine in the world. NDCG is adopted as our accuracy metric. For comparison, we also evaluate the accuracy and training speed of the state-of-the-art parallel GBRT(denoted as H-GBRT) [13] and the original parallel GBRT algorithm (denoted as ORIGINAL-GBRT) [9].

Both H-GBRT and KH-GBRT uses approximation strategies but ORIGINAL-GBRT does not. All the algorithms are implemented on the OpenMP or MPI programming models.

5.1   Platforms and Benchmarks

We conduct experiments on a cluster with 10 computing nodes. One node is reserved to act as the master, and the left 9 nodes are used as workers. Each node has two Xeon Quad 2.4 GHz processors, 64 GB memory and two 2 TB 7200 RPM SATA hard disks. The nodes are connected with 1 Gb/s Ethernet. All the nodes run on RHEL6 operating system and Ext3 file system. OpenMPI v1.8.3 and OpenMP carried by GCC 4.4.4 are installed on this cluster.

We adopt two widely-used Learning To Rank benchmark datasets, the Microsoft LETOR [8] and the YahooLTR benchmark, to evaluate the performance of the algorithms. The LETOR dataset contains 723,412 samples with 135 features. The dataset from Yahoo! LTR Challenge 2011 [4] has 473,134 samples with 699 features. Both datasets consist of training and testing datasets.

5.2   Performance Analysis

Accuracy Analysis. We first evaluate the accuracy of GBRT algorithms. The NDCG@10 of our algorithm KH-GBRT is compared with the H-GBRT [13] and the ORIGINAL-GBRT [9] on both LETOR and YahooLTR datasets. We also run our KH-GBRT without using the kernel density estimation (using the approximation method in [1] instead) to evaluate the effect of the kernel density estimation optimization.

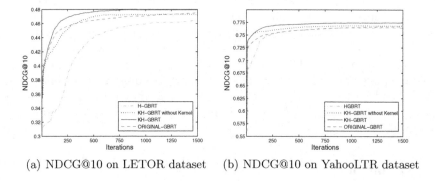

(a) NDCG@10 on LETOR dataset   (b) NDCG@10 on YahooLTR dataset

Fig. 1. NDCG@10 on LETOR and YahooLTR dataset

All the GBRT algorithms have the same configurations, which contain 1500 trees of depth 5, learning rate or shrinkage is 0.02 and the minimum number of the instances in leaf node is 10. For the histogram-based algorithms (KH-GBRT and H-GBRT), the number of bins that each worker creates for the histogram is 25 and the number of candidate split points is 500. The results are shown in Fig. 1(a) and (b) respectively. We can see that KH-GBRT outperforms H-GBRT and ORIGINAL-GBRT. This is due to the better generalization ability of KH-GBRT which can better avoid the overfitting problems. Especially, KH-GBRT achieves an obvious accuracy improvement over H-GBRT since the kernel-based probability density curve is closer to the actual density curve. By comparing KH-GBRT without using kernel density approximation, we observe around 1 % increase in NDCG@10 on LETOR and YahooLTR set respectively. This indicates that using the kernel density estimation optimization brings an obvious improvement in accuracy. The results also demonstrate that our algorithm has a faster convergence speed.

Training Speed Analysis. In this subsection, we evaluate the training speed of the KH-GBRT algorithm on parallel platforms. For performance comparison, we also evaluate the training speed of H-GBRT, which is the state-of-the-art parallel GBRT algorithm [13]. The ORIGINAL-GBRT is much slower than both KH-GBRT and H-GBRT, thus we leave it out in our figures.

We first study the performance on multi-core environment. One multi-core computing node and the LETOR dataset are used for this group of experiments. We trained 100 trees with the number of processors varying from 1 to 8. The bin number and the number of candidate split points are set 25 and 500 respectively. The learning rate is 0.02. As shown in Fig. 2(a), our algorithm always runs faster than the H-GBRT algorithm. It costs about 60 % of the time H-GBRT costs on average, achieving around 1.5 times of speedup compared to the H-GBRT algorithm. This is because KH-GBRT has lower time complexity than H-GBRT. In the multi-core machine, as the number of CPU cores increases from 1 to 8, our algorithm shows a speedup of almost 7, achieving the near-linear scalability on the multi-core parallel platform.

We then evaluate the performance of training time when the size of datasets increases. We construct the training sets of different sizes by replicating the LETOR sets several copies. We trained 100 regression trees of depth 5. The number of bins is 25 and the learning rate is 0.02. In Fig. 2(b), we can see that both methods gain the near-linear data scalability, but the time cost of our algorithm KH-GBRT is much less than H-GBRT and increases slower than H-GBRT.

Then, we evaluate the performance of KH-GBRT in the distributed environment. We train 500 trees of depth 5. The learning rate is 0.02 and the number of bins is 50. We first evaluate the performance when the number of training machines increases. As shown in Fig. 3(a), KH-GBRT has a faster training speed than H-GBRT. When the number of the computing nodes increases from 1 to 9, the time cost of KH-GBRT reduces from 32,230 s to 3,951 s with a speedup of 8.15, which is a near-linear speedup. While the time cost of H-GBRT reduces from 47,232 s to 6,255 s with a speedup of 7.55. We can see that with 9 computing nodes, the training time cost of KH-GBRT is about 63 % of H-GBRT, achieving

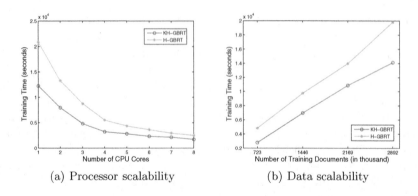

(a) Processor scalability   (b) Data scalability

Fig. 2. Scalability in multi-core environment

1.58 times of speedup. While the average time cost is 65 % of the time cost of
H-GBRT when the number of nodes varies from 1 to 9, achieving 1.54 times of
speedup.

Also, we evaluate the data salability of our methods. We construct the training sets with different sizes by replicating the LETOR set several copies. We
trained 50 regression trees of depth 5. The number of bins is 25 and the learning rate is 0.02. Figure 3(b) illustrates that both methods scale well with large
datasets, but the time cost of KH-GBRT increases slower than H-GBRT.

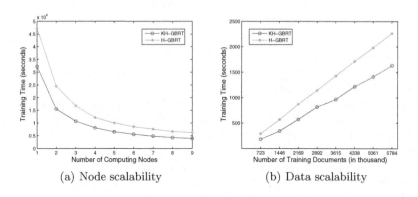

(a) Node scalability   (b) Data scalability

Fig. 3. Scalability in distributed environment

5.3   Performance in Large Scale Real-World Applications

Besides evaluating on the public LTR benchmarks, we also evaluate our algorithm on the large scale realistic data from Baidu search engine for Learning To
Rank. Even a slight improvement in training speed or accuracy would save a
lot of resource and benefit billions of people on such a large real-world application. Experiments in this subsection are conducted on the production cluster at

Baidu. Each computing node is equipped with an Intel Xeon CPU E5-2420, each with 32 GB memory and 6 physical cores with the frequency of 1.9 GHz. Two real-world datasets are adopted. One of them contains about 20,000,000 samples and the other contains about 80,000,000 samples. They both have 36 features.

Accuracy Analysis. We evaluate the NDCG accuracy and training speed of the KH-GBRT algorithm on the dataset with 20 million training samples under 8 workers. We train 500 trees with each with the depth of 5. The learning rate is 0.5 and the number of bins of histogram varies from 5 to 25. For comparison, we evaluate the existing Baidu's GBRT implementation (denoted as Baidu-GBRT), which is an optimized distributed GBRT but not open, under the same training configurations and hardware environment. Table 1 shows that our algorithm is very competitive compared with Baidu-GBRT. It even achieves slightly better performance on each NDCG accuracy than Baidu's existing GBRT solution. As for the training time, KH-GBRT only costs about half of the time of Baidu-GBRT, which would save a lot of resources in real-world production scenarios.

Table 1. NDCG performance comparison on Baidu's real-world datasets

Model	NDCG@1	NDCG@3	NDCG@5	Time(s)
Baidu-GBRT	0.6268	0.6244	0.6347	7,716
KH-GBRT(5bin)	0.6297	**0.6254**	**0.6355**	**3,711**
KH-GBRT(10bin)	0.6294	0.6248	0.6344	3,802
KH-GBRT(15bin)	0.6290	0.6245	0.6348	3,811
KH-GBRT(20bin)	**0.6302**	0.6253	0.6348	3,834
KH-GBRT(25bin)	0.6289	0.6247	0.6352	3,866

Training Speed Analysis. In this subsection, we compare the speedup performance of our algorithm with Baidu-GBRT. First, we evaluate the performance when the number of training machines increases. The dataset adopted in this group of experiments contains 80 million training samples. The GBRT model is trained with 50 trees of depth of 5 with the learning rate 0.5. KH-GBRT constructs 5 bins in each histogram, as this configuration shows better NDCG accuracy performance on Baidu datasets. The number of training nodes varies from 1 to 8. The results are shown in Fig. 4(a). We can see that the training time of our algorithm decreases from 7,693 s to 2,335 s when the number of training nodes increases from 1 to 8. In fact, as we can see from Fig. 4(a) that, Baidu-GBRT fail to handle the data with 2 nodes because of the lack of memory. With 8 machines, the time cost of KH-GBRT is around 60 % of Baidu-GBRT, achieving 1.6 times of speedup compared to it.

We also evaluate the performance on training sets with different sizes varying from 10 million to 80 million. Again, we train 50 trees with depth of 5. The learning rate is 0.5 and the number of bins in histogram is 15. From Fig. 4(b), we can see that both our algorithm and Baidu-GBRT scale well as the size of datasets increases. KH-GBRT runs faster than Baidu-GBRT. The time cost of our algorithm increases from 206 s to 1,493 s when the size varies from 10 million to 80 million. As for Baidu-GBRT, the time cost increases from 379 seconds to 3,549 s. The time cost of KH-GBRT is about 40 % of the time cost of Baidu-GBRT, achieving 2.5 times of speedup compared to Baidu-GBRT. Also, the average time cost of KH-GBRT is about 47 % of the time cost of Baidu-GBRT when the data size varies from 10 million to 80 million, achieving a speedup of about 2.13.

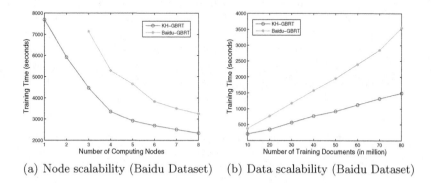

(a) Node scalability (Baidu Dataset)   (b) Data scalability (Baidu Dataset)

Fig. 4. Scalability on Baidu dataset

6 Conclusion and Future Work

Learning to rank is one of the critical techniques used in information retrieval systems, while GBRT is a widely-used algorithm in web search ranking [13]. In this paper, we present a parallel algorithm for efficiently training GBRT on large scale datasets. We propose a novel KMeans-Based histogram construction algorithm and combine it with the kernel density estimation technic for higher efficiency and accuracy. The experimental results show that our algorithm out-performs the state-of-the-art parallel GBRT algorithm on training speed and accuracy under the public LTR benchmark datasets and the Baidu's large-scale realistic datasets. In the further, we plan to explore more approximation methods for many other large scale machine learning tasks.

Acknowledgments. This work is funded in part by Jiangsu Province Industry Support Program (BE2014131), China NSF Grants (No. 61572250 & No. 61223003) and Baidu *the most valuable topics* Open Research Project.

References

1. Ben-Haim, Y., Tom-Tov, E.: A streaming parallel decision tree algorithm. J. Mach. Learn. Res. (JMLR) **11**, 849–872 (2010)

2. Burges, C., Shaked, T., Renshaw, E., Lazier, A., Deeds, M., Hamilton, N., Hullender, G.: Learning to rank using gradient descent. In: Proceedings of the 22nd International Conference on Machine Learning (ICML), pp. 89–96. ACM (2005)
3. Cao, Z., Qin, T., Liu, T.Y., Tsai, M.F., Li, H.: Learning to rank: from pairwise approach to listwise approach. In: Proceedings of the 24th International Conference on Machine Learning (ICML), pp. 129–136. ACM (2007)
4. Chapelle, O., Chang, Y.: Yahoo! learning to rank challenge overview. In: Proceedings of JMLR: Workshop and Conference on Yahoo! Learning to Rank, pp. 1–24 (2011)
5. Dean, J., Ghemawat, S.: Mapreduce: simplified data processing on large clusters. Commun. ACM 51(1), 107–113 (2008)
6. Friedman, J.H.: Greedy function approximation: a gradient boosting machine. Ann. Stat. 29(5), 1189–1232 (2001)
7. Hang, L.: A short introduction to learning to rank. IEICE Trans. Inf. Syst. 94(10), 1854–1862 (2011)
8. Liu, T.Y., Xu, J., Qin, T., Xiong, W., Li, H.: Letor: benchmark dataset for research on learning to rank for information retrieval. In: Proceedings of SIGIR 2007 Workshop on Learning To Rank for Information Retrieval, pp. 3–10 (2007)
9. Mohan, A., Chen, Z., Weinberger, K.Q.: Web-search ranking with initialized gradient boosted regression trees. In: JMLR: Workshop and Conference Proceedings, pp. 77–89 (2011)
10. Panda, B., Herbach, J.S., Basu, S., Bayardo, R.J.: Planet: massively parallel learning of tree ensembles with mapreduce. Proc. VLDB Endowment 2(2), 1426–1437 (2009)
11. Shafer, J., Agrawal, R., Mehta, M.: Sprint: a scalable parallel classi er for data mining. In: Proceedings of the 1996 International Conference Very Large Data Basesm (VLDB), pp. 544–555. Citeseer (1996)
12. Srivastava, A., Han, E.H., Kumar, V., Singh, V.: Parallel formulations of decision-tree classification algorithms. In: Proceedings of the 1988 International Conference on Parallel Processing (ICPP), pp. 237–244. IEEE (1998)
13. Tyree, S., Weinberger, K.Q., Agrawal, K., Paykin, J.: Parallel boosted regression trees for web search ranking. In: Proceedings of the 20th International Conference on World Wide Web(WWW), pp. 387–396. ACM (2011)
14. Valizadegan, H., Jin, R., Zhang, R., Mao, J.: Learning to rank by optimizing ndcg measure. In: Bengio, Y., Schuurmans, D., Lafferty, J., Williams, C., Culotta, A. (eds.) Advances in Neural Information Processing Systems 22 (NIPS), pp. 1883–1891. Curran Associates Inc., Red Hook (2009)
15. Wu, Q., Burges, C.J., Svore, K.M., Gao, J.: Ranking, boosting, and model adaptation. Tecnical report, MSR-TR-2008-109 (2008)
16. Zaharia, M., Chowdhury, M., Das, T., Dave, A., Ma, J., McCauley, M., Franklin, M.J., Shenker, S., Stoica, I.: Resilient distributed datasets: a fault-tolerant abstraction for in-memory cluster computing. In: Proceedings of the 9th USENIX Conference on Networked Systems Design and Implementation (NSDI), pp. 2–12. USENIX Association (2012)
17. Zheng, Z., Zha, H., Zhang, T., Chapelle, O., Chen, K., Sun, G.: A general boosting method and its application to learning ranking functions for web search. In: Advances in Neural Information Processing Systems (NIPS), pp. 1697–1704 (2008)

DBSCAN-M: An Intelligent Clustering Algorithm Based on Mutual Reinforcement

Yin Li[1(✉)], Chuyuan Guo[2], Ronghua Shi[1], Xiaoqun Liu[3],
and Yan Mei[4]

[1] School of Information Science and Engineering,
Central South University, Changsha 410083, China
{liyin2012, shirh}@csu.edu.cn
[2] School of Software Engineering, Central South University,
Changsha 410075, China
gcytime@foxmail.com
[3] Dongting Lake Water Resources Administration Bureau
of Hunan Province, Changsha 410083, China
lxql1488@163.com
[4] College of Network Education, Central South University,
Changsha 410083, China
sugar24@sohu.com

Abstract. An intelligent clustering algorithm named DBSCAN-M is proposed for the purpose of data mining, which improves the recognition rate of noise under the circumstance of high noise density forming new clusters. The proposed algorithm is a synthesis of density clustering theory from DBSCAN (Density-Based Spatial Clustering of Applications with Noise) and mutual reinforcement from HITS (Hypertext Induced Topic Search) within search engine technology. The core points and clusters in the data set are mutually reinforced, thereby the capability of accurate identification of the noise is enhanced beneath high noise density. An algorithmic model was established, and simulations are taken by the WEKA software with real data sets from the University of California. Results showed that the proposed algorithm can obtain a more accurate recognition of the noises contrasting with the usual DBSCAN algorithm.

Keywords: DBSCAN · Noise clustering · HITS · Mutual reinforcement

1 Introduction

The Internet of Things (IoT) provided advanced and intelligent services to the world, and tremendous data were produce simultaneously in recent years. Data mining (DM) techniques have been widely used in many fields [1], and it has already become an important part in IoT [2]. DBSCAN (Density-Based Spatial Clustering of Applications with Noise) is a density-based clustering algorithm, which is different from the hierarchical clustering method, it defines clusters as the maximum collection of points with density connectivity, and the region that has sufficient density can be divided into clusters [3]. One of the DBSCAN applications is finding noise. The purpose of testing

© Springer International Publishing Switzerland 2015
G. Wang et al. (Eds.): ICA3PP 2015, Part II, LNCS 9529, pp. 66–77, 2015.
DOI: 10.1007/978-3-319-27122-4_5

is to find the points which have special behavior or unusual properties compared with the most other objects within the data set.

Two character parameters are used in the DBSCAN execution, which are MinPts and Eps. The DBSCAN algorithm distinguish the clusters by the predefined parameter MinPts, when the number of noise is greater than the threshold of MinPts, a new cluster is formed, thus the identification rate of outliers begin to decline if the noises form a new cluster. Aiming at this shortcoming of DBSCAN, an improved algorithm adopting the HITS (Hypertext Induced Topic Search) from the ranking algorithm in search engine technology is proposed. The HITS make mutual reinforcement between the Authority page and the Hub page, which method is introduced and improved in our clustering algorithm named DBSCAN-M. This novel approach solves the problem of noises at high density forming new clusters, and the problem usually confuses the distinguish result of the noise from the normal ones. This approach also extends the application scope of search engine ranking algorithms in DM. Beneath the stable external environment, DBSCAN-M computes on the data points and the clusters with mutual reinforcements, thus the newly formed noise cluster is taken into secondary or multiple assessments, ultimately the accuracy and reliability of outlier data mining are improved remarkably. Experiments are taken based on the real data sets, and the simulation results show that the proposed approach has great performance comparing with the origin DBSCAN algorithm.

The contributions of this paper for DBSCAN-M algorithm are as follows.

(1) The mutual reinforcement mechanism is applied to the regular points and clusters, which greatly improves the recognition rate of noises even they formed new clusters with high density.
(2) The proposed algorithm can be calculated according to the internal characteristics of the given data, thereby the reliance on the input parameters is reduced.

2 Related Work

Many researchers have made intensive studies on the DBSCAN algorithm [4–6], and they obtained a lot of achievements. While there are still some deficiencies need to be settled, for instance, DBSCAN algorithm is often obsessed with how to choose the appropriate values of Eps and MinPts for efficient and accurate calculation. Another problem of noise recognition is more obvious since one of the basis for evaluating the point as a noise is based on the value of MinPts. If the noise density is greater than MinPts and forms a new cluster, DBSCAN will be confused and make a wrong conclusion.

In the aspect of noise identification, Feng P. J. et al. [7] used numbers of different parameters of Eps for clustering, then chose one of the most optimal results. This approach solves the problem of automatically selecting parameters of Eps, while the time complexity increases.

Birant D et al. [8] and Koteshwariah C B et al. [9] studied based on the ability of non-spatial and spatial data to discover clusters of objects, and the noise can be found in different clusters density exist. However, results from the data warehouse are relatively large, more powerful computing capacity is required.

Smiti Abir et al. [10] studied the DBSCAN algorithm by using fuzzy set theory, the results of the method showed that it was not only efficient in handling noises, but also able to assign one data point into more than one cluster. While the results did not address the problem of accumulated noise in some particular applications.

The massive data generated by the IoT are considered of huge potential value, and DM can be applied to this area to obtain the hidden valuable information. Feng Chen et al. [11] and Shah M et al. [12] gave a systematic way to review DM in knowledge and application aspects, a brief review of the features of DM for IoT usage is given, including classification, clustering, association analysis, time series analysis and outlier analysis.

3 Motivational Factors

3.1 DBSCAN Algorithm

The DBSCAN algorithm was proposed by Martin Ester [13], which is one of the most common clustering algorithms. It is designed to discover clusters of arbitrary shape as well as to distinguish noises. The core concept of the algorithm is that, within the predefined radius (Eps) surrounding each core object of the cluster, the number of data objects must be greater than the other predefined value (MinPts). The main phases of DBSCAN are as follows. Object p is been chosen randomly from the object set D then inspection begins, if p is a core object, all the density reachable objects satisfied the given parameters of Eps and MinPts should be identified, and a new cluster is created. On the contrast, the object p is not a core subject, it will be considered as a noise temporarily. Then another object in the data set will be chosen randomly and the same steps will be performed until all object processing finished. In terms of noise finding, most of the definitions about DBSCAN algorithm are defined as follows [13, 14].

Definition 1: Eps-neighborhood
To the given data object p, Eps neighborhood is defined that p as the core and the Eps for the area radius, i.e.

$$N_{Eps} = \left\{ q \in D | dist(p, q) < E_{ps} \right\} \tag{1}$$

$dist(p, q)$ represents the distance of D between the object p and object q.

Definition 2: Core Point
Core Point is a point if it has more than a specified number of points within the radius of Eps. These points are at the interior of a same cluster.

Definition 3: Directly Density-Reachable
Object p is directly density-reachable from the object q if the object p and q are met

$$p \in E_{ps}(q) \tag{2}$$

and

$$N_{Eps}(q) > MinPts \tag{3}$$

Definition 4: Density-Reachable

To the given data set D, if there exist a chain of objects p1, p2, p3, …, and pn, where $p_1 = q$, $p_n = p$, for $p_i \in D$ if p_{i+1} is directly density-reachable from p_i beneath the conditions $(E_{ps}, MinPts)$, then object p defined as density-reachable from object q.

Definition 5: Cluster and Noise Point

All the density reachable objects from an arbitrary core point and the core itself constitute a cluster.

A noise point is a point that is not a core point or not belongs to any cluster.

As shown in Fig. 1, MinPts is set to 3 and A represents a core point. Point B from point C is density-reachable belongs to the same cluster. Obviously, point N is a noise, it is not a core point or density-reachable from any point in the former cluster.

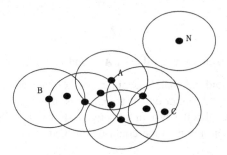

Fig. 1. Schematic diagram of the DBSCAN algorithm

3.2 HITS Algorithm

The HITS algorithm was proposed by Dr. JM Kleinberg of Cornell University in 1997 [15]. It evaluates the quality of web pages by two feather weights of the Authority and the Hub. The algorithm analyzes the Hub on the basis of valuation of Authority from each page, then a comprehensive assessment result of the page was given.

The HITS was also defined as Hubs and Authorities [16], which is an algorithm of web page and link analysis [17]. Currently, it has been used as a link analysis algorithm by Teoma search engine (www.teoma.com).

The Hub and Authority pages are the most fundamental definitions of HITS algorithm [18]. The authority page refers to the web page which is highly associated with a certain area, for instance, Google in the search engine and Facebook in the social networking. The Hub page contains a lot of high-quality Authority web page links, such as the origin Yahoo navigator. The core concept of HITS algorithm is mutual reinforcement between Authority pages and Hub pages. In other words, the higher the quality of the Hub is, the quality of their Authority links are better, and vice versa. By iterative calculations of this mutually reinforcing relationship, the high quality Hub and Authority pages could be found as a natural consequence.

The details of HITS algorithm are shown as follows.

(1) $A(i)$ and $H(i)$ indicate the value of Authority and Hub of a web page separately.
(2) For the expansion set, it is difficult to examine which pages are of high Authority quality or high Hub quality, each page has a potential possibility. Thus two weights of each page are set up, to record the possibilities of being a high quality of Authority page and Hub page respectively.
(3) The weights of Authority and Hub are been calculated in each iteration. The authority weight of page $A(i)$ is the sum of all the Hub weight pointing to the page $A(i)$, i.e.

$$A(i) = \sum H(i) \tag{4}$$

And the Hub weight of the page $A(i)$ is the sum of the Authority weights of all pointed pages in the page $A(i)$, i.e.

$$H(i) = \sum A(i) \tag{5}$$

At the end of the iteration, the value of $A(i)$ and $H(i)$ should be normalized.

(4) Repeat step (3), and calculate the differences of the two weights between the present round and the former one, if the changes of weights is within a tolerance, it could be deduced that the system turns into a steady state, i.e., the $A(i)$ and $H(i)$ are convergence and the iteration could be finished.

4   DBSCAN-M Algorithm

4.1   Limitations of DBSCAN

There are some limitations of DBSCAN algorithm, which are shown as follows.

(1) It is sensitive to the input parameters of Eps and MinPts. It is difficult to determine the parameters of Eps and MinPts [19, 20]. And if the choosing is inappropriate, the quality of clustering will be decreased.
(2) Since the parameters of Eps and MinPts are globally unique, when the data are uneven distributed, there will have minor possibility of high clustering quality. Due to the Eps is used globally, the neighborhood sizes of all the objects in the data set are consistent, therefore it is inappropriate to determine the Eps depending on the denser or the sparser cluster when the data density and distribution are uneven.
(3) In case the number of noises is greater than the MinPts forming a new cluster, the recognition rate of DBSCAN decreases, which is shown in Fig. 2.

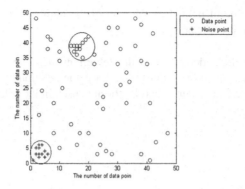

Fig. 2. Noise cluster

Based on the descriptions above, the existing improvements cannot accurately indicate the noises in the event that there are too many noises to form a new cluster. In this paper, we propose a novel clustering approach, which derived from the DBSCAN algorithm by importing mutual reinforcement from HITS in the field of search engine. The approach enhances the interaction between the points of a cluster and the cluster itself, and ultimately improves the recognition rate of noises. This novel approach is named of DBSCAN-M algorithm.

4.2 Theoretical Basis

Reasonable adjusting for the numerical calculations of the clusters and the points is an effective approach in the case of a large amount of noises. The fundamental concept of the DBSCAN-M algorithm is as follows. Referencing the mutual reinforcement mechanism between the Authority and the Hub pages in the HITS algorithm, the points and the cluster are calculated mutually, and the cluster would be treated as noise one if the weight of it is less than a certain value.

Cluster analyses by the DBSCAN-M solve the problem of how to identify the noises accurately in high-density, meanwhile, enhance linkages between the points and the cluster. The flow chart of the DBSCAN-M algorithm is shown in Fig. 3.

4.3 Mutual Reinforcement

In order to better explain the fundamental concepts of the DBSCAN-M algorithm, two definitions are introduced here, where C represents the current cluster, and P stands for the center point of the cluster.

Definition 6: The weight of the cluster C is the sum of the weights of other clusters relative to the present cluster.

Definition 7: The value of point P is the sum of the number difference between the other clusters and the present one.

Two equations could be derived from the definitions mentioned above, where W is the number of points in the current cluster, and d is the position of the center point of the current cluster too. The distance that the formula used in the calculation is from the Euclidean Metric.

The formula for C_i,

$$C_i = W_i * \sum \Delta d_i \tag{6}$$

The formula for P_i,

$$P_i = \sum \Delta W_i \tag{7}$$

The mutual reinforcement between the points and the cluster is achieved by iteration of the two equations above. After each round of iteration, normalizing of the present P_i should be taken as follows,

$$P_i = P_i / \sqrt{\sum [P_i]^2} \tag{8}$$

If the difference between the present weight and that of the former iteration hasn't significant variation, the system could be considered with a steady state, and the iteration would be terminated. Ultimately, we can rank the obtained clusters and the one with the lowest weight is the noise.

It worthy of being noticed that, the initial values of the Authority and the Hub of the HITS are not provided, and it would be convenient to set them of 1 to facilitate the calculation. Nevertheless, the calculations are based on the center point and the cluster in the DBSCAN-M algorithm, the initial values can be set as follows. The initial value of P is the position of the center point in the multi-dimensional space, and the initial value of C is the number of points for each cluster.

4.4   Algorithm Phases

In the DBSCAN-M algorithm, a cluster can be uniquely determined by the core object after the characteristic parameters was given. The pseudo-code of the algorithm is shown below.

Algorithm 1. The DBSCAN-M algorithm. Input: the proportion of each cluster, location of the center of each cluster, radius Eps and the minimum number of points required to form a cluster, i.e., MinPts. By calculation of mutual gain, each cluster gets a rational weight. Output: the weight of each cluster.

```
procedure DBSCAN(D,Eps,MinPts)
  Initialize C
  Repeat P
    mark P as having been visited
    N = getNeighbors(P,Eps)
    if sizeof(N) < MinPts
      labeled P as noise
    else
      C = next cluster
      call ExpandCluster(P,N,C,Eps,MinPts)
    Return DBSCAN-M(P,N,C,Eps,MinPts)
ExpandCluster(P,N,C,Eps,MinPts)
  add P to the cluster C
  for each P' in N
    if Not visited P'
      mark P' as having been visited
      N' = getNeighbors(P',Eps)
      if sizeof(N') >= MinPts
        N = N∪N'
    if P' not belongs to any cluster
      Add P' to Cluster C
call MUTUALGAIN(P,N,C,Eps,MinPts)
  P[0] = {D_i | Center of each cluster in the entire space}
  C[0] = {W_i | The number of points for each clustering}
  P_0[] = {0}
  C_0[] = {0}
  while i < N
    P_0(i) = getWeightSub(C,i)
    C_0(i) = getScoredSub(P,i)
    P_0(i) = P_0(i) / sqrt(Σ[P_0(i)]^2)
    While count < M
      PTmp = P0.copy(), CTmp = C0.copy()
      For j from 1 to length do
        P_0(j) = getWeightSub(CTmp,j)
        C_0(j) = getScoredSub(P,PTmp,j)
        P_0(i) = P_0(i) / sqrt(Σ[P_0(i)]^2)
      count--
    P_min = sort(P_0)
Return (P_min,C_position)
```

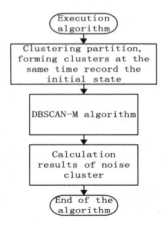

Fig. 3. The flow chart of DBSCAN-M

5 Experimental Studies

The real data used in the simulation are from the Center for Machine Learning and Intelligent Systems at the University of California (http://archive.ics.uci.edu/). The data sets used in our study are Iris and Wine. The operating system is Linux of Ubuntu14. 04, and the algorithm is implemented by Weka (Waikato Environment for Knowledge Analysis) and Java 7.

Table 1 shows the comparison between the DBSCAN-M and the DBSCAN algorithm on noise recognition under the same condition. The more conspicuous comparison between the two algorithms is given in Fig. 4.

Table 1. Data of the simulation based on Iris

MinPts	Eps	Number of added noises	Recognition results of DBSCAN	Recognition results of DBSCAN-M
9	0.04	0	11	11
9	0.04	3	14	14
9	0.04	6	17	17
9	0.04	9	20	20
9	0.04	12	19	23
9	0.04	15	22	26
9	0.04	18	15	29
9	0.04	21	13	32

From Table 1 and Fig. 4 we can conclude that, the results of noises recognition are consistent whether from the DBSCAN or the DBSCAN-M algorithm if the number of noise is less than the MinPts. However, if the number of noises is greater than the MinPts, the recognition capability of the DBSCAN begin to decline since the noises are greater enough to form a new cluster, fortunately, the DBSCAN-M algorithm distinguishes the noises as always.

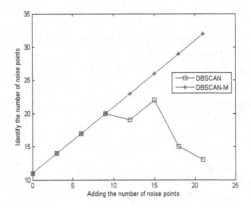

Fig. 4. Performance comparison between the two algorithms

For the sake of verifying the effectiveness of the proposed algorithm, the data set named Wine from the same source was used in another simulation. Figure 5 shows the comparison results between the DBSCAN-M and the DBSCAN algorithm on noise recognition with the same parameters. According to the data sampling and statistical analysis from the results presents above, it can be seen that, the noise identification of the DBSCAN algorithm begins to decline if the number of noises exceeds a certain threshold, and the clustering result will not be sufficient accurate. On the contrary, the DBSCAN-M algorithm uses a mechanism of mutual reinforcement between the cluster and the points within the cluster, and the possibility of forming a new cluster by high density noises is suppressed effectively.

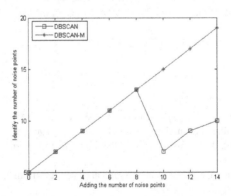

Fig. 5. Performance comparison between DBSCAN-M and DBSCAN algorithm

The comprehensive contrasts of noise recognition between the two algorithms are shown in Table 2.

Data from Table 2 show that the noise recognition rates of the DBSCAN-M algorithm improve from the original one by a percentage of 146.18 % and 89.86 % underneath different datasets respectively.

Table 2. Comprehensive contrast

Dataset	Algorithm	MinPts	Eps	Proportion of noise	Promotion rate
Iris	DBSCAN	9	0.04	7.60 %	\
Iris	DBSCAN-M	9	0.04	18.71 %	146.18 %
Wine	DBSCAN	8	0.05	5.03 %	\
Wine	DBSCAN-M	8	0.05	9.55 %	89.86 %

6 Conclusions

Cluster analysis is one of the data mining problems studied widely. In this paper, a novel algorithm based on the DBSCAN algorithm is proposed aiming at enhancing the noise recognition. The algorithm is a clustering approach of importing mutual reinforcement and name by DBSCAN-M. The fundamental concept of the algorithm is that using a mechanism of mutual reinforcement between the points and the cluster that points belongs to. Experimental results show that when the noises are at high-density and form a new cluster, the performance of noise recognition of the DBSCAN-M is much better than that of DBSCAN.

Along with the developments of data mining techniques, the applications become more and more flexible and the challenges are increasing. Many applications require interdisciplinary knowledge to obtain a better solution. A combination of the search engine and the data mining technology solves the problem of static data analysis in data mining. The DBSCAN-M algorithm establishes a foundation of noise recognition underneath the circumstance that the noises form a new cluster with high density.

Acknowledgements. This work was supported by the Hunan Provincial Natural Science Foundation of China under Grant 14JJ5009, and the Post Doctoral Foundation of Central South University, China.

References

1. Liu, Z.H., Jiang, Z.Q., Zuo, R.S.: Study of fussy clustering of engineering geological environment with GIS. J. China Univ. Min. Technol. **13**, 196–200 (2004)
2. Liu, J., Yan, Z., Yang, L.T.: Fusion–an aide to data mining in internet of things. Inf. Fusion. **23**, 1–2 (2015)
3. Chen, M.S., Han, J., Yu, P.S.: Data mining: an overview from a database perspective. Knowl. Data Eng. **8**, 866–883 (1996)
4. Knorr, E.M., Ng, R.T.: A unified notion of outliers: properties and computation. In: Proceedings of the KDD 1997, pp. 219–222. AAAI Press, Phoenix (1997)
5. Zhang, Y., Liu, J., Li, H.: An outlier detection method based on probability. Comput. Eng. **3**, 47–55 (2013)
6. Liang, B.: A hierarchical clustering based global outlier detection method. In: 5th IEEE International Conference on Bio-Inspired Computing: Theories and Applications (BIC-TA), pp. 1213–1215. IEEE Press, New York (2010)

7. Feng, P.J., Ge, L.D.: Adaptive DBSCAN-based algorithm for constellation reconstruction and modulation identification. In: Radio Science Conference, pp. 177–180. IEEE Press, New York (2004)
8. Birant, D., Kut, A.: ST-DBSCAN: an algorithm for clustering spatial–temporal data. Data Knowl. Eng. **60**, 208–221 (2007)
9. Koteshwariah, C.B., Kisore, N.R. Ravi, V.: A fuzzy version of generalized DBSCAN clustering algorithm. In: Proceedings of the Second ACM IKDD Conference on Data Sciences, pp. 128–129. ACM Press (2015)
10. Smiti, A., Eloudi, Z.: Soft DBSCAN: Improving DBSCAN clustering method using fuzzy set theory. In: 6th International Conference on Human System Interaction (HSI), pp. 380–385. IEEE Press, New York (2013)
11. Chen, F., Deng, P., Wan, J., et al: Data mining for the internet of things: literature review and challenges. Int. J. Distrib. Sens. Netw. vol. 2015, p. 14, 501, Article id. 431047 (2015)
12. Shah, M.: Big Data and the Internet of Things. arXiv preprint (2015). arXiv:1503.07092
13. Ester, M., Kriegel, H.P., Sander, J., Xu, X.: A density-based algorithm for discovering clusters in large spatial databases with noise. In: Proceedings of the KDD 1997, pp. 226–231, AAAI Press, Phoenix (1996)
14. Han, J., Kamber, M., Pei, J., Kamber, M., Pei, J.: Data mining: concepts and techniques, 3rd ed. San Francisco. **29**, S103–S109 (2001)
15. Kleinberg, J.M.: Authoritative sources in a hyperlinked environment. J. ACM (JACM) **46**, 604–632 (1999)
16. Ding, C., He, X., Husbands, P., Zha, H., Simon, H.D.: Pagerank, hits and a unified framework for link analysis. In: Proceedings of the 25th Annual International ACM SIGIR Conference on Research and Development in Information Retrieval, pp. 353–354. ACM Press (2002)
17. Flake, G.W., Lawrence, S., Giles, L.C., Coetzee, F.M.: Self-organization and identification of web communities. Comput. **35**, 66–70 (2002)
18. Chakrabarti, S., Dom, B.E., Kumar, S.R., Raghavan, P., Rajagopalan, S., Tomkins, A., et al.: Mining the web's link structure. Comput. **32**, 60–67 (1999)
19. Mitra, S., Nandy, J.: KDDClus: a simple method for multi-density clustering. In: SKAD 2011-Soft Computing Applications and Knowledge Discovery, pp. 72–76 (2011)
20. Parimala, M., Lopez, D., Senthilkumar, N.C.: A survey on density based clustering algorithms for mining large spatial databases. Int. J. Adv. Sci. Technol. **31**, 59–66 (2011)

An Effective Method for Gender Classification with Convolutional Neural Networks

Hao Zhang[✉], Qing Zhu, and Xiaoqi Jia

School of Software Engineering, Beijing University of Technology,
Beijing 100124, China
{zhanghao.py,jiaxiaoqi}@emails.bjut.edu.cn, ccgszq@bjut.edu.cn

Abstract. A gender classification system uses a given image from human face to tell the gender of the given person. An effective gender classification approach is able to improve the performance of many other applications, including image or video retrieval, security monitoring, human-computer interaction and so on. In this paper, an effective method for gender classification task in frontal facial images based on convolutional neural networks (CNNs) is presented. Our experiments have been shown that the method of CNNs for gender classification task is effective and achieves higher classification accuracy than others on FERET and CAS-PEAL-R1 facial datasets. Finally, we built a gender classification demo, where input is the scene image per frame captured by the camera and the output is the original scene image with marked on detected facial areas.

Keywords: Gender classification · Gender recognition · Face detection · Convolutional neural networks · Deep learning

1 Introduction

It is exceedingly critical for us to make the information visualization in communication with others. Not only are we able to identify who his/her is, but also acquire the other information, for instances, gender, age, ethnicity, even mental state when we look at the person's face. It is not difficult task for individual beings, but a big challenge for machines. Gender classification plays a prominent role on many research areas, including images or videos retrieval, human-computer interaction, robotics vision, security monitoring, demographics studies and so on.

A computer system with the capability of gender classification has profound prospect in basic and applied research areas. Although the field of face recognition have been explored by a great deal of researchers, only a few studies on gender classification have been reported. The gender classification process can reduce half of the search space in face recognition, which is favorable for face identification with preprocessing step.

An effective and feasible method for gender classification in facial images has been presented in this paper, which can achieve a better precision for this task.

© Springer International Publishing Switzerland 2015
G. Wang et al. (Eds.): ICA3PP 2015, Part II, LNCS 9529, pp. 78–91, 2015.
DOI: 10.1007/978-3-319-27122-4_6

In addition, other methods for gender classification in face images, including feature extraction and classification, are also presented and compared. Our experiments show that the method in this paper enables to acquire the higher accuracy for gender classification task.

2   Related Works

Xia et al. [1] combined shape and texture features in their experiment. They used Random Forest on the FRGC-2.0 dataset with 10-fold cross-validation and achieved the accuracy of 93.27 %. Timotius et al. [2] built a gender classifier with the edge orientation histogram, which is estimated on image pixels, and achieved the accuracy of 84.2 % on the VISiO Lab face database. Shan [3] adopted a compact Adaboost algorithm to learn the better description with local binary pattern (LBP) histogram feature and obtained the accuracy of $94.40 \pm 0.86\%$ on the LFW database [4]. Jabid et al. [5] proposed a novel texture descriptor, local direction pattern (LDP), to detect gender via facial image for gender recognition task, and achieved accuracy of 95.05 % on FERET facial dataset. Habid et al. [6], who relied on the movement track of the video frame sequences, presented a gender classification algorithm based on LBP feature with boosting algorithm in the time-spatial domain and achieved high precision on CRIM, Vid-TIMIT and Cohn-Kanade video face databases. Principal component analysis (PCA) via non-linear support vector machine (SVM), representing those images as eigenvector in low-dimensional subspace, was applied in gender classification by Kumari et al. [7] in their experiment, which achieved the accuracy of 92 % on the indian face database.

In China, the effective method proposed by Li et al. [8], based on AdaBoost algorithm to combine facial and hair information for gender recognition, achieved accuracy of $95.1\pm0.5\%$ on FERET and $95.0\pm0.8\%$ on BCMI datasets. Zhang [9] used VG-TSA algorithm with SVM to recognize gender on face image in the videos. Chu et al. [10] randomly cut the detected face image and distinguished gender with support subspace, which made it successful on face gender recognition task with accuracy of 91.13 % on the FERET dataset. Chen et al. [11] proposed an iterative learning algorithm which combined active appearance models (AAM) with SVM, and obtained the great improvement on the IMM face database [12].

3   Convolutional Neural Networks

This section describes the feature extraction, the architecture of classification model, and the dropout regularization in our experiments.

3.1   Architecture

Convolutional neural networks (CNNs) are comprised of a series of convolutional and subsampling layers sequentially, and then followed by one or more fully connected layers in multi-layers perceptron network. CNNs represent the multi-stage Hubel-Wiesel architecture, which extract local features with high resolution and turn them into a lower resolution combined more complex features.

The lower layers consist of alternative layers: convolutional layers and pooling layers. Each convolutional layer presents a two-dimensional discrete convolutional operation on its source image with a given kernel (filter) and applies a nonlinear transfer function. The objective of pooling layers is that reducing the size of the input map thought averaging or summarizing neurons from a small spatial neighborhood. The upper layers, however, are fully connected and correspond to a traditional multi-layers perceptron networks, as illustrated in Fig. 1.

In CNNs, such as LeNet-5 proposed by LeCun et al. [13], shift-invariance is implemented thought subsampling layers. A small non-overlapping receptive fields in these layers receive input neurons of the previous layer. Each neuron calculates the sum of its inputs by a training coefficient, and adds a bias. At last, the intermediate results can be trained through a nonlinear transfer function.

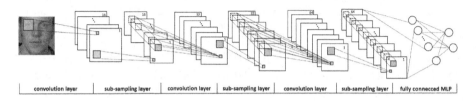

Fig. 1. Convolutional neural networks architecture.

3.2   Convolutional Layers

The purpose of the convolutional layer is that extracting underlying patterns covered within local regions of the input images throughout the dataset, which convolves by a filter over the input image pixels and computes the inner-product with the kernel and pixels at every position of the image.

The input to a convolutional layer is $\mathbf{x}_i$, where $\mathbf{x}_i \in \mathbb{R}^{w \times h}$ is the $w \times h$ matrix, which is corresponding to the pixels of input map i (image with width w and height h).

The convolutional layer will have k kernels with $m \times n$ size, where m and n is smaller than the width and height of the image respectively. The size of the filters, which are convolved with the image to engender k feature maps with $(w - m + 1) \times (h - n + 1)$ size, leads to the local connected structure.

In convolutional layer, the feature maps in the previous layer need to be convolved with learnable kernels and pass through the activation function to figure out the output feature map. Each output map can be combined with multiple input maps through convolutions. Apparently, we have that

$$\mathbf{a}_j^{(l)} = f \left(\sum_i^k \mathbf{k}_{ij}^{(l)} * \mathbf{a}_i^{(l-1)} + b_j^{(l)} \right) \tag{1}$$

where $*$ is convolutional operator, l represents the layer in the networks, $\mathbf{a}_i^{(l-1)} = \mathbf{x}_i$ when $l = 2$ (the 1st layer in the network is data input layer, and the 2nd layer is convolutional layer), $\mathbf{k}_{ij}^{(l)} \in \mathbb{R}^{m \times n}$ is the kernel of the l-th layer in the networks between the i-th input map and the j-th output map, $f(\cdot)$ is non-linear transfer function to activations, such as hyperbolic tangent function.

An additive bias b_j is given at each output map, but for a specific output map, the input maps will be convolved with different kernels distinctly. In other words, if both the j_1-th output map and the j_2-th output map sum over the i-th input map, then the kernels are applied to the i-th input map, which is different from the j_1-th and j_2-th output maps.

3.3 Pooling Layers

The objective of pooling [14] layers is to acquire spatial invariance through scaling down the resolution of the feature maps. And then, each map needs to be subsampled typically with mean or max pooling over $p \times q$ adjoining regions, where p and q is the size (width and height respectively) of patches in the pooling layer. In general, we have that:

$$\mathbf{a}_j^{(l)} = g\left(\mathbf{a}_i^{(l-1)}\right), \forall i \in R_j \tag{2}$$

where R_j is the j-th pooling region with $p \times q$ size in the i-th input map.

Two kinds of conventional operators for $g(\cdot)$ can be chosen: average and max operation. The former takes the arithmetic mean of the elements in each pooling region:

$$\mathbf{a}_j^{(l)} = \frac{1}{|R_j|} \sum_{i \in R_j} \mathbf{a}_i^{(l-1)} \tag{3}$$

but the largest element is picked up via the max operator in each pooling region:

$$\mathbf{a}_j^{(l)} = \max_{i \in R_j} \mathbf{a}_i^{(l-1)} \tag{4}$$

Both two kinds of pooling operators have own disadvantages when training deep convolutional networks. When it comes to the average pooling, all elements in a pooling region need to be took fully into account, even though many of them have low magnitude. While max pooling does not suffer from these weaknesses, we are able to find it easily to overfit the training set in practice, making it difficult to generalize well to the test instances. In feedforward propagation, the pooling regions with $p \times q$ size are scaled down as a single value. And then, this single value attains an error calculated by backwards propagation from the previous layer. This error is then just feedforwarded to the place where it comes from. Since it only comes from the one place within the region of $p \times q$ size, the back-propagated errors from max-pooling layers are considerable sparse.

3.4   Regularization

For regularization, we apply dropout [15] regularization on the hidden layer with a constraint on l_2-norms of the weight vectors. Dropout enables to prevent over-fitting thought dropping units out randomly with a probability p in the network. For instance, setting to zero with a probability p of the hidden units during feed-forward and back-propagation in the network. That is, given the hidden layer, also called perceptron layer (after pooling layer), $\mathbf{a}^{(l-1)} = [a_1, \ldots, a_h]$, instead of using

$$\mathbf{a}^{(l)} = f\left(\mathbf{w} \cdot \mathbf{a}^{(l-1)} + b\right) \tag{5}$$

but for output unit $\mathbf{a}^{(l)}$ in feedforward propagation, dropout represents

$$\mathbf{a}^{(l)} = f\left(\mathbf{w} \cdot \left(\mathbf{a}^{(l-1)} \circ r\right) + b\right) \tag{6}$$

where $\circ$ is the element-wise multiplication operator, and $r \in \mathbb{R}^h$ is a masking vector of Bernoulli random variables with probability p of being 1. At training time, the gradients are able to be updated only through the unmasked units via back-propagation. At test phase, the weight vectors we have learned enbale to be scaled by p such that $\hat{\mathbf{w}} = p\mathbf{w}$, where $\hat{\mathbf{w}}$ is employed without dropout in the test procedure. In addition, we constrain l_2-norms of the weight vectors by rescaling $\mathbf{w}$ such that $||\mathbf{w}||_2 = s$ whenever $||\mathbf{w}||_2 > s$ after a gradient descent step.

4   Experiments

This section describes the datasets, data preprocessing steps, detailed hyperparameters, as well as the training procedure in our experiments.

4.1   Datasets and Computers

Our experiments were carried out on the FERET [16] dataset and CAS-PEAL-R1 [17] formal subsets, labeled by ourselves, as described in Table 1. FERET face database dataset consists of 1351 8-bit grayscale images of human from 193 people (108 males and 85 females for each 7 images), heads with views ranging from frontal to left and right profiles. CAS-PEAL-R1 formal subsets made up 1040 Chinese face images from 208 people (119 males and 89 females for each 5 images).

Table 1. Summary statistics for the facial datasets.

Dataset	#images	#people	#males	#females	Each
FERET	1351	193	108	85	7
CAS-PEAL-R1	1040	208	119	89	5

We used up to a workstation machine with Ubuntu 14.04 for our experiments. It has 2 Intel Core CPUs, each for 8 cores (Intel(R) Core(TM) i7-5960X CPU at 3.00 GHz), 32 GB memory and a GPU with GeForce GTX TITAN Z. (6 GB memory). Our experiments below are carried out on GPU with Theano 0.7.0.

4.2 Data Preprocessing

The facial images in the datasets are preprocessed before model training. There are some preprocessed steps as follows.

Gray-Scale. Firstly, the color images, if they have 3 color channels, are converted into grayscale images as follows.

$$\hat{x}_{ij} = 0.299x_{ij}^{(R)} + 0.587x_{ij}^{(G)} + 0.114x_{ij}^{(B)} \tag{7}$$

where $x_{ij}^{(R)}$, $x_{ij}^{(G)}$ and $x_{ij}^{(B)}$ are the pixels of R, G, B channels.

Face Detection. Secondly, histogram equalization is used for adjusting facial image intensities to enhance contrast. And then, we need to detect face area in the image using Harr-likes features with Adaboost method [18] and cut the detected areas. What's more, we are able to resize the images, outputs in the previous step, to 80×80 on FERET dataset and 100×100 on CAS-PEAL-R1 dataset.

Normalization. Ultimately, data normalization, a function map transformed $0{\sim}255$ into $0{\sim}1$, can be used in these datasets. The formula is shown in the following:

$$\hat{x}_{ij} = \frac{x_{ij} - \min(\mathbf{x})}{\max(\mathbf{x}) - \min(\mathbf{x})} \tag{8}$$

where are $\hat{x}_{ij}$ is normalized value, proceeding from original pixel x_{ij} of $\mathbf{x}$.

The visualised samples of facial image on FERET and CAS-PEAL-R1 datasets after preprocessing has been shown in Fig. 2.

4.3 Hyperparameters and Training

The CNN architecture with dropout regularization [15] and two kinds of learning algorithms have been implemented by ourselves with Theano. For all datasets, we randomly split all data via 20 %–80 % as training set and test set separately. Learning algorithms at training procedure has been carried out through Stochastic Gradient Descent (SGD) [19] over mini-batched with learning rate decay update rule and ADADELTA [20] method.

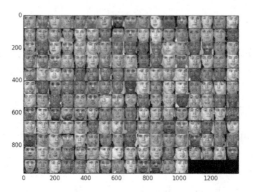

(a) FERET dataset

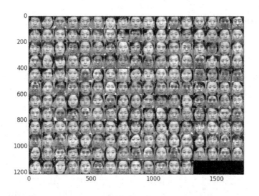

(b) CAS-PEAL-R1 dataset

Fig. 2. Face image samples visualization after preprocessing on FERET and CAS-PEAL-R1 dkatasets.

Networks Structure. The exact network architecture on FERET and CAS-PEAL-R1 datasets in our experiment have been listed in Tables 2 and 3. Taking FERET dataset for example, the size of input layer is 80 × 80, and followed by convolution with max-pooling layers many times, increasing the number of kernels and reducing the size of patch. Ultimately, flattening the output in the pervious layer, concatenating by fully connected layers with dropout regularization and making classification via softmax layer. The fourth column in the Tables 2 and 3, namely #params, means the number of parameters we need to learn, for instance, 0.4K is equal to 16 × 5 × 5.

For convolution layers, the number of kernels are increased with network going deeper. But for pooling layers, we need to acquire spatial invariance by scaling down the size of the feature maps with max-pooling over given contiguous

Table 2. CNN architecture parameters on FERET.

Type	Kernel size	Output size	#params
input	-	80×80	-
convolution	$16@5 \times 5$	$16@76 \times 76$	0.4 K
max-pooling	$16@2 \times 2$	$16@38 \times 38$	0.4 K
convolution	$32@5 \times 5$	$32@34 \times 34$	0.8 K
max-pooling	$32@2 \times 2$	$32@17 \times 17$	0.8 K
convolution	$64@3 \times 3$	$64@15 \times 15$	0.57 K
max-pooling	$64@3 \times 3$	$64@5 \times 5$	0.57 K
flatten	-	1600	-
dropout(0.2)	-	1600	-
fully connected	-	256	409 K
dropout(0.5)	-	256	-
softmax	-	2	0.5 K

regions. Apparently, the loss function of our network is negative log-likelihood in output layer as follows.

$$\mathcal{L}(\theta = \{W^1, b^1, \ldots, W^l, b^l\}) = -\frac{1}{|\mathcal{D}|} \sum_{i=0}^{|\mathcal{D}|} \log(P(Y = y^{(i)} | x^{(i)}, \theta)) \qquad (9)$$

where θ is the parameters we need to learn in this network. W^i and b^i is represented by the weight matrix and bias in the i-th hidden layer respectively, as well as $\mathcal{D}$ stands for the samples of training dataset, so that $|\mathcal{D}|$ means the number of training data.

Learning Algorithm. In our experiments, two kinds of learning algorithms, SGD [19] and ADADELTA [20], have been used to optimize the loss function and obtained the optimal parameters in the training step.

A stochastic gradient trainer with momentum μ and learning rate α updates parameter θ at step t by blending the current velocity v with the current gradient $\frac{\partial \mathcal{L}}{\partial \theta}$. Besides, we make the learning rate decreased at every step gradually, so the learning decay rate γ is no more than zero and the gradient update rule is followed by Eqs. (10)–(12). (For more training details, please refer to the article [19].)

$$v_{t+1} = \mu v_t - \alpha_t \frac{\partial \mathcal{L}}{\partial \theta} \qquad (10)$$

$$\theta_{t+1} = \theta_t + v_{t+1} \qquad (11)$$

$$\alpha_{t+1} = \alpha_t \gamma \qquad (12)$$

The ADADELTA method uses the same general strategy as all first-order stochastic gradient methods, in the sense that these methods make small parameter

Table 3. CNN architecture parameters on CAS-PEAL-R1.

Type	Kernel size	Output size	#params
input	-	100×100	-
convolution	$16@5 \times 5$	$16@96 \times 96$	0.4 K
max-pooling	$16@2 \times 2$	$16@48 \times 48$	0.4 K
convolution	$32@5 \times 5$	$32@44 \times 44$	0.8 K
max-pooling	$32@2 \times 2$	$32@22 \times 22$	0.8 K
convolution	$64@5 \times 5$	$64@18 \times 18$	1.6 K
max-pooling	$64@3 \times 3$	$64@6 \times 6$	1.6 K
flatten	-	2304	-
dropout(0.2)	-	2304	-
fully connected	-	256	589 K
dropout(0.5)	-	256	-
softmax	-	2	0.5 K

adjustments iteratively using local derivative information. The difference with ADADELTA is that as gradients are computed during each parameter update, an exponentially-weighted moving average (EWMA) gradient value, as well as an EWMA of recent parameter steps, are maintained as well. And the update rule is followed by Eqs. (13)–(16). (For more training details, please refer to the article [20].)

$$g_{t+1} = \rho g_t + (1 - \rho)\left(\frac{\partial \mathcal{L}}{\partial \theta}\right)^2 \tag{13}$$

$$v_{t+1} = \frac{\sqrt{x_t + \epsilon}}{\sqrt{g_{t+1} + \epsilon}} \frac{\partial \mathcal{L}}{\partial \theta} \tag{14}$$

$$x_{t+1} = \rho x_t + (1 - \rho)v_{t+1}^2 \tag{15}$$

$$\theta_{t+1} = \theta_t - v_{t+1} \tag{16}$$

Parameters Settings. In our experiment, $tanh(\cdot)$ activation function has been used for convolutional layers and fully connected layers, and setting dropout rates (p) of 0.2 and 0.5 for flatten layers and fully connected layers, initial bias b set 0 and initial weight matrix $W \sim U\left[-\sqrt{\frac{6}{I+O}}, \sqrt{\frac{6}{I+O}}\right)$ for each layer, where I and O is represented by the feature maps of input and ouput in the hidden layer respectively.

For SGD trainer, initial learning rate α_0 of 0.01, learning decay rate γ of 0.998 and mini-batch size of 30 for stochastic gradient descent learning algorithm. But for ADADELTA trainer, decay constant ρ of 0.95 and constant ϵ of 10^{-6} should been set. These hyperparameters have been selected through a grid search on the FERET and CAS-PEAL-R1 datasets.

4.4   Results and Comparation

As can be seen in Fig. 3, the results have been demonstrated as follows. On the one hand, the cost value with learning rate decay method has smoothly declined and gradually stabilized on all datasets when the epoch increased. In contrast, the cost value has a large number of shaking in the first few epochs and gradually kept stable on all datasets with Adadelta method.

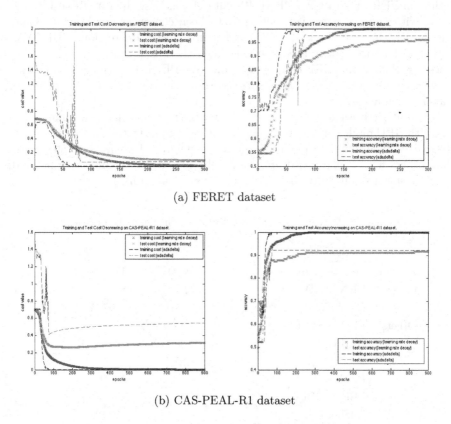

(a) FERET dataset

(b) CAS-PEAL-R1 dataset

Fig. 3. Cost decreasing and accuracy increasing of training set and test set on FERET and CAS-PEAL-R1 datasets.

On the other hand, the accuracy rates increases smoothly with epoch increased. The misclassification rates of test data, as described by Eq. (17), achieves 4.07 % at the 259th epoch on FERET and 8.33 % at the 825th epoch on CAS-PEAL-R1 with SGD learning algorithm. And the error rates obtains 2.23 % at the 82th epoch on FERET and 6.67 % at the 75th epoch on CAS-PEAL-R1 with ADADELTA learning algorithm.

$$\epsilon = \frac{1}{|\mathcal{D}|} \sum_{i}^{|\mathcal{D}|} I\{y_i \neq \hat{y}_i\} \tag{17}$$

where $I(\cdot)$ is the indicator function, which is that $I\{a\,false\,statement\} = 0$ and $I\{a\,true\,statement\} = 1$. And then, y_i is the label of image $\mathbf{x}_i$, corresponsively, $\hat{y}_i$ is the label of predication, $|\mathcal{D}|$ is the number of test data sets.

In training such networks, the cost value stops decreasing after a few epochs and remains at a level lower than that of learning rate decay method, which achieves a great performance util convergence.

Accordingly, we compared with mainly different methods for gender classification on FERET and CAS-PEAL-R1 datasets, as described in Table 4. Image pixels with logistic regression method have been chosen as our baseline. Compared with these methods which included in Logistic Regression, RBF-SVM, C.H.O, Adaboost and Stacked-Autoencoders, the misclassification rates of our works are 2.23 % on FERET and 6.67 % on CAS-PEAL-R1, which is lower than previous works. Our works have achieved the great improvements with higher classification accuracy.

In addition, it is exceedingly decreased for the training time-consuming problem with GPU mode compared to CPU mode, as demonstrated on Tables 5 and 6. No matter what the datasets are, training time with GPU mode is 150× faster than other (with CPU mode) approximately. It is a very competitive method, which perform significantly better than their contemporaries.

Table 4. Test error rates on classification with different approaches.

	Methods	FERET	CAS-PEAL-R1
Baseline	Logistic regression	14.00 %	11.50 %
Ours	CNN (SGD)	4.07 %	8.33 %
	CNN (ADADELTA)	**2.23 %**	**6.67 %**
Others	LDP + SVM [5]	4.95%	-
	(C.H.O)[8]	4.90 ± 0.5%	-
	SubSVM [10]	8.87%	-
	Pixels + RBF-SVM [21]	-	14.04 %
	LBP + RBF-SVM [21]	-	20.55 %
	Adaboost [21]	-	15.90 %
	Autoencoder + RBF-SVM [22]	14.66 %	16.37 %
	Stacked-autoencoders [22]	9.98 %	11.71 %

5   Application to Gender Recognition from Camera

Finally, we carried out the CNNs model, which were trained and tuned on hyperparameters by ourselves, to build a application for gender classification with facial images.

Image acquisition on natural scene is captured by camera. And then, the whole image is preprocessed to acquire the area about human face, as described

Table 5. Average execution time per epoch on FERET dataset.

Methods	Data	Theano CPU	Theano GPU
CNN (SGD)	Training	65.690 s	0.351 s
	Test	3.979 s	0.023 s
CNN (ADADELTA)	Training	66.174 s	0.358 s
	Test	2.923 s	0.022 s

Table 6. Average execution time per epoch on CAS-PEAL-R1 dataset.

Methods	Data	Theano CPU	Theano GPU
CNN (SDG)	Training	59.067 s	0.408 s
	Test	3.195 s	0.022 s
CNN (ADADELTA)	Training	59.602 s	0.401 s
	Test	3.106 s	0.021 s

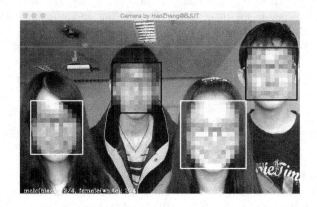

Fig. 4. Application of gender classification based on CNNs model.

in Sect. 4.2. Next step, the facial area of image as 2d signal inputs is put into the CNNs model, which has been trained parameters previously, included the weight matrix and bias for each layer, the kernels for each convolutional layer, and the patch size for pooling layer, the dropout rates for perceptron layers and so on. At last, we get the outputs from the model, which enables to distinguish male from female on facial images, and label on the original image. The rectangle with black lines on face represents male, and the white one stands for female, as illustrated in Fig. 4.

6 Conclusion

An effective and feasible method for gender classification in facial images has been presented in this paper. The underlying gender descriptors on face would need to be general, invariant to pose, illumination, expression, and image quality. Our works demonstrate that CNNs model can learn from many samples to distinguish gender effectively on facial images. Adadelta method, to tune the learning rate automatically, is able to make convergence rapidly and acquire the much lower misclassification rates in our works.

The ability, to present a remarkable improvement in gender classification, attests to the potential of such coupling to become significant in other vision domains as well. Finally, this method has been applied in the gender recognition system in order to build a application to predict the gender with facial images captured by camera.

In the next step, we still need to improve the accuracy for classification performance and focus on high-precision recognition under the influence of different positions and orientations.

Acknowledgments. This research is partially supported by Beijing Natural Science Foundation (Grant 4152008). Hao is supported by the Foundation of Science and Technology of Beijing University of Technology (Grant ykj-2013-9341). We sincerely thank the anonymous reviewers for their thorough reviewing and valuable suggestions. In addition, the authors would also give warm thanks to Yutong Yu for the data labelling works, and Lei Wang and Zhiqiang Wang for their comments and discussions.

References

1. Xia, B., Ben Amor, B., Huang, D., Daoudi, M., Wang, Y., Drira, H.: Enhancing gender classification by combining 3D and 2D face modalities. In: 2013 Proceedings of the 21st European Signal Processing Conference (EUSIPCO), pp. 1–5, September 2013
2. Timotius, I.K., Setyawan, I.: Using edge orientation histograms in face-based gender classification. In: 2014 International Conference on Information Technology Systems and Innovation (ICITSI), pp. 93–98, November 2014
3. Shan, C.: Learning local binary patterns for gender classification on real-world face images. Pattern Recogn. Lett. **33**(4), 431–437 (2012). Intelligent Multimedia Interactivity
4. Huang, G.B., Mattar, M., Lee, H., Learned-Miller, E.: Learning to align from scratch. In: NIPS (2012)
5. Jabid, T., Kabir, M.H., Chae, O.: Gender classification using local directional pattern (LDP). In: 2010 20th International Conference on Pattern Recognition (ICPR), pp. 2162–2165, August 2010
6. Hadid, A., Pietikainen, M.: Combining appearance and motion for face and gender recognition from videos. Pattern Recogn. **42**(11), 2818–2827 (2009)
7. Kumari, S., Sa, P.K., Majhi, B.: Gender classification by principal component analysis and support vector machine. In: Proceedings of the 2011 International Conference on Communication, Computing and Security, ICCCS 2011, pp. 339–342. ACM, New York (2011)
8. Li, B., Lian, X.-C., Lu, B.-L.: Gender classification by combining clothing, hair and facial component classifiers. Neurocomputing **76**(1), 18–27 (2012). Seventh International Symposium on Neural Networks (ISNN 2010) Advances in Web Intelligence

9. Zhang, M.: Design and implementation of video-based face gender recognition system using manifold learning. Master's thesis, University of Electronic Science and Technology (2013)
10. Chu, W.-S., Huang, C.-R., Chen, C.-S.: Gender classification from unaligned facial images using support subspaces. Inf. Sci. **221**, 98–109 (2013)
11. Chen, H., Wei, W.: Support vectort aam based iterative learning algorithm for gender classification. J. Zhejiang Univ. (Eng. Sci.) **39**(12), 1989–2011 (2005)
12. Nordstrøm, M.M., Larsen, M., Sierakowski, J., Stegmann, M.B.: The IMM face database - an annotated dataset of 240 face images. Technical report, Informatics and Mathematical Modelling, Technical University of Denmark, DTU, Richard Petersens Plads, Building 321, DK-2800 Kgs. Lyngby, May 2004
13. Lecun, Y., Bottou, L., Bengio, Y., Haffner, P.: Gradient-based learning applied to document recognition. Proc. IEEE **86**(11), 2278–2324 (1998)
14. Zeiler, M.D., Fergus, R.: Stochastic pooling for regularization of deep convolutional neural networks. CoRR, abs/1301.3557 (2013)
15. Srivastava, N., Hinton, G., Krizhevsky, A., Sutskever, I., Salakhutdinov, R.: Dropout: a simple way to prevent neural networks from overfitting. J. Mach. Learn. Res. **15**, 1929–1958 (2014)
16. The defense advanced research team: the facial recognition technology (feret) database. Technical report, United States Department of Defense (1996)
17. Gao, W., Cao, B., Shan, S., Chen, X., Zhou, D., Zhang, X., Zhao, D.: The CAS-PEAL large-scale chinese face database and baseline evaluations. IEEE Trans. Syst. Man Cybern. Part A Syst. Hum. **38**, 149–161 (2008)
18. Lienhart, R., Maydt, J.: An extended set of haar-like features for rapid object detection. In: Proceedings of the 2002 International Conference on Image Processing, vol. 1, pp. I-900–I-903 (2002)
19. Rumelhart, D.E., Hinton, G.E., Williams, R.J.: Learning representations by back-propagating errors. In: Neurocomputing: Foundations of Research, pp. 696–699. MIT Press, Cambridge (1988)
20. Zeiler, M.D.: ADADELTA: an adaptive learning rate method. CoRR, abs/1212.5701 (2012)
21. Lu, L.: A study of gender classification and age estimation based on face image. Ph.D. thesis, Shanghai Jiao Tong University (2010)
22. Zhang, H., Zhu, Q.: Gender classification in face images based on stacked-autoencoders method. In: 2014 7th International Congress on Image and Signal Processing (CISP), pp. 486–491, October 2014

AQUAdex: A Highly Efficient Indexing and Retrieving Method for Astronomical Big Data of Time Series Images

Zhi Hong[1], Ce Yu[2(✉)], Ruolei Xia[2], Jian Xiao[1], Jie Wang[2],
Jizhou Sun[2], and Chenzhou Cui[3]

[1] School of Computer Software, Tianjin University, Tianjin 300050, China
{hongzhi,xiaojian}@tju.edu.cn
[2] School of Computer Science and Technology, Tianjin University,
Tianjin 300050, China
yuce@tju.edu.cn, ruoleixia@163.com, {wang_jie,jzsun}@tju.edu.cn
[3] National Astronomical Observatories, Chinese Academy of Sciences,
Beijing 100012, China
ccz@bao.ac.cn

Abstract. In the era of Big Data, scientific research is challenged with handling massive data sets. To actually take advantage of Big Data, the key problem is to retrieve the desired cup of data from the ocean, as most applications only need a fraction of the entire data set. As the indexing and retrieving method is intrinsically connected with specific features of the data set and the goal of research, a universal solution is hardly possible. Designed for efficiently querying Big Data in astronomy time domain research, AQUAdex, a new spatial indexing and retrieving method is proposed to extract Time Series Images form Astronomical Big Data. By mapping images to tiles (pixels) on the celestial sphere, AQUAdex can complete queries 9 times faster, which is proven by theoretical analysis and experimental results. AQUAdex is especially suitable for Big Data applications because of its excellent scalability. The query time only increases 59 % while the data size grows 14 times larger.

Keywords: Spatial index · Pseudo-sphere index · Astronomy big data · Time series images · FITS File

1 Introduction

Big Data is increasingly attracting attention from both the academia and the industry. With the incredible growth of computational power and storage capacity, Big Data has unlocked more possibilities that fundamentally changes the way that we used to see and interact with data.

It does not, however, come with no challenges attached. A major problem with Big Data is that there could be an ocean of data, but only a cup of that data is useful for a specific need. This is especially true in the field of astronomy research. Considering the technological advancement of telescope CCDs

© Springer International Publishing Switzerland 2015
G. Wang et al. (Eds.): ICA3PP 2015, Part II, LNCS 9529, pp. 92–105, 2015.
DOI: 10.1007/978-3-319-27122-4_7

and the sizeable number of ongoing sky survey projects, Big Data has become a real challenge in the field of astronomy. [5] Storage space taken up by astronomy observation data has long past the terabytes (TB) scale and is speeding towards the petabytes (PB) scale. Chinese Virtual Observatory (China-VO), for instance, has accumulated about 100 TB of data from observatories located across China [8]. But in order to thoroughly study a celestial body (e.g. a star, a galaxy, etc.), astronomers need Time Series Images of the target. Time Series Images are a collection of images covering the same area of the sky but taken at different times by one or more telescopes. [11] They are of great importance because they offer astronomers a chronological view of what happened over time in a certain area of the sky.

Usually, extracting Time Series Images involves a lot of manual work by the researcher. In this paper, AQUAdex, (**A**ccelerating **Q**uery **U**sing **A**rea pixelization inde**x**ing), is proposed to automatically and efficiently extract Time Series Images from Astronomy Big Data. AQUAdex saved the user from querying a enormous starcatalog database and manually picking out desired images.

Our contributions include creating a highly efficient method for indexing and fast retrieving Time Series Image files from Astronomy Big Data. Our method allows easy appending of new information into existing indices and also scales nicely for large data sets, which makes it especially suitable for handling Big Data. The number of records in our index is only 1/1000 to 1/10000 of that of a traditional starcatalog. Besides, we have also extended the ability of an existing tool, HEALPix, to match each image to one or more zones in the sky, thus further improves the query performance and make it a breeze querying Astronomy Big Data.

The paper is structured as follows. Section 1 introduces the background of our work while Sect. 2 shows existing work related to Big Data is scientific research. Section 3 focuses on our approach and offers some theoretical analysis that are proved by experimental results in Sect. 4. The last section draws a conclusion to our work and brings this paper to an end with a vision for further research opportunities.

2   Related Work

2.1   Existing Workflow of Extracting Time Series Images

Time Series Images [5] are usually extracted from existing observation data archives published by institutions where the observations were conducted. One advantage of working with astronomy data is that they have a standard file format, FITS (Flexible Image Transport System), which has been adopted by the astronomy community since the 1980s. Metadata of the image, including the name of target celestial body, the time of the observation, etc., are stored in ASCII format in the header of the FITS file and are easily readable.

Here's a simple example showing the process of extracting Time Series Images. As shown in Fig. 1, there are four images, the observation time `OBS-TIME` of which are shown in Table 1. The goal is to find the Time Series Images that both covered

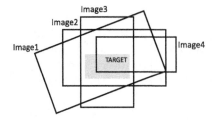

Fig. 1. Searching for time series images

Table 1. Timestamps of the four images

FILE	OBS-TIME
Image1	2014-03-01 20:05:05
Image2	2014-03-05 22:22:30
Image3	2014-04-01 23:00:00
Image4	2014-03-10 21:30:33

the target area (in grey) and were taken between 2014-03-01 00:00:00 and 2014-03-31 23:59:59. Examining these four files one by one, it is easy to find that Image 3&4 are not qualified because they were either not taken during the desired time period or did not cover the entire desired area. Thus the result Time Series Images shall include Image 1&2.

The existing workflow for finding time series images requires a lot of manual work. The user need to query a large database ("the starcatalog") to find relevant images, and then download the images to the local machine for further analysis. Currently, when an image is captured by an optical telescope, the information of each celestial body in the image will be extracted and inserted into a the starcatalog as a record. The problem, however, is that the number of objects in a single image can easily reach 10^3 or even 10^4, so the number of rows in the database is usually 3 or 4 orders of magnitude higher than the number of the files. Its no surprise that one starcatalog may contain billions of records, which makes it extremely slow to query.

Even after an astronomer has got the results from the time-consuming query, it can be quite difficult to get the original image files. Technically speaking, the starcatalog should include the information of the original image file for each record, so that each record can be traced back to its origin, but in reality, sometimes such information is just non-existent. Another problem is that the original image, albeit containing the star, may not cover the entire desired area around the star (i.e., the star is near the edge of the image). This is due to the fact that the starcatalog only includes features about stars in the image and does not have information of the image as a whole (such as its size). In the current workflow, astronomers have to manually check each file they have got from querying the starcatalog to make sure the images indeed cover the desired area.

2.2 Related Work on Querying Big Data

As mentioned earlier, a number of ways have been put forward to handle large amounts of scientific data. NoSQL is one of the most popular methods used to deal with such problem. Several examples are:

– Hadoop, which is based on the MapReduce model, is widely used in Big Data applications like data warehouse, data mining, etc. [13]

- SciDB, which is designed specially to work on multi-dimensional data, have already been applied to the storage of astronomical images [7,12,15]
- Hadoop-GIS, which is capable of efficient spatial queries, is used in map applications as well as in medical image processing [1,2].

Its impractical, nevertheless, to apply the NoSQL method to solve our problem because of its high storage cost. [1–3] all requires importing raw data files into some specific file system, but as raw files are generally required to be kept in all conditions in astronomy, this kind of method would effectively require at least doubling the storage space. Whats worse, astronomy data are no exception to the 20–80 rule (i.e. 80 % of the queries focuses only on 20 % of the data), which makes it even less cost-efficient to duplicate the entire data. What is needed here is an method that will keep the original data intact and requires as little overhead as possible. In fact, there are some work that have made an effort to query directly on the raw data files [9,14,16].

- SDS/Q, which specializes in processing HDF5 data, takes advantage of bitmap indices to locate pieces of data in a single file [6]
- PostgresRAW, which apparently is based on the PostgreSQL Relational DBMS, supports queries on a starcatalog file as large as 12 GB [3,4].

Unfortunately, none of these is really suitable for querying tons of astronomy image files. [4,5] both attempt to mitigate the aforementioned problem by allowing querying directly on data files, yet not without drawbacks. [4] only works on HDF5 data, which is not compatible with the FITS format of astronomy images. [5] does support the FITS format, but is limited to ASCII data only, and has no support for image data.

3 Introducing AQUAdex

3.1 Analysis of the Problem

The problem of extracting Time Series Images from Astronomy Big Data can be expressed formally as follows.

Problem: Given a set of FTIS image files S, a pair of coordinates (x_c, y_c), a size of the desired images $(l_x \times l_y)$, and a time frame (t_1, t_2), find all files in S that

- cover an area whose centroid is at (x_c, y_c) and have a size of at least l_x by l_y
- are created (observed) at or after t_1 but no later than t_2
- are sorted in chronological order

The general architecture of our innovation is shown in Fig. 2. The data set would be scanned once to build indices, then the query engine can take an area of the sky and a time period as inputs, and return all images that (a) cover that area and (b) was taken during that time period as the result. Ultimately, a command line-based, SQL-like, easy-to-use tool is provided to the end user. The query syntax is as follows.

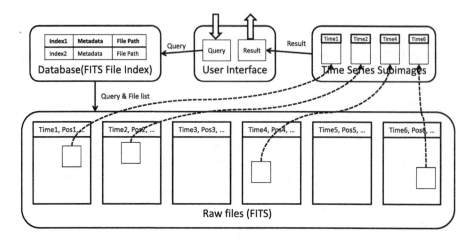

Fig. 2. Overall architecture

```
SELECT {subimage|rawimage}
FROM {DataSourceList}
WHERE {center_RA, center_DEC, X_size, Y_size, Begin_Time, End_Time}
```

The user needs to name the `datatsource` that he'd like to search in, give a target area (descripted by `center_RA`, `center_DEC`, `X_size`, and `Y_size`), and specifiy a time period of the data (`begin_Time`, `end_Time`).

From the discussion in Sect. 2.1, it is clear that starcatalogs are unfit for extracting time series images from existing data archives. Searching among billions of records in a starcatlog is prohibitively time-consuming, and end users still have to manually pick out the really useful images.

To accelerate this process, we focus on the image files, instead of the stars in them, and create a new file indexing method to accelerate queries of time series images.

3.2 A Direct Indexing Method

FITS files, as aforementioned, have headers in which the files' metadata are stored. For images produced by optical telescopes, the coordinates (RA, Dec) of the target celestial body is always included in the header. The size of the images from the same telescope is usually fixed as it is determined by the field of view (FOV) of that telescope.

Given the coordinates and the relative position of a point in the image, as well as the length and width of the image, it seems pretty intuitive to make an index consisting of the coordinates and the sizes. (Table 2) Then, with the help of B-Tree indexing and efficient range query abilities provided by many DBMSs, finding out which files has covered the desired area of sky seems like a piece of cake, right? Sadly, no. As shown in Fig. 3, the images are usually not perfectly

Table 2. A direct index of the image files

FILE	RA	Dec	Length	Width	OBS-TIME
Image1	67.34	27.33	3.5	2.0	2014-03-01 20:05:05
Image2	98.12	34.67	3.5	2.0	2014-03-05 22:22:30
Image3	33.50	78.21	3.5	2.0	2014-04-01 23:00:00
					...

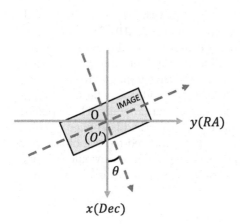

Fig. 3. Each image may have a rotation angle θ

Fig. 4. Partition of the celestial sphere [10]

aligned with the RA, Dec axes but have an angle θ. This angle is influenced by the geological location of the telescope as well as its posture when capturing the image, thus it would vary from image to image. Taking this varying rotation angle into account effectively nullify the B-Tree index built on the RA and Dec columns because each row must be checked individually to calculate its actual covered area using its own rotation angle, hence no matter what indices are used, for every query command a traversal of all the records is always needed. Its apparent that this method is still pretty inefficient.

3.3 AQUAdex

One major contribution of AQUAdex is introducing the idea of sky partitioning (pixelizaiton) into Astronomy Big Data indexing and creating a new spatial indexing method to replace the B-Tree indexing. The core idea of our solution is to assign each image with one or more PIXEL_IDs according to its covered area of the sky. The images with the same PIXEL_IDs are grouped together so that when querying for images covering a target area, only the files that are in the same group with the target area are selected. Then the selected files are checked one by one to see whether they covers the entire target area using their respective θ.

The spatial index of AQUAdex is built on the basis of HEALPix, which is an acronym for Hierarchical Equal Area isoLatitude Pixelization of a sphere. [10] The parameter N reflects the level of partition. The base partition (N=1) divides the sphere surface into 12 equal sized pixels numbered in binary from 0001 to 1100. In the next level of partition (N=2), each pixel in the base level is further divided into four equal-sized sub-partitions, thus pixel 0101 would have four sub-pixels 010100, 010101, 010110, and 010111. (Fig. 4) This is a problem for calculating all the PIXEL_IDs for a given area because two neighboring pixels are not necessarily numbered sequentially.

AQUAdex solved this problem by dichotomy (Algorithm 1). First, to find all the pixels crossed by the sides of the image area, the PIXEL_ID of the endpoints and the midpoint of a side are computed. Then compare the midpoints PIXEL_ID to each of the endpoints. If the two IDs are different and not adjacent [17], then the process will be done again on the segment from the endpoint to the middle point. In this way all the pixels crossed by the four sides can be discovered. Then there is the possibility that the area might contain some whole pixels, which cannot be found in the previous step. A similar method is applied to solve this. The PIXEL_IDs of the centroid of the area are compared to each of the four vertexes. If they are not equal and not adjacent, the same process would be done to the sub-area from the vertex to the centroid. Algorithm 1 has a linear time complexity of $O(n)$.

Table 3. AQUAdex, a spatial index of the image files

FILE	PIXEL_ID	RA	Dec	θ	OBS-TIME
Image1	001001	67.34	27.33	23	2014-03-01 20:05:05
Image2	000110	98.12	34.67	55	2014-03-05 22:22:30
Image3	010001	33.50	78.21	103	2014-04-01 23:00:00
				...	

The index building function is shown in Algorithm 2. In AUQAdex, the spatial index mapped the images to their corresponding HEALPix pixels. Each row in the index table has six columns (Table 3). FILE is original files location. PIXEL_ID is the ID of the pixel that image covered. If an image covers multiple pixels, then it will have one record for each pixel that it covers. RA and DEC are the coordinates of the center of image. THETA is the rotation angle θ. At last, OBS-TIME is the timestamp of the observation. The indices are stored in a relational database so that a Hash index can be built on the PIXEL_ID column. This process is described in Algorithm 2. Because it needs to go through all the files in the given data set one by one using a for loop, Algorithm 2 has a time complexity of $O(n)$. When choosing the HEALPix partition level N properly, most image would cover only 1 to 2 pixels, thus the size of the index table and overhead of building the index should be much less than scanning for all the stars in all the images and build a starcatalog.

Algorithm 3 describes the querying process. When a query arrives, the corresponding PIXEL_ID(s) of the target area are calculated first. Then all the records in the index whose PIXEL_ID match the target PIXEL_ID(s) got picked out. Because the PIXEL_ID column has a Hash index, this steps time complexity is $O(1)$. In this step, only the images that have the same PIXEL_ID with the target area are selected so that the amount of data for the next step is greatly reduced. The next step is almost identical to that of the simple indexing method, that is, to check for each of the selected records whether they covered the entire target area by calculating their actually covered area using their respective θ. Only the images that covered the entire target area are returned in the result. This step clearly has a time complexity of $O(n)$. Combining the two steps together, Algorithm 3 has a time complexity of $O(an)$, where $\alpha < 1$ and α has a positive correlation with the number of files that have the same PIXEL_ID with the target area. The parameter c is also influenced by the choice of the HEALPix Partition level N. N would certainly affects the speed of both the indexing building and querying process.

If N is too small, meaning the size of each pixel is relatively large, more images would fall into same pixel and have the same PIXEL_ID with the target, thus the hash selection on PIXEL_ID will return more files to be checked in the next step, which would slows down the query. If N is too large, then each image may cover several pixels. Therefore, it would take more time to build the index, and the query performance would be affected as well because it would take more time to calculate the pixels covered by the target area. The optimal choice of the partition level N should be inversely proportional to the image size. With each level of sub-partition, one pixel will be divided into four equal-sized sub-pixels. The level N should increase by 1 if the images width and length both doubled. If the image is in rectangular shape (i.e. not square), the best choice of N should be based on the longer side because N depends on the number of pixels that the image may cover. The size of the target area, on the other hand, shouldn't make a big difference of the choice of N because it cannot exceed the size of the original image.

The last step of the query is to determine whether the target area is entirely covered by the image. To do so, some axis-transformation calculations are performed. The target area is defined as a center point $C_T(x_T, y_T)$ and a size of $l_{xT} \times l_{yT}$, the image area is defined as $C_I(x_I, y_I)$ and a size of $l_{xI} \times l_{yI}$. V_{Ti} and $V_{Ii}(i = 1, 2, 3, 4)$ are the vertexes of the target and the image area, respectively (Fig. 3).

Next, C_T are converted to the O' system.

$$C_T' = (x_T \cdot \cos \theta - y_T \cdot \sin \theta, \quad x_T \cdot \sin \theta + y_T \cdot \cot \theta) \tag{1}$$

Similarly, C_I is converted to C_I', V_{Ti} and V_{Ii} are converted to V_{Ti}' and V_{Ii}'. Then check the following inequalities

$$x_I' - \frac{l_{xI}}{2} \leqslant \min(x_{Vi}') \leqslant \max(x_{Vi}') \leqslant x_I' + \frac{l_{xI}}{2} \quad (i = 1, 2, 3, 4) \tag{2}$$

$$y_I' - \frac{l_{yI}}{2} \leqslant \min(y_{Vi}') \leqslant \max(y_{Vi}') \leqslant y_I' + \frac{l_{yI}}{2} \quad (i = 1, 2, 3, 4) \tag{3}$$

If any of the inequalities are not satisfied, the image in question should be removed from the result set.

Algorithm 1. CalculateCoveredPixels(Area A)

1: Set S = ∅
2: **for** each side of the given area **do**
3:    pid1, pid2 = the PIXEL_ID for each endpoints. Insert pid1, pid2 into S
4:    **if** pid1 ≠ pid2 **then**
5:        divide this segment at its midpoint
6:        **for** each of the two new segments **do**
7:            go to Line 2
8:        **end for**
9:    **end if**
10: **end for**
11: pidc = the PIXEL_ID of the centroid of the area
12: pidv[i] = the PIXEL_ID of the four vertexes of the area (i=1,2,3,4)
13: insert pidc, pidv[i] (i = 1 to 4) into S
14: **for** i = 1 to 4 **do**
15:    **if** pidc ≠ pid[i] **then**
16:        find the sub-area A' of which the vertex i and the centroid are two vertexes on the new diagonal
17:        CalculateCoveredPixels(A')
18:    **end if**
19: **end for**
20: **return** S

Algorithm 2. Build_AQUAdex (FITS_File_Collection C)

1: **for** each file F in C **do**
2:    read RA, Dec, θ, Obs-Time from F's header
3:    Set S = CalculateCoveredPixels (F)
4:    **for** each PIXEL_ID in S **do**
5:        insert record (F, PIXEL_ID, RA, Dec, θ, Obs-Time) into index
6:    **end for**
7: **end for**
8: build Hash index on the PIXEL_ID column

All source codes of the aforementioned algorithms are publicly available at the Paper Data system of China-VO [18].

4   Experimental Results

The data set used in our experiments are from actual observations conducted during the first three months of 2014 using the AST3 Telescope in Mohe, China.

Algorithm 3. QueryForTimeSeriesImages(Target_Area T)

1: Set ST = PIXEL_IDs covered by T
2: Result R = SELECT file FROM index WHERE PIXEL_ID IN ST AND
   begin_Time < obstime < end_Time
3: **for** each file F in R **do**
4:    convert T to F's coordinate system
5:    **if** F doesn't cover the entire target area **then**
6:       remove F from R
7:    **end if**
8: **end for**
9: return R

Our test PC is equipped with an Intel i7-4970 CPU (4 cores@3.6 GHz), 16 GB
of RAM, and two HDDs, one (1 TB) for the Ubuntu operating system, the other
(3 TB) for storing the data set. The index tables are stored in PostgreSQL DBMS
(v9.4). A relational database is chosen over the more modern non-relational databases (such as MongoDB) because relational databases provide highly efficient
equality comparisons using Hash indices (on the PIXEL_ID colum) as well as
excellent range query abilities using B-Tree indices (on the Obs-Time column).

4.1   Building Spatial Index

In this series of experiment, indices are built for eight data sets, the sizes of which
increases from 100 to 1400 gigabytes (GB). For each data set we measured the
time used to create its index. The results are shown in Table 4.

Table 4. Overhead of building the spatial index

Data Size (GB)	100	200	400	600	800	1000	1200	1400
Time(s)	19.126	42.813	92.207	141.519	210.332	271.456	321.104	331.446

As we can see from the results, the index building time, in principle, increases
linearly as the data set grows. This is due to the indexing building function
(Algorithm 1) having a time complexity of $O(n)$. Building index for 1 TB of
data takes about 4.5 min, which, considering that the index building is just a
one-time thing, is pretty acceptable in real life usage.

4.2   The Optimal Partition Level

To find out the relationship among the partition level N, the size of the original
images, and the size of the target area, the following series experiments are
conducted.

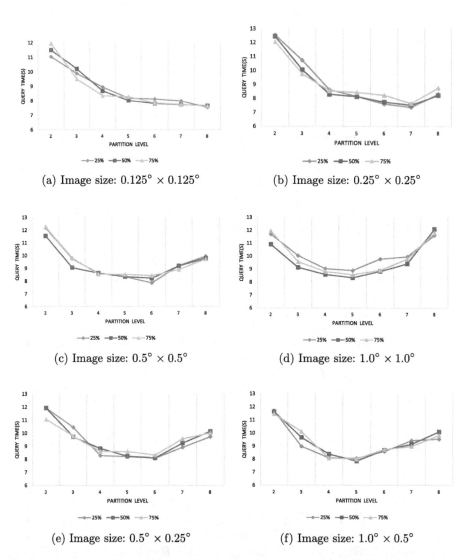

Fig. 5. Exploring the relationship among partition level, image size, and target area size. These figures show that partition level N should decrease by 1 when the original image size quadruples, and the size of the query target area has negligible influence on the query performance. For rectangular images (not square) the longer side plays the dominating role in choosing N

In the experiments, a same number of images with sizes of $0.125° \times 0.125°$, $0.25° \times 0.25°$, $0.5° \times 0.5°$, $1.0° \times 1.0°$, $0.5° \times 0.25°$, and $1.0° \times 0.5°$ are used as the test data. ($1.0° \times 1.0°$ is a pretty large image in astronomy). The HEALPix partition level increases from 2 to 8, so seven indices are built for each type of original image size. To test the influence of the size of target area on query performance, the size of the query target area are set to 25 %, 50 %, and 75 % of the original image size. 1000 random queries are generated for each combination of target size and image size. The queries are executed using all the seven indices. So we can see what partition level works best for each image size and target size combination.

The results are presented in Fig. 5, which shows that as the image size increases, the most suitable partition level N (i.e. the level in which the queries took the least time to complete) decreases. More specifically, the experiments corroborate our theory that the best partition level N should subtract 1 when the original image size quadruples. Figure 5 (e) and (c) have the same optimal N. Figure 5 (f) and (d) also have the same optimal N. This shows that for rectangular images, the longer side is the deciding factor when choosing N.

Another point the experiments demonstrated here is that the target size of queries has negligible effects on the performance. As can be seen in Fig. 5, all the three lines almost overlapped with each other in every graph.

4.3   Scalability

In this part, the scalability of our method is tested by executing one thousand query commands on multiple data sets with increasing sizes. Based on the experiment results of Sect. 4.2, the partition level N here is set to 5 to allow for best performance. Our innovative method is compared with the direct indexing

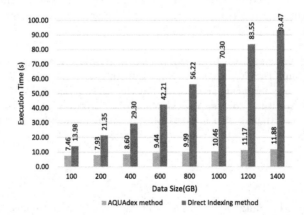

Fig. 6. Compared with the direct indexing method, AQUAdex showed excellent scalability. The query time only increased by 59 % when the data size has grown 1400 %. In all tests, our method only took a fraction of the time needed by the direct indexing method to complete the same task.

method introduced in Sect. 3.2, The execution time is used to measure the efficiency of the above two methods. The results are shown in Fig. 6. Our method demonstrated excellent scalability comparing to the direct indexing method. The query time only increased by 59 % when the data size has grown 1400 %. In all tests, our method only took a fraction of the time needed by the direct indexing method to complete the same task.

5   Conclusion and Future Work

In this paper, AQUAdex,an innovative spatial indexing and querying big data sets of astronomy image files is presented. AQUAdex increases the query speed significantly by introducing the idea of partitioning the sky into pixels so that each image would belong to one or more pixels. Experimental results shows that AQUAdex can accelerate the query up to 9 times faster. What's more, experimental results also demonstrated excellent scalability as the query time only increased by 59 % when the data size grows 14x larger. The algorithms of the index building, querying and pixel computation functions are presented, with the source code made publicly available online. Theoretical analysis has been provided to discuss the optimization of relevant parameters. The experimental results has corroborated the theory and testified that our method have achieved great efficiency while managed to maintained the overhead well within the acceptable range.

Moreover, AQUAdex can be easily adapted to other applications aside from extracting Time Series Images in astronomy. Generally speaking, any application that needs to query data that can be projected onto a sphere surface could benefit from it, such as the high dimensional data in digital map and remote sensing applications, etc.

For future work, reducing the index building time as well as the index size is worth investigating, and further increasing the scale of data set might bring new interesting challenges to AUQAdex.

Acknowledgments. This work was supported in part by National Natural Science Foundation of China (NSFC) through grant 61303021, U1531111 and U1231108. The data set used in the experiments are provided by the AST3 team of NAOC. The authors wish to express gratitude to Ms. Yiyi Gao and Ms. Xingyu Xu for their insightful suggestions. Sincere thanks also goes to Mr. Jie Wen for helping putting the final touches in place.

References

1. Aji, A., Wang, F., Saltz, J.H.: Towards building a high performance spatial query system for large scale medical imaging data. In: Proceedings of the 20th International Conference on Advances in Geographic Information Systems, pp. 309–318. ACM (2012)

2. Aji, A., Wang, F., Vo, H., Lee, R., Liu, Q., Zhang, X., Saltz, J.: Hadoop GIS: a high performance spatial data warehousing system over mapreduce. Proc. VLDB Endow. **6**(11), 1009–1020 (2013)
3. Alagiannis, I., Borovica, R., Branco, M., Idreos, S., Ailamaki, A.: NoDB: efficient query execution on raw data files. In: Proceedings of the 2012 ACM SIGMOD International Conference on Management of Data, pp. 241–252. ACM (2012)
4. Alagiannis, I., Borovica, R., Branco, M., Idreos, S., Ailamaki, A.: NoDB in action: adaptive query processing on raw data. Proc. VLDB Endow. **5**(12), 1942–1945 (2012)
5. Berriman, G.B., Groom, S.L.: How will astronomy archives survive the data tsunami? Commun. ACM **54**(12), 52–56 (2011)
6. Blanas, S., Wu, K., Byna, S., Dong, B., Shoshani, A.: Parallel data analysis directly on scientific file formats. In: Proceedings of the 2014 ACM SIGMOD International Conference on Management of Data, pp. 385–396. ACM (2014)
7. Brown, P.G.: Overview of SciDB: large scale array storage, processing and analysis. In: Proceedings of the 2010 ACM SIGMOD International Conference on Management of data, pp. 963–968. ACM (2010)
8. China-VO: Data explorer of China virtual observatory. http://explorer.china-vo.org
9. Ivanova, M., Kersten, M., Manegold, S.: Data vaults: a symbiosis between database technology and scientific file repositories. In: Ailamaki, A., Bowers, S. (eds.) SSDBM 2012. LNCS, vol. 7338, pp. 485–494. Springer, Heidelberg (2012)
10. NASA: Jet propulsion laboratory healpix homepage. http://healpix.jpl.nasa.gov/
11. Ng, M.K., Huang, Z.: Data-mining massive time series astronomical data: challenges, problems and solutions. Inf. Softw. Technol. **41**(9), 545–556 (1999)
12. Planthaber, G., Stonebraker, M., Frew, J.: EarthDB: scalable analysis of MODIS data using SciDB. In: Proceedings of the 1st ACM SIGSPATIAL International Workshop on Analytics for Big Geospatial Data, pp. 11–19. ACM (2012)
13. Richter, S., Quiané-Ruiz, J.-A., Schuh, S., Dittrich, J.: Towards zero-overhead static and adaptive indexing in hadoop. VLDB J. **23**(3), 469–494 (2014)
14. Silva, V., de Oliveira, D., Mattoso, M.: Exploratory analysis of raw data files through dataflows. In: 2014 International Symposium on Computer Architecture and High Performance Computing Workshop (SBAC-PADW), pp. 114–119. IEEE (2014)
15. Stonebraker, M., Brown, P., Poliakov, A., Raman, S.: The architecture of SciDB. In: Bayard Cushing, J., French, J., Bowers, S. (eds.) SSDBM 2011. LNCS, vol. 6809, pp. 1–16. Springer, Heidelberg (2011)
16. Tian, Y., Alagiannis, I., Liarou, E., Ailamaki, A., Michiardi, P., Vukolić, M.: DiNoDB: Efficient large-scale raw data analytics. In: Proceedings of the First International Workshop on Bringing the Value of Big Data to Users (Data4U 2014), p. 1. ACM (2014)
17. Zhao, Q.: Research on high-efficient massive data oriented astronomical crossmatch. Ph.D. thesis, Tianjin University (2010)
18. Hong, Z.: Source code of the algorithms in this paper. http://paperdata.china-vo.org/Hong.Zhi/2015/ICA3PP/AQUAdex/AQUAdex_Zhi.cpp

SAKMA: Specialized FPGA-Based Accelerator Architecture for Data-Intensive K-Means Algorithms

Fahui Jia, Chao Wang$^{(\boxtimes)}$, Xi Li, and Xuehai Zhou

School of Computer Science,
University of Science and Technology of China, Hefei 230000, China
fahuijia@mail.ustc.edu.cn,
{cswang,llxx,xhzhou}@ustc.edu.cn

Abstract. In the era of BD explosion, poses significant challenges in the processing speed due to huge data volume and high dimension. To address this problem, we design a hardware implementation of K-means based on FPGA, named SAKMA, which can accelerate the whole algorithm in hardware and can be easily configured via parameters. What's more, the accelerator makes the data size unlimited and can solve the problem about frequent off-chip memory access in a certain extent. Taking into account the hardware resource and power consumption, the SAKMA architecture adopts novel methods to accelerate the algorithm, including pipeline, tile technique, duplication parallelism, and hardware adder tree structures. In order to evaluate the performance of accelerator, we have constructed a real hardware prototype on Xilinx ZedBoard xc7z020clg484-1 FPGA. Experimental results demonstrate that the SAKMA architecture can achieve the speedup at 20.5 × with the affordable hardware cost.

Keywords: K-means algorithm · FPGA · Tile technique · Pipeline · Adder tree · Factors

1 Introduction

In the era of BD explosion, the enterprise has brought unprecedented opportunities, but also challenges one after another. From the BD, we can get important information that can predict the future trend or can reflect some relations between data. So the speed of Mining information is more and more important. However, BD makes the process time longer and longer. So algorithm acceleration becomes a hot research in BD explosion. For example, some people designs the heterogeneous cloud framework for BD Genome Sequencing to accelerate algorithm [1]. Some people adopts the method of designing the FPGA based accelerators for BD [2]. Some people accelerates algorithm by GPU. In a word, in the era of BD, the research on algorithm is more and more important.

K-means clustering is a popular technique for partitioning a data set into subsets of similar features [3]. Especially in the era of BD explosion, due to its simplicity and efficiency, it has been applied in numerous fields, such as Machine Learning, Image Processing and Data Mining. Many researchers have done the study to accelerate k-means on FPGA. However, Some hardware accelerators are limited by the size of

G. Wang et al. (Eds.): ICA3PP 2015, Part II, LNCS 9529, pp. 106–119, 2015.
DOI: 10.1007/978-3-319-27122-4_8

data, the number of Cluster and dimension of data and some other accelerators to make the data size unlimited often result in frequent off-chip memory access. As we know, frequent off-chip memory access takes much time and has posed significant contributions on the speedup. In the BD era, the above scenario occurs more frequently due to the two main reasons:

- The data volume is explosive as well as the number of centroid. However on-chip memory is significantly constrained. Therefore it is very important to explore the space locality of the dataset.
- With respect to the task level parallelism, much more on-chip memory will be consumed, because we have to use data redundant to realize parallelism. So the ability to store data and centroid should be discovered. Due to off-chip memory access, the frequently memory access will drag down the speedup.

To tackle this problem, in this paper, we present a k-means accelerator based on FPGA, named SAKMA, which can solve frequent off-chip memory access. We claim the following contributions:

- We present an accelerator for k-means based on FPGA, which can be easily configured via different parameters and expand the data size that is applicable to be processed at hardware accelerators.
- We propose a novel method to solve frequent off-chip memory access. The required data are divided into small blocks that can be stored as cache on-chip.
- We evaluate the performance and analyze the hardware cost of the accelerator, which could be useful to leverage the trade-off among the metrics.
- We measure the impact on speedup and give a conclusion by analyzing the experimental results.

The remainder of this paper is organized as below. In Sect. 2 we summarize the relate work. Then Sect. 3 illustrates the Architecture and methodologies. In Sect. 4 we present the experimental results and give the conclusion about the impact of some factors on speedup. Finally Sect. 5 concludes the paper.

2 Motivation and Related Work

K-means clustering is one of the unsupervised computational methods used to group similar objects into smaller partitions called clusters so that similar objects are grouped together [4, 5]. The goal is to find the optimal partition which minimizes the objective function given in (1) where Cj is geometric center (centroid) of the cluster Sj.

$$J(\{S_j\}) = \sum_{j=1}^{K} \sum_{x_i \in S_j} \left\| x_i - C_j \right\|^2 \tag{1}$$

As to the method to similarity measure, we adopt the Manhattan metric to calculate the similarity. The distance formula is shown in (2). The specific process of the algorithm is shown as below.

$$D(P, C) = \sum_{i}^{n} |P - C| \tag{2}$$

```
Initialization for mean[k] array
Loop(N)
    For each point of the data set
        For each centroid in the classes
            Dist[i] = dist(point[j],mean[i]);
        End for
        Shortest = Dist[0];
        Label = 0;
        For each element in the Dist array
            If Dist[i] < shortest
                Shortest = Dist[i];
                Label = i;
            End if
        End for
        Sum[label] += shortest;
        Count[label]++;
    End for
    mean[i] = sum[i] / count[i];
End Loop
```

2.1 Motivation

Based on the above steps, the algorithm will consume much more time when the data set and the number of centriods increase. In addition, it will lead to frequent off-chip memory access due to small on-chip memory. As a result, we design an accelerator based on FPGA for k-means algorithm. The main motivation of this paper has three folds:

- This paper is to present a hardware accelerator which can be easily configured via parameters, therefore the flexibility and scalability can be significantly improved.
- This paper proposes a method to avoid the frequent off-chip memory accesses when the data size and centroid size are very large.
- This paper tackles the impact on speedup for K-means and gives the corresponding detailed analysis.

2.2 Related Work

In 2000, Dominique Lavenier at Los Alamos National Laboratory implemented systolic array architecture of K-means clustering on a number of FPGA boards [6]. This paper only implemented the calculation of the distance between point and centroid on

FPGA, while other work done by the CPU. The accelerator obtained a speedup of is about 15x [7, 8]. This approach was effective in allowing for any data size to be processed, however, the disadvantage was the communication overhead between the host and the FPGA [9].

In 2001, Michael Estlick et al. implemented K-means in hardware using software/hardware co-design [10]. The algorithm was partitioned in two parts. In that case, distance calculation was implemented in hardware in purely fixed point and the new means was calculated in the host to avoid consuming hardware resources. The hardware implementation achieved a speedup of $50 \times$ more than 500MHZ Pentium III host processor [11]. However, sometimes the fixed point will lose precision. Perhaps it can perform well for one dataset, but not suitable for other datasets. This is the disadvantage of the fixed point.

In 2003, Venkatesh Bhaskaran implemented a parameterized implementation of K-means algorithm on FPGA [12]. The whole algorithm is implemented on FPGA and his research achieved a $500 \times$ speedup over Matlab implementation. His design was only tested on several clusters and the board used did not have any memory capability. So it is limited to the data size that can be processed at one time and it is the limitation of the design.

In 2011, H. Hussain implemented K-means Algorithm based on FPGA for Bioinformatics Application: An Accelerated Approach to Clustering Microarray Data [6]. That research implemented five K-means core on Xilinx Virtex4 XC4VLX25 FPGA, and tested them on a sample of real Yeast Microarray dataset. His design achieved about $51.7 \times$ speedup. The design adopted the fixed point and it may make the precision lost. In addition, it did not address frequent off-chip memory access.

In 2012, Zhongduo Lin designed a K-means accelerator on FPGA for high-dimensional data using triangle inequality [13]. The accelerator had a remarkable speedup for high dimension data processing. The experimental results demonstrated that the hardware can achieve 55-fold speedup compared to software for 1024 MNIST. In his design, it also did not address the off-chip memory.

3 SAKMA Hardware Implementation

3.1 General Architecture

Figure 1 presents the general architecture of SAKMA which consists of two parts: the PS (Processing System) in software and the PL (Processing Logic) in hardware. Every part has its own block memory to store the input volumes. The two parts are interconnected through AXI4-Lite bus for demonstration. Specific function of the block in every part will be introduced respectively:

In the PS part, the DDR block is responsible for the storage of the data set and initial centroids of the cluster. The ARM block is in charge of the control signal and transmits data between DDR block and DMA controller block.

In the PL part, DMA Controller block transmits data between ARM and IP Core. The AXI Timer is used to calculate the running time of the algorithm in hardware. The AXI-interconnect is responsible for the connection between DMA Controller block and AXI Timer block. The IP Core implements the K-means algorithm based on FPGA.

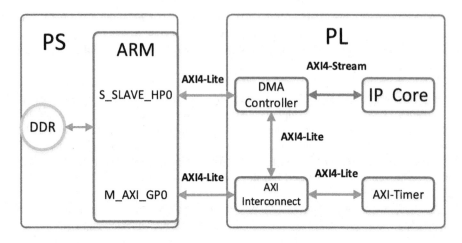

Fig. 1. The General architecture of SAKMA

3.2 IP Core Design Flow

The whole algorithm is divided four steps. The first step is to calculate the distances between one point and all centroids. The second step is to compare the distances and find the cluster centroid which has the shortest distance than other centroids. The third step is to partition point into corresponding cluster and accumulate the sum of the point in the same cluster. The last step is to recompute the new centroids by the arithmetic average method. Figure 2 gives the algorithm flow.

From the Fig. 2, we can know the detailed architecture of the SAKMA IP Core. The IP Core consists of multiple input arrays, several Functional Units (Cal_Dist, Compare, Acc, and Division), three input arrays (points, clusters, Parameters) and one output arrays. In addition, the IP Core integrates a number of BRAM Memory space to store intermediate results. The DMA controller transmits data into the input array from external DDR main memory, which firstly gets the parameters and then configures the IP Core according to the user's requirements. In the next, the IP Core starts to work and finally the output results are sent to DDR. Figure 2 presents the interconnect architecture including two same function unit, so it is able to handle the distance calculation with parallel execution. The parallelization degree depends on the real time a requirement from the application, as well as the chip area constraints. Due to that the off-chip memory access will affect the performance significantly, A detailed introduction for the tile technique is presented to solve the problem [14].

```
Calculation distance
for(i = 0;i < N; i++) {
      for(j = 0; j < K; j++) {
            Dist(i,j) = distance(point(i),Mean(j));
      }
}
```

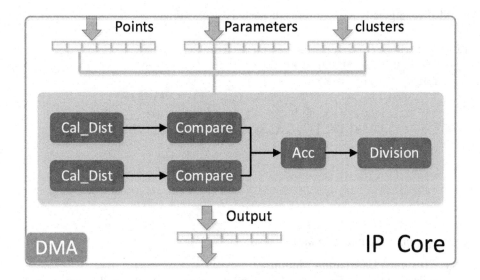

Fig. 2. Hardware IP core architecture in SAKMA

Above program code presents the original code of distance calculation. We observe that every centroid can be reused after N-1 distance calculations (N is the number of the point). When N is becoming larger, the reuse of centroid is also significant. However the chip cannot store all centroids simultaneously. So it will lead to frequent off-memory access, which results in fetching the same centroid for different points.

To solve the problem, we tile loops of both point and centroid and define each tiled block to calculate the distances between Ti point and Tj centroids. The tiled code of distance calculation is presented in the below. Tiling significantly reduces the reuse of centroid to avoid the frequent off-chip memory access. For example, assume N is 60000 and K is 2000, while the chip only can store 1000 centroids. So through original code every point needs 2 times off-chip memory accesses. The number of off-chip memory access is 2*60000. If we tile the loops with 1000 points and 1000 centroids, the 1000 points only need 2 times off-chip memory accesses. Off-chip memory access will be reduced to 2*60 times. Assuming that the data size is N, memory storage capacity of FPGA is K and the cluster number is M, the difference between original code and tiled code in term of off-chip memory access times can be shown in (3), (4). (3) is on behalf of off-chip memory access times resulting from original code and (4) delegates off-chip memory access times of tiled code. This two expressions show that

$$\frac{M}{K} * N \tag{3}$$

$$\frac{M}{K} * \frac{N}{K} \tag{4}$$

the tiled code greatly reduces off-chip memory access times.

```
Tiled code of distance calculation
 for(i = 0; i < N/T; i++) {
    for(j = 0;j < K/S; j++) {
        For(ii = i * T; ii < (i + 1) * T; ii++){
            For(jj = j * T; jj < (j+1) * S; jj++){
            Dist(i,j) = distance(point(ii),Mean(jj));
            }
        }
    }
 }
```

3.3   Specific Functional Modules

3.3.1   Distance Calculation Module

The module is to calculate the similarity and it consists of some small function units (Vector SUB, Vector ABS, Adder Tree, Accumulate). Vector SUB and Vector ABS functions make some dimensions of data can be calculated in parallel. Adder Tree makes the sum process more efficient. Accumulate function is to calculate the final distance. The detailed content is shown Fig. 3.

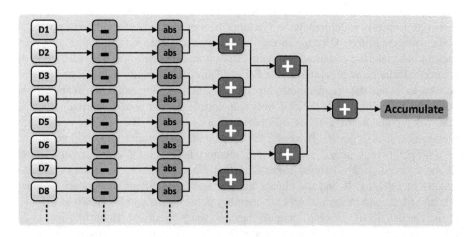

Fig. 3. Distance calculation module

Some dimensions of point and centroid can be got in parallel to calculate the absolute value. Unlimited by the hardware resource, we designed that every 16 dimensions of data can be calculated in parallel in Vector SUB and Vector ABS operations. Then adopt the corresponding adder Tree to calculate the sum of 16 dimensions. For example, when the dimension is 128, we can calculate the first 16 dimensions and then do the work in the same method for other dimensions; so as to finally we calculate all dimensions and get the final result in the Accumulate operation. In this process, we adopt pipeline method to process the batch calculation.

3.3.2 Comparison Module

After distances calculation, the next step is to find the shortest value among the calculated distances. In order to accelerate this process, we use the comparison tree to find the cluster centroid which has the shortest distance to point than other centroids. Then store the label of the corresponding cluster to prepare for the next step. The comparison tree is shown in Fig. 4. Every two distances in Dist_array are compared to find the smaller distance. At the same time the comparison will give the flag of the centroid which has smaller distance than another one. Then the next layer will continue to compare the distances by the data received from this layer. The comparison is paralleled in every layer and finally we get the index of the cluster centroid that has the shortest distance to point than other centroids. The index is one input of Acc Module. If the number of clusters is more than the designed compare units, we adopt pipeline method to batch the compare operations.

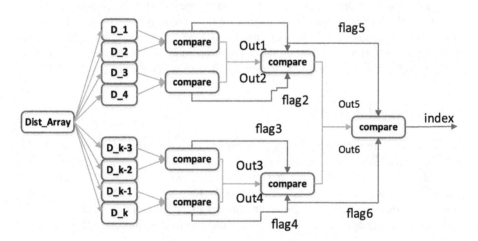

Fig. 4. Comparison module

3.3.3 Acc Module and Division Module

The Acc Module takes the index received from the Compare Module as the cluster label. Then according to the label, find the corresponding cluster counter and add 1 to its value. Finally, sum the point in the same cluster with accumulator in the cluster. When all points are processed, Division Module will start to recompute new centroids for the next iteration. Figure 5 shows the process flow for Acc Module and Division Module.

Due to that every point has multiple dimensions, so the accumulator is to sum for vectors. The add operations of all dimensions complete in one cycle. In other words,

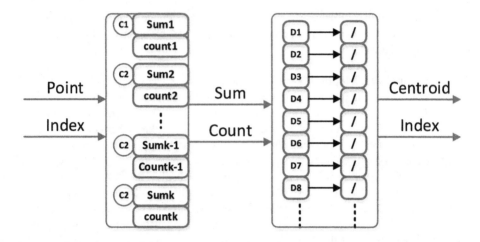

Fig. 5. Acc module and division module

these add operations operate in parallel. Similarly, the division process is same with this one. In the Division Module, the inputs are the sum array and count array and the output are new centroid and index of cluster. As long as receiving the input data, all dimensions of the sum will operate the division operation in the same time. After all new centroids are recomputed next iteration will start automatically.

4   Experimental Results

The test data is real biological data set with 20 k vectors. In order to evaluate the hardware accelerator, we generated a synthetic data set of vectors whose elements were randomly selected from 0 to 1 using the mersenne twister, which is a widely used pseudorandom generator with an extraordinarily long cycle of 219.937-1 [15]. We generated some data sets with different dimensions or different number of vectors. These data sets are applied to test the design and the factors impacting the speedup.

4.1   Software Implementation

The k-means algorithm is tested on an Intel(R) Core(TM)2 Duo 2.33 GHz CPU, with 4 GB RAM running on Ubuntu 12.04 system. When the number of clusters is set to 300, the average execution time of the algorithm for 10 times is 0.307813 s when the data consists of 10000 points and every point have 32 dimensions. This result is based on initial centroids predefined and given as an input of the k-mean algorithm. Then we tested several data sets with different data size, dimension and K parameter to analyze these factors impact on the speedup.

4.2   Hardware Platform and Experimental Results

In order to evaluate the performance metrics of the design on FPGA, we have built a platform on Xilinx ZedBoard based on ZYNQ-7000 architecture, equipped with xc7z020clg484-1 FPGA chip. According to the hardware design, we have implemented one IP Core to test speedup when the data set owns 10000 float points. The hardware resource occupied by our IP Core is given in Table 1.

Table 1. Occupied hardware resource chart

Logic	used	Available	Utilization
BRAM_18K	176	280	62%
DSP48E	110	220	50%
FF	28784	106400	27%
LUT	39023	53200	73%

Previous works use fixed point implementation, but we used float point operations to promote the design performance. In hardware the execution time about the whole algorithm is 238.86 s. As a result, comparing with software we achieved a speedup of 23.01x. Compared with other state-of-the-art methods, for example, GPU, although we only achieve $0.2 \times$ speedup, our design can reduce the energy by 401x.

When the data size and centroid size are very large the tile technique will reduce the off-chip memory access to improve the speedup. Figure 6. shows the comparison result between original code and tiled code. The x-axis delegates the K parameter, y-axis indicates the speedup. Purple column refers to tiled code, while the red column refers to original code. When K parameter value is 20, the original code do not need to access off-chip memory. Therefore the speedup of original code is the same with tiled code. When the K parameter value is 40 or 60, the difference is remarkable. In addition, the speedup of tiled code increases as the K parameter value grows. But on the contrary, the speedup of original actually reduces. These results demonstrate that frequent off-chip memory access really has a significant impact on the performance, tiled code indeed avoid frequent off-chip memory access and improve the speedup. Meanwhile, the reduction of off-chip memory access can also reduce power consumption.

The speedup is influenced by many factors and we tested some factors to get the performance metrics. Firstly we verified the data size and get some figures in Fig. 7. The x-axis refers to data size, while the y-axis indicates speedup ratio. Figure 7.

Shows that when the data size grows from 500 to 4000, the speed up increases as the data size grows. when the data size grows from 4000 to 6000 the speedup keeps flat in general. It demonstrates when the data size is small the speedup grows as the growth of data size, while when data size increases to a certain scale the speedup remains flat. Through the analysis, we explore that when the data size is small the time spent on other aspects that cannot be overlooked, while when the data size grows large enough, the data processing takes up major time. So the speedup keeps consistent.

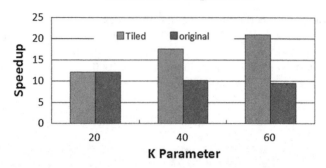

Fig. 6. Tiled code VS original code

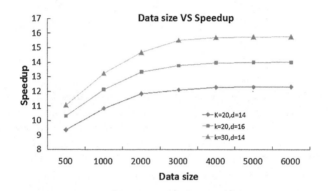

Fig. 7. Data size VS speedup

Secondly we tested factor with the K parameter, which indicates the number of the class or cluster. As is illustrated in the Fig. 8, x-axis refers to K parameter, y-axis indicates speedup. These results mean that as K parameter grows the speedup Increases as well. Due to hardware resource restriction, we cannot completely parallel some operations and the best solution is to partly parallel some operations. Finally, as the

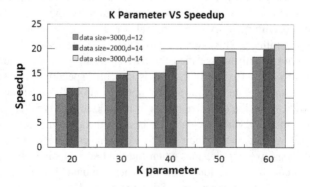

Fig. 8. K parameter VS speedup

growth of clusters, the off-chip memory access times will increase, which makes the speedup increase more slowly.

Finally, we tested the impact of dimension parameter on speedup. The detailed results are shown in Fig. 9. The x-axis delegates the speedup, and the y-axis represents the dimension parameter. We take the red cylinders as an example, the speedup increases from 12.10 × to 16.863 × as the growth of dimension. When the dimension is 14 the speedup is 12.10x. When dimension is 22, the speedup increased to 16.863, which means that the dimension grows with the increase of the speedup.

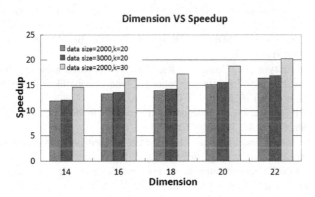

Fig. 9. Dimension VS speedup

5   Conclusion

In this paper, we have presented SAKMA, a specialized high efficient hardware accelerator based on FPGA for K-means algorithms. We adopted float point to get a speedup promotion with an affordable hardware cost. In order to avoid frequent off-chip memory access, the paper presents a tiled technique to divide large volume of memory blocks into small tiles that can be buffered on-chip. Finally, performance metrics (data size, dimension parameter, K parameter) were tested to analyze the impact on the speedup. The design is tested on Xilinx xc7z020clg484-1 ZedBoard and the software implement is on Intel(R) Core(TM) 2 Duo 2.33 GHz CPU, with 4 GB RAM running on Ubuntu 12.04 system. Experimental results demonstrate that its speedup is satisfying for large volume size, high dimensions data with avoiding frequent off-chip memory accesses.

There are some future directions worth pursing. As we know, the limited hardware resource reduces the speedup. If we can demonstrate a point in some short bytes of prime numbers [16], which can not only reduce the use of BRAM but also improve efficiency. In the future work, this is our main direction for K-means accelerator based on FPGA.

Acknowledgments. This work was supported by the National Science Foundation of China under grants (No. 61379040, No. 61272131, No. 61202053), Jiangsu Provincial Natural Science Foundation (No. SBK201240198), Open Project of State Key Laboratory of Computer Architecture, Institute of Computing Technology, Chinese Academy of Sciences (No. CARCH 201407), and the Strategic Priority Research Program of CAS (No. XDA06010403).

References

1. Wang, C., Li, X., Chen, P., Wang, A., Zhou, X., Yu, H.: Heterogeneous cloud framework for big data genome sequencing. IEEE/ACM Trans. Comput. Biol. Bioinform. **12**(1), 166–178 (2015)
2. Wang, C., Li, X., Zhou, X.: SODA: software defined FPGA based accelerators for big data, pp. 884-887 (2015)
3. Winterstein, F., Bayliss, S., Constantinides, G.A.: FPGA-based K-means clustering using tree-based data structures. In: 23rd International Conference on Field Programmable Logic and Applications (FPL) 2013, pp. 1–6 (2013)
4. Macgregor, P.F., Squire, J.A.: Application of microarrays to the analysis of gene expression in cancer. Clin. Chem. **48**, 1170–1177 (2002)
5. Akay, M.: Genomics and Proteomics Engineering in Medicine and Biology (IEEE Press Series in Biomedical Engineering). John Wiley & Sons, New York (2007)
6. Lavenier, D.: FPGA implementation of the k-means clustering algorithm for hyper spectral images. In: Los Alamos National Laboratory LAUR (2000)
7. Lavenier, D.: FPGA implementation of the K-means clustering algorithm for hyper spectral images. In: Los Alamos National Laboratory, LAUR # 00-3079, pp. 1-18 (2000)
8. Gokhale, M., Frigo, J., McCabe, K., Theiler, J., Wolinski, C., Lavenier, D.: Experience with a hybrid processor: K-means clustering. J. Supercomput. **26**, 131–148 (2003)
9. Hussain, H.M., Benkrid, K., Seker, H., Erdogan, A.T.: FPGA implementation of K-means algorithm for bioinformatics application: an accelerated approach to clustering microarray data. In: 2011 NASA/ESA Conference on Adaptive Hardware and Systems (AHS), pp. 248-255 (2011)
10. Estlick, M., Leeser, M., Theiler, J., Szymanski, J.J.: Algorithmic transformations in the implementation of K-means clustering on reconfigurable hardware. In: Proceedings of the 2001 ACM/SIGDA Ninth International Symposium on Field Programmable Gate Arrays, pp. 103–110 (2001)
11. Theiler, J., Leeser, M.E., Estlick, M., Szymanski, J.J.: Design issues for hardware implementation of an algorithm for segmenting hyper spectral imagery. In: Descour, M.R., Shen, S.S. (eds.) Imaging Spectrometry VI, vol. 4132, pp. 99–106. The International Society for Optical Engineering, Bellingham, WA (2000)
12. Bhaskaran, V.: Parameterized Implementation of K-means Clustering on Reconfigurable Systems Citeseer (2004)
13. Lin, Z., Lo, C., Chow, P.: K-means implementation on FPGA for high-dimensional data using triangle inequality. In: 22nd International Conference on Field Programmable Logic and Applications (FPL) 2012, pp. 437–442 (2012)
14. Daofu Liu, T.C., Liu, S., Zhou, J., Zhou, S., Temam, O., Feng, X., Zhou, X., Chen, Y.: Pudiannao: a polyvalent machine learning accelerator. In: Proceedings of the 20th ACM International Conference on Architectural Support for Programming Languages and Operating Systems (ASPLOS 2015) (2015)

15. Ichikawa, K., Morishita, S.: A simple but powerful heuristic method for accelerating k-means clustering of large-scale data in life science. IEEE/ACM Trans. Comput. Biol. Bioinf. **11**(4), 681–692 (2014)
16. Childs, L., Childs, L.N.: A Concrete Introduction to Higher Algebra, vol. 1. Springer, New York (1979)

HDCat: Effectively Identifying Hot Data in Large-Scale I/O Streams with Enhanced Temporal Locality

Jiahao Chen[1], Yuhui Deng[1,2(✉)], and Zhan Huang[1]

[1] Department of Computer Science, Jinan University,
Guangzhou 510632, People's Republic of China
[2] State Key Laboratory of Computer Architecture,
Institute of Computing Technology, Chinese Academy of Sciences,
Beijing 100190, People's Republic of China
cm2243@foxmail.com, {tyhdeng,thz}@jnu.edu.cn

Abstract. Hot data is very important for optimizing modern computer systems. For example, the identified hot data can be employed to extend the lifespan of flash memory. However, it is very challenging to effectively identify hot data with low memory consumption and low runtime overhead. This paper proposes a Hot Data Catcher (HDCat) which can effectively identify hot data in large-scale I/O streams by leveraging enhanced temporal locality. HDCat only maintains a hot data queue and a candidate hot data queue to record the data access pattern by tracking limited data set, thus effectively reducing the memory consumption. Furthermore, HDCat adopts a D-bit counter and a recency-bit to leverage both the frequency and recency contained in the data stream. Additionally, HDCat can significantly reduce the conversion between hot data and cold data. Real traces are used to evaluate the proposed approach. Experimental results demonstrate that HDCat significantly outperforms the state-of-the-art Multi-hash algorithm and the two-level LRU algorithm.

Keywords: Hot data · Identifying hot data · Large-scale · Temporal locality · Hot data identification algorithm

1 Introduction

Hot data is very important for optimizing modern computer systems. The traditional hot data identification algorithms simply recorded the occurrences of the data items and ignore the volume of the corresponding data set. Therefore, most of the traditional approaches employed to identify hot data incured large memory consumption [4] or a high runtime overhead [1]. Additionally, these approaches did not consider the temporal locality which has a significant impact on the hot data identification [2,12]. This is because the recently accessed data is more likely to be accessed again in the near future. In order to overcome this

© Springer International Publishing Switzerland 2015
G. Wang et al. (Eds.): ICA3PP 2015, Part II, LNCS 9529, pp. 120–133, 2015.
DOI: 10.1007/978-3-319-27122-4_9

problem, Hsieh et al. [8] proposed a multiple hash function framework to identify hot data. This algorithm used multiple hash functions and a Boolean filter
to capture the frequency information of data access pattern. Furthermore, it
employed a counter to accurately capture the frequency information. However,
the exponential decay mode adopted in the algorithm (i.e. every time all the
counters are reduced by half) made it hard to capture the temporal locality of
the data access pattern.

Hot data identification methods can be applied in different scenarios. Caching
is typical scenario [5,7,10]. By caching hot data in advance, we can significantly
improve the corresponding system performance.When the hot data is transferred
to cold data, in order to make room for the other data to cache, it has to write
the data back to flash memory. Due to the characteristics of flash memory that
it cannot be updated in place, the data from memory cannot be directly over
write the original data, and it will be written to another clean storage space.
The old data should erase in advance, and the erasing operation in flash memory is in block units to implement, which makes the data stored in the same
block need to be copied to other clean data space. If the conversion between hot
and cold data arises frequently, it will greatly increase the number of erasing
operation in flash memory [9,13]. However, the flash memory can be written
out by a finite number of erasing operation, thus it will greatly reduce the service life of flash memory [6,15]. In addition, erasing operation ($500\,\mu s$) [14] was
expensive in flash memory compared with the read ($25\,\mu s$) and write ($200\,\mu s$)
operation. Thus, frequent conversion between hot and cold data will lead to frequent erasing operation as well as an unpredictable delay to system. In general,
reducing the number of conversion between hot and cold data will help reduce
the number of erase operation on flash memory as well as prolong its service life
and prevent unpredictable delay in system. Although there have been a lot of
researches on flash memory and its optimization, seldom from the perspective of
hot data identification algorithm to prolong the service life of the flash memory
and improve its performance.

This paper proposes a Hot Data Catcher (HDCat) to effectively identify hot
data by leveraging a recency-bit and a D-bit counter. The key idea is that:
1. Update the D-bit counter of item according to its recency bit ·which will
lead to a result that the recently access data (recency bit = 1)will increase its
heat value a bit faster than the item has not been accessed for a period of
time(recency bit = 0). 2. Filtering mechanism based on the recency information,
when the algorithm needs to eliminate an item, it first chooses the lowest counter
item with a negative recency bit. In this case, an item with a positive recency
bit will not be eliminated even though its counter is lower. 3. Our trembling
mechanism and the two level structure, these feature are in order to reduce
the run time overhead and the memory consumption respectively. Experimental
results demonstrate HDCat that can effectively improve the accuracy of hot
data identification, while maintaining low memory overhead and low runtime
overhead, and significantly reducing the conversion between hot data and cold
data.

The rest of this paper is organized as follows. Section 2 introduces the related work. Section 3 presents the design and operation of the hot data catcher. Section 4 shows the experimental results. Finally, Sect. 5 summarizes and concludes the paper.

2 Related Work

2.1 Bloom Filter

The main goal of bloom filters (BFs) is recording information with a low storage overhead. For BFs, space efficiency is a very important factor. Therefore, it often maximizes the space efficiency at the expense of correctness. Even if an element does not belong to a given set, BFs may also give a wrong positive answer, and judge the element included in the set. This is called false positive. However, the basic BFs do not cause false negative problem, if we give an element belonging to a set, it will generate a right answer. We can modify some parameters (i.e., BF size, the number of hash functions and the number of unique elements) of BFs to reduce the probability of false positive.

2.2 D-bit Counter

The information a simple Boolean record is too limited, and cannot meet the demand of information we have on many occasions, but the use of plastic variables to record data will takes up too much storage space, a D-bit counter will be an acceptable compromise.

D-bit counter is a D bits array, which can record the data range from zero to $2^D - 1$. We first set all bits in counter to 0, whenever the corresponding element appears, the entire counter value is incremented by 1. When the entire counter value exceeds $2^D - 1$, we will stop adding 1 operation. D-bit counter also includes a B-most Significant Bits, which we call threshold. When all the bits after the B-most Significant Bits are 0, we can judge the frequency of data does not exceed the threshold. Otherwise, the data will be regard as exceed the given threshold. In general, D-bit counter is a structure that can provide sufficient accuracy as well as space efficiency. The algorithm we proposed and the famous Multiple Hash Function have employed this structure. Subsequent chapters will introduce more detail.

In hot data identification, we are concerned about the data access pattern but not the detail access information. For example, we need to know whether a data accessed frequently, or to be exact, we want to know whether the occurrence of this data exceeds a given threshold. However, once we know that a data access frequency exceeds the thresholds, we generally do not care about the specific number of request. We do not need to use an integer variable to record the complete access information. In this scenario, D-bit counters satisfy our needs well, and provide space efficiency.

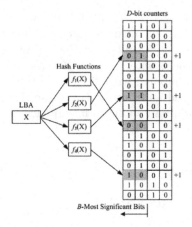

Fig. 1. Multiple hash function framework. Here D = 4 and B = 2.

2.3   Hot Data Identification Algorithms

In order to decrease the memory consumption of hot data identification, Chang and Kuo [1] proposed a two-level LRU algorithm (TLL) including a hot data list and a candidate hot data list. Both two lists have a fixed length and are LRU lists. Whenever a request arrives, TLL checks if the corresponding LBA is in the hot list. If it hits the hot list, then the data will be regarded as a hot data. Otherwise, the data is treated as cold data. If the data is not in the hot list but in the candidate list, then the data is promoted to the hot list. If the data is not in both lists, they are inserted to the candidate list. This two-level LRU algorithm has better space efficiency than FMS, because it only needs to record the access information of hot data and the candidate data, instead of recording all of the data access information. Unfortunately, it has another problem. Its performance relies heavily on the length of the two lists. In other words, a short list can reduce memory overhead, but it would improperly degrade hot data to the candidate list. This will decrease the accuracy of identification. Another disadvantage of this algorithm is that, it incurs a high run-time overhead when running the algorithm.

Recently, Hsieh et al. [8] proposed another algorithm called multiple hash function framework (MHF) to identify hot data (Fig. 1). This MHF adopts multiple hash functions and a D-bit counter. MHF records the data access information by incrementing the corresponding counters. It updates the data access information by periodically dividing the counter by 2. If a bit after the B-most significant bits is set to 1, the corresponding counter returns 1. Otherwise, it returns 0. Similar to the method of bloom filters, MHF also adopts K independent hash functions. If all K-bit positions (from the k-hash functions) are set to 1, the data is regard as a hot data. For example, as shown in Fig. 1, the assumption is that the algorithm uses 4-bit counters and adopts 2 as its most significant bit, then 4 will be its hot threshold. In this example, we map the address of the data X with 4 hash functions (f1, f2, f3, f4) and we then get 4 values: 0010, 0100, 1111, 1001. Here only the counter corresponding to f2 returns 0, but it is enough to judge data X as a cold data. Due to the ageing mechanism, this algorithm decreases all the counters by a half with 1-bit right shifting after a specified time interval. Compared with other algorithms, MHF achieves a relatively low memory overhead and run-time overhead.However, it does not catch recency information appropriately due to its exponential decrement of all LBA counters.

3   HotData Catcher

3.1   Overview of Hot Data Catcher

As shown in Fig. 2. HDCat consists of a hot list and a candidate hot list to identify hot data. Each item on the list contains a recency bit and a D-bit counter. Initially, both lists are empty. All the data items are treated as cold data. When a new data item arrives, HDCat first checks whether it is on the two lists. If any list contains the data item, the corresponding value of the D-bit counter will be increased. If a data item is on the candidate list and its D-bit counter is bigger than a given hot threshold, this data item will be promoted to the hot list. If the hot list is full, a data item on the hot list will be demoted to the candidate hot list by leveraging a filtering mechanism. If the two lists do not contain the new data item, a data item on the candidate list will be evicted and the new data item will be recorded on the candidate hot list.

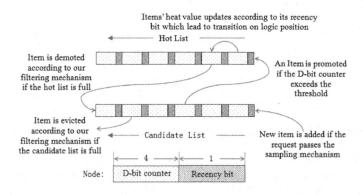

Fig. 2. D-bit counters with recency bit in two-level structure

Each item on the list contains a recency bit and a D-bit counter. The D-bit counter is used to store the access frequency. It is in the range of 0 to $2^D - 1$. The recency bit is adopted to identify whether the associated item is recently accessed. Both the D-bit counter and the recency bit are initialized to zero. If the recency bit is 0, it indicates that the item has not been visited for certain a period of time. When an item on the list is accessed, the D-bit counter will be increased by 1, and the recency bit will be changed to 1. This indicates that the corresponding item has just been visited. If the recency bit is 1, and the associated item has been accessed within a short period of time, we increase the associated D-bit counter by 2. If the value of a D-bit counter exceeds $2^D - 1$, we cannot get the exact access frequency. However, HDCat only needs to know whether the D-bit counter exceeds a given threshold but not an exact number of occurrences. This feature makes D-bit obtain high accuracy of identification with a low storage overhead. If the D-bit counter overflows, a freezing approach [14] is adopted to handle this issue. The approach does not increase the counter value any more even if the corresponding data is access again. The D-bit counters are not simply storing the occurrences of data, but the heat value which represents frequency as well as recent information of the access pattern. According to the mechanism of HDCat, even if the occurrences of two data items are equal, but one focuses on the past, another one focuses on the recency, the two data items will get different heat value. This is reasonable for a real scenario of hot data identification. Additionally, we believe that a data item continuously accessed for a short period of time is a better candidate of hot data than a data item referenced within a long period of time. This scenario will generate different heat values for the two data items when using HDCat. For example, if a data item has been visited repeatedly over a short period of time, this data is more likely to become a hot data. Therefore, the recency bit of the data item will be set to 1 and its heat value will grow fast. HDCat employs an aging mechanism to handle this issue where the D-bit counter does not simply increase with the increase of its occurrence, but becomes less and less as time goes by. Algorithm 1 summarizes the working process of HDCat using pseudo-code. When a new data item arrives, there are three different scenarios which handle the new data item differently. (1) If the data item is on the hot list, the D-bit counter of data item is increased by 1. If the recency bit of the data item is 0, it will be changed to 1. Otherwise, if the recency bit of the data item is already set to 1, the D-bit counter will be added 2 indicating that this data item has recently been accessed. (2) If the new data item is not on the hot list but on the candidate hot list, HDCat will deal with the data item like step one. Furthermore, if the D-bit counter of the data item exceeds a given threshold, this date item will be promoted to the hot list. If the hot list is full, one data item on the list will be demoted using the filtering mechanism to make space. (3) If the new data item is not on the two lists, HDCat will perform a sampling mechanism. If it passes the sampling mechanism, the data item will be inserted to the candidate hot list. Otherwise, the data item will be discarded.

3.2   Design of Hot Data Catcher

In order to effectively identify hot data, HDCat involves three important components including a filtering mechanism, a sampling mechanism and an aging mechanism. The data structures used to record data access information include

---

Algorithm 1. Hot Data Catcher

Data: Request for item
Result: Hot or Cold data classification of the item
1 **begin**
2   A Request for an item x is issued;
3   **if** *HotList Hit* **then**
4   Increase its coounter according to its recency bit;
5   Set the recency bit to 1;
6   Classify x as hot data;
7   **else**
8   //HotList Miss;
9   **if** *CandidateList Hit* **then**
10   Increase its counter according to its recency bit;
11   Set the recency bit to 1;
12   **if** *Counter greater than HotThreshold* **then**
13   //promote to HotList;
14   **if** *HotList is not full* **then**
15   Promote x to the HotList;
16   **else**
17   //Need to evict item;
18   find the evict data y with our filtering mechanism;
19   demote y to the CandidateList;
20   **else**
21   //CandidateList Miss;
22   **if** *Pass the sampling test* **then**
23   **if** *CandidateList is full* **then**
24   find the evict item y with our filtering and remove it;
25   Insert x into the CandidateList;
26   **else**
27   Skip further processing of the x;
28 **end**

---

one recency bit and a D-bit counter, where D is equal to 4 in our experiment. The recency bit divides the data of list Lx ($x \in 0, 1$, L0 represents the hot list, L1 represents the candidate hot list) into two sets S1 and S0 ($S1, S0 \subseteq Lx$ and $S1 \bigcup S0 = Lx$). S1 represents a data set that the recency bit of the data is 1 and the data has been recently visited. S0 represents the remaining data.

Filtering Mechanism. When Lx is full and a new data item has to be inserted into this list, it invokes the filtering mechanism. The filtering mechanism can be divided into two parts. The first part is selecting the data item that has the minimum value of the 4-bit counter in S0 and removing it. This indicates that if $S0 \notin \varnothing$, the data item s will be removed from $S0\{s \mid (\forall v)s, v \in S0 \wedge s.counter \leq v.counter\}$. If there is no data item with the recency bit setting to 0, the second part will select a data item from S1. Similarly, the data item with the minimal counter value is selected. This means, if $S0 \in \varnothing$, the data item s will be removed from $S1\{s \mid (\forall v)s, v \in S1 \wedge s.counter \leq v.counter\}$. After finishing the filtering process, the recency bits of all data items are changed to 0 except the newly added one. The data item removed from hot list will be inserted into the candidate hot list. If the candidate hot list is full, we will perform the filtering mechanism on the candidate hot list with the same process. This is the conversion between hot and cold data.

Since the filtering mechanism has to traverse the whole list, this run-time overhead may lead to a performance degradation of the system. In order to alleviate this problem, the filtering mechanism locates a data item that the associated heat value (the value of 4-bit counter) is less than a threshold instead of finding the data item with the minimum heat value. Once the data item is located, the traversal process will be stopped. This applies to the candidate hot list as well. In the worst case, traversing the whole list may not be able to locate a qualified data item, we take the data item which has the minimum heat value across the whole list. Since we only consider the data items with high heat value, this simple optimization can significantly reduce the runtime overhead with a negligible impact on the accuracy of hot data identification.

Sampling Mechanism. If a forthcoming data item is not on the both lists, but it would be inserted to the candidate hot list, a sampling mechanism is triggered to handle this scenario. The mechanism puts the forthcoming data item on the candidate hot list with a certain probability. The goal of this mechanism is avoiding the frequent conversion between hot data and cold data, thus further reducing the runtime overhead of the algorithm. For example, we can insert a new data item to the candidate hot list with a 50 % probability. This mechanism will not change the probability that a frequently accessed data item is inserted to the candidate hot list. Since the data is frequently accessed, the opportunity of passing this sampling is also bigger than other data. However, this simple sampling mechanism helps HDCat discard those infrequently accessed data at a very early stage. Therefore, it reduces not only memory consumption, but also computational overhead. If a data item passes the sampling mechanism, the data will be inserted to the candidate hot list. If the candidate list is full, HDCat will employ the filtering mechanism to remove a data item from the candidate hot list. Combing with the D-bit counter and recency bit, the HDCat can achieve very high accuracy of hot data identification with low runtime overhead and memory consumption.

Aging Mechanism. HDCat employs an aging mechanism to update the data access information. It cuts all the values of the D-bit counters by half within a fixed period of time, thus updating the data access information. Therefore, even if one data item is frequently accessed in the past, as long as it is no longer

Table 1. System parameters and values

System parameters	HDCat	MHF	TLL
Number of counter	2^{12}	2^{13}	2^{12}
Counter size	4	4	N/A
Decay	$2^{12}/(1\text{–}20\,\%)$	$2^{13}/(1\text{–}20\,\%)$	$2^{12}/(1\text{–}20\,\%)$
Number of hash function	N/A	2	N/A
Hot threshold	4	4	N/A
Number of levels	2	N/A	2

Table 2. Workload characteristics

Workloads	Total requests	Trace features	(Read:Write)	Total request blocks
hm	4,602,527	Hardware monitoring	R : (43.4 %) W : (56.6 %)	82,310,381
wdev	1,326,264	Test webserver	R : (17.3 %) W : (82.7 %)	23,727,666
rsrch	1,655,022	Research projects	R : (16.3 %) W : (83.7 %)	27,636,758

frequently visited over a certain period of time, this data item will eventually become a cold data and be demoted from the hot list. The aging mechanism of HDCat employs M arrays, each array consists of a 4-bit BF as the counter. Its decay period is N. It indicates that after N requests, the aging mechanism will be invoked. This decay period must ensure that the hash table sizing M can accommodate all the N requests within this period, where $N \leq M/(1 - R)$, R represents the hot ratio of the data access pattern, R=20 % [8]. As long as we have determined the capacity of the M hash table arrays, we can find out the corresponding decay period N. The decay period of HDCat is set as N that is defined as 4096 in our experiment.

4   Evaluation

4.1   Evaluation Environment

In order to evaluate the performance behavior of HDCat, we designed two state-of-the-art schemes including a Multi-hash function (MHF) [8] and a two-level LRU (TLL) scheme [1] for comparison. Table 1 summarizes the parameters used by the three schemes. For a fair evaluation, we adopt the same decay interval (4,096 write requests) and an identical aging mechanism for all the three schemes. Three real traces are used to evaluate the schemes. The traces are collected from the core servers in Microsofts data centre at block level by using event tracing for Windows [11]. The time length of the three traces are all 144 h. Table 2 shows the characteristics of three traces, where HM tracks the data access pattern of hardware monitoring, WDEV collects the data accesses of a test web server and RSRCH logs the disk activities of a research projects. Each record in the traces includes timestamp, request type, data address offset, data block size. Each request in the traces consists of several sectors which are equal 512 Bytes. For example, if the offset field of a request is 1001, and the size is 1024, this indicates that the request can be divided into two sector requests, and the block address of the actual request are 1001 and 1002, respectively.

In our experiments, we replay the whole traces in terms of the timestamp. Furthermore, a typical cache simulator is designed to evaluate the schemes. Hit ratio is employed as a very important metric to devaluate the schemes. In the condition that each algorithm can cache the same amount of data blocks, higher hit ratio indicates better performance of the corresponding scheme. In addition to the hit ratio, we also compare the conversions between hot and cold data across the three schemes.

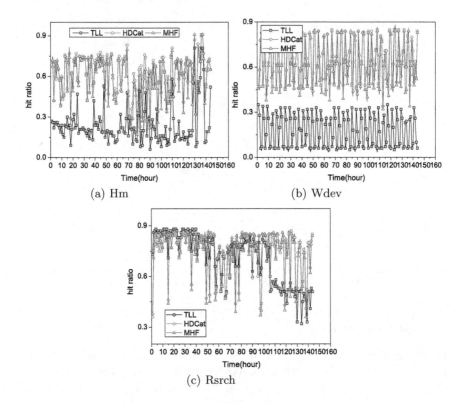

(a) Hm

(b) Wdev

(c) Rsrch

Fig. 3. Hit ratio of three algorithms with different traces

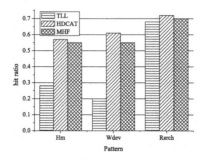

Fig. 4. Total hit ratio of three algorithms with three traces

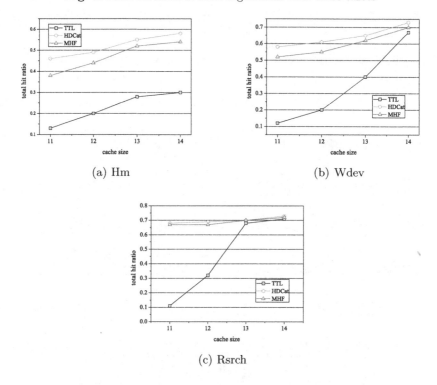

(a) Hm   (b) Wdev

(c) Rsrch

Fig. 5. Total hit ratio under different cache capacity

4.2   Experimental Result

Evaluating Hit Ratio. Figure 3 shows the hit ratio of three schemes when using three different traces, where X axis represents time length, and Y axis indicates the hit ratio. The experimental results show that both HDCat and MHF have a much higher hit ratio than that of TLL. This is because the accuracy of hot data identification depends on the length of the two lists when using TLL. Since we use a small Cache capacity in our experiments, the length of lists used

to record data items is limited. Furthermore, From the figure, we can also see
that the hit ratios of TLL are lagged far behind that of HDCat and MHF when
using HM trace and WDEV trace. This is because HM and WDEV have very
large address space, which results in very low spatial locality. Therefore, the
performance of TLL is tightly correlated with the spatial locality contained in
the traces. Figure 4 summarizes the total hit ratio of the three schemes with
three different traces. It indicates that HDCat significantly outperforms MHF
and TLL.

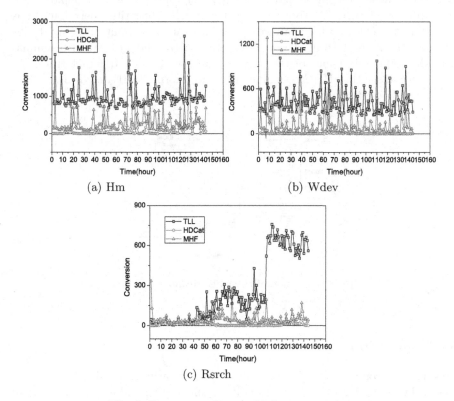

(a) Hm   (b) Wdev

(c) Rsrch

Fig. 6. Frequency of hot/cold data conversion

Figure 5 shows the impact of cache capacity on the hit ratio of three different
schemes, where X axis represents the size of cache capacity. (e.g. number 12 represents that the size of cache is $2^{12} = 4096$.). It demonstrates that TLL performs
worst, and the hit ratio of TLL grows significantly with the increase of Cache
capacity. This confirms that the performance of TLL algorithm is very dependent on its list length (cache size). Although both HDCat and MHF achieve very
good performance, Fig. 5 also implies that HDCat achieves a better performance
than MHF across different cache capacity.

Evaluating the Conversion of Hot/Cold Data. Even with the same hit ratio, different algorithms may still have a different read/write frequency due to the conversions between hot data and cold data. Figure 6 shows the number of conversions between hot data and cold data when using different schemes and different traces, where the X axis represents time length (144 h in our experiment) of replaying traces, and the Y axis represents the number of conversions. The statistics are calculated every one hour. The figures demonstrate that HDCat incurs the minimal number of conversions across the three traces. This feature can be leveraged by many applications. For example, if HDCat is deployed for flash memory, it will effectively reduce the number of write operations, thus extending the effective life span of the flash memory without reducing its hit ratio. Furthermore, HDCat is more stable than MHF and TLL. We also summarizes the total conversions of the three schemes with three different traces. In Fig. 7 we can see that HDCat significantly outperforms MHF and TLL.

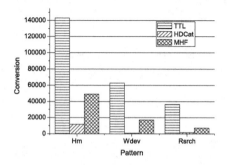

Fig. 7. Total conversion of three algorithms with three traces

5   Conclusion

This paper proposes and designs a hot data identification algorithm called HDCat by leveraging the combination of a D-bit counter and a recency bit. Real traces are employed to evaluate HDCat against two state-of-the-art schemes including a multi-hash function method and a two-level LRU approach. Experimental results demonstrate that HDCat can accurately capture the temporal locality of data access patterns and achieve a high hit ratio with low cache capacity and runtime overhead. Furthermore, HDCat significantly reduces the number of conversions between hot and cold data, thus decreasing the number of write operations. Therefore, HDCat is a very good candidate method for optimizing the performance the reliability of flash memory. Furthermore, we believe HDCat can be applied to many scenarios to optimize the computer systems.

Acknowledgments. This work is supported by the National Natural Science Foundation (NSF) of China under Grant (No. 61572232, and No. 61272073), the key program of Natural Science Foundation of Guangdong Province (No. S2013020012865), the Open Research Fund of Key Laboratory of Computer System and Architecture, Institute of Computing Technology, Chinese Academy of Sciences (CARCH201401), and the Fundamental Research Funds for the Central Universities, and the Science and Technology Planning Project of Guangdong Province (No. 2013B090200021).

References

1. Chang, L.P., Kuo, T.W.: An adaptive striping architecture for flash memory storage systems of embedded systems. In: IEEE Real-time Embedded Technology Applications Symposium, pp. 187–196 (2002)
2. Chang, L.P., Kuo, T.W.: Efficient management for large-scale flash-memory storage systems with resource conservation. ACM Trans. Storage 1(4), 381–418 (2005)
3. Chang, L.P., Kuo, T.W., Lo, S.W.: Real-time garbage collection for flash-memory storage systems of real-time embedded systems. ACM Trans. Embed. Comput. Syst. 3(4), 837–863 (2004)
4. Chiang, M.L., Paul, C.H.L., Chang, R.C.: Managing flash memory in personal communication devices. In: Proceedings of the 1997 International Symposium on Consumer Electronics (ISCE 1997), pp. 177–182 (1997)
5. Debnath, B., Subramanya, S., Du, D., Lilja, D.J.: Large block clock (lb-clock): a write caching algorithm for solid state disks. In: IEEE International Symposium on Modeling, Analysis Simulation of Computer and Telecommunication Systems, MASCOTS 2009, pp. 1–9 (2009)
6. Deng, Y.: What is the future of disk drives, death or rebirth? ACM Comput. Surv. 43(3), 194–218 (2011)
7. Deng, Y., Wang, F., Na, H.: EED: energy efficient disk drive architecture. Inf. Sci. 178(22), 4403–4417 (2008)
8. Hsieh, J.W., Chang, L.P., Kuo, T.W.: Efficient identification of hot data for flash memory storage systems. ACM Trans. Storage (TOS) TOS Homepage 2, 22–40 (2006)
9. Jo, H., Kang, J.U., Park, S.Y., Kim, J.S., Lee, J.: FAB: flash-aware buffer management policy for portable media players. IEEE Trans. Consum. Electron. 52(2), 485–493 (2006)
10. Kim, H., Ahn, S.: BPLRU: a buffer management scheme for improving random writes in flash storage. In: FAST, pp. 239–252 (2008)
11. Narayanan, D., Donnelly, A.: Write off-loading: practical power management for enterprise storage. Trans. Storage 4(3), 1–23 (2008)
12. Park, D., Debnath, B., Du, D.: CFTL: a convertible flash translation layer adaptive to data access patterns. In: SIGMETRICS, pp. 365–366 (2010)
13. Park, S.Y., Jung, D., Kang, J.U., Kim, J.S., Lee, J.: CFLRU: a replacement algorithm for flash memory. In: CASES 2006: Proceedings of the 2006 International Conference on Compilers, Architecture, pp. 234–241 (2006)
14. Parkz, D., Nam, Y.J., Debnath, B., Du, D.H.C., Kim, Y., Kim, Y.: An on-line hot data identification for flash-based storage using sampling mechanism. ACM SIGAPP Appl. Comput. Rev. 13(1), 51–64 (2013)
15. Zhang, L., Deng, Y., Zhu, W., Zhou, J., Wang, F.: Skewly replicating hot data to construct a power-efficient storage cluster. J. Netw. Comput. Appl. 50, 168–179 (2015)

LuBase: A Search-Efficient Hybrid Storage System for Massive Text Data

Debin Jia[1,3,4], Zhengwei Liu[2,5], Xiaoyan Gu[1(✉)], Bo Li[1], Jingzi Gu[1],
Weiping Wang[1], and Dan Meng[1]

[1] Institute of Information Engineering,
Chinese Academy of Sciences, Beijing 100093, China
{jiadebin,guxiaoyan}@iie.ac.cn
[2] Inspur Group Co., Ltd., Beijing 100085, China
[3] National Engineering Laboratory for Information Security Technologies,
Chinese Academy of Sciences, Beijing 100093, China
[4] University of Chinese Academy of Sciences, Beijing 100049, China
[5] State Key Laboratory of High-end Server Storage Technology,
Beijing 100085, China

Abstract. Recent years have witnessed a great deal of enthusiasm devoting to big data analytics systems, some of them, with the property of high scalability and fault tolerance, are extensively used in real productions. However, such systems are mostly designed for processing immutable data stored in HDFS, not suitable for real-time text data in NoSQL database like HBase. In this paper, we propose a search-efficient hybrid storage system termed LuBase for large-scale text data analytics scenarios. Not just a novel hybrid storage system with fine-grained index, LuBase also presents a new query process flow which can fully employ pre-built full-text index to accelerate the execution of interactive queries and achieve more efficient I/O performance at the same time. We implemented LuBase in a data analytics system based on Impala. Experimental results demonstrate that LuBase can reap huge fruits from Lucene index technique and bring significant performance improvement for Impala when querying HBase.

Keywords: Massive text data · Lucene · HBase · Hybrid storage system · Impala

1 Introduction

With increasingly rapid development and popularization of Internet, the volume of text data generated daily online is becoming extremely large. As an effective programming model to deal with the large data sets, Apache Hadoop [1] has been widely used. As one of its important parts, HDFS (Hadoop distributed file system) [2] is designed and optimized for storing massive files with a write-once read-many access model. Admittedly, it works well on storing static data

© Springer International Publishing Switzerland 2015
G. Wang et al. (Eds.): ICA3PP 2015, Part II, LNCS 9529, pp. 134–148, 2015.
DOI: 10.1007/978-3-319-27122-4_10

which means the data supposed to be immutable after written into HDFS. However, for scenarios with some properties need to be updated frequently, such as accumulating repost times of a microblog message, HDFS cannot handle well.

Built on top of HDFS, HBase [3] can break this limitation. By virtue of column-oriented storing model and supporting update operation, it has been widely known as a distinguished distributed NoSQL database used for massive data storage with update columns. As a key-value database, the unique key of each record in HBase is automatically sorted in lexicographic order, which induces high performance for searching by row key. However, it is significantly expensive for HBase to process non-key column search, especially for keyword search on the non-key text columns, as the whole table needs to be scanned row by row to find the target records.

To search keyword on text data, plenty of methods emerge successively, of which Apache Lucene [4] as a text search library is suitable for applications that need full-text search functionality. With the powerful analyzer and inverted index technology, Lucene can perform keyword search operation more efficiently than other indexing methods. Furthermore, Lucene offers many powerful features, such as scalable incremental indexing, rich query types and multiple-index searching with merged results. In fact, Lucene has been widely integrated into plenty of text search systems as the de facto standard of search libraries.

Motivated by the aforementioned observations, in this paper, we proposed a new hybrid storage system named LuBase, which integrated Lucene into HBase, for analyzing large-scale text data. It takes fully advantage of HBase to store massive textual records with some update columns. Furthermore, it makes fully use of Lucenes merits to build index for immutable columns which can improve the performance of full-text search.

The contributions of this paper can be summarized as follows:

(1) We proposed a search-efficient hybrid storage system with new query processing flow termed LuBase, which combines Lucene with HBase by indexing non-key immutable columns to support efficient data analysis.
(2) Based on Impala, we constructed a data analytics system to validate the feasibility of LuBase by comparing with native Impala over HBase.
(3) The intensive experiments demonstrated that LuBase can help Impala achieve better performance and less amount of I/O in processing queries with relatively low selectivity.

The paper is structured as follows. We introduce the related work in Sect. 2. Section 3 describes the framework and implementation of LuBase, and experiments are described in Sect. 4. Section 5 is the conclusion and future work.

2   Related Work

Existing solutions for equipping HBase with index consist of ITHBase [5], IHBase [6], Lily [7], Hindex [8] and CCIndex [9]. As the earlier secondary index solution for HBase, ITHBase creates an extra table to store index and uses the indexed columns as new rowkeys. But it is not compatible with the official version of HBase. IHBase is an extension of HBase core which supports faster scan at the expense of larger RAM consumption. Therefore, it is incapable of processing large datasets because it relies on the memory capacity. Lily is a data management platform combining data storage, indexing and search with online usage tracking, audience analytics and content recommendations. To provide rich functionality, it unifies Hadoop, HBase and Solr into a data platform, which makes it extremely complicated. Furthermore, Lily doesnt provide SQL query interface and cannot be integrated with modern query engine easily. Hindex is an open source project providing secondary index on HBase. It is implemented on specific version of HBase, which makes it tight coupled with certain version and difficult to upgrade to the latest HBase version. CCIndex is another solution proposed by Zhou et al., which creates one index table for each indexed column and stores all the records in every index table. The design concept of CCIndex is easy to understand, but it consumes much more additional storage space, which makes it not fit for big data scenarios with many columns to be indexed. To achieve efficient search on text data, Gao et al. proposed a searching framework based on Lucene full-text indexes implemented as HBase tables [10]. But it is designed to use in a high-performance computing environment and no testing results are provided.

Some efforts have been made to investigate storage solutions in cloud platforms to provide better service [11]. On top of storage layer, SQL-on-Hadoop system has become a hot trend for big data analysis, which uses SQL-like query language and process data stored in distributed storage system like NoSQL databases. In the following part, we will review several acknowledged representatives.

Apache Hive [12] is a native Hadoop data warehouse system that provides a mechanism to query data by using a SQL-like language termed HiveQL. As the pioneer SQL-on-Hadoop system, Hive has made great contributions to big data analysis field for its ease of use. MapReduce [13] is a programming model and an associated implementation for big data processing. However, system based on MapReduce may takes a long time to run all the computing tasks [14]. Due to the employment of MapReduce as its underlying processing framework, Hive suffers from inefficient execution process. As a new module in Apache Spark, Spark SQL [15] integrates relational processing with Sparks functional programming API. Spark greatly benefits from in-memory computation on large scale data by using Resilient Distributed Datasets (RDDs). As for querying HBase, Spark SQL uses HadoopRDD in Spark Core to execute queries in memory, which can avoid writing mid-results into disk. Although this fact makes Spark SQL faster than Hive, it cannot hide the truth that for queries over HBase, Spark SQL is still difficult to use and has high latency result from limited pushdown capabilities and MR-like iterative computations.

Inspired by Google Dremel [16], Impala is an open-source, fully-integrated MPP SQL engine designed specifically to leverage the flexibility and scalability of Hadoop [17]. As a remarkable candidate among the new emerging SQL-on-Hadoop systems in recent years, Impala discards MapReduce and exploits a shared-nothing MPP database architecture. Like Hive and Spark, Impala also supports HDFS or HBase as data source. Previous studies [18] demonstrated that, Impala provides a significant performance advantage over Hive when the workloads dataset fits in memory. When executing queries over HBase, Impala calls the HBase client API via Java Native Interface (JNI) to fetch results. This process does not read HFiles directly, which may lead to considerable extra communication overhead. Limited to this, it is wise to use HBase table for queries that return a single row or a range of rows, not queries that scan the entire table to avoid performance bottleneck. This limitation leads to Impalas unimpressive performance over HBase. But most importantly, Impala has an advanced architecture that attracts our attention, so we decide to implement LuBase mode based on it. Here we want to introduce some details about Impalas architecture.

Impala has three main components, i.e., Impalad, Statestore, and Catalog service.

Impalad is a daemon process, which typically runs on each HDFS datanode for the purpose of data locality. It is responsible for processing SQL queries. Impala supports multiple client interfaces such as JDBC, ODBC programs and Impala shell. There are three components in Impalad: query planner, query coordinator and query executor. They all play important roles in query processing flow. When the client submits a query to an Impalad daemon in the cluster, this daemon process plays the role of coordinator for current query. During the process of execution, the coordinator is engaged in distributing plan fragments to other nodes, collecting partial results, and returning the summarized results to the client.

Statestore service is represented by statestored process, whose goal is track the health of each Impala daemon and distribute that information among the cluster. When a node becomes unavailable, all the other nodes will be informed. And then the following tasks wont be allocated to this node. When the Statestore node becomes offline, all the Impalad nodes still run as before until it recovers. The Statestore service is also engaged in disseminating metadata updates to every Impalad process, making DDL changes broadcasted among the cluster.

Catalog service employs itself in managing the metadata in system and distributing any change about it. When a DDL command is executed in an Impalad node, the result will be reflected in the Metastore and spread among the cluster through Catalog service. For example, an update operation on a database or table will lead to a change to system catalog, which will be broadcast to every node via Statestore service.

3   LuBase System Design and Implementation

Section 3.1 overviews the internal structure and features of LuBase storage system. Section 3.2 presents the query processing flow in LuBase mode by introducing a data analytics system based on Impala. At last, Sect. 3.3 introduces the SQL Language Enhancement by LuBase.

3.1 LuBase Storage System

As described in Sect. 1, since high performance of non-key-column query and
partial data updating functionality are desirable in our workload, we designed
and implemented LuBase storage system to solve these problems. As its name,
LuBase means combination of Lucene and HBase, which fully takes advantages of
excellent full-text search capability of Lucene and high scalability and reliability
of HBase.

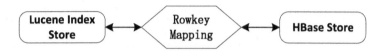

Fig. 1. Internal structure of LuBase storage layer

Internal Structure. Figure 1 shows the internal structure of LuBase storage
that consists of two main components to store indexes and original data respectively. The update columns of data records have to be stored in HBase, because
HBase has better update performance. Typically user can store the immutable
part of data together with its index in Lucene, which makes data retrieval procedure faster than that stored in HBase. Since the most efficient way to locate
records in HBase is using rowkey or key range, the rowkey mapping module acts
as the broker to link the immutable part with corresponding update part of a
record. In a word, LuBase is a hybrid storage system that stores update part
of data in HBase and immutable part in Lucene with indexes, and the rowkey
mapping component links up them.

Index Storage Mode. The number of index files for each LuBase table could
be adjusted according to the table size during data loading phase. Actually it is
a tricky point that fewer index files produce less read worker threads but lead
to more time spent on searching each file, while more index files fits for large
table to speed up index searching process. Furthermore, how to distribute index
files is also a point worthy of notes. For a large table, there may be many sizable
index files, which can be distributed among many compute nodes in the cluster
to lessen the processing workload of each node and to gain concurrency in index
searching phase. During the experiments, we found that when the data volume is
relatively small (e.g., less than 1 million), there is hardly no difference between
distributed and centralized modes in response time. However, when the data
volume rises to tens of million, distributed mode turns out to be obviously faster
than centralized.

Table Properties in LuBase. To use LuBase storage mode, the corresponding
HBase table must be created in advance. When a new record is inserted into this
table, the data loading service will automatically build index on its immutable

Table 1. Available properties in LuBase mode.

Property	Scope	Value domain	Description
datastore	Table	Lucene/LuBase	Table store mode
isLubaseTable	Table	true/false	Whether table is a LuBase table
isUpdateColumn	Column	true/false	Whether column is updatable, if true, it will be stored in HBase
isIndexed	Column	true/false	Whether build index on it
isAnalyed	Column	true/false	Whether analyze it
isStored	Column	true/false	Whether it stores in Lucene, if false, it will be stored in HBase

columns according to the table configuration. Since the immutable columns of a table are mostly stored in Lucene and the update columns must be located in HBase, mapping service module will generate mapping data to combine the static part with the updatable part of a same record.

User can create a LuBase table by specifying datastore property with the value LuBase. In addition, you can also declare which column to be stored in HBase and whether this column should be indexed, analyzed or stored by Lucene. Detail informations about all the properties in LuBase mode are as shown in Table 1.

3.2 Data Analytics System and Query Processing Flow

To perform comprehensive evaluation for LuBase mode, we construct a data analytics system by modifying Impala from ground up to adapt it for LuBase storage mode. By integrating LuBase and Impala, the system gains the abilities of storing massive real-time text data records and performing SQL queries on them. In the rest part of this paper, we use name LuBase system as the alias of the analytics system based on Impala and LuBase, which matches CDH system consist of Impala and HBase.

LuBase System Architecture. Figure 2 shows the high-level architecture of the LuBase system. Each layer is described as follows.

The bottom layer of the system is data loading service responsible for loading external data into LuBase store and generating index data at the same time. Raw data may be stored in plain text files, which can be used to extract records. Next, it transfers the data into LuBase storage layer.

As the key part of system, LuBase layer absolutely takes charge of storing massive datasets and Lucene indexes on specified columns. It also provides index searching APIs for upper layer to filter irrelevant data records.

The work of Impala (the single quotation mark means the modified version by us that supports LuBase mode) layer is query processing, which includes query analyzing, query plan generation and execution. Details of this process will be discussed in the following part.

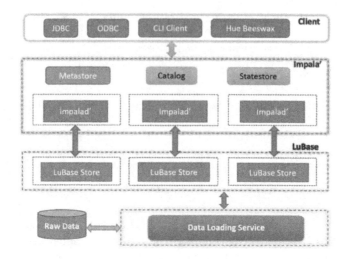

Fig. 2. Architecture of data analytics system based on LuBase and Impala

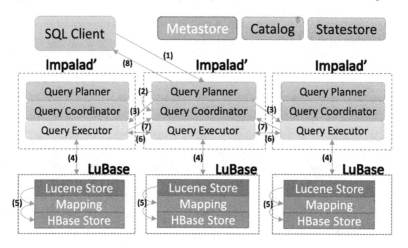

Fig. 3. LuBase query processing flow

The top layer of the system is the client that can connect to the service and submit queries. Since the system is constructed based on Impala, which is compatible with Hive, it supports as many types of clients as Hive and Impala. The client could be a JDBC/ODBC program, CLI client shell or the Hue beeswax interface.

Query Processing Flow. Not only act as a storage layer, LuBase also has its own query processing flow with full use of Lucene index. To make Impala support querying over LuBase store, we modified its initial work flow. Figure 3 shows the newly designed LuBase query processing flow.

As is shown in Fig. 3, the flow mainly contains eight steps.

- Step 1: A SQL client submits the query statement to an Impalad node in the cluster. And this daemon becomes the coordinator for this query;
- Step 2: The Query Planner component validates the correctness of this query, then parses it into a logical plan and finally compiles the plan into a number of distributed plan fragments, which would be delivered to the Query Coordinator. In these fragments, predicates about immutable, indexed columns can be extracted to be used by index searching worker threads;
- Step 3: When the Query Coordinator receives these plan fragments, it delivers them to other nodes according to the data distribution and coordinates their parallel execution;
- Step 4: Once the Query executor begins to execute a fragment, it will search the local index data stored in its own storage;
- Step 5: The query predicates (if exist) about indexed immutable columns will be transformed into Lucene index search conditions that can be used to locate related data records quickly. After finishing index searching procedure, LuBase uses the results (rowkey list) to locate corresponding HBase records and return needed columns;
- Step 6: If necessary, Query Executor can also collaborate with others when there is a join operation;
- Step 7: The query coordinator collects all the results from every executor;
- Step 8: Finally, the coordinator sends the result to the client.

As the step 5 states, LuBase mode can take advantages of Lucenes full-text search ability to speed up the query process when there are predicates about immutable columns.

Query Plan Generation and Execution. When processing a query, the query planner component will parse query predicates, and then extract the part about immutable columns, which will be then transformed into Lucene index search conditions. Afterwards, Lucene index searcher can locate target records according to the search conditions. After Lucene search procedure, rowkey list mapping service will find their row keys, which are finally delivered to HBase to locate target records.

Here we use a sample query statement to show the difference of query plan between official Impala and LuBase. The query is shown as follow:

SELECT SUM lo_extendedprice **AS** revenue
FROM lineorder, date
WHERE lo_orderdate = d_datekey
AND d_year = 1993
AND lo_discount **BETWEEN** 1 **AND** 3
AND lo_quantity < 25;

Figure 4(a) and (b) shows the logical plans generated by Impala and LuBase for above sample query respectively. There are two HBaseScan nodes as leaves of the tree in Fig. 4(a), which contains predicates for constructing HBase scan filters. When the data volume becomes extremely large, HBase scanner with

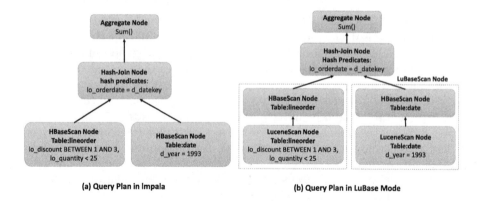

Fig. 4. Internal structure of LuBase storage layer

multiple non-key column filters may lead to a long response time. In contrast, two LuBaseScan nodes are emerged in Fig. 4(b) which have extra LuceneScan nodes. A LuceneScan node is responsible for locating target rowkeys according to column predicates by taking advantages of pre-built indexes. Benefiting from the powerful Lucene index technique, data retrieval in LuBase becomes exceedingly faster than that in Impala, which will be shown in the next section.

3.3   SQL Language Enhancement

Highly compatible with HiveQL, Impala supports a host of SQL statements and data types from HiveQL. Furthermore, we introduce a new operator SEARCH to enhance the text search functionality, which benefits from Lucene search framework. The syntax of this operator is:

> **SEARCH**() = columnName: keyWord$_1$ **OP** keyWord$_2$

In the above clause, columnName represents the target column where the operator applies, and the keyWord$_1$ and keyWord$_2$ are values for matching. The OP is a logical connective which can be OR, AND or NOT. For example, if you want to retrieve all records that contain key word Turing or Clarke in column name of table tbl_test, the SQL query statement may like this:

> **SELECT** * **FROM** tbl_test **WHERE** SEARCH() = name: Turing OR Clarke

The significant difference between equal (i.e., =) and SEARCH operator is that the former is used for retrieving exact match records while SEARCH can be used for fuzzy matching. Also different from LIKE, the SEARCH clause doesnt need any wildcard and will be transformed into Lucene index search conditions. With the native support of analyzer, Lucene can help LuBase perform better in full-text fuzzy search.

4   Evaluation

Since LuBase system is implemented based on Impala, the performance evaluation experiments were conducted between official Impala over HBase and the proposed system to validates the feasibility of LuBase.

4.1   Experiment Environment

We setup an experimental cluster with 8 compute nodes connected by Gigabits Ethernet to run all the testing queries. Each node has an AMD Opteron(tm) Processor 6132 HE CPU with 32 cores, 64 GB memory and 1 TB disks.

We conduct the query performance experiments over two workloads in which the biggest table has about 6 and 60 million rows generated by SSBM benchmark (Star Schema Benchmark) [19]. SSBM is designed to measure performance of database products in support of classical data warehousing applications, which is based on the TPC-H benchmark [20]. The SSBM benchmark consists of 13 queries in four groups that involve one large fact table and four dimension tables. It also does well in providing functional coverage and selectivity coverage by using only a small number of query flights, which makes it simple to do multi-dimensional query performance evaluation.

To avoid the detrimental effect of cache, we clear each nodes cache before every test. Each query case will be run 3 times and the average execution time is considered as the final result.

4.2   Performance Evaluation

According to the fact that there are typically few columns which are supposed to be updatable in a real social network record, we assume that most of the columns present in testing queries are immutable which need to be indexed. The experiments workflow is as follows:

(1) Use SSBM tools to generate raw data at given scale;
(2) Run custom programs to generate rowkeys for every table;
(3) Load data into HBase tables and build indexes for immutable columns of every table at the same time;
(4) Run each testing query in Impala and LuBase system respectively, record the response time.

Firstly we compared the count query latency of LuBase with Impala, and the result is shown in Fig. 5. As the result shown, Impalas latency is mainly in positive correlation with the size of target table, while LuBase can always finish counting within 1 s. This result can be explained by the fact that Impala counts an HBase table by a full-table scan operation. Differently, LuBase can directly return the sum of each index files pre-count value by Lucene.

Considering the facts that SSBM is not tailored for querying over HBase and Impala would take a pretty long time to run these 13 queries which very

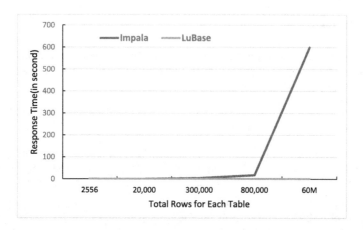

Fig. 5. Count query latency comparison over 60M workload

likely lead to a timeout exception, we modified these queries by reduce their selectivity properly to make them runnable for Impala. One of the test queries looks like this:

SELECT SUM(lo_extendedprice * lo_discount) **AS** revenue
FROM lineorder, datee
WHERE lo_orderdate=d_datekey **AND** lo_quantity $\leq (5)$
AND lo_discount **BETWEEN** 1 **AND** 3;

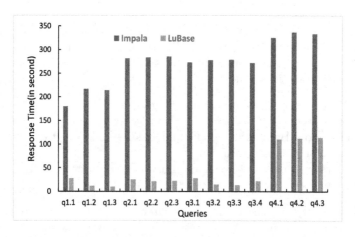

Fig. 6. SSBM benchmark performance comparison over 6M workload

The comparisons of all 13 query response times over 6M workload are shown in Fig. 6. As can be seen in the figure, LuBase outperforms Impala across all queries in the workload. The performance advantage of LuBase over Impala ranges from 2.9x to 21.4x in all query groups. The biggest difference appears in q1 and q3 groups, the greatest gap here results from the maximization of Lucene indexs superiority. With the group number growing, the complexity of corresponding queries increases, which means joining more tables and covering more records. Until q4 group, the gap becomes smallest, as these queries has higher selectivity that counteracts part of the positive effect of index and lead to more communication and I/O overhead.

Figure 7 compares the amount of I/O between LuBase and Impala. The amount of I/O in LuBase consist of disk I/O for index searching and HDFS I/O for data retrieval, while Impala just has HDFS I/O. As shown in this figure, LuBase has much lower amount of I/O than Impala. Limited to the fact that Impala directly call HBase interface to filter data in region servers after read raw data from HDFS, its I/O performance is almost determined by the size of table, which can also explain why its response times for all queries are approximately equal in Fig. 6. Benefiting from powerful Lucene index technique, LuBase can effectively filter data by searching index in advance and give HBase guide lines to avoid reading undesirable raw data from HDFS. Furthermore, the index file size is roughly just 20–30 % the size of data indexed. Based on this fact, LuBase has more efficient I/O performance than Impala.

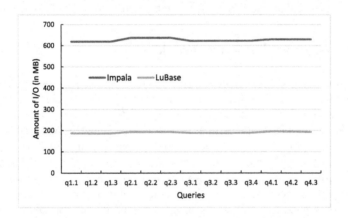

Fig. 7. Amount of I/O comparison over 6M workload

4.3   Index Storing Mode Test

Figure 8 focuses on exploring the impact of index storing mode on query response time in LuBase. The results suggest that distributing index files to more compute nodes help gain better query response performance in most test cases. The reason behind this result is that distributed index store can lighten searching workload in each node and reap huge fruits from parallel index searching among multi nodes, which helps accelerate the query execution process. At the same time, the negative effect from distributed mode may lead to more network traffic. In most of our testing cases except q4 group, the growing overhead of network traffic

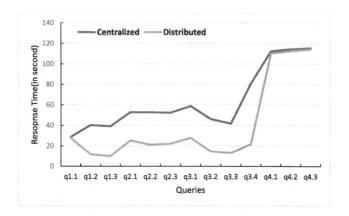

Fig. 8. Comparison of response times between different index storing modes

is far less than the improvement for search process from distributed mode, so we got better query performance in distributed mode. As for the q4 group, the gap becomes pretty small because these 3 queries concentrate on several specific index files which makes them hardly benefit much from parallel searching.

5   Conclusion and Future Work

With the booming growth of social network data, storing and searching requirements about them has become an extremely tough nut to crack. In this paper, we propose a search-efficient hybrid storage system termed LuBase for realtime text data analytics. According to the comprehensive evaluation, despite that it takes about 10 % extra time to build indexes during data loading phase, LuBase system achieves significant performance improvement and less amount of I/O compared with the system based on official Impala. Furthermore, in theory, LuBase can be generalized as a common resolution for most query engines over HBase that need fast full-text search functionality on non-key columns. So LuBase also can be integrated with other SQL query engine besides Impala to build more efficient text data analytics system.

More performance test over real-world datasets such as Weibo or SMS messages data is our next focus in future work. Additional work should be done to optimize the query performance in high selectivity scenarios. Making full use of HBase coprocessor feather to speed up aggregated query execution is also part of our plan. More practical experiences and lessons should be given.

Acknowledgments. This work is partially supported by National HeGaoJi Key Project under grant numbered 2013ZX01039-002-001-001, the National KeJiZhiCheng Project under grant numbered 2012BAH46B03, and "Strategic Priority Research Program" of the Chinese Academy of Sciences under grant numbered XDA06030200.

References

1. Hadoop: Open-source implementation of MapReduce. http://hadoop.apache.org/
2. Shvachko, K., Kuang, H., Radia, S., Chansler, R.: The hadoop distributed file system. In: Proceedings of the 2010 IEEE 26th Symposium on Mass Storage Systems and Technologies (MSST), pp. 1–10. IEEE (2010)
3. Apache HBase. http://hbase.apache.org/
4. Apache Lucene: The de facto standard for search libraries. http://lucene.apache.org/
5. ITHBase. https://github.com/hbase-trx/hbase-transactional-tableindexed
6. IHbase, An extension of HBASE core which support faster scans at the expense of larger RAM consumption. https://github.com/ykulbak/ihbase/
7. Lily. http://www.lilyproject.org/lily/index.html
8. Hindex: Secondary Index for HBase. https://github.com/Huawei-Hadoop/hindex
9. Zou, Y., Liu, J., Wang, S., Zha, L., Xu, Z.: CCIndex: a complemental clustering index on distributed ordered tables for multi-dimensional range queries. In: Ding, C., Shao, Z., Zheng, R. (eds.) NPC 2010. LNCS, vol. 6289, pp. 247–261. Springer, Heidelberg (2010)
10. Gao, X., Nachankar, V., Qiu, J.: Experimenting lucene index on HBase in an HPC environment. In: HPCDB 2011 Proceedings of the First Annual Workshop on High Performance Computing Meets Databases, pp. 25–28. ACM (2011)
11. Esposito, C., Ficco, M., Palmieri, F., Castiglione, A.: Smart cloud storage service selection based on fuzzy logic, theory of evidence and game theory. IEEE Trans. Comput. (1), p. 1 (2015) (in press)
12. Thusoo, A., Sarma, J.S., Jain, N., Shao, Z., Chakka, P., Anthony, S., Liu, H., Wyckoff, P., Murthy, R.: Hive - a warehousing solution over a map-reduce framework. In: Proceedings of the VLDB Endowment, vol. 2, pp. 1626–1629. VLDB Endowment (2009)
13. Dean, J., Ghemawat, S.: MapReduce: simplified data processing on large clusters. In: OSDI 2004: Sixth Symposium on Operating System Design and Implementation, vol. 51, pp. 107–113. ACM, New York, USA (2008)
14. Pavlo, A., Paulson, E., Rasin, A., Abadi, D.J., DeWitt, D.J., Madden, S.: A comparison of approaches to large-scale data analysis. In: SIGMOD 2009 Proceedings of the 2009 ACM SIGMOD International Conference on Management of data. pp. 165–178. ACM, New York, USA (2009)
15. Armbrust, M., Xin, R.S., Lian, Ch., Huai, Y., Liu, D., Bradley, J.K., Meng, X., Kaftan, T., Franklin, M.J., Ghodsi, A., Zaharia, M.: Spark SQL: relational data processing in spark. In: ACM SIGMOD Conference 2015, Melbourne, Victoria, Australia (2015)
16. Melnik, S., Gubarev, A., Long, J.J., Romer, G., Shivakumar, S., Tolton, M., Vassilakis, T.: Dremel: Interactive analysis of web-scale datasets. In: VLDB 2010, 36th International Conference on Very Large Data Bases, pp. 330–339. VLDB Endowment (2010)
17. Kornacker, M., Behm, A., Bittorf, V., Bobrovytsky, T., Ching, C., Choi, A., Erickson, J., Grund, M., Hecht, D., Jacobs, M., Joshi, I., Kuff, L., Kumar, D., Leblang, A., Li, N., Pandis, L., Robinson, H., Rorke, D., Rus, S., Russell, J., Tsirogiannis, D., Milne, S.W., Yoder, M.: Impala: a modern, open-source SQL engine for hadoop. In: CIDR (2015)

18. Floratou, A., Minhas, U.F., Ozcan, F.: SQL-on-Hadoop: full circle back to shared-nothing database architectures. In: Proceedings of the VLDB Endowment, vol. 7, pp. 1295–1306. VLDB Endowment (2014)
19. O'Neil, P., O'Neil, E., Chen, X., Revilak, S.: The star schema benchmark and augmented fact table indexing. In: Nambiar, R., Poess, M. (eds.) TPCTC 2009. LNCS, vol. 5895, pp. 237–252. Springer, Heidelberg (2009)
20. TPC-H: An ad-hoc, decision support benchmark. http://www.tpc.org/tpch/

Enhancing Parallel Data Loading for Large Scale Scientific Database

Hui Li[1,2(✉)], Hongyuan Li[1,2], Mei Chen[1,2], Zhenyu Dai[1,2],
Ming Zhu[3], and Menglin Huang[3]

[1] Department of Computer Science, Guizhou University, Guiyang 550025, China
{cse.HuiLi,gychm,cse.zydai}@gzu.edu.cn
[2] Guizhou Engineering Laboratory of ACMIS, Guiyang 550025, China
[3] National Astronomical Observatories, Chinese Academy of Sciences, Beijing 100016, China
{mz,huangmenglin}@nao.cas.cn

Abstract. The rapidly increased data size make large scale scientific database often have a huge time delay between loading data into the system and ready for receiving query request. To solve this problem, we proposed an efficient parallel data loading approach named FASTLoad. It is designed to maximize the given resource (e.g., network bandwidth, main memory) utilization for optimizing the data loading in large scale array model based scientific database system. To verify the efficiency of FASTLoad, we implemented it in our Adaptable Data Loading System and evaluate its performance over various sizes of large scientific data sets. Our experimental results show that the performance of FASTLoad can be 4 to 6 times fast than the built-in loading techniques of states-of-the-arts array model based scientific database system.

Keywords: Data loading · Scientific database · Array model · Massive data · Database cluster

1 Introduction

In the big data era, large scale scientific data have been generated in various research fields, e.g., bioinformatics, meteorology, astronomy survey, and so on [1, 10, 11]. Before conduct data analysis over these data sets, data needs to be loaded into database system. As the increase of data size, the time delay between loading data into the system and ready for receiving query request tends to be very long. Furthermore, since the modern scientific database system, e.g., SciDB [2], tends to employ array model to meet the requirements of complex analytical tasks, which make lots of relational model based parallel database's data loading techniques become inappropriate. Therefore, there is an urgent requirement for the loading techniques that is capable to make the array model based scientific database system can efficiently ingest the given data.

To solve this problem, array database researchers proposed many technical solutions. For instance, a novel technology named NoDB [3–5], which enable that users can use a select statement over the raw data to query the results without loading data set into a database [6]. Furthermore, a novel database physical operator named SCANRAW [7]

© Springer International Publishing Switzerland 2015
G. Wang et al. (Eds.): ICA3PP 2015, Part II, LNCS 9529, pp. 149–162, 2015.
DOI: 10.1007/978-3-319-27122-4_11

is developed for in-situ processing over raw files, which integrates data loading and external tables seamlessly while preserving their advantages. It have been implemented into DataPath system [8] for further evaluation. In technical view, SCANRAW is inappropriate for array model based scientific database like SciDB, due to the data generate in scientific areas often with hundreds of dimensions. Furthermore, SCANRAW currently only supports single-query optimal execution. And it is very difficult to execute two or more SQL statement on a series of shared data file concurrently. When these task involves with complex lock operations [9] and costly joins, the performance of SCANRAW often tends to degrade significantly.

Although modern scientific database system, e.g., SciDB has a built-in parallel data loading functionality which implemented in its "loadcsv.py" script, due to it adopted the traditional approach originally from relational model based database systems, SciDB cannot always achieve satisfactory performance in array model based scientific database cluster, especially in the circumstance when the data size and data dimensionality are very large. In order to optimize this procedure, we proposed an enhanced parallel data loading approach named FASTLaod for array model based scientific database cluster, the major idea of FASTLoad is that it employs a speculative partition technique before loading data into database cluster in parallel, and we implement it in our advanced data loading system named Adaptable Loading System which has a built-in simple but efficient scheduling capability.

The rest of this paper is organized as follows: in Sect. 2, we give a brief introduction of preliminary knowledge of array model based scientific database, and outline the key features of the typical array model based scientific database SciDB. In Sect. 3, we describe the preliminary knowledge of FASTLoad algorithm. In Sect. 4, we present the details of the FASTLoad and the framework of our Adaptable Loading System. Experimental results are shown in Sect. 5. We conclude this paper and briefly outline the future work in Sect. 6.

2   Preliminary Knowledge of the Scientific Database SciDB

With the advancement of scientific areas, various scientific data are generated in an explosive growing trend [10, 11]. To meet the requirements of various complex analytical tasks, array model has been the trend of scientific data management and analytics. For the array based analytical software tools such as Matlab, which also used in scientific data processing, it is preferable for the small size of data which can be loaded into main memory, and it is always hard for the users to use it to manage and analyze large-scale data. Meanwhile, it is also too complex and inefficient for scientists to use the traditional database such as SQL Server, MySQL, Oracle to store and analyze array data [12–14], since the intrinsic characteristics of these database system are based on relational model, which have not optimized the execution process for array based data storage and scientific analysis. Furthermore, the scalability of relational model based distributed and parallel database also limited its application in scientific areas.

To solve above issues, a group of researchers in database area led by M. Stonebraker have collected and deeply analyzed a series of needs for the management and analysis of scientific data, and devoted into developing an array model based distributed database system named by SciDB [15–17]. Its architecture is shown in Fig. 1. There are two types of nodes in SciDB cluster. Coordinate node is responsible for coordinating query activity in addition to participating in query execution, while worker node is the server that only participates in query execution. In SciDB cluster, Postgres database is employed to store the metadata of SciDB cluster.

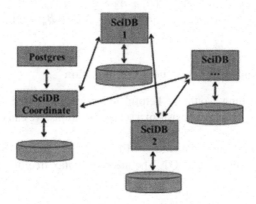

Fig. 1. Architecture of SciDB

SciDB is an open-source database system, our FASTLoad and Adaptable Loading System are implemented to coupling with it, thus we also present some preliminary features of it. SciDB supports mathematical multidimensional array operations [18]. Its basic unit is a cell, every cell contains the same type of data. A cell can be one or more mathematical array [19]. The representative features of SciDB can be characterize as following.

Firstly, the scope of a transaction in SciDB is a single statement. Each statement involves many operations on one or more arrays. Ultimately, the transaction stores the result into a destination array.

Secondly, SciDB implements array-level locking [20]. Locks are acquired at the beginning of a transaction and are used to protect arrays during queries. Locks are released upon completion of the query. If a query aborts, pending changes are undone at all instances in the system catalog, and the database is returned to a prior consistent state [21].

Thirdly, SciDB support append operations. It uses a "no overwrite" storage model, which means every time you update data in an array, SciDB creates a new array version [22]. Therefore, when inserting a series of new data into an existing array, it will cause the data being redistributed into a new version of the array, thus additional overheads incurred.

3 Preliminary Knowledge of FASTLoad

3.1 Preliminary Knowledge for Set Theory

A and B is a set. Then A and B must have the following properties [28].

$A = A_1 \cup A_2 \cup \ldots \ldots \cup A_n$ while $A_1, A_2, \ldots \ldots, A_n$ is all of subsets of A.

If $A_i \cap A_j = \Phi$ when $i \neq j$, then we have

$A = A_1 + A_2 + \ldots \ldots + A_n$

$A - B = (A_1 + A_2 + \ldots \ldots + A_n) - (A_1 + A_2 + \ldots \ldots + A_n) \cap B$

$A \times B = (A_1 + A_2 + \ldots \ldots + A_n) \times (B_1 + B_2 + \ldots \ldots + B_n)$ while $B_1, B_2, \ldots \ldots, B_n$ is all the subsets of B.

3.2 Preliminary Knowledge for Query Optimization

Accelerating data loading would be helpful to optimize query execution. Since an execution procedure of a query consists of a set of operations, we can use the conclusion of Sect. 3.1.

A simple SQL query statement is like "SELECT …… FROM ArayName WHERE ……". Which can be regarded as Q1. The abstract syntax tree of Q1 is presented as Fig. 2:

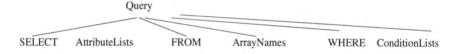

Query

SELECT   AttributeLists   FROM   ArrayNames   WHERE   ConditionLists

Fig. 2. Abstract **syntax tree of Q1**

The abstract syntax tree of Q1 is not the tree that indicates the process of the database engine execute a query. In this paper, our optimization do not involve with the execution process. Towards queries like Q1, optimizations for *AttributeLists*, *ArrayNames* and *ConditionLists* may lead the performance improvement of query processing. If we split a large table or an array into a series of smaller ones, then the executions can be accelerated in many scenarios due to the query can be divide into a series of SQL statements and executed in parallel. This performance enhancement may be significantly, especially when the disk I/O and network I/O bottleneck have not incurred during coordination of sub queries execution.

Let's use Q1 as an example. In order to execute it faster we split the table *ArrayName* into smaller ones that each one have a different sections of this table. Assume they are *ArrayName_1*, *ArrayName_2*, …, *ArrayName_n*.

Therefore, when we execute Query 1, we actually run several statements as follows.

SELECT …… FROM ArayName_1 WHERE ……
SELECT …… FROM ArayName_2 WHERE ……
……
SELECT …… FROM ArayName_n WHERE ……

We denote a more complex query like "*SELECT ...... FROM ArayName1 AS A1 JOIN ArrayName2 AS A2 WHERE ......*" as Q2.

If the tables involve in Q2 is too large to load it into memory, Q2 will executed slow even its execution is failed. Some optimization policy is to decrease the data size the join operation involves and execute it in a nested loop manner, but if the SQL statement doesn't have a limited condition, this policy may still become inefficient in some scenarios.

Suppose we turn a large table into smaller ones that can be efficiently loaded and assume they are $A_1, A_2,......, A_n, B_1, B_2,......, B_n$.

Since the *join* operation can be denoted as a certain type of Cartesian Product [29] in nature. According to the set theory mentioned in Sect. 3.1, we have:

$$
\begin{aligned}
A \times B &= (A_1 \cup A_2 \cup ... \cup A_n) \times (B_1 \cup B_2 \cup ... \cup B_n) \\
&= (A_1 + A_2 + ... + A_n) \times (B_1 + B_2 + ... + B_n) \\
&= A_1 \times B_1 + ... + A_1 \times B_n + ... + A_n \times B_1 + ... + A_n \times B_n
\end{aligned}
$$

Since join operation involves smaller size of data is relative easy to achieve better optimization and performance, and we can control the size of data and distribute it into both table A and table B, therefore these smaller join operations have a significant potential to execute in parallel.

In our FASTLoad approach, we employ above strategy and write an external parser to quickly find which smaller table contains the data in the original large logical table.

3.3   Analysis of Data Load Theory

There are many invisible factors will explicitly affect the performance of loading data into database system [30], and network I/O is one of a major factor to the efficiency of distributed parallel database system. Assume the data file size is S, the network transfer speed is V, the number of the machine nodes, including both the physical machines and the virtual machines, denotes as N, the data compression ratio is denote as R. Thus the ideal time needed for data loading time t is as Eq. 1.

$$
t = \frac{R \cdot S}{V \cdot N} \tag{1}
$$

Let's give a concrete illustration for above formula. In our experimental evaluation, the maximum network bandwidth is about 26 M/s, which means that V is a limited parameter which has the maximum size. For simplicity, we assume R is near 1 due to the data is hard for further compression. Furthermore, we found that SciDB can only load data with its Coordinate Node, and the number of SciDB Coordinate Node is only one, which means N is also set as 1. Then the ideal policy shows that the cost time of the best data loading method is near linear grow with the data size.

Based on above analysis, we can know that, if the data reading speed lower than network bandwidth, it will cost more time. The fast way to load a data file is to split it in a series of smaller ones which can be loaded into main memory, and then load it in parallel.

As mentioned in Sect. 3.2, the data partitioning method will also optimized the execution of a query. This idea is simple but useful, and will smooth the growth curve of data loading overheads.

4 Methodology of FASTLoad

In this section, we will briefly describe the architecture of our Adaptable Loading System, and present the detail of our FASTLoad approach.

4.1 Architecture of the Proposed Adaptable Loading System

In order to efficiently integrate our FASTLoad approach and coupling work with SciDB cluster, we design and implement Adaptable Data Loading System, a.k.a. ADLS. The data loading procedures can be divided into two types.

If the user asks the load system to load data immediately, then the data file information is transferred into System Coordinate with a flag suggesting that this data must be imported into cluster immediately. Then the System Coordinate waits for the FAST-Load subsystem being free. Whenever the subsystem is available, the data loading task will be executed immediately.

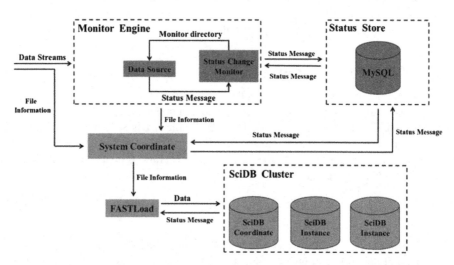

Fig. 3. Architecture of Adaptable Loading System

If the user doesn't urgently need to use the data immediately and tolerant it in a task queue, the data will be transferred into the monitor engine. It means the data streams are represent as files according to the administrator's setting of the maximum records of a partitioned data file. Assume it denote as n. When a file in this data streams has more than n records, the data will be split into multiple files to conform to the n tuples limitation. Meanwhile the file status are stored at the Status Store subsystem. The file status and the file information are associated with each other. Then the file information including the loading order are sent to the System Coordinate subsystem, and the System Coordinate subsystem will call FASTLoad subsystem to import data into database cluster according to the order in the task queue.

Both the two types of procedures will sent the status of the loaded data file to the Status Store subsystem. In both procedures, the data partition employ our extended SQL parser to determine how to split the data into smaller ones. During data loading, we also optimize the data partitioning to avoid the main memory bottleneck. Once the loading failed, the data loading procedure will repeat until it reached the threshold.

The System Coordinate subsystem is a simple scheduler employ the FIFO (First in First Out) strategy. That means the loading order is same as the order of data file loading request which received by the System Coordinate subsystem. When the loading process failed, the order of the file is still same as before, which means the ongoing task will not suspend. For instance, a task in the data loading queue with an order denotes as X, when it failed, the data loading task with the order (X + 1) will not be scheduled, the failed process will try again. If it still fails and repeated the maximum allowed times, then the task information and failure message will be sent to the Status Store subsystem, and available for the administrator for further investigation.

The proposed FASTLoad approach is implemented in the FASTLoad component of Fig. 3, the architecture of FASTLoad subsystem is illustrated as Fig. 4.

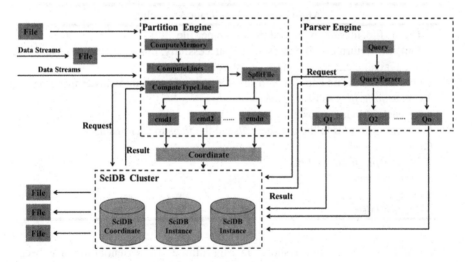

Fig. 4. Architecture of FASTLoad component

The FASTLoad component consists of three parts. The partition engine responsible for splits the data file into the smaller ones with specified size, it plays an important role in the FASTLoad method. First, it obtain the metadata of data file from the Status Store or the file itself. Based on the metadata, the partition engine can obtain the data type of every column, the number of records and the size of the file, and then it split the data file into multiple small ones to make it can be fit into the available main memory. After that, the partition engine will ask SciDB nodes invoke its built-in load function ("loadcsv.py") to load the splitted files in parallel. The Parser Engine is started to work whenever user raises a query request, which means it does the parser job, and it determine how to split the query into several sub queries. For example, the data in array A is loaded into SciDB cluster by three worker nodes, and the corresponding sub dataset in these worker nodes are denote as a, b, c. When we execute the AQL statement "select * from A", the parser engine will determine to split this query into three sub queries, i.e., "select * from a", "select * from b" and "select * from c". In our current implementation, the Coordinator only employ the simple FIFO strategy for task schedule, more advanced schedule techniques will be adopted in the future. The principle of the FASTLoad approach is described in Sect. 4.2. It aims to ensure each load process not only runs parallel but also is optimized by efficiently utilize the available main memory.

4.2   The FASTLoad Algorithm

The *LoadData* algorithm revise the built-in data loading policy of SciDB [31] which implemented in its source file "lodacsv.py". The communication pipeline between instances is restricted to FIFO, which is simple for implementation and shows a good performance. The procedures of *LoadData* is show as Algorithm 1:

Algorithm 1.   LoadData Algorithm

Input: file, number of record limitation per file
Output: Return true if data is loaded successfully, otherwise return false
1 Get available cluster instances and store it as a list
2 Split the candidate data file into smaller ones and send into cluster instances
3 Create *split files* as FIFO pipe
4 **for** each instance in instance list **do**
5   send *split files* to the instance   //send the flags to each instance
6 **try**
7   Load *split files* parallel
8   return true;
9 **except**
10   return false;

The FASTLoad Algorithm is shown in Algorithm 2. The essential idea has been presented in Sect. 3.3. And compared with other databases, SciDB does support append operations, but these operations will cause data redistribution and incur expensive overheads. Lines 2–13 describe the load policy when the free memory is smaller than the file size. Among them, lines 3–5 is used to obtain the total number of records, the size of the tuples and the maximum size of all the properties. For example, if each line in the data file stores n column which have int32, int8 etc., the maximum size of all the properties means 5 (bytes). Lines 6–10 split the data file and then call the *LoadData* for data loading. Lines 14–21 show the load procedures when the available memory is bigger than the file size. Lines 16–21 list the detailed steps of loading data.

Algorithm 2. FASTLoad Algorithm

Input: file, number of record limitation per file, assemble rate r (default 0.01), chunk size C, memory usage mu (default 90%)

Output: Return true if data is loaded successfully, otherwise return false

1 Obtain the size of the data file S1, the size of free main memory S2;
2 **if** S1> S2 **then**
3   obtain the size of the first line as $d1$
4   obtain the total number of lines in the data file as nl
5   obtain the maximum size of all the properties in a line and denotes as $d2$
6   **if** $|d1\text{-}S1/nl|\leqslant r$ **then**
7   compute the available number of lines as $N = int(S2/d1/C \times mu) \times C$
8   **else**
9   compute the available number of lines $N = int(S2/d2/C \times mu) \times C$
10   split every N lines of the data file and associate metadata into a *map* structure
11   //Note: map.key = the length of the file map.value=file
11   **for** *map* in Map **do**
12   *LoadData(map.value, map.key)* // LoadData Algorithm
13 **else**
14   obtain the total number of lines in the data file nl
15   **if** $nl<C$ **then**
16   *Loaddata(file, n1)*
17   **else**
18   obtain the available number of lines $N=int(n1/C) \times C$
19   split the file into two files: $f1$ *(include N data lines) and file2*
20   *LoadData(file1, N)*
21   *LoadData(file2, n1-N)*

5 Evaluation

In this section, we will present the experimental evaluation between the proposed FASTLoad approach and SciDB's built-in parallel data loading technique, which is implemented in its source file "loadcsv.py".

5.1 Experimental Setup

In our evaluation, all the experiments are conducted over 15 KVM (Kernel-based Virtual Machine) [23–27] virtual machines. Each virtual machine has a virtualized 4-core CPU, 50 GB swap space and 1 TB disk storage. The virtual machine to host the SciDB coordinator has 40 GB main memory, while the 14 worker node of SciDB cluster has 8 GB main memory. All the virtual machines are run over two physical machine who has two 2.0 GHz Intel(R) Xeon(R) E5-2620 CPU (each CPU has 6 cores with 12 thread process). The two physical machines have a total of 192 GB memory and 14 TB hard disk space. The stable network transportation speed between every two virtualized nodes is about 22 MB/s. The version of SciDB is 14.3.

5.2   Loading Environment

In order to compare the FASTLoad approach with SciDB's build-in data loading technique [31], we employ nine different sizes of data set for performance evaluation. These data sets are extracted from the ninth data release of Sloan Digital Sky Survey (SDSS) [32]. The data size and number of records in above nine data sets are tabulated in Table 1, each tuple of the data has 519 column. The raw file format for data loading is CSV while the raw data file type of SDSS is MDF (SQLServer data file).

Table 1. Overview of Data sets

Data set ID	Data size	Number of tuples
1	1.1G	80000
2	11G	800000
3	22G	160000
4	33G	240000
5	43G	320000
6	54G	400000
7	65G	480000
8	76G	560000
9	86G	640000

5.3   Results and Performance Analysis

In this experiment, we compare FASTLoad with the data loading method employed in SciDB cluster by evaluate the effect of data size to both approaches. The detailed experimental results are depicted in Fig. 5. Furthermore, we evaluate the data transfer overheads and the memory overheads of both approaches, the results are shown in Figs. 6 and 7.

From Fig. 5, we can found that, towards the data sets among the 1st data set to the 4th data set, the parallel loading performance of FASTLoad and SciDB's built-in techniques is nearly identical. A more clearly view of this experimental data is shown as Fig. 7. It means, in our cluster environment, when the data size is smaller than 33 GB, although the overheads are adhere to a nearly line growth, the performance difference of these two approach is relative small.

As to the relative large data set from the 5th data set (43 GB) to the 9th data set (86 GB), the performance gap between FASTLoad and SciDB's built-in technique can be explicitly observed. And we can know that the FASTLoad approach can achieve 4 to 6 times fast than its competitor. Even when conduct the experiment over the 5th data set who only have 43 GB data, FASTLoad still fast than the other one with hundreds of seconds.

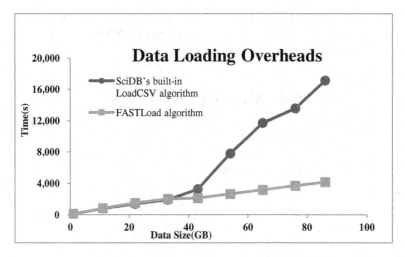

Fig. 5. Overheads of parallel data loading

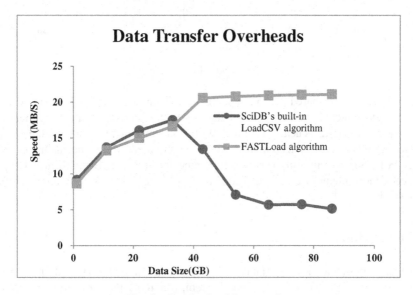

Fig. 6. Overheads of data transfer

As to the evaluation of data transfer speed, the result is shown in Fig. 6, the FastLoad algorithm performs behave better with the rapid increase of the data size. From the 1st data set to the 4th data set, the average data transfer speed between the two methods is almost identical. As the data size grows, the descent of the data transfer speed of SciDB's built-in technique is quite swift, meanwhile, the FASTLoad algorithm finally keep a nearly constant transfer speed. From the 5th data set (43 GB) to the 9th data set (86 GB), the transfer speed of FASTLoad achieves 4 to 6 times better than SciDB's built-in data load technique. Even when conduct the experiment over the 5th data set who only have 43 GB data the gap between the two is also big.

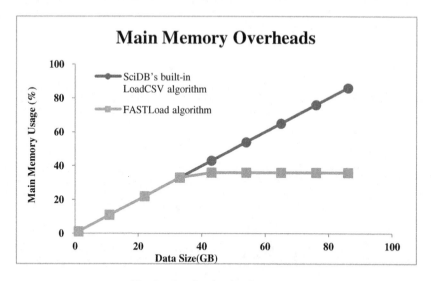

Fig. 7. Overheads of main memory

In Fig. 7, we compared the main memory utilization between FASTLoad and SciDB's built-in technique. From the 1st data set to the 4th data set, the used memory size of the two methods is nearly identical. As the data size increase, the main memory usage of SciDB's built-in technique become larger, meanwhile, the main memory utilized by FASTLoad algorithm keeps nearly same. It means SciDB's built-in technique may needs more memory than FASTLoad to ensure it can successfully complete the loading task.

6   Conclusions

This paper proposed an advance data loading approach named FASTLoad, it has been implemented into the Adaptable Loading System, which has the capability to coupling work with the array model based modern scientific database cluster SciDB. The experimental results show that, FASTLoad can achieve 4 to 6 times of performance improvement when the loaded data size is really large.

In the future, we will continuously optimize the implementation of system coordinator engine with more comprehensive schedule capability, which can make the parallel data loading become more robust and have better throughput. And we also have a plan to enhance the techniques used in SCANRAW, we will make revision on it to make it can be fit into array model based scientific data base cluster, which will make scientific database system like SciDB have better in-situ data processing capability.

Acknowledgments. This work was supported by the China Ministry of Science and Technology under the State Key Development Program for Basic Research (2012CB821800), Fund of National Natural Science Foundation of China (No. 61462012, 61562010, U1531246), Scientific Research Fund for talents recruiting of Guizhou University (No. 700246003301), Science and Technology Fund of Guizhou Province (No. J [2013]2099), High Tech. Project Fund of Guizhou Development and Reform Commission (No. [2013]2069), Industrial Research Projects of the Science and Technology Plan of Guizhou Province (No. GY[2014]3018) and The Major Applied Basic Research Program of Guizhou Province (No. JZ20142001, No. JZ20142001-05).

References

1. Hey, T., Tansley, S., Tolle, K. (eds.): The Fourth Paradigm: Data-Intensive Scientific Discoveries. Microsoft Research, Redmond (2009)
2. Cudre-Mauroux, P., Kimura, H., et al.: A demonstration of SciDB: a science-oriented DBMS. VLDB **2**, 1534–1537 (2009)
3. Alagiannis, I., Borovica, R., Branco, M., Idreos, S., et al.: NoDB in action: adaptive query processing on raw data. VLDB **5**, 1942–1945 (2012)
4. Alagiannis, I., Borovica, R., Branco, M., Idreos, S., et al.: NoDB: efficient query execution on raw data files. In: SIGMOD (2012)
5. Blanas, S., Wu, K., Byna, S., Dong, B., Shoshani, A.: Parallel data analysis directly on scientific file formats. In: SIGMOD (2014)
6. Witkowski, A., Colgan, M., Brumm, A., Cruanes, T., Baer, H.: Performant and Scalable Data Loading with Oracle Database 11g (2011)
7. Cheng, Y., Rusu, F.: Parallel in-situ data processing with speculative loading. In: SIGMOD (2014)
8. Arumugam, S., Dobra, A., Jermaine, C., et al.: The DataPath system: a data-centric analytic processing engine for large data warehouses. In: SIGMOD (2010)
9. Lock (computer science). http://en.wikipedia.org/wiki/Lock_(computer_science)
10. Duggan, J., Stonebraker, M.: Incremental elasticity for array databases. In: SIGMOD/PODS 2014 (2014)
11. Szalay, A.S.: The sloan digital sky survey. Comput. Sci. Eng. **1**(2), 54–62 (1999)
12. Dobos, L., Szalay, A., Blakeley, J., Budavári, T., Csabai, I., Tomic, D., Milovanovic, M., et al.: Array Requirements for Scientific Applications and an Implementation for Microsoft SQL Server
13. Widmann, N., Baumann, P.: Efficient execution of operations in a DBMS for multidimensional arrays. In: Proceedings of the SSDBM 1998, Capri, Italy, pp. 155–165, July 1998
14. Thakar, A.R., Szalay, A.S., Kunszt, P.Z., Gray, J.: Migrating a multiterabyte archive from object to relational databases. Comput. Sci. Eng. **5**(5), 16–29 (2003)
15. Stonebraker, M., Becla, J., DeWitt, D., Lim, K.-T., Maier, D., Ratzesberger, O., Zdonik, S.: Requirements for science databases and SCIDB. In: CIDR 2009 Conference. Asilomar, CA, USA, January 2009
16. Brown, P., et al.: Overview of SciDB: large scale array storage, processing and analysis. In: SIGMOD 2010, pp. 963–968 (2010)
17. Cudre-Mauroux, P., Kimura, H., Lim, K.-T., Rogers, J., Simakov, R., et al.: A demonstration of SciDB: a science-oriented DBMS. In: VLDB 2009, pp. 1534–1537 (2009)
18. Mathematical multidimensional array. http://en.wikipedia.org/wiki/Array_data_structure

19. Agrawal, R., et al.: Modeling multidimensional databases. In: Proceedings of the ICDE 1997, Birmingham, pp. 232–243, April 1997. [2]
20. Lock (database). http://en.wikipedia.org/wiki/Lock_(database)
21. Soroush, E., Balazinska, M., Wang, D.: ArrayStore: a storage manager for complex parallel array processing. In: SIGMOD (2011)
22. Seering, A., Cudre-Mauroux, P., et al.: Efficient versioning for scientific array databases. In: International Conference on Data Engineering (ICDE) (2012)
23. Virtualization, October 2012. http://en.wikipedia.org/wiki/Virtualization
24. Kernel based virtual machine. http://www.linux-kvm.org/page/Main_Page
25. Hypervisor: http://en.wikipedia.org/wiki/Hypervisor
26. Virtualization support through KVM. Linux: 2.6.20 Kernel release notes, 05 February 2007. http://kernelnewbies.org. Accessed 16 June 2014
27. X86 virtualization. http://en.wikipedia.org/wiki/X86_virtualization
28. Set (mathematics). http://en.wikipedia.org/wiki/Set_(mathematics)
29. Cartesian product. http://en.wikipedia.org/wiki/Cartesian_product
30. Abouzied, A., Abadi, D.J., Silberschatz, A.: Invisible loading: Access-driven data transfer from raw files into database systems. In: EDBT/ICDT (2013)
31. Planthaber, G., Stonebraker, M., Frew, J.: EarthDB: scalable analysis of MODIS data using SciDB. In: ACM SIGSPATIAL BIGSPATIAL 2012 (2012)
32. Gray, J., Szalay, A.S., Thakar, A.R., Kunszt, P.Z., Stoughton, C., Slutz, D., vandenBerg, J.: Data mining the SDSS SkyServer database. MSR-TR-2002-01 (2002)

Tradeoff Between the Price of Distributing a Database and Its Collusion Resistance Based on Concatenated Codes

Thach V. Bui[1,2]([✉]), Thuc D. Nguyen[3], Noboru Sonehara[1,2],
and Isao Echizen[1,2]

[1] Department of Multidisciplinary Sciences, School of Informatics,
SOKENDAI (The Graduate University for Advanced Studies),
1560-35 Kamiyamaguchi, Hayama, Kanagawa Prefecture 240-0115, Japan
{bvthach,sonehara,iechizen}@nii.ac.jp
[2] National Institute of Informatics, 2-1-2 Hitotsubashi,
Chiyoda-ku, Tokyo 101-8430, Japan
[3] Faculty of Information Technology, Ho Chi Minh City University of Science,
225 Nguyen Van Cu Street, District 5, Ho Chi Minh City, Vietnam
ndthuc@fit.hcmus.edu.vn

Abstract. The purchasing of customer databases, which is becoming more and more common, has led to a big problem: the use of purchased databases to mount a collusion attack, which is when purchasers of a database illegally combine their versions of it in order to de-anonymize the private information it contains. However, the purchasing of customer database is only available in the black market. In this paper, we first investigated the relationship between the price of distributing a database and its collusion resistance. A fingerprint is embedded in database so that illegal distributors can be identified. The fingerprints are constructed on the basic of concatenated codes. After the fingerprint is embedded, the price of distributing the database and its collusion resistance are modelled as decreasing functions. The less expensive the database is, the less collusion resistance the database owner deals with. There are upper and lower bounds for the collusion capabilities. To the best of our knowledge, this scheme is unique in that the tradeoff between the price of distributing a database and its collusion resistance is based on a mathematical model. Second, we propose a guideline to sell customer database legally with profit and risk evaluation.

Keywords: Database distribution · Guideline · Price evaluation · Collusion resistance · Coding theory · Mathematical model

1 Introduction

We are living in the era of a social, economic, and technological revolution [1]. Gantz and Reinsel [5] estimated that the amount of information created and

© Springer International Publishing Switzerland 2015
G. Wang et al. (Eds.): ICA3PP 2015, Part II, LNCS 9529, pp. 163–182, 2015.
DOI: 10.1007/978-3-319-27122-4_12

replicated on the Internet would be about 7.9 zettabytes[1] by 2015. This amount was estimated to be about 40 zettabytes in 2020. Moreover, companies in many sectors are gathering and storing vast amounts of information and increasing their use of Big Data[2] and analytics [27–29]. People are sharing a lot of personal information, such as their preferences online without realizing it, making it easier for companies to collect personal information. And the number of people using social networks continues to grow. Facebook, for example, had about 890 million daily active uses in 2014 [31]. In 2012, there were 1.2 trillion searches made by Google users [32]. That means the amount of information Google and Facebook collect a vast amount of information about their users every day. Such information enables companies to orientate new products for the market.

Financial Times [2] addressed that there exists "the multibillion-dollar data broker industry profits from the trade of thousands of details about individuals". It also provided a calculator to calculate your personal data worth. It is a bad news that a personal data worth is suggested to be not exceed $1. The Guardian [3] reported that a man named Shawn Buckles sold his personal data for € 238. Moreover, The Guardian pointed out that a company prefer to purchase a bundle of at least 1,000 persons for a business. That means the more data brokers collects, the more money they get. Forbes [4] also informed about the black market for personal information. Therefore, purchasing database containing customer information has become a big business (Fig. 1).

Many countries and organizations have thus taken steps to protect privacy. For example, the European Union enacted the EU Directive on Data Privacy in 1995, and the United Kingdom enacted the Data Protection Act three years later. These laws require the control of information in the processing of personal data, i.e., data about a living and identifiable individual. They require that personal data be used only for authorized and lawful purposes. This means that any other use of such data, such as retention for longer than necessary, use for other purposes without permission, and redistribution, should be detected to enable punishment of the offender. In May 2014, the White House [1] released a report on Big Data in which the authors stated that "data services" or "data brokers" collect data for many sources, analyse that data, and then sell the data for a profit. This selling of data is problematic because it can result in personal information being spread worldwide. Although the GLBA of 1999 and the HIPAA of 1996 require that data be anonymized before publishing to prevent data brokers from re-identifying persons in the released data, U.S. legislators now are drafting new laws for targeting the purchased data problem. Much research has been done on protecting data privacy [9,11,12] by using k-anonymity technique in

---

[1] A zettabyte is 1,000,000,000,000,000,000,000 bytes. Imagine that every person in Vietnam (population of 92.5 million in 2014) took a digital photo every second of every day for over three months. All of those photos put together would equal about one zettabyte.

[2] Big Data is a term that refers to "large, diverse, complex, longitudinal, and/or distributed datasets generated from instruments, sensors, Internet transactions, email, video, click streams, and/or all other digital sources available today and in the future" [30].

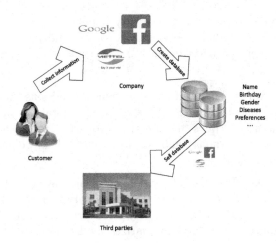

Fig. 1. Model of database creation and distribution

which if attacker attempts to link explicitly identifying information to a person, its content maps the information to at least k persons. Most of the research has focused on preventing identification of individuals from information contained in the data.

Although aimed at protecting customer privacy, the legislation mentioned above still allows companies to sell customer databases, which we call *database distribution*. There are two main problems in the distribution of databases that have been k-anonymity: how to evaluate the price of distributing a database and how to prevent purchasers from illegally combining their version in order to get the de-anonymize it. We call such purchasers *colluders* and such attacks *collusion attack*. Willenborg and Kardaun [15] first proposed adding fingerprints to a database and thereby creating various distinguishable versions of the database, making it possible to identify an illegal distributor. However, the algorithm used to create fingerprints is not deterministic and can be used only for identifying specific records. Schrittwieser et al. [14] and Kieseberg et al. [6] also proposed schemes for embedding fingerprints based on k-anonymity into databases. Their aim was to design fingerprints that are secure against collusion attack.

Coding Theory is the study of the properties of codes and their suitability for various applications. A code is a set of codewords, and each codeword is a string over a finite field. A code has block length, dimension, and the minimum distance. A code could be generated by concatenating two codes using concatenation technique (defined later). For each code, researchers try to balance *its relative distance* (the ratio of the minimum distance to block length) and *its code rate* (the ratio of dimension to block length). The larger the relative distance (code rate), the smaller the code rate (relative distance).

In this paper, our goals are to:

– Propose a guideline for database owners to sell their database legally with profit and risk evaluation.

– Determine who discloses the database they bought.
– Determine the relationship between price of a database and its collusion attack, prove upper and lower bounds for the collusion capabilities based on concatenated codes.

By using the codewords generated by concatenated codes as fingerprints for a database, we can connect the price of distributing a database and its collusion resistance. Concatenated codes also provide properties to trace the database owner who purchased a database embedded by them. Then, we propose a guideline based on these results.

Outline of the Paper: The rest of the paper is organized as follows: Sect. 2 presents related work. Section 3 presents preliminaries. Section 4 presents our proposed scheme. Section 5 describes analysis on price and collusion resistance of database distribution. Section 6 summarizes the key points.

2   Related Work

2.1   k-anonymity

In the medical health field, patient records are extremely important for doctors and also researchers, and most hospitals create, maintain, then publish databases containing patient information. GLBA and HIPAA require that a database be anonymized before it is published. However, even after removing identity attributes such as name, social security number, and home address, Samarati and Sweeney [13] and Sweeney [10] showed that they could identify people by using *quasi-identifiers* (QIs) that is defined as a subset of attribute that can uniquely identify each tuple in a database. For example, a pair (Gender, Country) is a QI in Table 1. To prevent such identification, they developed a k-anonymity concept, i.e. each record cannot be distinguished from $k - 1$ other records using quasi-identifiers. To support its development, they created *generalization level* concept. Generalization level is a term that mentions about a level that an attribute is anonymized to in order to reduce the quality of the attribute. For example, the next generalization level of {Male, Female} is {Person}. The actual gender cannot be identified on the basis of the "Person" information, and no information can be obtained from {Person}. An example of generalization levels is shown in Fig. 2.

2.2   Traitor Tracing

Agrawal and Kiernan [20] developed an algorithm for watermarking relational databases that uses a private key held by the data owner to form a pattern of specific values at certain bit position of certain attributes of certain tuples. However, this scheme depends on the primary key attributes. A year later, Li et al. [18] constructed a virtual primary key that differs from tuple to tuple to overcome this point. Their fingerprint scheme can embed and detect arbitrary bit-string marks in relations. Some attacks such as adding, deleting, shuffling, and colluding with other recipients of relation are considered to prove robustness of the

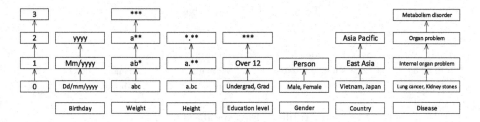

Fig. 2. Generalization strategies for seven attributes

proposed scheme. Guo et al. [19] introduce a two-level fingerprinting scheme to protect valuable numeric relational data. A secret key is used to embed a unique fingerprint to identify each recipient. The scheme can verify the extracted fingerprint and give a numerical confidence level. Schrittwieser et al. [14] also presented an algorithm for creating unique fingerprints of microdata sets that are partially anonymized using k-anonymity techniques. This algorithm generalizes several attributes of the dataset into an certain anonymity and data precision level. Different generalization patterns are considered to be fingerprints, and an unique fingerprint can be assigned to each user. Users can therefore be classified into groups on the basis of their data precision levels.

2.3 Database Distribution

A company that provides services to customers can also collect information on their customers. This information is quite important to both that company and other companies for making and releasing new products. There is thus a market for customer information, i.e. for **database distribution**. However, if the database owner sells the original database of customer information, the owner will have nothing to sell next time. Thus, they should reduce the quality of the database before selling it.

Before selling a database, the owner can reduce the quality of the data and make it possible to identify an illegal buyer of the database. Such a scheme was introduced by Bui et al. [16,17]. A fingerprint characterized by a vector is embedded into the database. Each attribute of the database is associated with an entry of the vector. The value of an entry is the generalization level of the associated attribute. For example, consider the database in Table 2. Because the *Birthday, Weight,* and *Height* attributes are associated with 1, 1, 1, respectively, all data for these three attributes is generalized to the first level. This creates a fingerprint for use in identifying an illegal buyer.

We use five databases (shown in Tables 1, 2, 3, 4 and 5) in our examples: the original database without a fingerprint embedded (Table 1) and anonymized databases with a fingerprint embedded (Tables 2, 3, 4 and 5).

2.4 Perfect Collusion

The most harmful damage occurs when colluders recreate the original database (Table 1) by combining their versions of the database. We call such attack

Table 1. Original database

0	0	0	0		0	0	0	0	0
Birthday	Weight	Height	Education level	Gender	Country	Blood type	Status	Disease
23.5.1998	50	1.72	Undergraduate	M	Vietnam	A	Single	Lung cancer
11.7.1988	70	1.67	Graduate	M	Japan	B	Married	Kidney stones

Table 2. First database

1	1	1	0	0	0	0	0	0
Birthday	Weight	Height	Education level	Gender	Country	Blood type	Status	Disease
5.1998	5*	1.*	Undergraduate	M	Vietnam	A	Single	Lung cancer
7.1988	7*	1.*	Graduate	M	Japan	B	Married	Kidney stones

Table 3. Second database

0	0	0	1	1	1	0	0	0
Birthday	Weight	Height	Education level	Gender	Country	Blood type	Status	Disease
23.5.1998	50	1.72	Over 12	Person	East Asia	A	Single	Lung cancer
11.7.1988	70	1.67	Over 12	Person	East Asia	B	Married	Kidney stones

Table 4. Third database

0	0	0	1	1	2	0	0	0
Birthday	Weight	Height	Education level	Gender	Country	Blood type	Status	Disease
23.5.1998	50	1.72	Over 12	Person	Asia	A	Single	Lung cancer
11.7.1988	70	1.67	Over 12	Person	Asia	B	Married	Kidney stones

Table 5. Fourth database

0	0	1	1	1	1	0	0	0
Birthday	Weight	Height	Education level	Gender	Country	Blood type	Status	Disease
23.5.1998	50	1.*	Over 12	Person	East Asia	A	Single	Lung cancer
11.7.1988	70	1.*	Over 12	Person	East Asia	B	Married	Kidney stones

perfect collusion. Perfect collusion was also addressed by Samarati [12], Kieseberg et al. [6], Bui et al. [17] in different ways named reducing generalization level or complimentary attack. Kieseberg et al. [6] developed a scheme that keeps a database secure against the combined efforts of colluders to reduce the generalization level. However, the number of fingerprints is much less than the number of attributes of the original database, so colluders can obtain some attributes without generalization. Therefore, this approach is impractical for database owners wanting to sell a customer database. Bui et al. [17] pointed out perfect collusion when using Non-Adaptive Group Testing as a fingerprint code. The research described above did not investigate the tradeoff between the price of distributing a database and its collusion resistance. Moreover, perfect collusion is not surveyed well in that work.

2.5   Data Precision Metric

In this paper, we evaluate the price of a database based on its information loss. Generalization results in the loss of information. For example, the second and third databases (Tables 3 and 4) have different levels of generalization. Since the second database has less generalization than the third one, its quality is better. Because the embedding fingerprint technique is based on anonymizing *attributes*, not by using tuples as conventionally done, the conventional metrics are not suitable for evaluating the information loss due to anonymization using this technique. We thus investigate the use of three alternative metrics: Samarati, Precision, and Modified Discernability.

Samarati Metric. The Samarati Metric [12] is defined as a sum of generalization levels. It is easy to calculate and helps one imagine information loss. However, it often fails to distinguish the difference between two different levels.

For example, the generalization vectors for the third and fourth database are $c_3 = (0\ 0\ 0\ 1\ 1\ 2\ 0\ 0\ 0)$ and $c_4 = (0\ 0\ 1\ 1\ 1\ 1\ 0\ 0\ 0)$. Although $sum(c_1) = sum(c_1) = 4$, the information loss differs between these two databases. Only **three** attributes of the third database were anonymized while the **four** of the fourth database were anonymized.

Precision Metric. Sweeney [9] proposed a metric that depends on the maximum generalization depth possible for an attribute. If an attribute has more than one level of generalization, the weight of the generalization is defined by

$$\frac{\text{Number of levels generalized}}{\text{Number of possible generalization levels}}$$

Because a database is supposed to a generalization vector $x = (x_1, x_2, \ldots, x_n)$, the Precision Metric of the database is defined as:

$$Prec(x) = 1 - \frac{\sum \frac{x_i}{\text{Number of possible generalization levels of } x_i}}{n}$$

For example, if an entry for the "Birthday" attribute is 5.1998, its weight is $1/2$ because there are three levels of the "Birthday" attribute: {dd/mm/yyyy, mm/yyyy, yyyy}. For example, although the precision values for the third and fourth databases are equal to 0.78, only **three** attributes of the third database were anonymized while **four** attributes of the fourth database are anonymized. This means that the information loss of these two databases differs. The Precision Metric cannot distinguish the difference.

Modified Discernability Metric (DM*). El Emam et al. [11] slightly adjusted the original Discernability Metric. A class is a group that each person in it cannot be distinguished from others. Suppose we have N classes and n_i is the number of elements of the ith class. In this case, the DM* Metric is

$$DM^* = \sum_{i=1}^{N} n_i^2$$

It reflects the change in any element in a class. However, if a class has many levels of generalization, it does not reflect the change well. The DM* metric is thus unsuitable for the technique we use because we would not be able to discern any differences due to the large number of databases being compared.

For example, if the DM* metric was used for the first, second, third, and fourth databases, which have only one class and each class has only two elements (two records), the DM* of these four databases would be $2^2 = 4$ even though they are quite different!

3   Preliminaries

In this section, we present preliminaries related to Coding Theory.

3.1   Coding Theory

Coding theory has a long history and has been around since computer was invented. Researchers in coding theory develop models on transmitting a signal from a source to another sources and study properties of codes and their fitness for specific applications. It has mostly been applied in engineering because codes are designed to reduce errors when a signal transmitted. In recent years, Coding theory is now being applied in other fields such as data stream [26]. There are several fundamental definitions and theorems in coding theory.

Definition 1. *(Hamming distance) The Hamming distance between two strings x and y of the same length over an alphabet Σ, denoted $\Delta(x, y)$, is defined as the number of positions at which the two strings differ, i.e. $\Delta(x, y) \stackrel{\text{def}}{=} |\{i|x_i \neq y_i\}|$.*

Definition 2. *(Hamming weight) The Hamming weight of a string x over an alphabet Σ, denoted $wt(x)$, is defined as the number of non-zero symbols in the string, i.e. $wt(x) \stackrel{\text{def}}{=} |\{i|x_i \neq 0\}|$. We define $sum(x) = \sum |x_i|$ ($\sum$ is an operation over Z^+). If x is a binary string, $wt(x) = sum(x)$.*

We define $wt(x, y)$ as $\Delta(x, y)$, i.e. $wt(x, y) = \Delta(x, y)$. For example, if $c_1 = (1\ 1\ 1\ 0\ 0\ 0\ 0\ 0\ 0)$ and $c_2 = (0\ 0\ 0\ 1\ 1\ 1\ 0\ 0\ 0)$, $wt(c_1) = 3$ and $wt(c_1, c_2) = 6$.

Definition 3. *(Code) An error correcting code C of length n over a finite alphabet Σ is a subset of Σ^n. The elements of C are called the codewords in C. If $|\Sigma| = q$, we say that C is a q-ary code. Specially, when $q = 2$, we call C a binary code. A code is an encoding map $\mathcal{E}$ so that it maps the message set $\mathcal{M}$ which is identical to $\{1, 2, \ldots, |C|\}$ to codewords belonging to Σ^n ($|C|$ is the total number of codewords of the code C). The code is the image of the encoding map.*

We now introduce a family of codes that is usually used in various applications. We call them linear codes.

Definition 4. *(Linear code) If an alphabet Σ is a field and $C \subset \Sigma^n$ is a subspace of Σ^n, C is said to be a linear code.*

From this time, we only use linear codes for our definition. A linear code C could be constructed by a *generator matrix*, which consists of columns so that these columns span C.

Definition 5. *(Generator matrix and encoding) Let $C \subseteq \Sigma^n$ be a linear code of dimension k over an alphabet Σ, $\Sigma = \mathcal{F}_q$ and have a generator matrix $G \in \mathcal{F}_q^{n \times k}$. A linear code has an encoding map $E : \mathcal{F}_q^k \to \mathcal{F}_q^n$ which is a linear transformation $x \mapsto Gx$.*

A linear code C is often referred as $[n, k, d]_q$, where n is block length, k is dimension, d is the minimum distance, and q is alphabet size. Sometimes, if q and d is clear from context, we only refer C as $[n, k]$. A $[n, k, d]_q$ code has q^k codewords.

For a code C, We denote w_{min} and w_{max} as the minimum Hamming weight and the maximum Hamming weight of all codewords of C. We also denote w_j as the Hamming weight of the jth codeword of C.

Definition 6. *A w_{min}-weight code $[n, k, d]_q$ is a code that the Hamming weight of all codewords is at least w_{min}.*

The most important thing about a code is the relationship between its **code rate** and its **relative distance**. After defining these two concepts, we will present some fundamental results for the relationship between the code rate and relative distance.

Definition 7. *(Code rate) The rate of a code $C \subseteq \Sigma^n$, is defined as $R(C) \overset{\text{def}}{=} \frac{\log |C|}{n \log |\Sigma|}$. If C is a $[n, k, d]_q$ code, $R(C) = \frac{k}{n}$.*

Definition 8. *(Relative distance) The minimum distance of a code C is defined as the minimum Hamming distance between two distinct codewords of C. That is,*

$$\Delta(C) \overset{\text{def}}{=} \min_{c_1, c_2 \in C,\ c_1 \neq c_2} \Delta(c_1, c_2)$$

The relative distance of C, denoted $\delta(C)$, is $\frac{\Delta(C)}{\text{the block length of } C}$. If C is a $[n, k, d]_q$ code, $\delta(C) = \frac{d}{n}$.

For simplicity, we refer to $R(C)$ as R and $\delta(C)$ as δ. We use the Singleton bound as a simple bound to indicate the relationship between the code rate and relative distance.

Theorem 9. *(Singleton bound) Let C be a code of block length n and minimum distance d over an alphabet of size q. Then $|C| \le q^{n-d+1}$. In particular, if C is a $[n, k, d]_q$ code, $R \le 1 - \delta + o(1)$.*

However, this bound is not good in some cases. Gilbert [24] and Vashamov [25] gave a tighter bound for R and δ over a finite field F_q.

Theorem 10. *(Gilbert-Varshamov bound) For every q and $\sigma \in [0, 1 - \frac{1}{q}]$, there exists an infinite family C of q-ary codes with rate $R \geq 1 - h_q(\delta) - o(1)$ where*

$$h_q(\delta) = \delta \log_q \frac{q-1}{\delta} + (1-\delta) \log_q \frac{1}{1-\delta}$$

However, the use of the Gilbert-Vashamov bound is limited to q-ary codes. For binary codes, we use another bound, the Hamming bound, which is tighter than the Gilbert-Vashamov bound.

Theorem 11. *(Hamming bound) Let C be a binary code of block length n and minimum distance d. Then*

$$|C| \leq \frac{2^n}{\sum_{i=0}^{\lfloor \frac{d-1}{2} \rfloor} \binom{n}{i}}$$

In asymptotic term,

$$R \leq 1 - h_2(\delta/2) + o(1)$$

where

$$h_2(\delta/2) = \frac{\delta}{2} \log \frac{2}{\delta} + (1 - \frac{\delta}{2}) \log \frac{1}{1 - \delta/2}$$

A code achieves the Hamming bound is called a **perfect code**. So far, only Hamming codes have achieved the Hamming bound. However, their minimum distance is only 3, so they are not suitable for actual applications due to their limited error-correction capabilities. Researchers have thus tried to design binary codes that asymptotically meet the Hamming bound.

Because only binary codes could meet the Hamming bound, we use binary codes for the rest of the paper. In this paper, we use a fingerprint and a codeword interchangeably.

3.2   Reed-Solomon Codes and Concatenated Codes

Reed-Solomon (RS) codes, named after the co-inventors, [22], are widely used in many fields [23]. A $[n, k, d]_q$-code C, $1 \leq k \leq n \leq q$, is a subset $C \subseteq [q]^n$ of size q^k. Because RS codes are constructed using polynomial method, they have several useful properties. First, they are *maximum distance separable* codes. In particular, A $[n, k, d]_q$- RS code has a minimum distance of $d = n - k + 1$. Second, RS codes can be generated by using a generator matrix over $\mathcal{F}_q$. Forney [21] described the basic idea of *concatenated codes*. Concatenated codes are constructed by using an *outer code* $C_{out} : [q]^{k_1} \rightarrow [q]^{n_1}$, where $q = 2^{k_2}$, and a binary *inner code* $C_{in} : \{0,1\}^{k_2} \rightarrow \{0,1\}^{n_2}$. Suppose we have two codes: C_{out} of length n_1, dimension k_1 and distance Δ_1 and C_{in} of length n_2, dimension k_2 and distance Δ_2. Suppose further that the alphabet of the second codes is 2 and the alphabet of the first codes is 2^{k_2}. The concatenated codes $C = C_{out} \circ$

C_{in} is defined as follows. Consider a message $m \in \left(\{0,1\}^{k_2}\right)^{k_1}$. Let $C_{out}(m) = (x_1, \ldots, x_{n_1})$. Then, $C_{out} \circ C_{in}(m) = (C_{in}(x_1), C_{in}(x_2), \ldots, C_{in}(x_{n_1}))$. C has length $n = n_1 n_2$ with message length $k_1 k_2$ and a minimum distance at least $\Delta_1 \Delta_2$. C's size is $(n_1 n_2) \times 2^{k_1 k_2}$. C has $2^{k_1 k_2}$ codewords.

If we receive a vector $r = (r_1, \ldots, r_{n_1})$, where r_i are elements of 2^{k_2}, finding an element of C_{out} such that it is sufficiently close to r is the best way to decode r. Forney proposed an efficient algorithm that can find a codeword of C_{out} that is sufficiently close to r on the basis of probabilistic method. In our scheme, this algorithm is used to identify illegal distributors of different versions of a database.

For the rest of the paper, we use C as a concatenated code constructed by a C_{out} code $[n_1, k_1, d_1]_{2^{k_2}}$ and a w_{min}-weight C_{in} code $[n_2, k_2, d_2]_2$ using concatenation technique. k_1 and k_2 are the largest numbers such that $k_1 \leq n_1 - d_1 + 1$ and $k_2 \leq n_2 \ d_2 + 1$.

4 Proposed Scheme

In this section, we present regulatory compliance for distributing personal information, fingerprint embedding and extracting, price of distributing a database and its collusion resistance, and a guideline for distributing personal information.

4.1 Regulatory Compliance

In accordance with the EU Directive on Data Privacy, the Data Protection Act in the United Kingdom, BLBA and HIPAA in U.S., if database owners would like to sell their customer information, they have to anonymize the identities of the customers. The well known technique widely used is k-anonymity. The second technique is to remove all QIs. For example, suppose that there are only two QIs {Gender, Country} and {Birthday, Gender, Weight} in a database. If we remove *Gender* attribute from a database, the database consists of {Country} and {Birthday, Weight}. Then, there is no quasi-identifier in the database. Removing all QIs is addressed by Motwani and Ying [7], and Lodha and Thomas [8]. They presented efficient algorithms for finding and removing all QIs.

Since database owners have much information about their customers, removing some attributes to make a database having no quasi-identifier is not a problem. Let's consider the example of the original database in Table 1. Since the names are not included, a buyer cannot identify the person corresponding to each record. This is not a problem however as the buyer is interested only in the information for making their products attractive to customers. For example, a health-related company could use the {23.5.1998, 50 kg, 1.72 m, Undergraduate, Male, Vietnam, A, Single, Lung cancer} information to create certain products or services:

- lung cancer drugs (on the basis of {*Lung cancer*}).
- lung cancer treatment for undergraduate students (on the basis of {*Lung cancer, 23.5.1998, Undergraduate*}).

– lung cancer treatment for undergraduate students in a developing country (on the basis of {*Lung cancer, 23.5.1998, Undergraduate, Vietnam*}).

In summary, to comply regulatory, database owners have to anonymize their databases or remove all quasi-identifiers in their databases.

4.2 Embedding and Extracting Phases

Using a fingerprinting code C generated from $C_{out} : [q]^{k_1} \rightarrow [q]^{n_1}$, where $q = 2^{k_2}$, and $C_{in} : \{0,1\}^{k_2} \rightarrow \{0,1\}^{n_2}$ as defined in Subsect. 3.2, we will explain how a fingerprint is embedded in and extracted from a database. These processes ares based on those previously described [17] with some slight modifications based on Forney's [21] algorithm. A codeword x is embedded as a fingerprint in each database using Algorithm 1.

Algorithm 1. Algorithm for embedding fingerprint (codeword x) in database

---

Step 1. Choose a codeword of C for the database. Associate each entry of the codeword with an attribute of the database.
Step 2. Replace each non-zero entry with one having the desired level of generalization.
Step 3. Generalize each attribute of the database in accordance with the generalization level of the associated attribute.

The fingerprint is extracted using Algorithm 2.

Algorithm 2. Algorithm for extracting fingerprint (codeword x) from database

---

Step 1. (Initiation) Set x as the codeword associated with the database from which the fingerprint is to be extracted.
Step 2. (Get owner's fingerprint) If the jth attribute differs from the jth attribute of the original database for at least 50 % of the positions, $x(j) = 1$.
Step 3.
for $i = 1 : 1 : n_1$ **do**
   Let y_i be the message of C_{in} minimizing $e_i = \Delta(C_{in}(y_i), x((i-1) \times n_2 : i \times n_2 - 1))$.
end for
Step 4. Set $w_i = \min \left[e_i, \frac{d}{2} \right]$
Step 5.
for $j = 1 : 1 : n_2$ **do**
   Set $y'_i = \#$ with probability $\frac{2w_i}{d}$. Use an unambiguous error and erasure decoder to decode y'. If the output is sufficiently close to r in term of the Hamming distance, output c, else continue.
end for

The first, second, third, and fourth databases are examples of codeword embedding and extracting.

Table 6. Impact of different metrics

Node	Samarati	Precision	DM*	Proposed metric
(1 1 1 0 0 0 0 0 0)	3	0.85	4	0.33
(0 0 0 1 1 1 0 0 0)	3	0.83	4	0.33
(0 0 0 1 1 2 0 0 0)	4	**0.78**	4	0.31
(0 0 1 1 1 1 0 0 0)	4	**0.78**	4	0.25

4.3   Price of Distributing a Database and Its Collusion Resistance

As we discuss in Subsect. 2.5, the Samarati Metric, Precision Metric, and Modified Discernability Metric are not suitable for evaluating the price of database distribution. Therefore, we define a new metric. Each database is represented by an unique codeword. The information loss of a database depends on its codeword. We define a price of a database as follow.

Definition 12. *Suppose that fingerprint f is embedded in database* DB. *The price of distributing the database is given by a function:*

$$price(DB) \stackrel{\text{def}}{=} \frac{1}{wt(f) + \frac{sum(f) - wt(f)}{sum(f)}} \tag{1}$$

This function adapts to the number of levels of generalizations in a column of the database. We will prove several useful properties of Eq. 1 in subsequent sections.

For the sake of explanation, we give an example for this definition. Each of the five databases (Tables 1, 2, 3, 4, and 5), each database is equivalent to a unique codeword. The codewords of the first, second, third, and fourth databases are:

$$c_1 = (1\ 1\ 1\ 0\ 0\ 0\ 0\ 0\ 0),\ c_2 = (0\ 0\ 0\ 1\ 1\ 1\ 0\ 0\ 0)$$
$$c_3 = (0\ 0\ 0\ 1\ 1\ 2\ 0\ 0\ 0),\ c_4 = (0\ 0\ 1\ 1\ 1\ 1\ 0\ 0\ 0)$$

According to Definition 12, the prices of distributing the first, second, third, and fourth databases are $\frac{1}{3}, \frac{1}{3}, \frac{4}{13}$, and $\frac{1}{4}$, respectively. Because the first and second databases have the same level of generalization (their codewords have the same Hamming weight), they have the same price. Although the codewords in the second and third databases have the same Hamming weight, the generalization level of the $6th$ attribute of each database is different. The $6th$ attribute of the third database is more general than the $6th$ attribute of the second one. Therefore, the price of distributing the third database is less than that of distributing the second one, $(\frac{4}{13} \leq \frac{1}{3})$. Table 6 gives an example on the data precision of the data in Tables 2, 3, 4 and 5 based on Samarati, Precision, DM* and proposed metrics.

Since colluders want the original database (Table 1) but can buy only the fingerprinted databases, they combine their versions of the database to recreate the original one. In this example, they could do this if and only if they had the first and second databases. That is, we could achieve perfect collusion. Let us formally define such an attack.

Definition 13. *Given a vector set C, suppose that every $x \in C$, $x \in \{0,1\}^n$. C is called **perfect collusion** if $\prod_{i \in C, i=1}^{|C|} x_{ij} = 0$ for all $j = 1, \ldots, n$.*

If colluders achieve perfect collusion by combining databases, they can recreate the original database. Our aim is to estimate the probability of such an attack.

4.4   Guideline for Distributing a Database

We present a guideline for distributing a database. When selling a database, risk is a collusion resistance of the database. Database owners, who want to sell their customer information legally with profit and risk evaluation should follow the following guideline:

1. (Regulatory compliance) Anonymize their customers' identities.
2. (Traitor tracing) Use a fingerprint code having tracing properties to embed into the anonymized database they will sell.
3. (Price and risk evaluation) Analyse the properties of the fingerprint code they used to evaluate price and risk.

5   Analysis

5.1   Price of Distributing a Database

Here we discuss several properties of the measurement of the price of distributing a database defined in Subsect. 4.3. It is easy to prove the following theorem.

Theorem 14. *Suppose that a codeword a and a codeword b of a code C are embedded in databases A and B, respectively. If $wt(a) \leq wt(b)$ and $sum(a) \leq sum(b)$ then $price(A) \geq price(B)$.*

This theorem leads to the following corollary.

Corollary 15. *Suppose that a codeword of C is embedded in database A. If the code rate of C increases, the price of A increases.*

Proof. In accordance with Singleton bound, $\delta(C) \leq 1 - R(C) + \frac{1}{\text{block length of } C}$. Therefore, if $R(C)$ increases, $\delta(C)$ decreases. Because the block length of C is unchanged, if $\delta(C)$ decreases, the Hamming weight of each codeword of C decreases. Thus, the price of A increases.

5.2   Lower and Upper Bounds

Embedding a codeword into a database might not change all the attributes. These unchanged attributes are a weakness that colluders exploit to achieve perfect collusion. Here we define these attributes and describe their properties.

Definition 16. *If an attribute is not changed after embedding, it is called an **unchanged attribute**.*

The following theorem states that colluders can exploit unchanged attributes by combining several versions of a database.

Theorem 17. *(Lower bound) Suppose a fingerprinting code C is constructed using a C_{out} code $[n_1, k_1, d_1]_{2^{k_2}}$ and a w_{min}-weight C_{in} code $[n_2, k_2, d_2]_2$. If colluders combine at least $\frac{n_1 w_{min} - 1}{(n_1 - d_1 + 1)(n_2 - d_2 + 1)}$ databases, there exists at least an unchanged attribute.*

Proof. According to the Singleton bound, two codewords of C_{in} and C_{out} agree at most $n_1 - d_1 + 1$ and $n_2 - d_2 + 1$ positions, respectively. Then, two codewords of C agree at $(n_1 - d_1 + 1)(n_2 - d_2 + 1)$ positions at most. The Hamming weight of each codeword of C is $n_1 w_{min}$. Therefore, if colluders combine at least $\frac{n_1 w_{min} - 1}{(n_1 - d_1 + 1)(n_2 - d_2 + 1)}$ databases, there is at least one unchanged attribute.

Theorem 18. *(Universal upper bound) Suppose a fingerprinting code C is constructed using a C_{out} code $[n_1, k_1, d_1]_{2^{k_2}}$ and a w_{min}-weight C_{in} code $[n_2, k_2, d_2]_2$. If $w_{min} > \frac{n_2}{2}$, colluders cannot achieve perfect collusion.*

Proof. Set w_j as the Hamming weight of the jth column of C C_j. The Hamming weight and the length of C_j of C are $n_1 w_j$ and $n_1 n_2$, respectively. Since $w_j \geq w_{min} > \frac{n_2}{2}$, $n_1 w_j \geq \frac{n_1 n_2}{2}$. This means that the Hamming weight of an arbitrary column is larger than the half size of that column. Therefore, two columns have to agree at least one position containing 1. Thus, colluders cannot achieve perfect collusion.

Now we present a tighter upper bound for perfect collusion if colluders have a certain number of databases (the proof is given in Appendix A).

Theorem 19. *(Tight upper bound) Suppose a fingerprinting code C is constructed using a C_{out} code $[n_1, k_1, d_1]_{2^{k_2}}$ and a w_{min}-weight C_{in} code $[n_2, k_2, d_2]_2$. Suppose that colluders have $c = |C|$ databases. The probability of perfect collusion is at most*

$$\left(1 - \left(\frac{w_{min}}{n_2}\right)^c\right)^{n_1 n_2} \tag{2}$$

The above probability is the largest if and only if C_{in} is a constant codeword weight code.

Theorem 19 leads to the following corollary.

Corollary 20. *If the relative distance of C_{in} increases (decreases), the probability of perfect collusion decreases (increases).*

Proof. In accordance with Corollary 21, if the relative distance of C_{in} increases (decreases), w_{min} increases (decreases). Therefore, the probability of perfect collusion decreases (increases).

We prove the following lemma before proving Corollary 20.

Lemma 21. *If the relative distance of C increases (decreases), the Hamming weight of each codeword of C increases (decreases).*

Table 7. Comparison between proposed solution and existing works.

	Regulatory compliance	Traitor tracing	Perfect collusion	Practical use
Sweeney [9,10], Samarati [12], Samarati and Sweeney [13]	$\checkmark$	–	–	$\checkmark$
Li et al. [18], Guo et al. [19], Agrawal and Kiernan [20]	–	$\checkmark$	$\times$	$\checkmark$
Bui et al. [16,17]	$\times$	$\checkmark$	$\times$	$\checkmark$
Kieseberg et al. [6]	$\times$	$\checkmark$	$\checkmark$	$\times$
Proposed solution	$\checkmark$	$\checkmark$	$\checkmark$	$\checkmark$

Proof. Given that $y_1 = C_{out}(x_1 G_{in})$ and $y_2 = C_{out}(x_2 G_{in})$ are two codewords of C and that $\Delta(C) = \Delta(y_1, y_2)$, $n_1 w_{min} \Delta(C) = \Delta(0, y_1 - y_2) = n_1 wt(y_0)$, where $y_0 = (x_1 - x_2)G$. Therefore, if the relative distance of C increases (decreases), the Hamming weight of each codeword of C increases (decreases).

We summarize our results with the following theorem (The proof appears in Appendix A).

Theorem 22. *Suppose a fingerprinting code C is constructed using a C_{out} code $[n_1, k_1, d_1]_{2^{k_2}}$ and a w_{min}-weight C_{in} code $[n_2, k_2, d_2]_2$. And suppose that an unique codeword of C is embedded in each database and C_{in} could be changed. Thus, the lower the price of distributing a database is, the less collusion resistance the database owner deals with.*

5.3 Comparison

In this subsection, we compare our proposed solution with existing solutions in terms of regulatory compliance, traitor tracing, and perfect collusion, and practice in Table 7. We denote $\checkmark$ as "achieved", $\times$ as "not achieved", – as "not considered". It has shown that our proposed solution guarantees all criteria.

6   Conclusion

We have shown that there is a the relationship between price and collusion resistance. The higher the price of distributing a database is, the less collusion resistance deals with. Then, we presented a new metric for evaluating the price of distributing a database which matches our intuition. Finally, we proposed a guideline for database owner who wants to sell their customer information with profit and risk evaluation.

Future work includes investigating concatenated codes generated from probabilistic out and inner codes and finding the minimum attributes of quasi-identifiers such that, if we delete them, the database has no quasi-identifiers.

A   Omitted Proofs from Sect. 5

Proof of Theorem 19

Proof. Set $n = n_1 n_2$. Since C is a matrix of $n_1 n_2 \times 2^{k_1 k_2}$, each codeword of C has a length of $n_1 n_2$. Each database is represented by a codeword of C. Since the Hamming weight in a codeword is $n_1 w$, each entry of a codeword is randomly assigned to 1 with probability $p_j = \frac{n_1 w_j}{n_1 n_2} = \frac{w_j}{n_2}$.

Colluders achieve perfect collusion if $\prod_{i \in C, i=1}^{|C|} x_{ij} = 0$ for all $j = 1, \ldots, n$. The probability of a row contains at least one 0 is:

$$1 - \prod_{i=1}^{c} p_{j_i} = 1 - \frac{\prod_{i=1}^{c} w_{j_i}}{n_2^c} \leq 1 - \left(\frac{w_{min}}{n_2}\right)^c \tag{3}$$

The probability of n rows whose each row containing at least one 0 each is:

$$\left(1 - \prod_{i=1}^{c} p_{j_i}\right)^n \leq \left(1 - \left(\frac{w_{min}}{n_2}\right)^c\right)^{n_1 n_2} \tag{4}$$

When C_{in} is a constant codeword weight code, $w_{min} = w_{max} = w_i$. Therefore, the Eq. 4 holds.

Proof of Theorem 22

Proof. In accordance with Definition 12, the price of distributing a database is

$$\frac{1}{wt(\text{a codeword}) + 1} < price(\text{a database}) = \frac{1}{wt(\text{a codeword}) + \frac{sum(\text{a codeword}) - wt(\text{a codeword})}{sum(\text{a codeword})}}$$

$$< \frac{1}{w_{min}} \tag{5}$$

Since C has $2^{k_1 k_2}$ codewords, the total price of distributing databases embedded with these codewords is

$$\sum_{i=1}^{2^{k_1 k_2}} \frac{1}{wt(\text{a codeword}) + \frac{sum(\text{a codeword}) - wt(\text{a codeword})}{sum(\text{a codeword})}} < 2^{k_1 k_2} \times \frac{1}{n_1 w_{min}}$$

Since the number of attributes of the database is unchanged, the block length of C_{in} is unchanged. Suppose that there is another w'_{max}-weight code $C'_{in}\ [n_2, k'_2, d'_2]_2$. The price of distributing the database when using C' generated using C_{out} and C'_{in} is:

$$\sum_{i=1}^{2^{k_1 k'_2}} \frac{1}{wt(\text{a codeword}) + \frac{sum(\text{a codeword}) - wt(\text{a codeword})}{sum(\text{a codeword})}} > 2^{k_1 k'_2} \times \frac{1}{n_1 w'_{max} + 1}$$

To complete our proof, we prove that if the price of distributing the databases when using C' is larger than the price of distributing the databases when using C, $k_2 > k'_2$. Indeed, we have:

$$2^{k_1 k_2} \times \frac{1}{n_1 w_{min}} > \sum_{i=1}^{2^{k_1 k_2}} \frac{1}{wt(\texttt{a codeword}) + \frac{sum(\texttt{a codeword}) - wt(\texttt{a codeword})}{sum(\texttt{a codeword})}} \quad (6)$$

$$> \sum_{i=1}^{2^{k_1 k'_2}} \frac{1}{wt(\texttt{a codeword}) + \frac{sum(\texttt{a codeword}) - wt(\texttt{a codeword})}{sum(\texttt{a codeword})}} \quad (7)$$

$$> 2^{k_1 k'_2} \times \frac{1}{n_1 w'_{max} + 1} \quad (8)$$

$$\Rightarrow 2^{k_1(k_2 - k'_2)} > \frac{n_1 w_{min}}{n_1 w'_{max} + 1} \quad (9)$$

We consider three cases:

1. If $k_2 < k'_2$,

$$2^{k_1(k_2 - k'_2)} \le \frac{1}{2^{k_1}} < \frac{1}{n_1} < \frac{n_1 w_{min}}{n_1 w'_{max} + 1} \quad (10)$$

because $0 < w_{min}, w'_{max} \le n_2 \le n_1$. It is contradicted to inequality 6.
2. If $k_2 = k'_2$, $d_2 = d'_2$ because k_2 and k'_2 are the largest numbers such that $k_2 \le n_2 - d_2 + 1$ and $k'_2 \le n_2 d'_2 + 1$. Therefore, the price of distributing the databases when using C' is equal to the price of distributing the databases when using C. It is contradicted to our hypothesis.
3. If $k_2 > k'_2$, the inequality 6 holds.

Thus, if the price of distributing the databases when using C' is larger than the price of distributing the databases when using C, $k_2 > k'_2$. If $k'_2 < k_2$, $d'_2 > d_2$.

According to Corollary 20, if the relative distance of C_{in} increases (decreases), the probability of perfect collusion decreases (increases). According to Corollary 15, if the code rate of C_{in} increases, the price of distributing databases using C increases. Therefore, the lower the price of distributing a database, the less collusion resistance the database owner deals with.

References

1. White House. Big Data: Seizing Opportunities, Preserving Values (2014)
2. Financial Times. Digital hunter-gatherers (2013). http://www.ft.com/intl/cms/s/0/f840dbc0-d34f-11e2-b3ff-00144feab7de.html#axzz3eS2n1CZx
3. The Guardian. How much is your personal data worth? (2014). http://www.theguardian.com/news/datablog/2014/apr/22/how-much-is-personal-data-worth
4. Forbes. The black market price of your personal info (2010). http://www.forbes.com/2010/11/29/black-market-price-of-your-info-personal-finance.html

5. Gantz, J., Reinsel, D.: The digital universe in 2020: big data, bigger digital shadows, and biggest growth in the far east. IDC iView: IDC Analyze Future **2007**, 1–16 (2012)
6. Kieseberg, P., Schrittwieser, S., Mulazzani, M., Echizen, I., Weippl, E.: An algorithm for collusion-resistant anonymization and fingerprinting of sensitive microdata. Electron. Markets **24**(2), 113–124 (2014)
7. Motwani, R., Xu, Y.: Efficient algorithms for masking and finding quasi-identifiers. In: Proceedings of the Conference on Very Large Data Bases (VLDB), pp. 83–93 (2007)
8. Lodha, S.P., Thomas, D.: Probabilistic anonymity. In: Bonchi, F., Malin, B., Saygın, Y. (eds.) PInKDD 2007. LNCS, vol. 4890, pp. 56–79. Springer, Heidelberg (2008)
9. Sweeney, L.: Achieving k-anonymity privacy protection using generalization and suppression. Int. J. Uncertain., Fuzziness Knowl.-Based Syst. **10**(05), 571–588 (2002)
10. Sweeney, L.: k-anonymity: a model for protecting privacy. Int. J. Uncertain., Fuzziness Knowl.-Based Syst. **10**(05), 557–570 (2002)
11. El Emam, K., Dankar, F.K., Isaa, R., Jonker, E., Amyot, D., Cogo, E., Corriveau, J.-P., et al.: A globally optimal k-anonymity method for the de-identification of health data. J. Am. Med. Inform. Assoc. **16**(5), 670–682 (2009)
12. Samarati, P.: Protecting respondents' identities in microdata release. IEEE Trans. Knowl. Data Eng. **13**(6), 1010–1027 (2001)
13. Samarati, P., Sweeney, L.: Protecting privacy when disclosing information: k-anonymity and its enforcement through generalization and suppression. Technical report, SRI International (1998)
14. Schrittwieser, S., Kieseberg, P., Echizen, I., Wohlgemuth, S., Sonehara, N., Weippl, E.: An algorithm for k-anonymity-based fingerprinting. In: Shi, Y.Q., Kim, H.-J., Perez-Gonzalez, F. (eds.) IWDW 2011. LNCS, vol. 7128, pp. 439–452. Springer, Heidelberg (2012)
15. Willenborg, L., Kardaun, J.: Fingerprints in microdata sets. In: CBS (1999)
16. Bui, T.V., Nguyen, B.Q., Nguyen, T.D., Sonehara, N., Echizen, I.: Robust fingerprinting codes for database. In: Aversa, R., Kołodziej, J., Zhang, J., Amato, F., Fortino, G. (eds.) ICA3PP 2013, Part II. LNCS, vol. 8286, pp. 167–176. Springer, Heidelberg (2013)
17. Bui, T.V., Nguyen, B.Q., Nguyen, T.D., Sonehara, N., Echizen, I.: Robust fingerprinting codes for database using non-adaptive group testing. Int. J. Big Data Intell. **2**(2), 81–90 (2015)
18. Li, Y., Swarup, V., Jajodia, S.: Fingerprinting relational databases: schemes and specialties. IEEE Trans. Dependable Secure Comput. **2**(1), 34–45 (2005)
19. Guo, F., Wang, J., Li, D.: Fingerprinting relational databases. In: Proceedings of the ACM Son Applied Computing, pp. 487–492. ACM (2006)
20. Agrawal, R., Kiernan, J.: Watermarking relational databases. In: Proceedings of the 28th International Conference on VLDB, pp. 155–166 (2002)
21. Forney Jr., G.D.: Concatenated codes. DTIC Document (1965)
22. Reed, I.S., Solomon, G.: Polynomial codes over certain finite fields. J. Soc. Ind. Appl. Math. **8**(2), 300–304 (1960)
23. Wicker, S.B., Bhargava, V.K.: Reed-Solomon Codes and Their Applications. Wiley-IEEE Press, New York (1999)
24. Gilbert, E.N.: A comparison of signalling alphabets. Bell Syst. Tech. J. **31**(3), 504–522 (1952)

25. Varshamov, R.R.: Estimate of the number of signals in error correcting codes. Dokl. Akad. Nauk SSSR **117**(5), 739–741 (1957)
26. Rosvall, M., Bergstrom, C.T.: Maps of random walks on complex networks reveal community structure. Proc. Natl. Acad. Sci. **105**(4), 1118–1123 (2008)
27. McAfee, A., Brynjolfsson, E.: Big data: the management revolution. Harvard Bus. Rev. **90**, 60–68 (2012)
28. Varian, H.R.: Big data: new tricks for econometrics. J. Econ. Perspect. **28**, 3–27 (2014)
29. Wu, X., Zhu, X., Wu, G.-Q., Ding, W.: Data mining with big data. IEEE Trans. Knowl. Data Eng. **26**(1), 97–107 (2014)
30. NSF-NIH Interagency Initiative. Core techniques and technologies for advancing big data science and engineering (BIGDATA) (2012)
31. Google. http://investor.fb.com/releasedetail.cfm?ReleaseID=893395
32. Google. http://www.google.com/zeitgeist/2012/#the-world

A MapReduce Reinforced Distributed Sequential Pattern Mining Algorithm

Xiao Yu[1], Jin Liu[1(✉)], Xiao Liu[2(✉)], Chuanxiang Ma[3], and Bin Li[4]

[1] State Key Laboratory of Software Engineering,
Computer School, Wuhan University, Wuhan 430072, China
xiao.yu213@yahoo.com, jinliu@whu.edu.cn
[2] Shanghai Key Laboratory of Trustworthy Computing,
East China Normal University, Shanghai 200241, China
xliu@sei.ecnu.edu.cn
[3] School of Computer Science and Information Engineering,
Hubei University, Wuhan 430062, China
mxc838@hubu.com
[4] Economics and Management School,
Wuhan University, Wuhan 430072, China
binli.whu@whu.edu.cn

Abstract. Redesign and reimplementation of traditional sequential pattern mining algorithms on distributed computing frameworks are essential for dealing with big data. Along the way, the critical issue is how to minimize the communication overhead of the distributed sequential pattern mining algorithm and maximize its execution efficiency by balancing the workload of distributed computing resources. To address such an issue, this paper proposes a MapReduce reinforced distributed sequential pattern mining algorithm DGSP (Distributed GSP algorithm based on MapReduce), which consists of two MapReduce jobs. The "two-jobs" structure of DGSP can effectively reduce the communication overhead of the distributed sequential pattern mining algorithm. DGSP also enables optimizing the workload balance and the execution efficiency of distributed sequential pattern mining by evenly partitioning the database and assigning the fragments to Map workers. Experimental results indicate that DGSP can significantly improve the overall performance, scalability and fault tolerance of sequential pattern mining on big data.

Keywords: Sequential pattern mining · Big data · Distributed GSP · MapReduce · Reinforced algorithm

1 Introduction

Sequential pattern mining is an important data mining technique that has been widely applied to various applications, such as customer purchase behaviors, Web access pattern prediction, disease diagnosis, network intrusion detection and so on [1]. In these domains, analyzing and mining of big data for novel insights has become a routine task. Traditional sequential pattern mining algorithms are inefficient in dealing with big

© Springer International Publishing Switzerland 2015
G. Wang et al. (Eds.): ICA3PP 2015, Part II, LNCS 9529, pp. 183–197, 2015.
DOI: 10.1007/978-3-319-27122-4_13

data. So there is a trend to redesign and reimplement these algorithms under a distributed computing framework that is better suited for dealing with big data.

Among the recent efforts for building a suitable distributed computing framework for dealing with big data, MapReduce is a popular framework that utilizes machine clusters to handle huge amount of data [2]. MapReduce abstracts computation problems through a map function and a reduce function: the former processes a key/value pair to generate a set of intermediate key/value pairs; the latter merges all intermediate values associated with the same intermediate key [2]. The challenges of solving the task of sequential pattern mining on a distributed platform like MapReduce usually include: (1) how to satisfy the validity of distributed algorithms; (2) how to balance the workloads of distributed computing platforms; (3) how to avoid useless results in local computing nodes; (4) how to reduce the time of aggregating local sequential patterns and getting the final result. For the first challenge, a distributed sequential pattern mining algorithm should compute the support of a candidate sequential pattern over the entire set of sequence database, which actually is partitioned into some database fragments residing on different computing nodes. For the second challenge, balanced workload of the computing nodes guarantees an efficient performance of distributed sequential pattern mining. For the third challenge, in a distributed platform, if the sequence database is partitioned over several computing nodes, useless local sequential patterns from local computing nodes imply inefficient search for desired sequential pattern. In the most serious case, the items contained in some local sequential patterns are not included in global 1-sequential pattern. So how to avoid useless results as early as possible in each worker node is also an important issue. For the last challenge, the local sequential patterns generated by each worker node needs to be aggregated to obtain global sequential patterns. The support count computation of the local patterns for obtaining the global sequential patterns is also time-consuming. How to reduce the time of aggregating local sequential patterns and getting the final result is also important. Considering the above challenges, the critical issue is how to minimize the communication overhead of the distributed sequential pattern mining algorithm and maximize its execution efficiency by adjusting workload balance of distributed computing platforms [3, 4]. This is because most typical distributed sequential pattern mining approaches take an iterative computing job to satisfy their validity [5–8]. Take MapReduce for example, the k-sequential pattern is generated in parallel by the k-th job and passed to the computing job to generate $k + 1$ sequential pattern [6–8]. Master worker has to schedule jobs to initialize each MapReduce jobs, which is pure overhead to the mining task. In most cases, the communication overhead is big because each MapReduce job needs to read the outputs in HDFS (Hadoop Distributed File System) from which the previous MapReduce job writes. Moreover, even if the communication overhead in execution is not prominent, the unbalanced workload may still impair the performance of the distributed sequential pattern mining [3]. Take MR-Prefixspan as an example, it corresponds to a prefixed sequence and parallel constructs the corresponding projected databases in each Map worker to obtain sequential patterns [9]. Reduce workers cannot start until all the Map workers have finished. Because the size of projected databases in each Map worker is various, the computing time of each Map worker is also different. Reduce workers have to wait for the slowest Map worker thus resulting pure waiting overhead.

The major difficulties in handling the issue mentioned above lie in two aspects: the one is to minimize the communication and scheduling overhead while satisfying the validity of distributed sequential pattern algorithm; the other is to balance the workload of each Map worker for distributed sequential pattern mining.

Accordingly, this paper proposes a distributed sequential pattern mining algorithm based on Map-Reduce programming model, named DGSP (Distributed GSP algorithm based on Map-Reduce). DGSP is mainly derived from the related work GSP [10] proposed by Srikant. The main idea of our work is that: unlike traditional iterative distributed algorithms [6–8], our algorithm contains only two MapReduce jobs, which significantly reduces the communication and scheduling overhead. For the "two-jobs" structure of DGSP, the first job executes the algorithm WordCount [11] based on MapReduce to get global 1-sequential pattern for avoiding useless results as early as possible in Map workers. For the second job, the Master worker partitions a sequence database into n same size fragments for workload balancing and assigns these fragments to Map workers. Each Map worker uses global 1-sequential pattern to generate candidate 2-sequential pattern and executes algorithm GSP that scans database fragments in memory to generate local sequential patterns. The Reduce worker merges local sequential patterns generated by Map workers to obtain the global sequential patterns.

The main tasks of our work involve: (1) reviewing and analyzing original GSP algorithm to extend it to distributed sequential pattern mining algorithm. (2) proposing DGSP, i.e., the novel MapReduce reinforced sequential pattern mining algorithm, to realize sequential pattern mining on big data; (3) analyzing the time complexity and communication overhead of DGSP; (4) conducting experiments on test datasets to verify whether DGSP can significantly improve the overall performance of sequential pat-tern mining on big data.

Compared with its rivals, the contributions of the proposed DGSP algorithm mainly include:

(1) DGSP can overcome the high communication and scheduling overheads of traditional distributed sequential pattern mining algorithms while still guaranteeing the validity of the distributed algorithm;
(2) DGSP can balance the workload of Map workers to significantly improve the overall performance of the distributed sequential pattern mining.
(3) DGSP can abandon useless local computing results in time to optimize the performance of the distributed sequential pattern mining.

The remainder of this paper is organized as follows. Section 2 presents the related work. Section 3 reviews the traditional GSP algorithm and then Sect. 4 proposes our novel DGSP algorithm. Section 5 conducts the analysis on time complexity and communication overhead. Section 5 demonstrate the experimental results which show that the proposed DGSP can significantly improve the overall performance, scalability and fault tolerance of sequential pattern mining on big data. Finally, Sect. 6 addresses the conclusion and points out the future work.

2 Related Work

In this section, we briefly review traditional sequential pattern mining algorithm running on a single machine and then focus on the distributed algorithms. Traditional sequential pattern mining algorithms can be categorized into three main types: Apriori-based [10, 12, 13], projection-based [14, 15] and vertical format-based [16].

AprioriAll [12] is the earliest sequential pattern mining algorithm proposed by Agrawal and Srikant. The following year they generalized the problem to include time constraints, user-specified time window, user-defined taxonomy, and presented improved algorithm GSP [10]. To quickly find all sequential patterns in large dataset, SPAM [13] utilizes a novel depth-first search strategy combined with a vertical bitmap representation of the entire database which needs completely fit into main memory with efficient support counting. The biggest drawback of the Apriori-based algorithms is multiple scans of database to discover all sequential patterns. FreeSpan [14], PrefixSpan [15] utilize the construction of projected databases and don't require candidate generation to discover sequential pattern. But if the minimal support is low, they need to generate large number of projected databases in sequential pattern mining. SPADE [16] uses efficient lattice search techniques and simple join operations to discover sequential pattern in only three database scans. However, the transformation into vertical format requires both time and more memory space. These algorithms running on a single processor struggle to dealing with big data in a time constraint, although the performance of these algorithms has been gradually enhanced. To overcome the challenge, searchers have proposed several distributed sequential pattern mining algorithms.

Two parallel formulations of a serial sequential pattern discovery algorithm based on tree projection are proposed in [5]. FMGSP [17] uses a lexicographic sequence tree and an efficient pruning strategy to obtain the global sequential patterns. The work in [18] presents two efficient Apriori implementations of Frequent Itemset Mining (FIM) that utilize new-generation graphics processing units. The work in [19] presents paralleled GSP algorithm for graphics processing units. These parallel algorithms are mainly implemented on shared memory systems or multiprocessor systems, thus requiring huge development and maintenance efforts.

MapReduce programming model on the cloud provides new ideas for the implement of the distributed algorithms. DPSP [6] is the first sequential pattern algorithm for progressive databases based on MapReduce. In this algorithm, the input data is divided into many progressive windows and it performs the process of candidate generation on many worker nodes independently. After the candidate patterns are generated, each worker node assembles supports of candidate sequential patterns. SPAMC [7], which is derived from the prior SPAM algorithm, utilizes an iterative MapReduce framework to efficiently generate and prune candidate patterns when constructing the lexical sequence tree. BIDE-MR [8] is the parallel implementation of BIDE algorithm on MapReduce to mine closed sequential pattern. It iteratively assigns the tasks of closure checking and pruning to different nodes in cluster. After one round of map-combine-partition-reduce, the closed frequent sequences with round-specific length and the candidates for the next round of computation are generated. One major drawback of these algorithms is that it needs to proceed through numerous rounds of MapReduces jobs, which will easily cause high communication and scheduling overhead. MR-PrefixSpan [9] is derived from PrefixSpan. Mining tasks in MR-PrefixSpan are decomposed to many small tasks, the Map function is used to mine each Prefix-Projected sequential pattern, the Reduce function processes intermediate results of each prefix by means of specification to obtain global sequential patterns. One major drawback of MR-PrefixSpan is unbalanced workload of Map workers, because the size of projected databases in each Map worker is different, the computing time of each Map worker is also different.

3   A Review of GSP

Definition 1: Let $I = \{i_k, k = 1, 2, \ldots, m\}$ be a set of m different items. We call a subset $X \subset I$ an itemset. A sequence is an ordered list of itemsets. We denote a sequence $S = <s_1, s_2, \ldots, s_n>$, where $s_i \subset I$. The number of items contained in S is defined as the length of a sequence. A sequence with length l is called an l-sequence.

Definition 2: A sequence database D is a set of tuples (Sid, S), where Sid is a sequence-id, S is a sequence. The number of sequences in D is defined as $|D|$.

Definition 3: A sequence $\alpha = <a_1, a_2, \ldots a_n>$ is contained in another sequence $\beta = <b_1, b_2, \ldots b_m>$ where $a_i \subset I, b_i \subset I$ if there are integers $1 \leq j_1 < j_2 < \ldots <j_n \leq m$ such that $a_1 \subset b_{j1}, a_2 \subset b_{j2}, \ldots, a_n \subset b_{jn}$. If sequence α is contained in sequence β, then we call α a subsequence of β, and β contains α.

Definition 4: The support count of a sequence S in a sequence database D is defined as the number of sequences that contain S, and the support of a sequence S is defined as the percentage of sequences that contain S. The support of S in D is denoted by $sup_D(S)$. Given a minimal support ξ, a sequence S is called a sequential pattern on D if $sup_D(S) \geq \xi$. A sequential pattern with length k is called a k-sequential pattern and defined as L_k. We will divide the original sequence database D into n database fragments $D_1, D_2, \ldots D_n$ below. The sequential pattern with minimal support ξ in D_i is called local sequential pattern. The local sequential pattern with length k is defined as LL_k.

The sequential pattern mining problem can be then defined as following. Given an input sequence database D and a minimal support ξ, find all sequences patterns with support equal to or bigger than ξ in D.

The basic structure of the GSP algorithm for finding sequential pattern is as follows. The algorithm makes multiple database passes. In the first pass, all single items are counted to find L_1. From L_1, a set of candidate 2-sequences (C_2) are formed, and another pass is made to identify their frequency to find L_2. The L_2 are used to generate the candidate 3-sequence (C_3), and this process is repeated until no more frequent sequences are found. There are two main steps in candidate generation.

Join Phase. C_k are generated by joining L_{k-1} with L_{k-1}. A sequence s_1 joins with s_2 if the subsequence obtained by dropping the first item of s_1 is the same as the subsequence obtained by dropping the last item of s_2. The candidate sequence generated by joining s_1 with s_2 is the sequence s_1 extended with the last item in s_2.

Prune Phase. We delete candidate sequence, at least one of whose subsequence is not frequent.

The time complexity of the first database pass to generate L_1 is $O(|D|*L)$, where L is the maximum length of the sequences. In the further passes, the time complexity of join phase is $O(|L_k|*|L_k|)$, the time complexity of prune phase is $O(|C_k|)$, the time complexity of scanning the sequence database to generate sequential pattern is $O(|D|*|C_k|)$. In the worst of condition, the time complexity of GSP algorithm is $T(GSP) = O(|D| * L) + O(\sum_{k \geq 2} |L_k| * |L_k| + |C_k| + |D| * |C_k|)$.

4   DGSP Algorithm

The above analysis shows that the time complexity of GSP mainly focuses on scanning the database repeatedly. When sequence database cannot be entirely loaded in main memory, GSP requires scanning the sequence database stored in disk repeatedly thus IO overhead is huge. To avoid the barrier, the paper proposed the DGSP algorithm based on MapReduce.

DGSP algorithm partitions a sequence database into n same size database fragments, each of which has the same number of sequences. So it enables the balanced workload of worker node to significantly improve the overall performance. The

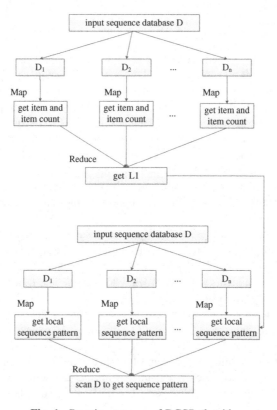

Fig. 1. Running process of DGSP algorithm

database fragments also need to be able to be stored in main memory for only scanning the database fragments in main memory, thus reducing the IO overhead. Figure 1 demonstrates the running process of DGSP. DGSP includes two MapReduce jobs, which can effectively reduce the communication and scheduling overheads.

The first MapReduce job executes algorithm WordCount [11] based on MapReduce to get global 1-sequential pattern for avoiding useless results as early as possible in Map workers. It mainly includes two steps as follows.

Step 1: Master worker distributes n same size database fragments to Map workers. Each Map worker counts the items in the database fragments to get the local support count of items.

Step 2: Reduce worker merges all items and the local support count of the items to find the item with the minimal support, that is L_1.

The Map function and Reduce function of the first MapReduce job is as follows.

Algorithm 1. Map function of the first MapReduce job

Input
D_i: the database fragments
Output
<key, value>: key is the item, value is the the local support count of the item on each Map worker
```
1:for each sequence S in D_i
2:   increment the count of all items that are contained
in S;
3:end for;
4:output<the item, the local support count of the item
on each Map worker>;
```

Algorithm 1. Reduce function of the first MapReduce job

Input
<key, values>: key and values come from the Map function
ξ: the minimal support
Output
<the item, the support count of the L_1>
```
1:sum=0;
2:for each value in values
3:   sum+=value;
4:   if(sum>ξ*|D_i|)
5:      output<the item, sum>;
6:end for;
```

Lemma 1: Let original sequence database D be partitioned into n same size database fragments, denoted as $D = \{D_1, D_2, ..., D_n\}$. The sequential pattern with minimal support ξ in D_i is called local sequential pattern. Sequential pattern L_k of the original sequence database is a subset of the union of all local sequential patterns LL_k of the database fragments.

Proof by contradiction: Assume sequential pattern S of the original sequence database is not a local sequential pattern of any database fragments. Let x_i be the support count of S on the i-th sequence database, then the support count of X on the original sequence database is $\sum_{i=1}^{n} xi$. If S is not a local sequential pattern of any database fragments, then the support count of S on each sequence database is less than the minimal support of each database fragment, that is $x_i < \xi *(|D|/n)$, so $\sum_{i=1}^{n} xi < n*\xi *(|D|/n) = \xi *|D|$. This contradicts the assumption. So sequential pattern L_k of the original sequence database is a subset of the union of all local sequential patterns LL_k of the database fragments.

According to Lemma 1, the second MapReduce job can find all sequential patterns. It mainly includes two steps as follows.

Step 1: Master worker partitions n same size database fragments to Map workers. Each Map worker uses global I-sequential pattern to generate candidate 2-sequential pattern, and then execute the original GSP algorithm to scan database fragments in main memory to generate local sequential patterns. Because the n database fragments are the same size, it guarantees the computing time of each Map worker is almost equal, thus keeping the workload balanced.

Step 2: Reduce worker merges all local sequential patterns generated by Map workers. For the local sequential patterns which don't exist in every Map worker, Reduce worker scans the original sequence database to calculate the support of them and obtains the final sequential patterns. And for the local sequential patterns exist in every Map worker, Reduce worker only needs to merge the support counts of the local sequential patterns, thus reducing the time of gaining global sequential patterns.

The Map function and Reduce function of the second MapReduce job is as follows.

Algorithm 2. Map function of the second MapReduce job

Input
D_i: the database fragments
L_I: the global I-sequential pattern
ξ: the minimal support
Output
<key, value>: key is the LL_k, value is the support count of LL_k

```
1:C₂= genCandidate (L₁)
2:for each sequence S in Dᵢ
3:   increment the count of all candidates in C₂ that are
contained in S;
4:   LL₂ =candidates in C₂ with ξ*|Dᵢ|;
5:end for
6:for(k=3; LLₖ₋₁≠ ∅; k++) do
7:   Cₖ =genCandidate (LLₖ₋₁);
8:   for each sequence S in Dᵢ
9:      increment the count of all candidates in Cₖ that
are contained in S;
10:    LLₖ =candidates in Cₖ with ξ*|Dᵢ|;
11:   end for
12:output<LLₖ, the support count of LLₖ>;
13:end for
```

Algorithm 2. Reduce function of the second MapReduce job

Input

<key, values>: key and values come from the Map function

ξ: the minimal support

Output:<L_k, the support count of L_k>

```
1:if(values.size==n)//n is the number of Map workers
2:   sum=0;
3:   for each value in values
4:      sum+=value;
5:      output(key,sum);
6:   end for
7:else
8:for each sequence S in D
9:   increment the count of key that is contained in S;
10:end for
11:if(the support count of LLk>=ξ*|D|)
12:   output(key, the support count of key);
```

Compared with distributed sequential pattern mining algorithms that adopt iterative MapReduce jobs, DGSP contains only two MapReduce job, so the communication and scheduling overhead is small.

5   Experiment and Result Analysis

The experimental platform is a Hadoop [20] cluster of 5 machines (1 Master, 4 DataNodes). Each machine has two single-core processors and 8 GB memory; Software configuration is on Centos 6.6 and Hadoop 2.4. We evaluate the performance of the proposed algorithm DGSP and compare it with the algorithm GSP on four datasets: C20D10k, C20D150k, accidents, pumsb. Dataset C20D10k and dataset C20D150k are generated by the IBM Generator [21]. D is the number of sequences in the dataset; C is the average number of itemsets per sequence. Dataset pumsb and dataset accidents dataset are taken from Frequent Itemset Mining Dataset Repository [22]. Dataset pumsb is the census data for population and housing which contains 49046 sequences. Dataset accidents is the anonymized traffic accident data which contains 340,183 sequences.

Experiment 1: In this experiment, we analyze the running time of DGSP and GSP for different minimal support in Hadoop cluster (1 Master and 4 DataNodes) and in a single-machine environment. The experimental results are shown in Fig. 2a, b, c, d.

Because the running time of DGSP mostly focuses in Map workers of the second MapReduce job, we also analyze the running time of Map workers in the second MapReduce job to test whether DGSP enables the balanced workload of Map workers to achieve optimal performance. The mean and variance of running time of Map workers in the second MapReduce job are presented in Table 1a, b, c, d.

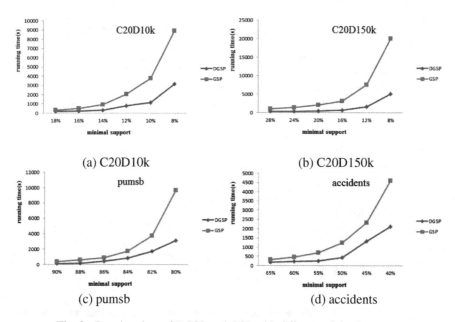

(a) C20D10k   (b) C20D150k

(c) pumsb   (d) accidents

Fig. 2. Running time of DGSP and GSP with different minimal support

Table 1. Statistics of the running time of Map workers in the second MapReduce job

Minimal support	Worker 1 time(s)	Worker 2 time(s)	Worker 3 time(s)	Worker 4 time(s)	Mean	Variance
18 %	78	103	112	114	101.75	14.32
16 %	130	157	171	187	161.25	20.93
14 %	219	246	252	287	251	24.22
12 %	930	946	981	1001	964.5	28.00
(a) C20D10k						
Minimal support	Worker 1 time(s)	Worker 2 time(s)	Worker 3 time(s)	Worker 4 time(s)	Mean	Variance
28 %	115	128	135	144	130.5	10.59
24 %	194	197	200	207	199.5	4.82
20 %	298	304	305	307	303.5	3.35
16 %	477	644	671	688	620	84.04
(b) C20D150k						
Minimal support	Worker 1 time(s)	Worker 2 time(s)	Worker 3 time(s)	Worker 4 time(s)	Mean	Variance
90 %	45	45	50	50	47.5	2.5
88 %	85	89	91	97	90.5	4.33
86 %	384	401	412	427	406	15.70
84 %	455	478	488	497	479.5	15.66

(*Continued*)

Table 1. (*Continued*)

Minimal support	Worker 1 time(s)	Worker 2 time(s)	Worker 3 time(s)	Worker 4 time(s)	Mean	Variance
(c) pumsb						
Minimal support	Worker 1 time(s)	Worker 2 time(s)	Worker 3 time(s)	Worker 4 time(s)	Mean	Variance
65 %	58	60	60	61	59.75	1.09
60 %	99	120	131	136	121.5	14.22
55 %	165	169	169	171	168.5	2.18
50 %	307	307	312	313	309.75	2.77
(d) accidents						

Result Analysis: As we can see in Fig. 2, the running time of both DGSP and GSP will increase along with the decrease of minimal support because the smaller the minimal support is, the more sequential patterns there will be. DGSP adopts the parallel mining tasks for n same size database fragments, it reduces the running time. So the performance of DGSP is more stable along with the decrease of minimal support. As we can see in Table 2, variance analysis indicates that DGSP enables the balanced workload of Map workers to achieve optimal performance.

Experiment 2: In this experiment, we test the running time of DGSP with different number of DataNodes. We conduct the experiment on C20D10 k with 10 % minimal support, C20D150k with 12 % minimal support, pumsb with 80 % minimal support and accidents with 40 % minimal support. The experimental results are shown in Fig. 3.

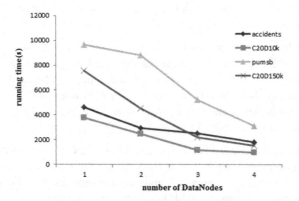

Fig. 3. Running time of DGSP with different number of DataNodes

Result Analysis: In Hadoop cluster, the running time is proportionally decreased with the number of DataNodes increasing. Because the running time is affected by data transmission between machines, it will not be fully proportional to the number of Datanodes. Nevertheless, it can be observed that more machines can greatly enhance the efficiency performance, meaning that DGSP has good scalability in MapReduce platform.

Experiment 3: In this experiment, we generate five synthetic datasets each containing 50k to 250k input sequences. We analyze the running time of DGSP and GSP for different size of test datasets in Hadoop cluster (1 Master and 4 DataNodes) and in the single machine environment. The experimental results are shown in Fig. 4.

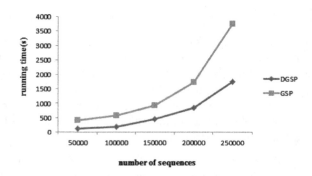

Fig. 4. Running time of DGSP and GSP with different number of sequences

Result Analysis: When scale of dataset increases, the running time of DGSP and GSP will increase proportionally to the size of the dataset. But for DGSP, as shown in Fig. 4, its running time only increases slightly along the size of the dataset because of the distributed sequential pattern mining strategy.

Experiment 4: In this experiment, we test the reliability of DGSP. We conduct the experiment on C20D10k with 10 % minimal support, C20D150k with 16 % minimal support, pumsb with 84 % minimal support and accidents with 50 % minimal support. When a DataNode is shut down in Hadoop cluster (1 Master and 4 DataNodes), test DGSP algorithm whether it can run normally and gains the right result. The experimental results are shown in Fig. 5.

Result Analysis: In the single machine, if a machine fails to work, the whole mining task of GSP algorithm will fail. When a DataNode fails to work in the Hadoop cluster, DGSP can still complete the mining task and gain the right result, although the overall running time increases. It shows DGSP has good fault tolerance.

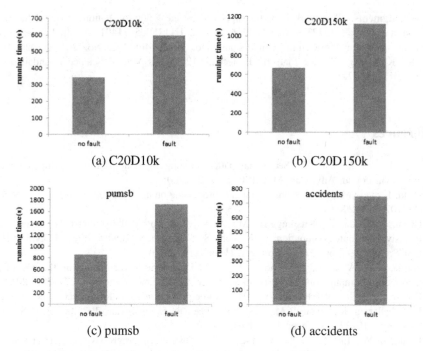

Fig. 5. Running time of DGSP with no fault and fault

6 Conclusion and Future Work

Currently, there are many efforts dedicated to the redesign and reimplementation of traditional sequential pattern mining algorithms on a distributed computing framework that is better suited for dealing with big data. However, they usually overlooked the problem of how to minimize the communication overhead of the distributed sequential pattern mining algorithm and maximize its execution efficiency given unbalanced workload. To address such a problem, in this paper, we proposed a reinforced distributed sequential pattern mining algorithm based on MapReduce. Compared with its existing rivals, the "reinforcement" of DGSP embodies at least two aspects: its "two-jobs" structure effectively reduces communication overhead of the distributed sequential pattern mining algorithm; it maximizes the execution efficiency of distributed sequential pattern mining by evenly partitioning the database to guarantee balanced workload. The experimental results indicated the feasibility and the effectiveness of the proposed DGSP. In the future, we will try to improve the performance of our distributed sequential pattern mining algorithms by employing the Spark [23] RDD framework that has an advanced DAG (Directed Acyclic Graph) excution engine and supports in-memory computing.

Acknowledgments. This work is partly supported by the grants of National Natural Science Foundation of China (61572374, 61070013, 61300042, U1135005, 71401128), the Fundamental Research Funds for the Central Universities (No. 2042014kf0272, No. 2014211020201), Shanghai Knowledge Service Platform Project (ZF1213) and Natural Science Foundation of HuBei (2011CDB072).

References

1. Han, J., Pei, J., Yan, X.: Sequential pattern mining by pattern-growth: principles and extension. Found. Adv. Data Min. **180**, 183–220 (2005)
2. Dean, J., et al.: MapReduce: simplified data processing on large clusters. Commun. ACM **51** (1), 107–113 (2008)
3. Groot, S., Goda, K., Kitsuregawa, M.: A study on workload imbalance issues in data intensive distributed computing. In: Kikuchi, S., Sachdeva, S., Bhalla, S. (eds.) DNIS 2010. LNCS, vol. 5999, pp. 27–32. Springer, Heidelberg (2010)
4. Sarma, A.D., Afrati, F.N., Salihoglu, S., et al.: Upper and lower bounds on the cost of a map-reduce computation. In: Proceedings of the VLDB Endowment, pp. 277–288 (2013)
5. Guralnik, V., Garg, N., Karypis, G.: Parallel tree projection algorithm for sequence mining. In: Sakellariou, R., Keane, J.A., Gurd, J.R., Freeman, L. (eds.) Euro-Par 2001. LNCS, vol. 2150, pp. 310–320. Springer, Heidelberg (2001)
6. Huang, J.-W., Lin, S.-C., Chen, M.-S.: DPSP: distributed progressive sequential pattern mining on the cloud. In: Zaki, M.J., Yu, J.X., Ravindran, B., Pudi, V. (eds.) PAKDD 2010. LNCS, vol. 6119, pp. 27–34. Springer, Heidelberg (2010)
7. Chen, C.C., Tseng, C.Y., Chen, M.S.: Highly scalable sequential pattern mining based on MapReduce model on the cloud. In: 2013 IEEE International Congress on Big Data, pp. 310–317 (2013)
8. Yu, D., Wu, W., Zheng, S., Zhu, Z.: BIDE-based parallel mining of frequent closed sequences with MapReduce. In: Xiang, Y., Stojmenovic, I., Apduhan, B.O., Wang, G., Nakano, K., Zomaya, A. (eds.) ICA3PP 2012, Part II. LNCS, vol. 7440, pp. 177–186. Springer, Heidelberg (2012)
9. Wei, Y.Q., Liu, D., Duan, L.S.: Distributed PrefixSpan algorithm based on MapReduce. In: 2012 International Symposium on Information Technology in Medicine and Education, pp. 901–904 (2012)
10. Srikant, R., Agrawal, R.: Mining sequential pattern: generalizations and performance improvements. In: Apers, P., Bouzeghoub, M., Gardarin, G. (eds.) EDBT 1996. LNCS, vol. 1057, pp. 1–17. Springer, Heidelberg (1996)
11. WordCount. http://wiki.apache.org/hadoop/WordCount
12. Agrawal, R., Srikant, R.: Mining sequential pattern. In: 11th International Conference on Data Engineering, pp. 3–14 (1995)
13. Ayres, J., Gehrke, J., Yiu, T., et al.: Sequential pattern mining using a bitmap representation. In: Proceedings of the Eighth ACM SIGKDD International Conference on Knowledge Discovery and Data Mining, pp. 429–435 (2002)
14. Han, J., Pei, J., Mortazavi-Asl, B., et al.: FreeSpan: frequent pattern-projected sequential pattern mining. In: Proceedings of the 6th ACM SIGKDD International Conference on Knowledge Discovery and Data Mining, pp. 355–359 (2000)
15. Pei, J., Han, J., Pinto, H.: PrefixSpan: mining sequential pattern efficiently by prefix-projected pattern growth. In: 17th International Conference on Data Engineering, pp. 215–224 (2001)

16. Zaki, M.: SPADE: An efficient algorithm for mining frequent sequences. Mach. Learn. **41** (2), 31–60 (2001)

17. Zhang, C., Hu, K., Liu, H.: FMGSP: an efficient method of mining global sequential pattern. In: 4th International Conference on Fuzzy Systems and Knowledge Discovery, pp. 761–765 (2007)

18. Fang, W., Lu, M., Xiao, X., et al.: Frequent itemset mining on graphics processors. In: Proceedings of the 5th International Workshop on Data Management on New Hardware, pp. 34–42 (2009)

19. Hryniow, K.: Parallel pattern mining - application of GSP algorithm for graphics processing units. In: 13th International Carpathian Control Conference, pp. 233–236 (2012)

20. Hadoop Website. http://hadoop.apache.org/

21. SPMF. http://www.philippe-fournier-viger.com/spmf/index.php?link=datasets.php

22. Frequent Itemset Mining Dataset Repository. http://fimi.ua.ac.be/data/

23. Spark Website. https://spark.apache.org/

SHDC: A Fast Documents Classification Method Based on Simhash

Liang Gu[1,2(✉)], Peng Yang[1,2], and Yongqiang Dong[1,2]

[1] School of Computer Science and Engineering,
Southeast University, Nanjing 211189, China
{guliang,pengyang,dongyq}@seu.edu.cn
[2] Ministry of Education, Key Laboratory of Computer Network
and Information Integration (Southeast University), Nanjing 211189, China

Abstract. In recent years, there have been vast research and remarkable progresses in automatic documents classification which becomes a research focus in information retrieval and data mining field gradually. These studies have achieved some success while still having very great limitations to deal with abundant features of documents. Things get worser especially in the big data environment, where the documents amount is considerably huge. In order to address these challenges, we propose a fast method called Simhash based document classification (SHDC) in this paper. In the method, we first compress the vast features of documents into a certain dimension to reduce the computation, and then generate the features of each category according to the documents belonging to them. At last, we parallelize the most computational expensive step, the feature extraction of documents and categories using the Apache Spark. To show the performance of SHDC, we give theoretic analysis of it and conduct a series of experiments on a real world dataset to evaluate the feasibility and performance of our method. Results show that our method (SHDC) outperform other methods in classification precision and temporal efficiency. Meanwhile, SHDC possesses good scalability as the number of computation nodes increases.

Keywords: Documents classification · Simhash · Feature · Big data · Spark

1 Introduction

The classification of documents into predefined categories has witnessed a booming interest in these years, on account of the dramatically increased availability of digital documents and the subsequent need to manage them. It plays a significant role in many applications e.g. web searching, Email filtering, relevance feedback, personalized recommendation and others. The performance of classification methods can be weighed by two critical criterions, precision and speed. The former focuses on if the documents are classified into the proper category while the latter concerns more about the efficiency of the methods especially in the online or big-data environment. According to these targets, researchers have put forward many methods including SVM [1, 2], Bayes [3, 4], linear classification [5], and kNN [6], etc.

Among the above methods, SVM possesses better performance in precision by overcoming the negative factors (e.g., sample distribution, redundant features and

© Springer International Publishing Switzerland 2015
G. Wang et al. (Eds.): ICA3PP 2015, Part II, LNCS 9529, pp. 198–212, 2015.
DOI: 10.1007/978-3-319-27122-4_14

over-fitting problem) via constructing a hyperplane or set of hyperplanes in a high or infinite dimensional space and minimizing the functional margin. Besides that, SVM has a better generalization ability compared to other methods. However, due to its complex model, SVM needs lots of time and memory and converges slowly on large datasets. Although some improving methods are proposed to cope with this problem, they cannot solve it fundamentally.

Different from SVM, the models of other methods such as Bayes, linear classification and kNN are simple relatively, thus converging at a faster speed. To obtain a better performance, researchers also proposed many improved methods. [7] proposes a self-adaptive attribute weighting method for Naive Bayes classification using immunity theory in Artificial Immune Systems to search optimal attribute weight values and hence improves classification accuracy. [8] makes an effort to combine principal component analysis (PCA) and linear discriminant analysis (LDA) to feature reduction. The experimental results show that the combination method performs well in classification ability and speed. Different from them, [9] presents a scalable non-linear feature mapping method based on a deep neural network pretrained with Restricted Boltzmann Machines for improving kNN classification in a large-margin framework. The proposed method in [9] can be used for both classification and supervised dimensionality reduction possessing a better performance than linear large-margin kNN. These proposed methods either combine existing methods or use some techniques to optimize them. As a consequence, the improving methods can achieve good performance under some conditions. However, generally speaking, they tend to perform better than SVM in speed while lacking competitiveness mildly in classification precision.

Due to the limitations of existing classification methods including SVM, Bayes and others, a new fast and effective method is required to satisfy the demand of the big data environment. Hashing methods can perform highly efficient data processing and have gained great success in many data mining applications such as content-based image retrieval [10, 11], near-duplicate detection [12, 13], etc. Hashing methods project high-dimensional objects to low-dimensional ones and retain the object inherent features [14].

In this paper, we assume that documents belong to the same category should have similar features and the features of the categories can be generated by dealing with the features of the documents belonging to it.

With this assumption, in this paper, we propose a Simhash based documents classification method (SHDC) for fast and effective documents classification. Unlike SVM, Bayes and other methods, SHDC projects the vast documents features into a certain dimension by Simhash technique and generates the features for each category for the following classification process. Moreover, due to the urgent need of dealing with massive documents, we also propose the parallelization strategy for SHDC in big data environment considering its particular advantage. To evaluate our method, we compare it with several typical methods on a large dataset and conduct experiments on the cluster to show its performance with parallelization.

The remainder of this paper is organized as follows. Section 2 briefly provides useful preliminaries. In Sect. 3, we describe our proposed SHDC and its parallelization.

Section 4 evaluates the performance of SHDC via experiments performed on a large dataset, followed by a conclusion in Sect. 5.

2 Preliminaries

To provide a technical context for the discussion, we begin with preliminaries related to our proposed method, including Simhash, TF-IDF and the Spark parallel computing method.

2.1 Simhash

Simhash (SH) is an interesting hashing technique, which is first coined in 2002 by Charikar [14]. SH uses random projections as hash functions to generate compact representation of high-dimensional vectors. Its main characteristic distinguished from other hash methods is that similar objects tend to have similar hash values. For an object w, the hash function can be specified as,

$$h(w) = sign(v^t w) = \begin{cases} +1 & \text{if } v^t w \geq 0 \\ -1 & \text{otherwise} \end{cases} \tag{1}$$

where v^t is the transpose of vector v generated randomly.

2.2 TF-IDF

Term frequency inverse document frequency (TF-IDF) is a numerical statistic that is intended to reflect the importance of a word w to a document d in a collection or corpus D, considering its frequency in the particular document and in the whole corpus [15]. TF-IDF is the product of two statistics, term frequency and inverse document frequency.

In the case of the term frequency, various ways can be adopted to determine its exact value. Among these ways, an augmented frequency has a stable performance due to its preventing the bias towards longer documents as,

$$tf(w, d) = 0.5 + \frac{0.5 \times f(w, d)}{\max\{f(v, d) : v \in d\}} \tag{2}$$

where $f(w, d)$ represents the frequency of word w in the document d and v is the most frequent word.

IDF is used to measure how much information the word w provides, i.e., whether the word is common or rare across D. IDF can be illustrated as follows,

$$idf_{(w,D)} = \log \frac{|D|}{|\{w \in d, d \in D\}| + 1} \tag{3}$$

where $|D|$ is the total number of the corpus and $|\{w \in d, d \in D\}|$ is the number of documents which contains the word w. The denominator is designed to cope with the condition when $|\{w \in d, d \in D\}|$ equals 0.

Once the $tf(w, d)$ and $idf_{w,D}$ are figured out, the final step is to coute the TF-IDF value as,

$$tfidf_{(w,D)} = tf(w, d) \times idf_{w,D} \tag{4}$$

2.3 Spark Parallel Computing Framework

Spark is a distributed computing framework developed at Berkeley AMPLab [16]. It accelerates the big data process by a series of features. The fundamental feature that especially benefits the iterative computations is its in-memory parallel execution model in which data will be loaded into memory from hard disk or Hadoop file system (HDFS). This feature is based on a new distributed memory abstraction, i.e., resilient distributed datasets (RDD) which is an immutable collection of data records [17]. Moreover, Spark provides a variety of built-in operations to transform one RDD to another RDD and caches the contents of the RDDs in memory on the worker nodes, making data reused substantially faster. The operations provided by Spark not only contains map and reduce which are the representative operations of Hadoop, but also some encapsulation of transformations like flatmap, sort, filter and group. All these elements improve the processing performance considerably.

3   The SHDC Method

In this section, we present our proposed SHDC method and its parallelization on Spark. The key point is that how to design the vectors representing each document and category and make the classification more efficient. In addition, to facilitate our discussion, we summarize symbols and notations used in this paper in Table 1.

Specifically, SHDC can be divided into two stages, including feature vector extraction and category determination as showed in Fig. 1. In this paper, the vector of an object (a document or category) is defined as: for object x, $V_x = (f_1, f_2, ..., f_n)$. f_i is the ith feature of the x. In Fig. 1, V_x represents the vector of the document to be classified and $V_1 \sim V_m$ represent the vectors of m categories. The function Sim can be any similarity or correlation function for figuring out the similarity between vectors. In this paper, we adopt the Pearson correlation coefficient (PCC). It should be noted that most computation of SHDC takes place in the stage of feature vector extraction.

3.1 Feature Vector Extraction

As mentioned above, our proposed SHDC can be divided into two stages, feature vector extraction and category determination. Most computation of SHDC takes place

Table 1. Basic Symbols and Notations

Notations	Descriptions
w	Word
d	Document
D	Corpus containing many documents
WordSegment	Split the documents to word strings
$tf(w,d)$	The tf value of word w in document d
$idf_{(w,D)}$	The idf value of word w in corpus D
$tfidf_{(w,D)}$	The tfidf value of word w in corpus D
n	The number of the features compressed for the d or D
$ifvalue$	The data type in final feature vector
V_{ti}	The vector containing tfidf value of each word
h_w	The hash value bits of word w
Hash(w)	The hash function
V_{hb}	The vector containing the hash value of each word
V_c	The vector representing each category c
indicator(w, d)	The flag indicating if word w appears in d

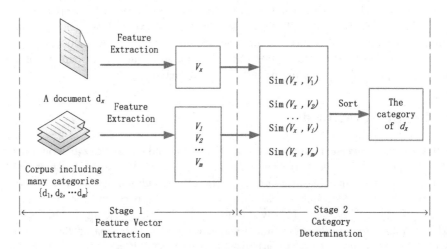

Fig. 1. The SHCD method

in the stage of feature vector extraction. In this section, we introduce the basic and parallelized feature vector extraction respectively.

Basic Feature Vector Extraction. The detail of basic feature extraction algorithm is illustrated in Algorithm 1. In Algorithm 1, we mainly introduce the process of feature extraction for the corpus. As to a document, the algorithm process is identical to the process for corpus expect for line 18 to line 19 and line 24 $\sim$ 26, where the vector V_c should be replaced by V_d.

We first compute the weights of each word in documents by the TF-IDF method, which is one of the best-known methods for specifying the weight of each word in

Information Retrieval (Phase A). Then, the hash bits of each word are computed, which are the basis of Simhash. In this paper, we adopt the classic MD-5 algorithm (Phase B). At last, based on the previous result, we figure out the feature vectors of each document and each category (Phase C).

Algorithm 1. Basic Feature Extraction Algorithm
Input: D, *ifvalue*, n
Output: V_c (feature vectors of each category)

/* **Phase A** Compute $tfidf_{(w,D)}$ for each word w */
1. Foreach d in D
2.   WordSegment(d)
3.   Compute $tf(w,d)$
4.   Compute $idf_{(w,D)}$
5.   Compute $tfidf_{(w,D)}$
6.   Put $tfidf_{(w,D)}$ in vector V_{ti}
7. EndForeach
  /* **Phase B** Compute $h_w(n$ bits) for each word w */
8. Foreach d in D
9.   While (w in d)
10. h_w= Hash(w)
11.   Put into vector V_{hb}
12.   EndWhile
13. EndForeach
  /* **Phase C** Compute V_c for each category c. If *ifvalue* == 0, the type of the element in V_c is Boolean, or the type is Double   */
14.   Foreach d in D
15.   While (w in d)
16.   For k = {1, 2, ..., h_w.length()}
17.   If (h_w (k) == 0)
18. V_c (k) = V_c (k) - $V_{ti}(w)$
19.   Else V_c (k) = V_c (k) + $V_{ti}(w)$
20.   EndFor
21.   EndWhile
22.   If (*ifvalue* == 0)
23.   For k = {1, 2, ..., V_c.length()}
24.   If (V_c (k) > 0)
25. V_c (k) = 1
26.   Else V_c (k) = 0
27.   EndFor
28.   EndIf
29. EndForeach

At this stage, we have two significant parameters, n and *ifvalue*. n represents the hash bits number and has a great influence on the performance of SHDC. The other parameter *ifvalue* is an option of element type of the vector, boolean or double, to provide an interface controlling the accuracy and convenience of category determination. To be specific, when the option, i.e., the parameter *ifvalue* is "TRUE", the element of vector V_c is in double type, and SHDC will be more accurate. While in the other case, when *ifvalue* is "FALSE", we change the element of V_c to "0" when it is negative and change it to "1" when it is positive. By this mean, SHDC will be more convenient to determinate the categories because we just need to count the same bits between vectors. However, at the same time, the accuracy is slightly weakened than the former case. More detailed information about the parameters will be presented in the experiment part.

Parallelized Feature Vector Extraction on Spark. To improve the scalability and efficiency of SHDC in big data environment, we attempt to implement it on Spark platform. Due to the fact that the feature extraction consumes most of the computing resources, our parallelization scheme mainly targets this stage. The algorithm is as shown in Algorithm 2.

This algorithm mainly consists of three phases. The first phase is to preprocess the documents (word segment) and cache them into the RDD for subsequent processing by a series operations of SparkContext. Each line in this raw RDD represents a document with words split. At the second phase, we compute the *n*-bit hash bits h_w for each word and transform the raw RDD to the tfidf RDD by the map and reducedByKey transformations. Each line in the tfidf RDD denotes a document with the tfidf values of each word. The third phase aims to compute the feature vector for each category. We load the tfidf data from the RDD and adjust the vector *Vc* continually according to the tfidf value of each word until all the documents are traversed. Then the feature vectors of each category are finally figured out.

In particular, the computations of each document are independent relatively. This trait of SHDC makes it more convenient to distribute the process tasks to nodes and hence brings the efficient parallelization.

Algorithm 2. Parallelized Feature Extraction Algorithm

Input: *D*, *ifvalue*, *n*

Output: V_c (feature vectors of each category)

/* **Phase** 1 Process corpus *D* and read the processed
documents into the RDD   */

1. Foreach *d* in *D*
2.   WordSegment(*d*)
3.   Save as HDFS file
4. EndForeach
5. Create a Sparkcontext
6. Read file from HDFS to a Spark RDD named *RDD*(raw)
7. *RDD*(raw) = *RDD*(raw).map(_.split(" ")).toSeq
8. *RDD*(raw).cache()
   /* **Phase** 2 Compute h_w(*n* bits) for each word *w* and
   transform *RDD*(raw) to *RDD*(tfidf)   */
9.   Foreach *w* in *d*
10.   *w* => (*w*, 1)
11.   indicator(*w*, *d*) = 1
12. h_w= Hash(*w*)
13.   EndForeach
14.   *RDD*(tf) = (*w*, 1).reducedByKey(_+_)

15. For(w in D)
16.   For(d in D)
17.   If(indicator(w, d) = 1)
18.   indicator(w, d) => (w, 1)
19.   EndIf
20.   EndFor
21. EndFor
22. RDD(idf) = (w, 1).reducedByKey(_+_)
23. RDD(tfidf) = RDD(tf) * RDD(idf)
    /* **Phase** 3 Compute V_c for each category c. If *ifvalue* == 0, the type of the element in V_c is Boolean, or the type is Double   */
24. RDD(tfidf).collect()
25. Foreach x in RDD(tfidf).collect()
26.   Foreach y in x
27.   If (tfidf(y) > 0)
28. h_w= Hash($y.getWord$)
29.   For j = {1, 2, ..., V_c.length()}
30.   If ($h_w(j)$ == 1)
31. $V_c(j) = V_c(j)$ + tfidf(y)
32.   Else $V_c(j) = V_c(j)$ - tfidf(y)
33.   EndIf
34.   EndFor
35.   EndIf
36.   EndForeach
37. EndForeach
38. If (*ifvalue* == 0)
39.   For k = {1, 2, ..., V_c.length()}
40.   If ($V_c(k)$ > 0)
41. $V_c(k)$ = 1
42.   Else $V_c(k)$ = 0
43.   EndFor
44. EndIf

3.2   Category Determination

Once we obtain the feature vectors of each document and category, at Stage 2 we focus on determining the category. The determination algorithm is illustrated in Algorithm 3. At this stage, we mainly attempt to compute the similarity between the feature vector of the document to be processed and the vectors of existing categories. Obviously, the target document will be classified into the category which has the largest similarity with it. The Sim function is the PCC method as illustrated in Eq. (6). For V_x and V_m, the vector of document x and category m, the similarity between them is,

$$\text{Sim}(V_x, V_m) = \frac{\sum_i (V_{x,i} - \bar{V}_x)(V_{m,i} - \bar{V}_m)}{\sqrt{\sum_i (V_{x,i} - \bar{V}_x)^2} \sqrt{\sum_i (V_{m,i} - \bar{V}_m)^2}} \tag{5}$$

where $V_{x,i}$ is ith feature of V_x, and $\bar{V}_x$ is the average of all the features in V_x

---

Algorithm 3. Category Determination Algorithm
Input: a document vector V_x and a set of vectors of each category, $V_1,\ldots V_m$
Output: the category V_x belongs to

---

1. num, sim = 0
2. For $i = \{1, 2, \ldots, m\}$
3.   If($Sim(V_x, V_m) > sim$)
4.   sim = (V_x, V_m)
5.   num = m
6.   End If
7. EndFor
8. Return m

3.3   Theoretic Analysis

In this section, we will give the theoretic analysis of our proposed SHDC to show its correctness and rationality. We will firstly introduce the hyperplane hashing method and its proof. Then, we will attempt to show that SHDC is fundamentally a hyperplane hashing problem and thus illustrating its correctness and rationality theoretically.

Hyperplane hashing method is proposed to solve the high-dimensional nearest neighbor problem. Let $v_1,\ldots, v_j$ be j random vectors with n dimensions. For a vector v with n dimensions, its f-bits hash value can be generated using Hyperplane hashing method with two critical steps: generate j random vectors and compute the dot product of the v and each random vector v_i, i.e., the value of the ith bit of the hash value sequence of v.

This method has been proved to be correct and effective. Note that the dot product between a vector and the random vector is used to figure out the projection of the vector over the random vector. The detailed proof can be found in [18]. For brevity, in this paper, we demonstrate the relation between SHDC and hyperplane hashing method as follows.

As illustrated above, in SHDC, we use the frequency of words in document as the features of it. For a document d including n features $f_1, f_2, \ldots, f_n$, it can be represented by a weight vector $w_d = (w_1, w_2, \ldots w_n)$ in which each element is the corresponding weight of the feature in d. Feature f_i can be hashed with common hash function and represented by a vector $h_{fi} = (h_{fi1}, h_{fi2}, \ldots, h_{fij})^T$ and our goal is to generate the j-bits simhash value for d. Assume that the j-bits simhash value of the document d can be represented by the vector $s_d = (s_{d1}, s_{d2}, \ldots, s_{dj})$, then, for element s_{di} in s_d, we will have

$$s_{di} = w_d \cdot v_i \qquad (6)$$

Essentially, in this equation, w_d is the weight vector of d. v_i is i^{th} vector from the j vectors with n dimensions and $v_i = (h_{f1i}, h_{f2i}, \ldots, h_{fni})$. That is to say, the ith vector is composed of all the ith hash value bits of the n features. By the computation of the dot product of the vector w_d and vectors u_i, we can obtain the ith bit of the simhash value of d. Obviously, this is the same as the second step of the hyperplane hashing method. Put it another way, the j vectors constructed by the hash values of features are exactly the random vectors generated in hyperplane hashing method.

4 Experimental Evaluation

In this section, experimental setup and experimental results for evaluating the performance of SHDC are presented. We use SogouC.reduced Dataset, a common dataset in document classification to conduct the experiments. This dataset contains nine categories and 1990 documents in each category.

The following aspects are evaluated in the experiments:

(1) Within-class and among-class similarity.
(2) Classification precision of SHDC and other typical methods.
(3) Running time of basic SHDC and other methods on a PC, running time of parallelized SHDC on the cluster (SHDC_cluster).
(4) Scalability Performance of SHDC_cluster while nodes number varies.

The experiments for basic SHDC are performed on a PC with an Intel Core i7-2600 CPU and 8 GB memory. While the cluster for evaluating the parallelization of SHDC consists of one master node and three slave nodes, where each node has 64 GB memory. When running the task, to improve the processing ability of slave nodes, we also make the master node work as a slave node, i.e., there will be four slave nodes available. The Spark platform is version 1.3.1.

Table 2. Within-class and Among-class Similarity of SHDC When *ifvalue* is False or True

n	32	48	64	80	96	112	128
W-false	0.098	0.095	0.096	0.097	0.097	0.101	0.104
A-false	0.019	0.021	0.028	-0.01	0.027	0.044	0.043
W-true	0.147	0.143	0.141	0.143	0.144	0.144	0.145
A-true	0.05	0.045	0.052	0.055	0.054	0.053	0.053

4.1 Within-Class and Among-Class Similarity

To evaluate the effectiveness of our proposed SHDC, we firstly vary the number of extracted feature n (from 32 to 128) and then measure the within-class and among-class similarity of SHDC under both conditions when *ifvalue* is false or true. The results can be observed in Table 2. From the table, it is not hard to infer that, SHDC may clearly differentiate the categories in all the cases (different *ifvalue* and n) due to the large gaps between within-class and among-class.

4.2 Classification Precision

Based on the results in the previous section, in this section, we firstly evaluate the performance of the proposed SHDC in terms of classification precision among different categories. Table 3 illustrates the condition when ifvalue is FALSE (SHDC_bits), i.e., the feature vector is composed of "0" and "1". The condition when ifvalue is TRUE (SHDC_values) is depicted in Table 4.

Table 3. Classification Precision of SHDC_bits (*ifvalue* is FALSE)

n \ CAT	32	48	64	80	96	112	128
1	0.688	0.667	0.681	0.809	0.821	0.837	0.842
2	0.575	0.622	0.631	0.68	0.732	0.784	0.825
3	0.611	0.64	0.682	0.721	0.767	0.814	0.853
4	0.609	0.652	0.694	0.729	0.774	0.821	0.865
5	0.601	0.591	0.602	0.681	0.733	0.765	0.792
6	0.645	0.655	0.671	0.777	0.811	0.839	0.841
7	0.637	0.64	0.656	0.761	0.792	0.816	0.828
8	0.594	0.61	0.657	0.683	0.735	0.781	0.829
9	0.622	0.652	0.666	0.711	0.752	0.78	0.813
avg	0.620	0.637	0.66	0.728	0.769	0.804	0.832

Table 4. Classification Precision of SHDC_values (*ifvalue* is TRUE)

n \ CAT	32	48	64	80	96	112	128
1	0.717	0.728	0.73	0.753	0.835	0.876	0.921
2	0.701	0.709	0.727	0.745	0.763	0.812	0.865
3	0.638	0.701	0.723	0.737	0.772	0.834	0.881
4	0.576	0.67	0.691	0.692	0.767	0.817	0.869
5	0.673	0.697	0.688	0.691	0.749	0.807	0.859
6	0.726	0.749	0.756	0.781	0.835	0.886	0.932
7	0.725	0.728	0.747	0.772	0.825	0.881	0.929
8	0.653	0.687	0.716	0.718	0.797	0.823	0.875
9	0.689	0.715	0.749	0.765	0.829	0.864	0.905
avg	0.678	0.709	0.725	0.739	0.797	0.844	0.893

From Tables 3 and 4, we can observe that as the number of extracted feature n increases (from 32 to 128), the classifications of SHDC in both occasions become more and more precise. Besides that, the SHDC_values tends to have a better classification result than SHDC_bits. The essence behind this phenomenon is that to SHDC_bits, we turn the feature value from double number to boolean type. Furthermore, features with different double values may have the same boolean values. Hence we lose some semantic information in this process.

To investigate the efficiency of SHDC furthermore, we then compare it to two typical methods: SVM-based method [2] and Bayes-based method [7]. The SHDC result is obtained when n equals 128. Comparison results are showed in Fig. 2. As we can see in the figure, SHDC_values outperforms the other methods in all categories. Although SVM based method shows higher precision than Bayes based method and even than SHDC_bits sometimes, its precision is roughly three percent lower than SHDC_values at average.

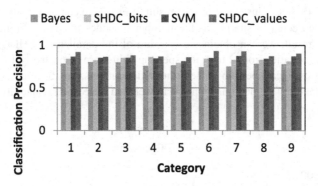

Fig. 2. Precision comparison of SHDC with other methods

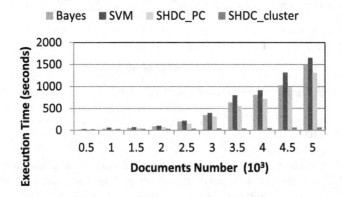

Fig. 3. Running time of different methods

4.3 Running Time Comparison of Different Methods

Figure 3 shows the running time of different methods with corpuses containing different numbers of documents from SogouC.reduced Dataset. As SHDC_value cost more time than SHDC_bits, to show the superiority of SHDC, we compare SHDC_value with other methods, renamed as SHDC_PC. In particular, the SHDC_cluster in Fig. 3 denotes the parallelized SHDC performed on cluster with four nodes. As illustrated in the figure, SHDC_PC outperforms SVM-based and Bayes-based methods in execution speed. Besides that, although SHDC_cluster consumes even more time than other methods when the dataset is small, its superiority becomes more and more remarkable as the size of the dataset scales up. When the corpus contains 5000 documents, SHDC_cluster is approximately 23 times faster than Bayes-based method and 25 times faster than SVM-based method.

4.4   Scalability Performance of Parallelized SHDC

The experiments in this section mainly focus on the scalability performance of parallelized SHDC (SHDC_cluster). From the result in Fig. 4 we can intuitively see that, the execution time decreases sharply as the number of nodes increases. Furthermore, by analysing the result, we can obtain the speedup of the parallelized SHDC. When the number of nodes varies from 2 to 4, the speedup values are respectively 1.68, 2.38 and 3.02, close to the ideal speedup values (the node numbers, i.e., 2, 3 and 4). All these results show that SHDC method can perform well and have good scalability in big data environment.

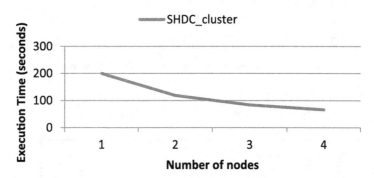

Fig. 4. Scalability performance of parallelized SHDC of datasets containing 5000 documents

5   Conclusion

In this paper, we have proposed a Simhash based documents classification method, named SHDC for efficient documents classification. The main idea of SHDC is to project the large amount of document features into a certain dimension using Simhash technique and generate the features of each category for classification. Moreover, to improve the scalability and efficiency of SHDC in big data environment, we also propose the parallelization strategy for it in Spark platform. Besides that, we give theoretical analysis of SHDC to illustrate its rationality. Finally, the experimental results demonstrate that SHDC significant improves the classification precision and speed over existing methods and shows good scalability in big data environment.

Our future work will focus on optimizing the extraction of the documents features and the presentation vector for each category to improve the classification precision. We also plan to study the data transformation of RDD to speed up the method furthermore.

Acknowledgments. This work is supported by National High Technology Research and Development Program (863 Program) of China under grant no. 2013AA013503, the National Science Foundation of China under grants No. 61472080, No. 61272532, the Consulting Project of Chinese Academy of Engineering under grant 2015-XY-04 and Collaborative Innovation Center of Novel Software Technology and Industrialization.

References

1. Forman, G.: BNS feature scaling: an improved representation over tf-idf for svm text classification. In: Proceedings of the 17th ACM Conference on Information and Knowledge Management, pp. 263–270 (2008)
2. Zhang, W., Yoshida, T., Tang, X.: Text classification based on multi-word with support vector machine. Knowl.-Based Syst. **21**(8), 879–886 (2008)
3. Andrés-Ferrer, J., Juan, A.: Constrained domain maximum likelihood estimation for naive Bayes text classification. Pattern Anal. Appl. **13**(2), 189–196 (2010)
4. Zhang, W., Gao, F.: An improvement to naive bayes for text classification. Procedia Engineering **15**, 2160–2164 (2011)
5. Kauermann, G., Ormerod, J.T., Wand, M.P.: Parsimonious classification via generalized linear mixed models. J. Classif. **27**(1), 89–110 (2010)
6. Zhang, X., Song, Q.: Predicting the number of nearest neighbors for the k-NN classification algorithm. Intell. Data Anal. **18**(3), 449–464 (2014)
7. Wu, J., Pan, S., Zhu, X., Cai, Z., Zhang, P., Zhang, C.: Self-adaptive attribute weighting for Naive Bayes classification. Expert Syst. Appl. **42**(3), 1487–1502 (2015)
8. Ali, J.B., Saidi, L., Mouelhi, A., Chebel-Morello, B., Fnaiech, F.: Linear feature selection and classification using PNN and SFAM neural networks for a nearly online diagnosis of bearing naturally progressing degradations. Eng. Appl. Artif. Intell. **42**, 67–81 (2015)
9. Min, R., Stanley, D., Yuan, Z., Bonner, A., Zhang, Z.: A deep non-linear feature mapping for large-margin knn classification. In: Proceedings of 9th IEEE International Conference on Data Mining, pp. 357–366 (2009)
10. Kulis, B., Jain, P., Grauman, K.: Fast similarity search for learned metrics. IEEE Trans. Pattern Anal. Mach. Intell. **31**(12), 2143–2157 (2009)
11. Ke, Y., Sukthankar, R., Huston, L., Ke, Y., Sukthankar, R.: Efficient near-duplicate detection and sub-image retrieval. ACM Multimedia **4**(1), 5 (2004)
12. Manku, G.S., Jain, A., Das Sarma, A.: Detecting near-duplicates for web crawling. In: Proceedings of the 16th International Conference on World Wide Web, pp. 141–150 (2007)
13. Costa, G., Manco, G., Ortale, R.: An incremental clustering scheme for data de-duplication. Data Min. Knowl. Disc. **20**(1), 152–187 (2010)
14. Charikar, M.S.: Similarity estimation techniques from rounding algorithms. In: Proceedings of the 34th Annual ACM Symposium on Theory of Computing, pp. 380–388 (2002)
15. Hong, T.P., Lin, C.W., Yang, K.T., Wang, S.L.: Using TF-IDF to hide sensitive itemsets. Appl. Intell. **38**(4), 502–510 (2013)

16. Zaharia, M., Chowdhury, M., Franklin, M.J., Shenker, S., Stoica, I.: Spark: cluster computing with working sets. In: Proceedings of the 2nd USENIX Conference on Hot Topics in Cloud Computing, vol. 10, p. 10 (2010)
17. Zaharia, M., Chowdhury, M., Das, T., Dave, A., Ma, J., McCauley, M., Stoica, I.: Resilient distributed datasets: a fault-tolerant abstraction for in-memory cluster computing. In Proceedings of the 9th USENIX Conference on Networked Systems Design and Implementation, p. 2 (2012)
18. Har-Peled, S., Indyk, P., Motwani, R.: Approximate nearest neighbor: towards removing the curse of dimensionality. Theory Comput. **8**(1), 321–350 (2012)

Identification of Natural Images and Computer Generated Graphics Using Multi-fractal Differences of PRNU

Fei Peng[1]([✉]), Yin Zhu[1], and Min Long[2]

[1] School of Computer Science and Electronic Engineering,
Hunan University, Changsha 410082, China
eepengf@gmail.com, zhuyinyin2009@qq.com
[2] College of Computer and Communication Engineering,
Changsha University of Science and Technology, Changsha 410014, China
longm@qq.com

Abstract. Comparing with computer generated graphics, natural images have higher self-similar and have more delicate and complex texture. Thus, the distribution of multi-fractal dimensions and singular index of natural images general have large variation range. Based on this, multi-fractal spectrum features of photo response non-uniformity noise (PRNU) are used for the identification of natural images and computer generated graphics. 9 dimensions of texture features including the square of the maximum difference in fractal dimension (SMDF), the square of the maximum difference in the singularity indices (SMS) and the variance of fractal dimensions (VF) are extracted from LL, LH, HL sub-bands of PRNU after wavelet decomposition. The identification is accomplished by using LIBSVM classifier. Experimental results and analysis indicate that it can obtain an average identification accuracy of 99.69 %, and it is robust against resizing, JPEG compression, rotation and additive noise.

Keywords: Forensic science · Source identification · Multi-fractal feature · Photo response non-uniformity · Natural images · Computer generated graphics

1 Introduction

With the rapid development of Internet, image processing technologies have been widely used in our daily life. Image editing software, such as Photoshop, MAYA, 3D MAX, Poser, Softimage XSI etc., are very popular, and they are implemented to edit, modify and retouch images for different purposes. As it brings convenience to us, it may also produce negative affect to our society. If high realistic computer generated graphics are used for court evidences, news report, research results and other important fields, it may lead to serious consequences. Therefore, the study of source forensics between natural images and computer generated graphics is of great importance. Compared with computer generated graphics, natural images generally have higher self-similar as well as delicate and complicated texture. Based on this, the difference of multi-fractal features between natural images and computer generated graphics are investigated, and 9 dimensions of features are extracted from the sub-bands of PRNU

© Springer International Publishing Switzerland 2015
G. Wang et al. (Eds.): ICA3PP 2015, Part II, LNCS 9529, pp. 213–226, 2015.
DOI: 10.1007/978-3-319-27122-4_15

after wavelet decomposition. The features are used for the identification of natural images and computer generated graphics.

The rest of the paper is organized as follows. The related works are introduced in Sect. 2. The characteristics of multi-fractal spectrum, the characteristics of PRNU and feature extraction are presented in Sect. 3. The proposed identification method is described in Sect. 4. Experimental results and analysis are provided in Sect. 5. Finally, some conclusions are drawn in Sect. 6.

2   Related Works

2.1   Image Processing Based on Fractal Theory

In 1970s, the concept of fractal was put forward by mathematician Mandelbrot, which compensates the limitation of integer dimension in the description of different objects [1]. Fractal theory provides a new prospective to observe objects, and can represent their diversity and complexity. After that, Peli found that natural images exhibit fractal characteristics [2]. From then on, fractal theory was used for image processing, and has wide application in various fields including astronomy, geography, medicine and computer science.

Fractal dimension is an effective method for describing the texture features of images. Fractal dimension and topological tree characteristics had been implemented for image classification by using linear classifier and the nearest neighbor classifier [3], which effectively improved the identification accuracy of drip paintings. A writer identification method was proposed by Chaabouni et al. based on the extraction of fractal and multi-fractal features from the images of Arabic words [4]. The identification is accomplished by using k-nearest neighbor classifier. In [5], multi-fractal spectrum was used for tissue image classification and retrieval. The results show its efficiency and good discriminating capability. Besides, fractal dimension was also integrated with intensity feature for the segmentation of natural images [6]. The combination of different features provides the segmented results similar to the ones by a human visual system.

2.2   Image Source Identification Based on Fractal Dimension

In recent years, fractal dimension has been implemented for the identification of natural images and computer generated graphics [7–10]. Ng et al. pointed out that the natural image is not smooth and the texture is complex. Moreover, it has a unique Gamma correction during the image acquisition process, while the computer generated graphics are composed by simple geometric models [7]. Based on this rationale, fractal dimension with the best scale and differential geometric features with the intermediate scale are used to represent the differences of them. With 192 dimensions of features, it obtained an average identification accuracy of 83.5 %. After that, Pan proposed a method to discriminate natural images and computer generated graphics by using fractal geometry [8]. 20 dimensions of fractal dimension features and 10 dimensions of general dimension features are extracted as identification features. By using a SVM classifier, an average identification accuracy of 92 % was obtained. A blind identification method for photorealistic computer graphics based on fractal dimensions was proposed in [9]. Fractal dimensions are extracted from image's gradient image, prediction error matrix and the whole image in HSV (Hue, Saturation, Value) color space. By using 41 dimensions of features and LIBSVM classifier, an average detecting accuracy of 92 % was obtained. In order to further improve the identification accuracy, Peng et al. proposed an image source identification method based on three aspects of hybrid features [10]. Statistical features in the spatial and wavelet domain, fractal dimension features in the spatial and wavelet domain, and statistical characteristics, fractal dimension, median of RGB (red, green, blue) channels in sensor pattern noise. With 48 dimensions of features and LIBSVM classifier, the identification accuracy for natural images was 97.3 %, but that for computer generated graphics was only 91.28 %.

2.3 Image Source Identification Based on Multi-fractal Features

As fractal dimension is an overall characteristic of the image, it cannot effectively represent the complex structure of the image from microcosmic point of view. In order to overcome this shortcoming, multi-fractal is proposed to describe the characteristics of image. In 2004, multi-fractal spectrum is used by Li et al. for analyzing material structure [11]. It provides a quantitative analysis and explanation of material structure from multi-fractal perspective. After that, Pu et al. proposed to apply multi-fractal features for image recognition [12]. With 8 dimensions of features, it can achieve an average identification accuracy of 80 % on an image database containing 3 categories, with a total of 200 images.

Recently, multi-fractal features have been implemented for the identification of natural images and computer generated graphics. Peng et al. proposed to identify photographic images and photorealistic computer graphics using multi-fractal spectrum features of PRNU [13]. 8 dimensions of multi-fractal spectrum features are extracted from the sub-bands of PRNU after wavelet decomposition. By using a LIBSVM classifier, it can obtain an average identification accuracy of 99 % for computer generated graphics, and that for natural images is 98.99 %.

Except identification of natural images and computer generated graphics based on fractal and multi-fractal features, some methods based on statistical features in wavelet transform domain [14, 15], space domain [16] and contourlet transform domain [17] were also put forward, and reasonable performance was achieved.

From the above analysis, it can be seen that multi-fractal features are indeed effective for the identification of natural images and computer generated graphics. Here, based on the work in [13], the multi-fractal spectrum of PRNU after wavelet decomposition is deeply investigated, and some more distinguishable multi-fractal features are extracted to discriminate natural images and computer generated graphics.

3 PRNU and Its Multi-fractal Spectrum

3.1 Extraction of PRNU

PRNU is described as a digital fingerprint of natural images, and it is a kind of sensor noise produced during the generation of the natural image [18–20]. A pixel value is composed of the ideal pixel value, multiplicative noise and additive noise, which can be described as:

$$Y = f((1+k) \cdot I) + N \tag{1}$$

where Y represents the actual pixel value, I represents the ideal pixel value which reflects the natural scene, N represents all kinds of additive noise during the generation of the image, $f(\cdot)$ represents a variety of camera processing, k represents PRNU coefficient, and represents multiplicative noise, namely the theoretical expression of PRNU.

In order to extract the PRNU, the image is first pre-processed by a Gaussian high-pass filter to filter out additive noise with Gaussian distribution. It can be described as:

$$I' = I - G(I) \tag{2}$$

where $G(\cdot)$ is a Gaussian high-pass filter, and I' is an image without additive noise. As the natural image's acquisition process is mainly focused on the center of the camera, it means that the center block generally contains the most of the information. Thus, the extraction of PRNU is executed on the center block of the image. Here, I'_c with a size of 256×256 are extracted from I'. PRNU are respectively extracted from R, G, B three channels according to:

$$DWT(n) = DWT(I'_c) - F(DWT(I'_c)) \tag{3}$$

where $DWT(\cdot)$ represents the discrete wavelet transform and $F(\cdot)$ represents a wiener filter.

Since PRNU is generally contaminated in the process of camera processing, it is enhanced in wavelet domain by using a mathematical model proposed in [21]. The enhancement operation is described as:

$$n_e = DWT^{-1}(F_e(DWT(n))) \tag{4}$$

where $F_e(\cdot)$ represents the enhancement operation, $DWT^{-1}(\cdot)$ represents an inverse discrete wavelet transform, and n_e represents the enhanced PRNU.

3.2   Multi-fractal Spectrum of PRNU

Given an image I, it is first partitioned into $\sigma \times \sigma$ non-intersect blocks, and the probabilistic testing function of each block is defined as:

$$P_i(\sigma) = \frac{\sum_{c_i(\sigma)} I(m,n)}{\sum I(m,n)} \tag{5}$$

where $c_i(\sigma)$ represents the ith block, $I(m,n)$ represents the pixel of the image. $\sum_{c_i(\sigma)} I(m,n)$ represents the sum of the pixels in the ith block, $\sum I(m,n)$ represents the sum of pixels in the whole image.

The normalized probability measure of the qth order moment of the block is defined as:

$$u_i(q, \sigma) = \frac{p_i^q(\sigma)}{\sum p_i^q(\sigma)} \tag{6}$$

For a given image block, $u_i(q, \sigma)$ is decreased with the increase of q because of $p_i(\sigma) < 1$. When $\sigma \to \infty$, singularity exponent and multi-fractal spectrum [22] can be simplified as:

$$\begin{cases} \alpha(q) & = & \lim\limits_{\sigma \to 0} \dfrac{\sum u_i(q,\sigma) \times \ln(p_i(\sigma))}{\ln(\sigma)} \\ f(\alpha(q)) & = & q\alpha(q) + \tau(q) = \lim\limits_{\sigma \to 0} \dfrac{\sum u_i(q,\sigma) \times \ln u_i(q,\sigma)}{\ln(\sigma)} \end{cases} \tag{7}$$

where $\tau(q) = -\lim\limits_{\sigma \to 0} \dfrac{\ln \sum p_i^q(\sigma)}{\ln(\sigma)}$. $\alpha(q)$ and $f(\alpha(q))$ can be calculated by using the least square matching algorithm with difference σ.

As indicated in [23], Eq. (7) satisfies the requirements of singularity exponent and multi-fractal spectrum, so it can be naturally obtained $df/d\alpha = q$. Thus, Eq. (7) satisfies the criterion for multi-fractal spectrum.

Based on the above analysis, PRNU has the characteristic of the multi-fractal spectrum.

3.3   Feature Extraction

In order to select effective identification features, some natural images and computer generated graphics are randomly selected for analysis. Here, four groups of natural images and computer generated graphics with similar contents are shown in Fig. 1. When computer multi-fractal spectrum as c(1)–c(4) in Fig. 1, $\sigma = 2^1, 2^2, 2^3, \ldots, size(I)$, q is arranged from $[-1,1]$ and the interval is 0.1.

As seen from Fig. 1, the range of singularity exponents of natural images is generally larger than those of the computer generated graphics. Meanwhile, the fluctuating interval of fractal dimension of natural images is larger than that of computer generated graphics. This phenomenon indicates that the texture of the computer generated graphics is simpler and smoother than that of the natural image.

Based on this, three kinds of features are extracted from the multi-fractal spectrum of PRNU.

(1) Square of the maximum difference in fractal dimension (SMDF)

The maximum difference in fractal dimension of image reflects the change degree of the image texture, and the square operation will highlight this difference. It is defined as:

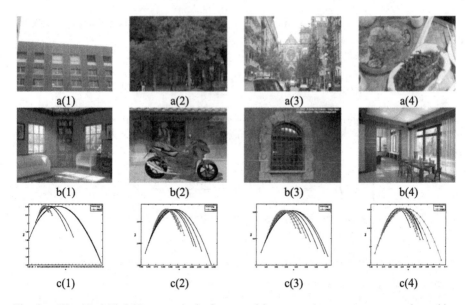

Fig. 1. a(1)–a(4), b(1)–b(4) respectively for natural images and computer generated graphics, c(1)–c(4) are fractal spectrum from LL, LH, HL sub-bands

$$\Delta_{SMDF} = (f(\text{max}) - f(\text{min}))^2 \tag{8}$$

where $f(\text{max})$ represents the maximum fractal dimension of these fractal dimensions after calculate the multi-fractal spectrum, and $f(\text{min})$ represents the smallest fractal dimension.

(2) Square of the maximum difference in singularity indices (SMS)

The difference between the singularity indices corresponding to the maximum and minimum fractal dimensions reflects the difference of the inhomogeneity of probability measure on a fractal structure, and the square operation will highlight the difference. Thus, SMS is selected as a feature for identification, and it is defined as:

$$\Delta_{SMS} = (\alpha(f(\text{max})) - \alpha(f(\text{min})))^2 \tag{9}$$

where $\alpha(f(\text{max}))$ represents the singularity indices corresponding to the maximum fractal dimensions, and $\alpha(f(\text{min}))$ represents the singularity indices corresponding to the minimum fractal dimensions.

(3) Variance of the fractal dimensions (VF)

As seen from Fig. 1, natural image and computer generated graphic have significant difference in the multi-fractal dimensions. Here, the variance between fractal dimensions is extracted as an identification feature, and it is defined as:

$$\Delta_{VF} = \text{var}(f) \tag{10}$$

where $\text{var}(f)$ represents variance of fractal dimension.

Δ_{SMDF}, Δ_{SMS} and Δ_{VF} of the images in Fig. 1 are listed in Table 1.

Table 1. Characteristics value of natural images and computer generated graphics

		a(1)	a(2)	a(3)	a(4)	b(1)	b(2)	b(3)	b(4)
LL	$\Delta_{SMDF}(10^{-4})$	13.53	46.37	41.48	8.53	0.46	0.37	1.23	0.45
	$\Delta_{SMS}(10^{-4})$	47.14	170.35	157.87	29.27	1.71	1.38	4.56	1.70
	$\Delta_{VF}(10^{-4})$	1.04	3.60	3.34	0.65	0.04	0.03	0.11	0.04
LH	$\Delta_{SMDF}(10^{-4})$	6.25	2.88	3.78	2.76	0.78	1.41	0.99	0.94
	$\Delta_{SMS}(10^{-4})$	24.26	11.55	15.39	10.58	3.05	5.46	3.90	3.72
	$\Delta_{VF}(10^{-4})$	0.58	0.29	0.40	0.26	0.08	0.13	0.10	0.09
HL	$\Delta_{SMDF}(10^{-4})$	2.01	2.58	2.34	1.35	0.42	0.64	0.70	1.03
	$\Delta_{SMS}(10^{-4})$	7.87	10.40	9.48	5.24	1.64	2.52	2.73	4.01
	$\Delta_{VF}(10^{-4})$	0.20	0.27	0.25	0.13	0.04	0.06	0.07	0.10
HH	$\Delta_{SMDF}(10^{-4})$	1.48	4.78	3.22	3.74	2.23	2.78	7.76	4.59
	$\Delta_{SMS}(10^{-4})$	5.65	16.50	10.74	14.59	8.80	10.92	31.35	18.71
	$\Delta_{VF}(10^{-4})$	0.14	0.36	0.24	0.37	0.22	0.27	0.78	0.48

where LL, LH, HL, HH each represent proximate component, horizontal component, vertical component and diagonal component after wavelet decomposition.

As seen from Table 1, it can be found that Δ_{SMDF}, Δ_{SMS} of the natural image are generally larger than those of the computer generated graphics in LL, LH, HL sub-bands. However, the difference in HH sub-band is subtle. Thus, 3 dimensions of features are extracted from LL, LH, HL sub-bands, respectively. Thus, 9 dimensions of features are extracted from PRNU.

4   Description of the Proposed Scheme

The identification processes include feature extraction (as shown in Fig. 2) and classification (as shown in Fig. 3).

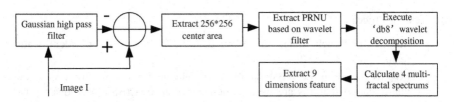

Fig. 2. Feature extraction process

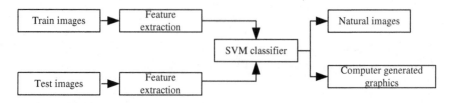

Fig. 3. Classification process

4.1   Feature Extraction

Step 1: Given an image I, Gaussian high-pass filter is first done to I according to Eq. (2), and then I' is obtained;

Step 2: A center block with a size of 256 × 256 is extracted from R, G, B channels respectively. According to Eq. (3), $DWT(n)$ is obtained;

Step 3: Enhancement is done to $DWT(n)$ and then get the enhanced PRNU n_e in RGB color space;

Step 4: 2-dimensions one-level wavelet decomposition with 'db8' is performed to the grayscale version of n_e and the multi-fractal spectrum is calculated from LL, LH, HL sub-bands, respectively;

Step 5: Δ_{SMDF}, Δ_{SMS} and Δ_{VF} are extracted from the multi-fractal spectrum. Thus, 9 dimensions of identification features are extracted.

4.2   Classification

The image database is partitioned into training dataset and testing dataset with a certain ratio. The training dataset is used to train the LIBSVM classifier to get the best classification model. The testing dataset is used to test the identification accuracy by using the classification model. In the experiment, the label of the natural images is 1, while the label of the computer generated is −1. The process can be described as follows:

(1) Training process

> **Step 1:** For each image in training dataset, 9 dimensions of identification features are extracted;
>
> **Step 2:** All extracted identification features are used to train LIBSVM, and 5 fold cross validation is executed to find the optimal parameters and obtain the classification model.

(2) Testing process

> **Step 1:** For each image in testing dataset, 9 dimensions of identification features are extracted;
>
> **Step 2:** Based on the classification model obtained in the training process, the identification features are used as odd the input of LIBSVM to discriminate whether they are natural images or computer generated graphics.

5   Experimental Results

Experiments are performed on MATLAB R2010a, python and gnuplot. The image database include 3000 natural images (800 of them are from the image library of Columbia University [24], and the others are from Dresden Image Database) and 3000 computer generated graphics (1200 of them are from Columbia University Image Database [24], 1200 of them are from the Dresden Image Database [25], and the others are from our image library). LIBSVM classifier is used for classification. To guarantee the randomness of the experiments, the image database is randomly divided into a training dataset with 4500 images and a testing dataset with 1500 images, and the experimental results are the average of five randomized trials. The experimental results are listed in Table 2.

Table 2. Identification accuracies of natural images and computer generated image

No	1	2	3	4	5	AVG
Accuracy (%)	99.40	99.87	99.67	99.73	99.80	99.69

Here, AVG represents the average identification accuracy of 5 trials. As seen from Table 2, an average classification accuracy of 99.69 % is achieved, which indicates the good performance of the proposed scheme.

5.1   Performance Analysis

(1) Comparative analysis

Experiments are done to compare the performance of different identification methods based on multi-fractal features [8, 10, 13], statistical features in wavelet transform domain [15, 16], statistical features in contourlet transform domain [17]. The experimental results are listed in Table 3.

Here, AC represents the average identification accuracy, and AUC represents the area of ROC curve. The ROCs of different methods are shown in Fig. 4.

As seen from Fig. 4, it can be found that the AUC of the proposed method is the largest one among the methods, which indicates its good identification performance. The detailed AUC values are listed in Table 3. The average identification accuracy of the proposed method is 99.69 %, which outperforms those of the existing methods in [8, 10, 13, 15–17]. Comparing to the methods in [8, 10, 13, 15–17], both PRNU features and multi-fractal spectrum features are considered in this paper. The results illustrated the effectiveness of the multi-fractal spectrum features of PRNU in discriminating natural images and computer generated graphics.

(2) Analysis of the sensitivity of the classifiers

In order to analyze the sensitivity of the proposed method to different classifiers, linear discriminant analysis (LDA) classifier is used for the comparison. The experimental results are listed in Table 4.

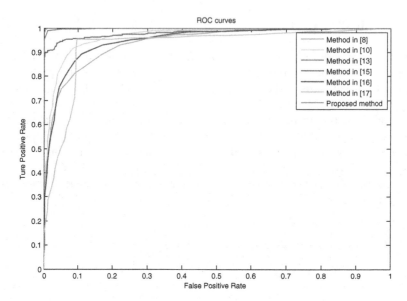

Fig. 4. Comparison of the ROC curves

Table 3. Comparison of experimental results

	[8]	[10]	[13]	[15]	[16]	[17]	Proposed
Feature dimensions	30	48	8	216	234	16	9
AC (%)	87.62	94.29	98.99	92.93	90.64	90.28	99.69
AUC		0.9422	0.9587	0.9978	0.9699	0.9495	0.9265	0.9986

Table 4. Experimental results of different classifier

No	1	2	3	4	5	AVG
LIBSVM (%)	99.40	99.87	99.67	99.73	99.80	99.69
LDA (%)	99.07	98.53	98.40	98.80	99.20	98.80

In LDA linear classifier, high-dimensional samples are projected to the optimal discriminant vector space, which is aimed to reduce the feature dimension and obtain the maximum distance between different categories and the minimum distance within the same category. As seen from Table 4, the average identification accuracy of LDA is only 0.89 % lower than that of LIBSVM classifier with the same training dataset and testing dataset, which indicates that the proposed method is not sensitive to different classifiers.

(3) Analysis of the sensitivity of the size of image center block

As the experimental results depend on the size of center block, comparative experiments are done to image center block with different sizes. The results are listed in Table 5.

Table 5. Experimental results of different image center block size

	Full-size	512 × 512	256 × 256	128 × 128	64 × 64	32 × 32
Accuracy (%)	99.99	99.87	99.80	99.20	96.93	92.27
time (s)	278.58	13.85	7.59	6.08	5.59	5.11

As seen from Table 5, the identification accuracies are decreased as the sizes of the image center block are decreased, which indicates that the size of image center block is relative to the identification accuracy. The main reason is that the texture information of the image is positive proportional to the size of it. When the size is 512 × 512, the identification accuracy is only 0.7 % higher than that of the size of 256 × 256, but the time consumption is nearly twice of it. In order to achieve a balance between the performance and the efficiency, the size of the image center block is recommended as 256 × 256.

(4) Analysis of the ratio between training set and testing set

The ratio between training dataset and testing dataset also have significant influence on the identification results. Here, different ratios are used to evaluate the identification performance. The experimental results are listed in Table 6.

Table 6. Experimental results of sample distribution ratio

Training set:Testing set	1:3	1:2	1:1	2:1	3:1
Accuracy (%)	99.36	99.25	99.70	99.70	99.80

As seen from Table 6, the identification accuracies are varied from 99.25 % to 99.80 % at different ratios. However, the differences are small. It can be found that the proposed method is not sensitive to the ratio between training set and testing set. At the same time, the experiment can achieve the best identification accuracy when the ratio is 3:1, so this ratio is adopted in this paper.

(5) Analysis of robustness

In order to analyze the robustness of the proposed method, different post-processing operations, such as resizing, JPEG compression, rotation and additive Gaussian white noise are made to the images in the experimental dataset. The experimental results are listed in Table 7.

As seen from Table 7, the identification accuracies are all above 99 % when different operations such as adding additive noise, rotation and JPEG compression with different parameters are performed to the testing images. However, the identification accuracy is reduced to 97.4 % when the resizing factor is 1.5, while the identification accuracy can be kept up to 99 % when the resizing factor varied from 0.25 to 1.2. The main reason is that the image size expansion means that an interpolation operation will be performed to the image. As a result, the complex texture structure of natural images will become smooth and simple, which leads to similarity to computer generated

Table 7. Robustness analysis of experimental results

Post-processing operations	Parameters		Accuracy (%)
Resizing	Scaling factor	1.50	97.40
		1.20	99.00
		0.50	99.87
		0.33	99.87
		0.25	99.67
JPEG compression	Quality factor	90	99.67
		80	99.27
		70	99.80
		60	99.67
		50	99.87
		40	99.60
Rotation	Rotation angle	180	99.87
		150	99.60
		120	99.93
		90	99.33
		60	99.73
		30	99.33
Additive noise	SNR	70	99.87
		60	99.80
		50	99.80
		40	99.73
		30	99.60
		20	99.80

graphics. Meanwhile, the size reduction still can keep the complex texture structure of the natural images. From the results listed in Table 7, the proposed method is robust against resizing, JPEG compression, rotation and adding Gaussian white noise.

6   Conclusions

Based on the characteristics of multi-fractal spectrum and PRNU, a more effective method is proposed to identify natural images and computer generated graphics. The experimental results show that the proposed method can achieve very high identification accuracy with only 9 dimensions of features. Furthermore, it is robust against JPEG compression, rotation and additive noise. Our future work will be concentrated on the research of how to improve the identification accuracy of the scaled images.

Acknowledgments. This work was supported in part by project supported by National Natural Science Foundation of China (Grant No. 61572182, 61370225), project supported by Hunan Provincial Natural Science Foundation of China (Grant No. 15JJ2007), supported by the Scientific Research Plan of Hunan Provincial Science and Technology Department of China (2014FJ4161).

References

1. Mandelbrot, B.B.: How long is the coast of Britain. Science **156**(3775), 636–638 (1967)
2. Peli, E.: Contrast in complex images. J. Opt. Soc. Am. A. **7**(10), 2032–2040 (1990)
3. Irfan, M., Stork, D.G.: Multiple visual features for the computer authentication of Jackson Pollock's drip paintings: beyond box counting and fractals. In: SPIE 7251. Image Processing: Machine Vision Applications II, vol. 7251. SPIE (2009)
4. Chaabouni, A., Boubaker, H., Kherallah, M., Stork, D.G.: Fractal and multi-fractal for arabic offline writer identification. In: IEEE International Conference on Pattern Recognition, pp. 3793–3796. IEEE (2010)
5. Mukundan, R., Hemsley, A.: Tissue image classification using multi-fractal spectra. Int. J. Multimedia Data Eng. Manage. **1**(2), 62–75 (2010)
6. Maeda, J., Novianto, S., Miyashita, A., Saga, S., Suzuki, Y.: Fuzzy region-growing segmentation of natural images using local fractal dimension. In: 14th IEEE International Conference on Pattern Recognition, vol. 2, pp. 991–993. IEEE (1998)
7. Ng, T.T., Chang, S.F., Hsu, J., Xie, L.: Physics-motivated features for distinguishing photographic images and computer generated graphics. In: 13th Annual ACM International Conference on Multimedia, pp. 239–248. ACM (2005)
8. Pan, F., Chen, J.B., Huang, J.W.: Discriminating between photorealistic computer graphics and natural images using fractal geometry. Sci. China Series F: Inf. Sci. **52**(2), 329–337 (2009)
9. Lv, Y., Shen, X.J., Wan, G., Chen, H.P.: Blind identification of photorealistic computer generated graphics based on fractal dimensions. In: International Conference on Computer, Communications and Information Technology, Atlantis Press (2014)
10. Peng, F., Liu, J., Long, M.: Identification of natural images and computer generated graphics based on hybrid features. Int. J. Digital Crime and Forensics **4**(1), 1–16 (2012)
11. Li, P., Hu, K.L., Wang, B.H.: Design and application about computing program of material multi-fractal spectrum. J. Nanjing Univ. Aeronaut. Astronaut. **36**(1), 77–81 (2004)
12. Pu, X.Q.: Image Recognition Research Based on Multi-Fractal. Northwestern University, Xi'an (2009)
13. Peng, F., Shi, J.L., Long, M.: Identifying photographic images and photorealistic computer generated graphics using multi-fractal spectrum features of PRNU. In: IEEE International Conference on Multimedia and Expo, pp. 1–6. IEEE (2014)
14. Chen, W., Shi, Y., Xuan, G.: Identifying computer generated graphics using HSV color model and statistical moments of characteristic functions. In: IEEE International Conference on Multimedia and Expo, pp. 1123–1126. IEEE (2007)
15. Lyu, S., Farid, H.: How realistic is photorealistic. IEEE Trans. Sig. Proc. **53**, 845–850 (2005)
16. Shi, Y., Chen, W., Xuan, G., Su, W.: Computer graphics identification using genetic algorithm. In: 19th International Conference on Pattern Recognition, pp. 1–4. IEEE (2008)
17. Wang, R.D., Fan, S.J., Zhang, Y.P.: Classifying computer generated graphics and natural imaged based on image contour information. J. Inf. Comput. Sci. **9**(10), 2877–2895 (2012)
18. Lukas, J., Fridrich, J., Goljan, M.: Digital camera identification from sensor pattern noise. IEEE Trans. Inf. Forensics Secur. **1**(2), 205–214 (2006)
19. Li, C.T., Li, Y.: Color-decoupled photo response non-uniformity for digital image forensics. IEEE Trans. Circuits Syst. Video Technol. **22**(2), 3052–3055 (2010)
20. Dehnie, S., Sencar, T.: Digital image forensics for identifying computer generated and digital camera images. In: IEEE International Conference on Image Processing, pp. 2313–2316. IEEE (2006)

21. Li, C.T.: Source camera identification using enhanced sensor pattern noise. IEEE Trans. Inf. Forensics Secur. **5**(2), 280–287 (2010)
22. Li, H.F.: The Study on Multi-fractal Theory and Application in Image Processing. Northwestern Polytechnical University, Xi'an (2004)
23. Zhou, W.X., Wang, Y.J.: Geometrical characteristics of singularity spectra of multi-fractals: I. Classical Renyi definition. J. East China Univ. Sci. Technol.: Nat. Sci. Ed. **26**(4), 385–389 (2000)
24. Columbia dvmm research lab columbia photographic images and photorealistic computer generated graphics dataset [db/dl] (5 February 2005) [12 August 2008]
25. Dresdem image database. http://forensics.inf.tudresden.de/ddimgdb/locations

Feature Selection Method Based on Feature's Classification Bias and Performance

Jun Wang[1,2], Jinmao Wei[1,2(✉)], and Lu Zhang[1,2]

[1] College of Computer and Control Engineering, Nankai University,
Tianjin 300071, China
[2] College of Software, Nankai University, Tianjin 300071, China
{junwang,luzhang}@mail.nankai.edu.cn, weijm@nankai.edu.cn

Abstract. Feature selection is one of the most important dimension reduction technologies for big data issues. Common feature evaluation criteria measure feature with a global score. There are two shortcomings of this strategy, i.e., partially predominant features submerged and classification redundancies for multi-features estimated inappropriately. In this paper, a new feature selection method based on *Classification Bias* and *Classification Performance* is proposed. Classification bias describes feature's inclination for recognizing instances to each class. And classification performance measures the consistency of classification bias with prior classification information for assessing feature's classification ability. Thus feature is reconstructed as classification performance vector. This vectorization representation of feature's classification ability is beneficial for those partially predominant features winning out. Also multi-features' classification redundancies are easily measured in the new space. Experimental results demonstrate the effectiveness of the new method on both low-dimensional and high-dimensional data.

Keywords: Dimension reduction · Feature selection · Classification bias · Classification performance · Redundancy reduction

1 Introduction

For big data problems, feature selection becomes more important for its effectiveness in reducing dimensionality [1]. It aims at choosing a subset of features for decreasing the size of the structure as well as improving prediction accuracy [2]. Discriminative features are preferred, and evaluation criteria are employed to evaluate their performances. *Mutual Information* (*MI*) [3,4] quantifies how much information is shared by two variables via measuring the divergence of their distributions. Another sequence of probability based criteria is *Information Gain* [5] and its variant *Symmetrical Uncertainty* (*SU*) [6]. Some statistical indices are also utilized for measuring feature's dependency with class, such as *Chi-square Statistic* (*X2*), *T Statistic*, *Gini Index*, etc. *Pearson Correlation Coefficient* (*COR*) is one of the most popular criteria among them. Its variant is *Max Information Compression Index* (*MICI*) [7]. Other criteria, like

© Springer International Publishing Switzerland 2015
G. Wang et al. (Eds.): ICA3PP 2015, Part II, LNCS 9529, pp. 227–240, 2015.
DOI: 10.1007/978-3-319-27122-4_16

Fisher Score [8], *Laplacian Score* [9], and *SPFS* [10], evaluate features via their capabilities in preserving sample similarities.

Feature dependency with the target class and feature redundancy between each other are two key points for feature selection [6,11–13]. Common feature evaluation criteria usually assign each feature with a unified univariate value for assessing its global classification ability [14]. However, there are shortcomings for such evaluation strategy both in measuring feature dependency and feature redundancy. As far as feature dependency is concerned, this strategy commonly forsakes *partially predominant* features. Figure 1 illustrates this problem. It's obvious that none of the feature a_1 and a_2 can split the instance space accurately. Feature a_1 can separate class 1 from class 3 with a certain value, but can't discriminate the instances belonging to class 2. The contrary situation happens to feature a_2. It's also demonstrated in Fig. 1(d) and (e) with histograms. However, instances can be correctly recognized in the space constructed by two features as shown in Fig. 1(c) and (f). It means that two boundaries determined respectively by two features in the space can discriminate all instances belonging to different classes. This attributes to their superior and complementary discriminative abilities specific to different classes. Such abilities are submerged by unified evaluation scores.

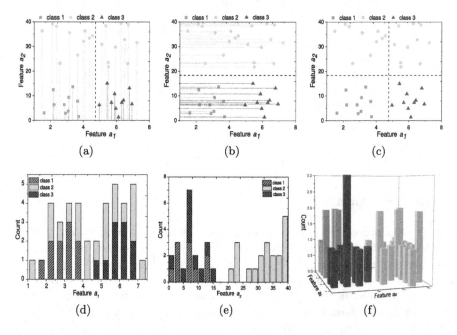

Fig. 1. 2-dimensional instances projected on two features: (a) and (b) are instances' projections on feature a_1 and a_2, and (c) is their separations in the subspace constructed by two features. (d), (e), and (f) are histograms of the three classes respectively projected on a_1, a_2, and the subspace.

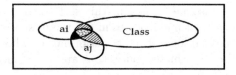

Fig. 2. Correlation of feature $\mathbf{a}_i$ and $\mathbf{a}_j$ in recognizing the class: red point part is their shared classification information, black part is the shared information unrelated with the class, and the shadow parts are two features' independent classification information given respectively (Color figure online).

Secondly, feature redundancy measured via common criteria is also a global value. So multivariate redundant information can't be measured appropriately. Take the popular criterion *MI* for example. Suppose feature subset $\mathbf{S}_M = \{\mathbf{a}_1, \mathbf{a}_2, ..., \mathbf{a}_M\}$. Its feature redundancy is commonly calculated as:

$$Redundancy(\mathbf{S}_M) = \sum_{\mathbf{a}_i, \mathbf{a}_j \in \mathbf{S}_M} I(\mathbf{a}_i; \mathbf{a}_j), \tag{1}$$

where $I(\mathbf{a}_i; \mathbf{a}_j)$ is the mutual information given by feature $\mathbf{a}_i$ and $\mathbf{a}_j$. This measurement is utilized by many popular *MI* based feature selection methods [11,13]. In fact, it's not the actual information for $\mathbf{S}_M$ in recognizing the target class. It is demonstrated in Fig. 2 via venn diagram, where the red point part should be counted excluding the black part, i.e., $I(\mathbf{a}_i; \mathbf{a}_j) - I(\mathbf{a}_i; \mathbf{a}_j | \mathbf{class})$. Strictly speaking, the accurate total redundant classification information is

$$Redundancy(\mathbf{S}_M, \mathbf{class}) = \sum_{\mathbf{a}_i \in \mathbf{S}_M} I(\mathbf{class}; \mathbf{a}_i) - I(\mathbf{class}; \mathbf{a}_1, ..., \mathbf{a}_M). \tag{2}$$

Estimating the latter term of Eq. (2), in which very complicated joint probabilities are involved, is much difficult and time exhausting [15]. So it's intractable for common criteria to measure the multi-feature redundancy for classification.

Aiming at the above problems, a new feature evaluation method is proposed in this paper. *Classification Bias* (*CB*) estimates the possibilities of instances classified to each class when a feature is provided as the observation feature. A feature is discriminative if it assigns a high *CB* weight to the instance's true class as well as low *CB* weights to the other classes. *Classification Performance* (*CP*) measures the consistency of *CB* with prior classification information. It focuses on individual feature's classification ability for a certain class. Thus feature dependency and feature redundancy for classification are both explicitly represented via *CP* vectors rather than unified evaluation values. The proposed method is expected to find the features especially predominant in recognizing some classes. Also the complicated estimation of multi-features' classification redundancy is simplified by measuring the difference of vectors.

The rest of the paper is organized as follows: *Classification Bias* and *Classification Performance* are defined in Sect. 2. Comparisons with popular feature evaluation criteria are also performed in this section. Section 3 presents *CPS* algorithm which searches optimal features in *CP* vector space. Compared experimental results are recorded for testing its performance in both low-dimensional and high-dimensional data. Finally conclusions are drawn in Sect. 4.

2   Feature's Classification Ability

2.1   Classification Bias

Suppose data set $\mathbf{X} = \{\mathbf{x}_j\}_{j=1}^{N}$ characterized by features $\{\mathbf{a}_i\}_{i=1}^{D}$ and classified to classes $\{\mathbf{\Omega}_k\}_{k=1}^{C}$. For class $\mathbf{\Omega}_k$, its instance number is denoted as N_k, center vector $\mu_k = [\mu_{k1}, ..., \mu_{ki}, ..., \mu_{kD}]^T$, where $\mu_{ki} = \frac{1}{N_k} \sum_{\mathbf{x}_j \in \mathbf{\Omega}_k} x_{ji}$, and dispersion vector $\mathbf{\Sigma}_k = [\Sigma_{k1}, ..., \Sigma_{ki}, ..., \Sigma_{kD}]^T$, where $\Sigma_{ki} = \frac{1}{N_k-1} \sum_{\mathbf{x}_j \in \mathbf{\Omega}_k} (x_{ji} - \mu_{ki})^2$.

Definition 1 (Classification Bias, *CB*). *Feature $\mathbf{a}_i$'s classification bias for classifying instance $\mathbf{x}_j$ to class $\mathbf{\Omega}_k$ is defined as:*

$$CB_i(\mathbf{x}_j, \mathbf{\Omega}_k) = \frac{\ln \max_{m=1,...,C} d_i(\mathbf{x}_j, \mu_m) - \ln d_i(\mathbf{x}_j, \mu_k)}{\ln \max_{m=1,...,C} d_i(\mathbf{x}_j, \mu_m) - \ln \min_{m=1,...,C} d_i(\mathbf{x}_j, \mu_m)}, \tag{3}$$

where $d_i(\mathbf{x}_j, \mu_k)$ is the Mahalanobis distance between $\mathbf{x}_j$ and μ_k at the ith dimension, defined as:

$$d_i(\mathbf{x}_j, \mu_k) = \sqrt{\frac{(x_{ji} - \mu_{ki})^2}{\Sigma_{ki}}}, \quad i = 1, ..., D, j = 1, ..., N, k = 1, ..., C. \tag{4}$$

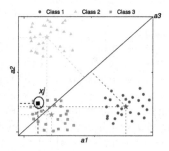

Fig. 3. Instances classified to three classes are projected respectively along the direction of feature $\mathbf{a}_1$, $\mathbf{a}_2$ and $\mathbf{a}_3$.

Figure 3 gives an illustration for *CB*. Each star represents the respective class center. It's noted that the distances of the instance $\mathbf{x}_j$ to μ_k ($k = 1, 2, 3$) are varied when different features are concerned. When instances project on $\mathbf{a}_1$, $\mathbf{x}_j$

is nearer to μ_2 than to the other two class centers. This is denoted by CB as $CB_1(\mathbf{x}_j, \Omega_2) > CB_1(\mathbf{x}_j, \Omega_3) > CB_1(\mathbf{x}_j, \Omega_1)$. So $\mathbf{x}_j$ is more likely classified to Ω_2 when projected on $\mathbf{a}_1$, although this is inconsistent with $\mathbf{x}_j$'s true class information. It's same for $\mathbf{a}_2$. However, $\mathbf{x}_j$ can be correctly discriminated when projected on $\mathbf{a}_3$, which is denoted as $CB_3(\mathbf{x}_j, \Omega_3) > CB_3(\mathbf{x}_j, \Omega_2) > CB_3(\mathbf{x}_j, \Omega_1)$. In fact $\mathbf{a}_3$ is most superior in discriminating the instances belonging to Ω_3 but inferior in the other two classes. $\mathbf{a}_1$ and $\mathbf{a}_2$ have the same properties respectively to Ω_1 and Ω_2. This characteristic is taken as Theorem 1:

Theorem 1. *Suppose* $\mathbf{X}$ *submits to the Gaussian distribution. Let* $p_i(\mathbf{x}_j|\Omega_k)$ *denote the probability of* $\mathbf{x}_j$ *classified to* Ω_k *at the ith dimension. Then* $CB_i(\mathbf{x}_j, \Omega_k)$ *is positively correlated to* $p_i(\mathbf{x}_j|\Omega_k)$.

Proof. $\because$ $\mathbf{X}$ submits to the Gaussian distribution,
$\therefore p_i(\mathbf{x}_j|\Omega_k) = \frac{1}{\sqrt{2\pi}h} \exp\left(-\frac{(x_{ji}-\mu_{ki})^2}{2h^2}\right)$. Let $h = \sqrt{\Sigma_{ki}}$. Then
$p_i(\mathbf{x}_j|\Omega_k) = \frac{1}{\sqrt{2\pi\Sigma_{ki}}} \exp\left(-\frac{(x_{ji}-\mu_{ki})^2}{2\Sigma_{ki}}\right) = \frac{1}{\sqrt{2\pi\Sigma_{ki}}} \exp\left(-\frac{1}{2}d_i^2(\mathbf{x}_j, \Omega_k)\right)$.
$\therefore p_i(\mathbf{x}_j|\Omega_k)$ is negatively correlated to $d_i(\mathbf{x}_j, \Omega_k)$.
According to Definition 1, $CB_i(\mathbf{x}_j, \Omega_k)$ is also negatively correlated to $d_i(\mathbf{x}_j, \Omega_k)$.
$\therefore CB_i(\mathbf{x}_j, \Omega_k)$ is positively correlated to $p_i(\mathbf{x}_j|\Omega_k)$. □

Every feature $\mathbf{a}_i$ in the data set corresponds to a *Classification Bias Matrix* $\mathbf{CM}_i$ whose elements are calculated by Eq. (3). The matrix records the possibilities of all the instances belonging to different classes provided by $\mathbf{a}_i$:

$$\mathbf{CM}_i \triangleq \left[\mathbf{CM}_i^1, ..., \mathbf{CM}_i^k, ..., \mathbf{CM}_i^C\right], \mathbf{CM}_i^k = [CB_i(\mathbf{x}_1, \Omega_k), ..., CB_i(\mathbf{x}_N, \Omega_k)]^T. \tag{5}$$

The vector $\mathbf{CM}_i^k$ represents $\mathbf{a}_i$'s classification bias as to Ω_k, i.e., the possibility of each instance belonging to Ω_k at the ith dimension. The jth row of $\mathbf{CM}_i$ represents $\mathbf{a}_i$'s classification bias to classify instance $\mathbf{x}_j$ to different classes. It's negatively correlated to $\mathbf{x}_j$'s Mahalanobis distance to each class center.

2.2 Classification Performance

For evaluating a feature's classification abilities to different classes, *Classification Performance* is defined by measuring the consistency of CB with instance's prior classification information:

Definition 2 (Classification Performance, CP). *Suppose* $\mathbf{DS}_k = [\mathbf{d}_k^1, ..., \mathbf{d}_k^m, ..., \mathbf{d}_k^C]^T$ *is the distance vector between* Ω_k *and other classes at the ith dimension, where* $\mathbf{d}_k^m = \sqrt{\frac{(\mu_{ki}-\mu_{mi})^2}{\Sigma_i}}, m = 1, ..., C$. $\Lambda_k = [\lambda_1, ..., \lambda_j, ..., \lambda_N]^T$, *where*
$\lambda_j = \begin{cases} 0, & \mathbf{x}_j \in \Omega_k \\ 1, & \mathbf{x}_j \notin \Omega_k \end{cases}, j = 1, ..., N$. *Then Feature* $\mathbf{a}_i$ *'s classification performance for class* Ω_k *is defined as:*

$$CP_i(\Omega_k) = p(\Omega_k) \cdot \|\mathbf{DS}_k\|_1 \cdot \|\mathbf{CM}_i^k - \Lambda\|_2^2, \quad i = 1, ..., D, k = 1, ..., C. \tag{6}$$

CP in Eq. (6) has three terms. The first term $p(\mathbf{\Omega_k})$ is the prior probability of class $\mathbf{\Omega}_k$. Here class imbalance is taken into consideration [16]. When evaluating a feature's classification ability to different classes, the class containing a majority number of inner-class instances is considered superiorly. Also this term is crucial when determining feature's generalized classification ability to all the classes.

The second term focuses on the inter-class scatter. It's a distance measurement for revealing the scatter of the instances from different classes. It is noted that Eq. (6) merely measures the scatter between $\mathbf{\Omega}_k$ and the other classes. The feature maximizing this scatter is regarded most helpful to discriminate $\mathbf{\Omega}_k$.

The last term is a variant of the *Quadratic Loss Function*, which is widely used for estimating the prediction error. For further explaining Eq. (6), *Quadratic Loss of Discriminating a Class* is given:

Definition 3 (Quadratic Loss of Discriminating a Class, QLC). *As feature $\mathbf{a}_i$ serves as the predictor, the quadratic loss of discriminating class $\mathbf{\Omega}_k$ is defined as:*

$$QLC_i(\mathbf{\Omega_k}) = \sum_{j=1}^{N} (p_i(\mathbf{x}_j|\mathbf{\Omega_k}) - \beta_j)^2, \ \beta_j = \begin{cases} 1, & \mathbf{x}_j \in \mathbf{\Omega}_k \\ 0, & \mathbf{x}_j \notin \mathbf{\Omega}_k \end{cases}, \quad (7)$$

where $p_i(\mathbf{x}_j|\mathbf{\Omega}_k)$ is the prediction probability of $\mathbf{x}_j$ to $\mathbf{\Omega}_k$ at the ith dimension.

QLC is actually a special case of *QLF*. It focuses on the prediction error of discriminating a certain class. Theorem 2 given next points out the relationship between *CP* and *QLC*:

Theorem 2. *$CP_i(\mathbf{\Omega_k})$ is negatively correlated to $QLC_i(\mathbf{\Omega_k})$,$i = 1, ..., D$,$k = 1, ..., C$.*

Proof. $\because \beta_j = \begin{cases} 1, & \mathbf{x}_j \in \mathbf{\Omega}_k \\ 0, & \mathbf{x}_j \notin \mathbf{\Omega}_k \end{cases}$, and $\lambda_j = \begin{cases} 0, & \mathbf{x}_j \in \mathbf{\Omega}_k \\ 1, & \mathbf{x}_j \notin \mathbf{\Omega}_k \end{cases}$, $\therefore \beta_j + \lambda_j = 1, j = 1, ..., N$.

$\therefore QLC_i(\mathbf{\Omega_k}) = \sum_{j=1}^{N} (p_i(\mathbf{x}_j|\mathbf{\Omega_k}) + \lambda_j - 1)^2$.

Let $f \triangleq \|\mathbf{CM}_i^k - \mathbf{\Lambda}_k\|_2^2 = \sum_{j=1}^{N} (CB_i(\mathbf{x}_j, \mathbf{\Omega_k}) - \lambda_j)^2$.

According to Theorem 1, $CB_i(\mathbf{x}_j, \mathbf{\Omega}_k)$ is positively correlated to $p_i(\mathbf{x}_j|\mathbf{\Omega}_k)$.

Meanwhile $0 \le p_i(\mathbf{x}_j|\mathbf{\Omega}_k) \le 1$, and $0 \le CB_i(\mathbf{x}_j, \mathbf{\Omega}_k) \le 1$.

$\therefore f$ is negatively correlated to $QLC_i(\mathbf{\Omega_k})$.

According to Definition 2, $CP_i(\mathbf{\Omega_k}) \propto f$.

$\therefore CP_i(\mathbf{\Omega_k})$ is negatively correlated to $QLC_i(\mathbf{\Omega_k})$. $\qquad \square$

Theorem 2 demonstrates that a feature with larger *CP* value to a certain class makes less prediction error to it. *CP* prefers to the feature which can not only separate the inner-class instances from the outer-class ones but also maximize this separation. Obviously, it depends on the consistency of feature's *CB* with instances' prior classification information to $\mathbf{\Omega}_k$. Maximal value of the third term in Eq. (6) is achieved when the possibilities of Ω_k's inner-class instances classified to Ω_k are maximized and possibilities of the outer-class instances classified to it are minimized. In this case, prediction error $QLC_i(\Omega_k)$ is minimized.

Since CP describes feature's discriminative ability for different classes, each feature $\mathbf{a}_i$ can be reconstructed as a CP vector:

$$\varepsilon_i \triangleq [CP_i(\Omega_1), CP_i(\Omega_2), ..., CP_i(\Omega_C)]^T . \tag{8}$$

Prior classification information is incorporated into the construction of the new space. So feature dependency with the target class is represented explicitly via vector. Each element of the vector is the corresponding feature's discriminative ability for each class. It contributes to finding the partially predominant features.

2.3   Comparison and Analysis

This section compares CP with some popular feature evaluation criteria. GCP defined next simply employs ℓ_1-norm of the CP vector for measuring feature's generalized classification ability. A high GCP score indicates the feature's predominant ability to discriminate a majority of classes.

Definition 4 (Gross Classification Performance, GCP). *Feature $\mathbf{a}_i$'s gross classification performance is defined as:*

$$GCP_i = \|\varepsilon_i\|_1 = \sum_{k=1}^{C} |CP_i(\Omega_k)|, \quad i = 1, ..., D. \tag{9}$$

Five popular feature evaluation criteria are compared with GCP, i.e., COR, $MICI$, $X2$, MI, and SU. Four data sets in Table 1 are tested, including two low-dimensional UCI data [17] and two high-dimensional microarray expression data [18]. The class number ranges from 2 to 6, i.e., binary-class and multi-class problems are both involved. Each criterion respectively selects top 50 optimal features. It's noted that $D < 50$ for Statlog, so its feature subset size reaches up to D. The selected subsets are compared according to different measure indices: (1) *Representation Entropy* [19], (2) *Inconsistency Rate* [20], (3) *Kruskal-Wallis Test* [21] and (4) *Fisher Discriminant Criterion* [8]. The first two indices are inversely proportional to the subset' classification performance. A discriminative subset achieves

Table 1. Four groups of test data sets

Data set	D	C	N
Statlog	36	6	4435
Hill-Valley	100	2	606
SRBCT	2308	4	63
Breast	9216	5	54

lower score under these indices. Whereas the last two indices are proportional to the performance.

Comparisons are shown in Figs. 4, 5, 6 and 7. Four measurement indices measure the feature subsets from different statistical aspects. Their experimental results are commonly diverse or even opposite. It means that the subset is deemed superior under some indices, but maybe inferior under the other ones. For example, the feature subsets selected by *COR* and *MICI* perform well in *Inconsistency Rate* on Statlog in Fig. 4(b). This indicates that the two subsets preserve more consistency information with the original data as compared with other criteria. However, their class separabilities are defeated by the other ones in Fig. 4(d). Thus only one index isn't sufficient for testifying subset's performance. In summary, experimental results demonstrate that *GCP* is comparably effective in different indices. It's effective not only for low-dimensional data but also for high-dimensional ones. So it's capable of selecting features in a univariate evaluation criterion used model.

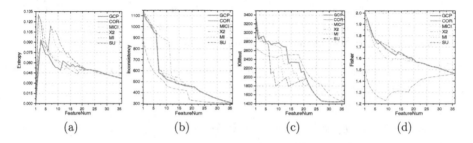

Fig. 4. Comparisons between *GCP* and other feature evaluation criteria on Statlog data: (a), (b), (c) and (d) correspond to four different measure indices of the feature subsets: *Representation Entropy, Inconsistency Rate, Kruskal-Wallis Test* and *Fisher Discriminant Criterion*.

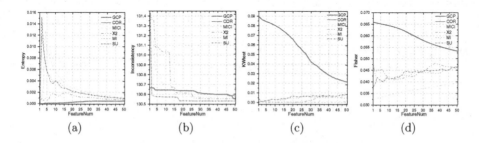

Fig. 5. Comparisons between *GCP* and other feature evaluation criteria on Hill-Valley data: (a), (b), (c) and (d) correspond to four different measure indices of the feature subsets: *Representation Entropy, Inconsistency Rate, Kruskal-Wallis Test* and *Fisher Discriminant Criterion*.

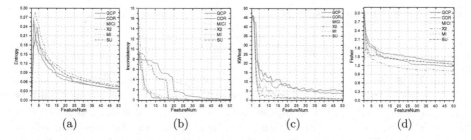

(a)   (b)   (c)   (d)

Fig. 6. Comparisons between *GCP* and other feature evaluation criteria on SRBCT data: (a), (b), (c) and (d) correspond to four different measure indices of the feature subsets: *Representation Entropy, Inconsistency Rate, Kruskal-Wallis Test* and *Fisher Discriminant Criterion.*

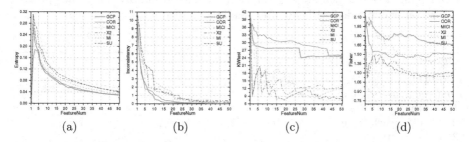

(a)   (b)   (c)   (d)

Fig. 7. Comparisons between *GCP* and other feature evaluation criteria on Breast data: (a), (b), (c) and (d) correspond to four different measure indices of the feature subsets: *Representation Entropy, Inconsistency Rate, Kruskal-Wallis Test* and *Fisher Discriminant Criterion.*

3   Feature Selection in *CP* Vector Space

3.1   *CPS*

Models constructed by top-k features are commonly below expectation. A primary reason is that the high degree of feature redundancy is neglected [22]. However, multi-features' classification redundancies are difficult to be estimated utilizing common evaluation criteria. A novel feature selection method *CPS* (*Classification Performance Based Selection*) is proposed. It searches features in *CP* vector space by reducing multi-features' classification redundancies.

    CPS seeks features excellent in recognizing different classes and least redundant with each other. Feature redundancy measured in *CPS* exploits a direct way, i.e., Mahalanobis distance. Suppose candidate feature subset $\mathbf{S} = \{\mathbf{a}_1, \mathbf{a}_2, ..., \mathbf{a}_K\}$. Then *CPS* selects K^* features from $\mathbf{S}$ for constructing the optimal subset $\mathbf{S}^*$ via maximizing the objective function:

$$CPS: \quad \underset{\mathbf{a}_i, \mathbf{a}_j \in \mathbf{S}^*, |\mathbf{S}^*| = K^*}{\arg\max} \sum d^2(\varepsilon_i, \varepsilon_j), \tag{10}$$

where $d(\varepsilon_i, \varepsilon_j)$ is the distance between the CP vectors of feature $\mathbf{a}_i$ and $\mathbf{a}_j$:

$$d(\varepsilon_i, \varepsilon_j) = \sqrt{(\varepsilon_i - \varepsilon_j)^T (\mathbf{\Sigma}^*)^{-1}(\varepsilon_i - \varepsilon_j)}, \qquad (11)$$

where $\mathbf{\Sigma}^*$ is the gross dispersion matrix of the K candidate CP vectors.

Equation (10) is a multi-feature redundancy reduction measurement, and its maximization is equivalent to minimizing multi-feature classification redundancies. CP vectors at far distances indicate their significant differences in recognizing classes. Furthermore, the computation of Eq. (10) is easily accomplished. So estimating the complicated multi-feature redundancy is solved in CPS.

An efficient and effective greedy searching scheme, *Sequential Forward Search*, is used in CPS in Algorithm 1. It includes one feature at a time, and the feature with maximal GCP calculated by Eq. (9) is selected primarily. Then the optimal feature set is expanded with features maximizing Eq. (10).

Algorithm 1. *CPS* algorithm

Require: $\mathbf{X} = \{\mathbf{a}_1, \mathbf{a}_2, ..., \mathbf{a}_D\}$, K, K^*
Ensure: $\mathbf{S}^* = \{\mathbf{a}_1^*, \mathbf{a}_2^*, ..., \mathbf{a}_{K^*}^*\}$
 1: **begin**
 2: calculate each feature's CP vector via Eq. (3) and (6);
 3: **for** $k = 1$ to C **do**
 4:     calculate N_{fk} via Eq. (12);
 5:     select top-N_{fk} feature $\mathbf{a}_1', \mathbf{a}_2', ..., \mathbf{a}_{N_{fk}}'$ according to $CP_i(\mathbf{\Omega}_k), i = 1, ..., D$;
 6:     $\mathbf{S} = \mathbf{S} \bigcup \{\mathbf{a}_1', \mathbf{a}_2', ..., \mathbf{a}_{N_{fk}}'\}$; //candidate subset
 7: **end for**;
 8: select feature $\mathbf{a}_1^*$ from $\mathbf{S}$ with maximal GCP calculate via Eq. (9);
 9: $\mathbf{S}^* = \mathbf{S}^* \bigcup \{\mathbf{a}_1^*\}$, $\mathbf{S} = \mathbf{S} \setminus \{\mathbf{a}_1^*\}$;
10: **for** $j = 2$ to K^* **do**
11:     select feature $\mathbf{a}_j^*$ from $\mathbf{S}$ maximizing Eq. (10);
12:     $\mathbf{S}^* = \mathbf{S}^* \bigcup \{\mathbf{a}_j^*\}$, $\mathbf{S} = \mathbf{S} \setminus \{\mathbf{a}_j^*\}$;
13: **end for**;
14: **end**;

It's noted that a candidate feature subset $\mathbf{S}$ is involved in CPS. There are two reasons for its necessity. First, it promises partially predominant features selected. CPS is a redundancy reduction based algorithm, and an inferior feature is perhaps selected if it is much irrelevant with the other features. So a candidate subset is needed. Second, a relatively small size of $\mathbf{S}$ promises more efficient searching process. Thus at the beginning of CPS, features are ranked according to their CP weights to different classes. Top-K features are selected to $\mathbf{S}$, The number of the features selected for $\mathbf{\Omega}_k$ depends on $\mathbf{\Omega}_k$'s prior probability:

$$N_{fk} = [K \times p(\mathbf{\Omega}_k)], \qquad (12)$$

where $[\cdot]$ is the rounding operation.

3.2   Experiment and Analysis

Eight groups of data sets in Table 2 are tested, including four UCI data and four microarray data. The UCI data are benchmark data. Their feature numbers are much smaller than the instance numbers. The latter four microarray data [10,18] are suitable for testing the effectiveness of the algorithms on high-dimensional data. All the raw data are continuous. For testing the performances of the compared methods, four groups of data sets have been discretized [13].

Table 2. Test data sets

Data set	D	C	N	Type
Gas	128	6	13910	Discrete
Arrhythmia	279	16	452	Continuous
Isolet	617	26	7797	Discrete
Multiple Features	649	10	2000	Continuous
TOX-171	5748	4	171	Discrete
Leukemia	7129	3	72	Continuous
CLL-SUB-111	11340	3	111	Continuous
Cancers	12533	11	174	Discrete

Four popular feature selection methods are compared with *CPS*. *MIFS* [11] and *mRMR* [13] select features on the basis of *Mutual Information*. Features most relevant to class and least redundant with each other are favored. *CBF* [6,12], is a correlation based selection method. Here *Pearson Correlation Coefficient* is used for measuring the correlation and *Sequential Forward Search* is performed. *Relief-F* [23] measures the differences between the inner-class and outer-class instances. Features maximize such differences are assigned high weights.

Each method adopts top 50 features for comparing, i.e., K^* increases from 1 to 50. For *CPS*, K is set as 100. Four classifiers, Naive Bayes (NB) classifier, Sequential Minimal Optimization (SMO) classifier, K-Nearest Neighbor (KNN) classifier, and C4.5 Decision Tree (DT) classifier, are built for estimating classification accuracies. Their aggregated 10-fold cross-validation classification accuracies for 10 times are compared in Table 3. It records the maximal accuracy of each classifier, so each method's performance in the best case is compared. One-tailed Welch t-test between the compared results and the best one in each column is conducted for testing the significance of the difference. The last row of each table shows the average accuracy of all the test data for each method.

Compared to the other tested methods, the performances of *CPF* are comparable or superior. Concerning the average classification accuracies, it's shown that SMO classifier achieves relatively better performance than the other three classifiers. Whereas DT classifier performs relatively inferior. It should be pointed

Table 3. Comparisons of the classification accuracies of different classifiers built by the selected features via each feature selection method (%): 10-fold cross-validation accuracies for 10 times are recorded, and the best result and those not significantly worse than it are highlighted in bold (one-tailed Welch t-test with 0.05 confidence level).

(a) Naive Bayes classifier

Dataset	MIFS	mRMR	CBF	Relief-F	CPS
Gas	53.09±0.23	53.52±0.24	52.37±0.14	52.68±0.19	**54.76±0.19**
Arrhythmia	58.68±0.62	68.49±0.74	62.06±0.56	66.44±0.62	**69.25±0.68**
Isolet	57.22±0.22	62.90±0.23	63.66±0.10	60.92±0.31	**77.81±0.23**
Multiple Features	72.04±0.14	94.64±0.14	93.59±0.17	86.19±0.19	**96.35±0.17**
TOX-171	78.69±0.76	76.50±1.58	70.21±2.98	67.33±1.45	**81.96±0.85**
Leukemia	94.34±0.61	**98.61±0.74**	94.75±0.88	97.22±0.76	98.14±0.56
CLL-SUB-111	78.59±1.50	80.03±1.38	80.98±1.13	69.72±1.31	**86.80±0.78**
Cancers	90.51±0.68	88.94±0.92	67.55±1.75	71.92±2.57	**92.96±1.15**
Avg.	*72.90*	*77.95*	*73.15*	*71.55*	*82.25*

(b) Sequential Minimal Optimization classifier

Dataset	MIFS	mRMR	CBF	Relief-F	CPS
Gas	61.64±0.22	64.50±0.16	64.54±0.16	**70.79±0.14**	69.02±0.11
Arrhythmia	55.96±0.66	70.33±0.39	63.82±0.28	**71.02±0.53**	70.40±0.53
Isolet	58.01±0.48	69.91±0.38	65.74±0.27	70.58±0.41	**81.87±0.31**
Multiple Features	75.14±0.50	97.76±0.10	95.73±0.29	93.24±0.13	**98.19±0.14**
TOX-171	73.98±1.03	81.98±1.17	76.57±1.86	80.73±1.48	**85.10±1.10**
Leukemia	97.68±0.65	97.55±0.64	97.55±0.60	97.70±0.72	**98.49±0.43**
CLL-SUB-111	79.72±2.50	84.99±0.96	**93.48±0.74**	81.42±1.17	88.73±0.63
Cancers	87.63±1.02	87.67±0.74	71.45±1.77	71.56±1.80	**88.87±0.92**
Avg.	*73.72*	*81.84*	*78.61*	*79.63*	*85.08*

(c) K-Nearest Neighbor classifier

Dataset	MIFS	mRMR	CBF	Relief-F	CPS
Gas	64.12±0.18	67.25±0.18	68.43±0.18	**74.56±0.18**	72.48±0.14
Arrhythmia	52.42±0.97	64.96±0.67	59.39±0.80	59.26±0.45	**68.37±1.17**
Isolet	50.09±0.43	61.31±0.16	49.51±0.19	61.69±0.50	**69.84±0.26**
Multiple Features	76.85±0.43	95.12±0.15	91.61±0.46	90.94±0.23	**97.06±0.12**
TOX-171	69.12±1.41	75.83±2.22	70.83±1.25	**76.58±0.99**	76.35±1.06
Leukemia	**97.17±0.57**	95.85±0.61	86.47±0.79	**97.27±0.81**	97.24±0.59
CLL-SUB-111	80.97±1.33	81.80±1.20	75.74±1.92	78.20±1.02	**88.09±0.87**
Cancers	79.54±0.85	82.38±2.59	63.99±0.66	69.24±1.61	**90.26±1.04**
Avg.	*71.29*	*78.06*	*70.75*	*75.97*	*82.46*

(d) C4.5 Decision Tree classifier

Dataset	MIFS	mRMR	CBF	Relief-F	CPS
Gas	63.64±0.13	65.92±0.17	67.23±0.15	**73.78±0.17**	71.48±0.15
Arrhythmia	56.04±0.38	**71.00±0.40**	64.02±1.28	**71.01±1.26**	70.03±0.49
Isolet	52.00±0.28	64.23±0.20	51.63±0.17	64.82±0.50	**73.34±0.25**
Multiple Features	71.80±0.54	**95.08±0.32**	89.29±0.27	90.09±0.30	94.37±0.26
TOX-171	69.64±1.16	69.90±1.94	52.60±2.16	64.63±1.28	**72.47±1.19**
Leukemia	90.73±1.41	94.36±1.41	79.62±1.92	94.29±1.07	**95.83±0.82**
CLL-SUB-111	70.84±1.91	74.67±1.34	67.34±3.27	69.64±1.16	**75.85±1.16**
Cancers	72.74±1.77	77.69±2.85	56.45±1.55	61.20±2.17	**85.26±0.96**
Avg.	*68.43*	*76.61*	*66.02*	*73.68*	*80.25*

out this is not a common phenomenon on some single tested data sets. Arrhythmia data demonstrates this situation. The accuracies of a majority of compared methods on this data is higher for DT classifier than for others.

The classification accuracies of *MIFS* and *mRMR* are closely related to the estimations of different probabilities. A small estimation error will influence the feature evaluation. It is especially complicated on continuous data. *CPS* is a distance based method, with no need for the probability estimation. It is available for instances under arbitrary distributions. On the other hand, the computation of distance is commonly faster than probability estimation. So *CPS* is more efficient than the information based methods.

For *CBF*, features' inner-correlations with each other and outer-correlation with class are both composite evaluation values. *CPS* describes these correlations via vectors, which facilitates measuring feature redundancy specific to each class. Also it conduces to those partially discriminative features winning out. *Relief-F* assigns features most separable for classes with higher weights. So in fact it's a maximal dependence strategy, and feature redundancy is neglected. *CPS* takes both dependence and redundancy into consideration, which helps for achieving better performance on the test data.

4 Conclusion

Two challenging issues in feature selection, how to find the partially predominant features and how to estimate multi-feature classification redundancy, are discussed in this paper. A new feature selection method concerning classification bias and classification performance is expected to tackle both problems. Features are reconstructed as discriminative ability vectors. This facilitates the partially predominant features more likely to be selected. Multi-feature classification redundancy is also properly measured by merely determining the differences of vectors. These advantages conduce to the effectiveness of the new feature selection algorithm *CPS* in both low-dimensional and high-dimensional data.

Acknowledgments. This work was partially supported by the National Natural Science Foundation of China (61070089), the Science Foundation of Tianjin (14JCYBJC15700), and the National 863 Project of China (2013AA013204).

References

1. Guyon, I., Elisseeff, A.: An introduction to variable and feature selection. J. Mach. Learn. Res. **3**, 1157–1182 (2003)
2. Hindawi, M., Benabdeslem, K.: Local-to-global semi-supervised feature selection. In: Proceeding 22nd CIKM, pp. 2159–2168 (2013)
3. Brown, G., Pocock, A., Zhao, M.J., Luján, M.: Conditional likelihood maximisation: a unifying framework for information theoretic feature selection. J. Mach. Learn. Res. **13**, 27–66 (2012)

4. Vinh, N.X., Chan, J., Romano, S., Bailey, J.: Effective global approaches for mutual information based feature selection. In: Proceeding 20th SIGKDD, pp. 512–521 (2014)
5. Sharma, A., Imoto, S., Miyano, S.: A top-r feature selection algorithm for microarray gene expression data. IEEE/ACM Trans. Comput. Biol. Bioinform. **9**(3), 754–764 (2012)
6. Yu, L., Liu, H.: Feature selection for high-dimensional data: A fast correlation-based filter solution. In: Proceeding 20th ICML, pp. 856–863 (2003)
7. Mitra, P., Murthy, C.A., Pal, S.K.: Unsupervised feature selection using feature similarity. IEEE Trans. Pattern Anal. Mach. Intell. **24**(3), 301–312 (2002)
8. Gu, Q., Li, Z., Han, J.: Generalized fisher score for feature selection. In: Proceeding 28th UAI, pp. 266–273 (2012)
9. Zhu, L., Miao, L., Zhang, D.: Iterative Laplacian score for feature selection. In: Liu, C.-L., Zhang, C., Wang, L. (eds.) CCPR 2012. CCIS, vol. 321, pp. 80–87. Springer, Heidelberg (2012)
10. Zhao, Z., Wang, L., Liu, H., Ye, J.: On similarity preserving feature selection. IEEE Trans. Knowl. and Data Eng. **25**(3), 619–632 (2013)
11. Battiti, R.: Using mutual information for selecting features in supervised neural net learning. IEEE Trans. Neural Netw. **5**(4), 537–550 (1994)
12. Hall, M.A.: Correlation-based feature selection for machine learning. PhD thesis, Dept. Computer Science, Waikato Univ., Hamilton, New Zealand (1999)
13. Peng, H., Long, F., Ding, C.: Feature selection based on mutual information criteria of max-dependency, max-relevance, and min-redundancy. IEEE Trans. Pattern Anal. Mach. Intell. **27**(8), 1226–1238 (2005)
14. Tang, J., Alelyani, S., Liu, H.: Feature selection for classification: a review. In: Data Classification: Algorithms and Applications. CRC Press, Chapman (2014)
15. Herman, G., Zhang, B., Wang, Y., Ye, G., Chen, F.: Mutual information-based method for selecting informative feature sets. Pattern Recognit. **46**(12), 3315–3327 (2013)
16. Wasikowski, M., Chen, X.W.: Combating the small sample class imbalance problem using feature selection. IEEE Trans. Knowl. and Data Eng. **22**(10), 1388–1400 (2010)
17. Bache, K., Lichman, M.: UCI machine learning repository, Univ. California, School of Information and Computer Science, Irvine. http://archive.ics.uci.edu/ml
18. Wei, J.M., Wang, S.Q., Yuan, X.J.: Ensemble rough hypercuboid approach for classifying cancers. IEEE Trans. Knowl. and Data Eng. **22**(3), 381–391 (2010)
19. Rao, V.M., Sastry, V.N.: Unsupervised feature ranking based on representation entropy. In: Proceeding 1st RAIT, pp. 421–425 (2012)
20. Dash, M., Liu, H.: Consistency-based search in feature selection. Artif. Intell. **151**(1), 155–176 (2003)
21. Ochiai, S., Kato, M.P., Tanaka, K.: Re-call and re-cognition in episode re-retrieval: a user study on news re-finding a fortnight later. In: Proceeding 23rd CIKM, pp. 579–588 (2014)
22. Lin, H.Y.: Feature selection based on cluster and variability analyses for ordinal multi-class classification problems. Knowl.-Based Syst. **37**, 94–104 (2013)
23. Kononenko, I.: Estimating attributes: analysis and extensions of RELIEF. In: Proceeding 7th ECML, pp. 171–182 (1994)

Enriching Document Representation with the Deviations of Word Co-occurrence Frequencies

Yang Wei[1,2], Jinmao Wei[1,2(✉)], and Zhenglu Yang[1,2]

[1] College of Computer and Control Engineering, Nankai University,
Tianjin 300071, China
weiyang_tj@outlook.com, {weijm,yangzl}@nankai.edu.cn
[2] College of Software, Nankai University, Tianjin 300071, China

Abstract. Recent strategies have been proposed to reveal the semantic relatedness between documents by enriching a document with the relatedness of all the words in the given document collection to the document. By restricting the relatedness to the expected frequencies that each word will occur in the document, the traditional weighted sum of word vectors is proved to give the upper bounds of the expected frequencies. Duplicate counts usually exist during the sum of the word vectors, which weaken the discriminativeness of the enriched document vectors. The strategy which gives the lower bounds of the expected frequencies is also obtained by keeping the maximum values of the word vectors on each dimension. Together with the lower bounds and the deviations of word co-occurrence frequencies, a novel method is proposed to remove the duplicate counts existing in the upper bounds. As a result, the proposed method smooths the generated document vectors better than the weighted sum strategy. Substantial experiments verify that the document clustering incorporated with the proposed method achieves a significant performance improvement compared with the existing strategies.

Keywords: Document representation · Document enrichment · Word co-occurrences · Word relatedness · Document clustering

1 Introduction

Measuring the semantic relatedness between documents is an important issue because it is the basis for many applications, such as document summarization, web search, text analysis, and so forth. The bag-of-words (BOW) model [10] is a common approach to represent documents in these domains for its simplicity, efficiency and acceptable accuracy. With BOW, the similarity between two documents mainly depends on the ratio of the common words shared by them. Wherefore BOW often fails to identify the semantic relatedness between documents composed of different words.

© Springer International Publishing Switzerland 2015
G. Wang et al. (Eds.): ICA3PP 2015, Part II, LNCS 9529, pp. 241–254, 2015.
DOI: 10.1007/978-3-319-27122-4_17

Our intuitive idea is to reveal the semantic relatedness between documents by enriching a document with the relatedness of the dimensions to the document, which is inspired by the semantic representations for words [5,11,16] that pragmatics can reveal semantics. By representing words as vectors, the relatedness of the dimensions to a word is evaluated with their co-occurrences with the word. Since the relatedness between words cannot be obtained directly from the dimensionality reduction methods of word representation [3,6] or the distributed representation for words [16], the distributional representation in the feature space of BOW [5,11] is used as the statistical foundation. The relatedness of the dimensions to a document is then estimated with the combination of the distributional word vectors.

Regarding each word vector as an abstractive concept, the idea of combining word vectors to represent documents is similar in spirit to those mapping documents into lower feature spaces [3,7,9,13] based on the assumption that documents with similar meanings share similar concepts. Significant improvements have been achieved with those methods. Nevertheless, the parameters, especially dimension of the space, are often difficult to be decided.

With the distributional representation, the dimensions are fixed as the distinct words in a document collection, and researchers mainly focus on the constructing of word vectors; the combination scheme of the word vectors is confined to the weighted sum [2,8,12,18]. Hence the relatedness of a word to a document is the average of the co-occurrence frequencies between the word and the original words in the document. However, such combination scheme has already been proved to hinder its usage on representing the semantic meanings of phrases [17]. By restricting the relatedness of a word to a document to the expected frequency that the word will occur in the document, we demonstrate that the weighted sum strategy gives the upper bound of the expected frequency. As shown in Example 1, a word may co-occur with several words at the same time, the sum of the co-occurrence frequencies between the word and the other words usually contains duplicate counts. As the common words are more likely to co-occur with others, their relatedness to a document will be overestimated more than the relatedness of the other words according to the duplicate counts. The imbalanced overestimation weakens the role of the other words, which further decreases the discriminativeness of the enriched document vectors.

Example 1. For a word segment $v_1 - v_2 - v_3$, the sum of the pairwise co-occurrence frequencies between v_1 and v_2, and v_2 and v_3, is two, while the real frequency of v_2 is one. Duplicate counts exist during the sum of the co-occurrence frequencies.

We also obtain the lower bound of the expected frequency by keeping the maximum value of the co-occurrence frequencies between the word and the original words in the document. A novel method is then proposed to estimate the amount of the duplicate counts in the sum of the co-occurrence frequencies by considering the lower bound and the deviation of the co-occurrence frequencies. By eliminating the duplicate counts, the proposed method obtains more smoothing power than the weighted sum strategy. Experimental results show that significant improvements have been achieved with the proposed method.

The remainder of this paper is organized as follows: Sect. 2 provides some backgrounds on document representation. The novel method is proposed in Sect. 3. The experimental results are shown in Sect. 4. The conclusion is drawn in Sect. 5.

2   Related Work

Formally, if there is a document collection D with n documents and m distinct words in it, the set of the m words constitute the vocabulary V, and each word in V is denoted as v. Then $\forall d \in D$, the document vector generated with BOW is:

$$\Phi_{\text{bow}} : \mathbf{d} = (\nu_1, \nu_2, \cdots, \nu_m) \in \mathbb{R}^m, \tag{1}$$

where ν_x is the frequency of the word v_x in the document vector $\mathbf{d}$. ν_x could be the raw frequency of v_x in d, namely, $c_{v_x|d}$. While it is usually re-weighted with the popular $\text{tf} \cdot \text{idf}$ weighting scheme:

$$\nu_x = \text{tf}_{v_x|d} \cdot \text{idf}_{v_x} = \frac{c_{v_x|d}}{\sum_{y=1}^{m} c_{v_y|d}} \cdot (1 + \log_2(\frac{n}{n_{v_x}})), \tag{2}$$

where n_{v_x} is the number of the documents in which v_x occurs. $\text{tf}_{v_x|d}$ is called the Term Frequency of v_x in d, and idf_{v_x} is the Inverse Document Frequency of v_x in the whole corpus.

Since BOW cannot figure out similar documents composed of different words, the Context Vector Model (CVM) tries to reveal the meanings of documents with the weighted sum of the distributional word vectors [2,8,12,18].

$\forall v_x \in V$, its word vector is usually defined as [4,19]:

$$\mathbf{v}_x = (\frac{c_{v_x,v_1|D}}{c_{v_x|D}}, \frac{c_{v_x,v_2|D}}{c_{v_x|D}}, \ldots, \frac{c_{v_x,v_m|D}}{c_{v_x|D}}), \tag{3}$$

where $c_{v_x,v_y|D}$ is the co-occurrence frequency between v_x and v_y in D, and $c_{v_x|D}$ is the frequency that v_x occurs in D. Generally, the meanings of words should be independent of the corpus size, so $c_{v_x|D}$ is introduced to give the basic context of a word [5]. The values in the word vector measure the relatedness of the words in V to the target word.

The co-occurrence frequencies can be estimated with several methods [5,11,15]. We choose the one used in the weighted sum of the word vectors for document representation [2]:

$$\frac{c_{v_x,v_y|D}}{c_{v_x|D}} = \frac{\sum_{a=1}^{n} \frac{c_{v_x|d_a}}{\sum_{z=1}^{m} c_{v_z|d_a}} \cdot \frac{c_{v_y|d_a}}{\sum_{z=1}^{m} c_{v_z|d_a}}}{\sum_{a=1}^{n} (\frac{c_{v_x|d_a}}{\sum_{z=1}^{m} c_{v_z|d_a}} \sum_{b=1,b \neq x}^{m} \frac{c_{v_b|d_a}}{\sum_{z=1}^{m} c_{v_z|d_a}})}. \tag{4}$$

Together with all the word vectors generated with (4), an $m \times m$ matrix is obtained, which is called *context matrix*:

$$\mathbf{V} = (\mathbf{v}_1, \mathbf{v}_2, \ldots, \mathbf{v}_m). \tag{5}$$

Then the new document vector generated with CVM is:

$$\Phi_{\text{cvm}} : \mathbf{d}' = \mathbf{dV} = \sum_{x=1}^{m} \nu_x \mathbf{v}_x \in \mathbb{R}^m. \tag{6}$$

With CVM, the corresponding word vectors of the words belonging to d will be assigned non-zero weights with the weighting scheme used to generate the document vector of BOW. As a result, the value of any word in $\mathbf{d}'$ is defined as the average relatedness of the word to the original words in d.

Billhardt [2] has compared the effects of using the schemes tf and tf · idf to estimate the weights of the word vectors, and further exploited the deviations of the co-occurrence frequencies in the word vectors to estimate the weights:

$$\text{dev}_{v_x} = 1 + \frac{\sum_{y=1}^{m} \left| \frac{\frac{c_{v_x,v_y|D}}{c_{v_x|D}}}{\text{mean}(\mathbf{v}_x)} - 1 \right|}{m}, \tag{7}$$

where $\text{mean}(\mathbf{v}_x)$ is the average of all the values in $\mathbf{v}_x$. Then $\nu_x = \text{tf}_{v_x|d} \cdot \text{dev}_{v_x}$.

In the common sense, specific words, which have occurred in only a few of documents, are very possible to be topic related. The weighting schemes tf · idf and tf · dev highlight the effects of the specific words by smoothing the weights of the word vectors, thus can help to improve the discriminativeness of the generated document vectors. However, the smoothing effect is achieved indirectly by verifying the specificities of the original words in a document. The proposed method gives a detailed consideration of the specificities of all the words in the document collection directly to smooth the generated vector of a document.

3   Document Enrichment

3.1   The Upper and Lower Bounds

Our intuitive idea is similar to CVM, that for any document, all the related words in the document collection should have non-zero values due to their relatedness to the original words in the document. Instead of giving the strategy to estimate the relatedness of a word to the document directly, we attempt to find the "co-occurrence frequency" between the word and the document, which is inspired by the success that co-occurrences between words can reveal the semantic meanings of words [5,11,15]. We restrict the "co-occurrence frequency" between the word and the document to the expected frequency that the word will occur in the document.

Definition 1. $\forall d \in D$, the document vector of d is:

$$\mathbf{d}' = (E_{v_1|d}, E_{v_2|d}, \cdots, E_{v_m|d}) \in \mathbb{R}^m,$$

where $E_{v_y|d}$ is the expected frequency that the word v_y ($v_y \in V$) will appear in d under the occurrences of the original words in d.

Generally, $\frac{c_{v_x,v_y|D}}{c_{v_x|D}}$ is regarded as the conditional probability $P(v_y|v_x)$. Hence the expected co-occurrence frequency, $E_{v_x,v_y|d}$, that v_y will co-occur with v_x in d under the occurrence of v_x is obtained:

$$E_{v_x,v_y|d} = c_{v_x|d}P(v_y|v_x) = c_{v_x|d}\frac{c_{v_x,v_y|D}}{c_{v_x|D}}. \tag{8}$$

Without loss of generality, suppose the first k words in V are those occurred in d. The expected co-occurrence frequency of v_y with several original words in d is:

$$\forall 1 \leq i < j \leq k, y = 1, \ldots, m, E_{v_i,\ldots,v_j,v_y|d} = c_{v_i,\ldots,v_j|d}P(v_y|v_i, \ldots, v_j). \tag{9}$$

With the expected co-occurrence frequencies, the expected frequency of v_y under the occurrences of the original words in d could be obtained inductively:

$$\text{if } k = 1, E_{v_y|d} = E_{v_1,v_y|d}; \tag{10}$$

$$\text{if } k = 2, E_{v_y|d} = E_{v_1,v_y|d} + E_{v_2,v_y|d} - E_{v_1,v_2,v_y|d}. \tag{11}$$

As shown in Example 1, the frequency of v_2 could be obtained by eliminating the duplicate counts for v_2 during the sum of the co-occurrence frequencies. Hence $c_{v_2} = c_{v_1,v_2} + c_{v_2,v_3} - c_{v_1,v_2,v_3}$. Similarly, $E_{v_1,v_2,v_y|d}$ has been counted twice with the sum of the expected co-occurrence frequencies.

$$\text{Inductively, } \forall k = 1, ..., m, E_{v_y|d} = \sum_{x=1}^{k} E_{v_x,v_y|d} - \sum_{1 \leq i < j \leq k} E_{v_i,v_j,v_y|d}$$

$$+ \sum_{1 \leq x < i < j \leq k} E_{v_x,v_i,v_j,v_y|d} + \cdots + (-1)^{k-1}E_{v_1,v_2,\ldots,v_k,v_y|d}. \tag{12}$$

With (12), $E_{v_y|d}$ will not be calculable unless the required expected co-occurrence frequencies are given. Unfortunately, this information seems unavailable under current conditions, for it still remains uncertain to define the semantic co-occurrence between two words [5]. It would be more difficult to define the semantic co-occurrence among more than two words. Instead, we give the following assumptions to simplify the calculation of $E_{v_y|d}$.

Proposition 1. *Assume* $\forall 1 \leq i < j \leq k, y = 1, \ldots, m, E_{v_i,\ldots,v_j,v_y|d} = 0$.

Then all the items in (12) will equal zero except the first one:

$$E_{v_y|d} = \sum_{x=1}^{k} E_{v_x,v_y|d}. \tag{13}$$

As shown in Fig. 1(a), Proposition 1 corresponds to the situation that no more than one original word will co-occur with v_y in d at the same time.

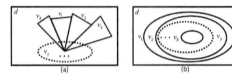

Fig. 1. Schematic diagrams of the propositions, where the dashed ellipses stand for the expected frequency of $v_y, y = 1, \ldots, m$, and the solid ellipses (or triangles) stand for the frequency of the original word $v_x, x = 1, \ldots, k$.

Proposition 2. *Assume* $\forall 1 \leq i \leq j \leq k, y = 1, ..., m,$

$$E_{v_i,\cdots,v_j,v_y|d} = \min\{c_{v_i|d}, \ldots, c_{v_j|d}, E_{v_y|d}\}.$$

Specifically, if $i = j$,

$$E_{v_i,v_y|d} = \min\{c_{v_i|d}, E_{v_y|d}\}.$$

Hence we have:

$$
\begin{aligned}
E_{v_i,\ldots,v_j,v_y|d} &= \min\{c_{v_i|d}, \ldots, c_{v_j|d}, E_{v_y|d}\} \\
&= \min\{\min\{c_{v_i|d}, E_{v_y|d}\}, \ldots, \min\{c_{v_j|d}, E_{v_y|d}\}\} \\
&= \min\{E_{v_i,v_y|d}, \ldots, E_{v_j,v_y|d}\}. \tag{14}
\end{aligned}
$$

Taken (14) into (12), the items in (12) will offset each other and leave the maximum expected co-occurrence frequency of v_y with some original word in d:

$$E_{v_y|d} = \max\{E_{v_1,v_y|d}, \ldots, E_{v_k,v_y|d}\}. \tag{15}$$

As shown in Fig. 1(b), Proposition 2 corresponds to the situation that all the words in the same document co-occur with each other.

In practice, $\forall 1 \leq i \leq j \leq k, y = 1, \ldots, m,$

$$0 \leq E_{v_i,\ldots,v_j,v_y|d} \leq \min\{c_{v_i|d}, \ldots, c_{v_j|d}, E_{v_y|d}\}.$$

Hence,

$$\max_{x=1}^{k}\{E_{v_x,v_y|d}\} \leq E_{v_y|d} \leq \sum_{x=1}^{k} E_{v_x,v_y|d}. \tag{16}$$

3.2   Eliminating the Duplicate Counts

In the previous section, we obtain the upper and lower bounds of the expected frequency of a word in a document. Since the assumptions required by the bounds cannot hold in most cases, a more general assumption will be given in this section to approach the exact expected frequency by eliminating the duplicate counts.

According to (11), $\forall 1 \leq i < j \leq k$, the expected frequency of v_y under the occurrences of v_i and v_j in d is,

$$E_{v_y|v_i,v_j,d} = E_{v_i,v_y|d} + E_{v_j,v_y|d} - E_{v_i,v_j,v_y|d}. \tag{17}$$

$E_{v_i,v_j,v_y|d}$ is the duplicate counts to calculate the expected frequency of v_y under the occurrences of the two original words in d. While according to (12), $\sum_{x=1}^{k} E_{v_x,v_y|d} - E_{v_y|d}$ is the overall duplicate counts to calculate the expected frequency of v_y under the occurrences of all the original words in d. We assume intuitively that the overall duplicate counts increase along with the growth of the local duplicate counts under the occurrences of any two original words.

Proposition 3. *Assume* $\sum_{x=1}^{k} E_{v_x,v_y|d} - E_{v_y|d} \propto \sum_{i=1}^{k-1} \sum_{j=i+1}^{k} E_{v_i,v_j,v_y|d}.$

Without loss of generality, suppose the expected co-occurrence frequencies between v_y and the original words in d are organized in ascending order, namely,

$$E_{v_1,v_y|d} \leq E_{v_2,v_y|d} \leq \cdots \leq E_{v_k,v_y|d}. \tag{18}$$

Since the conditional probabilities of words are determined by the inherent relatedness between them, the conditional probabilities could be regarded as constants. Therefore,

$$E_{v_i,v_j,v_y|d} = E_{v_i,v_y|d} P(v_j|v_i,v_y) \propto E_{v_i,v_y|d}. \tag{19}$$

Similarly, $E_{v_i,v_j,v_y|d} \propto E_{v_j,v_y|d}$. We choose $E_{v_i,v_y|d}$ for $E_{v_i,v_y|d} \leq E_{v_j,v_y|d}$. Hence we have,

$$\sum_{x=1}^{k} E_{v_x,v_y|d} - E_{v_y|d} \propto \sum_{i=1}^{k-1} \sum_{j=i+1}^{k} E_{v_i,v_j,v_y|d} \propto \sum_{i=1}^{k-1} \sum_{j=i+1}^{k} E_{v_i,v_y|d}$$

$$= \sum_{i=1}^{k-1} (k-i) E_{v_i,v_y|d} = \sum_{i=1}^{k} (k-i) E_{v_i,v_y|d}. \tag{20}$$

Dividing all the items in (20) by $\sum_{x=1}^{k} E_{v_x,v_y|d}$, we can obtain:

$$1 - \frac{E_{v_y|d}}{\sum_{x=1}^{k} E_{v_x,v_y|d}} \propto \sum_{i=1}^{k} \frac{(k-i) E_{v_i,v_y|d}}{\sum_{x=1}^{k} E_{v_x,v_y|d}}. \tag{21}$$

Namely,

$$\frac{E_{v_y|d}}{\sum_{x=1}^{k} E_{v_x,v_y|d}} \propto \sum_{i=1}^{k} \frac{\sum_{x=1}^{k} E_{v_x,v_y|d}}{(k-i) E_{v_i,v_y|d}} \propto \sum_{i=1}^{k} \left| \frac{\sum_{x=1}^{k} E_{v_x,v_y|d}}{k} - E_{v_i,v_y|d} \right|. \tag{22}$$

Let $\omega_{v_y|d} = \frac{E_{v_y|d}}{\sum_{x=1}^{k} E_{v_x,v_y|d}}$, the expected frequency of v_y is then obtained with:

$$E_{v_y|d} = \omega_{v_y|d} \sum_{x=1}^{k} E_{v_x,v_y|d}. \tag{23}$$

We give the following two steps to estimate $\omega_{v_y|d}$ based on (22). Firstly, let

$$\omega_{v_y|d} = 1 + \frac{\sum_{i=1}^{k} \left| \frac{\sum_{x=1}^{k} E_{v_x,v_y|d}}{k} - E_{v_i,v_y|d} \right|}{\sum_{x=1}^{k} E_{v_x,v_y|d}}. \tag{24}$$

Then the corresponding parameters of all the words constitute the parameter vector for d:

$$\boldsymbol{\omega}_d = (\omega_{v_1|d}, \omega_{v_2|d}, \cdots, \omega_{v_m|d}). \tag{25}$$

Secondly, $\forall \omega_{v_y|d} \in \boldsymbol{\omega}_d$, let

$$\omega_{v_y|d} = \begin{cases} \left(\dfrac{\omega_{v_y|d}}{\|\boldsymbol{\omega}_d\|_\infty}\right)^\beta & (\dfrac{\omega_{v_y|d}}{\|\boldsymbol{\omega}_d\|_\infty})^\beta \geq \dfrac{E_{v_k,v_y|d}}{\sum_{x=1}^k E_{v_x,v_y|d}} \\ \dfrac{E_{v_k,v_y|d}}{\sum_{x=1}^k E_{v_x,v_y|d}} & \text{else,} \end{cases} \tag{26}$$

where β is introduced to smooth the values in $\boldsymbol{\omega}_d$, and $E_{v_k,v_y|d}$ is the maximum expected co-occurrence frequency claimed in (18).

Converting the final parameter vector to an $m \times m$ diagonal matrix $\boldsymbol{\Omega}_d$, where the item in the i-th row and column of $\boldsymbol{\Omega}_d$ corresponds to the i-th item in $\boldsymbol{\omega}_d$, the method to generate the enriched document vector of d is therefore:

$$\Phi_{\text{ecvm}} : \mathbf{d}' = \mathbf{d}\mathbf{V}\boldsymbol{\Omega}_d. \tag{27}$$

The proposed method is called the Extension of the traditional CVM, ECVM in short. The traditional CVM defined in (6) is equivalent to the strategy defined in (13), which gives the upper bounds of the expected frequencies of each word in d. Compared ECVM with CVM, the significant difference is the introducing of the parameters to eliminate the duplicate counts in the upper bounds. By tuning the smoothing parameter β, ECVM boils down to CVM when $\beta = 0$.

When β tends to the positive infinity, $(\dfrac{\omega_{v_y|d}}{\|\boldsymbol{\omega}_d\|_\infty})^\beta \ll \dfrac{E_{v_k,v_y|d}}{\sum_{x=1}^k E_{v_x,v_y|d}}$, hence $\omega_{v_y|d} \equiv \dfrac{E_{v_k,v_y|d}}{\sum_{x=1}^k E_{v_x,v_y|d}}$. ECVM comes down to the lower bound strategy defined in (15) consequently.

In (19), we estimate the overall duplicate counts conservatively with the smaller expected co-occurrence frequencies (We choose $E_{v_i,v_y|d}$ to estimate the duplicate counts rather than $E_{v_j,v_y|d}$ for $E_{v_i,v_y|d} \leq E_{v_j,v_y|d}$). The ratio of the duplicate counts is probably to be less estimated. In other words, the expected frequency is overestimated. So it's reasonable to make β greater than one to reduce the overestimation.

4   Experiments

4.1   Experimental Setup

In this section, we conduct the performance evaluation using the TDT2 and the Reuters datasets[1]. The TDT2 dataset consists of data extracted from six sources, including two newswires (APW, NYT), two radio programs (VOA, PRI) and two television programs (CNN, ABC). Those documents appearing in two or more categories are removed, and the categories with more than 10 documents

---

[1] www.cad.zju.edu.cn/home/dengcai/Data/TextData.html.

are kept, thus leaving us with 10,021 documents in total. The Reuters dataset contains 21,578 documents which are grouped into 135 classes. Those documents with multiple category labels are discarded, and the categories with more than 10 documents are selected. This leaves us with 8,213 documents in total. Table 1 provides the statistics of the datasets.

Table 1. Statistics of the Datasets

	TDT2	Reuters
No. docs. used	10021	8213
Avg. doc. length	182	68
No. words used	36771	18933
Avg. word freq	51	30
No. clusters	56	41
Avg. cluster size	179	200

The performance of the pairwise similarity evaluation is an important index to verify the qualities of the representations for documents. Generally, with good representation, the similarities between semantically related documents should obtain high scores, while the similarities between unrelated documents should obtain low scores. This is consistent with the purpose of the clustering task that similar documents are organized into the same group, while dissimilar documents are organized into different groups. Therefore, we evaluate our algorithms on document clustering problem with the k-means clustering algorithm. The cosine of document vectors is chosen to be the similarity measure. The evaluation of the similarities between documents directly affects the results of k-means, thus can reflect the qualities of the representation methods for documents. The document representation methods to be compared include:

1st. The popular BOW method and the Non-negative Matrix Factorization based document representation (NMF) method [20], which were once tested with the above corpora, are used as the baselines to evaluate the proposed method.

2nd. The traditional CVM incorporated with the weighting scheme tf, tf$\cdot$ idf, and tf$\cdot$ dev is performed to verify the improvement of our method. The corresponding versions of CVM are denoted as CVM-TF, CVM-TFIDF, and CVM-TFDEV, respectively.

3rd. The proposed ECVM method is tested incorporated with the simple tf weighting scheme to measure the frequencies of the original words in a document.

Document vectors generated with the algorithms listed above are used as the input of the k-means clustering algorithm.

Two metrics are adopted to evaluate the performance of document clustering, the accuracy (AC) [20] and the normalized mutual information (NMI) [1,20]. Given a document vector $\mathbf{d}_a$, let r_a and l_a be the cluster label and the label provided by the document collection, respectively. AC is defined as follows:

$$AC = \frac{\sum_{a=1}^{n} \delta(l_a, map(r_a))}{n}, \tag{28}$$

where n denotes the total number of documents in the test, $\delta(l_a, map(r_a))$ is the delta function that equals one if $l_a = map(r_a)$ and equals zero otherwise, and $map(r_a)$ is the mapping function that maps each cluster r_a to the equivalent label from the document collection. The best mapping can be found by using the Kuhn-Munkres algorithm [14].

Let n_l be the number of documents in class l, n_r be the number of samples in cluster r, and $n_{l,r}$ be the number of samples in class l and cluster r, then:

$$NMI = \frac{\sum_{l,r} n_{l,r} log \frac{n n_{l,r}}{n_l n_r}}{max(\sum_l n_l log \frac{n_l}{n}, \sum_r n_r log \frac{n_r}{n})}. \tag{29}$$

It is easy to check that NMI ranges from 0 to 1. Since the cluster number is predefined as the number of the classes in the document collection, NMI $= 1$ if cluster r is identical to class l, and NMI $= 0$ if the two sets are independent.

4.2   Performance Evaluations

The clustering results are shown in Table 2. ECVM was performed with $\beta = 4$ on both datasets. The evaluations were conducted with the class numbers ranging from two to ten. For each given class number, 50 test runs were performed on different randomly chosen classes and the average performance is reported in the table. Hence the evaluation was conducted on 900 different datasets actually. These experiments reveal a number of interesting points:

1st. The best performances are achieved with CVM and ECVM on both datasets, respectively. This demonstrates that a better representation could be obtained by enriching a document with the expected frequencies that all the words in the given document collection will occur in the document.

2nd. The superiority of ECVM to the versions of CVM indicates the effectiveness on eliminating the duplicate counts during the sum of the expected co-occurrence frequencies for each word.

3rd. The weighting schemes tf$\cdot$idf and tf$\cdot$dev also improve the performance of CVM, but less significant than ECVM. This demonstrates that ECVM gives the better representation for documents than CVM-TFIDF or CVM-TFDEV. The improvement is achieved by giving more consideration to the specificities of all the words in the document collection for every document, which will be further discussed in the following section.

4.3   Further Comparison Between CVM and ECVM

The superiority of ECVM is demonstrated by the experimental results. The theoretical difference between CVM and ECVM is further discussed in this section.

The formula used to estimate $\omega_{v_y|d}$ in (24) is similar to the weighting scheme dev_{v_x} defined in (7). In fact, dev_{v_x} is the deviation of $\frac{c_{v_x,v_y|D}}{c_{v_x|D}}$, for $y = 1, \ldots, m$. While $\omega_{v_y|d}$ is the deviation of $E_{v_x,v_y|d}$ for $x = 1, \ldots, k$.

Table 2. Clustering Results on the TDT2 and the Reuters Datasets

No. class	2	3	4	5	6	7	8	9	10	Avg.
TDT2-AC										
BOW	0.938	0.882	0.834	0.778	0.762	0.708	0.653	0.651	0.613	0.758
NMF	0.866	0.804	0.755	0.705	0.699	0.681	0.608	0.611	0.578	0.701
CVM-TF	0.967	0.916	0.889	0.840	0.838	0.823	0.780	0.783	0.754	0.843
CVM-TFIDF	0.964	0.923	0.885	0.849	0.838	0.826	0.783	0.785	0.775	0.848
CVM-TFDEV	**0.972**	0.921	0.895	0.857	0.847	0.824	0.791	0.778	0.756	0.849
ECVM	0.969	**0.927**	**0.923**	**0.859**	**0.862**	**0.843**	**0.810**	**0.794**	**0.760**	**0.861**
TDT2-NMI										
BOW	0.807	0.771	0.739	0.691	0.716	0.668	0.629	0.648	0.622	0.699
NMF	0.687	0.678	0.667	0.625	0.661	0.648	0.593	0.616	0.596	0.641
CVM-TF	0.883	0.809	0.792	0.737	0.766	0.757	0.720	**0.731**	0.709	0.767
CVM-TFIDF	0.875	0.813	0.786	0.737	0.762	0.749	0.710	0.718	**0.710**	0.762
CVM-TFDEV	0.881	0.811	0.799	0.747	0.769	0.757	**0.725**	0.727	0.708	0.770
ECVM	**0.889**	**0.816**	**0.823**	**0.749**	**0.773**	**0.761**	0.725	0.727	0.701	**0.774**
Reuters-AC										
BOW	0.825	0.692	0.652	0.588	0.589	0.539	0.469	0.447	0.480	0.587
NMF	0.828	0.712	0.683	0.580	0.582	0.535	0.448	0.457	0.490	0.591
CVM-TF	0.840	0.758	0.705	0.633	0.631	0.591	0.528	0.543	0.540	0.641
CVM-TFIDF	0.847	0.761	0.725	0.638	0.628	0.578	0.537	0.567	0.541	0.647
CVM-TFDEV	0.844	0.760	0.717	0.629	0.634	0.592	0.524	0.538	0.556	0.644
ECVM	**0.880**	**0.765**	**0.754**	**0.660**	**0.670**	**0.629**	**0.576**	**0.592**	**0.578**	**0.678**
Reuters-NMI										
BOW	0.428	0.409	0.483	0.428	0.482	0.460	0.393	0.393	0.478	0.439
NMF	0.436	0.410	0.509	0.424	0.485	0.449	0.362	0.391	0.464	0.437
CVM-TF	0.531	0.517	0.548	0.473	0.519	0.488	0.415	**0.447**	0.500	0.493
CVM-TFIDF	0.547	0.536	0.581	0.476	0.513	0.476	0.405	0.437	0.492	0.496
CVM-TFDEV	0.533	0.525	0.568	0.473	0.517	0.485	0.414	0.445	0.504	0.496
ECVM	**0.575**	**0.544**	**0.611**	**0.486**	**0.544**	**0.502**	**0.423**	0.444	**0.512**	**0.516**

Usually, words with big idf or dev values must appear in only a few of documents therefore are regarded as high specificity. The frequencies of the original words in d with high specificities are enhanced by multiplying idf or dev. The enhancement increases the weights of the corresponding word vectors in CVM, for $\mathbf{d}' = \sum_{x=1}^{m} \nu_x \mathbf{v}_x$. Relatively, the weights of the word vectors belonging to the words with low specificities are reduced. This mechanism abandons many duplicate counts because the words with low specificities have more chance to co-occur with other words. It's clear that the ratio of the removed duplicate

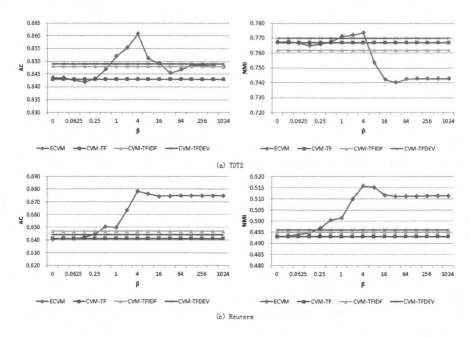

(a) TDT2

(b) Reuters

Fig. 2. The performance of ECVM with the different values for β.

counts is the same for all the m words in $\mathbf{d}'$, as they share the same idf or dev values corresponding to the original words in d.

All in all, CVM incorporated with idf or dev only considers the specificities of the original k words in d. ECVM estimates the specificities of the m words in $\mathbf{d}'$ based on the expected co-occurrence frequencies, which considers both of the values in the word vectors and the frequencies of the original words in d. For each document, m specific parameters are generated respectively. ECVM gives a detailed consideration of the specificities of all the m words for each document.

Besides, the well-known functionality of idf is to smooth the document vectors generated with BOW. Since the values of the words with low specificities are usually bigger than the values of the words with high specificities in the document vector generated with CVM, ECVM subtracts much more scores from the words with low specificities than the words with high specificities, the differences between the values of the words are therefore decreased. ECVM also achieves the functionality of smoothness. This is the practical effect of eliminating the duplicate counts, and ECVM is expected to have more smoothing power according to the above discussion.

4.4 Parameter Selection

The parameter β is essential to ECVM. Figure 2 shows how the performance of ECVM varies with the parameter β. The horizontal axis is the value of β, and the vertical axis denotes the corresponding average performance.

According to (26), ECVM boils down to the lower bound strategy when β tends to the positive infinity. Figure 2 shows that ECVM converges to the lower bound strategy when $\beta \geq 2^8$ on TDT2, and when $\beta \geq 2^6$ on Reuters. Since the sum of the expected co-occurrence frequencies of a word with the original words in a long text is usually larger than the one in a short text, the difference between the upper and lower bounds of the expected frequency of the word in the long text is larger than the one in the short text. Therefore, ECVM converges slower on TDT2 than on Reuters, as the documents in TDT2 are much longer than those in Reuters according to Table 1.

The performance of ECVM is very stable with respect to the parameter β. ECVM achieves consistent good performance with the values for β ranging from 2^0 to 2^2 on TDT2 and from 2^0 to the positive infinity on Reuters. The results support the analysis in Sect. 3.2 that the expected frequencies of each word are overestimated with the proposed method, so β should be greater than one to reduce the overestimation.

Besides, the consistent good performance on Reuters when the value for β grows demonstrates that the lower bound strategy defined in (15) is more suitable on Reuters than the upper bound strategy given by CVM. The lower bound strategy holds on the assumption that all the words in the same document co-occur with each other. This assumption is more sensible when the document is short. This agrees with the statistical result that the documents in Reuters are much shorter than those in TDT2 as shown in Table 1. On the contrary, setting β to large values is not suitable for long texts.

5   Conclusion

In this paper, we present a novel document representation method called the Extension of the traditional Context Vector Model, ECVM in short. ECVM represents a document with the expected frequencies that all the distinct words in the given document collection will appear in the document. The traditional CVM measures the expected frequency of a word with the accumulation of the expected co-occurrence frequencies of that word with the original words in the document. ECVM obtains more accurate expected frequency by eliminating the duplicate counts during the accumulation. As a result, ECVM has more smoothing power than the traditional CVM. The substantial experiments on document clustering show that ECVM provides a better representation in the sense of semantic meaning.

There is a parameter β which reduces the overestimation of the expected frequencies with our ECVM model. ECVM boils down to the traditional CVM when $\beta = 0$. A suitable value for β is critical to our algorithm. Although we have proven that β should be greater than one, it still remains unclear how to tune β efficiently.

Acknowledgments. This work was supported by the National Natural Science Foundation of China under grant 61070089, the Science Foundation of TianJin under grant 14JCYBJC15700, and the National 863 Project of China under Grant No. 2013AA013204.

References

1. Andrews, N.O., Fox, E.A.: Recent developments in document clustering. Computer Science, Virginia Tech., Tech. report (2007)
2. Billhardt, H., Borrajo, D., Maojo, V.: A context vector model for information retrieval. J. Am. Soc. Inform. Sci. Technol. **53**(3), 236–249 (2002)
3. Blei, D.M., Ng, A.Y., Jordan, M.I.: Latent dirichlet allocation. J. Mach. Learning Res. **3**, 993–1022 (2003)
4. Blunsom, P., Grefenstette, E., Hermann, K.M., et al.: New directions in vector space models of meaning. In: Proceedings of the 52nd Annual Meeting of the Association for Computational Linguistics (2014)
5. Bullinaria, J.A., Levy, J.P.: Extracting semantic representations from word co-occurrence statistics: a computational study. Behav. Res. Meth. **39**(3), 510–526 (2007)
6. Bullinaria, J.A., Levy, J.P.: Extracting semantic representations from word co-occurrence statistics: stop-lists, stemming, and SVD. Behav. Res. Meth. **44**(3), 890–907 (2012)
7. Cai, D., He, X., Han, J.: Locally consistent concept factorization for document clustering. IEEE Trans. Knowl. Data Eng. **23**(6), 902–913 (2011)
8. Cheng, X., Miao, D., Wang, C., Cao, L.: Coupled term-term relation analysis for document clustering. In: The 2013 International Joint Conference on Neural Networks (IJCNN), pp. 1–8. IEEE (2013)
9. Deerwester, S.C., Dumais, S.T., Landauer, T.K., Furnas, G.W., Harshman, R.A.: Indexing by latent semantic analysis. JASIS **41**(6), 391–407 (1990)
10. Harris, Z.S.: Distributional structure. Word **10**(23), 146–162 (1954)
11. Iosif, E., Potamianos, A.: Unsupervised semantic similarity computation between terms using web documents. IEEE Trans. Knowl. Data Eng. **22**(11), 1637–1647 (2010)
12. Kalogeratos, A., Likas, A.: Text document clustering using global term context vectors. Knowl. Inf. Syst. **31**(3), 455–474 (2012)
13. Le, Q.V., Mikolov, T.: Distributed representations of sentences and documents. In: Proceedings of the 31st International Conference on Machine Learning, W&CP, vol. 32. JMLR (2014)
14. Lovász, L., Plummer, M.: Matching Theory Annals of Discrete Mathematics, vol. 29. North-Holland, Amsterdam (1986)
15. Lund, K., Burgess, C.: Producing high-dimensional semantic spaces from lexical co-occurrence. Behav. Res. Meth. Instrum. Comput. **28**(2), 203–208 (1996)
16. Mikolov, T., Chen, K., Corrado, G., Dean, J.: Efficient estimation of word representations in vector space. arXiv preprint (2013). arXiv:1301.3781
17. Mitchell, J., Lapata, M.: Composition in distributional models of semantics. Cogn. Sci. **34**(8), 1388–1429 (2010)
18. Rungsawang, A.: DSIR: the first trec-7 attempt. In: TREC, pp. 366–372. Citeseer (1998)
19. Turney, P.D., Pantel, P., et al.: From frequency to meaning: vector space models of semantics. J. Artif. Intell. Res. **37**(1), 141–188 (2010)
20. Xu, W., Liu, X., Gong, Y.: Document clustering based on non-negative matrix factorization. In: Proceedings of the 26th Annual International ACM SIGIR Conference on Research and Development in Informaion Retrieval, pp. 267–273. ACM (2003)

Big Data Analytics and Visualization with Spatio-Temporal Correlations for Traffic Accidents

Xiaoliang Fan[1], Baoqin He[1], Cheng Wang[1], Jonathan Li[1(✉)],
Ming Cheng[1], Huaqiang Huang[1], and Xiao Liu[2,3]

[1] Fujian Key Laboratory of Sensing and Computing for Smart City,
School of Information Science and Engineering, Xiamen University,
Xiamen 361000, China
xfb_fxl@xm.gov.cn, {315441777,514187809}@qq.com,
{cwang,junli,chm99}@xmu.edu.cn
[2] Shanghai Key Laboratory of Trustworthy Computing,
East China Normal University, Shanghai 200062, China
xliu@sei.ecnu.edu.cn
[3] School of Information Technology,
Deakin University, Melbourne, VIC 3125, Australia

Abstract. Big data analytics for traffic accidents is a hot topic and has significant values for a smart and safe traffic in the city. Based on the massive traffic accident data from October 2014 to March 2015 in Xiamen, China, we propose a novel accident occurrences analytics method in both spatial and temporal dimensions to predict when and where an accident with a specific crash type will occur consequentially by whom. Firstly, we analyze and visualize accident occurrences in both temporal and spatial view. Second, we illustrate spatio-temporal visualization results through two case studies in multiple road segments, and the impact of weather on crash types. These findings of accident occurrences analysis and visualization would not only help traffic police department implement instant personnel assignments among simultaneous accidents, but also inform individual drivers about accident-prone sections and the time span which requires their most attention.

Keywords: Big data analytics · Accident occurrence analysis · Crash type analysis · Spatio-temporal correlations · Visualization

1 Introduction

Big Data analytics and visualization have been driving nearly every aspect of society, including mobile services, intelligent transportation, manufacturing, financial services, life sciences, and physical sciences [1, 2]. Despite significant development and advancement in vehicle technology and transportation engineering over the last 50 years, traffic accidents are still one of the major accidental causes of deaths and injuries worldwide [3]. For example, there are 700 ~ 800 traffic accidents daily in Xiamen, a middle size city with over 3 million populations in China. Accident data seems not to be a big data scenario due to its "small" volume. However, accident data analyses face

© Springer International Publishing Switzerland 2015
G. Wang et al. (Eds.): ICA3PP 2015, Part II, LNCS 9529, pp. 255–268, 2015.
DOI: 10.1007/978-3-319-27122-4_18

typical big data challenges as well: (1) it is necessary to analyze accidents data very rapidly (i.e., "velocity" feature of big data). The occurrence of an accident would generate both potential traffic congestions and secondary accidents. For example, even a very small accident may cause big traffic congestion in rush hours at crowded segments; and (2) it is quite difficult to mine the value of accident data (i.e., "value" feature of big data), especially in the spatio-temporal view precisely. For example, when and where to occur which type of accidents is nearly unpredictable.

The analysis and prediction of accident occurrences are research areas of considerable interest for a long time [4, 5]. Comprehensive works have been investigated to find the most important risks and variables that might contribute to accident occurrences [10]. However, the limitations of previous works are [16–19]: (1) they considered temporal and spatial view separately; and (2) it is rare to analyze accident occurrences quantitatively in spatio-temporal visualization.

In this paper, we propose a novel accident occurrences analytics and visualization method in spatio-temporal dimension to foresee when and where an accident with a certain crash type will happen consequentially by whom. The abundant sources of 38,674 accident records come from Xiamen City in China from October 2014 to March 2015. First, we analyze the spatial and temporal view of accident occurrences. Second, we illustrate spatio-temporal visualization results through two case studies in multiple road segments, and the impact of weather on crash types.

The remainder of this paper is organized as follows. Section 2 introduces the related works. Section 3 analyzes accident occurrences in spatio-temporal view. Section 4 illustrates the accident big data analytics results and visualization in two case studies. Finally, the general conclusion is drawn in Sect. 5.

2 Related Works

2.1 Accident Occurrences Analysis

The assessment and prediction of the occurrence of accidents as well as how to deal with this risk are research areas of considerable interest for a long time. Comprehensive surveys could be found to investigate the most important risks and variables that might contribute to accident occurrences [4, 5, 17]. Later, several models focus on the impact of temporal and spatial patterns on accident occurrences separately. Lord and Geedipally [6] studied the effects of modeling single- and multivehicle crashes, separately and jointly. Classification and regression tree has been used to perform variable selection [7]. Furthermore, Park and Harghani [14] investigated a primary incident's impact on secondary incidents. However, previous works mainly considered temporal or spatial view separately. Thus the analysis of spatio-temporal correlations on accidents is still an open issue.

2.2 Crash Types Analysis

In order to reduce accident occurrences and minimize the severity of crashes, various crash type models have been studied to reveal the mechanisms of crash occurrences.

Qin et al. [8] implemented a Bayesian framework to predict crash occurrences in relation to the hourly exposure by crash types. Four crash types were analyzed: (1) single-vehicle, (2) multivehicle same direction, (3) multivehicle opposite directions, and (4) multi-vehicle intersecting directions. Moreover, several other works [9] have also focused on propensity of crash types by developing safety performance functions for highway intersections. Furthermore, four features are widely considered as main factors that cause accidents in different crash types [10]: *geometric factors* (i.e., number of lanes, grade, road segments); *weather* (i.e., rains, snow), *traffic* (i.e., speed, volume), and *driver characteristics* (i.e., age, sex, driving years). However, existing works mainly discuss the features above in the qualitative dimension, while it is rare to analyze the spatio-temporal view quantitatively. In this paper, we focus on the impact of weather on crash types in terms of spatio-temporal visualization.

2.3 Accident Visualization

Wang et al. [11, 15] presented an interactive system for visual analysis of urban traffic congestion based on GPS trajectories. Pack et al. [12] studied incidents visualization from sensors data. Specifically, they designed a linked view interface to visualize the spatial, temporal and multi-dimensional aspects of accidents. Piringer et al. [13] proposed an automatic method to detect and prioritize different types of events by surveillance videos in a tunnel and marked them in space and time. We focus on accident occurrences and crash types analysis in the spatio-temporal dimensions, considering the impact of weather on the spatio-temporal visualization. No such accident data analysis has been studied before in the accident visualization community.

3 Accident Occurrences Analytics in Temporal and Spatial View

3.1 Datasets and Data Pre-processing

When a traffic accident was reported to Xiamen Intelligent Transport Control Center (ITCC), Traffic Accident Management System (TAMS) would initialize an accident record, including several initial information such as accident location (road name, longitude, latitude, and zone ID), number of vehicles, and accident time. In addition, during the accident response period, new information about this accident was continually added to the previous accident record, mostly details such as vehicle type and driver characteristics (i.e., age, sex, driving years). In this paper, we use the following four datasets for accident occurrences and crash-type analysis:

- *Dataset_1* consists six months of **accident data** from October 2014 to March 2015 in Xiamen, totally 38,674 records. Each record has 112 fields, indicating when, where and how the crash occurred.
- *Dataset_2* describes **accident vehicles and drivers** in Xiamen. Each record includes fields such as who were involved in this accidents as well as information on driver characteristics (e.g., age, sex, driving years). The timespan of this dataset is also from October 2014 to March 2015.

- *Dataset_3* is the **weather forecasting data** in Xiamen from October 2014 to March 2015, crawled from the website[1].
- *Dataset_4* is the **road networks** of Xiamen. It contains administrative region, expressway, urban main roads, branch roads, etc.

The pre-processing phase consists of two steps:

- **Road Network Processing.** We first improved the road network quality by filtering out irrelevant roads, merging and splitting ways, and correcting errors. Second, we extracted road segments, crossings and regions from road networks. Specifically, urban arterial roads are divided into 144 segments by traffic lights and road crossings. In addition, we marked 98 road crossings based on the road segments, in which the crossing is a circle with 150 meters. Therefore, we constructed three layers: road segments, road crossings and regions.
- **Accident Data Cleaning and Pre-processing.** Three raw datasets (Dataset_1, Dataset_2 and Dataset_3) are fused that fields with little correlations to accident occurrences are deleted. Therefore, we extracted 15 fields from three datasets. Other preprocessing methods include data integration, conversion and reduction.

Table 1 shows the summary descriptive statistics for part of variables in the above three datasets. Various variables are described in Table 1, such as weather (rain, no rain), rush hour, daytime (day, night), crash position (front, right, left, rear, right front, left front, right rear, left rear), accident liability (full responsibility, without fault), sex, age, driving years, crash type (single-vehicle, side-wipe, rear-end), and location type (segment, crossing, others).

3.2   Temporal View

The accident occurrences are widely considered to represent the temporal periodical pattern. For example, few hours may have more accidents than other time span. Figure 1 shows the temporal view of accident occurrences in the periodical pattern. Specifically, Fig. 1(a) and (b) describe the peridical pattern in weekdays and weekends in separate charts. First, weekdays are shown to have obvious morning and evening peak, while such peaks are not repeatable in the weekend (e.g., less accidents happened during the weekend). In addition, this phenomenon is highly corresponding to the traffic conges-tion. For instance, when the traffic flow reached the early peak in the morning, accident occurrences were at the early peak accordingly. Second, Fig. 1(c) is the overlay chart of the periodical pattern, and the supplementary comment is that the early peak in the weekend is both smaller and more postponed than those in the weekdays.

In summary, the early and evening peak of accidents is strongly correlated to the peak of traffic flows in urban arterial roads. For example, the early and evening peak of traffic flows is also similar in weekdays, while weakened and postponed in weekends.

---

[1] Weather forecasting website, http://lishi.tianqi.com/xiamen/index.html.

Table 1. Descriptive statistics for the variables in three datasets

Variables	Type	Coding	Descriptive Statistics (29425)
Weather	Binary	1 = Rainy day 0 = Non-rainy day	21.1 % (6222) 78.9 % (23203)
Rush hour	Binary	1 = Rush-hour traffic 0 = Non-rush-hour traffic	28.2 % (8310) 71.8 % (21115)
Daytime	Binary	1 = Daytime 0 = Night	86.5 % (25438) 13.5 % (3987)
Crash position	Nominal	1 = front 2 = right 3 = left 4 = rear 5 = right front 6 = left front 7 = right rear 8 = left rear	21.0 % (6181) 13.9 % (4095) 14.6 % (4302) 15.8 % (4648) 12.7 % (3727) 10.4 % (3067) 4.8 % (1423) 6.7 % (1982)
Accident liability	Binary	1 = full responsibility 0 = without fault	54.3 % (15988) 45.7 % (13437)
Sex	Binary	1 = male 0 = female	17.1 % (5031) 82.6 % (24316)
Age	Continuous	Driver's age	Mean = 36.18; Std Dev. = 8.981
Driving years Crash type Location type	Continuous Nominal Nominal	0 = Single-vehicle crash 1 = Side-wipe crash 2 = Rear-end crash 0 = Road segment 1 = Road crossing 2 = Others	Mean = 2.46; Std Dev. = 1.817 3.4 % (1009) 69.4 % (20413) 27.2 % (8003) 58.2 % (17133) 31.9 % (9388) 9.9 % (2904)

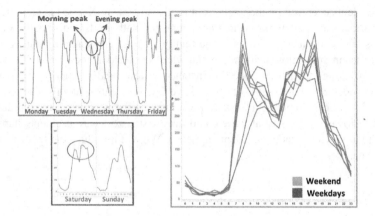

Fig. 1. Temporal view of accident occurrences: the periodical pattern in six months: (a) separate charts by weekdays; (b) separate charts by weekend; and (c) the overlay chart.

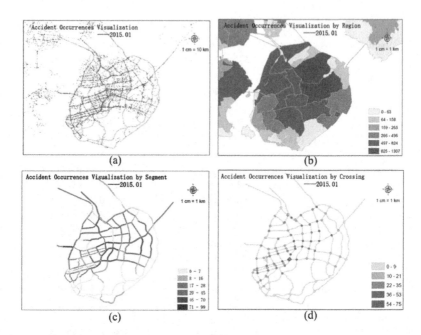

Fig. 2. Spatial view and visualization of accident occurrences for one month with different granularities: (a) coordinates of each accident; (b) by region; (c) by road segment; and (d) by crossing.

3.3 Spatial View

The spatial view and visualization of accident occurrences in January 2015 is presented with different granularities in Fig. 2. Figure 2(a) shows the latitude and longitude coordinates of each accident, and totally 5682 accident occurred in January. Figure 2(b) describes the spatial view of accident occurrences by administration region of the traffic police (the deeper the color, the more the accident in the region). Figure 2(c) shows where accidents occurred on the totally 144 road segments in Xiamen Island, including the four bridges and one tunnel which are connected with the Island. Finally, Fig. 2(d) illustrates the accident occurrences in the totally 99 road crossings in Xiamen Island.

There is an indication that the spatial view of accident occurrences meets the condition of long-tail distribution. For instance, a few road segments and crossings have many accidents while most of others have few accidents spatially. The result will help traffic polices implement instant personnel assignments among simultaneous accidents. However, the spatial view could only visualize where accidents happened, but don't know when exactly accident happened. We will introduce the spatio-temporal view in Sect. 4.1.

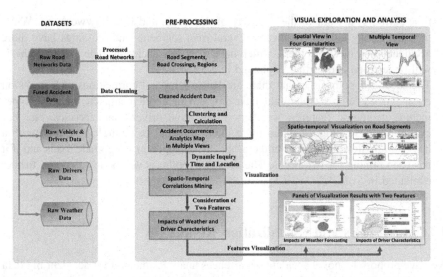

Fig. 3. The design methodology of accident occurrences analytics and visualization with spatio-temporal correlations. We use four datasets (left); in the preprocessing step (center), we extract road segments, crossing and regions from road networks, then clean the data from fused accidents data; and in the visual exploration and analysis step (right), we visualize the results in spatio-temporal view, integrated with the impact of two features on crash types.

3.4   Design of Accident Occurrences Analytics with Spatio-Temporal Correlations

Figure 3 shows the design methodology of accident occurrences analytics and visualization. Our visual analysis work consists of three phases. The first phase is data collection and fusion (left in Fig. 3). Second, in the preprocessing phase (center in Fig. 3), we start from the input data, and extract road segments, crossing and regions from road networks that fit our model. Finally in the third phase of visual exploration and analysis (right in Fig. 3), we visualize the results in spatio-temporal view, integrated with the impact of two features on crash types. The methodology will be implemented in Sect. 4 as two case studies. Plus, we use the Tableau Desktop V8.3[2] software for visualization.

3.5   Hypotheses

Based on the review of the state of the art in Sect. 2, we propose the following two hypotheses, which will be explained and testified in Sect. 4:

- The first hypothesis is that there are various spatio-temporal patterns for accident occurrences. For example, the temporal periodical pattern indicates that the accident occurrences would accumulate on certain time period(s) while decrease during other

---

[2] Tableau Desktop 8.3, www.tableau.com.

time period(s) in hour of the day, day of the week, and weekday/weekend. While the spatial long-tail pattern means several road segments and crossings have more accidents than most of others, which have very few accidents. The first hypothesis will be testified and further explained in Sect. 4.1.

- The second hypothesis is that there are spatio-temporal correlations of features on crash types Features that might have implicit or explicit impacts on crash types include geometric features, weather, traffic flow, driver characteristics, etc. For example, sideswipe crashes are more likely to occur in multiple-lane road with a heavy traffic flow, while rear-end crashes often happen in steep grade roads and if it has been raining for two hours. The second hypothesis will be testified and further explained in Sect. 4.2.

4 Case Studies and Visualization Results

We have proposed a novel accident occurrences analytics method for accident big data in multiple views. The following two cases will demonstrate the spatio-temporal visualization results in multiple road segments (Sect. 4.1), and the impact of weather on crash types (Sect. 4.2).

4.1 Case I: Accident Occurrences Visualization on Multiple Road Segments

On the road segment level, as shown in Fig. 4(b), we use a table to represent temporal accidents occurrences analytics for six month. The table contains seven rows representing days of the week from Monday to Sunday, and each row contains 24 columns (i.e., 24 h a day). Thus, each cell represent number of accidents occurred at an hour of the day. Specifically, the darker color indicates the more accidents at the hour of the day.

Through road segments classification, Fig. 4 shows the distinguished spatio-temporal patterns on six selected road segments in Xiamen Island. First, as shown in Fig. 4(a), each segment presents its distinguished temporal pattern in accident occurrences visualization. We believe that such differences are mainly due to the following factors correlated to the segment:

- **Commuting hours:** Fig. 4(b) shows a main bridge which links the Xiamen Island to outsides on weekdays, with both a morning peak when people go to work from home, and an evening peak when people go back home after work.
- **Tourist attractions:** Fig. 4(c) shows on segments next to two biggest tourist attractions in Xiamen (i.e., "Gulangyu Island" and "ZhongShan Road", accidents often happen at weekends. In fact, Xiamen is one of the famous tourist destinations nationwide on weekends and holiday.
- **Schools and Shopping malls:** Fig. 4(d) and (f) show two road segments with very different behaviors: as shown in Fig. 4(d), morning accident peaks often come earlier near primary schools, because parents bring children to school before they drive to work on weekdays; while as described in Fig. 4(f), evening accident peaks

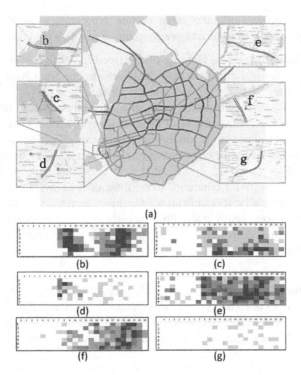

Fig. 4. Distinguished spatio-temporal patterns on six selected road segments in Xiamen Island: (a) each of six road segments has its distinguished temporal patterns in a global view; (b) accidents on Haicang bridge connecting Xiamen island with outside often occur at commuting hours on weekdays; (c) accidents near tourist attractions often happen on weekends; (d) accidents next to primary schools and accident-prone segments also are apt to happen on weekdays with earlier morning peak; (e) accidents could occur at almost any time span in the city downtown and most serious accident-prone segments; (f) accidents near shopping mall are likely to happen during evening peaks; and (g) accidents occurred very occasionally on expressways such as "Chenggong expressway".

were always postponed close to shopping malls, because people are likely to go shopping or have a dinner after work.

- **Accident-prone segments:** Fig. 4(e) shows that on arterial roads in the city downtown, which are also accident-prone segments, accidents could occur at almost any time span. This finding is coherent to the traffic flows at congestion-prone segments.
- **Expressways:** as shown in Fig. 4(g), accidents occurred very occasionally on expressways such as "Chenggong expressway". Because expressways usually have smooth traffic condition.

Furthermore, we could further analyze crash types with spatio-temporal view based on classification results from Fig. 4. Figure 5 shows three pie charts, which indicates different portions of crash types on three selected road segments (see Fig. 4(b), (d), and

(e) respectively). Specifically, the green portion represents rear-end crashes, blue represents single-vehicle crashes and orange represents side-wipe crashes:

- Figure 5(a) shows that on the Haicang Bridge (see Fig. 4(b)), rear-end crashes takes the largest portion while there is few single-vehicle crashes, because this type of road segments are normally straight without forks.
- Figure 5(b) indicates that it is likely to occur single-vehicle crashes on this segment (see Fig. 4(d)). The characteristics of these road segments are both a narrow road and there are not isolated strips between vehicles lanes and pedestrian/bicycle lanes.
- Figure 5(c) shows that in the busy arterial road segments, it is opt to occur side-wipe crashes (see Fig. 4(e)). The complicated road networks, multiple crossings and zebra crossing collectively contribute to the difficulties in driving through this type of segments. Especially, it is difficult for the driver to avoid side-wipe crashes at a turning. Furthermore, heavy traffic flows at early and evening peaks make the risk of side-wipe crashes even worse, because of frequent lane changes and cut-into-line in this circumstance.

Figure 5 collectively suggests that it is likely to occur side-wipe crashes at crossings, while rear-end crashes often happen at road segments. In summary, through the first case on spatio-temporal view of accident occurrences analysis, both traffic polices and drivers could explore different accident occurrence patterns with our visualization results.

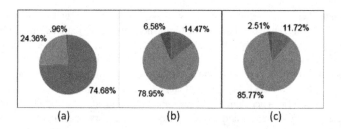

Fig. 5. The percentage of different crash types in three segments (see Fig. 4(b), (d), and (e) respectively) (Color figure online)

4.2 Case II: Crash Types Visualization with the Feature of Weather

Figure 6 presents visualization results of crash-type analysis with the feature of weather. The panel contains four views: map view (Fig. 6(a)), temporal view (Fig. 6(b)), weather view (Fig. 6(c)) and crash-type view (Fig. 6(d) and (e)). In addition, Fig. 6(f) shows various filters, which provide dynamic visual statistics and fast combination queries on demand. Data filters include spatial and temporal queries, and the selection of weather and crash-type. **From the spatial aspect,** three selection shapes could be used: circle, rectangular and lasso (Fig. 6(g)). We could also select road segments, crossings and regions through shape filters. **From the temporal aspect,** a three-level temporal filter could be used from date, week and time in Fig. 6(b). Therefore, we could build complex scenarios by the combination of atomic queries. For example, we could analyze and

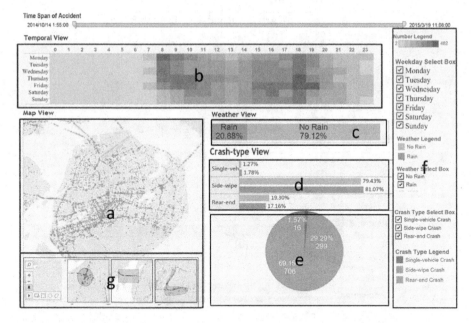

Fig. 6. Crash Types Analysis and Spatio-temporal Visualization on Weather: (a) map view of accident occurrences; (b) temporal view of accident occurrence; (c) percentage distribution on weathers; (d) percentage distribution on crash-type by weathers; (e) percentage distribution on crash-type; (f) (g) selection shapes on data filter.

visualize the results of when and where are likely to occur which type of crash in the rainy day.

To further illustrate the impact of weather on crash types, we select three segment types: four bridges (left picture in Fig. 7(a)), an arterial road (center picture in Fig. 7(a)) and several branch roads (right picture in Fig. 7(a)). Specifically, there is no intersection or ramp on the bridges, while there are zebra crossings and crossings on arterial roads. It seems that there is no connection between weather and accident occurrences, but it's meaningful when we consider temporal feature and cash-types.

The visualization results have the following indications:

- Most accidents are rear-end crashes on the bridges (65.30 %, 81.67 %). On the contrary, most accidents are side-wipe crashes on arterial roads (79.43 %, 81.07 %) and branch roads (78.26 %, 88.81 %). The main reasons for these results are: (1) the traffic condition is normally fluent with high speed on the bridge, which might result in rear-end crashes due to speeding behaviors; (2) there is always congestion in urban arterial roads, which increases the risk for side-wipe crashes if there are frequent lane changes at the crossings and turns; and (3) it is unavoidable that narrow branch roads could induce side-wipe crashes.

- Weather is likely to have more impact on accidents for bridges, next for branch roads, but doesn't have obvious influence on arterial roads. Because percentages of side-wipe crashes and rear-end crashes change more than 15 % when it rains on

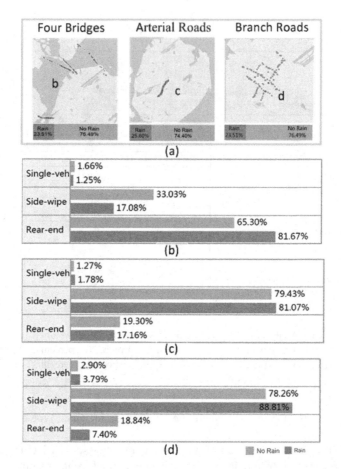

Fig. 7. The impact of weather on crash types, which has different influence on crash types: (a) three selected typical types of road segments; (b) the influence of weather on bridges; (c) the influence of weather on arterial roads; (d) the influence of weather on branch roads.

bridges, about 10 % on branch roads, and less than 3 % on the arterial roads. When we focus on the rear-end crashes, it seems that a heavy and long-lasting rain would decrease the rear-end crashes on the bridges (65.30 %, 81.67 %), but increase the possibility of side-wipe crashes on the branch roads (18.84 %, 7.40 %). On the rainy days, there are slippery ground and speed cars on bridges.

5   Conclusion

Given the massive traffic accident records in urban arterial roads, accident occurrence analysis is known to identify the main factors that contribute to crash type, crash position and severity. However, due to heterogeneous case-by-case nature of traffic accidents, the difficulty to analyze such traffic big data quantitatively has led to minimal effects in previous works. Especially, previous works have a major shortage in the lack of considering spatio-temporal correlations in accident occurrences analytics.

By analyzing the traffic accident data from October 2014 and March 2015 in Xiamen, China, we propose a novel accident occurrence analysis and visualization method in both spatial and temporal dimensions, in order to predict when and where an accident with a certain crash type will happen sequentially by whom. Despite the significant progress of spatio-temporal visualization in accident occurrences, there still remain numerous avenues to explore. Our future works include the consideration of geometrics features (number of lanes, grade, etc.) in spatio-temporal correlations mining in crash types analysis. For example, sideswipe crashes are likely to happen on multiple lanes, while rear-end crashes are often seen in road segments with steep grade.

Acknowledgments. This work is supported by the grants from Natural Science Foundation of China (No. 61300232, No. 61300042); Ministry of Education of China "Chunhui Plan" Cooperation and Research Project (No. Z2012114, Z2014141); Funds of State Key Laboratory for Novel Software Technology, Nanjing University (KFKT2014B09); Fundamental Research Funds for the Central Universities (lzujbky-2015-100); and China Telecom Corp. Gansu Branch Cuiying Funds (lzudxcy-2014-6). The authors acknowledge Xiamen Intelligent Transport Control Center (ITCC) for providing the data.

References

1. Jagadish, H.V., Gehrke, J., Labrinidis, A., Papakonstantinou, Y., Patel, J., Ramakrishnan, R.: Big data and its technical challenges. Commun. ACM **57**(7), 86–94 (2014)
2. Wu, X., Zhu, X., Wu, G., Ding, W.: Data mining with big data. IEEE Trans. Knowl. Data Eng. **26**(1), 97–107 (2014)
3. WHO: World Report on Road Traffic Injury Prevention. World Health Organization, Geneva (2004)
4. Hauer, E.: Speed and safety. Transp. Res. Rec. **2103**(2103), 10–17 (2009)
5. Ma, J., Kockelman, K.M., Damien, P.: A multivariate Poisson-lognormal regression model for prediction of crash counts by severity, using Bayesian methods. Accid. Anal. Prev. **40**(3), 964–975 (2008)
6. Lord, D., Geedipally, S.: Investigating the effect of modeling single-vehicle and multi-vehicle crashes separately on confidence intervals of Poisson–gamma models. Accid. Anal. Prev. **42**(4), 1273–1282 (2010)
7. Yu, R., Abdel-Aty, M.: Utilizing support vector machine in real-time crash risk evaluation. Accid. Anal. Prev. **51**(2), 252–259 (2013)
8. Qin, X., Ivan, J., Ravishanker, N., Liu, J., Tepas, D.: Bayesian estimation of hourly exposure functions by crash type and time of day. Accid. Anal. Prev. **38**(6), 1071–1080 (2006)
9. Jonsson, T., Lyon, C., Ivan, J., Washington, S., van Schalkwyk, I., Lord, D.: Investigating differences in the performance of safety performance functions estimated for total crash count and for crash count by crash type. Transp. Res. Rec. J Transp. Res. Board **137**(2102), 115–123 (2009)

10. Yu, R., Abdel-Aty, M.A., Ahmed, M.M., Wang, X.: Utilizing microscopic traffic and weather data to analyze real-time crash patterns in the context of active traffic management. IEEE Trans. Intell. Transp. Syst. **15**(1), 205–213 (2014)
11. Wang, Z., Lu, M., Yuan, X., Zhang, J., de Wetering, H.: Visual traffic jam analysis based on trajectory data. IEEE Trans. Vis. Comput. Graph **19**(12), 2159–2168 (2013)
12. Pack, M., Wongsuphasawat, K., VanDaniker, M., Filippova, D.: Ice–visual analytics for transportation incident datasets. In: IEEE International Conference on Information Reuse Integration, pp. 200–205. IEEE Press, New York (2009)
13. Piringer, H., Buchetics, M., Benedik, R.: Alvis: situation awareness in the surveillance of road tunnels. In: IEEE Conference VAST, pp. 153–162. IEEE Press, New York (2012)
14. Park, H., Haghani, A: Real-time prediction of secondary incident occurrences using vehicle probe data. Transp. Res. Part C Emerg. Technol. (2015). doi:10.1016/j.trc.2015.03.018
15. Wang, Z., Yuan, X.: Urban trajectory timeline visualization. In: IEEE International Conference on BigComp. IEEE Press, New York (2014)
16. Zhang, G., Yau, K.W., Zhang, X.: Analyzing fault and severity in pedestrian–motor vehicle accidents in China. Accid. Anal. Prev. **73**(73), 141–150 (2014)
17. Zhang, G., Yau, K.W., Zhang, X.: Risk factors associated with traffic violations and accident severity in China. Accid. Anal. Prev. **59**(10), 18–25 (2013)
18. Tak, S., Kim, S., Yeo, H.: Development of a Deceleration-Based Surrogate Safety Measure for Rear-End Collision Risk. IEEE Trans. Intell. Transp. Syst. **16**(5), 2435–2445 (2015)
19. Lin, L., Wang, Q., Sadek, A.W.: A novel variable selection method based on frequent pattern tree for real-time traffic accident risk prediction. Transp. Res. Part C Emerg. Technol. **55**, 444–459 (2015)

A Novel APP Recommendation Method Based on SVD and Social Influence

Qiudang Wang[1], Xiao Liu[1,2(✉)], Shasha Zhang[1], Yuanchun Jiang[3],
Fei Du[3], Yading Yue[4], and Yu Liang[4]

[1] Shanghai Key Laboratory of Trustworthy Computing, East China Normal
University, Shanghai 200062, China
xliu@sei.ecnu.edu.cn
[2] School of Information Technology, Deakin University, Melbourne, VIC 3125,
Australia
[3] School of Management, Hefei University of Technology, Hefei 230009, China
[4] Knowledge Discovery Team, Department of Social Networks Operation,
Tencent Inc., Shenzhen 518057, China

Abstract. The market for Mobile Applications (APP for short) is perhaps the most thriving sector nowadays in the software industry with about 4 million APPs around the world. APP recommendation is playing an increasingly important role in every APP store to enhance user experience and raise revenue. Existing recommendation strategies are mainly based on user's individual information while their social relations are often neglected. However, it is an intuitive knowledge that users tend to be affected by their friends' recommendation in the choice of APPs. Therefore, it is worth investigating whether and how social influence can be employed for APP recommendation. In this paper, to answer the above question, we propose a novel APP recommendation method based on SVD (Singular Value Decomposition) algorithm and social influence which is defined by an extended CD (Credit Distribution) model. The experimental results based on the real-world datasets from Tencent APP Store demonstrate that our proposed method with social influence can achieve a better recommendation results than conventional SVD based algorithm without social relations.

Keywords: Recommendation · Social network · Mobile applications · SVD

1 Introduction

Browsing and shopping online has already become part of people's everyday life. As there is no shop assistant to recommend products in person, online recommendation powered by backend recommendation algorithms becomes the major if not the only way to help customers to choose and promote products selling online. Recommendation algorithms are often regarded as one of the most important competitiveness for E-Commerce companies such as Alibaba, Amazon, eBay, Taobo and JD [1]. Recommendation algorithms have been intensively studied by the researchers in the area of data mining, machine learning, information retrieval and also marketing science. Recent years have witnessed a dramatic increase in the market for mobile applications

© Springer International Publishing Switzerland 2015
G. Wang et al. (Eds.): ICA3PP 2015, Part II, LNCS 9529, pp. 269–281, 2015.
DOI: 10.1007/978-3-319-27122-4_19

(APP for short). Leading APP stores such as Google Play and Apple APP Store have well over 1 million APPs each and the whole market is estimated to have over 4 million APPs as in 2015 [2]. Popular Android app stores in China includes Baidu App Store, Tencent APP Store, Qihoo 360 Mobile Assistant, Wandoujia, and 91 Mobile Assistant [3]. These APPs cover almost every aspects of our everyday life. For example, the Tencent APP Store has over 50 types of APPs such as music, reading, video, entertainment, social network and so on. It has a cumulative 64 million daily app downloads as reported in 2014.

Given such a huge number of options, it is very difficult and in most cases very time-consuming for users to search, compare and find out the most suitable APPs. Meanwhile, it is also a very challenging task for the APP store to recommend the right APPs to the users. To tackle this problem, most existing strategies are based on the conventional "Collaborative Filtering" (CF) type of methods which mainly utilize user's personal information such as his/her APP download history, times of usage, and also their ratings for different APPs [4]. CF based algorithms, either item-based or user-based, have been widely applied in both traditional E-Commerce websites and APP stores. However, the statistics show that the success rate for online recommendation (e.g. the so called clickthrough rate) is often less than 0.1 %. Even for Facebook which is regarded as the most successful social network company in online advertisements, the average clickthrough rate is often less than 0.3 % [5]. According to many studies, the problem with user's download history is obvious since the action of download an APP does not necessarily mean that the user likes it. In many cases, users just download an APP because it is free and they want to have a try. Meanwhile, as the storage for mobile devices is getting much larger and cheaper, there are many APPs on users' mobile devices which are seldom used but they just do not bother to delete them. As for the APP ratings, the problem of data sparsity is very common and difficult to handle. According to [6], the density of the users' ratings data is often less than 1 % in most recommender systems as people tend to rate a product only when it is very good or very bad.

Recently, the investigation of recommendation with social relations has been attracted widely attention. Traditional recommender systems only utilize user's personal information and assume that all users are independent to each other. However, in the real-world, we often ask our friends for recommendation on some specific products as we normally have a high confidence on the products recommended by our trusted friends. In addition, social information such as the friends' download, usage and ratings about a specific type of products can help to address the "cold-start" and data sparsity problem for fresh users. Therefore, how to employ user's social relations for recommendation is becoming a very hot topic and promising direction for recommender systems. For example, the work in [7] proposed a probabilistic graphical model which fuses the user-item matrix with the users' social trust networks. Some studies employ Web 2.0 applications to collect various kinds of social context information such as users' social trust network and tags issued by users or associated with items. There are already some preliminary results showing that better recommendations can be achieved with social integrated collaborative filtering algorithms than those without. However, no specific results on APP recommendation have been reported so far.

In general, recommendation frameworks with social relations can be designed with at least the following three steps: (1) to create a new or adopt a user's existing social network; (2) to define the social influence among users; (3) to design the recommendation algorithm based on the above social information. As the work in this area is still at its infancy, most existing studies are with general models and algorithms which are not dedicated to APPs. In this paper, we focus on the recommendation of mobile applications. Specifically, we propose a novel APP recommendation method based on SVD (Singular Value Decomposition) algorithm [6] and social influence defined by an extended CD (Credit Distribution) model [8]. Our method is evaluated with the real-world dataset from an Android APP Store running by Tencent Inc. (http://www. tencent.com/en-us/index.shtml) which is the second largest social network company after Facebook. The experimental results have shown our method can achieve better performance than conventional SVD based algorithms without social relations.

The remainder of this paper is organized as follows. Section 2 presents the related work. Section 3 proposes our novel APP recommendation method. Section 4 demonstrates the experimental results based on Tencent APP Store. Section 5 addresses the conclusions and points out the future work.

2 Related Work

Recently, APP recommendation is emerging as one of the most popular topics in recommender systems due to the rapid growth in the number of mobile applications. SimApp which works as a detector for similar APPs is based on their semantics and the classification results can help APP recommendation [9]. The work in [10] proposes an Actual-Tempting (AT) model under the basic assumption that downloaded APPs demonstrated the sense of satisfaction and new APP download can be predicted with a tempting value. Based on the AT model, recommendation of a new APP may be given only when its temptation is higher than the satisfaction of old ones. This model has better performance than the traditional recommendation methods that only utilize user interests, e.g., Collaborative Filtering (CF) based methods. Furthermore, some methods utilize context information such as time and location to provide users with more accurate recommendation [11, 12]. However, most existing recommender systems are based on individual information such as user profile or geographical information rather than user's social attributes.

Collaborative filtering (CF) and content-based recommendation (CBR) belong to the most popular conventional recommendation approaches. Item-based CF [6] and User-based CF [13] make recommendation based on item similarity and user similarity respectively where the similarity is calculated on the user-item matrix. Data sparsity is a notorious challenge in CF. APPJoy system proposed in [14] adopted item-based CF given its better ability in handling data sparsity compared with user-based CF [13].

Singular Value Decomposition (SVD) is a widely used algorithm which can implement collaborative filtering. SVD finds hidden features which can implicitly connects users and items, and gets the closeness values of user-feature and item-feature through learning. It uses matrix factorization to decompose the User-Item matrix into a user matrix and an item matrix. Algorithms related to matrix factorization like SVD predefine a function in order to predict ratings of users, and the variables in the prediction function will be learned through stochastic gradient descent [15]. In this paper, we first exploited ALS-WR which is a specific implementation of the SVD algorithm as proposed in [4] to handle APP recommendation on large-scale dataset as ALS-WR is more scalable than SVD. Additionally, in order to gain user rating matrix, our work employed social influence which will be discussed in the next section.

Nowadays, researchers pay much more attention on social attributes as more and more people utilizing social network for personalized activities. It is recognized that social influence is very important on social recommendation. The study on user influence propagation on social networks has aroused the interest of many researchers. Influence propagation can be used to search for a subset of users with significant impact on social networks. In [16], probabilistic nature which can speed up estimation of social influence spread is appended and the work on social influence can be divided into three aspects: the first aspect is on the influence model, the second aspect is on the social influence propagation and the third aspect is about the selection of seed nodes in order to get the maximal influence with minimal cost. Moreover, some researchers distinguished the social influences according to different topics. In order to measure social influence based on different topics on large scale networks, Topical Affinity Propagation (TAP) model was proposed in [17]. TAP has the capability of modelling different social influence on the topic-level by utilizing existing topic-models as well as network structures. Some methods incorporated social context to achieve more accurate recommendation. For example, a method combines matrix factorization and information of social context was provided in [18]. This method was also designed for solving the problem of data sparsity. However, the authors in [18] incorporated social context information such as social tags while we in this paper employ the user action logs on App download and usage.

Recently, some works on influence propagation are based on social graphs with influence probabilities. The work in [19] provided methods to compute influence probabilities on edges of social network from user action logs and proposes several models for social possibility determination, e.g., Continuous Time (CT) Models and Discrete Time (DT) Models (an improved version of CT model). In comparison, DT model is more scalable than CT model which is much more time-consuming for training. The proposed method tries to predict whether a user will make a certain action at a specific time or not. In the meanwhile, social influence measurement should be modified in consideration of different platforms. For example, the work in [20] proposed three influence evaluation methods based on Twitter which is a well-known Microblog application. The work in [21] defines the social influence as the similarity or correlation between users, but it does not provide a specific method for influence measurement. The work in [8] introduced a model named CD (Credit Distribution) to address influence maximization by learning and predicting influence propagation on a social network. In this paper, we also investigate the measurement of social influence (to quantify the impact between individuals) based on social graph and action logs. Specifically, we are interested in actions related to APP download and usage. To the best of our knowledge, there is so far no work dedicated to APP recommendation which combined SVD algorithm with social influence.

3 APP Recommendation Based on SVD and Social Influence

As mentioned above, current recommendation should not only consider personal information but also social relations. In this paper, we propose a model named influence-based recommendation (denoted as IR). It is defined by using the function $f(u,i)$ as follows:

$$f(u,i) = \alpha*(\widehat{pr_{ui}}/\max(\widehat{pr_u})) + \beta*(\widehat{ir_{ui}}/\max(\widehat{ir_u})) \tag{1}$$

This function indicates the possibility of user u to download APP i where $\widehat{pr_{ui}}/\max(\widehat{pr_u})$ stands for user preference rating. From the review of personal preference of user u to APP i, $\widehat{pr_{ui}}$ denotes the user u's predicted usage frequency on APP i. $\max(\widehat{pr_u})$ represents the predicted maximum usage frequency of user u. $(\widehat{ir_{ui}}/\max \widehat{ir_u})$ represents for social influence rating which considers the influence and APP i's download ratio among friends of user u, $\widehat{ir_{ui}}$ indicates the influence of friends around user u to download APP i, and $\max(\widehat{ir_u})$ is the maximum value of user u's friend's influence to download any APPs. The detailed formula for $\widehat{pr_{ui}}$ and $\widehat{ir_{ui}}$ will be given in the following section. α and β are important coefficients with values in the range of [0,1] and $\beta = 1 - \alpha$.

In the following, we first introduce user preference prediction model and then incorporate it with friends' influences into the download possibility prediction. Table 1 summarizes the notation used here.

Table 1. Notations

Notation	Explanation
q_u	User u's feature vector
p_i	APP i's feature vector
$\widehat{pr_{ui}}$	User u's predicted usage frequency on APP i
$\widehat{ir_{ui}}$	User u's friends' influence to download APP i
r_{ui}	User u's real usage frequency on APP i
P	$P = [p_u]$ is the user feature matrix
Q	$Q = [q_i]$ is APP feature matrix
R	Usage frequencies matrix
n_{p_i}	The number of APP used by user u
n_{qj}	The number of users used APP i

3.1 Usage Preference Prediction

The usage frequency can directly and effectively represents a user's preference for an APP. Generally speaking, the higher the usage of an APP, the user is more likely to prefer this APP. Meanwhile, we also need to consider when an APP was used. For example, if an APP was used frequently about a year ago but it is not used anymore for recent few months, its value for preferen prediction will be decreased significantly.

Therefore, in this paper we try to choose the most recent usage frequency to train our prediction model and use usage frequency to denote user preference.

Given a usage frequencies matrix $R = \{r_{ui}\}_{n*m}$ (n users to m APPs), the element r_{ui} denotes the historical frequency of APP i . used by user u. The missing frequency, if user u has not used APP i before, can be predicted with the following formula:

$$\widehat{pr_{ui}} = q_u^T * p_i \tag{2}$$

Here q_u^T represents the user u's feature vector and p_i means the APP i's feature vector. The goal of our model is to compute $\widehat{pr_{ui}}$ for user u's every unused APP, and minimizing the RMSE (root mean squared error) on test dataset. In [4], the problem of RMSE minimization is formulated as finding p_u and q_i that minimize the loss function $L(P, Q)$:

$$L(P, Q) = \sum_{u, i \in I} (r_{ui} - p_u^T q_i)^2 + \lambda (\sum_u n_{p_u} ||p_u||^2 + \sum_i n_{qi} ||q_i||^2) \tag{3}$$

Where $P = [p_u]$ is the user feature m.tx, where $p_u \subseteq \mathbb{R}^{n_f}$ for all $i = 1\ldots\ldots n_p$, n_p is the number of users, and $Q = [q_i]$ is APP feature matrix, where $q_i \subseteq \mathbb{R}^{n_f}$ for all $i = 1\ldots\ldots n_q$, n_q is the number of APPs, here n_f is the dimension of the feature space. Besides n_{p_u} and n_{qi} represents the number of APP used by user u and the number of users used APP i respectively.

The $L(P, Q)$. minimization problem can be transformed into solving the equation $\frac{\partial L(P,Q)}{\partial p_u} = 0$ and $\frac{\partial L(P,Q)}{\partial q_i} = 0$ [4]. In this way, we can discover the relation between P and Q (as shown in Formulas 4 and 5) and then interactively solve the value of P and Q (as shown in Algorithm 1).

$$Q = P * R^T * \left(P * P^T + \lambda * \sum_u n_{p_u} * E\right)^{-1} \tag{4}$$

$$P = Q * R^T * (Q * Q^T + \lambda * \sum_i n_{qi} * E)^{-1} \tag{5}$$

Algorithm 1
Input: P, Q
Output: P, Q
1: initialize Q
2: **For** (i=0; i< maxIterations; i=i+1)
3: $P = Q * R^T * (Q * Q^T + \lambda * \sum_j n_{qj} * E)^{-1}$
4: $Q = P * R^T * \left(P * P^T + \lambda * \sum_i n_{p_i} * E\right)^{-1}$
5: **End For**

Q is initialized by assigning the average usage frequency for every APP as the first row, and random numbers within the range of maximum and minimum usage frequency for the remaining entries. The maxIterations stands for the number of maximum iterations which can be specified according to the available time for training. More details will be presented in Sect. 4 for the experiments.

3.2 Incorporating Social Influence

As discussed above, social influence is a key factor in APP recommendation. Therefore, after investigating the influence propagation models in previous work, we define a new social influence model and apply it to the APP recommendation scenario. Specifically, we use social influence and download rate of a user's friends to compute the possibility a user may download an APP under social influence. This is because a user is more likely to download an APP when friends with higher influence to him/her have already downloaded the APP. $\widehat{ir_{ui}}$ represents such a possibility and is defined as follows:

$$\widehat{ir_{ui}} = \sum\nolimits_{v \in F_u} D(v, i) * \gamma(v, u) \tag{6}$$

Where, F_u. indicates a set of users v, and v is reachable to user u in the social network. $D(v, i)$ with an value of either 0 or 1 represents whether user v used APP or not. $\gamma(v, u)$ is v's influence on u. Next, we will introduce the influence model and specify formula for $\gamma(v, u)$.

3.2.1 Data-Based Influence Diffusion Model (DID Model)

Unlike most previous work, we learn the edge probabilities from real data that is inspired by the idea of the work in [8]. Both our experimental results and those shown in [8] have demonstrated that if the probabilities are not learned from real data, the risk of choosing poor quality seeds will be increased. Here, the set of seeds is first introduced in the influence maximization problem [22] which is to find k "seed" nodes in the network such that by activating them we can maximize the expected influence spread.

As shown in Fig. 1, a social network G is demonstrated where nodes are users and edges are labeled with influence probabilities among users. As can be seen from Fig. 1, the computation of social influence consists of two parts, one is direct user influence

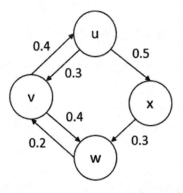

Fig. 1. Social network graph

and the other is indirect (or cascaded) user influence. Direct influence means the user v and user u are connected directly. Cascaded user influence means that although u do not have direct connection with w, u can propagate his/her influence to w through x, so that u can still have a hidden influence on w.

Cascaded user influence is calculated based on the result of direct user influence. Here, we first define direct user influence (Fig. 2).

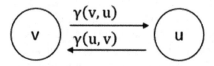

Fig. 2. Direct influence graph

The influence between two users is not symmetrical, we use $\gamma(v, u)$ to denote the influence of v on u. In this paper, v's infence on u is estimated by the following function:

$$\gamma(v, u) = \exp(-100/(\text{mutufriend}_{v,u} + \sum_{i \in I_{u,v}} \text{mutuAPP}_{u,i} + 1)). \tag{7}$$

Here, $\text{mutufriend}_{v,u}$ is the number of common friends of u and v. Let $I_{u,v}$ represents the set of APP i that both user u and user v have downloaded and used, and $\text{mutuAPP}_{u,i}$ indicates the usage frequency of user u on APP i.

Furthermore, we define cascaded user influence. Take user u and user w in Fig. 1 as an example. $\gamma(u, w)$ is defined as follows.

$$\gamma(u, w) = \gamma(u, v) * \gamma(v, w) + \gamma(u, x) * \gamma(x, w) - \gamma(u, v) * \gamma(v, w) * \gamma(u, x) * \gamma(x, w) \tag{8}$$

$\gamma(u, v) * \gamma(v, w)$ indicates u influence w through the path u- > v- > w, similarly, $\gamma(u, x) * \gamma(x, w)$ represents u influence w by the path u- > x- > w. To composite the result of the two paths, we adopt the inclusion-exclusion principle as shown in Formula 9.

$$P_1 \cup P_2 = P_1 \cup P_2 - P_1 \cap P_2 \tag{9}$$

Generally speaking, if user u has n paths to reach w, its influence on w is defined as follows:

$$\gamma(u, w) = |P_1 \cup P_2 \cup \ldots \cup P_n|$$
$$= \sum_{1 \leq i \leq n} |P_i| + \sum_{1 \leq i \leq j \leq n} |P_i \cap P_j| + \sum_{1 \leq i \leq j \leq k \leq n} |P_i \cap P_j \cap P_k| \tag{10}$$

Where P_i denotes the influence of u on w through the Path i.

4 Evaluation

In this section, we will demonstrate the experimental results for the evaluation of our novel APP recommendation algorithm based on social influence. Our experiments consist of two parts, the first part is to evaluate the social influence model and the second part is to evaluate the recommendation algorithm.

Our experiments are conducted on real datasets provided by Tencent as part of our collaborative project supported by CCF-Tencent Open Fund. Tencent is the second largest social network company after Facebook. Tencent's many services include social network, web portals, e-commerce, and multiplayer online games. Its most well-known software product is the instant messenger Tencent QQ, and also recently its Mobile chat service WeChat. Tencent runs an Android app Store named Tencent App Store. As shown in Fig. 3, Tencent App Store has both desktop and mobile versions, and it can

(a)   Desktop Version

(b)   Mobile Version   (c) List of Apps used by Friends

Fig. 3. Tencent app sotre

also get accessed through the website (http://sj.qq.com/). One of the most distinctive features about Tencent App Store is that after you login with your QQ ID, you will see the list of APPs used by your QQ friends. This is actually the major sector where our studies on APP recommendation with social influence can be applied and tested online. But at this stage, we can only employ offline datasets for evaluation purposes.

The datasets are generated from the offline database for Tencent APP Store. We start with the random selection of 10 K users and then search for their direct linked friends. After that, we are able to build a social network with about 300 K users. Finally, based on their user ID, we can query their APP download and usage information. In our experiments, all datasets have been anonymized according to Tencent's strict data protection standard to ensure no personal information can be obtained. The three main tables provided by Tencent are listed as follows. The first one is t_intimacy (uid, aid, intimacy) which shows how many time an APP has been used in the recent one month, the second is t_friend(uid, fid, mutufrd_cnt) which shows how many common friends two users share, and the third is t_appdowload(uid, aid, time) which shows the downloaded Apps and their download time. Detailed descriptions of these data are shown in Table 2 as follows.

Table 2. Description of datasets

Columns	Data types
uid:user ID	bigint
aid:APP ID	bigint
intimacy:the times uid used aid for recent one month	bigint
fid:user ID	bigint
time(t_friend):the time uid and fid become friend	String
time(t_appdowload):the time uid download aid for recent one month	datetime

In our experiments, we use t_intimacy $-$ t_intimacy $\cap$ t_appdowload as usage frequencies matrix R (as in Sect. 3.1) to train the user and APP feature matrix, and use t_intimacy and t_friend to build the social influence network, finally we take t_appdowload as our test data set.

As mentioned above, our experiment is composed of two parts. The first part is to verify our DID model (as in Sect. 3.2.1). We evaluated the activation probability of our model and compared with that of LT (Linear Threshold) Model. Here, a user's activation probability is defined as the number of users he or she is able to activate diving the number of total users. Specifically, for LT model, edge probabilities (direct user influence) are defined as $\gamma(v, u) = 1/N_u$, where N_u is the number of u's direct friends. The truncation threshold λ is the average value of edge probabilities. If v' s influence on u is over λ, we say that v activates u. In the experiment we run LT model for one thousand times. For DID model, edge probabilities are defined as in Eq. (10), the threshold λ is also the average value of edge probabilities. The result is showed in Fig. 4. We select top ten users with the activation probability as the seed set for both DID model and LT model. Obviously, DID model performs better than LT model (Figs. 4 and 5).

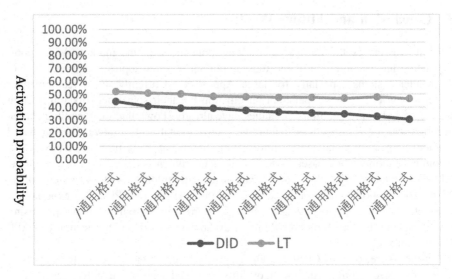

Fig. 4. Activation probability of top 10 users with DID and LT models

	iterations	Hit rate
ALS-WR	10	0.123%

	iterations	β	Hit rate
IR	10	0.4	0.125%
		0.7	0.130%
		1	0.125%

	iterations	Hit rate
	100	0.193%

iterations	β	Hit rate
100	0.4	0.553%

Fig. 5. APP recommendation results for traditional ALS-WR and our IR algorithm

The second part of our experiment is to test our influence-based recommendation algorithm (denoted as IR) and compare with that of ALS-WR [4] recommendation algorithm. Here, β is the proportion of influence rating $\widehat{ir_{ui}}$, introduced in Sect. 4. We employ both algorithms to recommend 10 APPs to every user. Under the same iterations, the hit rate of our IR based algorithm is higher and the highest hit rate can achieve 0.553 % which is much higher than that of 0.3 % as reported for Facebook's online advertisement mentioned earlier. In general, the results shown in Fig. 4 verify that our IR based recommendation algorithm can achieve much higher accuracy in APP recommendation than ALS-WR, especially when number of iterations reaches 100. Clearly, longer training time can help to significantly improve the performance of both algorithms but ours can gain a much better improvement. Meanwhile, the choice of β does not have much impact on the performance of our recommendation algorithm.

5 Conclusion and Future Work

As fast growing in the number of mobile applications in the market, App recommendation has become one of the most important research topics in the area of recommender systems especially for large App stores. Currently, most recommender systems only utilize users' personal information but their social network information was neglected. Some preliminary studies have already shown that the recommendation accuracy can be improved by integrating conventional collaborative filtering based methods with some social context information. In this paper, we proposed a novel APP recommendation method based on SVD and social influence. Specifically, we adopt the ALS-WR algorithm which is more scalable than traditional SVD and extended the Credit Distribution model for social influence on the use of APPs. The experiments conducted on the real-world datasets from Tencent App Store have shown promising results on both the activation probability of the social network and the accuracy of APP recommendation.

In the future, besides CF based algorithms, we can further investigate the performance of other recommendation algorithms enhanced with social influence. In addition, the social influence model especially the selection of seed users can be applied to APP advertisement as a kind of social influence propagation.

Acknowledgements. The research work reported in this paper is partly supported by CCF-Tencent Open Fund CCF-TencentRAGR20140109, National Natural Science Foundation of China (NSFC) under No. 61300042, No. 71490725, No. 71302064, No. 71371062, National Key Basic Research Program of China (2013CB329600), Research Fund for the Doctoral Program of Higher Education of China (Project 20120111120029), and Shanghai Knowledge Service Platform Project No. ZF1213.

References

1. Research and Markets, The World's Leading E-commerce Companies 2014. http://www.researchandmarke-ts.com/research/dtxzvc/the_worlds. Accessed 1 July 2015
2. Statista, Number of Apps Available in Leading App Stores as of July 2015. http://www.statista.com/statistics-/276623/number-of-apps-available-in-leading-app-stores/. Accessed 1 July 2015
3. Tech in Asia, 10 Alternative Android App Stores in China. https://www.techinasia.com/10-android-app-stores-china-2014-edition/. Accessed 1 July 2015
4. Zhou, Y., Wilkinson, D., Schreiber, R., Pan, R.: Large-scale parallel collaborative filtering for the netflix prize. In: Fleischer, R., Xu, J. (eds.) AAIM 2008. LNCS, vol. 5034, pp. 337–348. Springer, Heidelberg (2008)
5. Business Insider, Clickthrough Rate and Cost-per-click on Facebook for Selected Sectors. http://www.businessinsider.com.au/chart-of-the-day-facebook-ctr-cpc-per-sector-2011-1. Accessed 1 July 2015
6. Sarwar, B., Karypis, G., Konstan, J., Riedl, J.: Item-based collaborative filtering recommendation algorithms. In: Proceedings of the 10th International Conference on World Wide Web, pp. 285–295 (2001)

7. Ma, H., Yang, H., Lyu, M.R., King, I.: SoRec: social recommendation using probabilistic matrix factorization. In: Proceedings of the 2008 ACM International Conference on Information and Knowledge Management, pp. 931–940 (2008)
8. Amit, G., Bonchi, F., Lakshmanan, L.V.S.: A data-based approach to social influence maximization. Proc. VLDB Endowment 5(1), 73–84 (2011)
9. Chen, N., Hoi, S.C.H., Li, S., Xiao, X.: SimApp: a framework for detecting similar mobile applications by online kernel learning. In: Proceedings of the Eighth ACM International Conference on Web Search and Data Mining, pp. 305–314 (2015)
10. Yin, P., Luo, P., Lee, W., Wang, M.: App recommendation: a contest between satisfaction and temptation. In: Proceedings of the Sixth ACM International Conference on Web Search and Data Mining, pp. 395–404 (2013)
11. Davidsson, C., Moritz, S.: Utilizing implicit feedback and context to recommend mobile applications from first use. In: Proceedings of the 2011 Workshop on Context-Awareness in Retrieval and Recommendation, pp. 19–22 (2011)
12. Girardello, A., Michahelles, F.: AppAware: which mobile applications are hot? In: Proceedings of the 12th International Conference on Human Computer Interaction with Mobile Devices and Services, pp. 431–434 (2010)
13. Herlocker, J.L., Konstan, J.A., Borchers, A., Riedl, J.: An algorithmic framework for performing collaborative filtering. In: Proceedings of the 22nd Annual International ACM SIGIR Conference on Research and Development in Information Retrieval, pp. 230–237 (1999)
14. Yan, B., Chen, G.: AppJoy: personalized mobile application discovery. In: Proceedings of the 9th International Conference on Mobile Systems, Applications, and Services, pp. 113–126 (2011)
15. Ma, C.: A guide to singular value decomposition for collaborative filtering. Technical report. http://www.csie.ntu.edu.tw/~r95007/thesis/svdnetflix/report/report.pdf. Accessed 1 July 2015
16. Zhang, M., Dai, C., Ding, C., Chen, E.: Probabilistic solutions of influence propagation on social networks. In: Proceedings of the 22nd ACM International Conference on Information & Knowledge Management, pp. 429–438 (2013)
17. Tang, J., Sun, J., Wang, C., Yang, Z.: Social influence analysis in large-scale networks. In: Proceedings of the 15th ACM SIGKDD International Conference on Knowledge Discovery and Data Mining, pp. 807–816 (2009)
18. Ma, H., Zhou, T.C., Lyu, M.R., King, I.: Improving recommender systems by incorporating social contextual information. ACM Trans. Inf. Syst., pp. 219–230 (2011)
19. Goyal, A., Bonchi, F., Lakshmanan, L.V.S.: Learning influence probabilities in social networks. In: Proceedings of the 3rd ACM International Conference on Web Search and Data Mining, pp. 241–250 (2010)
20. Cha, M., Haddadi, H., Benevenuto, F., Gummadi, K.P.: Measuring user influence in twitter: the million follower fallacy. In: Proceedings of International AAAI Conference on Weblogs & Social (2010)
21. Anagnostopoulos, A., Kumar, R., Mahdian, M.: Influence and correlation in social networks. In: Proceeding of ACM SIGKDD International Conference on Knowledge Discovery & Data Mining, pp. 7–15 (2008)
22. Kempe, D., Kleinberg, J., Tardos, E.: Maximizing the spread of influence through a social network. In: Proceedings of the 9th ACM SIGKDD International Conference on Knowledge Discovery & Data Mining, pp. 137–146 (2003)

SHB⁺-Tree: A Segmentation Hybrid Index Structure for Temporal Data

Mei Wang$^{(\boxtimes)}$ and Meng Xiao

School of Computer Science and Technology,
Donghua University, Shanghai 201620, China
wangmei@dhu.edu.cn, chaumont0317@163.com

Abstract. Temporal index provide an important way to accelerate query performance in temporal database. However, the current temporal index can not support the variety of queries very well, and it is hard to take account of both the efficiency of query execution and the index construction as well as maintenance. This paper propose a novel segmentation hybrid index SHB⁺-Tree for temporal data. First the temporal data in temporal table deposited is separated to fragments according to the time order. In each segment, the hybrid index is constructed which is a combination of temporal index and object index, and the temporal data is shared by them. By employing the segmented storage strategy and bottom-up index construction approaches for every part of the hybrid index, it greatly improves the performance of construction and maintenance. The experimental results on benchmark data set verify the effectiveness and efficiency of the proposed method.

Keywords: Temporal data · Temporal index · SHB⁺-Tree index · Segmented storage · Bottom-Up

1 Introduction

In the era where data are being produced over time and shared in an unprecedented pace, mining the information in the data has become increasingly crucial. Temporal information is the natural and basic description for the development and changes of real-world objects, and almost everything has explicit or implicit temporal features. While the traditional snapshot database always records the information in a given specific time, it is difficult to reflect the dynamic changes of real world sufficiently and accurately. The need for temporal data management and retrieval shows increasingly urgent in most modern database systems today.

Temporal data management has already attracts wide concerns in both academic and industrial fields. Tang [1] proposed the concept of bi-temporal data at an earlier time. In this work, each tuple of the temporal table carries two time intervals $[start_t, end_t)$ and $[start_v, end_v)$, representing transaction time and valid time (a.k.a system time and application time, respectively). He also proposed to take time interval as a key, which makes a breakthrough in tradition databases which only take digit or character as a key. In this basis, many temporal database prototypes have been implemented, such as TimeDB [2] and TempDB [3]. Under the impetus of the above

© Springer International Publishing Switzerland 2015
G. Wang et al. (Eds.): ICA3PP 2015, Part II, LNCS 9529, pp. 282–296, 2015.
DOI: 10.1007/978-3-319-27122-4_20

research and real applications, ISO/IEC published the edition of the SQL standard in December 2011, SQL: 2011 [4, 5], which has an important new functionality to create and manipulate temporal tables. In the meantime, many popular commercial databases such as Oracle [6], IBM DB2 [7], SAP HANA [8] have also included temporal features. With the developments of temporal databases, some key technologies in the traditional database have been re-examined. As an important way to accelerate query performance, index has received great attentions. Some index structures have been proposed to support different temporal query operations such as temporal join [9, 10], temporal aggregation [11, 12] and time travel [13].

The existing temporal index technologies are always extensions of traditional B⁺-Tree or R Tree. The Time Index [14] is one of the earliest temporal indexing methods, which maps temporal relation to a multi-dimensional space. So the current index such as B-tree can be readily adopted to support temporal operations. However, such kind of methods suffer low efficiency when data size increases. As the data size reached TB or PB level, the cost of index construction and maintenance is extremely expensive. In addition, almost every method does not support all type of temporal operations and these methods do not work efficiently on modern hardware and architectures. In the latest study, SAP HANA [15] proposed a novel index structure called Timeline Index. The proposed Timeline index can support different kinds of temporal operations as well as is easy to construct and maintain by adopting the sample sequential structure. However, when using the Timeline Index to process a query, it need to do a linear scan of the index table. When the data size becomes large, the cost of continual liner scan is very expensive.

In addition, in the current temporal databases, the proposed index structures focus on fast retrieval on the temporal attributes. Specifically the corresponding query is about "**what happened in a given time period**" (**Denoted as Temporal Query**). However, for many practical applications, users also pay close attention to the objects that they are interested in, in this case the query is more likely as "**what the given object happened in the given time period**" (**Denoted as Object Query**). For the second kind of query, it is difficult to avoid the linear scanning of the whole records in the process of query execution for the current temporal index structures. Although by building a traditional secondary index can reply "what the given object happened" more efficiently, the cost of update for the secondary index is very huge as the objects change over time.

To deal with the above problems, in this paper, we propose a novel segmentation hybrid index on temporal data. In the proposed method, the temporal data is deposited to segment by chronological order firstly, and then in each segment the local hybrid structure with temporal index and object index is created where both indexes share the same local segment data. Furthermore, the bottom-up index construction approach is incorporated in the proposed method to improve the performances of construction and maintenance of the index structure. The contributions of the proposed method are: (1) we propose a hybrid temporal index structure, where the temporal index and object index share the same local data, which can support both Temporal Query and Object Query more effectively compared with the previously temporal indexes. (2) By segmenting the temporal data before and incorporating the bottom-up construction approach, the performance of construction and maintenance of the index has been improved significantly. (3) The experiments have been conducted on benchmark data sets verify the effectiveness and the efficiency of the proposed method. Specifically, compared with Timeline index, the SHB$^+$-Tree (Segmentation Hybrid B$^+$-Tree) index performs excellent in the Object Query, the cost of query time for the SHB$^+$-Tree is reduced to 10 percent of the Timeline index.

The remainder of this paper is organized as follows. Section 2 gives an overview of existing work on temporal data management and temporal index technologies. Section 3 presents the SHB$^+$-Tree Index. Section 4 describes SHB$^+$-Tree and the algorithms on how to process different kinds of temporal operators using the SHB$^+$-Tree in detail. Section 5 provides the experimental results. Section 6 contains conclusions and possible avenues for future research.

2   Related Work

2.1   Traditional Database and Index

Traditional relational database is attribute-tuple two-dimensional structure [16], it is suitable for processing the permanent stability data. However, it is important to know that the traditional database only saves a snapshot instead of the complete history. The snapshot cannot reflect the historical changes of the object, and it is hard to meet the real-time requirements for the industrial applications. Temporal database is a DBMS which support time dimension. The Temporal DB can describe not only the information at some point, but also the history and future of the data. A first important direction of work is to model and organize temporal data. Index technology is one of the key technologies to improve the query efficiency of mass data, and the research of index has attracted the attention of researchers in recent years.

Traditional database has rules to create indexes. (1) Create an index on the column that are joined in queries frequently, and it is not a foreign key. (2) Create an index on the column that are sorting or grouping frequently. (3) Create an index on the column that used in the conditional expression frequently and has more different values. For this reason, the traditional index can support the query such as what the object do very well. However, as time goes on, there are constant updates on the temporal database, which makes the cost of update and maintenance of the index expensive. Therefore, a large body of researches on indexes created on the temporal attribute has established.

2.2   Temporal Indexing Technology

In order to accelerate query performance in temporal database, various data structures have been proposed for different temporal data models. Since most of these index structures were developed in the mid-to-late '90s, they are designed for hard-disk efficiency, optimizing the number of I/O operations for updates and queries. The Time Index [14] is one of the earliest temporal indexing methods. Technically, the Time Index is a B+-Tree over versions, and provides explicit support for multiple temporal operations. The multi-version B-tree [17] is one of the most advanced temporal indexing methods. It provides an index for both key- and time- dimensions with optimal I/O behavior. The Timeline Index [15] used to process different kinds of temporal queries on this index structure proposed by SAP HANA. The main temporal operations are temporal aggregation, time travel and temporal join. Several general-purpose temporal index structures exist, but they only support one particular kind of temporal operations, even though there is a demand for all kinds of operators. In addition, these index structures are focus on the query about the time domain, which can carry out the query such as what happened in the given time period, which limit adoption in object-related query demand.

3   SHB⁺-Tree Index

This section describes the data structures and basic principles of the SHB+-Tree Index. Some definitions are provided at first. Then the index structure and the query processing by using the proposed index are introduced in detail.

3.1   Definitions

Definition 1: Temporal Data is data with temporal attributes.

Definition 2: Time interval (Period) indicates the duration of a transaction, including its start time and end time. Instead of adding a period type, we add period definitions as metadata to tables. A period definition is named table component, identifying a pair of columns that capture the period start and the period end time.

Definition 3: Version_IDs are the timestamps used in the time period, monotonically increasing and scoped at the level of a database.

Same as Timeline, for each table, our temporal data model keeps the current version of the table (Current Table) and the whole history trajectory of the table (Temporal Table) in separate structures. Tables 1 and 2 illustrate the examples of a Current Table and a Temporal Table. This example models a small banking application with customer names and their account balance. Table 2 shows that the new customer Alice was inserted by Transaction 101. Transaction 102 created customer Ann and Transaction 103 created Grace. In addition, Transaction 103 updated the Alice record (identified by ROW_ID 1) and creating a new version of the Alice record (identified by ROW_ID 4). Transaction 105 created two new customers (Bob and Gary) and Transaction 106 and Transaction 107 deleted the accounts of Ann, Alice and Gary. Table 1 shows the current state of the table after all these transactions have been applied; Table 2 captures the whole history.

Table 1. Current table

Name	Balance
Grace	$300
Bob	$200

Table 2. Temporal table

ROW_ID	Name	Balance	Start	End
1	Alice	$100	101	103
2	Ann	$500	102	107
3	Grace	$300	103	∞
4	Alice	$600	103	106
5	Bob	$200	105	∞
6	Gary	$300	105	106

3.2   SHB$^+$-Tree Index Data Structure

It is obvious that the scale of the temporal table increases over time, it is necessary to design an efficient index to accelerate the operations. In order to avoid the huge cost of updating and maintaining the index caused by the data increase, we propose to divide the time-ordered temporal data into two or more successive segments. On each segment, the SHB+-Tree index is designed and created for the Temporal Table to support both kinds of query operations (Object Query and Temporal Query). Figure 1 illustrates an example of SHB+-Tree Index structure for Table 2.

As shown in Fig. 1, the whole SHB+-Tree could be divided into five layers from bottom to top. Layer 1 and layer 2 belong to the temporal Index support Temporal Query, layer 2 and the remaining 3 layers belong to the object index support Object Query.

In the tree structure, layer 2 is a shared layer, which is the transaction sequence layer. Each data item in this layer records the state of the transaction in each row. The number in each data item is the ROW_ID in the temporal table. If the transaction corresponding to this ROW_ID are happened, flag "+" is put behind the ROW_ID, else, flag "-" is put behind the ROW_ID in the case of update or delete. For example, according to Fig. 1 and Table 2, the first data item of layer 2 is <"1", "+">, which means the first row in the temporal table is valid at version 101, as well, the third data item is <"1", "-">, which means the first row in the temporal table is invalid at version 103. All the transactions must be ordered according to the system time.

Layer 1 is the time trajectory layer, each data item in this layer records the discrete time version and the rows which could be "seen" by this version. This is achieved by storing the end offset for each version in layer 2. For example, according to Fig. 1, the first data item <"101", "1"> means Version 101 only sees the first data item in layer 2. The third data item <"103", "5"> indicates Version 103 corresponds to the first 5 data items in layer 2.

Layer 3 to layer 5 are layers contained internal nodes, which is an improvement of a B$^+$-Tree where sparse coefficient equals to 0. The nodes in the index will be filled, so that the utilization ratio is improved and the number of tree node is also reduced. The internal nodes in these layers are composed by <Key, P>, where Key represents the object in the temporal table in layer 4 and layer 5, and it also represents the Version_IDs in layer 3. P represents the pointer associated between the node and its child node.

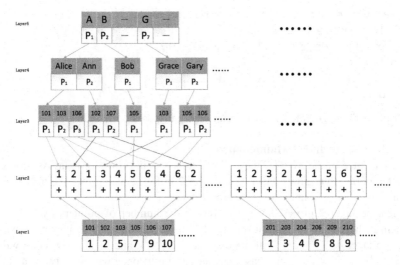

Fig. 1. The structure of SHB+-Tree index

3.3 SHB+-Tree Index Construction and Maintenance

3.3.1 SHB+-Tree Index Construction

As mentioned above, the Temporal table is increased over time, so it is infeasible to create and maintenance an object index by using the traditional "insert/split" method. So the bottom-up construction approach for every part of the hybrid index has adopted in the proposed method, which greatly improves the performance of construction and maintenance. There is a premise that we must sort the data in ascending order of Version_ID. And then fulfill the node of the upper layer, until the whole tree is established.

The algorithm of constructing the SHB+-Tree Index is as follows:

```
Function Create Index
Input: Temporal Table
Output: Index of SHB+-Tree
create an empty balance tree A to store version
for row in temporal table:
insert_to_balancetree (row, A);
end for
create an empty list B to store event list
for row in temporal table:
insert_to_list (row, B, A);
end for
create an empty list C to store leaf node of SHB+-Tree
for node in list B:
insert_to_leaf_node (node, C);
end for
sort list C based on key
```

```
create an empty list D to store son node of SHB⁺-Tree
for leaf_node in list C
insert_to_son_node (lead_node, D);
end for
merge list D into a root node E;
return;
```

Based on the segmented data, we can efficiently create the index.

3.3.2   SHB⁺-Tree Index Maintenance

The maintenance of the SHB+-Tree index is aimed at inserting for data. As time goes on, the temporal table grows, layer 1 and layer 2 in Fig. 1 also grow. We only need to maintain the layer 3 to layer 5 for inserting data.

When the layer 2 grows, layer 3 increases the number of pointers by bottom-up approach. If there is no space to insert, the leaf node will split, and a new node will be inserted to layer 4. Similarly, leaf node splits in layer 4, and then a new node will be inserted to layer 5. In the worst case, we need to insert once with spilt twice and new insert three times, so the time complexity of maintenance is $\mathcal{O}(1)$.

4   Query Implementation Based on SHB⁺-Tree Index

4.1   Object Query

The Object Query is designed to answer the question like "what the given object happens in the given time period".

Example. What is the account balance of all customers whose name start with "A" at time point 105? This query can be expressed as follows:

```
Select balance
From TemporalTable te
Where te.name like 'A%'
As of timestamp '105'
Group by name;
```

Figure 2 shows how such Object Query can be accelerated by using the object index of SHB+-Tree. For the sake of simplicity, we use a separated representation of the object index to illustrate. To execute the query, we scan the object index to find the "A", then we can find the names start with "A" based on the pointers. Following the pointers, we keep searching the time version from left to right until the version more than 105, then stop scanning. We adopt the previous version as results, obtain the ROW_ID in the temporal table and take the balance value. If we want take the result of Alice, we can scan the index until time version 106, then obtain 103 as a result. According to the pointers from 103, we can find two ROW_IDs, however, the first one is an invalid ROW_ID, then take the other one as the final result.

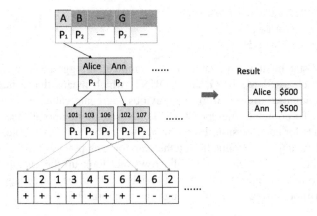

Fig. 2. An example of the object query

The algorithm of the Object Query is as follows:

```
Function object query
Input: SQL Query
Output: set of result
create temp result list A;
for i in root node
if node i fit the constraint of object
    for j in node i
        if node j fit the constraint of object
            insert V_j into A;
        end if
    end for
end if
end for
create result list B;
for i in A
if i fit the constraint of version
    insert i into B;
end if
end for
return B;
```

4.2 Temporal Query Based on SHB⁺-Tree Index

Temporal Query is designed to answer the question like "what happened in a given time period".

Example. What is the total sum of the account balances of all customers at each point in time? This query can be expressed as follows:

```
Select SUM(Balance) as sum
From TemporalTable te
Group by te.Version_ID();
```

The query statement is equivalent to the cumulative aggregates in the temporal aggregation, such as SUM, AVG, and COUNT, which means that a new aggregate value can be computed directly from the previous aggregate value. Figure 3 illustrates this approach. To compute a temporal SUM, we scan the temporal index to find the valid ROW_IDs for each version. Furthermore, we keep a single variable, sum, which keeps track of the aggregate value during the scan for each point in time. For each entry of the temporal index, we check the valid rows and look up the customer's balance from the temporal table, and adjust the sum variable reflects the correct aggregate value for each point time during the scan through the temporal index.

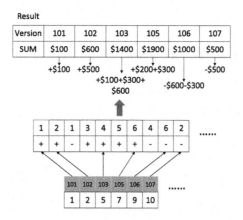

Fig. 3. An example of the temporal query

The algorithm of the Temporal Query is as follows:

```
Function temporal query
Input: SQL Query
Output: set of result
create result list A;
for i in timeline
if node i fit the constraint of version
    for j in node i
        if node j fit the constraint of object
            insert V_j into A;
        end if
    end for
end if
end for
return B;
```

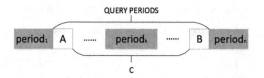

Fig. 4. Query over segments

4.3 Query Over Segments

If the time period involved in the query is distributed in different segments, it is called Query over segments. As shown in Fig. 4, the query period involves three different segments, we use A, B, C to represent the three segments respectively. In the Query of Periods, we follow the rules as shown in 4.1 or 4.2 in each segment. At last, we combined the single results together to get the final result. In the process of reality, we can use the parallel technology in the distributed environment to improve the efficiency of query greatly.

4.4 Summary

In conclusion, users have the flexibility to choose the retrieval mode according to their different requirements. (1) We can search the index from top to bottom when the user want to retrieve information associated with object. (2) If the query focus on the temporal dimension, we can search the index by employing bottom-up approach. (3) The most complex query class is the so-called Query over Segments. We can combine the Object Query with the Temporal Query together, and search in the different index blocks. With these 3 methods, we can meet the diversity needs of users efficiently.

5 Experiments

This section presents the results of experiments that access the performance of the SHB +-Tree Index from the following three aspects: (1) the query performance by using SHB +-tree for Q1 and Q2 are testified respectively. The query related to a single time period and multiple time periods are both examined. In each case, the SHB + -Tree Index is compared to the Timeline Index; (2) the time efficiency for index construction and maintenance are testified; (3) the space consumption is examined in the experiments.

5.1 Software and Hardware Used

As shown in Table 3, all experiments were carried out in the following experiment environment.

Table 3. The test environment and configuration

Configuration category	Configuration item	Configuration
Hardware configuration	CPU	Intel(R) Core(TM) i5-2400 CPU @ 3.10 GHz
	RAM	4G
Software configuration	OS	Windows7
	Development environment	Visual Studio 2010

5.2 Dataset

There is no standard benchmark for temporal databases. We obtain the temporal extensions of the TPC-H benchmark [18] by adopting the recent technology. We also generate the historical temporal data by executing TPC-C transactions [19]. A technical report describes the method in more detail. We adjust the Scaling Factor to control the size of the datasets. The dataset properties are illustrated in Table 4.

Table 4. Dataset properties

Dataset	SF_0	SF_H	|lineitem|	#version
Tiny	0.01	0.01	0.3Mio	0.2Mio
Small	0.1	0.1	3.4Mio	2.2Mio
Medium	1	1	34Mio	22Mio

SF_0: Scaling factor of dbgen tool creating Version 0.

SF_H: Number of update transactions, it determines the number of versions in the benchmark database.

Given the widely varying cost of temporal operators and specific implementations, we set three different database scaling factors.

5.3 Experimental Results and Analysis

5.3.1 Experiment 1: Object Query

Figure 5 illustrates the running time to execute the Object Query according to the example of Sect. 4.1 based on the SHB+-Tree Index and Timeline Index respectively. SHB+-Tree Index obviously outperforms Timeline Index. The gap becomes larger when the amount of data increases, the main reason is that there is no object index in the Timeline Index, so it needs to scan the temporal table after finding the right time. The cost of scanning temporal table will be depend on the size of time version. Its time complexity is approximately (n). While in our method, we can return the results according to the object index structure, so the time complexity for SHB+-Tree Index is just $\mathcal{O}(\log(n))$.

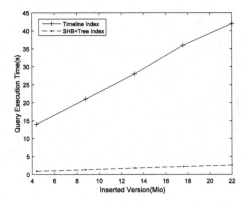

Fig. 5. Object query execution time (s)

5.3.2 Experiment 2: Temporal Query

This section testify the performance of the Temporal Query according to the example of Sect. 4.2. The queries about a single index block and multiple index blocks are both examined. The running time by using the SHB+-Tree Index and Timeline Index respectively in both cases are illustrated in Fig. 6(a) and (b).

For a single index block, the results of the SHB+-Tree Index and Timeline Index has shown minor difference according to Fig. 6(a). Instead for multiple index blocks, the SHB+-Tree Index is much better than Timeline Index, which is because the multiple segmentation of the SHB+-Tree Index can be scanned in parallel, the searching efficiency can be boosted correspondingly. As the data size increases, the performance difference becomes larger according to Fig. 6(b). In addition, the performance of the query related to one segment is better than the query related to multiple segments, because we need to merge the results from the segments, which has some time consumption.

5.3.3 Experiment 3: Index Construction

Because the bottom-up construction approach is adopted in the proposed method, we need to sort the data by time series of start time and end time before construction. Then

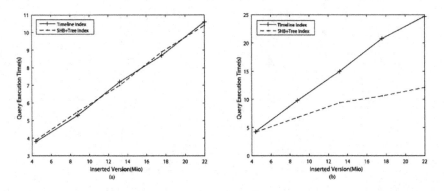

Fig. 6. (a) Temporal query execution time (s) (b) query over segments execution time (s)

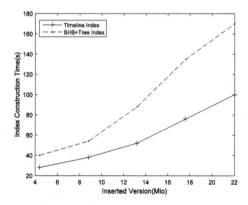

Fig. 7. Index construction time (sec)

data will be divided into blocks. The time for constructing a new SHB+-Tree Index data structure is illustrated in Fig. 7. From the figure, it can be seen the time for constructing the tow indexes all grow linearly as the amount of data increases. Obviously, the time for constructing the SHB+-Tree Index is always more than the time for construction the Timeline Index. At the size of Large, the time for constructing the SHB+-Tree Index is almost 50 % more than the time for constructing the Timeline Index, that is because one more scanning of temporal table for object Index construction. However, since the time to construct to timeline is less and the index construction is only once, such result can be accepted.

5.3.4 Experiment 4: Space Consumption

This experiment shows the memory consumption of the SHB$^+$-Tree Index. Since the proposed index structure consists of two index structures to support both the Temporal Query and Object Query, so the space consumption is larger than original timeline index. However, we construct the SHB$^+$-Tree Index by employing bottom-up approach, so the B$^+$-tree nodes are filled in fully populated. The nodes utilization rate is 100 %. The space is greatly reduced for the tree index structure. We measure the

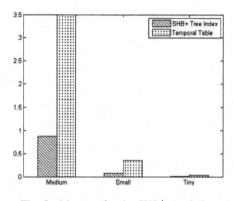

Fig. 8. Memory for the SHB$^+$-tree index

space consumption for Table 4 on three different datasets. As shown in Fig. 8, with the increasing size of dataset, the memory consumption of the SHB$^+$-Tree Index is increasing too. We show the memory consumption of the temporal table in Medium size, which is 3.5 GB, and the size of the SHB$^+$-Tree Index is 0.88 GB, which is approximately 25 % of the table memory consumption. For Timeline Index, the size is 0.38 GB, which is approximately 10 % of the table memory consumption.

6 Conclusion and Forecast

This paper presented a novel, versatile index structure for temporal tables called SHB+-Tree Index. The structure is universal, thereby supporting the variety of the queries. By employing the block storage strategy and bottom-up index construction approach for every part of the hybrid index, greatly improves the performance of construction and maintenance. And it is space-efficient, typically the size is only a small percentage of the size of a temporal table. Most importantly, the SHB+-Tree Index is fast.

Currently, we can construct the SHB$^+$-Tree Index on a single machine. We can study the characteristics of distributed system and realize the distributed index in the future.

Acknowledgments. This work was supported by the Fundamental Research Funds for the Central Universities and DHU distinguished Young Professor Program No. B201312.

References

1. Tang, C.J.: The background, characteristics and representative researchers of temporal database. Comput. Sci. **26**(2), 27–29 (1999)
2. TimeDB – A temporal relational DBMS. http://www.timeconsult.com/software/software.html
3. Tang, Y., Guo, H., Ye, X.: Design and implementation of TempDB. In: Tang, Y., Ye, X., Tang, N. (eds.) Temporal Information Processing Technology and Its Application, pp. 261–279. Springer, Heidelberg (2010)
4. Kulkarni, K., Michels, J.E.: Temporal features in SQL: 2011. ACM Sigmod Rec. **41**(3), 34–43 (2012)
5. Zemke, F.: What is new in SQL: 2011. ACM SIGMOD Rec. **41**(1), 67–73 (2012)
6. Rajamani, R.: Oracle total recall/flashback data archive. An Oracle White Paper 12 (2007)
7. Saracco, C.M., Nicola, M., Gandhi, L.: A matter of time: temporal data management in DB2 for z/OS (2012)
8. Färber, F., May, N., Lehner, W., et al.: The SAP HANA database–an architecture overview. IEEE Data Eng. Bull. **35**(1), 28–33 (2012)
9. Gao, D., Jensen, C.S., Snodgrass, R.T., et al.: Join operations in temporal databases. VLDB J. **14**(1), 2–29 (2005)
10. Zhang, D., Tsotras, V.J., Seeger, B.: Efficient temporal join processing using indices. In: Proceedings of the 18th International Conference on Data Engineering, pp. 103–113. IEEE (2002)

11. Böhlen, M.H., Gamper, J., Jensen, C.S.: Multi-dimensional aggregation for temporal data. In: Ioannidis, Y., Scholl, M.H., Schmidt, J.W., Matthes, F., Hatzopoulos, M., Böhm, K., Kemper, A., Grust, T., Böhm, C. (eds.) EDBT 2006. LNCS, vol. 3896, pp. 257–275. Springer, Heidelberg (2006)

12. Kline, N., Snodgrass, R.T.: Computing temporal aggregates. In: Proceedings of the Eleventh International Conference on Data Engineering, pp. 222–231. IEEE (1995)

13. Stonebraker, M.: The Design of the Postgres Storage System. Morgan Kaufmann Publishers, Burlington (1987)

14. Elmasri, R., Wuu, G.T.J., Kim, Y.J.: The time index: an access structure for temporal data. In: Proceedings of the 16th International Conference on Very Large Data Bases, pp. 1–12. Morgan Kaufmann Publishers Inc (1990)

15. Kaufmann, M., Manjili, A.A., Vagenas, P., et al.: Timeline index: a unified data structure for processing queries on temporal data in SAP HANA. In: Proceedings of the 2013 ACM SIGMOD, pp. 1173–1184. ACM (2013)

16. Huang, N.: Research and implementation technology of temporal database management system. Comput. Knowl. Technol. Sch. Commun. **8**(11), 7402–7403 (2013)

17. Becker, B., Gschwind, S., Ohler, T., et al.: An asymptotically optimal multiversion B-tree. VLDB J. **5**(4), 264–275 (1996)

18. Al-Kateb, M., Crolotte, A., Ghazal, A., Rose, L.: Adding a temporal dimension to the TPC-H benchmark. In: Nambiar, R., Poess, M. (eds.) TPCTC 2012. LNCS, vol. 7755, pp. 51–59. Springer, Heidelberg (2013)

19. Funke, F., Kemper, A., Krompass, S., Kuno, H., Nambiar, R., Neumann, T., Nica, A., Poess, M., Seibold, M.: Metrics for measuring the performance of the mixed workload CH-benCHmark. In: Nambiar, R., Poess, M. (eds.) TPCTC 2011. LNCS, vol. 7144, pp. 10–30. Springer, Heidelberg (2012)

Fusion-Cache: A Refactored Content-Aware Host-Side SSD Cache

Xian Chen[✉], Wenzhi Chen, and Zhongyong Lu

College of Computer Science and Technology,
Zhejiang University, Hangzhou 310000, China
{chenxiancool,chenwz,lzy6032}@zju.edu.cn

Abstract. For the merits of high I/O performance and low energy consumption, SSDs have been widely deployed as the host-side cache devices for backend storage to improve the hosted virtual machines' I/O performance. But in today's host-side SSD cache, the cache behavior and flash memory are managed individually, without knowing each other's internal information. This semantic gap not only makes host-side cache inefficient, but also shortens cache device's lifetime. Additionally, prior studies point out that host-side cache contains much duplicate data. This will further worsen the situation. In this paper, we try to refactor the cache architecture by integrating the management of cache behavior and flash memory to remove the semantic gap. Moreover, data deduplication is applied to improve the usage efficiency of cache device. Compared with conventional host-side caches, experiments show our proposed cache architecture can generate great improvements on I/O performance and device's lifetime.

Keywords: Host-side SSD Cache · Data deduplication · Cache replacement strategy

1 Introduction

Compared with HDD, flash-based solid state drive (SSD) has many advantages, such as low access latency, high I/O throughput and low energy consumption. Due to such merits, SSDs have been widely deployed in today's cloud computing centers. Usually, for price and performance reasons, they are used as cache devices in the host server side for backend storage to improve the I/O performance of the hosted virtual machines. This cache-based storage architecture can also reduce the I/O traffic between the host server and the backend storage server, which in turn improves host servers' remote access performance [1]. However, for host-side SSD cache, there are still some challenges. **(1)** The pressure faced by SSD cache device is much greater than that by normal SSD storage device. Besides, SSD device has limited erase/program cycles (typically 10K-100K). Thus, it is much easier for SSD cache device to be worn out. **(2)** In traditional host-side SSD cache, cache behavior and flash memory are managed individually. The cache module is usually placed inside host system and it manages the cache behaviors such as the insertion and eviction of cache blocks. Flash

G. Wang et al. (Eds.): ICA3PP 2015, Part II, LNCS 9529, pp. 297–314, 2015.
DOI: 10.1007/978-3-319-27122-4_21

memory is managed inside SSD device by a software layer called flash translation layer (FTL). This separated management mechanism has several drawbacks. It generates redundant address translation layers in the I/O stack. One is in the cache module to translate the backend storage address to the SSD logical address and the other is in FTL to translate the SSD logical address to SSD physical address. The redundant translation layers not only consume more memory space, but also increase the data access latency. In addition, the separated management mechanism causes semantic gap between the cache management module and the flash management module, which can significantly reduce the cache's performance and shorten SSD device's lifetime. (3) As shown in [2–4], there are many duplicate data blocks in host-side SSD cache. This is because many virtual machines can be hosted on the same physical server and most of them are running same or similar operating systems, libraries and applications. These redundant data blocks greatly prevent the cache device from being efficiently used. (4) Because the memory in host server is usually very large and most of the hot data is cached in memory, the data locality at the disk I/O level is very poor. Traditional cache management policies may not be suitable for host-side SSD cache and even degrade the overall I/O performance [5].

To tackle the problems discussed above, we propose a refactored content-aware host-side SSD cache architecture, which we named fusion-cache. Fusion-cache refactors the I/O stack of host-side SSD cache by moving FTL from device to host system and tightly integrating it with the cache management module. This can remove the overhead caused by the redundant translation layer and the semantic gap between cache management and flash memory management can be bridged. Additionally, to remove the duplicate data blocks in SSD cache and improve its usage efficiency we try to apply data deduplication in fusion-cache. An effective cache replacement strategy is also proposed to better balance the cache hit ratio and garbage collection overhead. Experimental results show fusion-cache can significantly improve the overall I/O performance. Moreover, the cache device's lifetime can be greatly prolonged and the I/O traffic between host server and backend storage server can also be drastically reduced.

The rest of the paper is organized as follows. We will introduce the background and motivation in Sect. 2. Then the system design of fusion-cache will be presented in Sect. 3. Section 4 will give a detailed evaluation on the performance. Related work and the difference with ours will be shown in Sect. 5. Finally, the conclusion and future work will be presented in Sect. 6.

2   Background and Motivation

In today's cloud computing center, data is usually stored in distributed storage system or dedicated storage servers, and workloads are deployed on dedicated computing servers in the form of virtual machines. When we start a virtual machine, we need to fetch its data content from the backend storage (distributed storage system or dedicate storage server), and run it on the computing server which is usually called the host server. Because I/O requests from virtual machine need to go through the network between the host server and the storage server, the I/O performance suffers a big degradation compared with the direct-attached storage. To alleviate this situation, one high-speed SSD is usually attached to the host server, acting as the cache for backend low-speed storage, and usually it is called host-side SSD cache.

Generally, host-side SSD cache is based on commodity product. Cache module and SSD device are managed independently. SSD device is used by the cache module as a normal fast storage device, and its internal functional features are hidden behind the exposed interface, e.g. SATA, SAS and PCI-E. But SSD device is very different from other fast storage devices. It cannot perform in-place updates and has a limited lifespan. To tackle the two shortcomings, SSD device periodically performs garbage collection and wear-leveling internally. Garbage collection recycles the invalid pages and provide clean erased block for future write requests. Wear-leveling makes all the blocks written evenly. Because garbage collection and wear-leveling may change the data content's physical address, an address translation table is needed. In addition, manufacturers usually provide a certain amount of over-provisioned flash space in SSD to assist garbage collection and wear-leveling. This space is called OP space and it cannot be used by user. The cache module inside host-side SSD cache is responsible for the logical cache management. It decides what data should be cached, how to organize the cached data and which data block should be replaced when the cache device is full. There is also an address mapping table in the cache module to map backend storage address to SSD logical address.

Even though host-side SSD cache can improve the virtual machines' I/O performance, there are some mismatches in its internal management. (1) There are two address translation layers, one is in the cache module and the other is in FTL inside SSD device. The two translation layers not only consume more memory space, but also increase the data access path length and data access latency. (2) There is semantic gap between the cache module and flash management module. Cache module can access SSD device only by the three storage interface, i.e. read, write and trim. And the SSD device has no idea about the above cache behaviors. It just receives I/O requests and responds to them, no different from the situation when it is used as a storage device by file systems. But in practice, the pressure faced by SSD device when it is used as a cache device is much higher than that when it is used as a storage device. It is much easier for SSD-based cache device to wear out. Thus, host-side SSD cache should try its best to reduce the write operations to SSD device, and getting help from the above cache module may be a feasible choice. (3) It is hard to tune the OP space size to balance cache hit rate and garbage collection overhead. If the OP space is enlarged, the garbage collection overhead will be decreased. Accordingly, the space used for cache will be reduced and the cache hit ratio will also be decreased. The overall cache performance is influenced by both cache hit ratio and garbage collection overhead. It is hard to find the optimal configuration of the OP space size for one workload, and the configuration is usually heuristic, let alone find a configuration which can be suitable for different workloads [6].

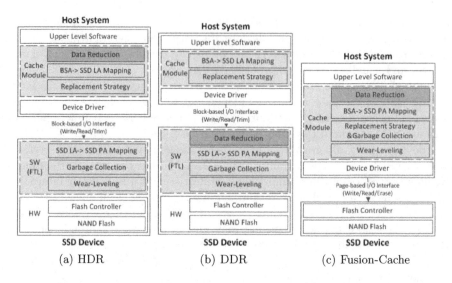

Fig. 1. Different content-aware SSD cache architectures. (a) host-side data reduction (HDR); (b) Device-side data reduction (DDR); (c) Fusion-cache; BSA denotes backend storage address; LA denotes logical address; PA denotes physical address.

Another feasible and effective way to reduce write operations is performing data reduction. Work in [2] shows that there is a substantial degree of duplication in dynamic workloads, and performing data deduplication in host-side SSD cache can reduce the data footprint by as much as 67 %. This can be further translated into higher cache hit ratio and less SSD writes.

There are two typical methods to conduct data reduction in host-side SSD cache as depicted by Fig. 1(a) and (b). The first one is performing data reduction in the cache module without any modification to SSD device. The second method is to perform data reduction in FTL inside SSD device, and the cache module just performs normal cache operations. But both of the two methods have their weak points. **Firstly**, in the two content-aware cache architectures, cache module and SSD device are managed separately. So they both have the drawbacks listed by (1) (2) (3) as discussed above. **Secondly**, there are many limitations when we perform data reduction inside SSD device which usually has limited memory space and computing power. As shown in work [7–9], to minimize the negative impact of data reduction operations on device's I/O performance, compromises have to be made between data deduplication ratio and data access latency. In addition, specific hardware logic is proposed to be added into SSD device to accelerate the data reduction operation [9]. But it also increases the complexity of hardware design. Restricted by the narrow I/O interface, the device cannot leverage the unused computing power in the host system. This will lead to the unbalanced resource usage between host system and the SSD device. **Thirdly**, the saved storage space by data reduction cannot be efficiently used. For HDR in Fig. 1(a), the saved space is only used as cache space. This can expand the effective cache space size and the cache hit ratio will be improved. But the garbage collection overhead is not changed, without getting any benefit from data reduction. One feasible optimization is to set aside a part of the cache space as the additional OP space. Yeah, this can reduce the garbage collection overhead, but the workload and its deduplication ratio are dynamically changing. It's very hard to determine how much of the saved storage space should be used as the cache space and how much is used as the additional OP space. For DDR in Fig. 1(b), the situation is just the opposite. All the saved storage space can only be used as the OP space, which can improve the efficiency of garbage collection and wear-leveling. However, the cache module in host system cannot notice any changes in the device, and the cache hit ratio will not be influenced by data reduction.

Based on the above analysis, we recommend refactoring the conventional content-aware cache architectures. The refactored content-aware cache architecture is depicted by fusion-cache in Fig. 1(c). There are several modifications in fusion-cache. **Firstly**, it moves FTL from device to host system just as Fusion-io Company did in its SSD products [10]. This modification has many advantages. It can reduce the design complexity of SSD device and make it easier to interact with upper software. In addition, in host system side, resource allocation is more flexible and the computing capability is more powerful. Powerful computing is very important especially for time-consuming data reduction operations. **Secondly**, fusion-cache tightly integrates cache module and FTL, removing redundant translation layer. This modification can shorten the data access path and remove the semantic gap between cache management and flash management. Fusion-cache can synthesize the cache behaviors and the storage features of NAND Flash to improve the overall cache performance. **Thirdly**, based on the above two modifications, fusion-cache can get enough information to make a better decision on the usage of the saved storage space by data reduction. Then the overhead caused by garbage collection and cache misses can be minimized. The details of fusion-cache will be presented in Sect. 3.

3   System Design of Fusion-Cache

Figure 2 presents the detailed architecture of fusion-cache. On the whole, fusion-cache contains three big components, i.e. address mapping table, data deduplication engine and cache management module. Address mapping table maps backend storage address to corresponding SSD physical address. Any data which will be written into cache must go through data deduplication engine. Data deduplication engine can recognize and remove the duplicate cache writes. In cache management module, we integrate cache eviction into garbage collection. This can significantly remove the page copy overhead caused by garbage collection. Even though data compression can further save more storage space, it will generate data blocks with different sizes, which will make cache management more complex. In current version of fusion-cache, we only consider data deduplication, and we will try to apply data compression in fusion-cache in future.

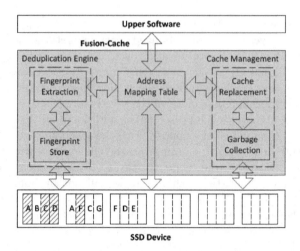

Fig. 2. System architecture of fusion-cache

For fusion-cache is designed as a write-back cache, all writes will be cached in SSD cache until they are evicted out and flushed back to backend storage. Log-based metadata update mechanism is deployed to guarantee the persistency of cached data. When host server suffers from a crash, the dirty cached data can also be flushed back to backend storage by another server, without losing any cached updates.

When upper software issues a read request to backend storage, we first search the address mapping table. If it is hit, then we fetch the requested data from cache device and return it to upper software. Otherwise, we need to fetch the data from backend storage and insert it into cache device. If the request is a write operation, data deduplication engine will extract the fingerprint of the written data, and then use it to search the fingerprint store. The fingerprint store stores all the fingerprints of cached data blocks. If it is hit in fingerprint store, this means cache device has already cached one data block which has the same data content with the written data. Then we only need to modify the address mapping table to map the requested address to the physical address of the duplicated data block, eliminating one SSD write operation. Otherwise, we need to find a free cache block to store the written data.

Even though we do not present wear-leveling related operations in Fig. 2, we think wear-leveling is very important especially for SSD cache device. We assume that wear-leveling can be implemented independently, working as a separate thread or process which can monitor the wear condition of flash blocks inside SSD device and shuffle hot/cold data to even erase operations among the flash blocks. In the following subsections, we will describe the details of fusion-cache from four aspects, i.e. metadata management, data deduplication engine, cache replacement strategies, cache persistency and consistency.

3.1   Metadata Management

Fusion-cache moves FTL from device to host system, and integrates it with the cache management module. This removes redundant address translation layer. Only one address translation layer is needed to be implemented in fusion-cache. As depicted in Fig. 2, the address translation table directly maps the backend storage address to the physical page address inside SSD device. This can shorten data access path and reduce access latency. Because nearly every I/O request needs to access the address translation table, the organization of address translation table is very important to the overall cache performance. In fusion-cache, we organize the address translation table as a hash table for its low lookup latency, and always place it in host memory. To make fusion-cache able to tolerate host system hardware/software crashes and avoid the long cache warm-up time, we also store the address translation table in a specific place in SSD device and use a log-based update mechanism to guarantee the its consistency.

The cache granularity in fusion-cache is the physical flash page which is usually 4 KB. The reason is three fold. **Firstly**, fusion-cache is a combination of cache module and FTL. It needs to manage both the cache behaviors (e.g. cache replacement) and the flash memory. Page-based cache granularity can simplify the design of fusion-cache. **Secondly**, page-based cache granularity can generate higher data deduplication ratio compared with block-based cache granularity. Yeah, page-based cache granularity also needs more memory space to store fingerprints in content-aware caches. But the recency feature of fingerprints shown in [7,9] can help to significantly optimize the memory usage (up to 80 % as shown in Sect. 4.3). **Thirdly**, in host system, memory is also managed with page-based granularity and storage I/O requests are usually multiple of the page size. Page-based granularity can simplify the processing of I/O requests from upper software.

3.2   Data Deduplication Engine

Data deduplication engine is a very import component in fusion-cache. It has a big influence on cache's efficiency and availability. The identification method of duplicate data must be efficient and precise. As presented in Fig. 2, Data deduplication engine contains two sub-components, i.e. fingerprint extraction module and finger-print store module. Fingerprint extraction module leverages cryptographic hash function to extract the fingerprint of written data, and use it to represent the whole written data block. For the high precision, we choose to use SHA-1 [11] as the fingerprint extraction method. SHA-1 is a widely used cryptographic hash function and its collision probability is extremely low, about 10^{-9} to 10^{-17} [8] which can be treated as practically unlikely. New techniques to further reduce the collision probability to as low as 10^{-46} have also been shown to be feasible [12]. Therefore, like prior work in [7–9,13,14], we also assume SHA-1 is collision-free. In addition, fusion-cache focuses on providing a framework for applying data deduplication in host-side SSD cache, leaving great flexibility on the design of fingerprint extraction module. We can change to use other fingerprint extraction method as long as it is better than SHA-1.

Fingerprint store stores the fingerprints of data blocks which have already been written into cache device. For low access latency, fingerprint store is placed in host memory when cache is active. We can discard the fingerprint store or persist it in a specific place in cache device when cache is unloaded. The difference is that, if the fingerprint store is discarded, we need to reconstruct it by the incoming I/O requests when the cache device is reused, and this may influence the cache performance in the early stage. One concern about the fingerprint store is the memory overhead. If the cache device is large, the memory overhead will be big. For example, if the cache device is 128 GB and each item in fingerprint store needs 24 bytes to store fingerprint (20 bytes) and corresponding physical page address (4 bytes). Then, the total memory overhead is about 768 MB which is really a bit big. But not all the fingerprints can make contribution to data reduction. Only a small amount of fingerprints (about 10–20 %) are highly duplicated as shown in [7] and our following experiments. In fusion-cache, we organize fingerprint store as a hash table and manage it with a recency-based replacement mechanism. Because only the hot fingerprints are maintained in fingerprint store, the memory overhead can be significantly reduced without big influence on the data deduplication ratio.

3.3   Cache Replacement Strategies

In fusion-cache, cache management and flash management are mixed together. However, there are some similarities between the two modules. To guarantee only hot data blocks are cached, cache module needs to do data replacement when cache is full. Similarly, FTL needs to perform garbage collection on the invalid pages when there is no free page for incoming write request. If the cold valid flash pages inside the victim block can be evicted out in garbage collection, the data copy overhead can be reduced. Based on the silent eviction mechanism borrowed from [15], we further design four cache replacement strategies. Note that, in fusion-cache, there is no clear demarcation between cache size and OP size, and cache size is dynamically changing.

- **SE-Invalid.** When performing garbage collection, we select the flash block which has the most invalid pages as the victim block. If the victim block has valid pages, we will evict them out from cache, whether they are clean or dirty.
- **SE-LRU.** We select the least recently used flash block as the victim block, and evict its valid pages out from cache if any in the victim block.
- **CCR.** When performing garbage collection, we first check if the total number of flash pages used as cache space has exceeded the predefined threshold. If not, it means there is sufficient OP space for garbage collection, and then we perform general garbage collection. The flash block containing the most invalid pages is selected as the victim block and its valid pages are copied to new places. If the number of flash pages used as cache space has exceeded

the predefined threshold, it means cache has occupied too many flash pages and OP space is not sufficient for garbage collection. Then we select the least recently used block as the victim block and evict its valid pages from cache.

- **GCR.** When performing garbage collection, we first select the flash block which has the most invalid pages as the victim block. And then check if its invalid pages have exceeded the predefined threshold. If so, it means only a few pages inside victim block are valid and the corresponding page copy overhead will be small. Thus, we will do normal garbage collection in this situation. If the number of invalid pages in victim block does not exceed the threshold, it means the OP space is not sufficient for garbage collection. Then we select the least recently used flash block as the new victim block and evict its valid pages form cache.

For all the four replacement strategies, we have to flush the evicted dirty pages back to the backend storage. As presented above, SE-Invalid and SE-LRU do not limit the OP space size to a specific value or a range. So they do not need any users' involvement to tune some parameters for better cache performance. Because they evict all the valid pages inside victim block regardless of whether there is sufficient OP space, the page copy overhead can be reduced. But this will also reduce the cache hit ratio, especially when the OP space is already sufficient for garbage collection. CCR and GCR try to make a balance between garbage collection overhead and cache hit ratio, but their focuses are different. CCR sets a threshold for the total number of flash pages used as cache space and wants to guarantee that the cache hit ratio will not be largely influenced by the eviction of valid flash pages inside victim block. This is reasonable, but the threshold value is sensitive to workload's characteristic. It's hard to choose a threshold value which can be efficient for all workloads. GCR further refines the garbage collection overhead. It sets a threshold for the total number of invalid pages in the victim block. For garbage collection overhead, the number of invalid pages inside victim block is more representative than the number of pages used as OP space. Compared with CCR, GCR can make a better balance between garbage collection overhead and cache hit ratio. As shown in the following experiments, GCR can get the best performance among the four cache replacement strategies and its threshold is insensitive to workload's characteristic.

3.4 Cache Persistency and Consistency

For fusion-cache is designed as a write-back cache, it is important to make the metadata (address translation table) persistent to tolerate software/hardware crashes in host system. Additionally, persisting metadata can also reduce the long cache warm-up time when cache device is reused. In fusion-cache, the metadata is stored in a specific place in cache device. To make the metadata consistent with the data in cache, we deployed a log-based update mechanism. For any updates to the metadata, we first log the update to cache device or other non-volatile storage device, and then change the metadata in memory. When cache suffers a host system crash, we can replay the update logs on the old metadata stored in cache device to reconstruct the up-to-date view of the data in cache. This guarantees that all the updates which have been cached will not be lost in host system crash.

If there are many updates to the metadata before a system crash, then the recovery will be very time consuming. To alleviate this situation, we can use checkpoint mechanism to periodically merge metadata update logs into cache device, making the log size not exceed a specific length. Another optimization is based on the observation that only dirty data can influence the correctness of host-side cache. Thus, we can log metadata updates only for dirty data to reduce the cache consistency overhead. The corresponding side effect is that some clean cache blocks may be lost in the recovered/reused cache, but this does not influence the cache's correctness and availability.

4   Evaluation

To evaluate the performance of fusion-cache, we construct a trace-driven simulator based on FlashSim [16] which is a widely used simulator in flash related research area. FlashSim can simulate the internal architecture inside a SSD device, e.g. bus, package, die, plane, block and page. We add a cache module to FlashSim and modify it to support data deduplication. The detailed configurations are listed in Table 1, among which flash memory is based on a product from Micron [17] and the backed storage latency is based on a HDD product form Seagate [18]. In the following experiments, we use SHA-1 as the fingerprint extraction function, and its latency is about 25 μs on our experiment platform (one Intel I7-3770 processor and 8 GB RAM). The traces used here are from FIU [19] and to the best of our knowledge they are the only publicly available traces with both requested address and data content. These traces are collected from three different platforms and the duration is 3 weeks. The web workload is from a virtual machine running two web servers. The home workload is from a file server that serves the home directories of department's research group. The mail

Table 1. Simulator configurations

	Items	Configuration
Flash Memory [17]	Flash Page Size	4 KB
	Pages per Block	64
	Blocks per Plane	512
	Read Time	50 μs
	Write Time	900 μs
	Erase Time	3 ms
HDD [18]	Read Time	3.4 ms
	Write Time	3.9 ms
Others	SHA-1 Hashing (4 KB)	25 μs

Table 2. Workload statistics. Duplication ratio is based on both reads and writes.

Workload	Total Requests	Writes (%)	Duplication Ratio (%)	Working Set Size (GB)	Sequential Ratio (%)
web	14294158	78.2	57.13	2.09	76.16
home	17836701	95.93	33.94	6.43	49.45
mail	458005630	88.7	89.97	57.30	89.11

server is from an email server that serves user INBOXes for the entire computer science department at FIU. Table 2 gives the detailed statistics, from which we can find the three workloads are all write intensive and mail workload has higher duplication ratio and sequential ratio.

In the following experiments, we will first evaluate the performance gains achieved by applying data deduplication in host-side cache and compare the performance of different content-aware cache architectures. Then, we will present and analyze the performance of fusion-cache with different cache replacement strategies. Finally we will evaluate the sensitivity of cache performance on fingerprint store size.

4.1   With/Without Data Deduplication

To clearly understand the benefits of removing duplicate data blocks in host-side SSD cache, we compare three content-aware cache architectures (HDR, DDR and fusion-cache) and one traditional flash cache architecture (TFC) which does not apply data deduplication. Additionally, we choose the performance of workloads without SSD cache as the baseline, which is denoted by NC in the following performance figures. The size of SSD device is set to 1 GB and the OP space size is tuned from 0 to 70 % of the whole SSD size. Note that, in this subsection, the cache replacement strategies used in TFC, HDR and DDR are based on LRU and fusion-cache is based on GCR with the threshold set to 0.8.

Figure 3 presents the average I/O performance of three workloads on different cache architectures. Because cache space and OP space are managed together inside fusion-cache and there is no obvious demarcation between them, we do not need to set OP size for fusion-cache. Thus, its performance line is flat. From Fig. 3, we find that, **(1)** compared with NC, there is performance improvement in nearly all cases except when the OP space size is set too small ($< 10\%$) or too large ($> 70\%$). This is because too large or too small OP space size can cause big garbage collection overhead or low cache hit ratio. **(2)** content-aware cache architectures can always generate better I/O performance than TFC. This means applying data deduplication in host-side SSD cache is of great help to improve cache's efficiency. **(3)** OP space size has a big influence on the performance of all the cache architectures except fusion-cache, and the optimal configuration of OP space size varies with the running workload and selected cache architecture. For example, for web workload, the optimal OP size is about 35 % for TFC, 0 for DDR and 20 % for HDR. But for home workload, the optimal OP size is

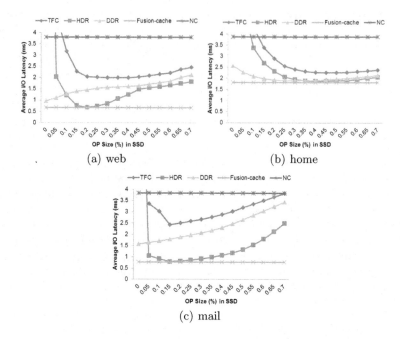

Fig. 3. Average I/O latency of three workloads on different cache architectures.

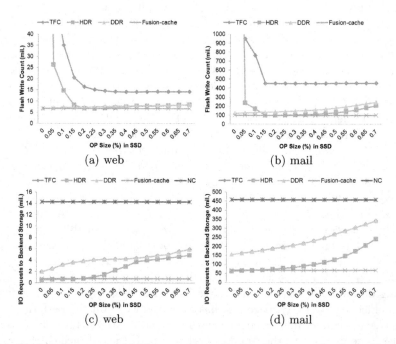

Fig. 4. Flash write count and I/O requests to backend storage of web workload and mail workload on different cache architectures.

changed to 45 % for TFC, 25 % for DDR and 40 % for HDR. This result presents a good evidence for that it is really very hard to achieve the optimal cache performance by manually tuning the OP size. As a compromise, in practice, manufacturers usually set aside about 15 % of the SSD size as the OP space. This configuration is good in most cases as shown in Fig. 3, but there is still a lot of room for performance improvement in some situations, e.g. in home workload. (4) Different from HDR, DDR can achieve its best performance when the OP space size is set to 0 for web workload and mail workload. This is because for the two workloads, the cache hit ratio is sensitive to cache size. When OP space size is set very small, most of the SSD space is used to improve the cache hit ratio. Besides, data deduplication inside SSD device can generate spare storage space to supplement the OP space to reduce the garbage collection overhead. Thus, the overall cache performance will be improved. (5) Fusion-cache can achieve the best I/O performance for all the three workloads. Even compared with the best performance of TFC, fusion-cache can still generate a big reduction on the average I/O latency, about 66.45 % for web workload, 20 % for home workload and 68.16 % for mail workload. All the performance gains achieved by fusion-cache are due to its integrated management of cache behaviors and flash memory, removing the semantic gap between the two components. Besides, the reasonable usage mechanism for the saved storage space by data deduplication is also very important to improve the cache's performance.

Figure 4 presents the flash write count and the total number of I/O requests redirected to backend storage for web workload and mail workload. Flash write count means the total number of write operations inside flash device, and it represents the wear condition of SSD device. If a read request is not found in cache, then it will be redirected to backend storage. When the cache is full, any dirty data evicted from cache will also be flushed back to backend storage. The two parts of requests consist of the I/O traffic between host server and the backend storage server. For both flash write count and the number of I/O requests redirected to backend storage, a lower value is better.

As depicted by Fig. 4, similar to average I/O performance, OP space size also has a big influence on the two metrics for TFC, HDR and DDR. Performing data deduplication can significantly reduce the flash write count as well as the I/O traffic redirected to backend storage. For example, for web workload, fusion-cache can reduce the flash write count by about 52 % and the number of I/O requests redirected to backend storage by about 62.4 %. For mail workload, the corresponding reduction ratios are 78 % and 58 %. Note that, all the reduction is based on the comparison with TFC with the optimal configuration of OP space size. Another interesting thing is that TFC and DDR have the same number of redirected requests. This is because the number of redirected I/O requests is determined by the cache size and the cache replacement strategy, while TFC and DDR have the same cache module inside host system.

4.2 Different Cache Replacement Strategies

We design four cache replacement strategies for fusion-cache as discussed in Sect. 3.3. In this subsection, we will evaluate the efficiency of the four replacement strategies and the sensitivity of their performance on the configuration of their thresholds. For SE-Invalid and SE-LRU, there is no threshold. Thus, their performance lines in Fig. 5 are flat. For CCR, there is a threshold for the total number of flash pages used as cache space. It tries to guarantee the cache hit ratio will not be very bad. Similar to CCR, GCR sets a threshold on the number of invalid flash pages inside the selected victim flash block. GCR tries to make the overhead of each garbage collection operation as small as possible.

In this experiment, we set SSD size to 1 GB, and tune the thresholds from 0.5 to 0.9. As presented by Fig. 5, SE-Invalid always achieves the worst performance. This is reasonable, because it only guarantees the number of evicted flash pages is the smallest in each garbage collection operation, ignoring the access characteristic of each cached page. SE-LRU can get the performance comparable with CCR and GCR in most cases except for web workload. The reason is that the cache size (1 GB) for web workload is relatively larger than the other two workloads as shown in Table 2. Besides, SE-LRU always evicts out the valid flash pages in the selected victim block from cache, without considering whether the OP space is sufficient. This will reduce the number of cached items and influence

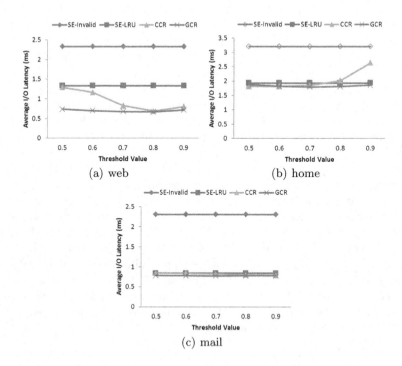

Fig. 5. Average I/O latency of three workloads on fusion-cache with different cache replacement strategies.

the cache hit ratio especially when the cache size is large. Compared with GCR, CCR is more sensitive on its threshold value. When the threshold is set too low, it will degrade to SE-LRU. And if the threshold is set too high, the overall cache performance will be influenced by the garbage collection overhead. The features of CCR can be clearly depicted by Fig. 5(a) and (b). Based on the fine-grained control over the garbage collection overhead, GCR can achieve the best performance for all the three workloads. Additionally, its performance is insensitive on workload characteristics as shown in Fig. 5. We recommend using GCR as the cache replacement strategy in fusion-cache.

4.3 Sensitivity of Cache Performance on Fingerprint Store Size

In this subsection we evaluate the sensitivity of cache performance on fingerprint store size. Because the total trace number in mail workload is huge and simulation on it is very time-consuming, we only use web workload and home workload in this experiment. For the two workloads, the SSD is configured to 1 GB, 512 MB and 256 MB. Here, the fingerprint store size is defined as the ratio of the number of fingerprints stored in the fingerprint store and the number of all the flash pages in SSD device. We tune the fingerprint store size from 0 to 1.0. When the fingerprint store size is set to 0, it means data deduplication is not applied. When the fingerprint store size is set to 1.0, it means the fingerprints of all the cached data blocks are maintained in memory. Then, the deduplication ratio will be higher, but this will also incur high memory overhead.

As shown in Fig. 6, the performance of fusion-cache will be improved when the fingerprint store size is increased. But the performance will be insensitive on the fingerprint store size when it is larger than 0.2. This means we can only maintain 20 % of the fingerprints for data deduplication in memory. Then the memory space occupied by fingerprint store can be reduced by 80 %, without significantly influencing the cache performance.

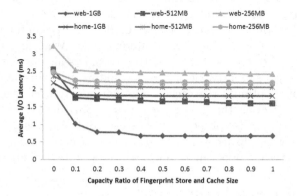

Fig. 6. Average I/O latency of fusion-cache with different fingerprint store sizes.

5   Related Work

While FTL can hide the internal operations of SSD from host system and improve the SSD device's compatibility, it also results in redundant address translation layers and causes additional performance overhead. To reduce this overhead, many methods have been proposed. Work in [20] proposed a new device interface for SSD device to make it support nameless writes. Then the upper file system can directly use SSD device's physical address, eliminating the internal translation for SSD device's logical address. In [21], Lee et al. refactored the I/O architecture of log structured file system (LFS) by integrating FTL with the storage space management in LFS. This can remove redundant garbage collection operation and improve file system's performance. The two works are focusing on the performance of file system, while our work focuses on cache-based storage system. Similar to [20], in [15] Zhang et al. proposed to extend the device interface of SSD to make SSD a dedicated cache device which they called SSC. Yang et al. also conducted extensive experiments to evaluate the impact of different cache mechanisms, GC policies and device configurations on hit rate and writes/erases to SSC in [22]. Even though SSC can remove the redundant address translation layer, the cache administration is still separate from flash management, while in fusion-cache the two components are tightly integrated.

Work in [2] laid the foundation for applying data reduction in host-side SSD cache. It shows there is a substantial degree of duplication in host-side cache device, up to 67 % in some situations. Different from our work, work in [7–9] performed data deduplication inside SSD device. In our experiments, we have given the comparison between them and fusion-cache. Work in [3,4] is similar with ours, they also apply data reduction in host-side SSD cache. But they are focusing on the cache management, without much consideration about the internal operations inside SSD device. While in fusion-cache, we try to consider both the two components, and provide a more effective cache management scheme.

There are also some works to improve the cache performance by optimizing the cache replacement strategy. Work in [23] presented a self-tuning cache management algorithm, which they named LARC. LARC can filter out seldom accessed blocks and prevent them from entering cache. Work in [24] proposed a hierarchical adaptive replacement cache that considers all the four factors of a cache block's status, i.e. dirty, clean, recency and frequency. Different from our work, these works optimize the cache performance only from the cache layer, also without considering the internal features of SSD device. Recently, many outstanding works are also proposed on host-side SSD cache, such as [5,25,26]. Even though they are focusing on the different aspects from our work, many good ideas from these works can be borrowed to optimize fusion-cache.

6   Conclusion and Future Work

Host-side SSD cache is widely used to improve the hosted virtual machines' I/O performance. But in traditional host-side SSD cache, the cache module and the flash memory are managed individually. This can cause semantic gap between the two components, and reduce the cache's usage efficiency. To alleviate this situation, we propose fusion-cache, in which the flash translation layer is moved from device to host system and tightly integrated with the cache module. Furthermore, we apply data deduplication in fusion-cache to expand its effective cache space and an efficient cache replacement strategy is also proposed to improve its cache efficiency. Experimental results show fusion-cache can significantly improve the I/O performance, prolong cache device's lifetime and reduce the I/O traffic between the host server and the backend storage server.

Fusion-cache is designed as a write-back cache in host server, without considering much about data consistency between host-side cache and backend storage. It cannot be used in a shared storage where several host servers share the same backend data. We will address this drawback in future, and then fusion-cache will upgrade to a big distributed host-side SSD cache. It can globally manage all the cache devices and improve the overall cache utilization and efficiency.

Acknowledgments. We would like to thank the anonymous reviewers for their hard work for this conference. We also appreciate the constructive comments and suggestions from the members of ARC Lab in Zhejiang University.

References

1. Arteaga, D., Zhao, M.: Client-side flash caching for cloud systems. In: 7th International Systems and Storage Conference, pp. 1–11. ACM (2014)
2. Feng, J., Schindler, J.: A deduplication study for host-side caches in virtualized data center environments. In: IEEE 29th Symposium on Mass Storage Systems and Technologies, pp. 1–6. IEEE (2013)
3. Li, C., Shilane, P., Douglis, F., Shim, H., Smaldone, S., Wallace, G.: Nitro: a capacity-optimized SSD cache for primary storage. In: USENIX Annual Technical Conference, pp. 501–512. USENIX Association (2014)
4. He, W., Xiao, N., Liu, F., Xing Y., Chen. B.: Adaptive Data Reduction Scheme for SSD-based Host-side Caches in VDI Storage. 2013
5. Kim, H., Koltsidas, I., Ioannou, N., Seshadri, S., Muench, P., Dickey, C.L., Chiu, L.: How could a flash cache degrade database performance rather than improve it? lessons to be learnt from multi-tiered storage. In: 2nd Workshop on Interactions of NVM/Flash with Operating Systems and Workloads. USENIX Association (2014)
6. Oh, Y., Choi, J., Lee, D., Noh, S.H.: Caching less for better performance: balancing cache size and update cost of flash memory cache in hybrid storage systems. In: 10th USENIX Conference on File and Storage Technologies. USENIX Association (2012)
7. Chen, F., Luo, T., Zhang, X.: CAFTL: A content-aware flash translation layer enhancing the lifespan of flash memory based solid state drives. In: 9th USENIX Conference on File and Storage Technologies. USENIX Association (2011)
8. Gupta, A., Pisolkar, R., Urgaonkar, B., Sivasubramaniam, A.: Leveraging Value Locality in Optimizing NAND Flash-based SSDs. In: 9th USENIX Conference on File and Storage Technologies. USENIX Association (2011)

9. Kim, J., Lee, C., Lee, S., Son, I., Choi, J.: Deduplication in SSDs: model and quantitative analysis. In: IEEE 28th Symposium on Mass Storage Systems and Technologies. IEEE (2012)

10. Batwara, A.: Leveraging host based flash translation layer for application acceleration. http://www.flashmemorysummit.com/English/Collaterals/Proceedings/2012/20120821_TB11_Batwara.pdf

11. FIPS 180-4. Secure hash standard. National Institute of Standards and Technology (2012)

12. Primmer, R., D'Halluin, C.: Collision and preimage resistance of the Centera content address. arXiv preprint (2013). arXiv:1306.6020

13. Quinlan, S., Dorward, S.: Venti: A New Approach to Archival Storage. In: USENIX Conference on File and Storage Technologies. USENIX Association (2002)

14. Black, J.: Compare-by-Hash: A Reasoned Analysis. In: USENIX Annual Technical Conference. USENIX Association (2006)

15. Saxena, M., Swift, M.M., Zhang, Y.: Flashtier: a lightweight, consistent and durable storage cache. In: 7th ACM European Conference on Computer Systems, pp. 267–280. ACM (2012)

16. FlashSim. https://github.com/MatiasBjorling/flashsim

17. Datasheet of MT29F32G08CBABA. Micro Technology (2008)

18. Cheetah 15K.7: Highest capacity, performance and reliability in 3.5-inch mission-critical storage. http://www.seagate.com/files/docs/pdf/datasheet/disc/cheetah-15k.7-ds1677.3-1007us.pdf

19. Koller, R., Rangaswami, R.: I/O deduplication: utilizing content similarity to improve i/o performance. ACM Trans. Storage **6**, 1–14 (2010)

20. Zhang, Y., Arulraj, L.P., Arpaci-Dusseau, A.C., Arpaci-Dusseau, R.H.: Deindirection for flash-based SSDs with nameless writes. In: 10th USENIX Conference on File and Storage Technologies. USENIX Association (2012)

21. Lee, S., Kim, J., Arvind, M.: Refactored design of i/o architecture for flash storage. Comput. Archit. Lett. **14**(1), 70–74 (2014)

22. Yang, J., Plasson, N., Gillis, G., Talagala, N.: HEC: improving endurance of high performance flash-based cache devices. In: 6th International Systems and Storage Conference. ACM (2013)

23. Huang, S., Wei, Q., Chen, J., Chen, C., Feng, D.: Improving flash-based disk cache with lazy adaptive replacement. In: IEEE 29th Symposium on Mass Storage Systems and Technologies, pp. 1–10. IEEE (2013)

24. Fan, Z., Du, D.H., Voigt, D.: H-ARC: a non-volatile memory based cache policy for solid state drives. In: 30th Symposium on Mass Storage Systems and Technologies, pp. 1–11. IEEE (2014)

25. Meng, F., Zhou, L., Ma, X., Uttamchandani, S., Liu, D.: vCacheShare: automated server flash cache space management in a virtualization environment. In: USENIX Annual Technical Conference. USENIX Association (2014)

26. Koller, R., Mashtizadeh, A.J., Rangaswami, R.: Centaur: Host-side SSD caching for storage performance control. In: 12th IEEE International Conference On Autonomic Computing, pp. 51–60. IEEE (2015)

A Novel Storing and Accessing Method of Traffic Incident Video Based on Spatial-Temporal Analysis

Yaying Zhang[✉] and Yinyin Zhu

Key Laboratory of Embedded System and Service Computing,
Tongji University, Shanghai 201804, China
{yaying.zhang,1333805}@tongji.edu.cn

Abstract. Hadoop Distributed File System (HDFS) is a reliable and scalable data storage solution. However, it has great weakness in storage of the numerous small files. A merging method of small video files containing traffic incidents is proposed to improve the HDFS storage efficiency of small files. As traffic incident videos can be classified in terms of time and the crossroad where the incident happens, the proposed method merges video files together by time and region (usually adjacent crossroads). Indexing mechanism has been improved in later searching for small video files. The whole HDFS file block related to specific incidents will be read out to local cache. The experimental results show that when accessing for traffic incidents by region in certain period, the average search time and the memory load of HDFS NameNode will be effectively reduced.

Keywords: Traffic incident videos · HDFS · Small files merge · Inverted index · Fast retrieval

1 Introduction

Video surveillance is an important application in intelligent traffic systems. In most modern urban traffic surveillance systems, smart video cameras are usually mounted at crossroads to monitor the road traffic status, i.e. vehicle queue length detection, traffic incident detection and vehicle tracking. Each camera captures video data continuously. The traffic video contains huge amount of those with normal traffic monitoring stream data and a small part of those with unexpected traffic incidents. In the real traffic scenario, the latter one is paid much more attention. Thus, it is unreasonable for these two kinds of video data to be stored in the same way. Traditional traffic monitoring system mainly employed storage servers to store all data as video streaming. The operator would later have to manually play back the video to look for a certain specific traffic incident. These storage systems cannot distinguish the traffic incident data from all the video streaming data. Nowadays, smart cameras with capabilities of incident detection could make a structured description about the incident [1]. Research in transmitting videos which contain incidents in higher resolution and for those not containing incidents in lower resolution to save the network bandwidth has been carried out [2, 3]. Thus, the small video files which contain incidents are retrieved and recorded separately in small size files. Therefore, research on the storing and accessing method of massive amounts of traffic incident videos in small size has its practical

G. Wang et al. (Eds.): ICA3PP 2015, Part II, LNCS 9529, pp. 315–329, 2015.
DOI: 10.1007/978-3-319-27122-4_22

significances in real traffic scenarios, i.e. tracking hit-and-run vehicles and analyzing the traffic incidents in certain urban district for the traffic police departments. How to efficiently store huge amounts of small videos containing traffic incidents and later fast fetch certain incident videos to play back have become an important topic in intelligent transportation surveillance system.

Hadoop has great advantages in scalability, robustness, calculated performance and cost, and has become the mainstream big data analysis platform of the current Internet applications [4]. Hadoop stores data in Hadoop Distributed File System (HDFS) [5–7] which is a file access model with the function of "write once and read many". Traffic video data are generated in real time and are written in sequence without modification and its feature matches well with HDFS. However, HDFS is designed for optimizing large file streaming access patterns and neglect storing and accessing small files. Small files in this paper refer to the video clip file which contains traffic incidents lasting for seconds or minutes, thus the file size is always less than 10 MB. As every file, directory and block in HDFS is represented as an object in the NameNode's memory, each of which occupies about 150 bytes. With small incident files coming continuously, more and more memory of NameNode will be occupied, the memory capacity of the machine which supports the NameNode may become the key point. Furthermore, the number of incidents on some crossroad at a certain period of time is usually more than one. If they are not merged and stored in the same block, reading through them will cause lots of seeks and switching from block to block or even DataNode to DataNode, all of which is an inefficient data access pattern. Storing and Accessing large amounts of small files have become a recognized challenge in both industrial and academic field [8–11]. In [12], Hadoop Archive was used to implement the mergers of small files to improve the storage efficiency of metadata. In [13, 14], the storage mechanism which was appropriate for the files of WebGIS and PPT was proposed to improve the efficiency of storing and accessing of small files. In [15], a new kind of file merging method was proposed to optimize the I/O performance of the system, and to improve the performance of distributed file system. Merging algorithm based on time and file size was proposed in [16], which improves the storage efficiency of cloud storage platform. A freestanding cache structure of small files had been designed to increases I/O cache of small files to improve the performance of Lustre [17].

Despite the variety of existing small file merging strategy, no method has considered about the specific features inherent in traffic incident videos, i.e. occurrence time, time and region correlation, and its real-time feature. Therefore, the average speed of searching for incident video files using existing methods is always slow. Due to the weakness in utilizing existing small file merging strategy to store real-time traffic incident videos, this paper proposes a new storing and accessing method of traffic incident small video files, which aims at fast search and lighter memory load of NameNode.

2   Problem Statement

2.1   Problem Overview

The road network and camera mounted on the crossroads can be self-explained in Fig. 1.

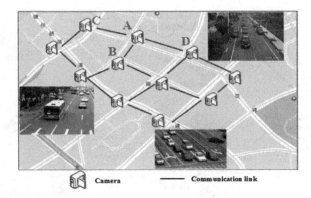

Fig. 1. Road network and cameras

In road network with smart cameras, cameras are always monitoring road traffic status. When it detects incidents, it will transmit the video containing the incident for storage and for later retrieval. Generally people are always interested in incidents with certain areas i.e. places where they live or work. Traffic police departments also concern about areas they are in charge of. These areas always could be represented by multiple adjacent crossroads. Normally neither general public nor policeman would be interested in incidents only on one particular crossroad i.e. crossroad A. They would also consider its adjacent crossroads B, C or D. Furthermore time is also an important consideration. People pay much more attention to incidents on peak hours rather than holidays. Based on these above observations, we merge the small video files containing incidents in terms of area and time for later fast retrieval.

The overall architecture of traffic incident file storing and accessing system is shown in Fig. 2. It consists of smarts cameras capturing traffic incident video data, a dispatcher which dispatches incident files to storing clients by region, several storing clients to store incoming incident videos temporarily and then merging them and build index, an index store to keep index, HDFS clusters storing incident videos permanently, search clients, and a server to response search requests.

Our method is shown in Fig. 3. We first merge massive amounts of real-time traffic incident videos collected by smart cameras by crossroad and time, generating merged files. Then we improve inverted index mechanism to create index for the merged files. Finally, we have a fast searching method for later incident file retrieval.

2.2 Basic Terminology Definitions

To simplify later illustration, the following terminologies are defined.

Definition 1 (*Crossing Number*): the *Crossing Number* is a unique serial number to identify the crossroad. It is an 11-digit number. i.e. 59565108098, 59565108097. We will use crossing and crossroad interchangeably in this paper.

Definition 2 (*Name of Small Incident File*): The *name of Small Incident File* has the format as Crossing Number-start time-end time. Among them, the *Crossing Number* is determined by the crossroad where the traffic incident happens. start time is the time when the traffic incident begins, and end time is the time when the traffic incident ends.

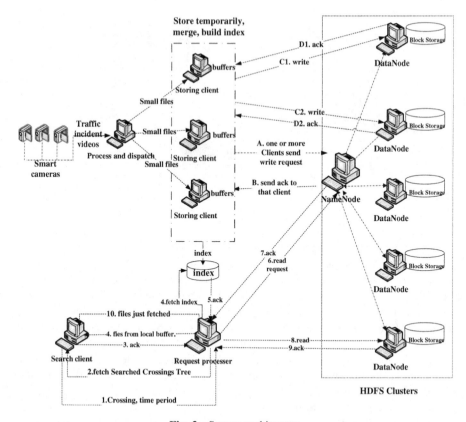

Fig. 2. System architecture

For example, 59565108098-20141128073205-20141128073217 is an incident file that describes an incident that had taken place on crossroad 59565108098 at 7:32 am on Nov, 28, 2014 and the incident lasted for 12 s.

Definition 3 (*Centered Crossing Number*): System client in Fig. 2 has a number of local storage buffers, i.e. buffer[0], buffer[1], ... The *Centered Crossing Number* of each buffer is defined as the *Crossing Number* of the first small file coming to the buffer. The local buffers are used to store small incident files temporally. For example, for buffer[0], the small incident file, named as 59565108098-20141128073205-20141128073217, is the first one that arrived at buffer[0], and then its *crossing number* 59565108098 is taken as the *centered crossing number* of buffer[0]. For each local buffer, if it is nonempty, it already had a *centered crossing number*. It is mainly used to determine whether a new coming incident video file can be stored temporally in a certain buffer or not.

Definition 4 (*Merged File Name*): The name of merged file has the format as serial number-starting time-ending time. The serial number here refers to the *Crossing Number* of the first small file in the buffer, which is the incident video file that first happened and so first arrived at the buffer. Furthermore, the small files in the buffer would be merged in the order that they had arrived at the buffer. starting time refers to

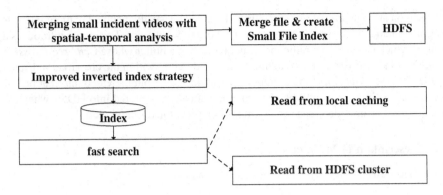

Fig. 3. Storing and accessing method

Table 1. Index of small file

Crossing number	Incident time	File size	Offset
59565108098	20141128070201 ∼ 20141128070212	3 MB	0 MB
59565108064	20141128070310 ∼ 20141128070327	1 MB	3 MB
……	……	……	……

the beginning time of the first small video file. ending time refers to the end time of the last small video file. For Example, the file 59565108098-20141128070110-2014112 8070118 is the first arrival in one buffer. File 59565108067-20141128070500-2014112 8070512 is the last arrival in this buffer. Then, when files are merged in this buffer, resulting merged file name is 59565108098-20141128070110-20141128070512.

Definition 5 (*Small File Index Table*): the *Small File Index Table* is used to store the metadata of each small incident file as in Table 1. With this index, the incident file would be conveniently located. When fetching incident files of a crossroad in certain period from local client cache, the *small file index table* is read to determine which small files should be fetched out. *Small File Index* and merged file are stored together in the HDFS clusters. When fetching the merged files from HDFS, the *small file index* is also retrieved to the local cache. The offset in Table 1 represents the starting position of the small file in the merged file.

Definition 6 (*Crossings To Be Searched*): The crossroads that are in a certain distance range of the crossroad where the user wants to search incidents.

Definition 7 (*Searched Crossings Tree*): We use the Trie structure to store the *crossing numbers* which have been searched. Note that the *crossing numbers* which have been searched come from *Crossings To Be Searched*.

3 Merging Method of Small Incident Videos with Spatial-Temporal Analysis

3.1 Basic Idea

In urban intelligent traffic systems, the smart cameras transfer traffic incident video files to system clients continuously as in Fig. 2. The videos contain metadata information about the location and the time of traffic incidents happened. Usually, people lay more interests on traffic incidents in a specific region instead of the whole city. This paper introduces a method which receives the traffic incident videos, find a buffer whose *Centered Crossing Number* is in some distance (we define a threshold value) within the crossroad indicated by the *Crossing Number* of the current incident video, and put the video into that buffer. All the videos in a buffer will be merged automatically and stored into HDFS when the buffer is full, or no video reaches any more in a predefined time period.

3.2   Description of Merging Method

A detailed description of our merge method is shown as follows.

```
Input: Real time small traffic incident video files which are generated continuously.
Output: Small incident files merged and stored into HDFS clusters.
1 Initialize the buffer number. Allocate buffers and initialize Centered Crossing Number of each buffer to null
2 if (an incident video file is at System client node) then
3     for i =1 to buffernumber
4         calculate the distance d between the incident file's Crossing Number and buffers' Centered Crossing
          Number
5         if (d<distanceThreshold) then
6             total file size of buffer+= file size of current incident file
7             if (total file size of buffer > the block size (64MB default)-2KB) then//incident file can't put into
              //buffer[i] due to buffer size, 2KB here is reserved to store small file index
8                 merge the files in buffer[i] with Small File Index (Table 1) to be a merged file;
9                 name the merged file and store into HDFS cluster;
10                clear buffer[i];
11                clear the Centered Crossing Number of buffer[i] (set to null);
12                set bufferEmptyflag of this buffer and set total file size of this buffer to 0
13            else
14                put current incident file into buffer[i];
15                break;
16            end if
17        end if
18    end for
19    if (i== buffernumber+1) then //cannot find a buffer (current not empty) to put the incident file
20        check whether there is empty buffer exist
21        if (empty buffer exists) then
22            find the first empty buffer
23            put the current incident file into buffer[firstEmptyBufferFlag];
24            set buffer's Centered Crossing Number as the incident file's Crossing Number;
25            update firstEmptyBufferFlag to the next available empty buffer
26        else
27            locate the least recently used buffer;
28            merge the files in the buffer as well as the Small File Index to be a merged file
29            name the merged file and store into HDFS;
30            clear the buffer.
31            put the current incident file into this buffer.
32            reset buffer's Centered Crossing Number as the incident file's Crossing Number;
33        end if
34    end if
35 end if
```

Here we consider one worse situation: a traffic incident happened at a crossroad, but since then for a long time no incident happened in this crossroad and in its distance threshold, leading to an occasion that a local buffer is not empty and its total file size cannot reach the block size (64 MB default)-2 KB after a long time. Therefore, files in this buffer may not be merged and written to HDFS clusters in a long period. This will affect the search for this incident since this incident file has not been available before it has been merged and written to HDFS. We cannot look up a traffic incident that has not been stored in the HDFS clusters. To avoid this, we set a LastUpdateTime when a new small file is placed in a local buffer. We monitor the nonempty buffers. If the differentials between system current time and the LastUpdateTime of nonempty buffer exceed the time threshold, the small files in this buffer together with its *Small File Index* will be merged and sent to the HDFS cluster for storage mandatorily.

3.3   Improved Inverted Index Strategy

In traffic surveillance system, a video file containing traffic incident normally has size of no more than 10 MBs. When the buffer is full or has waited for a very long time, HDFS Client will merge them into a large file, and send it to HDFS for storage. In order to decrease the time cost on searching for particular incidents, index tree will be built for newly-merged video files. When users search for particular incident, the system will count out index keys by target time and merge them, getting the merged paired values, which are the names of merged files that are to be fetched. This is an improved version of inverted index.

Inverted index [18] is suitable for key-value structured data, where the key is the target word and the value is the location. It is called inverted index because location is searched by particular word. Files with inverted index is called inverted file.

When accessing the incident file after it had been merged and stored in the HDFS clusters. The Mapping from *Crossing Number*-half hour to Name of merged files is used. This is a map of key-value pairs. *Crossing Number*-half hour is the key, and Name of merged files is the value. *Crossing Number*-half hour is expressed like { ......, 59565108098-20141128080000-20141128083000,   59565108098-20141128083000-20141128090000,   59565108098-20141128090000-20141128093000, ...}. For every half hour, an index is created for the merged files that are stored in HDFS cluster during the past half hour. The name of merged file will be added into one or more values through analyzing the three parts of the merged file name separated by the hyphen. For example, the name of one merged file is 59565108098-20141128062803-2014112 8071220, flagged as MFN. It can be determined that the time of MFN has an overlap with   20141128060000-20141128063000,   20141128063000-20141128070000   and 20141128070000-20141128073000. Therefore, we add the MFN into the values whose paired key is 59565108098-20141128060000-20141128063000, 59565108098-20141 128063000-20141128070000 and 59565108098-20141128070000-20141128073000.

As shown in Fig. 4, for each merged file, as long as its occurrence time has an overlap with the time period of the key of index, its name will be appended into the paired value of the keys above. When searching for incident videos at a crossroad in a period of time, usually, index keys which are worked out by the period of time above are to be merged, resulting the names of merged files which are to be fetched from HDFS.

The improved inverted index method includes index creation and index merging as follows:

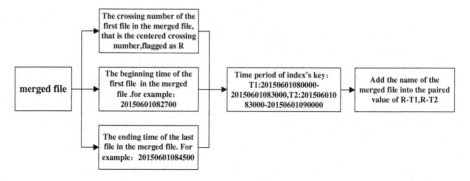

Fig. 4. Index creation

(a) Index creation

Step 1: When a merged file is sent to HDFS for storage, we append the name of this merged file to a variable, named as mergedFilesName, which records the names of merged files in the past half an hour.

Step 2: At half and whole hour, according to the mergedFilesName in step 1, index for the merged files is created. For each merged file name, refer to its second and third parts to get the periods of time that have an overlap with the merged file. The periods of time above refer to the part of index key. Append the merged file name into the value as long as the time part of the paired key has an overlap with the time part of the merged file name.

(b) Index merging

Step 1: All *centered crossing numbers* which are to be searched are obtained by the crossroad provided by user.

Step 2: By the period of time input and the *centered crossing numbers* acquired in step 1, keys will be worked out, and the resulting paired values are the names of merged files that are to be searched.

When searching for traffic incidents, given the crossroad, starting time and ending time, a threshold will be used to determine the crossings to be searched. With the starting time and ending time, for example, the starting time is 7:10 am on November 28, 2014, the ending time is at 8:20 am on November 28, 2014, merge all the corresponding values in the *Crossings To Be Searched*-20141128070000-20141128073000, *Crossings To Be Searched*-20141128073000-20141128080000 and *Crossings To Be Searched*-20141128080000-20141128083000. The duplicate ones will be removed and the names of merge files that to be fetched could be obtained.

3.4   Fast Searching Method

Given crossroad where the user wants to search incidents, named as *crossing wanted* (*CW*), start time t_1 and end time t_2, all crossroads within the range of *CW* are set as *Crossings To Be Searched*. Search them from *Searched Crossings Tree* (as in

Definition 7) which are *crossing numbers* having been searched. If all *Crossings To Be Searched* are in the *Searched Crossings Tree*, it means that all videos waiting for searching are already fetched to local storage cache before. We only need to read them by *Small File Index Table* (as in Table 1). If not, the system will compute and merge the index keys through start and end time to get the value, which are the names of merged files. These file names can be used to retrieve corresponding files from HDFS clusters. If no file name is found, this means that all videos are fetched to local storage before.

This search method is processing as in Fig. 5.

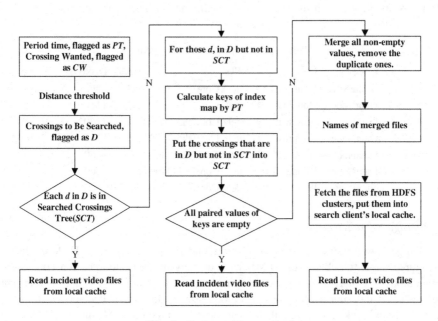

Fig. 5. Fast searching method

Step 1: Given *Crossing Wanted*, *CW*, starting time t_1, ending time t_2, work out crossings that are in the distance threshold by *CW*. Set these crossings as *Crossings to Be Searched*, D. Check *Crossings to Be Searched* from *Searched Crossings Tree*. For each d in D, if all d are in *Searched Crossings Tree*, all incident videos that you want to search are in local cache and go to step 4.

Step 2: for each crossing in *Crossings To Be Searched* but not in *Searched Crossings Tree*, calculate keys of index map by t_1 and t_2 as in Sect. 3.3. If paired values of keys are not null, add the crossings that are in *Crossings To Be Searched* but not in *Searched Crossings Tree* into *Searched Crossings Tree* and go to step 3. Otherwise, if all paired values of keys are null or empty, then put the crossings that are in *Crossings To Be Searched* but not in *Searched Crossings Tree* into *Searched Crossings Tree* and go to step 4.

Step 3: Merge all non-empty values and remove the duplicate ones. The result is the names of merged files that are to be searched. Then, fetch the files from HDFS clusters according to the filenames, and put them into local cache.

Step 4: By *Small File Index Table*, read incident video files from local cache.

4 Experiments and Result Evaluation

The experiment environment we set is shown as in Table 2. The experiment simulates the smart cameras generating real-time video data. The experiment is aimed mainly to test users' average search time as well as the memory usage of the NameNode.

Table 2. Experimental environment

Node	OS	CPU	RAM	Disk(G)
NameNode	Ubuntu12.04	Intel®Core™i5-3230	4G	500
DataNode1	Ubuntu12.04	Intel®Core™i5-2400	2G	1160
DataNode2	Ubuntu12.04	Intel®Core™i5-2400	2G	1160
DataNode3	Ubuntu12.04	Intel®Core™i5-2400	2G	225
DataNode4	Ubuntu12.04	Intel®Core™i5-2400	2G	160
DataNode5	Ubuntu12.04	Intel®Core™i5-2400	2G	160
client	Win7	Intel®Core™i5-3230	4G	500

A. Average Search Time

Compare with users' average search time under four strategies: 1. Hadoop cluster configured with a block size of 10 MB without merging. 2. Hadoop cluster configured with a block size of 10 MB with our merging method 3. The existing small file merging method HAR merging strategy witch a block size of default. 4. Hadoop cluster configured with a block size of default with our merging method. HAR method is Hadoop Archive method which is used widely in merging small files. It can also be used in our proposal, but it is less efficient in the situation of our proposal. The experiment uses 1000 crossroads of Beijing as the site of the incidents. It uses multi threads to generate real-time traffic incident video data which take place in those 1000 crossings. Three groups of experiments respectively query 10 times, 50 times and 200 times. A search is to access for traffic incident video files at a crossroad at a certain time period. Each set of the search is in accordance with the users' interested crossroads' incidents, that is, crossings of search in each group of experiment are roughly distributed in an area.

The average search time is the total time divided by the number of search. The experimental results show in Fig. 6. It indicates that with the increasing of the number of queries, the access method put forward in this paper reduces the user's average search time. Using Hadoop cluster configured with a block size of 10 MB without using our merging method to store and fetch small incident files, firstly all filenames will be got and analyzed to estimate which incidents occurred on the crossroad and at the time period of the query. Then, the traffic incident files which satisfy the query conditions will be fetched. However, there is no need to analyze all filenames using Hadoop cluster configured with a block size of 10 MB with using our merging method to store and fetch small incident files on a crossroad at a certain time period.

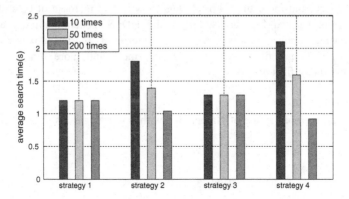

Fig. 6. Average search time

Small file merging method, HAR merging method (hadoop archive method), is a method which has not taken the characteristics of traffic incident videos into consideration, so those traffic incident videos happened on adjacent crossroads are usually stored dispersedly in different block or even different DataNode. Moreover, in this case, if we want to fetch traffic incident videos at a certain crossroad and period, then these actions will be performed. Firstly, all _masterIndex will be iterated to get all _index (_masterIndex and _index are index files of files. They are generated when using HAR method to merge files, _masterIndex is first-level index to locate _index file which finally would find the specific small file wanted). Then those _index will be traversed to get the DataNode and block's position as well as the offset and the size of traffic incident file. Finally, the traffic incident files which satisfy the query conditions will be fetched. In addition, incident videos at a crossing over a period of time are usually more than one. When fetching, HDFS Client usually need to constantly fetch from one block to another block, decreasing the query efficiency.

The query efficiency of the proposed method is higher than HAR merging method and method with no merging. But if the number of query is small, leading to some incident videos which has been fetched out not to be later used, the user's average search time will rise instead. The proposed method could be used for the traffic police department to store and search traffic incident videos. When traffic policemen track the hit-and-run vehicle by looking up surveillance videos or analyze the characteristics of traffic incidents in certain urban district, the search will not be limited to few crossings. On the other hand, the policemen normally don't deal with the case or analyze the characteristics of incidents only once, and they will go on after a time, they need to search and watch those videos again. Aiming at this situation, the method proposed in this paper actually decreases the average search time.

As shown in Figs. 7 and 8, as time passes, the average search time of strategy 1 and strategy 3 significantly increased. For strategy 1, with the increase of running days of the storing system, more and more files are stored in the HDFS, thus when fetching incidents generated on a crossing at a certain time period, more filenames will be got and analyzed, costing more time. For strategy 3, with the increase of operation time, more and more merged files are stored in the HDFS, generating more and more _masterIndex and _index. As it is necessary to traverse all _masterIndex and _index to determine which small files are to be fetched, more and more time will cost in traversing the index files above.

B. *Memory Usage*

We test the memory usage of NameNode with six strategies as showed in Table 3 as follows.

Table 3. Six strategies

Strategies	Description
Strategy 1	A Hadoop cluster configured with a block size of 10 MB without merging
Strategy 2	A Hadoop cluster configured with a block size of 10 MB with our merging method in the best situation
Strategy 3	A Hadoop cluster configured with a block size of 10 MB with our merging method in the worst situation
Strategy 4	Using the existing small file merging method HAR merging strategy witch a block size of default
Strategy 5	A Hadoop cluster configured with a block size of default with our merging method in the best situation
Strategy 6	Hadoop cluster configured with a block size of default with our merging method in the worst situation

We respectively measure the memory usage of NameNode before storing files and after completing storing files in HDFS. Our method is tested in the best case and worst case. The best case is that when an incident happens at a certain crossroad, a while later other incidents happen at crossroads which are in the distance threshold of the cross-road above. The result is that total file size in buffers can reach close to the block size (64 MB default) in time threshold. In this situation, all incident video files will be merged into large files before stored into HDFS in time, making the great performance of memory usage of NameNode. The worst case is that when an incident happens at a certain crossroad, and with a long time passed, no other incidents happen at crossroads which are in the distance threshold of the crossroad above. In this situation, each buffer may have only one small video file. However in order to enable users to search real-time incident video files, we won't keep the buffers ever waiting for incident videos. Once the time threshold of nonempty buffers reaches, the small file in the buffer will be stored into HDFS, making the low performance of memory usage of NameNode.

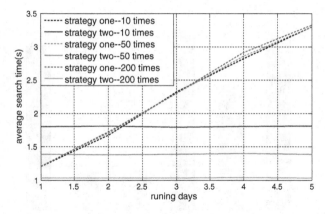

Fig. 7. Average search time of strategy 1 and strategy 2

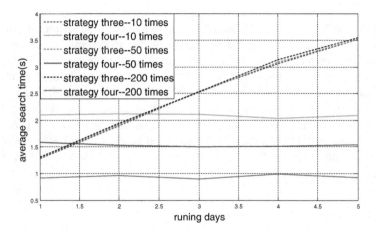

Fig. 8. Average search time of strategy 3 and strategy 4

Experiment selects 1000 crossroads of Beijing. We use multithreading to generate 60000 small files, simulating real-time incident scenarios. Among them, the number of files with size of 1M, 2M, 3M, 4M, 5M and 6M are 10000 respectively. The HDFS uses default replications. The Hadoop is restarted before and after doing experiments.

The experimental results are showed as follows in Fig. 9.

The y-coordinate represents the difference between the memory usages of the NameNode before and after files are stored into the HDFS under six strategies respectively.

The result indicates that, in the best case, the memory load of NameNode is lower when using our merging method to optimize Hadoop cluster with a block size of 10 MB or default to store small traffic incident files and is almost equal in the worst case. This is because all small files can be merged into larger files with a size of nearly the block size (64 MB default) in the best case. Due to the merge, the number of files

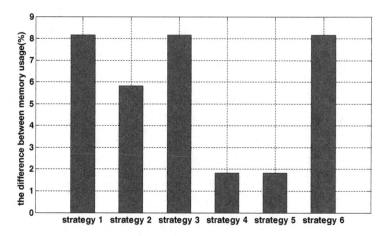

Fig. 9. Memory usage of NameNode

that sent to HDFS for storage is substantially reduced, and metadata information that is installed in the memory of NameNode reduces. In the worst case, small file in each buffer has not been merged with enough other small files before stored into HDFS, due to this, the number of files stored into HDFS is not reduced, leading to metadata information installed in the memory of NameNode equal with that of the no merging method. The memory load of NameNode of our merging method is almost equal with that of HAR merging method when using the equal size of blocks. In general, the efficiency of our merging method to the storage and access for large amounts of small traffic incident files is better than the HAR merging method or Hadoop method without merging.

5   Conclusion

This paper embarks from the actual application scenario, to overcome the weakness that HDFS is not well-suited for storing a large number of small files. In order to make users quickly searching for the incident videos in this scenario, a new storing and accessing method of traffic incident video based on the time and spatial properties is put forward in this paper. Verified by the experiment, this method can make users' average search time reduced and can comparably effectively decrease the possibility of the memory bottlenecks of NameNode.

Acknowledgments. This research was supported by the International Science and Technology Cooperation Program of China (2012DFG11580).

References

1. Zhang, Q.: The development and application of cloud storage technology in video surveillance. China Secur. Prot. 53–58, August 2013
2. RFC3550-IETF R T P. A transport protocol for real-time applications. Internet Eng. Task Force (2003)
3. Feng, S.: Research and Implementation on Video Transmission and Access Technology of Traffic Events. Tongji University, Shanghai (2013)
4. Apache Hadoop (2012). http://hadoop.apache.org
5. Shvachko, K., Kuang, H., Radia, S., et al.: The hadoop distributed file system. In: 2010 IEEE 26th Symposium on Mass Storage Systems and Technologies (MSST), pp. 1–10 (2010)
6. Cai, B., Chen, X.: Hadoop Internals: In-depth Study of Common and HDFS, pp. 216–217. China Machine Press, Beijing (2013)
7. Wu, W.: Design of the cloud storage model for video monitoring. Shanxi Sci. Technol. 35–37 (2012)
8. Dong, J., Chen, G., Wang, W., et al.: Msfss: a storage system for mass small files. In: 11th International Conference on Computer Supported CooperativeWork in Design (CSCWD), pp. 1087–1092. IEEE, Melbourne, Australia (2007)
9. Mohandas, N., Thampi, S.M.: Improving hadoop performance in handling small files. In: Abraham, A., Mauri, J.L., Buford, J.F., Suzuki, J., Thampi, S.M. (eds.) ACC 2011, Part IV. CCIS, vol. 193, pp. 187–194. Springer, Heidelberg (2011)
10. Zhang, W.Z., Lu, G.Z., He, H., Zhang, Q.Z., Yu, C.L.: Exploring large-scale small file storage for search engines. J. Supercomputing (2015). doi:10.1007/s11227-015-1394-z
11. Gohil, P., Panchal, B., Dhobi, J.S.: A novel approach to improve the performance of hadoop in handling of small files. In: 2015 IEEE International Conference on Electrical, Computer and Communication Technologies (ICECCT), pp. 1–5 (2015)
12. Mackey, G., Sehrish, S., Wang, J.: Improving metadata management for small files in HDFS. In: Proceedings of 2009 IEEE International Conference on Cluster Computing and Workshops, pp. 1–4. IEEE Press, Piscataway (2009)
13. Liu, X., Han, J., Zhong, Y., et al.: Implementing WebGIS on hadoop: A case study of improving small file I/O performance on HDFS. In: 2009 IEEE International Conference on Cluster Computing and Workshops, pp. 1–8. IEEE Press, Piscataway (2009)
14. Dong, B., Qiu, J., Zheng, Q., et al.: A novel approach to improving the efficiency of storing and accessing small files on hadoop: a case study by PowerPoint files. In: Proceedings of the 2010 IEEE International Conference on Services Computing, pp. 65–72 (2010)
15. Mohandas, N., Thampi, S.M.: Improving hadoop performance in handling small files. In: Abraham, A., Mauri, J.L., Buford, J.F., Suzuki, J., Thampi, S.M. (eds.) ACC 2011, Part IV. CCIS, vol. 193, pp. 187–194. Springer, Heidelberg (2011)
16. Zheng, Z., Zhao, S., Zhang, X., Wang, Z., Lu, L.: Cloud storage management technology for small file based on two-dimensional packing algorithm. In: Wong, W.E., Zhu, T. (eds.) Computer Engineering and Networking. LNEE, vol. 277, pp. 847–853. Springer, Heidelberg (2014)
17. Qian, Y., Yi, R., Du, Y., et al.: Dynamic I/O congestion control in scalable lustre file system. In: IEEE 29th Symposium on Mass Storage Systems and Technologies (MSST), pp. 1–5. IEEE, Lake Arrowhead, USA (2013)
18. Nguyen, B.V., Pham, D., Ngo, T.D.: Integrating spatial information into inverted index for large-scale image retrieval. In: 2014 IEEE International Symposium on Multimedia (ISM), pp. 102–105. IEEE (2014)

Arbitrary-Length Jacket-Haar Transforms

Guibo Liu[1]([✉]), Dayong Luo[1], Geli Lv[1], Ying Guo[1], and Moonho Lee[2]

[1] School of Information Science and Engineering, Central South University,
Changsha 410083, China
lgbtrs2006@126.com
[2] Institute of Information and Communication, Chonbuk National,
Jeonju 561-756, South Korea

Abstract. Recently, motivated by Haar transform and Jacket transform, Jacket Haar transform has been successfully generalized, but unfortunately, it is not available in the case where the length N is not a power of 2. In this paper, with the new proposed generation methods, the arbitrary-length Jacket-Haar transform can be constructed capriciously. Meanwhile, just like the original Haar transform, the presented arbitrary-length Jacket-Haar transform has fast algorithm and can be decomposed into the 2-point generalized Haar transforms, the general form of which is also successfully derived. Subsequently, the proposed Jacket-Haar transform has been applied to the electrocardiogram (ECG) signal analysis, and simulation results show that the new proposed transform is more efficient than FFT in signal reconstruction.

Keywords: Jacket transform · Haar transform · Jacket-Haar transform · Fast algorithm · Kronecker product

1 Introduction

The Hadamard matrix and its generalizations are orthogonal matrices with many applications in signal transforms and data processing [1–4]. The Jacket matrix, motivated by the center weighted Hadamard matrix [5], is a special matrix with its inverse matrix being determined by the element or block-wise inverse of the original matrix [6,7]. Its corresponding transforms have been extensively investigated and applied in many fields, such as signal processing [8,10], encoding design [9,13], wireless communication [20], image compression [11], cryptography [12], Quantum information system [14], and so on. Furthermore, several interesting matrices, such as Hadamard matrix, DFT matrix and skew matrix, all belong to the Jacket matrix family [15]. Besides all, lots of commonly used matrices, such as unitary matrices, Hermitian matrices, and so on, have close relations with Jacket matrices.

In recent years, literatures relevant to Jacket matrices and its transforms mainly involve explorations of new category of Jacket transform matrices and exploitations of their practical applications. In the later aspect, block Jacket transforms have been tentatively applied to Big-Data processing [16,17] and

© Springer International Publishing Switzerland 2015
G. Wang et al. (Eds.): ICA3PP 2015, Part II, LNCS 9529, pp. 330–343, 2015.
DOI: 10.1007/978-3-319-27122-4_23

emerging new-generation mobile communication [19]. On the other hand, new Jacket transforms, such as fractional Jacket transforms [18], parametric Jacket transforms [20], Toeplitz Jacket transforms, and so on, have been gradually proposed.

Also, the Haar matrix, which is useful for localized signal analysis, edge detection, OFDM, filter design and electrocardiogram (ECG) analysis, has been generalized into Jacket Haar matrix [21], whose entries can be 0 and $\pm 2^k$ compared with the entries of the original Haar matrix being 1, -1, and 0. Although 2^k-point Jacket Haar matrices are successfully defined in [21], there is still a problem how to define the arbitrary length Jacket-Haar transform just like arbitrary-length Walsh-Jacket transform [22]? Unfortunately, until this paper, the method to solve this problem is still absent, so focus of this paper is to place on arbitrary point Jacket Haar transforms. Compared to the existing literatures, contributions are listed as follows: (1) The structure of the arbitrary-length Jacket-Haar transform matrix is presented for the first time. (2) Methods for obtaining arbitrary-length Jacket Haar transform matrices by using the Jacket Harr matrices with size 2 are successfully derived. (3) Corresponding fast algorithm and actual application of arbitrary length Jacket Haar transforms are also proposed.

The rest of this paper is organized as follows. In Sect. 2, the elegant structure of Jacket-Haar transform is given, followed by the general form of Jacket-Haar transform with size 2. In Sect. 3, with the new proposed generation algorithm, the $(2M + 1)$-point Jacket-Haar transform can be derived from the $(M + 1)$-point Jacket-Haar transform. Together with the generation algorithm for the $(2M)$-point Jacket-Haar transform, arbitrary point Jacket-Haar transform can be derived successfully. The fast algorithm and application of the Jacket-Haar transform will be shown in Sect. 4. Finally, the conclusion is drawn.

2   Structure of Jacket-Haar Transform

Definition 1. The Haar transform is defined as

$$
\mathbf{H_2} = \begin{bmatrix} 1 & 1 \\ 1 & -1 \end{bmatrix}, \ \mathbf{H_N} = \begin{bmatrix} \mathbf{H_{N/2}} \otimes [1,1] \\ \mathbf{I_{N/2}} \otimes [1,-1] \end{bmatrix}, \tag{1}
$$

where N must be a power of 2. $\mathbf{I_{N/2}}$ denotes the $N/2$ point identity matrix and $\otimes$ means the Kronecker Product. The inverse of the Haar transform $\mathbf{H}_N^{-1}$ is

$$
\mathbf{H}_N^{-1} = \mathbf{H_N^T D_N}, \tag{2}
$$

where $\mathbf{D_N} = diag\{d_1, d_2, \cdots, d_N\}$, $d_1 = d_2 = 1/N$, $d_n = 2^k/N$, and $2^k < n \le 2^{k+1} \le N$.

As in [22], the Walsh transform can be extended to a generalized Walsh transform with arbitrary length. Similarly, it is theoretically feasible to extend the Haar transform to a more generalized Haar transform with any size. In order to verify the correctness of the above judgement, Subsequently, definition of the generalized Haar transform named by the Jacket-Haar transform is firstly given.

Definition 2. Jacket-Haar transform is a discrete transform and it must satisfy three constraints listed below.

(1) If $\mathbf{\Psi_N}$ and $\mathbf{\Gamma_N}$ denote the forward and inverse N-point generalized Haar transform matrices, respectively, then all entries of the both matrices are $\pm 2^p$ or 0, where p is an integer. Besides, all elements of the first row of $\mathbf{\Psi_N}$ is non-negative.

(2) The point number of zero crossing of any row of $\mathbf{\Psi_N}$ is the same as the original Haar matrix. Namely, the zero crossing point number of any row of $\mathbf{\Psi_N}$ is one except the first row, where zero crossing point do not exist.

(3) It has a fast algorithm similar to the original Haar transform.

It is not hard to demonstrate that all the original Haar matrices meet the above three constraints, therefore, they can be seen as a special case of the Jacket-Haar transform matrices. All the elements of the Haar transform matrices are only $1, -1$ or 0, while at the same time the order of them must be a power of 2. However, Jacket-Haar transform relaxes the constraint and its elements can be chosen from $\pm 2^p$ or 0, where p defined as above. Since the multiplication of the powers of 2 can be computed by bit-shifting, the Jacket-Haar transform can still be implemented in an efficient way without multiplication. What's more, the Jacket-Haar transform is also more general than the Jacket transform, since the constraint that $\mathbf{\Gamma_N}(m, n) = \mathbf{\Psi_N}(n, m)/C$ where C is a constant, is not required.

Before discussing method for generating arbitrary-length Jacket-Haar transform, the Jacket-Haar matrices with size 2 are extensively discussed and corresponding general forms are successfully derived, based on which Jacket-Haar matrices with any relatively larger sizes can be obtained based on certain theorems presented in subsequent sections.

Theorem 1. Any 2-point Jacket-Haar transform matrices should conform the following forms,

$$\mathbf{\Psi_2}^{(1)} = \begin{bmatrix} a & 0 \\ c & -d \end{bmatrix}, \tag{3}$$

$$\mathbf{\Psi_2}^{(2)} = \begin{bmatrix} 0 & b \\ c & -d \end{bmatrix}, \tag{4}$$

or

$$\mathbf{\Psi_2}^{(3)} = \begin{bmatrix} a & b \\ c & -d \end{bmatrix}, ad = bc, \tag{5}$$

where

$$a > 0, b > 0, cd > 0, \tag{6}$$

with $a, b, c,$ and d are 0 or a power of 2.

Proof. It is straightforward that constraint (3) is always satisfied for the 2-point Jacket-Haar transform. Besides, the 2-point Jacket-Haar transform matrix $\mathbf{\Psi_2}$ can be generally denoted as follows,

$$\mathbf{\Psi_2} = \begin{bmatrix} a_1 & b_1 \\ c_1 & -d_1 \end{bmatrix}, \tag{7}$$

and its inverse is

$$\mathbf{\Gamma_2} = \frac{1}{a_1 d_1 + b_1 c_1} \begin{bmatrix} d_1 & b_1 \\ c_1 & -a_1 \end{bmatrix}. \tag{8}$$

According to constraint (1), a_1, b_1, c_1 and d_1 are 0 or a power of 2, so there exists,

$$a_1 d_1 + b_1 c_1 = \pm 2^p, \tag{9}$$

where p is defined as above, and

$$a_1 \geq 0, b_1 \geq 0. \tag{10}$$

Meanwhile owing to constraint (2), we can obtain

$$c_1 d_1 > 0. \tag{11}$$

So there exist three cases as follows: **Case 1**, if $b_1 = 0$, then it is easy to get that $a_1 > 0$ holds. So the 2-point Jacket-Haar transform possesses the form of Eq. (3). **Case 2**, if $a_1 = 0$, then similar to case 1, the 2-point generalized Haar transform has the form of Eq. (4). **Case 3**, if $a_1 b_1 > 0$, according to Eq. (9), we can obtain $(a_1 d_1)(b_1 c_1) > 0$. There exist two cases, and let us discuss them respectively. Case 1, if $a_1 d_1 = 2^m$ and $b_1 c_1 = 2^n$, supposing $a_1 d_1 = k(b_1 c_1)$, then $a_1 d_1 + b_1 c_1 = (1 + k)2^n$. Since (9) holds, k must be equal to 1. Case 2, if $a_1 d_1 = -2^m$ and $b_1 c_1 = -2^n$ hold, similar to case 1, we can also get $a_1 d_1 = b_1 c_1$. Therefore, the 2-point Jacket-Haar transform conforms Eq. (5). In a word, Theorem 1 holds. It suggests an elegant way to construct 2-point Jacket-Haar transform matrices.

3   Arbitrary-Length Jacket-Haar Transform

The general forms of the 2-point Jacket-Haar transform have been derived in the previous section. While in this section, two generalization algorithms are respectively proposed for obtaining arbitrarily long odd and even Jacket-Haar transform in the following subsections.

3.1   Generation Algorithm for Odd N

Theorem 2. If $N = 2M + 1$ is an odd integer, then we can use the generation algorithm presented below to derive the N-point Jacket-Haar transform from both the $(M + 1)$-point Jacket-Haar transform matrix and the M-point identity matrix. Suppose $\mathbf{\Psi_{M+1}}$ is an $(M + 1)$-point Jacket-Haar transform matrix and $\mathbf{\Gamma_{M+1}}$ denotes its inverse. The $n^{th}, n \in \{1, 2, \cdots, M + 1\}$ column of $\mathbf{\Psi_{M+1}}$ and the nth row of $\mathbf{\Gamma_{M+1}}$ are described by $\mathbf{v_n}$ and $\mathbf{u_n}$, respectively.

$$\mathbf{\Psi_{M+1}} = (\mathbf{v_1}, \mathbf{v_2}, \cdots, \mathbf{v_{M+1}}), \quad \mathbf{\Gamma_{M+1}} = (\mathbf{u_1}^T, \mathbf{u_2}^T, \cdots, \mathbf{u_{M+1}}^T) \tag{12}$$

Also suppose $\mathbf{\Psi}_{2,1}, \mathbf{\Psi}_{2,2}, \ldots, \mathbf{\Psi}_{2,n}$ are 2-point Jacket-Haar transform matrices and $\mathbf{\Gamma}_{2,1}, \mathbf{\Gamma}_{2,2}, \ldots, \mathbf{\Gamma}_{2,n}$ are their inverses, respectively. $\mathbf{v}_{1,n}$ and $\mathbf{v}_{2,n}$ are used to denote the first and second row of $\mathbf{\Psi}_{2,n}$, respectively. $\mathbf{u}_{1,n}$ and $\mathbf{u}_{2,n}$ are used to denote the first and second column of $\mathbf{\Gamma}_{2,n}$, respectively, So the following equations exist.

$$\mathbf{\Psi}_{2,n} = \begin{bmatrix} \mathbf{v}_{1,n} \\ \mathbf{v}_{2,n} \end{bmatrix}, \mathbf{\Gamma}_{2,n} = \begin{bmatrix} \mathbf{u}_{1,n} & \mathbf{u}_{2,n} \end{bmatrix},$$
$$\mathbf{v}_{1,n}\mathbf{u}_{1,n} = \mathbf{v}_{2,n}\mathbf{u}_{2,v} = 1, \mathbf{v}_{1,n}\mathbf{u}_{2,n} = \mathbf{v}_{2,n}\mathbf{u}_{1,n} = 0. \tag{13}$$

Moreover, suppose $\mathbf{e}_n$ denotes the nth column of the M-point identity matrix.

$$\mathbf{e}_n[n] = 1, \mathbf{e}_n[m] = 0, \text{ if } m \neq n. \tag{14}$$

Then the $(2M + 1)$-point generalized Haar transform can be derived as

$$\mathbf{\Psi}_{2M+1} = \begin{bmatrix} \mathbf{v}_1 \otimes \mathbf{v}_{1,1} , \cdots , \mathbf{v}_M \otimes \mathbf{v}_{1,M} & \mathbf{v}_{M+1} \\ \mathbf{e}_1 \otimes \mathbf{v}_{1,1} , \cdots , \mathbf{e}_M \otimes \mathbf{v}_{2,M} & 0 \end{bmatrix} \tag{15}$$

and the inverse $(2M + 1)$-point generalized Haar transform is

$$\mathbf{\Gamma}_{2M+1} = \begin{bmatrix} \mathbf{u}_1^T \otimes \mathbf{u}_{1,1}^T , \cdots , \mathbf{u}_M^T \otimes \mathbf{u}_{1,M}^T & \mathbf{u}_{M+1}^T \\ \mathbf{e}_1 \otimes \mathbf{u}_{2,1}^T , \cdots , \mathbf{e}_M \otimes \mathbf{u}_{2,M}^T & 0 \end{bmatrix}^T. \tag{16}$$

Proof. $\mathbf{\Psi}_{2M+1}\mathbf{\Gamma}_{2M+1}$ can be described as,

$$\mathbf{\Psi}_{2M+1}\mathbf{\Gamma}_{2M+1} = \begin{bmatrix} \mathbf{A}_{11} & \mathbf{A}_{12} \\ \mathbf{A}_{21} & \mathbf{A}_{22} \end{bmatrix}. \tag{17}$$

Since Eq. (13) exists, so $\mathbf{A}_{11}, \mathbf{A}_{12}, \mathbf{A}_{21}$ and $\mathbf{A}_{22}$ can be respectively calculated as,

$$\mathbf{A}_{11} = \sum_{k=1}^{M} [(\mathbf{v}_k\mathbf{u}_k) \otimes (\mathbf{v}_{1,k}\mathbf{u}_{1,k})] + \mathbf{v}_{M+1}\mathbf{u}_{M+1} = \sum_{k=1}^{M+1} (\mathbf{v}_k\mathbf{u}_k) = \mathbf{I}_{M+1}, \tag{18}$$

$$\mathbf{A}_{12} = \sum_{k=1}^{M} [(\mathbf{v}_k \otimes \mathbf{v}_{1,k})(\mathbf{e}_k^T \otimes \mathbf{u}_{2,k})] = \sum_{k=1}^{M} [(\mathbf{v}_k\mathbf{e}_k^T) \otimes (\mathbf{v}_{1,k}\mathbf{u}_{2,k})] = 0, \tag{19}$$

$$\mathbf{A}_{21} = \sum_{k=1}^{M} [(\mathbf{e}_k \otimes \mathbf{v}_{2,k})(\mathbf{u}_k \otimes \mathbf{u}_{1,k})] = \sum_{k=1}^{M} [(\mathbf{e}_k\mathbf{u}_k) \otimes (\mathbf{v}_{2,k}\mathbf{u}_{1,k})] = 0, \tag{20}$$

$$\mathbf{A}_{22} = \sum_{k=1}^{M} [(\mathbf{e}_k \otimes \mathbf{v}_{2,k})(\mathbf{e}_k^T \otimes \mathbf{u}_{2,k})] = \sum_{k=1}^{M} [(\mathbf{e}_k\mathbf{e}_k^T) \otimes (\mathbf{v}_{2,k}\mathbf{u}_{2,k})] = \mathbf{I}_M. \tag{21}$$

Hence,

$$\mathbf{\Psi}_{2M+1}\mathbf{T}_{2M+1} = \mathbf{I}_{2M+1}. \tag{22}$$

Furthermore, we can easily check that constraint (1) and constraint (2) are both satisfied. In fact, constraint (3) is also satisfied, therefore, Theorem 2 holds. According to the Theorem 2, Any $(2M + 1)$-point Jacket-Haar transform can be generated successfully.

3.2 Generation Algorithm for Even N

The above section surrounds generalization algorithm for Jacket-Haar transform matrices with odd N, while this section will continue to derive another generation algorithm for even N.

Theorem 3. If N is an even integer, then we can use the generation algorithm presented below to derive the N-point Jacket-Haar transform from both the M-point Jacket-Haar transform matrices and the M-point identity matrices, where $N = 2M$. The $(2M)$-point Jacket-Haar transform can be calculated as,

$$
\boldsymbol{\Psi}_{2\mathrm{M}} = \begin{bmatrix} \widehat{\mathbf{v}}_1 \otimes \mathbf{v}_{1,1} \, , \cdots , \widehat{\mathbf{v}}_{\mathrm{M}} \otimes \mathbf{v}_{1,\mathrm{M}} \\ \mathbf{e}_1 \otimes \mathbf{v}_{2,1} \, , \cdots , \mathbf{e}_{\mathrm{M}} \otimes \mathbf{v}_{2,\mathrm{M}} \end{bmatrix},
\tag{23}
$$

and the inverse can be computed as,

$$
\boldsymbol{\Gamma}_{2\mathrm{M}} = \begin{bmatrix} \widehat{\mathbf{u}}_1^T \otimes \widehat{\mathbf{u}}_{1,1}^T \, , \cdots , \widehat{\mathbf{u}}_{\mathrm{M}}^T \otimes \mathbf{u}_{1,\mathrm{M}}^T \\ \mathbf{e}_1 \otimes \mathbf{u}_{2,1}^T \, , \cdots , \mathbf{e}_{\mathrm{M}} \otimes \mathbf{u}_{2,\mathrm{M}}^T \end{bmatrix}^T,
\tag{24}
$$

where $\boldsymbol{\Psi}_{\mathrm{M}}$ is the M-point Jacket-Haar transform matrix and $\boldsymbol{\Gamma}_{\mathrm{M}}$ is its inverse. The $n^{th}, n \in \{1, 2, \cdots, M\}$ column of $\boldsymbol{\Psi}_{\mathrm{M}}$ and the nth row of $\boldsymbol{\Gamma}_{\mathrm{M}}$ are denoted by $\widehat{\mathbf{v}}_{\mathbf{n}}$ and $\widehat{\mathbf{u}}_{\mathbf{n}}$, respectively.

$$
\boldsymbol{\Psi}_{\mathrm{M}} = (\widehat{\mathbf{v}}_1, \widehat{\mathbf{v}}_2, \ldots, \widehat{\mathbf{v}}_{\mathrm{M}}),
\tag{25}
$$

$$
\boldsymbol{\Gamma}_{\mathrm{M}} = (\widehat{\mathbf{u}}_1^T, \widehat{\mathbf{u}}_2^T, \ldots, \widehat{\mathbf{u}}_{\mathrm{M}}^T)^T,
\tag{26}
$$

$$
\boldsymbol{\Psi}_{\mathrm{M}} \boldsymbol{\Gamma}_{\mathrm{M}} = \mathbf{I}_{\mathrm{M}},
\tag{27}
$$

other notations are defined the same as the Theorem 2.

Proof. The proof is similar to that of the Theorem 2, so omitted here for simplicity.

Example 1. A general 4-point Jacket-Haar transform

$$
\boldsymbol{\Psi}_4 = \begin{bmatrix} \alpha_1\alpha_2 & \alpha_1\beta_2 & \beta_1\alpha_3 & \beta_1\beta_3 \\ \mu_1\alpha_2 & \mu_1\beta_2 & -\nu_1\alpha_3 & -\nu_1\beta_3 \\ \mu_2 & -\nu_2 & 0 & 0 \\ 0 & 0 & \mu_3 & -\nu_3 \end{bmatrix},
\tag{28}
$$

can be obtained, where $\boldsymbol{\Psi}_{2,\mathbf{n}} = \begin{bmatrix} \alpha_n & \beta_n \\ \mu_n & -\nu_n \end{bmatrix}, n \in \{1, 2, 3\}$, are 2-point Jacket-Haar transforms. Especially, if $\alpha_n = \beta_n = \mu_n = \nu_n = 1$ exists, then $\boldsymbol{\Psi}_4$ is an original 4-point Haar transform matrix with $N = 4$ in Eq. (1).

Example 2. If $\Psi_3 = \begin{bmatrix} 4 & 1 & 2 \\ 8 & 2 & -4 \\ 8 & -2 & 0 \end{bmatrix}$, then we can get the 6-point Jacket-Haar transform

$$\Psi_6 = \begin{bmatrix} 4a_1 & 4b_1 & a_2 & b_2 & 2a_3 & 2b_3 \\ 8a_1 & 8b_1 & 2a_2 & 2b_2 & -4a_3 & -4b_3 \\ 8a_1 & 8b_1 & -2a_2 & -2b_2 & 0 & 0 \\ c_1 & -d_1 & 0 & 0 & 0 & 0 \\ 0 & 0 & c_2 & -d_2 & 0 & 0 \\ 0 & 0 & 0 & 0 & c_3 & -d_3 \end{bmatrix}, \tag{29}$$

where $\Psi_{2,n} = \begin{bmatrix} a_n & b_n \\ c_n & -d_n \end{bmatrix}, n \in \{1, 2, 3\}$, are 2-point Jacket-Haar transforms that satisfy the subsequent equation

$$a_n d_n + b_n c_n = \lambda_n, \tag{30}$$

where λ_n is a power of 2. The inverse 6-point Jacket-Haar transform is

$$\Gamma_6 = 2^{-3} diag\{2^{-2}\lambda_1^{-1}, 2^{-2}\lambda_1^{-1}, \lambda_2^{-1}, \lambda_2^{-1}, \lambda_3^{-1}, \lambda_3^{-1}\}$$
$$\times \begin{bmatrix} 2d_1 & d_1 & 2d_1 & 32b_1 & 0 & 0 \\ 2c_1 & c_1 & 2c_1 & -32a_1 & 0 & 0 \\ 2d_2 & d_2 & -2d_2 & 0 & 8b_2 & 0 \\ 2c_2 & c_2 & -2c_2 & 0 & -8a_2 & 0 \\ 2d_3 & -d_3 & 0 & 0 & 0 & 8b_3 \\ 2c_3 & -c_3 & 0 & 0 & 0 & -8a_3 \end{bmatrix}. \tag{31}$$

To sum up, by combining the Theorem 2 with the Theorem 3, we can success-fully construct arbitrarily long Jacket-Haar transform. When N is odd, we use the Theorem 2 to obtain the N-point Jacket-Haar transform from the $(M + 1)$-point Jacket-Haar transform, where $N = 2M + 1$. While N is even, we can choose the Theorem 3 to derive the N-point Jacket-Haar transform from the M-point Jacket-Haar transform, where $N = 2M$. For example, when $N = 10$, the value of M is 5 and the Theorem 3 is chosen. It means the 10-point Jacket-Haar trans-form can be derived from the 5-point Jacket-Haar transform. Furthermore, the 5-point Jacket-Haar transform can be generalized from the 3-point Jacket-Haar transform with the Theorem 2. Moreover, the 3-point Jacket-Haar transform can be constructed from the 2-point Jacket-Haar transform by using the Theorem 2. Therefore, the 10-point Jacket-Haar transform can be obtained from the 2-point Jacket-Haar transforms. Table 1 tells how to generate N-point Jacket-Haar trans-form for $N \in \{3, 4, \cdots, 20\}$. In fact, Jacket-Haar transform with any size can be derived from the 2-point Jacket-Haar transforms.

4 Fast Algorithms and Applications of Jacket-Haar Transform

4.1 Fast Implementation Algorithms

Arbitrary-length Jacket-Haar transform illustrated in above sections, can be decomposed into combination of the 2-point Jacket-Haar transforms, no matter

Table 1. Methods to generate the N-point generalized harr transform listed in the 1st column from the M-point generalized haar transforms listed in the 2nd column by using the theorems listed in the 3rd column.

N	M	METHODS
3	2	The Theorem 2
4	2	The Theorem 3
5	3	The Theorem 2
6	3	The Theorem 3
7	4	The Theorem 2
8	4	The Theorem 3
9	5	The Theorem 2
10	5	The Theorem 3
11	6	The Theorem 2
12	6	The Theorem 3
13	7	The Theorem 2
14	7	The Theorem 3
15	8	The Theorem 2
16	8	The Theorem 3
17	9	The Theorem 2
18	9	The Theorem 3
19	10	The Theorem 2
20	10	The Theorem 3

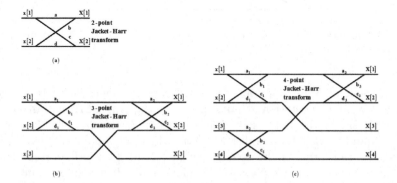

Fig. 1. The implementations of (a) the 2-point Jacket-Haar transform, (b) the 3-point Jacket-Haar transform and (c) the 4-point Jacket-Haar transform.

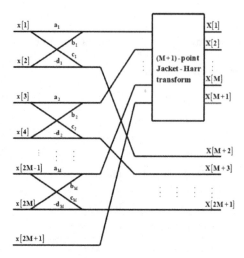

Fig. 2. Implementing the $(2M + 1)$-point Jacket-Haar transform by the $(M + 1)$-point Jacket-Haar transform.

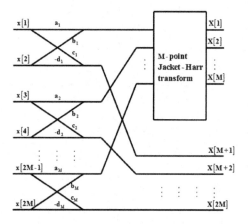

Fig. 3. Implementing the $(2M)$-point Jacket-Haar transform by the M-point Jacket-Haar transform.

what the value of N is. Moreover, Arbitrarily long N-point Jacket-Haar transform has fast implementation algorithms just as the original Haar transform.

Figure 1 shows the implementation structures of the 2-point, the 3-point and the 4-point Jacket-Haar transform, from which the 3-point and the 4-point Jacket-Haar transforms can be decomposed into 2 and 3 butterflies, respectively. When $N > 4$, we can decompose the N-point Jacket-Haar transform into combination of 2-point Jacket-Haar transforms by using recursively the methods illustrated as in Figs. 2 and 3. From Figs. 1 to 3, we can see clearly that the fast algorithms of the original Haar transform and the Jacket-Haar transform are extremely similar.

4.2   Applications in Signal Analysis

Just like the original Haar transform, the new proposed arbitrary-point Jacket-Haar transform can also be applied in signal analysis, edge detection, OFDM, filter design and electrocardiogram (ECG) analysis. In fact, all applications of the original Haar transform can be viewed as a special applications of the proposed arbitrary-point Jacket-Haar transform.

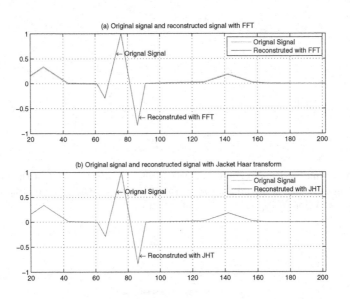

Fig. 4. A 202-length electrocardiogram(ECG) and reconstructed signal.

From Figs. 4 to 7, two simulations are arranged for comprehensive analysis with even and odd-point transform used, respectively. The length of the ECG signal in Fig. 4 is 202, which is not a power of 2. It is not convenient to analyze by using the original Haar transform directly, but it can be analyzed by the proposed arbitrary-point Jacket-Haar transform directly. In Fig. 5, we show the normalized mean square error (NMSE) of the reconstructed signal when using part of the coefficients of the 202-point generalized Haar transform.

$$\text{NMSE} = \frac{\|\mathbf{x_s} - \mathbf{x}\|^2}{\|\mathbf{x}\|^2} \tag{32}$$

$$\mathbf{y} = \mathbf{W_N}\mathbf{x}, \mathbf{x_s} = \mathbf{U_N}\mathbf{y_s}, \tag{33}$$

where $\mathbf{x}$ is the original signal, $\mathbf{W_N}$ and $\mathbf{U_N}$ are the forward and inverse Jacket-Haar transform matrices. The vector $\mathbf{y_s}$ preserves S coefficients of $\mathbf{y}$ and others are set to zero. In Fig. 6, we also show the NMSE of the reconstructed signal when using the 202-point fast Fourier transform (FFT). The results in Fig. 5

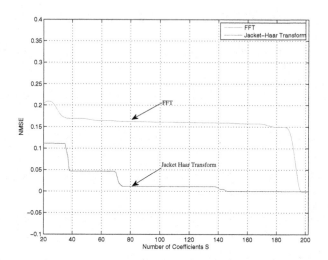

Fig. 5. The normalized mean square error(NMSE) when using part of the coefficients to reconstruct the ECG signal in Fig. 4. Red line: using the 202-point Jacket-Haar transform; green line: using the FFT (Color figure online).

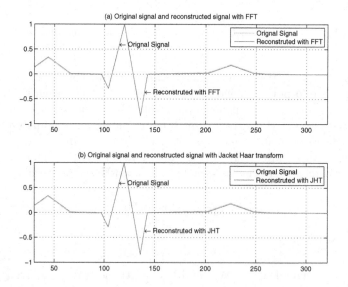

Fig. 6. A 321-length electrocardiogram(ECG) and reconstructed signal.

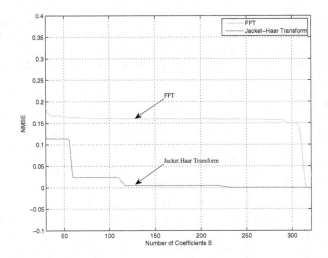

Fig. 7. The NMSE when using part of the coefficients to reconstruct the ECG signal in Fig. 6. Red line: using the 321-point Jacket-Haar transform; green line: using the FFT (Color figure online).

show that, with the Jacket-Haar transform, we can achieve less approximation error when using only S terms (S < 202) to expand the ECG signal.

In Figs. 6 and 7, another simulation experiment is also designed for comparison. The length of the ECG in Fig. 6 is 321 with Theorem 3 used for transform matrix constructed, which is not a power of 2. Figure 7 shows the NMSE of the reconstructed signal when using part of the coefficients of the 321-point Jacket-Haar transform compared with the 321-point FFT. Results also show that Jacket-Haar transform is more efficient for analyzing the ECG signal than FFT.

5   Conclusions

In this paper, we extend the Haar transform to generalized Haar transform named by Jacket-Haar transform, which overcomes the constraint that the number of points must be the power of 2. With the new proposed generalization algorithms, arbitrarily long Jacket-Haar transform can be derived successfully. Moreover, fast implementation algorithms similar to the fast algorithms of original haar transform are also introduced for Jacket-Haar transform with any even and odd size, respectively. After that, applications of this new proposed transform are also arranged for further study. Compared to the traditional FFT, simulation results show that Jacket-Haar transform is more efficient in signal reconstruction. In the near future, more properties of the Jacket-Haar transform and its practical applications may be further investigated.

Acknowledgment. This work was supported by the National Natural Science Foundation of China (61379153, 61272495), the New Century Excellent Talents in University, China (NCET-11-0510), and partly by the World Class University (R32-2010-000-20014-0), and Fundamental Research (2010-0020942, 2012-002521) NRF, Korea.

References

1. Rao, K.R., Ahmed, N.: Orthogonal transforms for digital signal processing. IEEE Trans. Syst. Man Cybern. **35**(1), 66–67 (1979)
2. Aung, A., Ng, B.P., Rahardja, S.: Sequency-ordered complex hadamard transform: properties, computational complexity and applications. IEEE Trans. Sig. Process. **56**(8), 3562–3571 (2008)
3. Wu, J., Wang, L., Yang, G.: Sliding conjugate symmetric sequency-ordered complex hadamard transform: fast algorithm and applications. IEEE Trans. Circuits Syst. I **59**(6), 1321–1334 (2012)
4. Pei, S.C., Wen, C.C., Ding, J.J.: Sequency-ordered generalized Walsh-Fourier transform. IEEE Trans. Sig. Process. **93**(4), 828–841 (2013)
5. Lee, M.H.: The center weighted Hadamard transform. IEEE Trans. Circuits Syst. **36**(9), 1247–1249 (1989)
6. Lee, M.H., Rajan, B.S., Member, S.: A generalized reverse jacket transform. IEEE Trans. Circuits Syst. II **48**(7), 684–690 (2001)
7. Zeng, G.H., Lee, M.H.: A generalized reverse block jacket transform. IEEE Trans. Circuits Syst. I **55**(6), 1589–1600 (2008)
8. Chen, Z., Lee, M.H., Song, W.: Arikan and alamouti matrices based on fast block-wise inverse jacket transform. EURASIP J. Adv. Sig. Proc. **37**(4), 1247–1249 (2013)
9. Jiang, X., Lee, M.H., Guo, Y.: Ternary codes from modified Jacket matrices. J. Commun. Netw. **13**(1), 12–16 (2011)
10. Guo, Y., Lee, M.H., Kim, K.J.: An explicit construction of fast cocyclic jacket transform on the finite field with any size. J. Adv. Sig. Process. **1**, 1–10 (2012)
11. Lee, M.H., Khan, M.H.A., Kim, K.J.: A fast hybrid Jacket-Hadamard matrix based diagonal block-wise transform. Sig. Process. Image Commun. **29**(1), 49–65 (2014)
12. Ma, W.P.: The Jacket Matrix and Cryptography. Chonbuk National University, Chonju (2004)
13. Song, W., Lee, M.H., Matalgah, M.M.: Quasi-orthogonal space-time block codes designs based on Jacket transform. J. Commun. Netw. **3**, 240–245 (2010)
14. Shi, R., Guo, Y., Lee, M.H.: Quantum codes based on fast pauli block transforms in the finite field. Quantum Inf. Process. **9**(5), 611–628 (2010)
15. Guo, Y., Liu, Y., Song, X.: A simple fast jacket transform for DFT based on generalized prime factor decomposing algorithm. In: IEEE Symposium on Business, Engineering and Industrial Applications, pp. 265–270 (2011)
16. Li, J., Yan, Y., Duan, W.: Tensor decomposition of Toeplitz Jacket matrices for big data processing. In: 2015 International Conference on Big Data and Smart Computing (BigComp), pp. 11–14. IEEE (2015)
17. Lee, M.H., Khan, M.H.A.: Big Data 'Fork': tensor product for DCT-II/DST-II/DFT/HWT. In: IEEE International Symposium on Broadband Multimedia Systems and Broadcasting (BMSB), pp. 1–6. IEEE (2014)
18. Mao, Y., Peng, J., Guo, Y.: On the fast fractional Jacket transform. Circuits Syst. Sig. Process. **33**(5), 1491–1505 (2014)
19. Lee, M.H., Zhang, X.D., Jiang, X.Q.: Fast parametric reciprocal-orthogonal jacket transforms. EURASIP J. Adv. Sig. Proc. **149** (2014)

20. Khan, M.H.A., Li, J., Lee, M.H.: A block diagonal jacket matrices for MIMO broadcast channels. In: IEEE International Symposium on Broadband Multimedia Systems and Broadcasting (BMSB), pp. 1–7. IEEE (2013)
21. Ding, J., Pei, S., Wu, P.: Jacket Haar transform. IEEE Int. Symp. Circuits Syst. **19**(5), 1520–1523 (2011)
22. Ding, J., Pei, S., Wu, P.: Arbitrary-length Walsh-Jacket transforms. In: APSIPA Annual Summit and Conference, Xi'an, China (2011)

Circulant Euler-Jacket Transform
and Its Applications Based on Fast Algorithm

Yang Zhang[✉], Geli Lv, Guibo Liu, and Ying Guo

School of Information Science and Engineering,
Central South University, Changsha 410083, China
zygoodkid@gmail.com

Abstract. Motivated by the elegant characteristics of the Euler theorem, we propose a novel Euler-Jacket matrix. This matrix has a circle-
limitation for exponential function and thus can be created by using
matrix operations with angle information. Especially, the inverses of the
yielded matrices equals the transpose of elements inverse. It corresponds
to the polynomial function, which is an unit operation of the orthogonal matrix in essence. The proposed matrix can be used to generate
higher-order Euler-Jacket matrices efficiently and hence other similar
real orthogonal matrices with fast algorithm. The proposed matrix is
much more concision and frank than direct-computation which means
Euler-Jacket transform is an efficient algorithm. Euler-Jacket transform
is proved to have stability and simplicity in digital image processing
simulation.

Keywords: Jacket transform · Euler transform · Circulant matrix ·
Euler-Jacket transform · Fast algorithm · Kronecker product

1 Introduction

Discrete orthogonal transforms have diverse efficient applications in signal and
image processing areas [1]. As well known, Discrete Fourier transform(DFT)
matrix [2,3], Hadamard matrix [4] and Haar matrix [5] are all representative
orthogonal matrices. Also, they belong to the much more general Jacket matrices, which were proposed by Lee et al. [6,7]. Jacket matrix is motivated by
the center weighted Hadamard matrix with a character that its inverse matrix
is determined by the element-wise of the matrix. Shown mathematically, let
$J = (j_{kt})$ be a matrix, if $J^{-1} = \left(j_{kt}^{-1}\right)^{T}$, then the matrix J is a Jacket matrix, where
T denotes the matrix transpose operation. Since inverse of the Jacket matrix
can be calculated easily, it is very helpful in signal processing [8], encoding [9],
telecommunication [10], cryptography [11], and quantum communication [12].

The Euler theorem is defined as a complex unit [13], i.e., $e^{i2\pi} = 1$. It has the
circle limitation with period 2π. Motivated by the fore-mentioned characteristics,
Jacket matrix with independent rows can be elegantly generated from an inherent
graph theoretic structure. It can be represented as a polynomial over Euler's

© Springer International Publishing Switzerland 2015
G. Wang et al. (Eds.): ICA3PP 2015, Part II, LNCS 9529, pp. 344–356, 2015.
DOI: 10.1007/978-3-319-27122-4_24

cyclic as the form $[A][B] = [B][A] = I_N$, where $B = e^{-i2\pi}$. Since circulant matrix can be eigen-decomposed by DFT, it becomes one of the most important matrices in signal processing. Therefore, our target is to construct a novel Euler-Jacket matrix, which can be fast generated with a Euler cyclic fashion. The block circulant Euler-Jacket matrix with highly practical value also owns fast algorithms based on Kronecker products of the identity matrix and successively lower-order block circulant inverse Jacket matrices.

The rest of the paper is organized as follows. Section 2 introduces the definition and related characteristics of Jacket matrix, Euler-Jacket matrix. Further more, in Sect. 3, block circulant Euler-Jacket matrices are put forward to construct higher-order Bose-Chaudhuri-Hocquenghem (BCH) matrices [14] and other similar orthogonal matrices. The inverses of the Euler-Jacket matrices are elements' inverses. we develop a fast algorithm for decomposition of the generalized circulant Euler-Jacket matrices. Circular matrices are important because they can be diagonal decomposed by the DFT, hence the linear equations that contain them can be quickly solved by using the fast Fourier transforms (FFT). The simulation of digital image processing with Euler-Jacket BCH matrices and Additive-White-Gaussian-Noise (AWGN) channels is proposed in Sect. 4. Finally, conclusions are drawn in Sect. 5.

2 Euler-Jacket Matrix

In this section, we introduce the definition of Jacket matrix, further more, put forward the Euler-Jacket matrix and its corresponding properties. Propose the large size with an elegant recursive relation based on the eigen-decomposition of Jacket matrix. Some examples are listed to explain the definition further vividly.

Definition 2.1. Let a square matrix $[J]_N = [j_{st}]_N$ whose elements are in field F which including real fields, complex fields and finite fields. The inverse matrix of $[J]_N$ can be easily obtained by calculating element-wise inverse, i.e., $[J]_N^{-1} = \frac{1}{C}[1/j_{st}]_N^T$, for $s, t = \{x \in Z | 1 \leq x \leq N\}$, where A is a nonzero constant. Then we call $[J]_n$ a Jacket matrix, such as

$$[J]_N = \begin{bmatrix} j_{0,0} & j_{0,1} & \cdots & j_{0,N-1} \\ j_{1,0} & j_{1,1} & \cdots & j_{1,N-1} \\ \vdots & \vdots & \ddots & \vdots \\ j_{N-1,0} & j_{N-1,1} & \cdots & j_{N-1,N-1} \end{bmatrix} \qquad (1)$$

and its inverse matrix is described as

$$[J]_N^{-1} = \frac{1}{A} \begin{bmatrix} 1/j_{0,0} & 1/j_{0,1} & \cdots & 1/j_{0,N-1} \\ 1/j_{1,0} & 1/j_{1,1} & \cdots & 1/j_{1,N-1} \\ \vdots & \vdots & \ddots & \vdots \\ 1/j_{N-1,0} & 1/j_{N-1,1} & \cdots & 1/j_{N-1,N-1} \end{bmatrix}^T, \qquad (2)$$

where T means matrix transpose.

Jacket matrix is symmetric with symmetric produce. Inference from the definition we achieve

$$\sum_{i=1}^{n} j_{si}^{-1} j_{ti} = \begin{cases} N, & s = t \\ 0, & s \neq t \end{cases} \tag{3}$$

where $s, t = \{x \in Z | 1 \leq x \leq N\}$. It is obvious that any two distinct rows in one Jacket matrix preserve good orthogonality. Fundamentally speaking, Jacket matrix is the generalization of Hadamard matrix [6], which means it is also a diagonal block-wise inverse matrix.

Definition 2.2. Let a Jacket matrix $[A]_N = [a_{st}]_N(s, t = \{x \in Z | 1 \leq x \leq N\})$ be represented as exponential form. If $[A]_N = S_N \Lambda_N S_N^T$, then Euler-Jacket matrix e^{iX_N} is defined as

$$e^{iX_N} = e^{i[A]_N} = S_N e^{i\Lambda_N} S_N^T, \tag{4}$$

where S_N is an eigenvector-based matrix given by $s_0, s_1, \cdots, s_{N-1}$ whose columns are normalized vectors. The inverse of e^{iX_N} is calculated as

$$e^{-iX_N} = S_N e^{-i\Lambda_N} S_N^T. \tag{5}$$

It is obvious that the eigenvector-based matrix S_N is orthogonal and Λ_N is the diagonal matrix with N nonzero elements, therefore the formula becomes

$$e^{iX_N} = S_N \begin{bmatrix} e^{i\lambda_0} & 0 & \cdots & 0 \\ 0 & e^{i\lambda_1} & \cdots & 0 \\ \vdots & \vdots & \ddots & \vdots \\ 0 & 0 & \cdots & e^{i\lambda_{N-1}} \end{bmatrix} S_N^T. \tag{6}$$

Proposition 2.1. If matrices X_N and Y_N are interchangeable, i.e., $Y_N X_N = X_N Y_N$, then

$$e^{iX_N + iY_N} = e^{iX_N} e^{iY_N} \tag{7}$$

Proof. Based on binomial theorem and $Y_N X_N = X_N Y_N$, original formula would be obtained as

$$e^{i(X_N + Y_N)} = \sum_{n=0}^{\infty} \frac{(iX_N + iY_N)^n}{n!}$$

$$= \sum_{n=0}^{\infty} \left[\sum_{l=0}^{\infty} \frac{(iX_N)^l (iY_N)^{n-l}}{l!(n-l)!} \right]. \tag{8}$$

On the other hand, by absolutely convergent series of multiplication theorem, the multiplication of two exponential matrix is shown as below

$$e^{iX_N} e^{iY_N} = \sum_{m=0}^{\infty} \frac{(iX_N)^m}{m!} \sum_{n=0}^{\infty} \frac{(iY_N)^n}{n!}$$

$$= \sum_{n=0}^{\infty} \left[\sum_{l=0}^{\infty} \frac{(iX_N)^l (iY_N)^{n-l}}{l!(n-l)!} \right]. \tag{9}$$

Combining with (8) and (9), (7) is proved to be true.

Proposition 2.2. The inverse matrix of e^{iX_N} equals to e^{-iX_N}.

Proof. In above proved Proposition (7), when $Y_N = -X_N$, it is evident that

$$e^{iX_N}e^{-iX_N} = e^{(iX_N + (-iX_N))} = e^0 = I. \tag{10}$$

Thus, $(e^{iX_N})^{-1} = e^{-iX_N}$ is proved to be true.

Proposition 2.3. Euler-Jacket matrix has the characteristic of periodicity, i.e., $e^{i(X_N + 2\pi I_N)} = e^{iX_N}$.

Proof. According to (7), the proposition is proved by

$$e^{i(X_N + 2\pi I_N)} = e^{2\pi i}(e^{iX_N}e^{I_N}) = e^{iX_N}. \tag{11}$$

Proposition 2.4. Euler-Jacket matrix has the characteristic of symmetry, i.e., $(e^{iX_N})^T = e^{iX_N}$. Also it has the characteristic of unitarity, i.e., $(e^{iX_N})^* = e^{-iX_N} = (e^{iX_N})^{-1}$, where the superscript * denotes the complex conjugation operation.

3 Block Circulant Euler-Jacket Matrix

For the given circulant matrix [15, 16],

$$[C]_{np} = \begin{bmatrix} c_0 & c_1 & \cdots & c_{n-1} \\ c_{n-1} & c_0 & \cdots & c_{n-2} \\ \vdots & \vdots & \ddots & \vdots \\ c_1 & c_2 & \cdots & c_0 \end{bmatrix}, \tag{12}$$

the matrix $e^{i[C]_{np}}$ is called as block circulant Euler-Jacket matrix. Block matrices c_i ($i = \{x \in Z | 0 \le x < n\}$) are Jacket matrices with uniform size $p \times p$. If each block has p common independent eigenvectors, such as block c_j has p nonzero vectors $\xi_1^{(j)}, \xi_2^{(j)}, \cdots \xi_p^{(j)}$ and its corresponding eigenvalues can be denoted as $\lambda_1^{(j)}, \lambda_2^{(j)}, \cdots, \lambda_p^{(j)}$. Then $[C]_{np}$ will have the eigenvalue which equals to $\lambda_k^{(0)} + \omega^j \lambda_k^{(1)} + \cdots + \omega^{(n-1)j}\lambda_k^{(n-1)}$, where $\omega = e^{\frac{2\pi}{n}i}$. The corresponding eigenvector is represented as $\eta_j \otimes \xi_k^{(j)}$, where $\eta_j = [1, \omega, \cdots, \omega^{(n-1)j}]$.

Example 3.1. Taking $n = 2$ with an arbitrary number p, there will be

$$[C]_{2p} = V_2 \begin{bmatrix} c_0 + c_1 & 0 \\ 0 & c_0 - c_1 \end{bmatrix} V_2^T, \tag{13}$$

where c_0 and c_1 are Jacket matrices with size $p \times p$ and $V_2 = \frac{1}{\sqrt{2}} \begin{bmatrix} 1 & 1 \\ 1 & -1 \end{bmatrix}$.

There is a detailed discussion on the typical block circulant Jacket matrix, BCH matrix [17], which is usually used in source-channel coding. The basic BCH matrix $[C]_2$ equals to $\begin{bmatrix} 1 & 1/2 \\ 1/2 & 1 \end{bmatrix}$. When $N = 4$, Real BCH matrix has a general form as below

$$[C]_4 \triangleq \begin{bmatrix} c_0 & c_1 \\ c_1 & c_0 \end{bmatrix}, \tag{14}$$

where $c_0 = [H]_2 = \begin{bmatrix} 1 & 1 \\ 1 & -1 \end{bmatrix}$ and $c_1 = \begin{bmatrix} 1 & -1 \\ -1 & -1 \end{bmatrix}$, respectively. Matrix $[C]_4$ can be decomposed as the block diagonal matrix

$$[C]_4 = \begin{bmatrix} 1 & 1 & 1 & -1 \\ 1 & -1 & -1 & -1 \\ 1 & -1 & 1 & 1 \\ -1 & -1 & 1 & -1 \end{bmatrix} \tag{15}$$

$$= (V_2 \otimes I_2) \begin{bmatrix} A_0 & 0 \\ 0 & A_1 \end{bmatrix} (V_2 \otimes I_2)^{-1},$$

where $V_2 = \frac{1}{\sqrt{2}} \begin{bmatrix} 1 & 1 \\ 1 & -1 \end{bmatrix}$. Block diagonal matrix is composed of c_0 and c_1 which can be shown as

$$\begin{bmatrix} A_0 & 0 \\ 0 & A_1 \end{bmatrix} = \begin{bmatrix} c_0 + c_1 & 0 \\ 0 & c_0 - c_1 \end{bmatrix}. \tag{16}$$

Through iterative algorithm, $[C]_N$ would be obtained.

$$[C]_N = [C]_2 \otimes [C]_{N/2}$$
$$= \begin{bmatrix} [C]_{N/2} & \frac{1}{2}[C]_{N/2} \\ \frac{1}{2}[C]_{N/2} & [C]_{N/2} \end{bmatrix} \tag{17}$$
$$= (V_2 \Lambda_2 V_2^T) \otimes (V_{N/2} \Lambda_{N/2} V_{N/2}^T)$$
$$= (V_2 \otimes V_{N/2})(\Lambda_2 \otimes \Lambda_{N/2})(V_2^T \otimes V_{N/2}^T),$$

where $N = 2^k, k = \{x \in Z | x \geq 3\}$ and $\Lambda_2 = \begin{bmatrix} \frac{3}{2} & 0 \\ 0 & \frac{1}{2} \end{bmatrix}$. Λ_2 is the eigenvalue of $[C]_2$ meanwhile corresponding eigenvector matrix is $V_2 = \frac{1}{\sqrt{2}} \begin{bmatrix} 1 & 1 \\ 1 & -1 \end{bmatrix}$. Generally speaking, $[C]_N$, V_N and Λ_N all have recursive relationship, they can be used to construct sparse matrix decomposition of $[C]_N$. $[C]_N$ is rewritten as

$$[C]_{2^k} = \prod_{m=1}^{k-1} (I_{2^{m-1}} \otimes V_2 \otimes I_{2^{k-m}}) \prod_{m=2}^{k-1} (I_{2^{k-m-1}} \otimes \Lambda_2 \otimes I_{2^m})$$

$$\cdot (I_{2^{k-2}} \otimes \Lambda_4) \prod_{m=1}^{k-1} (I_{2^{m-1}} \otimes V_2^T \otimes I_{2^{k-m}}), \tag{18}$$

where $k = \{x \in Z | x \geq 3\}$.

Through the conversion with Euler-Jacket transform, Euler-Jacket matrix $e^{i[C]_2}$ is shown as

$$e^{i[C]_2} = V_2 e^{i\Lambda_2} V_2^T = \begin{bmatrix} e^{i\frac{3}{2}} + e^{i\frac{1}{2}} & e^{i\frac{3}{2}} - e^{i\frac{1}{2}} \\ e^{i\frac{3}{2}} - e^{i\frac{1}{2}} & e^{i\frac{3}{2}} + e^{i\frac{1}{2}} \end{bmatrix}. \tag{19}$$

Also block circulant Euler-Jacket matrix $e^{i[C]_4}$ is

$$
\begin{aligned}
e^{i[C]_4} &= S_4 e^{i\Lambda_4} S_4^T \\
&= (V_2 \otimes I_2) \begin{bmatrix} e^{iA_0} & 0 \\ 0 & e^{iA_1} \end{bmatrix} (V_2 \otimes I_2)^T \\
&= (V_2 \otimes I_2) \begin{bmatrix} e^{i2} & 0 & 0 & 0 \\ 0 & e^{-i2} & 0 & 0 \\ 0 & 0 & 0 & e^{i2} \\ 0 & 0 & e^{i2} & 0 \end{bmatrix} (V_2 \otimes I_2)^T \\
&= \frac{1}{2} \begin{bmatrix} e^{i2} & e^{i2} & e^{i2} & -e^{i2} \\ e^{i2} & e^{-i2} & -e^{i2} & e^{-i2} \\ e^{i2} & -e^{i2} & e^{i2} & e^{i2} \\ -e^{i2} & e^{-i2} & e^{i2} & e^{-i2} \end{bmatrix}.
\end{aligned}
\tag{20}
$$

The inverse of (20) would be calculated by

$$
\begin{aligned}
(e^{i[C]_4})^{-1} &= (V_2 \otimes I_2) \begin{bmatrix} e^{-iA_0} & 0 \\ 0 & e^{-iA_1} \end{bmatrix} (V_2 \otimes I_2)^T \\
&= (V_2 \otimes I_2) \begin{bmatrix} e^{-i2} & 0 & 0 & 0 \\ 0 & e^{i2} & 0 & 0 \\ 0 & 0 & 0 & e^{-i2} \\ 0 & 0 & e^{-i2} & 0 \end{bmatrix} (V_2 \otimes I_2)^T \\
&= \frac{1}{2} \begin{bmatrix} e^{-i2} & e^{-i2} & e^{-i2} & -e^{-i2} \\ e^{-i2} & e^{i2} & -e^{-i2} & e^{i2} \\ e^{-i2} & -e^{-i2} & e^{-i2} & e^{-i2} \\ -e^{-i2} & e^{i2} & e^{-i2} & e^{i2} \end{bmatrix}.
\end{aligned}
\tag{21}
$$

Based on the characteristics of higher-order BCH matrix, when $N \geq 8$, the recursive relation form of Euler-Jacket matrix is shown as

$$e^{i[C]_N} = (V_2 \otimes V_{N/2})(e^{i\Lambda_2} \otimes e^{i\Lambda_{N/2}})(V_2 \otimes V_{N/2})^T. \tag{22}$$

When $N = 2^k$, the formula of fast algorithm becomes

$$
\begin{aligned}
e^{i[C]_{2^k}} &= \prod_{m=1}^{k-1} (I_{2^{m-1}} \otimes V_2 \otimes I_{2^{k-m}}) \prod_{m=2}^{k-1} (I_{2^{k-m-1}} \otimes e^{i\Lambda_2} \otimes I_{2^m}) \\
&\cdot (I_{2^{k-2}} \otimes e^{i\Lambda_4}) \prod_{m=1}^{k-1} (I_{2^{m-1}} \otimes V_2^T \otimes I_{2^{k-m}}),
\end{aligned}
\tag{23}
$$

where $k = \{x \in Z | x \geq 3\}$, spontaneously. The inverse matrix of $e^{i[C]_N}$ can be obtained by taking reciprocal of each element. As $e^{i[C]_N}$ is a symmetric matrix, the nonzero constant A in (2) equals to 4. So the matrix is further proved to be Jacket matrix.

Example 3.2. For $N = 8$ in (18), $e^{i[C]_8}$ is shown as

$$
\begin{aligned}
e^{i[C]_8} &= e^{i[C]_2} \otimes e^{i[C]_4} \\
&= \begin{bmatrix} (e^{\frac{3}{2}} + e^{\frac{1}{2}})e^{iX_4} & (e^{\frac{3}{2}} - e^{\frac{1}{2}})e^{iX_4} \\ (e^{\frac{3}{2}} - e^{\frac{1}{2}})e^{iX_4} & (e^{\frac{3}{2}} + e^{\frac{1}{2}})e^{iX_4} \end{bmatrix}.
\end{aligned}
\tag{24}
$$

Using (23), the eigen-decomposition method, we would obtain

$$
\begin{aligned}
e^{-i[C]_8} &= (V_2 \otimes I_4)(I_2 \otimes V_2 \otimes I_2)(e^{-i\Lambda_2} \otimes e^{-i\begin{bmatrix} A_0 & 0 \\ 0 & A_1 \end{bmatrix}}) \\
&\quad \cdot (V_2^T \otimes I_4)(I_2 \otimes V_2^T \otimes I_2).
\end{aligned}
\tag{25}
$$

Through two different methods, we would verify that

$$
e^{i[C]_8} e^{-i[C]_8} = I_8.
\tag{26}
$$

From the examples mentioned above, we can get the conclusion that block circulant Euler-Jacket matrices process simple operations and elegant implementation. Compared with multiplication computations of matrices, block circulant Euler-Jacket matrices have much smaller number of operation units. The computations of polynomial calculations for the matrix with order $N = 2^k$ have kN multiplications and $k/2N$ additions. The signal flow graph is shown in Fig. 1.

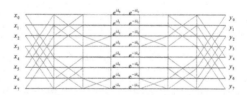

Fig. 1. The signal flow graph of 8-point Euler-Jacket transform. The fast implementation algorithm of the 8-point Euler-Jacket transform. The transform can be fully decomposed into the 2-point Euler-Jacket transforms.

Theorem 3.1. In generalized block circulant Euler-Jacket matrix $e^{iX_{np}}$, if each block matrix has p nonzero unit orthogonal eigenvectors and U_p is classical DFT matrix, we can obtain the general decomposition expression

$$e^{iX_{np}} = (V_n \otimes I_p) \prod_{j=1}^{m} (I_{np_1 \cdots p_{j-1}} \otimes F_{p_j} \otimes I_{p_{j+1} \cdots p_m}) e^{i\Lambda_{np}}$$

$$\cdot \prod_{j=1}^{m} (I_{np_1 \cdots p_{j-1}} \otimes F_{p_j}^T \otimes I_{p_{j+1} \cdots p_m})(V_n \otimes I_p)^T, \tag{27}$$

where $p = p_1 p_2 \cdots p_m$. In the above formula F_{p_i} is the DFT matrix with order p_i where $1 \le i \le m$.

Proof. If there exists p nonzero unit orthogonal eigenvectors ξ_1, ξ_2, $\cdots \xi_p$ in block matrix, we can get $c_j \xi_k = \lambda_k^{(j)} \xi_k$ for $j = \{x \in Z | 0 \le x < n\}$ and $k = \{x \in Z | 0 < x \le p\}$. Therefore block circulant Euler-Jacket matrix can be factorized as below

$$[C]_{np} = (V_n \otimes U_p)\text{diag}(\varphi_{01}, \cdots, \varphi_{0p}, \cdots, \varphi_{(n-1)1}, \cdots,$$

$$\varphi_{(n-1)p})(V_n \otimes U_p)^{-H}. \tag{28}$$

In [18], it is proved that if the size of DFT can be represented as the product of prime numbers, like $p = p_1 p_2 \cdots p_m$, then DFT matrix could be factorized as

$$U_p = F_{p_1} \otimes F_{p_2} \otimes \cdots \otimes F_{p_m}$$

$$= D_{p_1}^1 D_{p_2}^2 \cdots D_{p_m}^m, \tag{29}$$

where $D_{p_i}^i = I_{p_1} \otimes \cdots \otimes I_{p_{i-1}} \otimes F_{p_i} \otimes I_{p_{i+1}} \otimes \cdots \otimes I_{p_m}$. Hence, by combining with V_n and U_p, the lager size generalized block circulant Euler-Jacket matrix can be constructed in following formula

$$e^{iX_{np}} = (V_n \otimes U_p)e^{i\Lambda_{np}}(V_n \otimes U_p)^H$$

$$= (V_n \otimes I_p)(I_n \otimes U_p)e^{i\Lambda_{np}}(I_n \otimes U_p)^T(V_n \otimes I_p)^T$$

$$= (V_n \otimes I_p)(I_n \otimes D_{p_1}^1) \cdots (I_n \otimes D_{p_m}^m)e^{i\Lambda_{np}}$$

$$\cdot (I_n \otimes D_{p_m}^m)^T \cdots (I_n \otimes D_{p_1}^1)^T(V_n \otimes I_p)^T \tag{30}$$

$$= (V_n \otimes I_p) \prod_{j=1}^{m} (I_{np_1 \cdots p_{j-1}} \otimes F_{p_j} \otimes I_{p_{j+1} \cdots p_m}) e^{i\Lambda_{np}}$$

$$\cdot \prod_{j=1}^{m} (I_{np_1 \cdots p_{j-1}} \otimes F_{p_j}^T \otimes I_{p_{j+1} \cdots p_m})(V_n \otimes I_p)^T.$$

The inverse form of block circulant Euler-Jacket matrix would be obtained, naturally,

$$e^{-iX_{np}} = (V_n \otimes U_p)e^{-i\Lambda_{np}}(V_n \otimes U_p)^H. \tag{31}$$

The factorable block circulant Euler-Jacket matrix of large size can be decomposed with the proposed fast algorithm. Using the computations of Euler-Jacket matrix will simplify operations and implementation. Table 1 compares the computational complexity of algorithms of direction computation and fast algorithm.

Table 1. Computational complexity of different algorithms. DC, FA, ADD and MUL indicate direct computation, fast algorithm, number of additions and number of multiplications, respectively.

	DC	FA($N = 2^k$)	FA($N = np_1p_2 \cdots p_m$)
ADD	$(N-1)N$	kN	$\sum\limits_{j=1}^{m}(n+p_j-1)N$
MUP	N^2	$\frac{kN}{2}$	$[\frac{(n-1)^2}{n} + \sum\limits_{j=1}^{m}p_j]N$

According to the algorithm, generalized block circulant Euler-Jacket matrix of length $N = np = np_1p_2\cdots p_m$ requires at most $\sum\limits_{j=1}^{m}(n+p_j-1)N$ additions and $[\frac{(n-1)^2}{n} + \sum\limits_{j=1}^{m}p_j]N$ multiplications, respectively. The proposed block circulant Euler-Jacket matrix with size $N = 8 = 2^3$ requires 24 additions and 12 multiplications. Comparing with the direct computation, the proposed algorithm is obviously faster.

4 Applications in Image Processing

An image which is transferred over the Internet contains a large amount of information, such as personal privacy, economic interest and national security which is not enable to be recognized by illegal users [19]. It is a considerable issue to ensure the security of the image over the Internet. In this section, former proposed Euler-Jacket transform and inverse Euler-Jacket transform are used to perform the encryption and decryption of two-dimension images. The further analysis of the comparison between Euler-Jacket transform and classical Hadamard transform is shown below [20].

The Fig. 2 shows the schematic diagram of encryption algorithm. In the schematic, image is scrambled as a meaningless noise image through matrix transform. Therefore, matrix transform is useful to achieve the initial information hiding. To encrypt a 128×128 picture, the BCH Euler-Jacket matrix and typical Hadamard matrix with size 256 are constructed by fast algorithm. BCH Euler-Jacket fast algorithm is introduced in (23) and Hadamard matrix is constructed by

$$H_{128} = H_2^{\otimes 7}, \tag{32}$$

where $H_2 = \begin{pmatrix} 1 & 1 \\ 1 & -1 \end{pmatrix}$. Original image and encrypted images with Hadamard transform and Euler-Jacket transform are shown in Fig. 3, respectively. Figure 3(c) has a uniform distribution of high and low gray bar while Fig. 3(b) only has the random distribution. Thus, images which under Euler-Jacket transform are suitable for transmission with low complexity which is able to be compressed efficiently.

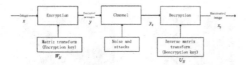

Fig. 2. The schematic diagram of encryption algorithm. The steps of encryption algorithm in general. Using Euler-Jacket transform to be encryption key.

In the process of Internet transmission the encrypted picture would encounter line noise, the malicious modification of hackers and a series of attacks. Therefore, the encryption algorithm must have the property of resisting attacks and noise in transmission schemes.

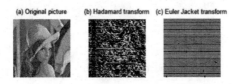

Fig. 3. The original and encrypted images. Image(a) is the original image, image(b) is the image through Hadamard transform, image(c) is the image under Euler-Jacket transform, respectively.

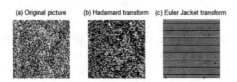

Fig. 4. Images under gaussian noise processing. Image(a) is the original image under gaussian noise processing, image(b) shows original image under gaussian noise processing after having been encrypted by Hadamard transform, image(c) shows original image under gaussian noise processing after having been encrypted by Euler-Jacket transform.

In Fig. 4, three pictures are shown under Additive-White-Gaussian-Noise(AWGN) whose Signal-to-Noise Ratio(SNR) is set to be 10 dB as the simulation with MATLAB. After decrypting with corresponding inverse transform, recovered images are illustrated in Fig. 5. This simulation shows Euler-Jacket transform is much more effective in resisting noise attacks while Hadamard transform generates image distortion in noise interference. Within a certain attacked range, Euler-Jacket transform encryption algorithm is still able to transmission basic information successfully.

(a) Hadamard transform   (b) Euler Jacket transform

Fig. 5. Decrypted images. Image(a) is the decryption of the Hadamard transform encrypted image, Image(b) is the decryption of the Euler-Jacket transform encrypted image.

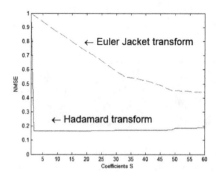

Fig. 6. NMSE of Euler-Jacket transform and Hadamard transform. The normalized mean square error(NMSE) when using part of the coefficients to decrypt images in Fig. 4. red dash line: using the 128-point Euler-Jacket transform; Blue solid line: using the 128-point Hadamard transform (Colour figure online).

A good encryption scheme should also be sensitive to the secret keys, and the key space should be large enough to make brute-force attacks infeasible. Research has been conducted during the situation that receiving terminal with wrong decryption matrix. Corresponding to Fig. 2, suppose there exists S coefficients of y in vector y_s and others are set to zero. The normalized mean square error(NMSE) of the image processing would be calculated as

$$NMSE = \frac{\|x_s - x\|^2}{\|x\|^2} \qquad (33)$$

The results in Fig. 6 show that, with Euler-Jacket transform, we can achieve the high security requirements. Euler-Jacket transform could not recover original information without correct decoding matrix in reality.

5   Conclusion

In this paper, we have presented a novel Euler-Jacket matrix. Through the application of block circulant Euler-Jacket matrices in both real BCH matrices and generalized circulant matrices, we can demonstrate that operations in

Euler-Jacket matrix are much more simple and more direct than ordinary matrix operations. Euler-Jacket matrix has the characteristics of periodicity, symmetry, unitarity and others. The inverses of these block circulant Euler-Jacket matrices equal to reciprocal of each element in matrices. Compared with direct computation, the proposed matrix has simple construction and fast computation for both forward and inverse matrix calculations. It has been realized in the field of image processing initially, which shows the great superiority. Proposed matrix would be further applied and made deeply studies in information theory, signal processing, encoding, image compression and many other research fields.

Acknowledgment. This work was supported by the National Natural Science Foundation of China (61379153, 61272495), the New Century Excellent Talents in University, China (NCET-11-0510), and partly by the World Class University (R32-2010-000-20014-0), and Fundamental Research (2010-0020942, 2012-002521) NRF, Korea.

References

1. Ahmed, N., Rao, K.R.: Orthogonal Transforms for Digital Signal Processing. Springer Science and Business Media, Heidelberg (2012)
2. Winograd, S.: On computing the discrete fourier transform. Math. comput. **32**(141), 175–199 (1978)
3. Rao, K.R., Yip, P.: Discrete Cosine Transform: Algorithms, Advantages, Applications. Academic press (2014)
4. Yarlagadda, R.K., Hershey, J.E.: Hadamard Matrix Analysis and Synthesis: With Applications to Communications and Signal/Image Processing. Springer Science and Business Media, US (2012)
5. Xiang, X., Zhou, J., Yang, J., Liu, L., An, X., Li, C.: Mechanic signal analysis based on the Haar-type orthogonal matrix. Expert Syst. Appl. **36**(6), 9674–9677 (2009)
6. Lee, M.H.: The center weighted Hadamard transform. IEEE Trans. Circuits Syst. **36**(9), 1247–1249 (1989)
7. Fan, C.-P., Yang, J.-F.: Fast center weighted Hadamard transform algorithms. IEEE Trans. Circuits Syst. II Analog Digital Signal Proc. **45**(3), 429–432 (1998)
8. Lee, M.H.: Jacket matrix and its applications to signal processing. In: 2011 IEEE 10th International Conference on Trust, Security and Privacy in Computing and Communications (TrustCom). IEEE, pp. 5–6, November 2011
9. Borissov, Y., Lee, M.H., Balakannan, S.: Jacket matrix construction using M-sequences. In: ISITC. IEEE, pp. 333–337, November 2007
10. Lin, C., Zhang, W., Guo, Y., Xu, Y.: Co-cyclic jacket matrix based optimal training design and placement for MIMO OFDM channel estimation. In: 2008 IEEE 4th International Conference on Circuits and Systems for Communications. IEEE, pp. 392–396, May 2008
11. Choe, C., Hwang, G.Y., Kim, S.H., Yoo, H.S., Lee, M.H.: Key agreement protocols based on the center weighted jacket matrix as a symmetric co-cyclic matrix. In: Gunsel, B., Jain, A.K., Tekalp, A.M., Sankur, B. (eds.) MRCS 2006. LNCS, vol. 4105, pp. 121–127. Springer, Heidelberg (2006)

12. Guo, Y., Peng, J., Lee, M.H.: Fast quantum codes based on Pauli block jacket matrices. Quantum Inf. Process. **8**(5), 361–378 (2009)
13. Lou, D.-C., Sung, C.-H.: A steganographic scheme for secure communications based on the chaos and Euler theorem. IEEE Trans. Multimedia **6**(3), 501–509 (2004)
14. Chien, R.T.: Cyclic decoding procedures for Bose-Chaudhuri-Hocquenghem codes. IEEE Trans. Inf. Theory **10**(4), 357–363 (1964)
15. Huckle, T.: Circulant and skewcirculant matrices for solving Toeplitz matrix problems. SIAM J. Matrix Anal. Appl. **13**(3), 767–777 (1992)
16. Vescovo, R.: Inversion of block-circulant matrices and circular array approach. IEEE Trans. Antennas Propag. **45**(10), 1565–1567 (1997)
17. Khalid, S., Khan, S., Application of compressed sensing on images via BCH measurement matrices. In: 2014 International Conference on Robotics and Emerging Allied Technologies in Engineering (iCREATE). IEEE, pp. 78–81 (2014)
18. Guo, Y., Mao, Y., Dong, S.P., Lee, M.H.: Fast dft matrices transform based on generalized prime factor algorithm. J. Commun. Networks **13**, 449–455 (2011)
19. Jinn-Ke, J., Yuh-Min, T.: On the security of image encryption method. Inf. Process. Lett. **60**(5), 261–265 (1996)
20. Annadurai, S.: Fundamentals of Digital Image Processing. Pearson Education India (2007)

Parallel and Distributed Algorithms

Deadline-Oriented Task Scheduling
for MapReduce Environments

Minghao Hu[✉], Changjian Wang, Pengfei You, Zhen Huang, and Yuxing Peng

National Laboratory for Parallel and Distributed Processing,
School of Computer Science, National University of Defense Technology,
Changsha 410072, China
{humh573,c_j_wang,ypfnudt,math_www,pengyuxing6}@163.com

Abstract. To provide timely results for 'Big Data Analytics', it is crucial to satisfy deadline requirements for MapReduce jobs in production environments. In this paper, we propose a deadline-oriented task scheduling approach, named *Dart*, to meet the given deadline and maximize the input size if only part of the dataset can be processed before the time limit. Dart uses an iterative estimation method which is based on both historical data and job running status to precisely estimate the real-time job completion time. By comparing the estimated time with the deadline constraint, a YARN-based task scheduler dynamically decides whether continuing or terminating the map phase. We have validated our approach using workloads from OpenCloud and Facebook on a cluster of 60 virtual machines. The results show that Dart can not only effectively meet the deadline but also process near-maximal data volumes even when the deadline is set to be extremely small and limited resources are allocated.

Keywords: MapReduce · Task scheduling · Deadline · Job completion time · Iterative estimation

1   Introduction

MapReduce [8], one of the most popular big data processing frameworks, along with its open-source implementation Hadoop [1], have been widely used to process 'Big Data Analytics'. In the production environment, MapReduce jobs with deadline constraints, often seen in the real-time SQL query, personalized advertisement recommendation, word frequency statistics and so on, are crucial for business applications. However, the rapid growth of data volumes, along with the limitation of cluster capacities and the concurrency of multiple running jobs have made it inevitable that deadline-bound jobs tend to operate on only a subset of their data in order to meet strict deadline constraints [2]. Since these jobs are spawned on large datasets and accuracy is proportional to the fraction of data processed, the natural goal of scheduling such jobs is *not only to satisfy deadline requirements but also to process as much data as possible to improve the accuracy* [9,10].

© Springer International Publishing Switzerland 2015
G. Wang et al. (Eds.): ICA3PP 2015, Part II, LNCS 9529, pp. 359–372, 2015.
DOI: 10.1007/978-3-319-27122-4_25

Lots of research efforts have been devoted to the problem of meeting deadlines [2,12,14]. Traditional schedulers [12,14] dynamically allocate resources to complete deadline-bound jobs before their deadlines. However, although these methods are capable of processing the entire dataset, missing deadlines could occur in two common situations. First, the job would fail in meeting its deadline even with maximal resource allocations as long as the user-defined deadline is set to be extremely small due to the urgency of the job. Second, since multiple deadline-bound jobs may run concurrently, missing deadlines could occur on a job if allocated resources are not enough for processing all its data before the deadline. Another kind of method such as the approximate query processing (AQP) system [2] executes an appropriately sized sample selected from the pre-constructed sample sets to meet the deadline. However, this kind of method may process a submaximal-sized sample because it simply assumes that the job completion time scales linearly with the sample size and the sample sets are statically computed before submitting the job.

To overcome the shortcomings of current solutions, a dynamic task scheduling method is required for terminating redundant map tasks as well as maximizing the input size if only part of the dataset can be processed before the deadline. Since when to terminate the extra map tasks must be confirmed, it requires us to estimate the job completion time based on the job running status, and then to compare the estimated value with the given deadline. However, the real-time estimation described here is complicated and difficult because the job completion time is dynamically changing with real-time input size, network bandwidth, available resources and so on, thus making it challenging to develop such a scheduling method.

In this paper, we propose a novel task scheduling approach for MapReduce environments, named *Dart*, which can efficiently satisfy the deadline requirement as well as maximize the input size if only part of the dataset can be processed. Given a specified deadline and limited resources, Dart iteratively calculates the duration of map, shuffle and reduce phases based on both the historical data and the job running status in order to precisely estimate the real-time job completion time. The task scheduler continues launching map tasks on workers so that the estimated time would approach but not exceed the deadline. Once the estimated time transcends the deadline, Dart terminates the map phase and finishes the remaining parts of the job. To support the termination, we develop our work based on a termination mechanism [15], which is capable of terminating the map phase once the user-defined condition is satisfied.

The main contributions of our work are as follows:

1. An iterative estimation method is introduced for that, given a job with previous execution, calculating the duration of map, shuffle and reduce phases based on the job running status and further estimating the real-time job completion time.
2. A YARN-based task scheduler is proposed to dynamically schedule map tasks on workers based on the estimated job completion time and the given deadline.

3. Comprehensive experiments have been conducted to demonstrate that our approach can not only effectively meet the deadline but also process near-maximal data volumes even when the deadline is set to be extremely small and limited resources are allocated.

The rest of this paper is organized as follows. Section 2 discusses related work. Section 3 describes the deadline-oriented task scheduling approach. Section 4 introduces the implementation of Dart. Section 5 shows the experimental results of our work. Finally, Sect. 6 concludes the paper.

2   Related Work

Meeting deadline requirements for MapReduce jobs has been an area of active research and plenty of recent works have been proposed [2,12,14]. Given a deadline-bound job, traditional resource management technique such as ARIA dynamically allocates appropriate resources to complete the job for achieving the deadline goal [14]. However, this kind of solutions can cause deadlines missed in two normal situations. First, for each deadline-bound job there exists a *minimum deadline threshold* (MDT) which is equal to the job completion time with *maximal resource allocations* (MRA). Obviously, the user-defined deadline given in current solutions should be no less than MDT, otherwise the job would miss its deadline even if it gets the maximal resources. Second, since the cluster capacities are limited and multiple submitted jobs may run concurrently, the resources allocated to the new deadline-bound job may be not enough for executing all the tasks before the time limit, thus failing in meeting the deadline requirement.

Approximate query process technique [2] executes jobs on an appropriately sized sample of data based on the deadline requirement. However, this kind of method may miss deadlines or process submaximal-sized data because errors are brought in due to the statically pre-computed sample sets and the simple assumption of linear relation between the job completion time and input size.

It is important to accurately estimate the job completion time in order to support meeting deadline requirements. The work presented in [11] estimates the progress of parallel queries by translating a MapReduce job into a directed acyclic graph (DAG), and using earlier debug runs of the same job on data samples to get the processing speeds for estimating the remaining time of the job. However, this approach would bring significant errors because that, it simply assumes that map (reduce) tasks of the same job share the same duration while the processing speed is dynamically changing with the input size. The work in [12] uses an online coarse-grained estimation method to calculate the job completion time, but it lacks the consideration of shuffle and reduce phases.

Early termination of map tasks is required when the estimated job completion time exceeds the given deadline. In [15], the author presents a termination mechanism which can terminate the remaining map tasks once the termination condition is satisfied. However, the termination condition is user-defined and therefore this method can not support meeting deadline requirements.

3   Deadline-Oriented Task Scheduling

3.1   Problem Statement

We are given a MapReduce job J consisting of M map tasks and R reduce tasks. Let us assume that the deadline is set to be small enough or limited resources are allocated to job J so that only part of all map tasks can be processed. We define k as the sum of real-time running and completed map tasks of J, which is proportional to the amount of processed data. T_J is denoted as job completion time and D is denoted as the deadline. For simplicity, we first assume that the job has uniform data distribution.

Given the above statement, our objective can be stated as follows: *endeavour to make T_J being less than D while maximizing k.*

In order to achieve the objective, we iteratively approach the optimal k. During runtime, the next map task is launched only if the estimated job completion time is less than the deadline, otherwise do not launch the task. Obviously, the main challenge of this method is how to estimate the job completion time while considering the next map task launched. To overcome this challenge, we design a novel iterative estimation method which is described below.

3.2   Iterative Estimation of Job Completion Time

Figure 1 shows a typical MapReduce job which has 6 map tasks and 3 reduce tasks. For clarity, we use a single bar to represent the shuffle phase and abstract the transmission of intermediate data. In Hadoop, the shuffle phase immediately begins after 5 % of map tasks are completed, and therefore it usually overlaps with the map phase. Each reduce task begins only after it has received the partitions shuffled from all map tasks.

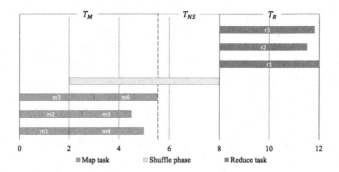

Fig. 1. A typical MapReduce job, which consists of map, shuffle and reduce phases, runs 12 time units.

From the figure we can see that, a MapReduce job consists of three phases: *map*, *shuffle* and *reduce*. Therefore we define T_M as the map phase duration,

T_{NS} as the non-overlapped shuffle phase duration and T_R as the reduce phase duration. Obviously, T_J can be calculated by the following equation:

$$T_J = T_M + T_{NS} + T_R \tag{1}$$

As long as we figure out T_M, T_{NS} and T_R, we can calculate T_J.

Map Phase Duration. Since we want to dynamically estimate the real-time duration of map phase, let us assume that J has already been executed for a period T_p and k map tasks have been scheduled. At this moment, the scheduler is ready to launch *the next map task* on the worker.

It has been observed that map task durations are generally stable [6]. Therefore, we define T_{map}^{avg} as the average duration of map tasks. Due to data locality [16], we further divide T_{map}^{avg} into *average duration of local map tasks* (denoted as T_{local}^{avg}) and *average duration of remote map tasks* (denoted as T_{remote}^{avg}).

We iteratively update a new T_M (denoted as T_M^n) everytime before scheduling the next map task, to represent the estimated map phase duration while considering the next map task launched. We also maintain an old T_M (denoted as T_M^o) to represent the last updated map phase duration. T_M^n is used to estimate the newest T_J. One potential T_M^n is $T_p + T_{map}^{avg}$, which means that the next map task is estimated to be the last completed one among current scheduled map tasks. The other situation is that T_M^n is equal to T_M^o, which may happen when an already running task is a remote map task while the next map task is node-local. Therefore, T_M^n is calculated as follows:

$$T_M^n = max(T_M^o, T_p + T_{map}^{avg}) \tag{2}$$

For example, Fig. 2(a) shows that when T_p is 3 time units, m3 is completed and the scheduler is ready to launch m6. At this moment, $k = 5$ and T_M^o is the estimated map phase duration before launching m5. Since T_M^n can be computed by Eq. 2, we can further calculate the new T_J. If $T_J < D$, then launch m6, update T_M^o as T_M^n and $k+ = 1$. Otherwise do not launch the task and keep T_M^o unchanged.

This procedure proceeds everytime scheduling the next map task. Besides, T_{local}^{avg} and T_{remote}^{avg} are first initialized based on historical job information and then updated once there is map task completed.

Non-overlapped Shuffle Phase Duration. In the shuffle phase, there usually exists three kind of bottlenecks which limit the shuffle performance [7]: the bottleneck in sender, the bottleneck in receiver and the bottleneck in network. The three bottlenecks lead to one simple characteristic: at least one link, whether it is the sender's link to the network, the contended links inside the network or the network's link to the receiver, is fully utilized during the shuffle phase. This characteristic is important for that, the overall transferring speed of shuffle phase would reach its upper bound and keep stable during the shuffle phase.

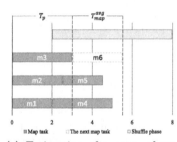
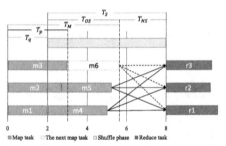

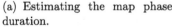

(a) Estimating the map phase duration.

(b) Estimating the non-overlapped shuffle phase duration.

Fig. 2. Estimating job completion time before scheduling the next map task.

Therefore, for a given J, we can define its *abstract average transferring speed*, which is denoted as B_J^{avg}.

As shown in Fig. 2(b), since T_{NS} is equal to *the overall shuffle phase duration* (denoted as T_S) minus *the overlapped shuffle phase duration* (denoted as T_{OS}), we can calculate T_{NS} by figuring out T_S and T_{OS}. T_S is the overall transferred data volumes divided by the average transferring speed. Let the average partition size of map task output be denoted as p. While the number of reduce tasks (denoted as R) is fixed, T_S can be calculated as $\frac{(k+1)\cdot p\cdot R}{B_J^{avg}}$. In addition, since the start time of shuffle phase (denoted as T_q) is available during runtime, T_{OS} is easily calculated as $T_M^n - T_q$. Finally, to get B_J^{avg}, the current transferred volumes are recorded (denoted as V_p). Then B_J^{avg} can be calculated as $\frac{V_p}{T_p - T_q}$.

In summary, T_{NS} can be calculated as follows:

$$T_{NS} = T_S - T_{OS} = \frac{(k+1)\cdot p\cdot R}{B_J^{avg}} - (T_M^n - T_q) \tag{3}$$

Reduce Phase Duration. In MapReduce job, the reduce task starts only after it has received all the volumes shuffled from map tasks. For the last reduce task, it starts only after the whole shuffle phase ends. Therefore we can calculate T_R as the execution time of the last reduce task, which is estimated to be *the average execution time of reduce tasks*.

Based on the analysis of previous work, a task's execution time depends on the input size, its computation complexity and available resources [3]. The input size is decided by the changing k at runtime. The computation complexity is unknown but is the same for all reduce tasks. Besides, we assume that the resources allocated to each reduce task are the same, which is reasonable in production environment.

To get the estimated T_R, we want to first figure out the relationship between k and the input size. Here we first define d as *the average input size of reduce tasks*. Because each map task transfers one partition to one reduce task, it is easy to calculate d as follows:

$$d = (k + 1) \cdot p \tag{4}$$

We then estimate $f(d)$, a variable denoting the average execution time of reduce tasks with given d, by running a series of sample reduce tasks with discrete $d \in [0, M \cdot p]$. However, multiple sample tasks may take a long time and add a significant delay if they are running during the job's execution. Therefore, we only estimate $f(d)$ offline, precomputing the distribution of $f(d)$ to accurately and quickly estimate T_R. Because the computation complexity and the allocated resources of sample tasks are the same as that of real reduce tasks, these sample results are close to real execution times.

Since $f(d)$ changes with d nonlinearly, giving a d to estimate $f(d)$ can be modelled as a *nonlinear regression problem* [4]. We find that using the power function $a \cdot d^b$ to represent $f(d)$ leads to accurate estimations in our experiment, where a and b are the unknown variables waiting to be calculated. Taking the logarithm of both sides of the equation, we can get $\ln(f(d)) = \ln(a) + b \cdot \ln(d)$. Notice that our model is then transformed into a linear regression problem where $Y = \ln(f(d))$ and $X = \ln(d)$. Therefore we apply the Least Square method to figure out $\ln(a)$ and b. Once obtaining the above variables, we can do the curve fitting of $f(d)$ so that given the specified k, T_R is calculated as follows:

$$T_R = a \cdot ((k + 1) \cdot p)^b \tag{5}$$

Algorithm 1. Task Scheduling Algorithm

Input: Job J, Containers C, Deadline D, k
1: **if** acceptEvent(available containers C are allocated) **then**
2:    Update T_p and B_J^{avg}
3:    **for** each available container $c \in C$ **do**
4:       **if** J has specified map task m on c **then**
5:          $T_J = \text{getEstimatedJCT}(k, m, c)$
6:          **if** $T_J < D$ **then**
7:             sendEvent(launch m on c)
8:             $k+ = 1$
9:          **else** $\{T_J > D$ **and** m is remote map task$\}$
10:             sendEvent(release c)
11:          **else** $\{T_J > D$ **and** m is local map task$\}$
12:             Terminate the remaining unlaunched map tasks
13:             Return k
14:          **end if**
15:       **end if**
16:    **end for**
17: **end if**

3.3 Dynamic Task Scheduling Algorithm

Knowing the estimated job completion time, we then need to design the task scheduling algorithm for allocating map tasks on workers.

As Algorithm 1 shows, once there are available containers for executing tasks, key parameters such as T_p and B_J^{avg} are updated and the job completion time is calculated by using the iterative estimation method (Line 1–5). The container is the abstract notion of resources such as memory and CPU. Next detailed scheduling decisions are made by comparing the estimated time with the given deadline (Line 6–13): if the job completion time is less than the deadline, then launch the map task on the worker with the specified container and $k+=1$; otherwise either release the assigned resources or terminate the remaining unlaunched map tasks and return the maximal k based on the data locality of map tasks. The terminating mechanism is a previous work [15], which can terminate the map phase when some user-defined conditions are satisfied and we integrate it into Dart.

Algorithm 2 shows the logic of workers. Once receiving the event of launching a task, the worker launches the task with the specified container. During the execution of tasks, the worker reports the status of running tasks to the scheduler periodically. When a map task is completed, the worker releases the container and sends the task-completed event along with task information to the scheduler.

Algorithm 2. Scheduling Logic of the Worker

Input: Map task m, Container c
1: **if** acceptEvent(launch m on c) **then**
2:     launchTask(m, c)
3: **end if**
4: **if** m on c is completed **then**
5:     sendEvent(m is completed)
6:     sendEvent(release c)
7:     Send p and T_{map}^{avg} to the scheduler
8: **end if**

---

4   Dart Implementation

We designed and implemented Dart prototype on top of Hadoop 2.2.0 [1]. We have added two extra components in the framework and modified the ApplicationMaster (AM) of Hadoop Yarn. The implementation consists of the following four main components which are shown in Fig. 3.

- **Task Sampler:** Before the job is launched, the task sampler runs multiple sample reduce tasks to get the distribution of the task's execution time with different input sizes. Then the results are sent to the job profiler to construct the whole profile information of the job.
- **Job Profiler:** The job profiler collects the statistic job profile information, such as the average duration of map tasks, the average partition size of map task and so on, from both the previous execution of jobs and the task sampler. After the job is initialized, it sends the information to the AM for initial scheduling.

- **Job Completion Time Estimator:** Given the job profile information, the JCT estimator calculates the job completion time by using the iterative estimation method.
- **Task Scheduler:** When the job is submitted, the task scheduler communicates with the ResourceManager (RM) by sending heartbeats periodically to request appropriate resources for executing tasks. When the scheduler receives available resources, it runs the task scheduling algorithm to dynamically launch map tasks. Once the termination condition is satisfied, the scheduler terminates the remaining unlaunched map tasks, returns the maximal k and finishes the rest of the job. Besides, the scheduler monitors the individual tasks and collects the real-time job profile information for more precise scheduling.

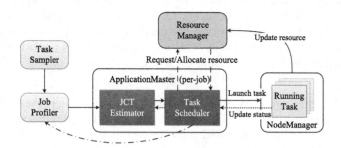

Fig. 3. The architecture design of Dart.

5 Evaluation

In this section we present the experimental results of Dart. We deploy Dart on a cluster consisting of 60 virtual machines (VM). Each VM contains 4 virtual cores and 8 GB RAM. The VM cluster is built based on 10 machines, each of which has four Intel Xeon CPU E5-2640 (2.50 GHz),64 GB of memory and 10 Gbps ethernet, using Linux.

5.1 Experimental Setup

WorkLoad. We use workload traces from Carnegie Mellon University's research cluster [13] and Facebook's production cluster [5] to evaluate our work. The trace of CMU includes more than 20-mouth logs and captures over a hundred thousand MapReduce jobs on a 64 node cluster, while the trace of Facebook is from a mix of batch jobs and captures over half a million jobs on a 3500 node cluster. To fit within our cluster, we use the same inter-arrival times, number of tasks and the task-to-rack mappings as in the traces. Finally, we get all jobs binned by

Table 1. Experimental configurations

Configurations	C1	C2	C3
δ	1	0.5	1
μ		0.95	1.6	1

the number of tasks, using three distinctions "Small" (<100 tasks), "Medium" (101–1000 tasks), and "Large" (>1001 tasks).

Next we convert these jobs to deadline-bound jobs as follows: for a MapReduce job J, we define δ as the ratio of actual resource allocations to MRA while μ is the ratio of the given deadline to MDT, so $\delta = 1$ means that J gets the *maximal resource allocations* and $\mu = 1$ means that the deadline of J is set to be the *minimum deadline threshold*. We further mark three main environmental configurations for implementing our experiments, which is shown in Table 1. Notice that C1 is the situation where the deadline is set to be too small to complete all tasks of the job even with maximal resources, C2 is the other situation where the resources are limited, and C3 is the ideal situation.

Baseline. We compare Dart with two existing methods. One is the state-of-the-art scheduling framework *ARIA* [14], which dynamically estimates and allocates the appropriate resources required for completing all tasks of the job within the deadline. The other is the *pre-selected sampling* (denoted as PS) [2], which produces several samples before the execution of job and the scheduler picks one appropriate sample to operate on for meeting the deadline.

5.2 Improvements in Meeting Deadlines

We first compare Dart with our baselines in meeting deadlines by running 140 jobs under the three environmental configurations described in Table 1. Each experiment is repeated at least five times and we plot the median values of results.

In Fig. 4(a), the x-axis shows the different environmental configurations while the y-axis shows the percentage of experiments that missed deadlines. The results show that Dart totally misses deadlines of only about 4.7 % of the jobs, while the performance of PS is a little worse. ARIA tries to allocate enough resources to complete all tasks of the job, which can achieve good performances in the ideal C3 but significantly causes deadlines missed in C1 and C2.

We further illustrate the results divided by the job size in C1 and C2. Figure 4(b) and (c) show that the gains compared to ARIA and PS in large jobs are pronounced compared to small and medium sized jobs. The reason is that, since the large jobs tend to have longer job completion time and multiple waves of map tasks, Dart can provide a more accurate estimation by using the iterative estimation method as the execution proceeds. ARIA also benefits from the large jobs because its dynamic estimation method is based on the

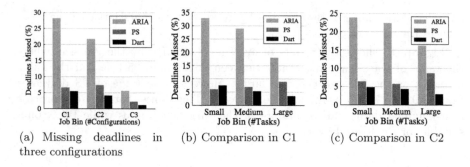

(a) Missing deadlines in three configurations

(b) Comparison in C1

(c) Comparison in C2

Fig. 4. Overall comparison of the percentage of deadlines missed.

coarse-grained multiple waves model. On the contrary, the performance of PS downgrades as the job size increases because it is more difficult to provide an appropriately sized sample which is statically built before the execution.

5.3   Improvements in Maximizing the Processed Data

Then we illustrate the ability of Dart in maximizing the processed data within given deadlines compared to PS. We only use the results in C1 and C2 and Fig. 5(a) summarizes our results. The x-axis shows the processed data relative to the maximal processed data within given deadlines, which is denoted as $\frac{k}{k_i}$: values below 100 % represent experiments that have not processed the maximal data volumes, values above 100 % represent experiments that process more than the maximal volumes, which means that they would have missed the deadlines. The y-axis shows the cumulative distribution function of Dart and PS.

Totally, Dart improves in processing more data than PS by about 14.2 %, and achieves an average $\frac{k}{k_i}$ of 90.8 %, which means that Dart is capable of processing near-maximal data volumes. Moreover, notice that although both Dart and PS have nearly the same fraction of values exceeding 100 %, Dart processes less

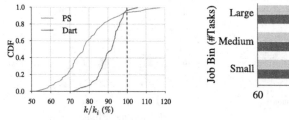

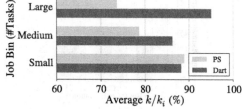

(a) Cumulative distribution function (CDF) of k relative to k_i

(b) Comparison of average k relative to k_i

Fig. 5. Overall comparison in maximizing the processed data.

exceeded data than PS. Besides, the figure also shows that Dart conspicuously reduces the variance of $\frac{k}{k_i}$.

Figure 5(b) shows the results of average $\frac{k}{k_i}$ divided by the job size, where the value of Dart maintains stable between 86.3 % and 95.1 %, and the value increases as the job size becomes larger. However, the value of PS decreases from 88.9 % to 73.7 % as the job size increases. This shows that Dart can process near-maximal data volumes despite of the various job sizes while PS is only suitable for small-sized jobs.

5.4 Estimation Accuracy

To understand why Dart can achieve such good performances, we evaluate the estimation accuracy of job completion time in Dart, while the baseline is the estimation method of ARIA. Figure 6(a) shows the overall estimation error of Dart and ARIA. Dart totally reduces the estimation error by 56.4 % compared to ARIA. Moreover, 80 % of jobs run by Dart has an estimation error which is less than 14.2 %, while the estimation errors of 80 % of ARIA's jobs are less than 34.3 %. The results show that Dart has a more accurate estimation of job completion time as well as efficiently reduces the variance in estimation error compared to ARIA.

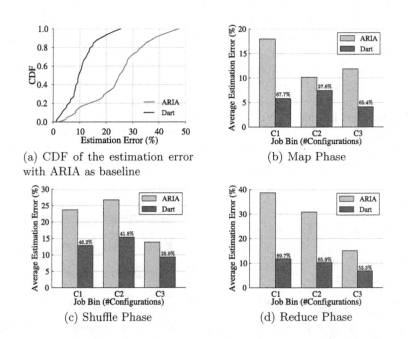

(a) CDF of the estimation error with ARIA as baseline

(b) Map Phase

(c) Shuffle Phase

(d) Reduce Phase

Fig. 6. Overall comparison of the estimation error. Numbers on the bar represent percentage reduction in estimation error by using Dart.

We further illustrate the average estimation error of detailed durations including map, shuffle and reduce phases. Figure 6(b) shows the results of map phase. We can see that Dart performs much better than ARIA in C1 and C3, reducing the average estimation error by 67.7 % and 65.4 % respectively. The reason is that, jobs in C1 or C3 have only one wave of map tasks because the maximal resources are allocated, in which situation the coarse-grained method of ARIA would calculate the duration of map phase as the average duration of map tasks, causing the estimated duration usually being smaller than the real value. In contrast, Dart estimates the duration of map phase based on the fine-grained iterative method and therefore can get a more accurate estimation.

Figure 6(c) shows the results of shuffle phase. We observed that Dart also performs better in all three configurations, reducing the error by 28.9 %–46.2 %, but not as good as the performances in map phase. It is probably because that Dart only uses a heuristic to do the estimation and there are a lot of uncertain factors influencing the shuffle phase, such as the changing network traffic, data skew and so on.

We finally evaluate our estimation method for reduce phase. The result in Fig. 6(d) shows that Dart reduces the average estimation error by 53.3 %–69.7 %. The main reason of such good performances is that: since the execution time of reduce tasks is dynamically changing with input size, Dart does not use previous information but runs samples in advance to do nonlinear regression, and then estimates the duration of reduce phase based on the regression model and real-time input of reduce tasks. On the contrary, ARIA uses statically historical information to estimate the dynamically changing duration, thus causing inaccurate estimations especially in C1 and C2.

6   Conclusion and Future Work

In this paper we have presented a deadline-oriented task scheduling approach, called Dart, for satisfying deadline requirements of MapReduce jobs while maximizing the amount of processed data despite of small deadlines and lack of resources. Dart makes dynamic scheduling decisions by comparing the estimated job completion time with the given deadline so as to process as much data volumes as possible before the deadline. To estimate the real-time job completion time, an iterative estimation method is used before scheduling map tasks. We have implemented Dart in Hadoop Yarn, and conducted comprehensive experiments on workloads from OpenCloud and Facebook. The results show that Dart successfully meet 96 % of given deadlines and processes near-maximal data volumes even when the given deadline is extremely small and limited resources are allocated.

Acknowledgments. This work is sponsored in part by the National Natural Science Foundation of China under Grant No. 61572510, the National Natural Science Foundation of China under Grant No. 61402490, and the National Basic Research Program of China (973) under Grant No. 2014CB340303.

This work is also supported by the National Basic Research Program of China under Grant No. 2011CB302601.

References

1. Hadoop: Open source implementation of MapReduce. http://hadoop.apache.org/
2. Agarwal, S., Mozafari, B., Panda, A., Milner, H., Madden, S., Stoica, I.: Blinkdb: queries with bounded errors and bounded response times on very large data. In: EuroSys, pp. 29–42 (2013)
3. Ananthanarayanan, G., Kandula, S., Greenberg, A., Stoica, I., Lu, Y., Saha, B., Harris, E.: Reining in the outliers in map-reduce clusters using mantri. In: OSDI, vol. 10, p. 24 (2010)
4. Bates, D.: Nonlinear Regression: Iterative Estimation and Linear Approximations. Wiley Online Library, New York (1988)
5. Chen, Y., Alspaugh, S., Katz, R.: Interactive analytical processing in big data systems: a cross-industry study of mapreduce workloads. In: VLDB, pp. 1802–1813 (2012)
6. Chen, Y., Ganapathi, A., Griggith, R., Katz, R.: The case for evaluating mapreduce performance using workload suites. In: MASCOTS (2011)
7. Chowdhury, M., Zaharia, M., Ma, J., Jordan, M., Stoica, I.: Managing data transfers in computer clusters with orchestra. In: SIGCOMM (2011)
8. Dean, J., Ghemawat, S.: Mapreduce: simplified data processing on large clusters. Commun. ACM 51(1), 107–113 (2008)
9. Garofalais, M., Gibbons, P.: Approximate query processing: taming the terabytes. In: VLDB (2001)
10. Lohr, S.: Sampling: Design and Analysis. Thomson (2009)
11. Morton, K., Balazinska, M., Grossman, D.: Paratimer: a progress indicator for mapreduce dags. In: SIGMOD, pp. 507–518 (2010)
12. Polo, J., Carrera, D., Becerra, Y., Torres, J., Ayguadé, E., Steinder, M., Whalley, I.: Performance-driven task co-scheduling for mapreduce environments. In: NOMS, pp. 373–380 (2010)
13. Ren, K., Kwon, Y., Balazinska, M., Howe, B.: Hadoop's adolescence: an analysis of hadoop usage in scientific workloads. In: VLDB (2013)
14. Verma, A., Cherkasova, L., Campbell, R.: Aria: automatic resource inference and allocation for mapreduce environments. In: ICAC (2011)
15. Wang, C., Peng, Y., Tang, M., Li, D., Li, S., You, P.: Mapcheckreduce: an improved mapreduce computing model for imprecise applications. In: Big Data, pp. 366–373 (2014)
16. Zaharia, M., Borthakur, D., Sen, S., Elmeleegy, K., Shenker, S., Stoica, I.: Delay scheduling: a simple technique for achieving locality and fairness in cluster scheduling. In: EuroSys, pp. 265–278 (2010)

Bitwise Data Parallelism with LLVM: The ICgrep Case Study

Robert D. Cameron[(✉)], Nigel Medforth, Dan Lin, Dale Denis,
and William N. Sumner

School of Computing Science, Simon Fraser University, Surrey, BC, Canada
{cameron,nmedfort,lindanl,daled,wsumner}@sfu.ca

Abstract. Bitwise data parallelism using short vector (SIMD) instructions has recently been shown to have considerable promise as the basis for a new, fundamentally parallel, style of regular expression processing. This paper examines the application of this approach to the development a full-featured Unicode-capable open-source grep implementation. Constructed using a layered architecture combining Parabix and LLVM compiler technologies, icGrep is the first instance of a potentially large class of text processing applications that achieve high performance text processing through the combination of dynamic compilation and bitwise data parallelism. In performance comparisons with several contemporary alternatives, 10× or better speedups are often observed.

Keywords: Bitwise data parallelism · Dynamic compilation · ICgrep ·
MatchStar · Parabix transform · Regular expression · SIMD

1 Introduction

Although well-established technical standards exist for Unicode regular expressions [4], most of today's regular expression processing toolsets fail to support the full set of processing features even at the most basic level [11]. One of the fundamental issues is performance and so it makes good sense to consider the ways in which parallel processing approaches can help address the gap.

Efforts to improve the performance of regular expression matching through parallelization have generally concentrated on the use of SIMD, multicore or GPU technologies to accelerate multiple instances of independent matching problems. Scarpazza [10] used SIMD and multicore parallelism to accelerate small ruleset tokenization applications on the Cell Broadband Engine. Salapura [9] built on these techniques to accelerate business analytics applications using SSE instructions on commodity processors. Zu et al. [13] use GPU technology to implement NFA-based regular expression matching with parallelism devoted both to processing a compressed active state array as well as to handling matching of multiple packet instances.

Using parallel methods to accelerate matching of a single pattern on a single input stream is more difficult. Indeed, of the 13 dwarfs identified in the Berkeley

© Springer International Publishing Switzerland 2015
G. Wang et al. (Eds.): ICA3PP 2015, Part II, LNCS 9529, pp. 373–387, 2015.
DOI: 10.1007/978-3-319-27122-4_26

overview of parallel computing research, finite state machines (FSMs) are considered the hardest to parallelize (embarrassingly sequential) [1]. However, some success has been reported recently along two independent lines of research. The first focuses on data-parallel division of an input stream into separately processed segments on multiple cores. In this case, the challenge is to identify the appropriate starting state or states that need to be considered for all but the first segment. Mytkowicz et al. [8] use dynamic convergence and range coalescing to dramatically reduce the number of states in play at any point, while Zhao et al. [12] address the problem using principled speculation. The second line of research is based on Parabix technology: the use of short vector SIMD instructions (e.g., Intel SSE or AVX instructions) to process bit streams in one-to-one correspondence with input character streams. Following this approach, Cameron et al. [3] have recently prototyped a new bitwise data parallel algorithm that shows significant acceleration of regular expression matching performance compared to sequential implementations even on a single core.

These previous works in applying parallel methods to regular expression matching have generally focused on traditional ASCII-based matching problems. However, documents and data formats increasingly use Unicode, particularly in the form of UTF-8. W3Techs.com reports that the percentage of websites reporting UTF-8 as the character encoding has reached 84% as of May 2015. But regular expression matching over UTF-8 introduces complexities of variable-length encodings for characters. To process UTF-8 documents directly, Unicode regular expressions must generally undergo considerable state expansion to equivalent regular expressions over byte sequences. Alternatively, if the price is paid to first transcode a UTF-8 document to UTF-16, the problem of very large transition tables arises.

In this paper, we report on the use of the implementation of a full UTF-8 regular expression search tool, building on the bitwise data parallel methods of the Parabix framework combined with the dynamic compilation capabilities of LLVM [5]. The result is icGrep, a high-performance, full-featured open-source grep implementation with systematic support for Unicode regular expressions, fully implementing Unicode level 1 requirements of Unicode Technical Standard #18 [4]. As an alternative to classical grep implementations, icGrep offers dramatic performance acceleration in Unicode regular expression matching.

The main contributions reported here are the extension of the bitwise data parallel methods for regular expression matching to handle UTF-8 natively, validating the bitwise data parallel method with the first complete implementation in a useful tool, and introducing icGrep itself as research artifact. From the latter perspective, icGrep is significant in several ways. First, it allows the performance results reported here to be independently replicated. Secondly, it is a platform for further research into regular expression matching using bitwise methods and is indeed being used to investigate Unicode level 2 requirements in a project funded by Google. Finally, it is working example demonstrating the Parabix+LLVM framework, and useful for guiding further research into bitwise data parallel algorithms generally and how they may take advantage of evolving architectural features.

The remainder of this paper is organized as follows. Section 2 presents background material dealing with Unicode regular expressions, the Parabix framework and regular expression matching techniques using bitwise data parallelism. Section 3 addresses the issues and performance challenges associated with meeting Unicode regular expression requirements and presents extensions to the Parabix techniques that we have developed to address them. Section 4 describes the overall architecture of the icGrep implementation with a focus on the integration of Parabix and LLVM technologies. Section 5 evaluates the performance of icGrep on several types of matching problems with two contemporary competitors, pcre2grep and ugrep of the ICU (International Component for Unicode) software library. Section 6 concludes the paper with remarks on developing the Parabix+LLVM framework for other applications as well as identifying further research questions in Unicode regular expression matching with bitwise data parallelism.

2   Background

Unicode Regular Expressions. Traditional regular expression syntax is oriented towards string search using regular expressions over ASCII or extended-ASCII byte sequences. A grep search for a line beginning with a capitalized word might use the pattern "`^[A-Z][a-z]+`" ("extended" syntax). Here, "`^`" is a zero-width assertion matching only at the start of a line, "`[A-Z]`" is a character class that matches any single character in the contiguous range of characters from A through Z, while the plus operator in "`[a-z]+`" denotes repetition of one or more lower case ASCII letters.

While explicit listing of characters of interest is practical with ASCII, it is less so with Unicode. In the Unicode 7.0 database, there are 1490 characters categorized as upper case and 1841 categorized as lower case. Rather than explicitly listing the individual characters, then, it is more practical to use named character classes, such as Lu for upper case letters and Ll for lower case letters. Using these names, our search might be rewritten to find capitalized words in any language as "`^\p{Lu}\p{Ll}+`" (Perl-compatible syntax). The Unicode consortium has defined an extensive list of named properties that can be used in regular expressions.

Beyond named properties, Unicode Technical Standard #18 defines additional requirements for Unicode regular expressions, at three levels of complexity [4]. Level 1 generally relates to properties expressed in terms of individual Unicode codepoints, while level 2 introduces complexities due to codepoint sequences that form grapheme clusters, and level 3 relates to tailored locale-specific support. We consider only Unicode level 1 requirements in this paper, as most grep implementations are incomplete with respect the requirements even at this level. The additional level 1 regular expression requirements primarily relate to larger classes of characters that are used in identifying line breaks, word breaks and case-insensitive matching. Beyond this, there is one important syntactic extension: the ability to refine character class specifications using set intersection and subtraction. For example, [\p{Greek}&&\p{Lu}] denotes the class of upper case Greek letters, while [\p{Ll}--\p{ASCII}] denotes the class of all non-ASCII lower case letters.

Bitwise Data Parallel Matching. Regular expression search using bitwise data parallelism has been recently introduced and shown to considerably outperform methods based on DFAs or NFAs [3]. In essence, the method is 100 % data parallel, considering all input positions in a file simultaneously. A set of parallel bit streams is computed, with each bit position corresponding to one code-unit position within input character stream. Each bit stream may be considered an L-bit integer, where L is the length of the input stream. Matching is performed using bitwise logic and addition on these long integers.

Consider the following simplified definition of regular expressions. A regular expression may be a character class C or formed by composition. If R and S are regular expressions, then the concatenation RS is the regular expression standing for the set of all strings formed by concatenating one string from R and one string from S, $R|S$ is the alternation standing for the union of the sets of strings from R and S, and $R*$ is the Kleene-star closure denoting the set of strings formed from 0 or more occurrences of strings from R.

Character class streams, such as CharClass([d]) for the stream that marks the position of "d" characters and CharClass([a-z]) for the stream of lower case ASCII alphabetics are first computed in a fully data-parallel manner. Then the search process proceeds by computing *marker streams* that mark the positions of matches so far. Each bit in a marker stream indicates that all characters prior to the given position have been matched. The initial marker stream m_0 consists of all ones, i.e., $m_0 = 2^L - 1$, indicating that all positions are in play. Matching then proceeds in accord with the following equations.

$$\text{Match}(m, C) = \text{Advance}(\text{CharClass}(C) \wedge m)$$
$$\text{Match}(m, RS) = \text{Match}(\text{Match}(m, R), S)$$
$$\text{Match}(m, R|S) = \text{Match}(m, R) \vee \text{Match}(m, S))$$
$$\text{Match}(m, C*) = \text{MatchStar}(m, \text{CharClass}(C))$$
$$\text{Match}(m, R*) = m \vee \text{Match}(\text{Match}(m, R), R*)$$

Here, Advance is an operation that advances all markers by a single position.

$$\text{Advance}(m) = m + m$$

MatchStar finds all matches of character class repetitions in a surprisingly simple manner [3].

$$\text{MatchStar}(M, C) = (((M \wedge C) + C) \oplus C) \vee M$$

Interestingly, the MatchStar operation also has application to the parallelized long-stream addition itself [3], as well as the bit-parallel edit distance algorithm of Myers [7]. For repetitions of other regular expressions, the final recursive equation accounts for the repeated extension of current matches; this equation is applied until no new match positions result.

For example, Fig. 1 shows how the regular expression d[a-z]*ed is matched against some input text using bitwise methods. In this diagram we use periods to denote 0 bits so that the 1 bits stand out. In the first step the character class stream [d] is matched and the results shifted one position (Advance) to produce marker bitstream M_1. Five matches indicated by marker bits are now in play simultaneously. The next step applies the MatchStar operation to find all the matches that may then be reached with the Kleene-* repetition [a-z]* (M_2). This produces pending matches at many positions. However, there is no need to consider these matches one at a time using lazy or greedy matching strategies. Rather, the full marker stream M_3 of remaining possibilities after matching [e] is easily computed using bitwise logic and shift. The final step produces marker stream M_4 indicating the single position at which the entire regular expression is matched.

$$
\begin{array}{ll}
\text{input data} & \texttt{dead dreams defeated.} \\
M_1 = \text{Advance}(\texttt{[d]}) & \texttt{.1..1.1......1......1} \\
M_2 = \text{MatchStar}(M_1, \texttt{[a-z]}) & \texttt{.1111.111111.11111111} \\
M_3 = \text{Advance}(M_2 \wedge \texttt{[e]}) & \texttt{..1.....1.....1.1..1.} \\
M_4 = \text{Advance}(M_3 \wedge \texttt{[d]}) & \texttt{....................1}
\end{array}
$$

Fig. 1. Matching d[a-z]*ed using bitwise data parallelism

The Parabix toolchain [6] provides a set of compilers and run-time libraries that target the SIMD instructions of commodity processors (e.g., SSE or AVX instructions on x86-64 architecture). Input is processed in blocks of code units equal to the size in bits of the SIMD registers, for example, 128 bytes at a time using 128-bit registers. Using the Parabix facilities, the bitwise data parallel approach to regular expression search was shown to deliver substantial performance acceleration for traditional ASCII regular expression matching tasks, often 5× or better [3].

3   Bitwise Methods for UTF-8

As described in the following section, icGrep is a reimplementation of the bitwise data parallel method implemented on top of LLVM infrastructure and adapted for Unicode regular expression search through data streams represented in UTF-8. In this section, we present the techniques we have used to extend the bitwise matching techniques to the variable-length encodings of UTF-8.

The first requirement in implementing a regular expression processor over UTF-8 data streams is to translate Unicode regular expressions over codepoints to corresponding regular expressions over sequences of UTF-8 bytes or *code units.* The toUTF8 function does the work, transforming input expressions such as '\u{244}[\u{2030}-\u{2137}]' to the corresponding UTF-8 representation: \xE2((\x84[\x80-\xB7])|(([\x81-\x83][\x80-\xBF])|(\x80[\xB0-\xBF])))

UTF-8 Byte Classification and Validation. In UTF-8, bytes are classified as (1) individual ASCII bytes, (2) prefixes of two-, three-, or four-byte sequences, or (3) suffix bytes. In addition, we say that the *scope* bytes of a prefix are the immediately following byte positions at which a suffix byte is expected. Mismatches between scope expectations and occurrences of suffix bytes indicate errors (we omit other error equations for brevity). Two helper streams are also useful. The Initial stream marks ASCII bytes and prefixes of multibyte sequences, while the NonFinal stream marks any position that is not the final position of a Unicode character.

$$\text{ASCII} = \text{CharClass}(\texttt{[\x00-\x7F]})$$
$$\text{Prefix} = \text{CharClass}(\texttt{[\xC2-\F4]})$$
$$\text{Prefix3or4} = \text{CharClass}(\texttt{[\xE0-\xF4]})$$
$$\text{Prefix4} = \text{CharClass}(\texttt{[\xF0-\xF4]})$$
$$\text{Suffix} = \text{CharClass}(\texttt{[\x80-\xBF]})$$
$$\text{Scope} = \text{Advance}(\text{Prefix}) \vee \text{Advance}(\text{Prefix3or4}, 2) \vee \text{Advance}(\text{Prefix4}, 3)$$
$$\text{Mismatch} = \text{Scope} \oplus \text{Suffix}$$
$$\text{Initial} = \text{ASCII} \vee \text{Prefix}$$
$$\text{NonFinal} = \text{Prefix} \vee \text{Advance}(\text{Prefix3or4}) \vee \text{Advance}(\text{Prefix4}, 2)$$

Unicode Character Classes. Whereas ASCII character classes can be determined by simple bitwise logic at a single code unit position, the UnicodeClass stream for a given class involves logic for up to four positions. By convention, we define UnicodeClass(U) for a given Unicode character class U to be the stream marking the *final* position of any characters in the class.

Using these definitions, it is then possible to extend the matching equations to operate with Unicode character classes as follows.

$$\text{Match}(m, U) = \text{Advance}(\text{ScanThru}(m, \text{NonFinal}) \wedge \text{UnicodeClass}(U))$$
$$\text{Match}(m, U*) = \text{MatchStar}(m, \text{UnicodeClass}(U) \vee \text{NonFinal}) \wedge \text{Initial}$$

Here, we use the ScanThru [2] operation to move a set of markers each through the nonfinal bytes of UTF-8 sequences to the final byte position.

$$\text{ScanThru}(m, c) = (m + c) \wedge \neg c$$

Figure 2 shows this technique in operation in the case of advancing through byte sequences (each 3 bytes in length) corresponding to Chinese characters. To better demonstrate the process, we use ni3, hao and men to represent these characters. CC_{ni3} is the bitstream that marks character ni3 and CC_{hao} is the bitstream that marks character hao. We start with the marker stream m_0 initialized to Initial, indicating all positions are in play. Using ScanThru, we move to the final position of each character t_1. Applying bitwise AND with CC_{ni3} and advancing gives the two matches m_1 for ni3. Applying ScanThru once more advances to the final position of the character after ni3. The final result stream m_2 shows the lone match for the multibyte sequence ni3hao.

input data	ni3hao(Hello),ni3men(You),
CC_{ni3}	..1.............1.........
CC_{hao}	.....1....................
$m_0 = $ Initial	1..1..111111111..1..111111
NonFinal	11.11.........11.11.......
$t_1 = $ ScanThru(m_0, NonFinal)	..1..111111111..1..1111111
$m_1 = $ Advance($t_1 \wedge CC_{ni3}$)	...1.............1........
$t_2 = $ ScanThru(m_1, NonFinal)	.....1.............1......
$m_2 = $ Advance($t_2 \wedge CC_{hao}$)	......1...................

Fig. 2. Processing of a multibyte sequence ni3hao

Unicode MatchStar. The MatchStar(M, C) operation directly implements the operation of finding all positions reachable from a marker bit in M through a character class repetition of an ASCII byte class C. In UTF-8 matching, however, the character class byte streams are marked at their *final* positions. Thus the one bits of a Unicode character class stream are not necessarily contiguous. This in turn means that carry propagation within the MatchStar operation may terminate prematurely.

In order to remedy this problem, icGrep again uses the NonFinal stream to "fill in the gaps" in the UnicodeClass(U) bitstream so that the MatchStar addition can move through a contiguous sequence of one bits. In this way, matching of an arbitrary Unicode character class U can be implemented using MatchStar$(m, $ UnicodeClass$(U) \vee $ NonFinal$)$.

Predefined Unicode Classes. icGrep employs a set of bitstreams that are pre-compiled into the executable. These include all bitstreams corresponding to Unicode property expressions such as \p{Greek}. Each property potentially contains many code points, so we further embed the calculations within an if hierarchy. Each if-statement within the hierarchy determines whether the current input block contains any codepoints at all in a given Unicode range. At the outer level, the ranges are quite coarse, becoming successively refined at deeper levels. This technique works well when input documents contain long runs of text confined to one or a few ranges.

4   Architecture

Regular Expression Preprocessing. As shown in Fig. 3, compilation in icGrep comprises three logical layers: RegEx, Parabix and the LLVM layer, each with their own intermediate representation (IR), transformation and compilation modules. As we traverse the layers, the IR becomes more complex as it begins to mirror the final machine code. The layering enables further optimization based on information available at each stage. The RegEx Parser validates and transforms the input RegEx into an abstract syntax tree (AST). Successive RegEx Transformations exploit domain knowledge to optimize the regular expressions. The aforementioned `toUTF8` transformation also applies during this phase to generate code unit classes.

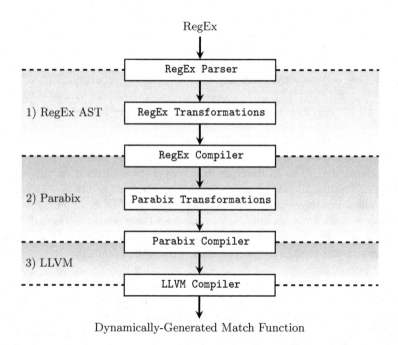

Fig. 3. icGrep compilation architecture

The next layer transforms this AST into the instructions in the Parabix IR. Recall that the Parabix layer assumes a transposed view of the input data. The *RegEx Compiler* first transforms all input code unit classes, analogous to non-Unicode character classes, into a series of equations over these transposed bitstreams. It next transforms the AST into Parabix instructions that use the results of these equations. For instance, it converts alternations into a sequence of calculations that are merged with ORs. The results of these passes are combined and transformed through typical optimization passes including dead code elimination (DCE), common subexpression elimination (CSE) and constant folding. These optimizations exploit redundancies that are harder to recognize in the RegEx AST itself.

The Parabix Compiler then directly converts the Parabix IR into LLVM IR. The LLVM Compiler framework provides flexible APIs for compilation and linking. Using these, icGrep dynamically generates a match function for identifying occurrences of the RegEx.

Dynamic Grep Engine. Figure 4 shows the structure of the icGrep matching engine. The input data is transposed into 8 parallel bit streams through the Transposition module. Using the 8 basis bits streams, the Required Streams Generator computes the line break streams, UTF-8 validation streams and the Initial and NonFinal streams needed to support ScanThru and MatchStar with UTF-8 data. The Dynamic Matcher, dynamically compiled via LLVM, retrieves the 8 basis bits and the required streams from their memory addresses and starts the matching process. During the matching process, any references to named Unicode properties generate calls to the appropriate routine in the Named Property Library. The Dynamic Matcher returns one bitstream that marks all the positions that fully match the compiled regular expression. Finally, a Match Scanner scans through the returned bitstream to select the matching lines and generate the normal grep output.

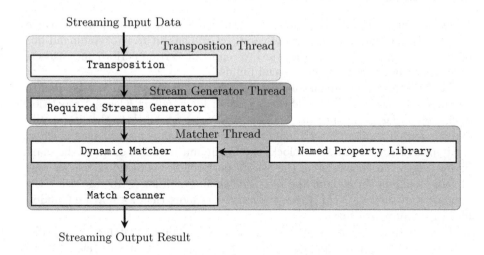

Fig. 4. Data flow in an icGrep execution

We can also apply a pipeline parallelism strategy to further speed up the process of icGrep. Transposition and the Required Streams Generator can be performed in a separate thread which can start even before the dynamic compilation starts. The output of Transposition and the Required Streams Generator, that is the 8 basis bits streams and the required streams, are stored in a shared memory buffer for subsequent processing by the Dynamic Matcher once compilation is complete. A single thread performs both compilation and matching using the computed basis and required streams. To avoid L2 cache contention, we allocate only a limited amount of space for the shared data in a circular buffer. The performance is dependent on the slowest thread. In the case that the cost of transposition and required stream generation is more than the matching process, we can further divide up the work and assign two threads for Transposition and the Required Streams Generator.

5   Evaluation

In this section, we report on the evaluation of icGrep performance, looking at three aspects. First, we discuss some performance aspects of icGrep internal methods, looking at the impact of optimizations discussed previously. Then we move on to a systematic performance study of icGrep with named Unicode property searches in comparison to two contemporary competitors, namely, pcre2grep released in January 2015 and ugrep of the ICU 54.1 software distribution. Finally, we examine complex expressions and the impact of multithreading icGrep on an Intel i7-2600 (3.4 GHz) and i7-4700MQ (2.4 GHz) processor.

5.1   Optimizations of Bitwise Methods

In order to support evaluation of bitwise methods, as well as to support the teaching of those methods and ongoing research, icGrep has an array of command-line options. This makes it straightforward to report on certain performance aspects of icGrep, while others require special builds.

For example, the command-line switch `-disable-matchstar` can be used to eliminate the use of the MatchStar operation for handling Kleene-* repetition of character classes. In this case, icGrep substitutes a while loop that iteratively extends match results. Surprisingly, this does not change performance much in many practical cases. In each block, the maximum iteration count is the maximum length run encountered; the overall performance is based on the average of these maxima throughout the file. But when search for XML tags using the regular expression `<[^!?][^>]*>`, a slowdown of more than 2× may be found in files with many long tags.

In order to short-circuit processing when no remaining matches are possible in a block, our regular expression compiler periodically inserts if-statements to check whether there are any marker bits still in play. To control this feature in dynamically generated code, the number of pattern elements between each if-test can be selected with the `-if-insertion-gap=` option. The default value in icGrep is 3; setting the gap to 100 effectively turns off if-insertion. Eliminating if-insertion sometimes improves performance by avoiding the extra if tests and branch mispredictions. For patterns with long strings, however, there can be a substantial slowdown.

The precompiled calculations of the various Unicode properties are each placed in if-hierarchies as described previously. To assess the impact of this strategy, we built a version of icGrep without such if-hierarchies. In this case, when a Unicode property class is defined, bitwise logic equations are applied for all members of the class independent of the Unicode blocks represented in the input document. For the classes covering the largest numbers of codepoints, we observed slowdowns of up to 5×.

5.2 Simple Property Expressions

A key feature of Unicode level 1 support in regular expression engines the support that they provide for property expressions and combinations of property expressions using set union, intersection and difference operators. Both `ugrep` and `icgrep` provide systematic support for all property expressions at Unicode Level 1 as well as set union, intersection and difference. However, in order to implement these operators with `pcre2grep`, we translated them into an equivalent form using lookbehind assertions.

We generated a set of regular expressions involving all Unicode values of the Unicode general category property (`gc`) and all values of the Unicode script property (`sc`). We then generated expressions involving random pairs of `gc` and `sc` values combined with a random set operator chosen from union, intersection and difference. All property values are represented at least once. A small number of expressions were removed because they involved properties not supported by pcre2grep. In the end 246 test expressions were constructed in this process.

We selected a set of Wikimedia XML files in several major languages representing most of the world's major language families as a test corpus. For each program under test, we performed searches for each regular expression against each XML document. Test cases were ranked by the percentage of matching lines found in the XML document and grouped in 5 % increments. Performance

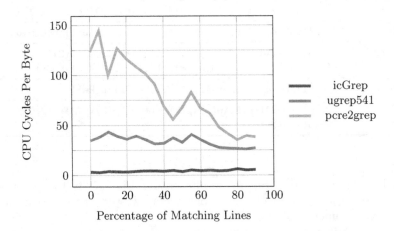

Fig. 5. Matching performance for simple property expressions

is reported in CPU cycles per byte on an Intel i7-2600 machine. The results are presented in Fig. 5.

When comparing the three programs, icGrep exhibits dramatically better performance, particularly when searching for rare items. The performance of both pcre2grep and ugrep improves (CPU cycles per byte decreases) as the percentage of matching lines increases. This occurs because each match allows them to bypass processing the rest of the line. On the other hand, icGrep shows a slight drop-off in performance with the number of matches found. This is primarily due to property classes that include large numbers of codepoints. These classes require more bitstream equations for calculation and also have a greater probability of matching. Nevertheless, the performance of icGrep in matching the defined property expressions is stable and well ahead of the competitors in all cases.

5.3   Complex Expressions

This study evaluates the comparative performance of the matching engines on a set of more complex expressions, shown in Table 1. The first two are alphanumeric (A.N.) expressions, differing only in that the first one is anchored to match the entire line. The third searches for lines consisting of text in Arabic script. The fourth expression is a published currency expression taken from Stewart and Uckelman [11]. An expression matching runs of six or more Cyrillic script characters enclosed in initial/opening and final/ending punctuation is fifth in the list. The last expression matches internationalized email names.

Table 1. Regular expressions

Name	Regular Expression
A.N. #1	`^[\p{L}\p{N}]*((\p{L}\p{N})|(\p{N}\p{L}))[\p{L}\p{N}]*$`
A.N. #2	`[\p{L}\p{N}]*((\p{L}\p{N})|(\p{N}\p{L}))[\p{L}\p{N}]*`
Arabic	`^[\p{Arabic}\p{Common}]*\p{Arabic}[\p{Arabic}\p{Common}]*$`
Currency	`(\p{Sc}\s*(\d*|(\d{1,3}([,.]\d{3})*))([,.]\d{2}?)?)|` `((\d*|(\d{1,3}([,.]\d{3})*))([,.]\d{2}?)?\s*\p{Sc})`
Cyrillic	`[\p{Pi}\p{Po}]\p{Cyrillic}{6,}[\p{Pf}\p{Pe}]`
Email	`([^\p{Z}<]+@[\p{L}\p{M}\p{N}.-]+\.(\p{L}\p{M}*){2,6})` `(>|\p{Z}|$)`

Table 2 shows the performance results on our Intel i7-2600 test machine, reporting seconds taken per GB of input averaged over 10 runs each on our Wikimedia document collection.

The most striking aspect of Table 2 is that both ugrep and pcregrep show dramatic slowdowns with ambiguities in regular expressions. This is most clearly

Table 2. Matching times for complex expressions (s/GB)

Expression	icGrep			
	SEQ	MT	pcre2grep	ugrep541
A.N.#1	2.4 – 5.0	2.1 – 4.4	8.2 – 11.3	8.8 – 11.3
A.N.#2	2.3 – 4.9	2.0 – 4.1	209.9 – 563.5	182.3 – 457.9
Arabic	1.5 – 3.4	1.2 – 2.6	7.5 – 270.8	8.9 – 327.8
Currency	0.7 – 2.1	0.4 – 1.4	188.4 – 352.3	52.8 – 152.8
Cyrillic	1.6 – 3.9	1.3 – 2.8	30.5 – 49.7	11.2 – 20.1
Email	3.0 – 6.9	2.7 – 6.4	67.2 – 1442.0	108.8 – 1022.3

illustrated in the different performance figures for the two Alphanumeric test expressions but is also evident in the Arabic, Currency and Email expressions. Contrastingly, icGrep maintains consistently fast performance in all test scenarios. The multithreaded icGrep shows speedup in every case but balancing of the workload across multiple cores is clearly an area for further work. Nevertheless, our three-thread system shows up to a 40 % speedup.

Table 3 shows the speedups obtained with icGrep on a newer Intel i7-4700MQ machine, considering three SIMD ISA alternatives and both single-threaded and multi-threaded versions. All speedups are relative to the base single-threaded SSE2 performance on this machine, which is given in seconds per GB in the first column. The SSE2 results are again using the generic binaries compiled for compatibility with all 64-bit processors. The AVX1 results are for Intel AVX instructions in 128-bit mode. The main advantage of AVX1 over SSE2 is its support for 3-operand form, which helps reduce register pressure. The AVX2 results are for icGrep compiled to use the 256-bit AVX2 instructions, processing blocks of 256 bytes at a time.

Table 3. Speedup of complex expressions on i7-4700MQ (σ)

Expression	Base	SEQ		MT		
	s/GB	AVX1	AVX2	SSE2	AVX1	AVX2
A.N. #1	2.76 (.65)	1.05 (.03)	1.25 (.08)	1.18 (.02)	1.19 (.03)	1.59 (.10)
A.N. #2	2.69 (.66)	1.05 (.02)	1.36 (.09)	1.20 (.03)	1.19 (.04)	1.80 (.11)
Arabic	1.82 (.39)	1.05 (.03)	1.15 (.08)	1.37 (.03)	1.37 (.04)	1.66 (.10)
Currency	1.04 (.30)	1.03 (.02)	1.04 (.06)	1.59 (.15)	1.61 (.14)	1.78 (.21)
Cyrillic	2.10 (.44)	1.06 (.02)	0.96 (.06)	1.27 (.02)	1.33 (.04)	1.23 (.09)
Email	3.57 (.87)	1.05 (.03)	1.37 (.14)	1.13 (.03)	1.16 (.04)	1.67 (.18)
Geomean	–	1.04	1.18	1.28	1.30	1.61

In each case, the use of three-operand form with AVX1 confers a slight speedup. The change to use 256 bits with AVX2 gives a further overall improvement, but some mixed results due to the limitations of 256 bit addition. Combining the AVX2 ISA with multithreading gives and average overall 61 % speedup compared to base.

6   Conclusion

icGrep demonstrates that predictable high-performance Unicode regular expression search can be achieved using a systematically parallel approach based on bitwise data parallelism. On modern commodity processors with SSE2 or better SIMD instruction sets, performance is dramatically better than that achievable using sequential state-transition methods based on DFAs, NFAs or backtracking. Multithread parallelism further enhances performance using a pipeline parallelism model.

Future research includes the investigation of regular expression matching techniques to handle Unicode level 2 and 3 requirements as well as the extension of optimization techniques to take advantage of MatchStar for more complex repetitions. Beyond regular expression matching, investigation of the bitwise data parallel model for other demanding Unicode processing tasks also seems worthwhile.

References

1. Asanovic, K., Bodik, R., Catanzaro, B.C., Gebis, J.J., Husbands, P., Keutzer, K., Patterson, D.A., Plishker, W.L., Shalf, J., Williams, S.W., et al.: The landscape of parallel computing research: a view from Berkeley. Technical report UCB/EECS-2006-183, EECS Department, University of California, Berkeley (2006)
2. Cameron, R.D., Amiri, E., Herdy, K.S., Lin, D., Shermer, T.C., Popowich, F.P.: Parallel scanning with bitstream addition: an XML case study. In: Jeannot, E., Namyst, R., Roman, J. (eds.) Euro-Par 2011, Part II. LNCS, vol. 6853, pp. 2–13. Springer, Heidelberg (2011)
3. Cameron, R.D., Shermer, T.C., Shriraman, A., Herdy, K.S., Lin, D., Hull, B.R., Lin, M.: Bitwise data parallelism in regular expression matching. In: PACT, pp. 139–150. ACM, New York (2014)
4. Davis, M., Heninger, A.: Unicode technical standard 18, Unicode regular expressions. The Unicode Consortium (2012)
5. Lattner, C., Adve, V.: LLVM: a compilation framework for lifelong program analysis & transformation. In: Code Generation and Optimization 2004, pp. 75–86. IEEE (2004)
6. Lin, D., Medforth, N., Herdy, K.S., Shriraman, A., Cameron, R.: Parabix: boosting the efficiency of text processing on commodity processors. In: High Performance Computer Architecture, pp. 1–12. IEEE (2012)
7. Myers, G.: A fast bit-vector algorithm for approximate string matching based on dynamic programming. J. ACM **46**(3), 395–415 (1999)
8. Mytkowicz, T., Musuvathi, M., Schulte, W.: Data-parallel finite-state machines. In: ASPLOS, pp. 529–542. ACM (2014)

9. Salapura, V., Karkhanis, T., Nagpurkar, P., Moreira, J.: Accelerating business analytics applications. In: HPCA, pp. 1–10. IEEE (2012)

10. Scarpazza, D.P.: Top-performance tokenization and small-ruleset regular expression matching. Int. J. Parallel Program. **39**(1), 3–32 (2011)

11. Stewart, J., Uckelman, J.: Unicode search of dirty data, or: how i learned to stop worrying and love Unicode technical standard # 18. Digit. Invest. **10**, S116–S125 (2013)

12. Zhao, Z., Wu, B., Shen, X.: Challenging the embarrassingly sequential: parallelizing finite state machine-based computations through principled speculation. In: ASPLOS, pp. 543–558. ACM (2014)

13. Zu, Y., Yang, M., Xu, Z., Wang, L., Tian, X., Peng, K., Dong, Q.: GPU-based NFA implementation for memory efficient high speed regular expression matching. In: PPoPP, pp. 129–140. ACM (2012)

Parallel Bloom Filter on Xeon Phi Many-Core Processors

Sheng Ni, Rentong Guo, Xiaofei Liao$^{(\boxtimes)}$, and Hai Jin

Services Computing Technology and System Lab, Cluster and Grid Computing Lab,
School of Computer Science and Technology, Huazhong University of Science and
Technology, Wuhan 430074, China
{xfliao,hjin}@hust.edu.cn

Abstract. Bloom filters are widely used in databases and network areas. These filters facilitate efficient membership checking with a low false positive ratio. It is a way to improve the throughput of bloom filter by parallel processing. Common many-core processors such as Xeon Phi can provide high parallelism. Thus, we build an iterative model to analyze memory access performance. This performance suggests that the bottleneck in the traditional design is mainly caused by synchronization cost and memory latency on many-core platforms. Therefore, we propose a *parallel bloom filter* (PBF), which is a lockless method involving input data preprocessing. This method reduces synchronization overhead and improves cache locality. We also implement and evaluate PBF on a Xeon Phi processor. Results show that the memory access performance is three times better than that of the counting bloom filter. PBF provides improved scalability, and the speedup ratio can reach a maximum of 80.7x.

Keywords: Bloom filter · Many-core processor · Cache coherence protocol · Xeon Phi · Scalability

1 Introduction

Bloom filters are important data collection structures that check memberships in large element sets with limited amounts of storage space [3]. The cost of space saving is associated with false positive errors. Such sets are unlikely to contain elements with positive query results and certainly do not contain elements with negative results. Bloom filters are widely used in the processing of massive data [6]. Most query operations are handled by a bloom filter in the main memory, thus significantly reducing on-disk database workload. Bloom filter optimization improves the performance of database applications by at least 10 % and considerably affects related research areas [5,12]. Therefore, a high-performance bloom filter must be designed.

The key performance indicators of bloom filters include throughput, memory consumption, and false positive ratio. In this study, we focus primarily on throughput. A significant method of boosting bloom filter throughput is by

© Springer International Publishing Switzerland 2015
G. Wang et al. (Eds.): ICA3PP 2015, Part II, LNCS 9529, pp. 388–405, 2015.
DOI: 10.1007/978-3-319-27122-4_27

processing requests in parallel. Such parallelization is appealing because the frequency and Dennard scaling are restricted by the current chip manufacturing process and high power consumption. Processors move from dual- or quad-core chips to cores with tens or hundreds of cores. The number of cores continues to grow. For instance, second-generation products of *Intel Many Integrated Core* (MIC) architecture are codenamed *Knight's Corner* (KNC) [21] and contain up to 61 cores. Processors with a large number of cores can exhibit excellent parallel performance. However, their interconnection structures and memory systems are complicated. Task granularity must be selected prudently and the system architecture understood comprehensively to achieve high performance. These requirements pose new challenges related to the performance optimization of traditional data structures and algorithms.

In this study, we design an efficient bloom filter kernel for many-core processors. The preliminary experiment results show that the throughput is not ideal. The theoretical analysis suggests that the majority of execution time is spent on synchronization operations and memory access during processing requests. Specifically, all hash operations in one membership request should be considered as one atomic operation to ensure the accuracy of results. Although many-core processors can host a large number of simultaneously running threads than multi-core processors can, more threads enter the wait state because of the current bloom filter design. This design cannot induce full parallel performance in many-core platforms. Moreover, the unbounded access on bit vectors also introduces cache synchronization overhead, that is, when one thread accesses a cache line connected to a remote core, then the thread must transfer data between two caches. This process is more costly than local cache access and is even slower than main memory access in certain cases.

To alleviate these bottlenecks, we propose a *parallel bloom filter* (PBF) for many-core platforms. This filter undergoes partition, sort, and response phases. Requests are distributed to hardware threads during the partition phase, and query/modified collisions on the same element between two threads are eliminated. Then, each thread processes a request in the corresponding sub-vector during the response phase. These methods reduce synchronization overhead and improve cache locality. We also evaluate PBF on KNC in terms of three aspects, namely, memory access performance, scalability, and simultaneous multithreading. The results show that PBF improves memory access performance by more than 3x and achieves a maximum speedup ratio of 80.7x.

We make the following specific contributions:

- We build a model to understand the performance of bloom filter, identify bottlenecks from traditional methods, and point out the way to improve throughput.
- We propose PBF to reduce synchronization overhead and improve cache locality. PBF provides better scalability than traditional designs do.
- We analyze the performance overhead of our method via theoretical approaches.

– We evaluate our proposed mechanism with realistic experiments. The results show that throughput improves by 38x in PBF over that in the traditional design.

The rest of this paper is organized as follows. Section 2 introduces the background of Xeon Phi processors and bloom filters. Section 3 analyzes the performance of a standard bloom filter with a theoretical method and discusses the bottlenecks. Section 4 illustrates the design details of our method, which is evaluated in Sect. 5. Section 6 concludes this paper.

2 Background and Related Work

2.1 Intel Xeon Phi Architecture

Xeon Phi is a many-core coprocessor based on the MIC architecture. In the latest KNC products, this architecture is composed of a maximum of 61 cores. Each core is a x86-based in-order core running at approximately 1 GHz and supports four-way *simultaneous multi-threading* (SMT). Such cores also include a 512 bit-wide vector processing unit that can process 16 single-precision or 8 double-precision elements per clock cycle. The parallelism of multiple instruction multiple data with a minimum memory bandwidth of 140 GB/s provides up to 1 TFLOP of double-precision performance in a single chip. Hence, Xeon Phi has been widely applied in high-performance computation.

To support the simultaneous computation and communication of a significant number of cores, three high-speed, ring-based bidirectional on-die interconnections are set. These interconnections consist of a data bus, a control bus, and an address bus. All of the cores with the caches, such as *tag directories* (TDs) and GDDR5 *memory controllers* (MCs), are interconnected with these rings. The KNC architecture is illustrated in Fig. 1.

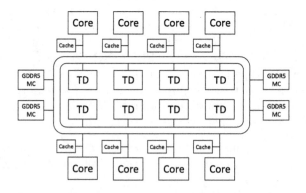

Fig. 1. Knight corner architecture

A KNC processor provides either 8 or 16 GB main memory. Each core has a 32 KB L1 cache and a 512 KB L2 cache. Unlike in multi-core architectures such as Sandy Bridge, which maintains cache coherence with the implementation of directory-based cache coherence protocols on the last level cache, KNC integrates *distributed tag directory* (DTD) into its structure. This directory assists in sending the referenced memory address to a correspondent TD on the ring when a core misses a private cache. Then, the TD initiates data transfer between the core connected to this cache line and the core that requires this line. If the cache line is not held by any core, then the request is sent to a MC. A well-designed hash function ensures that requests are evenly distributed to 64 TDs. The complicated process introduces additional overhead. Thus, reducing private cache miss rate improves overall performance.

It is convenient to migrate the code optimized for multi-core processor to co-processor. *Message passing interfaces* (MPIs) are also supported in common application program interfaces, such as OpenMP [13]. Xeon Phi can not only run in offloading mode controlled by a host as other co-processors but also can run independently in native mode. This characteristic enhances the flexibility of the programing on Xeon Phi.

Much academic work has been conducted on many-core processors. *Core-map count-based priority* (CMCP) [9,10] is a page replacement policy based on the number of CPU cores mapped. Many-core processors that apply this policy perform better than those that follow the *least recently used* (LRU) and first-in first-out policies. In addition, Ramos *et al.* built an intuitive performance model for a cache-coherent SMP system and proposed several optimized algorithms based on this model [22]. The follow-up evaluation showed that the performance of the modified algorithms improved by approximately four times. Liao *et al.* [16] studied a runtime system that supports collaborative scheduling with CPU and Xeon Phi. The overall speedup ratio can be improved by more than three times. To reduce the overhead introduced by coherence protocol, Wang *et al.* propose an approach to dynamically identify the shared memory blocks at cache block level [23]. This approach can on an average reduce the coherence overhead by 77 %.

2.2 Bloom Filter and Its Generalizations

Bloom filter are space saving data structures for checking of membership of elements. This structure consists of a m-bit vector. Each element x_i of set S is mapped by k independent hash functions $h_j(x_i)$ to the bit vector. The index range of this vector belongs to $[0, m)$. In the initial state, all bits in the bit vector are set to a value of zero. When an element is inserted into bloom filter, k hash functions generate k indices of bit vector. The value of these bits are set to one. As such, for a membership query, if k mapped bits are all one in value, the membership query result is positive, otherwise, the result is negative.

The cost of space saving lies in the errors generated in the query process results. The queried element may not exist in the set if the result is positive, because the bits with a value of one may all belong to the others elements with a low probability. The probability is *false positive ratio* (FPR). Obviously, the number of hash functions is positively related to FPR. By contrast, the number of inserted elements and the bit vector length are negatively related to FPR. This ratio can be calculated as [5]:

$$P_{FP} = \left(1 - \left(1 - \frac{1}{m}\right)^{kn}\right)^k \approx \left(1 - e^{\frac{-kn}{m}}\right)^k \tag{1}$$

where n indicates the number of inserted elements, m indicates the bit vector length, and k indicates the number of hash functions. The optimal k that minimizes FPR is obtained with:

$$k = \ln 2 \cdot \frac{m}{n} \tag{2}$$

In a standard bloom filter, a membership query introduces k memory accesses in the worst case. The common optimization method involves reducing the number of memory accesses, such as in the *Bloom-1 filter* [20]. It requires only one memory access. The k indices calculated by hash functions are mapped into a continuous block, and the block size is equal to the size of a cache line (64 B) that can be fetched by processors in one memory access.

Counting bloom filter (CBF) [8] are a generalization of bloom filters. CBFs provide delete operations. In CBFs, each bit in the vector represents a counter. The counter is used to record the number of the bits mapped by elements. These k-mapped counters increase in number if an element is inserted into CBF; these counters decrease in number if the element is deleted.

Many researchers have recently studied bloom filter extensively. Hao *et al.* proposed a partitioned hashing method [11] that maps keys into multiple groups and selects corresponding hash functions for each group. The FPR is reduced through this method. *dlCBF* [4] is a generalization of CBF that reduces memory consumption by 27 % and maintains FPR. Kirsch *et al.* implemented a bloom filter including two random hash functions without increasing FPR [15]. This bloom filter requires less computation and memory access. Bloom filters are also applied to new devices. *BloomFlash* [7] was designed for the SSD characteristics. It adopts the bulk-update method to reduce the random writes on flash. Moreover, the flash locality is improved by hierarchical vectors. Ma *et al.* implemented a bloom filter on the GPU [18] and built a performance model to quantify the tradeoffs between throughput and FPR. Yi *et at.* presents *Par-BF*[17] for dynamic data sets. Par-BF also applies multiple matching threads to achieve higher throughput. The main difference between their work with ours is Par-BF focuses on boosting single request, and our work focuses on boosting batch requests.

3   Theoretical Analysis

In this section, we design a standard counting bloom filter for many-core platforms, and analyze the performance using a theoretical method. We choose Xeon Phi as experiment platforms. The goals are to identify the bottlenecks in traditional design and to disclose the huge gap on programming methods between the multi-core processors with many-core processors.

3.1 Standard Bloom Filter

We design a CBF in a multi-thread environment. The key to achieve excellent parallel performance is by selecting the appropriate granularity for applications. Bloom filter can be parallelized in two aspects. First, tasks are assigned to threads in unit of hash functions. All threads compute the hash function of one or several requests simultaneously. For one membership query, barrier synchronization is necessary to ensure that all computations are completed before judging whether or not this element is in the set. This task-division approach increases communication overhead among threads after computation. Moreover, the number of threads is limited by the number of hash functions. Second, tasks are divided into threads in unit of requests. Each thread processes independent tasks. The extra synchronization overhead is avoided. Hence, we regard requests as task granularity.

During the parallel processing, the modification operations on vector bits may conflict with other modification operations or query operations. We implement spin locks on bit vectors to ensure the operations atomicity. The granularity of locks also affects processing performance. The use of coarse-grained locks limits scalability. Fine-grained locks provide improved scalability, but such locks also generate single critical section that can protect few bits. Thus, a single request requires additional lock operations. In the current study, we consider the number of locks that is equal to the number of hardware threads.

3.2 Memory Access Pattern

We must to analyze the memory access pattern to measure the overall memory system performance. One bloom filter request introduces k memory accesses. When one core of a many-core processor accesses the memory, three scenarios can occur: local cache hit, remote cache hit, and cache miss. Each scenario introduces different overheads. The overall requests throughput depends on the percentage of each scenario with its overhead. Hence, we design two experiments to obtain the performance indicators.

First, we conduct a synthetic experiment to determine the proportion of each scenario. The ratio of local cache hit is represented by R_L; the ratio of remote cache hit is denoted by R_R; and the ratio of cache miss is represented by R_M. We synthesize a group of random bloom filter requests sets, where each set contains different ratios of query, insert and delete requests. The ratios can be presented as $R_{Q,I,D}$. Each element in the requests has the same proportion. To ensure the correctness of delete operations, the existence of the item in the vector must be recognized before the corresponding bits are modified. All bloom filter requests are evenly distributed to threads by a mapping function, and the hash functions presumably map elements to each bit equally. The bloom filter vector is divided into multiple sub-vectors; the size of a sub-vector is equal to that of a cache line. When a thread accesses a sub-vector, the corresponding cache line is fetched from the local cache.

In our experiments, we simulate a C-core processor. The private cache of each core can contain N cache lines. Cache coherency is maintained via a directory-based Modified-Exclusive-Shared-Invalid protocol, which is widely used by multi- and many-core processors. Let parameters $N_{M,E,S,I}$ represent the number of each state cache lines in each state, the sum of the lines is determined by:

$$N = N_M + N_E + N_S + N_I \tag{3}$$

Moreover, N_V represents the number of valid cache lines:

$$N_V = N_M + N_E + N_S \tag{4}$$

The cache miss rate can be calculated as:

$$p_{miss} = 1 - \frac{N_V}{M} \tag{5}$$

Let the $p_{r,w}$ represent the proportion of the read and write operations respectively. These variables can by easily to calculated as:

$$
\begin{aligned}
p_r &= \frac{R_Q + R_D}{R_Q + R_I + 2R_D} \\
p_w &= \frac{R_I + R_D}{R_Q + R_I + 2R_D}
\end{aligned}
\tag{6}
$$

We build an iterative method to calculate expected number of cache lines in each state during processing. In consideration of the random input data, these expectations are equal in all cores. Suppose each core references a memory address and prefetches the corresponding cache line in each iteration. Operations on cache lines change the parameters. All parameters will converge to a stable value after numerous iterations.

We choose random replacement as the cache algorithm because the random input cannot utilize the locality. Furthermore, this replacement is simpler to design than the LRU algorithm is. Specifically, N_I increases when remote cores broadcast cache invalidations, and decreases when the invalid cache lines are evicted because of local cache miss. If N_I is less than 0 after one iteration, then the rate of invalid cache lines being evicted is greater than the increase rate. We define the absolute value of N_I as N_{evict}:

$$N_{evict} = p_{miss} - \frac{(C-1)p_w N_V^{(t-1)}}{M} - N_I^{(t-1)} \tag{7}$$

where N_{evict} represents the expected number of valid cache lines evicted when $N_I < 0$ in one iteration, otherwise $N_{evict} = 0$.

To calculate the other parameters conveniently, we define N_D as expected number of distinct cache lines in the global cache divided by C. N_D increases when the core reads a cache line that does not exists in the global cache, and decreases when local cache lines are evicted:

$$N_D^{(t)} = 1 + N_D^{(t-1)} \left(1 - \frac{C}{M} - \frac{N_{evict}}{N} \right) \tag{8}$$

N_M increases when the core writes a local cache line whose state is unmodified, and decreases when the modified cache lines are read/written by remote cores:

$$N_M^{(t)} = N_M^{(t-1)} \left(1 - \frac{C - 1 + p_w}{M} - \frac{N_{evict}}{N} \right) + p_w \tag{9}$$

N_E increases when the core reads a cache line that has not been fetched from the global cache, and decreases when the local exclusive cache lines are written by any core, or are evicted:

$$N_E^{(t)} = N_E^{(t-1)} \left(1 - \frac{C - 1 + p_w}{M} - \frac{N_{evict}}{N} \right) + p_r \left(1 - \frac{CN_D^{(t-1)}}{M} \right) \tag{10}$$

N_S increases when the core reads a remote cache lines, and decreases when the shared cache lines are either written by any cores, or are evicted:

$$N_S^{(t)} = N_S^{(t-1)} \left(1 - \frac{Cp_w}{M} - \frac{N_{evict}}{N} \right) + \frac{(C - 1)p_r N_D^{(t-1)}}{M} \tag{11}$$

The proportion of $R_{L,R,M}$ can be calculated as:

$$\begin{aligned} R_L &= \frac{N_V}{M} \\ R_R &= \frac{CN_D}{M} - R_L \\ R_M &= 1 - \frac{CN_D}{M} \end{aligned} \tag{12}$$

The iterative method will converge when the difference between the parameters $N_X^{(t)}$ with $N_X^{(t-1)}$ is less than 10^{-6}.

Second, we design an experiment to measure the latency of each scenario on the many-core processor Xeon Phi 5110P. The latency of the local cache L_L can be measured using a pointer-chasing benchmark. In this benchmark, a thread bound to one core traverses linked lists with different sizes and strides. We can obtain the latency of each cache level by adjusting the size. When the list can be held within the local cache, the latency of accessing local cache L_L is approximately 8.2 ns. Moreover, data is fetched from main memory and the latency L_M is roughly 280.0 ns when the size of the list is greater than 512 KB. This size is beyond the L2 cache of KNC. We use BenchIT [19] benchmark to measure the latency of remote cache L_R. The benchmark creates two threads T_0 on core 0 and T_1 on different cores. T_0 generates data with three types of coherency states M, E, S in its local cache and then measures the latency of the T_1 reading the data produced by T_0. The results are shown in Table 1.

The latency of accessing the remote cache is approximately 240 ns. The result differs significantly from the results of the other scenario. No distinct relationship is detected between latency and the distance of cores or coherency state, hence we choose the mean value of L_R at 240.4.

Table 1. Latency in nanoseconds

	Modified	Exclusive	Shared	RAM
Local		8.2		280.0
Core 1	245.1	238.2	240.7	
Core 15	239.3	239.4	241.0	
Core 30	242.5	238.4	239.1	

The average latency of memory access can be calculated as:

$$L = L_L \times R_L + L_R \times R_R + L_M \times R_M \qquad (13)$$

We implement a 60 MB bloom filter. This bloom filter is processed by a 60-core processor. Each core contains a 512 KB private cache and the proportion of write operations is 20 %. Hence $N = 8192$ and $M = 983040$ when the size of one cache line is 64 B and $p_w = 0.2$. Under such a condition, L is equal to 263.51 ns, which is close to the value of L_M. This finding implies that standard bloom filter cannot exploit locality effectively.

4   Design

In this section, we propose a PBF, that runs on many-core processors with improved scalability and high throughput. Unlike in the traditional method, partition and sort phases are introduced into our design. In partition phase, all requests are divided into distinct sets. The order of requests is disrupted during this phase. To ensure the sequential consistency of results, each set of requests is sorted based on the timestamp in the sort phase. Finally, threads acquire request sets and respond to these requests in the sub-vectors of the threads themselves.

4.1   Partition Phase

The input of partition phase is a batch of requests, and the output is multiple request sets. The number of sets is equal to the number of threads. Requests are divided into different threads by using the hash function h_0, which is called the partition function on the key of elements. Each thread processes only process the elements divided by itself; therefore, the size of the memory space accessed by the single thread decreases. This finding suggests that partition can improve scalability and locality significantly.

The two common partition methods are the share buffer and multi-pass partition methods [2,14]. To conveniently clarify the methods in detail, we suppose that m requests are arranged in an array order by a timestamp. These requests are partitioned into n sets by t threads. The generated request sets are n arrays, which are allocated in advance.

Share Buffer Method. This method creates a total of n buffers in total. When a thread writes an output buffer, the thread must acquire the tail index of the array in an atomic operation, such as the *__sync_fetch_and_add*. Then, the data are written. This method does not consume additional memory, but instead introduces synchronization overhead. This overhead is composed of two parts. The first part is the idle time spent waiting to acquire locks. The second part is the cache consistency overhead. An example is shown in Fig. 2. This piece of OpenMP code can be executed serially. When we increase the number of threads N, the execution time also multiplies although the total number of loops remains the constant. The main reason for the degraded performance is that numerous RFO operations are triggered on an interconnect bus when multiple threads write the memory chunk of a lock frequently.

```
1  #pragma parallel for num_threads(N)
2  for (int i = 0; i < M; i++) {
3      pthread_spin_lock(&lock);
4      //empty critical section
5      pthread_spin_unlock(&lock);
6  }
```

Fig. 2. A case of acquire/release lock in parallel

Multi-pass Partition Method. This method is *offline*, unlike the methods described above. Thus, the entire input must be available before partitioning, and two or more times scans are required [14]. In our design, the requests arrive in batches, and the partition method receives a batch of requests each time. During the first pass of method, each thread gets a continuous block of request arrays, and counts the number of elements for each partition in the block. The numbers of each partition as counted by different threads are stored in an array. We can obtain the offset that each thread begins to write by calculating the prefix sum of this array. After the calculation, each thread writes the requests from its own block into output buffers at a corresponding offset during the second pass. This method also voids contentions between two threads and introduces fewer cache and *translation lookaside buffer* (TLB) misses than the share buffer method does. However, the multi-pass process requires two scans which increases computational overhead.

4.2 Sort Phase

A batch of requests is divided equally to all threads in the design of standard bloom filter on many-core. The query and modify requests to an element are spread across different threads. When all threads execute actions concurrently, the order of thread execution would affect the query request results. This situation may introduce false negative and false positive errors. In our design, all requests of one element are divided into single partitions. The requests in each partition buffer are assigned to different orders by using various partition methods. Hence, after partition phase, we sort each partition buffer by a timestamp of requests for this program after the partition to satisfy the sequential consistency. These sort processes can be parallelized easily, and we bind each sort process on a specific hardware thread.

4.3 Response Phase

In our design, the bloom filter vector is composed of t sub-vectors, whose length is denoted by w. Each thread acquires an exclusive sub-vector and processes a partition of requests on the thread. Moreover, we modify the hash functions. The new functions introduce $k - 1$ memory accesses per request on the sub-vector instead of the entire vector. During one membership check, the standard bloom filter generates $k \cdot \log_2(w \times t)$ hash bits. The bloom filter for many core processors uses $\log_2 t$ bits generated by h_0 to first locate the sub-vector. The rest of the hash functions $h_{1,2,...,k}$ generate $(k - 1) \cdot \log_2 w$ bits to locate the counters.

Our design decreases the size of the memory space accessed by a single thread and eliminates the overlap of memory areas among threads. The operations on the same memory block are executed sequentially, therefore locks need not to be used to prevent conflicts between operations in same element. As in the sort phase, each response process is bound on a specific hardware thread. To improve cache locality and minimize cache pollution, we apply the software prefetch instructions to read requests and to write results.

4.4 Analysis

In this section, we analyze the performance of bloom filter on many-core processors. In our design, we reduce the range of memory access per hardware thread and eliminate the overlap memory areas shared by multiple threads. Therefore, the actual vector size for each request decreases. The use of the exclusive sub-vector increases the local cache hit ratio, and reduces the average latency of memory access in the response phase.

FPR. Let F present the false positive event. X is a random variable for the number of elements mapped in the same sub-vector, and x is a constant in the range of $[0, n]$. We can calculate the conditional probability F when $X = x$ as follows:

$$P(F|X = x) = \left(1 - \left(1 - \frac{1}{m/t}\right)^{x(k-1)}\right)^{k-1} \tag{14}$$

Suppose the partition function can divide elements into each sub-vector equally, hence, X follows the binomial distribution $B(n, \frac{1}{t})$. The probability of X is:

$$P(X = x) = \binom{n}{x} \left(\frac{1}{t}\right)^x \left(\frac{t-1}{t}\right)^{n-x} \tag{15}$$

Hence, we can derive the *FPR*:

$$
\begin{aligned}
P_{FP} &= \sum_{x=0}^{n} \left(P(F|X=x) \cdot P(X=x) \right) \\
&= \sum_{x=0}^{n} \left(1 - \left(1 - \frac{t}{m}\right)^{x(k-1)} \right)^{k-1} \cdot \binom{n}{x} \left(\frac{1}{t}\right)^{x} \left(\frac{t-1}{t}\right)^{n-x}
\end{aligned}
\tag{16}
$$

In Fig. 3, we compare the FPRs of CBF and PBF when we choose $m = 3866624$, $t = 59$ and $k = 10$. The horizontal axis load factor represents the ratio of the vector length to the number of inserted elements. The FPR of PBF is significantly lower than that of CBF when the load factor is in the range of $[0.073, 1]$. In addition, the FPR of PBF is slightly higher than that of CBF when the load factor is in the of range of $[0, 0.073]$, and the maximum deviation is less than 3.5×10^{-5}.

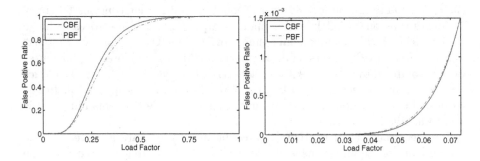

Fig. 3. The false positive ratio of CBF and PBF

Average Memory Access Latency. In PBF, each thread processes requests on an exclusive sub-vector. The transmission of cache lines between two threads is eliminated. Therefore, we must modify our iterative method to measure the latency in the new design. In the previous experiments, no distinctive relationship is identified between latency and coherency. Therefore, we apply only N_V and N_I to measure the proportion of each scenario with new method. Specifically, N_I decreases when the invalid cache lines are evicted. The N_{evict} is defined as:

$$
N_{evict} = N_I^{(t-1)} \frac{C-M}{M}
\tag{17}
$$

This variable represents the expected number of valid cache lines evicted when $N_I < 0$ in one iteration, otherwise $N_{evict} = 0$. N_V increases when the core references a line that does not exist in the local cache and decreases when local cache lines are evicted:

$$
N_V^{(t)} = N_V^{(t-1)} \frac{M-C}{M} + 1
\tag{18}
$$

Average memory access latency L can be measured via Eq. 13. Moreover, latency is affected by vector size and cache capacity. This condition is similar to that described in Sect. 3, and L is equal to 141.80 ns. This result indicates that our method improves the memory access performance effectively.

5   Evaluation

In this section, we evaluate the performance of PBF. First, we introduce the evaluation environment and method. The experiments emphasize three aspects, including memory access performance, scalability, and the SMT effect. Finally, we compare PBF with CBF on realistic datasets, and the reason behind the performance gap is analyzed.

5.1   Evaluation Setup

The experiments are performed on a Xeon Phi 5110P that contains 60 cores. Each core runs on 1.05 GHz and supports 4-way SMT. The co-processor has a private cache of 32 MB and a main memory of 8 GB GDDR5. *Manycore Platform Software Stack* (MPSS) version 3.2.3 is used in this study. Moreover, all source codes is complied by Intel C++ Compiler XE 15.0.0.090 with -O2 flag. To reduce the performance effect from TLB miss, 2 MB is used as the page size. In the performed experiments, 59 cores are used at most, while the remaining core is used to handle system calls.

Internet traces from CAIDA [1] are obtained, which are gathered by the passive monitor Equinix-SanJose in 2014, and test sets are generated from the IP flows. Each test set is divided into two parts. The first part only contains insert requests to initialize the bloom filter vector. After the initialization, the fill rate of the bloom filter is about 0.2. The second part contains 16 M requests, including 60 % query requests, 20 % insert requests and 20 % delete requests.

5.2   Memory Access Performance

To compare the memory performance between PBF and CBF, we need to eliminate the performance impact introduced by locks in CBF. More specifically, the wrong results are ignored, and the code of the *lock/unlock* operations in CBF is deleted. The average execution time of the response phase in PBF and the total execution time of CBF using 59 cores are plotted in Fig. 4.

Experiment results verify the theoretical analysis findings postulating that the memory access performance of PBF is considerably higher than that of CBF. The execution time of CBF is approximately 1.10 s as a result of the poor cache hit rate. This time is marginally affected by an increase in vector size. In PBF, each sub-vector can fit into the L1 cache when the vector is smaller than 0.9 MB. Computation time is the main component of execution time. When the vector is larger than 0.9 MB and is smaller than roughly 26 MB, the sub-vector and temporary data can fit into the L2 cache. Execution time increases rapidly and

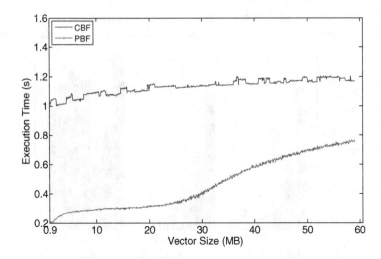

Fig. 4. The execution time of CBF and PBF with various size of vector

remains stable at approximately 0.28 s. When the vector is larger than 26 MB, the sub-vector and temporary data cannot fit into the L2 cache. Cache miss rate increases as vector size increases. Memory latency becomes the main component of execution time. Hence, it is much helpful to improve throughput by building a bloom filter fitted into cache.

5.3 Scalability

In this section, we compare the performance of PBF with that of CBF in an environment with various numbers of cores. The execution times of CBF and PBF are shown in Fig. 5. Moreover, the time of the partition and sort phases are counted in the overhead. We also present the calculated speedup ratio in Table 2.

CBF is scalable when a small number of threads is applied. However, speedup ratio does not increase significantly with an increase in the number of cores. This lack of increase is caused by the cost of lock acquisition which offsets the performance improvement introduced by parallel processing. The result of PBF with share buffer partition method is similar to that of CBF. We use the synchronization primitives in the partition phase. Hence, overhead may also increase although we add more threads. The PBF processed with the multi-pass partition method reports a speedup ratio of 43.92x when we adopt a large number of threads. Nonetheless, execution time is longer than that recorded when the share buffer partition method is applied in certain case because computation overhead is increased by the use of the multi-pass partition method. Therefore, the application of lockless methods in many-core platforms enhances performance.

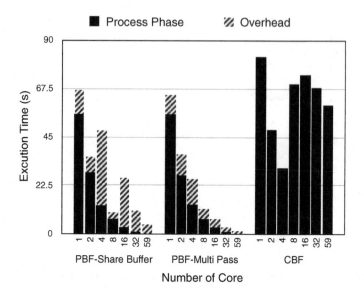

Fig. 5. The execution time with various number of cores

Table 2. The speedup of CBF and PBF

	CBF	PBF-share buff	PBF-multi pass
1	82.09 (1.00)	66.66 (1.00)	64.56 (1.00)
2	48.04 (1.70)	35.38 (1.88)	36.95 (1.75)
4	30.43 (2.70)	48.16 (1.38)	25.49 (2.53)
8	69.19 (1.19)	9.75 (6.84)	10.85 (5.95)
16	73.64 (1.11)	25.70 (2.59)	6.88 (9.38)
32	67.57 (1.21)	10.58 (6.30)	3.00 (21.52)
59	59.44 (1.38)	4.13 (16.14)	1.47 (43.92)

5.4   The Impact of SMT

Common SMT technologies include Hyper-Threading, which is an effective way
of utilizing hardware resources. SMT can hide the latencies of lock acquisition
and memory by switching contexts. In this section, we evaluate the execution
time of PBF on a 30 MB vector with 59 cores with two to four ways SMT, as
depicted Fig. 6. The execution time of the partition phase is reduced by 85 %
when the share buffer partition method is adopted and two or more threads
used in one core. The PBF processed with the multi-pass partition method
displays a maximum speedup ratio of 80.7x with three-ways SMT. The main
contribution of the multi-pass partition method to performance improvement is
through the hiding of memory latency, therefore, execution time is reduced by
only approximately 35 %. Additionally, the execution time of the process phase

increases when we employ more than three threads per core. The proportion of memory latency in the process phase is small when a vector fits into the cache. Hence, the process phase can be considered as a computation-intensive task. This task cannot exploit SMT effectually.

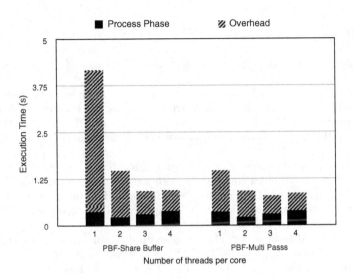

Fig. 6. SMT experiments of PBF

6 Conclusion and Future Work

Exploiting more and more parallelism is current research trend. Developers are greatly challenged in terms of designing high-performance applications on increasingly complex processors. In this study, we first build an iterative model to analyze the memory performance of bloom filters. The bottleneck in standard design is caused by the inefficient utilization of cache locality and the cost of lock acquisition. We then design a PBF that undergoes partition, sort and response phases.

We also evaluate CBF and PBF on many-core processors. The memory access performance of PBF improves by more than three times. In addition, PBF exhibits improved scalability. The speedup ratio reaches a maximum of 80.7x when we use 177 threads. Finally, performance is mainly improved by reducing the amount of data shared among threads on many-core processors.

In the future, we plan to design a key-value store database based on many-core co-processors. This database supports complex database operations. Additionally, the cooperative process with CPUs will be incorporated to improve the overall throughput further.

Acknowledgments. This paper is supported by National High-tech Research and Development Program of China (863 Program) under grant No. 2012AA010905, National Natural Science Foundation of China under grant No. 61322210, 61272408, 61433019, Doctoral Fund of Ministry of Education of China under grant No. 20130142110048.

References

1. CAIDA: The cooperative association for internet data analysis. http://www.caida. org/data/
2. Balkesen, C., Teubner, J., Alonso, G., Özsu, M.T.: Main-memory hash joins on multi-core CPUs: tuning to the underlying hardware. In: Proceedings of the 29th IEEE International Conference on Data Engineering (ICDE), pp. 362–373 (2013)
3. Bloom, B.H.: Space/time trade-offs in hash coding with allowable errors. Commun. ACM **13**(7), 422–426 (1970)
4. Bonomi, F., Mitzenmacher, M., Panigrahy, R., Singh, S., Varghese, G.: An improved construction for counting bloom filters. In: Azar, Y., Erlebach, T. (eds.) ESA 2006. LNCS, vol. 4168, pp. 684–695. Springer, Heidelberg (2006)
5. Broder, A., Mitzenmacher, M.: Network applications of bloom filters: a survey. Internet Math. **1**(4), 485–509 (2004)
6. Broder, A.Z., Mitzenmacher, M.: Using multiple hash functions to improve IP lookups. In: Proceedings of the IEEE INFOCOM, pp. 1454–1463 (2001)
7. Debnath, B.K., Sengupta, S., Li, J., Lilja, D.J., Du, D.H.: Bloomflash: bloom filter on flash-based storage. In: Proceedings of the International Conference on Distributed Computing Systems (ICDCS), pp. 635–644 (2011)
8. Fan, L., Cao, P., Almeida, J., Broder, A.Z.: Summary cache: a scalable wide-area web cache sharing protocol. IEEE/ACM Trans. Netw. (TON) **8**(3), 281–293 (2000)
9. Gerofi, B., Shimada, A., Hori, A., Ishikawa, Y.: Partially separated page tables for efficient operating system assisted hierarchical memory management on heterogeneous architectures. In: Proceedings of the 13th IEEE/ACM International Symposium on Cluster, Cloud, and Grid Computing (CCGrid), pp. 360–368 (2013)
10. Gerofi, B., Shimada, A., Hori, A., Masamichi, T., Ishikawa, Y.: CMCP: a novel page replacement policy for system level hierarchical memory management on many-cores. In: Proceedings of the 23rd International Symposium on High-performance Parallel and Distributed Computing (HPDC), pp. 73–84 (2014)
11. Hao, F., Kodialam, M.S., Lakshman, T.V.: Building high accuracy bloom filters using partitioned hashing. In: Proceedings of the 2007 ACM International Conference on Measurement and Modeling of Computer Systems (SIGMETRICS), pp. 277–288 (2007)
12. Huang, K., Zhang, J., Zhang, D., Xie, G., Salamatian, K., Liu, A.X., Li, W.: A multi-partitioning approach to building fast and accurate counting bloom filters. In: Proceedings of the 27th IEEE International Symposium on Parallel and Distributed Processing (IPDPS), pp. 1159–1170 (2013)
13. Jeffers, J., Reinders, J.: Intel Xeon Phi Coprocessor High Performance Programming. Newnes, Boston (2013)
14. Kim, C., Sedlar, E., Chhugani, J., Kaldewey, T., Nguyen, A.D., Blas, A.D., Lee, V.W., Satish, N., Dubey, P.: Sort vs. hash revisited: fast join implementation on modern multi-core CPUs. Proc. VLDB Endowment **2**(2), 1378–1389 (2009)

15. Kirsch, A., Mitzenmacher, M.: Less hashing, same performance: building a better bloom filter. In: Azar, Y., Erlebach, T. (eds.) ESA 2006. LNCS, vol. 4168, pp. 456–467. Springer, Heidelberg (2006)

16. Liao, X., Xiang, X., Jin, H., Zhang, W., Lu, F.: Hostosink: a collaborative scheduling in heterogeneous environment. In: Sun, X., Qu, W., Stojmenovic, I., Zhou, W., Li, Z., Guo, H., Min, G., Yang, T., Wu, Y., Liu, L. (eds.) ICA3PP 2014, Part I. LNCS, vol. 8630, pp. 214–228. Springer, Heidelberg (2014)

17. Liu, Y., Ge, X., Du, D.H., Huang, X.: Par-BF: a parallel partitioned bloom filter for dynamic data sets. In: Proceedings of the 2014 International Workshop on Data Intensive Scalable Computing Systems (DISCS), pp. 1–8 (2014)

18. Ma, L., Chamberlain, R.D., Buhler, J.D., Franklin, M.A.: Bloom filter performance on graphics engines. In: Proceedings of the International Conference on Parallel Processing (ICPP), pp. 522–531 (2011)

19. Molka, D., Hackenberg, D., Schöne, R., Müller, M.S.: Memory performance and cache coherency effects on an Intel Nehalem multiprocessor system. In: Proceedings of the 18th International Conference on Parallel Architectures and Compilation Techniques (PACT), pp. 261–270 (2009)

20. Qiao, Y., Li, T., Chen, S.: One memory access bloom filters and their generalization. In: Proceedings of the IEEE INFOCOM, pp. 1745–1753 (2011)

21. Rahman, R.: Intel Xeon Phi Coprocessor Architecture and Tools: The Guide for Application Developers. Apress, Berkeley (2013)

22. Ramos, S., Hoefler, T.: Modeling communication in cache-coherent SMP systems: a case-study with Xeon Phi. In: Proceedings of the 22nd International Symposium on High-Performance Parallel and Distributed Computing (HPDC), pp. 97–108 (2013)

23. Wang, H., Wang, R., Luan, Z., Qian, X., Qian, D.: Improving multiprocessor performance with fine-grain coherence bypass. SCIENCE CHINA Inf. Sci. 58(1), 1–15 (2015)

A List Scheduling Algorithm for DAG-Based Parallel Computing Models

Hao Fu, Ce Yu$^{(\boxtimes)}$, Jizhou Sun, Mengmeng Wang, and Jun Du

School of Computer Science and Technology, Tianjin University,
Tianjin 300072, China
{haofu,yuce,jzsun,mmwang,tjudujun}@tju.edu.cn

Abstract. Task scheduling on multiprocessor system is a well-known problem in area of parallel computing. For this problem, many static scheduling algorithms have been reported. But in most static algorithms, only one attribute of tasks is considered when constructing a ready list, which consists of all ready tasks, and there is no evaluation for different task attributes.

In this paper, a list scheduling algorithm for DAG-based parallel computing models is proposed. It is mainly designed for reducing the scheduling length of applications with regular DAG models. Eight task attributes in the DAG model are evaluated, and corresponding rules are presented, which will be used in constructing the ready list. And when scheduling tasks, its start time and communication cost on idle processors are taken into consideration. Experimental results show that the proposed algorithm can achieve a significant performance improvement, which is up to 142%.

Keywords: CAEST · CAEST scheduling algorithm · DP algorithms · Scheduling algorithm · List scheduling algorithm

1 Introduction

Scheduling is a key problem in parallel computing. The basic goal of scheduling is to dispatch tasks to processor elements reasonably and optimally. Most of scheduling problems have been proved to be NP-hard [1,2]. In order to study these problems, researchers always make several simple assumptions [3,4]. But the scheduling problem is still NP-hard, even in a very simple situation. Besides, polynomial time algorithms are available in some special cases. One is to schedule tasks with a tree structure task graph onto any number of processors. Another is to schedule tasks with a random task graph onto two processors. All tasks in both cases take uniform computing time [5,6]. Even within the two cases mentioned above, communication cost between tasks is ignored. And it has been proved that these two scheduling problems are NP-hard when communication cost is taken into account [7].

Many parallel application can be described as node- and edge-weighted directed acyclic graph (DAG) model. List scheduling algorithms for this model

G. Wang et al. (Eds.): ICA3PP 2015, Part II, LNCS 9529, pp. 406–419, 2015.
DOI: 10.1007/978-3-319-27122-4_28

can always be divided into two part: construction of a ready list and allocation of ready tasks. When constructing the ready list, many list scheduling algorithms just use one task attribute as the priority, which can simplify the construction of ready list. But when two or more tasks are assigned with the same priority, there is no reasonable strategy to break the tie. In this paper, we select and evaluate eight widely used task attributes, and rank them according to their influences on the scheduling length of applications. Algorithms adopting these rules may be more complex than others in the stage of constructing ready list, but it can offer a better result. While compared with dynamic scheduling algorithm, static scheduling algorithm has smaller complexity. So we propose a new static scheduling algorithm for DAG-based parallel computing models named Communication-aware Earliest Start Time (CAEST) scheduling algorithm, which is mainly designed for applications with regular DAG models. By taking all the eight rules into consideration to construct the list of ready tasks and making use of start time and communication time of tasks on idle processor elements, we can get a significant improvement on the scheduling length.

The remainder of this paper is organized as follows. Section 2 lists the related works. Section 3 introduces the DAG data driven model. Section 4 presents a detailed definition used in this paper. The introduction to CAEST algorithm is given in Sect. 5. And Sect. 6 presents experimental results. Section 7 concludes this paper and discusses the future works.

2   Related Work

The scheduling problem is still a hot topic in computer science, on which many significant works have been done. Recent years, with the emergence and development of various emerging disciplines, numbers of researches are devoted to the scheduling problem, such as researches on generic algorithm, artificial neural network, and artificial intelligence.

As for the scheduling model part, scientists have tried creating algorithms with data structure like tree, graph and fork-join pair. At present, several typical task scheduling models, which are also known as the task graph, are based on the graph theory. For example, (1) Task Interaction Graph (TIG) model, (2) Task Precedence Graph (TPG) model [8], (3) DAG model. Strictly, the DAG model is just a special TPG model, and is widely used in describing many problems. In most scheduling problems, the DAG model and the TPG model are regarded as identical. Based on the DAG model, a programming model named DAG data driven model is presented in [9], which is introduced in Sect. 3 in detail.

For static scheduling problems, most algorithms use the technology based on list scheduling [10,11]. In the list scheduling algorithm, a scheduling list of ready tasks is established first, and all these ready tasks are sorted in a particular order according to their attributes. Then the system should repeat following steps till the scheduling of all these tasks is completed: (1) choosing a task from the ready list; (2) scheduling this task onto a processor element. The priority of a task can be determined by various ways, such as Critical Path(CP), Longest Path (LP), Highest Level First (HLF), and Longest Processing Time (LPT) [12–14]. But how to find a suitable priority, there is no introduction before. In this paper, we evaluate eight attributes to find reasonable priorities for constructing ready list.

There have been several approaches to the tasks allocating problem in a multiprocessor system. Sih, G.C. and Lee, E. A. proposed an algorithm named Dynamic Level Scheduling (DLS) [15], which uses an attribute called *dynamic level* (DL) as its priority to construct ready list. Earliest Time First Algorithm (ETF) [16] is given by Jing-Jang Hwang and Yuan-Chieh Chow etc. M. Y. Wu and D. D. Gajski presented Modified Critical Path algorithm (MCP) [17], and it takes the as late as possible start time (ALAP) of a node as priority. Insertion Scheduling Heuristic algorithm (ISH) mentioned in [18] uses *static b-level* as its priority. In CAEST algorithm mentioned in this paper, more than one attribute are considered, which is based on our attributes evaluation. When scheduling nodes on the list, earliest start time of this nodes on all available processor elements is taken and communication cost is used to break ties.

3   DAG Data Driven Model

In bioinformatics and scientific computing, DAG model is often used to describe the data dependencies and precedence relationship between tasks. Each node in this model represents a task and each directed edge represents the dependency between two tasks. Nodes with zero indegree are current computable tasks. A simple DAG diagram is provided in Fig. 1. Nodes in this figure represent tasks of a parallel application, and directed edges represent the communication relationship or precedence constraints between nodes.

Inspired by the simplicity of parallel programming and the purpose of reusability, the DAG data driven model is presented in [9], and shown in Fig. 2. It is composed of three modules: User Application Module, DAG Pattern Module, and DAG Runtime System Module. Several steps that the programmer needs to follow are presented in the user application module. The DAG pattern module

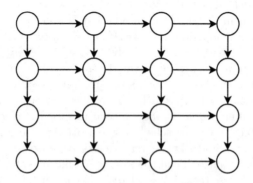

Fig. 1. A simple DAG diagram

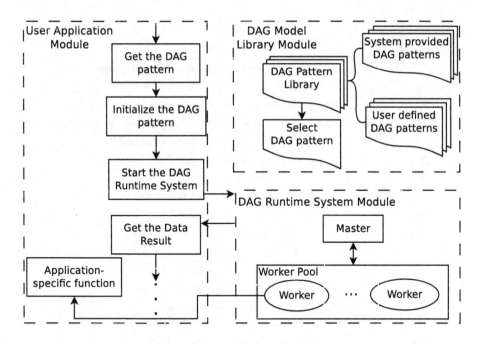

Fig. 2. The DAG data driven model diagram

establishes a DAG pattern library, in which there are lots of DAG patterns provided by the system or defined by users. The DAG runtime system module is responsible for the task allocation and scheduling algorithms according to a specific application. All these three modules are closely corelated. And CAEST scheduling algorithm is based on this model and mainly used to schedule ready tasks in the DAG runtime system module.

Based on the DAG data driven model, the High Performance Computing Lab of Tianjin University has developed two runtime systems named EasyPDP [19] and EasyHPS [20], respectively. And we presented an implementation of the proposed CAEST algorithm based on the EasyHPS system, and the experimental results is shown in Sect. 6.

4 Definitions

4.1 DAG Model

A directed acyclic graph (DAG) is denoted as $G = (V, E, \tau, c)$, where $V = \{v_1, v_2, ..., v_n\}$ represents a set of n tasks, E represents the relationship and the precedence constraints between tasks and $e_{i,j} = e(v_i, v_j) \in E$ represents task v_j only can start computing after former task v_i is completed, $\tau = \{\tau_1, \tau_2, ..., \tau_n\}$ is the set of computation time of each task and $\tau_i \in \tau$ represents the computation time of task v_i, $c = c(i, j)$ represents the communication time of a message from task v_i to task v_j. Specially, if task v_i and task v_j are scheduled onto the same

Table 1. Notation

Symbol	Definition
v_i	The node number of a node in the task graph
τ_i	The computation time of task v_i
$e(v_i, v_j)$	The precedence relationship between v_i and v_j
$c(v_i, v_j)$	The communication time of the directed edge from node v_i to v_j
ct	Number of worker threads on one node
CCR	Communication-to-computation Ratio
SL	Schedule length
$FT(v_i, P_j)$	The finish time of node v_i on target processor P_j
$Proc(v_i)$	The processor accommodating node v_i
EST	The earliest start time of a task
EFT	The earliest finish time of a task
LST	The latest start time of a task
LFT	The latest finish time of a task
PTN	The predecessor task number of a task
STN	The successor task number of a task
CT	The computation time of a task
CP	Critical path
Exp_X_Y	Experiment using Y threads on X nodes

processor element, the communication between them is 0. The communication-to-computation-ratio (CCR) of a parallel program is defined as its average edge weight divided by its average node weight [21]. Notations used throughout the paper is given in Table 1.

4.2   Scheduling of the DAG Model

In a general scheduling, based on the DAG model, the target cluster system is assumed to have an arbitrary topology of processing elements. And the goal of the scheduling algorithm is to determine task dispatching and execution order based on a certain strategy and distributes tasks to process elements to get an optimal result.

Specifically, scheduling a task graph $G = (V, E, \tau, c)$ onto p processors is a function f. Function f maps each task to a processor t and determines its beginning time. In a formal method, scheduling can be expressed as follows.

$$f : V \rightarrow \{1, 2, ..., p\} \times [0, \infty)$$

$f(v) = (P, t)$, where $v \in V$, means the system schedules task v onto processor P and its beginning time is t. The schedule length is defined as $max_i\{FT(v_i)\}$ across all processors. The goal of CAEST algorithm is to minimize $max_i\{FT(v_i)\}$.

If scheduling system wants to schedule $v_i \in V$ onto p processors and the total communication time can be determined, the SL of a program is as follows.

$$SL = \sum_{i=1}^{k} CT(v_i) + \sum_{i,j}^{k} real\_c(v_i, v_j)$$

$CT(v_i)$ represents the computation time of task v_i, and $real\_c(v_i, v_j)$ represents the communication cost of a real message passing from v_i to v_j, which is the part cannot overlap with computation of other tasks.

5   The CAEST Scheduling Algorithm

5.1   Construction of the Scheduling Ready List

In most priority-driven list scheduling algorithm, one particular attribute is taken as the priority and tasks scheduling is based on it. When two tasks are assigned with the same priority, most algorithms randomly choose a task to schedule. Obviously, the random scheduling method is not an useful way to shorten the schedule length. For using task attributes better to schedule tasks objectively and orderly, the relationship between attributes and completion time must be studied. Steps to schedule tasks are : (1) tasks are sorted by the attribute with the biggest influence on the completion time; (2) if there is an equality of influence after the last step, the attribute with smaller influence than the former one will be adopted to sort tasks, and so on. And task attributes used and evaluated in this paper are $CP, LST, EFT, STN, CT, LFT, EST$, and PTN, which is widely used.

In order to evaluate importance of attributes to the SL, a number of different parallel problems are generated randomly, and the parallelism of each question ranges from 2 to 256. The algorithm to test the attributes is shown in *Algorithm 1*.

Algorithm 1. The algorithm used to evaluate task attributes

Require: *Eight task attributes*;
Ensure: *Corresponding scheduling length of all problems*;
 1: push all eight node into the parameter list named *para_list*;
 2: **while** *para_list* is not empty **do**
 3:    pop out an attribute from *para_list*;
 4:    select and schedule ready tasks on by this attribute;
 5:    store its *scheduling length* in the time table
 6: **end while**
 7: rank the time table in order of descending *scheduling length*;

Based on the experimental results, the rank of all these eight attributes and the corresponding values is as follows.

- The task is in the critical path;
- The latest start time of the task is lower than others;

- The earliest finish time of the task is higher than others;
- The successor task number is bigger than others;
- The computation time of the task is lower than others;
- The latest finish time of the task is lower than others;
- The earliest start time of the task is higher than others;
- The predecessor task number is smaller than others.

If the ready tasks can be ranked and scheduled based on these rules, SL of an application should be shortened.

5.2   Scheduling Ready Tasks

In this paper, it is assumed that if successors of a task are scheduled onto the same processor, this task only need deliver a message to them for once. The network bandwidth is assumed to be unlimited, and there can be several messages transmitting through the same link and the jam and queuing delay can be ignored.

Inputs of CAEST algorithm are task graph with computation time and communication time and physical connection diagram of nodes. A physical diagram is given as an example in the Fig. 3. The edge weight represents communication time to pass one message between two connected processor elements.

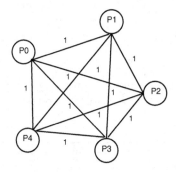

Fig. 3. A physical connection diagram

Outputs of CAEST algorithm are start time of tasks, nodes which tasks will be scheduled onto, source and target nodes of messages, start time of each communication.

The algorithm is described *Algorithm* 2. When scheduling ready tasks onto idle processors, the task with lowest EST will be dispatched first. If several tasks have the same EST, communication cost will be used to break ties.

If we assumed that the number of tasks is n and the number of processors is p. Under this assumption, the complexity of the Floyd-Warshall algorithm is $O(p^3)$. For every task, the time needed to look up a suitable processor is $O(n \times p)$, and the complexity of the process to compute the attributes of tasks

---

Algorithm 2. The CAEST algorithm

Require: $Task\ graph\ G\ =\ (V, E, \tau, c), V\ =\ v_1, v_2, ..., v_n; Physical\ connection$
$diagram; Number\ of\ finished\ node\ finished = 0;$
Ensure: $Scheduling\ results$
1: compute the communication cost between processors using *Floyd-Warshall* algorithm;
2: push the entry node v_1 into ready list;
3: **while** $finished \neq n$ **do**
4:　**if** ready list is not empty **then**
5:　　get a task from ready list;
6:　　lookup idle processors for the task;
7:　　**if** get idle processors **then**
8:　　　compute the *EST* of the current task on all these processors;
9:　　　**if** no equal *EST* **then**
10:　　　　choose the processor with the lowest *EST*;
11:　　　**else**
12:　　　　choose the processor with lower communication cost;
13:　　　**end if**
14:　　**else**
15:　　　update the state of processors;
16:　　**end if**
17:　**else**
18:　　Update the task graph;
19:　　lookup new ready tasks;
20:　　sort tasks using rules mentioned in section A;
21:　　push ready tasks into ready list;
22:　**end if**
23: **end while**

---

and to push the ready tasks into ready list is $O(n^2)$. So, the complexity of CAEST algorithm is

$$O(p^3) + O(n \times (p \times n + n^2)) = O(p^3) + O(p \times n^2 + n^3).$$

In most cases, n is bigger than p, so the complexity of CAEST is $O(n^3)$.

6　Experiments

6.1　Implementation Using the EasyHPS System

In this paper, we choose the EasyHPS system as a basic runtime environment to measure the performance of CAEST scheduling algorithm with regular task graphs. The computation time of tasks and the topology of processors are not needed in the former system, which uses dynamic scheduling algorithm. But in the system using CAEST scheduling algorithm, these information must be given as the foundation of the scheduling system before starting to schedule tasks. Steps to initialize the new runtime system are showed as follows.

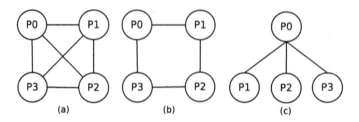

Fig. 4. Three common physical topologies of processors provided by the improved EasyHPS system. (a) Full connection; (b) Ring connection; (c) Star connection.

First, after selecting the DAG model, users are also required to set the task graph in details. Second, users need to choose a suitable physical topology according to the environment where the system running in. The modified EasyHPS system provides three common topologies of processors. They are mesh topology, ring topology and star topology as illustrated in Fig. 4.

When users finish initialization, the system starts to schedule tasks using the algorithm mentioned in the Sect. 5. And this process is proceeded in the data block level. In other words, tasks in the task graph are the tasks after data partitioning. The scheduling job is finished by the process 0. After completing the algorithm, the scheduling result in process 0 will be sent to all other processes.

After finishing the scheduling algorithm, each process begins to do the computation. Each process has its own task queue that stores all the tasks scheduled onto it. Whenever the process finishes the computation of a task, the system will execute the corresponding method to determine whether it needs to send messages and give processes that messages are passed to. Also, the process will check whether the needed messages from other processes are received. If not, it will wait for the messages from the routing process.

Compared with the former scheduling algorithm, the modified EasyHPS system changes the process pool to a fixed number of processes in the process level. But in the thread level, it is the same as the former system and uses a dynamic scheduling algorithm. System puts computable tasks into task queue of the thread pool. An idle worker will then fetch a task from the queue only if the queue is not empty and starts to compute.

On fault-tolerant mechanism, the modified system uses the same Timeout Fault-Tolerant Mechanism, in both process level and thread level, as before. When the threshold of a task is exceeded, the system chooses to abandon the task and recomputes it. Additional information of this mechanism can be found in reference [20].

6.2   Experiments with Regular DAG Model

The Smith-Waterman algorithm is a typical dynamic programming algorithm in bioinformatics, which can be divided into parallel tasks with strong data dependency between them. The function of it is to find the sequence alignment. There are two methods. One is the Smith-Waterman algorithm with Linear and

Affine Gap penalty (SWLAG) and the other is the Smith-Waterman algorithm with General Gap penalty (SWGG).

We implement these two methods, CAEST algorithm and the former algorithm, in the EasyHPS system respectively and use the historical statistics information of the system to initialize the input of CAEST algorithm.

Experiments are performed on an Tianhe-1A high-performance computer. Every node of this supercomputer is multi-core SMP server, which has an Intel Xeon 5670 multi-core processor and 24 GB memory. It has a two-stage infiniband quad data rate (QDR) as its communication network. The EasyHPS system is implemented in C language and uses the MPICH 1.4.1 library and the POSIX thread library.

The EasyHPS system uses master/slave mode both in process level and thread level. Because the limitation of the hardware, a process in the system can create 11 threads at most in thread level. We defined Exp_X_Y as an experiment using Y threads on X multi-core nodes. For each experiment, one multi-core node is used to do the task scheduling in process-level, while the other $(X-1)$ nodes are used to do the computation using one thread to do the task scheduling on thread-level. Therefore, EasyHPS use $Y - 2 \times X + 1$ which are distributed on $(X-1)$ computing nodes to do the computing for Exp_X_Y. If EasyHPS is deployed on N nodes, the total number of cores used is $N + (N-1) + ct \times (N-1)$, where the 1st N describes the sum of scheduling threads in process-level and the 2nd $(N-1)$ describes the number of scheduling threads in thread-level. As mentioned above, there is $1 \leq ct \leq 11$. System uses 4–14 threads on 2 nodes, or 10–40 threads on 4 nodes. There are 4 experiments using 2, 3, 4 and 5 nodes called $Exp\_2\_K_2(4 \leq K_2 \leq 14)$, $Exp\_3\_K_3(7 \leq K_3 \leq 27)$, $Exp\_4\_K_4(10 \leq K_4 \leq 40)$, and $Exp\_5\_K_5(13 \leq K_5 \leq 53)$, respectively.

The OLD-EasyHPS/CAEST ratio is defined as evaluation index, which represents the time ratio of the system with the former scheduling algorithm to the system with CAEST scheduling algorithm. If the ratio is higher than 1.0, it means that CAEST algorithm is better. In order to ease the difficulty of observation, there is the 1.0 baseline in graphs. Lengths of genome sequences used in all experiments are the same, which is 10000, and the size of the data block for each thread is 10. Sizes of the data block for each process (donated as $process\_partition\_size$) used in every two experiments are 200 and 500, respectively. For each size of $process\_partition\_size$, it is run on 2, 3, 4 and 5 nodes separately. The number of threads on each node increases by 2 every time in the rank of the total number of threads. Corresponding OLD-EasyHPS/CAEST ratios are shown from Figs. 5, 6, 7, 8, 9, 10, 11 and 12.

As we can see from the curve graphs given above, almost all of the OLD-EasyHPS/CAEST ratios are greater than 1.0. It means that the EasyHPS system adopting CAEST scheduling algorithm can achieve a significant speedup.

Under the same experimental environment and program parameters, the performance of the SWLAG algorithm is better than the performance of the SWGG algorithm using CAEST algorithm. And it means that CAEST scheduling algorithm does better in the scheduling of a DP algorithm with a regular DAG model than in that with an irregular DAG model.

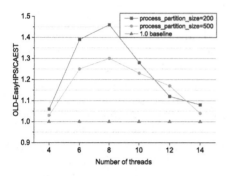

Fig. 5. SWLAG on 2 computing nodes

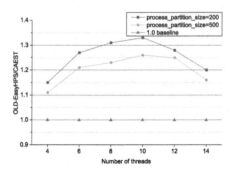

Fig. 6. SWGG on 2 computing nodes

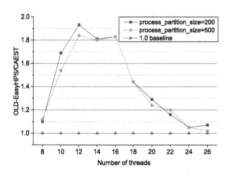

Fig. 7. SWLAG on 3 computing nodes

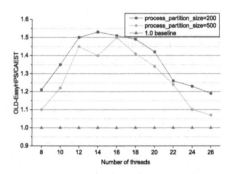

Fig. 8. SWGG on 3 computing nodes

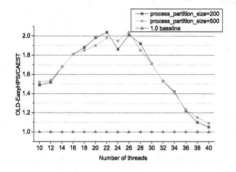

Fig. 9. SWLAG on 4 computing nodes

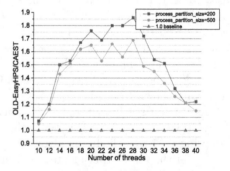

Fig. 10. SWGG on 4 computing nodes

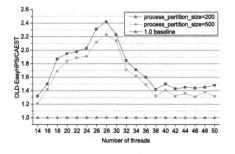
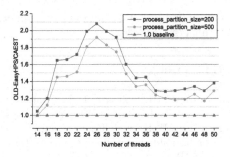

Fig. 11. SWLAG on 5 computing nodes

Fig. 12. SWGG on 5 computing nodes

When the number of nodes where programs run on is different, the corresponding ratio curve is different. But all curves increase first and then decrease. It means that under each number of nodes, there is a thread number, which makes CAEST scheduling algorithm get the best performance.

For the SWLAG and SWGG, the performance of CAEST algorithm gets better when the *process_partition_size* changes from 200 to 500. When the *process_partition_size* is 200, the size of the task graph is $(10000 \div 200) \times (10000 \div 200) = 50 \times 50$, while the size is $(10000 \div 500) \times (10000 \div 500) = 20 \times 20$ when the *process_partition_size* is 500. And it can be concluded that the algorithm would get a better performance when the partition of the task graph is fine-grained.

7 Conclusion

In this paper, a new scheduling algorithm named Communication-aware Earliest Start Time (CAEST) scheduling algorithm, which is mainly designed for parallel applications with regular DAG models, is presented. This algorithm takes eight task attributes into account to construct ready list, and makes use of the earliest start time and communication cost to schedule tasks onto processors. To verify the performance of CAEST algorithm on scheduling tasks with regular task graphs, an implementation based on EasyHPS runtime system has been developed. Results demonstrate that it can achieve a performance improvement up to 142 %. Therefore, this algorithm can effectively reduce the scheduling length of application and provides a new method to select a ready task from several tasks with the same value under selecting strategy using only one attribute. However, cost of selecting a ready task will increase in this algorithm. But, in situations that the computation and communication cost of tasks take up most of the time, this algorithm will perform better.

In the future work, it will be helpful to design an efficient scheduling algorithm in thread level, and made an assumption in the physical topology of CAEST algorithm. It is also necessary to simulate the network environment considering that the network bandwidth is always limited in reality.

Acknowledgments. This work was supported by National Natural Science Foundation of China (No. 61303021).

References

1. Garey, M.R., Johnson, D.S.: Computers and Intractability: A guide to the theory of NP-Completeness. WH Freeman & Co., San Francisco (1979)
2. Kohler, W.H., Steiglitz, K.: Characterization and theoretical comparison of branch-and-bound algorithms for permutation problems. J. ACM (JACM) **21**(1), 140–156 (1974)
3. Bruno, J., Coffman Jr., E.G., Sethi, R.: Scheduling independent tasks to reduce mean finishing time. Commun. ACM **17**(7), 382–387 (1974)
4. Gonzalez Jr., Mario, J.: Deterministic processor scheduling. ACM Comput. Surv. (CSUR) **9**(3), 173–204 (1977)
5. Hu, T.C.: Parallel sequencing and assembly line problems. Oper. Res. **9**(6), 841–848 (1961)
6. Sethi, R.: Scheduling graphs on two processors. SIAM J. Comput. **5**(1), 73–82 (1976)
7. Grama, A.: Introduction to Parallel Computing. Pearson Education, London (2003)
8. Roig, C., Ripoll, A., Senar, M.A., et al.: A new model for static mapping of parallel applications with task and data parallelism. In: Proceedings of the International Parallel and Distributed Processing Symposium, IPDPS 2002, Abstracts and CD-ROM, p. 8. IEEE (2001)
9. Tang, S., Yu, C., Lee, B.S., et al.: Adaptive data refinement for parallel dynamic programming applications. In: 2012 IEEE 26th International Parallel and Distributed Processing Symposium Workshops & PhD Forum (IPDPSW), pp. 2220–2229 (2012)
10. Björnfot, L., Lundqvist, K., Wall, G., et al.: Distribution of tasks within a centrally scheduled local area network. In: Toussaint, M. (ed.) Ada in Europe. LNCS, vol. 887, pp. 421–432. Springer, Heidelberg (1994)
11. Buyya, R., Paprazycki, M.: Clustering Computing. Prentice Hall, Upper Saddle River (2000)
12. Gerasoulis, A., Yang, T.: A comparison of clustering heuristics for scheduling directed acyclic graphs on multiprocessors. J. Parallel Distrib. Comput. **16**(4), 276–391 (1992)
13. Wang, F., Mok, A., Emerson, E.A.: Formal specification of asynchronous distributed real-time systems by APTL. In: Proceedings of the 14th International Conference on Software Engineering, pp. 188–198. ACM (1992)
14. El-Rewini, H., Lewis, T.G.: Parallel and Distributed Computing. Manning Publications Co., Greenwich (1999)
15. Sih, G.C., Lee, E.: A compile-time scheduling heuristic for interconnection-constrained heterogeneous processor architectures. IEEE Trans. Parallel Distrib. Syst. **4**(2), 175–187 (1993)
16. Hwang, J.J., Chow, Y.C., Anger, F.D., et al.: Scheduling precedence graphs in systems with interprocessor communication times. SIAM J. Comput. **18**(2), 244–257 (1989)
17. Wu, M.Y., Gajski, D.D.: Hypertool: a programming aid for message-passing systems. IEEE Trans. Parallel Distrib. Syst. **1**(3), 330–343 (1990)
18. El-Rewini, H., Lewis, T.G., Ali, H.H.: Task Scheduling in Parallel and Distributed Systems. Prentice-Hall Inc., Upper Saddle River (1994)

19. Tang, S., Yu, C., Sun, J., et al.: EasyPDP: an efficient parallel dynamic programming runtime system for computational biology. IEEE Trans. Parallel Distrib. Syst. **23**(5), 862–872 (2012)
20. Du, J., Yu, C., Sun, J., et al.: EasyHPS: a multilevel hybrid parallel system for dynamic programming. In: 2013 IEEE 27th International Parallel and Distributed Processing Symposium Workshops & PhD Forum (IPDPSW), pp. 630–639 (2013)
21. Kwok, Y.K., Ahmad, I.: Static scheduling algorithms for allocating directed task graphs to multiprocessors. ACM Comput. Surv. **31**(4), 406–471 (1999)

One-to-One Disjoint Path Covers on Mesh

Manyi Du[1], Jianxi Fan[1], Yuejuan Han[2], and Cheng-Kuan Lin[1](✉)

[1] School of Computer Science and Technology,
Soochow University, Suzhou 215000, China
cklin@suda.edu.cn
[2] Center of Information Development and Management,
Soochow University, Suzhou 215000, China

Abstract. We propose a new definition to describe the characteristics of a graph. A graph G is strong k^*-connected if there is a r^*-container between any two distinct vertices u and v of G with $r \leq \min\{deg(u), deg(v), k\}$. The strong spanning connectivity of graph G, $s\kappa(G)$, is the maximal value of G satisfies (a) G is strong $s\kappa(G)^*$-connected and (b) $s\kappa(G) \leq \Delta(G)$ where $\Delta(G)$ is the maximal degree of G. Similarly, strong spanning laceability of bipartite graph G, is denoted by $s\kappa^L(G)$. A mesh with m rows and n columns is denoted by $M_{m,n}$. Let m be any even integer and n be any integer. In this paper, we show that $s\kappa^L(M_{m,n}) = 3$ if $\min\{m, n\} \geq 4$.

Keywords: Disjoint path cover · Strong spanning connectivity · Mesh · Container

1 Introduction

With the rapid development of hardware devices, large multi-processor networks consisting of thousands of processors are becoming more common. Such a multi-processor interconnection network can be seen as a graph where the vertices and edges represent processors and communication channels, respectively [4,10,15]. As we all know, the topology of multi-processor network is an important factor to system performance. For example, if the diameter of the graph is smaller, the communication performance of the system is better. Meanwhile, the disjoint path problem is one of the important factors to the improvement of routing performance.

Routing is a process of transmitting messages among vertices/processors. Its efficiency and reliability are very important for the performance of the system. They can be enhanced by employing internally vertex-disjoint paths (disjoint paths for short), because they are used to speed up the transfer of a large amount of data by splitting the data over several vertex-disjoint communication paths [3]. The vertex-disjoint paths can be used to avoid congestion, accelerate transmission rate, and provide alternative transmission routes [10]. Additional benefits of adopting such a vertex-disjoint routing scheme are the enhanced robustness to

© Springer International Publishing Switzerland 2015
G. Wang et al. (Eds.): ICA3PP 2015, Part II, LNCS 9529, pp. 420–433, 2015.
DOI: 10.1007/978-3-319-27122-4_29

vertex failures and the enhanced capability of load balancing [14,19]. The benefits of disjoint paths make them play an important role in the study of routing,
reliability, and fault tolerance in parallel and distributed systems [7–9,20,21].

A k-container $C(u, v)$ of a graph G is a set of k disjoint paths between u and
v [5,18]. It is a k^*-container if it contains all vertices of G [2]. The k^*-container
problem can be applied in many ways such as full utilization of network nodes,
software testing, database design, and code optimization [1,16,17]. A graph G is
k^*-connected if there exists a k^*-container between any two distinct vertices of
G. The spanning connectivity of G, $\kappa^*(G)$, is the maximal value satisfies that G
is k^*-connected for every $1 \leq k \leq \kappa^*(G)$. A graph G is super spanning connected
if $\kappa^*(G) = \kappa(G)$ where $\kappa(G)$ is the connectivity of G. A bipartite graph G is
k^*-laceable if there exists a k^*-container between any two vertices from different
partite set of G. The spanning laceability of a bipartite graph G, $\kappa^{*L}(G)$, is
the maximal value satisfies that G is k^*-laceable for every $1 \leq k \leq \kappa^{*L}(G)$. A
bipartite graph G is super spanning laceable if $\kappa^{*L}(G) = \kappa(G)$. There have been
many articles on the k-container problem for many well-known networks, e.g.,
Lin et al. [12,13] for pancake graphs and hypercube-like networks, Shih and Kao
[19] for k-ary n-cubes, Chang et al. [2] for hypercubes, Li et al. [11] for tori.

According to the definition of spanning connectivity, it is easy to
see that $\kappa^*(G) \leq \min\{\kappa(G), \delta(G)\}$ where $\delta(G)$ is the minimal degree
of G. Let H be a graph with $V(H) = \{a, b, c, d, e\}$ and $E(H) =$
$\{(a, b), (a, c), (a, d), (a, e), (b, c), (b, d), (c, d), (c, e), (d, e)\}$ as Fig. 1.

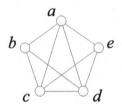

Fig. 1. Graph H

Table 1 shows that the $\kappa^*(H) = 3$ since $\kappa(H) = 3$. Table 2 shows that there is
a 4^*-container between any two distinct vertices p and q with $\{p, q\} \subset \{a, c, d\}$.
The definition of the spanning connectivity cannot completely describe the characteristics of H. Thus, we propose a new definition to describe the characteristics
of a graph. A graph G is strong k^*-connected if there is a r^*-container between
any two distinct vertices u and v of G with $r \leq \min\{deg(u), deg(v), k\}$. The
strong spanning connectivity of graph G, $s\kappa(G)$, is the maximal value of G satisfies (a) G is strong $s\kappa(G)^*$-connected and (b) $s\kappa(G)^* \leq \Delta(G)$ where $\Delta(G)$ is the
maximal degree of G. Thus, we have $s\kappa(H) = 4$. A bipartite graph G is strong
k^*-laceable if there is a r^*-container between any two distinct vertices u and v
from different partite set of G with $r \leq \min\{deg(u), deg(v), k\}$. The strong spanning laceability of bipartite graph G, $s\kappa^L(G)$, is the maximal value of G satisfies
(a) G is strong $s\kappa^L(G)^*$-laceable and (b) $s\kappa^L(G) \leq \Delta(G)$.

Table 1. k^*-container of graph H with $k \in \{1, 2, 3\}$

x to y	1^*-container	2^*-container	3^*-container
a → b	$\{\langle a,e,d,c,b\rangle\}$	$\{\langle a,b\rangle, \langle a,e,d,c,b\rangle\}$	$\{\langle a,b\rangle, \langle a,c,b\rangle, \langle a,e,d,b\rangle\}$
a → c	$\{\langle a,b,d,e,c\rangle\}$	$\{\langle a,c\rangle, \langle a,b,d,e,c\rangle\}$	$\{\langle a,c\rangle, \langle a,b,c\rangle, \langle a,e,d,c\rangle\}$
a → d	$\{\langle a,b,c,e,d\rangle\}$	$\{\langle a,d\rangle, \langle a,b,c,e,d\rangle\}$	$\{\langle a,d\rangle, \langle a,e,d\rangle, \langle a,b,c,d\rangle\}$
a → e	$\{\langle a,b,c,d,e\rangle\}$	$\{\langle a,e\rangle, \langle a,b,c,d,e\rangle\}$	$\{\langle a,e\rangle, \langle a,d,e\rangle, \langle a,b,c,e\rangle\}$
b → c	$\{\langle b,a,e,d,c\rangle\}$	$\{\langle b,c\rangle, \langle b,a,e,d,c\rangle\}$	$\{\langle b,c\rangle, \langle b,d,c\rangle, \langle b,a,e,c\rangle\}$
b → d	$\{\langle b,a,e,c,d\rangle\}$	$\{\langle b,d\rangle, \langle b,a,e,c,d\rangle\}$	$\{\langle b,d\rangle, \langle b,c,d\rangle, \langle b,a,e,d\rangle\}$
b → e	$\{\langle b,a,c,d,e\rangle\}$	$\{\langle b,a,e\rangle, \langle b,c,d,e\rangle\}$	$\{\langle b,a,e\rangle, \langle b,c,e\rangle, \langle b,d,e\rangle\}$
c → d	$\{\langle c,e,a,b,d\rangle\}$	$\{\langle c,e,d\rangle, \langle c,a,b,d\rangle\}$	$\{\langle c,a,d\rangle, \langle c,b,d\rangle, \langle c,e,d\rangle\}$
c → e	$\{\langle c,a,b,d,e\rangle\}$	$\{\langle c,e\rangle, \langle c,a,b,d,e\rangle\}$	$\{\langle c,e\rangle, \langle c,a,e\rangle, \langle c,b,d,e\rangle\}$
d → e	$\{\langle d,b,a,c,e\rangle\}$	$\{\langle d,e\rangle, \langle d,b,a,c,e\rangle\}$	$\{\langle d,e\rangle, \langle d,c,e\rangle, \langle d,b,a,e\rangle\}$

Table 2. 4^*-container of graph H

x to y	4^*-container
a → b	none
a → c	$\{\langle a,c\rangle, \langle a,b,c\rangle, \langle a,d,c\rangle, \langle a,e,c\rangle\}$
a → d	$\{\langle a,d\rangle, \langle a,b,d\rangle, \langle a,c,d\rangle, \langle a,e,d\rangle\}$
a → e	none
b → c	none
b → d	none
b → e	none
c → d	$\{\langle c,d\rangle, \langle c,a,d\rangle, \langle c,b,d\rangle, \langle c,e,d\rangle\}$
c → e	none
d → e	none

In this paper, we discuss the k^*-container problem of mesh networks. The rest of this paper is organized as follows. In Sect. 2, we introduce some necessary definitions and notations. In Sect. 3, we show the necessary condition of k^*-container in $M_{m,n}$. In Sect. 4, we show that $s\kappa^L(M_{m,n}) = 3$ for every even integer m and for every integer n with $\min\{m, n\} \geq 4$. Conclusions and future work are discussed in the final section.

2   Definitions and Preliminaries

For the definitions and notations of graph theory, we follow [4]. Let G be a simple undirected graph which is composed of a vertex set V and an edge set E. Two vertices x and y in V are adjacent if and only if $(x, y) \in E$. Let u be a vertex in graph G, we use $N_G(u)$ to denote the set of vertices adjacent to u. The *degree* of a vertex x in G, denoted by $deg_G(x)$, is the number of vertices adjacent to x. A *path* $P = \langle x_1, x_2, \ldots, x_k \rangle$ with $k \geq 2$ in G is a sequence of distinct vertices and any two subsequent vertices in P are adjacent. The length of P, $len(P)$, is the number of edges in it. The *distance* between vertex x and vertex y, denoted by $d(x, y)$, is the length of the shortest path between x and y. A graph G is *bipartite* if its vertex set can be partitioned into two subsets V_1 and V_2 such that every edge joins a vertex of V_1 and a vertex of V_2.

A *mesh* with m rows and n columns, denoted by $M_{m,n}$, is a graph with $V(M_{m,n}) = \{(i, j) | 0 \leq i \leq m-1 \text{ and } 0 \leq j \leq n-1\}$ and $E(M_{m,n}) = \{((i, j), (i+1, j)) | 0 \leq i \leq m - 2 \text{ and } 0 \leq j \leq n - 1\} \cup \{((i, j), (i, j + 1)) | 0 \leq i \leq m - 1 \text{ and } 0 \leq j \leq n - 2\}$. We set $A_{m,n} = \{(i, j) | (i, j) \in V(M_{m,n}) \text{ and } (i + j) \text{ is even}\}$ and $B_{m,n} = \{(i, j) | (i, j) \in V(M_{m,n}) \text{ and } (i + j) \text{ is odd}\}$. We have $|A_{m,n}| = |B_{m,n}|$ if m or n is an even integer, and $|A_{m,n}| = |B_{m,n}|+1$ if both m and n are odd integers. Moreover, $A_{m,n} \cup B_{m,n} = V(M_{m,n})$. We set $R(x : y, z)$ being a path as $\langle (x, z), (x + 1, z), \ldots, (y, z) \rangle$ if $x < y$ and $\langle (x, z), (x - 1, z), \ldots, (y, z) \rangle$ if $x > y$, and $R(a, b : c)$ being a path as $\langle (a, b), (a, b + 1), \ldots, (a, c) \rangle$ if $b < c$ and $\langle (a, b), (a, b - 1), \ldots, (a, c) \rangle$ if $b > c$. Meanwhile, we set $Q(a : a + 1, c : d)$ being a path as $\langle (a, c), (a + 1, c), (a + 1, c + 1), (a, c + 1), \ldots, (a, d - 1), (a + 1, d - 1), (a + 1, d), (a, d) \rangle$ if $c < d$, and $Q(a : b, c : c + 1)$ being a path as $\langle (a, c), (a, c+1), (a+1, c+1), (a+1, c), \ldots, (b-1, c), (b-1, c+1), (b, c+1), (b, c) \rangle$ if $a < b$. Similarly, we set $Q(a : b, c : c - 1)$ being a path as $\langle (a, c), (a, c - 1), (a + 1, c - 1), (a + 1, c), \ldots, (b - 1, c), (b - 1, c - 1), (b, c - 1), (b, c) \rangle$ if $a < b$.

Lemma 1. [6] *In $M_{m,n}$ with $m \geq 4$ and $n \geq 4$, there is a hamiltonian path from s to t for each $s \in A_{m,n}$ and each $t \in B_{m,n}$ if $|A_{m,n}| = |B_{m,n}|$. Otherwise, there is a hamiltonian path from s to t for each $s \in A_{m,n}$ and each $t \in A_{m,n}$ if $|A_{m,n}| = |B_{m,n}| + 1$.*

3 Necessary Condition

Theorem 1. *Let m and n be any two odd integers with $\min\{m, n\} \geq 3$. If there is a k^*-container between x and y in $M_{m,n}$, then both x and y are in $A_{m,n}$ and $k = 1$, or in $B_{m,n}$ and $k = 3$.*

Proof: Let $\{P_1, P_2, \ldots, P_k\}$ be a k^*-container between x and y in $M_{m,n}$. We have the following cases.

Case 1. $x \in A_{m,n}$ and $y \in A_{m,n}$. We have that $|(V(P) - \{x, y\}) \cap A_{m,n}| = |(V(P) - \{x, y\}) \cap B_{m,n}| - 1$ for any path P between x and y. Then, we have $|A_{m,n}| = |\{x, y\}| + \sum_{i=1}^{k} |(V(P_i) - \{x, y\}) \cap A_{m,n}| = |\{x, y\}| + \sum_{i=1}^{k} (|(V(P_i) - \{x, y\}) \cap B_{m,n}| - 1) = 2 + |B_{m,n}| - k \neq |B_{m,n}| - 1$ if $k \neq 1$. So, there is only a 1^*-container between x and y.

Case 2. $x \in B_{m,n}$ and $y \in B_{m,n}$. We have that $|(V(P) - \{x, y\}) \cap A_{m,n}| - 1 = |(V(P) - \{x, y\}) \cap B_{m,n}|$ for any path P between x and y. Then, we have $|B_{m,n}| = |\{x, y\}| + \sum_{i=1}^{k} |(V(P_i) - \{x, y\}) \cap B_{m,n}| = |\{x, y\}| + \sum_{i=1}^{k} (|(V(P_i) - \{x, y\}) \cap A_{m,n}| - 1) = 2 + |A_{m,n}| - k \neq |A_{m,n}| - 1$ if $k \neq 3$. So, there is only a 3^*-container between x and y.

Case 3. Either $x \in A_{m,n}$ and $y \in B_{m,n}$, or $x \in B_{m,n}$ and $y \in A_{m,n}$. We have that $|(V(P)-\{x,y\}) \cap A_{m,n}| = |(V(P)-\{x,y\}) \cap B_{m,n}|$ for any path P between x and y. Then, we have $|B_{m,n}| = |\{x,y\} \cap B_{m,n}| + \sum_{i=1}^{k} |(V(P_i)-\{x,y\}) \cap B_{m,n}| = |\{x,y\} \cap A_{m,n}| + \sum_{i=1}^{k} |(V(P_i)-\{x,y\}) \cap A_{m,n}| = |A_{m,n}| > |A_{m,n}|-1$. So, if either $x \in A_{m,n}$ and $y \in B_{m,n}$, or $x \in B_{m,n}$ and $y \in A_{m,n}$, there is no k^*-container between x and y with any integer k. □

Theorem 2. *Let m be an even integer and let n be a integer with $\min\{m,n\} \geq 4$. If there is a k^*-container between x and y with $k \neq 2$, then x and y are in distinct vertex partite sets.*

Proof: Suppose that x and y are in same vertex partite set. Without loss of generality, we assume that $\{x,y\} \subset A_{m,n}$. We have that $|(V(P) - \{x,y\}) \cap A_{m,n}| = |(V(P)-\{x,y\}) \cap B_{m,n}|-1$ for any path P between x and y. Suppose that there is a k^*-container $\{P_1, P_2, \ldots, P_k\}$ of $M_{m,n}$ between x and y where $\cup_{i=1}^{k} V(P_i) = V(M_{m,n})$. Then, we have $|A_{m,n}| = |\{x,y\}| + \sum_{i=1}^{k} |(V(P_i) - \{x,y\}) \cap A_{m,n}| = |\{x,y\}| + \sum_{i=1}^{k} (|(V(P_i)-\{x,y\}) \cap B_{m,n}|-1) = 2 + |B_{m,n}| - k \neq |B_{m,n}|$ if $k \neq 2$. So, if there is a k^*-container between x and y with $k \neq 2$, then x and y are in distinct vertex partite sets. □

4 k^*-container of $M_{m,n}$

Lemma 2. *For any two distinct vertices u and v in $A_{3,3}$, there is a 1^*-container of $M_{3,3}$ between u and v. For any two distinct vertices u and v in $B_{3,3}$, there is a 3^*-container of $M_{3,3}$ between u and v.*

Proof: The 1^*-container of $M_{3,3}$ between u and v with $\{u,v\} \in A_{3,3}$ in dotted line is given in the following Fig. 2, and the 3^*-container of $M_{3,3}$ between u and v with $\{u,v\} \in B_{3,3}$ is given in the following Fig. 3. □

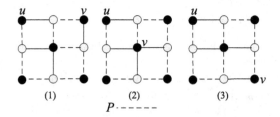

Fig. 2. The 1^*-container of $M_{3,3}$ between u and v

Theorem 3. *Let m and n be any two odd integers with $\min\{m,n\} \geq 3$. For any two distinct vertices u and v in $A_{m,n}$, there is a 1^*-container of $M_{m,n}$ between u and v.*

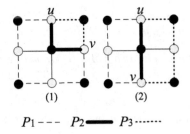

$$P_1 \text{---} \quad P_2 \text{━━━} \quad P_3 \cdots$$

Fig. 3. The 3^*-container of $M_{3,3}$ between u and v

Proof: By Lemma 1, this theorem holds on $\min\{m, n\} \geq 4$. Thus, we consider that $m = 3$ or $n = 3$. Without loss of generality, we assume that $m = 3$. We prove this case by induction on n. By Lemma 2, this theorem holds on $m = 3$ and $n = 3$. Thus, we show that it is true for $n \geq 5$ as follows. We set $u = (u_i, u_j)$ and $v = (v_i, v_j)$. Without loss of generality, we assume that $u_j \leq v_j$. According to whether there exist two columns outside u and v in the case of $M_{3,n}$, we have the following two cases.

Case 1. There exist two columns outside u and v in the case of $M_{3,n}$. Without loss of generality, we assume that the two columns are the rightmost two columns. That is, $\{u, v\} \cap \{(x, y) \mid 0 \leq x \leq 2 \text{ and } n - 2 \leq y \leq n - 1\} = \emptyset$. Next, we set $a_1 = (0, n - 3)$, $a_2 = (1, n - 3)$ and $a_3 = (2, n - 3)$. By the induction hypothesis, there exists a path P between u and v which covers all vertices except the vertices in the two columns. Since $deg_{M_{m,n}}(a_2) = 3$ and $a_2 \in B_{m,n}$, $\langle a_1, a_2 \rangle$ or $\langle a_2, a_3 \rangle$ is a part of path P.

We set $P = \langle u, R_1, x, y, R_2, v \rangle$ where $\{x, y\} = \{a_1, a_2\}$ if $\langle a_1, a_2 \rangle$ is a part of path P and $\{x, y\} = \{a_2, a_3\}$ otherwise. Note that $R_1 = \emptyset$ if $u = x$ and $R_2 = \emptyset$ if $v = y$. Then we set $Q_1 = \langle (0, n - 2), (0, n - 1), (1, n - 1), (2, n - 1), (2, n - 2), (1, n - 2) \rangle$, $Q_2 = \langle (1, n - 2), (2, n - 2), (2, n - 1), (1, n - 1), (0, n - 1), (0, n - 2) \rangle$, $Q_3 = \langle (1, n - 2), (0, n - 2), (0, n - 1), (1, n - 1), (2, n - 1), (2, n - 2) \rangle$, and $Q_4 = \langle (2, n - 2), (2, n - 1), (1, n - 1), (0, n - 1), (0, n - 2), (1, n - 2) \rangle$. Thus, $\langle u, R_1, x, Q, y, R_2, v \rangle$ forms a 1^*-container of $M_{3,n}$ between u and v where $Q = Q_1$ if $x = a_1$ and $y = a_2$, $Q = Q_2$ if $x = a_2$ and $y = a_1$, $Q = Q_3$ if $x = a_2$ and $y = a_3$, and $Q = Q_4$ if $x = a_3$ and $y = a_2$.

Case 2. There are not two columns outside u and v in the case of $M_{3,n}$. In other words, u lies on the leftmost two columns and v lies on the rightmost two columns.

In this case, we set $a = (0, n - 3)$. By the induction hypothesis, there exists a path P between u and a which covers all vertices except the vertices in the rightmost two columns. So, we can set $P = \langle u, R, a \rangle$. Then we set $Q_1 = \langle (0, n - 2), (1, n - 2), (2, n - 2), (2, n - 1), (1, n - 1) \rangle$, $Q_2 = \langle (0, n - 2), (0, n - 1), (1, n - 1), (1, n - 2), (2, n - 2) \rangle$, and $Q_3 = \langle (0, n - 2), (0, n - 1), (1, n - 1), (2, n - 1), (2, n - 2) \rangle$. Depending on the different position of v, the 1^*-container P'

of $M_{3,n}$ between u and v is $\langle u, R, a, Q_1, v \rangle$ if $v = (0, n-1)$, $\langle u, R, a, Q_2, v \rangle$ if $v = (2, n-1)$, and $\langle u, R, a, Q_3, v \rangle$ if $v = (1, n-2)$.   □

Theorem 4. *Let m and n be any two odd integers with $\min\{m, n\} \geq 3$. For any two distinct vertices u and v in $B_{m,n}$, there is a 3^*-container of $M_{m,n}$ between u and v.*

Proof: Take the numbers of m and n into account, we have the following two cases.

Case 1. $m = 3$ or $n = 3$. Without loss of generality, we assume that $m = 3$. We prove this case by induction on n. By Lemma 2, this theorem holds on $m = 3$ and $n = 3$. Thus, we show that it is true for $n \geq 5$. We set $u = (u_i, u_j)$ and $v = (v_i, v_j)$. Without loss of generality, we assume that $u_j \leq v_j$. According to whether there exist two columns outside u and v in the case of $M_{3,n}$, we have the following two cases.

Case 1.1. There exist two columns outside u and v in the case of $M_{3,n}$. This case is very similar with case 1 in Theorem 3.

Case 1.2. There are not two columns outside u and v in the case of $M_{3,n}$. In other words, u lies on the leftmost two columns and v lies on the rightmost two columns.

In this case, we set $a = (1, n-3)$, $b_1 = (0, n-3)$, $b_2 = (1, n-4)$ and $b_3 = (2, n-3)$. By the induction hypothesis, there exist three disjoint paths P_1', P_2' and P_3' between u and a which cover all vertices except the vertices in the rightmost two columns. So, we can set $P_i' = \langle u, R_i, b_i, a \rangle$ with $1 \leq i \leq 3$ (it is possible that $R_i = \emptyset$). Depending on the different position of v, the 3^*-container $\{P_1, P_2, P_3\}$ of $M_{3,n}$ between u and v are shown as follows.

If $v = (0, n-2)$, then we set $P_1 = \langle u, R_1, b_1, v \rangle$, $P_2 = \langle u, R_2, b_2, a, (1, n-2), v \rangle$, and $P_3 = \langle u, R_3, b_3, (2, n-2), R(2 : 0, n-1), v \rangle$.

If $v = (2, n-2)$, then we set $P_1 = \langle u, R_1, b_1, (0, n-2), R(0 : 2, n-1), v \rangle$, $P_2 = \langle u, R_2, b_2, a, (1, n-2), v \rangle$, and $P_3 = \langle u, R_3, b_3, v \rangle$.

If $v = (1, n-1)$, then we set $P_1 = \langle u, R_1, b_1, (0, n-2), (0, n-1), v \rangle$, $P_2 = \langle u, R_2, b_2, a, (1, n-2), v \rangle$, and $P_3 = \langle u, R_3, b_3, (2, n-2), (2, n-1), v \rangle$.

Case 2. $m \geq 5$ and $n \geq 5$. According to the symmetry, we can get the case of $M_{s,t}$ by rotating the case of $M_{t,s}$. So, if there exist two columns or two rows outside u and v in the case of $M_{m,n}$, the case is similar with case 1.1. Otherwise, the position of u must be $(0, 1)$ or $(1, 0)$ and the position v must be $(m-2, n-1)$ or $(m-1, n-2)$. We set $a = (1, 1)$ and $b = (m-2, n-2)$. Obviously, no matter $u = (0, 1)$ or $(1, 0)$, a is neighbor vertex of u. Similarly, b is neighbor vertex of v. Because $m - 2 \geq 3$ and $n - 2 \geq 3$, there exists a path P' between a and b which covers all internal vertices by Theorem 3 and we set $P' = \langle a, R, b \rangle$. Suppose that $u = (0, 1)$, depending on the different position of v, the 3^*-container $\{P_1, P_2, P_3\}$ of $M_{m,n}$ between u and v are shown as follows.

If $v = (m-2, n-1)$, then we set $P_1 = \langle u, R(0 : m-1, 0), R(m-1, 1 : n-1), v \rangle$, $P_2 = \langle u, R(0, 2 : n-1), R(1 : m-3, n-1), v \rangle$, and $P_3 = \langle u, a, R, b, v \rangle$.

If $v = (m-1, n-2)$, then we set $P_1 = \langle u, R(0 : m-1, 0), R(m-1, 1 : n-3), v \rangle$, $P_2 = \langle u, R(0, 2 : n-1), R(1 : m-1, n-1), v \rangle$, and $P_3 = \langle u, a, R, b, v \rangle$.

If $u = (1, 0)$, the case is similar with above. □

Lemma 3. *Let m be an even integer and let n be any integer with $\min\{m, n\} \geq 4$. For any vertex u in $A_{m,n}$ and for any vertex v in $B_{m,n}$, there is a 3^*-container of $M_{m,n}$ between u and v.*

Proof: Take the parity of n into account, we have the following two cases.

Case 1. n is an even integer. When $m = 4$ and $n = 4$, depending on the position of u and v, there exist six cases of $M_{4,4}$. The 3^*-container $\{P_1, P_2, P_3\}$ of $M_{4,4}$ between u and v are given in the following Fig. 4.

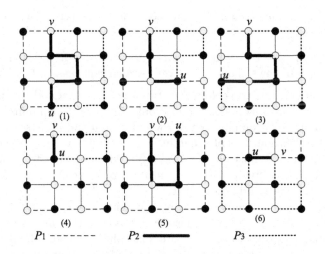

Fig. 4. The 3^*-container of $M_{4,4}$ between u and v

We would like to prove it in two cases which are divided according to if there exist two columns or two rows outside u and v. However, when $u = (0, 2)$ and $v = (0, n-3)$, as shown in the following Fig. 5, there exist two columns outside u and v in the $M_{4,n}$ with $n \geq 6$. We take the rightmost two columns as example. Obviously, there is not a 3^*-container of the $M_{4,n-2}$ consisting of the other $n-2$ columns because $deg_{M_{4,n-2}}(v) = 2$. We call those two columns *fake columns*. It is the same for the leftmost two columns and we can not take rows into account because we discuss from $m \geq 4$. So, the $M_{4,n}$ is a case which can not be obtained from the induction basis and the 3^*-container $\{P_1, P_2, P_3\}$ of the $M_{4,n}$ between u and v are shown as follows.

If $n = 6$, then we set $P_1 = \langle u, v \rangle$, $P_2 = \langle u, (1, 2), (1, 1), R(2, 1 : 4), (1, 4), (1, 3), v \rangle$, and $P_3 = \langle u, (0, 1), R(0 : 2, 0), R(3, 0 : 5), R(2 : 0, 5), (0, 4), v \rangle$.

If $n \geq 8$, then we set $P_1 = \langle u, Q(0 : 1, 3 : n-4), v \rangle$, $P_2 = \langle u, (1, 2), (1, 1), R(2, 1 : n-2), (1, n-2), (1, n-3), v \rangle$, and $P_3 = \langle u, (0, 1), R(0 : 2, 0), R(3, 0 : n-1), R(2 : 0, n-1), (0, n-2), v \rangle$.

According to the symmetry, we can get the case of $M_{s,t}$ by rotating the case of $M_{t,s}$. Assuming that the theorem holds for $m-2$ and $n-2$, for some $m \geq 6$ and $n \geq 6$, thus we show that it is true for m and n. According to whether there exist two columns or two rows outside u and v in $M_{m,n}$ and whether they are fake, we have the following two cases.

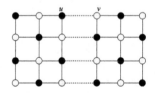

Fig. 5. The $M_{4,n}$ which can not be obtained from the induction basis for case 1

Case 1.1. There exist two columns or two rows outside u and v and they are not fake columns or rows. This case is very similar with case 1.1 in Theorem 4.

Case 1.2. There are not two columns or two rows outside u and v or there exist two columns or two rows outside u and v but they are fake columns or rows.

If there are not two columns or two rows outside u and v, we set $u = (u_i, u_j)$ and $v = (v_i, v_j)$. Without loss of generality, we assume that $u_i \leq v_i$ and $u_j \leq v_j$. Then, the position of u must be (1,1) and the position of v must be (m-1,n-2) or (m-2,n-1). So, we can divide the $M_{m,n}$ into $M_{m-2,n}$ and $M_{2,n}$ or $M_{m,n-2}$ and $M_{m,2}$ that u and v are in different parts.

If there exist two columns or two rows outside u and v but they are fake columns or rows. Without loss of generality, we assume that $m \geq 4$ and $n \geq 6$, $u = (0,2)$ and the leftmost two columns are fake columns. Then, the position of v may be $(0, n-3)$ or v is located in the rightmost two columns. If $v = (0, n-3)$, then m must be 4 and it is the special case shown above. Otherwise, there exist two rows outside u and v and they are not fake rows. If v is located in the rightmost two columns, then we can divide $M_{m,n}$ into $M_{m,n-2}$ and $M_{m,2}$ that u and v are in different parts.

According to the symmetry, without loss of generality, we assume that we can divide the $M_{m,n}$ into $M_{m-2,n}$ and $M_{2,n}$ such that $u \in V(M_{m-2,n})$ and $v \in V(M_{2,n})$. If $v_i = m-1$, we set $a = (m-3, v_j)$, $b_1 = (m-3, v_j-1)$, $b_2 = (m-4, v_j)$ and $b_3 = (m-3, v_j+1)$. By the induction hypothesis, there exist three disjoint paths P_1', P_2' and P_3' between u and a which cover all vertices in $M_{m-2,n}$ and we set $P_i' = \langle u, R_i, b_i, a \rangle$ with $1 \leq i \leq 3$. So, the 3*-container $\{P_1, P_2, P_3\}$ of $M_{3,n}$ between u and v are shown as follows.

$$\begin{cases} P_1 = \langle u, R_1, b_1, R(m-2, v_j-1 : 0), R(m-1, 0 : v_j-1), v \rangle \\ P_2 = \langle u, R_2, b_2, a, (m-2, v_j), v \rangle \\ P_3 = \langle u, R_3, b_3, R(m-2, v_j+1 : n-1), R(m-1, n-1 : v_j+1), v \rangle \end{cases}$$

If $v_i = m-2$ and $v_j \leq n-3$, we set $a = (m-3, v_j+1)$, $b_1 = (m-3, v_j)$, $b_2 = (m-4, v_j+1)$ and $b_3 = (m-3, v_j+2)$. By the induction hypothesis, there exist three disjoint paths P_1', P_2' and P_3' between u and a which cover all vertices in $M_{m-2,n}$ and we set $P_i' = \langle u, R_i, b_i, a \rangle$ with $1 \le i \le 3$. So, the 3*-container $\{P_1, P_2, P_3\}$ of $M_{m,n}$ between u and v are shown as follows.

$$\begin{cases} P_1 = \langle u, R_1, b_1, v \rangle \\ P_2 = \langle u, R_2, b_2, a, (m-2, v_j+1), v \rangle \\ P_3 = \langle u, R_3, b_3, R(m-2, v_j+2 : n-1), R(m-1, n-1 : 0), \\ \qquad R(m-2, 0 : v_j - 1), v \rangle \end{cases}$$

If $v_i = m-2$ and $v_j = n-1$, we set $a = (m-3, v_j - 1)$, $b_1 = (m-3, v_j - 2)$, $b_2 = (m-4, v_j - 1)$ and $b_3 = (m-3, v_j)$. The 3*-container $\{P_1, P_2, P_3\}$ of $M_{m,n}$ between u and v can be easily got like above.

Case 2. n is an odd integer. When $m = 4$ and $n = 5$, depending on the position of u and v, there exist twenty-one cases of $M_{4,5}$. The 3*-container of $M_{4,5}$ between u and v are given in the following Fig. 6.

However, as shown in the following Fig. 7, there exist three cases which can not be obtained from the induction basis.

Case 2.1. The 3*-container $\{P_1, P_2, P_3\}$ of the $M_{4,n}$ with $n \ge 7$ in Fig. 7(a) between u and v when $u = (0, 2)$ and $v = (3, n-3)$ are shown as follows.

$$\begin{cases} P_1 = \langle u, Q(0 : 3, 1 : 0), R(3, 2 : n-4), v \rangle \\ P_2 = \langle u, R(0, 3 : n-3), Q(0 : 3, n-2 : n-1), v \rangle \\ P_3 = \langle u, Q(1 : 2, 2 : n-4), (1, n-3), (2, n-3), v \rangle \end{cases}$$

Case 2.2. The 3*-container $\{P_1, P_2, P_3\}$ of $M_{m,5}$ with $m = 6$ in Fig. 7(b) between u and v when $u = (2, 4)$ and $v = (3, 0)$ are shown as follows.

$$\begin{cases} P_1 = \langle u, (1, 4), R(0, 4 : 0), (1, 0), (2, 0), v \rangle \\ P_2 = \langle u, (3, 4), (4, 4), R(5, 4 : 0), (4, 0), v \rangle \\ P_3 = \langle u, (2, 3), R(1, 3 : 1), (2, 1), (2, 2), (3, 2), (3, 3), R(4, 3 : 1), (3, 1), v \rangle \end{cases}$$

The 3*-container $\{P_1, P_2, P_3\}$ of $M_{m,5}$ with $m \ge 8$ in Fig. 7(b) between u and v when $u = (2, 4)$ and $v = (m-3, 0)$ are shown as follows.

$$\begin{cases} P_1 = \langle u, (1, 4), R(0, 4 : 0), (1, 0), (2, 0), Q(3 : m-4, 0 : 1), v \rangle \\ P_2 = \langle u, Q(3 : m-4, 4 : 3), R(m-3 : m-1, 4), R(m-1, 3 : 0), (m-2, 0), v \rangle \\ P_3 = \langle u, (2, 3), R(1, 3 : 1), (2, 1), R(2 : m-3, 2), (m-3, 3), R(m-2, 3 : 1), \\ \qquad (m-3, 1), v \rangle \end{cases}$$

Case 2.3. The 3*-container $\{P_1, P_2, P_3\}$ of $M_{m,5}$ with $m = 6$ in Fig. 7(c) between u and v when $u = (2, 0)$ and $v = (3, 0)$ are shown as follows.

$$\begin{cases} P_1 = \langle u, v \rangle \\ P_2 = \langle u, (1, 0), R(0, 0 : 4), R(1 : 5, 4), R(5, 3 : 0), (4, 0), v \rangle \\ P_3 = \langle u, (2, 1), R(1, 1 : 3), (2, 3), (2, 2), (3, 2), (3, 3), R(4, 3 : 1), (3, 1), v \rangle \end{cases}$$

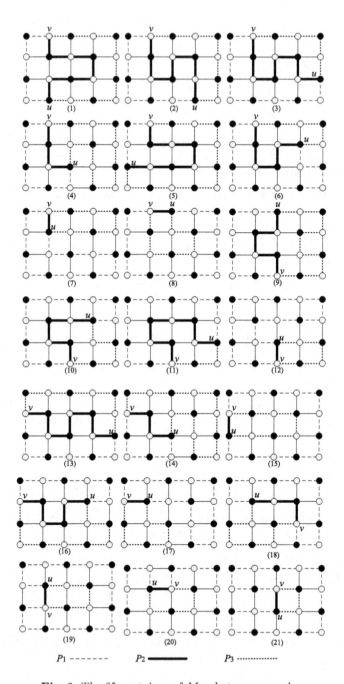

Fig. 6. The 3*-container of $M_{4,5}$ between u and v

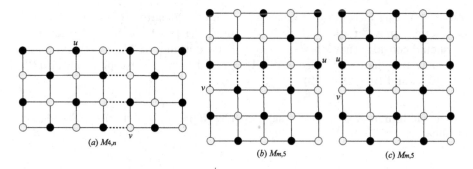

Fig. 7. The three cases which can not be obtained from the induction basis for case 2

The 3*-container $\{P_1, P_2, P_3\}$ of $M_{m,5}$ with $m \geq 8$ in Fig. 7(c) between u and v when $u = (2,0)$ and $v = (m-3,0)$ are shown as follows.

$$
\begin{cases}
P_1 = \langle u, Q(3:m-4,0:1), v \rangle \\
P_2 = \langle u, (1,0), R(0,0:4), R(1:2,4), Q(3:m-4,4:3), R(m-3:m-1,4), \\
\quad\quad R(m-1,3:0), (m-2,0), v \rangle \\
P_3 = \langle u, (2,1), R(1,1:3), (2,3), R(2:m-3,2), (m-3,3), R(m-2,3:1), \\
\quad\quad (m-3,1), v \rangle
\end{cases}
$$

We use the cases of $M_{4,5}$ as induction basis and assume that the theorem holds for $m-2$ and $n-2$, for some $m \geq 6$ and $n \geq 7$, thus we show that it is true for m and n. The next is similar with case 1. □

Lemma 4. *The $M_{m,n}$ is hamiltonian if m or n is an even integer.*

Proof: Without loss of generality, we assume that $m = 2t$ is an even integer for some $t \geq 1$. We set $P = R(m-1:1,0)$, $P_{2i} = R(2i, 1:n-1)$ and $P_{2i+1} = R(2i+1, n-1:1)$ for every $0 \leq i \leq t-1$. Then $\langle (0,0), P_0, P_1, P_2, \ldots, P_{2t-1}, P, (0,0) \rangle$ forms a hamiltonian cycle of $M_{m,n}$. □

Theorem 5. *For any even integer m and for any integer n with $\min\{m,n\} \geq 4$, $s\kappa^L(M_{m,n}) = 3$.*

Proof: By Lemmas 1, 3 and 4, $M_{m,n}$ is strong 3*-laceable. Suppose that $u = (1,1)$ and $v = (2,1)$. Let $\{P_1, P_2, P_3, P_4\}$ be a 4*-container of $M_{m,n}$ between u and v. Since $N_{M_{m,n}}(u) = \{(0,1), (1,0), (2,1), (1,2)\}$ and $N_{M_{m,n}}((0,0)) = \{(0,1), (1,0)\}$, $(0,0) \notin \bigcup_{i=1}^{4} V(P_i)$. That is, there is no 4*-container of $M_{m,n}$ between u and v. Thus, $s\kappa^L(M_{m,n}) = 3$. □

5 Conclusion

In this paper, we propose a new definition to describe the characteristics of a graph G, called strong spanning connectivity, denoted by $s\kappa(G)$. Similarly, strong spanning laceability of bipartite graph G, is denoted by $s\kappa^L(G)$. For any even integer m and for any integer n with $\min\{m, n\} \geq 4$, $s\kappa^L(M_{m,n}) = 3$. Next, we should consider that whether there is a 4^*-container of $M_{m,n}$ between u and v for any two distinct vertices u in $A_{m,n}$ and v in $B_{m,n}$ except $(1,1)$, $(1,n-2)$, $(m-2,1)$ and $(m-2, n-2)$.

Acknowledgments. This work is supported by National Natural Science Foundation of China (No.61572337, No.61572340).

References

1. Asdre, K., Nikolopoulos, S.D.: The 1-fixed-end point path cover problem is polynomial on interval graphs. Algorithmica **58**(3), 679–710 (2010)
2. Chang, C.-H., Lin, C.-K., Huang, H.-M., Hsu, L.-H.: The super laceability of the hypercubes. Inf. Process. Lett. **92**, 15–21 (2004)
3. Day, K., Al-Ayyoub, A.E.: Fault diameter of k-ary n-cube networks. IEEE Trans. Parallel Distrib. Syst. **8**(9), 903–907 (1997)
4. Hsu, L.-H., Lin, C.-K.: Graph theory and interconnection networks. CRC Press, New York (2008)
5. Hsu, D.F.: On container width and length in graphs, groups, and networks. IEICE Trans. Fundam. Electron. Commun. Comput. Sci. **E77-A**(4), 668–680 (1994)
6. Itali, A., Papadimitrion, C.H., Czwacfiter, J.L.: Hamiltonian paths in grid graphs. SIAM J. Comput. **11**(4), 676–686 (1982)
7. Lai, C.-N.: Optimal construction of all shortest node-disjoint paths in hypercubes with applications. IEEE Trans. Parallel Distrib. Syst. **23**(6), 1129–1134 (2012)
8. Lai, C.-N.: Two conditions for reducing the maximal length of node-disjoint paths in hypercubes. Theoret. Comput. Sci. **418**, 82–91 (2012)
9. Lai, C.-N.: An efficient construction of one-to-many node-disjoint paths in folded hypercubes. J. Parallel Distrib. Syst. **74**(4), 2310–2316 (2014)
10. Lai, C.-N.: Constructing all shortest node-disjoint paths in torus networks. J. Parallel Distrib. Syst. **75**, 123–132 (2015)
11. Li, J., Liu, D., Yang, Y., Yuan, J.: One-to-one disjoint path covers on multidimensional tori. Int. J. Comput. Math. **92**(6), 1114–1123 (2014)
12. Lin, C.-K., Huang, H.-M., Hsu, L.-H.: The super connectivity of the pancake graphs and the super laceability of the star graphs. Theoret. Comput. Sci. **339**(2–3), 257–271 (2005)
13. Lin, C.-K., Tan, J.J.M., Hsu, D.F., Hsu, L.-H.: On the spanning connectivity and spanning laceability of hypercube-like networks. Theoret. Comput. Sci. **381**(1–3), 218–229 (2007)
14. Liu, C., Yarvis, M., Conner, W.S., Guo, X.: Guaranteed on-demand discovery of node-disjoint paths in Ad hoc networks. Comput. Commun. **30**(14–15), 2917–2930 (2007)
15. McHugh, J.A.M.: Algorithmic graph theory. Prentice-Hall, Englewood Cliffs (1990)
16. Ntafos, S.C., Hakimi, S.L.: On path cover problems in digraphs and applications to program testing. IEEE Trans. Software Eng. **5**(5), 520–529 (1979)
17. Park, J.-H., Kim, H.-C., Lim, H.-S.: Many-to-many disjoint path covers in hypercube-like interconnection networks with faulty elements. IEEE Trans. Parallel Distrib. Syst. **17**(3), 227–240 (2006)

18. Park, J.-H., Ihm, I.: Single-source three-disjoint path covers in cubes of connected graphs. Inf. Process. Lett. **113**(14–16), 527–532 (2013)
19. Shih, Y.-K., Kao, S.-S.: One-to-one disjoint path covers on k-ary n-cubes. Theoret. Comput. Sci. **412**(35), 4513–4530 (2011)
20. Wu, R.-Y., Chen, G.-H., Kuo, Y.-L., Chang, G.J.: Node-disjoint paths in hierarchical hypercube networks. Inf. Sci. **177**(19), 4200–4207 (2007)
21. Xiang, Y., Stewart, I.A.: One-to-many node-disjoint paths in (n, k)-star graphs. Discrete Appl. Math. **158**, 62–70 (2010)

Parallel Computing Method for HRV Time-Domain Based on GPU

Jie Wang, Weihao Chen, and Gang Hou[⊠]

School of Software Technology, Dalian University of Technology,
Economic and Technological Development Zone, Dalian 116600, China
{Wangjie1003,Endeavour35,hg.dut}@163.com

Abstract. HRV (Heart rate variability, which has a function of prediction for cardiovascular disease) contains a wealth of medical information, rapid extraction and procession of these signals will bring an important meaning for the prevention of heart diseases. Physionet open source project provides a good platform for the research and development of HRV, which also provides demonstration tools for the calculation of HRV. The characteristics of medical signal are real-time and have large volume of data. Conventional serial methods are difficult to meet the requirements of biomedicine, and the parallel method based on multi-core CPU is larger communication overhead. In this paper, we designed some parallel algorithms for the calculation of HRV in time-domain based on the strategy of parallel reduction, compared and analyzed the various optimization methods, and received the highest 38 times speedup compared with serial method.

Keywords: GPU · HRV · Parallel · Reduction · Time-domain

1 Introduction

Cardiovascular disease is one of the major diseases that threaten human life [1], which has features of high incidence, high morbidity, and high mortality. World Health Organization statistics shows that about 17 million people worldwide died of all types of cardiovascular disease each year. For the diagnosis of heart diseases, treatment and prevention is still the huge challenge of medical profession.

ECG (Electrocardiogram) [2] diagnosis is a very important way for cardiovascular disease diagnosis, which has a high value [3, 4] for the identification of all types of arrhythmias, suggesting atrial, ventricular hypertrophy, the diagnosis of myocardial infarction, myocarditis and other diseases. With the deepening of HRV study, physiological and pathological information that it contains will be further revealed, which will make HRV contains more space and value of application. Currently, heart rate variability analysis method [5, 6] contains time-domain analysis, frequency-domain analysis, time-frequency analysis and nonlinear analysis. Time-domain analysis is the easiest way of measuring heart rate variability signal, which is a method of statistical analysis. Researchers discrete RR interval changes based on the method of trend analysis by statistics. Analysis in time-domain is simple, intuitive and easy for the acceptance of the clinicians, and has accumulated a lot of experience.

© Springer International Publishing Switzerland 2015
G. Wang et al. (Eds.): ICA3PP 2015, Part II, LNCS 9529, pp. 434–443, 2015.
DOI: 10.1007/978-3-319-27122-4_30

Medicine signal characteristics: informative, randomness and noise background are strong, which makes it require long time for the measurement of biomedical signal. HRV time-domain analysis in general should be a long-term of at least 24 h, especially for acute myocardial infarction (AMI) prognosis, so it is extremely important for the rapid processing of mass of HRV data. GPU is widely used in biomedicine [7–9], and the calculation methods used for HRV and optimization are very necessary.

2 The Current Status of Research

2.1 Open Source Project of PhysioNet

In order to promote the exchange and cooperation in medical field, the US National Institutes of Health (NIH) funded, Massachusetts Institute of Technology (MIT) jointly BethIsrael Deaconess Medical Center in Boston, etc. established a web-based complex physiological and biomedical signal resources website PhysioNet (www.physionet.org) since 1999, to facilitate the exchange of research data and analysis software, and encourage extensive collaboration between researchers. Physionet medical researchers can apply them to their own research, to validate and assess the range of practical algorithms.

A signal data of PhysioBank database consists of multiple files, a major component consists of three parts: the header file, data file and comment file, while the header file (.hea) is essential document among them. As shown in Fig. 1, website also provides analytical tools that can be used to calculate various HRV parameters. The open-source project provides a good platform for the cooperation and exchange of biomedical science development.

2.2 Prospects of GPU in Biomedicine

Speed and accuracy [10] are the key index of signal evaluation, which is more and more important. With the increasing amount of data to be processed, especially for situation that requires 24-hour monitoring and real-time processing, the execution time will increase as the amount of data gradually extend.

Applications of GPU in biomedicine are widespread. Saha and Desai [11] made a real-time analysis of huge amount of data generated by multichannel body sensor

Fig. 1. The data structure of signals

networks such as Electroencephalogram (EEG), Electrocardiogram (ECG), Electromyography (EMG) and Functional-MRI (fMRI), which is critical for the deployment of these technologies. Processing these multichannel data sets using complex signal processing algorithms such as Grassberger and Procaccia (GP) algorithm to compute Correlation Dimension (D2) is resource intensive. Using massively parallel computing infrastructure comprising of Graphical Processing Units (GPU) and Multicore Processing nodes for parallelizing such huge data dependent problems is an apt use of the resource (Tables 1 and 2).

Table 1. The result comparison A

ECG sample	Computing infrastructure	No. of samples	Time taken for all samples	Speedup for complete data
MIT BIH 101	Sequential C Code	5120	60.4998	1
		10240	283.752	1
	MPI/Thread Hybrid	5120	3.32361	18.20303826
		10240	17.8462	15.89985543
	GPU Implementation#1	5120	14.837	4.077630249
		10240	91.12	3.11404741
	GPU Implementation#2	5120	6.28	9.633726115
		10240	96.25	2.948072727

Table 2. The result comparison B

ECG sample	Computing infrastructure	No. of samples	Time taken for one iteration of "r"	Speedup for one iteration
MIT BIH 101	Sequential C Code	5120	0.43	1
		10240	1.59	1
	MPI/Thread Hybrid	5120	0.42	1.023809524
		10240	1.49	1.067114094
	GPU Implementation#1	5120	0.0086	50
		10240	0.045	35.3333333
	GPU Implementation#2	5120	0.0086	50
		10240	0.045	35.3333333

The authors took two different databases for this experiment, and tested the algorithms of Sequential C Code, MPI/Thread Hybrid, GPU implementation#1, GPU implementation#2. The two algorithms of GPU can get ideal speedup in one iteration, and have an obvious speedup when compared with algorithm of sequential C code.

The implementation results of traditional serial method is slow, which is hard to deal with HRV parameters for the calculation of large amounts of data, and is difficult

Table 3. Time-domain parameters formula

$$AVNN = \frac{\sum_{i=1}^{N} R_i}{N} \tag{1}$$

$$SDNN = \sqrt{\frac{\sum_{i=1}^{N}(R_i - \bar{R})^2}{N}} \tag{2}$$

$$SDANN = \sqrt{\frac{\sum_{i=1}^{N}(aR_i - \overline{aR})^2}{N}} \tag{3}$$

$$SDNNIDX = \frac{SDNNi}{Num} \tag{4}$$

$$rMSSD* = \sqrt{\frac{\sum_{i=1}^{N}(R_i - R_{i-1})^2}{N}} \tag{5}$$

$$pNN50 = \frac{NN_{>50}}{TotalNN} \times 100\% \tag{6}$$

to meet the medical requirements for real-time detection. Aiming at the characteristics of HRV parameters in time-domain, a parallel strategy of reduction will be applied. The experiment showed that it could achieve good acceleration when compared with traditional serial algorithm (Table 3).

3 Serial Analysis of Time-Domain of HRV

Parameters in time-domain of HRV are calculated above, the calculation processes based on the above formula is shown as follows:

Step 1: Get files of PhysioBank database of corresponding disease;
Step 2: Call QRS detection program [12];
Step 3: Generate document of RR interval sequence;
Step 4: Read file and compute time-domain parameters;
Step 5: Output the results.

According to the calculation process, it is easy to write the appropriate serial computing program. But there are lots of plus operations in the calculation of time-domain, and it is difficult to meet the requirements of real time ECG analysis when operating a large amount of data. So optimization of this part is crucial.

4 Parallel Calculation of Time-Domain HRV

4.1 Parallel Optimization Principle

In the calculation of time-domain HRV, a number of data encryption and storage will be performed. Speed and accuracy are the key indicators to evaluate signal processing algorithm, especially in the field of biomedical.

Parallel reduction [13] is a common and important optimization method, which can be applied to more than one thread blocks and guarantee GPU processors in a busy state. By dividing calculations into multiple kernels, global synchronization operation will be avoided, communication overhead will be reduced too (Fig. 2).

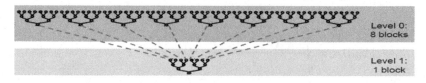

Fig. 2. Parallel reduction method

4.2 Strategy of Reduction

These are applets of the calculation of HRV in time-domain. THREAD_NUM is 512, which is the block Dimension. At first, the data is stored in an array vec1 in global memory. When the applet starts, data will be copied to the array vec, which is allotted by every block. At the end of every applets, the data in the first thread of each block will be copied to nnCounter that is allotted in global memory.

Sequential Addressing.

```
__shared__ int vec[THREAD_NUM]; //call for the shared momory for 512
vec[index] = vec1[id];      //threads, and copy the data form global
   __syncthreads();          // memory to shared memory
 for(int i=blockDim.x/2;i>0;i/=2){
   if(index < i)
     vec[index]+= vec[index+i];
        __syncthreads();
 }
 if(threadIdx.x == 0)     //add the sum of blocks to the first thread
   nnCounter[blockIdx.x] = vec[0];
```

Shared memory is second only to register, and has a faster execution. In this part of optimization, every vector will be stored in shared memory of the block. By the judgment of (index < i) for each thread, bank conflict will be avoided by the thread discontinuously.

First Add During Global Load.

```
__shared__ float vec[THREAD_NUM];
int id = blockIdx.x * (blockDim.x*2) + threadIdx.x;
int index = threadIdx.x;
vec[index] = vec1[id]+vec1[id+blockDim.x]; //two blocks
__syncthreads();                                    //add together
for(int i=blockDim.x/2;i>0;i/=2){
  if(index < i)
    vec[index]+= vec[index+i];
      __syncthreads();
}
if(threadIdx.x == 0)
  vec0[blockIdx.x] = (int)vec[0];
```

Drawbacks of the above optimization algorithm are that half threads will be idle during each cycle. In order to reduce idle threads as much as possible, addition operations will be done when accessing global memory, so each block can use the same threads to complete twice operations of statue summing elements.

Unroll The Last Warp. The execution unit of GPU thread is warp, each warp thread within no synchronization. So when there are only 32 threads of a warp need to added, other warps will execute null branch. Warp synchronized will not be needed because of the sequential consistency, and when blockDim.x $\geq$ 32, operations will be operated based on reduce2.

```
__device__ void warpReduce1(volatile int* vec,int index)
{
  vec[index]+=vec[index+32]; //unroll the warp
  vec[index]+=vec[index+16];
  vec[index]+=vec[index+8];
  vec[index]+=vec[index+4];
  vec[index]+=vec[index+2];
  vec[index]+=vec[index+1];
}
```

Complete Unrolling. CPU execution cycle is an inefficient recycling portion, which can be fully extended. When the number of threads in each block is n-th power of 2, the efficiency of the code will be higher.

```
vec[index] = vec1[id]+vec1[id+blockDim.x];
__syncthreads();
if(blockDim.x>=512){
  if(index<256){
    vec[index]+=vec[index+256];}
  __syncthreads();}
if(blockDim.x>=256){
  if(index<128){
    vec[index]+=vec[index+128];}
  __syncthreads();}
if(blockDim.x>=128){
  if(index<64){
    vec[index]+=vec[index+64];}
  __syncthreads();}
if(index<32)
  warpReduce1(vec,index);
if(threadIdx.x == 0)
  vec0[blockIdx.x] = vec[0];
```

Multiple Adds/Threads.

```
__shared__ int vec[THREAD_NUM];
int id = blockIdx.x * (blockDim.x*2) + threadIdx.x;
int index = threadIdx.x;
int gridSize = blockDim.x*2*gridDim.x;
vec[index] = 0;
while(id < MAX_PEAK)  // MAX_PEAK is all threads number
{
  vec[index] = vec1[id]+vec1[id+blockDim.x];
  id += gridSize;
}
__syncthreads();
```

Loop reading of the global memory and copying data to shared memory. In this cycle, vast majority of warps are able to maintain full load and is possible to improve efficiency.

5 Implementation of the Results and Analysis of HRV

5.1 Introduction of the Platform

The testing environment of parallel reduction was run in Linux, GPU is GeForce GTX460 of NVIDIA. GTX460 computing power of 2.1, memory 1G, memory interface

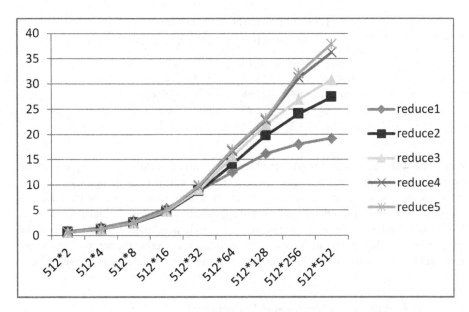

Fig. 3. According to the table to draw the appropriate line chart is as above.

256-bit, memory frequency 1848.00 MHz, a total of 336 CUDA [14, 15] Cores, GPU clocked at 1.40 GHz. Because GTX460 uses the latest Fermi architecture, so the number of threads is 1024. In order to make the code more portable, we allocate the maximum 512 threads per block (Fig. 3).

5.2   Analysis of the Results

Analysis of different sizes for each algorithm speedup situation Tables 4 and 5.

When the data size is less than 512 * 4, the result of GPU parallel optimization acceleration is not ideal, and the difference of the acceleration effect between various optimization methods is not great. So the acceleration effect of various optimization strategies is not ideal when the data set is small, and the difference between them is small too.

When the data size increases to 512 * 64, the acceleration effect gap between them is able to reflect. The strategy of first add of reduce2 has greatly improved when

Table 4. Points table with speedup A

	512*2	512*4	512*8	512*16	512*32
reduce1	0.79	1.58	2.87	5.38	8.92
reduce2	0.62	1.22	2.42	4.55	8.78
reduce3	0.62	1.22	2.47	4.78	9.03
reduce4	0.64	1.28	2.5	5.03	9.74
reduce5	0.64	1.27	2.5	4.94	10.02

Table 5. Points table with speedup B

	512*64	512*128	512*256	512*512
reduce1	12.56	16.15	18.06	19.2
reduce2	14.1	19.77	24.08	27.35
reduce3	15.42	21.88	26.97	30.81
reduce4	16.77	22.75	31.22	36.23
reduce5	17.2	23.11	32.14	37.91

compared with strategy that used shared memory only, and the accelerating effect will be improved further when unrolling the last warp or unroll them completely.

From the above figure, we can also analyze that with the node-by-fold increasing in the size, speed node ratio does not increase exponentially, but is gradually leveled off. From the trend of reduce1, we can see that each acceleration policies have the appropriate stability threshold. To make the algorithm accelerate further, we can use the new architectures such as Kepler hardware, or optimize the transmission bandwidth.

5.3   The Complexity of the Parallel Reduction

Parallel reduction will perform Log(N) steps, each step S does $N/2^2$ independent ops, step complexity is O(logN); For $N = 2^D$ perform $\sum_{S\in[1...D]} 2^{D-S} = N - 1$ operations, work complexity is O(N). It is work-efficient, and it does not perform more operations than a sequential algorithm; With P threads physically in parallel (P processors), time complexity is O(N/P + logN), in a thread block, N = P, so O(logN).

6   Conclusion and Future Work

HRV as an important index for cardiovascular and cerebrovascular disease, quick and accurate are crucial. This article designed and implemented the calculation of time-domain of HRV parameters, which received nearly 35 times speedup. For different ECG database, according to the characteristics of each parameter calculation, using the appropriate strategy of parallelization can bring great improvement for the calculation of the various parameters.

GPU distributed computing model promotes the development of the top super-computers. MPI enables CUDA extend to compute thousands of nodes. At the same time, commercial-grade GPU clusters and cloud computing platform provides a full range of resources for users and organizations. We designed some HRV parallel computing methods based on GPU, and analysis the speedup of each algorithm. With the rapid increase of medical data, combining with GPU and distributed computing, taking advantage of GPU cluster analysis process will greatly improve the calculation of HRV and other mass medical data.

Acknowledgments. This paper was supported by National Nature Science Foundation of China (No. 61472100) and Fundamental Research Funds for the Central Universities, China (No. DUT14QY32).

References

1. Thayer, J.F., Yamamoto, S.S., Brosschot, J.F.: The relationship of autonomic imbalance, heart rate variability and cardiovascular disease risk factors. Int. J. Cardiol. **141**, 122–131 (2010). Elseiver
2. Bansal, D., Singh, V.R.: Algorithm for online detection of HRV from coherent ECG and carotid pulse wave. Int. J. Biomed. Eng. Technol. (IJBET) **14**, 333–343 (2014). Inderscience Publishers Ltd
3. Ferrari, E., Imbert, A., Chevalier, T., et al.: The ECG in pulmonary embolism: predictive value of negative T waves in precordial leads—80 case reports. CHEST J. **113**, 537–543 (1997). American College of Chest Physicians
4. Zhou, Q.: ECG heart beat modeling and analysis to identify. PhD thesis of Zhejiang University, Biomedical Engineering and Instrument Science, Zhejiang University, Zhejiang, pp. 5–10 (2004)
5. Mohan, A., et al.: Design and development of a heart rate variability analyzer. J. Med. Syst. **36**, 1365–1371 (2012). Springer
6. Jeppesen, J., Fuglsang-Frederiksen, A., Brugada, R., et al.: Heart rate variability analysis indicates preictal parasympathetic overdrive preceding seizure-induced cardiac dysrhythmias leading to sudden unexpected death in a patient with epilepsy. Epilepsia **55**, e67–e71 (2014). Wiley Online Library
7. Konstantinidis, E.I., et al.: Accelerating biomedical signal processing algorithms with parallel programming on graphic processor units. In: ITAB2009. IEEE, pp. 1–4 (2009)
8. Freiberger, M., et al.: The agile library for biomedical image reconstruction using GPU acceleration. Comput. Sci. Eng. **15**, 34–44 (2013). AIP Publishing
9. Costa, C.M., Haase, G., Liebmann, M., Neic, A., Plank, G.: Stepping into fully GPU accelerated biomedical applications. In: Lirkov, I., Margenov, S., Waśniewski, J. (eds.) LSSC 2013. LNCS, vol. 8353, pp. 3–14. Springer, Heidelberg (2014)
10. Konstantinidis, E.I., et al.: Accelerating biomedical signal processing algorithms with parallel programming on graphic processor units. In: Information Technology and Application in Biomedicine, ITAB. IEEE, pp. 1–4 (2009)
11. Saha, D.P., Desai, A.R.: Performance analysis of computing multichannel correlation dimension (D2) on multicore system and GPU. Researchgate.net
12. Tarvainen, M.P., et al.: Kubios HRV – heart rate variability analysis software. Comput. Methods Programs Biomed. **113**, 210–220 (2014). Elseiver
13. Harris, M.: Optimizing parallel reduction in CUDA. Presentation packaged with CUDA Toolkit, NVIDIA Corporation (2007)
14. NVIDIA Corporation, NVIDIA CUDA Programming Guide (2009)
15. http://developer.download.nvidia.com/compute/cuda/2_3/toolkit/docs/NVIDIA_CUDA_Programming_Guide_2.3.pdf

Accelerated Steiner Tree Problem Solving on GPU with CUDA

Christian Mathieu[1] and Matthias Klusch[2]([⊠])

[1] Computer Science Department, Saarland University, 66123 Saarbruecken, Germany
[2] German Research Center for Artificial Intelligence, 66123 Saarbruecken, Germany
klusch@dfki.de

Abstract. The Steiner Tree Problem in Graphs (STPG) is an important NP-hard combinatorial optimization problem arising naturally in many applications including network routing, social media analysis, power grid routing and in the context of the semantic web. We present the first parallel heuristics for the solution of the STPG for GPU with CUDA, and show that the achieved speedups for different kinds of graphs are significant compared to one of the fastest serial heuristics STAR.

Keywords: Graphs · Steiner tree · Parallel algorithms · GPU · CUDA

1 Introduction

The Steiner Tree Problem in Graphs (STPG) is one of the most important combinatorial optimization problems in computer science and defined as follows:

Definition 1. *Given a weighed graph $G(V,E)$ with node set V, edge set $E \subseteq V \times V$ and a nonnegative weight function $w : E \to \mathbb{R}^+$, a solution tree $S(V',E')$ is a connected acyclic graph with node set $V' \subseteq V$ and edge set $E' \subseteq E \cap (V' \times V')$. We extend the weight function w to solution trees as $w(S) = \sum_{e \in E'} w(e)$. The Steiner tree problem in graphs (STPG) is as follows: For a given terminal set $V_t \subseteq V'$, find a minimal-cost tree S in G that spans V_t. Minimal cost denotes that $w(S)$ is minimal among all possible solution trees in G spanning V_t. The vertices $v \in V_t$ are called terminal nodes, while the remaining vertices $v \in V' \backslash V_t$ are called non-terminal nodes*

The STPG and close variants of it are used in a wide range of applications, including wire routing in very-large-scale integration circuits (VLSI) [11], network routing in wireless networks [20], multicast routing [12] and power distribution in electric grids [8]. Large graph databases, especially in the context of social networks or the semantic web, grow ever more important. When close relationships between multiple entities are of interest, the STPG often arises naturally. Many of these applications deal with very large problem sizes.

However, solving the STPG optimally grows prohibitively expensive with increasing problem size: Deciding the existence of a Steiner tree below a given

© Springer International Publishing Switzerland 2015
G. Wang et al. (Eds.): ICA3PP 2015, Part II, LNCS 9529, pp. 444–457, 2015.
DOI: 10.1007/978-3-319-27122-4_31

cost is one of Karp's classical 21 NP-complete problems [14]. Thus, the optimization problem given in Definition 1 is NP-hard. In fact, there is essentially no known algorithm with worst-case time complexity better than exhaustive search, resulting in exponential runtime complexity. Due to the importance of the problem, there has been considerable effort into finding both serial [17, 23–25], distributed [12, 20] and parallel [22] heuristics approximating the optimal solution while offering far better runtime. On the other hand, there are also many implementations of other graph algorithms on GPU [10, 16, 26], including the Rectilinear Steiner Tree Problem [6]. However, to the best of our knowledge, there are no parallel heuristics for the STPG employing the GPU so far. To this end, we present the first parallel solution of the STPG for GPU with CUDA, called STP_CUDA [19], based on one of the fastest serial heuristics for the STPG, called STAR [15]. Our experimental evaluation shows that for different kinds of graphs, achieved speedup of STP_CUDA is significant compared to the reference implementation of STAR for CPU.

The remainder of this paper is structured as follows: NVIDIA's CUDA and Kasneci et al.'s STAR [15] are introduced in Sect. 2, while our parallel implementation is described in Sect. 3. Results of our practical evaluation are presented in Sect. 4, before we draw our final conclusions in Sect. 5.

2   Background

In this section, we briefly introduce CUDA and an approximated STP solver, called STAR [15], which serves as a basis of our parallel STP solving on GPU with CUDA, introduced in a subsequent section.

Approximated Solution with STAR. A very fast approximated STP solver called STAR [15] replaces the exhaustive search for a globally optimal solution with a subdivision approach that repeatedly recombines partial solutions using a shortest path heuristic. While unmodified STAR's worst case runtime is exponential, the authors also introduced the ϵ-*improvement rule* which is an early abort criterion skipping recombinations resulting in minimal improvements, thus guaranteeing termination in a limited number of iterations.

Using this optimization, STAR has a time complexity of $\mathcal{O}(\frac{1}{\epsilon} \frac{w_{max}}{w_{min}} mk(S))$ for improvement threshold ϵ, query terminal count k, graph node count n, graph edge count m and largest and smallest edge weight w_{max} and w_{min} [15]. S denotes the time complexity of the chosen search algorithm, which is $nlogn + m$ for the reference implementation. It has been shown that STAR approximates the optimal solution to a factor of $(1 + \epsilon)(4\lceil logk \rceil + 4)$.

During its execution, STAR broadly operates in two phases. It first constructs an arbitrary tree connecting all terminals using edges of the encompassing graph. This tree can be thought of as an initial candidate solution. It is found by performing a breadth-first search from each terminal node until a single node is reached by all of the searches. The path to the corresponding starting terminal of each search is then backtracked to build a tree spanning all terminals. This initial tree is then passed to the second phase, which tries to iteratively improve it. The key idea is to visualize a tree as a collection of non-branching paths of degree 2, called *loose paths*, which are connected to either nodes of degree ≥ 3 or terminal nodes. These crossroads where loose paths meet are called *fixed nodes*. This is illustrated in Fig. 1(a). Note that removing all *intermediate* (non-endpoint) nodes of a loose path from the tree decomposes the tree into two partitions, both of which are trees as well. Figure 1(b) shows the graph from Fig. 1(a) after removing loose path 3. STAR now attempts to find a better (lower cost) tree by following the following scheme:

- All loose paths in the currently best solution candidate tree are found
- The loose paths are sorted by descending length
- STAR attempts to replace the longest loose path not yet attempted
- To replace the loose path, it is cut out of the tree, and the shortest path from any node of the first partition to any node in the second partition is found. This is a regular multi-source multi-target shortest path search.
- If the two partitions and the shortest path between them form a cheaper tree than the current best, it is the new current best and STAR repeats these steps on the newfound tree.
- If the newfound tree is not strictly better, it is discarded and the next loose path attempted.
- If all loose paths have been attempted but none resulted in an improvement, then the currently best solution is returned as STAR's result. Note that this implies that the tree is a local optimum regarding STAR's heuristic.

A schematic overview of STAR's execution is shown in Fig. 2. Loose paths, fixed nodes and their role during tree partitioning are depicted in Fig. 1(a) and (b).

A pseudo-code listing of STAR is shown in Algorithm 1. *buildInitialTree()* denotes a first phase not depicted here, which connects all terminal nodes to a common tree. *partition()* returns the two partitions that result when removing all edges and intermediate nodes of *loosePath* from *tree*. By 'intermediate node' we mean all nodes of the path excluding the two end points (see Fig. 1). *findShortestPath()* in Kasneci et al's reference implementation is a straightforward bidirectional shortest path search based on Disjkstra's Algorithm. We will later replace it with one of two parallel implementations. For further information on the reference implementation, refer to [15].

Algorithm 1. STAR(graph, terminals)

```
bestTree := buildInitialTree(graph, terminals)
newTree := improveTree(graph, terminals, bestTree)
while newTree.cost < bestTree.cost do
    bestTree := newTree
    newTree := improveTree(graph, terminals, bestTree)
end while
return bestTree
```

Algorithm 2. improveTree(graph, terminals, tree)

loosePaths := getLoosePaths(terminals, tree)
for loosePaths ordered by descending length **do**
   (partitionA, partitionB) := partition(tree, loosePath)
   path := findShortestPath(graph, partitionA, partitionB)
   newTree := merge(partitionA, path, partitionB)
   if newTree.cost < tree.cost **then**
     return newTree
   end if
end for
return tree

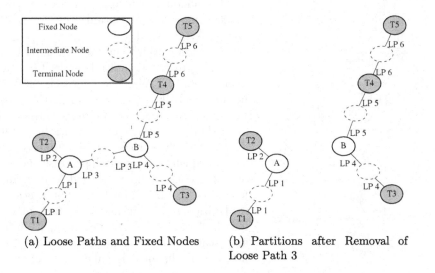

(a) Loose Paths and Fixed Nodes

(b) Partitions after Removal of Loose Path 3

Fig. 1. Partitioning of solution candidate tree

Parallel Processing with CUDA. In a GPU using NVIDIAs Compute Unified Device Architecture (CUDA), multiple cores are clustered into coherent units called streaming multiprocessors (SM). CUDA segrates parallely executed code into enclosed units called *kernels*. A kernel can be distributed across hundres of cores, executing tens of thousands of lightweight threads concurrently. To synchronize this vast amount of threads, a simple barrier synchronization model is employed. Since groups of 32 threads (called a *warp*) are executed in true SIMD fashion on one SM, divergent control flow is to be avoided within a warp to keep performance high. To keep costly global memory accesses to a minimum, threads on one SM can use a local memory called *shared memory* to cooperate with other threads within the same core (or more precisely: within a *block*, a logical unit clustering some threads guaranteed to reside within the same SM). The device is further capable of joining multiple memory accesses within a contiguous region of memory, a so called *coalesced* memory access. These hardware details necessitate adapted program design avoiding inefficient memory layout and playing to the strengths of the architecture.

3   Parallel STP_CUDA Algorithm

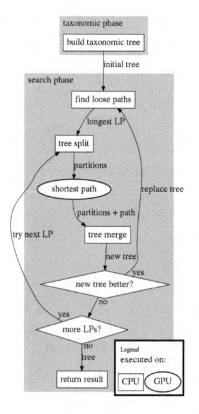

Fig. 2. STAR Overview

Since we found STAR's runtime on large graphs to be mostly dominated by the shortest path heuristic (Fig. 6), we replaced the serial implementation of Dijkstra's Algorithm [7] with two GPU-based parallel approaches. CUDA_N, the first of these, follows Martin et al.'s node-parallel approach closely [18], further employing an optimization found by Ortega-Arranz et al. [21].

The basic idea is to unroll DA's outer loop partially, processing multiple nodes from the queue at once. The second approach, CUDA_E, parallelizes Dijkstra's Algorithm further, traversing *edges* in parallel, not unlike Jia et al.'s algorithm for betweenness centrality [13]. This effectively unrolls DA's innermost loop as well, which traverses each processed nodes' outgoing edges. The general idea for parallelization is identical for both approaches:

Dijkstra's Algorithm keeps track of the length of the best known shortest path from any search source node to each reached node. This distance is called the *tentative distance*. During each iteration, the least tentative distance node (*min-node*) among unprocessed (not yet *settled*) nodes is found. Since Dijkstra's Algorithm forbids negative weight edges, no node can *relax* (i.e. update its tentative distance) a neighboring node to a tentative distance lower than its own. Since the min-node is by definition the least distance node not yet settled, it must have already converged to its true shortest path distance, since all other unsettled nodes have at least the same tentative distance and thus cannot reduce the min-node's tentative distance further. But the min-node is not necessarily unique. Depending on the edge weights in the graph, a potentially large number of nodes can be equally minimal at a given time. We call such nodes the F-set, since they are the *frontier* of nodes about to be settled (See Fig. 4). The order in which nodes in the F-set are processed does not matter, since all nodes in the F-set have converged to their final state, i.e. there is no interdependence among these nodes. It is thus possible to expand them concurrently, as long as we take care to resolve conflicts while updating neighbors.

Ortega-Arranz et al. further showed that this definition of the F-set can be expanded to certain *almost-minimal* nodes which must have converged to their true shortest path distance as well [21]. A node n_i is almost minimal if $d_i \leq d_{min} + min_j(w_{j,i})$, where d_i denotes the tentative distance of node i, $min_j(w_{j,i})$ denotes the least weight of any incident edge to i and d_{min} denotes the minimal tentative distance of any yet unsettled node. In other words, there is no node yet unsettled that could relax node i.

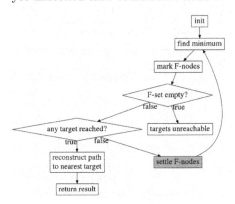

Fig. 3. Parallel Search Overview

Since this requires either processing all edge weights of each node in each iteration, or storing the minimal edge weight for each node, and since many of our graphs have uniform edge weights anyway, we opted to use Ortega-Arranz' *economical approach* instead. We only relax nodes in parallel when $d_i \leq d_{min} + w_{min}$ where w_{min} denotes the least weight of *any* edge in the graph. This is more conservative, but not dependent on the individual node's edge weights anymore. For uniform weight graphs, both approaches are equivalent.

To actually exploit this inherent parallelism, we proceed as follows: The graph is stored in GPU memory using a straightforward adjacency list representation. For each node, we store the offset of its first edge in the edge arrays. For each edge, we store source node index, target node index and weight. While storing the source node index might seem superfluous, it is very useful for our edge-parallel approach CUDA_E below. We further store the graphs minimal edge weight. The graph is initialized once and reused for subsequent searches and STAR invocations. Due to this, our algorithms are most useful for static graphs.

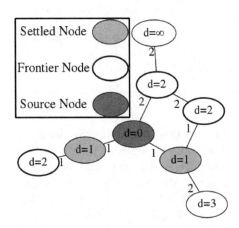

Fig. 4. Frontier Nodes of Search Fringe

During each search operation, tentative distances, F- and U-sets are initialised first and stored in form of a flag array. The F flag represents nodes that are about to be expanded (i.e. in the aforementioned *frontier*), whereas the U flag represents unsettled but visited nodes (i.e. potential candidates for the F-set during the next iteration). We then find the minimal tentative distance among U-nodes using a slightly modified parallel reduction [9]. We now mark all F-nodes, i.e. nodes n_i where $d_i \leq d_{min} + w_{min}$. If this results in no marked node, the target node(-s) must be unreachable and we abort (all possible paths are explored). If F-nodes were marked, we retrieve the least distance one. Note that, since F-nodes are equivalent to nodes Dijkstra's Algorithm might have settled in this iteration, we are done if such a target exists. If no target was F-marked, we settle all F-nodes. To avoid data races, neighboring distance values are updated using the atomicMin operator. Parallel settling of nodes is where CUDA_N differs the most from CUDA_E. The general scheme of the search operation is depicted graphically in Fig. 3 and as pseudo-code in Algorithm 3.

Algorithm 3. findShortestPath(graph, partitionA, partitionB)

$w_{min} := min\{w(i,j) \mid edge\ (i,j) \in graph\}$ # precalculated once

$\forall$ nodes $n \in graph : d(n) := \infty$

$\forall$ nodes $s \in partitionA : d(s) := 0$

$d_{min} := \infty$

$U := \{s \mid s \in partitionA\}$

$F := \{\}$

while true **do**

    $d_{min} := min_{n \in U}d(n)$ # parallel reduction [9]

    $F := \{n \mid (n \in U) \land (d(n) \leq d_{min} + w_{min})\}$ # parallel setting of flag array

    if $|F| = 0$ **then**

        return null   # no solution exists

    end if

    $t_{min} := arg\ min_{t \in F \cap partitionB}d(t)$ # any target about to be settled?

    if $t_{min}exists$ **then**

        return constructPath(t_{min})   # backtrack from target node

    end if

    settle(U, F, d)   # This is where CUDA_N and CUDA_E differ!

end while

Node-parallel variant CUDA_N of STP_CUDA. Our node-parallel approach CUDA_N differs from CUDA_E in the strategy chosen when settling nodes in parallel. The idea behind CUDA_N is to distribute F-nodes over available cores, where they are settled in parallel. A single node is always processed by a single thread. To avoid the overhead of managing queue structures, U and F nodes are marked in a global flag array. We distribute *all* graph nodes among available cores, skipping nodes not in the F-set. Each thread then iterates over all neighbors of its currently allotted node in series. If successful relaxation seems possible (we don't know whether other threads are just relaxing the same node!), an atomicMin operation is executed to synchronize parallel write access. This is safe, since neither edge weights nor F-node tentative distances are going to change, thus no read after write conflicts occur. As mentioned above, the entire approach is mostly equivalent to [18].

Algorithm 4. settle_N

---

for all n in parallel **do**
  if $n \in F$ **then**
    for each neighbor m **do**   # this is serial
      if $w(m) > w(n) + w(n,m)$ **then**
        $w(m) := w(n) + w(n,m)$ # synchronized with atomicMin()
      end if
    end for
  end if
end for

Edge-parallel variant CUDA_E of STP_CUDA. The node-parallel approach employed by CUDA_N above potentially suffers from poor load balancing when processing real-world ontologies, which often have a power-law distribution of edge degree. When nodes differ greatly in edge degree, the workload differs between individual threads as well. Remember: CUDA_N has a single thread settle a single F-flagged node. This thread thus needs to iterate over all outgoing edges of the node. Differing edge degree results in unequal workload between threads. Our second approach thus distributes work not on a per-node but on a per-edge basis. When settling nodes in parallel, *all* graph edges (belonging to F-set nodes or not) are distributed among threads. For each edge, the F flag of its source node is checked. If the F-flag is not set, the edge is skipped, otherwise the target node's distance is updated. This effectively parallelises the settling of each single node. While this incurs significant overhead due to repeated access to source nodes as well as processing of unneeded edges, it offers much more fine grained load balancing, thus utilizing available processors more efficiently. As above, conflicts are resolved using the hardware-supported atomicMin operator. Thread safety follows from the same argumentation as with CUDA_N above.

Algorithm 5. settle_E

---

for all edges (n,m) in parallel **do**   # rollout of inner loop of settle_N
  if $n \in F$ **then**
    if $w(m) > w(n) + w(n,m)$ **then**
      $w(m) := w(n) + w(n,m)$ # synchronized with atomicMin()
    end if
  end if
end for

---

4 Evaluation

Setting. All experiments below were executed using an Intel® Xeon® W5590 3.33 GHz CPU with 32 GB of DDR3-1333 main memory. The GPU-based components were executed using a Fermi-based Nvidia® GeForce® GTX590 card in standard memory configuration (i.e. 1536 MB of GDDR5 memory per GPU). While this card is a dual gpu card, only one GPU was employed during our tests. We compare the performance of three variants of STAR:

reference The purely CPU-based reference implementation, as defined by Kasneci et al. [15]. This implementation runs entirely host-sided and employs a straightforward serial implementation of Dijkstra's Algorithm [7] when searching for shortest paths.

cuda_n An implementation which performs the shortest path search *node*-parallel on GPU, i.e. distributing graph nodes among available threads. The implementation follows [21] closely.

cuda_e An implementation which performs the shortest path search *edge*-parallel on GPU, i.e. distributing graph edges among available threads, not unlike Jia et al.'s algorithm for betweenness centrality [13].

Both cuda_n and cuda_e perform the remaining components of STAR single-threaded on host side. To evaluate the performance of both parallel implementations as well as reference, we use object-relational queries in several large real-world ontologies. Test cases for each ontology were generated as follows:

– Each sample is a single object-relational query, defined by the set of terminal nodes and the ontology graph.
– The solution to a query is the resultant Steiner tree connecting the terminal nodes along edges of the ontology graph.
– Since query terminal count k affects runtime heavily, samples are generated for multiple values of k.
– k is set to increasing powers of two (starting with two), until main memory prohibits further increase (elaborated below).
– For each choice of k, 10 samples are generated.
– The query terminals of a given sample are chosen uniformly at random among all nodes of the ontology graph. If this results in an unsolvable instance (i.e. terminals are in disconnected components of the overall graph), the sample is discarded and a new sample generated until a valid sample is found.
– The evaluated algorithms all execute the same samples. The sample set is global, not per algorithm.
– The samples are executed by increasing k. Once at least one algorithm exceeds main memory during execution of a sample, all preceding samples of this k are discarded and no larger values of k are attempted. This is to ensure sample count is uniform among k, making runtime variance comparable.
– The protocolled performance metrics are wallclock runtime spent during execution and wallclock runtime spent during search. The former is defined as the time elapsed between issue of query until the resultant Steiner tree is returned. The latter is defined as the sum total of time spent inside shortest path searches during the former.
– We evaluate our parallel implementations regarding their *speedup* over reference as well as against each other. We define speedup of implementation i over implementation j as $\frac{t_j}{t_i}$, where t_i and t_j denote the measured runtime. If both implementations have equal runtime, this results in a speedup of 1.

- Time spent for creation of the ontology graph structure in memory does not affect runtime metrics. The graph is generated only once for each ontology and is considered part of the problem input. This includes both the graph representation in main memory as well as in GPU memory.

Table 1. Ontologies used for Runtime Testing

Ontology	$|N|$	$|E|$	mean edge degree	edge degree variance
OpenGalen	1.8M	8.7M	4.69	337k
IMDb	4.6M	29.8M	6.45	743
GeoSpecies	389k	4.1M	10.74	81k
Jamendo	484k	2M	4.32	48k

The ontologies chosen were (cf. Table 1):

OpenGalen An open source medical terminology, in development since 1990. The comparitively low edge count and high edge degree variance made it an interesting test case, since it introduced high branch divergence and poor load balancing for cuda_n. We used the OWL 2.0 based download of the entire GALEN ontology version 8, including Common Reference Model as well as all available extensions. [4]

IMDb The international movie database, a large database containing information about movies, television programs and video games. We built our test set using the plain text data files supplied by IMDb. We restricted the test set to the complete set of movies, actors, actresses, directors, producers and edges between those, as of 14th April 2014. The larger edge count and far lower edge degree variance provided an interesting contrast to OpenGalen above, since both favor the node parallel implementation cuda_n over the edge parallel cuda_e. [2]

GeoSpecies An ontology containing information about select plant and animal species, including their taxonomic relation and distribution area. Its lower edge and node count make it interesting to close the gap to the substantially smaller SteinLib test cases we will introduce below. [1]

Jamendo An ontology containing information about royalty free music tracks, records and the corresponding artists. It has about half the edge count of GeoSpecies and a comparable edge degree variance, further closing the gap to larger SteinLib test cases. [3]

For further information about the chosen ontologies, refer to Table 1. We further used SteinLib [5] test suites B, C, D and E to evaluate our implementation for high terminal count queries on small graphs. Since these queries are suboptimal for the parallelization approach chosen, they promise further insights into use cases where using our approach is *not* feasible. Figure 5(a) gives an overview how the SteinLib test cases and the ontology test cases compare in graph size and query terminal count. Note that both x and y-axis have been inverted to keep consistency with Fig. 5(b), (c) and (d), which had to be rotated to avoid occlusion of high-k values.

Results. Parallelizing the search operation of STAR promises substantial speedups when dealing with large graphs, especially at low query terminal counts. Figure 5(b) shows the speedup of CUDA_N over REFERENCE, while Fig. 5(c) shows the same information for our edge-parallel approach CUDA_E. Both approaches achieved a total runtime speedup over reference of over two orders of magnitude for the larger ontology based test cases and smaller terminal counts.

While the edge-parallel approach incurs overheads due to repeated calculations and additional edges it needs to iterate over, it still outperforms the node-parallel approach consistently, presumably due to better load balancing. This advantage is most pronounced for ontologies with high edge degree variance. Figure 5(d) shows the speedup of CUDA_E over CUDA_N. Note the prominent ridge for OpenGalen, an ontology with high edge degree variance, while speedup for the rather uniform IMDb is much more subtle.

For smaller graphs or queries with very high terminal count, the relative performance of both our parallel implementations suffers compared to the serial reference implementation. This has multiple reasons (cf. Fig. 2). STAR needs to perform a tree split and merge each time a loose path is processed. For high terminal counts, a large number of shortest path searches needs to be conducted, while the effort for each individual search often even sinks. A higher terminal count often results in a larger, more branched solution tree, thus reducing the average distance between tree nodes, resulting in earlier search termination. A smaller graph size on the other hand reduces the overall amount of nodes the search needs to process, resulting in lower search overhead as well. In both cases, the benefit of parallelizing the search is reduced due to the lowered contribution of search to total runtime. For sufficiently short searches, the CPU even outperforms the GPU. We verified these assumptions with synthetic power-law graphs generated according to the Barabasi-Albert model (initial graph size 3, connection factor 2). Figure 6 shows the time spent creating the initial tree, performing searches, and performing tree splits/merges for graphs of increasing node count.

Figure 6(a) shows results for a query terminal count of 4. The dominant factor contributing to runtime is clearly the time in shortest path searches, followed by the initial tree construction, which is a search as well. Effort for tree splits and merges is largely independent of graph size. This is unsurprising, since the size of the candidate solution tree is largely uneffected by graph size. In these graphs, the amount of nodes reachable along a path grows exponentially with path hop count (i.e. number of edges traversed). Contrast this with Fig. 6(b), which shows the results for queries with terminal count 128. The contribution of tree splits and merges increases significantly and now dominates time spent searching. This is not due to an increase in runtime per split/merge, but due to a higher amount of searches performed in total. The search effort for each

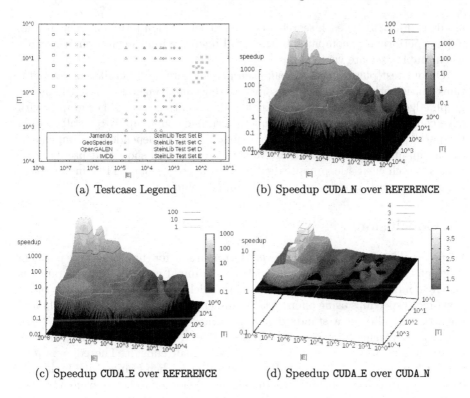

(a) Testcase Legend

(b) Speedup CUDA_N over REFERENCE

(c) Speedup CUDA_E over REFERENCE

(d) Speedup CUDA_E over CUDA_N

Fig. 5. Speedups

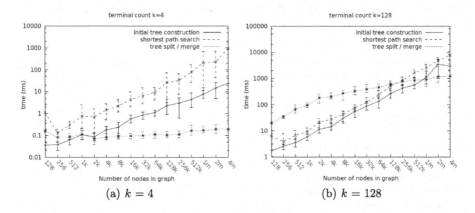

(a) $k = 4$

(b) $k = 128$

Fig. 6. STAR Component Scaling

individual search even decreases compared to the lower terminal count case, thus reducing opportunity for parallelism and runtime contribution of search itself. Since each kernel invocation on GPU adds a small constant runtime overhead and since both GPU-based approaches iterate over all graph nodes (for CUDA_N) or edges (for CUDA_E) each search step, a sufficiently high terminal count results in poor performance compared to the serial reference implementation, especially when graph sizes are very small.

On our test platform, the break-even point where both parallel implementations consistently outperform the serial reference implementation is at about 10^4 graph edges, as long as query terminal counts don't exceed 10. For graphs with edge count higher than about 10^5, query terminal counts up to 10^3 still favored the parallel implementations. This of course is heavily dependent on implementation, input graphs and hardware, but the results still show that parallelizing STAR's search heuristic promises substantial speedups for STPG instances in large graphs with moderate to small terminal counts.

5   Conclusions

While serial STAR itself is already a very fast heuristic for the Steiner tree problem in graphs, its runtime for queries with low terminal counts on large graphs is heavily dominated by its search heuristic. Parallelizing this search heuristic offers substantial speedups using affordable consumer graphics hardware. We evaluated both the viability of a standard node-parallel search approach and an edge-parallel improvement thereupon, and found both to be highly viable as long as graph sizes are large and query sizes are small enough. The edge-parallel approach promises much more robust performance when graphs with high edge degree variance are encountered. In our tests, both parallel implementations required graphs larger than about 10^4 edges to play to their strengths, limiting their feasibility on high-k problem instances in smaller graphs. Due to its more stable performance and consistently higher speedup, the edge parallel approach seems preferable to the node-parallel one.

Acknowledgement. This work was supported by the German ministry for education and research (BMBF) in the project INVERSIV under contract number 01IW14004.

References

1. http://lod.geospecies.org/
2. http://www.imdb.com/
3. https://www.jamendo.com/
4. http://www.opengalen.org/
5. http://steinlib.zib.de
6. Chow, W.K., Li, L., Young, E.F.Y., Sham, C.W.: Obstacle-avoiding rectilinear Steiner tree construction in sequential and parallel approach. Integr. VLSI **47**(1), 105–114 (2014)
7. Dijkstra, E.W.: A note on two problems in connexion with graphs. Numerische Mathematik **1**, 269–271 (1959)
8. Duan, G., Yu, Y.: Power distribution system optimization by an algorithm for capacitated Steiner tree problems with complex-flows and arbitrary cost functions. Electr. Power Energy Syst. **25**(7), 515–523 (2003)

9. Harris, M.: Optimizing parallel reduction in CUDA (2007). http://docs.nvidia. com/cuda/samples/6_Advanced/reduction/doc/reduction.pdf

10. Hong, S., Kim, S.K., Oguntebi, T., Olukotun, K.: Accelerating CUDA graph algorithms at maximum warp. In: Proceeding of 16th ACM Symposium on Principles and Practice of Parallel Programming, pp. 267–276. ACM, New York (2011)

11. Ihler, E., Reich, G., Widmayer, P.: Class Steiner trees and VLSI-design. Discrete Appl. Math. **90**(1–3), 173–194 (1999)

12. Jia, X., Wang, L.: A group multicast routing algorithm by using multiple minimum Steiner trees. Comput. Commun. **20**(9), 750–758 (1997)

13. Jia, Y., Lu, V., Hoberock, J., Garland, M., Hart, J.: Edge v. node parallelism for graph centrality metrics. In: GPU Computing Gems Jade Edition, 1st edn., chap. 2, pp. 15–30. Morgan Kaufmann, USA (2011)

14. Karp, R.M.: Reducibility among combinatorial problems. In: Complexity of Computer Computations, pp. 85–103 (1972)

15. Kasneci, G., Ramanath, M., Sozio, M., Suchanek, F.M., Weikum, G.: STAR: steiner-tree approximation in relationship graphs. In: Proceeding of IEEE International Conference on Data Engineering, pp. 868–879. IEEE, Washington DC (2009)

16. Katz, G.J., Kider, Jr., J.T.: All-pairs shortest-paths for large graphs on the GPU. In: Proceeding of 23rd ACM SIGGRAPH/EUROGRAPHICS Symposium on Graphics Hardware. Eurographics Association, pp. 47–55. ACM, Switzerland (2008)

17. Kou, L., Markowsky, G., Berman, L.: A fast algorithm for Steiner trees. Acta Informatica **15**(2), 141–145 (1981)

18. Martín, P.J., Torres, R., Gavilanes, A.: CUDA solutions for the SSSP problem. In: Allen, G., Nabrzyski, J., Seidel, E., van Albada, G.D., Dongarra, J., Sloot, P.M.A. (eds.) ICCS 2009, Part I. LNCS, vol. 5544, pp. 904–913. Springer, Heidelberg (2009)

19. Mathieu, C.: On approximated Steiner tree problem solving with CUDA. Bachelor thesis, Saarland University, Computer Science Department, Saarbruecken, Germany (2014)

20. Muhammad, R.: Distributed steiner tree algorithm and its application in ad hocwireless networks. In: Proceeding of International Conference on Wireless Networks, pp. 173–178 (2006)

21. Ortega-Arranz, H., Torres, Y., Llanos, D., Gonzalez-Escribano, A.: A new GPU-based approach to the shortest path problem. In: Proceeding of International Conference on High Performance Computing and Simulation, pp. 505–511 (2013)

22. Park, J.S., Ro, W., Lee, H., Park, N.: Parallel algorithms for Steiner tree problem. In: Proceeding of 3rd International Conference on Convergence and Hybrid Information Technology (ICCIT), vol. 1, pp. 453–455 (2008)

23. Rayward-Smith, V.J.: The computation of nearly minimal Steiner trees in graphs. Math. Educ. Sci. Technol. **14**(1), 15–23 (1983)

24. Robins, G., Zelikovsky, A.: Improved Steiner tree approximation in graphs. In: Proceeding of 11th Annual ACM-SIAM Symposium on Discrete Algorithms SODA, pp. 770–779. Society for Industrial and Applied Mathematics, USA (2000)

25. Takahashi, H., Matsuyama, A.: An approximate solution for the Steiner problem in graphs. Mathematica Japonica **24**, 573–577 (1980)

26. Zhong, J., He, B.: Medusa: Simplified graph processing on GPUs. IEEE Trans. Parallel Distrib. Sys. **25**(6), 1543–1552 (2014)

Self-Timed Periodic Scheduling
of Data-Dependent Tasks in Embedded
Streaming Applications

Xuan Khanh Do$^{(\boxtimes)}$, Amira Dkhil, and Stéphane Louise

CEA, LIST, PC172, 91191 Gif-sur-Yvette, France
{xuankhanh.do,amira.dkhil,stephane.louise}@cea.fr

Abstract. Developers increasingly use streaming languages to write embedded many-core applications that process large volumes of data with high throughput. Because they enable periodic scheduling, cyclo-static models of computation and their variants are well fitted to modern real-time applications. Nevertheless, most existing works have proposed periodic scheduling that ignore latency or can even have a negative impact on it: the results are quite far from those obtained under Self-Timed scheduling (STS). In this paper, we introduce a new scheduling policy noted Self-Timed Periodic (STP), which is an execution model combining self-timed scheduling with periodic scheduling: STS improves the performance metrics of the programs, while the periodic model captures the timing aspects. We evaluate the performance of our scheduling policy for a set of 10 real-life streaming applications. We find that in most of the cases, our approach gives a significant improvement in latency compared to the Strictly Periodic Schedule (SPS), and competes well with STS. The experiments also show that, for more than 90 % of the benchmarks, STP scheduling results in optimal throughput.

Keywords: Many-core systems · Real-time · Data-flow · Scheduling · Latency · IPC · Self-timed · Periodic

1 Introduction

There is an increasing interest in developing applications on multiprocessor platforms due to their broad availability and the appearance of many-core chips, such as the MPPA-256 chip from Kalray (256 cores) [8] or the SThorm chip from STMicroelectronics (64 cores). Given the scale of these new massively parallel systems, programming languages based on the data-flow model of computation have strong assets in the race for productivity and scalability. Nonetheless, as streaming applications must ensure *data-dependency constraints*, scheduling has serious impact on performance. Hence, multiprocessor scheduling for data-flow languages has been an active area and therefore many scheduling and resource management solutions were suggested.

© Springer International Publishing Switzerland 2015
G. Wang et al. (Eds.): ICA3PP 2015, Part II, LNCS 9529, pp. 458–478, 2015.
DOI: 10.1007/978-3-319-27122-4_32

The Self Timed Scheduling (STS) strategy (a.k.a. *as-soon-as-possible*) of a streaming application is a schedule where actors are fired as soon as data-dependency is satisfied. This scheduling policy is considered as the most appropriate for streaming applications modeled as data-flow graphs [16–18] because it delivers the maximum achievable throughput and the minimum achievable latency if computing resources are in sufficient number [3]. However, this result can only be true if we ignore synchronization times. Synchronization can be considered as a special case of communication, for which data are control information. Its role is to enforce the correct sequencing of actors firing and to ensure the mutually exclusive access to shared resources, and the time it takes should not be neglected.

Furthermore, STS does not provide guarantees on the availability of a given result in conformance with time constraints for real-time or cyber-physical systems. Due to the complex and irregular dynamics of self-timed operations, in addition to the synchronization overhead, many different hypotheses were suggested, like contention-free communication [16] or considering uniform costs for communication operations [3,17]. But neglecting subtle effects of synchronization is not a good practice with regards to real-life systems and hard real-time guarantees they could convey. In addition, using a predefined schedule of accesses to shared memory [13] makes run-time less flexible. Therefore, analysis and optimization of self-timed systems under real-time constraints remain challenging.

To cope with this challenge, periodic scheduling is receiving more attention for streaming applications [3,10,17] with its good properties (*i.e.*, timing guarantees, temporal isolation [7] and low complexity of the schedulability test). It was shown that interprocessor communication (IPC) overhead can be defined as a monotonically increasing function of the number of conflicting memory accesses in a given period of the schedule [10]. Moreover, periodic scheduling increases the latency significantly for a class of graphs called unbalanced graphs. A balanced graph is the one where the product of actor execution time and repetition is the same for all actors [2]. In contrast, an unbalanced graph is the one where such products differs between actors and in the real world, as execution times of processes can have large variations, unbalanced graphs are the usual cases.

In this paper, we show that the Strictly Periodic Schedule (SPS) model, firstly presented in [3], increases significantly the latency of unbalanced graphs and that it is possible to resolve this problem by using a new scheduling policy noted Self-Timed Periodic (STP) schedule. STP is a hybrid execution model based on mixing Self-Timed schedule and periodic schedule while considering variable IPC times. To illustrate the impact of the STP model on the performance, we present the following motivational example.

1.1   Motivational Example

In Fig. 1(a), we show a Cyclo-Static Dataflow (CSDF) [4] graph of an MP3 application implemented using the ΣC language of CEA LIST (see Sect. 5.1). CSDF graphs are directed graphs where a set of nodes referred to as computation

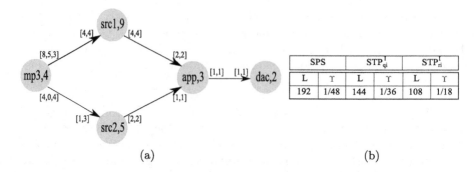

Fig. 1. (a) CSDF graph of the MP3 application. Numbers between square brackets are the number of data tokens produced or consumed by the FIFO channel. Numbers next to the name of each actor are its worst-case computation and communication time. (b) Latency (L) and throughput (Υ) metrics for the MP3 application under different scheduling schemes.

actors are connected by a set of edges which are communication First-In First-Out channels (FIFOs). In this application, the compressed audio is decoded by the *mp3* task into an audio sample stream. These samples are converted by the Sample Rate Converter (SRC) task, after which the Audio Post-Processing (APP) task enhances the perceived quality of the audio stream and sends the samples to the Digital to Analog Converter (DAC).

In CSDF graphs, each actor in the graph is executed through a periodically repeated sequence of sub-tasks. Any CSDF graph is characterized by two repetition vectors $\vec{q}$ and $\vec{r}$. Vector $\vec{q}$ is the minimal set of sub-tasks firings returning the data-flow graph to its initial state (all inputs are consumed) (see Sect. 3.1). For the example depicted in Fig. 1(a), $\vec{r} = [1, 2, 2, 4, 4]$ and $\vec{q} = [3, 4, 4, 8, 8]$, respectively in the order $mp3, src1, src2, app, dac$. To get q_i, we multiply r_i by the length of the consumption and production rates of a_i. For example, if $r_1 = 1$ then $q_1 = 3$ because actor *mp3* contains 3 sub-tasks. The worst-case computation and communication time of each actor is shown next to its name after a comma (*e.g.*, 4 for actor *mp3*). The graph is an example of an unbalanced graph since the product of actor execution time and repetition is not the same for all actors (*e.g.*, $3 \times 4 \neq 4 \times 9$). Let Υ and L denote the throughput (*i.e.*, rate) and latency of graph G, respectively, derived in Fig. 1(b) for the example of Fig. 1(a). The throughput and latency resulting from scheduling the actors of this graph as strictly periodic tasks is shown under the SPS column in Fig. 1(b). We see that the SPS model pays a high price in terms of increased latency and decreased throughput for the unbalanced graph. Instead, if the actors are to be scheduled as self-timed periodic tasks as introduced in this paper, then it is possible to achieve 25 % to 60 % improvement in latency compared to the SPS schedule. For our contribution, we propose two granularities of scheduling. This depends on whether we use q_i or r_i as the basic repetition vector of CSDF. For the proposed example, $STP_{r_i}^I$ gives better results and for latency and for throughput, it obtains the maximum throughput, as achieved by the STS model.

1.2   Paper Contributions

The contributions of this paper consists in four classes of STP schedules based on two different granularities and two types of deadline: implicit and constrained. Two first schedules, denoted $STP_{q_i}^I$ and $STP_{q_i}^C$, are based on the repetition vector q_i without including the sub-tasks of actors. Two remaining schedules, denoted $STP_{r_i}^I$ and $STP_{r_i}^C$, have a finer granularity by including the sub-tasks of actors. It is based on the repetition vector r_i. For unbalanced graphs, we show that it is possible to significantly decrease the latency and increase the throughput under the STP model for both granularities. We evaluate the proposed STP representation using a set of 10 real-life applications and show that it is capable of achieving significant improvements in term of latency (with a maximum of 96.6 %) compared to the SPS schedule and yielding the maximum achievable throughput obtained under the STS schedule for a large set of graphs.

The remainder of this paper is organized as follows. In Sect. 2, we represent a state of the art methods relative to the scheduling policies of CSDF graphs on multiprocessor systems. Section 3 introduces the background material needed for understanding the contributions of this paper. Section 4 present our main contribution: the STP schedule. Section 5 present our evaluation of the proposed scheduling policy. Finally, Sect. 6 ends the paper with conclusions.

2   Related Work

Latency is a useful performance indicator for concurrent real-time applications, and so is throughput. Minimizing or analyzing latency of a stream program requires to find an efficient scheduling policy which should be achieved by hiding communication latencies whenever possible, in parallel with minimizing the worst-case execution time (WCET) of each computation task. Ghamarian *et al.* propose a heuristic for optimizing latency under a throughput constraint [11]. It gives optimal latency and throughput results under a constraint of maximal throughput for all DSP and multimedia models. However, this approach uses Synchronous Data-flow (SDF) graphs which are less expressive than CSDF graphs in that SDF supports only a constant production/consumption rate on their edges, whereas CSDF supports varying (but predefined) production/ consumption rates. As a result, the analysis result in [11] is not applicable to CSDF graphs. In [5], Bodin *et al.* present a characterization of feasible periodic schedules associated with a CSDF. Two algorithms are deduced to approximately solve the evaluation of the maximum throughput of a CSDF and the buffer sizing with a throughput constraint. However, the throughput computed for instances with bounded buffers is quite far from the optimal achieved under self-timed schedule.

In [1], Ali *et al.* propose an algorithm for extracting the real-time properties of dataflow applications with timing constraints. However, the algorithm can only be applied on dataflow applications modeled as Homegeneous Synchronous Data-flow (HSDF) graphs, which are less expressive than CSDF and transformation of (C)SDF graphs into equivalent HSDF graphs use an unfolding process that replicates each actor possibly an exponential number of times.

Bouakaz *et al.* [6] propose a model of computation in which the activation clocks of actors are related by affine functions. That is the model is called Affine Dataflow (ADF) and extends the CSDF model. Based on this approach, they proposed an analysis framework to schedule the actors in an ADF graph as periodic tasks. A major advantage of their approach is the enhanced expressiveness of the ADF model. For most benchmarks, both CSDF and ADF achieve the same throughput and latency while requiring the same buffer sizes. However, in few cases, ADF results in reduced buffer sizes compared to CSDF [6].

In [3], Bamakhrama and Stefanov present a complete framework for computing the periodic task parameters using an estimation of worst-case execution time. They assume that each write or read has constant execution time which is often not true. Our approach is somewhat similar to [3] in using the periodic task model which allows to apply a variety of proven hard-real-time scheduling algorithms for multiprocessors. However, it is different from [3] in: (1) in our model, actors will no longer be strictly periodic but self-timed assigned to periodic levels, and (2) we treat the case variable execution time of actors due to synchronization and contention in shared resources.

3 Background

We introduce in this section the timed graph, system model and schedulability of a CSDF graph which are important points for understanding our contribution in Sect. 4.

3.1 Timed Graph

The timed graph is a more accurate representation of the CSDF graph, that associates to each sub-task or instance of an actor a computation time and a communication overhead. We consider the Timed graph $G = \langle A, E, \omega, \varphi \rangle$, where A is a set of actors, $E \subseteq A \times A$ is a set of communication channels, ω gives the worst-case computation time of each actor and φ is its communication time according to a scheduling policy. The set of actors is denoted by $A = \{a_1, a_2, ..., a_n\}$, where each actor represents one function that transforms the input data streams into output data streams. The communication channels carry streams of data and work as a FIFO queue with unbounded capacity. An atomic piece of data carried out by a channel is called a *token*. This channel is blocking read but scheduling ensures this condition is never reached.

Each actor $a_j \in A$ has an execution sequence of length τ_j, $[f_j(0), \cdots, f_j(\tau_j - 1)]$ which can be understood as follows: The n-th time that actor a_j is fired, it executes the code of function $f_j(n \bmod \tau_j)$ and each function is viewed as a *sub-task* of actor a_j. As a consequence, production and consumption are also sequences of length τ_j. The production of actor a_j on channel $e_u \in E$ is a sequence of constant integers $[x_j^u(0), \cdots, x_j^u(\tau_j - 1)]$. The n-th time actor a_j is fired, it produces $x_j^u(n \mod \tau_j)$ tokens on channel e_u. The consumption of actor a_k on channel $e_u \in E$ is also a sequence of constant integers $[y_k^u(0), \cdots, y_k^u(\tau_k - 1)]$. The firing rule of a cyclo-static actor a_k is evaluated as true for its n-th firing if and only if all input channels contain at least $y_k^u(n \mod \tau_k)$ tokens. The total number of tokens produced by actor a_j on channel e_u during the first n invocations, denoted by $X_j^u(n) = \sum_{l=0}^{n-1} x_j^u(l)$. Similarly, the total number of tokens consumed by actor a_k on channel e_u during the first n invocations, denoted by $Y_k^u(n) = \sum_{l=0}^{n-1} y_k^u(l)$.

For a Timed graph G, an *execution time vector* of G, denoted by $\overrightarrow{\omega} \in \mathbb{N}^N$, is a vector such that $\omega_i \in \overrightarrow{\omega}$ is the worst-case execution time (WCET) of actor $a_i \in A$. Similarly, a *communication time vector* of G, denoted by $\overrightarrow{\varphi} \in \mathbb{N}^N$, is a vector such that $\varphi_i \in \overrightarrow{\varphi}$ is the communication cost of actor $a_i \in A$ (*i.e.* worst-case time needed for reading and writing data tokens, *etc.*).

One of the most important properties of the CSDF model is the ability to derive at compile-time a schedule for the actors. Compile-time scheduling has been an attractive property of these dataflow models because it removes the need for a run-time scheduler. In order to derive a compile-time schedule for a CSDF graph, it has to be both *consistent* and *live*. A timed graph G is said to be live if and only if a deadlock-free schedule can be found.

Definition 1. *Given a connected CSDF graph G, a **valid static schedule** for G is a schedule that can be repeated infinitely on the incoming sample stream and where the amount of data in the buffers remains bounded. A vector $\overrightarrow{q} = [q_1, q_2, ..., q_n]^T$, where $q_j > 0$, is a **repetition vector** of G if each q_j represents the number of invocations of an actor a_j in a valid static schedule for G. A CSDF graph is called **consistent** if and only if it has a non-trivial repetition vector. For a consistent graph, there is a unique smallest non-trivial repetition vector which is designated as the repetition vector of the CSDF graph [14].*

Theorem 1 (From [4]). *In a CSDF graph, a repetition vector $\overrightarrow{q} = [q_1, q_2, ..., q_n]^T$ is given by*

$$\overrightarrow{q} = P \cdot \overrightarrow{r} \ , with \quad P = P_{jk} = \begin{cases} \tau_j, & if \ j = k \\ 0, & otherwise \end{cases} \tag{1}$$

P is a square matrix where the diagonal elements are equal to the number of sub-tasks. And, $\overrightarrow{r} = [r_1, r_2, ..., r_n]^T$, where $r_i \in \mathbb{N}^\star$, is a solution of the balance equation:

$$\Gamma \cdot \overrightarrow{r} = 0, \tag{2}$$

and where the topology matrix Γ, which specifies the connections between edges in directed multigraph, is defined by

$$\Gamma_{uj} = \begin{cases} X_j^u(\tau_j), & if \ task \ a_j \ produces \ on \ edge \ e_u \\ -Y_j^u(\tau_j), & if \ task \ a_j \ consumes \ from \ edge \ e_u \\ 0, & otherwise \end{cases} \tag{3}$$

Example 1. For the CSDF graph shown in Fig. 1(a)

$$\Gamma = \begin{bmatrix} 16 & -8 & 0 & 0 & 0 \\ 8 & 0 & -4 & 0 & 0 \\ 0 & 8 & 0 & -4 & 0 \\ 0 & 0 & 4 & -2 & 0 \\ 0 & 0 & 0 & 2 & -2 \end{bmatrix}, \vec{r} = \begin{bmatrix} 1 \\ 2 \\ 2 \\ 4 \\ 4 \end{bmatrix}, P = \begin{bmatrix} 3 & 0 & 0 & 0 & 0 \\ 0 & 2 & 0 & 0 & 0 \\ 0 & 0 & 2 & 0 & 0 \\ 0 & 0 & 0 & 2 & 0 \\ 0 & 0 & 0 & 0 & 2 \end{bmatrix}, and \ \vec{q} = \begin{bmatrix} 3 \\ 4 \\ 4 \\ 8 \\ 8 \end{bmatrix}$$

Algorithm 1. TIMED-GRAPH-LEVELS(G)

Require: Timed graph $G = \langle A, E, \omega, \varphi \rangle$
1: $i \leftarrow 1$
2: **while** $A \neq \emptyset$ **do**
3:     $V_i \leftarrow \{a_j \in A : \mathbf{prec}(a_j) = \emptyset\}$
4:     $E_i \leftarrow \{e_u \in E: \exists a_k \in V_i \text{ that is the source of } e_u\}$
5:     $A \leftarrow A \setminus V_i$
6:     $E \leftarrow E \setminus E_i$
7:     $i = i + 1$
8: **end while**
9: $\alpha \leftarrow i - 1$
10: **return** α disjoint sets $V_1, V_2, \ldots, V_\alpha$ where $\bigcup_{i=1}^{\alpha} V_i = \overset{\bullet}{A}$

3.2   Graph Levels

In this paper, we restrict our attention to acyclic CSDF graphs which account for most of the dataflow applications. An acyclic graph G has a number of levels, denoted by α. Different graph traversals types exist like topological, breadth-first, *etc.* Actors will be assigned to a set of levels $V = \{V_1, V_2, ..., V_\alpha\}$. The authors of [3] proposed a method, presented in Algorithm 1, based on assigning the actors in the graph according to precedence constraints. An actor a_i that belongs to level V_j in Algorithm 1 has a level index $\sigma_i = j$. Each actor $a_i \in A$ is associated with two sets of actors. The sets of actors are the successors set, denoted by $\mathbf{succ}(a_i)$, and the predecessors set, denoted by $\mathbf{prec}(a_i)$.

$$\begin{aligned} \mathbf{succ}(a_i) &= \{a_j \in A : \exists e_u = (a_i, a_j) \in E\} \\ \mathbf{prec}(a_i) &= \{a_j \in A : \exists e_u = (a_j, a_i) \in E\} \end{aligned} \qquad (4)$$

3.3   System's Model and Schedulability

This section presents the system's model and its schedulability analysis.

System's Model. A system Π consists of a set $\pi = \{\pi_1, \pi_2, ..., \pi_m\}$ of m homogeneous processors. The processors execute a level set $V = \{V_1, V_2, ..., V_\alpha\}$ of α periodic levels. A periodic level $V_i \in V$ is defined by a 4-tuple $V_i =$

$(S_i, \overset{\wedge}{\omega}_i, \overset{\wedge}{\varphi}_i, D_i)$, where $S_i \geq 0$ is the start time of V_i, $\overset{\wedge}{\omega}_i$ is the worst-case computation time (where $\overset{\wedge}{\omega}_i = \max_{k=1 \to \beta_i} \omega_k$ with β_i representing the number of actors in level V_i), $\overset{\wedge}{\varphi}_i \geq 0$ is the worst-case communication time of V_i under STP schedule and D_i is the relative deadline of V_i where $D_i = \max_{k=1 \to \beta_i} D_k$. A periodic level V_i is invoked at time $t = S_i + k\phi$, where $\phi \geq \overset{\wedge}{\omega}_i + \overset{\wedge}{\varphi}_i$ is the level period, and has to finish execution before time $t = S_i + k\phi + D_i$. If $D_i = \phi$, then V_i is said to have *implicit-deadline*. If $D_i < \phi$, then V_i is said to have *constrained-deadline*.

Schedulability Analysis. Actors (*i.e.*, tasks) in the Timed graph G are scheduled as *implicit-deadline* or *constrained-deadline* periodic tasks (depending on the STP approach being used) and assigned to levels. At run-time, they are executed in a *self-timed* manner. This is possible because actors of level $k + 1$ consume the data produced in level k. A necessary and sufficient condition for scheduling an asynchronous set of implicit-deadline periodic tasks $\Gamma \subseteq A$ on m processors is $U_{sum} \leq m$, where U_{sum} is the total utilization of Γ as defined in [7]. In this work, we consider only consistent and live CSDF graphs. A static schedule [18] of a consistent and live CSDF graph is valid if it satisfies the precedence constraints specified by the edges. Authors in [16] introduced a theorem that states the sufficient and necessary conditions for a *valid schedule*. However, this result was established for Synchronous Data-flow graphs where actors have constant execution times. In this context, our research uses the test introduced in [9] which allows the timing of firing to respect the firing rules of actors in a CSDF graph.

3.4   Strictly Periodic Schedule (SPS)

A *Strictly Periodic Schedule* [17] of a Cyclo-Static Dataflow graph is a schedule such that, $\forall a_i \in A$:

$$s(i, k) = s(i, 0) + \phi \times k, \tag{5}$$

where $s(i, k)$ represents the time at which the k-th iteration of actor a_i is fired and ϕ is an equal iteration period for every complete repetition of all the actors. In this paper, the latency resulting from the SPS approach is calculated by using the scheduling policy presented in [3]. The authors proved that it is possible to schedule actors of a graph G as strictly periodic tasks using periods given by the following equation:

$$\phi = q_1\lambda_1 = q_2\lambda_2 = \cdots = q_{n-1}\lambda_{n-1} = q_n\lambda_n, \tag{6}$$

where $q_i \in \overrightarrow{q}$ (The basic repetition vector of G) and $\lambda_i \in \mathbb{N}^N$, represents the period measured in time-units of actor $a_i \in A$, given by:

$$\lambda_i^{min} = \frac{Q}{q_i} \left\lceil \frac{\eta}{Q} \right\rceil \quad for \ a_i \in A, \tag{7}$$

where $\eta = \max_{a_i \in A}(\omega_i q_i)$ and $Q = lcm(q_1, q_2, \ldots, q_n)$ (*lcm* denotes the least common multiple operator).

4   Self-Timed Periodic Model

The effect of Self-timed Periodic (STP) scheduling can be modeled by replacing the period of the actor in each level by its worst-case execution time under periodic scheduling. The worst-case execution time is the total time of computation and communication parts of each actor. The period of each level i is the maximum time it needs to fire each actor $a_j \in V_i$, when resource arbitration and synchronization effects are taken into account. This is counted from the moment the actor meets its enabling conditions to the moment the firing is completed. There are 4 types of STP scheduling that we are interested in modeling as depicted in Table 1.

Table 1. Proposed STP schedules

Type/Repetition vector	q_i	r_i
$\phi = D_i$ (Implicit-Deadline)	$STP^I_{q_i}$	$STP^I_{r_i}$
$\phi > D_i$ (Constrained-Deadline)	$STP^C_{q_i}$	$STP^C_{r_i}$

STP_{X_i} refers to scheduling decisions using the different granularities offered by CSDF model:

- *Coarse-Grained Schedule:* coarse-grained description of STP schedule regards instances of actors by using $\overrightarrow{q}$ as the repetition vector. Each actor a_i is viewed as executing through a periodically repeating sequence of q_i instances of subtasks.
- *Fine-Grained Schedule:* fine-grained description of STP schedule regards smaller components (*i.e.*, sub-tasks of actors) of which the actors are composed by using $\overrightarrow{r}$ as the repetition vector.

4.1   Assumptions and Definitions

A graph G refers to an acyclic consistent CSDF graph. A consistent graph can be executed with bounded memory buffers and no deadlock. We base our analysis on the following assumptions:

A1. External sources in data-flow: The model is accomplished with interfaces to the outside world in order to explicitly model inputs and outputs (I/Os). A graph G has a set of input streams $I = \{I_1, I_2, ..., I_\Delta\}$ connected to the input actors of G, and a set of output streams $O = \{O_1, O_2, ..., O_\Lambda\}$ processed from the output actors of G. An actor $a_i \in A$ is defined, inter alia, with $E_i = (E^{in}_i, E^{out}_i)$ such that E^{in}_i and E^{out}_i represent the sets of input and output edges of a_i. A source and a sink nodes can be integrated as closures since they define limits of an application. These special nodes are defined as follows: $src \in A$, $E^{in}_{src} = \emptyset$ and $E^{out}_{src} = \{I_1, I_2, ..., I_\Delta\}$, $snk \in A$, $E^{in}_{snk} = \{O_1, O_2, ..., O_\Lambda\}$ and $E^{out}_{snk} = \emptyset$.

Definition 2. *For a graph G under periodic schedule, the worst-case communication overhead $\overset{\wedge}{\varphi}_j$ of any level $V_j \in V$ depends on the maximum number of accesses to memory m_{β_j} processed in the time interval $[(j-1) \times \phi, j \times \phi[$. In [10], the authors proved that $\overset{\wedge}{\varphi}_j$ is a monotonic increasing function of the number of conflicting memory accesses:*

$$\overset{\wedge}{\varphi}_j =\uparrow f(m_{\beta_j}), \quad \forall V_j \in V \tag{8}$$

A2. For periodic schedules, synchronization cost is constant, because periodic behavior guarantees that an actor $a_i \in V_j$, $\forall i \in [1, ..., \beta_j]$, will consume tokens produced at level $(j-1)$ [10]. This implies that actors of the same level can start firing immediately in the beginning of a given period because all the necessary tokens have already been produced.

Definition 3. *A graph G is said to be **matched input/output (I/O) rates graph** if and only if:*

$$\eta \mod Q = 0 \tag{9}$$

*If Formula (9) does not hold, then G is a **mismatched I/O rates graph**.*

Definition 4. *A graph G is called **balanced** if and only if:*

$$q_1\omega_1 = q_2\omega_2 = \cdots = q_n\omega_n, \tag{10}$$

*where $q_i \in \vec{q}$ is the repetition of actor $a_i \in A$ and ω_i is its worst-case computation time. If Eq. (10) does not hold, then the graph is called **unbalanced**.*

Definition 5. *An **actor workload** is defined as:*

$$W_i = v_i \times \omega_i, \tag{11}$$

where v_i is the ith component of the repetition vector used for STP schedule. For STP_{q_i}, $v_i = q_i$ and for STP_{r_i}, $v_i = r_i$. The maximum workload of level V_j is $\hat{W}_j = \max_{a_i \in V_j}\{W_i\}$.

Definition 6. *Let $p_{a \leadsto z} = \{(a_a, a_b), \ldots, (a_y, a_z)\}$ be an output path in a graph G. The latency of $p_{a \leadsto z}$ under periodic input streams, denoted by $L(p_{a \leadsto z})$, is the elapsed time between the start of the first firing of a_a which produces data to (a_a, a_b) and the finish of the first firing of a_z which consumes data from (a_y, a_z).*

Consequently, we define the maximum latency of G as follows:

Definition 7. *For a graph G, the maximum latency of G under periodic input streams, denoted by $L(G)$, is given by:*

$$L(G) = \max_{p_{i \leadsto j} \in P} L(p_{i \leadsto j}), \tag{12}$$

*where P denotes the set of all output paths in G. A path $p_{i \leadsto j} = (a_i, a_j)$ is called **output path** if a_i is a source node which receives an **input stream** of the application and a_j is a sink node which produces an **output stream**.*

Example 2. The CSDF graph shown in Fig. 1(a) has two output paths given by $P = \{p_1 = \{(mp3, src1), (src1, app), (app, dac), p_2 = \{(mp3, src2), (src2, app), (app, dac)\}$. This graph is also an example of an unbalanced graph since the product of actor execution time and repetition is not the same for all actors (*e.g.*, $3 \times 4 \neq 4 \times 9$).

4.2   Latency Analysis Under STP Schedule

A self-timed schedule does not impose any extra latency on the actors. This leads us to the following result:

Algorithm 2. GRAPH-LEVELS-STP-Ri(G)

Require: Timed graph $G = \langle A, E, \omega, \varphi \rangle$
1: $count_i \leftarrow 0$
2: $j \leftarrow 1$
3: $S \leftarrow \{a_1\}$ ▷ a_1 assumed to be the source actor;
4: **if** $count_i = q_i \; \forall a_i \in A$ **then**
5:      **break**
6: **else**
7:      $V_j \leftarrow \{a_i \in S : there\ are\ enough\ tokens\ in\ all\ input\ edges\ to\ fire\ a_i\ for\ r_i$ $times\}$
8:      $j \leftarrow j + 1$
9:      **for all** $a_i \in S$ **do**
10:          $count_i \leftarrow count_i + r_i$
11:          **if** $count_i < q_i$ **then**
12:              $S = S \bigcup \mathbf{succ}(a_i)$
13:              **goto** 4
14:          **else**
15:              **if** $count_i = q_i$ **then**
16:                  $S \leftarrow S \setminus \{a_i\}$
17:              **end if**
18:          **end if**
19:      **end for**
20: **end if**
21: $\alpha' \leftarrow j$ - 1
22: **return** α' disjoint sets $V_1, V_2, \ldots, V_{\alpha'}$

Definition 8. *(Periods of Levels in STP_{q_i}) For a graph G, a period ϕ, where $\phi \in \mathbb{Z}^+$, represents the period, measured in time-units, of the levels in G. If we consider $\vec{q}$ as the basic repetition vector of G in Definition 5, then ϕ is given by the solution to:*

$$\phi \geq \max_{j=1 \to \alpha} (\hat{W}_j + \overset{\wedge}{\varphi}_j) \tag{13}$$

Definition 8 defines the level period ϕ as the maximum execution time of all levels. Similarly, we define the schedule function for the finer granularity of

CSDF characterized by the repetition vector $\vec{r}$ if we consider $\vec{r}$ as the basic repetition vector of G in Eq. (13).

For STP_{q_i}, we use Algorithm 1 to find the levels of G. For STP_{r_i}, Algorithm 2 is used because this scheduling policy has a finer granularity and requires an algorithm which depends also on the precedence constraints and firing rules of actors. In this case, each actor a_i could only be fired for r_i times if there are enough tokens in all of their input edges.

An actor $a_i \in V_j$ is said to be a level-j actor. For STP_{q_i}, let ϕ denote the level period as defined in Definition 8, and let a_1 denote the level-1 actor. a_1 will complete one iteration when it fires q_1 times. Assume that a_1 starts executing at time $t = 0$. Then, by time $t = \phi \geq q_1\omega_1$ as defined in Definition 8, a_1 is guaranteed to finish one iteration in a self-timed mode (start the next sub-task immediately after the end of the precedent). According to Theorem 1, a_1 will also generate enough data such that every actor $a_k \in V_2$ can execute q_k times (*i.e.* one iteration). According to Definition 8, firing a_k for q_k times in a self-timed mode takes $q_k\omega_k$ time-units. Thus, starting level-2 actors at time $t = \phi$ guarantees that they can finish one iteration. Similarly, by time $t = 2\phi$, level-3 actors will have enough data to execute for one iteration. By repeating this over all the α levels, a schedule S_α (shown in Fig. 2) is constructed in which all actors $a_i \in V_j$ are started at *start time*, denoted $s_{i,j}$, given by:

$$s_{i,j} = (j-1)\phi \tag{14}$$

time	$[0,\phi)$	$[\phi,2\phi)$	$[2\phi,3\phi)$	$\ldots$	$[(\alpha-1)\phi,\alpha\phi)$
level	$V_1(1)$	$V_2(1)$	$V_3(1)$	$\ldots$	$V_\alpha(1)$
		$V_1(2)$	$V_2(2)$	$\ldots$	$V_{\alpha-1}(2)$
			$V_1(3)$	$\ldots$	$V_{\alpha-2}(3)$
				$\ldots$	$V_{\alpha-3}(4)$
				$\ldots$	$\ldots$
					$V_1(\alpha)$

Fig. 2. Initial phase of schedule S_α

$V_j(k)$ denotes level-j actors executing their k-th iteration. For example, $V_2(1)$ denotes level-2 actors executing their first iteration. At time $t = \alpha\phi$, G completes one iteration. It is trivial to observe from S_α that as soon as a_1 finishes one iteration, it can immediately start executing the next iteration since its input stream arrives periodically. If a_1 starts its second iteration at time $t = \phi$, its execution will overlap with the execution of the level-2 actors. By doing so, level-2 actors can start immediately their second iteration after finishing their first iteration since they will have all the needed data to execute one iteration in a self-timed mode at time $t = 2\phi$. Now, the overlapping can be applied α times to yield a schedule S_α as shown in Fig. 2. Starting from $t = \alpha\phi$, a schedule S_∞ can be constructed by pipelining the S_α schedule, as can be seen in Fig. 3.

time $[0,\phi)$	$[\phi,2\phi)$	...	$[(\alpha-1)\phi,\alpha\phi)$	$[\alpha\phi,(\alpha+1)\phi)$
level $V_1(1)$	$V_2(1)$	...	$V_\alpha(1)$	$V_\alpha(2)$
	$V_1(2)$	...	$V_{\alpha-1}(2)$	$V_{\alpha-1}(3)$
		...	$V_{\alpha-2}(3)$	$V_{\alpha-2}(4)$
		...	$V_{\alpha-3}(4)$	$V_{\alpha-3}(5)$
		...	...	...
			$V_1(\alpha)$	$V_1(\alpha+1)$

Fig. 3. Schedule S_∞ by pipelining the steady state S_α

The start time defined in Eq. (14) guarantees that actors at a given level will execute only when they have enough data to execute. Thus, schedule S_∞ shows the existence of a self-timed periodic schedule of G where every actor $a_j \in A$ is self-timed periodic with a period level equal to ϕ.

According to Definitions 6 and 7, latency is defined as the maximum time elapsed between the first firing of src actor in level V_1 and the finish of the first firing of snk actor in level V_α. Then, the graph latency $L(G)$ is given by:

$$L(G) = \max_{p_{i \leadsto j} \in P}(s_{snk,\alpha} + \hat{y}^u_{snk}\phi + D_\alpha - (s_{src,1} + \hat{x}^r_{src}\phi)) \tag{15}$$

where $s_{snk,\alpha}$ and $s_{src,1}$ are the earliest start times of the snk actor and the src actor, respectively, D_α is the deadline of snk and V_α, and $\hat{x}^r_{src}$ and $\hat{y}^u_{snk}$ represent the first non-zero production (consumption) sub-task of the src (snk) actor, such that for an output path $p_{src \leadsto snk}$ in which e_r is the first channel and e_u is the last channel, $\hat{x}^r_{src}$ and $\hat{y}^u_{snk}$ are given by:

$$\hat{x}^r_{src} = \min\{k \in N : x^r_{src}(k) > 0\} - 1 \tag{16}$$

$$\hat{y}^u_{snk} = \min\{k \in N : y^u_{snk}(k) > 0\} - 1 \tag{17}$$

Under the *implicit-deadline* model, $D_\alpha = \phi$ and under the *constrained-deadline* scheduling, $D_\alpha < \phi$. Using Eqs. (13) and (14), it is possible to obtain a simple version of Eq. (15) under the *implicit-deadline* model for acyclic CSDF graphs where production of src actor and consumption of snk actor taking place from the first firing of each node ($\hat{x}^r_{src} = \hat{y}^u_{snk} = 0$):

$$L_{STP^I_{q_i/r_i}} = (s_{snk,\alpha} + \phi) - s_{src,1} = \alpha \times \phi \tag{18}$$

Example 3. We illustrate in Fig. 4 different scheduling policies applied for the MP3 application shown in Fig. 1(a). This application has an execution vector $\vec{\omega} = [4,9,5,3,2]^T$ and a communication vector $\vec{\varphi}$ approximately equal to $\vec{0}$. The $mp3$ node is the src actor and dac is the snk actor. Applying Algorithm 1, the number of levels for $STP^I_{q_i}$ is $\alpha = 4$ and we have 4 sets: $V_1 = \{mp3\}$, $V_2 = \{src1, src2\}$, $V_3 = \{app\}$, $V_4 = \{dac\}$.

Applying Algorithm 2, the number of levels for $STP^I_{r_i}$ is $\alpha = 6$ and we have 6 sets: $V_1 = \{mp3\}$, $V_2 = \{mp3, src1, src2\}$, $V_3 = \{mp3, app\}$, $V_4 =$

$\{src1, src2, dac\}$, $V_5 = \{app\}$, $V_6 = \{dac\}$. Given $\overrightarrow{q} = [3, 4, 4, 8, 8]^T$ and $\overrightarrow{r} = [1, 2, 2, 4, 4]^T$, we use Eqs. (11) and (13) to find the period of levels $\phi = 36$ for $STP_{q_i}^I$ and $\phi = 18$ for $STP_{r_i}^I$.

This graph has two output paths given by $P = \{p_1 = \{(mp3, src1), (src1, app), (app, dac), p_2 = \{(mp3, src2), (src2, app), (app, dac)\}$. Finally, using Eq. (18), we have $L_{STP_{q_i}^I}(p_1) = L_{STP_{q_i}^I}(p_2) = 144$ and $L_{STP_{r_i}^I}(p_1) = L_{STP_{r_i}^I}(p_2) = 108$ as depicted in Fig. 4.

5 Experiments and Evaluations

In this section, we want to evaluate the scheduling policy described in Sect. 4 by performing an experiment on a set of 10 real-life streaming applications. The objective of the experiment is to compare the efficiency of our STP approach to their maximum achievable performance obtained via self-timed scheduling and the results achieved under strictly periodic scheduling.

The streaming applications used in the experiment are real-life applications which come from different domains (e.g., signal processing, video processing, mathematics, etc.). The benchmarks are described in details in Sect. 5.2.

5.1 $\varSigma C$ and MPPA Platform

Among these benchmarks, 4 are developed by CEA LIST and use $\varSigma C$ [12], a data-flow language designed in order to ensure programmability and efficiency on many-core. This programming language is built as an extension to C. It adds to C the ability to express and instantiate agents, links, behavior specifications, communication specifications and an API for topology building by using some new keywords like *agent*, *subgraph*, *init*, *map*, *interface*, ... The $\varSigma C$ programming model defines a superset of CSDF or a network of connected agents. In this context, an *agent* is an autonomous entity, with its own address space and thread of control. It has an interface describing a set of ports, their direction and the type of data accepted; and a behavior specification describing the behavior of the agent as a cyclic sequence of transitions with consumption and production of specified amounts of data on the ports listed in the transition.

These benchmarks are tested in the *MPPA - 256* [8] clustered architecture, from Kalray, comprising 256 user cores (*i.e.*, cores with fully processing power provided to the programmer for computing tasks) organized as 16 (4×4) clusters tied by a Network-on-Chip (NoC) with a torus topology. Each cluster has 16 user processors connected to a shared memory of 2 MB per cluster.

5.2 Benchmarks

We used benchmarks from different sources to check the efficiency of this scheduling in different architectures. The first source is the $\varSigma C$ benchmark which contributes 4 streaming applications. The second source is the SDF[3] benchmark which contributes 5 streaming applications [19]. The last source is the StreamIt

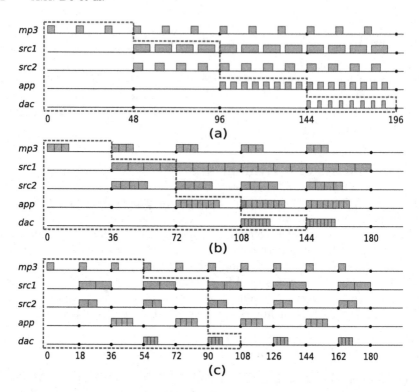

Fig. 4. Illustration of latency path for the MP3 application shown in Fig. 1(a): (a) SPS (b) $STP_{q_i}^I$ (c) $STP_{r_i}^I$. The dotted line represents a valid static schedule of the graph. An improvement of 25 % to 60 % in latency could be achieved by the $STP_{q_i}^I$ and $STP_{r_i}^I$ schedules compared to the SPS schedule.

benchmark [20]. In total, 10 applications are considered as shown in Table 2. The graphs are a mixture of CSDF (ΣC's applications) and SDF (StreamIt and SDF³ benchmark) graphs. The use of synchronous data-flow (SDF) models does not affect our scheduling policy because SDF, with static firing rules of actors, is a special case of CSDF model [4,15]. The fourth column (N) shows the number of actors in each application, the fifth column (Q) shows the least-common-multiple of the repetition vector elements (*i.e.*, $Q = lcm(q_1, q_2, \ldots, q_n)$) and the sixth column is the maximum of the product $q_i\omega_i$ used to calculate the end-to-end latency by Formula (11), (13) and (18).

The actors execution times of the ΣC benchmark are measured in clock cycles on the MPPA 256 cores, while the actors execution times of the SDF³ benchmark are specified by its authors for ARM architecture. For the StreamIt benchmark, the actors execution times are specified in clock cycles measured on MIT RAW architecture.

We use SDF³ tool-set for several purposes during the experiments. SDF³ is a powerful analysis tool-set which is capable of analyzing CSDF and SDF graphs to check for consistency errors, compute the repetition vector, compute the max-

Table 2. Benchmarks used for evaluation

Domain	No.	Application	N	Q	$\max(q_i\omega_i)$	Source
Signal processing	1	Discrete Cosine Transform (DCT)	4	12	1800	CEA LIST
	2	Fast Fourier Transform (FFT) kernel	4	6	900	
	3	Multi-Channel beamformer	4	12	7800	
Audio processing	4	Filter bank for multirate signal processing	17	600	113430	[20]
	5	MP3 audio decoder	5	24	36	CEA LIST
	6	Sample-rate converter used in CDs	6	23520	960	[19]
Video processing	7	H.263 video encoder	5	33	382000	
	8	H.263 video decoder	4	2376	10000	
Mathematics	9	Bipartite graph	4	144	252	
Communication	10	Satellite receiver	22	5280	1056	

imum achievable throughput, *etc.* In this experiment, we use SDF^3 to compute the minimum achievable latency of the graph and use it as a reference point for comparing the latency under the SPS and STP models. For StreamIt benchmark, the graph exported by this language is converted in the XML required by SDF^3. For ΣC applications, the ΣC compiler is capable of checking consistency errors and computing the repetition vector during its 4 stages of compilation [12]. The latency of its applications is calculated by using the execution times measured on the MPPA platform.

5.3   Latency Results

In these experiments, we compare the end-to-end latency resulting from our STP approach to the minimum achievable latency of a streaming application obtained via self-timed scheduling and the one achieved under strictly periodic scheduling. The STS latency is computed using the latency algorithm of the *sdf3analysis* tool from SDF^3 with auto-concurrency disabled and unbounded FIFO channel sizes.

Table 3 shows the latency obtained under STS, SPS, $STP_{q_i}^I$, $STP_{r_i}^I$, $STP_{q_i}^C$ and $STP_{r_i}^C$ schedules as well as the improvement of these policies compared to the SPS model. We report the graph maximum latency according to Formula (18). For SPS schedule, we used the minimum period given by Eq. (6). For STP schedule, we used the level period given by Definition 8. We see that the calculation of the STP schedule is not complicated because the graph is consistent and an automatic tool could be implemented to find this schedule.

Table 3. Latency obtained under STS, SPS, $STP_{q_i}^I$, $STP_{r_i}^I$, $STP_{q_i}^C$ and $STP_{r_i}^C$ schedules as well as the improvement of these policies compared to the SPS model.

Application	STS	SPS	$STP_{q_i}^I$	$Eff_{STP_{q_i}^I}$	$STP_{r_i}^I$	$Eff_{STP_{r_i}^I}$	$STP_{q_i}^C$	$Eff_{STP_{q_i}^C}$	$STP_{r_i}^C$	$Eff_{STP_{r_i}^C}$
DCT	2500	7200	5400	38.3	4500	57.5	3500	78.7	3200	85.1
FFT	23000	36000	27000	69.2	32000	30.8	23000	100.0	23000	100.0
Beamformer	9500	25200	23400	11.5	30000	-30.6	12100	83.4	13700	73.3
Filterbank	124792	1254000	1247730	0.6	1247730	0.6	309033	83.7	309033	83.7
MP3	48	192	144	33.3	108	58.3	88	2.2	72	83.3
Sample-rate	1000	141120	5760	96.6	5760	96.6	2439	99.0	2439	99.0
Encoder	664000	1584000	1528000	6.1	1528000	6.1	799000	85.3	799000	85.3
Decoder	23506	47520	40000	31.3	40000	31.3	25880	90.1	25880	90.1
Bipartite	293	576	504	25.4	504	25.4	369	73.2	369	73.2
Satellite	1314	58080	11616	81.9	11616	81.9	2377	98.1	2377	98.1

For the $STP_{q_i}^I$, we see that it delivers an average improvement of 39.4 % (with a maximum of 96.6 %) compared to the SPS model for all the applications. In addition, we clearly see that our $STP_{q_i}^I$ provides at least 25 % of improvement for 7 out of 10 applications. Only three applications (Filterbank, Beamformer and H.263 Encoder) have lower performance under our $STP_{q_i}^I$. To understand the impact of the results, we use the concept of *balanced* graph (see Definition 4). According to [2], periodic models increase the latency significantly for *unbalanced* graphs. For our approach, Definition 8 and Formula (18) indicate that if the product $q_i\omega_i$ is too different between actors, so the period of levels ϕ and the latency L become higher. For actors where this product is much smaller, wasted time in each level increases the final value of latency. This main reason prompt us to reduce these bad effects by using the constrained-deadline self-timed periodic schedule $STP_{q_i}^C$ and $STP_{r_i}^C$.

We also see that the *mismatched* I/O rates applications (*i.e.* with large Q such as Sample-rate, Satellite and Filterbank in Table 2) have higher latency under strictly periodic scheduling. This result could be explained using an interesting finding reported in [20]: *Neighboring actors often have matched I/O rates. This reduces the opportunity and impact of advanced scheduling strategies proposed in the literature.* This issue can be resolved by using our approach. In fact, for nearly balanced graphs (*i.e.*, graphs where the product $q_i\omega_i$ is not too different between actors) such as Sample-rate and Satellite, we have an improvement of 96.6 % and 81.9 %, relatively, for the end-to-end latency of each benchmark. For the remaining applications, the SPS model increases the latency on average by 2.5× compared to the STS latency while this rate for $STP_{q_i}^I$ is 2×.

For the $STP_{r_i}^I$ approach, we have an average improvement of 35.8 % compared to the SPS model for all the applications. For 8 out of 10 benchmarks, this scheduling policy give at least the result given by $STP_{q_i}^I$. Only two applications (Beamformer and FFT) have lower performance when using this scheduling policy. The main reason is that the $STP_{r_i}^I$ give a finer granularity based on the

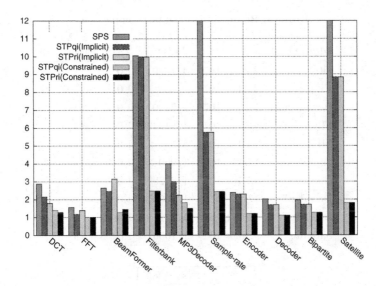

Fig. 5. Ratios of the latency under SPS, $STP^I_{q_i}$, $STP^I_{r_i}$, $STP^C_{q_i}$ and $STP^C_{r_i}$ to the STS latency. It must be noted that the Sample-Rate and Satellite programs have a ratio for SPS much larger than 12, but the graph is zoomed to display accurately the results for most of the programs.

repetition vector r_i. This means that if $\vec{r}$ is too close to $\vec{1}$, the sum of wasted time in each level will significantly increases the end-to-end latency.

For this reason, we extend our result by using 2 other constrained deadline approaches: $STP^C_{q_i}$ and $STP^C_{r_i}$. The constrained deadline model assigns for each task a deadline $D < \phi$, where ϕ is the period of levels. Figure 5 shows the ratio of the latency of 5 scheduling policies (including $STP^C_{q_i}$ and $STP^C_{r_i}$) to the minimum achievable latency (*i.e.*, STS latency). A ratio equal to 1.0 means that the $STP^C_{q_i}$ and $STP^C_{r_i}$ latency are equal to the STS latency. We see that the $STP^C_{r_i}$ model achieves nearly the minimum achievable latency for 7 graphs. In addition, it is worthy of note that these approaches have, on average, 86.4 % of improvement for $STP^C_{q_i}$ and 87.1 % for $STP^C_{r_i}$ compared to the SPS latency; it means that we have only 13.6 % and 12.9 %, respectively, degradation of latency compared to STS. This degradation is negligible for a schedule that guarantees periodic properties. However, using the constrained deadline model requires different schedulability analysis. Therefore, a detailed treatment of how to reduce the latency by using these approaches need further research in the future.

5.4 Throughput Results

In these experiments, we compare the throughput resulting from our STP approach to the maximum achievable throughput of a streaming application obtained via self-timed scheduling. Computing the throughput of the STS using SDF[3] is done using the algorithm *throughput* of the *sdf3analysis − (c)sdf* tool.

Table 4. Results of throughput comparison

Application	Υ_{STS}	$\Upsilon_{\mathrm{STP}^I_{q_i}}$	$\Upsilon_{\mathrm{STS}}/\Upsilon_{\mathrm{STP}^I_{q_i}}$
DCT	2.22×10^{-3}	4/1800	1.0
FFT	3.33×10^{-3}	3/900	1.0
Beamformer	5.13×10^{-4}	4/7800	1.0
Filterbank	8.81×10^{-6}	1/113430	1.0
MP3	2.22×10^{-1}	8/36	1.0
Sample-rate	1.04×10^{-3}	1/960	1.0
Encoder	4.73×10^{-6}	1/382000	1.8
Decoder	1.0×10^{-4}	1/10000	1.0
Bipartite	3.96×10^{-3}	1/252	1.0
Satellite	9.46×10^{-4}	1/1056	1.0

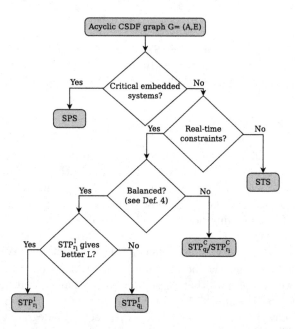

Fig. 6. Decision tree for real-time scheduling of CSDF applications. The STP scheduling could be used to reduce the end-to-end latency of real-time CSDF applications. In the case of unbalanced graphs, $STP^C_{q_i}$ and $STP^C_{r_i}$ give better results if the constrained deadline model is possible.

The last column of Table 4 shows the ratio of the STS schedule throughput to the $STP^I_{q_i}$ schedule throughput ($\Upsilon_{STS}/\Upsilon_{STP^I_{q_i}}$). Notice that the unit for the results in Table 4 is $\frac{1}{clock\ cycle}$. A result in seconds could be obtained by dividing these results by the value of one cycle (*e.g.* 2.5×10^{-9} s for MPPA 256 cores).

We clearly see that our STP delivers the same throughput as STS for 9 out of 10 applications. The only application have lower throughput is H.263 Encoder but overall, we demonstrated good results while ensuring high level of time determinism. This fact show one more advantage of using our STP framework.

5.5   Discussion: Decision Tree for Real-Time Scheduling of CSDF Applications

Based on the evaluation results in Sects. 5.3 and 5.4, we present a decision tree for selecting between different real-time scheduling policies that we propose for CSDF graphs in this paper. The decision tree is illustrated in Fig. 6. The first decision is to determine whether the application is safety-critical or not. If the application is safety-critical, then the SPS model, with its better temporal isolation property, is chosen to guarantee time constraints. If the application have simpler real-time constraints, $STP_{q_i}^I$ and $STP_{r_i}^I$ could be chosen, based on which granularity gives better result, to reduce the end-to-end latency while ensuring the maximum throughput obtained under the Self-Timed Scheduling. In the case of unbalanced graphs, $STP_{q_i}^C$ and $STP_{r_i}^C$ helps in further reducing latency if the constrained deadline model is possible.

6   Conclusions

In this paper, we showed that the actors of a streaming application modeled as CSDF graph, can be scheduled as self-timed periodic tasks. As a result, we conserved the properties of a periodic scheduling and at the same time improve its performance. We also showed how the different granularities offered by CSDF model can be explored to decrease latency. We presented an analytical framework for computing the periodic task parameters while taking into account inter-processor communication and synchronization overhead. Based on empirical evaluations, we showed that our STP approach reduces significantly the latency compared to the SPS model and delivers the maximum throughput achieved under the STS model. We summarized our results in the form of a decision tree to assist the designer in choosing the appropriate scheduling policy for acyclic CSDF graphs. As a future work, we want to improve our scheduling policy for STP model using the constrained deadline which requires different schedulability analysis.

References

1. Ali, H., Akesson, B., Pinho, L.: Generalized extraction of real-time parameters for homogeneous synchronous dataflow graphs. In: Proceedings of PDP (2015)
2. Bamakhrama, M.A., Stefanov, T.: Managing latency in embedded streaming applications under hard-real-time scheduling. In: CODES+ISSS, pp. 83–92 (2012)
3. Bamakhrama, M.A., Stefanov, T.: On the hard-real-time scheduling of embedded streaming applications (2012)

4. Bilsen, G., Engels, M., Lauwereins, R., Peperstraete, J.: Cyclo-static data flow. In: Proceedings ICASSP, vol. 5, pp. 3255–3258 (1995)
5. Bodin, B., Kordon, A.M., de Dinechin, B.D.: Periodic schedules for cyclo-static dataflow. In: ESTImedia, pp. 105–114 (2013)
6. Bouakaz, A., Talpin, J., Vitek, J.: Affine data-flow graphs for the synthesis of hard real-time applications. In: Proceedings of ACSD, pp. 183–192 (2012)
7. Davis, R.I., Burns, A.: A survey of hard real-time scheduling for multiprocessor systems. ACM Comput. Surv. **43**, 35 (2011)
8. De Dinechin, B.D., De Massas, P.G., Lager, G., Léger, C., Orgogozo, B., Reybert, J., Strudel, T.: A distributed run-time environment for the kalray MPPA-256 integrated manycore processor. Procedia Comput. Sci. **18**, 1654–1663 (2013)
9. Dkhil, A., Do, X., Louise, S., Rochange, C.: Self-timed periodic scheduling for cyclo-static dataflow model. ICCS. Procedia Comput. Sci. **29**, 1134–1145 (2014)
10. Dkhil, A., Louise, S., Rochange, C.: Worst-case communication overhead in a manycore based shared-memory model. In: Junior Researcher Workshop on Real-Time Computing, Nice (2013)
11. Ghamarian, A.H., Stuijk, S., Basten, T., Geilen, M.C.W., Theelen, B.D.: Latency minimization for synchronous data flow graphs. In: Proceedings of the 10th Euromicro Conference on Digital System Design Architectures. Methods and Tools, Washington, DC, USA, pp. 189–196 (2007)
12. Goubier, T., Sirdey, R., Louise, S., David, V.: ΣC: a programming model and language for embedded manycores. In: Xiang, Y., Cuzzocrea, A., Hobbs, M., Zhou, W. (eds.) ICA3PP 2011, Part I. LNCS, vol. 7016, pp. 385–394. Springer, Heidelberg (2011)
13. Khandelia, M., Bambha, N., Bhattacharyya, S.: Contention-conscious transaction ordering in multiprocessor DSP systems. IEEE Trans. Signal Process. **54**, 556–569 (2006)
14. Lee, E.A.: Consistency in dataflow graphs. IEEE Trans. Parallel Distrib. Syst. **2**, 223–235 (1991)
15. Lee, E.A., Messerschmitt, D.G.: Synchronous data flow. Proc. IEEE **75**(9), 1235–1245 (1987)
16. Moreira, O.: Temporal analysis and scheduling of hard real-time radios running on a multi-processor. Ph.D. Thesis, Technische Universiteit Eindhoven (2012)
17. Moreira, O.M., Bekooij, M.J.: Self-timed scheduling analysis for real-time applications. EURASIP J. Adv. Sig. Process. **2007**, 14 (2007). Article ID 83710
18. Sriram, S., Bhattacharyya, S.S.: Embedded Multiprocessors: Scheduling and Synchronization, 2nd edn. Marcel Dekker Inc., New York (2009)
19. Stuijk, S., Geilen, M., Basten, T.: SDF³: SDF for free. In: Proceedings of the Sixth International Conference on Application of Concurrency to System Design, pp. 276–278 (2006)
20. Thies, W., Amarasinghe, S.: An empirical characterization of stream programs and its implications for language and compiler design. In: Proceedings of the 19th International Conference on Parallel Architectures and Compilation Techniques, pp. 365–376 (2010)

A Novel Concurrent Generalized Deadlock Detection Algorithm in Distributed Systems

Wei Lu[1], Yong Yang[1]([✉]), Liqiang Wang[2], Weiwei Xing[1], and Xiaoping Che[1]

[1] School of Software Engineering, Beijing Jiaotong University, Beijing 100044, China
{wlu,12112088,wwxing,xpche}@bjtu.edu.cn
[2] Department of Electrical Engineering and Computer Science,
University of Central Florida, Orlando, FL 32816, USA
lwang@cs.ucf.edu

Abstract. Detecting deadlocks has been considered an important problem in distributed systems. Many approaches are proposed to handle this issue; however, little attention has been paid on coordinating concurrent execution of distributed deadlock detection algorithms. Previous approaches may report incorrect results (false negatives), and they are inefficient due to lack of proper coordination of concurrent execution. In this paper, we present a novel concurrent coordination algorithm for distributed generalized deadlock detection. The proposed algorithm aims to avoid false negatives and improve the performance when concurrently executing deadlock detection in a distributed system. Our algorithm adopts diffusion computation to distribute probe messages and employs priority-based method to coordinate concurrent algorithm instances. Priority carried in the received probe messages will be locally recorded by each initiator. Instead of being suspended by higher priority algorithm instances, lower priority algorithm instances can accomplish deadlock detection locally. The initiator with the highest priority will receive and collect all related resource requests information from lower priority instances in a hierarchical manner and perform global deadlock detection at last. We evaluate our algorithm on a bunch of event-driven simulations. The experimental results show that our approach can achieve better accuracy and efficiency compared to previous approaches.

Keywords: Distributed system · Deadlock detection · Concurrent coordination · False negative

1 Introduction

Problems of detecting deadlocks have been long considered important problems in distributed systems due to the vulnerability to deadlocks. A deadlock occurs when processes wait for resources held by other processes, such as data object in database systems, buffers in store-and-forward communication networks, or messages in message passing systems. The wait-for relationships are usually represented by WFG (Wait-for graph), a directed graph in which vertices represent

© Springer International Publishing Switzerland 2015
G. Wang et al. (Eds.): ICA3PP 2015, Part II, LNCS 9529, pp. 479–493, 2015.
DOI: 10.1007/978-3-319-27122-4_33

processes and edges indicate not granted resource requests between processes, in a distributed system [1–3].

Some researches have classified existing deadlock detection algorithms in terms of underlying resource request models [3–5]. For example, in the *p-out-of-q* (also called *generalized*) model, a process makes requests for q resources and remains idle until p out of the q resources are granted [6–8].

Deadlocks in the generalized model correspond to generalized deadlocks. Detection of generalized deadlock is rather difficult, because the resource dependent topology is more complex than those in other models. A *cycle* in the WFG is a necessary but not sufficient condition in the AND model, whereas a *knot* (which is a strongly connected sub-graph with no edge directed away from the sub-graph in a directed graph [9–11]) is a sufficient but not necessary condition for a generalized deadlock [12]. It become more complicated when several processes initiating the deadlock detection algorithm concurrently, e.g., a process might be involved in more than one instance and will be declared deadlocked and resolved by more than one algorithm instance. This problem can result in useless abortion, i.e., false deadlock resolution. Priority-based approach is often used to address the aforementioned problem; however, improper coordination of algorithm instances may cause false negative and poor performance.

To avoid false negatives and improve performance in concurrent execution of algorithm, we propose a novel concurrent coordination algorithm for distributed generalized deadlock detection. During the probe phase, each initiator will record the priority locally when receiving a probe message. After the probe phase, a hierarchical resource request report mechanism is exploited to construct a global WFG in the initiator with the highest priority.

Contributions of proposed algorithm are summarized as follows:

(1). The proposed algorithm can handle all kinds of aforementioned resource request models;
(2). Our algorithm can avoid false negatives of deadlock detection and provide better performance.

The rest of this paper is organized as follows. Related work is presented in Sect. 2. System models and definitions are described in Sect. 3. Section 4 details the proposed algorithm. Experiment results are shown in Sect. 5. At last, Sect. 6 gives conclusions and future works.

2   Related Work

2.1   Categories of Deadlock Detection Algorithms

Deadlock detection approaches can be classified in different ways according to classification criteria. *Singhal* [3] classified the deadlock detection in distributed systems into three types: centralized, decentralized, and hierarchical, according to the way in which WFG is maintained and how to detect cycles and knots. *Knapp* described three taxonomies based on theoretical principle: path pushing [14] (which is later disproved due to asynchronous snapshots at different sites [15]), probe-based (includes edge chasing and diffusing computing) [16], and global state detection, to detect deadlocks in distributed systems [2]. *Brzezinski* defined five types of resource request models: Single-Request, AND, OR [12,17], AND-OR, and generalized model (p-out-of-q) [18–22], based on the complexity of resource requests [3–5].

2.2 Review of Algorithms of Generalized Deadlock Detection

Centralized Deadlock Detection Algorithms. A process, acting as initiator, sends probe messages to its direct and indirect successor processes when it suspecting itself blocked in a defined time interval. All reply messages will be sent back directly to the initiator where a global WFG and deadlock detection will be constructed and performed.

The authors of [13] proposed a centralized algorithm in which an initiator send probe messages directly to all the processes reachable from itself, and replies from successor processes are sent back to the *initiator* process directly. The Initiator is in charge of constructing global WFG and detecting deadlocks.

The authors of [21] proposed a two-phases centralized algorithm. Unlike classical diffusion computation, the resource request is carried in the probe messages, and report messages are send to initiator directly rather than backward along the opposite direction of edges. The resource requests are equal distributed in each probe message, and the performance is improved in this manner.

The authors of [19,20] proposed a centralized algorithm to detect and resolve deadlocks in which the termination of the algorithm depended on either technique of weight distribution liked [1] or whenever a deadlock was detected. Reply messages carrying weight information will be delayed until all the probe messages have been received from all its predecessor processes. Message overhead will be minimized through merging weighted messages into one message. To decrease time complexity, the proposed algorithm performs reduction as soon as a reply message from an active process is received.

Decentralized Deadlock Detection Algorithms. Different with centralized approaches, no complete global WFG is constructed by the initiator node (site, process, and node will be used interchangeably throughout this paper) in decentralized approaches. Nevertheless, the WFG constituted in multiple sites in decentralized deadlock detection algorithms.

The paper [12,23] presented a one-phase decentralized algorithm for detecting generalized distributed deadlocks. The algorithm initiated by an initiator consists of outwards and inwards sweep. The outwards sweep induces a spanning tree and records WFG by propagating the probe messages. The inwards sweep performs a reduction in an up-tree direction started at an active node. An ECHO message will be replied by an active node when receiving probe messages. A PIP message, contains ids of nodes that sent PIP messages but reduces later and residual requirement conditions, will be replied when a node receiving the second and subsequent probe message if the state of this node is indeterminate at this instant. When a node that sent PIP message receiving ECHO or PIP message that makes it reduced would send ECHO message to its parent node in directed spanning tree. This algorithm performed reduction in a "lazy evaluation" manner.

The paper [22] proposed a semi-centralized algorithm for distributed generalized deadlock detection and resolution. They adopted hash table to save global ids, initiation time-stamp (hash key) of initiator, resource requests and phantom edges (hash value). The approach delays the phantom edge reply message reporting operating and combines it with common reply messages, and reply messages are in a reduction manner by reduction of request conditions of involved nodes.

Hierarchical Deadlock Detection Algorithm. Sites are arranged in a hierarchical way, and each site only responses for detecting deadlock that involves its child processes.

A hierarchical algorithm was proposed to detect deadlocks in distributed database system in [24]. They arranged all the resource controllers in a tree structure. Controllers were classified into two types: leaf-controllers and nonleaf-controllers. A leaf-controller responds to manage resources and collect part of the global TWF (Transaction Wait-For) that represent the wait-for relations of corresponding resources. Whenever there is a change of TWF occurs in a leaf-controller, the change will be propagated to its parent non-leaf controller to do deadlock detection locally.

The authors of [25] proposed a hierarchical deadlock detection algorithm different from [24]. A central control site is chosen among all sites, and the rest of sites will be divided into several clusters in which an inter-cluster control site will be selected by the central control site. The inter-cluster control site responds to detecting inner cluster deadlock and reports its detection results to the central control site. The global deadlocks will be detected by the central control site finally.

2.3 Previous Concurrent Coordination Strategies

Most of the previous works focused on performance improvement of single execution of the deadlock detection algorithm. Very few effort was paid on handling the practical and important problem: concurrent execution in which more than one node conduct concurrent deadlock detection in a distributed system. Priority-based approach was commonly used by most representative algorithm that address problem of concurrent execution [12,20–22]. They can be classified into mainly two categories: [12]-like and [21]-like.

The authors of [12] proposed a concurrent execution strategy in which high priority algorithm instance will suspend low-priority one. So, algorithm instance with lower priority cannot complete in this approach, and message overload (number and size) is high due to repeatedly sending probe messages by processes with lower priority. That is, a process will terminate the current algorithm instance to join a higher priority instance when it receives a probe message with a higher priority.

The authors of [21] proposed an improved approach to improve performance by equal distributing resource requests in probe messages to reduce the message size in the probe phase. In addition, a higher priority process will report an active state to a lower priority process when the higher priority process is receiving a probe message from the lower one. It is based on the assumption that processes with higher priority will always resolve the detected deadlocks. The lower priority algorithm can accomplish and do local deadlock detection and resolution after receiving enough resource request information [21].

The shortage of [12] is that repeatedly work of low-priority instance will be done by high priority instance again. And, false negatives might happen if a probe message is sent to a process with a higher priority by a process with a lower priority in an OR model [21].

To address the aforementioned shortages in previous approaches, we propose a novel concurrent coordination algorithm for generalized distributed deadlock detection by:

(1). Utilizing equal distribution of resource requests in probe messages to reduce the message size like [21];

(2). Reusing the information discarded by previous approaches to reduce message overhead, that is, lower priority initiator process's execution will not be suspended by higher ones any more;

(3). Recording priority of probe messages locally and adopting a hierarchical resource request report mechanism to collect global WFG to avoid false negatives.

3   Preliminaries

3.1   System Model

This paper follows the system model described in [12, 20–22]. A distributed system consists of various site communicating with each other by message passing to exchange messages or access resource. Messages are sent and received in a reliable way but their delay time is uncertain. A node has one of the following two states: *active* and *blocked*. In a generalized model a node is on *active* state when sufficient number of its resource requests are granted, otherwise it is on *blocked* state. Two kinds of messages, computation message and control message, are transmitted in the system. Computation messages are triggered by the execution of applications, and control messages are issued when the execution of deadlock detection algorithm. Both computation message and control message could be sent by an *active* process, however, a *blocked* process can only send control message.

3.2   Definitions of Deadlocks

Definition 1. *WFG is a directed graph $G(V, E)$, V denotes the set of all vertices and E is the set of directed edges.*

A generalized deadlock exists in a distributed system *iff* the resource request of processes can never be granted. Actually, the resource request of deadlocked processes consists of a sub-graph $D(N, K)$ in $G(V, E)$, and all resource requests belonging to each node in D will never be granted while the resource requests belonging to the node out of D is always satisfied.

Definition 2. *Let rc_i denote the resource conditions or requests of node i.*

For example, $rc_i = (j\&k)|l$ means node i becomes **active** if both node j and node k grant the request resources to i, or node l grants the request resource to node i.

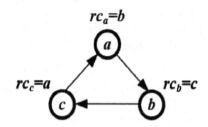

Fig. 1. Example of deadlocked WFG

Definition 3. *Let evaluate(rc_i) be a recursive operation based on the following:*

(1). evaluate(rc_i) = true for an active node i,
(2). evaluate(i) = evaluate(rc_i),
(3). evaluate($P \vee Q$) = evaluate(P) $\vee$ evaluate(Q),
(4). evaluate($P \wedge Q$) = evaluate(P) $\wedge$ evaluate(Q).

where P and Q are non-empty AND/OR expression of node identifiers.

Definition 4. *A sub-graph $D(N, K)$ involves a deadlock if the following conditions are satisfied:*

(1). evaluate(rc_i) = false, $\forall\ i \in D$.
(2). No computation message is under transmission between any nodes in D.

For example, $D(N, K)$ presents a WFG in which $K = \{\langle a, b \rangle, \langle b, c \rangle, \langle c, d \rangle\}$ and $N = \{a, b, c\}$ in Fig. 1. $evaluate(rc_a) = evaluate(a) = evaluate(b)$. State of node a is decided by node b, and other nodes are evaluated in a similar way.

4   Proposed Algorithm

In this section, we will omit describing the single execution of the proposed generalized deadlock detection algorithm, but detail the proposed algorithm used to coordinate the concurrent execution of deadlock detection algorithm instances.

In a distributed system, processes can be blocked concurrently, and all the blocked processes may initiate the deadlock detection algorithm after being blocked for a certain time interval. It will become more complex when more than one algorithm instance executing concurrently in a distributed system. Especially, a process is participating more than one algorithm instance. The proposed algorithm aims to handle the concurrent execution of deadlock detection algorithm to avoid false negatives and improve performance.

4.1   Informal Description of Concurrency Execution

The proposed algorithm adopts a priority-based approach like previous works to coordinate the concurrency execution. Instead of being suspended by higher priority instances, lower priority instances can continue executing even if encountering a higher priority instance in the proposed algorithm. The initiator will record both lower and higher priority in the probe messages when receiving a probe message with a different priority. The probe phase will complete when all initiator nodes finish local procedure. At last, the initiator with the highest priority will collect resource requests by receiving report messages from lower priority initiator nodes in a hierarchical manner.

A node initiates a deadlock detection algorithm instance by sending probe messages with a priority (denoted as its *id* for simple in this paper) and a weight value to its direct successor nodes when it suspects itself being blocked as **Algorithm** 1. The probe message will be propagated by nodes that receive the probe message and have not participated any other algorithm instance yet. Resource requests are distributed among all probe messages sent to successor processes. Probe message will be not propagated by the node that has participated an algorithm instance. There are three cases when a node receiving a probe message:

Case 1, the node has participated an algorithm instance and has a lower priority than received probe message as **Algorithm** 2;

Case 2, the node has participated an algorithm instance and has a higher priority than received probe message as **Algorithm** 2;

Case 3, it is a leaf node as **Algorithm** 3 **line** 4;

The node will record the priority in the probe message and send a REPORT message with its local current priority to the initiator process that propagates the probe message in both case 1 and case 2. The priority in the REPORT message will be also recorded locally or REPORT to the initiator of the instance that this node is participating now as **Algorithm** 5. In case 3, the node will send REPORT message to the initiator node directly.

A weight value will also be carried by the REPORT message and sent back to reply PROBE message. An algorithm terminates when the initiator receives all distributed weights and the sum of all the weight is 1. An initiator will complete its local deadlock detection algorithm if the sum of weight value is 1 as **Algorithm** 2 **line** 14 - **line** 23 and **Algorithm** 4. If a node is a leaf node (i.e., has no resource request from any other processes) or has the least priority, detection results (deadlocked and active) will be reported to the initiator that has the minimal priority in the set of initiators with priority higher than local priority as **Algorithm 7 line 10 - line 13**. Generally, a node will report its local detection results to the higher one after receiving REPORT messages from all processes have lower priority recorded locally. The process within the highest priority will receive all local detection results and resource requests, construct a global WFG, and perform global deadlock detection at last as **Algorithm 6**.

We also detect phantom edge, node i send a probe message to node j while a reply message is being transmitted to i by j in edge $i \rightarrow j$, during the deadlock detection procedure to avoid false results as **Algorithm 3**. Proposed algorithm will determine an edge is a phantom edge when the probe message is replied.

4.2   Formal Description of Concurrency Execution

Data types, message types and operations are formally defined as follows (Table 1).

Table 1. Date types, additional data types, message types, and operations at node i

Data type	Description
W	Weight value that is carried in PROBE and REPORT messages
rc_i	Resource request of node i
RC_i	Resource request that is collected by node i
IN_i	Ids of node that has requested resource to node i and has been not granted by node i
OUT_i	Ids of node that has been requested resource by node i and has been not granted resource to node i
$PROBE$	$PROBE(pri, i, RC_i, W)$ is sent by node i with priority (pri), resource request (RC_i), and WEIGHT (W)
$REPORT$	$REPORT(pri, i, RC_{(j)}, W, Pri_{cur})$ is sent by node j to initiator node that has a priority (pri) with local priority (Pri_{cur}), resource request (RC_j), weight (W)
$NOTIFY$	$NOTIFY(pri, Pri_{cur})$ is sent by node that has Pri_{cur} to initiator node that has pri
$SUBMIT$	$SUBMIT(pri, i, RC_i, Pri_{high}, Pri_{low})$ is sent by node i to initiator node has pri with resource request (RC_i), priority $(Pri_{high}$ and $Pri_{low})$ collected locally
$WEIGHT$	Sum of weight values in $REPORT$ messages (additional data type)
Pri_{high}	Set of priority that is higher that Pri_{cur} (additional data type)
Pri_{low}	Set of priority that is lower that Pri_{cur} (additional data type)
$max\{Pri_{high}\}$	The maximum value in Pri_{high}
$min\{Pri_{low}\}$	The minimum value in Pri_{low}
$|\{1, 2, ..., n\}|$	The size of a set

Algorithm 1. When node i initiating an deadlock detection algorithm instance

1: **for** $j \in OUT_i$ **do**
2:      Sending **PROBE**$(i, i, rc, \frac{1}{|OUT_i|})$ to node j;
3: **end for**

Algorithm 2. When a **non-leaf** node j receiving a $PROBE(pri, i, rc, w)$ message

1: **if** $i \rightarrow j$ is not a phantom edge **then**
2:      **if** $Pri_{cur}! = NULL$ and $Pri_{cur} > pri$ **then**
3:          $Pri_{low} := Pri_{low} \cup \{pri\}$;
4:          Sending **NOTIFY**(pri, Pri_{cur});
5:          **if** node j is not an initiator **then**
6:              Sending **NOTIFY**(Pri_{cur}, Pri_{cur});
7:          **end if**
8:      **else if** $Pri_{cur}! = NULL$ and $Pri_{cur} < pri$ **then**
9:          $Pri_{high} := Pri_{high} \cup \{pri\}$;
10:         Sending **NOTIFY**(pri, Pri_{cur});
11:         **if** node j is not an initiator **then**
12:             Sending **NOTIFY**(Pri_{cur}, Pri_{cur});
13:         **end if**
14:     **else if** $Pri_{cur}! = NULL$ and $Pri_{cur} == pri$ **then**
15:         **if** node i is an initiator **then**
16:             $WEIGHT := WEIGHT + w$;
17:             **if** $WEIGHT == 1$ and $Pri_{low} == \emptyset$ **then**
18:                 **Algorithm 7**;
19:             **end if**
20:         **else**
21:             Sending **REPORT**$(Pri_{cur}, Pri_{cur}, rc, w, Pri_{cur})$;
22:         **end if**
23:     **end if**
24:     **if** $Pri_{cur} == NULL$ **then**
25:         $Pri_{cur} := pri$;
26:         $RC_j := rc \cup rc_j$;
27:         $w' := \frac{w}{|OUT_j|}$;
28:         **for** $k \in OUT_k$ **do**
29:             Sending **PROBE**$(Pri_{cur}, j, \frac{RC_j}{|OUT_j|}, w')$ to node k;
30:         **end for**
31:     **end if**
32: **else**
33:     *Discarding the PROBE message (a phantom edge: $i \rightarrow j$)*;
34:     Sending **REPORT**$(pri, i, rc, w, \emptyset)$;
35: **end if**

5   Experiment

In this section, we evaluate the correctness and performance of the proposed algorithm and present the simulation results. False negative is mainly

Algorithm 3. When a **leaf** node j receiving a $PROBE(pri, i, rc, w)$ message

1: if $i \in IN_j$ then
2:     $Pri_{cur} := pri$;
3:     $RC_j := rc \cup rc_j$;
4:     Sending **REPORT**$(pri, i, RC_j, w, Pri_{cur})$;
5: else
6:     *Discarding the PROBE message (a phantom edge: $i \to j$)*;
7:     Sending **REPORT**$(pri, i, rc, w, \emptyset)$;
8: end if

Algorithm 4. When a node i receiving a $REPORT(pri', j, rc, w, pri'')$ message

1: $WEIGHT := WEIGHT + w$;
2: $RC_i := RC_i \cup rc$
3: if $pri'' ! = \emptyset$ then
4:     if $WEIGHT == 1$ and $Pri_{low} == \emptyset$ then
5:         Algorithm 7;
6:     end if
7: else
8:     $RC_i := RC_i / i \to j$;
9: end if

Algorithm 5. When a node i receiving a $NOTIFY(pri', pri'')$ message

1: if $Pri_{cur} > pri'$ then
2:     $Pri_{low} := Pri_{low} \cup \{pri'\}$;
3: else if $Pri_{cur} < pri'$ then
4:     $Pri_{high} := Pri_{high} \cup \{pri'\}$;
5: end if

Algorithm 6 . When a node i receiving a $SUBMIT(pri, j, RC_j, Pri'_{high}, Pri'_{low})$ message

1: $RC_i := RC_i \cup RC_j$;
2: $Pri_{high} := Pri_{high} \cup Pri'_{high}$;
3: $Pri_{tmp} := Pri_{tmp} \cup Pri'_{low}$;
4: if $Pri_{cur} == max(Pri_{cur})$ then
5:     if $Pri_{tmp} \cap Pri_{low} == Pri_{low}$ then
6:         Algorithm 7 (line 1-line 7) and terminating;
7:     end if
8: else
9:     if $Pri_{tmp} \cap Pri_{low} == Pri_{low}$ then
10:         Algorithm 7 (line 11-line 13) and terminating;
11:     end if
12: end if

considered as the correctness metric. The performance metrics mainly total message number and total message size of submitted messages in the life-cycle of

Algorithm 7. Locally deadlock detection procedure $LDD(RC_i)$

1: **for** $rc^j \in RC_i$ **do**
2:   **if** $evaluate(rc^j) == flase$ **then**
3:       $Deadlocked := Deadlocked \cup \{j\}$
4:   **else**
5:       $Active := Active \cup \{j\}$
6:   **end if**
7: **end for**
8: **if** $Pri_{cur} == max\{Pri_{high}\}$ **then**
9:   **Algorithm terminating**;
10: **else**
11:   $pri := min\{Pri_{high}\}$;
12:   Sending **SUBMIT**$(pri, i, RC_i, Pri_{high}, Pri_{low})$;
13: **end if**

algorithm. Especially, total message size is the number of resource request contained in a PROBE message.

5.1 Experiment Setup

Simulation programs are event-driven and written in Python2.7. Processes are used to simulate nodes in a distributed system, and network socket is used to implement message passing and simulate wait-for relationship between processes (nodes). The number of socket calls (e.g., socket.send() and socket.recv()) and the size of data that presents resource request are collected and compared. Each simulation result is the mean value obtained after running the program for 100 times. We choose two extreme resource request models: Single-Request and Generalized model, to perform simulation. Each process waits for another one process that has a lower id value (i.e., priority) in Single-Request model. In the Generalized model, each process waits for all the other processes excepting for itself. Six special cases are constructed manually in Fig. 2 to examine the correctness and efficiency of the distributed deadlock detection algorithms.

5.2 Simulation Results

Table 2 gives the quantitative comparison among [12, 21] and the proposed methods where notation "NFN" denotes no false negatives and notation "FN" denotes false negatives. The reason of false negative in [21] comes from the OR request model. Based on the assumption that higher priority algorithm instance will resolve the deadlock, detected deadlocks (e.g., a and c) in Fig. 2(d) can be resolved even if there is a false negative. However, no deadlocks will be detected in Fig. 2(e) and (f), because the edge $c \rightarrow d$ propagates the false negative result to sub-graph (a and c included). The proposed algorithm can detect all deadlocks in Fig. 2 without false negatives.

The value of x-axis represents the number of processes. The value of y-axis of left sub-figure in Figs. 3, 4, 5, and 6 means the total number of messages that

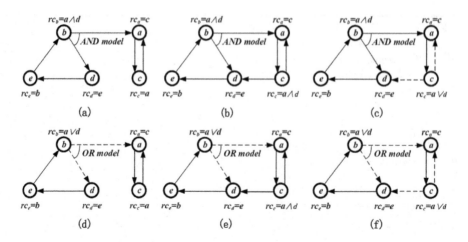

Fig. 2. Six WFGs of different resource request models

Table 2. Results of correctness simulations

	Fig. 2(a)	Fig. 2(b)	Fig. 2(c)	Fig. 2(d)	Fig. 2(e)	Fig. 2(f)
[12]-like	NFN	NFN	NFN	NFN	NFN	NFN
[21]-like	NFN	NFN	NFN	FN	FN	FN
Proposed	NFN	NFN	NFN	NFN	NFN	NFN

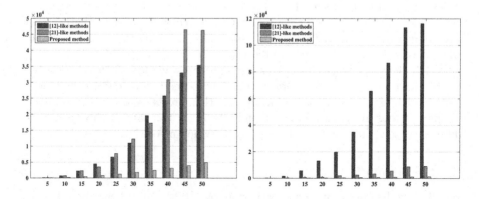

Fig. 3. All processes as initiator in Generalized model

are transmitted, and the value of y-axis of right sub-figure represents the total data size of transmitted messages.

From left sub-figures of Figs. 3, 4, 5, and 6, we can find that the proposed algorithm has better performance than [12,21] in the aspects of total number of message transmitted during the life-cycle of algorithm. [12,21] transmitting almost the same number of messages in the simulations, because they both used the strategy of suspending lower priority instance with higher one. Proposed

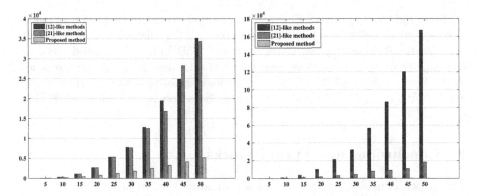

Fig. 4. 1/5 of processes as initiator in Generalized model

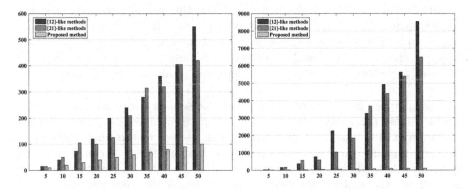

Fig. 5. All processes as initiator in Single-Request model

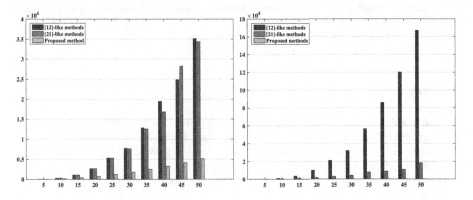

Fig. 6. 1/5 of processes as initiator in Single-Request model

method reduces the number messages by recording priority and report resource requests in the hierarchical report phase.

From right sub-figures of Figs. 3, 4, 5, and 6, we can find that [21]-like methods transmits smaller number of message size than [12]-like methods. The reason is equal distribution of resource requests in PROBE phase. Proposed methods has smaller number of message size than [21]-like methods, because proposed method avoid sending PROBE message by lower priority initiators when receiving PROBE messages from other initiators based on improvement of [21]-like methods.

6   Conclusions and Future Works

This paper focuses on the problem of coordinating the deadlock detection algorithm instances that executing concurrently in a distributed system. The proposed algorithm coordinates the execution of concurrent instances by recording priority of different algorithm instance and reporting resource requests in a hierarchical manner. The proposed algorithm can avoid false detection results (false negatives) and reduce the number and size of message transmitted during the life-cycle of a complete deadlock detection. Simulation results show that the proposed algorithm can report correct detection results and have better performance.

The approach presented in this paper can be seen as a very first step towards a solution for the problems of generalized distributed deadlock detection. A limitation exists in the current proposal with respect to the time efficiency of the algorithm. In the future, we will aim to improve the time complexity and apply the proposed algorithm to detect run-time deadlocks in real scenario, such as, MPI programs, network forwarding or distributed database systems.

Acknowledgements. This work was supported in part by National Natural Science Foundation of China (No. 61100143, No. 61272353, No. 61370128, No. 61428201), Program for New Century Excellent Talents in University (NCET-13-0659), Beijing Higher Education Young Elite Teacher Project (YETP0583).

References

1. Kshemkalyani, A.D., Singhal, M.: Efficient detection and resolution of generalized distributed deadlocks. IEEE Trans. Softw. Eng. **20**(1), 43–54 (1994)
2. Knapp, E.: Deadlock detection in distributed databases. ACM Comput. Surv. (CSUR) **19**(4), 303–328 (1987)
3. Singhal, M.: Deadlock detection in distributed systems. Computer **22**(11), 37–48 (1989)
4. Brzezinski, J., Helary, J.M., Raynal, M., Singhal, M.: Deadlock models and a general algorithm for distributed deadlock detection. J. Parallel Distrib. Comput. **31**(2), 112–125 (1995)
5. Singh, S., Tyagi, S.S.: A review of distributed deadlock detection techniques based on diffusion computation approach. Int. J. Comput. Appl. **48**(9), 28–32 (2012)
6. Chandy, K.M., Misra, J., Haas, L.M.: Distributed deadlock detection. ACM Trans. Comput. Syst. (TOCS) **1**(2), 144–156 (1983)

7. Edgar, K.: Deadlock detection in distributed databases. ACM Comput. Surv. (CSUR) **19**(4), 303–328 (1987)
8. Lee, S.: Efficient generalized deadlock detection and resolution in distributed systems. In: 21st International Conference on Distributed Computing Systems, pp. 47–54 (2001)
9. Gunther, K.: Prevention of deadlocks in packet-switched data transport systems. IEEE Trans. Commun. **29**(4), 512–524 (1981)
10. Gambosi, G., Bovet, D.P., Menascoe, D.A.: A detection and removal of deadlocks in store and forward communication networks. In: Performance of Computer-Communication Systems, pp. 219–229 (1984)
11. Cidon, I.: An efficient distributed knot detection algorithm. IEEE Trans. Softw. Eng. **15**(5), 644–649 (1989)
12. Kshemkalyani, A.D., Singhal, M.: A one-phase algorithm to detect distributed deadlocks in replicated databases. IEEE Trans. Knowl. Data Eng. **11**(6), 880–895 (1999)
13. Chen, S., Deng, Y., Attie, P., Sun, W.: Optimal deadlock detection in distributed systems based on locally constructed wait-for graphs. In: Proceedings of the 16th International Conference on Distributed Computing Systems, pp. 613–619. IEEE (1996)
14. Beeri, C., Obermarck, R.: A resource class independent deadlock detection algorithm. In: Proceedings of the Seventh International Conference on Very Large Data Bases, vol. 7, pp. 166–178 (1981)
15. Elmagarmid, A.K.: A survey of distributed deadlock detection algorithms. ACM SIGMOD Rec. **15**(3), 37–45 (1986)
16. Chandy, K.M., Ramamoorthy, C.V.: Rollback and recovery strategies for computer programs. IEEE Trans. Computers. (TC) **100**(6), 546–556 (1972)
17. Lee, S., Joo, K.H.: Efficient detection and resolution of OR deadlocks in distributed systems. J. Parallel Distrib. Comput. **65**(9), 985–993 (2005)
18. Selvaraj, S., Ramasamy, R.: An efficient detection and resolution of generalized deadlocks in distributed systems. Int. J. Comput. Appl. **1**(19), 1–7 (2010)
19. Srinivasan, S., Rajaram, R.: A decentralized deadlock detection and resolution algorithm for generalized model in distributed systems. Distrib. Parallel Databases **29**(4), 261–276 (2011)
20. Srinivasan, S., Rajaram, R.: An improved, centralised algorithm for detection and resolution of distributed deadlock in the generalised model. Int. J. Parallel Emergent Distrib. Syst. **27**(3), 205–224 (2012)
21. Lee, S.: Fast, centralized detection and resolution of distributed deadlocks in the generalized model. IEEE Trans. Softw. Eng. **30**(9), 561–573 (2004)
22. Tao, Z., Li, H., Zhu, B., Wang, Y.: A semi-centralized algorithm to detect and resolve distributed deadlocks in the generalized model. In: 2014 IEEE 17th International Conference on Computational Science and Engineering (CSE), pp. 735–740 (2014)
23. Kshemkalyani, A.D., Singhal, M.: Distributed detection of generalized deadlocks. In: Proceedings of the 17th International Conference on Distributed Computing Systems, pp. 553–560. IEEE (1997)
24. Menasce, D.A., Muntz, R.R.: Locking and deadlock detection in distributed data bases. IEEE Trans. Softw. Eng. **3**, 195–202 (1979)
25. Ho, G.S., Ramamoorthy, C.V.: Protocols for deadlock detection in distributed database systems. IEEE Trans. Softw. Eng. **6**, 554–557 (1982)

BiTEM: A Two-Tier Energy Efficient Resource Management Framework for Real-Time Tasks in Clusters

Wei Huang[1], Jin Shi[2], Zhen Wang[3], and Zhuzhong Qian[3](✉)

[1] School of Computer Engineering, Nanjing Institute of Technology,
Nanjing 211167, China
wweihuang@sina.com
[2] School of Information Management, Nanjing University, Nanjing 210023, China
shijin@nju.edu.cn
[3] State Key Laboratory for Novel Software Technology, Nanjing University,
Nanjing 210023, China
wangzhen@dislab.nju.edu.cn, qzz@nju.edu.cn

Abstract. Energy saving is a fundamental issue for clusters because huge energy consumption has profound impact on operating cost, system reliability and environment. Therefore, many techniques have been proposed to reduce energy consumption, among which, Dynamic Frequency and Voltage Scaling (DVFS) is recognized as an efficient technique. To save energy for DVFS-enabled clusters where independent real-time tasks are executed, we propose BiTEM which is a cooperative two-tier energy efficient management method including local DVFS control and global task scheduling. By using this method, the DVFS controller adjusts the frequencies of homogenous processors in each server at runtime based on the practical energy prediction. On the other hand, global scheduler assigns incoming tasks onto suitable processors on the designate servers based on the cooperation with the local DVFS controller. Each local DVFS controller responses minimum energy changes to the global scheduler to assist it in assigning tasks. The final evaluation results demonstrate the effectiveness of BiTEM on energy saving.

Keywords: Energy aware · DVFS · Task scheduling · Energy prediction · Datacenter

1 Introduction

Cloud computing provides solutions for most conceivable forms of applications but it also causes huge amounts of electric energy consumption. It is shown that servers consume about 0.5 % of world's total power usage in [7]. Processors (CPUs) account for the main part of power consumed by a server. Besides, the processor is the only component supports the low-power models while others can only be totally or partially turned off [1]. Therefore, using the dynamic nature of CPUs' power to reduce energy has become a hot research topic.

G. Wang et al. (Eds.): ICA3PP 2015, Part II, LNCS 9529, pp. 494–508, 2015.
DOI: 10.1007/978-3-319-27122-4_34

According to [5], the dynamic power consumption of CPU is proportional to the frequency and to the square of voltage. Most of modern processors support Dynamic Voltage and Frequency Scaling (DVFS), which enables processor's frequency and voltage to be dynamically adjusted. Scaling down the frequency and voltage can lower the power while may usually increase the execution time of tasks. It is hard and complex to determine how to reduce energy consumption by DVFS control. Serval works adapt the frequency and voltage according to the CUP utilization. Although these strategies can save some energy, they do not achieve energy minimization via frequency scaling. More energy can be saved if suitable DVFS policies are applied.

Several DVFS strategies such as these from [10,14] have been proposed in recent years to control processors' frequencies. Some of the policies adjust to the optimal frequency by predicting the influences of frequencies on performance and power consumption. On the other hand, the energy saving achieved by DVFS control limits on a single host, while distribution of tasks can also influence overall energy of a cluster and the appropriate energy-aware task scheduling can reduce overall energy. However, many researches only focus on the task scheduling on multi-processor or multi-cores in a server, or study the scheduling between servers.

In this paper, we propose a cooperative Two-Tier Energy Efficient Manage-Ment framework for real-time tasks, called *BiTEM* ($\underline{T, T, E, E, M, M}$), which is designed to save energy through local DVFS control and global task scheduling. On the local tier, we propose a novel way to find the best combinations of frequencies that consume the least energy based on the practical energy prediction. We take both the frequency-power and utilization-power relationship into consideration when forecasting energy consumption. On the global tier, by cooperating with local DVFS controller, the global task scheduler assigns a task to its favourite processor in a cluster that brings minimum energy change. In summary, the main contributions of this paper are as follows:

- We solve issues of energy prediction, frequency scaling and task allocation simultaneously. These three aspects perform their respective duties and have interrelation to the others for energy saving.
- We solve the energy minimization problem of frequency scaling in a novel way. We transform it to a node searching problem in directed graphs. We also prove that the optimal state which consumes the least energy can be found from an initial state that all processors' frequencies are maximum.
- We provide a novel scheduling algorithm, which can work in parallel and efficiently cooperates with local DVFS controller, for the problem of energy-aware task scheduling.

The rest of this paper is organized as follows. Section 2 introduces the framework of *BiTEM* and Sect. 3 introduces the task model and real-time task analysis. In Sect. 4, we introduce the energy prediction method and energy minimizing algorithm of local DVFS controller. The global task scheduling algorithm is presented in Sect. 5. In Sect. 6, we evaluate *BiTEM* through some experiments.

Section 7 introduces some related works. Finally, we conclude this paper in Sect. 8.

2   Overview

BiTEM can efficiently allocate independent real-time tasks and control the running speed of processors on each server. Figure 1 shows the framework of BiTEM which consists of two components in the *Local Manager* and three components in the *Dispatcher*.

Definition 1 (Host Model). *Let* $host_j = (U_j, F_j)$ *donate as resources of* j^{th} *host, where* U_j *and* F_j *are vectors that record the utilizations and frequencies of each processor.*

The *Task Analyzer* in Dispatcher receives and analyzes the information of incoming real-time tasks and sends them to other components when necessary. The *Host Monitor* is an assistant component which connects to each server and gathers the basic information of servers. The *Local Monitor* monitors the resources of a server and sends the basic information to Host Monitor when necessary. The basic information of servers are recorded in the *Host Model* (Definition 1). The main work mechanism of BiTEM to schedule a new task $task_n$ is described as follows:

(1) When $task_n$ comes, the Task Analyzer analyzes the basic information of $task_n$ and sends it to the Host Monitor and Global Scheduler (Sect. 5).
(2) When the Host Monitor receives the information of $task_n$, it selects a set of candidates who can load $task_n$ according to the basic information of servers and sends the set to the Global Scheduler.
(3) When the Global Scheduler receives the candidates and the basic information of $task_n$, it sends the task information to the servers who are in the candidate set.
(4) When a candidate receives the task information, the Local DVFS Controller (Sect. 4) will run to estimate the minimum energy change if $task_n$ is allocated to it according to the monitored information. Then the controller returns the result to the Global scheduler.
(5) When the Global Scheduler receives responses from all the candidates, it allocates the $task_n$ to the best server using our scheduling algorithm.

The collaboration among energy prediction, frequency scaling algorithm and task scheduler is the key feature of BiTEM. The basic information of tasks is also important because the energy prediction, frequency scaling and task allocation all use the information of tasks and the real-time task analysis will be introduced in the section.

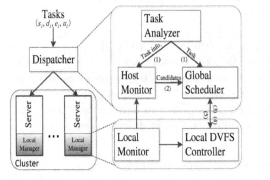

Fig. 1. Framework of BiTEM.

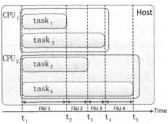

Fig. 2. An example of FSUs.

3   Real-Time Task Analysis

The independent real-time tasks and independent subtasks of distributed applications, are one of the most typical applications in cloud computing environments. These tasks usually have deadline constraints which is the major aspect of Service Level Agreements (SLAs). We first define the *Real-time Task Model* (Definition 2) to describe an independent real-time task.

Definition 2 (Real-Time Task Model). *Let $task_i = (s_i, d_i, e_i, u_i)$ describes i^{th} task, where s_i, d_i, e_i, u_i represent the start time, relative deadline, predicted execution time and the average utilization respectively.*

We designed the *Task Analyzer* to accept and analyze the incoming tasks. The real-time analysis is designed to distinguish the computation-intensive periods and CPU idle time. The average utilization of a task can reflect the computing requirements in some degree. Let $T_c(f)$, T_i represent computing time at frequency f and idle time respectively. We estimate the computing time $T_c(f_{max}) = e_i \cdot u_i$ and idle time $T_i = e_i \cdot (1 - u_i)$ for i^{th} task when a real-time task arrives. The *Task Analyzer* calculates the $T_c(f_{max})$, T_i and sends them as well as start time and deadline to Host Monitor and Global Scheduler.

The computing time of a task has a tight relation to the CPU frequency which shows a linear relationship, while the idle time of a task will barely change due to frequency scaling. Therefore, the running time of ith task running at frequency f can be expressed as:

$$T^i(f) = T_c(f_{max})\frac{f_{max}}{f} + T_i \tag{1}$$

When Local DVFS Controller predicts the energy consumption under different frequencies, the execution time of tasks can be calculated by Eq. (1) according to the basic task information provided by Task Analyzer.

4   Local DVFS Controller

The *Local DVFS Controller* plays an important role in BiTEM and it has two main functions. On the one hand, it predicts the energy consumption of a multi-processor server according to the processors' utilizations, frequencies and the execution time of tasks. On the other hand, based on the energy prediction, it runs **k-Phase energy Prediction (kPP)** algorithm to find the best combination of frequencies which consumes minimum energy in different scenarios.

4.1   Energy Prediction for Multi-processor Servers

The electric energy consumption is the integral of the active power with respect to time. Therefore, the power prediction is crucial to predict energy consumption of a server. Previous researches [5,6,8] provided several power predicting methods. However, they only considered the frequency-power or utilization-power relationship and the details of power prediction for multi-processor platforms were also ignored. In this paper, we provide a practical power predicting method for multi-processor servers which takes both utilization and frequency into consideration. We utilize the nature that homogenous processors consume the same power when they are under the same conditions to predict the power.

The power consumption of a server consists of two parts: static and dynamic power consumption. The static part includes the power consumption of main board, hard disks, fans etc. Let P_s represent the static power of a server when the system is not idle. The dynamic power of a processor can be expressed as:

$$P_{dynamic} \simeq A \times C \times V^2 \times f \tag{2}$$

where A is the percentage of active gates, C is total capacitance, V is supply voltage and f is the operating frequency. According to [5], the voltage has a linear relationship to frequency, so the dynamic power of a processor can be simplified as: $P_{dynamic} = \alpha \times f^3$, where α is a proportional coefficient. Processors also have static power and let P_{CPU_s} represent the static power of a processor. The power that all homogenous processors are fully utilized in the same frequency f can be expressed as:

$$P(f) = P_s + N_c(P_{CPU_s} + \alpha f^3) \tag{3}$$

where N_c is the number of processors. We want to eliminate the static power of processors, which is not easy to measure. For a given host, we can easily measure its maximum power which is $P_{max} = P_s + N_c(P_{CPU_s} + \alpha f_{max}^3)$. Therefore, we can estimate the power consumption of a server that all processors are fully utilized at the same frequency f:

$$P(f) = P_{max} - \alpha N_c(f_{max}^3 - f^3) \tag{4}$$

According to [2,6,8], the power consumption is also related to utilizations, which presents a linear relationship. Therefore, the power consumption of one homogenous CPU with frequency f and utilization u can be denoted as:

$$P_{CPU}(u, f) = \frac{1}{N_c}[P_{max} - P_s - \alpha N_c(f_{max}^3 - f^3)]u \tag{5}$$

Finally, the power of a homogenous multi-processor server can be expressed as:

$$P_{host} = P_s + \sum_{c=1}^{N_c} P_{CPU}^c \tag{6}$$

$$= P_s + \frac{1}{N_c}\sum_{c=1}^{N_c}[P_{max} - P_s - \alpha N_c(f_{max}^3 - F_{j,c}^3)]U_{j,c} \tag{7}$$

We can view the power of jth host as a function of utilizations and frequencies, presented as $P_{host}(F_j, U_j)$, where U_j and F_j are defined in Definition 1.

Definition 3 (Frequency Scaling Unit). *A time interval $[t_1, t_2)$ is a Frequency Scaling Unit (FSU) if 1) $\forall\ t \in [t_1, t_2)$, $NT(t) = NT(t_1)$ and $NT(t_1) \neq NT(t_2)$, 2) $NT(.)$ changes at t_1 and t_2, where $NT(t)$ represents the number of tasks at time t in a server.*

The energy consumption depends on both the power and the execution time. Therefore, we define the concept of *Frequency Scaling Unit* (FSU, Definition 3) to estimate the execution time of tasks and distinguish different periods of time when the numbers of tasks are different. The FSU represents a period of time when the number of tasks does not change. An example of FSU is shown in Fig. 2 which includes four FSUs. Assuming a task finishes at time t_2 and next task finishes at time t_3, then $T = t_3 - t_2$ is an FSU. If a task is allocated to the server at t_1 and the a task finished at t_2, $T = t_2 - t_1$ is also an FSU. It is obvious that the number of tasks in the host is equal to the number of FSUs if all tasks finish at the different times. We assume different tasks finish at the different times in a host in the rest of this paper.

If we set consistent frequencies for all processors in an FSU, the power state in this FSU is relatively stable because the workloads in this FSU is fixed. We know the length of this FSU, so the energy consumption in an FSU can be predicted conveniently and precisely by the equation: $E = P \times T$, where P and T represent power and time respectively. Based on the definition of FSU, power function and related notations in Table 1, the energy consumption of jth host to finish all the tasks can be predicted as follow:

$$E_j = \sum_{k=1}^{N_{j,p}} P_{j,k}(U_{j,k}, F_{j,k})T_{j,k} \tag{8}$$

where the power of host $P_{j,k}$ can be calculated by the Eq. (7) in different situations. The length of FSU can also be estimated under different frequencies by Eq. (1).

Table 1. Notations used in this paper

Notations	Definition
J_j	The set of jobs (tasks) in j^{th} host
C_j	CPU set of jth host
F_j	All possible combinations of frequencies for CPUs on j^{th} host
$F_{j,k}$	A combinations of frequencies for CPUs on j^{th} host in k^{th}
$U_{j,k}$	Utilizations of CPUs of jth host in k^{th} FSU
$U_{j,k}^c$	Utilization of cth CPU of jth host in k^{th} FSU
$T_{j,k}$	Time length of kth FSU of jth host
$N_{j,p}$	The number of FSU from the current time of jth host
$P_{j,k}(.)$	The power function of jth host in k^{th} FSU

4.2   KPP Algorithm for Energy Minimization

According to the analysis of energy prediction, if we adjust different frequencies in all FSUs, the execution time of tasks and power state of a server will be different, which causes different energy consumptions. We want to find the best combinations of frequencies for all the FSUs that consume the least energy on the promise of ensuring the SLAs of tasks in different statuses. For clearly describing the problem, we define $(F_{j,1}, F_{j,2}, ..., F_{j,|J_j|})$ as a *state* that possible combinations of frequencies for FSU 1 to $|J_j|$ using the notations in Table 1. If only one combination of frequencies in an FSU is different, we say they are neighbors. For example, if there are two states $s_1{:}(F_{j,1}, F_{j,2}, ..., F_{j,|J_j|})$ and $s_2{:}(F_{j,1}, F_{j,2}, ..., F'_{j,|J_j|})$, the combinations of frequencies for FSU $|J_j|$ in s_1 and s_2 are different while others are same, then s_1 and s_2 are neighbors. In addition, we define $E(s)$ as the energy cost function according to Eq. (8) if we scale the frequencies like s in each FSU. Let a node present a state and an edge (u, v) between two nodes present neighbourhood between u and v. The minimization problem is to find the optimal node that consumes the least energy without any violation of SLAs from an initial node in the constructed graph.

k-Phase energy Prediction algorithm (kPP): By predicting total energy of k FSUs for different states, the best state can be found moving from the initial state. There are $|F_j|$ possible combinations of frequencies in each FSU, so there may be $|F_j|^{|J_j|}$ possible states with different energy consumptions. Let FL_j represent the frequency levels of processors on j^{th} host, we have $|F_j| = |FL_j|^{|C_j|}$. We want to find the optimal state in these $|FL_j|^{|C_j||J_j|}$ possible states and ensure SLAs at the same time. Unfortunately, the searching space may be extremely huge if there are many tasks. Therefore, we provide two heuristic algorithms which are based on simulated annealing (SA) [11] and variable depth search (VDS) [9] respectively.

Simulated Annealing Based Heuristic Algorithm. By comparing energy consumption of a state to a random neighbor, we can find a better state which consumes less energy. The algorithm randomly selects an FSU r to change the frequencies of processors and generates a new state st in each iteration. If the random neighbor st violates SLAs for any one of tasks, the state is discarded and the algorithm enters into the next iteration (line 9). Otherwise, if predicted energy et of st is less than e, st is selected as compared state for next iteration. The algorithm also changes the state with the probability $exp(-\frac{(et-e)}{pT})$ suggested by Metropolis-Hastings [12] to give the possibilities to find optimal solution (line 11). The details of SA-based algorithm are presented in Algorithm 1.

Algorithm 1. SA based kPP algorithm

Input:
 A set of tasks and basic information of a host;
Output:
 The best state s;
1: $J_j = host_j.getTask(), F_j = host_j.getFreqSpace()$
2: Initialize the initial state s_i
3: $s = s_i, e = E(s_i), t = 0, k = |J_j|$
4: **while** $t < t_{max}$ or s doesn't change in l rounds **do**
5: $st = s, r = random(k)$
6: $F_{j,r} = random(F_j - s.get(r))$ /*Select a neighbor*/
7: $st.set(r, F_{j,r})$
8: If st violates SLAs of any task, then **go to** line 13
9: $et = E(st)$
10: **if** $et \leq e$ or $random() < exp(-\frac{(et-e)t}{pT})$ **then**
11:   $s = st, e = et$ /*Change states*/
12: **end if**
13: $t = t + 1$
14: **end while**
15: **return** s

Variable Depth Search Based Heuristic Algorithm. The details of VDS-based algorithm are shown in Algorithm 2. The VDS-based kPP algorithm selects the state that consumes least energy in a subset of neighbors and compares it to the current state. If the selected state consumes the less energy on the promise of ensuring the SLAs of all the tasks, the algorithm changes the state to the new state. The initialized state of VDS-based algorithm is same with the initialization of SA-based algorithm. The algorithm selects a subset of neighbors whose combinations of frequencies for FSU r are different (line 5–6). The combination of frequencies for FSU r that consumes the least energy will be selected (line 7) to generate a new state. The algorithm checks the SLAs violations of new state (line 9). If the energy cost of new state is less than the state in last iteration, the new state will be selected (line 10–12). The process will repeat t_{max} times or until s does not change in l iterations to find a better solution.

Algorithm 2. VDS based kPP algorithm

Input:
    A set of tasks and basic information of a host;
Output:
    The best state s;
1: $J_j = host_j.getTask(), F_j = host_j.getFreqSpace()$
2: Initialize s_i
3: $s = s_i, e = E(s_i), t = 0, k = |J_j|$
4: **while** $t < t_{max}$ or s doesn't change in l rounds **do**
5:    $st = s, r = random(k)$
6:    randomly select a subset $X \subseteq F_j$
7:    $x = argmin(E(st.set(r, x)))$, for all $x \in X$
8:    $st.set(r, x)$ /*Change combination of frequencies for FSU r to x*/
9:    If st violates SLAs of any task, then **go to** line 13
10:    **if** $E(st) \leq e$ **then**
11:        $s = st, e = et$ /*Change states*/
12:    **end if**
13:    $t = t + 1$
14: **end while**
15: **return** s

The Local DVFS Controller runs the kPP algorithm when the Global Scheduler asks it to predict the minimum energy and returns the results to Global Scheduler. This is one of the opportunities to run kPP algorithm. When the workload changes, the power state will also change. In addition, the execution time of tasks may have some errors which may lead to errors of energy prediction. Therefore, the algorithm also runs to obtain the best combinations of frequencies when a task finishes. We scale the frequencies for the first FSU according the results, which means that the algorithm only scales the CPUs' frequencies just for the first FSU while predicting the energy cost for k FSUs.

5   Global Scheduler

Different allocations of a new task may affect the overall energy consumption, because the new task executed on different servers will cause different energy consumptions. We want to find the appropriate scheduling to minimize total energy consumption of a cluster after performing this new task. We can obtain the different energy consumptions of different allocations if we ask each host to predict the minimum energy consumption. The energy minimization problem of task scheduling is to find a server to load new task $task_n$ which causes minimum energy consumption of the whole cluster. The minimum energy consumption of each server can be predicted on each server by kPP algorithm, represented by $EMIN_j$ for j^{th} host. If an incoming task is allocated to i^{th} host, $EMIN_i$ changes to be $EMIN'_i$ while the minimum energy consumptions of other servers do not change. Therefore, the minimum energy consumption of a cluster after allocating a new task can be expressed as:

$$E_{min} = EMIN_i' + \sum_{j \in H-\{i\}} EMIN_j$$

$$= \Delta EMIN_i + EMIN_i + \sum_{j \in H-\{i\}} EMIN_j \qquad (9)$$

$$= \Delta EMIN_i + \sum_{j \in H} EMIN_j$$

According to Eq. (9), we can select the host which brings minimum energy change to load the incoming tasks. We call the scheduling algorithm *Minimum energy Change (MC)* whose details are shown in Algorithm 3. The *Global Scheduler* sends the information of a task to a subset of hosts (line 2) who are selected by Host Monitor. Then each host predicts the minimum energy change and send it back to Global Scheduler. Each host also records the best processor to hold this task and the combination of frequencies (line 3). The Global Scheduler will select the server who causes minimum energy change to allocate a new task. When this task is really allocated to it, BiTEM schedules this task onto the best processor and adjust the best frequencies according to the recorded results.

Algorithm 3. Minimum energy change allocation

Input:
   A new task $task_n$;
Output:
   Designate host and processor for loading $task_n$;
1: *Host Monitor* selects a subset of active hosts that can load the task
2: notify the information of $task_n$ to all candidates
3: each host estimates the minimum energy change $\Delta EMIN_j$ if task is allocated to processor c of $host_j$
4: $host_j = argmin_{j \in H}(\Delta EMIN_j)$
5: **return** $host_j$

In a large scale data center, the mean task length can be acquired according to the historical data, and we can carefully select the size of candidate set to control the energy consumption of kPP algorithm as little as possible.

Table 2. Details of servers

Name	Dell PowerEdge R720
CPUs	Two Intel Xeon E5-2620 @2.1 GHz
Frequency steps (GHz)	1.20, 1.30, 1.40, 1.50, 1.60, 1.70, 1.80, 1.90, 2.00, 2.10
Memory	64G ECC DDR3
Disk	One 10 k SAS, 300 GB
Operation system	CentOS 6.5

6 Experimental Evaluation

6.1 Experiments in Real Environment

Our real experimental environment has three servers and a controller on a virtual machine. The power is measured by Aitek Power Analyzer AWE2101. Each R720 server whose details are shown in Table 2 runs the kPP algorithm to predict energy and control processors' speed. We combine the kPP algorithm with the random (Ran) and first-fit (FF) task scheduling. Meanwhile, the proposed global task assignment (MC) is also combined with the default DVFS controller Ondemand [13] (DEF) in Linux. We compare these six strategies to evaluate the performance of BiTEM on energy savings. For each task, its execution time is generated uniformly at random between a *minimum* and *maximum* execution time represented by ET_{min} and ET_{max} respectively. The deadline of a task is set from 1 to 1.5 times longer to its execution time randomly. Moreover, their utilizations requirements follow the normal distribution with $\mu = 0.75$ and $\sigma = 1$. In addition, the arriving times of tasks follow a Poisson distribution with different average rates.

In these experiments, the iteration times are 10000 for SA-based kPP and 1000 for VDS-based kPP and the number of neighbor in VDS-based kPP algorithm is 20. The results of SA-based and VDS-based algorithms are very close, so we show the results of VDS-based kPP algorithm in Fig. 3 whose legend represents different numbers of tasks. Meanwhile, the size of candidates in MC algorithm is equal to the number of servers. As we can see in Fig. 3, the energy savings of BiTEM can reach from 8 % to 17 % in the real environment with 3 servers.

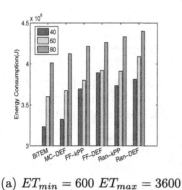
(a) $ET_{min} = 600 \ ET_{max} = 3600$

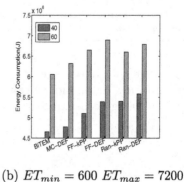
(b) $ET_{min} = 600 \ ET_{max} = 7200$

Fig. 3. Energy consumption of real system. The legend in the picture means the total numbers of arriving tasks.

6.2 Simulation Results

Due to the inaccessibility of a large scale datacenter, we conduct the simulations to evaluate BiTEM in a larger cluster. We model Dell R710 servers to service the dynamically arriving tasks. Meanwhile, the attributes of generated tasks are same with the attributes introduced in Sect. 6.1.

As we can see in Fig. 4(a) and (b), the local kPP algorithm can reduce energy consumption of a specific server compared to Ondemand strategy with a little more SLA violations when global scheduling algorithms are same. In addition, the influences of global scheduling algorithm is greater that the influences of local DVFS controller on energy savings when different scheduling algorithms are applied. The lengths of tasks in Fig. 4(c) are generated uniformly and randomly between 600 and 7200 s. The legend in Fig. 4(c) represents the arriving ratio of tasks in one minute. The results show an increasing tendency of the energy saving ratio with the increments of task numbers and the best result can reach about 28 %. In Fig. 4(d), we investigate the influence of lengths of tasks, tasks are generated in different lengths which are shown in the legend. As shown in Fig. 4(d), BiTEM can also save more energy when the tasks become more. At the same time, BiTEM performs better when the average execution time of tasks becomes longer, because the influence of local kPP algorithm itself becomes smaller and the effectiveness of frequencies scaling becomes more obvious. We evaluate the effectiveness of BiTEM in different scales of data centers ranging from 50 to 5000 servers with different features of arriving tasks. According to the results of Fig. 5, the BiTEM outperforms other strategies in different scales of datacenters, which can reach about 25 % energy savings. With the increasement of host numbers and task numbers, BiTEM performs stably in different scenarios.

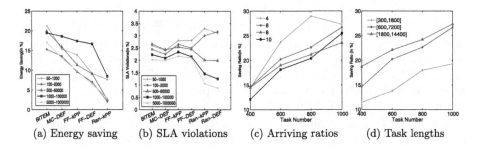

(a) Energy saving   (b) SLA violations   (c) Arriving ratios   (d) Task lengths

Fig. 4. Performance evaluation on different aspects.

7   Related Work

Reducing energy consumption has already been a critical issue in data center in recent years. There have been many researches that studied DVFS policies to decrease processors' power consumption in hosts. Some of them periodically adjust the frequency though evaluating the impacts of frequencies on performance. [14] monitores the utilizations of processors periodically and the frequency is decreased very carefully when there are observable impacts on execution time of tasks.

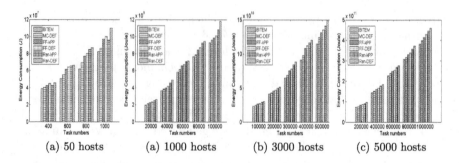

Fig. 5. Energy consumption of different scale of datacenters with different number of tasks.

Some researchers have studied the aspects of the tradeoff between performance and energy saving. Gandhi et al. [8] explore the problem of power allocation with a fixed power budget aiming to minimize average response time for HPC applications. The authors introduce queueing theoretic model to predict mean response time as a function of some parameters such as power-to-frequency relationship, arrival rate of requests, fixed power budget. However, the adaption cost which may have a significant impact on total energy system is not taken into consideration.

The DVFS can indeed reduce the energy consumption, but it is limited on CPUs. A lot of researchers developed the DVFS-based task scheduling algorithms among servers because the distributions of workloads will influence the overall energy. [15] proposed an energy aware strategy which schedule a set of tasks onto suitable physical machines. They adjust the supply voltage by utilizing slack time of non-critical jobs. [15] also discussed the tradeoff between energy consumption and scheduling length. Different to these works, we study the independent real-time tasks with deadline constraints in multi-processor systems.

In [3], the authors have developed dynamic resource provisioning and allocation problem with virtualized technique for energy-efficient cloud computing. [4] have presented a novel approach for power-efficient VM placement for the heterogeneous data centers by leveraging min-max and share features of the VMs based on the DVFS and soft scaling technique. Different to these previous researches, our task allocating algorithm cooperates the local DVFS controller to predict the energy consumption in different situations, the influence of frequency scaling to energy consumption is taken into account before allocation for saving more energy.

8 Conclusions

In this paper, we propose a cooperative two-tier energy efficient strategy to manage the task allocations and adapt frequencies scaling for saving energy. A frequency scaling algorithm is proposed based on the practical power and energy prediction. The global task scheduler collaborates with local DVFS controller to assign tasks and save overall energy. In addition, two heuristic algorithms are provided for searching the optimal solutions which predict minimum energy consumption. The time complexities of both the algorithms are acceptable with satisfactory results according to the experiments. Finally, the real experiment results justify the effectiveness of BiTEM.

Acknowledgments. This work is partially supported by the National Natural Science Foundation of China under Grant No. 61472181, 61100197, 61202113; Jiangsu College Natural Science Foundation under Grant No. 14KJB520016; Jiangsu Natural Science Foundation under Grant No. BK20151392. And this work is also partially supported by Collaborative Innovation Center of Novel Software Technology and Industrialization.

References

1. Beloglazov, A., Buyya, R., Lee, Y.C., Zomaya, A., et al.: A taxonomy and survey of energy-efficient data centers and cloud computing systems. Adv. Comput. **82**(2), 47–111 (2011)
2. Blackburn, M.A., Grid, G.: Five Ways to Reduce Data Center Server Power Consumption. Green Grid, USA (2008)
3. Buyya, R., Beloglazov, A., Abawajy, J.: Energy-efficient management of data center resources for cloud computing: a vision, architectural elements, and open challenges. arXiv:1006.0308 (2010)
4. Cardosa, M., Korupolu, M.R., Singh, A.: Shares and utilities based power consolidation in virtualized server environments. In: Integrated Network Management, IM 2009, pp. 327–334. IEEE (2009)
5. Elnozahy, E.N.M., Kistler, J.J., Rajamony, R.: Energy-efficient server clusters. In: Falsafi, B., VijayKumar, T.N. (eds.) PACS 2002. LNCS, vol. 2325, pp. 179–196. Springer, Heidelberg (2003)
6. Fan, X., Weber, W.D., Barroso, L.A.: Power provisioning for a warehouse-sized computer. ACM SIGARCH Comput. Archit. News **35**, 13–23 (2007)
7. Forrest, W.: How to cut data centre carbon emissions? Website, December 2008
8. Gandhi, A., Harchol-Balter, M., Das, R., Lefurgy, C.: Optimal power allocation in server farms. In: SIGMETRICS, vol. 37, pp. 157–168. ACM (2009)
9. Hromkovič, J.: Algorithmics for Hard Problems: Introduction to Combinatorial Optimization, Randomization, Approximation, and Heuristics. Springer Science & Business Media, Heidelberg (2013)
10. Hsu, C.H., Feng, W.C.: A power-aware run-time system for high-performance computing. In: Proceedings of the 2005 ACM/IEEE Conference on Supercomputing, p. 1. IEEE Computer Society (2005)
11. Kirkpatrick, S., Gelatt, C.D., Vecchi, M.P., et al.: Optimization by simulated annealing. Science **220**(4598), 671–680 (1983)
12. Metropolis, N., Rosenbluth, A.W., Rosenbluth, M.N., Teller, A.H., Teller, E.: Equation of state calculations by fast computing machines. J. Chem. Phys. **21**(6), 1087–1092 (1953)
13. Pallipadi, V., Starikovskiy, A.: The ondemand governor. In: Proceedings of the Linux Symposium, vol. 2, pp. 215–230 (2006)

14. Semeraro, G., Albonesi, D.H., Dropsho, S.G., Magklis, G., Dwarkadas, S., Scott, M.L.: Dynamic frequency and voltage control for a multiple clock domain microarchitecture. In: MICRO-35, pp. 356–367. IEEE (2002)
15. Wang, L., Von Laszewski, G., Dayal, J., Wang, F.: Towards energy aware scheduling for precedence constrained parallel tasks in a cluster with dvfs. In: CCGrid, pp. 368–377. IEEE (2010)

Multitask Oriented GPU Resource Sharing and Virtualization in Cloud Environment

Xingfang Zhao[1(✉)], Yujie Zhang[1], and Bing Su[2]

[1] College of Computer Science and Technology,
Nanjing University of Aeronautics and Astronautics, Nanjing 211106, China
{chiu,zyj_086}@nuaa.edu.cn
[2] School of Information Science and Engineering,
Changzhou University, Changzhou 213164, China
subing@cczu.edu.cn

Abstract. With the enrichment of hardware features and software development environment gradually maturing, GPU is widely applied in the field of general-purpose computing. As a high performance computing resource, GPU is introduced into Cloud Computing to improve its processing capability so as to provide a kind of high performance computing service. In this paper, a multi-GPU based dynamic allocation and management framework is built to achieve centralized management and on-demand allocation. This framework can discover computing nodes automatically and estimate the computing capacity of GPU dynamically to achieve the purpose of the rational allocation of GPU in cloud environments. A GPU load balancing algorithm based on dynamic multi-load-status, named DMLS-GPU, is provided for the calculation of integrated GPU load value and GPU allocation. The experimental results show that the virtualization performance overhead is inconsistent according to different task types. We verify the feasibility and effectiveness of DMLS-GPU in a multi-task oriented multi-GPU sharing system by comparing with randomized load assignment scheme, and the utilization of hardware resource and the throughput of the cluster systems have an improvement.

Keywords: GPGPU · Virtualization · Load balancing · Multi-load-status

1 Introduction

Graphics processing unit (GPU) has very high computational performance and relatively low cost, thus it occupies a very important position in high performance computing (HPC) [1]. Nowadays, HPC technology is no longer just in the field of scientific research, many applications in engineering has the demand of HPC when they meet the massive industrial data. GPU computing, as a low cost scheme widely used in enterprises and institutions, is a federation in science and engineering.

As a key technology of cloud computing, virtualization technology can integrate physical resource and converts them to dynamically scalable virtual resource, so as to achieve the goal of abstracting and managing the underlying heterogeneous hardware

© Springer International Publishing Switzerland 2015
G. Wang et al. (Eds.): ICA3PP 2015, Part II, LNCS 9529, pp. 509–524, 2015.
DOI: 10.1007/978-3-319-27122-4_35

resource in cloud platform effectively [2]. Introducing GPU into cloud infrastructure and the utilization of virtualization technologies for high performance computing applications make it possible for providing HPC service in cloud computing environment. Currently, GPU utilization is low due to the exclusive features of GPU as well as load imbalance in use. What's more, GPU resource management in cloud is an immature technology. The research on the management and sharing of multi-GPU in cloud computing environment is burgeoning.

To provide better support for multitask oriented HPC in cloud computing environment, this paper constructs a framework about resource management based on manifold resource features of GPU and dynamic on-demand resource allocation. It is a virtualization scheme in cloud environments which supports dynamic scheduling and multitask concurrent processing, and it also be a solution for the adaptation issues of general purpose computing in virtualized environments. Learned from the existing GPU virtualization technology, based on type and size of tasks the user submitted as well as GPU status, virtual resource management layer adopts centralized and flexible management mechanism to realize GPU resource requests, monitor, allocation and scheduling. The computing resource can be used concurrently, efficiently and transparently. It guarantees the performance and improves ease of use while reducing use cost too.

In order to keep multi-GPU load balance, a GPU load balancing algorithm based on dynamic multi-load-status is proposed, called DMLS-GPU. On the basis of the integrated load value LD_g, the algorithm selects the set of appropriate GPUs to be allocated. Which means the higher performance GPU has, the much task load is assigned to it. The principle of the algorithm is to make sure all of GPUs do their best. The research on multitask oriented GPU resource sharing and virtualization has great theoretical and practical significance for supercomputing, cloud computing, grid computing on a heterogeneous platform.

The remainder of this paper is organized as follows. We review related work in Sect. 2. The overall architecture of the system is described in detail in Sect. 3. In Sect. 4, a GPU load balancing algorithm based on dynamic multi-load-status (DMLS-GPU) is proposed. We present the experimental platform configuration and a comparative analysis of experimental results in Sect. 5. Finally, we conclude in Sect. 6.

2   Related Work

On virtualization technology, it is much easier for CPU virtualization rather than GPU virtualization. Because of the built-in timesharing mechanism of CPU, it can be very easy to implement process switching in CPU virtualization. In contrast, GPU usually runs a single task at a time and does not switch among processes [3], so the virtualization of GPU is more difficult. In addition, for the commercial considerations, GPU manufacturers do not provide open source library, as a result, GPU cannot be controlled by other system solutions, including virtualization hypervisor.

As GPU virtualization is still a bottleneck, both virtual manufacturers and academics are devoted to the development of GPU virtualization technology. The GPU virtualization terms can be divided into pass-through, partitioning, timesharing and live migration.

The five major virtualization technology vendors are VMware, Microsoft, Oracle, Citrix and Red Hat. Most of them support pass-through, besides the Citrix XenServer can support CUDA (Compute Unified Device Architecture) partitioning, the technology calls GRID. There are many works to do before sharing true virtual GPU hardware acceleration between multiple users.

For evading the seal of GPU computing in the driver layer, some GPU virtualization schemes are designed on software stacks layer in academia. Since CUDA is widely used in GPGPU, primarily proposed solutions are based on CUDA. There are vCUDA [4], Gvim [5], gVirtus [6], rCUDA [7], DS-CUDA [8], GridCUDA [9] and so on. All of these frameworks are based on distributed client-server architecture. The communication is between front end in a virtual machine and rear end in the privilege fields. The common form of GPU virtualization is that front ends intercept CUDA Application Program Interface (API) calls and forward to the rear end to execute. Different virtualization frameworks have different characteristics. For example, the latest rCUDA supports CUDA 6.5 and special communication mechanism for Ethernet and InfiniBand, gVirtus supports CUDA 3.2 and is optimized on KVM virtual machine, DS-CUDA supports CUDA 4.1 and does some communication optimize, V-GPU is a commercial tool that supports CUDA 4.0. Gvim, vCUDA and GridCuda only support obsolete versions of CUDA (1.1–2.3).

Amazon EC2 and IBM Computing on Demand already use GPU in cloud by pass-through, the GPUs are fixed allocation for each virtual machine and not on-demand allocation. In academics, some other schemes like Mars [10], VGRIS [11] and our previous work [12] are presented for sharing GPUs and making their load balance. Mars is a MapReduce runtime system accelerated with GPUs. VGRIS is a framework for scheduling virtualized GPU resources in cloud gaming, its main contributions are a set of API to support scheduling algorithms and the implement of three scheduling policies in cloud gaming. Our previous work provided a GPU virtualization framework with a simple scheduling policy, which developed former schemes. In this paper, our focus is to solve the load imbalance on GPU in cloud, the load evaluation criteria and load balancing algorithm is discussed detailedly.

3   System Architecture

3.1   System Requirements

Nowadays, the mainstream cloud resources sharing schemes are missing support for GPU. The system architecture in this paper introduces GPU into virtual machines by using dynamic libraries intercept method, so as to support GPU parallel programs development and remotely run on machines without GPUs. Virtual resource management layer receives tasks that multiple virtual machines submit, and schedules the physical GPUs in cloud in accordance with their load. The main targets of the system design are as follows: (1) Flexible functions of scheduling and management. Tasks are divided reasonably and distributed to the GPUs in cluster; (2) Transparency. CUDA programs can execute in cloud without any modification; (3) Platform independence. The GPU virtualization framework is not limited to a specific virtual machine manager (VMM) system; (4) Scalability. The platform can be adapted to GPU changes, whether the number of GPU increases when the platform expands or the GPU is revoked due to the hardware failure.

3.2   Overall Architecture

The overall architecture includes: User layer, Virtual Resource Management (VRM) layer and Computing Resources Service (CRS) layer (see Fig. 1).

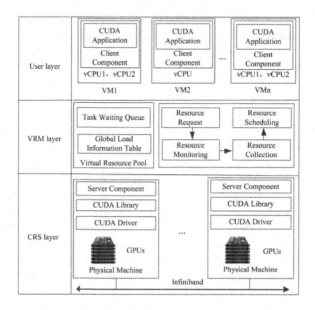

Fig. 1.   The architecture of multi-GPU virtualization

User Layer.   User layer, facing to CUDA applications, is a client program that supports functions such as viewing the running status of the job, interrupting jobs, cancelling jobs and so on. The dynamic API interception method used in the system makes the vast majority of CUDA applications run properly in the virtualized platform without any modification. A series of fake libraries provided in virtual machines replace the original CUDA API libraries and some CUDA related state is maintained to provide the virtual GPU (vGPU). Original CUDA has two dynamic libraries: libcudart.so and libcuda.so. They are corresponded to CUDA Runtime API and CUDA Driver API respectively. CUDA Runtime API is packaged based on CUDA Driver API, hiding some details of the implementation. That makes programming convenient and CUDA Runtime API more widely used. The main functions of User layer: (1) CUDA dynamic libraries API interception; (2) Locality examine for the dependency of functions; (3) Packaging and encoding the parameters along with the functions identifier; (4) Decoding the data got back from server and passing to the applications.

Virtual Resource Management (VRM) Layer. Virtual Resource Management layer, as a core module in unified virtualization platform, is mainly responsible for the management and scheduling of entire resources in the virtual resource pool, as well as monitoring of the entire system. The layer integrate server resources, storage resources and network resources to build a well-organized resource pools for dynamic management and allocation of equipment and resources through a variety of virtualization technologies. All resources realize unified, centralized, intelligent scheduling and management. VRM receives requests for GPU resources from User layer and manages GPU resources in the system uniformly. VRM's monitoring, collection and scheduling of GPU computing resources are at a higher logical level. A basic principle of scheduling is to make the virtual machines that send the resource requests give priority to call the local physical GPU. When local GPU resources are not able to meet the demand, the vGPUs are redirected to the physical GPUs on remote machines. When the workload on certain GPU is overload, the DMLS-GPU algorithm presented in Sect. 4 in detail is used to adjust the calculated load and to select the appropriate GPU by dynamical scheduling.

Computing Resources Services (CRS) Layer. Computing Resources Services layer faces to physical GPUs. Each node in CRS is connected over InfiniBand. The server components in CRS include complete CUDA libraries and drivers those are used to interact with the hardware directly, and manipulate physical GPUs to execute general purpose computing tasks. The server components can service multiple user programs which may come from several different virtual machines or the same virtual machine. In response to a user program request, a service thread is created on the server side, and each thread corresponds to one application. Each server components conducts unified management on local hardware resources and provides virtual computing resources for general purpose computing in accordance with the requirements of a virtual machine as well as the resource allocation tactics. The number of allocation threads depends on the physical resources, load balancing algorithm and user need. In addition, server components need to create worker threads, each GPU device has a thread to receive CUDA API and parameters in datagram from the CUDA program, the thread process the parameters to API-compliant interface definition as well. Applications that end normally inform server components to retrieve physical resources, then worker threads release.

3.3 Main Workflow

The workflow adopted in the architecture refers to MapReduce framework [13] which is widely used in cloud computing platforms. Our cluster system is built on Master/Slave model (Fig. 2). The system contains two types of node: a resource management node and multiple computing nodes. The resource management node (Master node) is responsible for receiving clients' tasks and managing computing nodes. Computing nodes (Slave nodes) perform tasks on GPU. Because of the need to support multiple tasks and heterogeneous GPU platform, considering the difference of each GPU's processing power and speed, computing resources in the system need to be allocated dynamically to maximize system utilization rate based on the real-time status of resources. Steps are as follows:

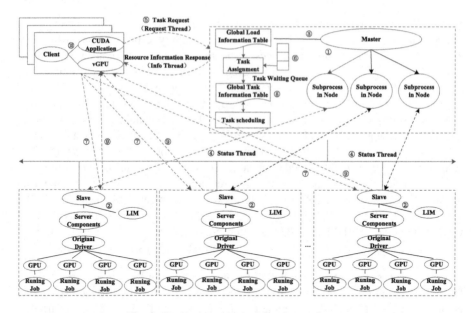

Fig. 2. Logical structure of the cluster system

When user programs first arrived at the system, the load values of GPU are updated to Master node firstly, next the right GPU resources are chosen for scheduling. After the system is running for a while, some tasks have been completed, and GPU load on each node is changing, the task assignment needs to re-adjust to a more rational and balanced status. The detailed steps are as below:

(1) Start Master node, monitor the resources requests from clients in virtual machines and the resources registration requests from the Slave nodes;

(2) Start Slave nodes, each Slave node runs a LIM (load information manager) process which is responsible for collecting the load information of local GPU devices and sending a registration request to the Master node within a specified time interval;

(3) Master node receives registration requests from Slave nodes to establish and maintain a status table (global load information table) for all GPUs in the system (Status thread), then return success message to Slave nodes.

(4) Slave nodes receive the success message for registration, and listen to the specified port at once;

(5) Start client module in virtual machine, when calls for GPU appears in the virtual machine, it will send a resource request to the Master node (Request thread);

(6) Master node receives the virtual machine client requests for resources, and put the task into a task queue, waiting to be assigned to apposite target node. Master node checks GPU state which was acquired in the global load information table, then assign the best matched GPU set to client modules according to the DMLS-GPU algorithm (Info thread);

(7) Virtual machine clients receive the distribution of GPU device resources, and establish a data connection with all of GPUs belonging to the set. The clients

intercept the CUDA API calls and sent them to selected GPUs by socket communication;

(8) Assigned results are updated to the global task information table. Tasks wait for scheduling by the scheduling module;
(9) Execute calls on GPU and return the results;
(10) Virtual machine clients receive the returned results.

Choice of the target node is based on global information of other nodes, so as to make the scheduling results more accurate. In addition, varied modules in every node have different functions including monitoring relevant data, collecting relevant information, and synchronizing preliminary results of the target nodes. Most of the scheduling processes are done in parallel on each node in the system. So the system has very good real-time performance and accuracy.

4 GPU Load Balancing Algorithm Based on Dynamic Multi-Load Status (DMLS-GPU)

To make full use of GPUs in cloud and solve the unbalanced resources allocation problem, a GPU load balancing algorithm based on dynamic multi-load-status is proposed. The GPU set for distribution is selected by minimum load values to make all GPUs do they can, which means higher performance GPUs take more task load.

4.1 GPU Load Evaluation

This part describes the key indicators which impact on the performance of GPU. Computational efficiency of GPU is roughly proportional to the product of computing/CUDA cores number and core frequency. The impact of the global memory size of GPU is also very large. If task's calculation scale is greater than available GPU global memory, the calculation cannot be completed in once, and there must be some additional communication overhead, so overhead of data transmission through PCIe also need to consider, computational efficiency of GPU is roughly proportional to the product of GPU memory frequency and memory bus width as well. Besides, network overhead in a cluster should not be ignored, GPU load is inversely proportional to the network bandwidth (NB). So the load information includes number of computing cores, core frequency, global memory, memory frequency, memory bus width and network bandwidth (NB), taking the size and complexity of tasks into account for load evaluation. GPU is scheduled based on the load information.

An integrated load value LD_g for all GPUs is settings at server:

$$LD_g = \sum_{i=1}^{N} \left(\alpha_1 * \frac{CN_i}{PN_g * PF_g} + \alpha_2 * \frac{Scale_i}{GM_g} + \alpha_3 * \frac{Scale_i/T_1}{BW_p} + \alpha_4 * \frac{Scale_i/T_2}{NB} \right) \quad (1)$$

Parameters are defined as shown in Table 1.

Table 1. Model parameters

Parameters	Meaning	Parameters	Meaning
LD_g	Comprehensive evaluation value of GPU load	i	Sequence number of a task
N	Tasks on GPU currently	NB(GBps)	Network bandwidth of a node
$Scale_i$	Scale of task i on GPU	T_1 (s)	Transmission time through PCIe
CN_i	FLOPS of task i	T_2(s)	Transmission time via network
PN_g	GPU cores number	GM_g	GPU global memory size
PF_g(GHz)	GPU core frequency	BW_p(GBps)	PCIe bandwidth
α_1	Weight of calculation intensity	α_2	Weight of global memory utilization rate
α_3	Weight of usage rate of memory bus width	α_4	Weight of usage rate of network bandwidth

Among them, the scale of task i named $Scale_i$ is got from the interface parameters and provided by CUDA applications. Master node maintains a global load information table, when each task is going to be assigned, the GPU set is determined according to the table. α_1, α_2, α_3, α_4 are the weight coefficients of key indicators to affect GPU performance, their values are determined according to the multiple attribute decision making method AHP, see Sect. 4.2. PN_g, PF_g, BWp, NB and GM_g are all provided by LIM in the Slave nodes. Different tasks have different values of CN_i, T_1 and T_2. The load information of GPUs updates at period T regularly, so the calculation of comprehensive load is also cyclical. The shorter is the period T, the more accuracy of GPU device status got, while the overhead is brought for the frequent calculation of load and the transmission. Experiments show that the time interval which is set to 1 s is reasonable for balance of the overhead and the effect of the system.

Master node returns the set of the minimum values of LD_g based on the dispatching principle of the CUDA task. The smaller the LD_g value is, the lighter the current GPU load is. Moreover, another scheduling principle is local priority, because of the communication mechanism of virtualization to reduce the overhead of data transmission. The GPU device information that Slave nodes submit includes the IP address of the server where the GPU is, GPU device number and GPU parameter information. Then sort the global load information table and select the less load GPU set. Assign the right number of GPU based on CUDA task needs.

4.2 Load Determination Based on Analytic Hierarchy Process (AHP)

Since GPU performance is determined by many factors, their impact on the overall performance is different. Therefore, each factor must be given weight of overall evaluation (important degree) at the time of comprehensive evaluation. Analytic Hierarchy Process (AHP) [14] proposed by Saaty is a mathematical decision-making technique which combines both qualitative and quantitative analysis method. As discussed above, multiple attributes are introduced to determine GPUs' load, then determine the load state according to the load value and artificially set threshold value. In order to calculate the weights of evaluation index, a pairwise comparison reciprocal matrix of judgment is constructed based on small amounts of qualitative information to calculate the weights by using hierarchical sorting method. Details are as follows:

Step 1. Establish hierarchy model
The problem is decomposed into components, which are grouped according to different attributes to create different levels. A hierarchical is arranged in accordance with the Goal level, Criteria level and Alternative level. The top level usually has one element, typically the intended goal or ideal results of problem, as shown in Fig. 3.

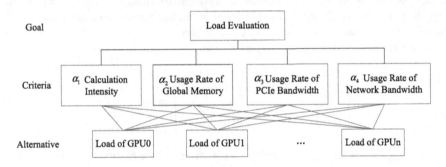

Fig. 3. Hierarchy model of load evaluation

Step 2. Build judgment matrix
One most important characteristic of AHP is that the appropriate importance levels of two schemes are form as pairwise comparison of criteria importance. For a criterion, compare all schemes by pairwise, and rate them according to the degree of importance. a_{ij} is the importance of the scheme a_i relative to a_j. Table 2 lists the 9 importance levels and their values that Saaty proposed.

Table 2. 1–9 scale table

a_i to a_j	Extremely important	Strongly important	Obviously important	Partially important	Equally important
Quantitative value	9	7	5	3	1

In AHP, in order to determine the values of α_1, α_2, α_3 and α_4, the normal 1–9 scale as shown in Table 2 is often used. For resources cost, GPU computing capacity is rather important than global memory utilization, so the value of 2 is assigned at the corresponding location; and GPU computing capacity is partially important than the memory bandwidth using rate, so assigns 3; it is obviously important than using rate of network communications bandwidth, so assigns value of 5; by analogy, the comparison matrix at the Criteria level is shown as (2):

$$A = \begin{bmatrix} a_{11} & a_{12} & a_{13} & a_{14} \\ a_{21} & a_{22} & a_{23} & a_{24} \\ a_{31} & a_{32} & a_{33} & a_{34} \\ a_{41} & a_{42} & a_{43} & a_{44} \end{bmatrix} = \begin{bmatrix} 1 & 2 & 3 & 5 \\ 1/2 & 1 & 2 & 4 \\ 1/3 & 1/2 & 1 & 2 \\ 1/5 & 1/4 & 1/2 & 1 \end{bmatrix} \tag{2}$$

with $a_{ij} = 1/a_{ji}$, and $a_{ij} > 0$ (i, j = 1, 2, 3, 4).

Step 3. Calculate the weights of evaluation index
Saaty obtained the values of weights through solving the eigenvectors of the maximum eigenvalue of A. In order to extract useful information from judgment matrix and achieve regularity cognition of things to provide decision-making the scientific basis, the weight vector of the judgment matrix needs to be calculated.

Calculate the eigenvectors of judgment matrix A according to step 2:

$$\begin{bmatrix} 1-\lambda & 2 & 3 & 5 \\ 1/2 & 1-\lambda & 2 & 4 \\ 1/3 & 1/2 & 1-\lambda & 2 \\ 1/5 & 1/4 & 1/2 & 1-\lambda \end{bmatrix} = 0 \tag{3}$$

Get $\lambda_{max} = 4.0211$, λ_{max} is the biggest eigenvalue of the matrix.
Set

$$\begin{bmatrix} 1-\lambda & 2 & 3 & 5 \\ 1/2 & 1-\lambda & 2 & 4 \\ 1/3 & 1/2 & 1-\lambda & 2 \\ 1/5 & 1/4 & 1/2 & 1-\lambda \end{bmatrix} \begin{bmatrix} \alpha_1 \\ \alpha_2 \\ \alpha_3 \\ \alpha_4 \end{bmatrix} = 0 \tag{4}$$

Eventually, the weight vector of evaluation index is:

$$\alpha = (\alpha_1, \alpha_2, \alpha_3, \alpha_4)^T = (0.509, 0.288, 0.204, 0.080)^T \tag{5}$$

Step 4. Conformance test
In actual scenes, thanks to the value orientation, grading skills and anisometry of importance rank assignment while the experts do the pairwise comparison, it's usually difficult to build a matrix that meet the consistency when the order of the matrix $n > 2$. However, the deviation of the matrix from the consistency condition

should have a degree, it is necessary to judge whether the matrix is acceptable, which is the connotation of the consistency test. In order to check the consistency of the judgment matrix, the consistency index CI, the random conformance rate CR and the mean random consistency index RI are needed.

Calculate the consistency index CI:

$$CI = (\lambda_{max} - n)/(n - 1) = 0.007 \tag{6}$$

By repeatedly calculating the eigenvalues of stochastic matrix, it takes the average value of eigenvalues as a mean random consistency index. Its value can be found according to the matrix order in Table 3 [15].

Table 3. Mean random consistency index of matrix

Matrix order	1	2	3	4	5	6	7	8	9
RI	0	0	0.52	0.89	1.12	1.26	1.36	1.41	1.46

Calculating random consistency rate CR. The ratio of the consistency index CI and the mean random consistency index RI of judgment called the random conformance rate is recorded as:

$$CR = CI/RI = 0.008 \tag{7}$$

The consistency of the judgment matrix is acceptable when the random conformance rate $CR \le 0.1$, otherwise the matrix need to be adjusted until the consistency of the judgment matrix is acceptable. At this point, we get a single rank order as shown in Table 4. Given in (7), $CR = 0.008 < 0.1$, so the results which pass the conformance test are acceptable.

Table 4. Single rank order of the weight of index at criteria level

Factor	Computing capacity	Memory resources	Memory bus bandwidth	Network bandwidth	Weight
Computing capacity	1	2	3	5	0.509
Memory resources	1/2	1	2	4	0.288
Memory bus bandwidth	1/3	1/2	1	2	0.204
Network bandwidth	1/5	1/4	1/2	1	0.080

5 Experiments and Analysis

5.1 Experimental Environment

The architecture of experimental system is: User layer (10 virtual machines), CRS layer (4 servers) and VRM layer (located at one of the servers). The CRS layer consists of four servers, each server is equipped with Intel Xeon (R) CPU E5410 (2.33 GHz), 32 GB of memory and 1 TB Hard Disk Drive (HDD) and contains 4 Tesla C2070 GPU, high-speed InfiniBand network is used for inter-server connection. Server components are deployed at the server side, and send the load registration request of GPU to the Master node within the specified time interval. User layer are 10 virtual machines which are on VMware Workstation. Every virtual machine is the same and their configuration is two vCPUs, 1G memory and 20 gigabytes of memory.

5.2 Virtualization Performance Analysis

In this part, the performance loss of virtualization is analyzed with the test programs chose from CUDA SDK. They can reflect different features of CUDA applications, such as I/O access, computational load and data size. Table 5 shows the comparison between the virtual environment and the non-virtualized environment. The Non-Virtualization column is that each CUDA program is running on physical machines and use physical GPUs directly for calculation, the performance of the CUDA programs at the situation is the best efficiency in the CUDA framework, the running time is used as the benchmark for evaluating the performance of virtual scheme.

Table 5. Comparison of virtualization environment and non-virtualization environment

Benchmark name	Data transfers	Category	Non-virtualization(s)	Virtuali-zation(s)	Norm.
alignedTypes(AT)	413.26 MB	memory	3.905	18.916	4.844
bandwidth Test(BT)	32.00 MB	memory	0.867	8.693	10.026
blackScholes(BS)	76.29 MB	memory	2.585	11.635	4.501
clock(CLK)	2.50 KB	calculation	0.278	0.312	1.122
matrixMul(MM)	79.00 KB	calculation	0.489	0.538	1.100

Experimental results show that, there are some different performance losses for different applications in the virtualization environment compared to non-virtualization environment. The overhead in virtualization environment is mainly divided into the following parts: VMM overhead (environment switch and virtual machine scheduling), the overhead of the pseudo library, socket transmission overhead, etc. Seen from Table 5, the execution time of I/O intensive tasks which have a large volume of data transmission such as AT and BS on virtualization environment beyond the non-virtualization environment situation of an order of magnitude. In contrast, when transfer data size is small, the performance of calculation intensive tasks like CLK and MM is close to non-virtualization environment situation. So the data transmission is the main performance bottleneck for the GPU virtualization.

5.3 Scalability Evaluation

In this paper, the architecture is required to discover computing devices automatically and GPU can join dynamically, GPU may increase with the continuous expansion of platform, a few nodes may be revoked due to the hardware damage. SimpleMultiGPU in CUDA SDK is used to verify the scalability of the architecture, the change of the task execution is observed when the amount of data is changing. Because the storage and computing capacity of a single GPU card is limited, the data change is that duplicate data is added into computing data to increase the amount of computation, and the data size is proportional to the number of GPU. Statistics the instruction number within unit time at the entire execution of computation task, so as to evaluate the scalability of the platform. As shown in Fig. 4, with the linear increase of the amount of data and the increase of GPU number, the number of computation instructions in unit time shows a linear growth trend, which means that the platform has good scalability.

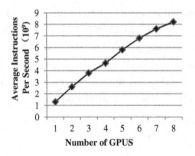

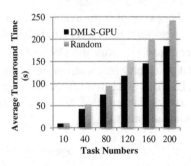

Fig. 4. Scalability test

Fig. 5. Task completion under GPU virtualization environment

5.4 System Performance Evaluation

In view of the scheduling algorithm, this paper verifies its feasibility and efficiency from two aspects. The first one is to use the same type of task, generate certain tasks randomly in the virtual machines and calculate the average turnaround time; the other is using a variety of different types of tasks, check the load status of the GPU devices with the time change.

For the first case, the DFT (Discrete Fourier transform) program written by authors is used for test. Within a certain period of time, the virtual machines generate a certain amount of DFT tasks randomly, the input points of the DFT tasks is 30000. Figure 5 shows the average turnaround time and a comparison of the task scheduling for the use of the DMLS-GPU algorithm and the use of the Random algorithm.

As can be seen from Fig. 5, with the increase number of submitted tasks, the turnover time of using DMLS-GPU algorithm is significantly less than that of using Random algorithm. One reason for this is that the GPU devices are selected randomly due to the random algorithm used by the master node in the actual environment but not rely on the real status of GPU. In some cases, multiple tasks will be accumulated on one or a few GPUs, therefore the later task needs to wait for the completion of task in front of it. In addition, the computing capacity of each GPU is not consistent in the actual situation. The Random algorithm can cause some GPU devices to be busy, while some GPU devices are idle. The DMLS-GPU algorithm, not only fully considers each GPU device's computing capacity, but also considers the number of tasks and the situation in the operation process of task, such as the floating point calculation speed peak of task, the size of actually used GPU global memory, the time of computing and transmission. The DMLS-GPU algorithm can not only calculate the actual load value of GPU, but also decrease the turnaround time of the task under the premise of balanced GPU load.

For the second case, the load status of the GPU device is monitored with the time variation of the different tasks of the device. Here we choose a DFT program on a single GPU device and a matrix multiplication program using two GPU devices. These two types of tasks are randomly generated on each virtual machine. The average load status of GPUs is listed in Table 6.

It's obvious that the average GPU utilization rate is higher when using the DMLS-GPU algorithm than that of Random algorithm. All utilization rates of GPUs reached more than 81 % with the DMLS-GPU and the variances is 2.5×10^{-3}. When using Random algorithm, these two indicators are 44 % and 6.37×10^{-3}. In summary, the DMLS-GPU algorithm makes the most of GPUs and keeps the load of each GPU in a relatively balanced state, and it's a significantly performance gains compared with the Random algorithm.

Table 6. Comparison of two schemes on GPU utilization rate

	Random	DMLS-GPU
Card0	56.40 %	82.57 %
Card1	68.23 %	83.95 %
Card2	53.06 %	95.02 %
Card3	44.81 %	81.03 %
Card4	55.62 %	82.57 %
Card5	67.01 %	80.08 %
Card6	53.93 %	91.76 %
Card7	45.93 %	83.91 %
Average	**55.62 %**	**85.11 %**

6   Conclusion

This paper first introduced a dynamic GPU resources allocation and management architecture based on multiple load features of GPU in cloud, the virtualization of GPU enable it to be shared between calculating nodes. The architecture is divided into User layer, VRM layer and CRS layer, and the workflow is also introduced in detail. The DMLS-GPU load balancing algorithm is proposed and the weights of features are analyzed by using AHP. Analysis the experimental results, the overhead of virtualization is different related to the task types, the feasibility and effectiveness of our algorithm is verified by comparing with the random algorithm when multiple tasks share GPUs, the utilization efficiency of server and the throughput of cluster system also are improved. In addition, there are still some problems to be ameliorated. MapReduce the framework adopts has the risk of single point of failure and the gap between the efficiency of GPU virtualization and the local's. In future work, the corresponding improvement will be made to make the system more perfect.

Acknowledgment. This work was supported by a grant from the National Natural Science Foundation of China (No. 61139002), the Jiangsu Province Science and Technology Support Program (No. BE2014135), and the Nanjing University of Aeronautics & Astronautics Graduate Students Innovation Experiment Cultivation Project. We appreciate the valuable comments from reviewers who made a great help.

References

1. Shen, W., Sun, L., Wei, D., Xu, W., Zhu, X., Yuan, S.: Load-prediction scheduling for computer simulation of electrocardiogram on a CPU-GPU PC. In: Proceedings of 2013 IEEE 16th International Conference on Computational Science and Engineering (CSE), pp. 213–218. IEEE Computer Society, Piscataway (2013)
2. Overby, E.: Process virtualization theory and the impact of information technology. Organ. Sci. **19**(2), 277–291 (2008)
3. Yeh, C.-Y., Kao, C.-Y., Hung, W.-S., Lin, C.-C., Liu, P., Wu, J.-J., Liu, K.-C.: GPU virtualization support in cloud system. In: Park, J.J.H., Arabnia, H.R., Kim, C., Shi, W., Gil, J.-M. (eds.) GPC 2013. LNCS, vol. 7861, pp. 423–432. Springer, Heidelberg (2013)
4. Shi, L., Chen, H., Sun, J., Li, K.: vCUDA: GPU accelerated high performance computing in virtual machines. IEEE Trans. Comput. **61**(6), 804–816 (2011)
5. Gupta, V., Gavrilovska, A., Schwan, K., Kharche, H., Tolia, N., Talwar, V., Ranganathan, P.: GViM: GPU-accelerated virtual machines. In: Proceedings of the 3rd ACM Workshop on System-Level Virtualization for High Performance Computing, pp. 17–24. ACM, New York (2009)
6. Giunta, G., Montella, R., Agrillo, G., Coviello, G.: A GPGPU transparent virtualization component for high performance computing clouds. In: D'Ambra, P., Guarracino, M., Talia, D. (eds.) Euro-Par 2010, Part I. LNCS, vol. 6271, pp. 379–391. Springer, Heidelberg (2010)
7. Duato, J., Pena, A.J., Silla, F., Mayo, R., Quintana-Ortí, E.S.: rCUDA: reducing the number of GPU-based accelerators in high performance clusters. In: 2010 International Conference on High Performance Computing and Simulation, pp. 224–231. IEEE, New York (2010)

8. Oikawa, M., Kawai, A., Nomura, K., Yasuoka, K., Yoshikawa, K., Narumi, T.M.: DS-CUDA: a middleware to use many GPUs in the cloud environment. In: 2012 SC Companion: High Performance Computing, Networking, Storage and Analysis, pp. 1207–1214. IEEE, New York (2012)

9. Liang, T.Y., Chang, Y.W.: GridCuda: a grid-enabled CUDA programming toolkit. In: 25th IEEE International Conference on Advanced Information Networking and Applications, pp. 141–146. IEEE, New York (2011)

10. Fang, W., He, B., Luo, Q., Govindaraju, N.K.: Mars: accelerating mapreduce with graphics processors. IEEE Trans. Parallel Distrib. Syst. 22(4), 608–620 (2011)

11. Qi, Z., Yao, J., Zhang, C., Yu, M., Yang, Z., Guan, H.: VGRIS: virtualized GPU resource isolation and scheduling in cloud gaming. ACM Trans. Archit. Code Optim. 11(2), 17:1–17:25 (2014)

12. Zhang, Y., Yuan, J., Lu, X., Zhao, X.: Multi-GPU parallel computing and task scheduling under virtualization. Int. J. Hybrid Inf. Technol. 8(7), 253–266 (2015)

13. Dean, J., Ghemawat, S.: Mapreduce: simplified data processing on large clusters. Commun. ACM 51(1), 107–113 (2008)

14. Saaty, T.L., Vargas, L.G.: The seven pillars of the analytic hierarchy process. In: Models, methods, concepts & applications of the analytic hierarchy process, vol. 34, pp. 27–46. Springer, US (2001). http://dx.doi.org/10.1007/978-1-4615-1665-1_2

15. Xiong, R., Luo, J., Song, A., Jin, J.: QoS preference-aware replica selection strategy in cloud computing. J. Commun. 32(7), 93–102 (2011). (in Chinese)

Solving Large Graph Problems in MapReduce-Like Frameworks via Optimized Parameter Configuration

Huanle Xu, Ronghai Yang$^{(\boxtimes)}$, Zhibo Yang, and Wing Cheong Lau

The Department of Information Engineering,
The Chinese University of Hong Kong, Hong Kong, China
{xh112,yr013,yz014,wclau}@ie.cuhk.edu.hk

Abstract. In this paper, we propose a scheme to solve large dense graph problems under the MapReduce framework. The graph data is organized in terms of blocks and all blocks are assigned to different map workers for parallel processing. Intermediate results of map workers are combined by one reduce worker for the next round of processing. This procedure is iterative and the graph size can be reduced substantially after each round. In the last round, a small graph is processed on one single map worker to produce the final result. Specifically, we present some basic algorithms like Minimum Spanning Tree, Finding Connected Components and Single-Source Shortest Path which can be implemented efficiently using this scheme. We also offer a mathematical formulation to determine the parameters under our scheme so as to achieve the optimal running-time performance. Note that the proposed scheme can be applied in MapReduce-like platforms such as Spark. We use our own cluster and Amazon EC2 as the testbeds to respectively evaluate the performance of the proposed Minimum Spanning Tree algorithm under the MapReduce and Spark frameworks. The experimental results match well with our theoretical analysis. Using this approach, many parallelizable problems can be solved in MapReduce-like frameworks efficiently.

Keywords: MapReduce · Graph problems · Parallel computing

1 Introduction

The amount of data worthwhile to be analyzed has grown at an astonishing rate in recent years. Although the processing power of commercially available servers has also grown at a remarkable pace over past decades, it remains woefully inadequate to deal with such huge amount of data. Malewicz et al. show that the World Wide Web graph can consist of billions of nodes and trillions of edges in [12]. Such graph data contributes a lot to the Big Data space. J. Leskovec et al. demonstrate that 9 different massive graphs from 4 different domains are growing over time and these graphs continue to become denser [10]. Under such a situation, it is beneficial to handle large dense graphs via parallel processing over multiple machines.

© Springer International Publishing Switzerland 2015
G. Wang et al. (Eds.): ICA3PP 2015, Part II, LNCS 9529, pp. 525–539, 2015.
DOI: 10.1007/978-3-319-27122-4_36

In the literature, there has been many works seeking parallelism to solve graph problems. However, most of those algorithms need to build a complicated communication model between parallel processors [3,4,13,15]. Today, the MapReduce framework in Google [2] and the open source project Hadoop[1] provide a very flexible way for developers to write parallel programs. Under this framework, different processors do not need to communicate with each other in a Map or Reduce phase.

In this paper, we present a method to solve a series of graph problems under the MapReduce framework. The primary idea is to encode the original graph into $< key, value >$ pairs where each key represents an edge and each value represents the corresponding metric. The encoded graph is managed by the Distributed File System (DFS) in terms of blocks and each block is assigned to an individual map worker. In this way, each map worker only processes a subgraph and outputs an intermediate result whose size is much smaller than the original input. These intermediate results from each map worker are then combined together to form a new graph. The resultant new graph is then fed as the input of the following MapReduce round. By repeating this procedure, the graph can finally be processed by one single machine.

Following the aforementioned process, it is natural to ask how to choose the two important parameters: the number of MapReduce rounds and the number of map workers in each round. We find these two parameters from the view of running-time optimization for graph algorithms under the MapReduce framework. To be more specific, we formulate an optimization problem to minimize the running time, whose solution determines the optimal values of these two parameters. Our proposed techniques can be applied to tackle various classical graph problems including Finding Minimum Spanning Tree, Connected Components and the Single Source Shortest Path on large graphs. To validate the efficacy of our scheme, we implement the proposed Minimum Spanning Tree (MST) algorithm as a showcase using our own private cluster. Empirical measurement results indicate that our theoretical analysis is valid and can be extended to a variety of parallelizable problems. In summary, the technical contributions of this paper include:

- We propose a method for solving large dense graph problems under the MapReduce framework. This method is also applicable to other frameworks such as Spark [19].
- Under our proposed scheme, we formulate a running time minimization problem whose solution determines the number of MapReduce rounds and the number of map workers in each round.
- To validate our theoretical analysis, we implement the MapRedcue-based MST algorithm in real clusters and conduct extensive experiments.

The rest of this paper is organized as follows. After reviewing the literature work for solving graph problems under parallel processing frameworks in Sect. 2, we

---

[1] http://hadoop.apache.org.

present the preliminaries of large graph problems and the MapReduce framework in Sect. 3. Section 4 discusses three classical graph problems to show how our proposed scheme can be used to solve various classical graph problems under MapReduce-like frameworks. We then present a mathematical model treating the running time performance as an optimization problem in Sect. 5. We implement the MapReduce-based Minimum Spanning Tree algorithm and show the experimental results in Sect. 6. Finally, Sect. 7 concludes our work.

2   Related Work

In the literature, designing graph algorithms under parallel processing frameworks has drawn a lot of attentions from both industry and academia.

To handle the issue of limited memory in a MapReduce cluster, Karloff et al. present a model of computation of MapReduce called $\mathcal{MRC}$ in [5]. This work describes a basic building block for many algorithms under the MapReduce framework and it focuses fitting a large dense graph on a machine with memory constraint. Following this framework, Lattanzi et al. propose several algorithms whose primary goal is to produce correct results with high probability even with limited memory [9]. In this paper, we adopt the same idea as [9], however, our work manages to optimize the running time of graph algorithms under MapReduce regardless of the memory restriction. In the meanwhile, our solution approach can guarantee the final correctness.Instead of studying the large dense graph, Spangler et al. present algorithms in MapReduce for sparse graph including maximal matching, approximate edge covering over grid graphs [16].

There also exist some graph algorithms which are problem-oriented under the MapReduce framework. For example, Xiang et al. propose several parallel schemes to partition a graph in [17] such that different worker nodes can compute the maximum cliques of different subgraphs independently. Kolda et al. implement a *wedge sampling* approach to efficiently and accurately estimate the clustering coefficient for massive graphs [6]. However, one limitation of these works is that they can only solve very specific problems.

Most of existing iterative algorithms under MapReduce(-like) model manages to minimize the number of rounds. Andoni et al. present algorithms that work in a constant number of rounds for geometric graphs under limited memory with unbounded computation power [1]. Though this model solves some specific graph-related problems including computing MST in a small number of rounds, it lacks of experimental results to show the efficiency of the algorithm. Kumar et al. proposes a sampling technique that aids in parallelization of sequential algorithms under the MapReduce framework [8]. The experimental results demonstrate that their proposed algorithms can reduce the number of rounds substantially comparing to the standard sequential algorithms. Going forward, Qin et al. introduce a scalable graph processing class to solve two graph problems (i.e., Finding Connected Components and Minimum Spanning Forest) with logarithmic number of rounds and linear communication costs per round [14].

Other than MapReduce, Pregel [12] and Graphlab [11] are also very popular programming platforms for solving graph problems. However, under these two platforms, different worker nodes need to communicate for information exchange very frequently. Under the Pregel framework, Yan et al. propose algorithms that require linear space, communication and computation per round with logarithmic number of rounds [18]. In contrast, our solution approach for solving large graph problems is easy to implement while keeping a low communication cost between different worker nodes.

3 Algorithm Design Framework

Let $G = (V, E)$ be an undirected graph where $|V| = n$ and $|E| = m$. Assume G is a $c - dense$ graph, i.e., $m = n^{1+c}$ where $0 < c \leq 1$. Consider an operation on the graph, h, namely, $h(G)$ is the targeting result. When n is very large and c is non negligible, directly operating h on the original graph with a single machine is time-consuming and may not be feasible due to the memory bottleneck. To tackle these issues, we design a MapReduce-based algorithm to compute $h(G)$.

Before going to the details of the graph algorithm design under the MapReduce framework, we first introduce the basics of the MapReduce programming model.

3.1 MapReduce Programming Model

Under the MapReduce framework, the input data for all applications are stored and organized on DFS (Distributed File Systems) in terms of blocks. Each block consists of multiple records in the form of $< key_1, value_1 >$. A MapReduce operation essentially includes two phases: Map and Reduce. In the map phase, each block is assigned to one map worker and the worker calls a map function to compute and generate an intermediate result. The intermediate results in the form of $< key_2, list(value_2) >$ are distributed to different reduce workers based on key_2s with the guarantee that records with the same key_2 are delivered to a unique reduce worker. During the reduce phase, each reduce worker executes the same reduce function to process these key-value pairs and the computation result is also stored on DFS. The map and reduce functions need to be defined in the application before submitted. One important feature with regard to MapReduce is that all workers in each phase can run in parallel. It's worthy to note that, one application may involve more than one MapReduce rounds where the output from the previous round is treated as input of the next round.

3.2 A General Graph Algorithm Design Framework in MapReduce

We represent the graph data with multiple $< key, value >$ records so that it can fit into the MapReduce programming model. To be more specific, we create a record, i.e., $< (v_i, v_j), w_{i,j} >$, for each edge $(v_i, v_j) \in E$ and associate this record with a metric $w_{i,j}$ which can be the edge weight, capacity, cost, etc. In the first MapReduce round, each block is assigned to one unique map worker which applies another function f to process the input data. In the reduce phase, only one reduce worker combines all intermediate results generated from map workers and applies the reduce function g to produce key value pairs with the form of $< (v_i, v_j), w_{i,j} >$. This procedure is repeated with multiple rounds and the output size is expected to be much smaller than the input size within each round. In the final round, the input data, which is denoted by G_l, can be processed by one map worker with Operation h. Moreover, to guarantee the correctness of these operations, $h(G_l)$ must be equivalent to $h(G)$.

3.3 Graph Algorithm Design Under Spark

Spark [19] is a fast and general engine for large-scale data processing with in-memory computing supported. To make it more efficient for iterative and inter-active jobs, Spark introduces an abstraction called resilient distributed datasets (RDD). Readers can refer to [19] for the detailed description. It's important to note that, the aforementioned operations can be readily implemented under Spark efficiently. To demonstrate this, we adopt the same data structure as the MapReduce framework. The algorithm is iterative, at the beginning of each iteration, one task is created for a RDD object and it applies Operation f on this RDD, which then transforms the original RDD into a new one. At the end of this iteration, these newly generated RDDs are merged together and further repartitioned into several small RDD objects, which are fed as the input of the subsequent iteration. Finally, at the last iteration, only one RDD is processed by a single task using Operation h.

4 Design Examples of Graph Algorithms

We adopt the MapReduce framework, which partitions the graph based on edges, to solve some basic graph problems such as Finding MST, Connected Components and Single-Source Shortest Path.

4.1 Finding the Minimum Spanning Tree

To compute MST on a single map worker, we adopt the Kruskal algorithm [7] whose major steps are illustrated as shown below.

1. Create a forest F, where each vertex in the graph is a separate tree;
2. Create a set E which contains all edges sorted in a non-decreasing order;
3. While E is nonempty and F is not yet connected:
    - Remove an edge with minimum weight from E;
    - If the removed edge connects two different trees, then adds it to the forest F.
4. Return F.

As shown in Algorithm 1, Kruskal algorithm can be correctly and efficiently implemented in a parallel and distributed manner. We adopt the framework proposed in Sect. 3.2 to partition a large dense graph into multiple small subgraphs such that each of them can be processed by a map worker. We then apply the Kruskal algorithm to find a MST for each subgraph. Since an MST contains at most $n-1$ edges, the graph size is therefore reduced substantially. In what follows, we merge the intermediate MSTs into a single graph. When the resultant graph is small enough to fit into the memory of a single machine, we compute the MST of this graph on one map worker and output the final result.

Since each mapper throws away the heaviest edge that satisfies the cycle property[2] at each iteration, these edges should not to be a part of any MST. As such, the aforementioned processes can generate the correct MST, as illustrated in the following lemma:

Algorithm 1. Finding Minimum Spanning Tree of Graph G(V, E)

1: **for** $|E| > \eta$ **do**
2:     **Partition**: partition a large graph into multiple sub-graphs.
3:     **Map Phase**: Each mapper i runs Kruskal algorithm on sub-graphs $G(V, E_i)$;
4:     **Reduce Phase**: Merge the intermediate MST into a smaller graph: $G(V, \bigcup_i S_i)$.
5:     **Re-Configure**: Configure the number of map workers m such that $\frac{|E|}{m} < \eta$.
6: **end for**
7: One mapper runs Kruskal algorithm on the resulting graph and return the result.

Proposition 1. *Algorithm 1 can output a correct Minimum Spanning Tree for any graph.*

Proof. For any cycle C in the graph, the edge with the highest weight in it cannot belong to an MST. In each round, the computation of any map worker is to delete the heaviest edges that are in some particular cycles. As such, these deleted edges do not belong to the final MST. Therefore, the remaining edges after each round are sufficient to produce the correct Spanning Tree. This completes the proof.

In the literature, there exists many work for parallelizing the MST algorithm in a multi-processors cluster. Most of them can speed up the processing while suffer from a high communication cost between processors [3,13]. As a comparison, the communication cost in our approach is low while the speedup is significant as characterized in the following sections.

4.2   Finding Connected Components

In recent years, there exist several works which manage to find the connected components in a large-scale graph under the MapReduce framework. For

---

[2] http://en.wikipedia.org/wiki/Spanning_tree.

instance, the algorithm proposed in [15] can find connected components in logarithmic rounds. However, the requirement of running on $O(n)$ machines makes it difficult to be implemented in practice.

Since computing MST does not destroy the connectivity of the whole graph, hence, Algorithm 1 can be readily applied to finding connected components in a graph. The only difference is that the result would be a forest containing multiple Spanning Trees instead of only one MST.

4.3   Finding the Single-Source Shortest Path

Finding the single-source shortest path (SSSP) between a pair of nodes on a weighted graph is a classical problem in Graph Theory. Here, we compute the SSSP by adopting the same method as discussed in Sect. 3.2. The graph data is partitioned into several blocks and each block is assigned to one map worker. To guarantee the correctness of the final result, every map worker deletes the edges whose wight are the heaviest in some particular cycles. Towards the end, a single node computes the shortest path on the resultant graph whose size is small enough.

5   Performance Optimization for Graph Problems Under the MapReduce Framework

The correctness of all graph algorithms presented in Sect. 4 are guaranteed regardless of the memory capacity of each machine in a cluster. People may naturally ask how these algorithms improve the performance comparing to the single instance case. When we implement the MapReduce-based MST algorithm in a real cluster, we observe that the performance in terms of running time is a function of the number of map workers as well as the number of MapReduce rounds. Therefore, there exist optimal solutions for these two parameters to minimize the running time. In this section, we propose a general framework to optimize the running time performance of parallel algorithms similar to fining MSTs under MapReduce-like frameworks.

We consider a parallelizable algorithm h whose time complexity is $g(x)$, where x is the input size. Each map worker produces an intermediate result with the size of $p(x)$ for an input, whose size is x. We assume the MapRedcue-based algorithm runs for k rounds. Therefore, the total running time of this algorithm can be formulated in the following equation:

$$f^k(l_1, l_2, \cdots, l_k) = g\left(\frac{x}{l_1}\right) + \sum_{i=2}^{k} g\left(\frac{p\left(\frac{x_{i-1}}{l_{i-1}}\right) l_{i-1}}{l_i}\right) \tag{1}$$

where l_i ($1 \leq i \leq k$) and x_i are the number of map workers and the input size in the ith round respectively. Following the computing framework in Sect. 4, l_k is equal to one. Due to the size of an output in each round is smaller than that in the previous round, it holds that $l_i < l_{i-1}$ for $2 \leq i \leq k$.

Our objective is to find appropriate values for k and $l_1, l_2, \cdots, l_k$ such that Eq. (1) is minimized, which yields the following optimization problem (P1):

$$\min_{l_1, l_2, \cdots, l_k} f^k(l_1, l_2, \cdots, l_k)$$
$$\text{s.t.} \quad l_i < l_{i-1}; \quad \forall \, 2 \leq i \leq k \qquad (2)$$
$$l_k = 1$$

We will solve this optimization problem in the next section using the MapReduce-based MST algorithm as a representative example. Although we only solve one specific problem, our solution approach can be applicable to a variety of parallelizable algorithms.

6   Performance Evaluation

In this section, we implement our proposed MST algorithm under MapReduce and Spark respectively. We begin by introducing the environment setup and then evaluate the running time with regard to the number of workers and MapReduce rounds. The solutions to Optimization Problem P1 are compared with the experimental results.

6.1   Environment Setup with MapReduce Framework

The graph data is distributed across our private cluster which has two master nodes and 4 slave nodes with 16 GB memory and 8-cores CPU each. Under our implementation, the weighted graph is randomly generated with $n = 10^7$ vertexes and $m = 7 \times 10^8$ edges. The size of the graph is 14 GB, which is difficult to be processed on one single machine. We generate the weight for each edge uniformly at random between [1,20000]. Although we only process a graph with such an order of magnitude, our algorithm is scalable to apply to graphs with much larger size.

6.2   Environment Setup with Spark Framework

Since our private cluster only deploys the MapReduce framework, we turn to Amazon EC2 for running the MST algorithm under Spark. This cloud-based cluster consists of 1 master node and 12 slave nodes. Each node is configured with the m1.large instance, i.e., 7.5 GB memory and 2-core CPU. In this experiment, the weighted graph is randomly generated with $n = 2.9 \times 10^6$ vertexes and $m = 1.5 \times 10^8$ edges. The weight of each edge is produced uniformly at random between [1,20000]. This graph keeps the same dense (i.e., c) as the graph in the previous experiment.

6.3 The Optimal Number of Workers in Two MapReduce Rounds

We first analyze the performance with respect to the number of workers when the large graph is processed within two rounds. In the following theoretical analysis, we only use MapReduce as the programming platform. Nevertheless, this analysis is also applicable to Spark. For ease of presentation, we will use the notations of map worker and worker node interchangeably in the rest of this paper.

Analytical Results. We denote by ι the number of machines used to run MST in the first round. In the second round, there is only one worker node to process the graph data and finds a correct MST.

In the first round, the size of the graph data allocated to each worker node is $\frac{m}{\iota}$. Therefore, the running time of a map worker in the first round can be characterized by:

$$f_1(\iota) = \frac{m}{\iota} \log \frac{m}{\iota} \tag{3}$$

After the first MapReduce round completes, each worker node finds a spanning tree whose size is at most $n - 1$. Thus, the size of the resultant graph generated by the first round is at most $(n - 1) \cdot \iota$. Hence, the running time in the second round is bounded by:

$$f_2(\iota) = (n - 1)\iota \cdot \log\left((n - 1)\iota\right) \tag{4}$$

And the total running time for the whole algorithm is $f(\iota) = f_1(\iota) + f_2(\iota)$. By setting the derivative of $f(\iota)$ to zero, we obtain the optimal value for ι which minimizes the total running time in the below:

$$\iota^* = \sqrt{m/(n - 1)} \approx \sqrt{m/n} \tag{5}$$

We illustrate the picture of $f(\iota)$ in Fig. 1(a) where $m = 7 \times 10^8$ and $n = 10^7$. It shows that, when ι is set to 8, the overall running time achieves its minimum. We further let $\iota = \sqrt{m/n}$, f^2 can be upper bounded by:

$$f^2 = 2\sqrt{mn} \log \sqrt{mn} \tag{6}$$

When the memory of the worker node is of size no less than the graph size. We can find an MST by using only one map worker with one MapReduce round. In this case, the running time is

$$r^1 = m \log m \tag{7}$$

Combine Eqs. (6) and (7), we have:

$$\frac{f^2}{r^1} \leq \frac{2\sqrt{mn} \log m}{m \log m} = 2\sqrt{\frac{n}{m}} \tag{8}$$

Following Eq. (8), we conclude that we can achieve a speedup of at least $\sqrt{\frac{m}{4n}}$ comparing to the single instance case by using $\sqrt{\frac{m}{n}}$ map workers in two MapReduce rounds. The analytical result is illustrated in Fig. 1(a) and the running time is normalized.

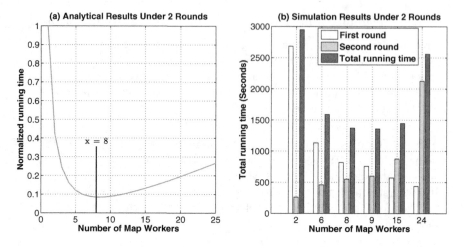

Fig. 1. The analytical and simulation results for the running time of MST algorithm in two MapReduce rounds where $m = 7 \times 10^8$, $n = 10^7$.

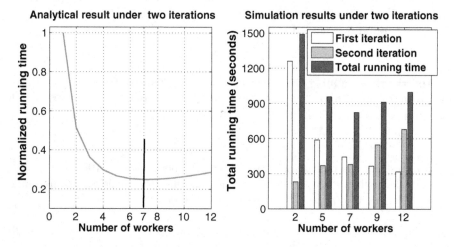

Fig. 2. The analytical and simulation results for the running time of MST algorithm under Spark with two iterations where $m = 1.5 \times 10^8$, $n = 2.9 \times 10^6$

Simulation Results. As illustrated in Fig. 1(b), the MapRedcue-based MST algorithm enjoys its optimal performance with 9 worker nodes in the first round. In contrast, Fig. 1(a) shows that the theoretical result attains its optima with 8 worker nodes. Given other factors that we do not take into consideration, the nuance (11s) between theoretical results and practical performance is reasonable.

Intuitively, there exists a trade-off between the first and second round. When the number of map workers in the first round becomes larger, each worker spends less time for computation on the graph data of a smaller size. Hence, it leads to less edges being deleted and a larger intermediate graph generated in the first round. As a result, it takes a longer time to find the final MST for the worker node in the second round. This intuition matches well with the observations from Fig. 1 that increasing the number of map workers in the first round results in a corresponding rise of the time spent in the second round.

The experimental result under the Spark framework is depicted in Fig. 2. It indicates that the optimal number of workers is 7 in the first iteration and the simulation result matches quite well with the theoretical result.

6.4   Deriving the Optimal Number of MapReduce Rounds

The number of MapReduce rounds is another important parameter which has a heavy impact on the running-time performance. When this number is too small, then in each round, all worker nodes need to process a large subgraph and thus take a long time. On the other hand, when the number of MapReduce rounds is very large, the overall running time is also significant though each node can work out the result within a short time.

With the above observations in mind, we aim to explore the relationship among the running time, the number of MapReduce rounds and map workers. In the following sections, we first present the analytical results and then conduct extensive simulations to evaluate the performance.

Analytical Results. The time complexity of Kruskal algorithm is $O(m \log m)$, where m is the number of edges. Substitute $g(m) = m \log m$ into Eq. (1), we derive the total running time of the MapReduce-based MST algorithm, which can be formulated as follows:

$$f^k(l_1, l_2, \cdots, l_k) = \frac{m}{l_1} \log \frac{m}{l_1} + \sum_{i=2}^{k} \frac{(n-1)l_{i-1}}{l_i} \log \frac{(n-1)l_{i-1}}{l_i} \qquad (9)$$

Further, we substitute Eq. (9) into P1 and derive an upper bound for the optimal value, which is illustrated in the following theorem :

Theorem 1. *For all* $k \geq 2$,

$$f^k \leq g^k \triangleq \frac{m}{l_1} \log \frac{m}{l_1} + (k-1)(n-1)l_1^{1/(k-1)} \log (n-1)l_1^{1/(k-1)} \qquad (10)$$

Proof. We prove this theorem by mathematical induction. For $k = 2$, this inequality can be satisfied as demonstrated in Subsect. 6.3. When $k = 3$, we have:

$$f^3 = \frac{m}{l_1} \log \frac{m}{l_1} + \frac{(n-1)l_1}{l_2} \log \frac{(n-1)l_1}{l_2} + (n-1)l_2 \log (n-1)l_2$$

Similar to Eq. (6), it holds that

$$f^3 \leq \frac{m}{l_1} \log \frac{m}{l_1} + 2(n-1)\sqrt{l_1} \log (n-1)\sqrt{l_1}$$

Hence, f^3 satisfy Inequality (10). Further, we assume that when $k = p$, all (f^i)'s (for $2 \le i \le p$) satisfy Eq. (10). Then, for $k = p + 1$, we get:

$$f^{p+1} = \frac{m}{l_1} \log \frac{m}{l_1} + \frac{(n-1)l_1}{l_2} \log \frac{(n-1)l_1}{l_2} + \sum_{i=3}^{p+1} \frac{(n-1)l_{i-1}}{l_i} \log \frac{(n-1)l_{i-1}}{l_i}$$

$$\le \frac{m}{l_1} \log \frac{m}{l_1} + \frac{(n-1)l_1}{l_2} \log \frac{(n-1)l_1}{l_2} + (p-1)(n-1)l_2^{1/(p-1)} \log (n-1)l_2^{1/(p-1)}$$

Further, we define h^{p+1}, which is a function of l_2, as follows:

$$h^{p+1}(l_2) = \frac{(n-1)l_1}{l_2} \log \frac{(n-1)l_1}{l_2} + (p-1)(n-1)l_2^{1/(p-1)} \log (n-1)l_2^{1/(p-1)} \quad (11)$$

By setting the derivative of $h^{p+1}(l_2)$ to zero, we derive the optimal solution to Eq. (11), which yields $l_2 = l_1^{\frac{p-1}{p}}$. Therefore, the optimal value of $h^{p+1}(l_2)$ can be characterized as $(h^{p+1}(l_2))^* = h^{p+1}(l_1^{\frac{p-1}{p}}) = p(n-1)l_1^{\frac{1}{p}} \log (n-1)l_1^{\frac{1}{p}}$. It follows that:

$$f^{p+1} = \frac{m}{l_1} \log \frac{m}{l_1} + h^{p+1}(l_2) \le \frac{m}{l_1} \log \frac{m}{l_1} + p(n-1)l_1^{\frac{1}{p}} \log (n-1)l_1^{\frac{1}{p}} \quad (12)$$

Hence, f^{p+1} satisfies Eq. (10). This completes the proof.

Based on the proof, it can be readily shown that the optimal solution satisfies the following condition:

$$l_{i+1} = l_i^{\frac{k-i-1}{k-i}} \quad \forall \, 1 \le i \le k - 1 \quad (13)$$

Further, we set the derivative of g^k to zero and get $l_1 = (\frac{m}{n-1})^{\frac{k-1}{k}}$. In the meanwhile, optimal value to P1 is upper bounded by:

$$(f^k)^* \le km^{\frac{1}{k}}(n-1)^{\frac{k-1}{k}} \log (m^{\frac{1}{k}}(n-1)^{\frac{k-1}{k}}) \quad (14)$$

Since $m = n^{1+c}$, we have:

$$(f^k)^* \approx (k+c)n^{1+\frac{c}{k}} \log n \quad (15)$$

Define $\xi(k) = (k+c)n^{1+\frac{c}{k}}$ and set the derivative of $\xi(k)$ to zero, we get $k \approx c \ln n$. When k is below $c \ln n$, $\xi(k)$ is an increasing function of k. On the other hand, when k is above $c \ln n$, $\xi(k)$ is a decreasing function. As such, $\xi(k)$ attains the minimum value when $k = c \ln n$. Moreover, l_{k-1} is above one due to the first constraint in P1, therefore, we have $(\frac{m}{n-1})^{\frac{1}{k}} \ge 2$, which is equivalent to $k \le c \log n$. Hence, we conclude that the optimal number of MapReduce rounds is $c \ln n$ and the corresponding number of worker nodes in each round is determined by Eq. (13).

We illustrate the running time as a function of the number of MapReduce rounds in Fig. 3 under $n = 10^7$ and $c = 0.2636$. In this case, the optimal number of MapReduce rounds is 4.

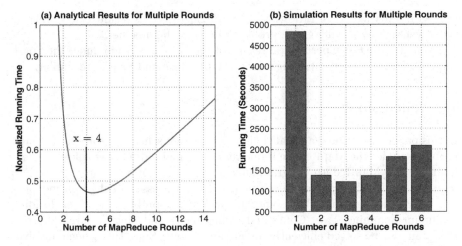

Fig. 3. The analytical and simulation results for the running time of MST algorithm related to the number of MapReduce rounds. $n = 10^7$ and $c = 0.2636$.

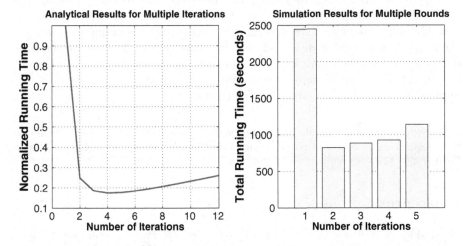

Fig. 4. The analytical and simulation results for the running time of MST algorithm where $n = 2.9 \times 10^6$ and $c = 0.2636$.

Simulation Results. The experiments result under the MapReduce framework are illustrated in Fig. 3(b). It shows that the minimum running-time is achieved under 3 MapReduce rounds other than 4 rounds. Considering other factors such as the overhead of job scheduling, memory, network delay in shuffle phase and I/O operation, this deviation is reasonable. Although the theoretical analysis does not quite fit well with the practical results, it still offers an useful guideline to enjoy a suboptimal performance. Moreover, Fig. 3(b) shows the computation under one round takes 3.52 times longer than that under two rounds, which fits well with our theoretical ratio (i.e., 4.18) in Eq. (8). This result exactly reflects the advantage by solving graph problems in a parallel manner.

We illustrate the experimental results of the MST algorithm under the Spark framework in Fig. 4. The findings under MapReduce and Spark are similar.

7   Conclusions

In this paper, we propose a parallel algorithm design scheme to solve large graph problems under the MapReduce framework. Our main idea is to exploit the flexibility of the MapReduce Programming model to partition a large graph into multiple small subgraphs and each map worker processes a subgraph independently. We demonstrate that some classical graph problems such as Finding Minimum Spanning Tree, Connected Components and Single-Source Shortest Path can also be solved efficiently under this scheme. Since this scheme involves multiple rounds, it fits well with the Spark framework as well.

To enjoy the optimal running-time performance, we formulate a running-time minimization problem and develop a mathematical tool to derive appropriate values for key parameters. More importantly, we implement the MapRedcue-base Minimum Spanning Tree algorithm as a representative example to evaluate the running-time performance. Both the experimental and the theoretical results demonstrate that the running-time is a function of the number of worker nodes as well as the number of MapReduce rounds. Our optimization framework is also applicable to a variety of parallelizable algorithms.

Acknowledgements. Huanle Xu and Ronghai Yang have contributed equally to this work. This project was partially supported by the Mobile Technologies Centre (MobiTeC), The Chinese University of Hong Kong.

References

1. Andoni, A., Nikolov, A., Onak, K., Yaroslavtsev, G.: Parallel algorithms for geometric graph problems. In: Proceeding of STOC, pp. 574–583 (2014)
2. Dean, J., Ghemawat, S.: MapReduce: simplified data processing on large clusters. In: Proceedings of OSDI, pp. 137–150, December 2004
3. Dehne, F., Gotz, S.: Practical parallel algorithms for minimum spanning trees. In: Proceedings of Seventeenth IEEE Symposium on Reliable Distributed Systems, pp. 366–371, October 1998
4. Israel, A., Itai, A.: A fast and simple randomized parallel algorithm for maximal matching. Inf. Process. Lett. (2012). abs/12035387
5. Karloff, H., Suri, S., Vassilvitskii, S.: A model of computation for MapReduce. In: Proceedings of SODA, pp. 938–948 (2010)
6. Kolda, T.G., Pinar, A., Plantenga, T., Seshadhri, C., Task, C.: Counting triangles in massive graphs with MapReduce. arXiv:1301.5887v3 (2013)
7. Kruskal, J.B.: On the shortest spanning subtree of a graph and the traveling salesman problem. Proc. Am. Math. Soc. **7**, 48–50 (1956)

8. Kumar, R., Moseley, B., Vassilvitskii, S., Vattani, A.: Fast greedy algorithms in MapReduce and streaming. In: Proceeding of SPAA, pp. 1–10 (2013)
9. Lattanzi, S., Moseley, B., Suri, S.: Fitering: a method for solving graph problems in MapReduce. In: SPAA, June 2010
10. Leskovec, J., Kleinberg, J., Faloutsos, C.: Graphs over time: densification laws, shrinking diameters and possible explanations. In: KDD (2005)
11. Low, Y., Bickson, D., Gonzalez, J., Guestrin, C., Kyrola, A., Hellerstein, J.M.: Distributed graphlab: a framework for machine learning and data mining in the cloud. Proc. VLDB Endow. 5(8), 716–727 (2012)
12. Malewicz, G., Austern, M.H., Bik, A.J., Dehnert, J.C., Horn, I., Leiser, N., Czajkowski, G.: Pregel: a system for large-scale graph processing. In: SIGMOD (2010)
13. Moussa, M.I.: A new parallel algorithm for computing MINIMUM SPANNING TREE. Int. J. Soft Comput. Math. Control 2(2) (2013)
14. Qin, L., Yu, J.X., Chang, L., Cheng, H., Zhang, C., Lin, X.: Scalable big graph processing in MapReduce. In: Proceeding of SIGMOD, pp. 827–838, June 2014
15. Rastogi, V., Machanavajjhala, A., Chitnis, L., Sarma, A.: Finding connected components in Map-Reduce in logarithmic rounds. Comput. Res. Repository (CoRR) 22(2), 77–80 (1986)
16. Spangler, T.: Algorithms for grid graph in MapReduce model. Thesis of master, December 2013
17. Xiang, J., Guo, C., Aboulnaga, A.: Scalable maximum clique computation using MapReduce. In: International Conference on Data Engineering, April 2013
18. Yan, D., Cheng, J., Lu, Y., Ng., W.: Practical Pregel algorithms for massive graphs. Technical report, September 2013
19. Zaharia, M., Chowdhury, M., Das, T., Dave, A., Ma, J., McCauley, M., Franklin, M.J., Shenker, S., Stoica, I.: Resilient distributed datasets: a fault-tolerant abstraction for in-memory cluster computing. In: NSDI (2012)

A Dynamic Extension and Data Migration Method Based on PVFS

Xiaoyu Zhang, Jie Tang$^{(\boxtimes)}$, Heng Gao, and Gangshan Wu

State Key Laboratory for Novel Software Technology, Department of Computer
Science and Technology, Nanjing University, Nanjing 210046, China
tangjie@nju.edu.cn

Abstract. With the development of the big data, The traditional file
system can no longer meet the demand of High Performance Computing
and Big Data. Parallel file systems are getting more and more popular in High Performance Computing. As a typical parallel file system,
PVFS has been widely used in big data computing area in recent years.
However with the increasing of computing scale, there exist the needs to
dynamic extend data nodes, which PVFS does not support at present.
This paper put forward a dynamic data node extension method as well as
the subsequent data migration algorithm based on PVFS. The algorithm
first adds a new data node automatically and transparently. After that,
the algorithm finds out the most loaded data node in the original file
system using a new load evaluation method and transfer the data into
the newly added data node to mitigate the imbalance of the system. The
experimental results show that our dynamic data node extension method
could improve the performance of PVFS and reduce the probability of
hot point effectively.

Keywords: Distributed file system · Parallel file system · PVFS ·
Dynamic extension · Data migration

1 Introduction

With the continuous development of High Performance Computing and Distributed Computing, the traditional storage system is no longer able to meet the I/O
requirements now. Parallel file system in High Performance Computing and Big
Data applications are getting more and more popular for its high performance,
availability and scalability. A typical parallel file system, PVFS [4–6], has been
widely used in Big Data computing applications, and achieved good results.

However, With the increase of computing scale, the cluster nodes must be
dynamically extended, which means that the file system needs to be expanded
dynamically. While PVFS has a nice parallelism in read/write performance,
it has deficiencies in the dynamic expansion, which is reflected in two aspects
below: First, the scalability of PVFS needs to be strengthened [4,15,16], which
means PVFS has no dynamic extension. PVFS use static configuration. The
system must be restarted after you add a new node in PVFS cluster. PVFS

© Springer International Publishing Switzerland 2015
G. Wang et al. (Eds.): ICA3PP 2015, Part II, LNCS 9529, pp. 540–552, 2015.
DOI: 10.1007/978-3-319-27122-4_37

configuration file (unlike Ceph, Hadoop, Lustre and other file systems)can not be edited manually, but is dynamically generated by pvfs2-genconfig program. Therefore, the generation of node IDs in PVFS is dynamic and unique each time. Second, PVFS has no load balancing mechanism [4,15,16]. Some program might cause the advent of hot spot node.

This paper presents a dynamic data node extension method as well as the subsequent data migration algorithm based on PVFS. The algorithm first adds a new data node automatically and transparently. After that, the algorithm find out the most loaded data node in the original file system using a new load evaluation method and transfer the data into the newly added data node to mitigate the imbalance of the system. The experimental results show that our dynamic data node extension method could improve the performance of PVFS and reduce the probability of hot point effectively.

The remainder of the paper is organized as follows: Sect. 2 introduces the related work about dynamically extension. Our dynamic extension and data migration algorithm is presented in Sect. 3. Section 4 describes the data migration algorithm framework. The experimental results and performance analysis of our algorithm are shown in Sect. 5. Finally, Summary and future work are drawn in Sect. 6.

2   Related Work

PVFS, developed by Clemson University is a parallel virtual file system, which is an open source parallel file system designed to run on linux. The design of PVFS fully embodies the characteristics of a parallel file system: provide high-performance of I/O [4]. PVFS currently has two versions: PVFS1 and PVFS2, PVFS in this paper is refers to the PVFS2 below.

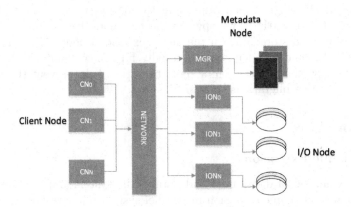

Fig. 1. PVFS system structure

Figure 1 describes the PVFS system structure. PVFS file system has three components: the client node (Client Node): provides file system interface to users;

the metadata node (Metadata Node): manages namespace and metadata, stores metadata; the data node (I/O Node): stores and manages data; nodes connected by the network, a physical node may have all functions of the above three components. File store in PVFS is divided into multiple sub-file in different nodes and can be concurrently access. A file is stored as metafiles and datafiles in PVFS. Datafiles are split across multiple I/O node, metafile stores the distribution and attributes of the file.

Dynamic extension [16] of distributed and parallel file systems has always been a hot research problem. Different distributed file system adopt different solution for this problem, while the solution also gives the relevant data migration algorithm. The next two paragraphs describes the typical solution of the dynamic extension problem in different distributed file system.

Ceph [1] uses an object-oriented storage architecture, it takes intelligent storage devices (Object Storage Devices: OSDs) to replace a traditional hard drive. OSDs might represents CPU, network, the local cache and the underlying disk or RAID which integrated these resources. A pseudo-random distribution algorithms (Pseudo-random data distribution function: CRUSH) used for system expansion and update in Ceph, CRUSH [1] algorithm uses a pseudo-random distribution of data, distributed to various OSDs [1] cluster maps are available through the cluster map marked.

GFS [2]: GFS converts dynamic extension problem to component failures problem. In the GFS, the component failure is common. GFS system must monitor its status uninterruptedly, detect component failure quickly and recover component failure timely. Furthermore, GFS maintain the consistency among files and its copies. When GFS extension, first add a node information to the configuration file, and reload the configuration. Thus for GFS, the dynamic extension problem is transformed into a node failure recovery problems. The system detect whether a new node on the line by heartbeat. After GFS expanded node, Mapreduce program [3] will be given priority in the below-average hard disk usage chunk server to stores the new copy. As the new node has no data, GFS will be given priority to storage file in the newly expanded node. Meanwhile, GFS will periodically load balancing and gradually fill a new chunk servers, rather than fill the new chunk servers in a short time that help prevent the new one overload. GFS data migrations through this strategy.

3 Algorithms

3.1 Dynamic Extension

Dynamic expansion of distributed and parallel file system [18] is always a hot research issues. Dynamic extension in parallel system refers to how to increase computing resources to meet the growing performance and functional requirements, or by reducing its resources to reduce costs, claimed that the system is scalable. There are three aspects in dynamic extension: (a) Functional and Performance: scalable parallel system should be able to provide more functionality or better performance after extension. (b) The cost of extension: Consideration

Extended spent must be reasonable. (c) Compatibility: after dynamic extension, the parallel computing system (software and hardware) still work after only small changes.

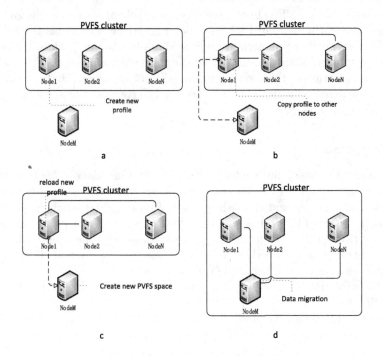

Fig. 2. Dynamic extension of PVFS

We proposes a new method to dynamic extend data nodes in PVFS. First of all, we rewrite the pvfs2-genconfig program and the related source code for adding a new function which allows the pvfs2-genconfig program read a configuration file and rebuild a new one based on the read one dynamically. As shown in Fig. 2, the algorithm is divided into four steps to complete the PVFS node expansion:

(a) A node is chosen randomly for re-building configuration file without shutting down the cluster by the new pvfs2-genconfig program, which inserts the new node information in configuration file and arrange a new handle to the new node. The new handle should not conflict with the original handles. The role of the new node in the PVFS is also decided.
(b) The node selected in first step sends the new configuration file to the others, including the new node.
(c) We rewrite the pvfs source code to support the original system nodes reload the configuration file and read the new node information without shutting down the cluster. The new node creates a new storage space and start PVFS deamon. Whether or not the expansion is successful is tested.

(d) If the expansion is successful, the system expansion is completed, the data migration algorithm starts after the expansion.

As we can see from the expansion process, the expansion process just adds a physical node into a PVFS cluster, regardless the role of the new node. Actually, the roles of the new node in PVFS are determined by user as his needed. The new node can be PVFS metadata node or datafile node or both of them. The dynamic extension algorithm only does the hardware expansion. The contents and the distribution of the file system are still not changed. There are no data stored in the extented node. Therefore, we need to consider the appropriate data migration algorithms next.

3.2   Stripe Size

In a parallel file system, hot spot might occur when imbalanced load happened. In a file system, load balance has two meanings: the distribution of data in the file system is balanced and the visiting load of each node is balanced.

The stripe size of PVFS has a greatly effect on the hot spot problem. Assume that a distributed file system has n_{node} node and each time a user will access file with size x, which is obedient to uniform distribution. A node is a hot spot only if the visiting time of this node is more than other nodes by C times. n_{visit} means the visit time of user. s_{block} means the PVFS stripe size. the max size of file in PVFS is l.

The probability density of x is:

$$f(x) = \frac{1}{s_{file}}(l > x > 0)$$

s_{file} represents the size of file, and C represents the visit times of the node more than other nodes.

Assume the size of data access meets the following conditions:

$$(i - 1) * s_{block} < x < i * s_{block}$$

Each node store s_{block} size data. Thus each access will visit i nodes in PVFS according to the conditions above.

The probability of one node visited is f when an access happen. The access from different users are independent. so $C = n_{visit} * f$

Since files are stored in PVFS node sequentially, the probability of the node on which stored the visited data is:

$$f_{file} = \int_{(i-1)*s_{block}}^{i*s_{block}} \frac{1}{s_{file}} dx$$

and this access will visit i nodes for the conditions above, the probability of the node visited is

$$f_{visit} = \frac{i}{n_{node}}$$

f_{visit}, f_{file} are independent, so $f = f_{visit} * f_{file}$, and present below, when $(i-1) * s_{block} < x < i * s_{block}$

$$f = \int_{(i-1)*s_{block}}^{i*s_{block}} \frac{1}{s_{file}} dx * \frac{i}{n_{node}}$$

we can accumulate f when the number of node is 0 up to n_{node}, the result is:

$$f = \sum_{0}^{n_{node}} \left(\int_{(i-1)*s_{block}}^{i*s_{block}} \frac{1}{s_{file}} dx * \frac{i}{n_{node}} \right)$$

After transformation, we can get the below formula:

$$f = \frac{s_{block}*(n_{node}-1)}{2 * s_{file}}$$

$$C = n_{visit} * \frac{s_{block}*(n_{node}-1)}{2 * s_{file}}$$

According to the above formulas, we can find a positive correlation between C and the stripe size in PVFS, which means we can control the stripe size in PVFS to reduce the probability of hot point.

3.3   Design Principles of Data Migration Algorithm

Data migration algorithm is the key part of the migration process, we analyze it from two aspect: the detail about migration algorithm itself and the application environment [11–13,17].

First, the system performance will be greatly affected by the distribution state of data migration algorithm, so we need to discuss the advantage and disadvantage between centralized and distributed migration algorithms. Generally distributed data migration algorithm has a good performance in scalability with respect to a centralized one because each node only need to decide itself. There is no single decision node in a distributed data migration algorithm, which means no single point failure. But on the other hand, if every decision node can only get part of the system information, the result of the distributed algorithms might not be the global optimal solution. Our situation is that the system has been extended one node just now, therefore the scalability of the data migration algorithms is not necessary, hence centralized algorithm is chosen.

Data migration algorithm will migrate a large file data from one node to others. Resources for the algorithm itself is little, which requires the algorithm make decisions in a short time and without much resource supported. It also limits the complexity of the algorithm. In a real environment, the system load of each original node are likely high, the new extended node is an idle node, so data migration algorithm arbitration can be set on the new node.

Second, data migration algorithm needs to be applied to different environments, there is a huge difference in the effect of the same migration design in the different environment [9]. So, to choose a suitable data migration algorithm based on the different environment is very important. Under the circumstances that PVFS just extended one node, and we need to migration data to the new node. So the design algorithms must be appropriate to consider this characteristics:

(a). As a highly efficient parallel file system, PVFS faced the user requirement and the goal of PVFS is to achieve a high speed when program read and write data and accelerating the program performance. Therefore, the main problem to be solved in the data migration is: After the migration, how could the distribution state of the data to meet the needs of users, plus allowing users to get a higher speed in accessing the data. The load of each node become a secondary consideration issues. When considering user requirements and hardware load capability, we take the user needs as our main purpose [15].

(b). We should choose those arguerments obtained by a simple method for the poor resources used. we should discover the existence of load unbalance based on the consideration of the complexity of the method implementation. Also, the data migration algorithm should try to make the distribution of the file in PVFS reasonable [14].

Considering the above reasons, we choose a centralized migration algorithm with the arbitration set on the extended node. The algorithm face to user needs [13], also hot issues will be considered, and ultimately improve the performance of data throughput.

4   The Framework of Data Migration Algorithm

Based on the data migration algorithm of the Sect. 3, we implement it with three subsystems: node detection module, migration arbitration subsystem, migration itself.

Node detection module: The goal of this module is to find the node congestion and load imbalances in this module. The most important thing is how to quantify a node load. Therefore, we design a performance monitoring module which running on each node for collecting node information as well as user operation and then feedback to the arbitration node.

Migration arbitration: This module is in charge for collecting data from every node in the system, generating a quantitative value for each node and making decision of what to migrate.

Migration: According to the arbitration result, migrate the selected files.

The algorithm module as shown in Fig. 3. The node detection module located on each node, the remaining modules located on the extended node.

We choose the following arguments for evaluation of the load of a node as follow:

The number of access of a file recently: c_{visit}, for the following reasons:

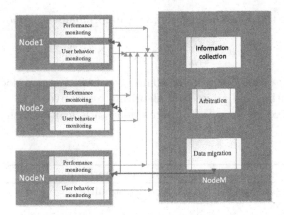

Fig. 3. Data migration algorithm

(a) According to the principle of locality, if a files has been accessed recently, it will be visited in the near future. Therefore migrating this file to a new node will receive higher benefits. And only a little access is the sequential access, which will easily leads to an unbalanced load in PVFS cluster and generates a hot spot node. Files in PVFS can be split into stripes in different sizes dynamically [14]. With this feature, during the file migration, we can reduce the probability of hot spot issues by reducing the file stripe size.

(b) PVFS system has cached data in datafile and metadata node. If a file is accessed recently, the file is cached in system memory. Select this file to migrate, the system can obtain files directly from memory, which is much faster than access files from hard disk.

File size s_{file}:

When selecting the files to migrate, we should consider the extra load generated from migrating file itself. Data migration is equal to a read and write operation. In order to minimize the impact on system performance, we should choose small files for migration.

Node load s_{load}:

we acquire load information through linux kernal functions. According to the above description, we decide if or not a file data should be migrated using three system feature values, i.e. network load, disk I/O throughput and load information through linux kernal functions. Because of a hot file or a hot spot is a relative result, during the choosing of hot spots, the computed feature values are sorted first, Then, the files need to be migrated are chosen according to the computed values. Similarly, the hot spot is the node with much greater load compared to other nodes in the System. Then to make the migration process according to file information [10].

According to the above description, we can formulate the following load evaluation formula:

$$\mu = \frac{\alpha}{s_{file}} + \beta * c_{visit} + \gamma * s_{load}$$

The data migration algorithm is composed of two parts: a node information statistical algorithm and arbitration algorithm respectively.

The pseudo codes of a node information statistical algorithm is shown as below:

Algorithm 1. Node information statistical algorithms

1: **procedure** INFORMATION STATISTICAL(input:null)
2:     **loop**
3:         **for all** $file \in PVFS$ **do**
4:             $C_{VisitOfFile}$ = file.getCvisit()
5:             S_{file} = file.getFileSize()
6:

$$InfoFile[file] = \frac{\alpha}{s_{file}} + \beta * C_{VisitOfFile}$$

7:             Send InfoOfFile to Arbitration node
8:         **end for**
9:         Send LoadOfNode to Arbitration node
10:         sleep(TimeThreshold)
11:     **end loop**
12: **end procedure**

The node information statistical algorithm is responsible for collecting information from each node: the number of access PVFS file, size of each file and the node load, then sending the information to the arbitration node.

The pseudo codes of arbitration algorithm is shown as below:

Algorithm 2. Arbitration algorithm

1: **procedure** ARBITRATION ALGORITHM(InfoOfFile,LoadOfNode)
2:     **loop**
3:         **for all** $file \in eachnode$ **do**
4:

$$InfoOfFile = \sum_{i=0}^{n} InfoOfFile_{eachnode}$$

5:         **end for**
6:         Load.add(loadOfNode)
7:         sort Load and InfoOfFile
8:         Choose file migrate by the load and InfoOfFile order.
9:         sleep(TimeThreshold)
10:     **end loop**
11: **end procedure**

The arbitration node accumulates the number of accesses from different nodes visiting the same file, and then chooses file to migrate according to the information collected. TimeThreshold in the algorithm is utilized to control the execution frequency of the algorithm.

According to the arbitration node algorithm, we don't take threshold method for deciding data transfer, but sort all node load evaluation value. Then we choose the highest load node for data migration. This mechanism guarantees data migration each time. It doesn't matter how to optimize α, β, γ in the load evaluation formula. Because it will only change the absolute value of evaluation function, and the relationship of size between each node load evaluation will not change. So we set value of α, β, γ equal to 1 in the next experiments.

5 Experiments

In this section, a series of experiments are carried on to verify our data migration method's effectiveness and efficiency. We do our experiments on a cluster with four nodes, each node has 2 2.1 GHz Intel Xeon E5-2620 processors, 64 GB of memory and a hard disk of 2 TB. The nodes of the cluster are connected by InfiniteBand [7,8] with bandwith 40 Gb/s, and the operating system is CentOs6.5.

First, we deploy PVFS in three nodes, then dynamic extend a new node in PVFS. We access data in PVFS using our reading program in the next twenty-five minites. The read speed of each node is shown in Fig. 4.

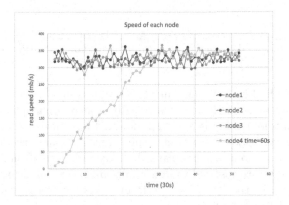

Fig. 4. Speed of read speed for each node when data migrate

The node 4 is the extented node as we can see. In our experiments, we execute the arbitration algorithm each 60 s, i.e. TimeThreshold equals to 60 s. We can see from the Fig. 4 that the speed of the node4 is growing while the others speed are stable.

Next, we discuss the affection of different values of TimeThreshold. Experimental results as shown in Figs. 5 and 6.

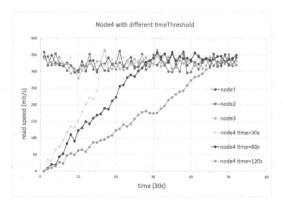

Fig. 5. Speed of each node with different data migration time

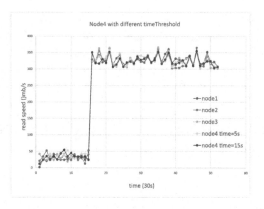

Fig. 6. Speed of each node with different data migration time

As shown in the Fig. 5. When TimeThreshold value is greater than 30 s, the speed of the extension node grows smoothly, the original nodes keep stable. When TimeThreshold value is less than 30 s in Fig. 6 below, the system of the reading speed is very poor in a period of time. This is because the data migration algorithms perform too frequently, caused a huge influence in the PVFS system. PVFS can not afford to respond to user requirements. So choosing TimeThreshold greater than 30 s, the PVFS can perform smooth migration, and ensure the needs of users at the same time.

Finally, we test our algorithm for hot spot issues. First, for a period of time, we make the program randomly read data in PVFS, then execute our data migration algorithm, perform the same operation, the results shown in Figs. 7 and 8.

As can be seen in the Fig. 7, before data migration, we randomly read file in PVFS and all data access stored in node 1. Node 1 become a hot spot node. In the Fig. 8, in the data migration process, the algorithm detects hot spot, and

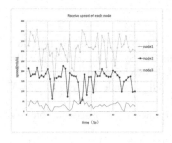
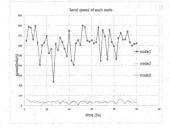

(a) Speed of network to receive   (b) Speed of network to send

Fig. 7. Speed of network before data migration

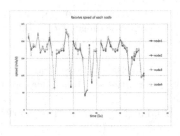
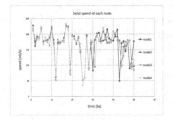

(a) Speed of network to receive   (b) Speed of network to send

Fig. 8. Speed of network after data migration

split file in the hot spot, and then distribute the file to other nodes. In Fig. 8, the send and receive amount of four nodes are balanced.

6   Conclusion

We present a dynamic node extension method based on PVFS, which can add a new node automatically and transparently. After that, we design a data migration method to find out the most loaded node in the original file system using a new load evaluation method and transfer the data into the newly added node to mitigate the imbalance of the system. Experiments prove it can effectively meets user demand, while reducing hot spot occurrence probability. However, our load evaluation method is a little simple and we do not consider the situation that more nodes added at a time. After the migration is completed, there still exist a hot spot potentially. So in the future work, we consider to design an algorithm dealing with node load reasonable and add more nodes at a time.

Acknowledgments. We would like to thank the anonymous reviewers for helping us refine this paper. Their constructive comments and suggestions are very helpful. This paper is partly founded by National Science and Technology Major Project of the Ministry of Science and Technology of China under grant 2011ZX05035-004-004HZ.

References

1. Weil, S.A., Brandt, S.A., Miller, E.L, et al.: Ceph: a scalable, high-performance distributed file system. In: Proceedings of the 7th Symposium on Operating Systems Design and Implementation, pp. 307–320. USENIX Association (2006)
2. Ghemawat, S., Gobioff, H., Leung, S.T.: The Google file system. ACM SIGOPS Operating Syst. Rev. **37**(5), 29–43 (2003)
3. Dean, J., Ghemawat, S.: MapReduce: simplified data processing on large clusters. Commun. ACM **51**(1), 107–113 (2008)
4. Haddad, I.F.: PVFS: A parallel virtual file system for linux clusters. Linux J. **2000**(80es), 5 (2000)
5. Kuhn, M., Kunkel, J.M., Ludwig, T.: Dynamic file system semantics to enable metadata optimizations in PVFS. Concurrency Comput. Pract. Experience **21**(14), 1775–1788 (2009)
6. Tantisiriroj, W., Son, S.W., Patil, S., et al.: On the duality of data-intensive file system design: reconciling HDFS and PVFS. In: Proceedings of 2011 International Conference for High Performance Computing, Networking, Storage and Analysis, p. 67. ACM (2011)
7. Wu, J., Wyckoff, P., Panda, D.: PVFS over InfiniBand: design and performance evaluation. In: Proceedings of the 2003 International Conference on Parallel Processing, pp. 125–132. IEEE (2003)
8. Pfister, G.F.: An introduction to the infiniband architecture. In: High Performance Mass Storage and Parallel I/O, chap. 42, pp. 617–632 (2001)
9. Hsiao, H.C., Chung, H.Y., Shen, H., et al.: Load rebalancing for distributed file systems in clouds. IEEE Trans. Parallel Distrib. Syst. **24**(5), 951–962 (2013)
10. Wang, K., Zhou, X., Li, T., et al.: Optimizing load balancing and data-locality with data-aware scheduling. In: 2014 IEEE International Conference on Big Data (Big Data), pp. 119–128. IEEE (2014)
11. Guoying, L., et al.: Data consistency for self-acting load balancing of parallel file system. In: Park, J.H.(James), et al. (eds.) Information Technology Convergence, Secure and Trust Computing, and Data Management. LNEE, vol. 180, pp. 135–143. Springer, Netherlands (2012)
12. Kobayashi, K., Mikami, S., Kimura H., et al.: The gfarm file system on compute clouds. In: 2011 IEEE International Symposium on Parallel and Distributed Processing Workshops and Phd Forum (IPDPSW), pp. 1034–1041. IEEE (2011)
13. Dong, B., Li, X., Xiao, L., et al.: Self-acting load balancing with parallel sub file migration for parallel file system. In: 2010 Third International Joint Conference on Computational Science and Optimization (CSO), vol. 2, pp. 317–321. IEEE (2010)
14. Jenkins, J., Zou, X., Tang, H., et al.: Parallel data layout optimization of scientific data through access-driven replication. Technical report-Not held in TRLN member libraries (2014)
15. Soares, T.S., Dantas, M.A.R., de Macedo, D.D.J., et al.: A data management in a private cloud storage environment utilizing high performance distributed file systems. In: 2013 IEEE 22nd International Workshop on Enabling Technologies: Infrastructure for Collaborative Enterprises (WETICE), pp. 158–163. IEEE (2013)
16. Huo, Y., Yang, K., Liang, H., et al.: Summary of parallel file system research. J. Chin. Comput. Syst. **29**(9), 1631–1636 (2008)
17. Zhang, C., Yin, J., et al.: Dynamic load balancing algorithm of distributed file system. J. Chin. Comput. Syst. **32**(7), 1424–1426 (2011)
18. Zhu, Y., Li, B., Sun, T., et al.: Parallel computing system scalability. Comput. Eng. Appl. **47**(21), 47–49 (2011)

Fast 3-Point Correlation Function Approximation on GPU

Chao Sun$^{(\boxtimes)}$, Mujin Yang, Ce Yu, and Jizhou Sun

School of Computer Science and Technology, Tianjin University,
Tianjin 300350, China
sch@tju.edu.cn

Abstract. The problem of 3-Point Correlation Function (3PCF) in astrophysics processes megabytes data with complex calculations, which is an important tool for calculating properties of heterogeneous systems, but its algorithmic complex is a notorious problem. The fast 3PCF Approximation algorithm can improve the efficiency by reduce the precision of result. In this paper, we are going to introduce a design of this algorithm on GPU, which is 13x speedup over a single CPU. Moreover, we will optimize it in the calculation details: converting the 3D arrays to 1D, padding 0s to arrays and shrinking the kernel array. Finally, this algorithm can achieve 27x speedup additional, and 347x speedup over a single CPU.

Keywords: GPU · CUDA · 3-Point Correlation Function (3PCF) · Recursive convolution for scalar fields (RCFS) · Fast Fourier Transform (FFT)

1 Introduction

The correlation functions are widely used tools for computation and analysis in many areas of astrophysics [9]. They are often used to quantify the clustering of objects in the universe (*e.g.* galaxies, quasars *etc.*) compared to a pure Poisson process. More recently, they have also been used to measure fluctuations in the Cosmic Microwave Background (CMB) [5]. On large scales, the higher-order statistics, such as the 3-Point Correlation Function (3PCF), is a valuable statistic for describing structure formation models. It contains information on cosmological parameters and detailed halo properties [10] that cannot be extracted from the 2-Point Correlation Function.

The n-Point Correlation Function (nPCF) of a scalar field $\rho(X)$ is a function of all possible arrangements of n points chosen from the system. For a system of N points, the brute force approach is intrinsically an $O(N^n)$ computation. For N of astronomical interest, such significant cost makes it impossible to compute by brute force the full correlation function of order n greater than two. Recent progress has been made in effort to speed up the computation of the nPCF, such as *Moore A. et al.*'s fast algorithm [6], *Zhang L.L. et al.*'s rapid algorithm [12] and

© Springer International Publishing Switzerland 2015
G. Wang et al. (Eds.): ICA3PP 2015, Part II, LNCS 9529, pp. 553–566, 2015.
DOI: 10.1007/978-3-319-27122-4_38

many other methods using the idea of kd-tree which is proposed by Bentley at 1975 [1]. These algorithms are all notorious for being computationally expensive. As a new way, Xiang Zhang proposed the Fast nPCF Approximation [13] to approximate calculating the nPCF problem with its computability in $O(N + nm^k \log m^k)$ where k is the number of dimensions and m is the number of areas in each dimension of the whole space. However, to get better accuracy, it needs to increase the value of m, which makes the calculation increasing rapidly. On the other hand, this algorithm is appropriate to be applied on parallel computing environments. *Yin Lingyan et al.*'s algorithm on MPI provided a method of dividing to small tasks using sub-blocks which uses a lot of CPUs to get a better accuracy [11].

Lately, high performance computer systems, such as supercomputer, have started to include GPUs, whose architecture fits the data parallel computing model best where a common processing kernel acts on a large data set [2]. Under this architecture, it is possible to parallelize the fast nPCF Approximation algorithm using GPUs. In this paper, we designed the algorithm of 3PCF ($n = 3$) on a GPU card. And, by studying the Fast Fourier Transform (FFT) [7] algorithm, we give some optimizations to the calculation details on GPU which can get 347 times faster than a single CPU core.

This paper is structured as follows. In Sect. 2, the Fast 3PCF Approximation algorithm is introduced. In Sect. 3, we present the algorithm on GPU. The experimental evaluation is proposed in Sect. 5. Then, we make some optimizations in Sect. 5. Finally, Sect. 6 concludes the paper with outlooks.

2   The Fast 3PCF Approximation Algorithm

The 3PCF ξ_3 of a scalar field $\rho(X)$ are defined as

$$\xi_3(s_1, s_2, s_3) = \langle \rho(X_1)\rho(X_2)\rho(X_3) \rangle \tag{1}$$

where s_i represents the spatial constraint between X_i and X_j with $j = i + 1$, $X_4 = X_1$. Here X_i represents a set of points in a k-dimensional space. The spatial constraints s_i are specified as a range of distance, such as:

$$s_i : r_{i_1} \leq \| x_i - x_j \| \leq r_{i_2}, \; x_i \in X_i \text{ and } x_j \in X_j. \tag{2}$$

where x_i is a single point in X_i, and x_j is a single point in X_j. r_{i_1} and r_{i_2} are the constraints of the distance between x_i and x_j.

By this definition, if we set the field quantity ρ as $\rho(x_i) = 1$, the expectation value of 3PCF is the amount of the tuples $\langle x_1, x_2, x_3 \rangle$ satisfy the spatial constraints $\langle s_1, s_2, s_3 \rangle$.

The Fast 3PCF Approximation proposed by Xiang Zhang are based on the definition of recursive convolution for scalar fields (RCSF), and it can be computed using various Fast Fourier Transform (FFT) algorithms.

2.1   Recursive Convolution for Scalar Fields

Using the recursive convolution, the global space should be partitioned into small areas. For each area $\mathbf{p}$, the function y_i is defined as the local sum of weighted value of the points in this area:

$$y_i(\mathbf{p}) = \sum_{x_i} 1\{x_i \in \mathbf{p}\} w(x_i)\rho(x_i) \tag{3}$$

Where $x_i \in X_i$ and $w(x_i)$ is the weight for point x_i. The notation $1\{x_i \in \mathbf{p}\}$ is a logic operator:

$$1\{x_i \in \mathbf{p}\} = \begin{cases} 1 \text{ if } x_i \in \mathbf{p} \\ 0 \text{ otherwise} \end{cases}. \tag{4}$$

As a matter of fact, $y_i(\mathbf{p})$ is a expression of the scalar $\rho(X_i)$, which consists of the weighted sum of the points in X_i.

Then, the kernel functions $\mathbf{f}$ are designed to be consistent with the spatial constraints in the 3PCF problem. For example, the f_i corresponding to s_i shown in formula 1 is

$$f_i(\mathbf{p}) = \begin{cases} 1 \text{ if } r_{i_1} \leq \| \mathbf{p} - \mathbf{0} \| \leq r_{i_2} \\ 0 \qquad \text{otherwise} \end{cases}. \tag{5}$$

where $\mathbf{0}$ is the center area of the global space. It is not a precise value of the formula $\| \mathbf{p} - \mathbf{0} \|$, that means this will make a inaccuracy to the result. To get more precise result, the size of the area should be devided smaller and the number of areas will be increase.

Base on the f_i and y_i, the RCSF noted as g_i has a recursive definition:

$$g_i(\mathbf{p}) = (g_{i-1} * f_{i-1})(\mathbf{p}) \cdot y_i(\mathbf{p}), \tag{6}$$

where $g_1(\mathbf{p}) = y_1(\mathbf{p})$. It can be recognized that g_i represents the sum of the weighted production of the scalar field $\rho(X)$ through X_1 to X_i, under corresponding spatial constraints.

By the definition, it can be concluded that an integral over g_i would compute the correlation value of the scalar satisfying the corresponding spatial constraints:

$$A_i = \int g_i(\mathbf{p}) d\mathbf{p}, \tag{7}$$

Where A_i is the sum of $\rho(i)$'s product for all points in tuples $\langle x_1, x_2, \cdots, x_i \rangle$ that satisfy the spatial constraints $\langle s_1, s_2, \cdots, s_{i-1} \rangle$. While the kernel functions $\mathbf{f}$ are not exactly consist with the spatial constraints, the result is an approximation. To get more accurate result, it is necessary to deeply partition the global space.

2.2   The Fast 3PCF Approximation

For the 3PCF, it need to calculate the correlation value satisfying the spatial constraints s_1, s_2 and s_3, which are closed loops form the starting point back to the starting point. Using RCFS, every point from X_1 would trace back to the

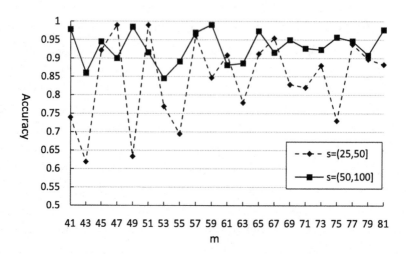

Fig. 1. The accuracy plot

same point in $X_4(X_1)$, so the 3PCF need to compute the results for all points in X_1. As the definition of the area $\mathbf{p}$ in RCSF is irrelevant to the size N of the point sets, the 3PCF Approximation processes with every area $\mathbf{p}$ individually.

This algorithm is an iterative procedure that iterates through every area $\mathbf{p_0}$ in y_1, setting $g_1(\mathbf{p}) = 1\{\mathbf{p} = \mathbf{p_0}\}$ and extracting $g_4(\mathbf{p_0})$ as the final result at $\mathbf{p_0}$. In RCSF iteration we can use FFT to accelerate the computing of $g_i(\mathbf{p})$, which reduces the computational complexity from $O(m^{2k})$ to $O(m^k \log m^k)$ where k is the number of dimensions and m is the number of the areas in each dimension of the whole space.

The accuracy of the result is closely related to the size of m. Figure 1 shows the relationship of the accuracy and the size of m on a set of real data, when $N = 10^5$, $k = 3$ and s choosing $(25, 50]$ and $(50, 100]$ with global range of $(-320, 320)$. It shows that the accuracy is still lower than 0.95 when the $m > 80$, while the execution time using 1 CPU core has already exceed 2 h when $m = 51$. It is not a sufficiently precise result.

3   Design on GPU

In this section, beginning with the feature to GPU, its architecture is finely suitable to parallel the fast 3PCF Approximation algorithm. Then we provided the detailed design and parallelization of the algorithm with the kernel part in CUDA.

3.1   Graphics Processors

Graphics processing units (GPUs) have evolved to massively parallel computational devices, containing hundreds of processing cores that can be used for general purpose computing beyond graphics rendering. The fundamental difference between CPUs and GPUs comes from how transistors are assigned to different tasks in the processor. A GPU devotes most of its area to a large array of Arithmetic Logic Units (ALUs).

The architecture of GPUs is based on a set of multiprocessors, each of which contains a set of stream processors operating on SIMD (Single Instruction Multiple Data) programs. For this reason, a GPU is ideal for parallel applications requiring high memory bandwidth to access different sets of data.

A unit of work issued by the host computer to the GPUs is called a *kernel*. A typical GPU *kernel* execution takes the following four steps: (i) the DMA controller transfers input data from host memory to device memory; (ii) a host program instructs the GPU to launch the *kernel*; (iii) the GPU executes threads in parallel; and (iv) the DMA controller transfers the results data back to the host memory from device memory. A *kernel* is executed on the device as many different threads organized in *thread blocks*, and each multiprocessor executes one or more *thread blocks*.

3.2   Design on GPU

Algorithm 1 shows the pseudo-code of the fast 3PCF Approximation Algorithm. In this program, All y_xs and f_xs and constructed at the beginning. Then, for all nonzero **p**s, calculate the result ($g_4(\mathbf{p_0})$) using FFT algorithm. To use FFT operation, the arrays f_i and g_i should be uniformed to the size of the result array in step (9). Assume the sizes of f_i and g_i are m^3 and n^3, the size of the result array gf_i is $(m + n - 1)^3$. For simplicity example, we use 2D arrays instead of the 3D arrays, whose sizes are 3^2 and 2^2:

$$A = \begin{bmatrix} 4 & 1 & 9 \\ 7 & 4 & 2 \\ 3 & 3 & 8 \end{bmatrix}, B = \begin{bmatrix} 0 & 1 \\ 4 & 2 \end{bmatrix},$$

so we get the size of the result array $(3 + 2 - 1)^2 = 4^2$. The uniformization of the two arrays are:

$$A' = \begin{bmatrix} 4 & 1 & 9 & 0 \\ 7 & 4 & 2 & 0 \\ 3 & 3 & 8 & 0 \\ 0 & 0 & 0 & 0 \end{bmatrix}, B' = \begin{bmatrix} 0 & 1 & 0 & 0 \\ 4 & 2 & 0 & 0 \\ 0 & 0 & 0 & 0 \\ 0 & 0 & 0 & 0 \end{bmatrix}.$$

So, we can image the uniformization of the 3D arrays. And the result will be transformed back in step (13).

In this algorithm, the converting using FFT (step 10) and inverse FFT (step 12) is the most time-consuming step, and the calculated amount increases rapidly when the size of the m grows. Nevertheless, the converting operation and the main processing steps is suitable for computing on GPUs. It is already have the library for executing FFT on GPUs called cuFFT [8], so the algorithm using GPU becomes a little easier.

Algorithm 1. The fast 3PCF approximation algorithm on CPU

1: Construct y_i from X_i, $i = 1, 2, 3, 4$
2: Construct f_i from s_i, $i = 1, 2, 3$
3: Initialize $result \leftarrow 0$
4: **for** area $\mathbf{p_0}$ in y_1 **do**
5:     **if** $y_1(\mathbf{p_0}) \neq 0$ **then**
6:         $g_1(\mathbf{p}) \leftarrow 1\{\mathbf{p} = \mathbf{p_0}\}$
7:         **for** $j = 1$ to 3 **do**
8:             $size \leftarrow$ size of $g_j \times f_j$
9:             Expand f_j and g_j's size to $size$
10:            Convert f_j and g_j using FFT
11:            $gf_j \leftarrow g_j \times f_j$
12:            Convert gf_j using inverse FFT
13:            Reduce gf_j's size to the original size
14:            $g_{j+1} \leftarrow gf_j \cdot y_j$
15:        **end for**
16:        $result \leftarrow result + g_4(\mathbf{p_0})$
17:    **end if**
18: **end for**

Algorithm 2. The fast 3PCF approximation algorithm on GPU

1: Construct y_i from X_i, $i = 1, 2, 3, 4$
2: Construct f_i from s_i, $i = 1, 2, 3$
3: Initialize $result \leftarrow 0$
4: Copy y_xs and f_xs to GPU Memory
5: **for** area $\mathbf{p_0}$ in y_1 **do**
6:     **if** $y_1(\mathbf{p_0}) \neq 0$ **then**
7:         $g_1(\mathbf{p}) \leftarrow 1\{\mathbf{p} = \mathbf{p_0}\}$
8:         Copy $g_1(\mathbf{p})$ to GPU Memory
9:         **for** $j = 1$ to 3 **do**
10:            $size \leftarrow$ size of $g_j \times f_j$
11:            (GPU)Expand f_j and g_j's size to $size$
12:            (GPU)Convert f_j and g_j using FFT
13:            (GPU)$gf_j \leftarrow g_j \times f_j$
14:            (GPU)Convert gf_j using inverse FFT
15:            (GPU)Reduce gf_j's size to the original size
16:            (GPU)$g_{j+1} \leftarrow gf_j \cdot y_j$
17:        **end for**
18:        Copy $g_4(\mathbf{p})$ from GPU Memory
19:        $result \leftarrow result + g_4(\mathbf{p_0})$
20:    **end if**
21: **end for**

To reduce the data transferring between the host memory and device memory, we transfer most of data outer the main loop process (step 5), leaving all the computing steps processed on GPU, shown on Algorithm 2. In the inner loop, the five operations are all parallelizable on GPU sequentially: step (12) and step (14) are the FFT processes, the FFT library cuFFT parallelizing them with all GPU threads cooperating in an efficient way; step (13) and step (16) are processes of multiplying two arrays and step (11) and step (15) are converting processes between arrays with different size, we distributed the compute tasks equally to the GPU threads by ourselves.

Base on the program on GPUs, we can partition all areas in y_1 into individual GPUs equally, so the tasks are divided into GPUs equally. The arrays f and y are needed to all processes on GPUs, so they transferred to all GPUs memory before the calculation starting. After computing finished, only the result is inevitably to transfer. During the whole programs, with a small amount data to transfer, it is possible to improve the performance using more GPUs.

4   Performance Evaluation

In this section, the performance of the algorithm on GPUs will be analyzed. All the following experiments in this and the next sections are using real data sets with $N = 10^5$, $k = 3$ and $s = (10, 100]$ with global range $(-320, 320)$, and running on the following systems:

- CPU: An Intel Xeon E5606, 2.13 GHz with 8 MB cache and 16 G memory.
- GPU: Tesla C2050 GPU with 448 CUDA cores, 3 G GDRR5 memory per GPU.

4.1   Acceleration on GPU

We compared the performance of our algorithm on GPU to the Xiang Zhang's algorithm on 1 CPU core. Figure 2 shows the tendency of the execution time with m from 11 to 51, which increasing rapidly with fluctuations. Figure 3 shows

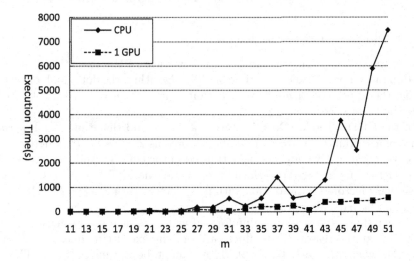

Fig. 2. Performances using GPU and CPU

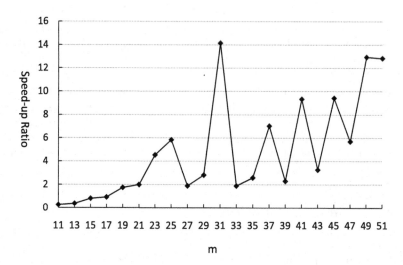

Fig. 3. The speedup ratio of the GPU algorithm (compared with CPU)

the speed up ratio, which shows that using GPU can get up to 13 times faster than CPU.

When $m \leq 17$, the condition of the speed up ratio lower than 1 is because of the transferring data between the host memory and device memory take more time than saved. After that, it can be found that the GPU algorithm is always faster than CPU even though under the worst condition.

With CPU algorithm, when m is bigger than 43, the execution time exceeds 1000 s and increasing rapidly up to 7473 s ($m = 51$) which is more than 2 h. However, using GPU which arrange all data to 448 CUDA cores for computing, it is much faster and completed in 582 s which is increasing gently.

4.2   Problems on Performance

Besides the acceleration, we can see obvious wave of the execution time and speedup ratio. For the execution time of CPU algorithm, the dots can look as two trends, the upper constituted by execution time with $m = ..., 31, 37, 45, 49, 51$ while the lower otherwise.

In the CUDA Toolkit Documentation [8], it is said that the cuFFT performance of any transform size that can be factored as $2^a * 3^b * 5^c * 7^d$ (where a, b, c, and d are non-negative integers) is optimized in the cuFFT. And the smaller the prime factor, the better the performance. While, the FFTW [3,4] in CPU have the similar factored optimization with more factors ($2^a * 3^b * 5^c * 7^d * 11^e * 13^f$) and it can be partially optimized.

Table 1 shows the size of the uniformed arrays as factored formation, so we can find that the reason of the fluctuation of the execution time. Considering $m > 29$, when $m = 31, 37, 45, 49, 51$, it cannot be optimized by FFTW, so

Table 1. Optimization of FFT with different ms (uSize represents the size of the uniformed arrays)

m	uSize	Optimized by CPU	Optimized by GPU
11	$21^3 = (3 * 7)^3$	yes	yes
13	$25^3 = (5^2)^3$	yes	yes
15	$29^3 = 29^3$	no	no
17	$33^3 = (3 * 11)^3$	yes	no
19	$37^3 = 37^3$	no	no
21	$41^3 = 41^3$	no	no
23	$45^3 = (3^2 * 5)^3$	yes	yes
25	$49^3 = (7^2)^3$	yes	yes
27	$53^3 = 53^3$	no	no
29	$57^3 = (3 * 19)^3$	partial	no
31	$61^3 = 61^3$	no	no
33	$65^3 = (5 * 13)^3$	yes	no
35	$69^3 = (3 * 23)^3$	partial	no
37	$73^3 = 73^3$	no	no
39	$77^3 = (7 * 11)^3$	yes	no
41	$81^3 = (3^4)^3$	yes	yes
43	$85^3 = (5 * 17)^3$	partial	no
45	$89^3 = 89^3$	no	no
47	$93^3 = (3 * 31)^3$	partial	no
49	$97^3 = 97^3$	no	no
51	$101^3 = 101^3$	no	no

the execution takes more time, while for cuFFT, it can only be optimized on $m = 41$, and it is the explanation to the results. There are a few declinations in the performance may be caused by processing 3D arrays which not be shown processing 1D arrays.

5   Optimizations for Algorithm

Besides parallelizing the algorithm of the fast 3PCF Approximation on GPUs, we studied the details of FFT algorithm and found that we can manually convert the 3D FFT arrays to 1D for faster running speed. What's more, we can arbitrarily extend or shrink the FFT arrays (remove leading and trailing zeros) and keep the right result. Considering this, firstly we convert the FFT arrays of f_i, g_i, and the fg_i to 1D, then padding some 0s to satisfy the cuFFT optimization. In additional, as there are lots of 0s in the f_i, we shrink it to reduce the calculation amount.

5.1   Converting 3D FFT Arrays to 1D

As studied the FFT algorithm, we know that it has the same result by convert the 3D FFT arrays to 1D. To manually convert the 3D FFT arrays to 1D, we need to calculate the result size of the 3D arrays, then add some 0s in the original 3D arrays, just like step (11) in the pseudo-code shown in Algorithm 2.

After the uniformization we can convert them to 1D sequentially, we also take the 2D arrays in the section *Design on GPU* as an example, the final 1D arrays for A and B is the flat form of the uniformization arrays:

$$A_{1D} = \begin{bmatrix} 4\ 1\ 9\ 0\ 7\ 4\ 2\ 0\ 3\ 3\ 8\ 0\ 0\ 0\ 0\ 0 \end{bmatrix},$$

$$B_{1D} = \begin{bmatrix} 0\ 1\ 0\ 0\ 4\ 2\ 0\ 0\ 0\ 0\ 0\ 0\ 0\ 0\ 0\ 0 \end{bmatrix}.$$

The reason to add 0s to the original 3D arrays is to insure that the products are gained from corresponding numbers and the result won't affect to other dimensions.

Using this method, we convert the 3D FFT arrays to 1D. The comparison of performances shown in Fig. 4, which indeed states that it can reduce the execution time. It is efficient obviously when $m = 41$ and 53, which is indeed optimized by cuFFT as we known from Table 1.

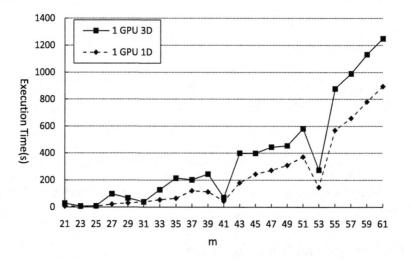

Fig. 4. Performances using 3D FFT arrays and 1D FFT arrays

And it is effective to resize the FFT 1D arrays than 3D arrays which using in the following optimizations.

5.2   Padding 0s to FFT Arrays

From the explanation above, we know the fluctuant of the execution time is because of the optimization in the cuFFT. As the running speed is associated

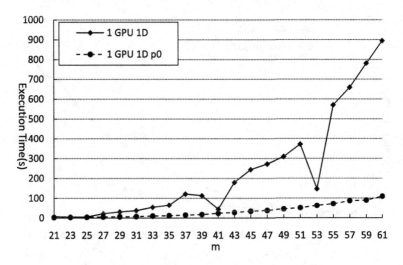

Fig. 5. The effect of padding 0s to FFT array

with the size of the FFT arrays and it can arbitrarily padding 0s in the FFT arrays, we extends the FFT arrays to get more powerful computing efficiency. For simplicity, we can extend the size of FFT arrays when $m = 43, 45, 47, 49, 51$ to the size when $m = 53$, that indeed make a little speedup.

Based on the FFT 1D arrays generated above, we padding some 0s for new size with more efficient performance. The Fig. 5 shows the comparison of this situation and the previous. It shows that this optimization almost speed up all the condition of m with a obviously acceleration.

Thanks to converting arrays to 1D, we can get efficient performance with padding fewer 0s, so more effective. To resize 3D arrays whose uniformed size is 73^3, we have to extend them to 75^3 using 3D arrays, but maybe we can extend them to $73^3 + 1608$ as 1D arrays, which is much smaller than 75^3. So, using 1D arrays must can achieve more efficient performance for almost all conditions.

5.3   Shrinking the Kernel Array

As the s_i is more smaller than the global space, it have lots of 0s in the f_i FFT array. It won't be removed when processing the FFT convert, but we can delete them manually, and the uniformed arrays' size will also be reduced. We also take the 2D arrays as an example, for an f_i array with its size 5^2 whose non-zero size is 3^2, the original array and the result may like:

$$f_i = \begin{bmatrix} 0 & 0 & 0 & 0 & 0 \\ 0 & 0 & 1 & 0 & 0 \\ 0 & 1 & 0 & 1 & 0 \\ 0 & 0 & 1 & 0 & 0 \\ 0 & 0 & 0 & 0 & 0 \end{bmatrix}, f_{result} = \begin{bmatrix} 0 & 1 & 0 \\ 1 & 0 & 1 \\ 0 & 1 & 0 \end{bmatrix}.$$

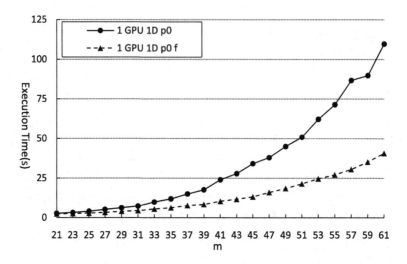

Fig. 6. The effect of shrink **f**

To shrink the kernel array **f**, we need to do it before converting to 1D array. Considering the 3D array **f** whose size is 51^3 and non-zero size is 15^3, the size can be reduced to 15^3 properly. After doing this, the uniformization will be performed, then converting to 1D arrays, and then padding 0s. The result of the optimizations is shown in Fig. 6. It also makes respectable speed up.

5.4   Brief Summarize

Now making all the optimizations, we surprisingly found that the execution with all the optimizations achieves up to 347 times faster than a single CPU core when

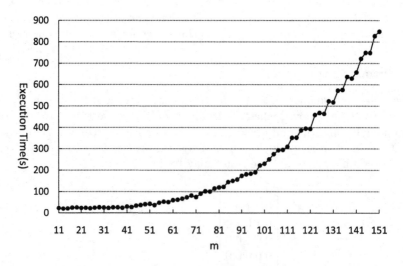

Fig. 7. The execution time of optimized program on GPU

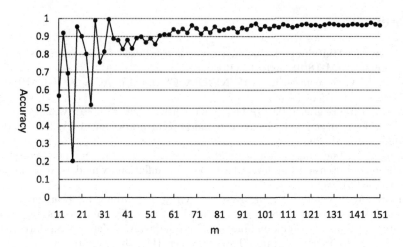

Fig. 8. The accuracy plot

$m = 51$. And the it will be more and more large according to the increasing of m and number of GPUs.

To acquire more accurate result, it is necessary to increase the size of m. Using the optimized algorithm, we get the result of $m = 151$ (it limited to the memory of the GPU) in 848 s which may take many days with a single CPU, and the accuracy reaches 0.96 stably shown in Figs. 7 and 8.

6   Conclusion

In this paper, we designed the Fast 3PCF Approximation algorithm on GPU card, which is 13 times faster than a single CPU. Then, we proposed some optimizations on the calculation details of cuFFT: converting the 3D arrays to 1D, padding 0s to arrays and shrinking the kernel array. The execution time achieves up to 347 times faster than the original program on a single CPU core. Furthermore, the result with accuracy 0.96 was worked out in 848 s. This is a worthful work for the astrophysics by measuring the large-scale structure the in a few time. In addition, the optimizations to the cuFFT are also available to other application, and possible to FFTW on CPU.

In the future, we intend to adjust this algorithm on multi-GPUs environment for computing more large data sets and produce more precise result. And, we will try to improve the algorithm to consider the memory limitation. After that, it is expected to release a toolkit for the 3PCF problem on GPUs.

Acknowledgments. The work is sponsored by the National Natural Science Foundation of China (61303021).

References

1. Bentley, J.: Multidimensional binary search trees used for associative searching. Commun. ACM **18**(9), 509–517 (1975)
2. Buck, I.: GPU computing with NVIDIA CUDA. In: ACM SIGGRAPH 2007 Courses, p. 6. ACM (2007)
3. FFTW: Fftw reference (2003). http://www.fftw.org/fftw2_doc/fftw_3.html
4. Frigo, M., Johnson, S.G.: The design and implementation of FFTW3. Proc. IEEE **93**(2), 216–231 (2005)
5. Gangui, A., Lucchin, F., Matarrese, S., Mollerach, S.: The three-point correlation function of the cosmic microwave background in inflationary models. arXiv preprint astro-ph/9312033 (1993)
6. Moore, A., Connolly, A., Genovese, C., Gray, A., Grone, L., Kanidoris II, N., Nichol, R., Schneider, J., Szalay, A., Szapudi, I., et al.: Fast algorithms and efficient statistics: N-point correlation functions. In: Banday, A.J., Zaroubi, S., Bartelmann, M. (eds.) Mining the Sky, pp. 71–82. Springer, Heidelberg (2001)
7. Moreland, K., Angel, E.: The FFT on a GPU. In: Proceedings of the ACM SIGGRAPH/EUROGRAPHICS Conference on Graphics Hardware, pp. 112–119. Eurographics Association (2003)
8. Nvidia, C.: CUDA toolkit documentation - cuFFT (2012). http://docs.nvidia.com/cuda/cufft/index.html
9. Peebles, P.: The Large-Scale Structure of the Universe. Princeton University Press, Princeton (1980)
10. Sefusatti, E., Scoccimarro, R.: Galaxy bias and halo-occupation numbers from large-scale clustering. Phys. Rev. D **71**(6), 063001 (2005)
11. Yin, L., Yu, C., Sun, J., Liu, X., Xiao, J., Sun, C.: Three-point correlation function parallel algorithm based on MPI. In: 2013 IEEE 10th International Conference on High Performance Computing and Communications and 2013 IEEE International Conference on Embedded and Ubiquitous Computing (HPCC_EUC), pp. 482–489. IEEE (2013)
12. Zhang, L., Pen, U.: Fast n-point correlation functions and three-point lensing application. New Astron. **10**(7), 569–590 (2005)
13. Zhang, X., Yu, C.: Fast n-point correlation function approximation with recursive convolution for scalar fields. In: 2011 IEEE Third International Conference on Cloud Computing Technology and Science (CloudCom), pp. 634–639. IEEE (2011)

Efficient Scheduling with Intensive In-Memory File Accesses Considering Bandwidth Constraint on Memory Bus

Lin Wu[2], Qingfeng Zhuge[1,2]([✉]), Edwin H.-M. Sha[1,2], and Zhilong Sun[2]

[1] Key Laboratory of Dependable Service Computing in Cyber Pyhsical Society, Ministry of Education, Chongqing 400044, China
[2] College of Computer Science, Chongqing University, Chongqing 400044, China
{wulin_cqu,qfzhuge,edwinsha,szllong}@cqu.edu.cn

Abstract. The latest trend in high performance computing and big data applications inspires new solutions of in-memory filesystems to achieve high throughput of file data accesses. However, new concerns arise because intensive in-memory file accesses can cause contention problem on memory bus. With existing schedulers, such as Complete Fair Scheduler (CFS) in Linux system, memory access intensive processes can excessively occupy memory bandwidth. As a result, the performance of a set of running processes is degraded. In this paper, we propose a scheduling algorithm to consider memory bandwidth consumption during scheduling and improve the completion time of a given working set. We first present the data to show that CFS can not efficiently handle a set of running processes involving intensive in-memory file accesses. Then, a heuristic algorithm is proposed to solve the scheduling problem with bandwidth consumption and execution time consideration. The scheduling algorithm is implemented and extensively experimented in Linux system. The experimental results show that the completion time is reduced up to 33.3 % compared with that generated by Linux scheduler CFS.

Keywords: In-Memory filesystem · Bandwidth contention · Scheduling · IO path · Completion time

1 Introduction

In high performance computing and big data applications, there is a growing trend of moving data sets to main memory with the goal of achieving high file accesses throughput. To exploit the benefits of memory system, a number of in-memory filesystems and main-memory databases are designed to fully utilize the memory bus to provide fast access to the file contents [1–4]. Since such systems are built upon the Non-Volatile Memory (NVM)/DRAM connected to memory bus, they have significant throughput improvement compared with data I/O on the traditional filesystems based on block devices [4–7]. As a result, processes requiring high-volume file accesses enjoy remarkable performance improvement.

© Springer International Publishing Switzerland 2015
G. Wang et al. (Eds.): ICA3PP 2015, Part II, LNCS 9529, pp. 567–580, 2015.
DOI: 10.1007/978-3-319-27122-4_39

However, memory bandwidth contention problem that can be caused by intensive in-memory file accesses has not been fully investigated. We study the impact of intensive in-memory file accesses on the system. Our study shows that processes can suffer performance degradation with existing linux Complete Fair Scheduler (CFS), because they can't get a fair share of memory bandwidth. Therefore, it is important to carefully study the scheduling strategy in system with intensive in-memory file accesses to avoid undesired performance degradation.

Many research works have reported the benefits obtained from in-memory filesystems, but few of these designs investigate the impact to the whole system. SCMFS [2] studied the impact of sharing system resources such as the memory bus, CPU cache and TLB, but no methods are proposed to deal with the problem. The designers of BPFS [1] discussed the possible traffic to Non-Volatile Memory can interfere with DRAM accesses and harm the overall system performance, but they only evaluated this impact on a simulated environment due to the lack of real-world hardware support for their proposed filesystem. The proposed filesystems can boost the application performance but no effective strategies have been developed to tackle the bus contention problem directly in a system using in-memory filesystems.

In this paper, we propose an approach to mitigate the bus contention problem. We motivate this approach with examples to show that the default Linux scheduler can't solve the problem when the system is loaded with processes requiring intensive in-memory file accesses. By taking into account the memory bandwidth consumption of the tasks, we can schedule tasks such that the accumulative bandwidth requirement does not exceed the memory bandwidth. In this way, bus contention problem can be avoided and the completion time of a given working set is reduced. This paper makes the following contributions:

1. We study the impact of intensive in-memory file accesses on system performance by analyzing bandwidth usage on memory bus.
2. We propose a polynomial-time heuristic algorithm to solve the scheduling problem considering memory bus bandwidth constraint. This technique can be integrated into Linux kernel to improve the system performance.

We implemented the proposed technique in Linux system with CFS and extensive experiments were conducted to evaluate the effectiveness of this strategy. The experimental results show that the completion time of a given working set is reduced up to 33.3 % compared to the Linux scheduler CFS. The rest of this paper is organized as follows: Sect. 2 gives the background information and problem definition. Section 3 provides a motivational example. Section 4 presents the heuristic algorithm. Section 5 shows the experimental evaluation of the proposed algorithm. This paper is concluded in Sect. 6.

2   Background and Problem Definition

In this section, we present background information and the system architecture upon which this work is built.

2.1 Architecture

The architecture we study in this paper has multiple processors, each processor has its own local cache. System memory is shared among all the processors through the common memory bus. The memory can be either DRAM, NVM or the combination of both DRAM and NVM. An in-memory filesystem is used in this system, all the file requests can be satisfied once they are initiated to the in-memory filesystem, since file operations are equivalent to memory access. Each processor can get any proportion of the system memory bandwidth as long as it does not exceed the bandwidth capacity of the whole system. The architecture of the system is depicted in Fig. 1.

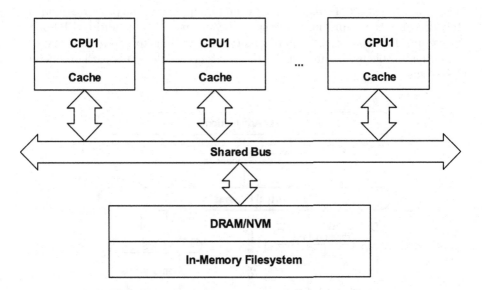

Fig. 1. The overview of system architecture.

We characterise the processes into two kinds by memory access patterns. One is Memory-access-intensive (MA-intensive) process, the other is Non-memory-access-intensive (Non-MA-intensive). The major difference between the two kinds of processes lies in the memory bandwidth requirement, An MA-intensive process usually occupies memory bus for a long time until its time slice is used up. For example, in a system using in-memory filesystem, applications that intensively access in-memory files can easily take up the whole memory bandwidth, such processes are MA-intensive. On the other hand, some kernel demons are Non-MA-intensive, they consume little memory bandwidth, either because the processor cache can service their requests or their bandwidth requirement is negligible compared with other processes.

2.2   CFS and Difference in File-Access Path

Complete Fair Scheduler[1] (CFS) is the default scheduler since the release of 2.6.23 kernel. Different from previous scheduler, CFS uses red-black tree to generate a "timeline" for future task execution. It uses the concept of "virtual runtime" to try to ensure fairness among all the tasks in the system.

Under the traditional I/O path, the processes initiating an I/O request have to wait until the data becomes available, I/O accesses to mainstream storage devices such as hard disk, RAID, SSD (either SATA-based or PCIe-based) trigger the system scheduler to switch out the requesting process in favor of another ready process in the system. Things are different when processes requesting data from in-memory filesystem. The operating system does not put these processes to sleeping state since the required data can be supplied to the processes immediately. Because the in-memory filesystem uses memory bus, traditional IO operations are all propagated to the memory bus, leading to severe memory bus contention problems. Figure 2 shows the difference in file access path of different filesystems.

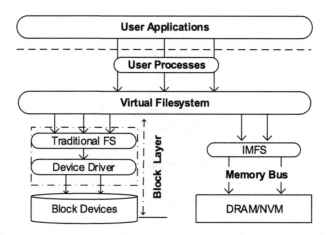

Fig. 2. The difference in file access path of different filesystems.

To sum up, on a system with in-memory filesystems, the I/O requests do not go through the traditional I/O path. All the processes are managed directly by Complete Fair Scheduler (CFS) and periodic scheduler in the run-time system [8]. CFS is designed to be fair to every task in the system in terms of CPU time, it lacks information of other system resource status such as bandwidth, as a result, bus contention arises due to the inefficient scheduling decision.

---

[1] http://en.wikipedia.org/wiki/Completely_Fair_Scheduler.

2.3   Problem Definition

Given a working set of n tasks consisting of MA-intensive and Non-MA-intensive tasks on a system using in-memory filesystem, $WS = \{t_1, t_2, \cdots, t_n\}$, for each task i, the execution time is C_i (measured in time slices) when this task is running alone with all available resources, the average memory bandwidth requirement of task i at time slice j is b_{ij} for each j in C_i. We assume that there is no data dependence among the tasks and that all the tasks are released simultaneously, which means that they are all ready to be scheduled at time slice 1. There are M processors in the system. The maximum available system bandwidth is B. Our goal is to find a task schedule such that the completion time of the working set is minimized with memory bandwidth constraints.

3   Motivational Example

In this section, we first present an experimental result that shows bus bandwidth contention can slow down other system processes even when there are free processors available. Then, we give a motivational example to show Complete Fair Scheduler (CFS) is ineffective to schedule tasks with intensive in-memory file accesses.

In a system with 4 logical processors, we ran one instance of *stream* program and one instance of *tar* program. The *stream* is modified to write a memory buffer to files located on ext4 filesystem on disk and an in-memory filesystem PMFS. *Stream* is memory-hungry, it can take up as much bandwidth as possible. The *tar* is co-scheduled with *stream*. When *stream* writes files on disk, the average utilization of the 4 processors is 23 %, 48 %, 1 %, and 2 % respectively, the average bandwidth utilization is 36 %. However, when *stream* writes files on PMFS, the average utilization of the processors is 85 %, 31 %, 1 %, and 2 %, the average bandwidth utilization is 92 %. As a consequence, *tar* is slowed down by 26 %. It shows that when CPU resource is still available, memory bus has already been fully occupied, which causes the slowdown of *tar*.

We now present a motivational example to show the weakness of CFS when there exists memory bandwidth contention. We refer the schedule with minimal completion time as the optimal schedule. Assume a system is equipped with 4 processors and the maximum bandwidth the system can provide is normalized to 15, there are 5 independent tasks in the working set, the execution time and bandwidth requirement of each task at every time slice is depicted in Table 1. Further assume that all the tasks are released simultaneously, and they are ready to be scheduled at time slice 1.

Because CFS tries to ensure that every task can get a fair share of CPU time without considering system resource usage, it is very likely that at some scheduling points, CFS chooses the tasks whose accumulated bandwidth requirement exceeds the maximum available system bandwidth, leading to system performance degradation caused by memory bandwidth contention. Besides, CFS does not put a processor to idle state if there are ready-to-run tasks in the system. We argue that this scheduling policy is not always suitable when the system memory

Table 1. Bandwidth requirement of each task

	Time slice					
Task	1	2	3	4	5	6
1	8	7				
2	6	9	3	1		
3	7	4	9	5		
4	3	5	1			
5	1	2	1	2	1	1

bus has already saturated. Figure 3 shows one possible scheduling sequence of CFS and the corresponding optimal scheduling sequence.

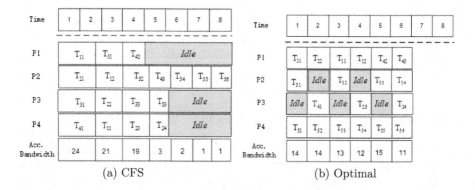

(a) CFS　　　　　　　　　　　(b) Optimal

Fig. 3. One possible schedule sequence and the optimal schedule sequence. The maximum bandwidth of the system is 15, CFS needs 8 time slices to finish execution of the given working set, while the optimal schedule takes only 6 time slices.

In Fig. 3, T_{ij} means the jth time slice of task i is selected to run. Since there are 4 processors available, when the working set is released, CFS randomly chooses ready tasks regardless of the bandwidth requirement of the selected tasks, so in the first four time slices, the accumulated bandwidth requirement exceeds the maximum system bandwidth. We assume that CFS continues to select the previously selected tasks so that they can get enough bandwidth resource to finish the work in the corresponding time slices. For simplicity, we further assume that the needed time slices linearly increase with accumulated bandwidth requirement. This assumption does not hold in real-world applications, because the context switch overhead and bandwidth contention can contribute extra time to the execution time of the work load. After the 5th time slice, four tasks have finished execution, the system is only lightly loaded with one task, leaving large part of the bandwidth and processor resource unused. To sum up, when the working set is scheduled with CFS, 8 time slices are required.

For the optimal schedule illustrated in Fig. 3(b), the tasks with low-bandwidth consumption are co-scheduled with high-bandwidth consumption tasks. When the memory bus saturates, we put one processor to idle state to avoid bandwidth contention, even there are ready tasks. In other words, we can schedule the working set with 6 time slices, and the optimal schedule can guarantee that there is no bandwidth contention at every time slice. The accumulated bandwidth requirement is evenly distributed among the execution of the working set.

From the motivational example presented above, it is clear that CFS cannot work effectively when the system memory bandwidth saturates. For example, in high performance computing and big data applications, when large data sets are moved to memory and an in-memory filesystem is used to manage the data, all the file operations (read and write) are delegated to data accesses through memory bus. When large number of tasks are accessing files on in-memory filesystem intensively, some tasks can saturate the memory bus, causing significant bandwidth contention. In this case, other system processes can not get a fair share of system bandwidth resource, thus slowing down their execution. In Sect. 5, We will present the experiment result to show how serious the problem can be. Based on the above analysis, we argue that new scheduling policy should be proposed to mitigate the bandwidth contention caused by intensive in-memory file accesses.

4 Bandwidth-Fit (B-Fit) Algorithm

In this section, we discuss the scheduling policy that must be considered when designing new scheduling strategy for systems including intensive in-memory file accesses processes. Then, we present the proposed scheduling algorithm.

According to the problem definition, Integer Linear Programming (ILP) can be used to get the optimal schedule with minimized completion time of a set of processes. While the ILP solution can give the optimum schedule for our problem, the exponential running time makes it unpractical to solve big problems. Thus, we propose a heuristic algorithm that runs in linear time, it is effective to produce a schedule close to the optimal result.

The essential idea of this algorithm is to select appropriate processes according to their memory bandwidth requirements and remaining execution time, so that the tasks with longest execution time can always be selected to run and the memory bus does not saturate during the next execution quantum. Besides, the scheduling algorithm should not favor one kind of process against another. This requirement is especially important when a system has many processes accessing in-memory filesystem, because those processes can easily saturate the memory bus, thus making other processes can not get a fair share of system resources.

In order to make intelligent scheduling decisions and ensure fairness among all the tasks, the scheduler maintains the following three queues:

1. Scheduling Sequences. This queue is used to hold the scheduling sequence of everytime slice, when a task is added to this queue, a processor can be allocated to it for execution in the next time slice.

Algorithm 4.1. B-Fit Algorithm

Input: Working set (WS), the execution time and bandwidth requirement (bwr) of
  each time slice of the task in the working set; the number of processors in the
  system M; the waiting threshold wt; the maximum system bandwidth B.

Output: The task schedule sequence (SS) with minimal final execution time.

1: Remaining bandwidth $rb \leftarrow B$
2: Number of selected tasks $n \leftarrow 0$
3: Ready Queue $RQ \leftarrow \phi$
4: Priority Waiting Queue $PWQ \leftarrow \phi$
5: **while** WS is not empty **do**
6:      Choose tasks from Priority Waiting Queue. (Algorithm 4.2)
7:      Sort tasks in Ready Queue according to the remaining execution time (ret) in
        descending order.
8:      Choose tasks from Ready Queue. (Algorithm 4.3)
9: **end while**

---

2. Ready Queue. When the working set is first released, all the tasks are put
   into this queue. All the tasks in this queue are sorted in descending order of
   remaining execution time. When the scheduling decision is made, the first task
   in this queue is always selected as long as there is enough system bandwidth.
3. Priority Waiting Queue. This queue is used to guarantee the fairness of the
   scheduling algorithm. When the system memory bus has saturated, no tasks
   can be picked up even if there are processors available. At every scheduling
   step, a running counter is kept for every task to denote how long the tasks in
   the waiting queue have been waiting. When this counter reaches a threshold
   value, this task is put into the priority waiting queue. The tasks in the priority
   queue have higher priority over other tasks in the ready queue, the scheduler
   first tries to pick up tasks in this queue to make tasks free of starvation.

   Algorithm 4.1. shows the strategy to get the desired schedule sequences. Algorithms 4.2. and 4.3. chooses tasks from Priority Waiting Queue and Ready Queue
respectively.

   At every scheduling step, any processor can be allocated to a certain task in
scheduling sequence. It is guaranteed that the accumulative bandwidth requirement does not exceed the maximum available system bandwidth. It is likely that
in some scheduling steps, not all the processors are loaded with tasks. In these
cases, the unused processors stay in idle state. By favoring the task with longest
execution time, we can get the minimum execution time of the working set.

   The B-Fit Algorithm is efficient in determining the schedule sequence of the
working set. It takes $O(n \log n)$ time to sort the ready queue and $O(M)$ time to
pick up tasks at every scheduling step. M is usually upper-bounded by constant.

5   Experiment

This section consists of two parts. The first part presents the experiments conducted to show how serious the memory bandwidth contention problem can be.

Algorithm 4.2. ChooseTaskFromPriorityWaitingQueue

Input: Working set (WS), the execution time and bandwidth requirement (bwr) of
    each time slice of the task in the working set; the number of processors in the
    system M; the maximum system bandwidth B.
Output: Task schedule sequence (SS).
 1: Remaining bandwidth $rb \leftarrow B$
 2: Number of selected tasks $n \leftarrow 0$
 3: **for** all task $t \in PWQ$ **do**
 4:    **if** $n < M$ and $rb > 0$ **then**
 5:      Move task t to SS
 6:      Update $t.ret$, rb, n
 7:      **if** $t.ret == 0$ **then**
 8:        Remove task t from WS
 9:      **end if**
10:      Update $t.waiting\_times$
11:    **end if**
12: **end for**

Algorithm 4.3. ChooseTaskFromReadyQueue

Input: Working set (WS), the execution time and bandwidth requirement (bwr) of
    each time slice of the task in the working set; the number of processors in the
    system M; the waiting threshold wt, the maximum system bandwidth B.
Output: Task schedule sequence (SS).
 1: Remaining bandwidth $rb \leftarrow B$
 2: Number of selected tasks $n \leftarrow 0$
 3: **for** all task $t \in RQ$ **do**
 4:    **if** $n < M$ and $rb > 0$ **then**
 5:      **if** More than one task has the same ret **then**
 6:        Move the previously executed task t to SS
 7:      **else**
 8:        Move task t from RQ to SS
 9:      **end if**
10:      Update $t.ret$, rb, n
11:      **if** $t.ret == 0$ **then**
12:        Remove task t from WS
13:      **end if**
14:    **end if**
15:    Update $t.waiting\_times$
16:    **if** $t.waiting\_times \geq wt$ **then**
17:      Move task t from SWS to PWQ
18:    **end if**
19: **end for**

The second part gives the results of evaluating the effectiveness of the proposed
scheduling algorithm, followed by detailed discussion of the experimental results.

5.1 Experimental Setup

The evaluation and analysis are performed on a dual core Intel Core i3 machine. The processor is configured to enable hardware hyperthreading and runs at 3.30 GHz. Each processor has 3 MB cache. This machine is equipped with 16 GB of main memory running at 1333 MHz and a 500 GB hard-disk running at 7200 rpm. The operating system is Ubuntu 14.04 with 3.11.0 kernel. This machine has two dual-channel mode memory interfaces, the memory interface is 64 bits wide, so the theoretical maximum memory bandwidth[2] of this machine is roughly 21.3 GB/s. However, the sustained memory bandwidth reported by STREAM [9] benchmark is 13292.7 MB/s. The in-memory filesystem is PMFS [5], the blocksize is 4 KB, we configured the PMFS to use 10 GB main memory.

5.2 Challenge of Using In-memory Filesystem

To investigate the impact of intensive in-memory file accesses imposed to the other system processes, we conducted extensive experiments to show the performance degradation when the system was under different degree of bandwidth contention. We created multiple working sets consisting of different instances of MA-intensive processes (*stream*) and Non-MA-intensive processes (*gcc*). The MA-intensive processes were designed to (1) continually read large chunk of data from PMFS to user buffer, (2) modify the buffer contents, and (3) write the buffer to PMFS. The aggregated data size varies from 1 GB to 64 GB. The Non-MA-intensive tasks read source files from disk to compile a *busybox* image with the default configuration. All the working sets were executed 5 times, and the completion time were averaged to get the average completion time of the working set. Figures 4 and 5 show the completion time of the working sets.

The experimental results show that when the number of MA-intensive processes is small (less than 4) and the data size doesn't exceed 16 GB, the MA-intensive processes have little impact to other processes. However, when there are more than two MA-intensive processes and the data size reaches more than 32 GB, the completion time of Non-MA-processes increases significantly. To a large extent, this is due to the severe bandwidth contention saturates the memory bus and CPU resource, making the Non-MA-intensive processes difficult to get a fair share of system resource. Because the Non-MA-intensive processes can relinquish CPU when reading files from ext4 filesystem, but the MA-intensive processes continue to execute until they are interrupted by the timer interrupt when their time slices are used up. Since MA-intensive processes are also CPU-intensive, the contention on CPU and bandwidth resource leads to the slowdown of the Non-MA-intensive processes.

5.3 Effectiveness of the Proposed Methods

We modified the *stream* benchmark program to allocate memory from PMFS using *mmap*, directing all the memory transactions to PMFS. Different instances

---

[2] http://en.wikipedia.org/wiki/Memory_bandwidth.

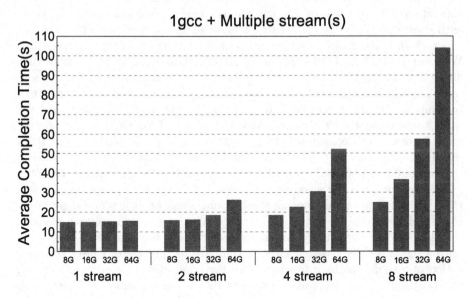

Fig. 4. Completion time of *gcc* when 1 instance of *gcc* is running with multiple *stream* benchmark.

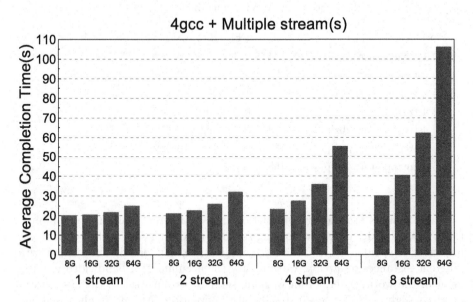

Fig. 5. Completion time of *gcc* when 4 instances of *gcc* is running with multiple *stream* benchmark.

of *stream* program were used to cause different degree of memory bandwidth contention. We chose several common data-intensive applications to co-schedule with *stream* program. We use *tar* to compress a Linux kernel source file directory to a tarball, this directory contains 2836 subdirectories and 44002 different files. We use *bzip* to extract a Linux source tarball, this tarball contains more than 40000 files and takes up around 500 MB disk space when extracted. We use *gcc* to compile a *busybox* image with the default configuration, there are about 2000 files to compile and link to get the final image. To get the profile information of the tasks, we use the CPU Performance Monitoring Unit (PMU) and *perf*[3] to get the memory bandwidth consumption information of every time slice [10,11]. PMU uses hardware counters to record transactions on memory bus of every process, this technique can be used to predict memory bandwidth usage of program [12].

We implemented the scheduling algorithm as a user-level program, on top of CFS. This program sends blocking/unblocking signals to the selected processes to control the execution of the applications. When a process receives a blocking signal, it invokes the *pause()* system call, which puts this process to sleep state until a signal is delivered that either terminates the process or causes the invocation of a signal-catching function[4]. All the applications have to register into this program so that it is possible to send the controlling signals to them. This program remains idle for most of its execution, and is waked up every 100 ms by timer interrupt, it sends signals to the corresponding processes according to the schedule sequences constructed by the heuristic algorithm.

Table 2. Performance comparison among different scheduling scheme.

Working set	CFS	B-Fit	ILP	B-Fit vs. CFS	B-Fit vs. ILP
(1) 1stream, 1tar, 1bzip, 1gcc	31	23.4	22.8	24.52 %	2.63 %
(2) 2stream, 1tar, 1bzip, 1gcc	36	28	25	22.22 %	12.00 %
(3) 2stream, 2tar, 2bzip, 2gcc	60	40	37	33.33 %	8.11 %
(4) 4stream, 1tar, 1bzip, 1gcc	52	36.6	40	25.77 %	−3.5 %
(5) 4stream, 2tar, 2bzip, 2gcc	73	51.2	49.2	29.87 %	−4 %
(6) 8stream, 2tar, 2bzip, 2gcc	113	94	-	16.81 %	-
(7) 8stream, 4tar, 4bzip, 4gcc	155	133	-	27.10 %	-

Table 2 shows the average completion time of different working set combinations. We defined 7 different working set, every working set consists of different instances of *stream, tar, bzip* and *gcc* applications. By loading the system with different instances of *stream*, we can vary the accumulative bandwidth requirement of the working set. From working set 1 to working set 7, the system can undergo slight to very severe bandwidth contention. All the applications are

---

[3] https://perf.wiki.kernel.org/index.php/Main_Page.
[4] http://linux.die.net/man/2/pause.

released at the same time, the waiting time threshold is set to 1 time slice (100ms). In all combinations, the heuristic algorithm and ILP can both reduce the execution time by 10 % to 30 %. For the first three working sets, ILP finds the optimal solution by searching all the combination of tasks. While for the fourth and fifth working set, the inputs are too large for the ILP to get the optimal result at a reasonable time, we ran the LINGO program for three hours and used the intermediate feasible solution as the ILP result. When the working set takes longer to finish execution, the ILP can not find a feasible schedule at a reasonable time, as in the last two working sets. In all cases, the heuristic algorithm can achieve near optimal results as ILP schedule.

6 Conclusion and Future Work

In this paper, we solve bus contention problem in a system using in-memory filesystem. We argue that Linux native scheduler CFS can not always produce the optimal schedule when the system memory bandwidth saturates. We present a heuristic algorithm that can produce schedule close to the optimal results. The proposed scheme was implemented in linux system as a user-level demon, we plan to incorporate the scheduling algorithm in linux kernel to enhance CFS, with the hope of posing less overhead to the whole system. Besides, we are going to evaluate the proposed approach with Big Data applications.

Acknowledgments. This work is partially supported by National 863 Program 2013AA013202, 2015AA015304, Chongqing High-Tech Research Program cstc2014yy kfB40007, NSFC 61472052, NSFC 61173014.

References

1. Condit, J., Nightingale, E.B., Frost, C., Ipek, E., Lee, B., Burger, D., Coetzee, D.: Better I/O through byte-addressable, persistent memory. In: Proceedings of the ACM SIGOPS 22nd Symposium on Operating Systems Principles, SOSP 2009, pp. 133–146. ACM (2009)
2. Wu, X., Reddy, A.L.N.: SCMFS: a file system for storage class memory. In: Proceedings of 2011 International Conference for High Performance Computing, Networking, Storage and Analysis, SC 2011. ACM (2011)
3. DeBrabant, J., Pavlo, A., Tu, S., Stonebraker, M., Zdonik, S.: Anti-caching: a new approach to database management system architecture. Proc. VLDB Endow. **6**(14), 1942–1953 (2013)
4. Kallman, R., Kimura, H., Natkins, J., Pavlo, A., Rasin, A., Zdonik, S., Jones, E.P.C., Madden, S., Stonebraker, M., Zhang, Y., Hugg, J., Abadi, D.J.: H-Store: a high-performance, distributed main memory transaction processing system. Proc. VLDB Endow. **1**(2), 1496–1499 (2008)
5. Dulloor, S.R., Kumar, S., Keshavamurthy, A., Lantz, P., Reddy, D., Sankaran, R., Jackson, J.: System software for persistent memory. In: Proceedings of the Ninth European Conference on Computer Systems, EuroSys 2014, pp. 15:1–15:15. ACM, New York (2014)

6. Zhuge, Q., Shi, L., Sha, E., Chen, X.: Designing an efficient persistent in-memory file system (2014). http://cacs.cqu.edu.cn/wp-content/uploads/2015/02/TR-2014-02-Designing-an-efficient-persistent-in-memory-file-system.pdf

7. Zhuge, Q., Shi, L., Jiang, W., Sha, E., Chen, X.: Designing an efficient persistent in-memory file system. In: 2015 IEEE Non-Volatile Memory Systems and Applications Symposium (NVMSA), August 2015

8. Yu, Y.J., Shin, D.I., Shin, W., Song, N.Y., Choi, J.W., Kim, H.S., Eom, H., Yeom, H.Y.: Optimizing the block I/O subsystem for fast storage devices. ACM Trans. Comput. Syst. **32**(2), 6:1–6:48 (2014)

9. Introduction to STREAM benchmark. http://www.cs.virginia.edu/stream/ref.html

10. Inam, R., Sjodin, M., Jagemar, M.: Bandwidth measurement using performance counters for predictable multicore software. In: 2012 IEEE 17th Conference on Emerging Technologies Factory Automation (ETFA), pp. 1–4, September 2012

11. Intel, Intel 64 and IA-32 Architectures Software Developer's Manual. http://www.intel.com/content/www/us/en/processors/architectures-software-developer-manuals.html

12. Wang, W., Dey, T., Davidson, J., Soffa, M.: Dramon: predicting memory bandwidth usage of multi-threaded programs with high accuracy and low overhead. In: 2014 IEEE 20th International Symposium on High Performance Computer Architecture (HPCA), pp. 380–391, February 2014

GPU-Accelerated Algorithm for Fast Computation of Biomolecular Isotopic Envelopes

Jingpeng Wang, Jie Huang$^{(\boxtimes)}$, Kaijie Xiao, and Zhixin Tian

School of Software Engineering, Tongji University, Shanghai 201804, China
`jingpeng.wang@outlook.com,`
`{huangjie,3852xkj,zhixintian}@tongji.edu.cn`

Abstract. To accommodate the new features of modern protein mass spectra with Nobel-prize-winner electrospray ionization, Zhixin Tian, et al. developed isotopic Mass-to-charge ratio and Envelope Fingerprinting (iMF) algorithm for in situ interpretation and database search of protein tandem mass spectra. The creation of the customized theoretical database of both proteins and their dissociation fragment ions requires efficient computation of isotopic envelopes. This paper presents a GPU-accelerated algorithm for rapid computation of isotopic envelopes on NVIDIA Compute Unified Device Architecture (CUDA) platform, which can achieve 17.6 speedup when computing isotopic distributions of 512 fragment ions with mass 27 kda on average on IBM Power 8 with NVIDIA Tesla K40 m. Through optimizations on both CUDA memory access and stream scheduling, we find out a proper solution with chunk size = 32 in each kernel and double buffer cache can just hide the latency of memory and solution with chunk size = 64 can achieve about 160 speedup on the same experiment environment. The experimental results show that parallel algorithm with GPU and multiple optimization strategies provide an effective method with high performance to calculate isotopic envelopes.

Keywords: GPU · CUDA · CUDA stream scheduling · Isotopic distribution · iMEF

1 Introduction

Since the mass measurement of an electron by Thomson [1], mass spectrometers have been used to analyze small inorganic, organic and large biological molecules. For these molecules, mass spectrometers measure their isotopic envelopes (iEs). Every iE consists of a certain number of isotopic peaks due to the presence of heavy isotopes. For large biological molecules (such as proteins), which are often analyzed by electrospray ionization (ESI) and carry multiple charges, the abundance of the isotopic peak is often very low due to the increased probability of multiple heavy isotopes.

Isotopic envelopes are directly used without deisotoping to identify biological molecules. An algorithm, isotopic mass-to-charge ratio (m/z) and envelope fingerprinting (iMEF) [2–4], was implemented in the ProteinGoggle search engine for top-down intact protein database searching and protein identification from tandem mass spectra [5].

© Springer International Publishing Switzerland 2015
G. Wang et al. (Eds.): ICA3PP 2015, Part II, LNCS 9529, pp. 581–591, 2015.
DOI: 10.1007/978-3-319-27122-4_40

However, the process of isotopic Mass-to-charge ratio and Envelope Fingerprinting (iMF) is very time consuming, especially the calculation of isotopic distribution of the molecules from ionization will cost lots of time when faced with high flux large molecules or fragment ions. This will hinder the application of top-down iEF [6] and related database searching. Considering that there exist lots of addition and multiplication in the algorithm, so it is very suitable for GPU acceleration.

During the past few years, graphical processing unit (GPU) has evolved into a flexible platform with highly parallelization for general computing. GPGPU researchers have achieved over an order of magnitude speedup over modern CPUs on some non-graphics problems. Initially, GPUs were programmed by low-level languages which restricts its application as computing workhorse. But with the release of the Compute Unified Device Architecture (CUDA) [7] of NVIDIA and the advent of GPUs consisting of multi-core processor with tremendous computational horsepower, programmers can use its parallel computing capabilities in real applications. Because the calculation of isotopic envelopes includes lots of addition and multiplication. It is very suitable to accelerate with GPU.

The main contribution of this paper is using CUDA and optimization strategies to accelerate the algorithm to calculate isotopic distributions. The architecture of this paper is as follows: Sect. 2 concentrates on the introduction of the algorithm to calculate isotopic distributions for iMEF. Section 3 mainly introduces the parallelization and optimization for the algorithm with CUDA. In Sect. 4 we conducted several experiments, collected related results and analyzed the corresponding results. The last section is conclusion and future work.

2 Algorithm to Calculate Isotopic Distributions for iMEF

2.1 Isotopic Peaks Distributions of Individual Elements

As a typical example, given an organic molecule

$$C_{1228}H_{1964}N_{340}O_{353}S_{13}$$

In this procedure, we firstly need to acquire the isotopic distribution of C_{1228}, H_{1964}, N_{340}, O_{353} and S_{13}.

The isotope distribution of individual elements in this chemical formula is generally acquired through polynomial expansion method. The algorithm is an iterative one based on polynomial expansion [8]. For a given molecular formula consist of isotopes of a single element, the isotopic distribution is described by the following product of polynomials:

$$(a_1 + a_2 + a_3 + \cdots)^m$$

where a_1, a_2, a_3, etc. represent the individual isotopes of the element in the molecule formula, and the exponents m are the number of atoms of this kind of element. Therefore, its isotopic distribution can be given by

$$(C^{12} + C^{13})^{1228}, (H^1 + H^2)^{1964}, (N^{14} + N^{15})^{340}, (O^{16} + O^{17} + O^{18})^{353} \text{ and}$$
$$(S^{32} + S^{33} + S^{34} + S^{36})^{353}$$

If the polynomial is fully expanded, it will consists of massive terms, the actual number of all the items will excess the maximum limit of computer when the input molecule is large enough, and thus some items need to be removed in each iterative step. The following is the detail procedure of the algorithm:

Initially, for a molecule consist of only one atom of element X, and it has its own isotopic distribution $\{X\} = \{X_1, X_2, \dots, X_m\}$. Then when another atom of element Y is added onto the molecule, assume its isotopic distribution $\{Y\} = \{Y_1, Y_2, \dots, Y_n\}$ and X and Y can be atoms of same elements, the peaks from $\{X\}$ and the peaks of $\{Y\}$ will be combined independently. Each peak X_i in set $\{X\}$ and each peak Y_j in set $\{Y\}$ can combine into a new peak, the mass of this peak is the sum of the mass of X_i and Y_j, the abundance of this peak is the product of the abundance of X_i and Y_j. The peaks combined from peak set $\{X\}$ and $\{Y\}$ form a new isotopic distribution $\{XY\}$ of the molecule XY.

Then, the generated isotopic distribution $\{XY\}$ will go through a merge operation, this step will traverse the entire generated peak set, and merge those peaks whose mass difference is less than K, which is usually set as $1.0 * 10^{-8}$. Once the mass difference between two peaks is less than the threshold value K, these two peaks will be merged into a new peak. The mass and possibility in this peak can be calculated according to the formula below (assume the mass of peak 2 is larger than the mass of peak 1).

$$M_P = M_{P1} + (M_{P2} - M_{P1}) * \frac{P_{P2}}{P_{P1} + P_{P2}}$$

$$P_P = P_{P1} + P_{P2}$$

where M_{P1} and M_{P2}, represent the mass of peak 1 and peak 2 respectively, and P_{P1} and P_{P2} represent the abundance of peak 1 and peak 2 respectively. M_P and P_P is the mass and abundance of the generated peak in merge manipulation.

At the end of this iteration, the isotopic distribution $\{XY\}$ will be sorted in a descending order of peaks' abundance, then we select top N (N is a threshold value, defined according to expected computational accuracy) peaks and remove residue other peaks. The top N peaks will form a new isotopic distribution of chemical formula XY, these peaks can be used in the next iteration.

Then in the final step of this algorithm, when all of the iterations are completed, the program need to filtrate the retrieved isotopic distribution, find out the peak whose abundance is the highest in the distribution as a benchmark, calculate the relative intensity of each peak inside the distribution according to the benchmark peak. The relative intensity RI can be calculated according to the formula below (P_P represents the abundance a peak P, P_{Pmax} represents the max abundance of the peak in the distribution).

$$RI_P = \frac{P_P}{P_{Pmax}}$$

If RI_P is lower than a threshold R (usually set as $1.0 * 10^{-4}$), the peak will be removed from the final isotopic distribution.

Generally, the isotopic distribution of individual elements has been acquired and stored in database (we use IBM Relational Database2 in experiment), which means that when we need to use these data, we do not need to compute them again, and also the size of these data is not large and will not cost much storage space.

Through this step of algorithm, we can get the isotopic distributions of individual elements in a given molecule or ion's formula.

2.2   Independent Assortment

We still take organic molecule $C_{1228}H_{1964}N_{340}O_{353}S_{13}$ as an example, in this step, for acquiring its isotopic distribution, we need to get the combined result by the independent assortment between the isotopic distributions of C_{1228}, H_{1964}, N_{340}, O_{353} and S_{13} calculated from step 1, here we denoted the isotopic distributions are $\{X_1, X_2, \ldots, X_m\}$, $\{Y_1, Y_2, \ldots, Y_n\}$, $\{Z_1, Z_2, \ldots, Z_o\}$, $\{U_1, U_2, \ldots, U_P\}$, $\{V_1, V_2, \ldots, V_q\}$. The independent assortment among different isotopic distributions is an operation to build a new array of isotopic peaks, the mass of each peak is

$$m\left(X_a\right) + m\left(Y_b\right) + m\left(Z_c\right) + m\left(U_d\right) + m(V_e)$$
$$(a \in (1,m), b \in (1,n), c \in (1,o), d \in (1,p), e \in (1,q))$$

The abundance of each peak is

$$p\left(X_a\right) * p\left(Y_b\right) * p\left(Z_c\right) * p\left(U_d\right) * p(V_e)$$
$$(a \in (1,m), b \in (1,n), c \in (1,o), d \in (1,p), e \in (1,q))$$

In the formula, m is the mass of isotopic peaks of individual elements, p is its abundance. When we retrieve the result of the independent assortment, repeat the filter operation in Sect. 2.1, and we could get the isotopic Mass-to-charge ratio (m/z) of the intact

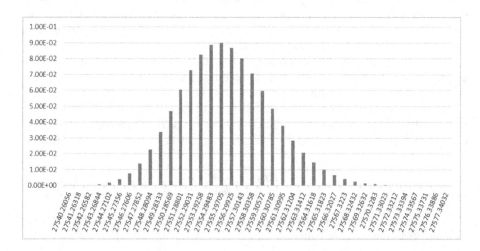

Fig. 1.   The X axis represents the mass of one peak while the Y axis represents the abundance

molecule. Below is the result of Mass-to-charge ratio (m/z) of organic molecule $C_{1228}H_{1964}N_{340}O_{353}S_{13}$ with charge state +1 (Fig. 1).

3   Parallel Implementation and Optimization with CUDA

In the experiment, the independent assortment among different isotopic distributions is a very time-costing procedure. In the process, there exists lots of addition and multiplication, which is a very suitable case for GPU acceleration.

Therefore, we conduct our experiments through allocating threads and blocks in GPU with CUDA APIs, here we use JCuda [9] wrapper to invoke CUDA kernels. Each GPU's block is responsible for calculating one chemical molecule's independent assortment among its different individual elements' isotopic peak distributions. After the manipulation in GPU, we filter out the peaks whose relative intensity is lower than 10^{-4} of the peak with maximum and merge the peaks whose mass difference is less than 10^{-8} and retrieve isotopic Mass-to-charge ratio (m/z).

First, we copy the mass and abundance data of each kind of individual element onto the GPU device, such as the mass and abundance of C_a, H_b, N_c, O_d, S_e, here we need to assume the largest possible number of a, b, c, d and e that may appear in the chemical formula, meanwhile, our copy operation will include all the mass and abundance data of $\{C_1C_2 \dots C_{amax}\}, \{H_1H_2 \dots H_{bmax}\}, \{N_1N_2 \dots N_{cmax}\}, \{O_1O_2 \dots O_{dmax}\}, \{S_1S_2 \dots S_{emax}\}$.

Then, we will need to denote each chemical formula in GPU, in this case, we mark a chemical formula such $C_aH_bN_cO_dS_e$ as a tuple as (a, b, c, d, e), and then copy an array of this kind of tuples onto GPU device. Each block focus on calculating the assortment result of one molecule formula (represented by one tuple), and a multiple nested loops in assortment (Detail code can be seen in **Code.** 1, variable cMax, sMax, hMax, nMax, oMax is the number of isotopic peaks array of C_a, H_b, N_c, O_d, S_e respectively, variable **cMass, sMass, hMass, nMass, oMass** is the mass of isotopic peaks of C_a, H_b, N_c, O_d, S_e respectively, variable **cP, sP, hP, nP, oP** is the abundance of isotopic peaks of C_a, H_b, N_c, O_d, S_e respectively, variable **massOutput** and **pOutput** is the mass and abundance of isotopic peaks of $C_aH_bN_cO_dS_e$) can be dismantled partially on each thread in the block.

Finally, the computing result will be transmitted from device to host, the size of result consist of peaks with mass and abundance data could be very large. For NVIDIA GTX 760 with 2 GB display memory, it can only calculate at most 512 chemical molecule's independent assortment in one kernel function.

Through a basic implementation on GPU with CUDA, we conduct several experiments on GPU. Firstly, we collect results on computing time of single GPU kernels and I/O time cost, here when the kernel executes once it will compute the assortment among isotopic peaks distribution of 512 molecules whose mass is about 27 kda. Through statistics, the time cost on each kernel is about 1.351 s on average on IBM Power 8 with NVIDIA Tesla K40 m and the time cost on I/O is 150 ms.

Considering that time cost on kernel execution is very long and there exists memory latency which will lead to GPU kernel delay, we tried some optimization to solve these problems, such as CUDA shared memory access optimization and CUDA stream scheduling.

```
Begin:
    int c=0;
    int sum=cMax*sMax*hMax*nMax*oMax;
    int x = blockIdx.x;
    for(int i=0;i!=cMax;i++){
        for(int j=0;j!=sMax;j++){
            for(int k=0;k!=hMax;k++){
                for(int l=0;l!=nMax;l++){
                    for(int m=0;m!=oMax;m++){
                        massOutput[sum*x+c] =
                            cMass[i]+sMass[j]+hMass[k]+nMass[l]+oMass[m]+
                            5*electronMass;
                        pOutput[sum*x+c]=cP[i]*sP[j]*hP[k]*nP[l]*oP[m];
                        c++;
                    }
                }
            }
        }
    }
End
```

Code. 1. The detail code to compute one isotopic envelope in a GPU block

3.1 CUDA Shared Memory Optimized

During the assortment among different isotopic distributions of individual elements, the thread in each block need to access (including reading and writing) the mass and abundance data on global memory, which causes the kernel execution cost a lot of time. Therefore, we use shared memory in kernel function to as a local storage for each molecule's isotopic distributions of its individual elements, look forward to accelerating the access of GPU memory.

According to NVIDIA's documentation [10], on-chip shared memory is much faster than local and global memory. Its latency is roughly $100 \times$ lower than uncached global memory latency. Shared memory is allocated per thread block, so all threads in the block have access to the same shared memory. Threads can access data in shared memory loaded from global memory by other threads within the same thread block. Hence we optimized our program with shared memory to accelerate the access of GPU memory.

We collect the time cost of CUDA shared memory optimized program. Through statistics, the time cost on each kernel is about 121 ms on average while the time cost on I/O is 151.15 ms on computing the assortment among isotopic distributions of individual elements of 512 molecules (mass is about 27 kda) on average on IBM Power 8 with NVIDIA Tesla K40. Obviously, the time cost of CUDA shared memory optimized program is much faster than the GPU program with global memory access.

3.2   CUDA Stream Scheduling

CUDA provides a programming model called CUDA stream with the ability to schedule multiple CUDA kernels simultaneously. One CUDA stream can encapsulate multiple kernels, and they have to be scheduled strictly following a particular order. However, kernels from multiple streams can be scheduled to run concurrently. The main purpose of using CUDA streams is to hide the memory latency: when kernel A is loading/writing data, kernel B can occupy the cores for computation. As a result, the cores in the Multi-processor reach better utilization.

In our previous program with CUDA shared memory optimized, we can find the time cost on kernel execution is less than the time cost on I/O on computing the assortment among isotopic distributions of individual elements of 512 molecules (mass is about 27 kda), which indicates that with CUDA stream scheduling applied, we can overlap the time cost on kernel execution and the time cost on I/O like a pipeline, meanwhile hide the memory latency and implements kernel concurrency. The snapshot of NVIDIA Visual Profiler on multiple kernels execution with default stream can be seen as follows (Fig. 2).

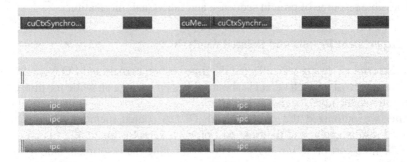

Fig. 2. The snapshot of GPU serial kernels from NVIDIA visual profiler.

From the snapshot, we can see memory latency exists during the process of data transmission from device to host. But because of that I/O time cost from device to host is longer than kernel execution, we conduct another solution to divide the computing of the assortment among isotopic distributions of individual elements of 512 molecules into several kernel chunks to find out a proper segmentation solution to satisfy that I/O time cost on data transmission from device to host is just equivalent to the time cost on a kernel execution.

Explicit chunk size we set in our experiment is 32, 64, 128, 256, and through the result of experiment we could find 32 is the proper chunk size which just satisfy that I/O time cost on data transmission from device to host is almost equivalent to the time cost on a kernel execution.

Besides this, we allocate 2 double buffers on host as pinned memory to store the GPU results (consist of large numbers of mass and abundance data) temporarily through Java nio APIs, with this channel, GPU device can communicate with host by Direct Memory Access (DMA), when one stream is executing kernels, the other one can write data to the buffers.

4   Experiment and Analysis

4.1   Experimental Environment Settings

The experimental settings of this paper are as follows:

- CPU:
  - IBM Power 8 Processor (20 cores, 160 threads in all)
- GPU:
  - NVIDIA Tesla K40 m
  - NVIDIA GTX 760 (The GPU is used to confirm the bottleneck of memory size)
- The version of Java virtual machine runtime is Java 8 Update 45.
- The version of CUDA runtime is 7.0.28.
- The operating system:
  - Power Linux.
- The dataset used in the experiment is from UniProt [11] and PeptideAtlas [12], which provides the scientific community with a comprehensive, high-quality and freely accessible resource of protein sequence and functional information.

4.2   Experiment Results and Related Analysis

In our experiment, firstly we collected the time cost on kernels and I/O from device to host. The time cost on each kernel is about 1.351 s on average on while the time cost on I/O is 150 ms, the time cost is 1.5 s in all.

After we optimized the program with CUDA shared memory mechanism, we collected results again, and the time cost on each kernel is about 121 ms on average while the time cost on I/O is 151.15 ms on computing the assortment among isotopic distributions of individual elements of 512 molecules (mass is about 27 kda), the time cost is 272.15 ms in all.

Then we use the CUDA shared memory optimized kernel function to further optimize with CUDA streams scheduling. We collected multiple results based on different chunk size (256, 128, 64, and 32). Detail snapshot taken from Visual Profiler can be seen in Figs. 3, 4, 5 and 6.

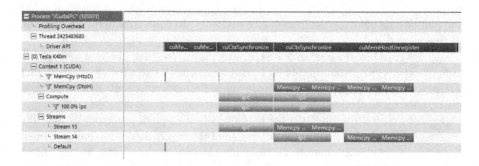

Fig. 3. Two CUDA streams encapsulated multiple kernels with chunk size = 256

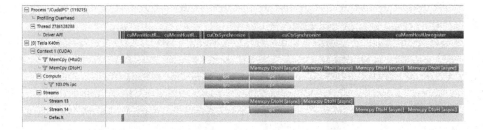

Fig. 4. Two CUDA streams encapsulated multiple kernels with chunk size = 128

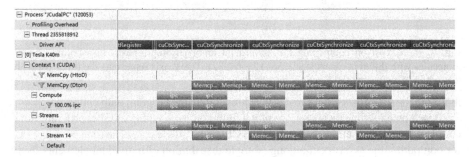

Fig. 5. Two CUDA streams encapsulated multiple kernels with chunk size = 64

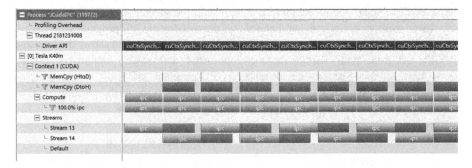

Fig. 6. Two CUDA streams encapsulated multiple kernels with chunk size = 32

From these snapshots, we can see that when chunk size = 32, the time cost during data transmission from device to host buffer is just less than the time cost on kernel executed once. Multiple kernels could execute concurrently on 2 streams, and the memory latency can be hided, at any time there always has one kernel executing and the other stream writing data to host pinned buffers.

We also compared the time cost on completing the assortment among isotopic peaks distribution of 512 molecules whose mass is about 27 kda in stream optimized programs with 4 different chunks respectively. The detailed time comparison can be seen in Fig. 7.

From the comparison of time cost on the same task, we could conclude that although the CUDA stream optimized program with chunk size = 32 can hide the memory latency completely, but its utilization of GPU is less than the program with chunk size = 64,

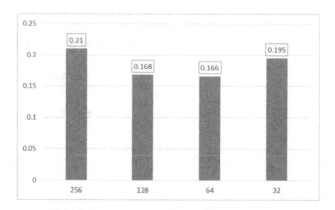

Fig. 7. Time cost on completing the assortment among isotopic peaks distribution of 512 molecules with different chunk size (256, 128, 64, 32). The Y axis represents the time cost with the unit in seconds, and the X axis is the chunk size.

therefore the time cost on the same task is longer than the program with chunk size = 64.

Based on experiments above, we plot a figure on the speedup of GPU programs and compared with serial algorithm on Power8 CPU with single core. The time cost on CPU for computing the assortment among isotopic distribution of individual elements from 512 molecules (whose mass is about 27 kda) is 26413 ms on average.

In the (Fig. 8), number 1 denotes the speedup of GPU program without shared memory optimized and stream optimized, number 2 represents the speedup of GPU program only with shared memory optimized, number 3 shows the speedup of GPU program with shared memory optimized and stream optimized (chunk size = 256), number 4 shows the speedup of GPU program with shared memory optimized and stream optimized (chunk size = 128), number 5 shows the speedup of GPU program with shared memory optimized and stream optimized (chunk size = 64), and number 6 shows the speedup of GPU program with shared memory optimized and stream optimized (chunk size = 32).

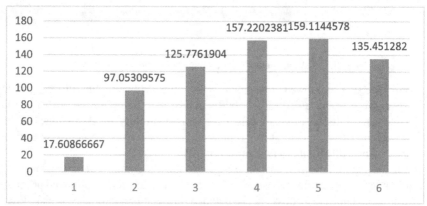

Fig. 8. The speedup of GPU programs

5 Conclusion and Future Work

According to the results from experiments, we can conclude that GPU accelerated algorithm to calculate isotopic distributions can dramatically improve the performance. With CUDA shared memory optimization, the GPU kernels accelerate its memory access, which brings a further improvement on the GPU program's performance. After that, scheduling CUDA streams and dividing the tasks into different chunk size can bring better performance, especially when the chunk size $= 64$, the speedup of GPU programs can reach about 160 compared with the time cost of serial algorithm on IBM Power 8 with NVIDIA Tesla K40m. It indicates that the powerful platform with GPU and multiple optimization strategy provide an effective method with high performance to calculate isotopic Mass-to-charge ratio for iMF, and make it possible to handle the bottleneck of iMEF.

Future work includes the aspects below but is not limited to: fully utilize the computing resources of Power 8 and implement cooperative parallelization between Power GPU and NVIDIA Tesla K40m; Using MPI to communicate between different CUDA contexts and collect the results of calculation on GPU clusters based on Open-POWER platform; Try to apply similar GPU solution and optimization for the searching and matching in isotopic Envelop Fingerprinting.

References

1. Thomson, J.J.: On the appearance of helium and neon in vacuum tubes. Science **37**, 360–364 (1913)
2. Li, L., Tian, Z.: Interpreting raw biological mass spectra using isotopic mass-to-charge ratio and envelope fingerprinting. Rapid Commun. Mass Spectrom. **27**(11), 1267–1277 (2013)
3. Tian, Z.: An analytical apparatus and method for biomolecule identification. Patent Application 201210146519.1 (People's Republic of China) (2012)
4. Tian, Z.: In: Proceedings of 60th ASMS Conference on Mass Spectrometry and Allied Topics, Vancouver, Canada, p. 107, 20–24 May 2012
5. Edwards, N.J.: Protein identification from tandem mass spectra by database searching. In: Bioinformatics for Comparative Proteomics, pp. 119–138. Humana Press, New York (2011)
6. Tian, Z., Tolic, N., Zhao, R., et al.: Enhanced top-down characterization of histone post-translational modifications. Genome Biol. **13**(10), R86 (2012)
7. Nvidia, C.U.D.A.: Zone (2015). https://developer.nvidia.com/cuda-zone
8. Yergey, J.A.: A general approach to calculating isotopic distributions for mass spectrometry. Int. J. Mass Spectrom. Ion Phys. **52**(2), 337–349 (1983)
9. JCUDA, Java. CUDA. http://www.jcuda.org/
10. Nvidia, C.: C Programming Guide v7.5. NVIDIA Corporation, Santa Clara (2015)
11. http://www.uniprot.org/
12. http://www.peptideatlas.org/

Cost-Efficient and Scalable Multicast Tree in Software Defined Networking

Shanshan Zhou, Hua Wang$^{(\boxtimes)}$, Shanwen Yi, and Fangjin Zhu

School of Computer Science and Technology, Shandong University,
Jinan 250101, China
ShanshanZhou@mail.sdu.edu.cn, wanghua@sdu.edu.cn

Abstract. Multicast can effectively reduce the cost of network resources, and Software Defined Networking (SDN) makes Steiner tree a feasible and promising way for multicast. However, multicast still suffers from a scalability problem when the number of groups is large since the flow table size is limited. In this paper, therefore, we propose the Degree-dependent Branch-node Weighted Steiner Tree (DBWST) problem, which is NP-hard. This problem aims to minimize the total cost of edges and branch nodes. The cost of a branch node is degree-dependent. We design an approximation algorithm, named Path-Vector based Harmony Search Algorithm (PVHS), to solve this problem. The path vector means a solution vector in a harmony and denotes the ordered set of nodes from source to a destination in the multicast tree. Globle and local optimization are combined appropriately. Simulation results on randomly generated topologies indicate that the trees obtained by PVHS are more cost-efficient and scalable over the existing ways.

Keywords: Multicast tree · Cost-efficient · Degree-dependent · Scalability · SDN

1 Introduction

In recent years, the technology of software defined networking (SDN) emerges and is becoming the leading technology behind many traffic engineering solutions. SDN is a network architecture where the data forwarding behavior of network elements is determined by a centralized controller. This separation of the control plane from the data plane allows network operators to gain a fine grain control over the actual way packets are forwarded, and thus better utilize their network [1]. SDN comprises two main components: SDN controller and SDN forwarding element [2]. SDN controller can adaptively set up different routes by centralized computation for traffic engineering [3] to improve the throughput of networks.

Multicasting is an efficient technique for point-to-multipoint (P2M) and multipoint-to-multipoint (M2M) communications and it can effectively reduce the cost of network resources. Multicast transmission is becoming more important due to the huge bandwidth consumption of various network-based applications, such as multi-party conferencing, distributed storage replication and software updates, to name a few [4, 5]. The central problem of multicast routing is to construct a minimum-cost

G. Wang et al. (Eds.): ICA3PP 2015, Part II, LNCS 9529, pp. 592–605, 2015.
DOI: 10.1007/978-3-319-27122-4_41

multicast tree that can satisfy certain QoS (quality of service) requirements, such as cost and delay. The base mathematical model of the minimum-cost multicast tree is the Steiner tree problem, which is NP-hard [6].

Since the construction of the Steiner tree is computation intensive and thus is difficult to be deployed as a distributed protocol on Internet. In contrast, it becomes feasible since the SDN controller can first finding the multicast tree and then store the forwarding information by adding flow entries to corresponding switches. The multicast routing states is maintained by a multicast routing table, which consists of a set of multicast forwarding entries directly used to control the forwarding of multicast packets in the on-tree switches. On the other hand, the SDN architecture can provide global visibility and the controller can find a better multicast tree leveraging the global topology information. SDN-enabled multicast mechanism is proposed in [7, 8].

However, multicast traffic engineering suffers from a scalability problem when the number of groups is large since the multicast algorithms require significant amount of memory space for maintaining the Multicast Forwarding Table (MFT) and high process time for executing the routing and forwarding decisions. In the SDN paradigm, considering the growing demands for a fast and efficient data plane, the general forwarding rules (e.g., OpenFlow [2, 9]) are implemented using expensive technology suchas TCAM (Trenary Content Aware Memory). In other words, the number of forwarding rules or the effective size of forwarding tables is limited in these expensive devices. Furthermore, once there are many small group multicasts with highly scattered receivers, each switch may consume massive resources to keep those multicast group states. It is expected that the bottleneck in the future networks would be the multicast-enabled routing nodes [10].

In order to overcome the scalability problem in terms of the number of multicast groups, lots of multicast routing or forwarding algorithms have been proposed in the past few decades. Bloom filter [11] is one of the most important ways to reduce the multicast routing states, which is used in the many of these propositions. In [10], an efficient multiple membership query algorithm called Scalar-pair Vectors Routing and Forwarding (SVRF) is proposed for the multicast scalability problem associated with software-defined datacenter, and can achieve remarkable performance in terms of memory consumption, processing time and hardware cost.

Branch forwarding technique [12] is a promising way to remedy the scalability problem of multicast communications. In this way, the forwarding states only need to be stored in the branch nodes rather than every node of a multicast tree. A branch node in a tree is the node with at least three incident edges. Between two neighboring branch nodes, packets are generally forwarded along the shortest path using a dynamically established unicast tunnel. The intermedia nodes no longer need to maintain the multicast forwarding entities. The previous works [12–15] have shown the promising reduction of multicast forwarding states. The unicast tunneling technique can be implemented in SDN by using the logic ports specified in the group table [2].

A Branch-aware Steiner Tree (BST) problem based on the branch forwarding technique is proposed in [16], which aims to minimize the bandwidth consumption and the number of forwarding entries maintained for the multicast tree. The algorithm BAERA (branch aware edge reduction algorithm) designed in this paper is scalable and computation-efficient but they ignored the impact of branch degree on the cost of branch nodes.

In this paper, we aim to obtain a cost-efficient and scalable multicast tree and propose the Degree-dependent Branch-node Weighted Steiner Tree (DBWST) problem using branch forwarding technique and considering the edge cost as well as the degree-dependent branch node cost. The DBWST problem is NP-hard. Finding a DBWST is very challenging. We apply the harmony search (HS) optimization to solve the problem and propose a path-vector based harmony search (PVHS) algorithm. Representation of solution space is one of the most important parts of designing a heuristic method. We proposed a path-vector representation for the tree. To the best of our knowledge, only Forsati et al. [17] applied harmony search algorithm based on node parent index for Steiner tree representation to solve multicast routing problem. We test our algorithm with shortest-path tree (SPT), PSOTREE [18] and BAERA [16].

The remainder of this paper is organized as follows. In Sect. 2, we present the formulation for degree-dependent branch-node weighted multicast tree problem. The path-vector based harmony search (PVHS) algorithm is described in Sect. 3. Section 4 gives the performance evaluation of our proposed algorithms on a variety of randomly generated topologies. Section 5 concludes the paper.

2 Problem Formulation

As mentioned above, the general forwarding rules are implemented using expensive technology (in terms of hardware cost and power). And in most practical applications, the cost associated with each node increase as the degree of the node increases. A node has to perform various processing for sending messages to each of its neighbors in the multicast tree, and that will consume more resources (such as memory consumption) and more processing time. Especially, the branch nodes assume a heavier responsibility of forwarding data packets to the destinations in the multicast tree. So, in this paper we consider the degree-dependent costs of the branch nodes. Based on the Branch-aware Steiner Tree (BST) problem in [16], we propose the Degree-dependent Branch-node Weighted Steiner Tree (DBWST) problem. This problem aims to minimize the resource consumption, including the cost of links as well as nodes (branch nodes, exactly), and the number of forwarding entries in the group tables on the multicast tree.

Consider an undirected graph $G = (V, E)$, where V denotes a set of vertices and E denotes a set of links, respectively. The link $e = (u, v) \in E$ denotes the edge from node $u \in V$ to the node $v \in V$ and is associated with a link cost $C(e) : E \mapsto R^+$, where R^+ are nonnegative numbers. Let $s \in V$ and $R \subseteq V - \{s\}$ be the source node the destination nodes respectively. The number of destination nodes $|R|$ is the group size. Let $T = (s, R)$ be a tree rooted at the source s and spanning all the destination nodes $r_i \in R$, $1 < i < |R|$. If the degree of node u is no less than three, then u is a branch node. Let binary variable β_u denote if u is a branch node in T. Then the total cost of the multicast tree T can be calculated as follows:

$$C(T) = \sum_{e \in T} C(e) + \sum_{u \in T} \beta_u \times C(u) \tag{1}$$

Generally, with the increasing of degree, the cost of a node may increase in different way, such as linearly or exponentially. Then the cost of a node can be defined as a function of the degree of the node and a weight w can be used to balance the tree cost and scalability. Let $d_T(u) \geq 1$ be the degree of branch node u in a multicast tree T. Then the cost of the node u in T can be defined as follows:

$$C(u) = w \times F(d_T(u)) \tag{2}$$

The DBWST problem is to find a tree $T = (s, R)$, such that the cost $C(T)$ of the tree is minimized. The DBWST problem includes the Steiner tree problem as a special case and thus the DBWST problem is also NP-hard.

3   The Path-Vector Based Harmony Search (PVHS) Algorithm

3.1   Overview

Harmony search (HS) [19] is a new meta-heuristic optimization method inspired from the music improvisation process where musicians improvise their instruments' pitches searching for a perfect state of harmony. A solution vector is analogy to a "harmony". Harmony Search includes five steps: initialization of the algorithm parameters, initialize the harmony memory, improvise a new harmony, update of the harmony memory and termination checking. The HS has been successfully applied to many optimization problems, such as [20–22, 23], presenting several advantages compared with other optimization methods [19].

The main idea of the path-vector based harmony search algorithm is to get iterative optimization of the multicast tree memory by imitating the improvisation process, during which the solution obtained is sufficiently random. The representation of the multicast tree memory is represented base on path vector. The PVHS algorithm mainly consists of three phases: initialization, improvisation and updating. More precisely, our algorithm initializes the parameters and constructs some random trees as the harmony memory firstly and then executes a number of iterations, each of which gets a new multicast tree by improvisation and updating the memory. If NI iterations have been executed, terminate the algorithm and output the best tree as the optimal solution. Table 1 shows the main PVHS algorithm for finding degree-dependent branch-node weighted Steiner trees. More details are given in the following sections.

3.2   The Path Vector Representation

The most important part of designing a algorithm is the representation of solution space. According the feature of HS, we propose the path-vector based representation. We encode the trees and describe harmony operations based on path vector, which is simple but practical. A path vector $P(s, r_i)$ means a solution vector and denotes the

Table 1. The PVHS algorithm

Algorithm: PVHS ($G, s, R, C(e), w$)

Input: Network $G = (V, E)$, source s, destination set R, edge cost $C(e)$, a nonnegative value w

Output: A degree-dependent branch-node weighted minimum-cost multicast tree T

$HMS, HMCR, PAR_{\max}, PAR_{\min}, NI$ //Initialization phase

For each node $u \in V$ **do**

  set $degree(u) \leftarrow 0$

End for

For i from 0 to HMS **do**

  $T_i \leftarrow$ **generateRandomTree** ($G, s, R, C(e), degree$)

  $HM_i \leftarrow$ **treeToPathVector** (T_i, s, R)

End for

Compute the best cost $C(T_{best})$ and worst cost $C(T_{worst})$ among the trees in HS

$P(s, R) \leftarrow \phi, gn \leftarrow 0$

While $gn < NI$ **do**   //improvisation phase

  For each $r_i \in R$ **do**

    If $U(0,1) < HMCR$ **then**

        $P(s, r_i) \leftarrow P_k(s, r_i)$ randomly selected for r_i from $\{P_1(s, r_i), P_2(s, r_i), ..., P_{HMS}(s, r_i)\}$

        If $U(0,1) < PAR$ **then**   // $U(0,1)$ is a random number between 0 and 1

          $P(s, r_i) \leftarrow$ **pathLocalAdjustment** ($P_k(s, r_i), C(e)$)

        End if

    Else then

        $P(s, r_i) \leftarrow$ **generateRandomPath** (G, s, r_i)

    End else

    $P(s, R) \leftarrow P(s, R) \cup P(s, r_i)$

  End for

  $T_{new} \leftarrow$ **pathVectorToTree** ($P(s, R), T_{new}$)   // repair by removing cycles and pruning

  updateHarmonyMemory ($HM, T_{new}, T_{best}, T_{worst}$)   //updating phase

  $gn \leftarrow gn + 1$

  $PAR(gn) \leftarrow PAR_{\min} + gn(PAR_{\max} - PAR_{\min}) / NI$

End while

Return T_{best}

---

ordered set of nodes from source node s to a destination node r_i in the multicast tree T, $P(s, r_i) = \{s, u, \ldots, v, r_i\}$. In a path vector, all the nodes are different with each other to guarantee there is no cycle.

As an example, Fig. 1 presents a multicast tree using solid line. Node s is the source node and c, e, f, h are the destination nodes. The path vector of node c is $P(s, c) = \{s, a, c\}$; the path vector of node h is $P(s, h) = \{s, a, d, g, h\}$. We can easily obtain all the path vectors according the multicast tree by a depth-first search.

The harmony memory is filled with HMS harmonies randomly generated in the solution space. According to the path vector representation, the harmony memory of

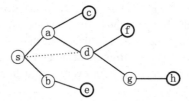

Fig. 1. A multicast tree of a graph

multicast trees can be denoted as follows:

$$
HM = \begin{bmatrix}
P_1(s, r_1) & P_1(s, r_2) & \ldots & P_1(s, r_{|R|}) & C(T_1) \\
P_2(s, r_1) & P_2(s, r_2) & \ldots & P_2(s, r_{|R|}) & C(T_2) \\
\ldots & \ldots & \ldots & \ldots & \ldots \\
P_{HMS}(s, r_1) & P_{HMS}(s, r_2) & \ldots & P_{HMS}(s, r_{|R|}) & C(T_{HMS})
\end{bmatrix} \tag{3}
$$

$P_k(s, r_i)$ denotes the path vector of destination node r_i in the multicast tree T_k and $C(T_1)$ denotes the cost of tree T_k in the harmony memory.

All trees can be represented by path vectors, however the combination of path vectors of all destinations cannot guarantee that the union of the paths in a tree, i.e., a subgraph without any cycle. In other words, the combination of path vectors of all destinations may not represent a valid solution. For this matter, we repair the solutions by removing the cycles and pruning the useless nodes.

3.3   Initialization Phase

In this phase, the algorithm first initializes the parameters including the harmony memory size (HMS), harmony memory considering rate (HMCR), pitch adjusting rate (PAR) and the number of improvisations (NI). In order to improve the performance of the algorithm, we use the variable PAR which changes dynamically with the generation number as expressed below:

$$PAR(gn) = PAR_{min} + \frac{(PAR_{max} - PAR_{min})}{NI} \times gn \tag{4}$$

PAR_{min} is the minimum pitch adjusting rate, PAR_{max} is the maximum pitch adjusting rate and gn is the iteration number.

For the initialization of harmony memory, we use a random depth-first based search algorithm, *generateRandomTree(G, s, R, C(e), degree)*, to generate random multicast trees. In the tree generation algorithm, a random node adjacent to the current node is selected. The node that is not in the path vector of all destinations will be pruned during the algorithm. When all destination nodes have been selected, the algorithm terminates.

Then each tree is covert to its associated path vector representation to initialize the harmony memory by *treeToPathVector(T_i, s, R)*. This process is implemented by traversing the path reversely. Suppose the destination node r_i is the current visited one, the algorithm will firstly find the node v which is in the tree and be adjacent by the destination node r_i, then set v as the current node and repeat the above process until the source s is found. Repeat this procedure for every destination. See in Table 2.

Table 2. Convert tree to path vectors

Algorithm: treeToPathVector(T_i, s, R)

For each destination $r_i \in R$ **do**
    $P(s, r_i) \leftarrow \Phi$
End for
For each destination $r_i \in R$ **do**
    $P(s, r_i) \leftarrow \{r_i\}$
    currentNode $\leftarrow r_i$
    While *currentNode* $\neq s$ **do**
        For each node $v \in T_i$
            If *edge*$(v, r_i) \in T_i$ **then**
                $P(s, r_i) \leftarrow \{v\} \cup P(s, r_i)$
                currentNode $\leftarrow v$
            End if
        End for
    End while
    $P(s, r_i) \leftarrow \{s\} \cup P(s, r_i)$
End for

3.4   Improvisation Phase

In the improvisation phase, three rules including memory consideration, pitch adjustment and random selection are implemented for the generation of the new path vector associated with every destination. The detail is described as following.

Memory consideration means that a path vector for a specific destination is selected from one of the path vectors associated with this destination in the memory with the rate of *HMCR*. If a random number bigger than *HMCR* is generated, the new path vector will be random generated by finding a random path from the source to the corresponding destination.

$$P(s,r_i) \leftarrow \begin{cases} P(s,r_i) \in \{P_1(s,r_i),\ldots,P_{HMS}(s,r_i)\} & \text{with probability HMCR} \\ random\ generated & \text{with probability } (1 - HMCR) \end{cases}$$

$$(5)$$

The function *generateRandomPath(G, s, r_i)* is used to generate a new random path vector based on depth first search. Table 3 demonstrates the algorithm. We obtain a path vector by generating a random sequence of candidate nodes repeatedly until there is a real path from the souce s to the destination r_i. The candidate nodes include all the other nodes in V except source s and the destination r_i.

Table 3. Generate a random path vector

Algorithm: generateRandomPath(G,s,r_i)

---

candidateNodes $\leftarrow V - \{s,r_i\}$

$P(s,r_i) \leftarrow \Phi$

While $P(s,r_i)$ is not a path from s to r_i **do**

   generate a random number $n, 0 \leq n \leq |V| - 2$

   generate a Node sequence $\{s,v_1,v_2,\ldots,v_n,r_i\}, v \in candidateNodes$

   $P(s,r_i) \leftarrow \{s,v_1,v_2,\ldots,v_n,r_i\}$

End while

Return $P(s,r_i)$

Every path vector obtained by the memory consideration is examined to determine whether it should be pitch-adjusted using the PAR parameter. Pitch adjustment corresponds to *pathLocalAdjustment(P_k(s, r_i), C(e))*, a simple local optimization of the path, which is demonstrated as follows:

$$pathLocalAdjustment(P_k(s, r_i), C(e)) \leftarrow \begin{cases} \text{Yes} & \text{with probability } PAR \\ \text{No} & \text{with probability } (1-PAR) \end{cases} \quad (6)$$

Consider a path $P(s, h) = \{s, a, d, g, h\}$ in Fig. 1, the local optimization process will select a node in the path vector, such as d, and replace $<d, g, h>$ with the shortest path from the destination node h to node d.

By the time when all the $|R|$ path vectors are generated, the algorithm $pathVectorToTree(P(s, R), T_{new})$ will superposition the paths and construct a new tree by removing the cycles by width first search and pruning useless nodes by depth first search. See in Table 4.

Table 4. Convert path vectors to tree

Algorithm : pathVectorToTree ($P(s, R), T_{new}$)

$T_{new} \leftarrow \Phi$
For each destination ri in R do
   $u \leftarrow$ predecessor node of r_i in $P(s, r_i)$
   $T_{new} \leftarrow T_{new} \cup edge <u, r_i>$
   While $u \neq s$
      $v \leftarrow u$
      $u \leftarrow$ predecessor node of u in $P(s, r_i)$
      $T_{new} \leftarrow T_{new} \cup edge <u, v>$
   End while
End for

3.5   Updating Phase

In this phase, the algorithm calculates the total cost of the new improvised tree according to the formula (1) and (2). The worst harmony in the HM will be replaced by the new improvised tree when the new tree is better than the worst. If the new tree replaces the worst one, the algorithm will compare it with the best one and if it has less cost than the best one recorded, it will replace that one as the best solution. The updating algorithm $updateHarmonyMemory(HM, T_{new}, T_{best}, T_{worst})$ is demonstrated in Table 5.

Table 5. Convert path vectors to tree

Algorithm: updateHarmonyMemory($HM, T_{new}, T_{best}, T_{worst}$)

Compute the cost $C(T_{new})$ of the new tree T_{new} according to the formula (1) (2)

if $C(T_{new}) < C(T_{worst})$ do

   Update the harmony memory by replacing T_{worst} with T_{new}

   if $C(T_{new}) < C(T_{best})$ do

      $T_{best} \leftarrow T_{new}$

   End if

End if

---

4 Simulation Results and Analysis

We use Waxman [24] model as our network topology generator. All of the topologies are generated randomly. We compare the performance of the PVHS algorithm with BAERA, PSOTREE (used for caculating Steiner trees) and the shortest-path tree (SPT) algorithm. The performance metrics include the total cost of the tree, the number of branch nodes and the running time. All algorithms are implemented withVisual C++ 6.0 and run on a machine withIntel Core i5-3470 CPU@3.20 Ghzand 4 GB memory, running Windows 7 operating system. We evaluate PVHS in both small topologies and large topologies.

4.1 Small Topologies

For small topologies, we used 50 random topologies with 40 nodes and 100 nodes respectively. The proportion of the multicast destination nodes is between 10 % and 50 %. The degree-dependent node cost function is supposed to increase linearly. All the results are the average results obtained on by running each algorithm 30 times on 50 topologies respectively. The number of improvisations (NI) is set as 40, PAR_{max} is set as 0.9 and PAR_{min} is set as 0.2.

As is shown in Fig. 2(a) and (b), the tree cost $C(T)$ grows as the group size increases in the two topologies with 40 nodes and 100 nodes respectively with $w = 50$, $HMS = 6$ and $HMCR = 0.85$. Nevertheless, PVHS outperforms PSOTREE algorithm and SPT since the total cost of branch nodes and edges is effectively reduced. PVHS gets better results than BAERA when there are more than about 15 destination nodes.

In regard to the harmony search algorithm, we should consider the performance respect to two parameters in the PVHS algorithm, HMS and $HMCR$. Firstly, we do experiments with 30 iterations and the topology size as 40 nodes. We get the variation

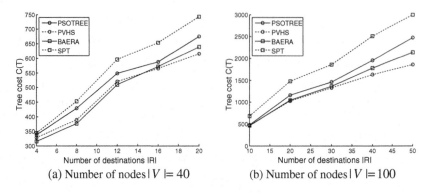

Fig. 2. Tree cost with varied destination number $|R|$

of tree cost with respect to *HMS* in Fig. 3. In our experiments, the solutions are very bad when harmony memory size is 2 and get stable when *HMS* is bigger than 8. For other settings, there should be another stable *HMS* for the algorithm.

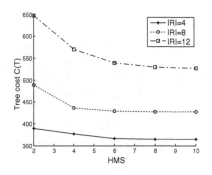

Fig. 3. Tree cost with various *HMS*

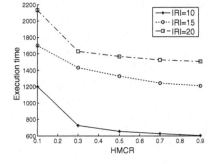

Fig. 4. Execution time with varied *HMCR*

In Fig. 4, the network has 50 nodes and *HMS* is set as 6. As can be observed from Fig. 4, *HMCR* has big effect to the convergence time. Indeed, the solution is also affected. When *HMCR* is lower than 0.5, the convergence speed is slow and the cost of the multicast tree is bad. Good performance can be get when *HMCR* is close to 0.9.

Figure 5 evaluates the impact of varied w with the network size $|V| = 40$, $HMS = 6$ and $HMCR = 0.85$. Obviously, we can see that the cost of tree becomes with the increase of w. The lines associated with the PVHS and BAERA algorithm can grow slowly than the others associated with PSOTREE and SPT as w becomes lager. This results shows that both the PVHS and BAERA can reduce the branch nodes effectively.

4.2   Large Topologies

In the following, we used 50 random topologies with 500 nodes and 1000 nodes respectively. The proportion of the multicast destination nodes is between 10 % and 50 % too. The degree-dependent node cost function is supposed to increase linearly. All the results are the average results obtained on by running each algorithm 30 times on 50 topologies respectively. The parameters are set same as on the small topologies.

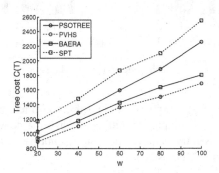

Fig. 5. Tree cost with varied w

Figure 5(a) and (b) evaluates the impact of multicast group size with $w = 40$. As is shown in Fig. 5, the number of branch nodes becomes larger as the destination number increases, since more branch nodes are in the tree. The number of branch nodes obtained by PVHS and BAERA are less than the other two algorithms. The reduction of the number of branch nodes means the less number of the flow table and it verifies the scalability of the both algorithm. It indicates that PVHS and BAERA are more scalable (Fig. 6).

In addition, the topology size affects the convergence speed importantly. Differently, the BAERA is computation-efficient while the PVHS algorithm converges very slowly when there are more than one thousand of nodes. For small real networks, PVHS has the advantage of getting more cost-efficient and scalable solutions. For Large topologies, BAERA has absolute advantage in computation than PVHS.

5   Conclusions

Software Defined Networking (SDN) makes Steiner tree a feasible and promising way for multicast. However, multicast suffers from a scalability problem when the number of groups is large since the flow table size is limited. In this paper, we propose the Degree-dependent Branch-node Weighted Steiner Tree (DBWST) problem for SDN and this problem has great significance for the cost-efficient and scalable multicast routing in SDN-enabled networks. This problem is NP-hard and we derived a path-vector based harmony search (PVHS) algorithm. PVHS outperforms other algorithms in reducing the total cost and reducing the number of branch nodes. Simulation

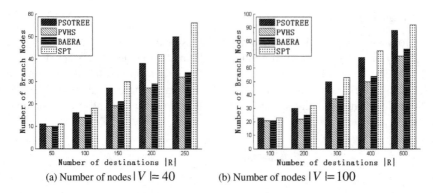

Fig. 6. Number of branch nodes with varied destination number $|R|$

results show that PVHS outperforms other algorithms with less total cost of edges and branches. But PVHS is not computation-efficient when the network has thousands of nodes. In the future, we will try to make effort in the improvement of the algorithm and evaluate the algorithm in SDN testbeds.

Acknowledgment. The study is supported by the Natural Science Foundation of Shandong Province (Grant No. ZR2015FM008; ZR2013FM029), the Science and Technology Development Program of Jinan (Grant No. 201303010), the National Natural Science Foundation of China (NSFC No. 60773101), and the Fundamental Research Funds of Shandong University (Grant No. 2014JC037).

References

1. Software-defined networking (SDN) definition. https://www.opennetworking.org/sdn-resources/sdn-definition
2. OpenFlow Switch Specification, Open Networking Foundation Std.1.4.0, Oct 2013
3. Agarwal, S., Kodialam, M., Lakshman, T.V.: Traffic engineering in software defined networks. In: IEEE Proceedings of INFOCOM, pp. 2211–2219 (2013)
4. Benslimane, A.: Multimedia Multicast on the Internet. ISTE, Wiley, London (2013)
5. Bianco, A., Giaccone, P., Giraudo, E.M., Neri, F., Schiattarella, E.: NXG07-3: multicast support for a storage area network switch. In: GLOBECOM, pp. 1–6, November 2006
6. Karp, R.M.: Reducibility among combinatorial problems. In: Complexity of Computer Computations, pp. 85–103 (1972)
7. Yu, Y., Zhen, Q., Xin, L., et al.: OFM: a novel multicast mechanism based on openflow. Adv. Inf. Sci. Serv. Sci. **4**(9) (2012)
8. Zhao, M., Jia, B., Wu, M., et al.: Software defined network-enabled multicast for multi-party video conferencing systems. In: IEEE International Conference on Communications (ICC), pp. 1729–1735 (2014)
9. McKeown, N., Anderson, T., Balakrishnan, H., Parulkar, G., Peterson, L., Rexford, J., Shenker, S., Turner, J.: OpenFlow: enabling innovationin campus networks. ACM SIGCOMM Comput. Commun. Rev. **38**(2), 69–74 (2008)

10. Jia, W.K., Wang, L.C.: A unified unicast and multicast routing and forwarding algorithm for software-defined datacenter networks. IEEE J. Sel. Areas Commun. **31**(12), 2646–2657 (2013)
11. Bloom, B.H.: Space/time trade-offs in hash coding with allowableerrors. Commun. ACM **13** (7), 422–426 (1970)
12. Tian, J., Neufeld, G.: Forwarding state reduction for sparse modemulticast communication. In: IEEE Proceedings of INFOCOM, pp. 711–719 (1998)
13. Yang, D.-N., Liao, W.: Optimal state allocation for multicast communications withexplicit multicast forwarding. IEEE Trans. Parallel Distrib. Syst. **19**(4), 476–488 (2008)
14. Stoica, I., Ng, T., Zhang, H.: Reunite: a recursive unicast approachto multicast. In: IEEE Proceedings of INFOCOM, pp. 1644–1653 (2000)
15. Wong, T., Katz, R.: An analysis of multicast forwarding state scalability. In: IEEE Proceedings of International Conference on NetworkProtocols, pp. 105–115 (2000)
16. Huang, L.H., Hung, H.J., Lin, C.C., et al.: Scalable and bandwidth-efficient multicast for software-defined networks. In: IEEE Global Communications Conference (GLOBECOM), pp. 1890–1896 (2014)
17. Forsati, R., Haghighat, A.T., Mahdavi, M.: Harmony search based algorithms for bandwidth-delay-constrained least-cost multicast routing. Comput. Commun. 2505–2519 (2008)
18. Hua, W., Xiangxu, M., Shuai, L., Hong, X.: A tree-based particle swarm optimization for multicast routing. Comput. Netw. 2775–2786 (2010)
19. Lee, K.S., Geem, Z.W.: A new meta-heuristic algorithm for continuous engineering optimization: harmony search theory and practice. Comput. Methods Appl. Mech. Eng. 3902–3933 (2005)
20. Jaberipour, M., Khorram, E.: A new harmony search algorithm for solving mixed–discrete engineering optimization problems. Eng. Optim. 507–523 (2011)
21. Nekooei, K., Farsangi, M.M., Nezamabadi-Pour, H., Lee, K.Y.: An improved multi-objective harmony search for optimal placement of DGs in distribution systems. IEEE Trans. Smart Grid 557–567 (2013)
22. Karahan, H., Gurarslan, G., Geem, Z.W.: Parameter estimation of the nonlinear muskingum flood-routing model using a hybrid harmony search algorithm. J. Hydrol. Eng. 352–360 (2013)
23. Wang, L., Yang, R., Xu, Y., Niu, Q., Pardalos, P.M., Fei, M.: An improved adaptive binary Harmony search algorithm. Inf. Sci. 58–87 (2013)
24. Waxman, B.M.: Routing of multipoint connections. IEEE J. Sel. Areas Commun. 1617–1622 (1988)

Parallel Data Regeneration Based on Multiple Trees with Network Coding in Distributed Storage System

Pengfei You[✉], Zhen Huang, Changjian Wang, Minghao Hu, and Yuxing Peng

College of Computer, National University of Defense Technology, Changsha 410073, China
hbypf@outlook.com,
{maosswu,wangcj,humh,pengyx}@sina.com

Abstract. Distributed storage systems can provide large-scale data storage and high data reliability by redundant schemes, such as replica and erasure codes. Redundant data may get lost due to frequent node failures in the system. The lost data is needed to be regenerated as soon as possible so as to maintain data availability and reliability. The direct way for reducing regeneration time is to reduce network traffic in regeneration. Compared with that way, tree-structured regeneration achieves shorter regeneration time by constructing better tree-structured topology to increase transmission bandwidth. However, some bandwidth of many other edges beyond the tree is not utilized to speed up transmission in tree-structured regeneration. In this paper, we consider to use multiple edge-disjoint trees to parallel regenerate the lost data, and analyze the total regeneration time. We deduce the formula about optimal regeneration time, and propose an approximate construction algorithm with polynomial time complexity for the optimal multiple regeneration trees. Our experiments shows, the regeneration time reduces 62 % compared with common tree–structured scheme, and the file availability reaches almost 99 %.

Keywords: Distributed storage systems · Data regeneration · Erasure code · Network coding · Overlay · P2P · Maximum spanning tree

1 Introduction

Distributed storage systems, such as Total Recall [15] and OceanStore [1] etc. are designed to provide large-scale storage services for users. They store data into a large number of storage nodes which may vary from cluster servers in data centers [5], to even ordinary computers in peer-to-peer networks. In such systems, departure and failure for storage node results in frequent data loss which is deemed as a normal state. Thus, data redundancy technology is needed to recovery data so as to keep data availability and reliability in the system [4].

Replica and erasure codes are two common redundancy technologies. Though replica is simple to apply, it requires large storage space [7]. For a (n, k) erasure code, where $n > k$, each data object is firstly divided into k blocks, and then these blocks are

G. Wang et al. (Eds.): ICA3PP 2015, Part II, LNCS 9529, pp. 606–620, 2015.
DOI: 10.1007/978-3-319-27122-4_42

encoded into n blocks. Erasure code is usually a Maximum Distance Separable (MDS) code, where the original data object can be constructed from any k blocks of n blocks [7]. It has been shown that MDS codes have optimal redundancy-reliability tradeoff because k blocks contain the minimum amount of information required to recover the original data [6], while replica needs more storage space. Therefore, erasure code becomes a more attractive redundancy solution in recent years, especially when data needed to store is very huge [3].

When a storage node fails in the system using erasure code, it will be recovered, which is called regeneration. In regeneration, a replacement node, called newcomer, receives coded data from active storage nodes, referred to as providers, and finally regenerate the lost data by encoding operations in it. The less time regeneration costs, the higher probability the regeneration can be finished with. To ensure data reliability and availability, the regenerate time is expected to be as little as possible [12]. The simplest way to reduce the regeneration time is to reduce the network traffic in the regeneration. Dimakis et al. [9] show that linear network coding can incur less regeneration traffic and the corresponding encoding scheme is given in [10].

Another way to reduce regeneration time is to improve network topology for data transmission in regeneration. Conventional regeneration process is performed on a simple *star-structured* topology [11], i.e. the newcomer downloads data directly from providers. Thus the regeneration time is limited by the path between the newcomer and the provider with the minimal bandwidth which is also called *bottleneck bandwidth* or *available bandwidth*, if the network of the storage system suffers from bandwidth heterogeneity. To increase bottleneck bandwidth, Li et al. [11, 12] take into account heterogeneity of bandwidth capacity between nodes and propose *tree-structured* topology to regenerate lost data. It constructs a maximum spanning tree (MST) based on an undirected complete graph network to maximize the minimal bandwidth among all end-to-end edges. The MST is proved an optimal topology and it achieves minimal regeneration time [11].

However, a MST has only k edges to regenerate the lost data, while many other edges of the undirected graph network are not used. In this paper, we try to reduce regeneration time by improving network topology and consider utilizing more edges effectively to regenerate the lost data by constructing multiple trees. We propose a regeneration scheme for optimal multiple parallel trees. In this scheme, we try to construct p trees ($p > 1$), and the lost data block is split into p fragments with different size propositions, each of them is regenerated by each tree respectively, then a formula about the final regeneration time and available bandwidths for p trees is deduced. We prove that the final regeneration time is optimal if the sum of available bandwidths for p trees is maximal, and these trees are called optimal multiple regeneration trees (OMRT). Further, we design an approximate construction algorithm with polynomial time complexity for the OMRT. The algorithm asymptotically increases bottleneck bandwidth for each tree by iteratively updating edge sets for edge-disjoint trees with swappable edge sequences so as to increase the total available bandwidths for all trees as much as possible.

Compared with MST, our method has two contributions. First, we parallel the regeneration by constructing multiple edge-disjoint trees, each of which is just responsible for a part of the lost block with different size proposition, and an optimal regeneration time formula is deduced. Second, we implement an asymptotical algorithm to construct optimal multiple regeneration trees whose total available bandwidth could be increased as much as possible so as reduce regeneration time significantly. We evaluate our scheme and the simulation results show that our scheme can reduce regeneration time at least by 62 % and improve data availability significantly compared with MST.

The reminder of the paper is organized as follows. In Sect. 2 we introduce the related work and some preliminaries. In Sect. 3, we present the parallel regeneration scheme for multiple trees and approximate construction algorithm for OMRT. The experiment results are showed in Sect. 4. Finally, we conclude the paper in Sect. 5.

2   Related Work

Compared with replica, erasure codes provide higher data availability and have been used in many distributed systems, such as Windows Azure [2], HDFS [3], etc. In order to maintain data availability and reliability, the system should regenerate lost data as soon as possible. There are two ways to reduce regeneration time for the lost data. One is to reduce network traffic incurred by coding, the other is to construct optimal network topology to increase bottleneck bandwidth for data transmission, such as tree-structured regeneration scheme [11, 12].

2.1   Erasure Codes

A common (n, k) erasure code, such as Reed–Solomon codes [7], stores redundant data for a file sized M bytes in n storage nodes, each node with M/k bytes data, where $n > k$. When a node fails, k providers participate in the regeneration, each of which transmits M/k bytes data to the newcomer. Ahlswede et al. [13] introduced the idea of network coding, and Accendanski et al. [8] showed linear network coding provides better data availability than common erasure codes. Duminuco et al. [14] proposed a new class of erasure codes, aiming to achieve the tradeoff between regeneration traffic and data reliability. Dimakis et al. showed that linear network coding can reduce the network traffic in the regeneration than common erasure codes [8]. They propose regenerating code, a new form of linear network coding which achieves optimal tradeoff between storage cost and network traffic. Wu *et al.* [10] propose minimum-storage regenerating (MSR) codes which is proved to incur minimal network traffic in the regeneration over all erasure codes.

2.2   Linear Network Coding and Regeneration

Linear network coding is proposed in [9, 16]. If a file is divided into k blocks with equal size, $B_1, B_2, ..., B_k$, a coded block C is a linear combination of the k blocks on a Galois field F_{2^q}. q bits are regarded as a symbol on F_{2^q} and a block is then a sequence of symbols on F_{2^q}. Thus we have

$$C = \sum_{i=1}^{k} a_i \cdot B_i, \tag{1}$$

where $(a_1, a_2, \ldots, a_k)^T$ is the randomly-generated encoding vector, $a_i \in F_{2^q}$, $i = 1$, $2, \ldots, k$. If q is large enough, any k coded blocks are sufficient to recover the original blocks with high probability. Given k coded blocks and their encoding vectors, we can reconstruct the original blocks by solving a linear system of k equations. All coded blocks have the same size and each storage node stores one coded block.

When regenerating one lost data block, a new node, called *newcomer*, is selected to replace the failed node. The newcomer should receive k' ($k' \geq k$) coded blocks, C_1, $C_2, \ldots, C_{k'}$ from k' active storage nodes, called *providers*, and get a new coded block C_0 as a linear combination of the received blocks:

$$C_0 = \sum_{i=1}^{k'} b_i \cdot C_i, \tag{2}$$

$b_i \in F_{2^q}$, $i = 1, 2, \ldots, k'$.

2.3   Network Model for Regenerating Lost Data

Assume linear network coding is applied to create redundancy in a distributed storage system. The original file with size of M is divided into k blocks and encoded into more than k coded blocks, each of which is M/k in size. Each storage node stores one coded block. Due to the node behaviors and the bandwidth cost, the number of providers is preferred to be small in the distributed storage system [14], thus k' is set to k in this paper. That is, a newcomer receives k coded blocks from k providers in regeneration. The node set is $V(k) = \{V_0, V_1, \ldots, V_k\}$, where V_0 denotes the newcomer and other nodes denote the providers. The end-to-end edge between V_i to V_j is denoted as (V_i, V_j). The edge set $E(k) = \{(V_i, V_j) \mid 0 \leq i, j \leq k, i \neq j\}$. $\omega(V_i, V_j)$ is the weight of (V_i, V_j), which denotes the available bandwidth between V_i to V_j. Therefore, the network model for regeneration is represented as an undirected complete graph $G(k) = \{V(k), E(k), \omega\}$.

2.4   Star-Structured Regeneration and Regeneration Tree

In an overlay storage network, links between storage nodes usually enjoy different available bandwidth. Conventionally the regeneration is carried out in a manner called star-structured regeneration, in which the newcomer receives coded blocks directly from each provider, thus the regeneration time depends on the edge with minimal bandwidth connecting to the newcomer. Fig. l(a) shows a star-structured regeneration in a network with symmetric links, in which the newcomer receives the coded blocks directly from the three providers. The regeneration will finish when the newcomer has received the coded block from provider A. That is, the regeneration time depends on the bandwidth bottleneck edge connecting to the newcomer and provider A, and the actual regeneration bandwidth is 10 KB/s.

Li et al. [11, 12] proposes tree-structured regeneration, which is mapped to a transmission tree based on network model $G(k)$. In the tree, the root node is the newcomer, the other nodes are providers. The child node sends data to its parent node, and the parent node encodes the received data with the data it stores and then sends the encoded data to its parent node as long as there are data available to send, rather than after the whole block is encoded. That is, the regeneration traffic is relayed by providers, thus the regeneration time depends on the bottleneck edge whose bandwidth is the minimal among the tree edges. The bandwidth of the bottleneck edge is called *available bandwidth* of the tree in this paper. Assume the available bandwidth is ω_a, and the regeneration time is t, then we have:

$$t = M/(k \cdot \omega_a) \tag{3}$$

In a tree-structured regeneration as showed in Fig. 1(b), bottleneck bandwidth link is the edge connecting to the newcomer and provider C, and the actual transmission rate during the regeneration process is 30 KB/s, which reaches higher speed than that in Fig. 1(a). Further, a maximum spanning tree (MST) is proved an optimal regeneration tree [11], which achieves maximal bottleneck bandwidth when regenerating single lost node, thus the regeneration time is minimal.

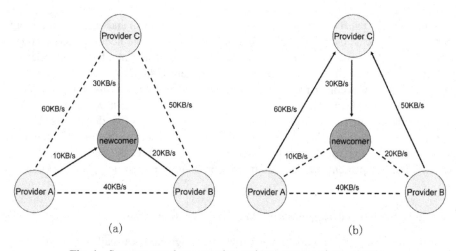

(a)   (b)

Fig. 1. Star-structured regeneration and tree-structured regeneration

3 Parallel Regeneration Scheme for Multiple Trees

In this section we present how to construct multiple parallel trees to fast regenerate data loss in the network model in Sect. 2. First, we show parallel regeneration scheme for multiple trees and the related optimization problem. Second, we analyze the challenge for constructing optimal multiple regeneration trees. Last we implement an approximate construction algorithm for the optimal multiple regeneration trees.

3.1 Regeneration Scheme for Multiple Trees

In the regeneration scheme, we use multiple edge-disjoint trees to parallel regenerate the single lost data block so as to reduce regeneration time, where each tree does not have any same edges with each other and regenerates each part of the block. For example, if two regeneration trees are constructed in the network model $G(k)$, the coded block in each provider can be divided into two parts and each part belongs to one of both trees. Each tree independently regenerates each part of the lost block, and the final regeneration time lies on the tree with more regeneration time.

Assume there exist p edge-disjoint parallel trees, $T_1, T_2, \ldots, T_p$ and each coded data block with size M/k is split into p pieces respectively, the size of each piece is $M_1, M_2, \ldots, M_p$ respectively. The available bandwidth of T_i is denoted as ω_i, $i = 1, 2, \ldots, p$. Since the p trees are edge-disjoint, the available bandwidth of each tree will not interfere with the other trees. Therefore, the total time for regenerating the lost data block is described as follows:

$$t = \max_{1 \leq i \leq p}\{\frac{M_i}{\omega_i}\} \tag{4}$$

Our objective is to reduce the total regeneration time t. If we want to minimize t, we can suppose each ω_i is constant and M_i is variable, since t is determined by M_i and ω_i which are independent mutually in Eq. (4). Then the problem is formulated as follows:

Problem 1: *Minimize:* $t = \max_{1 \leq i \leq p}\{\frac{1}{\omega_i} \cdot M_i\}$, subject to the conditions:

$$\sum_{1 \leq i \leq p} M_i = M/k \tag{5}$$

Lemma 1: Problem 1 has optimal solution $t_{\min} = \frac{M}{k \cdot \sum\limits_{1 \leq i \leq p} \omega_i}$ when $M_i = \frac{\omega_i}{\sum\limits_{1 \leq i \leq p} \omega_i} \cdot \frac{M}{k}$.

Proof: $t_i = \frac{1}{\omega_i} \cdot M_i = \frac{1}{\sum\limits_{1 \leq i \leq p} \omega_i} \cdot \frac{M}{k}, 1 \leq i \leq p$ when $M_i = \frac{\omega_i}{\sum\limits_{1 \leq i \leq p} \omega_i} \cdot \frac{M}{k}$. It shows the regeneration time for each tree t_i is the same. In this situation, $t_{\min}$ must be optimal. If not, there must be a set of t_i' and respective M_i which satisfy the following formula:

$$t_i' < t_{\min}, 1 \leq i \leq p \tag{6}$$

Denote $\theta_i = M_i/(\frac{M}{k}), 1 \leq i \leq p$, Eqs. (5) and (6) are equivalent to the following formulas respectively:

$$\sum_{1 \le i \le p} \theta_i = 1 \tag{7}$$

$$\frac{\theta_i}{\omega_i} < \frac{1}{\sum_{1 \le i \le p} \omega_i}, 1 \le i \le p \tag{8}$$

Equation (8) is equivalent to: $\theta_i < \frac{\omega_i}{\sum_{1 \le i \le p} \omega_i}, 1 \le i \le p$, then we have:

$$\sum_{1 \le i \le p} \theta_i < \frac{\sum_{1 \le i \le p} \omega_i}{\sum_{1 \le i \le p} \omega_i} = 1 \tag{9}$$

Evidently, Eq. (9) contradicts Eqs. (7) and (5). Therefore, Lemma 1 is proved.

Based on Eq. (4) and Lemma 1, minimizing the total regeneration time t for p multiple trees is equivalent to the problem as follows:

Problem 2: *Minimize:* $t = \frac{M}{k \cdot \sum_{1 \le i \le p} \omega_i}$.

3.2   Analysis for Optimal Multiple Regeneration Trees

Definitions: The **total available bandwidth** for multiple regeneration trees is $\omega = \sum_{1 \le i \le p} \omega_i$. The **Optimal Multiple Regeneration Trees (OMRT)** are multiple edge-disjoint trees whose total available bandwidth $\omega = \sum_{1 \le i \le p} \omega_i$ is maximal according to Problem 2.

There are many combinations for constructing p trees based on a graph and different combinations determine different total available bandwidths. For example, as shown in Fig. 2, the complete graph $G(3)$ has 6 combinations for constructing 2 edge-disjoint trees. In Fig. 2(1), the total available bandwidth for 2 trees is *min* $\{16,7,13\}$ + *min*$\{15,14,5\}$ = 7+5 = 12. In Fig. 2(2), it is *min*$\{16,15,13\}$ + *min* $\{14,7,5\}$ = 13 + 5=18.

Therefore, the construction for the OMRT is a discrete combinatorial optimization problem based on graph, since ω_i is the weight of the minimal edge for each tree T_i and these trees are disjoint mutually. To achieve the optimal solution, we may need to compare all the possible combinations. In the worst case the computation cost is $O(C_m^k \cdot C_{m-k}^k \cdot \ldots \cdot C_{m-(p-1)k}^k)$, which is very high. It shows efficient construction for the OMRT is very challenging. Therefore, constructing an approximate OMRT with polynomial time complexity to increase the total available bandwidth seems more feasible.

3.3   Approximate Construction Algorithm for the OMRT

There are some methods to construct multiple edge-disjoint trees [20, 21], but they only return any one combination of multiple trees or prove the edge-disjoint trees do not exist, and do not consider bottleneck edges' weight situation for trees, thus can not ensure the bottleneck edge for each tree is large enough.

We notice there are many edge-disjoint combinations with different total available bandwidths even for the same edge set of $G(k)$. As shown in Fig. 2, for the same edge set: $\{16, 15, 14, 13, 7, 5\}$, the total available bandwidth for the combination in Fig. 2(1) is 18, while it is 12 in Fig. 2(2). In addition, one combination can be generated from another combination by swapping some edges of each others, while keeping edge-disjoint. For example, the combination of two trees in Fig. 2(1) can be generated from that in Fig. 2(2) by swapping edge of weight 7 with that of weight 15 and 2 trees are still edge-disjoint. These points inspire us to iteratively construct combinations for edge-disjoint trees from an existing combination, by finding some swappable edge sequences among trees towards increase of total available bandwidth of multiple trees. In this section, we propose an approximate construction algorithm for the OMRT, in which the minimal edge for each tree is updated iteratively to reach maximal weight, thus the total available bandwidth for multiple trees is increased.

Mechanism and implementation for the algorithm

1. p edge-disjoint trees only needs $p \cdot (k\text{-}1)$ edges of m edges of $G(k)$, thus we first select the $p \cdot (k\text{-}1)$ edges with maximal weights from $G(k)$, which constitute p edge-disjoint trees, $T_1, T_2, ..., T_p$. This way ensures the bottleneck edges of all trees would be selected from a subset of $E(k)$ with maximal weights.
2. Based on the combination of $T_1, T_2, ..., T_p$, update iteratively minimal edge of T_1 by swapping with edges of other trees until the minimal edge of T_1 can not be increased by weight. Then update iteratively $T_2, T_3, ..., T_p$ one by one according to the same way. Finally, we achieve a combination of p edge-disjoint trees whose total available bandwidth could not be increased.
3. Key points of iterative update: when increasing the available bandwidth of one tree, the minimal edges of other trees should not be impacted and p trees should always be edge-disjoint. The way for updating tree T_i are as follows:
   (a) Remove the minimal edge e_i from T_i, then T_i becomes a forest of $G(k)$.
   (b) Starting from e_i, create a set of swappable edge sequences among all other trees and T_i, in which each swapped edge is larger than the minimal edge of current tree. If this set of edge sequences do not exist, it is over.
   (c) When new minimal edge of T_i is found, then update all trees with swappable edges in the sequences and repeat (a).

The above mechanism ensures the minimal edge for each tree is increased asymptotically by weight, thus increasing the total available bandwidth for multiple trees finally. The details for construction algorithm are shown in Algorithm 1.

Algorithm 1: Construction for Optimal Edge-disjoint parallel regeneration trees (OMRT)

Input: p, $G(k)=\{V(k),E(k),\omega\}$. Let $E(k)=\{e_1, e_2,...,e_n\}$, where $\omega(e_1)\geq\omega(e_2)\geq...\geq\omega(e_n)$, $|V(k)|=n$, $|E(k)|=m$ // p is the number of disjoint trees
Output: disjoint trees set TS = $\{T_1, T_2, ..., T_p\}$ with maximal bottleneck weight sum// T_i denotes the i-th tree and edges queue with length of $n-1$
Program:

```
1.  TS ← creating p disjoint trees in G(k) according to
    descending order of elements weight in E(k)
2.  for i←1 to p do
3.      if Tᵢ == ø then
4.          return ø
5.      end if
6.  end for
7.  for i←1 to p do
8.      adjust elements of Tᵢ in descending order by
        weight, where Tᵢ(1) ≥Tᵢ(2) ≥...≥Tᵢ(n-1)
9.  end for
10. for i←1 to p do
11.     while(true) do
12.         mark every edges in all trees as unlabeled
13.         remove Tᵢ(n-1) from Tᵢ
14.         SwappedQue ← adding Tᵢ(n-1)
15.         'swap' ←0 // successful swapping symbol
16.         while(SwappedQue is not empty) do
17.         remove the next edge e from SwappedQue
18.         for j←1 to p do
19.             if({e}∪Tⱼ is tree && ω(e)>ω(Tⱼ(n-1)))
    then
20.                 'swap'←1
21.                 break
22.             end if
23.             if (ω(e)<ω(Tⱼ(n-1))) then
24.                 continue
25.             end if
26.             SwappedSet← the edges of Tⱼ which
                form a cycle with e
27.             if (SwappedSet ≠ ø) then
28.             L←every edge of SwappedSet
29.             label any unlabeled edges in L with e
30.             SwappedQue←adding any just labeled edges
31.             end if
32.         end for
33.         end while
34.         if ('swap' == 0) then
35.             Tᵢ←{Tᵢ(n-1)}∪Tᵢ
36.             break
37.         end if
38.         update each tree using the labeled edges
39.         adjust order of e by weight in Tᵢ
40.     end while
41. end for
42. return {T₁, T₂, ..., Tₚ}
```

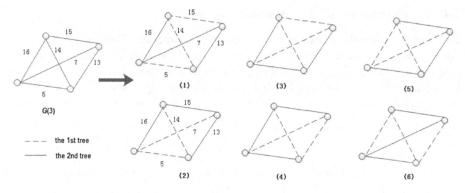

Fig. 2. Different combinations for 2 edge-disjoint trees in $G(3)$

Algorithm 1 consists of 3 parts as follows:

1. Initialization: in Line 1, we use the algorithm proposed in [21] to generate p edge-disjoint trees by testing edges of $G(k)$ in descending order by weight. This step aims to leave $p \cdot (k\text{-}1)$ maximal edges into edge set of p trees. The time complexity is $O(m \cdot \log m + p^2 \cdot k^2)$. From Line 2 to Line 7, set each tree empty if p trees do not exist. From Line 8 to Line 9, list edges of each tree in descending order by weight.

2. Asymptotic iteration in any tree (Line 11 to Line 40):

   (a) From Line 11 to Line 25, first remove the minimal edge of the tree, then uses it as the starting edge to produce suitable swappable edges for multiple trees. We remove edge swapping operations which could decrease the bottleneck bandwidth of other trees, thus the swappable edges are found in the direction where the minimal edge of the tree could finally be swapped by a larger edge. As shown in Line 16, the process continues until the desired edge is found.

   (b) In Line 26, we use the algorithm by finding cycle in [21] to label swappable edges with the edge in the label queue. The complexity is only $O(1)$, since a related data structure has been prepared in Initialization of step 1. From Line 27 to Line 30, add the desired edges into the label queue. Therefore, after Line 33, the label queue includes a set of swappable edge sequences. From Line 34 to Line 39, based on the label relation of edges among all trees in label queue, output the set of sequences which would increase the bottleneck bandwidth of the tree, then update each tree using the sequences. Last repeat step (a), as shown in Line 40. It will increase asymptotically the bandwidth of bottleneck edge of the tree until it can not be increased.

3. Choose next tree and repeat step 2.

From above steps, we calculate the complexity of algorithm is $O(m \cdot \log m + 2p^2 \cdot k^2)$, thus our method is practicable for constructing an approximate OMRT.

3.4   An Example for the Construction Algorithm

In this section, we take an example to present the construction algorithm. To make the process clearer and more intuitive, we just constructs 2 edge-disjoint trees: T_1 and T_2 based on network model of $G(5)$ in Fig. 3. The number crossing the edge is its weight. For simplicity, we use the weight number to denote the edge directly.

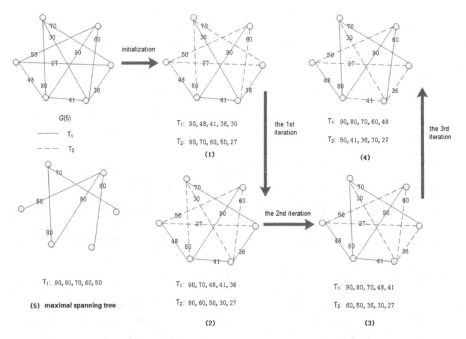

Fig. 3. Construction algorithm for 2 trees

First, T_1 and T_2 are created in initialization phase of the algorithm, as shown in Fig. 3(1). Second, update T_1 in 3 iterations, as show in Fig. 3(2), (3) and (4) respectively. The set of swappable edge sequences between 2 trees for each iteration is {30, 70}, {36, 80} and {41, 60} respectively. After 3 iterations, the minimal edge of T_1 can not be updated by larger edge, thus the update for T_1 stops. Third, update T_2 and its minimal edge has been maximal, then the algorithm is over.

Notice, in update for each tree, other trees are also updated by swappable edges. After many updates (or iterations), the weight of the minimal edge of each tree becomes maximal. If the number of edge-disjoint trees is more, the construction detail for the swappable edge sequences among trees would be more complex, thus not easy to present. Therefore, we just present the example for 2 trees.

In Fig. 3(5), we create the maximal spanning tree (MST) for $G(5)$, and available bandwidth is 50. While in Fig. 3(4) the total available bandwidth for 2 trees is $48 + 27 = 75$, then the bandwidth increment rate is up to 50 %. Therefore, compared with regular regeneration tree, our algorithm for constructing multiple trees can significantly increase regeneration bandwidth, thus further reduce regeneration time.

4   Experiment Evaluation

In this section, we compare regeneration performance of multiple trees with that of single tree and star-structured scheme in an event-based simulator which is based on the real data of available bandwidth [18] and node behaviors [19] measured in PlanetLab [17]. We evaluate three performance metrics as follows:

- **regeneration time**: how much time is spent from the start of a regeneration to the end;
- **probability of the successful regeneration**: the ratio of finished regeneration number to total started regeneration number;
- **data availability**: the ratio of data's available time to total simulation time. For (n, k) − linear network coding, data are available when there are at least k active storage nodes.

Each simulation covers 10^6 s and totally 200 nodes with the most frequent join/leave behaviors from the nodes in the trace file [18] in PlanetLab. The size of the original file is set to be 20 GB and $(5 + k, k)$-linear network coding is used. Then the file is divided into k blocks and the coded blocks are stored in $5 + k$ storage nodes. In the simulation at most 3 parallel regeneration trees can be constructed during the regeneration, and k varies from 5 to 15, which could make 3 edge-disjoint parallel regeneration trees exist. The simulation is repeated for 1000 times.

We run the simulation for multiple regeneration trees based on our algorithm, MST and star-structured regeneration respectively. The simulation results are shown in Figs. 4, 5 and 6.

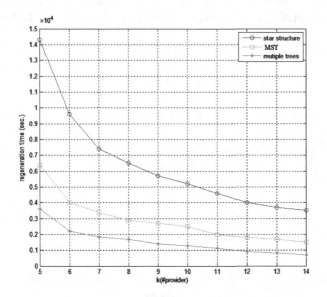

Fig. 4. Regeneration time

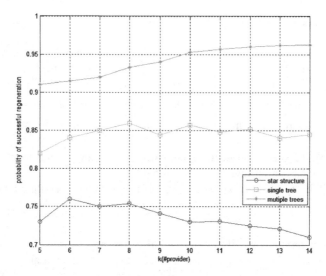

Fig. 5. Probability of successful regeneration

In Fig. 4, we can see that multiple trees for our algorithm can reduce the regeneration time by at least 62 % compared with single MST and reduce the time by at least 79 % compared with star-structure scheme. Because the number of links in the network increases with k, it is more likely to select the links with more available bandwidth when k is larger. Thus the curves all go down with the increasing of k.

In Fig. 5, multiple trees have the probability of successful regeneration more than 95 %, while only about 74 % of the regeneration processes using star-structured scheme and about 83 % of the regeneration processes using single MST success.

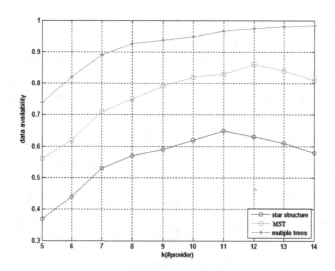

Fig. 6. Data availability

Moreover, when k is large, the probability of the successful regeneration process begins to reduce, because node departures are more likely to happen during the regeneration.

In Fig. 6, the file availability of star-structured scheme is only about 55 %, while that of single MST and multiple trees is about 82 % and 93 %. The file availability becomes higher with the increasing of k. When $k = 14$, the file availability of multiple trees is almost 99 %. It shows multiple trees regeneration has remarkable advantage for keeping high data availability.

5 Conclusion

In this paper, we present a parallel regeneration scheme for multiple edge-disjoint trees in distributed storage system using linear network coding. We deduce the optimal regeneration time for our regeneration scheme and then propose an approximate construction algorithm with polynomial time complexity for optimal multiple regeneration trees so as to reduce the regeneration time as much as possible. We evaluate the performance of our algorithm using real data measured in PlanetLab. The results show that our scheme can significantly reduce regeneration time, enhance probability of successful regeneration and improve data availability, compared with star-structured and MST regeneration scheme.

Acknowledgments. This research work is supported by National Basic Research Program of China under Grant No.2014CB340303, and The Program of National Natural Science Foundation of China under Grant No.61402514 and No.61402490, and Scientific Research Program of Hunan Provincial Education Department (No.12b012).

References

1. Rhea, S., Eaton, P., Geels, D., Weatherspoon, H., Zhao, B., Kubia towicz, J.: Pond: the OceanStore Prototype. In: FAST, pp. 1–14 (2003)
2. Huang, C., Simitci, H., Xu, Y., et al.: Erasure coding in windows azure storage. In: Proceedings of the 2012 USENIX Conference on Annual Technical Conference, pp. 2–2. USENIX Association, Boston, MA, USA (2012)
3. Sathiamoorthy, M., Asteris, M., Papailiopoulos, D., et al.: XORing elephants: novel erasure codes for big data. In: Proceedings of the 39th International Conference on Very Large Data Bases, pp. 325–336. VLDB Endowment (2013)
4. Ghemawat, S., Gobioff, H., Leung, S.-T.: The Google file system. In: SOSP, pp. 29–43 (2003)
5. Guo, C., Lu, G., Li, D., Wu, H., Zhang, X., Shi, Y., Tian, C., Zhang, Y., Lu, S.: BCube: a high performance, server-centric network architecture for modular data centers. In: Proceedings of ACM SIGCOMM 2009 conference on Data communication, pp. 63–74 (2009)
6. Weatherspoon, H., Kubiatowicz, J.D.: Erasure coding vs. replication: a quantitative comparison. In: Druschel, P., Kaashoek, M.F., Rowstron, A. (eds.) IPTPS 2002. LNCS, vol. 2429, p. 328. Springer, Heidelberg (2002)

7. Rodrigues, R., Zhou, T.H.: High availability in DHTs: erasure coding vs. replication. In: van Renesse, R. (ed.) IPTPS 2005. LNCS, vol. 3640, pp. 226–239. Springer, Heidelberg (2005)
8. Acedanski, S., Deb, S., Medard, M., Koetter, R.: How good is random linear coding based distributed networked storage?. In: Proceedings of 1st Workshop on Network Coding, pp. 1–6, Riva del Garda, Italy (2005)
9. Dimakis, A., Godfrey, P., Wainwright, M., Ramchandran, K.: Network coding for distributed storage systems. In: Proceedings of 26th INFOCOM, pp. 2000–2008 (2007)
10. Wu, Y., Dimakis, R., Ramch, K.: Deterministic regenerating codes for distributed storage. In: Allerton Conference on Control, Computing, and Communication, pp. 1–5, Urbana-Champaign, IL (2007)
11. Li, J., Yang, S., Wang, X., Xue, X., Li, B.: Tree-structured data regeneration with network coding in distributed storage systems. In: Proceedings of 17th IEEE International Workshop on Quality of Service (IWQoS), pp. 1–9 (2009)
12. Li, J., Yang, S., Wang, X., Li, B.: Tree-structured data regeneration in distributed storage systems with regenerating codes. In: Proceedings INFOCOM, pp. 1–9 (2010)
13. Ahlswede, R., Cai, N., Li, S.-Y., Yeung, R.: Network information flow. IEEE Trans. Inf. Theory 46(4), 1204–1216 (2000)
14. Duminuco, A., Biersack, E.: Hierarchical codes: how to make erasure codes attractive for peer-to-peer storage systems. In: Eighth International Conference on Peer-to-Peer Computing, pp. 89–98 (2008)
15. Bhagwan, R., Tati, K., Cheng, Y., Savage, S., Voelker, G.: Total recall: system support for automated availability management. In: Proceedings of NSDI 2001, pp. 25–25 (2004)
16. Ho, T., Koetter, R., Medard, M., Karger, D., Effros, M.: The benefits of coding over routing in a randomized setting. In: Proceedings of IEEE International Symposium on Information Theory, pp. 442–447 (2003)
17. Planetlab. http://www.planet-lab.org/
18. Banerjee, S., Lee, S.-J., Sharma, P., Yalagandula., P.: S3 (Scalable Sensing Service). http://networking.hpl.hp.com/scube/PLI
19. Stribling., J.: Planetlab All Pairs Ping. http://infospect.planet-lab.org/pings
20. Tarjan, R.E.: A good algorithm for edge-disjoint branching. Inf. Process. Lett. 51–53 (1974)
21. Roskind, J., Tarjan, R.E.: A note on finding minimum-cost edge-disjoint spanning trees. Math. Oper. Res. 701–708 (1985)

Maximize Throughput Scheduling and Cost-Fairness Optimization for Multiple DAGs with Deadline Constraint

Wei Wang$^{(\boxtimes)}$, Qingbo Wu, Yusong Tan, and Fuhui Wu

School of Computer Science, National University of Defense Technology,
Changsha 410073, China
wangwei0114@163.com, {qingbo.wu,yusong.tan,fuhui.wu}@nudt.edu.cn

Abstract. More and more application workflows are computed in cloud and most of them can be expressed by Directed Acyclic Graph (DAG). As Cloud resource providers, they should guarantee as many as possible DAGs be accomplished within their deadline when they face the over-step request of computer resource. In this paper, we define the urgency of DAG and introduce the MTMD (Maximize Throughput of Multi-DAG with Deadline) algorithm to improve the ratio of DAGs which can be accomplished within deadline. The urgency of DAG is changing among execution and determine the execution order of tasks. We can detect DAGs which will exceed the deadline by this algorithm and abandon these DAGs timely. Based on the MTMD algorithm, we put forward the CFS (Cost Fairness Scheduling) algorithm to reduce the unfairness of cost between different DAGs. The simulation results show that the MTMD algorithm outperforms three other algorithms and the CFS algorithm reduces the cost of all DAGs by 12.1 % on average and reduces the unfairness among DAGs by 54.5 % on average.

Keywords: Workflow scheduling · Deadline constrained scheduling · Multiple DAGs

1 Introduction

Currently in many areas, such as e-commerce, bioinformatics, atmospheric sciences, or information processing, all above can be expressed by a DAG (directed acyclic graph), which is composed of multiple task nodes. Some tasks can be executed concurrently, but at the same time, they have restrictions of data transmission [1]. In order to improve the efficiency of the processing, these task nodes often require a computing system which composed of multiple processing units or multiple computers. Since the size of computing growing rapidly, especially in scientific computing, it is impossible to complete the calculation with only one computer timely.

The development of grid and cloud computing technologies provides a good computing platform for these computing. Cloud computing is a high-throughput

© Springer International Publishing Switzerland 2015
G. Wang et al. (Eds.): ICA3PP 2015, Part II, LNCS 9529, pp. 621–634, 2015.
DOI: 10.1007/978-3-319-27122-4_43

computing paradigm, which uses a large data center to provide dynamic and extended virtualized computing resources via the Internet. Cloud computing provides infrastructure, platform or software as a service, so that users can select different service models under different circumstances [2]. IaaS (Infrastructure as a Service) model is the most common service that allows users to use the virtual IT resources including computing, storage and network services to compute on a leased cloud infrastructure. Users can deploy and execute applications on system which they selected, but they can not manage the cloud infrastructure.

Majority studies about DAG scheduling focus on single DAG scheduled on multiple resources. These studies raise different technologies to solve the single DAG application scheduling for different types of DAG applications, different resources and different scheduling targets, such as makespan minimization, throughput maximization, fairness schedule and resource allocation optimization etc. [1,3–8]. In addition, the workflow with restriction of deadline in the field of cloud computing also attracts researchers' attention. In a distributed cloud environment, cloud provider charges based on resource type, QoS (Quality of service) and total time of workflow. Users take into account economic factors and specify a deadline for application, so application should be accomplished before the deadline and do not need to be completed in the shortest time. At the same time, cloud providers only need to allocate appropriate resources to applications, thus reduce the fee of users' pay. To schedule these DAGs with deadline restriction, researchers put forward a number of algorithms [7,9–13]. The basic idea of these algorithms is to divide the deadline based on the task execution time. It sets a sub-deadline for each task and ensure that each task is completed in the respective sub-deadline, so the entire DAG scheduling can be completed within deadline. And for each task, it selects the cheapest resources and at the same time the task can be accomplished before the sub-deadline. However, this method mainly focuses on single DAG scheduling on a set of resources.

Many existing single DAG scheduling models can be used for multi-DAGs scheduling, such as a direct approach is scheduling multiple DAGs in turn using single DAG scheduling method, and another common approach is to put all DAG into one bigger DAG by add one entrance node and one exit node, then adopt single scheduling method to schedule this bigger DAG [14,15]. However, the biggest difference between DAG applications and multiple independent tasks is the data transfer relationship between tasks in DAG. No matter which method is adopted, the data transfer relationship always result in idle slots on the resources, thereby it leads to the reduction of throughput and resource utilization. If one DAG task uses free slots of other DAG tasks when multiple DAG are scheduled simultaneously, it will greatly enhance resource utilization and task throughput. So scheduling more DAG shared resources is becoming a research hotspot.

For cloud resource providers, their duty is to ensure that as many as possible DAGs can be accomplished before its deadline. All DAGs submit resource requests and the schedule order of DAG is determined according to the urgency of each DAG. Based on the throughput maximize, to reduce inequity between different users, the urgency of DAG, execution time, execution cost and other factors should also be considered. So the issue which is raised and addressed at this article includes two aspects: (1) Which scheduling policy should be taken to maximum throughput of multiple DAGs When these DAGs have various deadline constraints and share resources (2) Optimize scheduling algorithm to reduce inequity of users based on the maximum throughput.

The rest of this paper is organized as follows. Section 2 introduces the related work. Section 3 builds the system model and define problems. The maximize throughput scheduling and fair cost-optimizing for multiple DAGs are introduced in Sects. 4 and 5 respectively. Section 6 evaluates two scheduling algorithms and three other contrast algorithms. Section 7 concludes the paper and describes future works.

2 Related Work

Compared to single DAG scheduling in cloud environment, the study of scheduling algorithm of multiple DAGs shared resources is not so much. One of the most straightforward methods is to schedule every DAG in order according to single DAG scheduling algorithm and one DAG starts to execute only if the previous one executes completely. FCFS (first come first served) is one of this kind of algorithms and it schedules DAGs by the order of DAGs' arriving time. Round-Robin is also a method of scheduling multiple DAG, which chooses a top priority DAG according to the selection criteria by turn. Combination DAG [14,15] is used by the U. Honig and Z. Henan in homogeneous and heterogeneous environments respectively. The main idea of this algorithm is to make multiple DAG into one larger DAG by adding false entrance and exit nodes, then adop single DAG scheduling method to schedule the mixed DAG. Most optimization of multiple DAGs is using scheduling algorithm of single DAG. However, no matter which method is adopted, the data transfer relationship always results in idle slots on the resource. It will greatly enhance resource utilization and task throughput if one DAG task uses free slots of other DAG tasks when multiple DAGs are scheduled simultaneously.

Some related researches [6–9] are interested in DAG scheduling with deadline constraints and propose some solutions, but these solutions are primarily for single DAG scheduling, but not suitable for multi-DAG scheduling issues. For the multiple hybrid DAGs scheduling with deadline constraints, Georgios L [16,17] uses the EDF (Early Deadline First) method which was mentioned in the literature [18,19] scheduling multiple independent tasks with deadline constraints, to schedule multiple DAGs application. The scheduling order of DAG is determined by the deadline of each DAG, and the DAG with smallest deadline will be scheduled firstly. This algorithm will work well in the case of structure and the amount of tasks are similar between multiple DAGs, but in more cases, DAG structure varies and the deadline of DAG can't represent the urgency of DAG. For example, DAG A and DAG B which sharing resources are ready to be scheduled at the same time. The deadline of DAG A is 8 units of time and it needs 7 units of time to complete the DAG, while deadline of DAG B is 6 units of time and it need 2 units of time. The scheduling priority of B is larger than A according to EDF algorithm, DAG A starts to execute only when all tasks of DAG B are completed, then A will not be completed before its deadline. LLF (Least-Laxity-First) [20] is also a method to solve scheduling of multiple independent real-time tasks, LLF takes laxity, which is the difference between the deadline and period of its completion, as a measure of the urgency. However, the measure of LLF is an absolute amount, without taking into account structural differences between DAGs. This method will not well define the urgency of multiple DAGs if the structural differences between DAGs are large. Therefore, both EDF and LLF methods are not good measures of the degree of urgency among multiple DAG for they do not consider the structure between a plurality of DAGs.

MDRS (Scheduling for Multi-DAGs with Deadline based on Relative Stritness) method puts forward a new definition of relative strictness in the literature [21] by Tian, and relative strictness of each DAG is expressed as the ratio of the execution time of the remaining task and the time available. This method takes into account the structure of DAG and the measurement is not an absolute value but a relative value, so the measure is more accurate. But this approach also has shortcomings. If the relative strictness value of DAG A is little smaller than DAG B when they both have only one task and the remaining time of A to complete is much less than the remaining time of B, the task of A should start to execute only after the completion of B, but it may lead to the completed time of A exceed its deadline. We improve the scheduling algorithm of MDRS, taking into account not only the absolute value but also the relative value.

3   System Model and Problem Definition

A workflow application can be represented by a DAG: $G = (V, E, S, D)$, as shown in Fig. 1.

V is the set of v task and E is the set of communication edges between tasks. Each $e(i, j) \in E$ represents the task-dependency constraint and task j should start to execute after the complete execution of task i. S is the set of mapping of tasks to resources and it is the result of scheduling of multiple DAGs. Cloud providers schedule N DAGs: $(G_1, G_2, ..., G_N)$ with various deadlines. Deadlines of all DAGs are represented by $(d_{G_1}, d_{G_2}, ..., d_{G_i}, ...d_{G_N})$ and each structure of

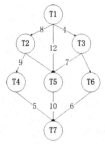

Task	M1	M2	M3
R1	20	24	18
R2	12	8	10
R3	15	9	17
R4	11	13	14
R5	15	21	18
R6	23	22	17
R7	7	6	14

Fig. 1. Application model and computation time matrix of the tasks in each processor

DAG can be completely different. Each DAG consists of various tasks and tasks belong to G_i can be expressed as $(task_{i,1}, task_{i,2}, ...task_{i,j}, ...task_{i,n_{G_i}})$ and we take $wl_{i,j}$ to express the workload of $task_{i,j}$ in this article. Applications share a set of R resources $(R_1, R_2, ...R_i, ...R_M)$ which have different computing capability. According to previous research [10–12] and the reality of data in cloud computing, the price of resource is proportional to the computing power ECU, and it means the economic cost of this resource is larger when the computing power of this resource is bigger. We define the unit price of resource M_i is p_{M_i} and the value has a positive correlation with its computing power. We can get the execution time and cost of task $task_{i,k}$ on resource M_j:

$$ET_{task(i,k)}^{M_j} = \frac{wl_{i,k}}{M_j.ECU} \tag{1}$$

$$Cost_{task(i,k)}^{M_j} = p_{M_j} * ET_{task(i,k)}^{M_j} \tag{2}$$

DAGs are submitted by different users, and its structure, size of tasks, and deadlines are arbitrary. All users want their DAG to be completed within limits and the payment as little as possible. Cloud resource providers face the multiple DAG requests, and they need to meet as many as possible DAGs requests and make as many as possible DAGs completed within the deadline. The scheduling priority of DAG needs to be determined according to the urgency of DAG. One DAG's execution is bound to affect other DAGs' execution when multiple DAGs are scheduled at the same time, and it may lead to other DAGs not being completed before the deadline. It will increase the ratio of DAG which can be completed within the deadline if we detect those DAGs which can not be completed within deadlines and discard them timely. It will reduce the waste of resources. When we have completed the scheduling of the DAG according to the degree of urgency, we can determine which DAG can be completed within the deadline and their execution time. If there are redundant time after they complete, it will be a reasonable optimization for algorithm if we measure the fairness between DAG and adjust the correspondence between tasks and resources. Therefore, we put forward MTMD (Maximize Throughput of Multi-DAG with Deadline) and CFS (Cost Fairness Scheduling) algorithm.

4   Throughput Maximizing for Multi-DAGs Scheduling with Deadline Constraint

If every task of DAG can be assigned to the resources with the shortest complete time, the complete time of all DAGs will be shortest and it will get a maximize throughput. HEFT [22] is a typical single DAG minimum execution time scheduling algorithm, and its implementation process consists of two phases:

– The first step is to determine the priority of each task. Calculate the upward rank of each task according to the formula:

$$rank_u(n_i) = \overline{w_i} + \max_{n_j \in succ(n_i)} (\overline{c_{i,j}} + rank_u(n_j)) \tag{3}$$

where $succ(n_i)$ is the set of immediate successors of task n_i, $\overline{w_i}$ is the average computation cost of task n_i and $\overline{c_{i,j}}$ is the average communication cost of $edge(i, j)$ for the exit task $rank_u(n_{exit}) = \overline{w_{exit}}$, so the upward rank represents the length of the longest path from task n_i to the exit node. Put all tasks into waiting list to be scheduled in descending order of the upward rank.

- The second step is to assign tasks to the resource. Select the task with the largest upward rank from the waiting list and compute the earliest completion time when tasks are assigned to each resource. Select the minimum completion time of resources assigned to the task. So HEFT method can guarantee the DAG has a shortest execution time.

To make as many as possible DAGs to be completed within the deadline, we need to arrange DAGs sort descending according to the urgency of DAGs waiting to be scheduled. When some tasks of DAG G_i have been assigned to resources, the rest tasks can be expressed as $un(G_i)$. We schedule these tasks according to the HEFT algorithm when some resources have been occupied, and the earliest start time of $un(G_i)$ can be expressed as st_{G_i} and the earliest completion time of $un(G_i)$ can be expressed as ft_{G_i}. So the makespan of $un(G_i)$ can be calculated as

$$mspan_{un(G_i)} = ft_{G_i} - st_{G_i} \tag{4}$$

With respect to the deadline, the available time is

$$rest_{un(G_i)} = d_{G_i} - st_{G_i} \tag{5}$$

And the remaining time after the accomplishment of DAG is

$$avail_{un(G_i)} = d_{G_i} - st_{G_i} \tag{6}$$

So the average time of remaining time of all DAGs is:

$$\overline{rest} = \frac{1}{N} \sum_{i=1}^{i=N} rest_{un(G_i)} = \frac{1}{N} \sum_{i=1}^{i=N} (d_{G_i} - ft_{G_i}) \tag{7}$$

We can definite the urgency of the remaining task is

$$R_{un(G_i)} = \frac{mspan_{un(G_i)}}{avail_{un(G_i)}} * \frac{\overline{rest}}{rest_{un(G_i)}} = \frac{ft_{G_i} - st_{G_i}}{d_{G_i} - st_{G_i}} * \frac{\frac{1}{N} \sum_{i=1}^{N} (d_{G_i} - ft_{G_i})}{d_{G_i} - ft_{G_i}} \tag{8}$$

MTMD method is an improvement over Tians MDRS method. Tian only considers the time required to complete DAG and available time, and we consider not only these two factors but also the remaining time. For example, both DAG A and DAG B have only one remaining task waiting to be scheduled, and both dispatch to the same resource by HEFT algorithm. Suppose $mspan_{un(G_A)} = 18$, $avail_{un(G_A)} = 24$, $mspan_{un(G_B)} = 2$, and $avail_{un(G_B)} = 3$. We will get the urgency according to MDRS algorithm

$$r_A = mspan_{un(G_A)}/avail_{un(G_A)} = 18/24 = 0.75$$

$$r_B = mspan_{un(G_B)}/avail_{un(G_B)} = 2/3 = 0.67$$

If we schedule DAG A firstly, it is obvious that DAG B can't be completed in time. The reason is that MDRS takes no count of remaining time after the execution of DAG. So we will improve the priority of urgency if the remaining time is not so much. According to our MTMD algorithm, we will get $R_A = 0.4375$, $R_B = 2.33$, B will be executed before A and A will also complete before its deadline. We put forward the Algorithm 1 according the urgency of reaming tasks.

Algorithm 1. Maximize Throughput of Multi-DAG with Deadline Algorithm

Input: $G_{unsche} \leftarrow G_i$: the DAG to be scheduled;
T_i: all tasks belong to G_i;
$Stask_{i,k} \rightarrow VM_j \leftarrow \emptyset$: the assignment of tasks.
Output: S
1: calculate $R_{all(G_i)}$ select the maximal $rank_u task_{i,k}$ from maximal $R_{all(G_i)}$ DAG
2: add $task_{i,k} \rightarrow VM_j$ to S, remove $task_{i,k}$ from T_i
3: **while** $(G_{unsche} \neq \emptyset)$ **do**
4:    calculate $R_{un(G_i)}$
5:    **if** $(d_{G_i} > ft_{G_i} | \forall G_{unsche} \neq \emptyset)$ **then**
6:       select the max $rank_u task_{i,k}$ from max $R_{un(G_i)}$ DAG
7:       add $task_{i,k} \rightarrow VM_j$ to S, remove $task_{i,k}$ from T_i
8:    **else if** $((\exists d_{G_i} = ft_{G_i}) \cap other(\forall d_{G_i} > ft_{G_i}))$ **then**
9:       schedule all tasks belong to DAG_i
10:      G_{unsche} remove G_i
11:      S .add all $task_i \rightarrow VM_j$
12:   **else if** $(\exists d_{G_i} < ft_{G_i})$ **then**
13:      roll back the last step; schedule all tasks belong to DAG_i
14:      **if** $(d_{G_i} < ft_{G_i})$ **then**
15:         abandon DAG_i roll back the until the first task belong to DAG_i
16:      **end if**
17:   **end if**
18: **end while**

The step of MTMD algorithm is executed as following:

– Select the first task which needs to be scheduled. There is no task assigned to any resources before scheduling, so the earliest start time of each DAG according to HEFT algorithm is 0. The calculation formula of urgency $R_{all(G_i)}$ becomes:

$$R_{all(G_i)} = \frac{ft_{G_i}}{d_{G_i}} * \frac{\frac{1}{N}\sum_{i=1}^{N}(d_{G_i} - ft_{G_i})}{d_{G_i} - ft_{G_i}} \tag{9}$$

Calculate the urgency of every DAG and select the task with the highest upward rank from the DAG with the highest R. Assigned the task to the resource by the HEFT algorithm.

- schedule follow-up tasks. Recalculate the urgency of remaining tasks $R_{un(G_i)}$ of all DAG, and choose the tasks with the highest upward rank from the DAG with the highest R. Assign the task to the resource which will complete the task earliest according to HEFT algorithm. Repeat this process until all DAG tasks are completed.

Using HEFT scheduling algorithm to calculate the makespan of every DAG will reflect each DAGs urgency directly when one or all of the resources have been occupied by some tasks. When we find that one DAG's minimize execution time of remaining tasks equals to the available time, we will schedule all the remaining tasks of this DAG firstly to make sure that this DAG will be completed before the deadline. There may exist a complex situation that we will find $d_{G_i} < ft_{G_i}$ when we calculate the urgency of the R. It means that the shortest execution time of remaining tasks less than the available time and this DAG will not be completed before the deadline. We will draw back the last assignment and then schedule all the remaining tasks of this DAG firstly. If this DAG will not be completed within deadline again then we will give up this DAG.

For a DAG with v tasks and the number of resources is m, the time complexity of HEFT algorithm is $O(v^2m)$. For the MTMD algorithm, we assume that the number of DAGs waiting to be scheduled is n. HEFT algorithm will be scheduled $2vn^2$ times if all DAGs can be completed within deadline and the complexity of MTMD is $O(n^2v^3m)$. If there is abandoned DAGs and in the most complicated condition, there is $(n-1)$ DAG needing to be abandoned, the HEFT algorithm will be scheduled $vn^2(n-1)$ times and the complexity of MTMD algorithm is $O(n^3v^3m)$. MTMD can offer a schedule for multi-DAGs within a power polynomial function.

5   Cost Fairness Optimization

We introduce the MTMD algorithm in the Sect. 4. To get the maximize throughput and make as many as possible DAGs to be completed before the deadline, we adapt HEFT algorithm to assign tasks to resources. HEFT algorithm is minimum completion time scheduling algorithm for single DAG, which will lead to a lot of DAGs completion time much smaller than its deadline. It is acknowledged that faster resources have higher unit costs. In order to make more DAGs to be completed in time, there exits unfairness among users. For example, the payment of DAG A is larger than DAG B but the workload of A is smaller than B, at the same time, the urgency of A is less than B. Users will not be satisfied with this scheduling if resource providers pay no attention to this unfairness of scheduling algorithm.

We can define the N DAGs which can be completed within their deadlines in the first stage of scheduling. They can be expressed as $co(DAG)$ and there are redundant time compared to their deadline. It means that we can cut down the payment of users by assigning some tasks to cheaper resources and ensuring that they are still able to be completed within their deadlines. To measure the fairness between multiple DAGs, one standard that we can accept is when the urgency degree is higher, the resource should be more efficient and the unit price of this source is higher. We use the ratio of the cost of unit workload and the urgency of DAG as a measure of fairness.

The cost optimization process based on the fairness is as follows: Add all tasks which have been selected by the first phase to the collection of waiting to be optimized and the collection of already being optimized is empty. Then determine the next scheduled task to be optimized based on the fairness standard. The optimized method of this task is selecting the resource which is cheaper than original resource and can cut down the unfairness value between DAGs. It is an obvious factor that this resource can make sure that $co(DAG)$ can be completed before the deadline. Transfer this task from the waiting collection to the already completed collection and this optimization process will be finished until the non-optimized set of tasks becomes empty. The following describes the relevant symbol and the definition of unfairness.

For every DAG belongs to $co(DAG)$, the payment according to MTMD algorithm is

$$\cos t(G_i) = \sum_{j=1}^{n_{G_i}} p_{M_{HEFT}} * t_{task_{i,j}, M_{HEFT}} \tag{10}$$

where $t_{task_{i,j}, M_{HEFT}}$ express the execution time of $task_{i,j}$ on resource M_{HEFT} and the $p_{M_{HEFT}}$ express the unit price of this resource. The workload of DAG can be represented as

$$workload(G_i) = \sum_{j=1}^{n_{G_i}} workload(task_{i,j}) \tag{11}$$

and the unfairness of each DAG can be represented as

$$F(G_i) = \frac{\cos t(G_i)/workload(G_i)}{M_{own}/d_{G_i}} \tag{12}$$

The Denominator measures the urgency of DAG and the numerator expresses the payment of unit workload. It is unfair if the urgency is very relaxed but the cost of unit workload is very high for user. The target of this cost optimization is to cut down the unfairness between applications and which is:

$$UNF = \sqrt{\sum_{i=1}^{N} \left(F(G_i) - \overline{F}\right)^2} \tag{13}$$

where $\overline{F}$ represent the average of $F(G_i)$. We choose the task to be optimized according to the value of $F(G_i)$ and judge the effect of optimization according to the value of UNF. The Algorithm 2 show the scheduling of fairness.

Algorithm 2. Cost Fairness Scheduling

Input: $G_{unoptimized} \leftarrow co(DAG)$
    $T_i \leftarrow$ all tasks belong to $co(DAG)$
    $S\{task_{i,k} \rightarrow VM_j\} \leftarrow \emptyset$ the assignment of tasks.
Output: S
  1: **while** ($G_{unoptimized} \neq \emptyset$) **do**
  2:    calculate the $F(G_i)$ of $G_{unoptimized}$
  3:    select the maximal $rank_u\ task_{i,k}$ from the maximal $F(G_i)$
  4:    calculate $R_{all(G_i)}$ select the maximal $rank_u task_{i,k}$ from maximal $R_{all(G_i)}$ DAG
  5:    $M_{i,j} \leftarrow$ the collection of cheaper resources
  6:    **while** ($M_{i,j} \neq \emptyset$) **do**
  7:      schedule all remaining tasks of $G_{unoptimized}$
  8:      **if** ($\exists d_{G_i} < ft_{G_i}$) **then**
  9:        remove this resource from $G_{unoptimized}$
10:      **else**
11:        calculate the UNF
12:      **end if**
13:    **end while**
14:    assign $task_{i,k}$ to the minimum UNF resource
15: **end while**

CFS algorithm optimizes the fairness of cost based on the MTMD algorithm and it optimizes DAGs which can be completed within their deadlines. We assume there is n_o DAGs can be completed within their deadlines and every DAGs has v tasks, and the number of resources is m. CFS algorithm will invoke MTMD algorithm $(n_o.v.m)$ times. So the complexity time of CFS is $O(n_o{}^3v^4m^2)$ and it also can offer a scheduling within a power polynomial function.

6 Performance Evaluation

6.1 The Competitive Algorithms

We introduce two algorithms in this article. The target of algorithm MTMD is to maximize the throughput and make as many as possible DAGs to be completed before deadlines. This algorithm will be compared with EDF, LLF, MDRS algorithm.

Table 1. Capability and price of available resource types.

RT	ECU	price	RT	ECU	price
rt_1	1.0	0.12	rt_6	3.5	0.595
rt_2	1.5	0.195	rt_7	4.0	0.72
rt_3	2.0	0.28	rt_8	4.5	0.855
rt_4	2.5	0.375	rt_9	5.0	1.0
rt_5	3.0	0.48			

The algorithms will be compared with MTMD are setting as following:

(1) EDF algorithm: the scheduling order is determined by the ascending of deadlines, and all tasks belong to DAG with the minimize deadline are execute firstly. Tasks belong to DAGs with larger deadline are inserted to the idle of resource.
(2) LLF algorithm: the scheduling order is determined by ascending of laxity of DAGs, and all tasks belong to DAG with the minimize laxity are execute firstly. Tasks belong to DAGs with larger ascending are inserted to the idle of resource.
(3) MDRS algorithm: assign the largest upward rank task of largest relative stringency to the resource of which will accomplish firstly.

The CFS algorithm is optimized on the base of MTMD algorithm. So it only needs to compare with the MTMD algorithm on the respect of payment and fairness.

6.2 Experimental Setup

In our experiments, we assume a service oriented environment offering 9 kinds different computation services, with different processing capabilities and prices as shown in Table 1. The average bandwidth of computation services is set to 20 MBps which is the approximate average bandwidth of services in Amazon $EC2$. There are 3 services for every kind of resource. For every experiment, there are 100 workflows waiting to be scheduled. The number of tasks which belong to every DAG and the deadline of every DAG are changing in different experiments. The minimum execution time of DAG is when it is scheduled by HEFT algorithm alone and the deadline of DAG is the multiple of this minimum execution time. We produce DAGs by a simulation and we set the number of DAGs is 100 in every experiment. There are 6 VMs for every kind of resource. The MTMD algorithm will be compared with these algorithms. The Comparative performance is the number of DAGs which will complete before their deadline. The Fig. 2 show the ratio of DAG which can be scheduled within deadline to all DAGs with different deadlines.

From the simulative result we can see that the performance of EDF and LLF algorithm is not as good as MDRS and MTMD algorithm for the reason that

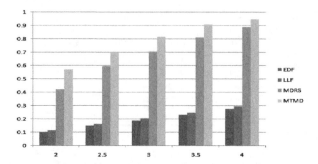

Fig. 2. The ratio of DAGs complete within deadline at different deadline

the last two algorithms can find DAGs which can't complete before deadline and abandon them timely. Whether the deadline is loose or urgent, MTMD algorithm will make more DAGs to be completed within deadline compared to the MDRS algorithm and the performance is better when the deadline is urgent.

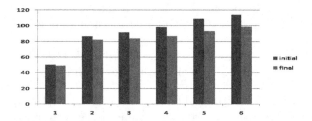

Fig. 3. The cost of DAGs with different VM resources

And for the CFS algorithm, it will compare with the MTMD algorithm for CFS algorithm optimizes DAGs which can be completed within deadline by MTMD algorithm so the number of scheduling DAGs by these two algorithms is equal. Figure 3 shows the total cost of DAGs when the number of every type VM changing from 1 to 6 and the Fig. 4 shows the unfairness before and after optimization. We can find that the cost of DAGs after optimization is less than before and the cost reduces rapidly when the size of every type VM is 1, because not all DAGs can be completed within deadline. We can get that the reduction of cost is 12.1 % on average after optimization from the simulation result. The unfairness increases with the increasing of VM resource before optimization and drops after optimization. It is due to the target of MTMD algorithm is to maximize throughput and it almost assigns tasks to the fastest resources. So the value of cost and unfairness are the maximal one among all experiment when the number of resources are the maximal. The CFS algorithm aims at the reduction of unfairness and the value of unfairness descends with the increasing of resources. The increase of unfairness before optimizing and the reduction of unfairness after optimizing lead to the unfairness descends rapidly with the increasing of VM resource and the CFS algorithm reduces unfairness among DAGs by 54.5 % on average.

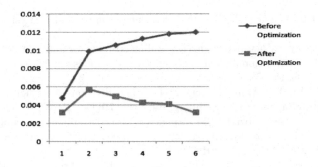

Fig. 4. The unfairness of DAGs with different VM resources

7 Conclusion

In this paper, we propose a maximize throughput algorithm for multi-DAGs named MTMD and a fair cost-optimize algorithm named CFS. We also make comprehensive comparison with 3 relative algorithms in the literature. Simulation results show that the MTMD algorithm performs better than the other overall and the performance is better when the deadline is urgent. The CFS algorithm can reduce the cost and unfairness among DAGs obviously and the unfairness descends rapidly with the increasing of VM resource. As future work, we intend to optimize these two algorithm to reduce the complexity time of them to improve the performance in the authentic cloud environment.

References

1. Zhao, H., Sakellariou, R.: Scheduling multiple DAGs onto heterogeneous systems. In: 20th International Parallel and Distributed Processing Symposium, IPDPS 2006, p. 14. IEEE (2006)
2. Hwang, K., Fox, G.C., Dongarra, J., et al.: Cloud Comptuing and Distributed System: From Parallel Processing to Web of Things. Machinery Industy Press, Beijing (2013)
3. Hnig, U., Schiffmann, W.: A meta-algorithm for scheduling multiple DAGs in homogeneous system environments. In: Proceedings of the Eighteenth IASTED International Conference on Parallel and Distributed Computing and Systems (PDCS 2006) (2006)
4. Bittencourt, L.F., Madeira, E.R.M.: Towards the scheduling of multiple workflows on computational grids. J. Grid Comput. **8**(3), 419–441 (2010)
5. Tian, G., Xiao, C., Zhusheng, X., et al.: Hybrid scheduling strategy for mulitple DAGs workflow in heterogeneous system. J. Softw. **23**(10), 2720–2734 (2012)
6. Arabnejad, H., Barbosa, J.: Fairness resource sharing for dynamic workflow scheduling on heterogeneous systems. In: 2012 IEEE 10th International Symposium on Parallel and Distributed Processing with Applications (ISPA), pp. 633–639. IEEE (2012)
7. Mao, M., Humphrey, M.: Auto-scaling to minimize cost and meet application deadlines in cloud workflows. In: Proceedings of 2011 International Conference

for High Performance Computing, Networking, Storage and Analysis, p. 49. ACM (2011)

8. Yu, Z., Shi, W.: A planner-guided scheduling strategy for multiple workflow applications. In: International Conference on Parallel Processing-Workshops, ICPP-W 2008, pp. 1–8. IEEE (2008)

9. Yuan, Y., Li, X., Wang, Q., et al.: Deadline division-based heuristic for cost optimization in workflow scheduling. Inf. Sci. **179**(15), 2562–2575 (2009)

10. Abrishami, S., Naghibzadeh, M., Epema, D.H.J.: Deadline-constrained workflow scheduling algorithms for Infrastructure as a service clouds. Future Gener. Comput. Syst. **29**(1), 158–169 (2013)

11. Yu, J., Buyya, R., Tham, C.K.: Cost-based scheduling of scientific workflow applications on utility grids. In: First International Conference on e-Science and Grid Computing, 8 p. 147. IEEE (2005)

12. Abrishami, S., Naghibzadeh, M., Epema, D.H.J.: Cost-driven scheduling of grid workflows using partial critical paths. IEEE Trans. Parallel Distrib. Syst. **23**(8), 1400–1414 (2012)

13. Liu, K., Jin, H., Chen, J., et al.: A compromised-time-cost scheduling algorithm in SwinDeW-C for instance-intensive cost-constrained workflows on cloud computing platform. Int. J. High Perform. Comput. Appl. **24**, 445–456 (2010)

14. Henan, Z., Sakellariou, R.: Scheduling multiple DAGs onto heterogeneous systems. In: Proceedings of the 20th International Parallel and Distributed Processing Symposium, Island of Rhodes, Greece, p. 159, 25–29 April 2006

15. Honig, U., Schiffmann, W.: A meta-algorithm for scheduling multiple DAGs in homogeneous system environments. In: Proceedings of the IEEE 18th IASTED International Conference on Parallel and Distributed Computing and System, pp. 147–152 (2006)

16. Stavrinides, G.L., Karatza, H.D.: Scheduling multiple task graphs with end-to-end deadlines in distributed real-time systems utilizing imprecise computations. J. Syst. Softw. **83**(6), 1004–1014 (2010)

17. Stavrinides, G.L., Karatza, H.D.: Scheduling real-time DAGs in heterogeneous clusters by combining imprecise computations and bin packing techniques for the exploitation of schedule holes. Future Gener. Comput. Syst. **28**(7), 977–988 (2012)

18. Baker, T.P.: An analysis of EDF schedulability on a multiprocessor. IEEE Trans. Parallel Distrib. Syst. **16**(8), 760–768 (2005)

19. Davis, R.I., Burns, A.: A survey of hard real-time scheduling for multiprocessor systems. ACM Comput. Surv. **43**(4), 1–44 (2011)

20. Oh, S.-H., Yang, S.-M.: A modified least-laxity-first scheduling algorithm for real-time tasks. In: Proceedings of the Fifth International Conference on Real-Time Computing Systems and Applications, pp. 31–36 (1998)

21. Tian, G.-Z., Xiao, C.-B., Xie, J.-Q.: Scheuling and fair cost-optimizing methods for concrrrent multiple DAGs with deadline sharing resources. Chin. J. Comput. **37**(7), 1067–1619 (2014)

22. Topcuoglu, H., Hariri, S., Wu, M.-Y.: Performance-effective and low-complexity task scheduling for heterogeneous computing. IEEE Trans. Parallel Distrib. Syst. **13**(3), 260–274 (2012)

Unified Multi-constraint and Multi-objective Workflow Scheduling for Cloud System

Fuhui Wu$^{(\boxtimes)}$, Qingbo Wu, Yusong Tan, and Wei Wang

School of Computer Science, National University of Defense Technology,
Changsha 410073, China
{fuhui.wu,qingbo.wu,yusong.tan,wei.wang}@nudt.edu.cn

Abstract. With the development of cloud computing, the problem of
scheduling workflow in cloud system attracts a large amount of
attention. In general, the cloud workflow scheduling problem requires
to consider a variety of optimization objectives with some constraints.
Traditional workflow scheduling methods focus on single optimization
goal like makespan and single constraint like deadline or budget. In this
paper, we first make a unified formalization of the optimality problem
of multi-constraint and multi-objective cloud workflow scheduling using
pareto optimality theory. We also present a two-constraint and two-
objective case study, considering deadline, budget constraints and energy
consumption, reliability objectives. A general list scheduling algorithm
and a tuning mechanism are designed to solve this problem. Through
extensive experimental, it confirms the efficiency of the unified multi-
constraint and multi-objective cloud workflow scheduling system.

Keywords: Cloud workflow scheduling · Multi-constraint · Multi-objective

1 Introduction

The workflow scheduling problem has been studied extensively over past years,
focusing on Multiprocessor system [1] and distributed environments like grids
[2] and clusters. The ever-growing data and computing requirement need higher
performance computing environment in order to execute these workflows in reasonable amount of time. With the development of cloud computing, large-scale
workflow applications are able to make benefit from the dynamically provisioned
resource instead of using a dedicated supercomputer.

In traditional systems, scheduling methods are usually classified as best effort
approach, with the only target of optimizing makespan. In contrast to best-effort
scheduling, QoS constrained workflow scheduling is studied to meet real world
application's requirements. A QoS constrained schedule tries to optimize some
objectives with constraints on other objectives. DTL [3], DBL [4], and DET
[5] are three heuristics that solve the deadline constrained workflow scheduling
problem. They solve the problem by distributing deadline over task partitions.
Abrishami et al. [6] presented partial critical path based scheduling algorithms,
which distribute deadline in PCP-wise way.

© Springer International Publishing Switzerland 2015
G. Wang et al. (Eds.): ICA3PP 2015, Part II, LNCS 9529, pp. 635–650, 2015.
DOI: 10.1007/978-3-319-27122-4_44

To address the budget constrained workflow scheduling problem, there are two main categories of solution. The first one is to implement budget constraint into *static* scheduling algorithms [7–9], which we categorize as one-time heuristic. The advantage of this category is the very small time complexity. Another category is back-tracking based heuristic. It starts with a schedule which has good performance under one of the two objectives considered (that is, makespan and budget), and then swaps tasks between resources trying to optimize as much as possible for the other objective. There are two approaches, "LOSS" and "GAIN" [10], implementing this idea. The "LOSS" approach starts with a schedule with optimal makespan, and repeats reassigning tasks to cheaper resource until the total cost is not over budget. While the "GAIN" approach starts with cheapest schedule, and repeats reassigning task to more expensive resource to gain more makespan optimization.

The workflow scheduling in service oriented environment also encounters with multiple objective requirements which are ofthen conflicting. One of the most straightforward way is to aggregate multi-objectives into a single objective [11, 12,15,26]. Wieczorek and Prodan et al. [16,17] used $\epsilon-$ approach to solve bi-criteria workflow scheduling problem. And Bessai et al. [18] and Yu et al. [19] used pareto approach to solve the multi-criteria optimization problem, which produces a set of non-dominated pareto front schedules.

As power is now widely recognized as a first-class design constraint for modern computing systems, the power management is another critical issue for clouds hosting thousands of computing servers. To optimize energy consumption of workflow scheduling, the most straight forward method is to generate a schedule using makespan best-effort algorithm firstly, and use DVS technique to optimize slack time of the generated schedule [20, 21]. Lee et al. [22] devised a novel objective function and a variant that effectively balance two goals of makespan and energy consumption minimization. Based on those two objective functions, they proposed a list scheduling heuristic and a tuning mechanism. Mezmaz et al. [23] and Yassa et al. [24] formalized the same problem as a multi-objective optimization problem, and solved it using meta-heuristic algorithms of genetic algorithm (GA) and particle swarm optimization (PSO) algorithm separately.

Due to hardware and software factors in cloud environment, it brings new challenge of reliability on workflow scheduling. To handle the performance fluctuation and failure problem, studies [25,26] addressed these problems when doing workflow scheduling.

Considering that all these works focus on customized constraints and objectives, we make a generalization of workflow scheduling with multi-constraint and multi-objective. We also instantiate the problem in a case of reducing energy consumption and enhancing reliability with constraints of deadline and budget. A list scheduling algorithm and a tuning mechanism are proposed.

2   MCMO Workflow Scheduling

2.1   System Model

A workflow is modeled by a directed acyclic graph (DAG): $G = (\mathcal{T}, \mathcal{E})$, where $\mathcal{T}$ consists of a set of tasks $\{t_1, t_2, ..., t_{|\mathcal{T}|}\}$ and $\mathcal{E}$ consists of a set of directed edges $\{e_i^j | (t_i, t_j) \in \mathcal{E}\}$ representing dependencies among tasks. Each task t is associated with multi-attribute of $<wl, ...>$, where wl is the key attribute of a task. The value, expressed as $t_{[wl]}$ of task t, denotes a certain amount of computation workload to be processed. And each edge e_i^j is also associated with multi-attribute of $<d, ...>$, where value $(e_i^j)_{[d]}$ denotes the size of date carried by e_i^j. A edge e_i^j also limits that t_j can start until t_i completes and all data from t_i has been received by t_j. Given a task graph, a task without any parent is called *entry* task, and a task without any child is called *exit* task.

The target system consists of a number of processors, hosts, or resources $\mathcal{P} = \{p_1, p_2, ..., p_{|\mathcal{P}|}\}$. Each processor $p \in \mathcal{P}$ is associated with multi-attribute of $<cap, pri, vsl, rel, ...>$, where $p_{[cap]}$ denotes the capability, $p_{[pri]}$ denotes the economic cost per time unit, $p_{[vsl]}$ denotes the voltage supply level, if dynamic voltage scaling (DVS) is enabled, $p_{[rel]}$ denotes the reliability of p, and etc. To construct a cloud system, a network system N is build for connecting processors. The key attributes of a network is the data transmission delay $N_{[dl]}$ and bandwidth $N_{[bw]}$ between processors.

2.2   MCMO Problem

Based on the system model, a schedule for a given DAG G is defined as: $S = <\mathcal{M}, O>$. Among a schedule S, $\mathcal{M}$ maps all tasks to processors, configured with available voltage supply. For task t, $m_t^{<p,v>}$ maps it to processor p, with voltage supply of v. In turn, $m_t^{<p,v>}$ is associated with multi-attribute $<st, ft, et, ...>$, where st denotes the start time, ft denotes the finish time, and et denotes the execution time of t on p, if the voltage supply is v. They are determined by the attributes of t and the environment it executes on. For a schedule S, multiple objectives of $O = <O_1, O_2, O_3, O_4, ...>$ are considered. Some common objectives include schedule length *makespan*, economic cost c, energy consumption e, reliability rel, and etc.

When scheduling a workflow application, there can be multiple constraints $C = <C_1, C_2, C_3, ...>$ on part of scheduling objectives $O_c = <O_1, O_2, O_3, ...>$, satisfying $O_c \subset O$. If a constraint C_i is strict, the constrained objective of a generated schedule should be better than C_i. Otherwise, the schedule is unacceptable. If a constraint C_i is not strict, a generated schedule, with worse objective than C_i, can be accepted by paying a certain amount of penalty.

3   Implementation of MCMO Using List Scheduling

In this section, an instantiation of MCMO problem is studied, and a local search method is proposed using list scheduling. This instantiation considers two constraints of execution time, denoted as deadline D, and economic cost budget B.

The scheduling objectives are reducing energy consumption (e) and improving reliability (rel).

3.1 Models and Formulation

A. Objective and Constraint Modeling

There are four objective $O = <O_1, O_2, O_3, O_4>$ considered in all, where $O_1, O_2,$ O_3, O_4 are customized as the schedule length *makespan*, economic cost c, energy consumption e, and reliability rel. Among these objectives, O_1 and O_2 are constrained by $C = <C_1, C_2>$, where C_1 is the execution deadline D, and C_2 is the economic budget B. O_3 and O_4 are non-constrained objectives, and are the optimization target for generated schedule.

In order to satisfy different service level, a cloud provider usually purchases heterogeneous hosts. In this paper, all hosts are assumed to be single processor configured. The processors own different properties in capability, price, voltage supply setting, and reliability. The processing capability of all processors is assumed to range from cap_{min} to cap_{max}. And the cloud system is assumed to be deployed in a single data center, with all processors connected by a homogeneous network N. Hence, the data transmission delay and bandwidth are the same. To reduce energy consumption, all processors are dynamic voltage scaling (DVS) enabled. The voltage supply level ($p_{[vsl]}$) configuration for a processor p is selectable from $\{vsl_0, vsl_1, vsl_2, vsl_3\}$ in Table 1. Each voltage supply level vsl_i configuration scales voltage supply v from $vsl_{i[min]}$ to $vsl_{i[max]}$. The relative speed and the voltage setting forms a 1-1 mapping relationship $rs_i(v)$ for each voltage supply level configuration vsl_i. For a processor p with voltage supply configured at v, the relative capability is calculated as: $p_{[rc]} = \frac{v}{(p_{[vsl]})_{[max]}} p_{[cap]}$, where $(p_{[vsl]})_{[max]}$ is maximal suppliable voltage of the voltage supply level configuration of processor p. And the economic cost per time unit is $\frac{\alpha(1+\alpha)}{2} pri_{max}$. The parameter α is the ratio of processing capability $p_{[cap]}$ of processor p to that of the fastest processor ($\frac{p_{[cap]}}{cap_{[max]}}$). Without lose of generality, the maximal price $pri_{[max]}$ of the fatest processing capability is normalized to 1. And the price $p_{[pri]}$ of processor p is $\frac{\alpha(1+\alpha)}{2}$.

Based on this model for cloud system, the execution time of a task t on a processor p, with voltage supplied at v, is calculated as:

$$(m_t^{<p,v>})_{[et]} = \frac{t_{[wl]}}{p_{[rc]}} = \frac{t_{[wl]}}{p_{[cap]}} \cdot \frac{(p_{[vsl]})_{[max]}}{v} \tag{1}$$

And the data transmission time from t_i to t_j is:

$$tt_{t_i}^{t_j} = \begin{cases} 0, & t_i \text{ and } t_j \text{ execute on the same processor} \\ N_{[dl]} + \frac{(e_i^j)_{[d]}}{N_{[bw]}}, & \text{otherwise} \end{cases} \tag{2}$$

Assuming the processors don't support time-shared task execution and preemption, there is at most one task executing on a processor at a time point. Using

Table 1. Voltage-relative speed configurations [22]

Conf.s / level	vsl_0		vsl_1		vsl_2		vsl_3	
	v	rs	v	rs	v	rs	v	rs
0	1.75	1.0	1.5	1.0	2.2	1.0	1.5	1.0
1	1.4	0.8	1.4	0.9	1.9	0.85	1.2	0.8
2	1.2	0.6	1.3	0.8	1.6	0.65	0.9	0.5
3	0.9	0.4	1.2	0.7	1.3	0.5		
4			1.1	0.6	1.0	0.35		
5			1.0	0.5				
6			0.9	0.4				

(1) and (2), the start time and finish time of a map of $m_{t_i}^{p_l}$ can be determined. And the schedule length of a schedule S is calculated as:

$$makespan = \max_{(m_{t_i}^{<p_l,v_j>}) \in S_{[\mathcal{M}]}} \{(m_{t_i}^{<p_l,v_j>})_{[ft]}\} \tag{3}$$

The economic cost of a schedule S is calculated as:

$$c = \sum_{(m_{t_i}^{<p_l,v_j>}) \in S_{[\mathcal{M}]}} (m_{t_i}^{<p_l,v_j>})_{[c]}$$

$$= \sum_{(m_{t_i}^{<p_l,v_j>}) \in S_{[\mathcal{M}]}} (m_{t_i}^{<p_l,v_j>})_{[et]} \cdot p_{l[pri]} \tag{4}$$

where, $(m_{t_i}^{<p_l,v_j>})_{[c]}$ i.e. the monetary cost of mapping task t_i to processor p_l, with voltage supply of v_j.

To model the energy consumption, we use a model of energy derived from the power consumption model in digital complementary metal-oxide semiconductor (CMOS) logic circuits [22]. The power consumption of a CMOS-based microprocessor is composed of capacitive, short-circuit and leakage power. Among them, the most significant factor is capacitive power (P_c), which is defined as:

$$P_c = AC_0 v^2 f \tag{5}$$

where, A is the number of switches per clock cycle, C_0 is the total capacitance load, v is the supply voltage, and f is the frequency. Equation 5 clearly indicates that the supply voltage is the dominant factor; therefore, its reduction would be most influential to lower power consumption. The energy consumption of a schedule S is calculated as:

$$e = \sum_{(m_{t_i}^{<p_l,v_j>}) \in S_{[\mathcal{M}]}} (m_{t_i}^{<p_l,v_j>})_{[e]}$$

$$= \sum_{(m_{t_i}^{<p_l,v_j>}) \in S_{[\mathcal{M}]}} AC_0 v_j^2 f \cdot (m_{t_i}^{<p_l,v_j>})_{[et]}$$

$$= C \sum_{(m_{t_i}^{<p_l,v_j>}) \in S_{[\mathcal{M}]}} v_j^2 \cdot (m_{t_i}^{<p_l,v_j>})_{[et]} \tag{6}$$

where, $(m_{t_i}^{p_l})_{[e]}$ is the energy consumption of mapping t_i to p_l, and C is a constant determined by hardware configuration.

In contrast to schedule length, economic cost, and energy consumption, reliability is a multiplicative objective. We assume processor failure to be statistically independent and follow a constant failure rate λ for each processor. We consider the reliability of a task as the probability of successful completion on mapped processor, modeled using an exponential distribution. The reliability of a schedule S is:

$$rel = \prod_{(m_{t_i}^{p_l}) \in S_{[\mathcal{M}]}} (m_{t_i}^{p_l})_{[rel]} = \prod_{(m_{t_i}^{p_l}) \in S_{[\mathcal{M}]}} e^{-p_{l[\lambda]} \cdot (m_{t_i}^{p_l})_{[et]}} \tag{7}$$

It is important to note that, the symbol e denotes the natural exponential, not energy consumption here.

B. Problem Formulation

Our customized multi-constraint and multi-objective scheduling problem can be formulated as:

$$minimize \ \{e\} \tag{8}$$
$$maximize \ \{rel\} \tag{9}$$

subject to,

$$makespan \leq D \tag{10}$$
$$c \leq B \tag{11}$$

3.2   List Scheduling for MCMO Optimization

In order to attain the objectives of minimizing energy consumption and maximizing reliability under constraints of execution deadline and economic budget, we design a local search based list scheduling algorithm. It tries to optimize objectives under sub-constraints at each scheduling step. To design a list scheduling algorithm, a task selection mechanism is designed to select a task at each scheduling step. In this list scheduling algorithm, all tasks are scheduled in accordance with their upward ranks [27], defined as:

$$rank_u(t_i) = \underline{et(t_i)} + \max_{t_j \in succ(t_i)} \{tt_{t_i}^{t_j} + rank_u(t_j)\} \tag{12}$$

The execution time denoted as $et(t_i)$ is calculated by scheduling task t_i to the fastest available processor at the highest voltage supply.

The second mechanism of the list scheduling algorithm is processor selection. For a selected task, a local optimal processor is selected. The local fitness of a task-processor mapping is defined using the pareto optimality theory. To implement this mechanism, the overall constraints should be distributed to every task. For total execution time deadline, it is distributed to tasks using the partial critical path (PCP) wise method proposed in [6]. All PCPs are determined recursively from the exit task t_{exit}. Then, tasks on the same PCP are distributed with sub-deadline in accordance with their computational workload. For overall monetary budget, it is also distributed to tasks in accordance with their computational workload. The difference is that, the deadline distribution is executed before task scheduling. While the budget distribution is executed after each scheduling step. After the scheduling of a task, the real monetary cost can be calculated. And the left budget is redistributed to unscheduled tasks.

Algorithm 1. MCMO List Scheduling

Input: G: a DAG to be scheduled;
    $\mathcal{P}$: available processors;
    D: the DAG execution time deadline;
    B: the affordable monetary budget.
Output: S: a generated schedule.
1: compute the upward ranks of all tasks of $\forall t_i \in \mathcal{T}$;
2: sort $\mathcal{T}$ in decreasing order of task upward rank;
3: distribute the overall deadline D to each task: $\forall t_i \in \mathcal{T}, t_i \leftarrow d(t_i)$;
4: $\mathcal{T}_a \leftarrow null, B_l = B$;   ▶ $\mathcal{T}_a$ stores already scheduled tasks
5: **for** $t_i \in \mathcal{T}$ **do**
6:    distribute a sub-budget to t_i from the left budget B_l: $b(t_i) = \dfrac{t_{i\,[wl]}}{\sum_{t_j \in (\mathcal{T}-\mathcal{T}_a)} t_{j\,[wl]}} \cdot B_l$

7:    $p' \leftarrow p_0; v' \leftarrow (p_{0\,[vsl]})_{[v_0]}$;
8:    **for** $p \in \mathcal{P}$ **do**
9:        **for** $v \in p_{[vsl]}$ **do**
10:           **if** $superior(p, v, p', v') = true$ **then**
11:               replace p' and v' with p and v;
12:           **end if**
13:        **end for**
14:    **end for**
15:    add $m_{t_i}^{p'}$ to S; add t_i to $\mathcal{T}_a$;
16:    update the left budget: $B_l = B_l - (m_{t_i}^{p'})_{[et]} \cdot p'_{[pri]}$;
17: **end for**
18: **return** S;

The overall list scheduling algorithm is depicted in Algorithm 1. It first initializes the upward ranks of all tasks of G using (12), and sort all tasks in decreasing order according to their upward ranks. Then, the overall deadline D is distributed to every task using the PCP wise method. After that, it iteratively scheduled sorted tasks to proper processors at line 5–17. During the scheduling, it uses $\mathcal{T}_a$ and B_l to store the already scheduled tasks and left budget. They are set by *null* and B initially. For a selected task, it first distributes a sub-budget to it at line 6. Then, it selects the most optimal processor and voltage supply from all processors and available voltage supplies. The optimal of a mapping of task to a voltage supply customised processor is determined by the *superior* function, which is an implementation of the pareto optimality. From the definition, a set of pareto optimal mappings, whose multi-dimensional objective values are at pareto frontier, will be taken as output at each scheduling step. To generate only one optimal mapping at each scheduling step, a common solution is to assign a weight to each dimension of all objectives. In the following, we demonstrate the details of superiority calculation assuming all objectives own the same weight.

Figure 1 shows the procedure of checking if mapping of t to p with voltage supply v is better than mapping of t to current optimal p' with voltage supply v', when scheduling task t.

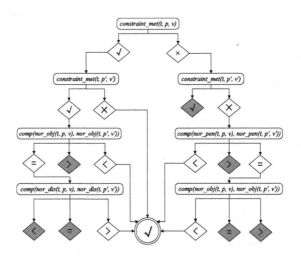

Fig. 1. The superiority of mapping of task to processor and voltage supply. If the mapping of $t \rightarrow <p,v>$ is better than $t \rightarrow <p',v'>$, it returns true at the double circled exit state. Otherwise, it returns false at the grayed exit state.

It first judges if the map of $m_t^{<p,v>}$ satisfies the step constraints, including sub-deadline and sub-budget constraints. A map of $m_t^{<p,v>}$ satisfies the step constraints if the following two conditions are met:

$$(m_t^{<p,v>})_{[ft]} \leq d(t) \tag{13}$$

$$(m_t^{<p,v>})_{[et]} \cdot p_{[pri]} \leq b(t) \tag{14}$$

If $m_t^{<p,v>}$ meets the step constraints, but $m_t^{<p',v'>}$ doesn't meet the step constraints, the procedure stops and returns true. On the contrary, if $m_t^{<p,v>}$ doesn't meet the step constraints, but $m_t^{<p',v'>}$ meets the step constraints, it stops and returns false. If both maps meet the step constraints, a normalized objective is designed to evaluate the optimality of non-constrained objectives. Both energy consumption objective and reliability objective are normalized by the maximal and minimal value among all available processors and voltage supplies. And the total normalized objective is calculated using the Euclidian distance to $(0,0)$ in (15). We assume that the weight of both objectives are customized the same, hence, their coefficient are 1. If a mapping consumes less energy and owns higher reliability, it is considered more superior.

$$nor\_obj(t,p,v) = \sqrt{(nor\_e(t,p,v))^2 + (nor\_rel(t,p,v))^2} \tag{15}$$

$$nor\_e(t,p,v) = \frac{(m_t^{<p,v>})_{[e]} - \min\limits_{\substack{v' \in p'_{[vsl]} \\ p' \in \mathcal{P}}} \{(m_t^{<p',v'>})_{[e]}\}}{\max\limits_{\substack{v' \in p'_{[vsl]} \\ p' \in \mathcal{P}}} \{(m_t^{<p',v'>})_{[e]}\} - \min\limits_{\substack{v' \in p'_{[vsl]} \\ p' \in \mathcal{P}}} \{(m_t^{<p',v'>})_{[e]}\}} \tag{16}$$

$$nor\_rel(t,p,v) = \frac{\max\limits_{\substack{v' \in p'_{[vsl]} \\ p' \in \mathcal{P}}} \{(m_t^{<p',v'>})_{[rel]}\} - (m_t^{<p,v>})_{[rel]}}{\max\limits_{\substack{v' \in p'_{[vsl]} \\ p' \in \mathcal{P}}} \{(m_t^{<p',v'>})_{[rel]}\} - \min\limits_{\substack{v' \in p'_{[vsl]} \\ p' \in \mathcal{P}}} \{(m_t^{<p',v'>})_{[rel]}\}} \tag{17}$$

If the normalized objective equals, the third case of pareto dominance is triggered for judgement. A normalized distance to step constraints is designed to evaluate the optimality of two mappings with the same normalized objective. The normalized distance is calculated as the Euclidian distance to step constraints:

$$nor\_dis(t,p,v) = \sqrt{(\max\{1 - \frac{(m_t^{<p,v>})_{[c]}}{b(t)}, 0\})^2 + (\max\{1 - \frac{(m_t^{<p,v>})_{[ft]}}{d(t)}, 0\})^2} \tag{18}$$

The mapping with larger distance means the task finish time is smaller and monetary cost is less. And it is superior in this case.

If both mappings violate step constraints, however, the procedure goes into the fourth case. It depends on a penalty metric defined as:

$$nor\_pen(t,p,v) = \sqrt{(\max\{\frac{(m_t^{<p,v>})_{[c]}}{b(t)} - 1, 0\})^2 + (\max\{\frac{(m_t^{<p,v>})_{[ft]}}{d(t)} - 1, 0\})^2} \tag{19}$$

The penalty is calculated as another Euclidian distance to step constraints as depicted in (19). A higher penalty denotes more violation of sub-deadline and sub-budget, hence it is less optimal. If the penalties of two mappings are equal, it compares the normalized objective of non-constrained objectives. Only mapping with smaller normalized objective is selected as optimal mapping.

Since each decision made at each scheduling step in Algorithm 1 tends to be local optimum, another tuning mechanism is proposed to refine the generated schedule from Algorithm 1. The overall tuning mechanism is depicted in Algorithm 2. For each task in $\mathcal{T}$, mapping to other combinations of processor and voltage supply are considered. For each combination, it produces a new schedule S'. Then, the current optimal schedule S will be replaced by S' if S' is superior to S. The superiority of two schedule is compared using the same procedure in Fig. 1. The procedure is only called after the new schedule has already generated. The step constraints are replaced by the over deadline and budget, and a schedule is said to meet constraints if (10) and (11) are satisfied. The normalized objective for a schedule S is calculated as:

$$nor\_obj(S) = \sqrt{(\frac{S_{[e]} - e_{min}}{e_{max} - e_{min}})^2 + (\frac{rel_{max} - S_{rel}}{rel_{max} - rel_{min}})^2} \qquad (20)$$

where, e_{max} and e_{min} denote the maximal and minimal energy consumption among all available schedules, and rel_{max} and rel_{min} denote the maximal and minimal reliability among all available schedules. They can be easily calculated. As the rel_{max} for example, it can be got by scheduling task to the most reliable processor at each scheduling step. And the normalized distance and normalized penalty of a schedule S is calculated as:

$$nor\_dis(S) = \sqrt{(\max\{1 - \frac{S_{[c]}}{B}, 0\})^2 + (\max\{1 - \frac{S_{[makespan]}}{D}, 0\})^2} \qquad (21)$$

$$nor\_pen(S) = \sqrt{(\max\{\frac{S_{[c]}}{B} - 1, 0\})^2 + (\max\{\frac{S_{[makespan]}}{D} - 1, 0\})^2} \qquad (22)$$

Algorithm 2. MCMO Tuning

1: **for** $t_i \in T$ **do**
2:    let p' be the processor satisfying: $m_{t_i}^{p'} \in S$; let $v' = p'_{[v]}$;
3:    **for** $p \in P$ **do**
4:       **for** $v \in p_{[vsl]}$ **do**
5:          generate a new schedule S' through replace $m_{t_i}^{p'}$ with $m_{t_i}^{p}$, $p_{[v]} = v$;
6:          **if** $superior'(S', S) = true$ **then**
7:             replace S with S';
8:          **end if**
9:       **end for**
10:   **end for**
11: **end for**

3.3 Time Complexity

The list scheduling algorithm is an extension of HEFT [27] algorithm. Hence, the time complexity is $O(|\mathcal{E}|N)$, where N is the number of processor and voltage supply combination. It equals to $\sum_{p \in P} |p_{[vsl]}|$, assuming $|p_{[vsl]}|$ denotes the number of configurable voltage supply of processor p. At the tuning procedure, there are $|T|$ times of new schedule generating. The worst case is to replace the first task in the sorted task list. The time complexity is $O(|\mathcal{E}|)$ to update the scheduling information of the new schedule. Hence, the worst time complexity of tuning procedure is $O(|T||\mathcal{E}|N)$, which is the total time complexity.

4   Experiment and Evaluation

This section presents the results obtained from our extensive evaluation for our algorithms.

4.1   The Competitive Algorithms

We implement three algorithms as competitive algorithms. The algorithm MCMO is the list scheduling of Algorithm 1, and MCMO-T is the list scheduling algorithm incorporated with tuning mechanism in Algorithm 2. We design two multi-constraint single-objective scheduling algorithms of MCE and MCR. Both algorithms consider two constraints of deadline and budget. The difference exists in the scheduling target. The MCE algorithm targets at reducing energy consumption, while the MCR algorithm targets at enhancing the reliability. We also implement a non-constraint multi-objective scheduling algorithm of MO. The MO algorithm targets at optimizing makespan, monetary cost, energy consumption, and reliability simultaneously. These algorithms are implemented through replacing the superiority judging procedure in Fig. 1. As the MO algorithm for example, because there are no constraint, the superiority of a mapping is determined by the normalized objective:

$$nor\_obj(t,p,v) = \sqrt{(nor\_ft(t,p,v))^2 + (nor\_c(t,p,v))^2 + (nor\_e(t,p,v))^2 + (nor\_rel(t,p,v))^2} \tag{23}$$

$$nor\_ft(t,p,v) = \frac{(m_t^{<p,v>})_{[ft]} - \min\limits_{p' \in \mathcal{P}} \{(m_t^{<p',v'>})_{[ft]}\}^{v' \in p'_{[vsl]}}}{\max\limits_{p' \in \mathcal{P}} \{(m_t^{<p',v'>})_{[ft]}\}^{v' \in p'_{[vsl]}} - \min\limits_{p' \in \mathcal{P}} \{(m_t^{<p',v'>})_{[ft]}\}^{v' \in p'_{[vsl]}}} \tag{24}$$

$$nor\_c(t,p,v) = \frac{(m_t^{<p,v>})_{[c]} - \min\limits_{p' \in \mathcal{P}} \{(m_t^{<p',v'>})_{[c]}\}^{v' \in p'_{[vsl]}}}{\max\limits_{p' \in \mathcal{P}} \{(m_t^{<p',v'>})_{[c]}\}^{v' \in p'_{[vsl]}} - \min\limits_{p' \in \mathcal{P}} \{(m_t^{<p',v'>})_{[c]}\}^{v' \in p'_{[vsl]}}} \tag{25}$$

4.2   Experimental Settings

The performance of our algorithms were thoroughly evaluated with randomly generated DAGs. We use a random graph generator described in [27]. To build weighted DAGs, the following input parameters are required.

- $|\mathcal{T}|$: The total number of tasks.
- α: This parameter defines the structure of a graph. The height of a graph is randomly generated from a uniform distribution with a mean value equal to $\frac{\sqrt{|\mathcal{T}|}}{\alpha}$. And the width for each level is randomly selected from a uniform distribution with mean value equal to $\alpha \cdot \sqrt{|\mathcal{T}|}$.

- *in_degree*: The input degree of a task.
- *ccr*: The communication to computation ratio.

In each experiment, the value of T, α, *in_degree*, and *ccr* are assigned from the corresponding sets in Table 2. For each combination of settings, 50 graphes are generated. Hence, the total number of generated graphes is $4 \times 3 \times 4 \times 3 \times 50 = 7200$.

Table 2. Experimental parameters

Parameter	Value
$|T|$	$\{50, 100, 200, 300\}$
α	$\{0.5, 1.0, 2.0\}$
in_degree	$\{2, 3, 4, 5\}$
ccr	$\{0.3, 1, 5\}$

In order to evaluate the impact of different deadline and budget level on our algorithms, we need to assign a deadline and a budget to a scheduling DAG. We firstly define the fastest schedule M_F, generated by HEFT algorithm, as the baseline. And the deadline of the DAG is set to be:

$$D = d_f \times M_F \tag{26}$$

The parameter of deadline factor d_f determines the slackness degree of the deadline. In our experiments, the deadline factor d_f is set among $\{2, 3, 5\}$ for each generated DAG.

To assign a budget to a DAG, another parameter of budget factor b_f from the set of $\{0.2, 0.5, 0.7\}$ is used. For a given budget factor b_f, the budget is calculated as:

$$B = c_{min} + b_f \times (c_{max} - c_{min}) \tag{27}$$

4.3   Comparison Metrics

Since a large set of workflows with different attributes are used, it is important to normalize the objectives of each workflow execution. Formally, the constrained objectives are normalized by the constraints, and non-constrained objectives are normalized by the maximal and minimal values of corresponding objectives. They are calculated as:

$$M = \frac{makespan}{D} \tag{28}$$

$$C = \frac{c}{B} \tag{29}$$

$$E = \frac{e - e_{min}}{e_{max} - e_{min}} \tag{30}$$

$$R = \frac{rel - rel_{min}}{rel_{max} - rel_{min}} \tag{31}$$

4.4   Experimental Results

All comparative results are shown in Figs. 2, 3, 4, 5 and 6. Figures 2, 3 and 4 compares the results of schedules with strict, normal, loose constraints separately. Figure 5 compares the results of schedules with strict deadline but loose budget constraints. And Fig. 6 compares the results of schedules with loose deadline but strict budget constraints. For each constraint setting, schedules for DAGs with different *ccr* setting are compared. From these results, we get that:

First, generated schedules are able to meet strict, normal, and loose constraints of both deadline and budget. In deadline loose but budget strict situation, the budget constraint can also be met as shown in Fig. 6. As the target of MCE algorithm is to minimize energy consumption, the results show that the key constraint of budget is met as shown in Figs. 3(b)(c) and 4(b)(c). The MCR algorithm enables enhancing reliability of generated schedules, however, the conflict constraint of deadline is still met in Fig. 6.

Second, the MCE algorithm generates schedules with the least energy consumption than other algorithms at the cost of reliability. Most results show that the schedules generated by MCE algorithm own the smallest reliability. On the other hand, the MCR algorithm generates schedules with the biggest reliability than other algorithms at the cost of energy consumption. Most results show that the schedules generated by MCR algorithm own the most energy consumption. The MCMO algorithm is able to generate schedules with energy consumption close to MCE algorithm, and reliability close to MCR algorithm. Moreover, the schedules generated by MCMO algorithm outperforms MO algorithm in both energy consumption and reliability. The optimality is at the cost of makespan and monetary cost.

Third, the tuning mechanism is able to further reduce energy consumption and enhance reliability of schedules generated by MCMO algorithm in most cases.

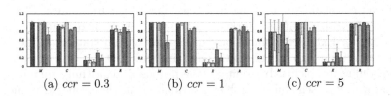

(a) $ccr = 0.3$ (b) $ccr = 1$ (c) $ccr = 5$

Fig. 2. $d_f = 2$, $b_f = 0.2$

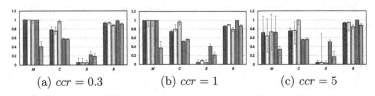

(a) $ccr = 0.3$ (b) $ccr = 1$ (c) $ccr = 5$

Fig. 3. $d_f = 3$, $b_f = 0.5$

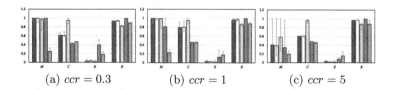

(a) $ccr = 0.3$ (b) $ccr = 1$ (c) $ccr = 5$

Fig. 4. $d_f = 5$, $b_f = 0.7$

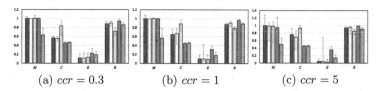

(a) $ccr = 0.3$ (b) $ccr = 1$ (c) $ccr = 5$

Fig. 5. $d_f = 2$, $b_f = 0.7$

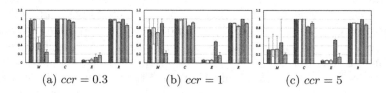

(a) $ccr = 0.3$ (b) $ccr = 1$ (c) $ccr = 5$

Fig. 6. $d_f = 5$, $b_f = 0.2$

5   Conclusion

In this paper, we devise a unified multi-constraint and multi-objective cloud workflow scheduling framework using Pareto optimality theory. A case that targets at reducing energy consumption and enhancing reliability with deadline and budget constraints is implemented according to the framework. The implementation is on basis of list workflow scheduling, with small time complexity of $O(|\mathcal{T}||\mathcal{E}|N)$. Extensive simulation experiments demonstrate that, the framework is powerful in expressing multi-constraint and multi-objective cloud workflow scheduling problems. In addition, the proposed algorithms are efficient in handling workflow scheduling problems formalized in the proposed framework. For future works, it is interesting to extends the framework to support other objectives. Moreover, as we use the most common weighting method, there are other weighting method to express propensity of user towards multi-constraint and multi-objective.

References

1. Kwok, Y.K., Ahmad, I.: Static scheduling algorithms for allocating directed task graphs to multiprocessors. ACM Comput. Surv. (CSUR) **31**(4), 406–471 (1999)

2. Yu, J., Buyya, R., Ramamohanarao, K.: Workflow scheduling algorithms for grid computing. In: Xhafa, F., Abraham, A. (eds.) Metaheuristics for Scheduling in Distributed Computing Environments. SCI, vol. 146, pp. 173–214. Springer, Heidelberg (2008)

3. Yu, J., Buyya, R., Tham, C.K.: Cost-based scheduling of scientific workflow applications on utility grids. In: First International Conference on e-Science and Grid Computing, pp. 8–15 (2005)

4. Yuan, Y., Li, X., Wang, Q., Zhang, Y.: Bottom level based heuristic for workflow scheduling in Grids. Chin. J. Comput. **31**(2), 282 (2008). Chinese Edition

5. Yuan, Y., Li, X., Wang, Q., Zhu, X.: Deadline division-based heuristic for cost optimization in workflow scheduling. Inf. Sci. **179**(15), 2562–2575 (2009)

6. Abrishami, S., Naghibzadeh, M., Epema, D.H.: Deadline-constrained workflow scheduling algorithms for infrastructure as a service clouds. Future Gener. Comput. Syst. **29**(1), 158–169 (2013)

7. Yu, J., Ramamohanarao, K., Buyya, R.: Deadline/budget-based scheduling of workflows on utility grids. In: Market-Oriented Grid and Utility Computing, pp. 427–450 (2009)

8. Zheng, W., Sakellariou, R.: Budget-deadline constrained workflow planning for admission control. J. Grid Comput. **11**(4), 633–651 (2013)

9. Arabnejad, H., Barbosa, J.G.: A budget constrained scheduling algorithm for workflow applications. J. Grid Comput. **12**(4), 665–679 (2014)

10. Sakellariou, R., Zhao, H., Tsiakkouri, E., Dikaiakos, M.D.: Scheduling workflows with budget constraints. In: Integrated Research in Grid Computing, pp. 189–202 (2007)

11. Li, J., Su, S., Cheng, X., Huang, Q.J., Zhang, Z.B.: Cost-conscious scheduling for large graph processing in the cloud. In: IEEE 13th International Conference on High Performance Computing and Communications (HPCC), pp. 808–813 (2011)

12. Garg, S.K., Buyya, R., Siegel, H.J.: Time and cost trade-off management for scheduling parallel applications on utility grids. Future Gener. Comput. Syst. **26**(8), 1344–1355 (2010)

13. Fard, H.M., Prodan, R., Barrionuevo, J.J D., Fahringer, T.: A multi-objective approach for workflow scheduling in heterogeneous environments. In: Proceedings of the 12th IEEE/ACM International Symposium on Cluster, Cloud and Grid Computing (CCGRID 2012), pp. 300–309 (2012)

14. Marler, R.T., Arora, J.S.: Survey of multi-objective optimization methods in engineering. Struct. Multi. Optim. **26**(6), 369–395 (2004)

15. Dogan, A., Ozguner, F.: Matching and scheduling algorithms for minimizing execution time and failure probability of applications in heterogeneous computing. IEEE Trans. Parallel Distrib. Syst. **13**(3), 308–323 (2002)

16. Wieczorek, M., Podlipnig, S., Prodan, R., Fahringer, T.: Bi-criteria scheduling of scientific workflows for the grid. In: IEEE 8th International Symposium on Cluster Computing and the Grid (CCGRID 2008), pp. 9–16 (2008)

17. Prodan, R., Wieczorek, M.: Bi-criteria scheduling of scientific grid workflows. IEEE Trans. Autom. Sci. Eng. **7**(2), 364–376 (2010)

18. Bessai, K., Youcef, S., Oulamara, A., Godart, C., Nurcan, S.: Bi-criteria workflow tasks allocation and scheduling in cloud computing environments. In: IEEE 5th International Conference on Cloud Computing (CLOUD), pp. 638–645 (2012)

19. Yu, J., Kirley, M., Buyya, R.: Multi-objective planning for workflow execution on grids. In: Proceedings of the 8th IEEE/ACM International Conference on Grid Computing, pp. 10–17 (2007)

20. Baskiyar, S., Abdel-Kader, R.: Energy aware DAG scheduling on heterogeneous systems. Cluster Comput. **13**(4), 373–383 (2010)
21. Cao, F., Zhu, M.M., Wu, C.Q.: Energy-efficient resource management for scientific workflows in clouds. In: IEEE World Congress on Services (SERVICES), pp. 402–409. IEEE (2014)
22. Lee, Y.C., Zomaya, A.Y.: Energy conscious scheduling for distributed computing systems under different operating conditions. IEEE Trans. Parallel Distrib. Syst. **22**(8), 1374–1381 (2011)
23. Mezmaz, M., Melab, N., Kessaci, Y., Lee, Y.C., Talbi, E.G., Zomaya, A.Y., Tuyttens, D.: A parallel bi-objective hybrid metaheuristic for energy-aware scheduling for cloud computing systems. J. Parallel Distrib. Comput. **71**(11), 1497–1508 (2011)
24. Yassa, S., Chelouah, R., Kadima, H., Granado, B.: Multi-objective approach for energy-aware workflow scheduling in cloud computing environments. Sci. World J. (2013)
25. Poola, D., Ramamohanarao, K., Buyya, R.: Fault-tolerantworkflowscheduling using spot instances on clouds. Procedia Comput Sci. **29**, 523–533 (2014)
26. Fard, H.M., Prodan, R., Barrionuevo, J.J.D., Fahringer, T.: A multi-objective approach for workflow scheduling in heterogeneous environments. In: 12th IEEE/ACM International Symposium on Cluster, Cloud and Grid Computing (CCGrid), pp. 300–309 (2012)
27. Topcuoglu, H., Hariri, S., Wu, M.Y.: Performance-effective and low-complexity task scheduling for heterogeneous computing. IEEE Trans. Parallel Distrib. Syst. **13**(3), 260–274 (2002)

Bi-objective Optimization Genetic Algorithm of the Energy Consumption and Reliability for Workflow Applications in Heterogeneous Computing Systems

Longxin Zhang[1,2,3], Kenli Li[1,2]([✉]), and Keqin Li[1,4]

[1] College of Computer Science and Electronic Engineering, Hunan University,
Changsha 410082, China
lkl@hnu.edu.cn
[2] National Supercomputing Center in Changsha, Hunan University,
Changsha 410082, China
[3] College of Computer and Communication, Hunan University of Technology,
Zhuzhou 412007, China
[4] Department of Computer Science, State University of New York, New Paltz,
NY 12561, USA

Abstract. Most recently existing studies pay too much attention on low energy consumption or execution time for tasks with precedence constraint in heterogeneous computing systems. In most cases, system reliability is more important than other performance metrics. Energy consumption and system reliability are two conflicting objectives. In this study, we present a novel bi-objective genetic algorithm (BOGA) to pursuit low energy consumption and high system reliability simultaneously. The proposed BOGA can offer the users more flexibility to submit their jobs to a data center. In the comparison with excellent algorithms multi-objective heterogeneous earliest finish time (MOHEFT) and Multi-objective Differential Evolution (MODE), BOGA is significantly better in terms of finding spread of compromise solutions.

Keywords: Multi-objective · Precedence constraint · Reliability · Scheduling · Workflow

1 Introduction

Modern data centers consume tremendous amount of power and produce huge amount of pollution. Take the Tianhe-2 (a heterogeneous computing system) for example, which located in National Supercomputer Center in Guangzhou (China), is the world's fastest supercomputer up to now (July 13, 2015). The power consumption of Tianhe-2 is 17,808 kW [1]. In addition, the high energy consumption also brings a negative impact to the system reliability. High performance on heterogeneous computing system attracts a large number of researchers. Many researchers have made numerous number of studies on different quality of service

© Springer International Publishing Switzerland 2015
G. Wang et al. (Eds.): ICA3PP 2015, Part II, LNCS 9529, pp. 651–664, 2015.
DOI: 10.1007/978-3-319-27122-4_45

of simple objective. When we focus on more than one objective simultaneously, the study would become more challenging. Boeres et al. [2] developed an efficient weighted bi-objective scheduling algorithm for heterogeneous systems. In order to devise matching and scheduling algorithms that account for both makespan and the failure probability and make a balance of them in a parallel application, Doğan and Özgüner [3] explored bi-objective scheduling algorithms for execution time-reliability trade-off in heterogenous computing systems. With respect to workflow scheduling in heterogenous environment, Fard et al. [4] proposed a four-objective case study comprising makespan, economic cost, energy consumption, and reliability based on ASKALON environment for Grid and Cloud computing. Durillo et al. [5] proposed a novel Multi-Objective Heterogeneous Earliest Finish Time (MOHEFT) list-based workflow scheduling algorithm, which is an extension of the Heterogeneous Earliest Finish Time (HEFT [6]) algorithm. In the beginning of the MOHEFT, higher quality initial population are generated under the state-of-the-art HEFT strategy. The MOHEFT is capable of computing a set of tradeoff optimal solutions in terms of makespan and energy efficiency. The Non-dominated Sorting Genetic Algorithm (NSGA-II) was presented by Deb et al. [7] in 2002. Zhang et al. [8] developed novel algorithms to maximize the system reliability with energy constrain in heterogenous systems. Due to the relative low time complexity and rapid convergence rate of NSGA-II, it has been used wisely in many fields which involves industry, transportation, finance and so on.

However, none of the above studies consider both the low energy consumption and high system reliability at the same time. Modern data centers need to provide a set of solutions with different performance metrics to meet diverse demands of the users, such as high system reliability and low energy consumption in different cases. This problem should be treated efficiently so that the algorithm with overall fine performance can be devised. By adopting the non-dominated ideal and Dynamical Voltage Frequency Scaling (DVFS) technology, a novel bi-objective genetic algorithm (BOGA) in the pursuit of low energy consumption and high system reliability simultaneously is developed in this study.

The rest of the paper is organized as follows. Section 1 describes the relative works about high performance research in heterogenous computing systems. Section 2 introduces the models used in this work. Section 3 shows basic conceptions about multi-objective optimization problems. Section 4 presents the algorithms developed in this work. Section 5 evaluates the performance of the compared algorithms. Section 6 gives the conclusion and future works.

2   Models

In this section, the models used in this paper are presented.

2.1   Workflow Model

A workflow application is usually modeled as a directed acyclic graph (DAG). A DAG, $W = (T, E)$, where T is a finite set of tasks $\tau_i (1 \leq i \leq n)$;

$E = \{(\tau_i, \tau_j, Data_{ij}) | (\tau_i, \tau_j) \in T \times T\}$, is the set of edges which denote task precedence constrains, where $Data_{ij}$ is the volume of the data transferred from activities τ_i to τ_j. $parent(\tau_i) = \{\tau_k | (\tau_k, \tau_i, Data_{ki} \in E)\}$ is used as the predecessor set of activity τ_i. All the activities should be completed before τ_i is released. As shown in Fig. 1, each directed arc is associated with a numeric label, which represents a data flow. Its' value denotes the communication cost, which indicates that the activity of data flow perform in different processors.

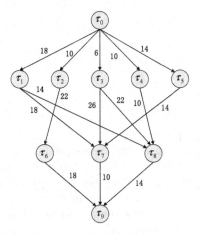

Fig. 1. A simple DAG

Table 1. Voltage-relative frequency pairs

Level	Pair 1		Pair 2		Pair 3	
	vol.	fre.	vol.	fre.	vol.	fre.
0	1.75	1.00	1.50	1.00	2.20	1.00
1	1.50	0.80	1.40	0.90	1.90	0.85
2	1.40	0.70	1.30	0.80	1.60	0.65
3	1.20	0.60	1.20	0.70	1.30	0.50
4	1.00	0.50	1.10	0.60	1.00	0.35
5	0.90	0.40	1.00	0.50		
6			0.90	0.40		

2.2 System Model

The system model consists of a set PE, which includes p heterogeneous cores/processors in a cluster. Each processor pe supports dynamic voltage frequency scaling (DVFS) technology, that is, each processor can work at several different speeds. For simplicity, we adopt the parameter configuration of processor reported in [8], in which each pe has f different available frequency levels (AFLs). Since the frequency switching overhead occupies only a insignificant part of time, it is ignored in the following study. The voltage-frequency pairs used in this study are shown in Table 1. In addition, the communication subsystem explored in this study comprises a set of fully connected processors, namely, each processor can communicate with any other ones at any time that is completely free of contention.

2.3   Power Model

We adopt the classic power model proposed in [9] to capture the system power in this study.

$$P = P_s + \hbar(P_{ind} + P_d) = P_s + \hbar(P_{ind} + C_{\mathit{eff}} f^\alpha), \tag{1}$$

where P_s is the static power consumption, P_{ind} refers to the frequency-independent active power, and P_d represents the frequency-dependent dynamic power. The static power term, including the power to maintain the basic circuits, keeps the clock working and the memory staying in sleep mode, can be removed only by turning off the whole system. P_{ind} is a constant, independent of system operation frequency (i.e., the power consumption occurs while accessing external devices like main memory, I/O, and so on), can be decreased to a very small value by setting the system to standby mode [10]. P_d is the dynamic power dissipation, the dominant component of energy consumption in widely popular CMOS technology. It can be given by $P_d = C_{\mathit{eff}} \cdot V_{dd}^2 \cdot f$, where C_{eff} is the effective loading capacitance, V_{dd} is the supply voltage, and f is the clock frequency. Since $f \propto v^\gamma$ ($0 < \gamma < 1$) [8], in other words, $v \propto f^{1/\gamma}$, we reckon that the frequency dependent active power consumption is $P_d \propto f^\alpha$, where $\alpha = 1 + 2/\gamma \geq 3$. In our studies, we have $P_d = C_{\mathit{eff}} f^\alpha$. And $\hbar$ indicates the system mode and represents whether active power consumption is occurred present. Particularly, $\hbar = 1$ signifies that the system is active currently. Otherwise, $\hbar = 0$ refers to a sleep mode that the system is in. In the context of this paper, all frequencies are normalized with respect to the maximum frequency $f_{\max}$ (i.e., $f_{\max} = 1.0$). And the energy consumption of task v_i can be calculated according to Eq. (2):

$$E_i(f_i) = P_{ind_i} \cdot \frac{c_i}{f_i} + C_{\mathit{eff}} \cdot c_i \cdot f_i^2, \tag{2}$$

where c_i is the computation cost of the task τ_i.

2.4   Reliability Model

As an application is running, a fault is hard to avoid due to the hardware failure, software bugs, devices work in a high temperature and so on. Accordingly, transient faults happen more frequently. Based on the previous study [8], the reliability model used in this study can be formalized as follows:

Definition 1. *The reliability of a task is the probability of executing the task successfully. If the transient fault follows a Poisson distribution, the reliability of node τ_i with the corresponding computation cost c_i is [9]*

$$R_i(f_i) = e^{-\lambda(f_i) \times \frac{c_i}{f_i}},$$ (3)

where f_i denotes the processing frequency, $\lambda(f) = \lambda_0 \cdot g(f) = \lambda_0 \cdot 10^{\frac{d(1-f)}{1-f_{min}}}$, d and λ_0 are two constants.

2.5   Problem Definition

The problem to be addressed in the study consists of scheduling the tasks of workflow applications in heterogenous computing system under the given certain constraints. The objectives are to minimize the energy consumption and probability of failure (POF, which equals to $1 - R$) while satisfying the shared deadline constraint of workflow tasks. This workflow scheduling problem can be formalized as follows:

$$\text{Minimize:} \quad F = (F_1, F_2)$$

$$F_1 = \min_{\tau_i \in T, \ f_j(\tau_i) \in PE} Energy\left(\tau_i, f_j(\tau_i)\right)$$

$$F_2 = \min_{\tau_i \in T, \ f_j(\tau_i) \in PE} POF\left(\tau_i, f_j(\tau_i)\right)$$

$$\text{subject to:} \ \ makespan(T) < D,$$ (4)

where D is the shared deadline of the entire tasks set T.

To meet the requirement of task scheduling, a prior order is established in this phase. Each task is set with its *URank*, which is computed recursively according to the following expression:

$$URank(\tau_i) = \overline{w_i} + \max_{\tau_j \in child(\tau_i)} \left(c_{i,j} + URank(\tau_j)\right),$$ (5)

where $child(\tau_i)$ is the set of immediate children of task node τ_i. The rank is computed recursively by traversing from the bottom to the top in a DAG. It is apparent to draw such a conclusion that $URank(\tau_{exit}) = \overline{w_{exit}}$.

3   Multi-Objective Optimization

In this section, some basic concepts of multi-objective optimization theory are introduced to understand this work better. Without loss of generality, Since any maximization problem can be transformed to a minimization problem, the goal of all the objectives can be defined as minimization problem.

we introduce concepts from the Multi-objective Optimization (MOP) theory for a better understanding of this work. Classically, multi-object optimisation problem can be formally defined as follows:

Definition 2. *MOP: Given a n-dimensional vector* $\vec{S} = [x_1, x_2, x_3, ..., x_n]$, *which minimizes the objective function* $\vec{F} = [f_1(\vec{S}), f_2(\vec{S}), f_3(\vec{S}), ..., f_m(\vec{S})]$.

For the particular problem in this study, n denotes the number of the task set T ($|T| = n$), and the i-th component of a solution $\vec{S}$ represents the resource on which task τ_i is released to execute. In the scenario of bi-object optimization problem, we obtain $m=2$, where $f_1(\vec{S})$ is the energy consumption and $f_2(\vec{S})$ is the POF.

As reported in our previous study [8], energy consumption and system reliability are two conflicting objects. It is impossible to achieve the minimum for both POF and energy consumption simultaneously. In such problems, there is no single optimal solution but rather a set of potential solutions. A solution is considered to dominate another solution if it is as good as the other and better in at least one object. Conversely, two solutions are considered to be non-dominated whenever neither of them dominates the other (one is better in energy saving and the other is better in system reliability).

Another important concept is the Pareto set which is a fine solution set. Pareto set consists of a set of non-dominated solutions, which captures a set of tradeoff solutions among different objects. Each solution in this pareto set denotes a distinct mapping of task to different processors with diverse energy consumption and POF. Pareto front can be used as a tool to help the user make the decision that choosing the kind of strategy of mapping the workflow tasks to resources.

4   Algorithm

The novel algorithm named Bi-objectives Genetic algorithm (BOGA) is devised in this section to address the workflow application scheduling problem in a heterogeneous cluster.

4.1   Encoding

In this approach, each chromosome comprises two components, which include the mapping string and the scheduling string. The scheduling string represents the topological sort of the DAG, which guarantees the precedence constrains. The length of chromosome equals to the number of the task set T ($|T| = n$). Let ch to be the scheduling string, that is, ch which is a vector of length $|T|$. It's clear that T_i appears only once in ch.

4.2   Initial Population

In the initial stage of BOGA, the quality of initial population is crucial. The strategy used in this stage should be efficient and has a relatively low time complexity. As we all known, some outstanding heuristic list scheduling algorithms, i.e., HEFT [6], Predict Earliest Finish Time (PEFT [11]) and so on, are proven to perform well in static task scheduling researches. In the priority establishing stage, these excellent strategies are selected randomly to generate distinct chromosomes.

4.3   Fitness Measure

A fitness function is used to measure the quality of the solutions according to the given optimization objectives. Two objects which include system reliability and energy consumption are two primary metrics in this study.

The energy consumption of a workflow application is measured by Energy Consumption (ECR), which can be expressed as following:

$$ECR = \frac{E_{total}}{\sum_{\tau_i \in CP} \min_{pe_j \in PE} \left\{ P_{ind_i} \cdot \frac{c_i}{f_i} + C_{eff} \cdot c_i \cdot f_i^2 \right\}}, \tag{6}$$

where E_{total} is the total energy consumption of the scheduled tasks, CP is the set of tasks in the critical path of the DAG.

A high system reliability problem can be transformed to a low probability of failure (POF). Hence, we use POF to measure the second objective in this study. Apparently, the POF can be defined as:

$$POF = 1 - R = 1 - \Pi_{i=1}^{n} R_i(f_i). \tag{7}$$

4.4   Selection

Applying the non dominated sorting reported in [12], each solution is set with a *rank* of non-dominated solutions. According to this *rank*, all of the feasible solutions are classified. The non-dominated level of each candidate solutions is established. The solutions with equal values of *rank* are put in the same level. The smaller value of the *rank* is, the higher priority of the solution which can maintain as a elitism to the next iteration is. For the particular objectives in this study, low POF and low energy consumption are the two main metrics. After the procedure of non-dominated sorting, it is not difficult to find that *rank*1 is at the inner position. From the inner to the outside, followed by *rank*2, *rank*3 and so on. The solutions in the inner levels are prior to the one in the outside levels when the solutions are selected as an elitism population to the next iteration.

To assess the quality of chromosome, i.e., the performance of both POF and energy consumption in the solution is very important. During each iteration of algorithm, twice populations ($2n$) are obtained after the mutation operation. The select operation is to choose the best n solutions from the candidate population (the size of which is $2n$). The rule of evaluate the solutions proceeds with the *rank* of solutions. The detailed rules of priorities selection are expressed as follows:

i. for the solutions in different levels, the non-dominated solutions with lower level are preferred.
ii. for the solutions in the same level, the solutions with large crowding distance are prior to the small ones.

4.5   One Point Crossover

The traditional crossover operation in genetic algorithm contains many kinds of strategies, such as One-point crossover, Multi-point Crossover, Uniform crossover cycle crossover and so on. However, these common strategies are not directly applied to the chromosomes of a DAG. The sequence of tasks on a chromosome must satisfy the precedence constraints of the task set. After the completion of the cross operation, the tasks of the chromosome representation must maintain the topology of the task graph to ensure the correctness of the crossover strategy. For DAG, the following will be a specific single point cross way.

Let $parent1$ and $parent2$ be the two random chromosomes in the population, they are also two feasible solutions to the workflow task of DAG. Accordingly, the order of genes in each of the two chromosomes satisfies the precedence constraint of the task graph. $parent1$ and $parent2$ are as the parents generation, after their one point crossover, two new chromosomes named $child1$ and $child2$ are generated. As shown in Fig. 2, let T ($|T| = n$) be the length of the chromosome, the one point crossover operation can be expressed as follows:

i. when the condition $0 \leq i \leq n - 1$ is met, two positive integers are picked up randomly as the crossover points.

ii. copy the genes in $parent1$ which locate before the crossover point i to the $child1$ in the same location. Namely when conditions $k < i$ and $0 \leq k \leq n - 1$ are satisfied, we have $child1_k = parent1_k$.

iii. mark the genes in $parent2$ which not appear in $child1$ currently and temporarily store them in the middle chromosome r_2. The length of r_2 is $n - i$.

iv. combine the r_2 from Step iii to the rear of $child1$.

v. for $parent2$, its one point crossover operations repeat as the steps mentioned above.

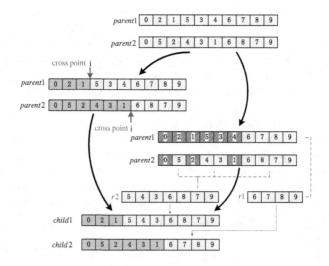

Fig. 2. One point crossover

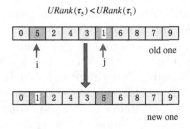

Fig. 3. Mutation

4.6 Mutation

In general, mutation operation includes Simple mutation, uniform mutation, Boundary mutation, Gaussian mutation and non-uniform mutation. Mutation operation can used to escape from local optima in order to explore better solutions to some extent. As mentioned above, $URank$ can maintain the topological order of the workflow tasks, i.e., the precedence constraints among tasks. As illustrated in Fig. 3, the strategy of mutation we used in this study is described as follows: Two positive integers i and j are selected randomly while satisfying the condition $0 \leq i < j \leq n-1$. When the $URank$ of the selected tasks τ_i and τ_j (corresponding to genes i and j in the candidate chromosome respectively) meet the inequality $URank(\tau_i) < URank(\tau_j)$, then the genes i and j can be swaped and a new chromosome is generated.

4.7 The Main Algorithm

Algorithm 1. BOGA

Require: A DAG $G =< V, E >$ and a set PE of DVS available processors.
Ensure: A pareto front which contains a set of schedule for G onto PE.
 1: initialize(population, POPULATION_SIZE)
 2: evaluate(population)
 3: GENERATION ← 1
 4: **while** GENERATION ≤ GENERATION_MAXIMUM **do**
 5:     parents ← select(population)
 6:     children ← one_point_crossover(parents)
 7:     mutation(children)
 8:     evaluate(children)
 9:     replace(population, children)
10:     update(archive, children)
11:     GENERATION ← GENERATION+1
12: **end while**

The pseudo code of BOGA is shown in Algorithm 1. In the initialization of population, the priority queue establish of some famous strategies such as

HEFT [6], PEFT [11] and so on can be used to create a feasible precedence queue. This operation can also improve the convergence speed of the algorithm. In BOGA, Step 2 calculates the entire energy consumption and POF for each individual when it is evaluated. Steps 5–11 repeats until the iteration circle reaches the specified maximum. Two parent individuals are selected randomly and the selected individuals are guaranteed to be different in Step 5. After Step 6, two new individuals are generated. In order to prevent the early convergence and escape from local optima, mutation operation devised for parallel tasks in Step 7 is employed to expand the solution space of this study. For the new generated individuals, only the one which dominates its parent can be selected to the next population. When BOGA proceeds to Step 10, the size of the current population is twice $(2N)$ of that of the initial population. Inspired by the fast and elitist multi-objective genetic algorithm reported in [12], the $2N$ individuals are processed with fast nondominated sorting and crowding-distance calculation. Then each individual is assigned with values of $rank$ and crowding-distance respectively. During the process of selection, the individual with a low $rank$ has a higher priority to be a elitist. And next is the one with a large crowding-distance value in the same $rank$ level. This process repeats until the size of elitists reaches N. The whole algorithm runs until the iterations reach at the upper bound. The latest N elitists of individuals are the pareto set. For a workflow with n nodes, e is the number of directed edges, let p processors schedule the n tasks. The complexity of the BOGA algorithm is $O(nlogn + (e + n)p)$.

5   Performances Evaluation

In this section, the experiment parameters configuration are shown. At last The experiment results are analysed.

5.1   Experimental Setting

In this section, some benchmarks which are used in workflow model are exploited to test BOGA. These workflows were designed to resolve some particular parallel numeric computation problems. These benchmarks include Parallel Gauss-Jordan Algorithm to solve systems of Equations [13], Parallel LU decompositions [13] and Discrete Laplace Transformation [14]. The detailed parameters are shown in Table 2.

Our experiments are carried out using a workstation at National Supercomputing Center in Changsha. It is equipped with an Intel Core i3-540 dual-core CPU, 8 GB DRAM, and 500 GB hard disk, respectively. The machine runs with Windows 7 (64 bit OS) SP1. The proposed algorithm is implemented in an open source framework jMetal [15], which is an object-oriented Java-based framework aimed at the development, experimentation, and study of metaheuristics for solving multi-objective optimization problems. The earliest version of jMetal is used to implement the multi-objective optimization problem of continuous functions. In the past two years, several researchers have developed it to solve the discrete optimization problem. The workflow scheduling problem developed in this study refers to a discrete and combinatorial multi-objective optimization problem in which each task has precedence constraint. In order to exhibit the performance of BOGA better, we compare the performance with another famous Multi-objective Differential Evolution (MODE) [16]. The MODE introduces a differential evolution ideal to solve the workflow scheduling in the global grid. Each algorithm iterates for 100 times. The benchmark used in this study involves three different types of workflows. Under these workflows in the benchmark, the minimum extent in each objective can be used to evaluate the quality of the proposed algorithms.

Table 2. Selected workflow models

Workflow	# Nodes	Reference	Note
T1	15	[13]	Gauss-Jordan Algorithm
T2	14	[13]	LU decomposition
T3	16	[14]	Laplace Transform

5.2   Experimental Analysis

According to the experimental parameters in Table 2, we use three heterogeneous processor configurations to schedule the three different type of workflow, i.e., T1, T2 and T3 respectively. When the commutation computation ration (CCR) is set to one, the comparisons of the three workflows under algorithms BOGA, MODE, MOHEFT are illustrated as Figs. 4, 5 and 6.

Figure 4 shows the Gauss-Jordan workflow under three kinds of algorithms. We can observe that the MODE based on the differential evolution idea finds a better pareto front compared with MOHEFT. As the value of ECR is above

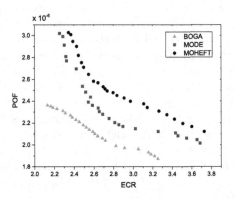

Fig. 4. Comparisons of Gauss-Jordan

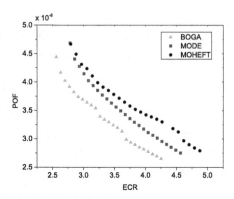

Fig. 5. Comparisons of Laplace

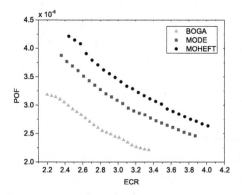

Fig. 6. Comparisons of LU

2.62, the POF of MOHEFT increases significantly. For BOGA, a fine initial population is obtain when famous list schedule algorithms such as HEFT and PEFT are employed. During each iteration of BOGA, the solutions in the population proceeds with non-dominated sorting and crowding distance operations to get non-dominated fronts. Then specific one point crossover and mutation operators for parallel tasks are employed, so that the generated individuals are invalid and they can reserve the most elitist individuals from its parent generations. Therefore, the BOGA could obtain the best pareto front in the comparisons with MODE and MOHEFT. In addition, the classical algorithms used in the beginning of BOGA greatly improve the efficiency of constructing the initial population, which has no impact on the time complexity of BOGA.

Likewise, as shown in Figs. 5 and 6, BOGA is consistent to perform well. The average indegree (or the average out degree) of T1, T2 and T3 are not the same, namely, the task set has different parallel degree. When the number of workflow are almost the same, the ECR and POF of the obtained pareto front under the three algorithms exist some difference.

6   Conclusion

The data center provides the users with different quality of service (QoS) such as maximum completion time, energy-saving effect, system reliability to satisfy their different requirements. This paper addresses the bi-objective of energy saving and system reliability for the workflow with precedence constraints in heterogenous system. BOGA is developed to obtain a fine pareto front. In the beginning of BOGA, some famous and efficient strategies are adopted to initial the population without bringing extra computation complexity. For the selection operation, the two objectives of both low energy consumption and low POF are used to determine the non-dominated solutions. The specific one point crossover are designed to generate new individuals without violating the precedence constraint. The selected solutions that fulfil the $URank$ constraint perform particular mutation operation, which can help the BOGA escape from local optima and explore new solution space. While entering to the next iteration, two operations include non-dominating sorting and crowding distance are performed, which can reserve the diversity of individuals. In the comparison with Modified MODE and MOHEFT, three kinds of workflows are exploited to assess the performance. The experiments show that the proposed BOGA algorithm significantly surpasses other algorithms in terms of system reliability and energy consumption.

One planned future research is to develop multiple objectives such as makespan, energy saving, and system reliability problem for workflow in heterogenous computing systems.

Acknowledgments. The research was partially funded by the Key Program of National Natural Science Foundation of China (Grant Nos. 61133005, 61432005), the National Natural Science Foundation of China (Grant Nos. 61370095, 61472124), the National Science Foundation for Distinguished Young Scholars of Hunan (Grant No. 12JJ1011), and the Research Foundation of Education Bureau of Hunan Province (No. 15C0400).

References

1. 2015. http://www.top500.org/
2. Boeres, C., Sardiña, I.M., Drummond, L.M.: An efficient weighted bi-objective scheduling algorithm for heterogeneous systems. Parallel Comput. **37**(8), 349–364 (2011)
3. Doğan, A., Özgüner, F.: Biobjective scheduling algorithms for execution time-reliability trade-off in heterogeneous computing systems. Comput. J. **48**(3), 300–314 (2005)
4. Fard, H.M., Prodan, R., Barrionuevo, J.J.D., Fahringer, T.: A multi-objective approach for workflow scheduling in heterogeneous environments. In: Proceedings of the 2012 12th IEEE/ACM International Symposium on Cluster, Cloud and Grid Computing (CCGRID 2012), pp. 300–309. IEEE Computer Society (2012)
5. Durillo, J.J., Nae, V., Prodan, R.: Multi-objective energy-efficient workflow scheduling using list-based heuristics. Future Gener.Comput. Syst. **36**, 221–236 (2014)

6. Topcuoglu, H., Hariri, S., Wu, M.-Y.: Performance-effective and low-complexity task scheduling for heterogeneous computing. IEEE Trans. Parallel Distrib. Syst. **13**(3), 260–274 (2002)
7. Wang, X., Yeo, C.S., Buyya, R., Su, J.: Optimizing the makespan and reliability for workflow applications with reputation and a look-ahead genetic algorithm. Future Gener.Comput. Syst. **27**(8), 1124–1134 (2011)
8. Zhang, L., Li, K., Xu, Y., Mei, J., Zhang, F., Li, K.: Maximizing reliability with energy conservation for parallel task scheduling in a heterogeneous cluster. Inf. Sci. **319**, 113–131 (2015)
9. Zhu, D., Melhem, R., Mossé, D.: The effects of energy management on reliability in real-time embedded systems. In: IEEE/ACM International Conference on Computer Aided Design ICCAD-2004, pp. 35–40. IEEE (2004)
10. Burd, T.D., Brodersen, R.W.: Energy efficient CMOS microprocessor design. In: Proceedings of the Twenty-Eighth Hawaii International Conference on System Sciences , vol. 1, pp. 288–297. IEEE (1995)
11. Arabnejad, H., Barbosa, J.: List scheduling algorithm for heterogeneous systems by an optimistic cost table. IEEE Trans. Parallel Distrib. Syst. **25**, 682–694 (2014)
12. Deb, K., Pratap, A., Agarwal, S., Meyarivan, T.: A fast and elitist multiobjective genetic algorithm: NSGA-II. IEEE Trans. Evol. Comput. **6**(2), 182–197 (2002)
13. Tsuchiya, T., Osada, T., Kikuno, T.: Genetics-based multiprocessor scheduling using task duplication. Microprocess. Microsyst. **22**(3), 197–207 (1998)
14. Wu, M.-Y., Gajski, D.D.: Hypertool: a programming aid for message-passing systems. In: IEEE Transactions on Parallel and Distributed Systems, vol. 1, pp. 330–343 July 1990
15. Durillo, J.J., Nebro, A.J.: jMetal: a java framework for multi-objective optimization. Adv. Eng. Softw. **42**(10), 760–771 (2011)
16. Talukder, A., Kirley, M., Buyya, R.: Multiobjective differential evolution for scheduling workflow applications on global grids. Concurrency Comput. Pract. Experience **21**(13), 1742–1756 (2009)

PE-TLD: Parallel Extended Tracking-Learning-Detection for Multi-target Tracking

Chenggang Zhou[1], Qiankun Dong[1], Wenjing Ma[2], Guoping Long[2], and Tao Li[1(✉)]

[1] College of Computer and Control Engineering, Nankai University, Tianjin 300350, China
litao@nankai.edu.cn
[2] Institute of Software, Chinese Academy of Sciences, Beijing 100190, China

Abstract. Multi-target tracking in video has been a research focus, with the combination of many fields, such as computer vision, artificial intelligence, pattern matching. In this paper, we present an efficient multi-target recognition and tracking algorithm based on TLD (Tracking-Learning-Detection), named PE-TLD. A new foreground extraction filter using ViBe is introduced to improve the speed and accuracy of detection. A new target recognition component is added, and core detector is improved. Based on that, we further implemented a parallel version, taking advantage of the state-of-the-art parallel computing techniques such as OpenMP and OpenCL, which runs efficiently on a system with both multi-core CPU and GPU. Experiments showed that PE-TLD is up to 5 times faster than the serial version. PE-TLD is an automatic multi-target recognition and tracking system, which is efficient enough to be deployed for real-time usage.

Keywords: Multiple target tracking · TLD · Detection · Vibe · GPGPU

1 Introduction

Video monitoring has been widely used in various areas. With a huge amount of video data being available, it is nontrivial to process those data. Normally, only video segments with certain targets are of interest. Therefore, capturing targets in video has been a focus of research, which involves both image processing and machine learning [1]. Two main techniques are used for target capturing, target detecting and target tracking. Study on this topic could be used not only for video analysis, but also for other applications, such as intellectual vehicle, extracting motion patterns from video to help investigation on bionic machines, etc.

Currently, target detection has been focusing on feature extraction (HOG [2], Sift [3], Haar-like feature [4], etc.) and classification (such as SVM) [5]. Features are extracted from different scales of the picture, and transformed into feature vectors. With some machine learning methods, the feature vectors are used to classify pictures.

Target tracking has also been intensively investigated. The main approaches are based on target features, template matching, or particle filter. Target tracking based on features is similar to target detection, which finds the same features from adjacent frames to pin the target. The approach based on template matching compares the pixels on two frames directly, and then finds out their similarity. It is time consuming and could not

© Springer International Publishing Switzerland 2015
G. Wang et al. (Eds.): ICA3PP 2015, Part II, LNCS 9529, pp. 665–677, 2015.
DOI: 10.1007/978-3-319-27122-4_46

handle light/shape change, but is simple and accurate. Particle filter based method introduces randomness to enhance the accuracy of tracking.

Among all the methods, TLD [6] is a wide used one, which combines target detection, tracking, and online learning. Traditional short term tracking algorithms could not deal with the cases when targets disappear or get transformed. TLD uses LK algorithm [7], a short term tracking algorithm, to do the tracking. With a carefully designed cascaded detection algorithm, it is able to detect target that disappear temporarily. Therefore, it could be used for long term target tracking. TLD has been used in a wide range of applications [8], and many researchers proposed improvement and optimizations to enhance its performance [9, 10].

Compared with single-target capturing, multi-target capturing is more challenging. Most research on this topic extends single-target capturing, and solves covering and separation problem with certain mechanisms. Some detect multiple targets in each frame, and mark them with some data management algorithms.

In this paper, we proposed a new algorithm, PE-TLD (Parallel Extended TLD), for multi-target tracking, and developed a parallel version to accelerate the processing. We added a vibe filter to improve precision and performance, and used HOG to detect new targets. We used openCL and openMP to accelerate the program on GPU and multicore CPUs. The parallel version obtained 2.5–5 times speedup on test videos.

The main contribution of this paper is as following.

- We propose a multi-target recognition and tracking algorithm E-TLD based on TLD, which can achieve effective multi-target tracking without performance loss.
- We developed PE-TLD, a parallel version of E-TLD. PE-TLD takes advantage of the state-of-the-art parallel computing techniques such as OpenMP on multi-core CPU and openCL on GPU, and demonstrates good performance.

The remainder of this paper is organized as follows. The background is introduced in Sect. 2. Sections 3 and 4 present the details of E-TLD for multi-target tracking and PE-TLD. Section 5 shows the results on random graphs and real-world applications. We conclude in Sect. 6.

2 Background

TLD algorithm was proposed for long term tracking of a single target. The main feature of TLD is the combination of two independent steps, tracking and detection, to resolve the object deformation and partial occlusion during tracking. The main procedure of TLD is shown in Fig. 1.

As shown in Fig. 1, TLD algorithm mainly consists of three steps, tracking, detection and feedback learning. Tracker and detector are initialized by a frame with a marked object. For each coming frame, the tracker uses a tracking algorithm based on Lucas-Kanade optical flow method [7, 11] to get a rectangle that covers the target object. Meanwhile, the detector detects each sliding window of frame by a well designed cascade detector, including variance filter, NCC filter and random forest classifier, to get another rectangle. Then the two rectangles resulted from tracking and detecting

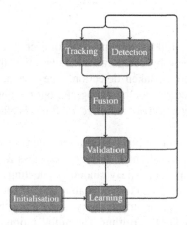

Fig. 1. Procedure of TLD algorithm

compose the final output, either one rectangle, or no rectangle. In case that the object may be partial occlusion, tracker and detector are running independently. In this way, if the objected is covered by a shelter, the detector would capture the object and recover the tracking process when the target gets out of the shelter. In long term tracking, the target object is prone to shape, light condition, physical dimension and other changes, resulting in tracking failure [12]. TLD introduced an improved online learning method named PN learning. PN learning can update the parameters and target model of detector using the tracking result of previous frame [13, 14]. Therefore, TLD could get a robust and stable output.

Our work further improved the performance of TLD with multi-targeting tracking. And out implementation on multi-core CPU and GPU parallel platform proves to be effective to accelerate TLD.

3   E-TLD

We proposed a revised TLD algorithm, named E-TLD, to support multi-target tracking, and further improve the precision and performance.

3.1   E-TLD Overview

In this section, the details of E-TLD algorithm are introduced. E-TLD algorithm makes the following improvements and expansion to TLD.

- A new filter named ViBe filter for foreground detection is added to enhance the origin detector.
- HOG and SVM training are used to recognize targets automatically.
- The data structures and implement are adjusted for long term multiple targets tracking.

In the following text, we describe the details of the three new features in E-TLD.

3.2   Vibe Filter

The detector of TLD runs a full tracking process for each detection window. Although TLD optimizes the detection by using cascaded classifier, there remain problems of excessive computation and mistaken detection. The variance filters can accomplish calculation in a short period of time by histogram, but the detection capability is very limited. Meanwhile, the detection of random forest filters is effective, but the calculation is time consuming.

ViBe is an efficient method for pixel-level foreground detection [15]. Since only the foreground need to be processed, the number of windows for the follow-up detection and calculation are reduced a lot [16]. By randomly selecting sample pixels that need to be replaced, ViBe can analog the pixel uncertainty in the video stream.

For the efficiency and calculation simplicity, ViBe algorithm is adopted as a part of the detector in the original TLD algorithm. The initialization of ViBe algorithm is also based on single frame, so the first frame used to initialize the detector and tracker can also be used to train the initial background model of ViBe, avoiding influencing other components of algorithm. E-TLD uses ViBe filter as the first phase of detection, as shown in Fig. 2. Only windows that got through the ViBe filter become the input of variance filter. ViBe filter works by these steps:

- Get the frame image, and update the background model.
- Expand the background model after corrosion to remove noise, select the foreground area over a certain size, and calculate bounding box of each region.
- Calculate the overlap rate between each foreground object and detection windows. Only the one whose overlap rate is greater than a certain threshold could pass.

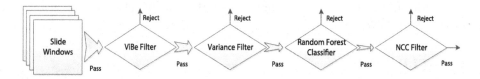

Fig. 2.   Detector with ViBe filter

ViBe filter can extract the prospect area of each target, and objects not belonging to the area must not be a target. As a result, ViBe filter can not only reduce the calculation for the next filters, but also help to improve the accuracy of detection.

3.3   Multi-target Tracking

To enable multi-target tracking, we apply the TLD process to each target individually. In doing this, there are several challenges.

First, the variance filter uses the C/2 as the threshold, where C is the variance of the target rectangle. When processing multiple targets, we use the minimum value of the variance of all the targets as the threshold. In this way, we could filter out as many slide windows as possible while maintaining the effectiveness of the algorithm. This value is updated after processing each frame.

Second, since each detector is only for one target, it is possible that the detector is still working after the target is already out of the detection area. This will result in useless computation. To avoid the extra computation, we inactivate a detector if the tracker for its target cannot track the target for a certain number (say, 50) of frames in a row. The status data is saved, in case that this detector is activated in future.

Third, in multi-target tracking, similar targets might get mixed, and occluded targets may appear again. To identify targets in those cases, we use the 3-channel color value in the frames. The color information is extracted from the results of the tracker and the potential windows provided by the detector. Then, a histogram is built by counting the number of pixels in each color interval (The color space is split into 27 intervals). By calculating the distance between the color features of this frame and the previous frame, we can obtain the tracking result. This method is not only effective for occluded and mixed targets, but also helpful in normal cases.

3.4 Automatic Target Recognition

As mentioned in the previous section, we use HOG to recognize targets. HOG is an image descriptor for detecting human targets [2]. Human targets have a lot of transformations, and could not be identified by traditional approaches. HOG constructs features by calculating histogram of gradient direction in certain areas. In this way, it could represent the contour and movement information, and is insensitive to the change of brightness and small skews.

HOG was designed for detecting pedestrians. However, because it is extensible enough, and is robust with certain transformations, it could be used for detecting other targets also. We use HOG together with SVM to construct the components for target identification. With this tool, we could enable multiple targets tracking in TLD. Since HOG also processes a frame by slide windows, it is inserted into the detector as an independent component, and use the data output by the ViBe filter.

4 PE-TLD

Based on E-TLD, we designed our parallel version PE-TLD. Since tracking and detecting could be done simultaneously, we launch two concurrent threads, one for the detector, and the other for the tracker. In the detector, the variance filter, random forest classifier, and NCC Filter are the three most time consuming components. Therefore, we use GPU and multi-threading to accelerate their execution. The parallelization scheme for the whole system is shown in Fig. 3. Since variance filter and random forest classifier could leverage data parallelism, they are implemented with OpenCL and executed on a GPU [17, 18]. On the other hand, NCC filter has complicated computation on each window, but the total number of windows is below 100. Therefore, it is more profitable to parallelize it with openMP on a multi-core CPU.

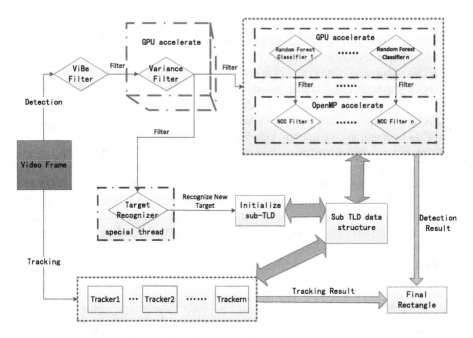

Fig. 3. PE-TLD overview

4.1 Variance Filter and Random Forest Filter on GPU

Variance filter and random forest filter are two performance hot spots in the TLD algorithm. They need to perform the same computation on a huge number of slide windows (possibly millions of windows), but the computation is not complicated. Therefore, it is very suitable to be done on a GPU, which has hundreds of cores. The procedure of executing these two components on GPU is shown in Table 1. First, the data of slide window and the images are copied to GPU memory. Then, we launch two kernels for variance filter and random forest filter respectively. Synchronization is needed between the kernels, for there are dependencies between these two filters. At last, the slide windows with high confidence degree would be calculated in parallel and final result would be copied back to host memory.

In order to adjust PE-TLD to other high-performance platforms (such as Intel Mic), we use OpenCL for the GPU code. Due to the complexity of multi-threaded operation and synchronization which may lead to performance loss, all targets to be tracked are packed together for unified transmission and computing, and then results are unpacked for each tracker.

Table 1. Detector with GPU acceleration

Input: ***B:* initialized slide windows (video with consecutive background)**
     ***J:* image of current frame**
     Q: **integrogram**
     ***R1,R2,* ... ,*Rn:* random forest classification trees corresponded to**
         target 1, 2, ... , n
 Output: *Z:* **collection of class numbers that each slide window most**
         probably belongs to

1.   Pack $R_1, R_2 \cdots R_n$ into a single array $\mathcal{R}$ 2.   Allocate memory for Z、B、J、Q、$\mathcal{R}$ on GPU   3.   Copy Z、B、J、Q、$\mathcal{R}$ from host memory to GPU memory   4.   Compute pixel variance of each slide window using B、J and Q. The ones that passed variance filter are stored in B_{var} on GPU   5.   Compute the classification result of each slide window for each random forest filter using B_{var} and $\mathcal{R}$. For each slide window, add the class number with the maximum confidence degree and store the results in Z 6.   Copy Z back to host memory

4.2 NCC with OpenMP

As the last filter in the detector of TLD, NCC filter holds the following features that different from other filters:

- The input slide windows are the ones that passed the previous filter, random forest filter. And NCC only chooses 100 slide windows with the highest confidence degree if the scale of input is too large.
- The calculations of input slide windows (at most 100) are independent.

As to typical GPUs, 100 parallel jobs seems to be much few, as a result of that the cores of GPU could not be occupied. In this case, lots of computing resources could be idle, and the advantages of computing cannot be demonstrated due to memory access latency could not be overlapped. On the other hand, the independent calculations of each input slide window are typically ideal for SIMD parallel. Therefore, the acceleration of NCC filter should use shared memory parallelism.

Over all, as to parallelism of NCC filter, OpenMP is a good choice, since OpenMP is a cross-platform, cross-language API that supports shared memory parallel programming [19]. The pseudo-code of NCC filter with OpenMP can be seen in Table 2. The calculation of each slide window in NCC is running in parallel using parallel for sentence of OpenMP. As to each slide window, if the calculation result meets the requirement of passing the filter, this slide window would be added to the collect of output in critical section.

Table 2. NCC Filter with OpenMP acceleration

Input: F: slide windows that passed random forest filter
Output: N: slide windows that passed NCC filter
1. N ← ∅
2. begin parallel **for**
3. for $(F_1 \cdots F_n)$
4. p_i ← getPattern (F_i)
5. ncc_i ← calcNCC (p_i)
6.   if $ncc_i \geq ncc\_threshold$
7.   begin critical section
8. N ← N ∪ { F_i}
9.   end critical section
10.   end if
11. end parallel **for**

5   Experiments

We tested PE-TLD on 4 publicly available videos, panda.mpg, car.mpg, carchase.mpg and pedestrian2.mpg [20], and 1 video that we shot by ourselves, people.mov. First, we tested the effectiveness and performance of the detector with ViBe filter. Then, we show how multiple targets are detected and tracked. In Sect. 5.3, we show the performance improvement imposed by different parallel mechanisms.

5.1   ViBe Filter for Detection

The effectiveness of detector with ViBe filter was tested on the video panda.mpg, and the result is shown in Fig. 4. The 4 windows in the figure are the original frame, the detection result of PE-TLD, the background model of ViBe and the foreground rectangles normalized from the background model. It can be seen that the areas that target may be located are limited in the selected foreground regions, reducing the input for next steps significantly.

To test the performance of detection with ViBe filter, we run the detector on two videos, panda.mpg and pedestrian2.mpg. Panda.mpg is a low resolution video with 320×240 pixels, while pedestrian2.mpg is a high definition video with 720×480 pixels. The running time of the original detector and detector with ViBe can be seen in Fig. 5. Experiment demonstrates that ViBe filter could improve the performance of detection by 1.4–1.7 times. As mentioned before, it reduced the number of sliding windows for the following filters, although it added an extra step at the beginning of the detector.

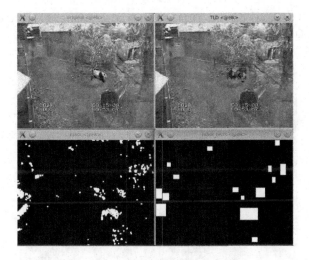

Fig. 4. Detection effect with ViBe filter

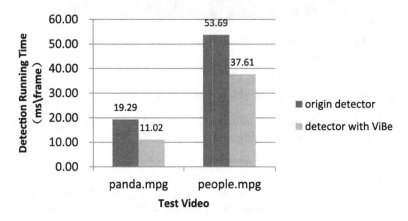

Fig. 5. Performance of detection

5.2 Multiple Targets Recognition and Tracking

The effect of multiple targets recognition and tracking is tested on carchase.mpg, a publicly available video.

HOG feature and SVM training are used in PE-TLD to recognize different targets, without dependence on manually specifying tracking target.

Figure 6 shows four frames during multiple targets tracking on carchase.mpg, which are Frame 20, 74, 160 and 167. The grey and blue rectangles are the regions that HOG recognized as targets. As Fig. 6 shows, the function of multiple targets tracking runs well. It is noteworthy that a target got partial occlusion in frame 160, and PE-TLD regained tracking in frame 167. Also, PE-TLD is able to track the object with only a part in Frame 74. It shows that PE-TLD keeps the good feature of long term tracking of the original TLD algorithm.

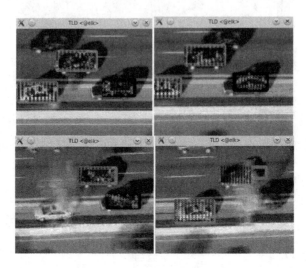

Fig. 6. Multiple target detection and tracking (Color figure online)

5.3   Performance Improvement of Parallelization

In this section, we demonstrate the effectiveness of using openCL on GPU and openMP to accelerate the execution of our program.

5.3.1   GPU Acceleration

We tested the performance of GPU accelerated variance filter and random forest filter with 3 videos, carchase.pmg, panda.pmg, and people.mov. The results are shown in

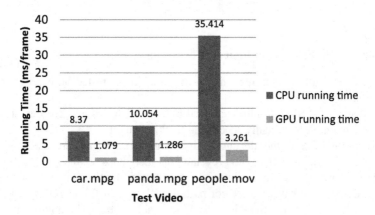

Fig. 7. Running time of detector with GPU acceleration

Fig. 7. It can be seen that the GPU version is more than 8 times faster than the CPU version. Due to the high parallelism of GPU, the speedup is especially obvious with people.mov, which is a high resolution video.

5.3.2 OpenMP Acceleration

As mentioned before, NCC filter was accelerated using OpenMP, because the processing of each input slide window is independent. Data parallelism with OpenMP could achieve good performance. A work station with 12 Intel Xeon CPU was chosen for the experiment. We tested the system with the number of slide window set as 25 and 100. The number of threads is set in the range [1, 48]. Experiment result is shown in Fig. 8. As can be seen in Fig. 8, launching about 30 threads could achieve the best performance. Compared to original sequential execution, NCC with OpenMP could get a speedup of 5 to 8.

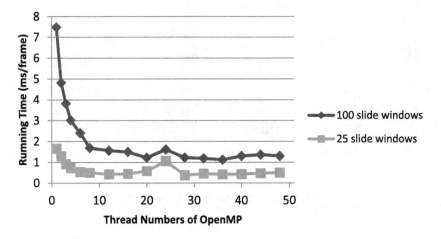

Fig. 8. Running time of detector with OpenMP acceleration

5.3.3 Overall Performance

Three videos with different features are adopted to test the overall performance of PE-TLD. Public video car.mpg is of low clarity and low resolution, and panda.mpg is of low clarity and high resolution, while people.mpg shot by us is of high clarity and high resolution. Two versions of PE-TLD are tested as shown in Fig. 9, one with only OpenMP acceleration, and the other with both OpenMP and GPU. Since the original TLD algorithm could only deal with single target, we compare the performance of the three versions only on single target detecting-tracking.

Overall, for the three test videos, PE-TLD can achieve better performance than original TLD, and the speedup ranges from 2.5 to 5. The following are our analysis.

NCC filter which is accelerated by OpenMP is the last filter of detection. If the targets were easy to recognize in the video, the slide windows that passed from previous filters would decrease, and the performance of acceleration would be relatively obvious. This can be seen from the experiment result on car.mpg and panda.mpg, in which the targets are easy to recognize.

As we can speculate from the procedure of PE-TLD, the running time of detector is positively correlated with the number of targets and the slide windows that need to be deal with. Especially for the variance filter and random forest filter in detector, perform-ance is almost in proportion to the number of slide windows. And this number is almost determined by the video resolution. Therefore, the filters that accelerated by GPU could achieve striking speedup on high resolution video people.mov as 4.52. If the video had higher resolution, we could assert that this speedup would be more remarkable.

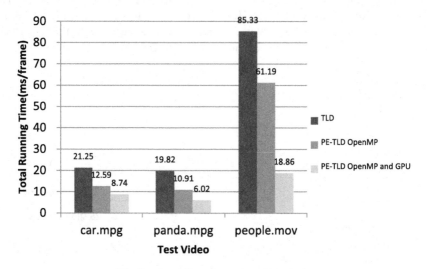

Fig. 9. Overall performance of PE-TLD

6   Conclusion

In this paper, we provide a multi-target recognition and tracking algorithm based on TLD and apply state-of-the-art parallel computing techniques to this algorithm. We showed the procedure of origin TLD and introduced ViBe filter and target auto recog-nition module into TLD as E-TLD. To improve the performance of E-TLD on high quality videos, the detection function of E-TLD was optimized by two typical parallel computing techniques, OpenMP and GPGPU. According to the different numbers of slide windows for each filter in detection, GPGPU was used to accelerate the previous filters while OpenMP was applied to the last filter. The experiment result showed the expected achievement and performance. E-TLD can efficiently handle multi-target tracking whereas the speedup of PE-TLD ranges from 2.5 to 5 on test videos.

Acknowledgments. This work is supported by the National Natural Science Foundation of China under Grant No. 61212005, 61303059, and the Natural Science Foundation of Tianjin, China under Grant No. 14JCTPJC00501.

References

1. Radke, R.J., Andra, S., Al-Kofahi, O., et al.: Image change detection algorithms: a systematic survey. IEEE Trans. Image Process. **14**(3), 294–307 (2005)
2. Tang, S., Andriluka, M., Schiele, B.: Detection and tracking of occluded people. Int. J. Comput. Vis. **110**(1), 58–69 (2014)
3. Zhou, Huiyu, Yuan, Yuan, Shi, Chunmei: Object tracking using SIFT features and mean shift. Comput. Vis. Image Underst. **113**(3), 345–352 (2009)
4. Sonka, M., Hlavac, V., Boyle, R.: Image processing, analysis, and machine vision. Cengage Learning (2014)
5. Tarabalka, Y., Fauvel, M., Chanussot, J., et al.: SVM-and MRF-based method for accurate classification of hyperspectral images. Geosci. Remote Sens. Lett. IEEE **7**(4), 736–740 (2010)
6. Kalal, Z., Matas, J., Mikolajczyk, K.: PN learning: bootstrapping binary classifiers by structural constraints. In: 2010 IEEE Conference on Computer Vision and Pattern Recognition (CVPR). IEEE (2010)
7. Bouguet, J.-Y.: Pyramidal implementation of the affine lucas kanade feature tracker description of the algorithm. Intel Corporation **5**, 1–10 (2001)
8. Kalal, Z., Mikolajczyk, K., Matas, J.: Face-tld: tracking-learning-detection applied to faces. In: 2010 17th IEEE International Conference on Image Processing (ICIP), pp. 3789–3792. IEEE (2010)
9. Xin, Z., Qiumeng, Q., Yongqiang, Y., et al.: Improved TLD visual target tracking algorithm. J. Image Graph. **18**(9), 1115–1123 (2013)
10. Hu, J., Hu, S., Sun, Z.: A real time dual-camera surveillance system based on tracking-learning-detection algorithm. In: 2013 25th Chinese Control and Decision Conference (CCDC), pp. 886–891. IEEE (2013)
11. Kalal, Z., Mikolajczyk, K., Matas, J.: Forward-backward error: automatic detection of tracking failures. In: 2010 20th International Conference on Pattern Recognition (ICPR). IEEE (2010)
12. Li, B., Yang, C., Zhang, Q., et al.: Condensation-based multi-person detection and tracking with HOG and LBP. In: 2014 IEEE International Conference on Information and Automation (ICIA), pp. 267–272. IEEE (2014)
13. Kalal, Z., Matas, J., Mikolajczyk, K.: Online learning of robust object detectors during unstable tracking. In: 2009 IEEE 12th International Conference on Computer Vision Workshops (ICCV Workshops). IEEE (2009)
14. Kalal, Z., Matas, J., Mikolajczyk, K.: PN learning: bootstrapping binary classifiers by structural constraints. In: 2010 IEEE Conference on Computer Vision and Pattern Recognition (CVPR). IEEE (2010)
15. Barnich, O., Van Droogenbroeck, M.: ViBe: a universal background subtraction algorithm for video sequences. IEEE Trans. Image Process. **20**(6), 1709–1724 (2011)
16. Huang, C., Li, Y., Nevatia, R.: Multiple target tracking by learning-based hierarchical association of detection responses. IEEE Trans. Pattern Anal. Mach. Intell. **35**(4), 898–910 (2013)
17. https://www.khronos.org/opencl
18. Nvidia. NVIDIA CUDA programming guide 6.5 (2014)
19. http://openmp.org/
20. https://github.com/arthurv/OpenTLD

Partitioning of Hypergraph Modeled Complex Networks Based on Information Entropy

Wenyin Yang[1,2], Guojun Wang[1,4(✉)], and Md Zakirul Alam Bhuiyan[1,3]

[1] School of Information Science and Engineering,
Central South University, Changsha 410083, China
csgjwang@csu.edu.cn
[2] School of Electronic and Information Engineering,
Foshan University, Foshan 528000, China
cswyyang@163.com
[3] Department of Computer and Information Sciences,
Temple University, Philadelphia, PA 19122, USA
zakirulalam@gmail.com
[4] School of Computer Science and Educational Software, Guangzhou University,
Guangzhou 510006, China

Abstract. Complex networks with nonuniform degree distribution characteristics are called scale-free networks, which can be divided into several natural imbalanced communities. Hypergraph is good at modeling complex networks, and balanced partitioning. But traditional hypergraph partitioning tools with balance constraints could not achieve good partitioning results for nature imbalanced datasets. In order to partition a complex network into "natural" structure, and reduce the interpart communication cost simultaneously, we make three contributions in this paper. First, we use an information entropy expression considering degree distribution to describe the complex networks. Second, we put forward a partitioning tool named EQHyperpart, which uses complex network information Entropy based modularity Q to direct the partitioning process. Finally, evaluation tests are performed on modern scale-free networks and some classical real world datasets. Experimental results show that EQHyperpart can achieve a tradeoff between modularity retaining and cut size minimizing of hypergraph modeled complex networks.

Keywords: Hypergraph · Partitioning · Complex network · Information entropy · Modularity

1 Introduction

A hypergraph, in mathematics, is a generalization of a graph, where an hyperedge, or net, can connect a group of vertices. Recent researches argued that hypergraphs are more powerful for modeling groups than usual graphs, in many domains [1–5], from programming models [1] to complex network [3] and network security [5], etc.

© Springer International Publishing Switzerland 2015
G. Wang et al. (Eds.): ICA3PP 2015, Part II, LNCS 9529, pp. 678–690, 2015.
DOI: 10.1007/978-3-319-27122-4_47

Partitioning is an important issue in both graph and hypergraph theories. Given a hypergraph H, k-way partitioning assigns vertex set V of H to k disjoint nonempty partitions $T(T_1, T_2, \ldots, T_k)$. Figure 1 illustrates an example of hypergraph partitioning. The k-way partitioning problem aims to minimize a given cost function of such an assignment. Pins allocation in VLSI(Very Large Scale Integration) design and computation load distribution in parallel computing are typical applications of hypergraph partitioning, in which the number of parts is known a priori, and balance constraint is desired. Multi-user operations in social networks [6] can also be modeled by hypergraph, and its partitioning can be adopted for user data allocation among a fixed number of servers to reduce the inter-user data access cost [4]. Minimum cut of hypergraph is more intuitive and effective than that of usual graph in some cases.

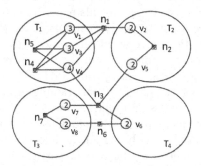

Fig. 1. Example of hypergraph partitioning. A hypergraph $H = (V, N)$ with vertex set $V=\{v_1, v_2, \ldots, v_8\}$ and hyperedge set $N=\{n_1, n_2, \ldots, n_7\}$ is partitioned into 4 parts.

hMETIS [7] is a common hypergraph partitioner for the above applications, which benefits load balancing while performing min-cut partitioning. Nevertheless, load balance constraint is not necessarily appropriate for all the applications. Because many "quasi-balanced" datasets may have natural clusters, Yaros [8] suggested a new partitioner named *hyperpart*, which introduced information entropy as a balance constraint for hypergraph partitioning. Compared to equal-sized partitioners, such as hMETIS and khMETIS [9], hyperpart is able to produce high quality partitions for imbalanced datasets. In other words, if the dataset is composed of groups with different sizes because of some natural characteristics, the fixed-part partitioning result of hyperpart would reserve the natural group members within a group to the utmost extent, even though it is imbalanced in size.

Data collection in complex networks, especially the scale-free networks, such as information network, social network, and biological network, is the very dataset mentioned above. Community structure is the nature partitioning result of these networks. Community structure detection moves towards the same fundamental objective of discovering groups with graph partitioning, but the number of parts is unknown in advance and is determined by the network itself [10]. It is argued that, to quantify the intuitive concept of the community structure, modularity would be better than simply counting the edges [10], and the same is true for hypergraph. Modularity is the most common method and measure, designed to estimate the strength of dividing a network into modules. Networks with a high modularity (a.k.a. Q value) have dense connections between the nodes within modules but sparse connections between nodes in different modules. When considering data storage, a scale-free complex network is required to be partitioned into fixed number of parts and simultaneously retain the community structure mostly to maintain the data locality, for the sake of decrease of cost induced by cross-part data access. This is an important goal of partitioning.

However, hyperpart cannot solve this problem properly, because its information entropy expression cannot reflect the scale-free features. In a scale-free network, the distribution of vertex degrees obeys the power law [11], that is, the network consists of a few hub vertices with a high degree and a great number of peripheral vertices with a low degree. In this paper, in order to reflect the scale-free characteristic and community structure feature, we suggest to use a complex network featured information entropy, which considers the vertex degrees rather than the vertex amounts of communities in the hyperpart. Then, Q values calculated based on this information entropy are used to direct the min-cut hypergraph partitioning process, therefore the partitioning results could maintain the modularity of complex networks and minimize cost function simultaneously.

The contributions of this paper are trifold. First, we propose a definition of EQ, i.e. the (modularity) Q value based on the information Entropy for hypergraph modeled complex networks. Second, a partitioning tool based on EQ, named *EQHyperpart*, is designed for hypergraph partitioning. It takes account of modularity maintaining, cut size minimizing and balance factors during partitioning the complex networks. Finally, experiments are conducted on datasets of classic real world networks and modern social network Facebook. Comparison results demonstrate that the proposed hypergraph partitioning method is effective for complex networks.

The remainder of this paper is organized as follows. In Sect. 2, we discuss related work and related definitions. We present the definition of scale-free information entropy and EQ in Sect. 3. Section 4 describes the algorithm of partitioner EQHyperpart in detail. Section 5 includes the experiment results and analysis. Finally, in Sect. 6, we give our conclusions and suggest future work.

2   Background and Related Work

2.1   Information Entropy

Entropy was firstly introduced as a thermodynamic concept in 1872 [12], and lately explored to information theory in 1948 [13]. The macro significance of entropy is a measure of the uniformity of system energy distribution, representing the object state is stable or not. The information entropy (more specifically, Shannon entropy) is used to characterizes the uncertainty about the source of information, and increases with more sources of greater randomness. The source can be characterized by the probability distribution of the samples drawn from it. When taken from a finite sample, Shannon defined the entropy H of a discrete random variable X with possible values $\{x_i | i = 1, \ldots, N\}$ and probability mass function $P(x_i)$ as (1), where b is the base of the logarithm used, and the unit of entropy is shannon (defined by IEC 80000-13) for $b = 2$.

$$H(X) = -\sum_{i}^{N} P(x_i) \log_b P(x_i). \tag{1}$$

2.2 Hypergraph Partitioning

With certain constraints like balance, the problem of optimally partitioning a hypergraph is known to be NP-hard [14]. Following KL algorithm [15], some direct k-way partitioning methods based on FM algorithm [16] and a multi-level framework [17] for hypergraph partitioning are proposed. For example, partitioning tools named hMETIS and khMETIS are designed to implement the multi-level framework via recursive bisection and direct k-way approaches, respectively. UMPa [18] is a multi-objective hypergraph partitioner also using multi-level. This framework is effective in reducing both execution time and cut size, but is limited to low levels of imbalance.

Lately, Yaros J.R. proposed to use information entropy in (2) as an imbalance constraint [8], and it enables the partitioner, named hyperpart, to find higher quality solutions for given levels of imbalance. In other words, the partitioning result is more similar to the actual partition result. However, $P(x_i)$ in (1) is assigned as $\frac{|V_i|}{|V|}$ in (2), where k denotes the number of parts, and $|V_i|$ denotes the number of vertex in part i, implying that it treats every node equally, without considering the node importance, which can be reflected by node degrees. Therefore, it cannot be applied to a complex network directly, which is characterized by the power law degree distribution.

$$E_u = -\sum_{i}^{k} \frac{|V_i|}{|V|} \log_b (\frac{|V_i|}{|V|}). \tag{2}$$

Hyperedge (i.e. net) cut is a standard cost function measuring the partition quality. Cut size refers to the number of nets in cut state, that is spanning more than one partition. Besides, the number of parts a cut net spans is referred as the Sum of External Degrees (SOED). The similar $K - 1$ measure has penalty of parts spanned outside the base part. For example, in Fig. 1, the cut size of net n_1 and n_3 is both 1, but SOED of n_1 and n_3 is 2 and 4 respectively, so the $K - 1$ cut size of them is 1 and 3, respectively. hMETIS aims to minimize cut size, while khMETIS is designed to optimize cut size or SOED. Typical objective of hypergraph partitioning is to minimize the necessary amount of interpartition communication. In this case, $K - 1$ cut size is the most suitable metric.

2.3 Community Detection

The community structure detector seeks to find naturally associated subgroups of complex networks. Modularity, a.k.a. Q value, the famous community detection result metric, is defined in (3), where k denotes the number of communities, e_{ii} stands for the ratio of number of edges inside community i to the total number of edges in the whole network, and e_{ij} stands for the ratio of number of edges between community i and j to the total number of edges in the whole network. To increase Q value, inner-connection should be higher and inter-connection should be lower.

$$Q = \sum_i^k (e_{ii} - (\sum_j^k e_{ij})^2). \tag{3}$$

Community structure detection methods, both for usual graphs [19–23] and hypergraph [2], explicitly admit the possibility that no good division of the network exists, but the goal of graph partitioning is usually to find the best division of the network regardless of whether a good division even exists [10]. Through skillfully integrating, community structure detection methods could help the graph partitioners to find a good division to the utmost in some way.

3   EQ in Hypergraph Modeled Complex Network

3.1   Definition of Entropy for Scale-Free Network

In complex networks, the degree distribution of scale-free networks follows the power law, indicating that the energy is unevenly distributed in these networks, which is so called *nonhomogeneity*. This property demonstrates that a scale-free network is a kind of *ordered* network, while scaled network, such as random network, belongs to *disordered* network. Entropy is made to measure the property of order.

Research on Barabàsi-Albert (BA) model [24] indicates that, the scale-free network is caused by the growing and preferential attachment mechanisms that the new nodes trend to connect with hub nodes. To be specific, when a new node tends to join a scale-free network, the probability of node i chosen to connect by the new node is decided by the degree of node i. Therefore, the degree of a node can be a basic metric to reflect the importance of a vertex in a network. Therefore, the importance of vertex i can be defined as by (4):

$$I_i = \frac{d_i}{\sum_{i=1}^N d_i}. \tag{4}$$

where N is the number of vertices in the network, and d_i is the degree of vertex i. We assume that $d_i > 0$, thus $I_i > 0$. The importance of vertices are different in an ordered network. But in a scaled network, importance of vertices are roughly equivalent. That is why a scaled network is called a disordered network. To quantitatively measure the order, network structure entropy is defined by (5):

$$E = -\sum_{i=1}^N I_i \log I_i. \tag{5}$$

It is easy to prove that, when the network is completely uniform, that is $I_i = 1/N$, E reaches the peak. When all the vertices connect to one hub vertex, say the first vertex, that is $d_1 = N - 1$, $d_j = 1$ ($j > 1$), E falls to the bottom, because the network is the most nonuniform.

3.2 Definition of Q Value Based on Entropy

From Sect. 3.1, we know that energy distributes unevenly in an ordered scale-free network, which is associated with community structures. It can be inferred that, the energy concentrates inside the community, leading to uneven distribution of the energy, resulting in the obvious community structure. We suggest to use EQ (Entropy-based Q value) to describe the community structure property for a scale-free network. The denser inside communities and the sparser among communities, then the greater Q value becomes, and the community structure would be more obvious. Inspired of this, we define EQ as the difference between Community Structure Entropy (CSE) and Inter-Community Entropy (ICE).

Community Structure Entropy (CSE). Base on the preferential attachment mechanisms of scale-free network, it can be inferred that, when the community structure is formed, the new node would choose a community to join, following the preferential mechanisms as well. In other words, the importance, say the quantity, of a community would determine the probability of new node's accession.

Let $Y = (y_1, y_2, \ldots, y_{|y|})$ be a variable of community, and $X = (x_1, x_2, \ldots, x_{|x|})$ be a variable of node. We define CSE as a conditional entropy $H(Y \mid X)$ by (6) to measure the uncertainty or the disorder situation of X, on the condition of already existing Y, where N is the total number of vertices, M is the total number of communities, and $P(x_i, y_j) = P(y_j|x_i)P(x_i)$ is the joint probability.

$$H(Y|X) = -\sum_{i=1}^{N}\sum_{j=1}^{M} P(x_i, y_j) \log P(y_j|x_i) = -\sum_{i=1}^{N}\sum_{j=1}^{M} P(y_j|x_i)P(x_i) \log P(y_j|x_i). \quad (6)$$

In the community structure entropy, $P(x_i)$ denotes the importance of a node i, which is evaluated by (4), and $P(y_j|x_i)$ represents the probability that community j contains node i. As we mentioned above, the probability that a node joins a community is determined by the importance of the community, therefore, $P(y_j|x_i)$ is defined as m_j/N, the proportion of node numbers of the community j to the total node numbers of the whole network. Thus, CSE is calculated by (7), where Z_{ij} is an assignment matrix. If node i is assigned to community j, then $Z_{ij} = 1$, otherwise 0.

$$E_{CS} = -\frac{\sum_{i=1, Z_{ij}=1}^{N} \sum_{j=1}^{M} d_i * (\frac{m_j}{N}) * \log(\frac{m_j}{N})}{\sum_{i=1}^{N} d_i}. \quad (7)$$

Inter-Community Entropy (ICE). ICE refers to the uncertainty among communities in scale-free networks. We focus the ICE of hypergraph modeled scale-free network in this paper. It's well known that multilevel partitioning framework is popular in many hypergraph partitioners, which is composed of three phases: coarsening, partitioning, and uncoarsing.

Hypergraph would be coarsened by merging vertices and/or edges through some heuristics algorithms. In an extreme case, a vertex-level hypergraph could be coarsened to a community-level one. Inspired by this, the communities can be viewed as super-vertices after coarsened, and the association among communities can be considered to be the cut hyperedges among communities. Hence, ICE can be defined as (8), where C is the current $K-1$ cut size of the hypergraph modeled network and M is the total number of communities.

$$E_{IC} = -C * (\frac{1}{M}) * \log \frac{1}{M}. \tag{8}$$

Entropy-Based Q Value. According to the idea of modularity (see Sect. 2.3), based on the definition of CSE and ICE, the entropy-based Q value is defined by (9):

$$EQ = E_{CS} - (E_{IC})^2. \tag{9}$$

4   Hypergraph Partitioning Algorithm Based on EQ

The hypergraph partitioning algorithm based on EQ, named as EQHyperpart, is designed based on the idea of khMETIS, the k-way counterpart of hMETIS, but the minimum cutsize metric is replaced by the maximum EQ. EQHyperpart comprises a sequence of operations depicted in Algorithm 1.

Firstly, after randomly distributing the pins of vertices, we compute the EQ value of the network, and the possible gains for each vertex as well (line 1). At the beginning of each iteration, we unfreeze all vertices to be ready for move (line 3). Then the algorithm enters the inner while loop (line 4–9). In this loop, we select the best move according to the compound conditions, including gain value, incremental EQ value, and the unbalance ratio (line 5–6). After performing the move of vertex v from FP part to the TP part and locking vertex v (line 7), we update the gain values and pin distributions in an incremental manner (line 8) and compute the new EQ value of the whole network (line 9). An iteration ends when there is no any unfreezed vertex, then we unwind sequences of executed moves back to the point where the partition with highest EQ value is seen (line 10). If the number of iteration exceeds the predetermined value, or we rolled back to the first move, indicating that no increase of EQ is possible for any further move, the outer loop terminates (line 11). Finally, the partitioned result with highest EQ value is output.

Algorithm 1. Algorithm of EQHyperpart

Input: hypergraph HG = (V, N), part number T, unbalance factor ε
Output: partitioned result P = $(P_1, P_2, \ldots, P_T)$ with highest EQ value
1: Initialize pin distributions, compute EQ value and gains for all possible moves from each vertex's current part to (T-1) other parts.
2: **repeat**
3:   Unfreeze all vertices.
4:   **while** there is any valid move **do**
5:     HGainList ← Select the highest gain moves that does not violate unbalance constraints.
6:     BestMove(v, FP, TP) ← Select the highest delta-EQ-value move in HGainList.
7:     Move vertex v from FP part to TP part, and freeze v.
8:     Update the gains of unfrozen neighbours of v and the pin distributions.
9:     Update EQ value.
10:   **end while**
11:   Rollback to the point when highest EQ value is seen.
12: **until** EQ did not increase in the last round or iteration number exceeds threshold.

---

5   Evaluation

In this section, we evaluate EQHyperpart by performing algorithms on several real-world datasets, with comparison to hMETIS, khMETIS, and hyperpart.

Three evaluation metrics are adopted in this paper: K-1 cut size, F-score, and the tradeoff ability. The K-1 cut size indicates the ability to decrease interpartition communication costs. F-score is used to assess the partitioners retaining capability of nature modularity features. The tradeoff ability is a comprehensive metric taking account of both the modularity retainment and cut size minimum capabilities.

5.1   Dataset

We consider five datasets in the experiment. Four classical real-world datasets, such as Karate club, dolphin social network, American college football and zoo, are obtained from Mark Newman's personal website [25] and UCI Network Data Repository [26], respectively. All of these four datasets offer the actual community numbers and partition details, enabling the F-score measurements. Another dataset is part of Facebook data, a recent popular social network, offered by SNAP (Stanford Network Analysis Project). The cut size comparisons are conducted on this dataset.

These five datasets would be modeled by hypergraph before being partitioned, according to the inherent characteristic or inner-association of each datasets. Moreover, the hypergraphs can be either unweighted or weighted, which take the degree as vertex weight. But the hyperpart partitioner only supports unweighted hypergraph partitioning. Table 1 describes the basic information of these datasets. Note that the UB-level here uses the unbalance metric of khMETIS.

Table 1. Real-world Dataset Characteristics.

Dataset	Vertices	Edges	Pins	Communities	$K-1$ cut size	UB-level*
Karate Club	34	78	190	2	11	41
Dolphin	62	159	380	2	10	12
American football	115	616	1347	12	347	36
Zoo	101	31	1616	7	119	185
Facebook	348 ~ 4039	11422 ~ 88234	23192 ~ 180507	Unidentified	Unidentified	Unidentified

5.2 Results and Analysis

$K-1$ **Cut Size within Balance Constraints.** To evaluate $K-1$ cut size at different balance level, we use a part of Facebook dataset mentioned in Sect. 5.1, which reflects the earlier stage of a scale-free network. The dataset is firstly modeled with weighted and unweighted hypergraphs. Then, four partitioners are performed on them respectively with different unbalance factors. For hMETIS, its UBFactor is varied from 1 to 50 in steps of 0.5. UBFactor of khMETIS and EQHyperpart is varied from 5 to 100 in steps of 1. Hyperpart's low entropy is varied from the high entropy to half the high entropy, in steps of 0.005. Finally, for each of these partitioners in each test, the partition result selected for comparison is the one with closest balance level to the EQHyperpart.

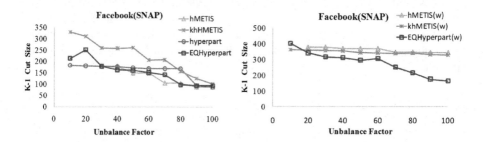

Fig. 2. Comparison of $K-1$ cut size with balance constraints.

Statistical results are shown in Fig. 2, where we display $K-1$ cut size at different balance levels. We observed that EQHyperpart highlights its advantages in the weighted network, because entropy based Q value is designed for nonuniform distributed scale-free network.

Modularity Features Retainment Ability. Real-world datasets, which the natural partitioning results (i.e. real communities) are known beforehand, would be used to evaluate the retainment ability of modularity features. we adopt the typical metrics in information retrieval system, including recall rate, precision rate, and F-score, as evaluation measures. To estimate these measures, we firstly match the partition $t \in T$ to the natural community $c \in C$ with the maximum degree of overlapping. Then a confusion matrix is built based on the part-community-match results. Given the confusion matrix, we can estimate for each community $c \in C$ the following quantities: $\alpha(c, T)$ defines the number of vertices correctly assigned to c, $\beta(c, T)$ defines the number of vertices incorrectly assigned to c and $\gamma(c, T)$ defines the number of vertices incorrectly not assigned to c. Then, the averaged recall is defined by (10) and the averaged precision is defined by (11). In order to consider these two measures comprehensively, the weighted harmonic mean of them, named F-Score, or F-Measure, calculated as (12), is widely used.

$$R(T) = \frac{\sum_c \alpha(c, T)}{\sum_c \alpha(c, T) + \gamma(c, T)}. \tag{10}$$

$$P(T) = \frac{\sum_c \alpha(c, T)}{\sum_c \alpha(c, T) + \beta(c, T)}. \tag{11}$$

$$F1 = \frac{2 * P(T) * R(T)}{P(T) + R(T)}. \tag{12}$$

Figure 3 illustrates the comparison of F-Measure at different designated balance levels, produced by four partitioners: hMETIS, khMETIS, hyperpart, and EQHyperpart, performing on four unweighted or weighted hypergraph modeled datasets.

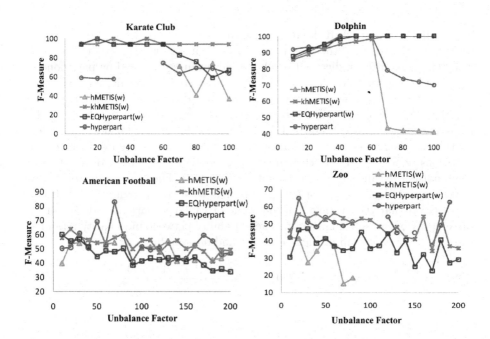

Fig. 3. F-Measure test results for classic datasets.

Several results should be noted specially as follows:

(a) When the unbalance levels get close to the points of true partitions, such as 16 in Karate club, 41 in dolphin, 33 in football and 185 in zoo dataset, EQHyperpart got extremely close to the best partitioner in F-Measure, implying that EQHyperpart is capable of keeping the modularity according to the nature characteristics of these networks.

(b) EQHyperpart performs better on the social network featured datasets. In dolphins dataset, EQHyperpart achieves full F-score on stricter unbalance level demand than other partitioners. In Karate club and American football dataset, the F-Measures of EQHyperpart and khMETIS are neck and neck. But in zoo dataset, the result of EQHyperpart is not so satisfying. This is because EQHyperpart is designed based on the generation mechanism of scale-free networks, but zoo is a typical dataset for classifying.

(c) Partition results on weighted datasets performs better than unweighted datasets, especially obvious in Karate club dataset. The reason for this is that the weight reflects the node importance, which affects the generation of communities, thus plays an important role in partitioning results of social featured networks.

(d) There are some data missed in test results of hMETIS and hyperpart, because they cannot produce partitioning results at certain balance levels.

To sum up, EQHyperpart is verified to be able to retain the modularity with the social network featured real world datasets under balance constraints.

Tradeoff Between Modularity and CutSize. Because we favour the increment of F-Measure, and the decrement of $K-1$ cut size, we quantify the tradeoff using (13), where $F1$ indicates the F1-Measure values produced by partitioners, C_{Real} and C_P refer to the $K-1$ cut size of true partition results for real-world datasets and the partition results produced by partitioners respectively. The a and b are weighting coefficients for these two factors, and $a + b = 1$. The related absolute values of four real-world network datasets are shown in Table 2. In Table 2, the number after data set names are unbalance values of their true partitions, F-S column lists the values from the first factor in (13), and C-Size column lists the values from the second factor in (13). The last row demonstrates the average tradeoff results for four partitioners when $a = 0.5$ and $b = 0.5$. It can be observed that the average tradeoff value of EQHyperpart exceeds the other three partitioners, showing that its tradeoff ability between modularity retaining and $K-1$ cut size minimizing is effective and outstanding.

$$TO = a * F1 * 100 - b * \frac{|(C_P - C_{Real})| * 100}{C_{Real}}. \tag{13}$$

Table 2. Tradeoff test results.

Dataset	hMETIS(w)			khMETIS(w)			EQHyperpart(w)			hyperpart		
	F-S	C-Size	TO	F-S	C-Size	TO	F-S	C-Size	TO	F-S	C-Size	TO
Karate Club(16)	100	0	100	94	9	85	100	0	100	58	45	13
Dolphin(41)	100	0	100	95	40	55	98	10	88	100	0	100
American football(33)	54	7	47	59	6	53	57	1	56	61	7	54
Zoo(185)	–	–	0	37	5	32	27	3	24	62	14	48
Average Tradeoff			62			56			**67**			54

6   Conclusion

For the sake of partitioning complex networks with scale-free characteristics, EQHyperpart is proposed in this paper, which is a hypergraph partitioning tool that uses information entropy based modularity Q to direct the low cost partitioning process. Comparison tests are performed on classical and latest popular real world datasets, such as Karate Club, Dolphin, and Facebook. We compared with today's leading partitioners, such as hMETIS, khMETIS, and newly proposed partitioner hyperpart. Results demonstrate that EQHyperpart outperforms the other partitioners in the ability of achieving lower $K - 1$ cut size with similar balance constraints, retaining the modularity at different balance levels, and the tradeoff between them, especially on the social network featured datasets. But the partitioning result on overlapping community, such as American Football, is unsatisfactory. As future work, improvement on performance and partitioning ability of EQHyperpart should be explored, in order to process different complex networks, including overlapping community scale-free networks.

Acknowledgments. This work is supported in part by the National Natural Science Foundation of China under Grant Numbers 61272151, 61472451, and 61402543, the International Science & Technology Cooperation Program of China under Grant Number 2013DFB10070, the China Hunan Provincial Science & Technology Program under Grant Number 2012GK4106, and the "Mobile Health" Ministry of Education - China Mobile Joint Laboratory (MOE-DST No. [2012]311).

References

1. Heintz, B., Chandra, A.: Beyond graphs: toward scalable hypergraph analysis systems. ACM SIGMETRICS Perform. Eval. Rev. **41**, 94–97 (2014)
2. Xie, Z., Yi, D.Y., Ouyang, Z.Z.: Hyperedge communities and modularity reveal structure for documents. Chin. Phys. Lett. **29**, 38902–38905 (2012)
3. Turk, A., Selvitopi, R.O., Ferhatosmanoglu, H., Cevdet, A.: Temporal workload-aware replicated partitioning for social networks. IEEE Trans. Knowl. Data Eng. **26**, 2832–2845 (2014)
4. Yang, W., Wang, G.: Directed social hypergraph data allocation strategy in online social networks. J. Chin. Comput. Syst. **36**, 1559–1564 (2015)

5. Guzzo, A., Pugliese, A., Rullo, A., Saccà, D.: Intrusion detection with hypergraph-based attack models. In: Croitoru, M., Rudolph, S., Woltran, S., Gonzales, C. (eds.) GKR 2013. LNCS, vol. 8323, pp. 58–73. Springer, Heidelberg (2014)
6. Waters, N.: Social Network Analysis. In: Fischer, M.M., Nijkamp, P. (eds.) Handbook of Regional Science, pp. 725–740. Springer, Heidelberg (2014)
7. George, K., Rajat, A., Vipin, K., Shashi, S.: Multilevel hypergraph partitioning: applications in VLSI domain. IEEE Trans. VLSI Syst. **7**, 69–79 (1999)
8. Yaros, J.R.: Imbalanced hypergraph partitioning and improvements for consensus clustering. In: 25th IEEE International Conference on Tools with Artificial Intelligence (ICTAI), pp. 358–365. IEEE Press, Herndon (2013)
9. George, K., Vipin, K.: Multilevel k-way hypergraph partitioning. In: 36th Design Automation Conference, pp. 343–348 (1999)
10. Newman, M.E.J.: Modularity and community structure in networks. Proc. Nat. Acad. Sci. **103**, 8577–8582 (2006)
11. Barabási, A., Bonabeau, E.: Scale-free networks. Sci. Am. **288**, 60–69 (2003)
12. Boltzmann, L.: Further studies on the thermal equilibrium of gas molecules. The Kinetic Theory of Gases. History of Modern Physical Sciences **1**, 262–349 (2003)
13. Shannon, C.E.: A mathematical theory of communication. Bell Syst. Tech. J. **27**, 379–423 (1948)
14. Borndörfer, R., Heismann, O.: The hypergraph assignment problem. Discrete Optim. **15**, 15–25 (2015)
15. Kernighan, B.W., Lin, S.: An efficient heuristic procedure for partitioning graphs. Bell Syst. Tech. J. **49**, 291–308 (1970)
16. Fiduccia, C., Mattheyses, R.: A linear-time heuristic for improving network partitions. In: 19th Conference on Design Automation, pp. 175–181 (1982)
17. Karypis, G., Aggarwal, R., Kumar, V., Shekhar, S.: Multilevel hypergraph partitioning: application in VLSI domain. In: 34th Proceedings of the ACM Annual Design Automation Conference, NewYork, pp. 526–529 (1997)
18. Deveci, M., Kaya, K., Ucar, B., Çatalyürek, Ü.V.: Hypergraph partitioning for multiple communication cost metrics: model and methods. J. Parallel Distrib. Comput. **77**, 69–83 (2015)
19. Newman, M.E.J., Girvan, M.: Finding and evaluating community structure in networks. Phys. Rev. E **69**, 292–313 (2004)
20. Newman, M.E.J.: Fast algorithm for detecting community structure in networks. Phys. Rev. E **69**, 279–307 (2004)
21. He, J., Chen, D.: A fast algorithm for community detection in temporal network. Physica A Stat. Mech. Appl. **429**, 87–94 (2015)
22. Brutz, M., Meyer, F.G.: A Modular Multiscale Approach to Overlapping Community Detection. Physics and Society. arXiv:1501.05623 (2015)
23. Deng, X., Wang, B., Wu, B.: Modularity modeling and evaluation in community detecting of complex network based on information entropy. J. Comput. Res. Develop. **49**, 725–734 (2012)
24. Barabási, A.L., Albert, R., Jeong, H.: Scale-free characteristics of random networks: the topology of the world-wide web. Phys. A Stat. Mech. Appl. **281**, 69–77 (2000)
25. Website of Mark Newman. http://www-personal.umich.edu/~mejn/netdata/
26. UCI Network Data Repository. http://networkdata.ics.uci.edu/

Improving Performance of Floating Point Division on GPU and MIC

Kun Huang[✉] and Yifeng Chen

Department of Computer Science, School of EECS,
Peking University, Beijing 100871, China
{h.k,cyf}@pku.edu.cn

Abstract. Floating point computing ability is an important concern in high performance scientific application and engineering computing. Although as a fundamental operation, floating point division (or reciprocal) has long been much less efficiency compared with addition and multiplication. Architectures like GPU and MIC even have no instruction for such division in the instruction level. This paper proposes a fast approximation algorithm to estimate the division of floating point numbers in IEEE 754 format based on existing instructions which in most cases are accurate enough for practical computing. It consists of a predicting step and an iterating step like most iterative numerical algorithm. The predicting step makes use of the property of IEEE 754 format to calculate estimation by only one integer subtraction instruction. The iterating step improves the accuracy by fast iterations in about ten instructions. This new algorithm is extremely easy to implement and shows a great performance in practical experiments.

Keywords: Computer arithmetic · IEEE 754 · Floating point division · Reciprocal · GPU · MIC

1 Introduction

The performance optimization of floating point operations in scientific applications is an essential concern on high performance computing systems. Benefiting from the continuous progress in microelectronics technology, floating point operations on modern processors have become increasingly efficient, which makes it possible to process larger scale computation.

However, most time when the great performance is mentioned is in fact talking about addition and multiplication. Compared with the addition and multiplication, as another one fundamental operation in arithmetic, floating point division (or reciprocal) is much less sufficient. Floating point division is obviously slower. The reason is that division is much more complex in logical design and even some architecture has no direct hardware support. In a typical workstation, the CPU's division unit has several times relay and cycles that of addition and multiplication.

© Springer International Publishing Switzerland 2015
G. Wang et al. (Eds.): ICA3PP 2015, Part II, LNCS 9529, pp. 691–703, 2015.
DOI: 10.1007/978-3-319-27122-4_48

This problem is even more outstanding on Graphics Processing Unit (GPU) and Intel® Many Integrated Core Architecture(MIC). GPU and MIC are the most typical hardware for many-core computing. In the latest 10 years, many-core architecture has been widely used in high performance computing systems for its high throughput on floating point computation.

Both GPU and Intel® MIC have no division unit for floating point numbers [6,8]. For the simplification of hardware design, they have no direct floating point division in the instruction level. Floating point division operation on these architectures is numerically implemented based on other basic instructions. On NVIDIA's K20 GPU card with CUDA support, the peak performance for the addition is 1.17 Tflops, while that of the build-in division is only 46.6 Gflops. Although CUDA also gives an intrinsic function __fdividef as an alternative division, however it is only for single precision division. On the Knight Corner architecture, a floating point division is composed of about 30 basic instructions involving complex numerical calculation and memory access. On MIC, the double precision floating point addition using vectorization has a peek performance of 500 Gflops while the corresponding division in Intel Short Vector Math Library (SVML) has only 18 Gflops.

Existing works to improve the performance of floating point division could be divided into two categories. One is to optimize hardware implementation. Hardware optimization means to redesign or improve the circuit or logic. It also means to upgrade the chips and use new hardware. It is quit restricted and cannot work for existing systems. Another is to develop new algorithm or approximation algorithm in the software ways based on existing hardware support. Software optimization is much more suited for current existing system and has better applicability. Most existing works are mainly focus on the hardware optimization [9–11].

This paper tries to solve the problem in software method. The motivation is very clear and simple, just reducing the number of instructions by iterating method and making the division become as fast as possible. Our contribution is to introduce a new approximation algorithm to calculate the division. it could improve the division on GPU and MIC dramatically in almost all practical cases. It is simple but powerful. It doesn't need table look-up or complex conditional check. It contains only basic instructions. It could be efficiently implemented in only about 10 instructions with the FMA support of GPU and MIC.

The paper is organized as follows. Section 2 describes our algorithm, which is divided into three parts– iterating, predicting and combining. Section 3 presents details experiment results on the performance and accuracy, followed by a short summary and conclusion in Sect. 4.

2   Algorithm and Implementation

Our algorithm is composed of two steps – *predicting* then *iterating*. The predicting step will give an initial estimation of the inverse. Based on the estimation, the iterating step will improve the precision iteratively. The work flow is just like most numerical iterative algorithm.

In order to facilitate understanding, the iterating step will be described first.

2.1   Iterating Step

The goal of the iterating step is to improve the precision based on an initial estimation. This is also a common and important step in most numerical calculation problems.

The most traditional iterating method in the numerical computation is Newton iterating method. Here we choose Goldschmidt division with the binomial theorem [3]. It has a very fast convergence rate and can be easily implement with the common FMA support on current many-core architectures.

Suppose y is an estimation to $\dfrac{1}{x}$, but not precise enough, that is

$$y \approx \frac{1}{x}. \tag{1}$$

Rewrite Eq. (1) it into another form

$$xy = 1 - \delta.$$

For that y is an estimation of $\dfrac{1}{x}$, δ will not be zero, but close to zero. It is reasonable to suppose $\delta \in (-1, 1)$. Then $\dfrac{1}{x}$ could be rewritten into the following formula in δ and y

$$\frac{1}{x} = \frac{y}{xy} = \frac{y}{1 - \delta}.$$

It means we can turn to the calculation of $\dfrac{1}{1 - \delta}$. Multiple both the numerator and the denominator by $1 + \delta$, and get

$$\frac{1}{1 - \delta} = \frac{1 + \delta}{(1 - \delta)(1 + \delta)} = \frac{1 + \delta}{1 - \delta^2}.$$

If repeating this trick to increase the order of δ in the denominator, the denominator will become increasingly close to 1 because of $\delta \in (-1, 1)$.

$$\begin{aligned}
\frac{1}{1 - \delta} &= \frac{1 + \delta}{1 - \delta^2} \\
&= \frac{(1 + \delta)(1 + \delta^2)}{1 - \delta^4} \\
&= \frac{(1 + \delta)(1 + \delta^2)(1 + \delta^4)}{1 - \delta^8} \\
&= \cdots
\end{aligned}$$

So we get

$$\frac{1}{1 - \delta} \approx (1 + \delta)(1 + \delta^2) \cdots (1 + \delta^{2^i}) \cdots \cdots$$

The general term $1 + \delta^{2^i}$ also approximates to 1 as i gets larger. Then we could get an estimation of $\dfrac{1}{1-\delta}$ by multiplying only some leading factors.

$$\frac{1}{1-\delta} \approx (1+\delta)(1+\delta^2)\cdots(1+\delta^{2^n})$$

We also get the corresponding estimation of $\dfrac{1}{x}$

$$\frac{1}{x} \approx y(1+\delta)(1+\delta^2)\cdots(1+\delta^{2^n}) \tag{2}$$

The absolute error is

$$
\begin{aligned}
error &= \frac{1}{x} - y(1+\delta)(1+\delta^2)\cdots(1+\delta^{2^n}) \\
&= \frac{1}{x} - \frac{1-\delta}{x} \cdot (1+\delta)(1+\delta^2)\cdots(1+\delta^{2^n}) \\
&= \frac{1}{x} - \frac{1-\delta^{2^{n+1}}}{x} \\
&= \frac{\delta^{2^{n+1}}}{x}
\end{aligned}
\tag{3}
$$

The relative error is $\delta^{2^{n+1}}$. The precision has a double exponential growth rate as n increases. If δ is close enough to zero, the estimation will quickly converge to a very small relative error as iterating. To understand it visually, supposing we has an initial estimation with the error $\delta = 0.1$, if we only calculate the first 4 items in Eq. (2), the result will have a relative error of 10^{-16}.

Equation 2 could be implemented as an iterative process which is listed in Algorithm 1.

Algorithm 1. Iterating Step

Input: x and an initial estimation y of $\dfrac{1}{x}$
Output: a much more precise estimation est
1: $est \leftarrow y$
2: $\delta \leftarrow 1 - xy$
3: **for** $i = 1$ to n **do**
4:     $est \leftarrow est + est \cdot \delta$
5:     $\delta \leftarrow \delta \cdot \delta$
6: **end for**

This iterating algorithm is very suited to modern high performance architecture. Fused Multiply Add (FMA) instruction set is supported on both general purpose GPU and Intel's MIC. These architecture has a corresponding instruction to calculate the form $A \leftarrow B \cdot C + D$. Each iteration step could be optimized into only two instructions.

2.2   Predicting Step

The iterating step gives an approach to improve the accuracy based on an inital estimation of the inverse. Theoretically, any value can be used as the initial estimation for Algorithm 1. But a relatively precise estimation can reduce the iterating steps to the final convergence. The predicting step will find such an estimation quickly.

A typical and straight-forward way is to use a look-up table based on the leading digits. However table look-up will cause divergent memory access in SIMD or SIMT execution model. On GPU and MIC it's an obvious great hurt for the performance. Another common way is using polynomial approximation. This method performs not well. In our attempt in polynomial approximation, the lower degree polynomial cannot get a precise enough result, while higher-degree polynomial will need much more complex calculation. It is impossible to get an expected balance between the iterating complexity and the estimation accuracy.

Inspired by a magic way to calculate the inverse square root of x in some computer video software, we find similar trick could also be applied to the reciprocal. The trick is to treat the floating point number as a fixed point integer and make a simple integer subtraction to acquire a relatively accuracy estimation for the inverse square root. We extend such integer subtraction to floating point reciprocal and combine it with iterating method described in Sect. 2.1.

A floating point number in IEEE 754 format [1] is represented as the following form. It is a signed multiplication of a normalization fraction in $(1,2)$ and a power of 2.

$$x = \pm 1.m \times 2^e \tag{4}$$

To keep things simple, the following discussion will only involve the non-negative case. The negative case will have a similar deduction and a same result.

Use the multiplication formula in Eq. 4 to rewrite the inverse of x with m and e. Calculate the logarithm of both y and $\frac{1}{x}$ in the form of IEEE 754 floating point number.

$$\frac{1}{x} = y$$
$$-\log x = \log y$$
$$-\log(2^{e_x}(1+m_x)) = \log(2^{e_y}(1+m_y))$$
$$-e_x - \log(1+m_x) = e_y + \log(1+m_y)$$

The logarithm operation is much more complex to calculate. So we consider to use a linear estimation $\log(1+p) = p + \Delta_p$ to replace the log function.

$$-e_x - \log(1+m_x) = e_y + \log(1+m_y)$$
$$-(e_x + m_x + \Delta_x) = e_y + m_y + \Delta_y \tag{5}$$

The sign bit (0 for positive numbers), the mantissa part and the exponent part are stored successively in 32 or 64 bits like Fig. 1. The following derivation

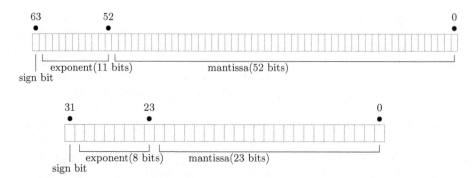

Fig. 1. IEEE 754 floating point format

process and experiments in Sect. 3 will only involve the double precision case. The single precision case is very similar.

If treating the mantissa part as an integer M, the exponent part as an integer E, m and e could be represented in M and E

$$e = E - 1023 \tag{6}$$

$$m = \frac{M}{2^{52}} \tag{7}$$

so the whole 64 bits could be treated as a 64 bit unsigned integer

$$x_{uint64} = E \cdot 2^{52} + M \tag{8}$$

After substituting Eqs. (6), (7) into Eq. (5), make more transformations.

$$- (e_x + m_x + \Delta_x) = e_y + m_y + \Delta_y$$

$$- (E_x - 1023 + \frac{M_x}{2^{52}} + \Delta_x)$$

$$= (E_y - 1023 + \frac{M_y}{2^{52}}) + \Delta_y$$

$$- (2^{52}E_x - 2^{52} \cdot 1023 + M_x + 2^{52}\Delta_x)$$

$$= (2^{52}E_y - 2^{52} \cdot 1023 + M_y) + 2^{52}\Delta_y$$

$$- (2^{52}E_x + M_x) + 2^{52}(1023 - \Delta_x)$$

$$= (2^{52}E_y + M_y) + 2^{52}(\Delta_y - 1023)$$

According to Eq. (8), $2^{52}E_x + M_x$ and $2^{52}E_y + M_y$ is the corresponding 64-bit integer of x and y

$$(2^{52}E_y + M_y) = -(2^{52}E_x + M_x) + 2^{52}(1023 - \Delta_x)$$
$$- 2^{52}(\Delta_y - 1023)$$
$$= 2^{52}(2046 - (\Delta_x + \Delta_y)) - (2^{52}E_x + M_x)$$
$$y_{uint64} = 2^{52}(2046 - (\Delta_x + \Delta_y)) - x_{uint64} \tag{9}$$

We use a constant value to estimate $\Delta_x + \Delta_y$ and minimize the maximal error of estimation when $m \in [0, 1)$. As

$$\Delta = \log(1 + m) - m \in [0, \delta_{max} \approx 0.0860] \tag{10}$$

when $m \in [0, 1)$, Δ_{max} is the optimal constant estimation to $\Delta_x + \Delta_y$

$$(\Delta_x + \Delta_y) - \Delta_{max} \in [-\Delta_{max}, \Delta_{max}] \tag{11}$$

The so the first term in Eq. (13)

$$2^{52}(2046 - \Delta_{max}) = 0x7FDE9F73AABB2400 \tag{12}$$

Thus we have a way to estimate the value of y by a integer subtraction

$$y_{uint64} \approx 0x7FDE9F73AABB2400 - x_{uint64} \tag{13}$$

As metioned in Sect. 2.1, the initial $\delta = xy - 1$ will decide how many rounds needs to iterate in Algorithm 1. δ for the y calculated by Eq. (13) can be calculated as follows.
We use the *log* function here again and calculate $\log(xy)$ first.

$$\log(xy) = \log x + \log y$$
$$= \log((1 + m_x) \cdot 2^{e_x}) + \log((1 + m_y) \cdot 2^{e_y})$$
$$= \log(1 + m_x) + e_x + \log(1 + m_y) + e_y$$

Equation (10) tells us that

$$m \leq \log(1 + m) \leq m + \Delta_{max} \tag{14}$$

This inequation can help to estimate the bound for $\log(xy)$.

$$\log(xy) = \log(1 + m_x) + e_x + \log(1 + m_y) + e_y$$
$$\leq m_x + \Delta_{max} + e_x + m_y + \Delta_{max} + e_y$$

After putting Eqs. (6) (7) (8) in, $\log(xy)$ becomes

$$\log(xy) \leq \frac{M_x}{2^{52}} + \Delta_{max} + E_x - 1023$$

$$+ \frac{M_x}{2^{52}} + \Delta_{max} + E_y - 1023$$

$$= \frac{M_x + E_x \cdot 2^{52}}{2^{52}} + \frac{M_y + E_y \cdot 2^{52}}{2^{52}} + 2\Delta_{max} - 2046$$

$$= \frac{x_{uint64} + y_{uint64}}{2^{52}} + 2\Delta_{max} - 2046$$

Because of Eq. (13), $x_{uint64} + y_{uint64} = \text{0x7FDE9F73AABB2400}$. Then we will get the upper bound of $\log(xy)$

$$\log(xy) \leq \frac{\text{0x7FDE9F73AABB2400}}{2^{52}} + 2\Delta_{max} - 2046$$

$$\approx 0.0859$$

In similar ways, we can calculate the lower bound of $\log(xy)$

$$\log(xy) \geq \frac{\text{0x7FDE9F73AABB2400}}{2^{52}} - 2046$$

$$\approx -0.0860$$

The initial estimation $\delta = 1 - xy = 1 - 2^{\log(xy)}$ will have a following bound

$$\delta \in [0.0560, 0.0580]$$

Furthermore, we can verify this result by experiments. The experiments will be discussed in Sect. 3. We will use the experimental result directly here, that the estimation error δ of Eq. (13) is no more than 0.06.

Similar estimation could be also derivated for 32-bit floating point number.

$$y_{uint32} \approx \text{0x7FF8D4FD} - x_{uint32} \tag{15}$$

2.3 Put Predicting and Iterating Together

As we metion in Sect. 2.2, the prediction method has a max error no more than 0.06. Considering that the IEEE754 double precision format has 52 significant binary bits (or 14 decimal digits) we only need no more than 5 iterations in Sect. 2.1 to increase the accuracy. More details about choosing and comparing the number of iterating steps will be discussed in Sect. 3.

Thus, we get the full algorithm as the following.

This algorithm could be easily implemented on GPU and MIC. Algorithm 3 is the code on Intel's Xeon Phi.

Algorithm 2. 10 instructions to calculate $\dfrac{1}{x}$

Input: x - a floating point number

Output: y - the estimation of $\dfrac{1}{x}$

1: $y_{uint64} \leftarrow$ **0x7FDE9F73AABB2400** $- x_{uint64}$
2: $y \leftarrow y_{float}$
3: $\delta \leftarrow 1 - xy$
4: $y \leftarrow y + y \cdot \delta$
5: $\delta \leftarrow \delta \cdot \delta$
6: $y \leftarrow y + y \cdot \delta$
7: $\delta \leftarrow \delta \cdot \delta$
8: $y \leftarrow y + y \cdot \delta$
9: $\delta \leftarrow \delta \cdot \delta$
10: $y \leftarrow y + y \cdot \delta$

Algorithm 3. 10 MIC instrinsic to calculate $\dfrac{1}{x}$

Input: x - a floating point number vector
Output: y - the reciprocal vector of x

1: __m512d y, delta;
2: union __m512i i; __m512d d; p;
3: p.d = x;
4: p.i = _mm512_sub_epi32(0x7FDE9F73AABB2400ULL, p.i);
5: y = p.d;
6: delta = _mm512_fnmadd_pd(p.d, x, _mm512_set1_pd(1.0));
7: y = _mm512_fmadd_pd(y, delta, y);
8: delta = _mm512_mul_pd(delta, delta);
9: y = _mm512_fmadd_pd(y, delta, y);
10: delta = _mm512_mul_pd(delta, delta);
11: y = _mm512_fmadd_pd(y, delta, y);
12: delta = _mm512_mul_pd(delta, delta);
13: y = _mm512_fmadd_pd(y, delta, y);

2.4 Limitations and Edge Cases

In IEEE 754 standard, some special binaries are reserved, including the positive infinity (0x7FF0000000000000ULL), negative infinity (0xFFF0000000000000ULL) and NaN(not a number, 0xFFF*************ULL, mantissa should not be all zero bits). These cases should be avoid.

What's more, in order to avoid floating point overflow results, the original number should not be 0x800*************ULL, which will cause the result too large to be represented in IEEE 754 format, which also could not be properly processed by the common standard division.

Equations (13) and (15) uses unsigned integer subtraction. However it is not totally the same as an 64-bit unsigned integer subtraction. The first bit of IEEE 754 format should be reserved for the sign bit. It means that the subtraction in fact should be a 63-bit integer subtraction. If we use 64-bit subtraction, borrowing from the first bit is not allowed here, otherwise, the sign bit will be not correct. In another words, this algorithm could not handle those floating point numbers whose last 63 bits are larger than 0x7FDE9F73AABB2400.

Summing up the above limitations, our algorithm works for 64-bit floating numbers in the range from 0x0000000000000000ULL to 0x7FBFFFFFFFFFFFFFULL and the range from 0x8010000000000001ULL to 0xFFBFFFFFFFFFFFFFULL approximatively. (In fact, the exact range is a little larger.) The excluded range is corresponding to those numbers whose absolutely value is extremely large or special form in IEEE 754.

Although our approximate algorithm is limited for some special cases, these two ranges have already covered most 64-bit floating numbers.

Above limitations also apply to single precision floating point numbers.

3 Experiment and Evaluation

We test our algorithm on NVIDIA's GPU and Intel's Xeon Phi. The test system is configured as Table 1. It is equipped with a NVIDIA K20 GPU card and an Intel Xeon Phi 5100 Series card.

Table 1. Experiment Setup

	GPU	MIC
Product Name	NVIDIA K20	Intel Xeon Phi 5100 Series
Number of Cores	2496	60
Clock rate/GHz	0.71	1.053
Compiler	CUDA 5.0	Intel Composer XE 2013.2.146

We have three tests, two for precision and one for performance.

3.1 The Precision of the Predicting Method

The initial estimation is a direct restriction and determinant to the final precision. Although we have made a detail mathematical analysis, but considering that floating point representation and operations have some intrinsic imprecision, we still need to test the predicting accuracy in practice carefully.

We multiply the original number and the predicted initial value with the algorithm in Sect. 2.2 and calculate its difference to 1.0. There are two sub-tests. One is for GPU and the other is for MIC. The tests enumerate 64-bit floating point number in the range mentioned in Sect. 2.4.

For the reason that the space of 64-bit floating point number is quite huge, only the first 44 bits are enumerated and the last 20 bits are randomly generated.

The test result is shown in Table 2.

Table 2. The maximal estimation error of the predicting step

	Initial estimation error $\delta = 1 - xy$
K20 GPU	5.08×10^{-2}
Intel MIC	6.14×10^{-2}

The test result shows that the estimation error for 64-bit floating point number in IEEE 754 format is not larger than 0.07. It means that there only needs no more than 4 iterations mentioned in Algorithm 1 to make the theoretical relative error decrease to $0.07^{2^4} \approx 3.323 \times 10^{-19}$, which is already less than the inherent relative error of IEEE 754 floating point number format.

3.2 The Precision of the Whole Algorithm

This experiment tests precision of the whole algorithm. This test runs a similar enumeration like Sect. 3.1. We test the relative error when iterating from 1 step to 5 steps compared with the standard division. The test result is shown in Table 3.

The IEEE 754 format double precision floating point number has 52 significant bits in the mantissa, which is corresponding to about 16 decimal significant digits after the decimal point. It also means that our result is accurately enough. The approximation algorithm is acceptable for most computing scenarios.

Table 3. The maximal relative error when iteration steps = 1,2,3,4,5

steps	GPU	MIC
1	2.58×10^{-3}	2.60×10^{-3}
2	6.68×10^{-6}	9.77×10^{-6}
3	2.22×10^{-16}	3.26×10^{-16}
4	2.22×10^{-16}	2.64×10^{-16}
5	2.22×10^{-16}	2.22×10^{-16}

3.3 The Peformance

We test the performance by repeating the calculation on a random pre-generate floating point number list. Each division iterates 4 steps like Algorithm 2. The experiment results are shown in Fig. 2.

Our algorithm acquires a performance of 117.7 GFlops on K20, while the built-in division implement of CUDA is only 46.6 GFlops. The algorithm on MIC acquires a performance of 37.6 Gflops, which is nearly twice of the Intel SVML which is only 18.0 Gflops.

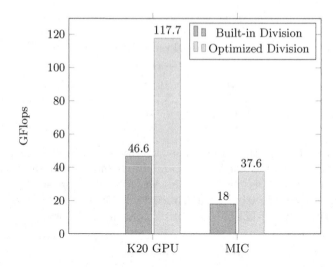

Fig. 2. The speedup of the optimized division on GPU and MIC

4   Conclusion

Due to the complexity implement of division on logical level, division is less efficient. This inefficiency is even worse on GPU and MIC, which may restrict the performance optimization on these platforms. In order to reduce the huge performance gap between floating point division and multiplication and addition, we have proposed a simple and fast approximate algorithm to calculate the reciprocal in IEEE 754 format. The core of the algorithm is to use an integer subtraction to acquire an initial estimation value and then iterate by Goldschmidt's iteration method. This algorithm could take advantage of GPU and MIC's FMA ability. It has a well performance on K20 GPU and Intel MIC.

Acknowledgments. We thank anonymous reviewers for comments and suggestions on the submitted version of this paper. Special thanks to the suggestions from members of the Parallel Software Group of EECS, Peking University.

This research is supported by the National HTRD 863 Plan under Grants No. 2012AA010902, 2012AA010903; and NSFC Grants No. 61170053, 61432018, 61379048.

References

1. IEEE standard for floating-point arithmetic: IEEE Std 754–2008, 1–70 (2008)
2. Flynn, M.J.: On division by functional iteration. IEEE Trans. Comput. **100**(8), 702–706 (1970)
3. Goldschmidt, R.E.: Applications of division by convergence. Ph.D. thesis, Massachusetts Institute of Technology (1964)
4. Granlund, T., Montgomery, P.L.: Division by invariant integers using multiplication. In: ACM SIGPLAN Notices, vol. 29, pp. 61–72. ACM (1994)

5. Hwang, K., Louri, A.: Optical multiplication and division using modified-signed-digit symbolic substitution. Opt. Eng. **28**(4), 284364–284364 (1989)
6. Jeffers, J., Reinders, J.: Intel Xeon Phi coprocessor high-performance programming. Newnes (2013)
7. Markstein, P.: Software division and square root using Goldschmidts algorithms. In: Proceedings of the 6th Conference on Real Numbers and Computers (RNC6). vol. 123, pp. 146–157 (2004)
8. NVIDIA: CUDA C programming guide. http://docs.nvidia.com/cuda/cuda-c-programming-guide/
9. Oberman, S.F.: Floating point division and square root algorithms and implementation in the AMD-K7 TM microprocessor. In: 14th IEEE Symposium on Computer Arithmetic, Proceedings, pp. 106–115. IEEE (1999)
10. Oberman, S.F., Flynn, M.J.: Design issues in division and other floating-point operations. IEEE Trans. Comput. **46**(2), 154–161 (1997)
11. Oberman, S.F.: Design issues in high performance floating point arithmetic units. Ph.D. thesis, Citeseer (1996)
12. Patterson, D.A., Hennessy, J.L.: Computer organization and design: the hardware/software interface. Newnes (2013)
13. Piñeiro, J.A., Bruguera, J.D.: High-speed double-precision computation of reciprocal, division, square root, and inverse square root. IEEE Trans. Comput. **51**(12), 1377–1388 (2002)
14. Sharangpani, H., Barton, M.: Statistical analysis of floating point flaw in the pentium processor. Intel Corporation (1994)
15. Soderquist, P., Leeser, M.: Division and square root: choosing the right implementation. IEEE Micro **17**(4), 56–66 (1997)
16. Wikipedia: Double-precision floating-point format. https://en.wikipedia.org/wiki/Double-precision_floating-point_format

UniDegree: A GPU-Based Graph Representation for SSSP

Changyou Zhang[1,2(✉)], Feng Wang[3], Kun Huang[2], Zhiyou Liu[2], and Yifeng Chen[2]

[1] Laboratory of Parallel Software and Computational Science, Institute of Software, Chinese Academy of Sciences, Beijing 100190, China
changyou@iscas.ac.cn
[2] HCST Key Lab, School of EECS, Peking University, Beijing 100085, China
[3] School of Computer, Beijing Institute of Technology, Beijing 100081, China

Abstract. GPU is the mainstream co-processor computers of heterogeneous architecture. Parallel graph algorithms are fundamental for many data-driven applications to be solved on heterogeneous clusters. SSSP (Single Source Shortest Path) algorithm is one of the most important one. We proposed a graph representation structure with unified vertex's degree. This method ensures the data block size consistency. And then, the transferring in memory on this representation makes the data reading in cohesion for CUDA thread blocks. Thirdly, vertex renumbering optimizes the locality of graph vertices to make the relaxing operation more efficient. With data of New York road, we implemented SSSP algorithms of delta-stepping on Nvida Tesla K20x GPU device. The experimental results show that the best unified-degree is approximate to the mode of vertex-degree of the graph. For example of the New York road map, all degrees were unified into 4-degree that results to the biggest speed-up of SSSP algorithm.

Keywords: GPU · Graph · SSSP · Degree · Unifying · Locality

1 Introduction

Generally, $G = (V, E)$ is a graph, where V is a set of nodes and E is a set of arcs. In the graph G, each edge is associated with a positive weight w. The problem of finding shortest path from V_s to V_t is a classical algorithm of graph. This algorithm is called SSSP (Single Source Shortest Path). Dijkstra is most popular algorithm, which is implemented in sequential and parallel [2–5].

In data-driven applications, graph is abstracted as the basic data model with very sparse, fine-grained data accesses. This requires a very high communication rate between many processors through inter-network. This communication mode is challenging for HPC platforms, especially GPU-based computer clusters. The Graph 500 [2] is a rating of supercomputer systems, focused on Data intensive loads. The benchmark used in Graph500 stresses the communication subsystem of the system, instead of counting double precision floating-point. It is based on a breadth-first

© Springer International Publishing Switzerland 2015
G. Wang et al. (Eds.): ICA3PP 2015, Part II, LNCS 9529, pp. 704–715, 2015.
DOI: 10.1007/978-3-319-27122-4_49

search in a large undirected graph (model of Kronecker graph with average degree of 16). There are two computation kernels in the benchmark: the first kernel is to generate the graph and compress it into sparse structures CSR or CSC (Compressed Sparse Row/Column); the second kernel does a parallel BFS search of some random vertices (64 search iterations per run). Single source shortest path search on these graphs is promoted as a new benchmark. The Graph500's goal is to promote awareness of complex data problems, instead of focusing on computer benchmarks like HPL (High Performance Linpack), which Top500 is based on.

According to the 45th edition of the twice-yearly TOP500 list of the world's most powerful supercomputers in June 2015 [1], for the fifth consecutive time, Tianhe-2, a supercomputer developed by China's National University of Defense Technology, has retained its position as the world's No. 1 system. That means the accelerator-based configuration is still mainstream of heterogeneous architectures of supercomputer. The Titan (at the second place) and the Piz Daint (at the sixth place) are equipped with Nvidia K20x GPU cards.

The remainder of this paper is organized as follows: Sect. 2 introduces the related works on GPU/CUDA programming properties and SSSP. Section 3 enumerates the graph representation methods by unifying vertex degrees. Section 3.4 illustrates the transposition scheme of graph data for cohesion reading on GPU. Section 4 develops experiments on performance of SSSP in new representation. Section 4.4 provides the discussion on the time cost on extra-processes. Section 5 makes a conclusion and further discussion.

2   Related Work

2.1   GPU/CUDA Properties

GPU (Graphics Processing Unit) card is a co-processor developed by Nvidia. A GPU consists of multiple multiprocessors. GPU provides different memory level named as, register memory, global memory, shared memory, constant memory and texture memory. Register memory is private memory for each thread. Global memory, constant memory and texture memory are accessible for the all thread present in a grid. Shared memory is local to the thread of the same block. Constant memory and texture memory are read only memory present in DRAM of the GPU device.

To conveniently programming on GPU, NVIDIA introduced CUDA (Compute Unified Device Architecture) in C/Fortran programming language. A CUDA program is composed of two parts, host code and device code. A host code is running on CPU. A device code is actually running on GPU, and it is called as kennel. In CUDA platform a set of instructions (kernel) executed on each thread of the GPU device. Threads are divided into blocks. Block is a collection of thread that can be run on each core of device in currently. A grid is a collection of blocks assigned to multiprocessor.

The architecture of GPU is most suited in algorithms with high computing intensity and regular data access pattern.

2.2   Graph Representation

Graph is represented in computer with a variety of structures, such as array, adjacency list, cross linked list, adjacency multi-lists.

Adjacency matrix and adjacency list are the two main data structure to represent a graph, adjacency matrix and adjacency list. If there are few edges between vertices, this is a sparse graph. For a large sparse graph, most of elements of this matrix are zero. This waste of memory causes no enough memory to load the whole graph to process, in case of the sparse graph. Adjacency list representation is the suitable structure to represent sparse graph.

Compact adjacency list is more popularly known as the compact sparse representation (CSR). In CSR, all the adjacency lists are packed into a single large array. An array E_a is used to store the adjacency lists where the list for vertex $i + 1$ immediately follows vertex i, for all the vertices in G. An array V_a stores the starting indices of the corresponding adjacency lists in E_a. Each of the indices of V_a acts as the vertex number of the graph. The key advantage of using this representation is that, the graph is stored in a continuous memory space and no long strides are required to go from a neighbor of a certain vertex. This helps in reducing the memory access irregularity and hence boosts the overall performance of the BFS implementation.

2.3   Single Source Shortest Path Algorithm

SSSP (single source shortest path) algorithm is widely used in data analysis. The most well-known serial algorithm is Dijkstra algorithm [5]. With Fibonacci heap [6], the time complexity is $O(|E| + |V|\log|V|)$. The Bellman-Ford algorithm computes single-source shortest paths in a weighted digraph [7]. In its basic structure, it is similar to Dijkstra's Algorithm, but instead of greedily selecting the minimum-weight node not yet processed to relax, it simply relaxes all the edges, and does this $|V| - 1$ times, where $|V|$ is the number of vertices in the graph.

To solve the parallel SSSP problem, U. Meyer and P. Sanders proposed a Delta-stepping algorithm for directed graph with uncertain weights [8]. The algorithm selected a set of vertices with distance within a limited range to parallel relaxation all out edges of these vertices. Delta-stepping algorithm improved the computational efficiency in label-correcting mode to achieve greater parallelism through redundant computing.

In classic GPU-based SSSP algorithm implementation, graph data are loaded in global memory. The bottleneck of this approach is that each relaxing operation has to access global memory with duplicate data. It does not take full advantage of the efficiency of shared memory. Efficient approach is to load sub-graph into shared memory. In sub-graph iterative process, data are read from shared memory. However, shared memory merely belongs to the corresponding CUDA block. Other CUDA blocks could not access this private data. Updates along boundary edges must be written back to the global memory to complete the communication between these blocks.

Δ-stepping algorithm is the parallelization of Dijkstra algorithm. Let v denotes vertices, $d(v)$ denotes the distance from vertex v to the source vertex s. The algorithm discovers proper vertices v with the distance $d(v)$ in the range of $i*\Delta$ and $(i + 1)*\Delta$ to save them into an array named Bucket[i]. Then relax each vertex of Bucket[i] in iteration, till the bucket is empty. When all the buckets are empty, algorithm terminates. Δ-stepping is a label-correcting algorithm. The relaxation times could not be pre-determined by the number of vertices and edges. The Δ value determines Bucket size. Different value provides a different degree of parallelism.

The relaxing operation is the core of Δ-Stepping algorithm implementation in CUDA. Each thread is responsible for a vertex. The heavy edge and light edge would be classified before the relax operation.

3   Graph Presentation with Unified Vertex Degrees

In high performance computing, the two common data structures are adjacency matrix and adjacency list. For a sparse graph, the adjacency list is often chosen. The adjacency list is a chain storage structure [10]. Each vertex points to a single linked list. For CUDA programming, a compact adjacency list often is used [11]. A graph with N vertices and M edges is represented as two arrays V_a and E_a, where V_a is an array with N elements to store each vertex information, and E_a is an array with M elements to store each edge information. Taking into account the special requirements of data access cohesive on GPU global memory, we unified the out-degree of each vertex and optimized memory with array.

The cohesion of data reading and writing is one of key points for GPU algorithm optimization. We designed a vertex degrees unifying approach. We do experiments of SSSP algorithm running on the New York map [9].

3.1   Graph Construction

The most common graph format in files is the edge set array. Each row in the file represents an edge. It consists of three values: the first one is the start vertex number, the second is the end vertex number, and the last one is the weight of this edge. Firstly, graph is temporarily stored in memory in two arrays. The first array is the degree array to store the degree of each vertex. The second array is an end_weight set used to store the edge's end vertex and the weight. At first, the degree array is initialized to zero and the end-weight array is allocated double the multiple of max degree of the graph and the number of vertex. Every vertex has double max degree spaces to store edge ends and weights in the second array. After reading an edge from the data file, we record the edge's end vertex number and weight at the end_weight array. The degree of the start vertex increases by one. Figure 1 illustrates the example graph G in (a) and the initial format of this graph is show in (b).

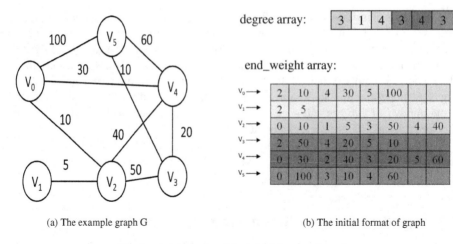

(a) The example graph G   (b) The initial format of graph

Fig. 1. An example of the initial format of graph

3.2 Unifying the Out-Degree of Vertices

The unifying approach is to check the degree of each vertex and compare it with a given number C. If the degree is less than C, the degree of vertex will be padded to; if it is greater than, vertex is split into several sub-vertices. Let the unified degree is C, the unifying process is listed as follows.

1. For all vertices, checking the degree of the *i-th* vertex degrees dv_i;
2. If dv_i is less than C, add C-dv_i meaningless edges;
3. If dv_i is greater than C, create a new vertex V_{N+1}. Sort all the edges of v_i according to the ID of neighbor vertex. Keep the smallest $C - 1$ vertex as V_i's neighbor. Vertex V_{N+1} add as the C-*th* edge, and set the weight as 0; Other neighbors are transferred from V_i to V_{N+1};
4. If any vertex is waiting, jump to step 2; else, finish.

For example, let $C = 3$, Fig. 1(a) illustrates the original graph, and Fig. 2 illustrate the out-degree unified graph G'. The blue vertices, V_6 and V_7, are new split vertices. V_6 is split from V_2 with weight = 0 to V_2; Vertex V_7 is split from V_4 with weight = 0 to V_4. V_1 only has one neighbor V_2, so add two meaningless vertices identified as −1, and weight = 0 to V_1. The degree of each vertex in the transformed graph G' is 3. Figure 3 illustrates the adjacency list of original graph, and Fig. 4 illustrates the adjacency list of transferred graph G'. The experiments show that this transformation does not affect the correctness of the shortest path solution.

In this paper, the graph is represented as compact adjacency list in array E_a. An edge is structured as <end vertex, weight>. Let $C = 4$, the graph is represented in memory as Fig. 5.

In Fig. 5, V_i denotes the *i-th* vertex, and E_j denotes the *j-th* edge. For example, V_0E_1 denotes that the 1st edge of 0# vertex is stored at this memory block. The maximum

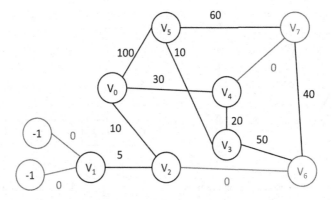

Fig. 2. G': the result of unifying out-degree of G (Color figure online)

	V_0			V_1	V_2			
end	2	4	5	2	0	1	3	4
weight	10	30	100	5	10	5	50	40
	V_3			V_4				V_5		
end	2	4	5	0	2	3	5	0	3	4
weight	50	20	10	30	40	20	60	100	10	60

Fig. 3. Adjacency list of G

	pad_0			pad_1			pad_2		
end	2	4	5	2	-1	-1	0	1	6
weight	10	30	100	5	0	0	10	5	0
	pad_3			pad_4			pad_5		
end	4	5	6	0	3	7	0	3	7
weight	20	10	50	30	20	0	100	10	60
	pad_6			pad_7					
end	2	3	7	4	5	6			
weight	0	50	40	0	60	40			

Fig. 4. Unified adjacency list of graph G'

V_0E_1	V_0E_2	V_0E_3	V_0E_4
V_1E_1	V_1E_2	V_1E_3	V_1E_4
V_2E_1	V_2E_2	V_2E_3	V_2E_4
V_3E_1	V_3E_2	V_3E_3	V_3E_4
......			
$V_{N-1}E_1$	$V_{N-1}E_2$	$V_{N-1}E_3$	$V_{N-1}E_4$
V_NE_1	V_NE_2	V_NE_3	V_NE_4

Fig. 5. Degree unified graph in compact adjacency list

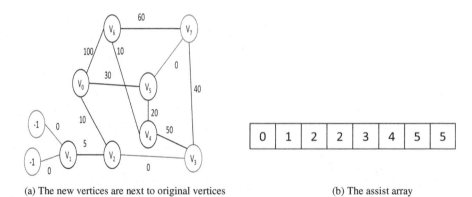

(a) The new vertices are next to original vertices   (b) The assist array

Fig. 6. New vertex are inserted next to original vertex (Color figure online)

number of vertex is $N' = N + X$. X is the number of new created vertices in degree unifying.

In this paper, the graph is represented as compact adjacency list in array E_a. An edge is structured as <end vertex, weight>. Let $C = 4$, the graph is represented in memory as Fig. 5.

In Fig. 5, V_i denotes the i-th vertex, and E_j denotes the j-th edge. For example, V_0E_1 denotes that the 1st edge of 0# vertex is stored at this memory block. The maximum number of vertex is $N' = N + X$. X is the number of new created vertices in degree unifying.

3.3 Renumber Vertices

In the process of unifying the out-degree of vertices, new vertices can be inserted into two places: one is at the rear of all the vertices; the other is that new vertex is inserted next the original vertices. The first one is as Fig. 2. In the second method, an assistant array is used to record the original vertex's corresponding vertex in the unified adjacency list.

Let the assistant array ass[] record the current vertex in unifying adjacency list. The initialized value of j is 0. The unifying process is listed as follows.

1. For all vertices, checking the degree of the i-th vertex degrees dv_i;
2. If dv_i is less than C, add $C-dv_i$ meaningless edges, ass[j] = i, j++;
3. If dv_i is greater than C, create a new vertex V_{j+1}. Sort all the edges of v_i according to the ID of neighbor vertex. Keep the smallest $C - 1$ vertex as V_j's neighbor. Vertex V_{j+1} add as the C-th edge, and set the weight as 0. Other neighbors are transferred from V_j to V_{j+1}. ass[j] = ass[$j + 1$] = i;
4. If any vertex is waiting, jump to step 2; else, finish.

In Fig. 6(a), The blue vertices, V_3 and V_7, are new split vertices from original V_2 and V_5. The assist array is as Fig. 6(b).

3.4   Graph Data Transposition

Solano-Quinde et al. [12] has found that threads in the same warp reading sequential memory data reduces large memory latency. In CUDA program implementation, each vertex is mapped to a thread. This mapping is illustrated in Fig. 7(a). Thread is responsible for accessing and operating data of this vertex. Each vertex contains four data area. This results in the interval of three-data-block between these threads. Therefore, we transpose this array to get the new array in Fig. 7(b).

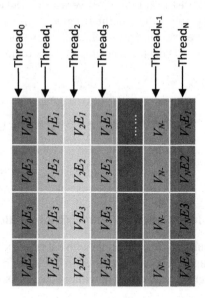

(b)after transposition

Fig. 7. The mapping between thread and vertex

4   The Experiments on SSSP

4.1   Introduction of Graph Data and Device

We choose New York road information in the 9th DIMACS Implementation Challenge
[9] - Shortest Paths to test the algorithms in this paper. New York graph has 264346
vertices and 733846 edges. The average degree is 5.552. The initialization of this algorithm includes reading map data from the graph file, out-degree unifying, and data
transposition. Each thread index is mapped to a vertex. SSSP algorithm runs on two
kinds of GPU devices, GTX 480 and Tesla K20xm.

4.2   Find the Best Value of C

On one hand, out-degree unifying could improve the cohesion of data access to optimize
the performance. On the other hand, the degree of the vertex is an important impact on
parallelism. Therefore, the unified degree, C, is vital to the algorithm performance.
Choosing unified degree C should consider the graph properties. Larger C gives higher
parallelism, but cause to much invalid padding vertex. This increases invalid work, and
will lead to poor performance. Based on the common sense that the crossroad is of four
directions, we guess $C = 4$ should be reasoning. In the process of unifying out-degree,
we choose to insert new vertex next to original vertex. We did experiments on $C = 2$,
$C = 3$, $C = 4$, $C = 5$ and graph without unified degree to discover the best value of C.
The experimental results are listed in Table 1. In Table 1, when $C = 4$, the running time
is the smallest one on both GPU device. The graph format of un-unified degree gets the
slowest speed.

Table 1.   SSSP running time (ms) on different value of C

Device	$C = 2$	$C = 3$	$C = 4$	$C = 5$	Un-unified degree
GTX 480	86.67	65.02	59.64	67.07	340.32
K20xm	129.21	83.92	73.44	83.28	215.54

4.3   Compare the Results of Data with/without Transposition

When $C = 4$, we test the running times of graph with data transposition and without data
transposition. The experimental results are listed in Table 2. Graph with data transposition nearly get twice higher speed than that without data transposition.

Table 2.   SSSP running time (ms) with/without data transposition

Device	Data transposition	Without data transposition
GTX 480	59.64	104.64
K20xm	73.44	120.67

4.4   The Time-Cost of Unifying the Out-Degree and Data Transposition

We also calculate time cost of unifying the out-degree of vertices and data transposition on host device. The host device is AMD Phenom(tm) II X4 960T processor with four cores and 4 GB of DDR3 memory. The time costs of unifying the out-degree of vertices and data transposition are affected by C. For when C is small, the count of vertex is large. When C is large, most out-degrees are invalid. The experimental results are listed in Table 3. From Table 3, we can find that when $C = 4$, the total running time of the processes of unifying the out-degree and data transposition is also the smallest.

Table 3. Unifying the out-degree and data transposition time (ms)

Process	$C = 2$	$C = 3$	$C = 4$	$C = 5$
Unifying the out-degree	31.10	28.85	27.78	31.75
Data transposition	7.79	8.68	9.06	13.16
Sum running time	38.89	37.53	36.84	44.91

4.5   The SSSP Running Time of Two Kinds of Graph in Different Renumbering Ways

In the process of renumbering vertices, there are two methods: one is to insert new vertex next to original vertex, we call it '$i + 1$'; another is to insert new vertex at the rear of all the vertices, which we call '$N + 1$'. Graph of these two kinds have different localities, so SSSP running times are different in these two graphs. GTX 480 is selected as the device. We list the results in Table 4. We can find that '$i + 1$' gets higher speed than '$N + 1$' in the same C.

Table 4. SSSP running time (ms) in different inserting methods

Insert position	$C = 2$	$C = 3$	$C = 4$	$C = 5$
$i + 1$	86.67	65.02	59.64	67.07
$N + 1$	214.64	111.41	62.50	70.02

4.6   Performance Analysis

From above experiments we can find that when $C = 4$, graph data with unifying the out-degree and data transposition in '$i + 1$' inserting way, SSSP get the highest speed. Although the process of unifying the out-degree and data transposition takes a little time on host CPU, the time is so little that the sum running time of all the processes is much smaller than that of original graph data. After unifying the out-degree, although the count of vertices increases, GPU can provide enough threads to calculate. Unifying the out-degree can avoid thread's long time waiting in block synchronization. After data transposition, threads in the same warp reading sequential memory data can reduce large memory latency.

As the data graph locality, we statics the difference value of vertices numbers on an edge. When $C = 4$, the difference value rate is shown in Fig. 8. The average of difference value of the edges' two vertex number of '$i + 1$' is 766, while the one of '$N + 1$' is 1382. We can find that graph renumbering in '$i + 1$' has higher rate of lower difference value. Graph renumbering in '$N + 1$' has larger rate of the highest difference value, for new vertices are inserted into the rear of all vertices. Vertices' distances and edges are store in the sequence of vertices number. So when renumbered in the way of '$i + 1$', vertex is linked to ones whose number is close to it. Graph in '$i + 1$' renumbering way has better locality than that in '$N + 1$' renumbering way. So cache hit rate of the former is much higher than latter. So graph in '$i + 1$' renumbering way get a higher speed in SSSP.

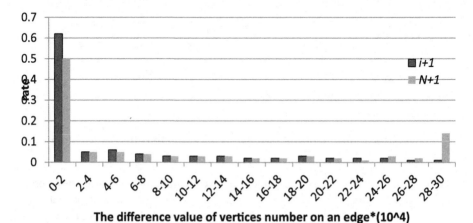

Fig. 8. The rate of edges with different value of the vertices number

5   Conclusion and Further Research

The character of graph parallel algorithms is redundant computation. This achieves higher parallelism to reduce computing time. We designed a method to unify vertex's out-degree to a constant value. This method ensures the balance works for GPU blocks threads. Every thread is allocated equal works to avoid long time waiting for the heaviest work load thread. The experimental results show that the unified out-degree gets a three times speed-up.

For SSSP algorithm, global synchronization with help of CPU and multi-revoke GPU kernel is very time-consuming. To minimize the kernel revoking times, proper graph partitioning and vertices reordering are available. A more efficient inter-block synchronization policy is vital to GPU-based SSSP algorithm.

Acknowledgements. This paper is supported by the Natural Science Foundation of China (61379048); Special Project of National CAS Union – The High Performance Cloud Service Platform for Enterprise Creative Computing; Special Project of Hebei-CAS Union

(Hebei, No. 14010015)–The Performance Optimization of Key Algorithms of Health Data Processing in Senile Dementia Analysis. The authors also would like to express appreciation to the anonymous reviewers for their helpful comments on improving the paper.

References

1. Top 500 List, June 2015. http://www.top500.org/list/2012/11/
2. Graph 500 List, November 2012. http://www.graph500.org/results_nov_2012
3. Angel, J.B., Flores, A.M., Heritage, J.S., et al.: The graph 500 benchmark on a medium-size distributed-memory cluster with high-performance interconnect, key facts. http://newsroom.fb.com/content/default.aspx?NewsAreaId=22. Accessed 23 November 2012
4. Karypis, G., Aggarwal, R., Kumar, V., Shekhar, S.: Multilevel hypergraph partitioning: application in VLSI domain. In: Proceedings of the 34th Annual Design Automation Conference, pp. 526–529 (1997)
5. Dijkstra, E.W.: A note on two problems in connexion with graphs. Num. Math. **1**, 269–271 (1959)
6. Fredman, M.L., Tarjan, R.E.: Fibonacci heaps their uses in improved network optimization algorithms. J. ACM (JACM) **34**, 596–615 (1987)
7. Bellman, R.: On a routing problem. Q. Appl. Math. **16**, 87–90 (1958)
8. Meyer, U., Sanders, P.: Δ-stepping: a parallelizable shortest path algorithm. J. Algorithms **49**, 114–152 (2003)
9. Nineth DIMACS implementation challenge - shortest paths. http://www.dis.uniroma1.it/challenge9/download.shtml
10. Harish, P., Vineet, V., Narayanan, P.: Large graph algorithms for massively multithreaded architectures. Technical report IIIT/TR/2009/74, International Institute of Information Technology Hyderabad, India (2009)
11. Harish, P., Narayanan, P.J.: Accelerating large graph algorithms on the GPU using CUDA. In: Aluru, S., Parashar, M., Badrinath, R., Prasanna, V.K. (eds.) HiPC 2007. LNCS, vol. 4873, pp. 197–208. Springer, Heidelberg (2007)
12. Solano-Quinde, L., Wang, Z.J., Bode, B., et al.: Unstructured grid applications on GPU: performance analysis and improvement
13. Singh, D.P., Khare, N.: Parallel implementation of the single source shortest path algorithm on CPU–GPU based hybrid system. Int. J. Comput. Sci. Inf. Secur. **11**(9), 74 (2013)
14. Singh, A.P., Sin, D.P.: Implementation of K-shortest path algorithm in GPU using CUDA. Procedia Comput. Sci. **48**, 5–13 (2015). (Original research article)

MTTF-Aware Reliability Task Scheduling for Heterogeneous Multicore System

Huaguo Liang[1,2], Yangyang Dai[2(✉)], Maoxiang Yi[2], Dawen Xu[2],
and Zhengfeng Huang[2]

[1] School of Computer and Information,
Hefei University of Technology, Hefei 230009, China
huagulg@hfut.edu.cn
[2] School of Electronic Science and Applied Physics,
Hefei University of Technology, Hefei 230009, China
mxyi902@hfut.edu.cn, zaneisdyy@gmail.com

Abstract. With silicon technology aggressively scaling, the aging-induced long-term reliability becomes the prominent problem of integrated circuits. The reliability of homogeneous multi-core system is improved and the aging is relieved through balancing the workload between cores. While for heterogeneous systems, this will increase the gap of original MTTF differences of each core. By considering the original diversity of MTTF, a MILP-based task scheduling method is proposed to balance the MTTF of whole system. Experimental results show that, compared to the workload balancing algorithms, our approach improve MTTF of system over 30 % on average.

Keywords: MTTF · Reliability · Aging effect · Task scheduling · Heterogeneous multicore system

1 Introduction

As silicon feature size continues shrinking, highly integrated multicore systems are increasingly adopted by industrial field. Chip interconnection of multicore system becomes increasingly denser, while long-term reliability becoming decreasing. TDDB (Time Dependent Dielectric Breakdown), NBTI (Negative Bias Temperature Instability), EM (Electromigration) and other wear-out mechanisms are becoming severe, leading the degradation of reliability. The lifetime or long-term reliability of a processor is usually measured by MTTF (mean time to failure) [1]. The MTTF of a processor could decline about 4X from 180 nm to 65 nm caused by aging effect, which will result in a destructive damage to the semiconductors [2].

Many researches and studies are focused on the transistor-level and gate-level aging effect [3, 4], however, little attention was paid on systematic level for mitigating degradation. For the enhancement of overall system reliability, some studies employed thermal-aware task scheduling to restrain the peak temperature or thermal gradient between cores [5, 6]. In terms of the relationship between leakage power and temperature, a thermal-aware task scheduling with power constraint technique is proposed to reduce the power dissipation [7]. Jin et al. proposed a NBTI-aware algorithm to

© Springer International Publishing Switzerland 2015
G. Wang et al. (Eds.): ICA3PP 2015, Part II, LNCS 9529, pp. 716–727, 2015.
DOI: 10.1007/978-3-319-27122-4_50

balance workload for multicore processor [8]. A dynamic zoning and corresponding task scheduling are applied for homogeneous multicore systems to extend MTTF and reduce failures of systems. Xie et al. proposed duplicating tasks on idle processors during system synthesis for cutting down soft error [9]. Considering the jointly correlation of wear-out mechanism, Wu et al. suggested that EM are dominated aging effect [10], while TDDB and NBTI have less effect on system-level reliability due to their interaction. Considering the MTTF model under Electromigration aging effect, a DVFS-based method was proposed to improve the reliability of embedded real-time system [11].

However, little study has taken account of the original diversity among MTTFs of the processors for reliability enhancement of multicore systems. In the heterogeneous system, different operational voltage/frequency or entirely different structures lead to the heterogeneity [12], resulting in the original MTTF of each processor in a heterogeneous multicore system is various before task running. Workload-balanced scheduling algorithms aren't applicable enough to enhance the reliability of heterogeneous multicore systems, and the least reliable processor will become the reliability bottleneck of the whole system, if its original MTTF is not considered before task running. In fact, [1] suggested that the least MTTF component is regarded as the MTTF of whole system.

So in a heterogeneous multicore system, the original diversity among MTTFs of involved heterogeneous processors must be taken account during task running and a MTTF-balance task scheduling is acquired for enhancing reliability of specific heterogeneous multicore system. This paper presents a MILP-based reliability-driven task scheduling algorithm to balance the MTTF of heterogeneous multicore systems. Based on the EM-aware reliability model (black model) of single processor in reference [12] and the absolute temperature model in references [7, 13], a reliability diversity model is deduced for the heterogeneous multicore systems, the variance of MTTF is adopted as the optimization target in this model. Based on this model, different EM-related impact factors on the MTTF-variance of the system are summarized, such as frequency, voltage and stress time etc.

Through this approach, the MTTF of heterogeneous multicore system is balanced during task running period. Experimental results on kinds of task graphs show that our method reduce the MTTF variance of a heterogeneous multicore system over 50 %, compared to the existing workload balance task allocation algorithm and system MTTF is extended over 30 %. The main contributions of this paper include:

- Based on the existing EM-aware MTTF model of a single processor, an optimization model for MTTF of multicore systems is proposed with voltage, frequency, stress time, power dissipation and other factors considered, which can be associated with task scheduling for heterogeneous system.
- The task scheduling problems on heterogeneous multicore system are formulated into MILP (Mixed-Integer Linear Programming) form to find optimal solution via balancing MTTF. The MTTF-variance is optimized as the basis to improve reliability of the whole system.

The remainder of this paper is organized as follows. Section 2 gives the establishment of optimization model for multicore system. Section 3 gives the proposed

MILP-based method. Experimental results are provided in Sect. 4. Finally, conclusion is in Sect. 5.

2 Preliminary

The overall reliability of the system is affected by amounts of factors, such as own structure, soft errors, wear-out mechanisms and etc. The reliability affected by aging is mainly investigated in this work and the MTTFs of processing cores are studied during task scheduling.

2.1 Problem Definition

Due to the core heterogeneity of a heterogeneous multicore system, the overhead of identical tasks is not neat while running on the different cores [12, 14, 15]. The problems studied in this work are as follows:

1. The primary attribute of a heterogeneous multicore system is that the overhead of same tasks running on the different cores is different.
2. Suppose that there is a set of n cores and a set of m tasks to be assigned, there is an execution time array $T = \{T_{i,j} | 1 \leq i \leq n, 1 \leq j \leq m;\}$, $T_{i,j}$ denotes that the execution time of task j running on the core i.
3. Similarly there is a power consumption array $P = \{P_{i,j} | 1 \leq i \leq n, 1 \leq j \leq m;\}$, $P_{i,j}$ denotes the power consumption of task j running on the core i.
4. Task scheduling strategy on heterogeneous multicore system is also a NP-complete problem.

2.2 MTTF Model for Electromigration

The MTTF model of whole system adopts the conclusion in reference [10]:

1. The EM effect domains the systematic wear-out than the interaction of TDDB and NBTI.
2. The least MTTF component is regarded as the MTTF of overall system.

Therefore, EM effect is taken as an example in our work, other reliability issues which caused by aging effect, such as NBTI and TDDB can also be analyzed by the similar flow in this paper.

In regard to the MTTF evaluation of single processor under EM aging effect, this paper adopts black model. The black model considers jointly effects of voltage, temperature and frequency on the MTTF. On this basis our own optimization model is derived out. According to the EM-aware MTTF model, many factors (e.g., absolute temperature, operational frequency and voltage) jointly affect the MTTF of a processor.

The systematic aging effect by EM effect is studied and The MTTF of whole system can be written as:

$$MTTF_{sys} = min[MTTF_i(C_i)] \tag{1}$$

C_i denotes the failure rate, Formula (1) suggested that $MTTF_{sys}$ is determined by the least $MTTF$.

In order to correctly capture the MTTF of a single processor under EM aging effect, several studies always adopt the black model [12].

$$MTTF_{EM} \propto (V_{dd} \cdot f \cdot pi)^{-2} \cdot e^{\frac{Ea}{kT}} \tag{2}$$

In the formula (2), V_{dd} is supply voltage, f is operational frequency, and pi is the transition probability of transistors in a clock cycle. T is the temperature. k is the Boltzmann's constant ($k = 8.617 \times 10^{-5} eV/K$) and Ea is a material related constant called activation energy.

2.3   Temperature and Power Model

The black model adopts fixed temperature. However, the temperature of a processor is jointly affected by the average power consumption and stress time. When processing a specific task, the absolute temperature of the processor can be concluded as formula (3) [13]:

$$T(t) = (P_{total} \cdot R + T_{amb})(1 - e^{-\frac{t}{RC}}) + T_{cur} \cdot e^{-\frac{t}{RC}} \tag{3}$$

T_{amb} and T_{cur} in formula (3) represent the ambient temperature and current temperature of processor respectively. P_{total} denotes the total power consumption. t is the stress time, R and C denote thermal resistance and capacitance respectively [10]. Formula (1) suggests that with stress time continues rising, it will has less effect on temperature, while average power consumption is increasingly becoming the dominated factor for temperature. The attribute of workload, including power dissipation and stress time, reflects in formula (3), which is associated with the task allocation and temperature of single processor.

Generally, total power consumption contains two parts:

$$P_{total} = P_{dyn} + P_{static} \tag{4}$$

P_{dyn} is the dynamic power contributed by average power of the task, which refers to E3S industrial standard given in TGFF [16]. More details will be represented in the Sect. 3. P_{static} is the leakage power. According to reference [13], static power dissipation could be approximated as linear relationship with temperature. $P_{static} = \alpha T + \Omega$, α and Ω are empirical constants. So the total power consumption can be expressed as:

$$P_{total} = P_{dyn} + \alpha T + \Omega \tag{5}$$

2.4   Optimal MTTF Model

Combining Eqs. (3) and (4), we can deduce that the temperature and power consumption is positive feedback relationship. Power consumption increases with temperature rising, and the increased power consumption will further result in the increase in temperature. So after long-running, the power consumption caused by workload should be paid more attention than the stress time for task scheduling strategy. The integration of formulation from (2) to (5) could be:

$$\ln(MTTF_{EM}) \propto -2\ln(V_{dd} \cdot f \cdot pi) + \frac{Ea}{k}\frac{1 - \alpha R + \alpha R e^{\frac{-t}{RC}}}{RP_{dyn} + R\Omega + T_{amb} + T_{cur} \cdot e^{\frac{-t}{RC}}} \qquad (6)$$

Formula (6) indicates that the MTTF of a single processor is mainly affected by two parts. One is the intrinsic factor, such as operational voltage and frequency. Another one is extrinsic factor (how it will be used), like ambient temperature and workload. Combined the formula (1), formula (6) can be extended to calculate the MTTF of whole system:

$$MTTF_{sys} = min_{i \in \theta}(MTTF_{EM,i}) \qquad (7)$$

Suppose that there is a heterogeneous system θ, $MTTF_{EM,i}$ stands for the MTTF of the *i-th* processing core. $MTTF_{sys}$ denotes the MTTF of whole system. The MTTF of least reliable core is regarded as the overall system.

Though many modern CPU employ DVFS technology, the diversity of processor cores is mainly considered in this work, and it is assumed that their operational frequency and voltage are fixed at runtime. The optimal MTTF model established is coarse-gained and statistical, however, our MILP method for balancing the MTTFs is still applicable for these DVFS system.

For a specific heterogeneous system, it is assumed that the operational voltage and frequency are fixed. Then the MTTF of whole system is chiefly affected by stress time t and dynamic power dissipation P_{dyn} according to formula (6). Both of them are caused by workload. In Sect. 3, a MILP-based task scheduling is proposed for searching the optimal task assignment for heterogeneous systems by balancing the MTTF of each core.

3   Optimal Solution

In this section, the MTTF-aware task scheduling problems is formulated into MILP (Mixed-Integer Linear Programming) form to find the optimal solution. A MILP problem always has three items: *objective function*, *variables* and *constraints* [17]. *Objective function* is the target that needs to be optimized, *variables* are what we search for and will be solved by the MILP, and *constraints* are formulations of task scheduling on heterogeneous multi-core systems in this paper.

3.1   MILP for Task Scheduling on Heterogeneous System

Objective function: Our goal is to minimize the variance of MTTF in multicore systems. In order to maximize the minimum MTTF of heterogeneous cores, the balance strategy is taken to reduce MTTF gap between cores. Suppose that a heterogeneous system contains i cores, MTTF variance is adopted to represent the difference between the individual cores:

$$\text{VAR}_{\text{MTTF}} = \frac{1}{i} \sum_{k=1}^{i} (MTTF_k - MTTF_{ave})^2 \tag{8}$$

$MTTF_k$ denotes the MTTF of the k-th core, $MTTF_{ave}$ represents the arithmetic mean of all MTTF of cores in the system. It should be ensured that the trend of MTTFs is convergent, and no weak ones will become the bottleneck of system reliability. Therefore, optimization goal is to minimize the MTTF variance:

$$\text{Minimize} \quad \text{VAR}_{MTTF} \tag{9}$$

Constraints: Workload can be regarded as a set of tasks, named task flow [8]. A task flow is always depicted by DAG (Directed Acyclic Graph) model as shown in Fig. 1. Each node $V_i \leftarrow$ represents a task that need to be executed, and each directed arc E_i denotes the precedence between tasks. As suggested in Fig. 1, the task V_4 shouldn't be executed until task V_2 and V_3 both have completed. If B_k is used to denote the beginning time of task V_k, V_k is the parent task of V_l. So the precedence relationship between task V_k and V_l can be easily expressed as following:

$$B_k + T_{i,k} \leq B_l \tag{10}$$

Task V_l can start execution after task V_k completed. $T_{i,k}$ denotes the execution time of task V_k scheduled to the specific core i. For a heterogeneous multicore system, different cores have different processing speed, unlike homogeneous one in which the cores have the identical frequency and the same execution time.

Variables: To affirm the core the task will be allocated, a matrix S is defined. S is a matrix with n rows and m columns, n is the total task number and m is the number of cores. If task V_i runs on core j, $S_{ij} = 1$, otherwise $S_{ij} = 0$. It is assumed that a task can only be assigned to one core:

$$S_{ij} = 0, 1; \tag{11}$$

$$1 \leq i \leq n; \ 1 \leq j \leq m; \tag{12}$$

$$\sum_{i=1}^{n} S_{ij} = 1; \tag{13}$$

Formula (12) denotes that the sum of all the elements in a column of the matrix should equals to 1, which forces the unique relationship between cores and tasks. The sum of all the elements in a row of the matrix is unlimited, which means that each core can execute several tasks sequentially.

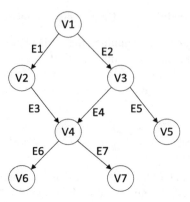

Fig. 1. DAG model of task flow

The following constraints are used for dynamic power consumption and task execution time respectively. For each core the MTTF is related to the total power consumption and stress time according to the model established in Sect. 2.

$$P_{dyn,i} = \sum_{j=1}^{m} \left(S_{ij} \cdot P_{i,j} \right) \tag{14}$$

$$T_i = \sum_{j=1}^{m} \left(S_{ij} \cdot T_{i,j} \right) \tag{15}$$

In formula (13), $P_{i,j}$ denotes the power consumption of task j running on the core i and $P_{dyn,i}$ stands for the dynamic power dissipation of core i. Similarly in formula (14), $T_{i,j}$ denotes the execution time of task j running on the core i and T_i stands for the total stress time of core i.

Other metrics such as the core utilization or some index measured the performance of our MILP are also closely related to the matrix S. But due to limited space, they are bypassed here.

After all, the entire MILP is as follows:

Objective:

$$\text{Minimize } VAR_{MTTF}$$

Subject to:

$$B_k + T_{kj} \leq B_l$$
$$S_{ij} = 0, 1; (1 \leq i \leq n, 1 \leq j \leq m)$$
$$\sum_{i=1}^{n} S_{ij} = 1;$$
$$P_{dyn,i} = \sum_{j=1}^{m} \left(S_{ij} \cdot P_{i,j} \right)$$
$$T_i = \sum_{j=1}^{m} \left(S_{ij} \cdot T_{i,j} \right)$$

In This MILP, the first constraint guarantees the precedence relationship of tasks. The second and third constraints reflect that the scheduling matrix forces the mapping relationship of tasks and cores. The last two constraints are to satisfy power dissipation and execution time needs of the proposed MTTF model. Moreover, this MILP method for balance MTTF is also adaptive to other MTTF models and it is easy to extend and add other parameters that need to be concerned, such as the communication cost or the utilization of cores.

3.2 Algorithm Implementation

The optimal solution can be achieved by solving the MILP. The linear program tool LINGO is used to solve our MILP and obtains possible solutions [17]. The global solver from LINGO combines a series of range bounding and range reduction techniques, a branch-and-bound framework is adopted to find global solutions.

However, the task scheduling is a NP-complete problem. For realistic workloads, the computational complexity is enormous. For all the experiments in this paper, the stopping criterion is set to 10^7 iterations or a local optimal solution is found when beyond the 10^7 iterations. Once a feasible task scheduling or a local optimal solution is found, the corresponding MTTFs of cores is recorded and the variance of MTTF is calculated. The ever best solution among the records is defined as our quasi-optimal solution for our MILP.

4 Experiments and Results

In this section, the MTTF of each core is obtained after running every task graph and the VAR_{MTTF} of each multicore system is computed. Meanwhile, the workload balance algorithms are implemented in this section for a comparison with our MILP-based method.

4.1 Experiment Setup

In this paper, task graphs used for experiment are randomly generated by TGFF tool [16]. The running time of each task is randomly selected from 2X to 12X of the execution time on 1 GHz processor, which can be set up in TGFF. The pioneers and successors constraints of every task are 2–3 respectively. To save experiment time, part of task graphs are selected as workload from the large task graphs generated by TGFF. Each task graph contains about $20 \sim 50$ tasks, and has different construction, total power dissipation and stress time.

Based on the proposed strategy, several random task flows generated by TGFF are chosen as our benchmarks and a heterogeneous quad-core system in [18] is adopted as our platform. Operating frequency of the four cores is set to 1.2 GHZ, 1.4 GHZ, 1.6 GHZ and 1.8 GHZ respectively.

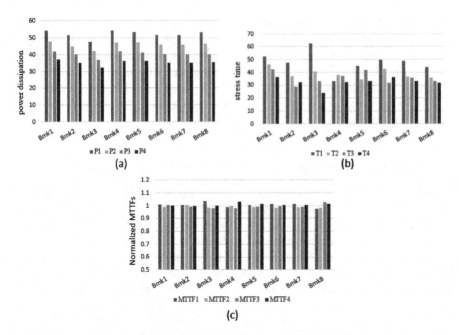

Fig. 2. Power consumption (a), stress time (b) and normalized MTTF (c) of cores after running our method.

4.2 Workload Verification

The stress time, power dissipation and MTTF of each core is obtained after running each benchmark respectively as shown in Fig. 3. The titles of abscissa axis, "*Bmk1*" to "*Bmk8*" denote the random task flows. The symbols from "*P1*" to "*P4*" denote power dissipation of the four cores, "*T1*" to "*T4*" represent the stress time of the four cores and "*MTTF1*" to "*MTTF4*" stand for the MTTF of the four cores. The MTTFs in Fig. 2(c) are the normalized MTTFs of cores, which are calculated by:

$$MTTF_{nor,k} = MTTF_k / MTTF_{ave} \qquad (16)$$

Figure 2 shows that our strategy makes power distribution relatively less for those cores the original MTTF of which is smaller. But stress time of each core seems not strictly accordance with this result. This phenomenon proves that due to the positive feedback between power dissipation and temperature, the tasks with higher power dissipation have greater impact on temperature than the ones with more stress time but less power dissipation.

It is observed that the stress time of core 1 on benchmark3 is abnormally high. This phenomenon is attributed by the loose structure of this task flow and the tasks in this benchmark is mainly with more stress time and less power dissipation.

4.3   MTTF-Variance Evaluation

In order to compare our algorithm with the workload balance algorithms, the following three basic approaches are considered:

(1) Power dissipation balance (abbreviated to "*Bal-Power*") represents that the scheduling algorithms try the best to allocate each core with the same power dissipation.
(2) Stress time balance (abbreviated to "*Bal-Time*"), indicates that the scheduling algorithms try to assign each core with the same working time.
(3) Temperature balance (abbreviated to "*Bal-Temp*") represents that the scheduling algorithms try to assign the tasks so that the temperature of each core is the same.

As shown in Fig. 3, the load balancing algorithm and our MILP-based method are running on the same sets of task flows, and the variance of the system MTTF are contrasted. Figure 3 shows that the method of this paper can significantly decrease the difference between cores and improve the overall reliability of the system. The average reduction of variance is over 50 %.

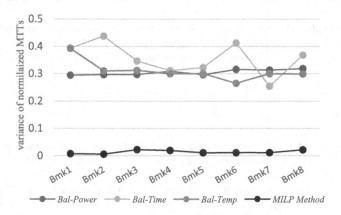

Fig. 3. Comparison of MTTF variance.

4.4   Compared with Workload Balance Algorithms

The above algorithms are running on the same set of task flows, where $MTTF$ and T denote MTTF of four cores and their temperature respectively. $MTTF_{sys}$ represents the MTTF of overall system. Table 1 shows that the *Bal-Power* and *Bal-Time* will lead to irregular temperature and cannot protect the least reliable core, while MILP-based method improves MTTF of systems over 30 % by balancing the MTTF between the cores. Compared with the *Bal-Temp*, our method increases the peak temperature of the system by about 3.2 %, but increases the MTTF of overall system by more than 30 %.

Table 1. Comparison between workload balance algorithm and MILP method.

Cores of	Bal-Power		Bal-Time		Bal-Temp		MILP Method	
system	$MTTF_{nor}$	T (k)	$MTTF_{nor}$	T (k)	$MTTF_{nor}$	T (k)	$MTTF_{nor}$	T (k)
Core 1	1.4273	349	1.3812	370	1.4788	349	1.0034	362
Core 2	1.1063	351	1.4099	341	1.0637	350	1.0074	354
Core 3	0.8029	352	0.7245	352	0.8200	350	0.9924	347
Core 4	0.6633	350	0.4843	356	0.6375	351	0.9968	341
$MTTF_{sys}$	0.6633		0.4843		0.6375		0.9924	

5   Conclusions

Regarding to the EM-aware MTTF model of single processor, an optimization model is concluded and proved, which can reflect the overall system reliability. Based on this optimization model, a MILP-based MTTF-diversity aware task scheduling method is presented for improving reliability. By balancing the MTTFs of each core, the MTTF-diversity of whole system can be reduced. The proposed method provides an effective reliability optimization solution for heterogeneous multicore systems.

Acknowledgments. This work is supported by National Natural Science Foundation of China (NSFC) under grant No. (61274036, 61371025, 61204027, 61106038 and 61574052) and Doctoral Foundation of Ministry of Education of china under grant NO. (20110111120012).

References

1. Srinivasan, J., Adve, S.V., Bose, P., Rivers, J.A.: The impact of technology scaling on lifetime reliability. In: 2004 International Conference on Dependable Systems and Networks, pp. 177–186. IEEE (2004)
2. Xiang, Y., Chantem, T., Dick, R.P., Hu, X.S., Shang, L.: System-level reliability modeling for MPSoCs. In: 2010 IEEE/ACM/IFIP International Conference on Hardware/Software Codesign and System Synthesis (CODES + ISSS), pp. 297–306. IEEE (2010)
3. Chen, X., Wang, Y., Yang, H., Xie, Y., Cao, Y.: Assessment of circuit optimization techniques under NBTI. IEEE Des. Test **30**(6), 40–49 (2013)
4. Vazquez-Hernandez, J.: Error prediction and detection methodologies for reliable circuit operation under NBTI. In: 2014 IEEE International Test Conference (ITC), pp. 1–10 (2014)
5. Coskun, A.K., Rosing, T.S., Whisnant, K.: Temperature aware task scheduling in multicore systems. In: Design, Automation, and Test in Europe, pp. 1–6 (2007)
6. Xie, Y., Hung, W.-L.: Temperature-aware task allocation and scheduling for embedded multiprocessor systems-on-chip (multicore system) design. J. VLSI Sig. Process. Syst. Sig. Image Video Technol. **45**(3), 177–189 (2006)
7. Yuan, L., Leventhal, S.R., Gu, J., Qu, G.: Talk: a temperature-aware leakage minimization technique for real-time systems. IEEE Trans. Comput.-Aided Des. Integr. Circ. Syst. **30**(10), 1564–1568 (2011)
8. Sun, J., Lysecky, R., Shankar, K., Kodi, A., Louri, A., Roveda, J.: Workload assignment considering NBTI degradation in multicore systems. ACM J. Emerg. Technol. Comput. Syst. **10**(1), 4 (2014)

9. Xie, Y., Li, L., Kandemir, M., Vijaykrishnan, N., Irwin, M.J.: Reliability-aware co-synthesis for embedded systems. In: IEEE International Conference on Application-Specific Systems, Architectures and Processors (ASAP), pp. 41–50 (2004)

10. Wu, K.C., Lee, M.C., Marculescu, D., Chang, S.C.: Mitigating lifetime underestimation: a system-level approach considering temperature variations and correlations between failure mechanisms. In: Design, Automation and Test in Europe Conference and Exhibition, pp. 1269–1274. IEEE (2012)

11. Kim, T., Zheng, B., Chen, H.-B., Zhu, Q., Sukharev, V., Tan, S.X.-D.: Lifetime optimization for real-time embedded systems considering electromigration effects. In: IEEE/ACM International Conference on Computer-Aided Design (ICCAD), pp. 434–439 (2014)

12. Huang, L., Yuan, F., Xu, Q.: On task allocation and scheduling for lifetime extension of platform-based mpsoc designs. IEEE Trans. Parallel Distrib. Syst. **22**(12), 2088–2099 (2010)

13. Wang, S., Chen, J.J.: Thermal-aware lifetime reliability in multicore systems. In: 11th International Symposium on Quality Electronic Design (ISQED), pp. 399–405. IEEE (2010)

14. Baruah, S.: Feasibility analysis of preemptive real-time systems upon heterogeneous multiprocessor platforms. In: Proceedings of the 25th IEEE International Real-Time Systems Symposium, pp. 37–46. IEEE Computer Society (2004)

15. Baruah, S.: Task partitioning upon heterogeneous multiprocessor platforms. In: 10th Real-Time and Embedded Technology and Applications Symposium, pp. 536–543. IEEE (2004)

16. Dick, R.P., Rhodes, D.L., Wolf, W.: TGFF: task graphs for free. In: International Workshop on Hardware/Software Codesign, pp. 97–101 (1998)

17. LINGO: The modeling language and optimizer. Lindo Systems inc. http://www.lindo.com

18. Liang, H., Li, J., Xu, D., Xu, X., Jin, S.: On enhancing electromigration-related reliability of heterogeneous MPSoC via task scheduling. J. Comput.-Aided Des. Comput. Graph. **27**(8), 1570–1577 (2015)

Author Index

Printed in the United States
By Bookmasters